WORD PROBLEMS II

STUDIES IN LOGIC

AND

THE FOUNDATIONS OF MATHEMATICS

VOLUME 95

NORTH-HOLLAND PUBLISHING COMPANY
AMSTERDAM · NEW YORK · OXFORD

WORD PROBLEMS II

The Oxford Book

Edited by

S. I. ADIAN

The Steklov Mathematical Institute
Moscow, USSR

W. W. BOONE

University of Illinois
Urbana, USA

G. HIGMAN

University of Oxford
Oxford, England

1980

NORTH-HOLLAND PUBLISHING COMPANY
AMSTERDAM · NEW YORK · OXFORD

ISBN: 0 444 85343 X

Published by:

North-Holland Publishing Company — Amsterdam · New York · Oxford

Sole distributors for the U.S.A and Canada:

Elsevier North-Holland, Inc.
52 Vanderbilt Avenue
New York, N.Y. 10017

Library of Congress Cataloging in Publication Data
Main entry under title:

Word problems II.

(Studies in logic and the foundations of mathematics ; v. 95)
"This book grew out of the working conference 'Decision problems in algebra' held in Oxford the summer of 1976."
Bibliography: p.
1. Groups, Theory of--Congresses. 2. Gödel's theorem--Congresses. I. Adian, S. I. II. Boone, William W. III. Higman, Graham. IV. Series.
QA171.W86 512'.22 79-15276
ISBN 0-444-85343-X

PRINTED IN THE NETHERLANDS

Dedicated to the memory of
Kurt Gödel (1906–1978)
in awe and affection

In angusto vivebamus,
si quicquam esset cogitationibus clausum.

Seneca, *Letters 55.11*

Photo by Alfred Eisenstaedt, courtesy Time-Life Books Inc.

Kurt Gödel (1906–1978)

INTRODUCTION

This book grew out of the working conference "Decision Problems in Algebra", held in Oxford the summer of 1976, under the auspices of the Science Research Council of the United Kingdom. This work is a sequel to the volume "Word problems: decision problems and the Burnside problem in group theory", which itself was the result of a similar working conference held in Irvine the summer of 1969.

The Oxford conference was organized by the editors of this volume. The secretary of the conference was Donald J. Collins, without whom the entire endeavour could not have been successfully carried out.

What is to be said about the present book? Like the Irvine book, a major intention is that it serves as a means of entry for the reader into the field of word problem. For this reason we have included various surveys; but, moreover, it is hoped that various articles which, while on the very borderline of advancing ideas, have still been presented in such a way as to be highly accessible to the working mathematician.

The field of "Word problems" would seem to have flourished between Irvine and Oxford. Unsolvability results have been sharpened in various ways. Thus, as explained in an expository article herein, various classical decision problems about groups have been attacked, but with the class of groups considered now restricted to some familiar variety; and in certain cases this has led to new unsolvability results — e.g., in the case of solvable groups. Now, too, the full story is known about the existence of word problems of the various finer degrees of Post. But positive results have not been lacking either. Indeed, we include an article solving the conjugacy problem for matrices with integer entries. (This was problem 22 of the Irvine book.)

A short article on algebraically closed groups appeared in the Irvine book, but in subsequent years, this has become a large area of inquiry both with regard to decision problems and with regard to purely algebraic questions. An in-depth study and a shorter paper are included. Much the same thing could be said about a focus of interest on simple groups within the word problem field, and we include an article on this matter also.

Small cancellation theory and generalizations (surveyed in the Irvine book) have truly come of age. We include two papers in the general area, one of which solves a well-known problem of Kurosch and Bjarni Jónsson.

A brief list of open questions is given as well.

We call the reader's attention to the note by J.L. Britton, "Erratum: The existence of infinite Burnside groups" in which he says that a mistake occurs in his article in the Irvine volume. This mistake was first noted in the book "The Burnside problem and identities in groups", by S.I. Adian (Nauka, Moscow, 1975), page 4. The existence of infinite Burnside groups of large odd exponent was proved in a joint article by P.S. Novikov and Adian in 1968. The much stronger proposition of the announcement of Novikov in 1959 must be regarded as not proved.

We wish to thank all the mathematicians who have helped us by refereeing individual articles, but to single out here, by name, only Gerhard Hesse for his especially valuable help in this regard.

Originally, this volume was intended as a Festschrift to mark the seventieth birthday of Kurt Gödel. Now, sadly, we can only dedicate it to his memory.

Sergei I. Adian
William W. Boone
Graham Higman

LIST OF CONTENTS

S.I. Adian, W.W. Boone, G. Higman, eds., Word Problems II
© North-Holland Publishing Company (1980) 1–16

MODULAR MACHINES, THE WORD PROBLEM FOR FINITELY PRESENTED GROUPS AND COLLINS' THEOREM

Stål AANDERAA and Daniel E. COHEN
University of Oslo and Queen Mary College, London

We shall define a class of machines which we call modular machines, related to Minsky machines [15] (these were called Γ-machines in the lecture by the first author on which this paper is based). These machines act on $\mathbf{N}^2$, the set of pairs of natural numbers, with a very simple transition function. It will then be almost immediate that any function computable by a modular machine is partial recursive. On the other hand, modular machines are defined in such a way that Turing-computable functions are computable by modular machines (which can also be regarded as a new way of Gödelising Turing machines). This provides a new proof that Turing-computable functions are partial recursive. It also provides an easy proof of the normal form theorem for partial recursive functions, since the data for a modular machine, being numerical in nature, can easily be encoded by a natural number with the decodings being primitive recursive. There will be a modular machine M_0 whose halting problem is unsolvable. Readers are invited to construct their own proof of the undecidability of elementary number theory using this machine M_0 and to see how it compares in difficulty with standard proofs. (Various results on the degrees of halting, word and confluence problems for modular machines, similar to known results for Turing machines, are proved in [9] but are not needed in this paper.)

However the main aim of this paper is not to apply modular machines in computability theory and logic, but to give some of their applications in group theory. In this and the following paper the group-theoretic results are all known, but the new proofs are very much easier than any previous proofs. We prove the following theorems.

Theorem A (Novikov–Boone). *There is a finitely presented group whose word problem is unsolvable.*

Theorem B (Collins). *For any recursively enumerable unbounded truth-table degree, there is a finitely presented group whose word problem has that degree.*

Theorem A was first proved by Novikov [16] and Boone [2] independently. The original proofs were somewhat complicated and lengthy, but were later simplified. In particular, Britton [5] made very important simplifications by proving results about HNN extensions. Lemma 4 of his paper is now referred to as Britton's Lemma and is a very important tool in combinatorial group theory, which will be used in our papers also. Our proof of Theorem A has the same basic idea as Britton's, but is very much easier because of the use of modular machines rather than Turing machines.

Other proofs of Theorem A are known. It can be proved using Higman's embedding theorem [0, 13]. A very different proof from any of the others has been given by McKenzie and Thomson [14].

A weaker form of Theorem B, with "unbounded truth-table degree" replaced by "Turing degree" was proved independently by Boone [3, 4], Clapham [6], and Fridman [11, 12]. Collins [10] was able to improve Boone's proof to obtain Theorem B itself.

In §1 we develop the theory of modular machines. Theorem A is proved in §2. In §4 we prove Theorem B, having obtained the relevant degree results for modular machines in §3. The paper following this used similar techniques to prove the Higman embedding theorem.

§1. Modular machines

We shall follow Turing and consider Turing machines as defined by quintuples $q_r a_i a_j q_s D$ (where a_i, a_j are letters, q_r, q_s are states, and D is one of the two symbols L, R) instead of the more common definition by quadruples due to Post. The two definitions are equivalent, a non-moving quadruple $q_r aa' q_s$ being replaced by a quintuple $q_r aa' q_{rsa} R$ (where q_{rsa} is a new auxiliary state) together with quintuples $q_{rsa} xx q_s L$ for all letters x. We shall use the word *configuration* rather than "instantaneous description". We write $uqav$ for the configuration with uav on the tape (u, v being words, a being a letter), the machine being in state q scanning letter a.

Let T be a Turing machine. We regard its alphabet as consisting of the natural numbers $0, 1, \ldots, n$ (where 0 is the blank) and its states as consisting of $n+1, \ldots, m-1$ and possibly 0.

Take a configuration $\cdots b_1 b_0 q a c_0 c_1 \cdots$. Define u, v by $u = \Sigma\, b_i m^i$, $v = \Sigma\, c_i m^i$. Minsky [15] represents this configuration by $(u, v, a, q) \in N^4$. It can also be represented by either of the pairs $(um + a,\ vm + q)$ or $(um + q,\ vm + a)$. We shall use whichever pair is most convenient at the time, sometimes using one pair and sometimes the other for the same configuration. Notice that both mappings from configurations to pairs are recursive. Also $P(T)=\{(\alpha,\beta)\in N^2;\ (\alpha,\beta)$ represents a configuration$\}$ is recursive and the map sending (α,β) to the corresponding configuration is partial recursive with domain $P(T)$.

Let $qaa'q'R$ be a quintuple of T. It is easy to see that (with u, v as above) one element of N^2 corresponding to the next configuration is $(um^2+a'm+q', v)$. Similarly if $qaa'q'L$ is a quintuple of T then $(u, vm^2+a'm+q')$ is a pair corresponding to the next configuration. This motivates the definition of a modular machine.

Definition. A modular machine M consists of an integer $m>1$, an integer n with $0<n<m$, and quadruples (a,b,c,R) and (a,b,c,L) such that $0\leq a,\ b<m,\ 0\leq c<m^2$, and, for each a, b, at most one quadruple begins with the pair a, b.

A configuration of M is an element (α,β) of N^2. Write $\alpha=um+a$, $\beta=vm+b$, where $0\leq a,\ b<m$. If no quadruple begins with a, b we call (α,β) *terminal.* If (α,β) is not terminal we say (α,β) *yields* (α',β'), written $(\alpha,\beta)\Rightarrow(\alpha',\beta')$, if either M has a quadruple (a,b,c,R) and $\alpha'=um^2+c$, $\beta'=v$ or M has a quadruple (a,b,c,L) and $\alpha'=u$, $\beta'=vm^2+c$. If $(\alpha_1,\beta_1)\Rightarrow(\alpha_2,\beta_2)\Rightarrow\cdots\Rightarrow(\alpha_k,\beta_k)$ we write $(\alpha_1,\beta_1)\rightarrow(\alpha_k,\beta_k)$.

We define a (partial) function $g_M: N\rightarrow N^2$ by $g_M(\alpha,\beta)=(\alpha',\beta')$ iff $(\alpha,\beta)\rightarrow(\alpha',\beta')$ and (α',β') is terminal. The class of functions $\{g_M;$ all $M\}$ is rather strange. For if g_M is somewhere defined, there is a pair a, b such that no quadruple begins with a, b. Then $g_M(\alpha,\beta)=(\alpha,\beta)$ if $\alpha\equiv a \pmod m$, $\beta\equiv b \pmod m$. We shall use the integer n (which has played no part as yet) to define input and output functions. The name "modular machine" is given because the action of M on a pair depends on its class modulo m.

For any $r\in N$ we can write r uniquely as $r=\Sigma_0^k b_j n^j$, $1\leq b_j\leq n$ (for $r=0$, take the empty sum). In a Turing machine with alphabet $0,1,\ldots,n$, this means that $b_k\cdots b_0$ is the tape description corresponding to r. Let $i_M: N\rightarrow N^2$ be given by $i_M r=(\Sigma\, b_j m^j, n+1)$.

Write $\alpha\in N$ as $\Sigma\, c_j m^j$, $0\leq c_j<m$, and take y with $c_y=0$ but $c_j\neq 0$ for $j<y$. Define $u_M: N^2\rightarrow N$ by $u_M(\alpha,\beta)=\Sigma_1^y a_j n^{j-1}$. Then $u_M g_M i_M$ is a partial function from N to N, which we call the function computed by M.

We shall associate with a Turing machine T a modular machine M such that M and T compute the same function. We shall use a slightly unusual definition of the function computed by T. The class of Turing computable functions is (without using their characterisation as partial recursive functions) easily seen to be the same for both definitions. The reader who prefers a more usual definition should change the definition of the input function i_M and the output function u_M accordingly.

Let T be a Turing machine with alphabet $0, 1, \ldots, n$, and states $n+1, \ldots, m-1$ and (perhaps) 0. Each $r \in N$ has a tape description as above. The output of a configuration will be the integer corresponding to the portion of the tape lying strictly between the scanned square and the first blank to its left. The function $f_T : N \to N$ computed by T is defined by $f_T r = s$ if T when started in state $n+1$ on the rightmost square of the description of r ultimately halts in a configuration with output s. Note that, if convenient, we may modify T so that whenever it halts the scanned square is blank.

We now define a modular machine M associated with T. M will have the integers m, n previously defined for T. M will have two quadruples $(a, q, a'm + q', R$ (or L)) and $(q, a, a'm + q', R$ (or L)) corresponding to each quintuple $qaa'q'R$ (or L) of T. The account preceding the definition of modular machines explaining how to associate members of N^2 with configurations of T makes it clear that M simulates T. Precisely, if (α, β) corresponds to C then (α, β) is terminal iff C is terminal, while if $C \Rightarrow C'$ then $(\alpha, \beta) \Rightarrow (\alpha', \beta')$ where (α', β') is a pair corresponding to C'. The definition of the functions computed by T and M now makes it clear that T and M compute the same function.

The numerical nature of M makes it obvious that the function computed by M is partial recursive, so we have a proof that Turing computable functions are partial recursive. We could also obtain the normal form theorem fairly easily by a Godel numbering of modular machines.

Define $H_0(M)$ to be $\emptyset$ if $(0,0)$ is not terminal for M and $H_0(M) = \{(\alpha, \beta); (\alpha, \beta) \to (0,0)\}$ if $(0,0)$ is terminal. It is obvious that $H_0(M)$ is r.e. For any r.e. set S there is a Turing machine T such that f_T is the (partial) characteristic function of S. Further we may assume that if $f_T r$ is defined then T halts on a blank tape (see [18], where T is constructed to simulate the action of a single-register machine computing the function). If M is the modular machine associated with T, plainly $H_0(M)$ is not recursive if S is not recursive. A stronger result is proved in §3.

§2. Unsolvability

We begin with an account of HNN extensions and Britton's Lemma for the reader who is unfamiliar with these topics. A knowledge of free groups and free products will be assumed.

Let A_i, A_{-i} (for i in some index set I which need not be countable) be subgroups of a group H. Let $\varphi_i : A_i \to A_{-i}$ be isomorphisms. Let G be the free product $H ** \langle p_i \rangle$ $(i \in I)$. Let N be the normal closure in G of the set of elements $p_i^{-1} a_i p_i (\varphi_i a_i)^{-1}$ for all i and all $a_i \in A_i$. The quotient group G/N is called the HNN extension of H with stable letters p_i and associated pairs of subgroups A_i and A_{-i}; it is usually written as $\langle H, p_i ; p_i^{-1} A_i p_i = A_{-i} \rangle$. Any element of G can be written as

$$h_0 p_{i_1}^{\varepsilon_1} h_1 \cdots h_{n-1} p_{i_n}^{\varepsilon_n} h_n,$$

where $n \geq 0$, $h_1, \ldots, h_n \in H$ and $\varepsilon_1, \ldots, \varepsilon_n = \pm 1$.

If for some r we have $i_r = i_{r+1}$, $\varepsilon_r + \varepsilon_{r+1} = 0$ and either $\varepsilon_r = -1$ and $h_r \in A_{i_r}$ or $\varepsilon_r = 1$ and $h_r \in A_{-i_r}$ we say this expression has a *pinch* (more precisely, that it has a p_{i_r}-pinch). In such a case the same element of G/N is represented by an expression with fewer p-symbols (since we can replace $p_i^{-1} a p_i$ with $a \in A_i$ by $\varphi_i a$ without altering the image) and we call this process *pinching out.*

We may now state Britton's Lemma (for a proof see [7] or [8]).

Britton's Lemma. *Any non-trivial element of G lying in N has a pinch.*

The following results are immediate consequences (and are all we need in this section; the full force of Britton's lemma is used in §4).

(I) H embeds in the HNN extension (by the map $H \to G \to G/N$; we regard this as inclusion).

(II) If K is a subgroup of H such that $\varphi_i (K \cap A_i) = K \cap A_{-i}$ for all i then $H \cap \langle K, p_i \text{ (all } i) \rangle = K$. For it is easy to check that if a pinch in G can be applied to an element of the subgroup $\langle K, p_i \text{ (all } i) \rangle$ of G the hypotheses ensure that the new element still lies in this subgroup. Hence any element of the subgroup $\langle K, p_i \rangle$ of G/N can be represented in a form without pinches. By Britton's Lemma it cannot lie in H if any p_i occurs, i.e. if it is in H it is in K. (It also follows that the map from the HNN extension of K with associated pairs $K \cap A_i$ and $K \cap A_{-i}$ to the group $\langle K, p_i \rangle$ is an isomorphism. This part is used in [0], not in this paper.)

(III) In the group $\langle H, p ; p^{-1} A p = A \rangle$, the isomorphism being the identity, $p^{-1} h p = h$ (with $h \in H$) only if $h \in A$.

Let A be the group $\langle t, x, y ; xy = yx \rangle = \langle t \rangle * \langle x, y ; xy = yx \rangle$, which is also an HNN extension of the free group $\langle t, x \rangle$ with stable letter y. Let $T = \langle t \rangle^A$ (the normal subgroup of A generated by t) and let $t(r, s) = y^{-s} x^{-r} t x^r y^s$. We easily obtain the following properties.

(i) T is free with basis $\{t(r,s)\}$. This follows from the Kuroš subgroup theorem, but is more easily proved directly by expanding a product of elements $t(r,s)$.

(ii) $T \cap \langle t(i,j), x^m, y^n\rangle$ has basis $\{t(r,s);\ r \equiv i \bmod m,\ s \equiv j \bmod n\}$. These elements are plainly contained in the subgroup, and any element of $\langle t(i,j), x^m, y^n\rangle$ is $ux^{\alpha m}y^{\beta n}$ for integers α, β and some element u of $\langle t(r,s);\ r \equiv i \bmod m,\ s \equiv j \bmod n\rangle$, whence the result.

(iii) The subgroups $\langle t(i,j), x^m, y^n\rangle$ for an $m, n \neq 0$ and any i, j are all isomorphic. For this subgroup is a conjugate of $\langle t, x^m, y^n\rangle = \langle t\rangle * \langle x^m, y^n\rangle$ which is isomorphic to A.

(iv) Let $m, n, m_1, n_1 \neq 0$ and i, j, i_1, j_1 arbitrary. Then the map $t(i,j) \mapsto t(i_1, j_1)$, $x^m \mapsto x^{m_1}$, $y^n \mapsto y^{n_1}$ induces isomorphisms of $\langle t(i,j), x^m, y^n\rangle$ with $\langle t(i_1,j_1), x^{m_1}, y^{n_1}\rangle$ and of $T \cap \langle t(i,j), x^m, y^n\rangle$ with $T \cap \langle t(i_1,j_1), x^{m_1}, y^{n_1}\rangle$. This is immediate from (iii) and (ii), the latter isomorphism sending $t(um+i, vm+j)$ to $t(um_1+i_1, vn_1+j_1)$.

Now let M be a modular machine with quadruples (a_i, b_i, c_i, R) for $i \in I$ and (a_j, b_j, c_j, L) for $j \in J$. Let $T(M) = \langle t(\alpha,\beta);\ (\alpha,\beta) \in H_0(M)\rangle$. Let $B(M)$ be the group $\langle A, r_i, l_j;\ r_i^{-1}t(a_i, b_i)r_i = t(c_i, 0),\ r_i^{-1}x^m r_i = x^{m^2},\ r_i^{-1}y^m r_i = y,\ l_j^{-1}t(a_j, b_j)l_j = t(0, c_j),\ l_j^{-1}x^m l_j = x,\ l_j^{-1}y^m l_j = y^{m^2}$ for all $i \in I$, $j \in J\rangle$. By (iii) this is an HNN extension of A with stable letters r_i, l_j.

(v) Let (a, b, c, R) be a quadruple of M with corresponding stable letter r. Then under the isomorphism of the associated subgroups their subgroups $T(M) \cap \langle t(a,b), x^m, y^m\rangle$ and $T(M) \cap \langle t(c,0), x^{m^2}, y\rangle$ are isomorphic. For by (iv) the isomorphism sends $t(\alpha,\beta)$ to $t(\alpha_1,\beta_1)$ where $\alpha \equiv a$, $\beta \equiv b \bmod m$ and $(\alpha,\beta) \Rightarrow (\alpha_1,\beta_1)$. Then $(\alpha,\beta) \in H_0(M)$ iff $(\alpha_1,\beta_1) \in H_0(M)$. The similar result holds for L.

(vi) $A \cap \langle T(M), r_i, l_j;\ \text{all } i, j\rangle = T(M)$. This follows from (II), using (v).

(vii) $\langle T(M), r_i, l_j;\ \text{all } i, j\rangle = \langle t, r_i, l_j;\ \text{all } i, j\rangle$.
We show $t(\alpha,\beta) \in \langle t, r_i, l_j\rangle$ for $(\alpha,\beta) \in H_0(M)$ by induction on the length of the computation. If (α,β) is terminal we have $\alpha = \beta = 0$ as $(\alpha,\beta) \in H_0(M)$. Let $(\alpha,\beta) \Rightarrow (\alpha_1,\beta_1)$, and let $\alpha \equiv a$, $\beta \equiv b \bmod m$ where (a, b, c, R) is quadruple with corresponding stable letter r (similarly for L and l). Then $t(\alpha_1,\beta_1) \in \langle t, r_i, l_j\rangle$ by induction and $r^{-1}t(\alpha,\beta)r = t(\alpha_1,\beta_1)$, giving the result.

Theorem 1. *Let $G(M) = \langle B(M), k;\ kt = tk,\ kr_i = r_ik,\ kl_j = l_jk,\ \text{all } i, j\rangle$. Then $G(M)$ is finitely presented and $H_0(M)$ is Turing reducible to the word problem for $G(M)$.*

Theorem A follows immediately, since we can choose M with $H_0(M)$ unsolvable.

Proof. $G(M)$ is plainly finitely presented. Also $G(M)$ is an HNN extension of $B(M)$ with stable letter k.

By (III), $kt(\alpha, \beta) = t(\alpha, \beta)k$ iff $t(\alpha, \beta) \in \langle t, r_i, l_j \rangle$. By (vii) and (vi) this holds iff $(\alpha, \beta) \in H_0(M)$, proving the theorem.

The most natural way of showing the existence of finitely presented groups whose word problem has arbitrary r.e. Turing degree would be to reduce the word problem for $G(M)$ to $H_0(M)$. $G(M)$ is nice enough for this to be possible, using the Bokut normal form; this is done in an unpublished paper by K. A. Kalforkoti. We shall prove a stronger result in §4.

§3. Modular machines revisited

It is frequently inconvenient to have two configurations of M corresponding to one of T. Suppose q is a state such that no quintuple ends with qL. Then if a configuration with state q occurs in a computation the corresponding element of N^2 is $(um + q, vm + a)$, with the previous notation. Consequently we need only associate this pair (and not the pair $(um + a, vm + q)$) with the configuration. Also corresponding to a quintuple $qaa'q'R$ (or L) we need take only one quadruple in M, namely $(q, a, a'm + q', R$ (or L)). Similarly if no quintuple ends with qR. In particular if T is a directed-state machine, i.e. no state q occurs both in a quintuple ending with qR and in one ending with qL, then we need only associate one pair with each configuration. Any Turing machine can be replaced by a directed-state machine computing the same function.

If q_0 is a state of the Turing machine T, and there is a quintuple beginning q_0a_0 define $H_0(T)$ to be $\emptyset$; if there is no such quintuple then the configuration C_0, of a blank tape in state q_0, is terminal, and we define $H_0(T)$ as $\{C; C \rightarrow C_0\}$.

We call the state q_0 *special* if the following conditions hold: no quintuple ends with q_0R, the only quintuples ending with q_0L are q^*aaq_0L for all a and some fixed state q^*, and no quintuple ends with q^*L. As above, in this case we only take one pair corresponding to configurations in states q_0 or q^*, and only take one quadruple of M corresponding to each quintuple starting with q_0 or q^*. For convenience when regarding states as integers, we take q^* as $m - 1$. Many complications occur because 0 may stand for the letter a_0 or the state q_0; requiring q_0 to be special is one way of managing the complications.

Theorem 2. (i) *Let T be a Turing machine with special state q_0 and let M be the associated modular machine. Then $H_0(T)$ and $H_0(M)$ have the same many-one degree.*

(ii) *Let d be an r.e. many-one degree, not that of N. Then there is a modular machine M_d with $H_0(M_d)$ of degree d.*

Proof. (i) $(0,0)$ is the unique pair corresponding to C_0. Since M simulates T, if (α, β) corresponds to C we have $C \in H_0(T)$ iff $(\alpha, \beta) \in H_0(M)$. Hence $H_0(T)$ is many-one reducible to $H_0(M)$, the function showing the reduction being $C \mapsto (\alpha, \beta)$ where (α, β) is chosen to be $(um + a, vm + q)$ if there are two possibilities.

The set $P(T)$ of pairs corresponding to configurations of T is recursive. Let $P^*(T) = \{(\alpha, \beta); (\alpha, \beta) \to (\alpha', \beta')$ for some $(\alpha', \beta') \in P(T)\}$. Plainly $H_0(M) \subseteq P^*(T)$. If $P^*(T)$ is recursive we can define a total recursive function π from N^2 to configurations of T as follows. If $(\alpha, \beta) \notin P^*(T)$ let $\pi(\alpha, \beta)$ be $q_0 a_0 a_1$ (which is not in $H_0(T)$, since it is terminal if $H_0(T) \neq \emptyset$). If $(\alpha, \beta) \in P^*(T)$, let (α', β') be the first pair in the computation starting from (α, β) which lies in $P(T)$ and let $\pi(\alpha, \beta) = C'$, the configuration corresponding to (α', β'). Then $C' \in H_0(T)$ iff $(\alpha', \beta') \in H_0(M)$ iff $(\alpha, \beta) \in H_0(M)$. Hence $(\alpha, \beta) \in H_0(M)$ iff $\pi(\alpha, \beta) \in H_0(T)$, as required.

Since $P(T)$ is recursive, to show $P^*(T)$ is recursive it is enough to show the following. $(\alpha, \beta) \in P^*(T) - P(T)$ iff

$\beta \equiv b \bmod m$ where $0 \leq b \leq n$,

$\alpha = um^{i+1} + qm^i + m^i - 1$ for some q with $n < q < m$ and some $i > 0$,

and, if i is the largest integer such that α can be written as above, then $(um + q, \beta m^i) \in P(T)$.

We prove this by induction on the number of steps needed to obtain an element of $P(T)$ starting from (α, β). Let $(\alpha, \beta) \Rightarrow (\alpha', \beta')$ where (α', β') satisfies conditions similar to the above. The quadruple which applies to (α, β) cannot correspond to a quintuple ending with q^*R (recall that q^* is represented by the integer $m - 1$, and no quintuple ends with q^*L). For such a quadruple leads to a pair whose first entry is congruent mod m^2 to $am + m - 1$ where $0 \leq a \leq n$, but α' is not of this form. The only other possibility is that in (α', β') the state-symbol is not $m - 1$ (occurring in α') but is 0 (occurring in β'). This means that the quadruple applied to (α, β) was $(m - 1, b, bm, L)$ for some b with $0 \leq b \leq m$. Hence $\beta \equiv b \bmod m$ and $\alpha = \alpha' m + m - 1$, so (α, β) has the required form.

We must start the induction by showing that if $((\alpha, \beta) \Rightarrow (\alpha', \beta')) \in P(T)$ then either $(\alpha, \beta) \in P(T)$ or (α, β) has the stated form.

Suppose the quadruple that applies is $(q, a, a'm + q', L)$ (other cases are similar). If $q' \neq 0$, and C' is the configuration corresponding to (α', β') it is easy to see that $C' = W_1 q' b a' W_2$ for some letter b and tape descriptions W_1, W_2. Then $(\alpha, \beta) \in P(T)$, corresponding to the configuration $W_1 bqa W_2$. If, however, $q' = 0$, when the quadruple can only be $(m-1, a, am, L)$ for some a, in addition to this case there is another one. We may regard q' as being the letter a_0 rather than a state. Thus we may have $\alpha' = um + q_1$ for some state q_1, and $\beta' = vm$; as $(\alpha', \beta') \in P(T)$ neither u nor v can be congruent mod m to an integer strictly between n and m. In this case $\alpha = \alpha' m + m - 1$ and $\beta = v$, giving the stated form of an element in $P^*(T) - P(T)$.

(ii) $H_0(M)$ is not many-one equivalent to N for any machine M, since if $H_0(M) \neq \emptyset$ then $(m, 0) \not\in H_0(M)$ as no quadruple begins with 0, 0. Also we can find M with $H_0(M) = \emptyset$. By (i) it is enough to find a Turing machine T_d with a special state such that $H_0(T_d)$ has many-one degree d for any other d.

The work of Borger [1] and Overbeek [17] show that $H_0(T)$ can be chosen to have any r.e. many-one degree (except that of N) for a Turing machine T defined by quadruples. This is explicit in [1] for a programmed Turing machine. Replacing program lines by the appropriate quadruples we get a Turing machine by quadruples whose configurations are bijective with those of the programmed machine. The work in [17] is already expressed in terms of quadruples; Lemma 5 of [17] shows that the halting problem may have any degree. If we add to the routine given there further subroutines clearing all the arguments it is easy to see that the resulting machine T has $H_0(T)$ of the required degree.

From the Turing machine T defined by quadruples we get, as explained earlier, a Turing machine T' defined by quintuples by adding auxiliary states q_{rsa} (indeed, a simpler set of auxiliary states may be used here; the full force of this labelling is only needed for other problems). Any configuration C of T can be regarded as a configuration of T' and $C \in H_0(T)$ iff $C \in H_0(T')$. T' has other configurations corresponding to the auxiliary states. If C' is such a configuration then $C' \Rightarrow C$, where C can be regarded as a configuration of T, and $C' \in H_0(T')$ iff $C \in H_0(T')$ iff $C \in H_0(T)$. Hence $H_0(T')$ and $H_0(T)$ are many-one equivalent.

Finally we obtain T_d by adding states to T'. Let $H_0(T')$ be defined in terms of the state q'_0. Obtain T_d from T' by adding states q^*, q_0 and quintuples $q^* a a q_0 L$ for all letters a and the quintuple $q'_0 a_0 a_0 q^* R$. Plainly a configuration C of T' is in $H_0(T')$ iff it is in $H_0(T_d)$. A configuration of T_d in states q^* or q_0 is in $H_0(T_d)$ iff it consists of a blank tape. Thus $H_0(T_d)$ and $H_0(T')$ are many-one equivalent, as required.

Remarks. 1. $H_0(T)$ and $H_0(M)$ are special halting problems. By contrast to Theorem 1, the general halting problem for M can have any r.e. Turing degree greater than that of T. A full account of these results is given elsewhere [9].

2. Instead of choosing the state $n+1$ as initial state and the state 0 as halting state we may, once having ensured that the machine only halts scanning 0, make 0 into the initial and final state (so no quintuple begins 00 but there is a quintuple beginning $0i$ for $1 \leq i \leq n$). This is useful in the proof of Higman's embedding theorem, and the details are given in the paper following [0].

§4. Truth-table degrees

Let M be a modular machine. We shall associate with M a finitely generated group whose word problem has the same truth-table degree as $H_0(M)$. There are several ways of doing this; indeed the group $G(M)$ of §2 is suitable. We shall use a different group, partly as an illustration of the techniques that can be used. It is convenient to regard M as acting on Z^2 instead of on N^2; $H_0(M)$ is unaltered by this change, as one may prove by induction on the length of the computation that if $(\alpha, \beta) \in H_0(M)$ with $\alpha, \beta \in Z$, then $\alpha, \beta \geq 0$.

Let $G_1(M) = \langle t_\alpha, k_\beta$ for $\alpha, \beta \in Z$; $t_\alpha k_\beta = k_\beta t_\alpha$ for $(\alpha, \beta) \in H_0(M)\rangle$. We sometimes write t, k for t_0, k_0 and $t(\alpha), k(\beta)$ for t_α, k_β to avoid complicated subscripts.

$G_1(M)$ may be regarded as an HNN extension with stable letters $\{k_\beta\}$ of the free group with basis $\{t_\alpha\}$ or as an HNN extension with stable letters $\{t_\alpha\}$ of the free group with basis $\{k_\beta\}$. It follows immediately that $t_\alpha k_\beta = k_\beta t_\alpha$ in $G_1(M)$ (if and) only if $(\alpha, \beta) \in H_0(M)$.

Let $G_2(M) = \langle G_1(M), x, y;\ x^{-1}t_\alpha x = t_{\alpha+1},\ y^{-1}k_\beta y = k_{\beta+1}$ for all $\alpha, \beta \in Z\rangle$. Since $\{t_\alpha\}$ and $\{k_\beta\}$ are bases for free subgroups of $G_1(M)$, we see that $G_2(M)$ is an HNN extension of $G_1(M)$ with stable letters x, y.

As before let M have quadruples (a_i, b_i, c_i, R) for $i \in I$ and (a_j, b_j, c_j, L) for $j \in J$. We obtain $G_3(M)$ by adding new generators $r_i (i \in I)$ and $l_j (j \in J)$ to $G_2(M)$ and corresponding relations $r_i^{-1}x^m r_i = x^{m^2}$, $r_i^{-1}y^m r_i = y$, $r_i^{-1}t_\alpha r_i = t_{\alpha_1}$, $r_i^{-1}k_\beta r_i = k_{\beta_1}$ for all pairs (α, β) to which (a_i, b_i, c_i, R) applies and yields (α_1, β_1) (more simply we have

$r_i^{-1}t(um+a_i)r_i = t(um^2+c_i)$, $r_i^{-1}k(vm+b_i)r_i = t(v)$) and the similar relations for l_j, interchanging x and y. We shall write G_1, G_2, G_3 instead of $G_1(M)$, $G_2(M)$, $G_3(M)$. We shall prove shortly that G_3 is an HNN extension of G_2.

From the two ways of regarding G_1 as an HNN extension of a free group we obtain both t_α-pinches and k_β-pinches. As G_2 is an HNN extension of G_1 we also have x- and y-pinches. Notice that if a word in the generators of G_2 has an x-pinch this means that it contains a subword $x^{-\varepsilon}ux^{\varepsilon}$ where $\varepsilon = \pm 1$ and u is a word in $\{t_\alpha, k_\beta\}$ which equals in G_1 a word in $\{t_\alpha\}$; this does not mean that u freely equals a word in $\{t_\alpha\}$.

(i) If a word in the generators of G_2 has an x-pinch then either it has an x-pinch of the form $x^{-\varepsilon}ux^{\varepsilon}$ with $\varepsilon = \pm 1$ where u is a word in $\{t_\alpha\}$ or it has a k_β-pinch for some β (and similarly for y).

For, as already remarked, it must have a subword $x^{-\varepsilon}ux^{\varepsilon}$ where u is a word in $\{t_\alpha, k_\beta\}$ which equals in G_1 a word v in $\{t_\alpha\}$. Either uv^{-1} freely equals 1 or uv^{-1} has a k_β-pinch for some β in which case so does u (as no k_β occurs in v).

(ii) G_3 is an HNN extension of G_2. To check the isomorphism conditions we have four cases to consider, one of which is the following (the others are similar).

Let W be a word in the symbols X, Y, T_p, K_q. Let (a, b, c, R) be a quadruple of M. If $W(x^m, y^m, t(pm+a), k(qm+b)) = 1$ in G_2 then $W(x^{m^2}, y, t(pm^2+c), k(q)) = 1$ in G_2.

We use induction on the length of W, which we may assume freely reduced. If W is non-trivial, $W(x^m, y^m, t(pm+a), k(qm+b))$ must contain a pinch. By (i) W freely equals either $W_1X^{-\varepsilon}UX^{\varepsilon}W_2$ where U is a word in $\{T_p\}$ and $\varepsilon = \pm 1$ or W freely equals $W_1K_q^{-\varepsilon}UK_qW_2$ where U is a word in those T_p for which $(pm+a, qm+b) \in H_0(M)$ (or a similar case with the roles of X and Y and of T_p and K_q interchanged). In the first case let $W' = W_1U'W_2$ where U' is obtained from U by replacing each T_p by $T_{p+\varepsilon}$; in the second case let $W' = W_1UW_2$. In both cases we find that $W(x^m, y^m, t(pm+a), k(qm+b)) = W'(x^m, y^m, t(pm+a), k(qm+b))$ and that $W(x^{m^2}, y, t(pm^2+c), k(q)) = W'(x^{m^2}, y, t(pm^2+c), k(q))$, so the result follows by induction.

The process of repeated HNN extension is called a *Britton tower.*

(iii) G_3 is finitely presented.

It is finitely generated, with generators t, k, x, y, r_i, l_j, since $t_\alpha = x^{-\alpha}tx^{\alpha}$ and $k_\beta = y^{-\beta}ky^{\beta}$. The infinitely many relations involving r_i (and similarly l_j) are consequences of four of them, namely $r_i^{-1}x^mr_i = x^{m^2}$, $r_i^{-1}y^mr_i = y$, $r_i^{-1}x^{-a_i}tx^{a_i}r_i = x^{-c_i}tx^{c_i}$, $r_i^{-1}y^{-b_i}ky^{b_i}r_i = k$. The remaining relations include $tk = kt$. However they are all consequences of this relation and the relations involving r_i and l_j. This follows by induction on the number of steps in the computation from (α, β) to $(0,0)$ since if $(\alpha, \beta) \Rightarrow (\alpha_1, \beta_1)$ using the quadruple (a_i, b_i, c_i, R) then the relations involving r_i show that r_i conjugates the commutator of $x^{-\alpha}tx^{\alpha}$ and $y^{-\beta}ky^{\beta}$ into the commutator of $x^{-\alpha_1}tx^{\alpha_1}$ and $y^{-\beta_1}ky^{\beta_1}$. Hence the former is trivial if the latter is.

(From this presentation we find a much easier expression for G_3 as a Britton tower, $G_3 \supseteq \langle t, x, y, r_i, l_j \rangle \supseteq \langle t, x, y \rangle$, the latter being free. This is easily seen to be a Britton tower, G_3 being obviously finitely presented, and the construction being analogous to that of §2. The construction given, however, makes questions of truth-table degrees easier to look at.)

Let W be a word in the generators of G_3. By a *reduction* of W we mean one of the following:

(I) Free reduction; also replacing $x^p . x^q$ by x^{p+q} if $p + q \neq 0$ and deleting $x^p . x^{-p}$; also similar reductions for y.

(II) If W freely equals $Ux^p t_\alpha^\varepsilon V$ where U does not end in x^θ, replacing W by $Ut_{\alpha-p}^\varepsilon x^p V$, and similarly for y and k_β.

(III) If W freely equals $Ur^{-1}W_0 rV$ where r is a stable letter corresponding to (a, b, c, R) and W_0 *freely* equals a word in x^m, y^m, $t(pm + a)$, $k(qm + b)$ (for all $p, q \in Z$), replacing W by UW_1V where W_1 is obtained from W_0 by replacing $x^m, y^m, t(pm + a), k(qm + b)$ by $x^{m^2}, y, t(pm^2 + c)$, $k(q)$; also similar replacements corresponding to r^{-1}, l and l^{-1}.

(IV) Replacing $Uk_\beta^\varepsilon t_\alpha^\theta V$ by $Ut_\alpha^\theta k_\beta^\varepsilon V$ or vice versa for *all* integers α, β. A reduction is called *correct* if it is of types (I), (II) or (III) or if it is of type (IV) with $(\alpha, \beta) \in H_0(M)$. A *reduction sequence* starting from W is a sequence $W = W_1, W_2, \ldots, W_n$ of distinct words such that W_{p+1} is a reduction of W_p for all p; a *correct reduction sequence* is one in which all reductions are correct.

Define the *weight* of W to be the sum of the following:
the number of occurrences of t_α, k_β, r_i, l_j and their inverses,
the number of occurrences of powers of x and y, and
the number of times a power of x precedes (not necessarily immediately) some t_α^ε (for $\varepsilon = \pm 1$) and similarly for y and k_β.

Plainly, reductions of types (I), (II), and (III) reduce the weight while type (IV) reductions preserve it. Since there is a bound on the number of type (IV) reductions which can be applied consecutively to W without getting a repetition, we see that only finitely many reduction sequences can start with W (indeed, there is a recursive function of W bounding their number).

Because we apply type (III) reductions only when W_0 freely equals a word in the relevant generators, and apply type (IV) reductions for all α, β, it is clear that the finite set $\{W'; W'$ is a reduction of $W\}$ depends recursively on W. The finite set $\{W'; W'$ occurs in a reduction sequence starting from $W\}$ will also depend recursively on W, as will $\{(\alpha, \beta) \in Z^2$; a type (IV) reduction involving t_α, k_β occurs in some reduction sequence starting from $W\}$. This set will be used to construct a truth-table depending recursively on W.

(iv) If a word in the generators of G_3 has a pinch it has a correct reduction sequence ending in a word of less weight. Such a sequence will be called a *weight-reducing* sequence or w.-r. sequence.

By (i) if there is an x- or y-pinch either a type (II) reduction applies or there is a t_α- or k_β-pinch. Suppose there is a k_β-pinch for some β_0 (the other case is similar). Then there is a subword $k_{\beta_0}^{-\varepsilon}Uk_{\beta_0}^{\varepsilon}$ where U is a word in those t_α with $(\alpha, \beta_0) \in H_0(M)$. Type (IV) correct reductions replace this subword by $Uk_{\beta_0}^{-\varepsilon}k_{\beta_0}^{\varepsilon}$ to which a type (I) reduction applies.

Let r be a stable letter corresponding to (a, b, c, R). Suppose the pinch is the subword $r^{-1}Wr$ (the other cases being similar). Then W equals in G_2 a word in x^m, y^m, t_α, k_β for $\alpha \equiv a \bmod m$, $\beta \equiv b \bmod m$. If W freely equals such a word we may apply a type (III) reduction to the original word, while the original word has a w.-r. sequence if W has. We use induction on the length of W to show that if W equals such a word and has no w.-r. sequence then it freely equals such a word. Suppose W has no w.-r. sequence. Then W has no pinch since it only involves x, y, t_α, k_β, and the result has been proved for such words. Let W equal W_1 in G_2, where W_1 is a word in $x^m, y^m, t_\alpha, k_\beta$ for $\alpha \equiv a$, $\beta \equiv b \bmod m$. We may assume W_1 has no pinch, since pinching out produces a shorter element in the same subgroup.

Let U and U_1 be the largest final segments of W and W_1 involving only t_α and k_β. Suppose there is cancellation in U_1U^{-1}. Then, for instance, $W = W't_{\alpha_0}$ where $\alpha_0 \equiv a \bmod m$ and W' is shorter than W. Then W' has no w.-r. sequence since W has none, and $W' = W_1t_{\alpha_0}^{-1}$. Hence, inductively, W' freely equals a word in $x^m, y^m, t_\alpha, k_\beta$ ($\alpha \equiv a$, $\beta \equiv b$). Then W will also freely equal such a word.

Suppose there is a k_β-pinch in U_1U^{-1} but no cancellation. Since U and U_1 have no pinches, W and W_1 must freely equal $W'k_\beta^{\varepsilon}V$ and $W_1'k_\beta^{\varepsilon}V_1$ where V, V_1 are words in $\{t_\alpha\}$ and $\beta \equiv b$ (since k_β occurs in W_1). The pinch now tells us correct type (IV) reductions take us from W to $W'Vk_\beta^{\varepsilon}$. This must be freely reduced, since it has no w.-r. sequence as W has none (and free reduction reduces weight). But then $W'V$ has no w.-r. sequence, equals in G_2 a word of the required form, and is shorter than W. Hence it freely equals such a word (by induction on length). Since $W'V$ is freely reduced and V involves only

$\{t_\alpha\}$, both W' and V, and hence W itself, must be as required. Similar aruments apply to a t_α-pinch.

As $W_1W^{-1} = 1$ in G_2 it must have a pinch. By (i) the only possibility left is that W and W_1 freely equal $W'x^qU$ and $W_1'x^{pm}U_1$ where U, U_1 are words in $\{t_\alpha\}$ (or similarly for y and k_β). U must be empty, else W has a type (II) reduction; we may also assume U_1 empty since a type (II) reduction applied to W_1 gives a word of the same form. If $q = pm$, as before W', and hence W, is as required. If $q \neq pm$ then $W_1'x^{pm-q}W^{-1}$ must have a pinch which can only be a pinch of a term $x^{\pm 1}$ in x^{pm-q} with a similar term in W_1' or W^{-1}. In the first case (by (i) as W_1 has no pinches) a further type (II) reduction could have been made in W_1; we may choose W_1 so that this is impossible. In the second case, for the same reason, a type (II) reduction could be made in W, contrary to hypothesis.

Lemma 3. *Let W be a word in the generators of G_3. If $W = 1$ in G_3 there is a correct reduction sequence starting at W and ending at* 1. *Conversely, if there is such a sequence then $W = 1$ in G_3.*

Proof. Each correct reduction is a consequence of the defining relations so $W = 1$ if there is such a sequence.

If $W = 1$ in G_3 and is non-trivial it must have a pinch. By (iv) there is a correct reduction sequence from W to W_1 where W_1 has smaller weight than W. This sequence shows that $W_1 = W$ in G_3, and the lemma follows by induction on weight.

The next lemma is used only for the Higman embedding theorem [0] but its proof fits in naturally here.

Lemma 4. *Let S be a subset of Z. If a word W equals in G_3 a word in $\langle k, t_\alpha(\alpha \in S)\rangle$ there is a correct reduction sequence from W to W_1 where W_1 freely equals a word in $\langle k, t_\alpha(\alpha \in S)\rangle$.*

Proof. It is enough to show that if W does not freely equal such a word then it has a w.-r. sequence. For if it has a w.-r. sequence ending in W' then $W' = W$ in G_3 and by induction on the weight there is a correct reduction sequence from W' to such a W_1, which gives a correct reduction sequence from W to W_1.

If W involves x, y, r_i, or l_j it must have a pinch since it equals an element of G_1. By (iv) it then has a w.-r. sequence.

Suppose W is a word in $\langle t_\alpha, k_\beta$ (all $\alpha, \beta)\rangle$ which equals in G_1 a word W_1 in $\langle k, t_\alpha(\alpha \in S)\rangle$. If W has a pinch it has a w.-r. sequence so we may assume it has no pinch. We may also assume that W_1 has no pinch, since pinching out gives an element of the same subgroup. Since $W_1 W^{-1} = 1$ in G_1 it must contain a cancellation or a pinch. We now proceed as in (iv).

Theorem B is an immediate consequence of Theorem 2 and Theorem 5 below.

Theorem 5. *$G_3(M)$ is a finitely presented group whose word problem has the same unbounded truth-table degree as $H_0(M)$.*

Proof. We have already shown that $G_3(M)$ is finitely presented.

$H_0(M)$ is one-one reducible to the word problem for $G_3(M)$ since $(\alpha, \beta) \in H_0(M)$ iff $x^{-\alpha} t x^{\alpha}$ and $y^{-\beta} k y^{\beta}$ commute in G_3.

We show how the word problem for G_3 is truth-table reducible to $H_0(M)$. Let W be a word in t, k, x, y, r_i, l_j. Our truth-table will have question columns corresponding to all pairs (α, β) occurring in type (IV) reductions in some reduction sequence starting at W. A line in the answer column will be "Yes" iff there is a reduction sequence ending in 1 all of whose relevant questions are answered by "Yes". This is a recursive construction, by the remarks on reduction sequences.

This construction gives a "Yes" somewhere in the answer column iff there is a correct reduction sequence starting at W and ending at 1. By Lemma 3 this holds iff $W = 1$ in G_3. This proves Theorem 5.

The crucial point that leads to truth-table reducibility rather than Turing reducibility is that we make reductions in a general situation, and only decide after all reductions are made whether or not they have been made correctly. If we had partial recursive functions which allowed us to make correct reductions, but (for instance) required us to determine if $(\alpha, \beta) \in H_0(M)$ or not before determining if $k_\beta^{-1} t_\alpha k_\beta$ could be replaced by t_α the procedure would only give Turing reducibility.

References

[1] E. Börger, A new general approach to the theory of the many-one equivalence of decision problems for algorithmic systems, Z. Math. Logik Grundlagen Math. (to appear).

[2] W.W. Boone, The word problem, Annals of Math. 70 (1959) 207–265.

[3] W. W. Boone, Word problems and recursively enumerable degree of unsolvability. A sequel on finitely presented groups, Annals of Math. 84 (1966) 49–84.

[4] W.W. Boone, Word problems and recursively enumerable degrees of unsolvability. An emendation, Annals of Math. 94 (1971) 389–391.
[5] J.L. Britton, The word problem, Annals of Math. 77 (1963) 16–32.
[6] C.R.J. Clapham, Finitely presented groups with word problems of arbitrary degrees of unsolvability, Proc. London Math. Soc. (3) 14 (1964) 633–676.
[7] D.E. Cohen, Residual finiteness and Britton's Lemma, J. London Math. Soc. (2) 16 (1977) 232–234.
[8] D.E. Cohen, Combinatorial group theory; a topological approach, Queen Mary College Lecture Notes, 1978.
[9] D.E. Cohen, Degree problems for modular machines (to appear).
[10] D.J. Collins, Truth-table degrees and the Boone groups, Annals of Math. 94 (1971) 392–396.
[11] A.A. Fridman, Degrees of unsolvability of identity in finitely presented groups, Soviet Math. 3 (1962) 1733–1737.
[12] A.A. Fridman, Degrees of unsolvability of the word problem for finitely defined groups (Izdatel'stvo Nauka, Moscow, 1967).
[13] G. Higman, Subgroups of finitely presented groups, Proc. Roy. Soc. A 262 (1961) 455–475.
[14] R. Mckenzie and R. J. Thompson, An elementary construction of unsolvable word problems in group theory, in Word Problems, Studies in Logic and the Foundations of Mathematics (North-Holland Publishing Co., Amsterdam, 1973).
[15] M.L. Minsky, Recursive unsolvability of Post' problem of 'Tag' and other topics in the theory of Turing machines, Annals of Math. 74 (1961) 437–455.
[16] P.S. Novikov, On the algorithmic unsolvability of the word problem in groups, Trudy Mat. Inst. Steklov 44 (1955).
[17] R. Overbeek, The representation of many-one degrees by decision problems of Turing machines, Proc. London Math. Soc. (3) 26 (1973) 167–183.
[18] J.C. Shepherdson and H.E. Sturgis, Computability of recursive functions, J. Ass. Computing Machinery 10 (1963) 217–256.

And also the immediately following paper in this volume. O.S. Aanderaa and D.E. Cohen, Modular machines and the Higman–Clapham–Valiev embedding theorem, in Word Problems II: The Oxford Book, Studies in Logic and the Foundations of Mathematics (North-Holland Publishing Co., Amsterdam, 1979).

S.I. Adian, W.W. Boone, G. Higman, eds., Word Problems II

MODULAR MACHINES AND THE HIGMAN–CLAPHAM–VALIEV EMBEDDING THEOREM

Stål AANDERAA and Daniel E. COHEN
University of Oslo and Queen Mary College, London

In this paper we use the modular machines introduced in [2] to give simple proofs of the following theorems.

Theorem A (Higman [5]). *Any finitely generated recursively presented group can be embedded in a finitely presented group.*

Theorem B (Valiev [10]). *Let C be a finitely generated recursively presented group. Then there is a finitely presented group containing C whose word problem has the same unbounded truth-table degree as the word problem for C.*

Since Higman's original proof of Theorem A, several other proofs have appeared [1, 3, 4, 6, 9]. Our proof is closest in spirit to that of Aanderaa [1]. As in [2], the use of modular machines instead of Turing machines greatly simplifies the proof.

Higman also showed (which is not difficult) that any finitely generated subgroup of a finitely presented group is recursively presented. He also observed that the existence of a finitely presented group with unsolvable word problem follows, by Theorem A, from the existence of a recursively presented group with unsolvable word problem, and that such a group is easy to find.

Theorem B was first proved by Valiev [10]. A weaker result, with Turing degree replacing truth-table degree, was proved earlier by Clapham [4].

Readers interested only in Theorem A should omit §1. They may omit §2 if they give their own proof of the following fact, shown in the middle of §2. *For any r.e. set S of words in the alphabet* $\{a_1, \ldots, a_n\}$ *there is a Turing machine T on* $a_0, a_1, \ldots, a_n$ *such that if W is not empty* $W \in S$ *iff the configuration with tape description W in state* q_0 *scanning the last square of W is in* $H_0(T)$. (Note the unusual features: q_0 is both the initial and the final state, and the last square of W is scanned.) The proof of Theorem A is contained in parts (i)–(iv) of §3.

§1. Some reduction lemmas

Let X be a (finite or countable) set of generators of a group H, and π the natural map from the free group $F = F(X)$ to H. A map f from H to H is called *recursive* if there is a recursive $\varphi : F \to F$ with $\pi\varphi = f\pi$. If X is infinite, changing the ordering of X could change recursiveness; in the applications there will always be a natural ordering of X. If X is finite, any homomorphism φ from F to F is recursive; if X is infinite, φ is recursive iff its restriction to X is recursive.

Lemma 1. *Let A be a subgroup of H, $f : H \to A$ a recursive map which is the identity on A. Then the membership problem for A is many-one reducible to the word problem for H.*

Proof. Take recursive $\varphi : F \to F$ with $\pi\varphi = f\pi$. Let $w \in F$. If $\pi w \in A$, $\pi\varphi w = f\pi w = \pi w$, while if $\pi w = \pi\varphi w$ we have $\pi w \in fH \subseteq A$. Hence $\pi w \in A$ iff $\pi\ (w^{-1}\varphi w) = 1$, which reduces the membership problem for A to the word problem for H.

Lemma 2. *Let A_i $(i = \pm 1, \ldots, \pm n)$ be subgroups of H, $f_i : H \to A_{-i}$ recursive maps which restrict to isomorphisms $A_i \to A_{-i}$ (the restrictions of f_i and f_{-i} being inverse). Let H^* be the HNN extension $\langle H, p_i;\ p_i^{-1}A_ip_i = A_{-i},\ i = 1, \ldots, n\rangle$. Then the word problem for H^* is truth-table reducible to the join of the word problem for H and the membership problems for A_i, $i = \pm 1, \ldots, \pm n$.*

Proof. Denote p_i^{-1} by p_{-i}. Let $\varphi_i : F \to F$ be maps with $\pi\varphi_i = f_i\pi$. (Note that f_i and φ_i need not be homomorphisms.) We use the methods of §3 of [2].

Let w be a word in X and the p_i $(i = \pm 1, \ldots)$. A *reduction* of w is one of the following:

(I) delete a subword $p_{-i}p_i$;

(II) delete a subword $p_{-i}up_i$, where $u \in F$; delete the whole of w if $w \in F$;

(III) replace a subword $p_{-i}up_i$ by φ_iu, where $u \in F$.

A reduction is *correct* if it is of type (I), of type (II) with the deleted subword equalling 1 in H, or of type (III) with $\pi u \in A_i$. A (*correct*) *reduction sequence* is a sequence $w_1, w_2, \ldots, w_k$ where w_{j+1} comes fom w_j by a (correct) reduction, $j = 1, \ldots, k-1$. Plainly there is a bound to the length of a reduction sequence starting at w, and there are only finitely many reduction sequences starting at w. We associate a truth-table recursively with w as follows. There will be a question column "$\pi u = 1$?" to each (sub)word u which is deleted in a type (II) reduction in a reduction sequence starting from w; there will be a question column "$\pi u \in A_i$?" for each u occurring in a type (III) reduction in some reduction sequence starting with w. In the answer column a line receives the answer "Yes" if the questions answered by "Yes" on this line include all the questions in some reduction sequence ending in 1. This means that there is a "Yes" in the answer column iff there is a correct reduction sequence from w to 1.

If there is such a correct reduction sequence then $w = 1$ in H^*, since each correct reduction corresponds to a relation of H^*. If $w = 1$ in H^* either $w \in F$ and $\pi w = 1$ or w contains a subword $p_{-i}p_i$ or w contains a pinch $p_{-i}up_i$ with $u \in F$ and $\pi u \in A_i$. In each case a correct reduction can be performed, yielding a word w' with w' equalling 1 in H^* and w' either trivial or with fewer p-symbols than w. Inductively, w' and hence w itself, has a correct reduction sequence ending in 1. Hence $w = 1$ iff the truth-table for w has a "Yes" in the answer column, giving the result.

Note that Lemmas 1 and 2 may be generalised slightly. In Lemma 1 we only require a recursive map φ with $\pi\varphi w \in A$ for all w and $\pi\varphi w = \pi w$ if $\pi w \in A$; then $\pi\varphi$ is a map from F to A which need not induce a map from H to A. In Lemma 2 we may take maps φ_i such that $\pi\varphi_i F \subseteq A_{-i}$ and φ_i induces the isomorphism from A_i to A_{-i} (but need not induce a map from H to A_{-i}).

Lemma 3. *Let A_i ($i = \pm 1, \ldots, \pm n$) be subgroups of H. Let $\varphi_i : F \to F$ be partial recursive functions such that φ_i induces an isomorphism from A_i to A_{-i} (and φ_{-i} induces the inverse isomorphism). Let θ_i be a recursive map from F to finite subsets of $\pi^{-1}A_i$ such that $\pi w \in \pi\theta_i w$ if $\pi w \in A_i$, and $\theta_i F \subseteq \operatorname{dom}\varphi_i$. Then the word problems for H and $H^* = \langle H, p_i;\ p_i^{-1}A_ip_i = A_{-i},\ i = 1, \ldots, n\rangle$ are truth-table equivalent.*

Proof. The proof combines and slightly generalises Lemmas 1 and 2.

Replace in the proof of Lemma 2 the reductions of type (III) by reductions of type (III′): replace $p_{-i}up_i$ by $\varphi_i v$ for some $v \in \theta_i u$. As θ_i is recursive and $\varphi_i v$ is defined for $v \in \theta_i u$ it is clear that $\{w';\ w'$ is a reduction of $w\}$ is a finite set depending recursively on w. The set of all reduction sequences starting from w is finite and depends recursively on w as do the finite sets $\{u;\ u$ is used in some reduction of type (II) in a reduction sequence starting from $w\}$ and (u, v); the pair (u, v) is used in a type (III′) reduction in a sequence starting from

w. A reduction of type (III′) is *correct* if $\pi v = \pi u$. Build a truth-table as before with columns corresponding to "$\pi u = 1$?" for u in a type (II) reduction in some sequence starting from w and "$\pi(uv^{-1}) = 1$?" for pairs (u, v) in such a type (III′) reduction. As before this provides a truth-table reduction of the word problem for H^* to the word problem for H. The word problem for H is trivially one-one reducible to that for H^*.

In Lemma 2 the existence of partial recursive isomorphisms from A_i to A_{-i} would enable us to perform pinches and so Turing reduce the word problem for H^* to the join of the word problems for H and the membership problems for $A_{\pm i}$ in H. The crucial feature that gives truth-table reducibility is that we have functions from H to A_{-i}. These enable us to perform reductions first and check correctness later.

Many similar results can be proved, in particular versions of Lemmas 2 and 3 for amalgamated free products. We will simply prove some results on solvable problems.

Lemma 4. *Let H, A_i and H^* be as before. Suppose the isomorphisms from A_i to A_{-i} are partial recursive. If the membership problems for $A_{\pm i}$ in H are solvable, then the membership problem for H in H^* is solvable. If, in addition, the word problem for H is solvable, so is the word problem for H^*.*

Remark. Frequently we are given partial recursive maps from Y_i to A_{-i}, which will always extend to partial recursive maps from $\langle Y_i \rangle$ to A_{-i}. If $\pi\langle Y_i \rangle = A_i$, and $\ker \pi$ is r.e. (i.e. H is recursively presented) this defines a partial recursive map from $\pi^{-1}A_i$ to A_{-i}, which is what we need.

Proof. Any element of H^* can be written as the product of elements of H and the stable letters (and their inverses). We can see if there is a subword $p_{-i}up_i$. If so, as the membership problem for A_i is solvable we can determine whether or not $u \in A_i$. If $u \in A_i$ we can replace $p_{-i}up_i$ by the corresponding element of A_{-i} (as the isomorphisms are partial recursive). This enables us to obtain recursively a reduced form for any element of H^*. An element of H^* equals 1 in H^* iff its reduced form lies in H and equals 1 in H.

Lemma 5. *Let A_1, A_2 be subgroups of H_1, H_2. Suppose there is an isomorphism from A_1 to A_2 which is partial recursive with partial recursive inverse. Let the membership problems for A_1 in H_1 and for A_2*

in H_2 be solvable. Let K_1 be a subgroup of H_1 with $A_1 \subseteq K_1$ and the membership problem for K_1 in H_1 solvable. Then the membership problems for H_1, K_1, and $\langle K_1, H_2 \rangle$ in the amalgamated free product $\langle H_1, H_2: A_1 = A_2 \rangle$ is solvable.

Proof. As in Lemma 4 we recursively find reduced forms for elements of the amalgamated free product. An element lies in H_1 iff its reduced form lies in H_1 (or in A_2). Because $K_1 \supseteq A_1$ an element lies in $\langle K_1, H_2 \rangle$ iff its reduced form consists of elements alternately from K_1 and H_2.

§2. Turing machines

Let S be an r.e. subset of N. It is proved by Overbeek (Lemma 5 of [7]) that there is a Turing machine (defined by quadruples) on the alphabet $\{0, 1\}$ whose halting problem is many-one equivalent to S. A glance at the construction shows that the machine halts on $q_1 01^r$ iff $r \in S$; also there is a halting state (i.e. a configuration is terminal iff its state is the specified one). It is easy to check that if $S \neq N$ and we add further subroutines clearing all registers and a final subroutine moving to the next blank square to the right (this latter is convenient but not necessary) we obtain a machine T_1 with halting state q_0 such that $H_0(T_1)$ (the problem of halting with a blank tape) has many-one degree that of S, while $r \in S$ iff $q_1 01^r \in H_0(T_1)$ (and T_1 does not halt on $q_1 01^r$ if $r \notin S$). The final subroutine (move to next blank right) ensures that there is only one quadruple involving q_0, which is $q00q_0$ for some state q.

Routine technical arguments (e.g. [8]) extend this result to an arbitrary alphabet. I.e., if S is a proper r.e. set of word in the alphabet $\{a_1, \ldots, a_n\}$ then there is a Turing machine T_1 on the alphabet $\{a_0, a_1, \ldots, a_n\}$ with the following properties: T_1 has a halting state q_0; only one quadruple involves q_0 and this is $qa_0a_0q_0$ for some state q; $H_0(T_1)$ is many-one equivalent to S; if T_1 halts on $q_1 a_0 W$ (where W is a word in $a_1, \ldots, a_n$) then $q_1 a_0 W \in H_0(T_1)$, and $q_1 a_0 W \in H_0(T_1)$ iff $W \in S$. For more details look at the discussion in [8] of machines on an arbitrary alphabet and translate the subroutines in Overbeek's machine (and his construction of machines computing total recursive functions) accordingly.

We wish to consider Turing machines defined by quintuples. These are obtained by adding auxiliary states corresponding to non-moving quadruples. We shall also need another modification.

Let T_1 be as above. Let T be defined by adding auxiliary states q_s^*

for each state q_s and two further states q', q''. The quintuples consist of $q_r a_i a_i q_s R$ (or L) corresponding to the quadruple $q_r a_i q_s R$ (or L), $q_r a_i a_j q^*_s R$ corresponding to $q_r a_i a_j q_s$, and for all s and i quadruples $q^*_s a_i a_i q_s L$, and finally quintuples $q_0 a_i a_i q' L$ for $i \neq 0$, $q' a_i a_i q' L$ for $i \neq 0$, $q' a_0 a_0 q'' R$ and $q'' a_i a_i q_1 L$ for all i. Note that q_0 is *special* in the sense of Theorem 2 of [2] and the remarks preceding it.

If T is started in state q_0 scanning the last square of W, and W is non-empty (if W is empty the tape is blank and the configuration is terminal) it will reach the configuration $q_1 a_0 W$; from this it will not halt if $W \notin S$ but will halt on a blank tape if $W \in S$.

A configuration in state q_r (for $r \neq 0$) will lie in $H_0(T)$ iff it is in $H_0(T_1)$ (note that T_1 only halts on a non-blank square if the configuration we start with is in state q_0). If the configuration C is in state q^*_s then $C \Rightarrow C_1$ with C_1 in state q_s; for $s \neq 0$ we have $C \in H_0(T)$ iff $C_1 \in H_0(T_1)$ (again because T_1 halts on blank squares the computation for T does not continue after it has simulated the computation for T_1). For configurations with state q_0 scanning a blank square or in state q^*_0 immediately to the right of a blank we can tell whether or not they are in $H_0(T)$. For any other configuration C we can recursively find a configuration C_1 with $C \rightarrow C_1$ and C_1 in state q_1 (all configurations between C and C_1 being in states q_0, q' or q''). Then $C \in H_0(T)$ iff $C_1 \in H_0(T_1)$. These remarks show that $H_0(T)$ is many-one equivalent to $H_0(T_1)$.

So we have found to any proper r.e. set S in the alphabet $a_1, \ldots, a_n$ a Turing machine T defined by quintuples such that (i) $H_0(T)$ is many-one equivalent to S and (ii) $W \in H_0(T)$ iff the configuration in state q_0 scanning the last square of W lies in $H_0(T)$ (the holding also for W empty). This machine is used in the next section, S being the set of relators of a recursively presented group.

§3. The embedding theorems

Let C be a non-trivial finitely generated recursively presented group. Let C be generated by $c_1, \ldots, c_n$. We regard a word in the letters $c_1^{\pm 1}, \ldots, c_n^{\pm 1}$ as a positive word in the letters $c_1, \ldots, c_{2n}$, where c_{n+i} denotes c_i^{-1}. Let $\mathcal{W}$ be the r.e. set of all relators of c. By §2 we may take a Turing machine T whose alphabet is $c_1, \ldots, c_{2n}$ and c_0 (blank) such that $H_0(T)$ is unbounded truth-table equivalent to $\mathcal{W}$ and such that a word w is in $\mathcal{W}$ iff the configuration with tape description w in state q_0 scanning the last square of w lies in $H_0(T)$ (note that $w = 1$ corresponds to the blank tape). As remarked in the introduction for the proof of Theorem A only the second of these two properties is needed, and readers may supply the proof of this property themselves if they do not wish to read §2.

Let M be the modular machine associated with T. Each word w defines an integer α, by regarding w as the representation in m-ary notation of α with $c_1, \ldots, c_{2n}$ being taken as the integers $1, \ldots, 2n$. The set I of integers represented by a word is recursive. For $\alpha \in I$ let w_α denote the corresponding word. In particular $w_0 = 1$ and, for $1 \leq i \leq 2n$, we have $w_i = c_i$ and $w_{\alpha m+i} = w_\alpha c_i$. If $\alpha \in I$ then $(\alpha, 0) \in H_0(M)$ iff $w_\alpha \in \mathcal{W}$ by the construction of M from T.

It was shown in §4 of [2] that the group $G_3 = G_3(M)$ constructed there is finitely presented.

We never refer to the quadruples of M explicitly so we can use letters a, b, c for generators of groups without fear of confusion. The notation used is chosen to be as close as is convenient to the notation in the proof of Theorem A by Aanderaa [1].

Let $H_3 = C^*G_3$. Let $H_4 = \langle H_3, b_i\ (i = 1, \ldots, n);\ b_i^{-1}c_jb_i = c_j\ (i, j = 1, \ldots, n),\ b_i^{-1}kb_i = kc_i^{-1}\ (i = 1, \ldots, n)\rangle$. Observe that if b_{n+i} denotes b_i^{-1} then we have $b_i^{-1}c_jb_i = c_j$ and $b_i^{-1}kb_i = kc_i^{-1}$ for $i, j = 1, \ldots, 2n$.

(i) H_4 is an HNN extension of H_3.

For the subgroups associated with b_i are both $C^*\langle k\rangle$, and the relevant map is a homomorphism which plainly has an inverse.

Let $H_5 = \langle H_4, d;\ d^{-1}kd = k\rangle$ and let $H_6 = \langle H_5, p;\ p^{-1}kp = k,\ p^{-1}t_\alpha p = t_\alpha w_\alpha(b)d$ for all $\alpha \in I\rangle$. Here if w is a word in the c_i, $w(b)$ denotes the corresponding word in the b_i; other similar notations will be used.

(ii) H_5 is (obviously) an HNN extension of H_4. Also H_6 is an HNN extension of H_5.

We must show that the subgroups $\langle t_\alpha, k\ (\alpha \in I)\rangle$ and $\langle t_\alpha w_\alpha(b)d, k\ (\alpha \in I)\rangle$ are isomorphic, with the named generators corresponding. The latter plainly maps to the former by the homomorphism of H_5 which maps G_3 identically and kills all the other generators.

From the construction of G_3 as a Britton tower we know that the former has defining relations $t_\alpha k = kt_\alpha$ for all α such that $\alpha \in I$ and $(\alpha, 0) \in H_0(M)$. Thus we have a homomorphism of the former to the latter provided $t_\alpha w_\alpha(b)dk = kt_\alpha w_\alpha(b)d$ for all such α. If $\alpha \in I$ we have $w_\alpha(b)dk = kw_\alpha(bc)d$ since $k^{-1}b_ik = b_ic_i$. Also $w_\alpha(bc) = w_\alpha(b)w_\alpha(c)$ since $b_ic_j = c_jb_i$ for all i, j. Since $w_\alpha(c) = 1$ iff $w_\alpha \in \mathcal{W}$ iff $(\alpha, 0) \in H_0(M)$ the required relations hold.

The last group needed is $H_7 = \langle H_6, a_1, \ldots, a_{2n};\ a_i^{-1}ta_i = t_i,\ a_i^{-1}xa_i =$

x^m, $a_i^{-1}pa_i = p$, $a_i^{-1}da_i = b_id$, $a_i^{-1}b_ja_i = b_j$ $(i = 1, \ldots, 2n;\ j = 1, \ldots, n)\rangle$. Notice that $a_i^{-1}b_ja_i = b_j$ will also hold for $j = n + 1, \ldots, 2n$.

(iii) H_7 is an HNN extension of H_6.

The corresponding associated subgroups which we must prove isomorphic are (for given i) $K = \langle t, x, b_j, d, p\ (j = 1, \ldots, n)\rangle$ and $L = \langle t_i, x^m, b_j, b_id, p\rangle$.

Recall that if B is a subgroup of a group A, and A^* is any HNN extension of A, then the group generated by B and the stable letters will be an HNN extension of B provided B meets the associated subgroups suitably (see, e.g., the remarks following Britton's Lemma in [2]). Also an HNN extension with trivial associated subgroups is just a free product.

It follows from these remarks that, since $\langle t, x\rangle \cap \langle k\rangle$ is trivial (and hence so is $\langle t, x\rangle \cap (C^*\langle k\rangle)$, the subgroup $\langle t, x, b_j\ (j = 1, \ldots, n)\rangle$ is free on these generators. In turn we find that $\langle t, x, b_j, d\ (j = 1, \ldots, n)\rangle$ is free on these generators. We next show that

$$\langle t, x, b_j, d\rangle \cap \langle k, t_\alpha w_\alpha(b)d\ (\alpha \in I)\rangle = \langle t_\alpha w_\alpha(b)d\ (\alpha \in I)\rangle.$$

For the former clearly contains the latter. Let h be in the former. In the homomorphism from H_5 to G_3 which is the identity on G_3 and kills the other generators h maps to an element $g \in \langle t, x\rangle \cap \langle k, t_\alpha\ (\alpha \in I)\rangle$ which equals $\langle t_\alpha\ (\alpha \in I)\rangle$ from the construction of G_3 (indeed this follows from the expression of G_2 as an HNN extension of G_1). Since h is the image of g under the map sending k to k and t_α to $t_\alpha w_\alpha(b)d$ we find that h is in the required subgroup.

From this and other similar properties we can identify K as the HNN extension with stable letter p of the group freely generated by $\{t, x, b_j, d\}$, the defining relations being (where $t_\alpha = x^{-\alpha}tx^{\alpha}$) $p^{-1}t_\alpha p = t_\alpha w_\alpha(b)d$ for all $\alpha \in I$. Similarly L is an HNN extension with stable letter p of the group freely generated by t_i, x^m, b_j, d, the relations being $p^{-1}t_\alpha p = t_\alpha w_\alpha(b)d$ for all $\alpha \in I$ with $\alpha \equiv i \bmod m$. Since $w_{\alpha m+i}(b) = w_\alpha(b)b_i$, the isomorphism condition is now easily checked.

(iv) H_7 is finitely presented.

Since G_3 is finitely presented it is clear that H_7 is finitely generated and is presented by: (I) the relations of C, i.e. $w_\alpha(c) = 1$ for all α with $\alpha \in I$ and $(\alpha, 0) \in H_0(M)$, (II) $p^{-1}t_\alpha p = t_\alpha w_\alpha(b)d$ for $\alpha \in I$, and (III) a further finite set of relations, namely, the relations of G_3, all the relations not in (II) which have been explicitly given in the construction of H_7, and the relation $p^{-1}tp = td$ (which also occurs in (II)).

We first show that the set of relations (I) follows from (II) and (III).

From (III) we have, for all $\alpha \in I$, both $k^{-1}p^{-1}t_\alpha pk = p^{-1}k^{-1}t_\alpha kp$ and $k^{-1}t_\alpha w_\alpha(b)dk = k^{-1}t_\alpha k w_\alpha(b)w_\alpha(c)d$. Hence, using (II), we find that $w_\alpha(c)=1$ if $k^{-1}t_\alpha k = t_\alpha$. But by definition of G_3, this holds as a consequence of the defining relations of G_3 provided $(\alpha,0)\in H_0(M)$. This gives the result.

Next we show that (II) follows from (III), proving H_7 is finitely presented. We first show inductively that, for $\alpha \in I$, $w_\alpha^{-1}(a)tw_\alpha(a)=t_\alpha$ and $w_\alpha^{-1}(a)dw_\alpha(a)=w_\alpha(b)d$ are consequences of (III). For these are true by definition if $0\leq\alpha\leq 2n$. Since $\beta>0$ is in I iff $\beta=\alpha m+i$ for some $\alpha\in I$ and $1\leq i\leq 2n$, it is enough to show that if these are true for α then they are true for $\alpha m+i$ $(1\leq i\leq 2n)$. Now $w_{\alpha m+i}(a)=w_\alpha(a)a_i$, so $w_{\alpha m+i}^{-1}(a)tw_{\alpha m+i}(a)=a_i^{-1}w_\alpha^{-1}(a)tw_\alpha(a)a_i = a_i^{-1}t_\alpha a_i$ (inductively) $= a_i^{-1}x^{-\alpha}tx^{\alpha}a_i = x^{-\alpha m}a_i^{-1}ta_ix^{\alpha m} = t_{\alpha m+i}$. Similarly $w_{\alpha m+i}^{-1}(a)dw_{\alpha m+i}(a)=a_i^{-1}w_\alpha^{-1}(a)dw_\alpha(a)a_i = a_i^{-1}w_\alpha(b)da_i = w_\alpha(b)b_id = w_{\alpha m+i}(b)d$.

Hence, as a consequence of (III) we have, for all $\alpha\in I$, $p^{-1}t_\alpha p = p^{-1}w_\alpha^{-1}(a)tw_\alpha(a)p = w_\alpha^{-1}(a)p^{-1}tpw_\alpha(a)=w_\alpha^{-1}(a)tdw_\alpha(a)=t_\alpha w_\alpha(b)d$, i.e. (II) follows from (III).

This completes the proof of Theorem A, since H_7, being obtained by a Britton tower (i.e. sequence of HNN extensions) from $C*C_3$, will contain C.

We now proceed to the proof of Theorem B. We use the same construction as above, and show that at each stage the degree of the word problem is preserved (by using the lemmas of §1). If H, H' are any groups we write $WP(H)\equiv WP(H')$ if H and H' have word problems which are unbounded truth-table equivalent.

(v) $WP(H_3)\equiv WP(C)$.

For by §4 of [2] the word problem for G_3 is truth-table equivalent to $H_0(M)$ which is many-one equivalent to $H_0(T)$ by Theorem 2 of [2]. Hence $WP(G_3)\equiv WP(C)$ by the construction of T. The result now follows from the analogue of Lemma 2 for free products (the details of this are left to the reader).

(vi) $WP(H_4)\equiv WP(H_3)$.

As already remarked, the associated subgroups are both $C*\langle k\rangle$. The isomorphisms plainly lift to partial recursive functions. We may now apply Lemma 3 (in the weak form where the maps θ map to elements rather than to subsets). The relevant maps send c_j to c_j $(j=1,\ldots,n)$, map all the finite set of generators of G_3 except k to the identity, and send k either to k or to kc_i^{-1}.

(vii) $WP(H_5) \equiv WP(H_4)$.

This is a very easy application of Lemma 3, the map θ being the homomorphism which kills all the generators except k.

(viii) $WP(H_6) \equiv WP(H_5)$.

For the only time we use the full force of Lemma 3. Let F_5, F_3 be the free groups on the generators of H_5 and G_3, $\pi : F_5 \to H_5$ the projection and $\rho : F_5 \to F_3$ the retraction (i.e. maps the generators of F_3 to themselves and maps the generators of F_5 not in F_3 trivially). Let U and V be the subgroups $\langle k, t_\alpha\ (\alpha \in I)\rangle$ and $\langle k, t_\alpha w_\alpha(b)d\ (\alpha \in I)\rangle$ of H_5. Let φ be the homomorphism from the subgroup $\langle k, t_\alpha\ (\alpha \in I)\rangle$ of F_5 into F_5 defined by $\varphi k = k$, $\varphi t_\alpha = t_\alpha w_\alpha(b)d$ (here t_α is the element $x^{-\alpha}tx^{\alpha}$ of F_5, and the homomorphism φ exists because the subgroup is free on the stated generators). As I is recursive, φ is partial recursive and $\rho\varphi w = w$ if $w \in \operatorname{dom}\varphi$. Plainly φ and ρ induce the isomorphisms between the associated subgroups U and V.

Refer to the discussion of reduction sequences in §4 of [2]. It is shown in Lemma 4 of that paper that if $w \in F_3$ with $\pi w \in U$ then there is a correct reduction sequence (in the sense of that section) from w to w' where w' is in the subgroup $\langle k, t_\alpha\ (\alpha \in I)\rangle$ of F_3; also $\pi w = \pi w'$ since the reductions are correct. For $w \in F_3$ let θw be the subset consisting of all words $w' \in \langle k, t_\alpha\ (\alpha \in I)\rangle$ which occur in some reduction sequence starting at w. By the above $\pi w \in \pi\theta w$ if $\pi w \in U$. Also θ is plainly recursive.

Extend θ to F_5 by defining θw to mean $\theta\rho w$ for any $w \in F_5$. Then θ has the required properties provided $\pi w = \pi\rho w$ whenever $\pi w \in U$. This certainly holds if $w \in F_3$, since then $\rho w = w$. If $w \notin F_3$ but $\pi w \in U$ there must be a pinch in w. Let w' be obtained from w by pinching out the relevant subword. It is easy to check that $\rho w' = \rho w$. Since $\pi w' = \pi w$ it follows by induction on the number of generators not in F_3 which occur in w that $\pi w = \pi\rho w$, as required.

Finally we must define θ' with $\pi w \in \pi\theta' w$ if $\pi w \in V$. We notice that $\theta w \subseteq \operatorname{dom}\varphi$ and define $\theta' w$ to be $\varphi\theta w$. If $\pi w \in V$ then $\pi\rho w \in U$. Hence we can find $w' \in \theta w = \theta\rho w$ with $\pi w' = \pi\rho w$. We have $\pi\varphi w' \in \pi\theta' w$ so we need only show $\pi\varphi w' = \pi w$. Since $\pi\varphi w' \in V$ and ρ induces an isomorphism from V to U we need only show $\pi\rho\varphi w' = \pi\rho w$, which is true since $\rho\varphi w' = w'$.

(ix) $WP(H_7) \equiv WP(H_6)$.

The isomorphisms between the associated subgroups K and L lift to partial recursive maps. By Lemma 3 it will be enough to find recursive maps from H_6 to K and L which are the identity on K and L. It will be enough to find a subgroup H_6' of H_6 containing K (and hence L) such that there is a retraction from H_6 to H_6' and to show that the membership problems for L in K and K in H_6' are solvable. For then a map (which is not a homomorphism) from H_6' to K can be defined to be the identity on K and trivial outside K, and this gives a map from H_6 to K by composing with the retraction.

Let H_6' be the subgroup of H_6 generated by t, x, d, p, b_j $(1 \leq j \leq n)$ and all the r- and l-symbols (which are among the generators of G_3). We obtain a retraction from H_6 to H_6' by killing the remaining generators. This retraction sends those defining relators of H_6 involving only the generators of H_6' to themselves and sends all other relators to the trivial relator. It follows that H_6' has as defining relators those defining relators of H_6 involving only the generators of H_6' (for H_6' is certainly a quotient of the group with the same generators and only these relators, but in addition H_6 and so H_6' maps to this latter group). In particular H_6' is an HNN extension of K with stable letters the r- and l-symbols; each associated subgroup is $\langle t_u, x^v \rangle$ for some integers u, v.

The required results have been proved by Kalorkoti (unpublished) using the Bokut normal form. The messy proof given here does not seem to admit much simplification.

It follows from Lemma 4 that the membership problem for K in H_6' is solvable if the membership problems for $\langle t_u, x^v \rangle$ in K are solvable for all u, v. The membership problem for $\langle t_u, x^v \rangle$ in $\langle t, x, b_j, d \rangle$ is clearly solvable, since the latter is free on the named generators. Hence it is enough to show that the membership problem for $\langle t, x, b_j, d \rangle$ (which we denote by K') in K is solvable.

Now K is in turn an HNN extension of K' with associated subgroups $\langle t_\alpha \, (\alpha \in I) \rangle$ and $\langle t_\alpha w_\alpha(b) d \;\, (\alpha \in I) \rangle$. Using Lemma 4 again it is enough to show the membership problems for these in K' are solvable. Now an element of K' is in the first of these iff (i) it is a word in t and x only, (ii) its exponent sum in x is zero, so that it can be written as a word in t_α (all α), and (iii) when so written it involves only those t_α with $\alpha \in I$. Since I is recursive, this is solvable. With the notation of part (viii) an element w of K' is in the second subgroup iff ρw is in the first subgroup and $w = \varphi \rho w$, showing that this problem is also solvable.

We still have to show that the membership problem for L in K is solvable. Now K is the amalgamated free product of the free group $\langle t, x \rangle$ with $\langle t_\alpha$ (all α), d, p, b_j $(1 \leq j \leq n) \rangle$, the amalgamated subgroup being $\langle t_\alpha \rangle$. Since $\langle t_\alpha, d, b_j, p \rangle$ is an HNN extension of the free group $\langle t_\alpha, d, b_j \rangle$, Lemma 5 and the previously proved results show that the membership problem for the subgroup $L' = \langle t_\alpha \text{ (all } \alpha),\ x^m, b_j$ $(1 \leqslant j \leqslant n),\ d, p\rangle$ in K is solvable.

Since $\langle x^m, t_\alpha \text{ (all } \alpha)\rangle$ is free on x^m and t_u $(1 \leqslant u \leqslant m)$ we may present L' as $\langle t_u, x^m, b_j, d, p;\ t_u^{-1} x^{vm} p x^{-vm} t_u = x^{vm} p d^{-1} w_{vm+u}^{-1}(b) x^{-vm}$ $(1 \leqslant j \leqslant n,\ 1 \leqslant u \leqslant m, \text{ all } v)\rangle$. Thus L' is an HNN extension of the free group $\langle x^m, b_j, d, p\rangle$ with several stable letters, and so is the amalgamated free product of HNN extensions with one stable letter. Since L is the subgroup of L' with the stable letter t_i, it follows from Lemma 5 that the membership problem for L in L' is solvable if the membership problems for the base group in each extension are solvable. A further application of Lemma 4 tells us that this holds if the membership problems for $x^{vm} p x^{-vm}$ (all v) and $x^{vm} p d^{-1} w_{vm+u}^{-1}(b) x^{-vm}$ (u fixed, all v) in the free group x^m, b_j, d, p are solvable. These problems are seen to be solvable in the same way as for t_α and $t_\alpha w_\alpha(b) d$ in K'.

These results complete the proof of (ix) and so prove Theorem B.

References

[1] S. Aanderaa, A proof of Higman's embedding theorem using Britton extensions of groups, in Word Problems. Studies in Logic and the Foundations of Mathematics (North-Holland Publishing Co., Amsterdam, 1973).

[2] S. Aanderaa and D.E. Cohen, Modular machines, the word problem for finitely presented groups and Collins' theorem, in Word Problems II: The Oxford Book, Studies in Logic and the Foundations of Mathematics (North-Holland Publishing Co., Amsterdam, 1979 (i.e. this volume)).

[3] C.R.J. Clapham, Finitely presented groups with word problem of arbitrary degrees of unsolvability, Proc. London Math. Soc. (3) 14 (1964) 637–676.

[4] C.R.J. Clapham, An embedding theorem for finitely generated groups, Proc. London Math. Soc. (3) 17 (1967) 419–430.

[5] G. Higman, Subgroups of finitely presented groups, Proc. Roy. Soc. A 262 (1961) 455–475.

[6] R.C. Lyndon and P.E. Schupp, Combinatorial Group Theory, Ergebnisse der Mathematik, Bd. 89 (Springer, Berlin–Heidelberg–New York, 1977).

[7] R. Overbeek, The representation of many-one degrees by decision problems of Turing machines, Proc. London Math. Soc. (3) 26 (1973) 167–183.

[8] J.C. Shepherdson and H.E. Sturgis, Computability of recursive functions, J. Ass. Computing Machinery 10 (1963) 217–256.

[9] M.K. Valiev, On a theorem of G. Higman, Algebra i logika, 8 (1969) 93–128.

[10] M.K. Valiev, On polynomial reducibility of the word problem under embedding of recursively presented groups in finitely generated groups, Lecture Notes in Computer Science, vol, 32 (Springer, Berlin, 1975), pp. 432–438.

S.I. Adian, W.W. Boone, G. Higman, eds., Word Problems II
© North-Holland Publishing Company (1980) 29–53

MALCEV'S PROBLEM AND GROUPS WITH A NORMAL FORM

L.A. BOKUT'*

Institute of Mathematics, Novosibirsk

Introduction

The following problem was known as Malcev's problem.

Does there exist an associative ring R, without zero divisors, which is not embeddable in a skew field whose multiplicative semigroup R^* of non-zero elements is embeddable in a group.

This problem occurred to A.I. Malcev in connection with his well-known work on embedding rings in skew fields and semigroups in groups (see [19]). In 1966 at the International Congress in Moscow it emerged that three authors had, independently, constructed examples of rings which solve Malcev's problem (see [5], [13], [18]). The solution given in Bokut' [5] to this problem leads to the notion of a group with standard basis, a notion which provides a uniform approach to certain well-known constructions in group theory.

This paper begins with a brief account of the solution in [5] to Malcev's problem and then goes on to provide the detailed definition of a group with standard basis, together with some examples.

§1. Malcev's problem

Let $k = GF(2)$ be the prime field of characteristic 2. Let Q be the semigroup with generators

$$a_i, \ b_i, \ c_i, \ s_i, \ t_i, \ v_j$$

where $1 \leq i \leq 4$, $0 \leq j \leq 1$, and with defining relations

(1) $a_i s_i = c_i v_0, \quad b_i s_{i+1} = c_i v_1, \quad b_i t_{i+1} = a_i t_i$

where $1 \leq i \leq 4$ and $s_5 = s_1$, $t_5 = t_1$.

---

* With D.J. Collins, Queen Mary College, London.

It is easy to show that the ring kQ contains no zero divisors and is not embeddable in a skew field. (The latter follows from the fact that if $kQ \subseteq D$, where D is a skew field, then the equality $(v_0^{-1}v_1)^4 = 1$ holds and hence $v_0 = v_1$, which is impossible.)

Theorem 1. *The semigroup $(kQ)^*$ is embeddable in a group.*

The proof of this theorem appears in Bokut' [8], [9]. The idea of the proof is as follows. Since Q is given by homogeneous relations, the ring kQ can be embedded in the ring $\overline{kQ}$ of infinite series. Then, to prove Theorem 1, it suffices to prove that the semigroup $(\overline{kQ})^*$ is embeddable in a group.

Now it follows from the results of [2] that the semigroup $(\overline{kQ})^*$ has a presentation of the form

$$(2) \qquad (\overline{kQ})^* = \langle \Gamma, \mathfrak{R};\ p_iX_{ij}p_j = p_kX_{kl}p_l,\ X_ip_i = p_iX_i' \rangle$$

where Γ is the group of units of the ring $\overline{kQ}$ (i.e. the set of all series with non-zero constant term), $\mathfrak{R}$ is a set of atoms of $\overline{kQ}$ consisting of one atom from each class of associated atoms (see [14] for terminology), the elements p with subscripts lie in $\mathfrak{R}$ and the elements X with subscripts belong to the group Γ.

We consider the corresponding group of quotients

$$(3) \qquad G((\overline{kQ})^*) = \mathrm{gp}\langle \Gamma, \mathfrak{R};\ p_iX_{ij}p_j = p_kX_{kl}p_l,\ X_ip_i = p_iX_i' \rangle$$

given by the same generators and defining relations as the semigroup (2). To establish Theorem 1 it is necessary to prove that two words in the alphabet of the semigroup (2) are equal in the group (3) if and only if they are equal in the semigroup (2).

The proof of this last assertion is carried out in the following manner.

Firstly we enlarge the initial system of defining relations of the group (3) by adding relations of the form

$$X_{ijkl}p_iX'_{ijkl}p_j^{-1}X''_{ijkl}p_kX'''_{ijkl}p_l^{-1} = p_kY'_{ijkl}p_l^{-1}Y''_{ijkl}p_iY'''_{ijkl}p_j^{-1}Y_{ijkl}$$

where $p \in \mathfrak{R}$, $X, Y \in \Gamma$. These additional relations are consequences of the initial defining relations and so we may write

$$(4) \qquad G((\overline{kQ})^*) = \mathrm{gp}\langle \Gamma, \mathfrak{R};\ \Phi \rangle$$

where Φ is the enlarged system of relations. Then we prove that every group word in the generators $\Gamma \cup \mathfrak{R}$ has a normal form, which is defined in terms of the presentation (4). It turns out that the process whereby a positive word in $\Gamma \cup \mathfrak{N}$ is reduced to normal form is carried out by means of transformations in the semigroup (2). This enables one to prove Theorem 1.

§2. Groups with standard basis

The process of constructing normal forms in the group $G((kQ)^*)$, given by (4), can be formalized and, in particular, the definition of a group with standard basis can be formulated. This was done in the papers [3], [4], and [6] of Bokut'. These papers also contain proofs that Novikov's groups $\mathfrak{A}_{p_1p_2}$ (see [20]) and Boone's groups $G(T, q)$ (see [10]) are groups with standard basis. This makes it possible to obtain many well-known properties of these groups (see [1] and [12]) in a uniform and relatively simple way. Furthermore, with the help of the same method, it was possible (Bokut' [7]) to prove that for any recursively enumerable Turing degree of unsolvability there exists a finitely presented group (of the kind $\mathfrak{A}_{p_1p_2}$) whose conjugacy problem is of the given degree. This last result was obtained, independently, by Collins [15].

We begin with the definition and some properties of groups with stable letters, following, by and large, P.S. Novikov's work [21].

If Σ is an alphabet, then by a *Σ-word* or a *word in Σ* (*on Σ, from Σ*) we shall always understand a group word constructed from this alphabet. For a fixed presentation $G = \langle \Sigma; \Phi \rangle$ of some group we write $X \in G$ if X is a Σ-word. Graphic equality of words will be denoted by the sign $\overset{\circ}{=}$ and definition or denotation by the sign $\rightleftharpoons$.

Let $\bar{G} = \langle \Sigma; \Phi \rangle$ be the group with generators Σ and defining relations Φ. The group

(5) $$G = \langle \Sigma, \mathfrak{P}; \Phi, A_i p_{m_i} = p_{n_i} B_i, \ i \in I \rangle$$

where $\Sigma \cap \mathfrak{P}$ is empty, $p_{m_i}, p_{n_i} \in \mathfrak{P}$ and A_i, B_i are Σ-words is the group with *stable letters* $\mathfrak{P}$ and *base group* $\bar{G}$. Groups with stable letters were first considered by G. Higman, B.H. Neumann and H. Neumann in their well-known paper [22]. Thus the group G is often called an HNN extension of the group $\bar{G}$. (We do *not* at present assume any conditions which ensure, for example, that $\bar{G}$ is naturally embedded in G although such conditions are often incorporated in the definition of HNN extension.)

The relations

(6) $$A_i^{-1} p_{n_i} = p_{m_i} B_i^{-1}, \qquad i \in I$$

are, of course, valid in G. We say that the letters p_m and p_n are *related* if the relations (5) and (6) contain, among them, a sequence of equalities

$$A_{i_k}^{\varepsilon_k} p_{n_{i_k}} = p_{n_{i_{k-1}}} B_{i_k}^{\varepsilon_k}, \ldots, A_{i_1}^{\varepsilon_1} p_{n_{i_1}} = p_{n_{i_0}} B_{i_1}^{\varepsilon_1}$$

where $p_m \mathrel{\overline{\underline{\circ}}} p_{n_{i_k}}$ and $p_n \mathrel{\overline{\underline{\circ}}} p_{n_{i_0}}$. When p_m and p_n are related via the above sequence, we use the notation

$$(7) \qquad \mathfrak{A}_{p_m p_n} \rightleftharpoons A_{i_1}^{\varepsilon_1} \cdots A_{i_k}^{\varepsilon_k}, \qquad \mathfrak{B}_{p_n p_m} \rightleftharpoons B_{i_1}^{\varepsilon_1} \cdots B_{i_k}^{\varepsilon_k}$$

In other words we use $\mathfrak{A}_{p_m p_n}$ and $\mathfrak{B}_{p_m p_n}$ as variables for pairs of words of the form (7). Obviously we always have $\mathfrak{A}_{p_m p_n} p_m = p_n \mathfrak{B}_{p_n p_m}$.

In the book [21], the words $\mathfrak{A}_{p_m p_n}$ and $\mathfrak{B}_{p_n p_m}$ in (7) are referred to as *occurring in the correspondence* L_p. We shall call the words (7) *connected.* For brevity we write

$$\mathfrak{A}_{p_n} \rightleftharpoons \mathfrak{A}_{p_n p_n}, \quad \mathfrak{B}_{p_n} \rightleftharpoons \mathfrak{B}_{p_n p_n}, \quad \mathfrak{A}_{p_m^{-1} p_n^{-1}} \rightleftharpoons \mathfrak{B}_{p_n p_m}, \quad \mathfrak{B}_{p_n^{-1} p_m^{-1}} \rightleftharpoons \mathfrak{A}_{p_m p_n}.$$

By the *extension system of relations* of the group G we mean the system of relations in (5) enlarged by the equalities

$$B_i^{-1} p_{n_i}^{-1} = p_{m_i}^{-1} A_i^{-1}, \qquad i \in I.$$

We now turn to the notion of *individuality* of letters. In using the extension system of relations of G, we perform transformations

$$XUY \to XVY$$

where either $U = V$ or $V = U$ is a member of the extension system of relations (or else a trivial relation of the kind $\sigma\sigma^{-1} = 1$, $pp^{-1} = 1$, $\sigma \in \Sigma$, $p \in \mathfrak{P}$). We say that the individuality of the letters in X and Y is preserved by the transformation. Further, if, for example, $U \mathrel{\overline{\underline{\circ}}} A_i p_{m_i}$ and $V \mathrel{\overline{\underline{\circ}}} p_{n_i} B_i$ or $U \mathrel{\overline{\underline{\circ}}} B_i^{-1} p_{n_i}^{-1}$ and $V \mathrel{\overline{\underline{\circ}}} p_{m_i}^{-1} A_i^{-1}$ we also say that p_{m_i} and p_{n_i}, or $p_{n_i}^{-1}$ and $p_{m_i}^{-1}$ have the same individuality. We define individuality for letters occurring in a sequence of transformations of the extension system of relations by transitivity. (For brevity we call such sequences *extension sequences.*)

We give three lemmas, which are explicitly or implicitly in Novikov [21], and which we shall use later.

Lemma 1. *Let there be given an extension sequence of the group* G

$$Wp_n^{\varepsilon} V \to W_1 p_{n_1}^{\varepsilon} V_1 \to \cdots \to W_k p_{n_k}^{\varepsilon} V_k$$

where $p_n^{\varepsilon}, p_{n_1}^{\varepsilon}, \ldots, p_{n_k}^{\varepsilon} \mathrel{\overline{\underline{\circ}}} p_m^{\varepsilon}$ *have the same individuality. Then for some connected words* $\mathfrak{A}_{p_m^{\varepsilon} p_n^{\varepsilon}}$ *and* $\mathfrak{B}_{p_n^{\varepsilon} p_m^{\varepsilon}}$ *the equalities*

$$W_k = W \mathfrak{A}_{p_m^{\varepsilon} p_n^{\varepsilon}}, \qquad V_k = \mathfrak{B}^{-1}_{p_n^{\varepsilon} p_m^{\varepsilon}} V$$

hold in G.

Lemma 2. *If in any extension sequence of G which starts with the word $Wp_n^{-\varepsilon}Up_m^{\varepsilon}V$ the letters $p_n^{-\varepsilon}$ and p_m^{ε} (strictly, letters of the same individuality as $p_n^{-\varepsilon}$ and p_m^{ε}) cancel one another, then $U = \mathfrak{A}_{p_m^{\varepsilon}p_n^{\varepsilon}}$ in G, for some $\mathfrak{A}_{p_m^{\varepsilon}p_n^{\varepsilon}}$.*

For the third lemma we need a definition. The system $\mathfrak{P}$ of stable letters of the group G is called *regular* if for any $p \in \mathfrak{P}$ and any two connected words $\mathfrak{A}_p$ and $\mathfrak{B}_p$ the condition

$$\mathfrak{A}_p = 1 \text{ in } \bar{G} \text{ if and only if } \mathfrak{B}_p = 1 \text{ in } \bar{G},$$

is satisfied. (This is often called the *isomorphism condition* for G and is assumed as part of the definition of HNN extension.)

Lemma 3 (Britton's lemma). *Let $\mathfrak{P}$ be a regular system of stable letters of the group G, with base group $\bar{G}$ and let W be a $(\Sigma \cup \mathfrak{P})$-word. If $W = 1$ in G then either W is a Σ-word and $W = 1$ in $\bar{G}$ or W contains a subword of the form*

(8) $$p_n^{-\varepsilon}Up_m^{\varepsilon}$$

where U is a Σ-word and for some $\mathfrak{A}_{p_m^{\varepsilon}p_n^{\varepsilon}}$

(8′) $$U = \mathfrak{A}_{p_m^{\varepsilon}p_n^{\varepsilon}} \quad \text{in} \quad \bar{G}.$$

A $(\Sigma \cup \mathfrak{P})$-word is called $\mathfrak{P}$-*reduced* if it has no subword (8) for which (8′) is satisfied.

We now embark on the definition of a group with standard basis. (Our account is a little different from that in [4].)

Let $G = \langle \Sigma ; \Phi \rangle$ be a group. Let us suppose that the given presentation of G satisfies the conditions:

SB 1) $\Sigma = \bigcup \Sigma_\alpha$, $0 \leq \alpha < \tau$, where τ is an ordinal and the sets Σ_α are non-empty and mutually disjoint.

SB 2) $\Phi = \bigcup \Phi_\alpha$, $0 \leq \alpha < \tau$ and, for every α, all the relations in Φ_α are of the form

(9) $$Ap_n = p_mB$$

where $p_n, p_m \in \Sigma_\alpha$ and A, B are non-empty words in $\bigcup_{\beta<\alpha} \Sigma_\beta$. (We allow the possibility that Φ_α is empty and our definition requires Φ_0 to be empty.)

We introduce the following notation:

$$\bar{\Sigma}_\alpha = \bigcup_{\beta<\alpha} \Sigma_\beta, \quad \bar{\Phi}_\alpha = \bigcup_{\beta<\alpha} \Phi_\beta, \quad \bar{G}_\alpha = \langle \bar{\Sigma}_\alpha ; \bar{\Phi}_\alpha \rangle,$$

$$G_\alpha = \bar{G}_{\alpha+1}.$$

Then G_α has stable letters Σ_α and base group $\bar{G}_\alpha$. The group G_0 is free on Σ_0. Thus G is obtained from a free group by a sequence of HNN extensions (taking ascending unions at limit ordinals). We shall see later that for Novikov's groups $\mathfrak{A}_{p_1p_2}$ and Boone's groups $G(T, q)$ the number τ is finite. For the group (4), and for other groups in [5] and [8], τ is infinite.

We distinguish in every word A and B, which appears in a relation (9) one letter (positive or negative). Thus every relation (9) is assumed to be in the form

$$A_1xA_2p_n = p_mB_1yB_2 \tag{10}$$

where x and y are the distinguished letters of A and B respectively. With each relation (10) we associate the following words of G_α:

$$\begin{array}{ll} x'\mathfrak{B}_{x'x}A_2p_n, & x'^{-1}\mathfrak{B}_{x'^{-1}x^{-1}}A_1^{-1}p_m \\ y'\mathfrak{B}_{y'y}B_2p_n^{-1}, & y'^{-1}\mathfrak{B}_{y'^{-1}y^{-1}}B_1^{-1}p_m^{-1} \end{array} \tag{11}$$

where x', x are both stable letters of some G_β, $\beta < \alpha$, y', y are both stable letters of some G_γ, $\gamma < \alpha$ and x, y are the distinguished letters in (10).

We now define, inductively, the sets of words C_α, $0 \leqslant \alpha < \tau$:

C 1) The set C_0 is the set of all freely reduced words in Σ_0.

C 2) Suppose, for some $\alpha \geqslant 0$ that the sets C_β, $\beta < \alpha$ have been defined and that C_β consists of words of G_β. Then the word

$$W \mathrel{\underline{\circ}} R_0p_{n_1}^{\varepsilon_1}R_1 \cdots p_{n_s}^{\varepsilon_s}R_s \tag{12}$$

where $s \geqslant 0$ (when $s = 0$, $W \mathrel{\underline{\circ}} R_0$), $p_{n_i} \in \Sigma_\alpha$ and R_i is a word in $\bar{\Sigma}_\alpha$, belongs to C_α if and only if the following conditions are satisfied:

(a) W is a (freely) reduced word;

(b) $R_i \in \bar{C}_\alpha = \bigcup_{\beta<\alpha} C_\beta$, $0 \leqslant i \leqslant s$;

(c) W contains no subword equal to a word (11) which is associated with a relation (10) from Φ_α.

We understand condition (c) to signify that W contains, for example, no subword $x'Ep_n$ where E is a $\bar{\Sigma}_\alpha$-word and $E = \mathfrak{B}_{x'x}A_2$ in $\bar{G}_\alpha$ (and similarly for other words from (11)).

Clearly the sets C_α form an ascending sequence

$$C_0 \subseteq C_1 \subseteq \cdots \subseteq C_\alpha \subseteq \cdots$$

We write $C = \bigcup C_\alpha$, $0 \leqslant \alpha < \tau$. We call elements of C *normal* words.

We say that the group $G = \langle \Sigma; \Phi \rangle$ is a group *with standard basis* if in addition to SB 1 and SB 2, the following condition SB 3 holds:

SB 3) For every α, $0 \leqslant \alpha < \tau$, the set C_α is a *basis* of the group G_α, that is, every word $X \in G_\alpha$ is equal to one and only one normal word $C(X) \in C_\alpha$.

We often call $C(X)$ the *normal form* of X. From condition SB 3, it follows that C is a basis of the whole group G. We note that any subword of a normal word is normal and that every letter p, p^{-1}, $p \in \Sigma$ constitutes a normal word. In addition, if Rp^ε, where $R \in \bar{C}_\alpha$, $p \in \Sigma_\alpha$, is normal and $U \in \bar{C}_\alpha$, then $Rp^\varepsilon U$ is normal. Furthermore, if Rp^ε and $Up_1^{\varepsilon_1}$ are normal words, where R, $U \in \bar{C}_\alpha$, $p, p_1 \in \Sigma_\alpha$ and $U \not\equiv 1$, then $Rp^\varepsilon Up_1^{\varepsilon_1}$ is normal.

In verifying condition SB 3 for our later examples we shall use the following lemma.

Lemma 4. *Let the conditions* SB 1 *and* SB 2 *be satisfied for the group* $G = \langle \Sigma ; \Phi \rangle$. *Let the relations of this presentation be fixed in the form* (10). *Then condition* SB 3 *is satisfied if and only if the following three conditions are simultaneously satisfied*:

SB 4) *each word* $X \in G_\alpha$ *is equal* (*in* G_α) *to some normal word* $C(X) \in C_\alpha$, $0 \leqslant \alpha < \tau$;

SB 5) *the set* Σ_α *is a regular system of stable letters for the group* G_α *with base group* $\bar{G}_\alpha$, $1 \leqslant \alpha < \tau$;

SB 6) *if* Rp_i^ε, $Tp_j^\varepsilon \in C_\alpha$, *where* p_i, $p_j \in \Sigma_\alpha$, R, $T \in \bar{C}_\alpha$ *and, for some* $\mathfrak{A}_{p_i^\varepsilon p_j^\varepsilon}$, $R = T\mathfrak{A}_{p_i^\varepsilon p_j^\varepsilon}$ *in* $\bar{G}_\alpha$ *then* $i = j$ *and* $R = T$ (*in* $\bar{G}_\alpha$).

Proof. Let condition SB 3 be satisfied. Then obviously SB 4 is satisfied.

We verify SB 5. To this end we pick some $\alpha \geqslant 1$, $p \in \Sigma_\alpha$ and connected words $\mathfrak{A}_p$, $\mathfrak{B}_p$ and prove, for example, that if $\mathfrak{A}_p = 1$ in $\bar{G}_\alpha$, then $\mathfrak{B}_p = 1$ in $\bar{G}_\alpha$. Then, in G_α, the equality $p = pC(\mathfrak{B}_p)$ holds, since $\mathfrak{B}_p = C(\mathfrak{B}_p)$ in $\bar{G}_\alpha$. Both sides of this equality are normal. Thus $C(\mathfrak{B}_p) \equiv 1$, i.e., $\mathfrak{B}_p = 1$ in $\bar{G}_\alpha$.

We verify SB 6. We have

$$Rp_i^\varepsilon = Tp_j^\varepsilon C(\mathfrak{B}_{p_j^\varepsilon p_i^\varepsilon})$$

and this is an equality between normal words. From the uniqueness assertion in SB 3 it follows that $i = j$ and $R = T$ in $\bar{G}_\alpha$.

Conversely, let us suppose that conditions SB 4–SB 6 are satisfied. We prove SB 3 by (transfinite) induction on α. Certainly C_0 is a basis of the free group G_0.

Suppose we have proved, for every $\beta < \alpha$, that C_β is a basis of G_β. We prove the same assertion for the index α. Let us note first of all that the normal words of G_α are, by our conditions, Σ_α-reduced. Suppose, to the contrary, that a normal word contains a subword $p_j^{-\varepsilon}Rp_i^\varepsilon$, where $p_i, p_j \in \Sigma_\alpha$, $R \in \bar{G}_\alpha$ and $R = \mathfrak{A}_{p_i^\varepsilon p_j^\varepsilon}$ in $\bar{G}_\alpha$. Then the words

Rp_i^ε and p_j^ε, which are certainly normal, satisfy the hypotheses of SB 6 whence $i = j$ and $R = 1$ in $\bar{G}_\alpha$. By the inductive assumption $R \mathrel{\bar{\circ}} 1$ and this contradicts the fact that a normal word is freely reduced.

Let us now consider two normal words of G_α

$$W \mathrel{\bar{\circ}} R_0 p_1^{\varepsilon_1} R_1 \cdots p_l^{\varepsilon_l} R_l, \qquad W_1 \mathrel{\bar{\circ}} S_0 q_1^{\delta_1} S_1 \cdots q_t^{\delta_t} S_t$$

where $l \geqslant 0$, $t \geqslant 0$, $R_i, S_j \in \bar{G}_\alpha$, $p_i, q_j \in \Sigma_\alpha$, $\varepsilon_i, \delta_j = \pm 1$. Suppose $W = W_1$ in G_α. Then we have

$$S_t^{-1} q_t^{-\delta_t} \cdots q_1^{-\delta_1} S_0^{-1} R_0 p_1^{\varepsilon_1} \cdots p_l^{\varepsilon_l} R_l = 1$$

in G_α. By virtue of Britton's lemma and the previous remark, we deduce that either $l = 0 = t$ and $R_0 \mathrel{\bar{\circ}} S_0$, or that $l, t > 0$ and $\varepsilon_1 = \delta_1$, $R_0 = S_0 \mathfrak{A}_{p_1^{\varepsilon_1} q_1^{\varepsilon_1}}$. From SB 6 it follows that $p_1 \mathrel{\bar{\circ}} q_1$ and $R_0 = S_0$ in $\bar{G}_\alpha$, i.e. $R_0 \mathrel{\bar{\circ}} S_0$. The proof of this assertion we need is completed by induction on l.

We make some remarks that we shall use later on.

Remark 1. Let $\alpha > 0$ and suppose that for each $\beta < \alpha$ the set C_β is a basis of G_β. We consider a reduced word W of the form (12) in which every R_i is normal. If W is not normal, then by condition C 2 it contains, for example, the subword

$$x' E p_n,$$

where $E \in \bar{G}_\alpha$ and $E = \mathfrak{B}_{x'x} A_2$ in $\bar{G}_\alpha$ (for some $\mathfrak{B}_{x'x}$). Since E is normal and so $E \mathrel{\bar{\circ}} C(\mathfrak{B}_{x'x} A_2)$. Thus condition C 2 is equivalent to the condition:

C 2') a reduced word W of the form (12) belongs to C_α if and only if every R_i is a normal word of $\bar{G}_\alpha$ and W contains no subword of the form

$$(13) \qquad \begin{array}{ll} x' C(\mathfrak{B}_{x'x} A_2) p_n, & x'^{-1} C(\mathfrak{B}_{x'^{-1}x^{-1}} A_1^{-1}) p_m, \\ y' C(\mathfrak{B}_{y'y} B_2) p_n^{-1}, & y'^{-1} C(\mathfrak{B}_{y'^{-1}y^{-1}} B_1^{-1}) p_m^{-1}, \end{array}$$

corresponding to a relation (10) from Φ_α.

Remark 2. In G_0, each word is transformed to its normal form by means of cancellations. Let us suppose that for some $\alpha > 0$, it is already proved, for every $\beta < \alpha$, that C is a basis of G and that rules for transforming words $R \in G_\beta$ into normal form have been formulated. Then the following constitute rules whereby a word

$$W \mathrel{\bar{\circ}} R_0 p_{n_1}^{\varepsilon_1} \cdots p_{n_s}^{\varepsilon_s} R_s$$

of the group G_α, where $s \geqslant 0$, $p \in \Sigma_\alpha$, $R_i \in \bar{G}_\alpha$, is transformed into normal form:

(a) transform each R_i into normal form, $0 \leqslant i \leqslant s$;

(b) make all possible cancellations of letters p_{n_i} in the word obtained from (a);

(c) exclude from the resulting word the leftmost occurrence of a word (13);

(d) return to (a).

We understand condition (c) to mean that one has to apply to the word under consideration a transformation of, for example, the kind

$$x'C(\mathfrak{B}_{x'x}A_2)p_n \rightarrow \mathfrak{A}_{xx'}A_1^{-1}p_mB.$$

Similar transformations are to be used for the other words from (13). We call the application of transformations (a)–(d) the process of reducing W to normal form in G_α.

In general this reduction process may not terminate in a finite number of steps. To realise the application of the given process in a finite number of steps it is necessary and sufficient that in reducing each word Rp_n^ε, where $R \in \bar{G}_\alpha$, $p_n \in \Sigma_\alpha$, only finitely many transformations (a) and (c) are applied.

Remark 3. The process described for reducing a word W of G_α to its normal form is some extension sequence of G_α beginning with W. Therefore we can refer to the individuality of letters $p^\varepsilon, p \in \Sigma_\alpha$ in this sequence of transformations. We shall say that p^ε is *cancelled* (*uncancelled*) according as a letter of the same individuality as p^ε is cancelled (remains uncancelled) when W is reduced to normal form. We note that Lemmas 1 and 2 can both be applied to the extension sequence of transformations whereby a word is reduced to normal form.

§3. Novikov groups

In this section we shall prove that a Novikov group $\mathfrak{A}_{p_1p_2}$ is a group with standard basis.

We give the definition of such a group $\mathfrak{A}_{p_1p_2}$, following [20]. Let

$$\Xi = \{a_1, \ldots, a_n, q_1, \ldots, q_\lambda, r_1, \ldots, r_\lambda, l_1, \ldots, l_\lambda\}$$

where n and λ are positive integers. We also consider the alphabet $\Xi^+ = \{a_j^+, q_i^+, r_i^+, l_i^+, 1 \leqslant j \leqslant n, 1 \leqslant i \leqslant \lambda\}$. Further we fix a system (A_i, B_i), $1 \leqslant i \leqslant \lambda$, of pairs of non-empty positive words in the alphabet

$\{a_1, \ldots, a_n\}$. Then we denote by $\mathfrak{A}_{p_1p_2} = G$ the group given in the alphabet

$$\Sigma = \Xi \cup \Xi^+ \cup \{p_1, p_2\}$$

by the following system of defining relations (the bold face italic letters are those which we distinguish in the relations)

$$\begin{array}{lll} & 1.\ \boldsymbol{q}_i a_j = a_j q_i \boldsymbol{q}_i & 1^+.\ \boldsymbol{a}_j^+ \boldsymbol{q}_i^+ = \boldsymbol{q}_i^+ q_i^+ \boldsymbol{a}_j^+ \\ & 2.\ \boldsymbol{r}_i r_i a_j = a_j \boldsymbol{r}_i & 2^+.\ \boldsymbol{r}_i^+ a_j^+ = a_j^+ r_i^+ \boldsymbol{r}_i^+ \\ & 3.\ l_i \boldsymbol{a}_j = \boldsymbol{a}_j l_i & 3^+.\ l_i^+ \boldsymbol{a}_j^+ = \boldsymbol{a}_j^+ l_i^+ \\ (14) & 4.\ A_i^+ p_1 A_i = q_i^+ \boldsymbol{l}_i^+ p_1 \boldsymbol{l}_i q_i & \\ & 5.\ \boldsymbol{r}_i^+ p_1 \boldsymbol{r}_i = p_1 & \\ & 6.\ B_i p_2 B_i^+ = r_i l_i p_2 \boldsymbol{l}_i^+ \boldsymbol{r}_i^+ & \\ & 7.\ \boldsymbol{q}_i p_2 \boldsymbol{q}_i^+ = p_2 & \end{array}$$

where $i = 1, 2, \ldots, \lambda$, $j = 1, 2, \ldots, n$ and $(a_{i_1} \cdots a_{i_k})^+ \rightleftharpoons a_{i_k}^+ \cdots a_{i_1}^+$.

We partition Σ and Φ into disjoint subsets:

$$\Sigma_0 = \{q_i, r_i, q_i^+, r_i^+, 1 \leqslant i \leqslant \lambda\}, \qquad \Sigma_1 = \{a_j, a_j^+, 1 \leqslant j \leqslant n\}$$

$$\Sigma_2 = \{l_i, l_i^+, 1 \leqslant i \leqslant \lambda\}, \qquad \Sigma_3 = \{p_1, p_2\};$$

$$\Phi_0 = \phi, \qquad \Phi_1 = \{(14.1), (14.2), (14.1^+), (14.2^+)\}$$

$$\Phi_2 = \{(14.3), (14.3^+)\}, \qquad \Phi_4 = \{(14.4) - (14.7)\}.$$

We view all the relations of the corresponding group G_α, $0 \leqslant \alpha \leqslant 3$, as being in the form

$$(15) \qquad A_1 x A_2 p_n = p_m B_1 y B_2$$

where $p_n, p_m \in \Sigma_\alpha$ and $A_1 x A_2$, $B_1 y B_2$ are $\Sigma_{\alpha-1}$-words. In each case x and y in (15) are the bold italic letters in (14) — making the obvious modifications to (14.4)–(14.7) so that they have the form (15).

We define the sets C_α, $0 \leqslant \alpha \leqslant 3$, as described in the previous section, and prove that C_α is a basis of G_α, $0 \leqslant \alpha \leqslant 3$. We shall use, in turn, the process of reducing to normal form given in Remark 2.

The set C_0 consists of all reduced words in Σ_0. It is clear that C_0 is a basis of G_0. The set C_1 consists of all reduced words of the form

$$W \boxeq U_0 x_1^{\varepsilon_1} U_1 x_2^{\varepsilon_2} \cdots x_k^{\varepsilon_k} U_k$$

where $k \geqslant 0$ (if $k = 0$ then $W \boxeq U_0$), $x_i \in \Sigma_1$, $U_i \in C_0$ and W contains no subword from the following list:

$$
(16) \qquad \begin{array}{l} q_i^{\varepsilon} a_j, q_i^{-2} a_j^{-1}, q_i a_j^{-1}, r_i^{2} a_j, r_i^{-1} a_j, r_i^{\varepsilon} a_j^{-1} \\ q_i^{+2} a_j^{+}, q_i^{+-i} a_j^{+}, q_i^{+\varepsilon} a_j^{+-i}, r_i^{+\varepsilon} a_j^{+}, r_i^{+} a_j^{+-1}, r_i^{+-2} a_j^{+-1}. \end{array}
$$

Let us verify conditions SB 4–SB 6 for $\alpha = 1$. We begin with SB 5. For the connected words $\mathfrak{A}_{a_j}$ and $\mathfrak{B}_{a_j}$ we have

$$
\mathfrak{A}_{a_j} = V(q_i, r_i^2), \qquad \mathfrak{B}_{a_j} = V(q_i^2, r_i)
$$

where $V(q_i, r_i^2)$ is a word in the arguments q_i, r_i^2, $1 \leqslant i \leqslant \lambda$ and $V(q_i^2, r_i)$ is the same word but in the arguments q_i^2, r_i. If $V(q_i, r_i^2)$ is reduced then, clearly, $V(q_i^2, r_i)$ is reduced. Hence SB 5 follows.

Next we show that every word of G_1 is equal to some normal word. By Remark 2 it suffices to prove that the process of eliminating subwords of the form (16) from a word Rp_n^{ε}, $R \in C_0$, $p_n \in \Sigma_1$ is finite. Suppose, for example, that $p_n^{\varepsilon} \circeq a_j$. In the transformations $q_i^{\varepsilon} a_j \rightarrow a_j q_i^{2\varepsilon}$ and $r_i^2 a_j \rightarrow a_j r_i$, the length of the word R is decreased. In the transformations $r_i^{-1} a_j \rightarrow r_i a_j r_i^{-1}$, the length of R does not increase and the number of negative letters in R is decreased. Therefore after finitely many such transformations Ra_j will be reduced to normal form. The argument is similar when $p_n^{\varepsilon} \circeq a_j^{-1}, a_j^{+}, a_j^{+-1}$.

Let us now verify SB 6. Let, for example, Ra_j and Ta_j be normal words and let $R = TV(q_i, r_i^2)$, where $V = V(q_i, r_i^2)$ is a reduced word. Suppose that $V \not\circeq 1$. If TV is reduced then R ends in q_i^{ε} or $r_i^{2\varepsilon}$ which is impossible since Ra_j is normal. Otherwise if V begins with q_i^{ε} then T ends with $q_i^{-\varepsilon}$ and thus Ta_j is not normal. Similarly if V begins with $r_i^{2\varepsilon}$, and $r_i^{2\varepsilon}$ can be cancelled in TV then Ta_j is not normal. So suppose only r_i^{ε} can be cancelled between T and V. If $V \not\circeq r_i^{2\varepsilon}$ then Ra_j is not normal while if $V \circeq r_i^{2\varepsilon}$ then either Ra_j or Ta_j is not normal according as $\varepsilon = -1$ or $\varepsilon = 1$. This condition is verified in an analogous way in the other cases.

Now let us consider the group G_2. From the equalities

$$
\mathfrak{A}_{l_i} = V(a_j), \quad \mathfrak{B}_{l_i} = V(a_j), \quad \mathfrak{A}_{l_i^{+}} = V(a_j^{+}), \quad \mathfrak{B}_{l_i^{+}} = V(a_j^{+}),
$$

it follows that $\{l_i, l_i^{+}\}$ is a regular system of stable letters. Then, by C 2′ (in Remark 1) the reduced word

$$
W \circeq U_0 x_1^{\varepsilon_1} U_1 \cdots x_k^{k} U_k
$$

where $k \geqslant 0$, $x_i \in \Sigma_2$, $U_i \in C_1$, is normal if and only if it contains no subword from the list:

$$
(17) \qquad \begin{array}{ll} a_j V(q_i^2, r_i) l_i^{\varepsilon}, & a_j^{-1} V(q_i, r_i^2) l_i^{\varepsilon} \\ a_j^{+} V(q_i^{+}, r_i^{+2}) l_i^{+\varepsilon}, & a_j^{+-1} V(q_i^{+2}, r_i^{+}) l_i^{+\varepsilon}, \end{array}
$$

where the V's are reduced words. To verify SB 4 in this situation it suffices, by Remark 2, to note that, for instance, after the transformation

$$Rl_i^{\varepsilon} \mathrel{\overline{\underline{\circ}}} R'a_jV(q_i^2, r_i)l_i^{\varepsilon} \rightarrow R'V(q_i, r_i^2)l_i^{\varepsilon}a_j$$

has been performed, $R'V(q_i, r_i^2)$ has fewer occurrences of the letter a_j than R.

Let us verify condition SB 6. Let Rl_i and Tl_i be normal words and let $R = TV(a_j)$, where $V(a_j) \mathrel{\overline{\underline{\circ}}} a_{j_1}^{\varepsilon_1}a_{j_2}^{\varepsilon_2}\cdots a_{j_s}^{\varepsilon_s}$ is a non-empty reduced word. We consider the process of reducing TV to normal form. If $a_{j_1}^{\varepsilon_1}$ is not cancelled in this reduction process then none of $a_{j_1}^{\varepsilon_1}, \ldots, a_{j_s}^{\varepsilon_s}$ will be cancelled. By Lemma 1 it follows, writing $\varepsilon = \varepsilon_s$ and $j = j_s$, that R must end in $a_j^{\varepsilon}E$ where $E = \mathfrak{B}_{a_j^{\varepsilon}}$.

We see immediately that Rl_i is not normal. If $a_{j_1}^{\varepsilon_1}$ is cancelled in the reduction process, then, by Lemma 2, T ends in $a_{j_1}^{-\varepsilon_1}E$, where $E = \mathfrak{B}_{a_{j_1}^{-\varepsilon_1}}$, and this contradicts the normality of Tl_i. Thus $V \mathrel{\overline{\underline{\circ}}} 1$ and SB 6 is verified.

Finally we consider G_3. By C 2′, the reduced word

$$W \mathrel{\overline{\underline{\circ}}} U_0x_1^{\varepsilon_1}U_1\cdots x_k^{\varepsilon_k}U_k,$$

where $k \geqslant 0$, $x_i \in \Sigma_3$ and $U_i \in C_2$, is normal if and only if it contains no subword from the list:

$$
\begin{array}{ll}
 & r_i^{+\varepsilon}p_1, \quad r_i^{\varepsilon}p_1^{-1}, \quad q_i^{\varepsilon}p_2, \quad q_i^{+\varepsilon}p_2^{-1}, \\
 & l_i^{+}V(a_j^{+})p_1, \quad l_i^{-1}V(a_j)p_1^{-1}, \\
(18) & l_i^{+-1}C(V(a_j^{+})q_i^{+-1}A_i^{+})p_1, \quad l_iC(V(a_j)q_iA_i^{-1})p_1^{-1}, \\
 & l_iV(a_j)p_2, \quad l_i^{+-1}V(a_j^{+})p_2^{-1}, \\
 & l_i^{-1}C(V(a_j)r_i^{-1}B_i)p_2, \quad l_i^{+}C(V(a_j^{+})r_i^{+}B_i^{+-1})p_2^{-1},
\end{array}
$$

where $1 \leqslant i \leqslant \lambda$, $1 \leqslant j \leqslant n$ and the V's are reduced words. The validity of SB 4 for the group G_3 follows from Remark 2 and the fact that eliminating subwords (18) from the word Rp_i^{ε}, where $R \in G_2$, either decreases the number of letters $l_i^{\varepsilon}, l_i^{+\varepsilon}$ in R or leaves fixed the number of these letters but decreases the number of letters $r_i^{\varepsilon}, r_i^{+\varepsilon}, q_i^{\varepsilon}, q_i^{+\varepsilon}$ in R.

Now we verify SB 5. The relations of G_3 which involve p_1 and p_2 can be presented in the form

$$E^+p_1E = p_1, \qquad Fp_2F^+ = p_2$$

where E, F are words in Ξ and $(x_{i_1}^{\varepsilon_1}\cdots x_{i_k}^{\varepsilon_k})^+ \rightleftarrows x_{i_k}^{+\varepsilon_k}\cdots x_{i_1}^{+\varepsilon_1}$. It remains to note that the mapping $U \rightarrow U^+$ defines an antiisomorphism of the group with generating set Ξ and defining relations (14.1)–(14.3) and the group with generating set Ξ^+ and defining relations (14.1$^+$)–(14.3$^+$).

Before verifying SB 6 we consider the elements $\mathfrak{A}_{p_1}$, $\mathfrak{B}_{p_1}$, $\mathfrak{A}_{p_2}$, $\mathfrak{B}_{p_2}$. In more detail these are

$$(19)\quad \begin{aligned} \mathfrak{A}_{p_1} &= V(A_i^{+-1}q_i^+l_i^+, r_i^+), & \mathfrak{B}_{p_1} &= V(A_iq_i^{-1}l_i^{-1}, r_i^{-1}) \\ \mathfrak{A}_{p_2} &= V(B_i^{-1}r_il_i, q_i), & \mathfrak{B}_{p_2} &= V(B_i^+r_i^{+-1}l_i^{+-1}, q_i^{+-1}) \end{aligned}$$

where we may assume that in the words V there are no adjacent inverse pairs $(A_i^{+-1}q_i^+l_i^+)^{-\varepsilon}(A_i^{+-1}q_il_i^+)^{\varepsilon}, r_i^{+-\varepsilon}r_i^{+\varepsilon}, \ldots, (q_i^{+-1})^{-\varepsilon}(q_i^{+-1})^{\varepsilon}$. We consider, for example, $\mathfrak{A}_{p_2} = V(B_i^{-1}r_il_i, q_i)$. Obviously this is normal if it contains no occurrences of l_i. On the other hand, if it does contain occurrences of l_i then it is, in fact, $\{l_i\}$-reduced. Suppose, for example, that V contains the subword

$$l_i^{-1}r_i^{-1}B_iW(q_j)B_i^{-1}r_il_i$$

and $r_i^{-1}B_iW(q_j)B_i^{-1}r_i = V_1(a_j)$, where W and V_1 are reduced. The normal forms (in G_1) of $r_i^{-1}B_iWB_i^{-1}r_i$ and V_1 must coincide graphically and so $C(r_i^{-1}B_iWB_i^{-1}r_i)$ contains no occurrences of letters q_j. But this happens only when $W \mathrel{\bar{\circ}} 1$ and then V contains an inverse pair, which we ruled out above.

Now, to verify SB 6, suppose that Rp_2 and Tp_2 are normal and that $R = TV(B_i^{-1}r_il_i, q_i)$, where V contains no adjacent inverse pairs $(B_i^{-1}r_il_i)^{-\varepsilon}(B_i^{-1}r_il_i)^{\varepsilon}$, $q_i^{-\varepsilon}q_i^{\varepsilon}$. If $V \mathrel{\bar{\circ}} V(q_i)$, then, since neither R and S can end in q_i^{ε}, it follows that $V \mathrel{\bar{\circ}} 1$. Let V contain an occurrence of a letter l_i^{ε}. We take the leftmost of such occurrences and suppose that this l_i^{ε} is cancelled in reducing TV to normal form. Two cases arise:

1) $\varepsilon = 1$. Then, by Lemma 2, we have

$$T \mathrel{\bar{\circ}} T_1l_i^{-1}T_2, \qquad T_2 \in G_1, \qquad V \mathrel{\bar{\circ}} V_1(q_j)B_i^{-1}r_il_iV_2$$

where $T_2V_1(q_j)B_i^{-1}r_i = V_3(a_j)$ in G_1. It follows that $T_2 \mathrel{\bar{\circ}} C(V_3(a_j)r_i^{-1}B_iV_4(q_j))$, where V_3 and V_4 are reduced words. The last equality shows that Tp_2 is not normal. (If $V_4 \not\mathrel{\bar{\circ}} 1$, then Tp_2 contains $q_j^{\varepsilon}p_2$ while if $V_4 \mathrel{\bar{\circ}} 1$, then Tp_2 contains $l_i^{-1}C(V_3(a_j)r_i^{-1}B_i)p_2$.)

2) $\varepsilon = -1$. Here we have

$$T \mathrel{\bar{\circ}} T_1l_iT_2, \qquad T_2 \in G_1, \qquad V \mathrel{\bar{\circ}} V_1(q_j)l_i^{-1}V_2$$

where $T_2V_1(q_j) = V_3(a_j)$. Thus $T_2 = V_3(a_j)V_4(q_j)$, with V_3, V_4 reduced and again Tp_2 is not in normal form. We conclude that the leftmost letter l_i^{ε} of $V(B_i^{-1}r_il_i, q_i)$ is not cancelled in reducing TV to normal form. But then, by Remark 3 and Lemma 1, the word $C(TV) \mathrel{\bar{\circ}} R$ ends in one of the following words:

$$l_iV_3(a_j)V_4(q_j), \qquad l_i^{-1}C(V_3(a_j)r_i^{-1}B_iV_4(q_j))$$

Arguing as above we show in both cases that Rp_2 is not in normal form.

The other cases occurring in the verification of SB 6 $(p_n^\varepsilon \bar{\circ} p_2^{-1}, p_1, p_1^{-1})$ are dealt with in an analogous way.

This completes the proof of the following theorem.

Theorem 2. *A Novikov group* $\mathfrak{A}_{p_1p_2}$ *is a group with standard basis.*

Corollary (See [1]). *The word problem in any Novikov group* $\mathfrak{A}_{p_1p_2}$ *is algorithmically solvable.*

To establish the corollary it suffices to inspect the list (16)–(19) of words which we eliminate in reducing to normal form and be convinced that the question of recognising whether an arbitrarily given word belongs to the indicated list is algorithmically solvable. In fact the only words in this list whose explicit form is not indicated are those words, for example, of the type $C(V(a_j)r_i^{-1}B_i)$. However, a normal word T is of this indicated form if and only if $C(TB_i^{-1}r_i) \bar{\circ} V(a_j)$ which fact one can always determine.

We derive from Theorem 2 the result of Novikov [20] concerning the conjugacy problem which may be unsolvable in a group $\mathfrak{A}_{p_1p_2}$. We recall the definition of a certain calculus introduced by Post. A *Post system* K is a pair $K = [\Sigma_0; \Phi_0]$ where Σ_0 is a finite alphabet and $\Phi_0 = \{(A_i, B_i);\ 1 \leqslant i \leqslant \lambda\}$ is a finite set of pairs of words from the alphabet Σ_0. By *elementary transformations* of K we mean the following transformations of words in the alphabet Σ_0:

(20) $\qquad X \to X, \qquad A_iX \to XB_i, \qquad XB_i \to A_iX$

where $(A_i, B_i) \in \Phi_0$.

Two words U and V (from Σ_0) are called *equivalent* in K, written $U \sim W$, if there exists a sequence of elementary transformations which transforms U into W. It is well known (see the references to Post and Markov in [20]) that there exists a Post system with unsolvable problem of equivalence.

With each Novikov group $\mathfrak{A}$, one can associate a Post system

$$K(\mathfrak{A}) = [\{a_1, \ldots, a_n\}; (A_i, B_i),\ 1 \leqslant i \leqslant \lambda]$$

Novikov's first theorem. *Let* X *and* Y *be positive words from* $\{a_i, 1 \leqslant i \leqslant n\}$. *If* $\mathfrak{B}_{p_1}X\mathfrak{A}_{p_2} = Y$ *in* $\mathfrak{A}_{p_1p_2}$, *then* $X \sim Y$ *in the corresponding Post system* $K(\mathfrak{A})$.

Proof. From the given condition we have

(21) $$V(A_i q_i^{-1} l_i^{-1}, r_j) X(a_j) W(B_i^{-1} r_i l_i, q_j) = Y(a_j)$$

where V and W are suitably reduced (see (19)). If $V \bar{\underline{\circ}} V(r_j)$, then $W \bar{\underline{\circ}} W(q_j)$ — otherwise the normal form of the left-hand side of (21) will contain letters l_i^ε, which is obviously impossible. In this case $V \bar{\underline{\circ}} 1$ and $W \bar{\underline{\circ}} 1$ because Y is in normal and contains no letters r_j^ε, q_j^ε. Then $X \bar{\underline{\circ}} Y$ and so $X \sim Y$ in $K(\mathfrak{A})$.

Now let V and W contain letters l_i^ε. Then the last letter l_i^ε of V has to be cancelled (in reducing the left-hand side of (21) to normal form) with the first letter $l_i^{-\varepsilon}$ of W. There are two alternative cases.

1) $\varepsilon = -1$. We have

(22) $$V \bar{\underline{\circ}} V_1 A_i q_i^{-1} l_i^{-1} V_2(r_j), \qquad W \bar{\underline{\circ}} W_1(q_j) B_i^{-1} r_i l_i W_2$$

and, by Remark 3 and Lemma 2, we obtain

(23) $$V_2(r_j) X W_1(q_j) B_i^{-1} r_i = U(a_j).$$

As the normal form of the left side of (23) cannot contain q_j or r_j we have $W_1 \bar{\underline{\circ}} 1$, $X \bar{\underline{\circ}} X_1 B_i$ and $V_2(r_j) X r_i = X_1$ in G_1. Substituting in (22) and (23) we obtain

$$V_1(A_i q_i^{-1} l_i^{-1}, r_j) A_i X_1 W'(B_i^{-1} r_i l_i, q_j) = Y$$

where V_1 and $W' \bar{\underline{\circ}} q_i^{-2|X_1|} W_2$ contain fewer occurrences of letters l_i^ε then do V and W respectively. (Here $|X_1|$ is the length of X_1.)

2) $\varepsilon = 1$. In the same way as above, we show that $X \bar{\underline{\circ}} A_i X_1$, and from (22) there follows the equality $V_1 X_1 B_i W_1 = Y$ where V_1 and W_1 contain fewer occurrences of letters l_i^ε.

The proof is completed by an obvious induction on the number of occurrences of letters l_i^ε in V.

Novikov's second theorem. *Let X and Y be positive words from $\{a_i, 1 \leq i \leq n\}$. Then the words $p_1 X p_2 X^+$ and $p_1 Y p_2 Y^+$ are conjugate in the group $\mathfrak{A}_{p_1 p_2}$ if and only if $X \sim Y$ in the corresponding Post system $K(\mathfrak{A})$.*

Proof. Write $E \bar{\underline{\circ}} p_1 X p_2 X^+$ and $D \bar{\underline{\circ}} p_1 Y p_2 Y^+$ and assume that E is conjugate to D in $\mathfrak{A}_{p_1 p_2}$. Let $\{E_k, 1 \leq k \leq N\}$ be the set of all words obtained from E by cyclic permutation of letters. Among all normal words U satisfying

(24) $$D = U E_k U^{-1},$$

for some k we choose a word U_0 in which the number of occurrences of $p_1^\varepsilon, p_2^\varepsilon$ is least. We claim that this chosen U_0 contains no occurrences of $p_1^\varepsilon, p_2^\varepsilon$. Suppose otherwise; if $U_0 \bar{\underline{\circ}} U_1 p_i^\varepsilon U_2$, where U_2 is p_i^ε-free, then we have

(25) $$D = U_1 p_i^{\varepsilon} U_2 E_k U_2^{-1} p_i^{-\varepsilon} U_1^{-1}.$$

Take $\varepsilon = -1$; as D contains only positive occurrences of p_1 and p_2, Britton's lemma applied to (25) yields

(26) $$E_k \overset{\circ}{=} E_1' p_i E_2', \qquad U_2 E_1' = \mathfrak{A}_{p_i}.$$

Substituting in (25), this yields

$$D = U_1 \mathfrak{B}_{p_i} E_2' E_1' p_i \mathfrak{B}_{p_i}^{-1} U_1^{-1}$$

and $C(U_1 \mathfrak{B}_{p_i})$ contains fewer occurrences of p_i^{ε} than U_0. This contradicts our choice of U_0.

Now we consider (24) with $U \overset{\circ}{=} U_0$. So we have

(27) $$U_0 E_k U_0^{-1} = p_1 Y p_2 Y^{+}.$$

Since U_0 has no occurrences of $p_1^{\varepsilon}, p_2^{\varepsilon}$ we can, without loss of generality assume that $E_k \overset{\circ}{=} p_1 X p_2 X^{+}$. Then Britton's lemma applied to (27) yields

$$\mathfrak{B}_{p_1} X \mathfrak{A}_{p_2} = Y$$

in $\mathfrak{A}_{p_1 p_2}$. It follows from Novikov's first theorem that $X \sim Y$ in $K(\mathfrak{A})$.

Conversely suppose $X \sim Y$ in $K(\mathfrak{A})$. Inductively it suffices to consider the two cases:

$$X \overset{\circ}{=} A_i X_1, \quad Y \overset{\circ}{=} X_1 B_i \quad \text{and} \quad X \overset{\circ}{=} X_1 B_i, \quad Y \overset{\circ}{=} A_i X_1.$$

Let, for example, the first of these occur. Then in $\mathfrak{A}_{p_1 p_2}$ we have

$$U p_1 A_i X_1 p_2 X_1^{+} A_i^{+} U^{-1} = p_1 X_1 B_i p_2 B_i^{+} X_1^{+}$$

where $U \overset{\circ}{=} (r_i^{+})^{-2|X_1|} l_i^{+-1} q_i^{+-1} A_i^{+}$. The second case is dealt with similarly and so the theorem is proved.

Novikov's second theorem shows that the equivalence problem for the system $K(\mathfrak{A})$ is reducible to the conjugacy problem for the group $\mathfrak{A}_{p_1 p_2}$. The converse reduction was established in [7] and the following result proved.

Theorem 3. *For any finitely presented semigroup Π one can construct a Post system $K(\Pi)$ such that*

1) *the word problem for Π is equivalent (in the sense of Turing reducibility) to the equivalence problem for $K(\Pi)$,*

2) *the equivalence problem for $K(\Pi)$ is equivalent (in the sense of Turing reducibility) to the conjugacy problem in the Novikov group $\mathfrak{A}_{p_1 p_2}$ for which $K(\Pi)$ is the corresponding Post system.*

From this theorem it follows that there exist finitely presented groups with conjugacy problem of arbitrary recursively enumerable Turing degree of unsolvability. As noted earlier, this last result was obtained independently by Collins [15].

§4. Boone groups

In this section, we shall prove that a Boone group $G(T,q)$, as defined in [10], is a group with standard basis and, using this fact, we shall derive some properties of such groups.

By a *special* semigroup, we understand a semigroup T with generators

$$s_b, q_a \qquad (b \in B, a \in A)$$

and defining relations

$$\Sigma_i = \Gamma_i, \qquad 1 \leq i \leq N$$

where Σ_i and Γ_i are *special* words, i.e. words of the form Sq_aS', where S and S' are (positive) $\{s_b\}$-words.

Let T be a special semigroup with a distinguished letter $q_1 = q$. We construct, for the pair (T,q), the following group $G(T,q)$. This group is generated by the set of elements

$$\Xi = \{s_b, q_a, k, t, x, y, l_i, r_i, b \in B, a \in A, 1 \leq i \leq N\}$$

and has the following defining relations (the bold face italic letters are to be distinguished):

$$
(28) \qquad
\begin{aligned}
&1.\ s_b\boldsymbol{y} = \boldsymbol{y}ys_b, &&\boldsymbol{x}s_b = s_bx\boldsymbol{x}\\
&2.\ s_b\boldsymbol{l}_i = y\boldsymbol{l}_iys_b, &&\boldsymbol{r}_is_b = s_bx\boldsymbol{r}_ix\\
&3.\ \Sigma_i = \boldsymbol{l}_i\Gamma_i\boldsymbol{r}_i,\\
&4.\ \boldsymbol{t}\boldsymbol{l}_i = \boldsymbol{l}_i\boldsymbol{t}, &&\boldsymbol{t}y = y\boldsymbol{t}\\
&5.\ \boldsymbol{r}_ik = k\boldsymbol{r}_i, &&\boldsymbol{x}k = k\boldsymbol{x}\\
&6.\ (q^{-1}tq)k = k(q^{-1}tq),
\end{aligned}
$$

where $b \in B$, $1 \leq i \leq N$ and Σ_i, Γ_i are the words from the defining system of equalities of the semigroup T.

We add to this system of relations the equalities

$$
(29) \qquad
\begin{aligned}
&4'.\ \boldsymbol{l}_iV(y)t = t\boldsymbol{l}_iV(y),\\
&6'.\ q^{-1}tqV(r_i,x)k = kq^{-1}tqV(r_i,x),
\end{aligned}
$$

where $V(y)$ and $V(r_i, x)$ are reduced words. The system of relations (28) and (29) we shall denote by Φ. Since each relation in (29) is easily seen to be a consequence of the relations (28), $\langle \Xi ; \Phi \rangle$ is still a presentation of $G(T, q)$, though now one with infinitely many relations. In our present approach the adjunction of these extra relations is essential to the definition of normal words.

Let us consider the following partitions of Ξ and Φ:

$$\Xi_0 = \{x, y\}, \qquad \Xi_1 = \{s_b, b \in B\}, \qquad \Xi_2 = \{l_i, r_i, 1 \leqslant i \leqslant N\}$$

$$\Xi_3 = \{q_a, a \in A\}, \quad \Xi_4 = \{t\}, \qquad \Xi_5 = \{k\},$$

$$\Phi_0 = \phi, \qquad \Phi_1 = \{(28.1)\}, \qquad \Phi_2 = \{(28.2)\},$$

$$\Phi_3 = \{(28.3)\}, \qquad \Phi_4 = \{(28.4), (29.4')\}, \quad \Phi_5 - \{(28.5), (29.6')\}.$$

These partitions define the groups G_α, $0 \leqslant \alpha \leqslant 5$, as explained in Section 2. (For reasons of convenience we change notation somewhat; instead of Σ we write Ξ, and so on.) We take all relations from Φ_α, $0 < \alpha \leqslant 5$ to be given in the form

$$A_1 z A_2 p_n = p_m B_1 u B_2$$

where $p_n, p_m \in \Xi_\alpha$, $A_1 z A_2$ and $B_1 u B_2$ are $\Xi_{\alpha-1}$-words, and z, u are distinguished letters in (28) and (29).

Let us construct the sets C_α, $0 \leqslant \alpha \leqslant 5$, and prove, for each α, that C_α is a basis of G_α. The group G_0 is free and C_0 is defined to be the set of reduced words in $\{x, y\}$. The group G_1 was essentially considered in the previous section. We note only that C_1 is the set of reduced words $W \mathrel{\underline{\circ}} U_0 x_1^{\varepsilon_1} U_1 \cdots x_k^{\varepsilon_k} U_k$, where $k \geqslant 0$, $U_i \in C_0$, $x_i \in \Xi_1 = \{s_b\}$, which contain no subwords

(30) $$y^2 s_b,\ y^{-1} s_b,\ y^{\varepsilon} s_b^{-1},\ x^{\varepsilon} s_b,\ x^{-2} s_b^{-1},\ x s_b^{-1}.$$

Now we consider G_2. By virtue of C 2′, the set C_2 consists of all the reduced words $W \mathrel{\underline{\circ}} U_0 x_1^{\varepsilon_1} U_1 \cdots x_k^{\varepsilon_k} U_k$, where $k \geqslant 0$, $U_i \in C_1$, $x_i \in \Xi_2 = \{l_i, r_i\}$, containing no subwords

(31) $$s_b V(y, x^2) l_i^{\varepsilon}, \qquad s_b^{-1} V(y^2, x) y^{\varepsilon} l_i^{-1}$$
$$s_b V(y, x^2) x^{\varepsilon_1} r_i, \qquad s_b^{-1} V(y^2, x) r_i^{\varepsilon}$$

where V, Vy^{ε}, Vx^{ε_1} and V are reduced words, $b \in B$ and $1 \leqslant i \leqslant N$.

Condition SB 4 is verified in a routine way — elimination of subwords (31) from Rp_n^{ε}, where $R \in C_1$, $p_n \in \Xi_2$, leads to a decrease in the number of letters $s_b^{\pm 1}$ in the word R. Condition SB 5 follows from the fact that

$$\mathfrak{A}_{l_i} = V(y^{-1}s_b) = ySy^{-1}, \qquad \mathfrak{B}_{l_i} = V(ys_b) = y^{-1}Sy$$

$$\mathfrak{A}_{r_i} = V(s_b x) = xSx^{-1}, \qquad \mathfrak{B}_{r_i} = V(s_b x^{-1}) = x^{-1}Sx$$

where S is a reduced $\{s_b\}$-word and the mapping $s_b \to s_b$, $x \to x^{-1}$, $y \to y^{-1}$ induces an automorphism of the group G_1. Condition SB 6 is verified in a routine way. For example, let Tl_i and Rl_i be normal with $R = T\mathfrak{A}_{l_i}$, i.e. $R = TySy^{-1}$ where S is a reduced word.

Let $S \cong s_{b_1}^{\varepsilon_1} \cdots s_{b_k}^{\varepsilon_k}$, $k \geq 1$. We consider two cases.

1) In reducing $TySy^{-1}$ to normal form, the letter $s_{b_1}^{\varepsilon_1} \cong s_b^{\varepsilon}$ is cancelled. Then by Lemma 2 and Remark 3, we obtain

$$T \cong T_1 s_b^{-\varepsilon} T_2, \; T_2 \in G_0, \; T_2 \cong C(\mathfrak{B}_{s_b^{-\varepsilon}} y^{-1})$$

This contradicts the fact that Tl_i is normal.

2) In reducing $TySy^{-1}$, the letter $s_{b_1}^{\varepsilon_1}$ is not cancelled. Then in reducing this word to normal form no letter of the word S is cancelled, and thus, by Lemma 1, the word $R \cong C(TySy^{-1})$ ends in $s_b^{\varepsilon} C(\mathfrak{B}_{s_b^{\varepsilon}} y^{-1})$, where $b = b_k$, $\varepsilon = \varepsilon_k$. This contradicts the fact that Rl_i is normal. Other possibilities ($p_n^{\varepsilon} \cong l_i^{-1}, r_i, r_i^{-1}$) are dealt with in an analogous way.

Let us consider the group G_3. Writing Σ_i and Γ_i in the forms

$$\Sigma_i \cong \Sigma_{i1} q_{n_i} \Sigma_{i2}, \qquad \Gamma_i \cong \Gamma_{i_1} q_{m_i} \Gamma_{i_2}$$

respectively, we rewrite the relations (28.3) as

(28.3′) $$\Sigma_{i1}^{-1} l_i \Gamma_{i1} q_{m_i} = q_{n_i} \Sigma_{i2} r_i^{-1} \Gamma_{i2}^{-1}.$$

Then, if $\mathfrak{A}_{q_m q_n}$ and $\mathfrak{B}_{q_n q_m}$ are connected words, we have

(32) $$\mathfrak{A}_{q_m q_n} \cong V(\Sigma_{i1}^{-1} l_i \Gamma_{i1}), \qquad \mathfrak{B}_{q_n q_m} \cong V(\Sigma_{i2} r_i^{-1} \Gamma_{i2}^{-1})$$

where we take a reduced word $V(x_i)$ in some new variables x_i, $1 \leq i \leq N$, and $\mathfrak{A}_{q_m q_n}$ and $\mathfrak{B}_{q_n q_m}$ are obtained from $V(x_i)$ by substituting $\Sigma_{i1}^{-1} l_i \Gamma_{i1}$ and $\Sigma_{i2} r_i^{-1} \Gamma_{i2}^{-1}$, respectively, for x_i. We shall call $V(x_i)$ the *diagram* of the words (32).

Let $\mathfrak{A}_{q_m q_n}$ have diagram $V(x_i)$, where $V(x_i)$ is reduced and non-empty. Then the projection of $\mathfrak{A}_{q_m q_n}$ on the alphabet $\{l_i\}$ is reduced and non-empty. This projection is a homomorphism from G_2 to the free group on $\{l_i\}$ and hence $\mathfrak{A}_{q_m q_n} \neq 1$ in G_2. By a similar argument the connected word $\mathfrak{B}_{q_n q_m} \neq 1$ in G_2 and SB 5 holds for G_3.

We note that the words $\mathfrak{A}_{q_m q_n}$, $\mathfrak{B}_{q_n q_m}$ are uniquely defined by the sequence of letters $l_i^{\varepsilon}, r_i^{\varepsilon}$ which appear in them. Specifically if $\mathfrak{A}_{q_m q_n}$ and $\mathfrak{B}_{q_n q_m}$ have diagram $V(x_i) \cong x_{i_1}^{\varepsilon_1} \cdots x_{i_k}^{\varepsilon_k}$, then we have

(33) $$\mathfrak{A}_{q_m q_n} \cong \mathfrak{A}(l_{i_1}^{\varepsilon_1}, \ldots, l_{i_k}^{\varepsilon_k}), \qquad \mathfrak{B}_{q_n q_m} \cong \mathfrak{B}(r_{i_1}^{-\varepsilon_1}, \ldots, r_{i_k}^{-\varepsilon_k}),$$

where

$$\mathfrak{A}(l_{i_1}^{\varepsilon_1},\ldots,l_{i_k}^{\varepsilon_k}) \rightleftharpoons (\Sigma_{i_1 1}^{-1} l_{i_1} \Gamma_{i_1 1})^{\varepsilon_1}\cdots(\Sigma_{i_k 1}^{-1} l_{i_k} \Gamma_{i_k 1})^{\varepsilon_k}$$

and

$$\mathfrak{B}(r_{i_1}^{-\varepsilon_1},\ldots,r_{i_k}^{-\varepsilon_k}) \rightleftharpoons (\Sigma_{i_1 2} r_{i_1}^{-1} \Gamma_{i_1 2}^{-1})^{\varepsilon_1}\cdots(\Sigma_{i_k 2} r_{i_k}^{-1} \Gamma_{i_k 2}^{-1})^{\varepsilon_k}.$$

For G_3, the verification of condition SB 4 is straightforward. We note only that C_3 consists of all reduced words $W \,\overline{\circ}\, U_0 q_{n_1}^{\varepsilon_1} U_1 \cdots q_{n_k}^{\varepsilon_k} U_k$, where $k \geq 0$, $U_i \in C_2$, which contain no subwords

$$\text{(34)}\qquad \begin{array}{ll} l_i C(y^{-1} S y \Gamma_{i_1}) q_{m_i}, & l_i^{-1} C(y S y^{-1} \Sigma_{i1}) q_{n_i} \\ r_i^{-1} C(x S x^{-1} \Gamma_{i2}^{-1}) q_{m_i}^{-1}, & r_i C(x^{-1} S x \Sigma_{i2}^{-1}) q_{n_i}^{-1} \end{array}$$

associated with the relations of (28.3′).

The verification of SB 6 is also straightforward. For example, let Rq_m and Tq_n be in normal form, where $R, T \in G_2$ and $R = T\mathfrak{A}_{q_m q_n} = T\mathfrak{A}(l_{i_1}^{\varepsilon_1},\ldots,l_{i_k}^{\varepsilon_k})$. Suppose $\mathfrak{A}_{q_m q_n} \not\equiv 1$; if $l_{i_1}^{\varepsilon_1}$ is cancelled in reducing $T\mathfrak{A}_{q_m q_n}$ to normal form, then, by Lemma 2, the word T ends in $l_{i_1}^{-1} C(y S y^{-1} \Sigma_{i_1 1})$ or in $l_{ik} C(y^{-1} S y \Gamma_{i_1 1})$, according as $\varepsilon_1 = 1$ or $\varepsilon_1 = -1$. In either case Tq_n is not normal. If $l_{i_1}^{\varepsilon_1}$ is not cancelled, then R ends in $l_{i_k}^{-1} C(y S y^{-1} \Sigma_{i_k 1})$ or $l_{i_k} C(y^{-1} S y \Gamma_{i_k 1})$ and Rq_m is not normal.

For the group G_4 we have

$$\mathfrak{A}_t = V(l_i, y), \qquad \mathfrak{B}_t = V(l_i, y)$$

where $V(l_i, y)$ is a reduced and hence normal word. The set C_4 consists of all reduced words $W \,\overline{\circ}\, U_0 t^{\varepsilon_1} U_1 \cdots t^{\varepsilon_k} U_k$, where $k \geq 0$ and $U_i \in C_3$, which contain no subwords

$$\text{(35)}\qquad y^{\delta} t^{\varepsilon}, \quad l_i C(y^{-1} S y V(y)) t^{\varepsilon}, \quad l_i^{-1} C(y S y^{-1} V(y)) t^{\varepsilon}$$

where $\delta = \pm 1$ and S, as usual, is a reduced $\{s_b\}$-word. Condition SB 5 is clear because $\mathfrak{A}_t = \mathfrak{B}_t$ while condition SB 4 follows from the fact that elimination of subwords (35) from Rt^{ε}, $R \in C_3$, either decreases the number of letters l_i^{ε} in R or decreases the number of letters y^{ε} in R.

To verify SB 6, consider, for example, Rt and St where $R = S\mathfrak{A}_t = SV(l_i, y)$, and $V(l_i, y)$ is reduced. Suppose $V(l_i, y) \not\equiv 1$; if $V(l_i, y) \,\overline{\circ}\, V(y)$ then either S or R ends in y^{δ} which is impossible. If $V(l_i, y)$ involves some l_i^{ε}, then considering, as usual, the first and last of the occurrences of these letters, we deduce that Rt or St contains a subword (35), which is impossible when Rt and St are normal.

Finally we consider G_5. Bearing in mind that we added relations (29.6′), strictly we have

$$\mathfrak{A}_k = W(q^{-1} t q V(r_i, x), r_i, x) = \mathfrak{B}_k\,;$$

of course we can write $W(q^{-1}tqV(r_i, x), r_i, x) = W'(q^{-1}tq, r_i, x)$. The set C_5 consists of all reduced words $W \overline{\underline{\circ}}\, U_0 k^{\varepsilon_1} U_1 \cdots k^{\varepsilon_s} U_s$, where $s \geqslant 0$ and $U_i \in C_4$, which contain no subwords

$$r_i^\delta k^\varepsilon, \quad x^\delta k^\varepsilon, \quad t^\delta C(W(l_i, y)qV(r_i, x))k^\varepsilon$$

where $\delta = \pm 1$. The verification of SB 4, SB 5 and SB 6 for G_5 is similar to that for G_4 and we omit these straightforward arguments.

We do, though, note precisely why the additional relations (29) are needed. Let Σ be a special word of T and suppose that $\Sigma = q$ in T. Then $\Sigma^{-1}t\Sigma k = k\Sigma^{-1}t\Sigma$ in G (see [10] or Lemma 6 below). If we had used only the relations (28) in our definition of normal form, then we would be forced to regard $\Sigma^{-1}t\Sigma k$ as normal since we are not able, in general, to show that $\Sigma = V(l_i, y)q$ in G. Since $k\Sigma^{-1}t\Sigma$ would also be normal, SB 6 would fail. The relations (29.6′) are added since, when $\Sigma = q$ in T, one can prove that $\Sigma = V(l_i, y)qW(r_i, x)$ in G_4.

Our conclusions above amount to the following result.

Theorem 4. *Any Boone group $G(T, q)$ is a group with standard basis.*

We shall now apply Theorem 4 to show that the word problem for $G(T, q)$ is equivalent to the problem of equality with q, for special words, in the semigroup T. For this we determine a number of properties of $G(T, q)$ (see [12], [17]).

Lemma 5. *The word problem for the group G_4 is solvable.*

Proof. We consider, in turn, the groups G_α, $0 \leqslant \alpha \leqslant 4$ and verify that, for each α, the basis C_α is effective in the sense that the process of reducing words to normal form is effective.

Since G_0 is free, its basis C_0 is clearly effective. The effectiveness of C_1 and C_2 follows from the fact that the words (30) and the words (31) are explicitly defined. By contrast the words (34) are not given in an explicit way. Suppose though, that we are given a normal word T. To decide, for example, whether or not there exists a word S such that $T \overline{\underline{\circ}}\, C(y^{-1}Sy\Gamma_{i1})$, it suffices to decide whether or not $C(yT\Gamma_{i1}^{-1}y^{-1})$ is an $\{s_b\}$-word and this can be done effectively. So C_3 is effective. In a similar way, we can decide of a normal word T of C_3 whether or not $T \overline{\underline{\circ}}\, C(y^{-1}Sy^n)$, for some reduced $\{s_b\}$-word S. For this occurs if and only if S is the projection of T on the alphabet $\{s_b\}$ and $C(S^{-1}yT) \overline{\underline{\circ}}\, y^n$. This shows that C_4 is effective and the lemma is proved.

Lemma 6. *Let Σ and Σ' be two special words of T. Then $\Sigma = \Sigma'$ in T if and only if there exist words $V(l_i, y)$ and $W(r_i, x)$ such that*

$$\Sigma = V(l_i, y)\Sigma' W(r_i, x) \tag{36}$$

in the group G_3.

Proof. Let $\Sigma = \Sigma'$ in T. Inductively, it suffices to consider the case when Σ is transformed into Σ' with the aid of one transformation of the type $\Sigma_i \to \Gamma_i$ or $\Gamma_i \to \Sigma_i$. Suppose, for example, that $\Sigma \overset{\circ}{=} S_1\Sigma_i S_2$ and $\Sigma' \overset{\circ}{=} S_1\Gamma_i S_2$. Then, applying relations (28.1)–(28.3) we see that $\Sigma = V(l_i, y)\Sigma' W(r_i, x)$ in G_3, for some words $V(l_i, y)$, $W(r_i, x)$.

We now prove the converse. Let the equality (36) hold. We suppose that

$$\Sigma \overset{\circ}{=} S_1 q_n S_2, \quad \Sigma' \overset{\circ}{=} S_1' q_m S_2', \quad V(l_i, y) \overset{\circ}{=} y^{n_0} l_{i_1}^{\varepsilon_1} \cdots l_{i_k}^{\varepsilon_k} y^{n_k},$$

and that V is reduced. By our assumption, the normal form of

$$y^{n_0} l_{i_1}^{\varepsilon_1} \cdots l_{i_k}^{\varepsilon_k} S_1' q_m \tag{37}$$

is of the form $S_1 q_n U$, where $U \in G_1$. However, by Remark 2, the normal form of (37) is obtained by eliminating words (34) which correspond to relations (28.3) of $G(T, q)$. Since each such elimination represents the application of a relation (28.3′), accompanied by use of the relations of G_1 except insertions of letters l_i, we obtain

$$y^{n_0} l_{i_1}^{\varepsilon_1} \cdots l_{i_k}^{\varepsilon_k} y^{n_k} S_1' = S_1 \mathfrak{A}(l_{i_1}^{\varepsilon_1}, \ldots, l_{i_k}^{\varepsilon_k}) \tag{38}$$

in G_1, where $\mathfrak{A}(l_{i_1}^{\varepsilon_1}, \ldots, l_{i_k}^{\varepsilon_k}) \overset{\circ}{=} \mathfrak{A}_{q_m q_n}$ and the diagram of $\mathfrak{A}_{q_m q_n}$ is reduced. From (36) and (38), it follows that

$$\mathfrak{B}(r_{i_1}^{-\varepsilon_1}, \ldots, r_{i_k}^{-\varepsilon_k}) S_2' W(r_i, x) = S_2. \tag{39}$$

From (39) and Britton's lemma (or the algorithm for reducing to normal form) we have

$$W(r_i, x) \overset{\circ}{=} x^{m_k} r_{i_k}^{\varepsilon_k} \cdots r_{i_1}^{\varepsilon_1} x^{m_0}.$$

We prove that $\Sigma = \Sigma'$ in T by induction on k. If $k = 0$, then $\Sigma \overset{\circ}{=} \Sigma'$. Let $k > 0$ and suppose, for example, that $\varepsilon_k = 1$. Then from (38) we have

$$l_{i_k} y^{n_k} S_1' q_m = l_{i_k} y^{-1} S y \Gamma_{i_k 1} q_m$$

where $q_m \overset{\circ}{=} q_{m_{i_k}}$ and S is a positive $\{s_b\}$-word. From a first reduction of the right-hand side of (36), we obtain

$$\Sigma = y^{n_0} l_{i_1}^{\varepsilon_1} \cdots l_{i_{k-1}}^{\varepsilon_{k-1}} y^{n_{k-1}} S \Sigma_{i_k 1} q_{n_{i_k}} \Sigma_{i_k 2} r_{i_k}^{-1} \Gamma_{i_k 2}^{-1} S_2' x^{m_k} r_{i_k}^{\varepsilon_k} \cdots r_{i_1}^{\varepsilon_1} x^{m_0}. \tag{40}$$

From (39), with $\varepsilon_k = 1$, it follows that

$$\Gamma_{i_k 2}^{-1} S'_2 x^{m_k} = xS'x^{-1}$$

where S' is a positive word, and thus $S'_2 \stackrel{\circ}{=} \Gamma_{i_k 2} S'$.

In this way we obtain, from (40),

$$\Sigma = y^{n_0} l_{i_1}^{\varepsilon_1} \cdots l_{i_{k-1}}^{\varepsilon_{k-1}} y^{n'_{k-1}} S \Sigma_{i_k 1} q_{n_{i_k}} \Sigma_{i_k 2} x^{m'_{k-1}} r_{i_{k-1}}^{\varepsilon_{k-1}} \cdots r_{i_1}^{\varepsilon_1} x^{m_0} \tag{41}$$

and $\Sigma' \stackrel{\circ}{=} S\Gamma_{i_k 1} q_{m_{i_k}} \Gamma_{i_k 2} S'$. The inductive assumption applied to (41) yields $\Sigma = S\Sigma_{i_k 1} q_{n_{i_k}} \Sigma_{i_k 2} S'$ in T and so $\Sigma = \Sigma'$ in T as required.

Lemma 7. *The problem of equality of an arbitrary word W of G_3 with a word of the form*

$$V(l_i, y)\Sigma W(r_i, x),$$

where Σ is special, is solvable.

Proof. If suffices to consider a normal word $Q \stackrel{\circ}{=} Q_1 q_m Q_2$ where $Q_1, Q_2 \in C_2$. Suppose that

$$Q = V(l_i, y)\Sigma W(r_i, x) \tag{42}$$

where $\Sigma \stackrel{\circ}{=} \Sigma' q_n \Sigma''$ is special and V, W are reduced. Among all equalities (42), for our given Q, we select one for which the $\{l_i\}$-length of V is least. Then we have

$$Q \stackrel{\circ}{=} C(V\Sigma W) \stackrel{\circ}{=} Q_1 q_m C(\mathfrak{B}_{q_m q_n} \Sigma'' W(r_i, x)) \tag{43}$$

where $Q_1 \stackrel{\circ}{=} Q_1(l_i, y, s_b)$ contains no letters s_b^{-1}, $\mathfrak{B}_{q_m q_n} \stackrel{\circ}{=} U(\Sigma_{i2} r_i^{-1} \Gamma_{i2}^{-1})$ and the diagram of this word is reduced. It follows from (42) that

$$Q_1 \mathfrak{A}_{q_n q_m} = V\Sigma'$$

where $\mathfrak{A}_{q_n q_m} \stackrel{\circ}{=} U(\Sigma_{i1}^{-1} l_i \Gamma_{i1})$.

We claim that $\mathfrak{B}_{q_m q_n} \Sigma'' W(r_i, x)$ is $\{r_i\}$-reduced. Let us suppose that this is not so and that, for example, $\mathfrak{B}_{q_m q_n}$ ends with $\Sigma_{i2} r_i^{-1} \Gamma_{i2}^{-1}$. Then $W(r_i, x)$ begins with $x^t r_i$, say $W \stackrel{\circ}{=} x^t r_i W_1(r_i, x)$, $\Sigma'' \stackrel{\circ}{=} \Gamma_{i2} S$ and $Sx^t = xSx^{-1}$. It follows from (43) that, when reducing $V\Sigma' q_n$ to normal form, the first transformation will be

$$l_i y^{-1} S_1 y \Gamma_{i1} q_n \to y S_1 y^{-1} \Sigma_{i1} q_{n_i} \Sigma_{i2} r_i^{-1} \Gamma_{i2}^{-1},$$

that is, $V \stackrel{\circ}{=} V_1(l_i, y) l_i y^k$, $\Sigma' \stackrel{\circ}{=} S_1 \Gamma_{i1}$ and $y^k S_1 = y^{-1} S_1 y$. Then (42) gives

$$\begin{aligned} Q &= V_1 l_i y^k S_1 \Gamma_{i1} q_n \Gamma_{i2} S x^t r_i W_1 \\ &= V_1 y^{k'} S_1 \Sigma_{i1} q_{n_i} \Sigma_{i2} S x^t W_1 \end{aligned}$$

and $V_1 y^{k'}$ has smaller $\{l_i\}$-length than V. This contradicts our choice and so our claim is proved.

Since $\mathfrak{B}_{q_m q_n} \Sigma'' W(r_i, x)$ is $\{r_i\}$-reduced, the characterisation of $\mathfrak{B}_{q_m q_n}$, in the form of the sequence of letters r_i^{ε} occurring therein, remains in the word $C(\mathfrak{B}_{q_m q_n} \Sigma'' W(r_i, x)) \equiv Q_2$ which we know. Thus $Q_2 \equiv R_0 r_{i_1}^{\varepsilon_1} \cdots r_{i_k}^{\varepsilon_1} R_k$, $k \geq 0$ and for some l, $0 \leq l \leq k$, $\mathfrak{B}(r_{i_1}^{\varepsilon_1}, \ldots, r_{i_l}^{\varepsilon_l})$ has the form $\mathfrak{B}_{q_m q_n}$, for some q_m. Furthermore the words

$$C(Q_1 \mathfrak{A}_{q_n q_m}), \qquad C(\mathfrak{B}_{q_m q_n}^{-1} Q_2)$$

contain no letters s_b^{-1}. These last conditions can be easily checked having found the normal forms of the respective words. Thus the lemma is proved.

Corollary 1 ([11], [17]). *The Turing degree of unsolvability of the word problem for the group $G(T, q)$ coincides with the degree of unsolvability of the problem of equality with q for special words in the semigroup T.*

Proof. The word problem for G_5 is reduced to the process for transforming words of G_5 into normal form. Since the word problem for G_4 is solvable the process is reduced to the problem of whether or not a word Q of the group G_3 is equal to a word of the form $V(l_i, y) q W(r_i, x)$. By Lemmas 6 and 7, this is reducible to the problem of equality with q for special words in T.

To prove the converse reduction, it suffices to note that $\Sigma = q$ in T if and only if $\Sigma^{-1} t \Sigma k = k \Sigma^{-1} t \Sigma$ in G_5. One part of this assertion follows from Lemma 6 and the other part from applications of Britton's lemma.

Since there exist special semigroups in which the problem of equality with q for special words has arbitrary Turing degree of unsolvability we have the following result.

Corollary 2 ([11], [16], [17]). *For an arbitrary recursively enumerable Turing degree of unsolvability, there exists a finitely presented group (namely a Boone group $G(T, q)$ for some semigroup T) with word problem of the given degree of unsolvability.*

In conclusion we should like to express our thanks to Professor W.W. Boone at whose invitation this article was written.

References

[1] S.I. Adjan, On the work of Novikov and his pupils concerning algorithmic questions in algebra, Trudy Matem. Inst. imeni V.A. Steklova AN SSSR 133 (1973), 23–32.

[2] L.A. Bokut', Factorisation theorems for some classes of rings without zero divisors, I. Algebra and Logic 4, No. 4 (1965), 25–52; II, Ibid. 5, No. 1 (1965), 5–30.

[3] L.A. Bokut', On a property of Boone's groups, Algebra and Logic 5, No. 5 (1966), 5–23; II, Ibid. 6, No. 1 (1967), 15–24.

[4] L.A. Bokut', On Novikov's groups, Algebra and Logic, 6, No. 1 (1967), 25–38.

[5] L.A. Bokut', On the embedding of rings in skew fields, Doklady AN SSSR 175, No. 4 (1967), 755–758.

[6] L.A. Bokut', Groups with a relative standard basis, Sib. Mat. Z. 9, No. 3 (1968) 499–521.

[7] L.A. Bokut', The degrees of unsolvability for the conjugacy problem for finitely presented groups, Algebra and Logic 7, No. 5 (1968) 4–70; 7, No. 6 (1968) 4–52.

[8] L.A. Bokut', Groups of fractions of multiplicative semigroups of certain rings, I, Sib. Mat. Z. 10, No. 2 (1969) 246–286; II, Ibid. 10, No. 4 (1969) 744–799; III, Ibid. 10, No. 4 (1969) 800–819.

[9] L.A. Bokut', On Malcev's problem, Sib. Mat. Z. 10, No. 5 (1969) 965–1005.

[10] W.W. Boone, The word problem, Ann. of Math. 70 (1959) 207–265.

[11] W.W. Boone, Word problems and recursively enumerable degrees of unsolvability. A first paper on Thue systems, Ann. of Math. 83 (1966) 520–571.

[12] W.W. Boone, Word problems and recursively enumerable degrees of unsolvability. A sequel on finitely presented groups, Ann. of Math. 84 (1966) 49–84.

[13] A.J. Bowtell, On a question of Malcev, J. Algebra 7 (1967) 126–139.

[14] P.M. Cohn, Free rings and their relations (Academic Press, London, New York, 1971).

[15] D.J. Collins, Recursively enumerable degrees and the conjugacy problem, Acta Math. 122 (1969) 115–160.

[16] C.R.J. Clapham, Finitely presented groups with word problems of arbitrary degree of unsolvability, Proc. Lond. Math. Soc. Series 3, 14 (1964) 633–676.

[17] A.A. Fridman, Degrees of unsolvability of the word problem for finitely presented groups (Nauka, Moscow, 1967).

[18] A.A. Klein, Rings nonembeddable in fields with multiplicative semigroups embeddable in groups, J. Algebra 7 (1967) 100–125.

[19] A.I. Malcev, Selected works, Vol. I (Nauka, Moscow, 1976).

[20] P.S. Novikov, Unsolvability of the conjugacy problem in the theory of groups, Izv. Akad. Nauk SSSR, Ser. Mat. 18 (1954) 485–524.

[21] P.S. Novikov, On the algorithmic unsolvability of the word problem in group theory, Trudy Mat. Inst. Steklov No. 44 (1955).

[22] G. Higman, B.H. Neumann and H. Neumann, Embedding theorems for groups, J. Lond. Math. Soc. 24 (1949) 247–254.

S.I. Adian, W.W. Boone, G. Higman, eds., Word Problems II
© North-Holland Publishing Company (1980) 55–69

DECISION PROBLEMS FOR RING THEORY

L.A. BOKUT'
Institute of Mathematics, Novosibirsk

In my talk I shall discuss the following questions concerning the theme of the title:

1. The word problem for Lie algebras.
2. Embeddings in simple associative algebras.
3. Associative algebras with one relation.
4. Finite approximation of algebras.
5. Free Lie algebras.
6. Alternative, Jordan, and Malcev rings.

I have not included the results on free associative algebras and associative division rings in my report, but have presented here some well-known theorems by P. Cohn, J. Bergman, A. Macintyre and others worth analysing in some detail. I do not touch upon constructive rings, because the theory of these rings is part of the general theory of constructive models (A.I. Malcev, Yu. L. Ershov and others).

§1. The word problem for Lie algebras

The first results on the word problem for finitely presented (f.p.) algebras

$$\langle a_1, \dots, a_n; f_1 = 0, \dots, f_m = 0\rangle_{\mathscr{X}}$$

in the given variety of linear algebras $\mathscr{X}$ belongs to A.I. Žukov (1950). He proved that if $\mathscr{X}$ is the class of all (non-associative) algebras over a field k, then the word problem in $\mathscr{X}$ is algorithmically solvable. A.I. Širšov published two papers in 1962. In the first he pointed out one simple algorithm "exclusions of the leading words of the defining relations" which solves the word problem in the class of all the algebras and in the class of commutative ($xy = yx$) or anti-commutative ($xy = -yx$) algebras. In the second paper Širšov obtained the first result on the word problem for Lie algebras — he proved the solvability of this problem for Lie algebras with one relation

$$\langle a_1, \dots, a_n; f = 0\rangle_{\text{Lie}}.$$

In the same paper Širšov proposed a composition method, which I will say more about below.

The status of the word problem for arbitrary f.p. Lie algebras was settled in 1972. I was able to prove

Theorem 1. *Let k be an arbitrary field. There exists an f.p. Lie algebra over field k with unsolvable word problem.*

I shall speak briefly about the idea of the proof. Let M be a recursively enumerable non-recursive set of natural numbers. Then the Lie algebra

$$\langle a, b, c, a_1, c_1; ab^n c = a_1 b_1^n c_1, n \in M \rangle,$$

where $ab^n c = (\cdots(ab)\cdots b)c$ has unsolvable word problem.

In this way, it suffices to prove that this (or some similar) Lie algebra is embeddable in a finitely presented Lie algebra. This is proved by means of Matijasevich's theorem on the existence of a Diophantine representation of the set M and uses the following simple analogy of one of Higman's lemmas.

Lemma. *Let A be an f.g. Lie algebra and let B be a Higman subalgebra A. Then the algebra*

$$\langle A, A^{(1)}; b = b^{(1)}, b \in B \rangle_{\mathrm{Lie}}$$

is embeddable in an f.p. Lie algebra.

Definition. $B <_H A$ if there exists the following diagram: $\exists K, L$ (K-f.p., L-f.g., $A, L \subseteq K$, $A \cap L = B$).

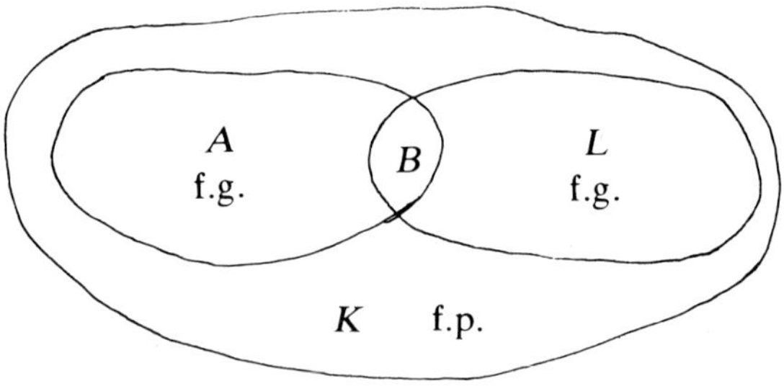

In this way it suffices to prove that every subalgebra $\langle ab^n c, n \in M \rangle$ is a Higman subalgebra of free Lie algebra $\langle a, b, c \rangle$.

At the present time a new proof of the theorem has been obtained by G.P. Kukin. Kukin has essentially simplified the construction of my paper and obtained the following proof. Let

$$\Pi = \langle u, v\,;\, A_i = B_i,\ 1 \leqslant i \leqslant n\rangle_{\mathrm{Sgp}}$$

be a semigroup with unsolvable word problem. Let us consider the Lie algebra

$$L(\Pi) = \langle x, y, u, v, a\,;\, xu = xv = yu = yv = 0,$$
$$ax = au,\ ay = av,\ aA_i = aB_i,\ 1 \leqslant i \leqslant n\rangle_{\mathrm{Lie}}$$

where, for example, $auvu^2 = (((au)v)u)u$. Then Kukin's lemma is:

Lemma. *Let* $A, B \in \langle u, v\rangle_{\mathrm{Sgp}}$. *Then*

$$A \underset{\Pi}{=} B \Leftrightarrow aA \underset{L(\Pi)}{=} aB.$$

One part of this lemma ($\Rightarrow$) is clear. If, e.g., $A = A'A_1A''$, $B = A'B_1A''$, then in $L(\Pi)$ because of the equalities

$$wxu = wux,\ wxv = wvx,\ wyu = wuy,\ wyv = wvy$$

we have:

$$aA'A_1A'' = aA_1A'(x, y)A'' = aB_1A'(x, y)A'' = aA'B_1A''.$$

In fact, the word problem for Π is Turing equivalent to the one for $L(\Pi)$, so that we have

Theorem 2 (G.P. Kukin). *For any r.e. Turing degree of unsolvability there exists an f.p. Lie algebra whose word problem is of the given degree.*

By means of Theorem 1 I obtained

Theorem 3. *Any Markov property α of f.p. Lie algebras is algorithmically unrecognizable. The problem of being isomorphic to any particular f.p. Lie algebra is algorithmically unsolvable.*

Of a number of open algorithmic problems for Lie algebras, the following problem of A.I. Širšov has the greatest interest: Is the word problem solvable in the class of solvable Lie algebras of given solvability step $n \geqslant 3$? For $n = 2$ the word problem is solvable. The analogous problem for groups was solved by V.N. Remeslennikov (1973, $n \geqslant 5$).

§2. Embeddings into simple associative algebras

The interest in embeddings into simple rings and algebras is supported by some internal questions (the study of simple algebras) as well as by external ones — comparison with theory of groups. I can distinguish at least three theorems, which, in this respect, have great influence. These are Higman–Neumann's theorem (1949) about embedding any group into a simple one, the Boone–Higman theorem (1974) on the algebraic characterization of f.g. groups with solvable word problem (f.g. $\leqslant$ simple r.p. $\leqslant$ f.p.), and P. Hall's theorem (1973) about embedding a group into a simple one, generated by four "abitrary" groups.

In 1962 I proved for associative rings and algebras the following

Theorem 1. *Any arbitrary associative algebra A can be embedded into a simple associative algebra $\mathfrak{A}$, in which any equation of the type $xay = b$, $0 \neq a$, $b \in \mathfrak{A}$ is solvable. If A is an algebra with a recursive basis, then $\mathfrak{A}$ is r.p. with solvable word problem. If A is a ring, then it is embeddable in a simple ring if and only if it has characteristic $p \geqslant 0$ (p is a prime number, or 0).*

Recently I proved the two following sharpenings of this theorem.

Theorem 2. *Let A, K_1, K_2, K_3 be arbitrary associative algebras over field k, $|A| \leqslant |K_1 * K_2 * K_3|$, $\dim K_1 * K_2 * K_3 \geqslant |k|$ (here $*$ is the operation of free product of algebras). Then the algebra A is embeddable in a simple associative algebra $\mathfrak{A}$ of the type $\mathfrak{A} = \langle K_1, K_2, K_3 \rangle$. If A, K_1, K_2, K_3 have recursive basis, then $\mathfrak{A}$ also has recursive basis (and solvable word problem).*

In particular, an arbitrary countable associative algebra is embeddable in a simple associative algebra with 3 generators.

Let K be an algebra over a field $k, \dim K = \alpha \geqslant \aleph_0$. Let us say that the algebra K satisfies condition (α), if

$$K = \bigcup_{n \geqslant 1} K^{(n)}, \; K^{(n)} \subset K^{(n+1)}, \; \dim K^{(n+1)}/K^{(n)} = \dim K^{(n)} = \alpha.$$

Theorem 3. *Let $A, K_1, \ldots, K_4$ be associative algebras over a field $k, \dim K_i = \alpha \geqslant |k|, \aleph_0$, $1 \leqslant i \leqslant 4$, $\dim A \leqslant \alpha$ and algebras K_i, $1 \leqslant i \leqslant 4$ satisfy condition (α). Then the algebra A is embeddable in a simple associative algebra $\mathfrak{A}$ of the type*

$$\mathfrak{A} = K_1 + \cdots + K_4.$$

In particular, algebras K_i with trivial multiplication satisfy the condition of the theorem. So, every algebra A is embeddable in a simple one which is the sum of the four algebras with trivial multiplication.

Theorem 4. *Every associative algebra can be embedded in a simple algebra* $\mathfrak{A} = N_1 + N_2 + N_3$, *when the* N_i *are nilpotent.*

O. Kegel (1964) proved, that if $B = N_1 + N_2$, where N_1, N_2 are nilpotent, then B is a nilpotent algebra.

Problem. Is every r.p. associative algebra embeddable in an f.p. associative algebra? The same question arises for Lie algebras.

As for embeddings into simple non-associative algebras and Lie algebras, there are the B. Neumann and P. Cohn theorems and my theorem as well (1962) on the embedding of an arbitrary Lie algebra into an algebraically closed Lie algebra.

I will say a few words concerning the methods of proof of the previous theorems. As I have already pointed out they follow from Širšov's work (1962) for Lie algebras. Let us reformulate the definition and the lemma by Sirsov for associative algebras. Let $F = k\langle X\rangle$ be a free associative algebra. The semigroup X can be linearly ordered (namely, lexicographically); denote by $\bar{f}$ the largest word of element $f \in k\langle X\rangle$. Let us define a composition $(f, g)_w$ of elements $f, g \in F$ with respect to a word $w \in \langle X\rangle_{\mathrm{Sgp}}$. Let

$$w = \bar{f}u = v\bar{g},\ l(w) < l(\bar{f}) + l(\bar{g}).$$

Then

$$(f, g)_w = \beta f u - \alpha v g,\ f = \alpha\bar{f} + \cdots,\ g = \beta\bar{g} + \cdots.$$

We have

$$\overline{(f, g)_w} < w.$$

Let $S \subseteq F = k\langle X\rangle$. The set S is closed with respect to the composition, if

$$(f, g)_w = \sum \alpha_i a_i s_i b_i,\ \alpha_i \in k,\ s_i \in S,\ \overline{a_i s_i b_i} < w$$

for every composition of elements $f, g \in S$.

Širšov's Lemma. *If* S *is a subset of free algebra* $F = k\langle X\rangle$ *closed with respect to the compositions, then in the associative algebra*

$\langle X; s_i = 0, s_i \in S\rangle$, *all the words from* X *which contain no subwords* $\bar{s}_i$, $s_i \in S$ *will serve as its base.*

§3. Associative algebras with one relation

The word problem for (associative) algebras with one relation was dealt with by several authors. S.I. Adyan (1960) proved the algorithmic solvability of the word problem for semigroups (hence, the same for algebras) with one relation of the type $A = 1$ and with the irreducible relation $A = B$ as well. In the paper by J. Levin and T. Levin (1968) the word problem was solved and there was proposed the Freiheitssatz for associative algebras

$$\langle x, y_1, \ldots, y_n; u = 0\rangle$$

with one relation, satisfying the conditions: 1) $F/\mathrm{Id}(u)$ is an algebra without zero divisors, where $F = k\langle x, y_1, \ldots, y_n\rangle$, 2) the least homogeneous part of element u doesn't lie in $k\langle y_1, \ldots, y_n\rangle$ (i.e. it contains x). In the paper by W. Dicks (1972) the solvability of the word problem was proved for associative algebras with one relation $u = 0$ satisfying the condition

$$\forall v \in F(uv \in F^* uF \Rightarrow v \in FuF),$$

where F^* is the set of polynomials with zero free members. I would like to give a more detailed description of the paper by V.N. Gerasimov (1976). Let $F = k\langle X\rangle$ be a free associative algebra with 1 over a field k, $d(x)$ the ordinary degree function, and F^n the set of homogeneous elements of degree $n \geqslant 0$ ($F^0 = k$). When considering the word problem it turns to be quite useful to have

Theorem 1 (V.N. Gerasimov). *Let f be an arbitrary homogeneous element of algebra F. Then the lattice subspaces*

$$\mathrm{Lat}(F^n f F^m, n, m \geqslant 0)$$

generated by subspaces $F^n f F^m$, are distributive.

Let us fix notations: $\bar{h}$ is the largest homogeneous part of element $h \in F$, $\bar{H} = \{\bar{h}, h \in H\}$, $H \subseteq F$. We consider a connection between Theorem 1 and the word problem. Let f be an element of the algebra F and $g \in \mathrm{Id}(f)$. Then in F there exists an equality

$$(1) \qquad \sum u_\lambda f v_\lambda = g,$$

where u_λ, v_λ are homogeneous elements. Let's assume that f satisfies the condition

$$(2) \qquad \bar{f}\bar{F} \cap \bar{F}\bar{f} = \overline{fF \cap Ff}$$

(here $\bar{F}$ is, of course, the set of all homogeneous elements of the algebra F). Condition (2), for example, is satisfied, if $\bar{f}$ has no proper two-sided divisors:

$$\bar{f} = xu = vx \Rightarrow x \sim 1 \quad \text{or} \quad x \sim \bar{f}.$$

From Theorem 1, using (2), one can easily derive the existence of representation (1) of the bounded degree

$$d(u_\lambda) + d(v_\lambda) \leqslant d(g) - d(f).$$

That means that the question of whether the element g belongs to the ideal $\mathrm{Id}(f)$ is reduced to the problem of the solvability of a finite system of linear equations (because the subspace $\Sigma_{n+m \leqslant d(g)-d(f)} F^n f F^m$ is finite-dimensional).

In this way, we obtain

Corollary 1. *If f is an element of the free algebra $k\langle X\rangle$, the largest homogeneous part of which contains no proper two-sided divisors, then in the algebra $\langle X; f = 0\rangle$ the word problem is solvable.*

This result contains Dicks' theorem mentioned above. In an analogous way one can prove

Corollary 2. *Let $f \in k\langle X\rangle$, $x_0 \in X$, $f \notin k\langle X\rangle \setminus \{x_0\}\rangle$, f_{x_0} — the largest homogeneous part of the element f with respect to x_0 and suppose that $\bar{f}_{x_0}$ has no proper two-sided divisors. Then the set $X \setminus \{x_0\}$ generates a free subalgebra in $\langle X; f = 0\rangle$.*

A special calculus is constructed to prove Theorem 1 in V.N. Gerasimov's paper with axioms and deduction rules which are as follows

$$\begin{matrix} \mathcal{A}_1 \searrow \\ \mathcal{A}_2 \nearrow \end{matrix} \mathcal{A}, \quad \mathcal{A}_1 \to \mathcal{A}.$$

where $\mathcal{A}$, $\mathcal{A}_1$, $\mathcal{A}_2$ are finite subsets of subspaces of a special kind. Two element sets $\{L_1, L_2\}$ of subspaces (which on account of the modularity generate the distributive lattice) are the axioms of this calculus. The deduction rules are such that if initial sets $\mathcal{A}_1$, $\mathcal{A}_2$ generate the distributive lattice of subspaces, then the conclusion set $\mathcal{A}$ has the same property. As a result, it is proved that any finite set of subspaces F^nfF^m is deducible; this is how the distributivity of the initial lattice is proved.

Problem. Let f be an arbitrary element of free algebra $F = k\langle X\rangle$. Is the lattice $\mathrm{Lat}(F^nfF^m, F^l, n, m, l \geqslant 0)$ distributive in the following sense: there exists an $n = n(f) \geqslant 2$, such that the identity $V \cap (\Sigma_{i=1}^n V_i) = \Sigma_{i=1}^n (V \cap \Sigma_{j\neq i} V_i))$ holds in the lattice?

From a positive solution of this problem immediately follows a positive solution of the word problem for associative algebras with one relation.

§4. Finite approximation

An algebra A over k is called finitely approximable, if it can be approximated by finite-dimensional algebras. It is easy to observe that any recursively presented finitely approximable algebra over a constructive field has solvable word problem.

The study of finitely approximable associative algebras was started in A.I. Malcev's work "Representations of infinite algebras" (1943). An algebra A over k is called representable, if A is embeddable in an algebra of matrices over any extension K of the field k. The representability of the algebra is equivalent to its finite approximability by algebras of bounded dimension. Of the results obtained by Malcev in this paper I shall point out only one:

Every f.g. commutative algebra is representable and therefore is finitely approximable.

Let $\mathfrak{M}$ be any variety of associative algebras. Let us call the variety $\mathfrak{M}$ locally representable (l.r.) (respectively, locally finitely approximable — l.f.a.), if any f.g. algebra from $\mathfrak{M}$ is representable (finitely approximable).

Because of this work by Malcev a natural problem arises: to describe (in terms of identities) l.r. and, separately, l.f.a. varieties of associative algebras.

The first progress towards the solution of this problem was made by V.T. Markov in 1975. Markov proved that the variety of Engel algebras

$$[[x, y], \dots, y] = 0$$

turns out to be l.r. (here $[x, y] = xy - yx$). The problem formulated above was finally solved by A.Z. Ananin. He proved

Theorem 1 (A.Z. Ananin). *Let k be an infinite field and let $\mathfrak{M}$ be a variety of associative algebras over the field k. Then the following conditions on $\mathfrak{M}$ are equivalent*

(1) *$\mathfrak{M}$ is l.r.,*

(2) *$\mathfrak{M}$ is l.f.a.,*

(3) *in $\mathfrak{M}$ an identity of the kind*

$$[[x, y], \ldots, y]z^n[[t, u], \ldots, u] = 0$$

holds.

The same varieties have several more remarkable properties: Conditions (1)–(3) are equivalent to the following conditions as well.

(4) (A.Z. Ananin, I.V. Lvov) $\mathfrak{M}$ is a locally weak Noether variety (i.e. in any f.g. algebra from $\mathfrak{M}$ the maximal condition for two-sided ideals holds).

It is clear that for the variety of associative commutative algebras over k Condition 4 is the Hilbert basis theorem.

(5) (Yu.N. Malcev) $\mathfrak{M}$ is a local Hopf variety (i.e. any f.g. algebra from $\mathfrak{M}$ is Hopfian).

The variety of commutative algebras is local Hopf. This was proved by A.I. Malcev in the work mentioned above.

Let us call a variety $\mathfrak{M}$ representable if every algebra from $\mathfrak{M}$ is representable in a matrix algebra over a commutative algebra. J. Levin proved (1972) that the variety $\mathfrak{M}([x, y][z, t] = 0)$ is representable.

Theorem 2 (A.Z. Ananin). *Every nilpotent variety is representable.*

This is a solution of one of L. Small's well-known problems, which he proposed at a conference on ring theory (Utah, 1971).

Theorem 3 (A.Z. Ananin). *Every group ring with a polynomial identity (PI — group ring) is representable.*

This is a solution of a problem in Passman's book in group rings.

§5. Free Lie algebras

In the theory of infinite-dimensional Lie algebras the theory of free Lie algebras and free products of Lie algebras occupies the main place at present. The foundations of this theory and some effective methods used in papers by other authors were created by A.I. Širšov. As in group theory, the study of free Lie algebras and free products of Lie algebras is connected very closely with decision problems.

1. Bases of free Lie algebras

The first method for constructing bases of free Lie algebras was given by M. Hall (1949). The general scheme of the construction of such bases was published by A.I. Širšov in 1962. This scheme was applied in my work (1964), in which bases of free polynilpotent Lie algebras were constructed. Namely, let $n_1, \ldots, n_k$ be positive integers, $L = k\langle X\rangle_{\mathrm{Lie}}$ be a free Lie algebra, $R = L/(((L^{n_1})^{n_2})\cdots)^{n_k}$ be the free polynilpotent Lie algebra corresponding to the sequence $\langle n_1, \ldots, n_k\rangle$. In the work mentioned, a basis $\mathfrak{A} = \mathfrak{A}' \cup \mathfrak{A}''$ of the algebra L is constructed such that $\mathfrak{A}'$ is a basis of the ideal $(((L^{n_1})^{n_2})\cdots)^{n_k}$ and the images of the words from $\mathfrak{A}''$ form a basis in the algebra R. So, R has a recursive basis.

Among all the bases proposed by A.I. Širšov, the most useful basis is the so-called Širšov basis of right words (1958). The basis has been used in Širšov's work to prove the following assertion.

Theorem 1 (A.I. Širšov). *An arbitrary Lie algebra with countable dimension is embeddable in Lie algebra with 2-generators.*

2. The intersection of finitely generated subalgebras of free Lie algebras

The following question was open for a long time: Is the intersection of two finitely generated subalgebras of a free Lie algebra again a finitely generated subalgebra? The analogous property of groups was proved by Howson (1954). Recently this question was solved positively by G.P. Kukin.

Theorem 2 (G.P. Kukin). *Let $L = k\langle X\rangle_{\mathrm{Lie}}$ be a free Lie algebra over an arbitrary field k. Then its f.g. subalgebras form a sublattice of the lattice of all subalgebras.*

In the case k has characteristic $p > 0$, this property was proved earlier in Kukin's work (1972).

3. The semigroup of the varieties of Lie algebras

Let k be a field of characteristic 0. Let Γ_{Lie} be the semigroup of Lie varieties. In 1967 V.A. Parfenov proved the following theorem, which is analogous to the well-known theorem by Neumann and Šmelkin for groups:

Theorem 3 (V.A. Parfenov). *The semigroup Γ_{Lie} of varieties of Lie algebras over a field of characteristic zero is a free semigroup with zero and unit.*

4. Subalgebras of free products of Lie algebras

Let L_i, $i \in J$ be Lie algebras over field k, let $L = \Pi^*_{i\in J} L_i$ be their free product. For a long time there existed the Kuros–Witt conjecture that any subalgebra $A \subseteq L$ has the following form:

$$A = F * \prod{}^* (A \cap L_i)$$

where F is a free Lie algebra. This conjecture was refuted by A.I. Širšov in 1962.

Theorem 4 (A.I. Širšov). *The Kuros–Witt conjecture is not true.*

The counter-example is the following pair:

$$L = \langle a \rangle * \langle b, c ; cb = b \rangle,$$

$$A = \langle ba, ca \rangle.$$

The problem stated by A.I. Širšov on the description of the subalgebras of free products of Lie algebras was solved by G.P. Kukin (1972) who proved the following theorem:

Theorem 5 (G.P. Kukin). *If $A \subseteq L = \Pi^*_{i\in J} L_i$ then*

$$A \cong \left[F * \prod_{i \in J}{}^* (A \cap L_i) \right] \Big/ N$$

where the generating elements of ideal N can be written out in terms of the multiplication table of algebras L_i.

In particular, if $A \cap L_i = 0$, then A is a free Lie algebra; the Cartesian subalgebra of the algebra L (the kernel of the natural homomorphism $\Pi^* L_i \to \Sigma L_i$) turns out to be the free subalgebra, etc.

5. Solvable Lie algebras with 2 generators

Recently G.P. Kukin proved the following theorem, which was open for a long time:

Theorem 6 (G.P. Kukin). *Any solvable countable-dimensional Lie algebra with solvability length n is embeddable in a solvable Lie algebra with 2 generators and solvability length $n + 2$.*

This result is analogous to the well-known theorem of Neumann for groups (1959). As in the case of groups, the result can be formulated for Lie algebras from an arbitrary variety.

§6. Alternative, Jordan and Malcev rings

Besides the classes of associative and Lie rings, the classes of alternative, Jordan and Malcev rings play a significant role in ring theory. Let us recall that the definitions of these classes are given by the following identities:

$$(x, x, y) = 0, \ (y, x, x) = 0 \quad \text{(alternative rings)},$$

(here $(x, y, z) = (xy)z - x(yz)$ is the associator),

$$xy = yx, \ (x^2y)x = x^2(yx) \quad \text{(Jordan rings)},$$

$$x^2 = 0, \ J(x, y, xz) = J(x, y, z)x \quad \text{(Malcev rings)}$$

(here $J(x, y, z) = (xy)z + (yz)x + (zx)y$ is the Jacobian).

Each of these classes of rings has a very rich internal theory and many connections with other fields of mathematics, so that the importance of studying these classes is clear.

In this section I shall briefly dwell upon the following questions, without any claim of completeness or depth.

1. Simple rings.
2. Finitely generated rings.
3. Free rings.

1. In the case of alternative and Malcev rings a situation takes place which is opposite to that mentioned in §3 for associative algebras and Lie algebras. Namely, in the case of alternative rings there is a well-known theorem, following from the work of Kleinfeld, that any simple alternative ring is either associative, or is the (8-dimensional) Cayley–Dickson algebra over its own centre. An analogous situation takes place for Malcev algebras.

Theorem 1 (V.T. Philippov). *Any central simple Malcev algebra is either a Lie algebra or 7-dimensional algebra $A^{(-)}$ which is adjoint to the Cayley–Dickson algebra A.*

Theorem 1 was obtained earlier for finite-dimensional Malcev algebras by E.N. Kuzmin (1968).

For Jordan rings the following question is still open: Is any simple

Jordan ring either a finite-dimensional algebra over its own centre or a special Jordan ring?

2. In the case of alternative rings any 2-generator ring is known to be associative (Artin). The following theorem shows that not every countable alternative ring is embeddable in a 3-generator alternative ring.

Theorem 2 (G.V. Dorofeev). *Any 3-generator alternative ring satisfies the non-trivial identity* $([x, y] \circ [u, v], z, t) = 0$ *where* $[x, y] = xy - yx$, $a \circ b = ab + ba$.

An interesting question was whether there exists a natural number n such that every countable ring is embeddable in an n-generator alternative ring. Recently this question was solved by I.P. Šestakov. He has proved

Theorem 3 (I.P. Šestakov). *There exists no natural number n, such that any countable generated alternative algebra is embeddable in an n-generator alternative algebra.*

Šestakov has also proved that the same theorem is true for Malcev algebras.

Theorem 4 (A.I. Širšov). *An arbitrary Jordan algebra over k with 2 generators is special.*

Here k is a commutative ring of operators containing 1 and the element 1/2; a Jordan algebra embeddable in an algebra $A^+ = \langle A, a \circ b = \frac{1}{2}(ab + ba)\rangle$ adjoint to an associative algebra A is called special.

Thus, not every countably generated Jordan algebra is embeddable in a Jordan ring with 2 generators.

3. I shall point out the following two theorems on free alternative rings. The first of them deals with the question, which is still open, about the existence of a simple effective basis in such rings.

Theorem 5 (A.I. Širšov). *In a free alternative ring* $k\langle X\rangle_{\mathrm{Alt}}$ *the set of* r_2*-words from X forms a linear system of generators of this ring (this system is dependent).*

Every word of the kind $((x_{i_1}x_{i_2})\cdots x_{i_n})$ (with the right order of brackets) is called a r_1-word from generators $X = \{x_i\}$; r_2-words are

r_1-words from r_1-words, i.e. the words of the kind $((v_1v_2)\cdots v_k)$, where v_i are r_1-words.

Theorem 6 (I.P. Šestakov). *The set of nilpotent elements of a free alternative ring $k\langle X\rangle_{\text{Alt}}$, where k is an integral domain, forms an ideal which coincides with the quasi-regular radical of this ring. There exists an algorithm for answering the question of whether an element $f\in k\langle X\rangle_{\text{Alt}}$ is nilpotent.*

It is known (Kleinfeld and Humm), that for $|X|\geqslant 4$ the quasiregular radical of the ring $k\langle X\rangle_{\text{Alt}}$ is non-zero (for $|X|=3$ this question is still open). K.A.Ževlakov (1972) proved that any element of the quasi-regular radical of a free alternative ring is nilpotent.

References

[1] A.Z. Ananin, Locally finitely approximated and locally representable varieties of associative algebras, 14th All-Union Student Conference, Novosibirsk, 1976, p. 15.
[2] L.A. Bokut, Embedding of Lie algebras in algebraically closed Lie algebra, Algebra and Logic 1, No. 2 (1962) 47–53.
[3] L.A. Bokut, Some embedding theorems for rings and semigroups, I, Sib. Mat. Z. 3, No. 4 (1963) 500–518.
[4] L.A. Bokut, Bases of free polynilpotent Lie algebras, Algebra and Logic 2, No. 3 (1963) 5–18.
[5] L.A. Bokut, Unsolvability of some algorithmic problem in the class of associative rings, Algebra and Logic 9, No. 2 (1970) 137–144.
[6] L.A. Bokut, Unsolvability of the word problem and of the subalgebra of finitely presented Lie algebras, Izv. Akad. Nauk Ser. Matem. 36, No. 6 (1972) 1173–1219.
[7] L.A. Bokut, Unsolvability of some algorithmic problems for Lie algebras, Algebra and Logic 13, No. 2 (1974) 145–152.
[8] L.A. Bokut, Embeddings in simple associative algebras, Algebra and Logic 15, No. 2 (1976) 117–132.
[9] V.N. Gerasimov, On distributive lattices of subspaces and the word problem for associative algebras with one relation, Algebra and Logic 15, No. 4 (1976) 384–435.
[10] G.P. Kukin, Primitive elements of free Lie algebras, Algebra and Logic 9 (1970) 458–472.
[11] G.P. Kukin, De carte subalgebras of free Lie products of Lie algebras, Algebra and Logic 9 (1970) 701–713.
[12] G.P. Kukin, Subalgebras of free products of Lie algebras, Algebra and Logic 11, No. 1 (1972) 59–86.
[13] G.P. Kukin, On the embedding of solvable Lie algebras in solvable Lie algebras with 2 generators, Algebra and Logic 14, No. 4 (1975) 414–421.
[14] I.V. Lvov, Maximality condition in algebras with identical relations, Algebra and Logic 8 (1969) 449–454.
[15] A.I. Malcev, Representations of infinite algebras, Matem. Sbornik 13 (55) (1953) 263–286.

[16] A.I. Malcev, Algorithms and recursive functions (Moscow, Nauka, 1967).
[17] A.I. Malcev, Introduction in the theory of algebraic systems (Moscow, Nauka, 1972).
[18] Yu. N. Malcev, Some properties of the varieties of the associative algebras products, Algebra and Logic 11, No. 6 (1972) 651–670.
[19] V.A. Parfenov, Varieties of Lie algebras, Algebra and Logic 6 (1967) 61–73.
[20] V.A. Parfenov, On one of the properties of ideals of free Lie algebras, Algebra and Logic 10 (1969) 940–944.
[21] A.I. Širšov, Subalgebras of free Lie algebras, Matem. Sbornik 33 (75), No. 2 (1953) 441–452.
[22] A.I. Širšov, On free Lie rings, Matem. Sbornik 45 (1968) 113–122.
[23] A.I. Širšov, Some questions of the theory of rings close to associative rings, Uspeki Matem. Nauk 13, No. 6 (1958) 3–20.
[24] A.I. Širšov, Some algorithmic problem for ε-algebras, Sib. Math. J. 3, No. 1 (1962) 132–137.
[25] A.I. Širšov, Some algorithmic problems for Lie algebras, Sib. Math. J. 3, No. 2 (1962) 292–296.
[26] A.I. Širšov, On one of the hypotheses of the theory of Lie algebras, Sib. Math. J. 3, No. 2 (1962) 297–303.
[27] A.I. Širšov, On the bases of free Lie algebras, Algebra and Logic 1, No. 1 (1962) 14–19.
[28] A.I. Širšov, Some algorithmic questions for solvable Lie algebras, Uspeki Matem. Nauki 17 (1962) 228.
[29] A.I. Širšov, On special J-Rings, Matem. Sbornik 38, No. 2 (1956) 149–166.
[30] A.I. Širšov, On some of non-associative nil-rings and algebraic algebras, Matem. Sbornik 4, No. 2 (1957) 381–394.
[31] G.V. Dorofeev, Alternative rings with 3 generators, Sib. Math. J. 4, No. 5 (1963) 1029–1048.
[32] K.A. Ževlakov, Quasi-regular ideals in finitely generated alternative rings, Algebra and Logic 11, No.2 (1972) 140–161.
[33] E.N. Kuzmin, Malcev algebras and their representations, Algebra and Logic 7, No. 4 (1968) 48–69.
[34] V.T. Philippov, On zero divisors and nil-elements in Malcev algebras, Algebra and Logic 14, No. 3 (1976) 204–214.
[35] I.P. Šestakov, Radicals and nilpotent elements of free Alternative algebras, Algebra and Logic 14, No. 3 (1975) 354–365.

S.I. Adian, W.W. Boone, G. Higman, eds., Word Problems II

ERRATUM: THE EXISTENCE OF INFINITE BURNSIDE GROUPS

J.L. BRITTON
Queen Elizabeth College, London

A mistake in my article [3] was pointed out by S. Adian [2]. However I have not investigated the nature of this mistake: I believe that what is now primarily needed is a much simpler proof, in which no attention is paid to the value of the lower bound A, of the result in question; namely, that there exists an A such that for all $m \geq 2$ and all odd integers $n > A$ the Burnside group $B(m, n)$ on m generators and with exponent n is infinite. (This was proved originally by Adian and Novikov [1] and subsequently by Adian [2].) Conceivably, such a proof might contain ideas from [1], [2] and [3].

It is possible that such a proof would also throw light on the outstanding unsolved problem in the field: is $B(m, 2^k)$ infinite for any $k \geq 1$? However I am inclined to pessimism since I believe that the answer is negative.

Reference

[1] P.S. Novikov and S.I. Adjan, On infinite periodic groups, Izv. Akad. Nauk SSSR, Ser. Mat. 32 (1968) 212–214, 224–251, 709–731.
[2] S.I. Adian, The Burnside problem and identities in groups, Nauka (1975).
[3] J.L. Britton, The existence of infinite Burnside groups, in Word Problems: Decision problems and the Burnside problem in group theory, Studies in Logic and Foundations of Mathematics (North-Holland Publishing Co., Amsterdam, 1973).

S.I. Adian, W.W. Boone, G. Higman, eds., Word Problems II
© North-Holland Publishing Company (1980) 73–80

ON SEMIFIR CONSTRUCTIONS

P.M. COHN
Bedford College, London

§1. Introduction

Free ideal rings or firs (the definition is recalled in §2) form an analogue of principal ideal domains, to which they reduce in the commutative case, and to obtain examples of firs one can use the weak algorithm and its variants. Semifirs form a wider class and it is less easy to construct semifirs (that are not also firs) directly. A possibility is to form direct limits or ultraproducts of firs, but a more interesting way is to start from n-firs, for the examples so obtained show that semifirs do not form an elementary class. This is in sharp contrast to the commutative case, where semifirs correspond to Bezout domains (an elementary class). After describing the necessary background in §§2–3 (including a 'small cancellation' theorem needed to construct n-firs) we examine the ultraproduct construction more closely. It turns out that a countable ultraproduct of n-firs for increasing n (with a non-principal ultrafilter) is always a semifir but never a fir, except in trivial cases. On the other hand, an uncountable ultraproduct may well be a genuine fir.

§2. Firs, semifirs, *n*-firs

Throughout, all rings are associative, with a unit-element 1 which is inherited by subrings and preserved by homomorphisms. Mostly our rings have a commutative field k as coefficient domain, i.e. they are k-algebras.

A free k-algebra on a set X, $k\langle X\rangle$ can be defined by a universal property, although often a more pragmatic definition (in terms of a normal form for its elements) is preferred. If we examine the sense in which relations in $k\langle X\rangle$ can be described as trivial, we are led to the following

Definition. Let R be a ring; a relation

$$(1)\qquad x.y = x_1y_1 + \cdots + x_ny_n = 0 \qquad (x_i, y_i \in R)$$

is said to be *trivial* if for each $i = 1, \ldots, n$ either $x_i = 0$ or $y_i = 0$. If there is an invertible $n \times n$ matrix P over R such that the transformed relation $xP^{-1}.Py = 0$ is trivial, the relation (1) is said to be *trivialized* by P.

It turns out that every relation in $k\langle X\rangle$ is trivializable in this way; this is proved by first showing that $k\langle X\rangle$ possesses a 'weak algorithm', an analogue of the Euclidean algorithm to which it reduces for commutative rings (cf. [8], Chapter 2). Next it is shown that in a ring with a weak algorithm all relations are trivializable. We shall not repeat the proofs, but to elucidate the connexion we quote the following result from [4] (cf. [8], Chapter 1):

Theorem 1. *Let R be a non-zero ring and $n \geq 1$, then the following conditions are equivalent*:

(a) *every relation* (1) *with at most n terms is trivializable,*

(b) *any right ideal of R generated by $m \leq n$ elements which are right linearly dependent over R can be generated by fewer than m elements,*

(c) *any right ideal on at most n generators is free, of unique rank.*

A non-zero ring satisfying these equivalent conditions is called an *n-fir*. By (a) this condition is left-right symmetric while (b) shows that the class of n-firs is elementary, i.e. it can be defined by a single elementary sentence. Thus for any $n \geq 1$, both the class of n-firs and its complement are closed under ultraproducts (cf. [5], Chapter 5).

It is easily checked that 1-firs are just (non-commutative) integral domains; for increasing n the n-firs form smaller and smaller classes until we reach *semifirs*, defined as n-firs for all n. From Theorem 1 we see that a ring R is a semifir if and only if every finitely generated right ideal is free, of unique rank. Thus semifirs can be defined by an infinite set of elementary sentences, so the class of semifirs is closed under ultraproducts. As we shall see later, its complement is not closed under ultraproducts, so the class of semifirs is not elementary. By contrast, in the commutative case a 2-fir is already a semifir (a commutative 2-fir is a Bezout domain, i.e. a domain in which every finitely generated ideal is principal), so the class of commutative semifirs is elementary.

Now a right fir (= free ideal ring) is defined as a ring in which every right ideal is free, of unique rank. Unlike semifirs right firs are no longer left-right symmetric (cf. [8], Chapter 2), so we must also define *left* firs, and by a *fir* we shall understand a left and right fir. In the commutative case firs reduce to principal ideal domains, while semifirs reduce to Bezout domains, as noted earlier. This remark already shows that the class of firs is not closed under ultraproducts, and so cannot be defined by a set of elementary sentences.

Examples of firs exist in profusion; they include (a) principal ideal domains (even non-commutative), (b) free algebras over a field, (c) free products (= coproducts) of skew fields.

Semifirs are a little harder to come by; as in the commutative case we can obtain them as direct limits of firs, or also as ultraproducts of firs. But now we can also form ultraproducts (or direct limits) of n-firs, for increasing n. For this method to be of use we shall need a source of n-firs; this is provided by a result to which we now turn.

§3. A 'small cancellation' theorem for rings

Our aim in this section is to describe a result which enables one to recognize from certain ring presentations that the ring defined is an n-fir. By definition this just means that every relation (1) of at most n terms is trivializable, and one would expect a condition for this to be expressed by saying that all the defining relations can be expressed as relations of $N > n$ terms with little interference, so that no non-trivializable relations of $\leq n$ terms can be deduced by cancellation. Such a theorem was proved in [7] (see also [6] for a special case). To state it we need some definitions.

Let k be any commutative field and let R be a k-algebra, generated by a set U; then R can be expressed as a homomorphic image of the free k-algebra $F = k\langle U\rangle : R = F/N$. On F we define a filtration v by assigning arbitrary positive integer values $v(u)$ to each $u \in U$, putting $v(u_1 \cdots u_r) = v(u_1) + \cdots + v(u_r)$ and for any $f = \Sigma\, \alpha_m m \in F$ writing

$$v\left(\sum \alpha_m m\right) = \max\{v(m) \mid \alpha_m \neq 0\},$$

where m runs over all products of u's and $\alpha_m \in k$. If the homomorphism $F \to R$ is denoted by $a \mapsto a^*$, then the filtration v can be defined on R by writing for $r \in R$,

$$v(r) = \inf\{v(a) \mid a^* = r\}.$$

We now turn to the defining relations. If one of them is linear, $\Sigma\, \alpha_i u_i + \beta = 0$ ($\alpha_i, \beta \in k$), we can use it to eliminate one of the generators, because k is a field. So we may assume that there are no linear relations. Now relations of higher degree may be expressed as relations of degree two, by introducing further generators. Thus the defining relations for R may all be taken to be of the form

$$(2) \qquad \sum_1^N x_i y_i - b = 0,$$

where $x_i, y_i \in U$ and b is an expression in the generators with no term having x_i as left factor. We shall assume that all defining relations are of the form (2) with the same value of N; this can always be achieved by incorporating supernumerary terms in b.

Now each element f of R can be expressed as a linear combination of products of the generators. Such an expression is said to be *in reduced form for the suffix 1* if no term contains a factor $x_1 y_1$ for any of the defining relations (2). Any $f \in R$ can be expressed in reduced form by writing down any expression for f and then applying the move

$$(3) \qquad x_1 y_1 \mapsto b - \sum_{\nu \neq 1} x_\nu y_\nu$$

arising from (2), for all the defining relations, wherever possible. Under suitable conditions a reduced form for the suffix 1 for f (not necessarily unique) is reached after a finite number of moves. If for each $f \in R$ there is just one reduced form we shall call it the *normal form* of f and denote it by $[f]_1$; we also say then that a normal form for the suffix 1 exists. In a similar way we can define a reduced and a normal form for the suffix ν ($\nu = 2, \ldots, N$) by using in place of (3) the move

$$x_\nu y_\nu \mapsto b - \sum_{\mu \neq \nu} x_\mu y_\mu .$$

Such a normal form will be denoted by $[f]_\nu$. Now we can state the result:

Theorem 2. *Let R be a k-algebra generated by a set U containing a family of distinct elements $(x_{i\nu})$ ($i \in I$, $\nu = 1, \ldots, N$), another family of distinct elements $(y_{\nu j})$ ($j \in J$, $\nu = 1, \ldots, N$) and possibly other elements z_h ($h \in H$). These generators are assigned positive integer values in any way such that $v(x_{i\nu}) = 1$ and $v(y_{\nu j})$ is independent of ν. Assume that R has a complete set of defining relations indexed by some subset of $I \times J$:*

$$\sum x_{i\nu} y_{\nu j} = b_{ij},$$

where b_{ij} is an expression of value $v(b_{ij}) \leq 1 + v(y_{\nu j})$ in U and it has no term of this value with any $x_{i'\nu}$ as left factor. Moreover, assume that a normal form exists for each $\nu = 1, \ldots, N$, satisfying

N_ν. *If fg is in normal form for ν and $v(g)>0$, then for any $h \in R$, the terms of highest value in $f[gh]_\nu$ are in normal form for ν.*

Then R is an n-fir, for all $n < N$

The proof consists in verifying that R satisfies a truncated form of the weak algorithm (($N-1$)-term weak algorithm, cf. [7]). In spite of its complexity the condition is a very natural one, easy to check in most concrete cases.

§4. Direct limits and ultraproducts

It is clear that any direct limit (over a directed system) of firs is again a semifir; more generally, a routine argument shows the truth of

Theorem 3. *Let $\{R_\alpha, f_{\alpha\beta}\}_I$ be a direct system of rings. Suppose that for each $n \geq 1$ there exists $\lambda_n \in I$ such that R_α is an n-fir for all $\alpha > \lambda_n$, then $\varinjlim R_\alpha$ is a semifir.*

This result enables one to construct semifirs from n-firs, but there is no guarantee that the limit will be non-trivial; it may well reduce to 0 or to the ground field k unless precautions are taken. For ultraproducts the situation is rather better.

We recall that in a fir each element not zero or a unit can be written as a product of a finite number of atoms (= unfactorable elements) and any two complete factorizations of c have the same number of factors; this is called the *length* of c, written $l(c)$. Moreover, the factors can be paired off into pairwise similar ones; the precise condition need not concern us here, it is expressed by saying that the ring is a *unique factorization domain*, or UFD for short. In the commutative case this reduces to the usual definition (cf. [8], Chapter 3). We also recall that a semifir is a UFD if and only if each non-unit $\neq 0$ can be written as a product of a finite number of atoms.

Theorem 4. *Let $\{R_\alpha\}_I$ be any family of rings and $R = \prod R_\alpha/D$ their ultraproduct with respect to a non-principal ultrafilter D. If for each $n \geq 1$, the set $\{\alpha \in I \mid R_\alpha$ is an n-fir$\}$ is in D, then R is a semifir. If moreover, I is countable, then R is either a skew field or not a fir.*

Proof. That R is a semifir is clear from the definition of ultraproduct, because n-firs form an elementary class. Now let $I = \mathbf{N}$ say; if the set $\{n \in \mathbf{N} \mid R_n$ is a field$\}$ is in D, then R is a field. Otherwise there exists

$N_0 \in D$ such that R_n is not field for all $n \in N_0$. Let $a_n \in R_n$ be neither 0 nor a unit for $n \in N_0$ and $a_n = 1$ for $n \notin N_0$, and consider $a = (a_n^n) \in \Pi R_n$. The image $\bar{a}$ of a in R is a non-unit, and it can be written as a product of n non-units, for each n. Hence R is not a UFD and a fortiori not a fir.

For uncountable index sets the situation can be very different, especially if we have an ω_1-complete ultrafilter. Here ω_1 denotes the first uncountable cardinal, and for any infinite cardinal d an ultrafilter D on a set I is called *d-complete* if the intersection of any set of fewer than d members of D belongs to D. This is the case if and only if, for any partition of I into fewer than d parts, one of the parts belongs to D (cf. [3] p. 180).

Theorem 5. *Let $\{R_\alpha\}_I$ be an uncountable family of firs and let D be an ω_1-complete non-principal ultrafilter on I, then the ultraproduct $R = \Pi R_\alpha / D$ is a unique factorization domain.*

Proof. As noted earlier, in a fir each non-zero element a has a finite length $l(a)$. Given $a = (a_\alpha) \in \Pi R_\alpha$, put $P_n = \{\alpha \in I \mid l(a_\alpha) = n\}$, $P_\infty = \{\alpha \in I \mid a_\alpha = 0\}$, then the P's form a partition of I into $\omega < \omega_1$ sets, hence one of them, say P_{n_1} lies in D, and a is a product of n_1 atoms (or $a = 0$). Thus R is a semifir in which each non-zero element has finite length, i.e. R is a UFD.

In the commutative case this result shows that an ultraproduct of an uncountable family of principal ideal domains with an ω_1-complete non-principal ultrafilter is again principal.

The same method of proof will show that under the conditions of the theorem R has ACC_n (i.e. the ascending chain condition on n-generator right ideals) for any n, but it is not known whether R is necessarily a fir. If however, each R_α is a ring with weak algorithm, then R will again have weak algorithm and hence be a fir.

§5. Examples

With the help of Theorem 2 it is easy to give examples of $(n-1)$-firs that are not n-firs. We simply take $2n$ generators x_i, y_i with the defining relation

$$x_1 y_1 + \cdots + x_n y_n = 0.$$

This is not trivializable (otherwise every n-term relation would be trivializable and every ring would be an n-fir!). But the conditions of Theorem 2 are satisfied, so we have an $(n-1)$-fir L_{n-1} say. If we take the ultraproduct of $L_1, L_2, \ldots$ with a non-principal ultrafilter, we obtain a ring which is an n-fir for all n, i.e. a semifir. Thus semifirs do not form an elementary class.

A slight modification shows that the class of rings embeddable in skew fields is not elementary. This problem, raised by Mal'cev [10] was answered in [9] using the compactness theorem. Here is a more direct proof: Let R_{n-1} be generated by $2(n^2+n)$ generators $a_{i\lambda}, b_{\lambda i}$ $(i = 1, \ldots, n,\ \lambda = 1, \ldots, n+1)$ with the defining relations

$$(4) \qquad \sum a_{i\lambda} b_{\lambda j} = \delta_{ij}, \quad \sum b_{\lambda i} a_{i\mu} = \delta_{\lambda\mu}.$$

In matrix terms we have an $n \times (n+1)$ matrix A and an $(n+1) \times n$ matrix B such that $AB = I$, $BA = I$. Thus R_{n-1} does not have invariant basis number (cf. [6]) and so is not embeddable in a skew field. But the relations (4) satisfy the conditions of Theorem 2 (cf. [6, 7]), hence R_{n-1} is an $(n-1)$-fir. Now the ultraproduct of all the R_n (with a non-principal ultrafilter) is a semifir, and by the results of [8], Chapter 7, is embeddable in a skew field. Therefore the class of rings embeddable in skew fields is not elementary, although, by general results of universal algebra (cf. [5, 10]) it can be defined by an infinite set of sentences. This can also be seen from the explicit form of the embeddability conditions given in [8].

In the last example we saw that when a relation such as $ab = 1$ is interpreted as a relation between $n \times n$ matrices, an $(n-1)$-fir results. This idea has been made precise and proved generally by G.M. Bergman [2]. His result (referring to square matrices only) may be stated as follows:

Let R be any k-algebra; if we take any presentation of R and interpret all relations as relations between $n \times n$ matrices, we obtain an $n \times n$ matrix ring over an $(n-1)$-fir.

Bergman gives two proofs, one based on results in [1], the other based on [7]. In this way one obtains a family of n-firs (for all n) from any given k-algebra; in general there is no way of making this family into a direct system, but by taking ultraproducts one can again obtain semifirs.

References

[1] G.M. Bergman, Modules over coproducts of rings, Trans. Amer. Math. Soc. 200 (1974) 1–32.

[2] G.M. Bergman, Coproducts and some universal ring constructions, Trans. Amer. Math. Soc. 200 (1974) 33–88.
[3] C.C. Chang and H.J. Keisler, Model theory, Vol. 73, Studies in logic (North-Holland Publishing Co., Amsterdam, 1973).
[4] P.M. Cohn, Free ideal rings, J. Algebra 1 (1964) 47–69.
[5] P.M. Cohn, Universal algebra (Harper and Row, New York, London, Tokyo, 1965).
[6] P.M. Cohn, Some remarks on the invariant basis property, Topology 5 (1966) 215–228.
[7] P.M. Cohn, Dependence in rings II. The dependence number, Trans. Amer. Math. Soc. 135 (1969) 267–279.
[8] P.M. Cohn, Free rings and their relations, LMS monographs No. 2 (Academic Press, London and New York, 1971).
[9] P.M. Cohn, The class of rings embeddable in skew fields, Bull. London Math. Soc. 6 (1974) 147–148.
[10] A.I. Mal'cev, Algebraic systems (Springer, Berlin, 1973).

S.I. Adian, W.W. Boone, G. Higman, eds., Word Problems II
© North-Holland Publishing Company (1980) 81–85

CONJUGACY AND THE HIGMAN EMBEDDING THEOREM

Donald J. COLLINS
Queen Mary College, London

The Higman embedding theorem asserts that if a finitely generated group has a recursively enumerable set of defining relations, then it can be embedded in a finitely presented group. Subsequently, Clapham showed that the Higman construction preserves the solvability of the word problem in the sense that if the original finitely generated group has solvable word problem, then so does the finitely presented group in which it is embedded.

Our purpose here is to show that the analogue of Clapham's theorem for the conjugacy problem is false.

Let $C = \langle c_1, c_2, \ldots, c_n;\ r = 1,\ r \in R\rangle$ be a finitely generated group with a recursively enumerable set R of defining relations. It is convenient to assume, as we may, that $R = R(c_i)$ is the normal subgroup of the free group $F(c_i) = F(c_1, c_2, \ldots, c_n)$ consisting of every relation of C.

As proved by Higman [4], C can be embedded in a finitely presented group G in the following manner.

Let $F(a_i)$ and $F(b_i)$ be free groups isomorphic to $F(c_i)$. From these form the amalgamated free product

$$H = (F(a_i) * F(b_i);\ R(a_i) = R(b_i)).$$

Then H can be embedded in a finitely presented group L. Next form the direct product $L \times C$ and finally the HNN extension

$$G = (L \times C, t;\ t^{-1}a_it = a_ic_i,\ t^{-1}b_it = b_i,\ i = 1, 2, \ldots, n).$$

Then G is, in fact, finitely presented.

We fix the above notation and are ambiguous, leaving the context to clarify, in our use of notation for an element of a free group and its image in a factor group.

Proposition 1. *Let $x(a_i) \in F(a_i)$ and suppose*
(a) *$x(a_i)$ is cyclically reduced in $F(a_i)$,*
(b) *$x(a_i)$ is not a proper power in $F(a_i)$,*
(c) *$x(a_i) \notin R(a_i)$.*

Then for any $u(c_i)$, *the subgroup of* C *generated by* $x(c_i)$ *contains* $u(c_i)$ *if and only if* $x(a_i)u(c_i)t^{-1}$ *and* $x(a_i)t^{-1}$ *are conjugate in* G.

Proof. Suppose $x(a_i)u(c_i)t^{-1}$ and $x(a_i)t^{-1}$ are conjugate in G. Then by Collins' Lemma (see [5]), they must be conjugate by an element $w(a_i, b_i)$. The conjugacy is then valid in the group

$$(H \times C, t;\ t^{-1}a_it = a_ic_i,\ t^{-1}b_it = b_i,\ i = 1, 2, \ldots, n).$$

From the equation

$$w(a_i, b_i)^{-1}x(a_i)u(c_i)t^{-1}w(a_i, b_i) = x(a_i)t^{-1}$$

we obtain, via the relations $t^{-1}a_it = a_ic_i$, $t^{-1}b_it = b_i$,

(1) $$w(a_i, b_i)^{-1}x(a_i)w(a_i, b_i) = x(a_i)$$

in H,

(2) $$u(c_i)z(c_i) = 1$$

in C, where $w(a_ic_i, b_i) = w(a_i, b_i)z(c_i)$ in $H \times C$.

As $x(a_i) \notin R(a_i)$ it follows from (1) and the structure of H as amalgamated free product that $w(a_i, b_i) \in F(a_i)$. Then from (a) and (b) in the hypotheses, we see that, for some integer m, $w(a_i, b_i) = x(a_i)^m$ in $F(a_i)$. This means that $z(c_i) = x(c_i)^m$ in C as required.

Conversely suppose that $u(c_i)x(c_i)^m = 1$ in C. A simple calculation verifies that

$$x(a_i)^{-m}x(a_i)u(c_i)t^{-1}x(a_i)^m = x(a_i)t^{-1}.$$

Corollary 2. *Let* C *have unsolvable power problem and solvable order problem. Let* C *be embedded in* G *via the Higman embedding. Then* G *has unsolvable conjugacy problem.*

Proof. Let X be the set of all cyclically reduced words of $F(c_i)$ that are not proper powers in $F(c_i)$ and do not lie in $R(c_i)$. Since C has solvable order problem this is a recursive set. On the other hand, since C has unsolvable power problem there is no algorithm to decide of an arbitrary element z of $F(c_i)$ and an arbitrary element x of X whether or not z lies in the cyclic subgroup of C generated by x. By Proposition 1 G must have unsolvable conjugacy problem.

We give another demonstration of the way in which the Higman embedding fails to preserve the solvability of the conjugacy problem.

Proposition 3. *Let x_k, y_k, $k = 1,2,3,4$ be elements of $F(c_i)$, none of which lies in $R(c_i)$. Let $w = w(a_i, b_i)$ be an element of the free product $F(a_i) * F(b_i)$. If*

$$w^{-1}x_1tx_2t^{-1}x_3tx_4t^{-1}w = y_1ty_2t^{-1}y_3ty_4t^{-1}$$

in G then, in C,

$$x_1 = y_1,\ z^{-1}x_2z = y_2,\ x_3 = y_3 \quad \text{and} \quad z^{-1}x_4z = y_4,$$

where $w(a_ic_i, b_i) = w(a_i, b_i)z(c_i)$ in $H \times C$.

Proof. The postulated equality must hold in the HNN extension

$$(H \times C, t;\ t^{-1}a_it = a_ic_i,\ t^{-1}b_it = b_i,\ i = 1, 2, \ldots, n).$$

Using t as stable letter, we see that $x_4w(a_ic_i, b_i)y_4^{-1}$ lies in the subgroup $\langle a_ic_i, b_i\rangle$. But then, clearly, $x_4w(a_ic_i, b_i)y_4^{-1} = w(a_ic_i, b_i)$. This gives $z^{-1}x_4z = y_4$ and

$$w(a_i, b_i)^{-1}x_1tx_2t^{-1}x_3w(a_i, b_i) = y_1ty_2t^{-1}y_3.$$

From this we obtain $x_3w(a_i, b_i)y_3^{-1} = w(a_i, b_i)$ and hence $x_3 = y_3$ and $w^{-1}x_1tx_2t^{-1}w = y_1ty_2t^{-1}$. A similar argument gives $z^{-1}x_2z = y_2$ and $x_1 = y_1$.

Corollary 4. *Let C have solvable conjugacy problem but suppose there is no algorithm to decide of two arbitrary pairs u_1, v_1 and u_2, v_2 of elements of $F(c_i)$ whether or not there exists z in $F(c_i)$ such that $z^{-1}u_1z = v_1$ and $z^{-1}u_2z = v_2$ in C. If C is embeddable in G via the Higman embedding then G has unsolvable conjugacy problem.*

Proof. Let x and y be elements of $F(c_i)$ such that $x \neq y$ in C and $x \neq 1$, $y \neq 1$ in C (i.e. $x \not\equiv y \bmod R(c_i)$ and $x, y \notin R(c_i)$). For any two pairs u_1, v_1 and u_2, v_2 of elements of $F(c_i)$, none of which lies in $R(c_i)$, it follows from Proposition 3 that if $xtu_1t^{-1}ytu_2t^{-1}$ and $xtv_1t^{-1}ytv_2t^{-1}$ are conjugate in G then there exists z in $F(c_i)$ such that $z^{-1}u_1z = v_1$ and $z^{-1}u_2z = v_2$ in C. Conversely, if such a $z = z(c_i)$ exists then the given words $xtu_1t^{-1}ytu_2t^{-1}$ and $xtv_1t^{-1}ytv_2t^{-1}$ are easily seen to be conjugate in G by $z(a_i)$.

Since C has solvable conjugacy problem it follows that even when the assumption that none of u_1, u_2, v_1, v_2 lies in $R(c_i)$ is added there is still no algorithm to decide whether or not there exists z such that $z^{-1}u_1z = v_1$ and $z^{-1}u_2z = v_2$ in C. Thus G must have unsolvable conjugacy problem.

Example. We specify a group in which the hypotheses of Corollary 4 are satisfied.

Let C have presentation (abandoning our systematic notation):

$$a_1,\ a_2,\ b_1,\ b_2,\ p_1,\ p_2,\ q_1,\ q_2,\ c_1,\ c_2,\ d_1,\ d_2,\ r_1,\ r_2,\ s_1,\ s_2;$$

$$p_1^{-j} b_1^j a_1 b_1^j p_1^j = r_1^{-j} d_1^j c_1 d_1^j r_1^j \qquad p_2^{-j} b_2^j a_2 b_2^j p_2^j = r_2^{-j} d_2^j c_2 d_2^j r_2^j$$

$$q_1^{-i} q_2^{-i} b_1^{f(i)} a_1 b_1^{f(i)} q_2^i q_1^i = s_1^{-i} s_2^{-i} d_1^{f(i)} c_1 d_1^{f(i)} s_2^i s_1^i$$

$$q_1^{-i} q_2^{-i} b_2^{f(i)} a_2 b_2^{f(i)} q_2^i q_1^i = s_1^{-i} s_2^{-i} d_2^{f(i)} c_2 d_2^{f(i)} s_2^i s_1^i$$

where i and j range through the positive integers and f is a one-to-one recursive function of the positive integers with non-recursive range.

Then C has solvable conjugacy problem and there exists z such that

$$z^{-1} b_1^j a_1 b_1^j z = d_1^j c_1 d_1^j \quad \text{and} \quad z^{-1} b_2^j a_2 b_2^j = d_2^j c_2 d_2^j$$

if and only if j lies in the range of f. We shall not give the arguments for this since they are standard and rather similar to the kind of argument given by Miller on pp. 46–54 of [5].

We conclude with some general remarks. There seems at present to be no hope of establishing the analogue of Clapham's theorem. To prove Higman's theorem one firstly achieves a kind of logical embedding in a finitely presented group (in our notation C is logically embedded in L since $w(a_i) = w(b_i)$ in L if and only if $w(c_i) = 1$ in C). Then, in Paul Schupp's graphic phrase, one performs the Higman "rope-trick" to achieve the actual group embedding. It follows from the author's paper [3] that at least for Aanderaa's version [1] of the Higman theorem, solvability of the conjugacy problem can be achieved for the logical embedding section of the construction. But, as we have seen, there are substantial difficulties in dealing with the "rope-trick" part. Furthermore, these difficulties seem to be more or less inevitable given the structure of the proof and probably a wholly new strategy will be needed to avoid them. For the present the most that can be hoped for is the isolation of conditions on C that are necessary and sufficient for the preservation of the solvability of the conjugacy problem in the Higman embedding.

References

[1] S. Aanderaa, A proof of Higman's embedding theorem using Britton extensions of groups, in: W.W. Boone, F.B. Cannonito and R.C. Lyndon (eds.), Word problems (North-Holland, Amsterdam, 1973).

[2] C.R.J. Clapham, An embedding theorem for finitely generated groups, Proc. Lond. Math. Soc. 3, 17 (1967) 419–430.
[3] D.J. Collins, Representation of Turing reducibility by word and conjugacy problems in finitely presented groups, Acta Math. 128 (1972) 73–90.
[4] G. Higman, Subgroups of finitely presented groups, Proc. Roy. Soc. Series A, 262 (1961) 455–475.
[5] C.F. Miller, On group-theoretic decision problems and their classification (Princeton, 1971).

S.I. Adian, W.W. Boone, G. Higman, eds., Word Problems II

SOME SOLVABLE WORD PROBLEMS

Trevor EVANS*
Emory University, Atlanta, Georgia

Introduction

This is a survey of some algorithms which have been used to solve decision problems (mainly word problems) in various varieties of algebras, e.g., lattices, commutative semigroups, quasigroups. Our interest is in algebraic properties which imply the existence of such algorithms. There is no attempt to be encyclopaedic but instead the emphasis is on examples of algorithms which have a universal algebra flavor.

In Section 1 we discuss the connection between embedding of partial algebras in a variety and the solvability of the word problem for finitely presented (f.p.) algebras in the variety. In Section 2 we consider algorithms based on finite separability properties. Finally, we look at some aspects of normal form theorems. We will work within a finitely presented variety **V**, i.e., a variety defined by a finite number of finitary operations and a finite set of identities, and by an *algebra*, we will always mean an f.p. algebra in such a variety.

§1. Partial algebras

Let **V** be an f.p. variety and let V^* be the variety with the same operation type as **V** but defined by the empty set of identities. For example, if **V** is the variety of commutative semigroups, V^* is the variety of groupoids. If Ω is the set of operations in a **V**-algebra, by a *partial* V^*-algebra $\mathcal{P} = (P, \Omega)$ we mean a set P of elements and, for each n-ary operation f in Ω, a mapping $\bar{f}: S \to P$ where $S \subseteq P^n$.

By a partial **V**-algebra, we mean a partial V^*-algebra $\mathcal{P} = (P, \Omega)$ such that the following conditions are satisfied.

(i) Insofar as the identities of **V** apply to $\mathcal{P}$, they are satisfied. That

* This research was supported in part by U.S. NSF Grant MCS76–06986.

is, if $u(x_1, x_2, x_3, \dots) = v(x_1, x_2, x_3, \dots)$ is one of the defining identities of V and if for any elements $a_1, a_2, a_3, \dots$ of P substituted for the variables in $u = v$, the partial Ω-operations of $\mathcal{P}$ allow both $u(a_1, a_2, a_3, \dots)$ and $v(a_1, a_2, a_3, \dots)$ to be computed, then the identity $u = v$ holds for these values.

(ii) The partial operations defined in $\mathcal{P}$ and the defining identities of V do not allow us to extend the domain of the partial operations of $\mathcal{P}$. In other words, if a substitution of elements of P for the variables in an identity $u = v$ of V enables us to compute one side as a_t and the other as $f(a_1, a_2, a_3, \dots)$, for some $f \in \Omega$ and $a_1, a_2, a_3, \dots$ in P, then $f(a_1, a_2, a_3, \dots) = a_t$ is already given as a value of the partial operation f.

We say that the *embeddability problem* is solvable for V if there is an algorithm for deciding whether any finite partial V-algebra (actually, we could just as well say "any finite partial V^*-algebra") can be embedded isomorphically in a V-algebra. The following theorem is proved in [4].

Theorem. *The embedding problem is solvable for the variety* V *if and only if the word problem is solvable for* V.

This theorem is useful in solving the word problem for two reasons.

(i) In the most favorable case, any finite partial V-algebra can be embedded in a finite V-algebra. This occurs more frequently than one would expect.

(ii) We may be able to give reasonable conditions on V or on partial V-algebras which imply a test for embeddability. For example, V may have the property that if a finite partial V-algebra is embeddable at all, then it can be embedded in a finite V-algebra.

If V has the property that any finite partial V-algebra can be embedded, then the algorithm for solving the word problem for an f.p. V-algebra goes as follows. Let $\mathcal{A}$ be a V-algebra given by generators $a_1, a_2, a_3, \dots$, and relations $r_i(a_1, a_2, a_3, \dots) = r'_i(a_1, a_2, a_3, \dots)$, $i = 1, 2, 3, \dots$. Let w_1, w_2 be two words in the generators of $\mathcal{A}$. We wish to decide whether $w_1 = w_2$ in $\mathcal{A}$.

We begin by introducing new generators $b_1, b_2, b_3, \dots$ for every word in the a_i which occurs as a subword of r_i, r'_i, w_1 or w_2. This enables us to rewrite the defining relations of $\mathcal{A}$ so that each relation is either of the form $b_i = b_j$ or $f(b_i, b_j, b_k, \dots) = b_t$ where f is an operation of $\mathcal{A}$.

Now, by direct applications of the identities of V and the defining relations of $\mathcal{A}$, we alternately remove redundant generators and introduce new relations of the form $f(b_i, b_j, b_k, \dots) = b_t$. We arrive at a presentation for $\mathcal{A}$ which has the form of a partial $\boldsymbol{V}$-algebra $\mathcal{P}$. In doing this, the b_i, b_j corresponding to w_1, w_2 may have been indentified, in which case we know that $w_1 = w_2$ in $\mathcal{A}$. On the other hand, b_i, b_j may remain distinct in $\mathcal{P}$. Since $\mathcal{P}$ can be isomorphically embedded in a $\boldsymbol{V}$-algebra, $b_i \neq b_j$ in the $\boldsymbol{V}$-algebra freely generated by $\mathcal{P}$ and so, isomorphically, $w_1 \neq w_2$ in $\mathcal{A}$. For more details see [3], [4].

The above procedure solves the word problem for the varieties of (i) lattices (ii) quasigroups, loops and many subvarieties of these which arise in the study of combinatorial designs [17]. In a number of papers (see, for example, [13]) Gluhov and Gvaramija have given conditions on varieties of quasigroups (and of other algebras) which imply that any finite partial algebra in the variety can be finitely embedded.

We can differentiate between the different kinds of embeddability of finite partial algebras in a variety $\boldsymbol{V}$ by the following conditions.

E_1: Any finite partial $\boldsymbol{V}$-algebra can be finitely embedded.

E_2: Any finite partial $\boldsymbol{V}$-algebra can be embedded (although not necessarily in a finite $\boldsymbol{V}$-algebra).

E_3: If a finite partial $\boldsymbol{V}$-algebra can be embedded, then it can be embedded in a finite $\boldsymbol{V}$-algebra.

Clearly, $E_1 \Leftrightarrow E_2 \wedge E_3$. One of the simplest examples of a variety $\boldsymbol{V}$ with property E_2 but neither E_1 nor E_3 is given by binary operations xy, $x\backslash y$ and the identity $x \cdot (x\backslash y) = y$. For details, see [17]. The situation is clarified by the following theorem [17]. (See also [2], [7].)

Theorem. *A variety* $\boldsymbol{V}$ *has the property* E_3 *if and only if every f.p.* $\boldsymbol{V}$*-algebra is residually finite.*

An f.p. residually finite algebra has a solvable word problem. (See [17], although the result is apparently first due to Malcev.) We repeat briefly the simple argument. Let $\mathcal{A}$ be an f.p. residually finite $\boldsymbol{V}$-algebra and let w_1, w_2 be words in the generators of $\mathcal{A}$. We enumerate all consequences of the defining relations of $\mathcal{A}$. If $w_1 = w_2$ in $\mathcal{A}$, it will appear in this enumeration. We also enumerate the finite $\boldsymbol{V}$-algebras which are homomorphic images of $\mathcal{A}$. If $w_1 \neq w_2$ in $\mathcal{A}$, then in one of these homomorphic images of $\mathcal{A}$ w_1 and w_2 will map onto distinct elements. Combining these enumerations, we have a procedure which, in a finite number of steps, will decide whether $w_1 = w_2$ in $\mathcal{A}$.

In the table below we list these embeddability properties for f.p. algebras in some familiar varieties. We note that the free algebras in all of the listed varieties other than inverse property loops and modular lattices are residually finite and hence have solvable word problem. It is not known whether free modular lattices are residually finite, i.e. have property E_3, nor is this known for inverse property loops.

Variety	E_1	E_2	E_3	W.P. solvable
Groups, rings semigroups, modular lattices	no	no	no	no
Abelian groups, commutative rings and semigroups	no	no	yes	yes
Quasigroups, loops, lattices	yes	yes	yes	yes
Inverse property loops	?	yes	?	yes
Non-associative rings	no	no	?	yes

For commutative rings and semigroups, residual finiteness (or E_3) at present provides the only procedure for solving the word problem for f.p. algebras.

Problems. 1. Prove that free modular lattices are not residually finite.

2. Prove that f.p. non-associative rings are residually finite.

3. Prove that finite partial inverse property loops can be finitely embedded. (Inverse property loops are one of the few varieties of loops which have been studied in detail but for which the finite embeddability property has not been verified.)

§2. Finite separability properties

An algebra $\mathscr{A}$ is residually finite if, for any two disjoint finite subsets S_1, S_2 of $\mathscr{A}$, there is a homomorphism of $\mathscr{A}$ onto a finite algebra such that the image of S_1 and S_2 are disjoint. There are numerous generalizations of this concept. If x is an element and $\mathscr{S}$ a subalgebra of $\mathscr{A}$, then $\mathscr{A}$ has the *finite separability property* (abbreviated to f.s.p.) if, for any $x \not\in \mathscr{S}$ there is a homomorphism α onto a finite algebra in which $x\alpha \not\in \mathscr{S}\alpha$. If $\mathscr{S}_1$, $\mathscr{S}_2$ are subalgebras, then $\mathscr{A}$ has the *subalgebra separability* property if for any such disjoint $\mathscr{S}_1$, $\mathscr{S}_2$, there is a finite homomorphic image of $\mathscr{A}$ such that the images of $\mathscr{S}_1$, $\mathscr{S}_2$ are disjoint. If $\mathscr{A}$ is a group, then it has the *conjugacy separability* property if for any elements x, y not conjugate in $\mathscr{A}$, there is a finite homomorphic image of $\mathscr{A}$ in which the images of x and y are not conjugate.

The relationship of such finite separability properties to algorithms for solving corresponding decision problems is obvious. We have given one example earlier — residual finiteness implies solvability of the word problem — a similar proof shows that finite separability of an element and an f.g. subalgebra implies solvability of the generalized word problem.

Free groups have the finite separability property for f.g. subgroups (M. Hall [14]), hence have solvable generalized word problem. So do free semigroups and free commutative semigroups (these are easy to show). In fact, free algebras in any variety defined by balanced identities (each variable in a defining identity $u = v$ occurs exactly the same number of times in u as in v). Surprisingly, however, free rings do not have the finite separability property. Let $\mathscr{R}$ be the free ring on one generator x and let $\mathscr{S}$ be the subring generated by $2x, 2x^2 + x$. Then $\mathscr{S} \neq \mathscr{R}$, i.e. $x \notin \mathscr{S}$. However, in any homomorphism α of $\mathscr{R}$ onto a finite ring, $x\alpha \in \mathscr{S}\alpha$. This result is due to K. Mandelberg [17].

The generalized word problem for free rings is apparently an open question. However, one can show, using methods similar to those of Mihailova [19] for groups, that the generalized word problem is unsolvable for $F \oplus F$, the direct sum of two copies of a free ring. Let $S = \langle g_1, g_2, \ldots, g_m;\ u_1 = v_1,\ u_2 = v_2,\ u_n = v_n\rangle$ be a semigroup with an unsolvable word problem and let F be the free ring generated by $g_1, g_2, \ldots, g_m$. In the direct sum $F \oplus F$, let S^* be the subring generated by (u_i, v_i), $i = 1, 2, \ldots, n$ and (g_i, g_i), $i = 1, 2, \ldots, m$. It is easy to prove that if u, v are monomials in F with coefficient one, then $(u, v) \in S^*$ if and only if $u = v$ in S. It follows that the G.W.P. is unsolvable for $F \oplus F$.

For the problem of deciding for a $\boldsymbol{V}$-algebra $\mathscr{A}$ whether two f.g. sub-algebras have a non-empty intersection, we appeal to the subalgebra separability property. For quasigroups (and various subvarieties) we can use the fact that any finite partial quasigroup can be finitely embedded to show that the variety of quasigroups has the subalgebra separability property [17].

There is an interesting contrast for this property between free semigroups and free commutative semigroups. Let $\mathscr{F}$ be an f.g. free semigroup and $\mathscr{S}_1$, $\mathscr{S}_2$ be disjoint f.g. subsemigroups of $\mathscr{F}$. By a standard result in the theory of finite automata, $\mathscr{S}_1$ and $\mathscr{S}_2$ can each be expressed as the union of congruence classes of some congruence of finite index on $\mathscr{F}$. (See, for example, [11].) The intersection of these two congruences is a congruence θ of finite index. In the quotient semigroup $\mathscr{F}/\theta$, the images of $\mathscr{S}_1$ and $\mathscr{S}_2$ will be disjoint. Now let $\mathscr{A}$ be the free commutative semigroup generated by g_1, g_2 and let $\mathscr{B}_1$, $\mathscr{B}_2$ be the subsemigroups generated by $\{g_1g_2, g_1g_2^2\}$ and $\{g_1, g_1^2g_2\}$ respectively. Although $\mathscr{B}_1 \cap \mathscr{B}_2 = \emptyset$ in $\mathscr{A}$, in any homomorphism of $\mathscr{A}$ onto a finite semigroup the images of $\mathscr{B}_1$ and $\mathscr{B}_2$ intersect (Garrett [12]).

We conclude this section with a decision problem which is known to be solvable [16] but for which it would be interesting to know whether there is an algorithm based on a finite separability property. Let $\mathscr{G}$ be a group. If, for any x, y in $\mathscr{G}$ such that x and y are not conjugate in $\mathscr{G}$, there is a homomorphism α of $\mathscr{G}$ onto a finite group such that $x\alpha$, $y\alpha$ are not conjugate in $\mathscr{G}_\alpha$, then $\mathscr{G}$ is conjugacy separable or *residually finite with respect to conjugacy*. Stebe [23] has shown that free groups are conjugacy separable. If we describe conjugacy separability in groups as finitely separating elements and conjugacy classes, it suggests the following generalization.

Let $\mathscr{A}$ be an algebra and $\mathscr{G}$ a group of automorphisms of $\mathscr{A}$. Does $\mathscr{A}$ have the finite separability property with respect to orbits of $\mathscr{G}$? A particularly interesting case of this concerns free algebras. Let $\mathscr{F}_n$ be an f.g. free algebra in a variety $\mathbf{V}$. Consider all homomorphisms of $\mathscr{F}_n$ onto n-generator finite algebras which are free in some subvariety of $\mathbf{V}$. If an element $x \in \mathscr{F}_n$ maps onto a primitive element in each such finite relatively free image, is x primitive in $\mathscr{F}_n$? (Here, *primitive* means an element of some free generating set.) We are actually asking here whether $\mathscr{F}_n$ has the finite separability property with respect to the orbits of its automorphism group. No examples of varieties $\mathbf{V}$ appear to be known in which $F_n(\mathbf{V})$ does not have this property but on the other hand only a few rather trivial examples, such as semigroups and groupoids, are known of varieties in which the free algebras do have this property.

Motivation for the above questions comes from the following theorem [17].

Theorem. *Let $\mathscr{F}_n$ be a residually finite free $\mathbf{V}$-algebra which also has the f.s.p. If $w_1, w_2, \ldots, w_n$ in $\mathscr{F}_n$ map onto a free generating set for every homomorphism of $\mathscr{F}_n$ onto a finite relatively free $\mathbf{V}$-algebra, then $w_1, w_2, \ldots, w_n$ is a free generating set of $\mathscr{F}_n$.*

From this, we obtain by a familiar argument

Theorem. *If $\mathscr{F}_n$ is a free $\mathbf{V}$-algebra on n generators which is residually finite and has the f.s.p., then there is an algorithm for deciding whether a set of n elements of $\mathscr{F}_n$ is a free generating set.*

This theorem applies to groups, semigroups, groupoids, quasigroups, loops, lattices.

It is tempting to conjecture that if each f.p. algebra in a variety $\boldsymbol{V}$ is residually finite (so that it has a large number of finite homomorphic images) then any two f.p. $\boldsymbol{V}$-algebras having the same homomorphic images are isomorphic. This is the case for abelian groups — unfortunately no other non-trivial example of this situation is known. A result of Pickel [21] states that if $H(\mathcal{A})$ is the set of finite homomorphic images of an f.g. nilpotent group $\mathcal{A}$, then there are only a finite number of f.g. nilpotent groups $\mathcal{B}$ such that $H(\mathcal{B}) = H(\mathcal{A})$. However, examples are known (Remeslennikov [22], Dyer [2]) of non-isomorphic f.g. nilpotent groups $\mathcal{A}$, $\mathcal{B}$ such that $H(\mathcal{A}) = H(\mathcal{B})$. Let us call an f.p. algebra in an f.p. variety ***V finitely determined*** if the set of its finite homomorphic images determines it uniquely (to within isomorphism). A similar argument to that used to show residual finiteness implies solvability of the word problem shows that the isomorphism problem is solvable for f.p. $\boldsymbol{V}$-algebras if every f.p. $\boldsymbol{V}$-algebra is finitely determined. However, as we remarked above, few examples of this situation are known. We conjecture, on rather flimsy evidence, that the varieties $\boldsymbol{V}$ of quasigroups with the property that every finite partial $\boldsymbol{V}$-quasigroup can be finitely embedded do have every f.p. algebra finitely determined. The variety of lattices is also another good candidate for this property.

A curious connection between the properties we have been discussing is that if the isomorphism problem is solvable for f.p. algebras in a variety $\boldsymbol{V}$ and if every such algebra is hopfian, then the word problem is solvable for f.p. $\boldsymbol{V}$-algebras. Let $\mathcal{A}$ be an f.p. $\boldsymbol{V}$-algebra and u, v words in the generators of $\mathcal{A}$. Let $\mathcal{A}_1$ be the algebra obtained from $\mathcal{A}$ by adding the additional defining relation $u = v$. Since $\mathcal{A}$ is hopfian, $u = v$ in $\mathcal{A}$ if and only if $\mathcal{A}$ and $\mathcal{A}_1$ are isomorphic.

Problems. 1. Solve the generalized word problem for free rings.

2. Prove that free lattices (or f.p. lattices) have the f.s.p. and the subalgebra separability properties.

3. Prove that w is a primitive element in an f.g. free group $\mathcal{F}_n$ if and only if w maps onto a primitive element in every homomorphism of $\mathcal{F}_n$ onto a relatively free finite group. Prove corresponding theorems for free loops and free quasigroups.

4. Let $\mathcal{A}$, $\mathcal{B}$ be two f.p. groupoids (or f.p. algebras in a variety $\boldsymbol{V}$ defined by the empty set of identities). Prove that if $\mathcal{A}$, $\mathcal{B}$ have the same sets of finite homomorphic images, then $\mathcal{A}$, $\mathcal{B}$ are isomorphic.

5. The same as Problem 4, for lattices.

6. It is known that residual finiteness of f.p. algebras in a variety $\boldsymbol{V}$ is not sufficient to prove the property described in 4 above for f.p. $\boldsymbol{V}$-algebras. Find finite separability properties on $\boldsymbol{V}$ which do imply this property.

§3. Normal form theorems

We recall the usual procedure for solving the word problem in a free group. Consider the set of all words in the generators and their inverses. We introduce *contractions* and *expansions* of words (deleting and inserting subwords gg^{-1}, $g^{-1}g$) and define two words to be *equivalent* if one can be transformed into the other by a finite sequence of expansions and contractions. It is easy to prove that every equivalence class $[w]$ contains a unique word $\bar{w}$ for which no contractions are possible, and that starting from any word in $[w]$ and applying contractions, we eventually arrive at $\bar{w}$. This word $\bar{w}$ is called the *normal form* (or *reduced form*) of any word in $[w]$. Clearly, when we have such a theorem we have a procedure for solving the word problem for F.

There are numerous varieties to which we can apply this method or some variation of it. The general setting is as follows. Let $\mathcal{A}$ be an algebra $\langle g_1, g_2, g_3, \dots ; r_1 = r_1', r_2 = r_2', \dots \rangle$ in a variety $\boldsymbol{V}$ defined by identities $v_i(x_1, x_2, x_3, \dots) = v_i'(x_1, x_2, x_3, \dots)$, $i = 1, 2, 3, \dots$. The elements of $\mathcal{A}$ are represented by *words* $w(g_1, g_2, g_3, \dots)$ built up from the generators and operations of $\mathcal{A}$. Two words u, u' are connected by an *elementary transformation* $u \leftrightarrow u'$ if one can be transformed into the other by an application of either a defining relation $r_i = r_i'$ of $\mathcal{A}$ or a defining identity $v_i = v_i'$ of V. Words u, u' are equivalent $u \equiv u'$ if one can be transformed into the other by a finite sequence of elementary transformations. The equivalence classes $[w]$ are the elements of $\mathcal{A}$ and the word problem for $\mathcal{A}$ consists of finding a method (or showing that one does not exist) which will decide when two words lie in the same equivalence class.

We may represent the situation by a graph. The points correspond to words and connecting segments to elementary transformations. The maximal connected components of the graph are the classes of equivalent words. We turn the graph into a directed graph by classifying the elementary transformations as either *contractions* or *expansions*. We write $u \to u'$ in the directed graph if we can get u' from u by a contraction. We attach a "weight" to each point, usually called the *length* $l(u)$ of the corresponding word. These weights can come from any well-ordered set although most frequently one uses the non-negative integers and we require that if $u \to u'$ then $l(u) > l(u')$. Our aim in doing this is to have in each connecting component exactly one point of minimum weight such that any directed path from any other point in the component ends at this "sink". This point will correspond to the *normal form* of every word in its equivalence class.

There is a general theorem of M.H.A. Newman [20] which enables us to achieve this desired end once we have assigned directions and weights in the graph. We require the resulting graph to satisfy the following *confluence property* (sometimes called the *Diamond Lemma*).

If $u \to u'$, $u \to u''$ are any two contractions of u, then there is a point u''' such that there are directed paths $u' \to \cdots \to u'''$, $u'' \to \cdots \to u'''$.

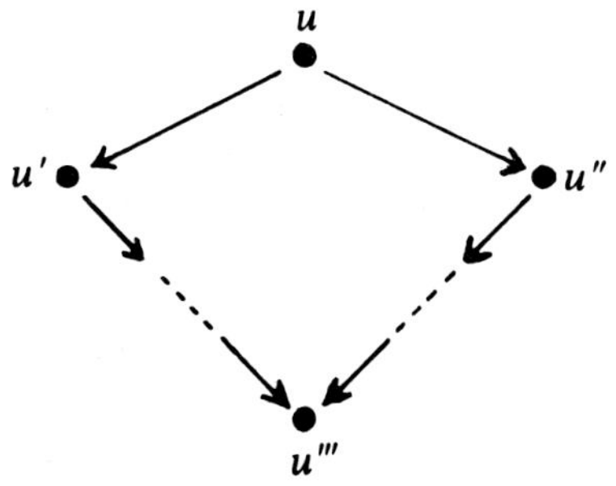

If this condition is satisfied it is an easy matter, using induction on the length $l(u)$ of u, to show that any sequence of contractions starting at a word u ends a unique normal form $\bar{u}$ of u. A simple induction on the number of elementary transformations connecting two words w, w' also enables us to show that words w, w' are equivalent iff they have the same normal form.

Thus, to use this approach to solve the word problem for algebras in a variety $\boldsymbol{V}$ we have to find an appropriate *length function* on words and we have to characterize the *contractions* of words so that we can prove that the confluence condition is satisfied. Once this is done, we may decide whether two words in an algebra are equivalent by comparing their *normal forms*.

Actually, what we have described is the bare bones of just one normal form approach to solving the word problem. In putting flesh on the bones, we may have to (even in the most direct application of this method)

(i) rewrite the defining relations so that they are in some special form (or consider only algebras whose relations can be put in this special form)

(ii) add redundant identities to the defining identities of $\boldsymbol{V}$.

Such adjustments (and others) may be necessary in order to obtain a confluence condition for the contractions. However, the above approach, with the refinements described, is sufficient to give a solution of the word problem for f.p. algebras in many different varieties. Some examples are given below.

Example 1. If $\boldsymbol{V}$ is a variety not satisfying any laws, then the word problem for free $\boldsymbol{V}$-algebras is trivial. For f.p. algebras in such a variety we rewrite the defining relations in the form $f(g_1, g_2, g_3, \ldots) = g_k$ (see [3]). Now, with the obvious definitions of *length* and *contraction*, the confluence condition holds.

Example 2. Let $\boldsymbol{V}$ be the variety of groupoids defined by the identity $xy \,.\, yz = y$, for all x, y, z. Let F be a free $\boldsymbol{V}$-algebra. If, using only the reduction $xy \,.\, yz \rightarrow y$, we try to prove that the confluence condition holds, then we fail but we do discover that the identities $x(xy \,.\, z) = xy$ and $(x \,.\, yz)z = yz$ are consequences of $xy \,.\, yz = y$.

We now try to verify the confluence condition using the contractions $xy \,.\, yz \rightarrow z$, $x(xy \,.\, z) \rightarrow xy$, $(x \,.\, yz)z \rightarrow yz$ where x, y, z are any words in the generators. This time, we are successful. This example illustrates a situation which occurs quite often — the confluence condition (if it holds) "generates" its own proof.

Example 3. Let $\boldsymbol{V}$ be the variety of quasigroups defined by three binary operations xy (multiplication), $x \backslash y$ (left-division), x/y (right-division) and the identities

$$x \,.\, (x \backslash y) = y, \quad (x/y) \,.\, y = x$$

$$x \backslash (xy) = y, \quad (xy)/y = x.$$

Let $\mathscr{A}$ be an f.p. $\boldsymbol{V}$-algebra generated by $g_1, g_2, g_3, \ldots$. In order to obtain the confluence property and hence, a normal form theorem, we first rewrite $\mathscr{A}$ in terms of generators $a_1, a_2, a_3, \ldots$ and defining relations of the form $a_i a_j = a_k$. Then we add the redundant identities

$$x/(y \backslash x) = y, \quad (y/x) \backslash y = x$$

to the defining identities of $\boldsymbol{V}$ and the redundant relations $a_i \backslash a_k = a_j$, $a_k / a_j = a_i$ for every defining relation $a_i a_j = a_k$.

Now we use as contractions $a_i a_j \to a_k$, $a_i \backslash a_k \to a_j$, $a_k / a_j \to a_i$, where $a_i a_j = a_k$ is a defining relation and $x(x\backslash y) \to y$, $(x/y)y \to x$, $x\backslash(xy) \to y$, $(xy)/y \to x$, $x/(y\backslash x) \to y$, $(y/x)\backslash y \to x$, where x, y are any words in the generators. The confluence condition holds and a normal form theorem results. See [5] for the use of this in studying the structure of f.p. algebras in various varieties of quasigroups and loops.

Actually, our original description of how we solve the word problem for free groups is not an example of the normal form approach we have described — it illustrates a generalization. When, in a free group, we define a word to be a string of generators and their inverses such as $g_1 g_2^{-1} g_3 g_3 g_2^{-1}$, the associative law (and the identities $(xy)^{-1} = y^{-1}x^{-1}$, $(x^{-1})^{-1} = x$) are sneaking in through the back door. Formally, we should define a word to be, for example, $((g_1 g_2^{-1})g_3)(g_2 g_3^{-1})^{-1}$. In writing $g_1 g_2^{-1} g_3 g_3 g_2^{-1}$ as a "word" we are identifying all words which are equivalent by using group identities which preserve length. In other words, the confluence condition using $xx^{-1} \to 1$, $x^{-1}x \to 1$ as reductions, is being applied to equivalence classes of words, rather than individual words, each equivalence class consisting of all words connected by the elementary transformations $(xy)z \leftrightarrow x(yz)$, $(x^{-1})^{-1} \leftrightarrow x$, $(xy)^{-1} \leftrightarrow y^{-1}x^{-1}$.

The general set-up is this. We have a variety $\boldsymbol{V}$ and a $\boldsymbol{V}$-algebra $\mathscr{A}$. With what seems to be the appropriate definition of *length* of a word, it may happen that some of the $\boldsymbol{V}$-identities preserve length and so cannot be used to shorten a word. We proceed by first considering an equivalence relation $\sim$ on words using only these length-preserving identities. We define contractions so that if $u \to u'$ and $u \sim v$, then there is a contraction $v \to v'$ where $u' \sim v'$. If this can be done, we have essentially defined contractions on $(\sim)$-equivalent classes of words. If we can now prove a confluence theorem for these contractions applied to the $(\sim)$-equivalence classes, then providing that we can recognize when words are $(\sim)$-equivalent, we have a solution of the word problem. An example of this procedure is used in [9] where the length-preserving identities are essentially generalized commutative laws for the operations.

We conclude this section with an example from group theory. The result is familiar — the normal form theorem for free products with an amalgamated subgroup — but the elementary transformations and length function used are not the familiar ones.

Let A, B be groups with subgroups A_1, B_1 which are isomorphic. We will identify A_1, B_1 according to the isomorphism and regard A, B as groups sharing a common subgroup $C = A \cap B$. We construct a group $A *_C B$, the generalized free product, as follows. The generators of $A *_C B$ are the elements $A \cup B$ and the defining relations are the multiplication tables of A and B.

By a *word*, we will mean a finite sequence $x_1x_2 \cdots x_n$ of elements of $(A \cup B) - \{e\}$ (e is the common neutral element of A and B). 1 denotes the empty word.

By an *elementary transformation* of a word we mean either a contraction or its inverse, where *contraction* is defined as follows.

We begin by choosing fixed left coset representatives for the subgroup C in the groups A and B. We take 1 as the coset representative of C and denote by x^* the left coset representative of C in A or B to which x belongs. Hence, $x = x^*c$ for some c in C. Let $w = x_1x_2 \cdots x_n$ where $x_i \in (A \cup B) - \{e\}$.

(i) If x_i belongs to $A - C$ or to $B - C$, then replacing x_i by x_i^*c where $x_i = x_i^*c$ in A or B, is a *contraction* of w.

(ii) If adjacent elements x_i, x_{i+1} in w belong to the same group A or B, and $x_ix_{i+1} = x = x^*c$ in that group, then replacing x_ix_{i+1} by x^*c is a *contraction* of w.

Thus, contractions have the effect of replacing elements of $A - C$ and $B - C$ by coset representatives and of shifting elements of C to the right. A *reduced* word in the free product of A and B with amalgamated subgroup C has the form $x_1^*x_2^* \cdots x_n^*c$ where the x_i^* are coset representatives from A and B, and c is either empty or in C.

We now introduce a *length* function with the right property. We define the empty word to have length (0, 0). If $w = x_1x_2 \cdots x_n$, we assign as its length an ordered pair of non-negative integers (p, q). Each x_i in C is given p-weight 1, each x_i which is a coset representative is given p-weight 3, all other x_i are given p-weight 5. We define p to be the sum of the p-weights. To each x_i which is in C we assign a q-weight the number of x_j's in w which are coset representatives and lie to the right of x_i in w. We define w to be the sum of the q-weights of w. We order lengths lexicographically.

It is a routine matter to check that the confluence condition holds and hence we obtain the usual normal form theorem that every element in the generalized free product can be written uniquely in the form $x_1^*x_2^* \cdots x_n^*c$.

Despite the simplicity of the procedure described in this section, it is enormously versatile. There is an extensive survey for other applications of the Diamond Lemma in a forthcoming expository paper by G. Bergman. P. Hall's expository paper [15] is a detailed study of an application of this technique. A number of examples are given in Knuth and Bendix [18].

Problems. 1. In the paper by Knuth and Bendix referred to above, there is a universal algebra version of the algorithm we have described for free algebras in a variety satisfying certain conditions. Can one extend the results of Knuth and Bendix to apply to varieties where some of the identities preserve length?

2. Is there a normal form theorem of the type we have described for free lattices? The usual solution of the word problem (Whitman [24]) involves explicit use of the order relation. The same question applies to f.p. lattices.

3. A version of the algorithm we have described for solving the word problem is used by the author (Trans. Amer. Math. Soc. 1963) to solve the isomorphism problem for some varieties of loops and quasigroups. Is there a universal algebra version of this?

References

[1] B. Banaschewski and E. Nelson, On residual finiteness and finite embeddability, Algebra Universalis 2 (1972) 361–364.
[2] J.L. Dyer, On the isomorphism problem for polycyclic groups, Math. Z. 112 (1969) 145–153.
[3] T. Evans, The word problem for abstract algebras, J. London Math. Soc. 26 (1951) 64–71.
[4] T. Evans, Embeddability and the word problem, J. London Math. Soc. 28 (1953) 76–80.
[5] T. Evans, On multiplicative systems defined by generators and relations, I. Normal form theorems, Proc. Cambr. Phil. Soc. 47 (1951) 637–649.
[6] T. Evans, The isomorphism problem for some classes of multiplicative systems, Trans. Amer. Math. Soc. 109 (1963) 303–312.
[7] T. Evans, Residual finiteness and finite embeddability. A remark on a paper by Banaschewski and Nelson, Algebra Universalis 2 (1972) 397.
[8] T. Evans, Identities and relations in commutative Moufang loops, J. of Algebra 31 (1974) 508–513.
[9] T. Evans, A decision problem for transformations of trees, Can. J. Math. 15 (1963) 584–590.
[10] T. Evans, Some connections between residual finiteness, finite embeddability and the word problem, J. London Math. Soc. (2), 1 (1969) 399–403.
[11] E. Engeler, Introduction to the Theory of Computation (Academic Press, New York, 1973).
[12] R. Garrett, Some problems concerning residual finiteness in algebras, Ph.D. Thesis, Emory University (in preparation).
[13] A.A. Gvaramija and M.M. Gluhov, A solution of the fundamental algorithmic problems in certain classes of quasigroups with identities, Sibirsk. Mat. Z. 10 (1969) 297–317 (Russian). English translation; Siberian Math. J. 10 (1969) 211–224.
[14] M. Hall, Jr., Coset representations in free groups, Trans. Amer. Math. Soc. 67 (1949) 421–432.
[15] P. Hall, Some word-problems, J. London Math. Soc. 33 (1958) 482–496.

[16] P.J. Higgins and R.C. Lyndon, Equivalence of elements under automorphisms of a free group, Mimeographed Notes, Queen Mary College, London.
[17] C. Lindner and T. Evans, Finite embedding theorems for partial designs and algebras (Les Presses de L'Universite de Montreal, 1977).
[18] D. Knuth and P. Bendix, Simple word problems in universal algebras, Proc. Conf. on Computational Problems in Abstract Algebra, Oxford, 1967.
[19] K.A. Mihailova, The occurrence problem for direct products of groups, Dokl. Akad. Nauk SSSR 119 (1958) 1103–1105 (Russian).
[20] M.H.A. Newman, On theories with a combinational definition of "equivalence", Ann. Math. 43 (1942) 223–243.
[21] P.F. Pickel, Finitely generated nilpotent groups with isomorphic finite quotients, Trans. Amer. Math. Soc. 160 (1971) 327–341.
[22] V.N. Remeslennikov, Finite approximability of groups with respect to conjugacy, Sibirsk. Mat. Z. 12 (1971) 1085–1099.
[23] P.F. Stebe, A residual property of certain groups, Proc. Amer. Math. Soc. 26 (1970) 37–42.
[24] P. Whitman, Free lattices, Ann. Math. 42 (1941) 325–330.

S.I. Adian, W.W. Boone, G. Higman, eds., Word Problems II
© North-Holland Publishing Company (1980) 101–139

SOLUTION OF THE CONJUGACY PROBLEM IN CERTAIN ARITHMETIC GROUPS

Fritz J. GRUNEWALD
University of Bielefeld (FRG)

The purpose of this paper is to give an algorithm which decides for two matrices $T, \hat{T} \in \mathrm{GL}_n(\mathbf{Q})$ whether there exists a matrix $X \in \mathrm{GL}_n(\mathbf{Z})$ such that:

$$XTX^{-1} = \hat{T}$$

This is problem 22 of the problem section of [1].

The algorithms we give can all be transformed into quite practical computer programs. They have as a general feature that one can always easily compute a bound for the number of steps necessary to complete the computation.

To explain our results we make the definitions:

Definition. Let $K_1 \subseteq K_2$ be two commutative rings with 1. For $T \in \mathrm{GL}_n(K_2)$ define:

$$\mathscr{C}_{K_1}(T) = \{X \in \mathrm{GL}_n(K_1) \mid XTX^{-1} = T\}$$

$\mathrm{GL}_n(K_1)$ being the group of invertible $n \times n$ matrices with entries in the ring K_1. n is a natural number. We of course consider $\mathrm{GL}_n(K_1)$ as being contained in $\mathrm{GL}_n(K_2)$. For $T, \hat{T} \in \mathrm{GL}_n(K_2)$ we write

$$T \sim_{K_1} \hat{T}$$

if and only if there is a $X \in \mathrm{GL}_n(K_1)$ with

$$XTX^{-1} = \hat{T}.$$

We write $\mathrm{SL}_n(K_2)$ for the group of $n \times n$ matrices with entries in K_2 of determinant 1.

We prove:

Theorem A. *Given two matrices, $T, \hat{T} \in \mathrm{GL}_n(\mathbf{Q})$, there is an algorithm for deciding whether*:

$$T \sim_{\mathbf{Z}} \hat{T}$$

If the answer is "yes" the algorithm constructs a conjugating matrix.

Another algorithm does the following:

Theorem B. *Given two matrices* $T, \hat{T} \in \mathrm{GL}_n(\mathbf{Q})$, *there is an algorithm for deciding whether there is a matrix* $X \in \mathrm{SL}_n(Z)$ *such that*

$$XTX^{-1} = \hat{T}$$

If the answer is "yes" the algorithm produces such an X.

We get Theorem B from Theorem A together with the following:

Theorem C. *Given* $T \in \mathrm{GL}_n(\mathbf{Q})$, *there is an algorithm for computing a finite set of generators of* $\mathscr{C}_{\mathbf{Z}}(T)$.

$\mathscr{C}_{\mathbf{Z}}(T)$ is an arithmetic group in the sense of [3]; a main theorem of this paper says that $\mathscr{C}_{\mathbf{Z}}(T)$ will be finitely generated.

As generalizations we mention some results on general and special linear groups over rings of algebraic integers. Let K be an algebraic number field, that is a finite extension of the field of rational numbers. We assume that K is given by a field generator ϑ together with its minimal polynomial over $\mathbf{Q}$.

Let $\mathcal{O}_K$ be the ring of algebraic integers in K. By algorithm A_6 listed in the last section of the paper it is possible to compute a $\mathbf{Z}$-basis for $\mathcal{O}_K$ together with a multiplication table for it. Almost a word for word translation (using $\mathcal{O}_K$ instead of $\mathbf{Z}$) gives now:

Theorem A′. *Given* $T, \hat{T} \in \mathrm{GL}_n(K)$, *there is an algorithm for deciding whether*:

$$T \sim_{\mathcal{O}_K} \hat{T}$$

If the answer is "yes" the algorithm computes a conjugating matrix.

A little more involved is:

Theorem B′. *Given* $T, \hat{T} \in \mathrm{Gl}_n(K)$, *there is an algorithm for deciding whether there is a matrix* $X \in \mathrm{SL}_n(\mathcal{O}_K)$ *such that*:

$$XTX^{-1} = \hat{T}.$$

If the answer is "yes" such an X may be computed.

Theorem B′ follows from:

Theorem C′. *Given $T \in \mathrm{GL}_n(K)$, there is an algorithm for computing a finite set of generators of $\mathscr{C}_{\mathcal{O}_K}(T)$.*

The groups $\mathrm{GL}_n(\mathcal{O}_K)$, $\mathrm{SL}_n(\mathcal{O}_K)$, $\mathscr{C}_{\mathcal{O}_K}(T)$ are again arithmetic groups in the sense of [3] as may be seen by "reduction to the ground field" in [24] Chapter I. Hence they are all finitely presented by [3], [3a]. Our algorithm therefore has some group-theoretic meaning. Presentations of some of them are computed in [21], [13], [14].

A more thorough look into the methods used here even leads to an effective algorithm for constructing a finite presentation for the $\mathscr{C}_{\mathcal{O}_K}(T)$ for a matrix $T \in \mathrm{GL}_n(K)$.

As an application to another type of arithmetic group we mention:

Corollary A. *Given $T, \hat{T} \in \mathrm{PGL}_n(K)$, there is an algorithm for deciding whether there is an $X \in \mathrm{PGL}_n(\mathcal{O}_K)$ with*

$$XTX^{-1} = \hat{T} \qquad \textit{in } \mathrm{PGL}_n(K)$$

and similarly:

Corollary B. *Given $T, \hat{T} \in \mathrm{PGL}_n(K)$, there is an algorithm for deciding whether there is an $X \in \mathrm{PSL}_n(\mathcal{O}_K)$ with*:

$$XTX^{-1} = \hat{T} \qquad \textit{in } \mathrm{PGL}_n(K).$$

Our method allows one to deduce Theorems A–C for **Z** replaced by an order in a (explicitly given) ring of algebraic integers or for an S-arithmetic ring if S is an explicitly given finite set of primes of the algebraic number field in question. The proof again is an almost word for word translation. It is also clear that Theorems A′–C′ decide the conjugacy problem in every subgroup of finite index in $\mathrm{GL}_n(\mathcal{O})$ or $\mathrm{SL}_n(\mathcal{O})$.

As a further generalization we mention the possibility of applying a quite similar procedure to $\mathrm{Sp}_{2n}(\mathbf{Z})$ or to $O_n(f, n)$ where f is an n-dimensional integral quadratic form, or to the group of matrices having entries in an order in a (explicitly given) finite dimensional skew field over **Q**, whose reduced norms lie in the unit group of an order in the center of the skew field. Details will appear elsewhere.

The particularly nice group-theoretic structure of $\mathrm{GL}_2(\mathbf{Z})$ and $\mathrm{SL}_2(\mathbf{Z})$ as amalgamated products of finite groups gives a more group-theoretic procedure for the decision problems in Theorems A and B (for $T, \hat{T} \in \mathrm{GL}_2(\mathbf{Z})$!). For this see for example [12], [13], [27], and for generalizations [11].

We have not tried to write out very effective algorithms, a lot of them depend highly exponentially on the data. But for dimensions 2 and 3 it is possible to modify the procedures (because there are not so many unipotent Jordan matrices) to actually obtain not too inefficient computer programs.

In the first part of the paper we give a number of effective reduction steps which will reduce our algorithm to a couple of algorithms known from algebraic number theory. These will be listed at the end of the paper.

I wrote this paper while doing a project on quite similar questions with Daniel Segal. I thank him very much for his advice. I also thank Professor J. Mennicke for help with an argument.*

A. Reductions

Before beginning, I want to mention that we often use a form of Gauss' algorithm:

Given a finitely generated free abelian group N with $\mathbf{Z}$-basis $n_1, \ldots, n_r$. Let $\{f_1, \ldots, f_s\}$ and $\{g_1, \ldots, g_t\}$ be two sets of elements in N, given in terms of the basis $n_1, \ldots, n_r$. Let:

$$N_1 = \langle \{f_1, \ldots, f_s\} \rangle$$

$$N_2 = \langle \{g_1, \ldots, g_t\} \rangle$$

be the subgroups generated by these two sets.

It is then effectively possible to compute the index:

$$|N_1 : (N_1 \cap N_2)|$$

and if it is finite to give a set of coset representatives for:

$$N_1/N_1 \cap N_2$$

For this see e.g. [5].

We will not always mention the use of this algorithm. We add some further definitions:

If R is a ring and ε a subset of R we put $\langle \varepsilon \rangle_R$ for the ideal generated by ε. We often leave the subscript R.

* (Added September 1977): After this paper was submitted in May 1977, Professor Adian informed me in September 1977 that similar results have been independently obtained by A. Sarkisjan.

Step I

Let n be a natural number. We are given two $n \times n$ matrices $T, \hat{T}$ with integer entries and both of determinant $\neq 0$. We hand these to algorithm A_3 which returns:

$$T = S + U \qquad \hat{T} = \hat{S} + \hat{U}$$

where S, $\hat{S}$ are rational semisimple matrices and U, $\hat{U}$ are rational nilpotent matrices. Furthermore we have:

$$SU = US \quad \text{and} \quad \hat{S}\hat{U} = \hat{U}\hat{S}.$$

These decompositions are clearly unique.

We now find a scalar matrix $k \cdot E_n$ where

$$E_n = \begin{pmatrix} 1 & & 0 \\ & \ddots & \\ 0 & & 1 \end{pmatrix}$$

is the n-dimensional unit matrix and where $0 \neq k \in \mathbf{Z}$, such that:

$$kE_n \cdot S,\ kE_n \cdot U \in M_n(\mathbf{Z})$$

$$kE_n\hat{S},\ kE_n\hat{U} \in M_n(\mathbf{Z}).$$

Put now:

$$T_1 = kE_n \cdot T \qquad \hat{T}_1 = kE_n \cdot \hat{T}$$

$$S_1 = kE_n \cdot S \qquad \hat{S}_1 = kE_n \cdot \hat{S}$$

$$U_1 = kE_nU \qquad \hat{U}_1 = kE_n\hat{U}$$

We find then:

Lemma 1. (1) $T \sim_{\mathbf{Z}} \hat{T} \Leftrightarrow T_1 \sim_{\mathbf{Z}} \hat{T}_1$.
(2) S_1, $\hat{S}_1$ *are semisimple with integer entries.*
(3) U_1, $\hat{U}_1$ *are nilpotent with integer entries.*
(4) $T_1 = S_1 + U_1$; $\hat{T}_1 = \hat{S}_1 + \hat{U}_1$.
(5) $S_1U_1 = U_1S_1$; $\hat{S}_1\hat{U}_1 = \hat{U}_1\hat{S}_1$.

These statements are obvious. Because of the uniqueness of the decomposition $T = S + U$ we get:

Lemma 2. $T_1 \sim_{\mathbf{Z}} \hat{T}_1 \Leftrightarrow$
(1) $\exists X \in \mathrm{GL}_n(\mathbf{Z})$ *with* $XS_1X^{-1} = \hat{S}_1$ *and*
(2) $\exists Y \in \mathscr{C}_{\mathbf{Z}}(\hat{S}_1)$ *with* $YXU_1X^{-1}Y^{-1} = \hat{U}_1$.

So, to decide the conjugacy problem we are essentially left with the two tasks:

I. Given two semisimple matrices S_1, $\hat{S}_1$ with integer entries and nonzero determinant, decide whether $S_1 \sim_{\mathbf{Z}} \hat{S}_1$ and if the answer is "yes" to produce a conjugating matrix X.

II. Given a semisimple matrix $\hat{S}_1$ with integer entries and two nilpotent matrices U_1, U_2 with integer entries and:

$$\hat{S}_1 U_1 = U_1 \hat{S}_1; \qquad \hat{S}_1 U_2 = U_2 \hat{S}_1$$

decide whether there is $X \in \mathscr{C}_{\mathbf{Z}}(\hat{S}_1)$ with

$$X U_1 X^{-1} = U_2.$$

We now define for any $n \times n$ matrix T with integer entries a $\mathbf{Z}[x_0]$-module, which as a $\mathbf{Z}$-module will be isomorphic to $\mathbf{Z}^n$. The operation of x_0 on $\mathbf{Z}^n$ is defined by:

$$x_0 \boldsymbol{v} = T \boldsymbol{v}^t$$

for any vector $\boldsymbol{v} \in \mathbf{Z}^n$. Here $\boldsymbol{v}^t$ is the transpose of $\boldsymbol{v}$. We call this module $\mathbf{Z}[T]$.

We obviously have:

Lemma 3. *Let $T_1, \hat{T}_1 \in M_n(\mathbf{Z})$, then $T_1 \sim_{\mathbf{Z}} \hat{T}_1 \Leftrightarrow \mathbf{Z}[T_1] \cong \mathbf{Z}[\hat{T}_1]$ as $\mathbf{Z}[x_0]$-modules.*

In Step II we shall reduce our problems I and II and the problem in Theorem C to the following two questions:

Let K be an algebraic number field and $\mathcal{O} \subseteq \mathcal{O}_K$ an order in the ring of integers of K (i.e. $\mathcal{O}$ is a subring of finite index in $\mathcal{O}_K$).

Ia. *Let M, $\hat{M}$ be two explicitly given $\mathbf{Z}$-torsion free, finitely generated $\mathcal{O}[y]/_{\langle y^l \rangle}$-modules, decide whether:*

$$M \simeq \hat{M}$$

as $\mathcal{O}[y]/_{\langle y^l \rangle}$-modules.

IIa. *Given a $\mathbf{Z}$-basis for $M \simeq \mathbf{Z}^n$, compute a (finite) set of generators for the group of $\mathcal{O}[y]/_{\langle y^l \rangle}$-module automorphisms, viewed as a subgroup of* $\mathrm{GL}_n(\mathbf{Z})$.

Step II.

This step gives reductions of our problems to more number-theoretic questions, which are then dealt with in Step III and Step IIIa.

We first compute the minimal polynomials $\min(S_1)$ and $\min(\hat{S}_1)$ by algorithm A_2. Both will be monic and will have integer coefficients. We assume that:

$$P(x) = \min(S_1) = \min(\hat{S}_1).$$

Otherwise the answer to our original question would be "no". We now split $P(x)$ by algorithm A_0:

(1) $$P(x) = P_1(x) \cdots P_r(x),$$

$P_i(x)$ being **Q**-irreducible, monic with integer coefficients for $i = 1, \ldots, r$. Our matrices being semisimple, the P_i will all be distinct. Put:

$$\tilde{P}_i(x) = \prod_{j \neq i} P_j(x)$$

for $i = 1, \ldots, r$. The polynomials $\tilde{P}_i(x)$ are coprime, so algorithm A_1 will give us polynomials $Q_1, \ldots, Q_r$ with integer coefficients and a natural number λ such that:

(2) $$Q_1\tilde{P}_1 + \cdots + Q_r\tilde{P}_r = \lambda$$

We now define:

$$R = \mathbf{Z}[x]/_{\langle P(x)\rangle}$$

where $\langle P(x)\rangle$ denotes the ideal generated by $P(x)$. The ring R decomposes:

(3) $$R \simeq \mathbf{Z}[x]/_{\langle P_1(x)\rangle} \times \cdots \times \mathbf{Z}[x]/_{\langle P_r(x)\rangle}$$

and we put $\mathcal{O}_i = \mathbf{Z}[x]/_{\langle P_i(x)\rangle}$ for $i = 1, \ldots, r$.

The polynomials $P_1, \ldots, P_r$ being **Q**-irreducible, monic with integer coefficients, the rings $\mathcal{O}_i$ are rings of algebraic integers.

We then find a natural number l such that:

$$U_1^l = \hat{U}_1^l = 0.$$

We define on $\mathbf{Z}[T_1]$ resp. $\mathbf{Z}[\hat{T}_1]$ now $R[y]/_{\langle y^l\rangle}$-module structures by:

$$x\mathbf{v} = S_1\mathbf{v}'$$

$$y\mathbf{v} = U_1\mathbf{v}' \quad \text{for all } \mathbf{v} \in \mathbf{Z}[\hat{T}_1]$$

with the corresponding definition for $\mathbf{Z}[\hat{T}_1]$. By Lemma 1 this definition leads to a ring operation of $R[y]/_{\langle y^l\rangle}$ on $\mathbf{Z}[T_1]$.

Putting everything so far together we get:

Lemma 4. *The following two statements are equivalent*:

(i) $\mathbf{Z}[T_1] \simeq \mathbf{Z}[\hat{T}_1]$ *as* $\mathbf{Z}[x_0]$*-modules*

(ii) $\mathbf{Z}[T_1] \simeq \mathbf{Z}[\hat{T}_1]$ *as* $R[y]/_{\langle y^l\rangle}$*-modules.*

We now decompose $\mathbf{Z}[T_1]$ and $\mathbf{Z}[\hat{T}_1]$ according to the decomposition (2). For this put:

$$M_i = \tilde{P}_i(x).\mathbf{Z}[T_1]$$
$$\hat{M}_i = \tilde{P}_i(x).\mathbf{Z}[\hat{T}_1].$$

The M_i and $\hat{M}_i$ are clearly $R[y]/_{\langle y^l \rangle}$-submodules of $\mathbf{Z}[T_1]$ and $\mathbf{Z}[\hat{T}_1]$. By a variant of Gauss' algorithm we are able to find $\mathbf{Z}$-bases in both M_i and $\hat{M}_i$. Equally we find a representation for the operations of x and y on these new bases. Put then:

$$M = M_1 + \cdots + M_r \subseteq \mathbf{Z}[T_1]$$
$$\hat{M} = \hat{M}_1 + \cdots + \hat{M}_r \subseteq \mathbf{Z}[\hat{T}_1]$$

Lemma 5. (i) *M, $\hat{M}$ are $R[y]/_{\langle y^l \rangle}$-submodules of $\mathbf{Z}[T_1]$ resp. $\mathbf{Z}[\hat{T}_1]$.*
(ii) *M_i, $\hat{M}_i$ are annihilated by $P_i(x)$ for $i = 1, \ldots, r$.*
(iii) *$|\mathbf{Z}[T_1]/_M| \leq \lambda^n$ and $|\mathbf{Z}[\hat{T}_1]/_{\hat{M}}| \leq \lambda^n$.*
(iv) *$M_i \cap (\Sigma_{j\neq i} M_j) = \langle 0 \rangle$, $\hat{M}_i \cap (\Sigma_{j\neq i} \hat{M}_j) = \langle 0 \rangle$. So M and $\hat{M}$ are direct sums of their submodules M_i and $\hat{M}_i$.*
(v) *M_i is a characteristic submodule of M for $i = 1, \ldots, r$ (i.e. normalized by any automorphism of M).*

Proof. Lemma 5 follows from our decomposition (2) and the fact that the polynomials $P_i(x)$ are distinct and $\mathbf{Q}$-irreducible.

We may consider then M_i, $\hat{M}_i$ as explicitly given $\mathcal{O}_i[y]/_{\langle y^l \rangle}$-modules. Furthermore M and $\hat{M}$ are given explicitly as $R[y]/_{\langle y^l \rangle}$-modules.

Lemma 6. *Let $\varphi : \mathbf{Z}[T_1] \to \mathbf{Z}[\hat{T}_1]$ be an $R[y]/_{\langle y^l \rangle}$-module isomorphism then:*

$$\varphi(M) = \hat{M}.$$

Proof. For any $v \in Z[T_1]$ we have:

$$\varphi(\tilde{P}_i(x) \cdot v) = \tilde{P}_i(x) \cdot \varphi(v),$$

hence φ even induces $R[y]/_{\langle y^l \rangle}$-module isomorphisms of the M_i and $\hat{M}_i$.

We now first decide whether the nicer $R[y]/_{\langle y^l \rangle}$-modules M and $\hat{M}$ are isomorphic. The following is clear:

Lemma 7. *The following two statements are equivalent:*
(i) *$M \simeq \hat{M}$ as $R[y]/_{\langle y^l \rangle}$-modules.*
(ii) *$M_i \simeq \hat{M}_i$ as $\mathcal{O}_i[y]/_{\langle y^l \rangle}$-modules for all $i = 1, \ldots, r$.*

We now go with our modules M_i, $\hat{M}_i$ together with their rings $\mathcal{O}_i[y]/_{\langle y^{l_i}\rangle}$ to Step III of this paper. We are supplied there with explicit $\mathcal{O}_i[y]/_{\langle y^{l_i}\rangle}$-module isomorphisms:

$$\gamma_i : M_i \to \hat{M}_i \qquad \text{for } i = 1, \ldots, r.$$

By our lemmata so far we are able to construct an $R[y]/_{\langle y^{l}\rangle}$-module isomorphism:

$$\gamma : M \to \hat{M}$$

by putting the information about the γ_i together. If the application of Step III to a pair of modules M_i, $\hat{M}_i$ yields that these are not isomorphic as $\mathcal{O}_i[y]/_{\langle y^{l_i}\rangle}$-modules, then our matrices T, $\hat{T}$ will certainly not be integrally conjugate.

We put now:

$$\hat{N} = \lambda \cdot \mathbf{Z}[\hat{T}_1]$$
$$N = \gamma(\lambda \mathbf{Z}[T_1])$$

We note that:

$$\lambda \mathbf{Z}[\hat{T}_1] = \hat{N} \subseteq \hat{M}$$

and

$$\gamma(\lambda \mathbf{Z}[T_1]) \subseteq \gamma(M) = \hat{M}.$$

$\hat{N}$ and N may be viewed as given by $\mathbf{Z}$-bases in terms of a fixed $\mathbf{Z}$-basis of $\hat{M}$.

Lemma 8. *The following statements are equivalent*:

(i) $\mathbf{Z}[T_1] \simeq \mathbf{Z}[\hat{T}_1]$ *as* $R[y]/_{\langle y^{l}\rangle}$*-modules.*

(ii) $\exists$ *an* $R[y]/_{\langle y^{l}\rangle}$*-module automorphism* $\kappa : \hat{M} \to \hat{M}$ *such that* $\kappa(N) = \hat{N}$.

Proof. Assume we have an $R[y]/_{\langle y^{l}\rangle}$-module isomorphism

$$\varphi : \mathbf{Z}[T_1] \to \mathbf{Z}[\hat{T}_1]$$

then $\varphi(M) = \hat{M}$ has already been observed. Furthermore we have:

$$\varphi(\lambda \mathbf{Z}[T_1]) = \lambda \mathbf{Z}[\hat{T}_1].$$

We take $\kappa = \varphi\gamma^{-1}$ Then κ is a $R[y]/_{\langle y^{l}\rangle}$-module automorphism of $\hat{M}$ with $\kappa(N) = \hat{N}$.

To prove the reverse direction we put $\varphi = \kappa\gamma$. Then $\varphi : M \to \hat{M}$ is a $R[y]/_{\langle y^{l}\rangle}$-module isomorphism with $\varphi\gamma^{-1}(N) = \hat{N}$ this means:

$$\varphi(\lambda \mathbf{Z}[T_1]) = \lambda \mathbf{Z}[\hat{T}_1].$$

We define:

(4) $$\varphi_0(\mathbf{v}) = \lambda^{-1}\varphi(\lambda\mathbf{v})$$

for all $\mathbf{v} \in \mathbf{Z}[T_1]$. φ_0 is evidently an $R[y]/_{\langle y^l \rangle}$-module isomorphism of $\mathbf{Z}[T_1]$ and $\mathbf{Z}[\hat{T}_1]$.

The formula (4) even gives a recipe of how to compute φ_0 from an explicitly given κ. We are now left with our nice $R[y]/_{\langle y^l \rangle}$-module $\hat{M}$ and two explicitly given abelian subgroups N and $\hat{N}$ both of finite index in $\hat{M}$ and we have to decide whether there is a $R[y]/_{\langle y^l \rangle}$-module automorphism:

(5) with
$$\kappa : \hat{M} \to \hat{M}$$
$$\kappa(N) = \hat{N}$$

To do this and to prove Theorem C, C′ we first construct a set of generators for the group of $R[y]/_{\langle y^l \rangle}$-module automorphisms $\hat{\Gamma}$ of $\hat{M}$. Our module $\hat{M}$ has a chosen $\mathbf{Z}$-basis, this enables us to view $\hat{\Gamma}$ as a subgroup of $\mathrm{GL}_n(\mathbf{Z})$. We will give finitely many matrices for the generators of $\hat{\Gamma}$. Let $\hat{\Gamma}_i$ be the group of $\mathcal{O}_i[y]/_{\langle y^l \rangle}$-module automorphisms of $\hat{M}_i$.

By our previous lemmata we know:

$$\hat{M} = \bigoplus_{i=1}^{r} \hat{M}_i$$

and each $\hat{M}_i$ is a characteristic $R[y]/_{\langle y^l \rangle}$-submodule of M. So:

$$\hat{\Gamma} = \hat{\Gamma}_1 \times \cdots \times \hat{\Gamma}_r$$

But from Step IIIa we know a finite set of generators for each individual $\hat{\Gamma}_i$.

We then compute the index:

$$|\hat{M} : (N \cap \hat{N})| = \lambda_2$$

Our $\mathbf{Z}$-basis of $\hat{M}$ gives us an explicit isomorphism:

$$\hat{M}/_{\lambda_2 \hat{M}} \cong (\mathbf{Z}/_{\lambda_2 \mathbf{Z}})^n$$

and a homomorphism:

$$\hat{\Gamma} \to \mathrm{GL}_n(\mathbf{Z}/_{\lambda_2 \mathbf{Z}})$$

Let $\hat{\Gamma}(\lambda_2)$ be the image and $\hat{\Gamma}[\lambda_2]$ be the kernel of this homomorphism. We know a set of generators of $\hat{\Gamma}(\lambda_2)$ in $\mathrm{GL}_n(\mathbf{Z}/_{\lambda_2 \mathbf{Z}})$ and we want to list all elements of $\hat{\Gamma}(\lambda_2)$. We may assume to be in possession of the order ($\leq (\lambda_2^{n^2})!$) and a multiplication table of $GL_n(\mathbf{Z}/_{\lambda_2\mathbf{Z}})$. We then employ:

Lemma 9. *Let G be a finite group of order m, and $H \leq G$ generated by $\gamma_1, \ldots, \gamma_s$. One can find all elements of H amongst the products of length $\leq m$ formed from the $\gamma_1, \ldots, \gamma_s$.*

Proof. To compute the length one adds up the number of occurrences of the generators γ_i. We claim that each element of H has an expression of length $\leq m$ in terms of the generators $\gamma_1, \ldots, \gamma_s$. This is so because any word of length $> m$ in the γ_i may be shortened in G; for among the first $m+1$ initial segments of such a word, at least two must take the same value in G.

To finish off our decision problem (5) put $\bar{N}$ and $\bar{\hat{N}}$ for the images of N resp. $\hat{N}$ in $(\mathbf{Z}/_{\lambda_2\mathbf{Z}})^n$. Obviously we get:

Lemma 10. *The following statements are equivalent*:

(i) *There is an $R[y]/_{\langle y^l \rangle}$-module automorphism*

$$\kappa : \hat{M} \to \hat{M}$$

with

$$\kappa(N) = \hat{N}$$

(ii) *There is an element*

$$\gamma \in \hat{\Gamma}(\lambda_2)$$

with

$$\gamma(\bar{N}) = \bar{\hat{N}}.$$

Being in possession of all elements of $\hat{\Gamma}(\lambda_2)$ we may decide (ii) of this lemma. Any preimage of a γ satisfying (ii) is then suitable as a κ in (i). The preimage is found as a word in the generators of $\hat{\Gamma}$. To prove theorems C, C′ we still have to find a set of generators for the group of $R[y]/_{\langle y^l \rangle}$-module automorphisms of $\mathbf{Z}[\hat{T}_1]$ which comes by our lemmata to the same as giving a set of generators for $\mathscr{C}_{\mathbf{Z}}(\hat{T}_1) = \mathscr{C}_{\mathbf{Z}}(\hat{T})$.

By our formula (4) in Lemma 8 this comes to the same as giving a finite set of generators for the group of $R[y]/_{\langle y^l \rangle}$-module automorphisms of $\hat{M}$ which leave $\hat{N}$ invariant. We call this group $\hat{\Gamma}_0 \subseteq \hat{\Gamma}$. Again we want matrices in $GL_n(\mathbf{Z}) \supseteq \hat{\Gamma}$ as generators for $\hat{\Gamma}_0 = \{\varepsilon \in \hat{\Gamma} \mid \varepsilon(\hat{N}) = \hat{N}\}$.

By our previous argument we find all elements $\bar{\varepsilon}_1, \ldots, \bar{\varepsilon}_t \in \hat{\Gamma}(\lambda_2)$ which satisfy:

$$\bar{\varepsilon}(\bar{\hat{N}}) = \bar{\hat{N}}.$$

$\varepsilon_1, \ldots, \varepsilon_t$ is a set of preimages in $\hat{\Gamma}$ for them. The ε_i can be found as words in the generators of $\hat{\Gamma}$. Secondly we can effectively solve the word problem in $\hat{\Gamma}(\lambda_2)$ by reduction mod λ_2. This enables us to define a set of coset representatives in terms of the generators of $\hat{\Gamma}$ for the quotient:

$$\hat{\Gamma}/_{\hat{\Gamma}[\lambda_2]}$$

together with an effective coset representative function. Algorithm A_5 will then construct a finite set of generators $\eta_1, \ldots, \eta_s$ of $\hat{\Gamma}[\lambda_2]$ as words in the generators of $\hat{\Gamma}$.

We then note that:

$$\hat{\Gamma}[\lambda_2] \subseteq \hat{\Gamma}_0$$

and find:

Lemma 11. *$\hat{\Gamma}_0$ is generated by $\varepsilon_1, \ldots, \varepsilon_t, \eta_1, \ldots, \eta_s$.*

We have proved now theorems A, C modulo the following Steps III and IIIa.

Step III

Let $P(x)$ be a monic, $\mathbf{Q}$-irreducible polynomial with integer coefficients, of degree m. Put:

$$\mathcal{O} = \mathbf{Z}[x]/_{\langle P(x)\rangle}$$

Let l be a natural number. Furthermore let M_1, $\hat{M}_1$ be two $\mathcal{O}[y]/_{\langle y^l\rangle}$-modules which are $\mathbf{Z}$-free of rank n. This step decides whether $M_1 \simeq \hat{M}_1$ as $\mathcal{O}[y]/_{\langle y^l\rangle}$-modules. If the answer is "yes" an isomorphism with respect to a given pair of $\mathbf{Z}$-bases in M_1, $\hat{M}_1$ is exhibited.

In this situation $\mathcal{O} = \mathbf{Z}[x]/_{\langle P(x)\rangle}$ is a ring of algebraic integers in an algebraic number field $K = \mathbf{Q}[x]/_{\langle P(x)\rangle}$ which is the quotient field of $\mathcal{O}$. Our fixed $\mathbf{Z}$-bases in M_1 and $\hat{M}_1$ enable us to define K-vector spaces $\mathbf{Q}M_1$ and $\mathbf{Q}\hat{M}_1$. Both $\mathbf{Q}M_1$ and $\mathbf{Q}\hat{M}_1$ carry an induced $K[y]/_{\langle y^l\rangle}$-structure. We are going to investigate certain nice subgroups of M_1 resp. $\hat{M}_1$; for this we make the following definition.

Definition. Let R_1 be a ring (commutative with 1). An $R_1[y]/_{\langle y^l\rangle}$-module M is called *standard of type* $\{d_0, \ldots, d_{l-1}\}$, where the d_i are nonnegative integers; if:

$$M \cong \left(\bigoplus_{\nu=1}^{d_0} R_1[y]/_{\langle y^l\rangle}\right) \oplus \left(\bigoplus_{\nu=1}^{d_1} R_1[y]/_{\langle y^{l-1}\rangle}\right) \oplus \cdots \oplus \left(\bigoplus_{\nu=1}^{d_{l-1}} R_1\right)$$

as $R_1[y]/_{\langle y^l\rangle}$-modules. We put in short $M \cong R_1\{d_0, \ldots, d_{l-1}\}$. For an $R_1[y]/_{\langle y^l\rangle}$-module M, we put $M^i = \{$kernel of the endomorphism y^i of $M\}$, with the convention $M^0 = \langle 0\rangle$.

We mention now the following easy characterization of standard modules:

Lemma 12. *Let M be an $R_1[y]/_{\langle y^l\rangle}$-module. The following two conditions are equivalent:*

(i) *M is standard.*

(ii) *$M^i/_{yM^{i+1}+M^{i-1}}$ is finitely generated free as R_1-module for $1 \leq i \leq l$.*

Proof.

(i) $\Rightarrow$ (ii) is obvious.

(ii) $\Rightarrow$ (i).

For each i there is a free R_1-submodule F_i of M, of rank $r(i)$ say, such that

$$M^i = (yM^{i+1} + M^{i-1}) \oplus F_i.$$

In particular, $M^l = F_l \oplus M^{l-1}$, and an inductive argument shows that for each i,

$$M^i = F_i \oplus yF_{i+1} \oplus \cdots \oplus y^{l-1}F_l \oplus M^{i-1}.$$

Therefore by a trivial induction:

$$M^l = \bigoplus_{i=1}^{l} \bigoplus_{j=0}^{i-1} y^j F_i.$$

But $\bigoplus_{j=0}^{i-1} y^j F_i \cong (R_1[y]/_{\langle y^i\rangle})^{r(i)}$, as $R_1[y]/_{\langle y^l\rangle}$-module since $F_i \subseteq M^i$ implies $y^i F_i = 0$.

Thus M is standard of type $\{r(l), \ldots, r(1)\}$ as claimed. It is also clear that explicit bases for the free R_1-modules $M^i/(yM^{i+1} \oplus M^{i-1})$ can effectively be lifted to R_1-bases of the F_i's, and thus yield an explicit isomorphism of M onto the standard module of the correct type.

We now go back to our original situation. Let $\mathcal{O}_K$ be the full ring of algebraic integers in K. Then $\mathcal{O} \subseteq \mathcal{O}_K$ and algorithm A_6 computes a $\mathbf{Z}$-basis $\{\omega_1, \ldots, \omega_n\}$ for $\mathcal{O}_K$ together with the index:

$$t = |\mathcal{O}_K : \mathcal{O}|.$$

We have $M_1 \subseteq \mathbf{Q}M_1$ and $\mathbf{Q}M_1$ carries a K-vector space structure. Hence it makes sense to say of an abelian subgroup N of M_1 that it is $\mathcal{O}_K$-stable, i.e., $\mathcal{O}_K N \subseteq N$. We now make the following definition.

Definition. An abelian subgroup N of M_1 is said to be good of level λ, λ being a natural number, iff:

(i) $|M_1 : N| \leq \lambda$.
(ii) N is $\mathcal{O}_K$-stable.
(iii) N is y-stable.
(iv) N is a standard $\mathcal{O}_K[y]/_{\langle y^l \rangle}$-module.

Lemma 13. *It is effectively possible to compute a natural number λ_3 such that the set of good subgroups of level λ_3 in M_1 is not empty.*

Proof. From linear algebra we know that any $K[y]/_{\langle y^l \rangle}$-module is of standard type. By a simple algorithm based on Lemma 12 we are able to pick a K-basis inside M_1 for the standard $K[y]/_{\langle y^l \rangle}$-module $\mathbf{Q}M_1$. So we have:

$$(6) \qquad \mathcal{O}\{d_0, \ldots, d_{l-1}\} \subseteq M_1 \subseteq \mathbf{Q}M_1 = K\{d_0, \ldots, d_{l-1}\}$$

if $\{d_0, \ldots, d_{l-1}\}$ is the type of the $K[y]/_{\langle y^l \rangle}$-module $\mathbf{Q}M_1$. By Gauss' method we compute the index λ_4 of the copy of $\mathcal{O}\{d_0, \ldots, d_{l-1}\}$ in M_1. We then multiply our previous K-basis by λ_4^{-1} and get:

$$(7) \qquad M_1 \subseteq \mathcal{O}\{d_0, \ldots, d_{l-1}\} \subseteq \mathcal{O}_K\{d_0, \ldots, d_{l-1}\} \subseteq \mathbf{Q}M_1 = K\{d_0, \ldots, d_{l-1}\}$$

Put now: $\lambda_3 = |\mathcal{O}\{d_0, \ldots, d_{l-1}\} : M_1|^n \cdot t^n$. Here n is the $\mathbf{Z}$-rank of M_1 and the index $|\mathcal{O}\{d_0, \ldots, d_{l-1}\} : M_1|$ is supposed to be computed from (7).

It would have been possible to define the notion of good submodules and to find a λ_3 without referring to the $K[y]/_{\langle y^l \rangle}$-module structure of $\mathbf{Q}M_1$ and an embedding (7). For this one must use Steinitz's theory in [18], [19]. This would have been more natural, but more complicated.

Lemma 14. *There are no more than $2^{(\lambda_3)^n}$ good subgroups of level λ_3 in M_1 (or $\hat{M}_1$). It is effectively possible to make a list of all of them:*

$$\{N_1, \ldots, N_s\},$$

each one together with an explicit $\mathcal{O}_K[y]/_{\langle y^l \rangle}$-module isomorphism:

$$\gamma_i : N_i \to \mathcal{O}_K\{d_0, \ldots, d_{l-1}\}.$$

$\{d_0, \ldots, d_{l-1}\}$ is here the type of the $K[y]/_{\langle y^l \rangle}$-module $\mathbf{Q}M_1$.

Proof. The first claim follows from the fact that for any good subgroup N of level λ_3 in M_1 we have:

$$\lambda_3 M_1 \leqslant N.$$

There order of $|M_1 : \lambda_3 M_1|$ is λ_3^n. We then list all abelian subgroups of index $\leqslant \lambda_3$. These will be only finitely many, again less than $2^{(\lambda_3)^n}$. Let N_0 be one of them, given by a $\mathbf{Z}$-basis in terms of our $\mathbf{Z}$-basis of M_1. To test whether N_0 is $\mathcal{O}_K$ stable it is enough to check whether:

$$\omega_i N_0 \subseteq N_0$$

for our $\mathbf{Z}$-basis of $\mathcal{O}_K$. The same method decides whether N_0 is y-stable. We end up with a finite list of $\mathcal{O}_K[y]$-submodules of M_1 of index $\leqslant \lambda_3$. Each one is (say) given by a $\mathbf{Z}$-basis and the operation of $\mathcal{O}_K[y]$ on it is given in terms of this $\mathbf{Z}$-basis: Let N be one of them. By algorithm A we compute $\mathbf{Z}$-bases for the groups N^i, $i = 0, \dots, l$. So we get a set of generators and relations for the groups

$$N^i /_{yN^{i+1} + N^{i-1}}.$$

The $\mathcal{O}_K$-module structure on them is given by a multiplication table for the ω_i, $i = 1, \dots, m$, our $\mathbf{Z}$-basis of $\mathcal{O}_K$. We hand these objects to algorithm A_{18}. It decides whether the

$$N^i /_{yN^{i+1} + N^{i-1}}$$

are free $\mathcal{O}_K$-modules. If they are free we get an $\mathcal{O}_K$-basis for each of them. The second part of the proof of Lemma 12 shows how to put this information together to obtain an explicit $\mathcal{O}_K[y]/_{\langle y^l \rangle}$-module isomorphism $\gamma : N \to \mathcal{O}_K\{d_0, \dots, d_{l-1}\}$.

Let now $\{N_1, \dots, N_{s_1}\}$ and $\{\hat{N}_1, \dots, \hat{N}_{s_2}\}$ be the sets of good subgroups of level λ_3 of M_1 and $\hat{M}_1$. γ_i, $\hat{\gamma}_i$ are the $\mathcal{O}_K[y]/_{\langle y^l \rangle}$-module isomorphisms

$$\gamma : N_i \to \mathcal{O}_K\{d_0, \dots, d_{l-1}\}$$

and

$$\hat{\gamma}_i : \hat{N}_i \to \mathcal{O}_K\{d_0, \dots, d_{l-1}\}.$$

We may clearly assume that the types of the $K[y]/_{\langle y^l \rangle}$-modules $\mathbf{Q}M_1$ and $\widehat{\mathbf{Q}M_1}$ are the same, otherwise the answer to our question would be "no".

For each $i = 1, \dots, s_1$ let:

$$\Delta_i = \lambda_3 M_1 \subseteq N_i$$

and correspondingly for $i = 1, \dots, s_2$ put:

$$\hat{\Delta}_i = \lambda_3 \hat{M}_1 \subseteq \hat{N}_i.$$

The Δ_i resp. $\hat{\Delta}_i$ are subgroups of N_i resp. $\hat{N}_i$ of finite (known) index.

Lemma 15. *The following two statements are equivalent:*
(i) *There is an $\mathcal{O}[y]/_{\langle y^t \rangle}$-module isomorphism:*

$$\gamma : M_1 \to \hat{M}_1.$$

(ii) *The set of good subgroups of $\hat{M}_1$ of level λ_3 is not empty. There are i, j with $1 \leq i \leq s_1$ and $1 \leq j \leq s_2$ and an $\mathcal{O}_K[y]/_{\langle y^t \rangle}$-module isomorphism:*

$$\kappa : N_j \to \hat{N}_j$$

with

$$\kappa(\Delta_i) = \hat{\Delta}_j.$$

Proof. (i) ⇒ (ii). Let $\gamma : M_1 \to \hat{M}_1$ be an $\mathcal{O}$-module isomorphism. Let $N \subseteq M_1$ be an $\mathcal{O}_K[y]/_{\langle y^t \rangle}$-submodule of M_1. We claim that

$$\gamma : N \to \gamma(N)$$

is an $\mathcal{O}_K$-module isomorphism. For this let $\omega \in \mathcal{O}_K$ and $\boldsymbol{v} \in N$. We put:

$$\boldsymbol{w} = \omega \cdot \gamma(\boldsymbol{v}) - \gamma(\omega \boldsymbol{v}) \in \mathcal{O}_K \cdot \hat{M}_1 \subseteq \mathbf{Q}\hat{M}_1.$$

Because $t\mathcal{O}_K \subseteq \mathcal{O}$ we get:

$$t\boldsymbol{w} = (t\omega)\gamma(\boldsymbol{v}) - \gamma((t\omega)\boldsymbol{v}) = \mathbf{0}.$$

Hence $\boldsymbol{w} = 0$. Put now:

$$\hat{N}_1 = \gamma(N_1).$$

By the above remark $\hat{N}_1$ is a good subgroup of $\hat{M}_1$. It is then clear that:

$$\gamma(\lambda_3 M_1) = \lambda_3 \gamma(M_1) = \lambda_3 \hat{M}_1.$$

(ii) ⇒ (i). Let $\kappa : N_i \to \hat{N}_j$ be the $\mathcal{O}_K$-module isomorphism. We define:

$$\gamma(\boldsymbol{v}) = \lambda_3^{-1} \kappa(\lambda_3 \boldsymbol{v})$$

for $\boldsymbol{v} \in M_1$. By our assumption we have:

$$\kappa(\lambda_3 \boldsymbol{v}) = \lambda_3 \boldsymbol{w}$$

for a $\boldsymbol{w} \in \hat{M}_1$. Hence γ defines an isomorphism of abelian groups between M_1 and $\hat{M}_1$. γ is clearly compatible with the $\mathcal{O}[y]/_{\langle y^t \rangle}$-module structures on both sides.

Having our lists of good subgroups

$$\{N_1, \ldots, N_{s_1}\} \quad \text{and} \quad \{\hat{N}_1, \ldots, \hat{N}_{s_2}\}$$

in M_1 and $\hat{M}_1$ together with the isomorphism γ_i, $\hat{\gamma}_i$ we end up with the following decision problem:

(8) Let Δ, $\hat{\Delta}$ be two abelian subgroups of $\mathcal{O}_K\{d_0, \ldots, d_{l-1}\}$ of finite index, given in terms of a Z-basis of $\mathcal{O}_K\{d_0, \ldots, d_{l-1}\}$; decide whether there is an $\mathcal{O}_K[y]/_{\langle y^l\rangle}$-module automorphism:

$$\gamma : \mathcal{O}_K\{d_0, \ldots, d_{l-1}\} \to \mathcal{O}_K\{d_0, \ldots, d_{l-1}\}$$

with

$$\gamma(\Delta) = \hat{\Delta}.$$

The decision procedure we shall describe will certainly exhibit such an automorphism, if there is any.

We write $\Gamma = \Gamma_{\mathcal{O}_K}\{d_0, \ldots, d_{l-1}\}$ for the group of $\mathcal{O}_K[y]/_{\langle y^l\rangle}$-module automorphisms of $M = \mathcal{O}_K\{d_0, \ldots, d_{l-1}\}$. By extending our $\mathbf{Z}$-basis of $\mathcal{O}_K$ we think of Γ as a subgroup of $\mathrm{GL}_n(\mathbf{Z})$. We are first going to construct a finite set of generators for Γ by giving certain matrices in $\mathrm{GL}_n(\mathbf{Z})$.

For each i between 1 and l we find an $\mathcal{O}_K$-free submodule F_i of M of $\mathcal{O}_K$ rank d_i such that:

$$M^i = (yM^{i+1} + M^{i-1}) \oplus F_i \qquad 1 \leq i \leq l.$$

We put:

$$\tilde{M} = \bigoplus_{i=1}^{l} F_i \subseteq M$$

We obviously have:

$$\tilde{M} \cong \mathcal{O}_K^{d_0} \oplus \cdots \oplus \mathcal{O}_K^{d_{l-1}}$$

as $\mathcal{O}_K$-modules.

Now let $\boldsymbol{\alpha} \in M$. Then there is a unique set of elements $\boldsymbol{\beta}_0, \ldots, \boldsymbol{\beta}_{l-1} \in \tilde{M}$ such that:

$$\text{(9)} \qquad \boldsymbol{\alpha} = \sum_{\nu=0}^{l-1} y^{\nu}(\boldsymbol{\beta}_\nu)$$

under the convention $y^0 = \mathrm{id}_M$.

Let $\tilde{\Gamma} = \mathrm{GL}_{d_0}(\mathcal{O}_K) \times \cdots \times \mathrm{GL}_{d_{l-1}}(\mathcal{O}_K)$. $\tilde{\Gamma}$ operates naturally on $\tilde{M}$. Let $\gamma \in \tilde{\Gamma}$ and $\boldsymbol{\alpha} \in M$.

Put then:

$$\gamma\boldsymbol{\alpha} = \sum_{\nu=0}^{l-1} y^{\nu}(\gamma(\boldsymbol{\beta}_\nu))$$

using expression (9). Elementary arguments show that now γ is an $\mathcal{O}_K[y]/_{\langle y^l\rangle}$-module automorphism of M. In fact we have defined a group monomorphism:

$$\varphi_1 : \tilde{\Gamma} \hookrightarrow \Gamma$$

We shall identify $\tilde{\Gamma}$ with its image in Γ.

Any $\mathcal{O}_K[y]/_{\langle y^l\rangle}$-module automorphism γ of M induces an $\mathcal{O}_K$-module automorphism of each:

$$M^i/_{(yM^{i+1}+M^{i-1})}$$

Let C be the subgroup of Γ which induces the identity automorphism on all of these quotients.

Furthermore put:

$$\tilde{H} = \bigoplus_{i=1}^{l} \mathrm{Hom}_{\mathcal{O}_K}(F_i, (yM^{i+1} + M^{i-1})).$$

We now define a map φ_2 of $\tilde{H}$ to C.

For this let $f \in \mathrm{Hom}_{\mathcal{O}_K}(F_i, (yM^{i+1} + M^{i-1}))$ and $\boldsymbol{\alpha} \in M$, we put:

$$\varphi_2(f)(\boldsymbol{\alpha}) = \sum_{\nu=0}^{l-1} y^\nu(\boldsymbol{\beta}_\nu) + \sum_{\nu=0}^{l-1} y^\nu(f(\boldsymbol{\beta}_\nu))$$

using the expansion (9) for $\boldsymbol{\alpha}$. By $f(\boldsymbol{\beta}_\nu)$ we understand f applied to the ith projection of $\boldsymbol{\beta}_\nu \in \tilde{M}$. This means $\varphi_2(f)$ centralizes all F_j with $i \neq j$. One easily sees that the so defined $\varphi_2(f)$ is an $\mathcal{O}_K[y]/_{\langle y^l\rangle}$-module automorphism of M. If $l > 1$ then φ_2 is not a group homomorphism. But we have:

Lemma 16. (i) *φ_2 is a surjective map from $\tilde{H}$ to C.*

(ii) *Let $h_1, \ldots, h_s$ be a set of generators for the abelian group $\tilde{H}$, then the $\varphi_2(h_1), \ldots, \varphi_2(h_s)$ generate C.*

(iii) *Γ is the semidirect product of C by $\tilde{\Gamma}$ if $\tilde{\Gamma}$ is assumed to be contained in Γ via φ_1.*

Proof. (i) Any $\mathcal{O}_K[y]/_{\langle y^l\rangle}$-module automorphism of M is determined by its values on $\tilde{M} \subseteq M$; if $\gamma \in C$ then for $\boldsymbol{\beta} \in F_i$,

$$\gamma(\boldsymbol{\beta}) = \boldsymbol{\beta} + \lambda_i(\boldsymbol{\beta})$$

with $\lambda_i(\boldsymbol{\beta}) \in (yM^{i+1} + M^{i-1})$. λ_i is clearly in $\mathrm{Hom}_{\mathcal{O}_K}(F_i, (yM^{i+1} + M^{i-1}))$, and $\gamma = \varphi_2(\lambda_1, \ldots, \lambda_l)$.

(ii) Let $\mathrm{Aut}_{\mathcal{O}_K}(M^i/_{M^{i-k-1}})$ be the group of $\mathcal{O}_K$-modules automorphisms of $M^i/_{M^{i-k-1}}$ for $i = 2, \ldots, l$; $k = 1, \ldots, i-1$. Each element of C

induces an element of this group. One easily sees that the composition map:

$$\begin{array}{ccc} \operatorname{Hom}_{\mathcal{O}_K}(F_i, M^{i-k}) & & C \to \operatorname{Aut}_{\mathcal{O}_K}(M^i/_{M^{i-k-1}}) \\ \wedge \mid & \nearrow \varphi_2 & \\ \operatorname{Hom}_{\mathcal{O}_K}(F_i, (yM^{i+1} + M^{i-1})) & & \end{array}$$

for each $k = 1, \ldots, i-1$ is a group homomorphism. (i) together with an obvious induction under the assumption that the automorphism in question already centralizes all F_j with $j > i$, finishes then (ii).

(iii) is obvious.

Both F_i and $(yM^{i+1} + M^{i-1})$ are free $\mathcal{O}_K$-modules. It is then easy to describe a finite set of generators for the group $\tilde{H}$ effectively. By algorithm A_{19} we may construct a finite set of generators for $\tilde{\Gamma}$. The maps φ_1, φ_2 are then explicit enough to deduce together with Lemma 16 a set of generating matrices for Γ in $GL_n(Z)$.

We now go back to our decision problem (8):

The first thing is to determine the index:

$$\lambda_5 = |\mathcal{O}_K\{d_0, \ldots, d_{l-1}\} : (\Delta \cap \hat{\Delta})|.$$

Our $\mathbf{Z}$-basis of $\mathcal{O}_K\{d_0, \ldots, d_{l-1}\}$ gives us an explicit reduction isomorphism:

$$\mathcal{O}_K\{d_0, \ldots, d_{l-1}\}/_{\lambda_5 \mathcal{O}_K\{d_0, \ldots, d_{l-1}\}} \xrightarrow{\sim} (\mathbf{Z}/_{\lambda_5 \mathbf{Z}})^n$$

of abelian groups. Let $\Gamma(\lambda_5)$ the image of Γ in $GL_n(\mathbf{Z}/_{\lambda_5\mathbf{Z}})$ via this homomorphism. Because we know a finite set of generators for Γ we know a set of generators for $\Gamma(\lambda_5)$. We may assume to be in possession of a multiplication table for the finite group $GL_n(\mathbf{Z}/_{\lambda_5\mathbf{Z}})$. The order of this group is certainly less than $(\lambda_5^n)!$ So by an argument used before we may list all elements of $\Gamma(\lambda_5)$. Let $\bar{\Delta}$ resp. $\bar{\hat{\Delta}}$ be the images of Δ or $\hat{\Delta}$ in $(\mathbf{Z}/_{\lambda_5\mathbf{Z}})^n$. We then obviously have:

Lemma 17. *The following statements are equivalent*:

(i) *There is an* $\mathcal{O}_K[y]/_{\langle y^l \rangle}$*-module automorphism*:

$$\gamma : \mathcal{O}_K\{d_0, \ldots, d_{l-1}\} \to \mathcal{O}_K\{d_0, \ldots, d_{l-1}\}$$

with

$$\gamma(\Delta) = \hat{\Delta}$$

(ii) *There is an element*

$$\kappa \in \Gamma(\lambda_5) \subseteq GL_n(\mathbf{Z}/_{\lambda_5\mathbf{Z}})$$

with

$$\kappa(\bar{\Delta}) = \bar{\hat{\Delta}}.$$

By the above remarks we know all the elements of $\Gamma(\lambda_5)$. There are not many things which are then easier than to decide the second condition of Lemma 17. Having found a κ satisfying this condition, any preimage of κ in Γ will then serve as γ. γ may be found as some expression in the generators of Γ.

Step IIIa

Let $P(x)$ be a monic, **Q**-irreducible polynomial of degree m with integer coefficients. Put:

$$\mathcal{O} = \mathbf{Z}[x]/_{\langle P(x)\rangle}$$

Let l be a natural number. Let M_1 be an $\mathcal{O}[y]/_{\langle y^l\rangle}$-module which is **Z**-free of rank n, with a fixed **Z**-basis. Let Γ_1 be the group of $\mathcal{O}[y]/_{\langle y^l\rangle}$-module automorphisms of M_1. The **Z**-basis in M_1 allows us to view Γ_1 as a subgroup of $\mathrm{GL}_n(\mathbf{Z})$. Step IIIa gives a finite set of generators for $\Gamma_1 \subseteq \mathrm{GL}_n(\mathbf{Z})$.

We use the terminology of Step III. We first compute a natural number λ_3 such that the set of good subgroups of level λ_3 in M_2 is not empty. We then compute a list:

$$\{N_1, \ldots, N_{s_1}\}$$

of all of them, together with explicit $\mathcal{O}_K[y]/_{\langle y^l\rangle}$-isomorphisms:

$$\gamma_i : N_i \rightarrow \mathcal{O}_K\{d_0, \ldots, d_{l-1}\} \qquad i = 1, \ldots, s_1$$

where $\{d_0, \ldots, d_{l-1}\}$, is the K-standard type of $\mathbf{Q}M_1$. Put again:

$$\Delta_i = \lambda_3 M_1 \subseteq N_i.$$

By the method described in Step III we decide for each pair:

$$(N_1, N_i) \qquad 2 \leq i \leq s_1$$

whether there is an $\mathcal{O}[y]/_{\langle y^l\rangle}$-module automorphism:

$$\varepsilon_i : M_1 \rightarrow M_1$$

with

$$\varepsilon_i : (N_1) = N_i.$$

Step III then gives us a finite list of ε_i's which we renumber to $\{\varepsilon_i, \ldots, \varepsilon_t\}$, to get:

Lemma 18. *Γ_1 is generated by the $\{\varepsilon_1, \ldots, \varepsilon_t\}$ together with*:

$$\{\varepsilon \in \Gamma_1 \mid \varepsilon(N_1) = N_1\}.$$

Proof. This follows from Lemma 15.

Using our isomorphism:

$$\gamma_1 : N_1 \to \mathcal{O}_K\{d_0, \ldots, d_l\}$$

We end up with the problem:

Give a set of generators for the group:

$$\Gamma_2 = \{\varepsilon \in \Gamma \mid \varepsilon(\Delta_1) = \Delta_1\} \tag{10}$$

where Γ is the group of $\mathcal{O}_K[y]/_{\langle y^l \rangle}$-module automorphisms of $\mathcal{O}_K\{d_0, \ldots, d_{l-1}\}$ and Δ_1 is a subgroup of finite index in $\mathcal{O}_K\{d_0, \ldots, d_{l-1}\}$.

At the end of Step III we showed how to give explicitly a finite set of generators for Γ. Knowing a set of generators for Γ_2 on a **Z**-basis of $\mathcal{O}_K\{d_0, \ldots, d_{l-1}\}$ we could rewrite the corresponding $\mathcal{O}[y]/_{\langle y^l \rangle}$-module automorphisms of M_1 by the method described in the proof of Lemma 15.

To deal with problem (10) we again put $M = \mathcal{O}_K\{d_0, \ldots, d_{l-1}\}$, and compute:

$$|M : \Delta_1| = \lambda_6$$

We put $\Gamma[\lambda_6] = \ker\{\Gamma \to \mathrm{GL}_n(\mathbf{Z}/_{\lambda_6\mathbf{Z}})\}$.

This homomorphism is defined by use of our **Z**-basis in M. The image of Γ in $\mathrm{GL}_n(\mathbf{Z}/_{\lambda_6\mathbf{Z}})$ was called $\Gamma(\lambda_6)$. Knowing all elements of $\Gamma(\lambda_6)$ we give a set of coset representatives for:

$$\Gamma/_{\Gamma[\lambda_6]}$$

in Γ. Because we are able to solve the word problem in $\Gamma/_{\Gamma[\lambda_6]}$ effectively by reduction mod λ_6 we have an effective coset representative function required by algorithm A_5. This algorithm then turns our set of generators for Γ into a set of generators $\{\eta_1, \ldots, \eta_v\}$ for $\Gamma[\lambda_6]$.

Next let $\bar{\Delta}_1$ be the image of Δ_1 in $(\mathbf{Z}/_{\lambda_6\mathbf{Z}})^n$. Knowing all elements of $\Gamma(\lambda_6)$ we make a list of:

$$\{\varepsilon \in \Gamma(\lambda_6) \mid \varepsilon(\bar{\Delta}_1) = \bar{\Delta}_1\}$$

This is a finite list with no more than $(\lambda_6^n)!$ members.

Let $\zeta_1, \ldots, \zeta_u$ be a set of preimages in Γ of all elements of this set. We are able to find them as expressions in terms of the generators of Γ. Any element γ of $\Gamma[\lambda_6]$ now satisfies:

$$\gamma(\Delta_1) = \Delta_1$$

and we obviously get:

Lemma 19. *Γ_2 is generated by $\eta_1, \ldots, \eta_v, \zeta_1, \ldots, \zeta_u$.*

This finishes the problem of Step IIIa.

Proof of Theorems A′, C′

A glance through Steps I and II shows that everything stays correct if one replaces **Z** by $\mathcal{O}_K$. One has to keep in mind that we consider $\mathcal{O}_K$ to be given by a **Z**-basis together with a multiplication table for this **Z**-basis. Steps III and IIIa may then be used as stated to obtain a proof of Theorems A′ and C′.

Proof of Theorems B, B′

We give our matrices T, $\hat{T}$ to the algorithm described in Theorem A and decide whether there is an $X \in \mathrm{GL}_n(\mathbf{Z})$ such that:

$$XTX^{-1} = \hat{T}$$

If there is none the answer to our question is "no" too. If the answer is "yes" we construct such an X by the same algorithm and compute the determinant of X. If $\det X = 1$ then we are in good shape. Otherwise we find the following two equivalent statements:

(i) $\exists Y \in \mathrm{SL}_n(\mathbf{Z})$ with $YTY^{-1} = \hat{T}$.

(ii) $\exists Y \in \mathscr{C}_{\mathbf{Z}}(T)$ with $\det Y = -1$.

Then we construct a set of generators $\zeta_1, \ldots, \zeta_s$ for the group $\mathscr{C}_{\mathbf{Z}}(T)$ by Theorem C and look whether:

$$\det(\zeta_i) = -1$$

for a generator ζ_i. The answer to our original question is then "yes" if and only if $\det(\zeta_i) = -1$ for at least one i.

The proof of Theorem B′ is slightly more involved. We again assume to have found an $X \in \mathrm{GL}_n(\mathcal{O}_K)$ with:

$$XTX^{-1} = \hat{T}$$

by Theorem A′. Put

$$u = \det X.$$

We then construct a set of generators $\{\zeta_1, \ldots, \zeta_s\}$ of the group $\mathscr{C}_{\mathcal{O}_K}(T)$, and put

$$\upsilon_i = \det \zeta_i \qquad \text{for } i = 1, \ldots, s$$

and $V = \langle \upsilon_1, \ldots, \upsilon_s \rangle \leq \mathcal{O}_K^*$. We then get the following two equivalent statements:

(i) $Y \in \mathrm{SL}_n(\mathcal{O}_K)$ with $YTY^{-1} = \hat{T}$.

(ii) $u \in V$.

To decide the second condition we express u and $\upsilon_1, \ldots, \upsilon_s$ in terms of our set of generators for $\mathcal{O}_K^*$ by the second part of algorithm A_8. Having done this we apply Gauss' method.

Proof of Corollaries A, B

Take two preimages $T_0, \hat{T}_0$ of T and $\hat{T}$ in $GL_n(K)$ and put:

$$a = \det T_0; \qquad \hat{a} = \det \hat{T}_0$$

We factorize then the polynomial:

$$X^n - \frac{\hat{a}}{a}$$

over K. By this method we find all zeroes $b_1, \ldots, b_r$ of this polynomial in K. For each zero put:

$$\tilde{b}_i = \begin{pmatrix} b_i & & 0 \\ & \ddots & \\ 0 & & b_i \end{pmatrix} \qquad i = 1, \ldots, r$$

and

$$T_i = T\tilde{b}_i \qquad i = 1, \ldots, r.$$

Then we find the following equivalent statements:

(i) $\exists X \in P\,GL_n(\mathcal{O}_K)$ with $XTX^{-1} = \hat{T}$ in $P\,GL_n(K)$.

(ii) $\exists 1 \leq i \leq r$ and $X \in GL_n(\mathcal{O}_K)$ with $XT_iX^{-1} = \hat{T}_0$.

Similarly:

(i) $\exists X \in P\,SL_n(\mathcal{O}_K)$ with $XTX^{-1} = \hat{T}$ in $P\,GL_n(K)$.

(ii) $\exists 1 \leq i \leq r$ and $X \in SL_n(\mathcal{O}_K)$ with $XT_iX^{-1} = \hat{T}_0$.

The second conditions may then be decided by applications of the algorithm from Theorems A′, B′.

B. Some algorithms

Let K be a finite extension field over the rational numbers $\mathbf{Q}$. We consider K to be known if we are given a $\mathbf{Q}$-irreducible polynomial $P(x)$ of degree m with rational coefficients and are told that K is generated as a field by a zero of $P(x)$, i.e.,

$$K \simeq Q[x]/\langle P(x)\rangle$$

as fields. By a suitable transformation

$$x \to \lambda x \qquad \lambda \in \mathbf{Z}$$

we may assume that $P(x)$ has integer coefficients and highest coefficient 1. Hence all zeroes of $P(x)$ are algebraic integers. We write

$\mathcal{O}_K$ for the full ring of algebraic integers in K. We consider $\mathcal{O}_K$ to be known if we have a **Z**-basis $\{\omega_1, \ldots, \omega_m\}$ for $\mathcal{O}_K$ in terms of the field generators $1, x, \ldots, x^{m-1}$, i.e.,

$$\begin{aligned}
\omega_1 &= c_{01} + c_{11}x + \cdots + c_{m-1,1} \cdot x^{m-1} \\
&\vdots \\
\omega_m &= c_{0m} + c_{1m}x + \cdots + c_{m-1,m} \cdot x^{m-1}
\end{aligned}$$

with $c_{ij} \in \mathbf{Q}$.

One of the following algorithms will compute such a **Z**-basis for $\mathcal{O}_K$. A lot of the following algorithms are taken from Steinitz's papers [19], [20]. We often have only written out why the reasoning of [19], [20] is effective.

For the algorithms given in section A of this paper we need only A_0–A_6 and A_{17}, A_{18}, A_{19} of the algorithms listed below.

Algorithm A_0

Let K be an algebraic number field and let $P(x) \in K[x]$ be a polynomial with coefficients in K. Algorithm A_0 splits $P(x)$ into irreducible factors:

$$P(x) = P_1(x) \cdot \cdots \cdot P_r(x).$$

$P_i(x)$ are K-irreducible for $i = 1, \ldots, r$. If $P(x)$ is monic with coefficients in the ring of algebraic integers $\mathcal{O}_K$ of K, then each $P_i(x)$ will be monic with coefficients in $\mathcal{O}_K$.

For this we use Kronecker's algorithm as described in [9].

Algorithm A_1

Let K be an algebraic number field. Given l polynomials $P_1, \ldots, P_l \in K[x]$, this algorithm decides whether $P_1, \ldots, P_l$ are coprime and if the answer is "yes" it produces polynomials $Q_1, \ldots, Q_l \in K[x]$ such that:

$$Q_1P_1 + \cdots + Q_lP_l = 1.$$

If the polynomials $P_1, \ldots, P_l$ have coefficients in the ring of algebraic integers $\mathcal{O}_K$ of K and if they are coprime, algorithm A_1 will compute the polynomials $Q_1, \ldots, Q_l$ with algebraic integer coefficients together with an element $\lambda \in \mathcal{O}_K$ such that

$$Q_1P_1 + \cdots + Q_lP_l = \lambda.$$

A repeated application of Euclid's algorithm in $K[x]$ will do the job of A_1.

Algorithm A_2

Let K be an algebraic number field and $T \in GL_n(K)$ for a natural number K. Algorithm A_2 computes the characteristic polynomial $\mathrm{char}(T)$ of T together with the minimal polynomial $\min(T)$.

Knowing the characteristic polynomial $\mathrm{char}(T)$ we factorize it by algorithm A_0. In the list of all divisors of $\mathrm{char}(T)$ we then find the polynomial of minimal degree which is satisfied by T.

Algorithm A_3

Let K be an algebraic number field. Let $T \in GL_n(K)$. Algorithm A_3 computes a semisimple matrix S and a nilpotent matrix U both with coefficients in K such that:

$$T = S + U$$

and

$$SU = US$$

We first compute the minimal polynomial $\min(T)$ of T by algorithm A_2. By successive factorisation of $\min(T)$ we construct a multiplication table for the normal extension field K_0 of K which is generated by all zeroes of $\min(T)$. By an algorithm of linear algebra we find $\gamma \in GL_n(K_0)$ such that

$$\gamma T \gamma^{-1} = J,$$

where $J \in GL_n(K_0)$ is in Jordan normal form.

How to decompose:

$$J = S_0 + U_0$$

with

$$U_0 S_0 = U_0 S_0$$

where U_0 is nilpotent and S_0 is semisimple is then evident. We put:

$$S = \gamma^{-1} S_0 \gamma, \qquad U = \gamma^{-1} U_0 \gamma.$$

A Galois-type argument then shows that both

$$S, U \in M_n(K).$$

For all this see [4] Chapter 7, §5.

Algorithm A_4

Let $M \simeq \mathbf{Z}^n$ be a free $\mathbf{Z}$-module with basis. Let A be an $n \times n$ matrix with integer entries representing an endomorphism with respect to this basis. Algorithm A_4 computes a $\mathbf{Z}$-basis for the kernel of A.

By elementary row and column operations (over the euclidian ring **Z**!) we find element $P, Q \in SL_n(\mathbf{Z})$ such that

$$PAQ = D$$

where D is a diagonal matrix.

Algorithm A_5 (Reidemeister–Schreier)

Given a finite set of generators $g_1, \ldots, g_r$ for a group G and a subgroup $H \leqslant G$ of finite index together with a set of coset representatives Y and an effective coset representative function

$$\Phi : G \to Y$$

A_5 computes a set of generators for H.

We use the method described in [6] Lemma 7.2.2.

Algorithm A_6

Let K be an algebraic number field with integeral generator ϑ. Let $\mathcal{O}$ be the subring of K generated by ϑ, this is the same as the **Z**-submodule of K generated by $1, \vartheta, \vartheta^2, \ldots, \vartheta^{m-1}$ where m is the degree of the minimal polynomial of ϑ. This algorithm computes a **Z**-basis

$$\begin{aligned} \omega_1 &= c_{01} + c_{11}\vartheta + \cdots + c_{m1}\vartheta^{m-1} \\ &\vdots \\ \omega_m &= c_{0m} + c_{1m}\vartheta + \cdots + c_{mm}\vartheta^{m-1} \qquad c_{i,j} \in \mathbf{Q} \end{aligned}$$

for the ring of algebraic integers $\mathcal{O}_K$ of K.

Furthermore the algorithm gives the index

$$|\mathcal{O}_K : \mathcal{O}| = t.$$

Let

$$\mathrm{Tr} : K \to \mathbf{Q}$$

be the trace of the field K. The trace of an element α of K is the trace of the linear automorphism, which is induced by multiplication with α. It can therefore be computed, for example, with our field basis $1, \vartheta, \ldots, \vartheta^{m-1}$. Let

$$B_K(\alpha, \beta) = \mathrm{Tr}(\alpha \cdot \beta)$$

be the trace form induced on K. If we first compute the matrix of B_K with respect to $1, \vartheta, \ldots, \vartheta^{m-1}$, we are able to give a complementary basis $\hat{\omega}_1, \ldots, \hat{\omega}_m$ for $1, \vartheta, \ldots, \vartheta^{m-1}$ with respect to B_K.

Let $\hat{\mathcal{O}}$ be the **Z**-module generated by $\hat{\omega}_1, \ldots, \hat{\omega}_m$. Then by [5] Chapter II, §2, Theorem 6:

$$\mathcal{O}_K \leqslant \hat{\mathcal{O}}$$

Next we list a set of coset representatives $\alpha_1, \ldots, \alpha_\nu$ for $\hat{\mathcal{O}}/\mathcal{O}$. Let $\alpha_1, \ldots, \alpha_\mu$ be those which are integral. This can be checked by computing the characteristic polynomials for the linear maps corresponding to the α's on K. Because the existence of an algebraic integer in a coset $\hat{\mathcal{O}}/\mathcal{O}$ would imply that any element of the coset is integral, we find

$$\mathcal{O}_K = \langle \mathcal{O}, \alpha_1, \ldots, \alpha_\mu \rangle$$

We then compute by Gauss' method a basis for $\mathcal{O}_K$ and the number t.

Algorithm A_7

Let K be an algebraic number field with ring of algebraic integers $\mathcal{O}_K$. Let n be a natural number. This algorithm lists a set of elements $\lambda_1, \ldots, \lambda_r \in \mathcal{O}_K$ with

$$|\mathcal{O}_K : \lambda_i \mathcal{O}_K| \leq n \qquad \forall i = 1, \ldots, r$$

such that for any $\lambda \in \mathcal{O}_K$ with

$$|\mathcal{O}_K : \lambda \mathcal{O}_K| \leq n$$

we can find a unit $u \in \mathcal{O}_K$ such that

$$\lambda = \lambda_i u$$

for some $i \in \{1, \ldots, r\}$.

Here we use the algorithm described in the book of Borevich–Shafarevich [5] Chapter II, §5.4.

Algorithm A_8

Let K be an algebraic number field with ring of algebraic integers $\mathcal{O}_K$ and let $\mathcal{O}_K^*$ be the unit group of $\mathcal{O}_K$.

(i) The first part of this algorithm gives a set of generators:

$$\zeta, u_1, \ldots, u_s$$

for the unit group of $\mathcal{O}_K$. $u_1, \ldots, u_s$ are a set of fundamental units and ζ is a root of unity.

(ii) Given a unit $u \in \mathcal{O}_K^*$ in terms of our $\mathbf{Z}$-basis of $\mathcal{O}_K$:

$$u = a_1\omega_1 + \cdots + a_m\omega_m \qquad a_i \in \mathbf{Z}$$

the second part finds $f, e_1, \ldots, e_s \in \mathbf{Z}$ with:

$$u = \zeta^f u_1^{e_1} \cdots u_s^{e_s}$$

(i): Let ϑ be a generator of K over $\mathbf{Q}$; we first compute the discriminant d of K, for example by obtaining a $\mathbf{Z}$-basis for $\mathcal{O}_K$. By [7]

§28.I the order of ζ is a divisor of $2|d|$. By algorithm A_0 we then decompose the polynomial:

$$X^{2|d|}-1$$

in K into irreducible factors. By this we find generators for the torsion group of $\mathcal{O}_K^*$. To find a set of fundamental units $\{u_1,\dots,u_s\}$ we employ the algorithm described in [5] Chapter II, §5. 3.

(ii): For the second part of this algorithm we have to explain Dirichlet's method in more detail. For a description of this method see [5] Chapter II, §5. We want to prove:

Let $u\in\mathcal{O}_K^*$ be a unit given in terms of the chosen $\mathbf{Z}$-basis of $\mathcal{O}_K$. There is an effectively computable number $c\in\mathbf{N}$ such that

$$(*)\qquad u\in\{\zeta^{e_0}u_1^{e_1}\cdot\dots\cdot u_s^{e_s}\,|\,|e_i|\le c,\ \forall i=0,\dots,s\}$$

where $\zeta, u_1,\dots,u_s$ is the set of generators computed in (i).

For this let $\sigma_1,\dots,\sigma_{r_1}$ be the distinct embeddings of K into $\mathbf{R}$ and $\tau_1,\dots,\tau_{r_2},\bar\tau_1,\dots,\bar\tau_{r_2}$ be the embeddings of k into $\mathbf{C}$ which do not map K entirely into $\mathbf{R}$. Put:

$$L: K\setminus\{0\}\to\mathbf{R}^{r_1+r_2}$$

$$L: a\to(\ln|\sigma_1(a)|,\dots,\ln|\sigma_{r_1}(a)|,\ln|\tau_1(a)|^2,\dots,\ln|\tau_{r_2}(a)|^2)$$

L is a homomorphism of the multiplicative group $K\setminus\{0\}$ into the additive group of $\mathbf{R}^{r_1+r_2}$. The image of $\mathcal{O}_K^*$ under L is a discrete lattice of dimension r_1+r_2-1 in $\mathbf{R}^{r_1+r_2}$. The kernel of L is exactly the group of roots of unity contained in $\mathcal{O}_K^*$. By the proofs of Lemma 1 and Theorem 2 of [5] Chapter II, §5 it is clear how to find effectively a rational number $c_1\neq 0$ such that:

$$B(c_1)\cap L(\mathcal{O}_K^*)=\langle\mathbf{0}\rangle$$

where:

$$B(c)=\{\mathbf{x}\in\mathbf{R}^{r_1+r_2}\,|\,\|\mathbf{x}\|={}_+\sqrt{\mathbf{x}\mathbf{x}'}\le c\}$$

is the (r_1+r_2)-dimensional euclidian ball of radius c. By approximating all zeroes of a minimal polynomial of a field generator of K in $\mathbf{C}$ up to the first decimal of their real and imaginary parts, we find for our explicitly given unit $u\in\mathcal{O}_K^*$ a rational number c_2 such that

$$u\in B(c_2).$$

In (*) we may then clearly put:

$$c=\max\left(2|d|,\frac{c_2}{c_1}+1\right)$$

To finish this algorithm we spread out each element of the finite set mentioned in (*) in terms of our **Z**-basis of $\mathcal{O}_K$ and look which element is equal to u.

Algorithm A_9

Let K be an algebraic number field, with ring of algebraic integers $\mathcal{O}_K$. Given r ideals $\mathbf{a}_1, \ldots, \mathbf{a}_r$ by **Z**-bases, which are pairwise coprime i.e.:

$$\langle \mathbf{a}_i, \mathbf{a}_j \rangle = \mathcal{O}_K \qquad \text{for } i \neq j$$

and elements $\theta_1, \ldots, \theta_r \in \mathcal{O}_K$. We give here an algorithm for determining an $x \in \mathcal{O}_K$ such that

$$\begin{aligned} x &\equiv \theta_1 \bmod \mathbf{a}_1 \\ &\vdots \\ x &\equiv \theta_r \bmod \mathbf{a}_r. \end{aligned}$$

We first determine a **Z**-basis for the ideal

$$\mathbf{a} = \mathbf{a}_1 \cap \cdots \cap \mathbf{a}_r.$$

This has as a consequence, that we explicitly know the order of $\mathcal{O}_K/\mathbf{a}$ and a multiplication table for the ring:

$$\mathcal{O}_K/\mathbf{a}.$$

In this finite ring we check for one element after the other whether it satisfies the corresponding conditions. The Chinese Remainder Theorem makes sure that we find an $\bar{x}$ in $\mathcal{O}/\mathbf{a}$ satisfying our congruences. As x we may take any preimage of $\bar{x}$.

Algorithm A_{10}

Let K be an algebraic number field, with ring of algebraic integers $\mathcal{O}_K$. Let $\mathbf{a}$ be an ideal of $\mathcal{O}_K$ given by a set of ideal generators or, which comes to the same (because we know a **Z**-basis of $\mathcal{O}_K$), by a **Z**-basis. Here we compute **Z**-bases for prime ideals $\mathbf{p}_1, \ldots, \mathbf{p}_r$ and natural numbers $e_1, \ldots, e_r$ such that:

$$\mathbf{a} = \mathbf{p}_1^{e_1} \cdot \cdots \cdot \mathbf{p}_r^{e_r}$$

By Gauss' method we know the order of the ring $\mathcal{O}_K/\mathbf{a}$. We are also given a multiplication table by reduction of our table for $\mathcal{O}_K$. We are then able to decompose:

$$\mathcal{O}_K/\mathbf{a} = R_1 \times \cdots \times R_r$$

effectively into a direct product of Artin local rings R_i. Let $\bar{\mathbf{p}}_i$ be the maximal ideal of R_i and e_i be the least natural number such that $\bar{\mathbf{p}}_i^{e_i} = \langle 0 \rangle$. Let:

$$\varphi_i : \mathcal{O}_K \to R_i$$

be the projection homomorphism, which we may consider to be known explicitly. Put

$$\mathbf{p}_i = \varphi_i^{-1}(\bar{\mathbf{p}}_i).$$

By algorithm A_5 we are able to compute a set of generators for the abelian groups $\mathbf{p}_i$. By Gauss' method we reduce these sets to **Z**-bases.

Algorithm A_{11}

Let K be an algebraic number field, with ring of algebraic integers $\mathcal{O}_K$. Let **a**, **b** be two ideals given by **Z**-bases. We decide here whether there is a $c \in K$ $(c \neq 0)$ with

$$c\mathbf{a} = \mathbf{b}.$$

If the answer is "yes" we determine such a c. In particular we decide whether ideals are principal, and in case they are, we give generators for them.

We determine first a $\lambda \in \mathbf{Z}$ with:

$$\lambda \mathbf{b} \subseteq \mathbf{a}.$$

A c satisfying $c\mathbf{a} = \mathbf{b}$ would then satisfy:

$$\lambda c \mathbf{a} = \lambda \mathbf{b} \subset \mathbf{a}.$$

Hence we get $\lambda c \in \mathcal{O}_K$. On the other hand putting:

$$\lambda_0 = |\mathbf{a} : \lambda \mathbf{b}|$$

we get:

$$|\mathcal{O}_K : \lambda c \mathcal{O}_K| = \lambda_0.$$

We now take the list of nonassociate elements $\gamma_1, \ldots, \gamma_s$ with

$$|\mathcal{O}_K : \gamma_i \mathcal{O}_K| = \lambda_0$$

computed by algorithm A_7 and check whether one of the numbers $\lambda^{-1}\gamma_i$, $i = 1, \ldots, s$, satisfies:

$$\lambda^{-1}\gamma_i \mathbf{a} = \mathbf{b}.$$

Algorithm A_{12}

Let K be an algebraic number field, with ring of algebraic integers $\mathcal{O}_K$. Let κ be the class number of $\mathcal{O}_K$ and J_K the ideal class group of $\mathcal{O}_K$. This algorithm computes κ together with ideals $\mathbf{a}_1, \ldots, \mathbf{a}_\kappa$ which lie in distinct classes. Furthermore a multiplication table for J_K is given.

Let m be the degree of K and D be the absolute discriminant of $\mathcal{O}_K$. From the proof of [5] Theorem 3 of Chapter II, §6 it follows that each ideal class of $\mathcal{O}_K$ contains an ideal $\mathbf{a}$ with

$$|\mathcal{O}_K : \mathbf{a}| \leq \left(\frac{2}{\pi}\right)^m \sqrt{|D|} = c.$$

We then list all subgroups of $\mathcal{O}_K$ of index $\leq c$. There are not more than $2^{(c^d)}$ of them. For each such subgroup we check whether

$$\omega_i N \subset N \qquad i = 1, \ldots, m$$

for our $\mathbf{Z}$-basis of $\mathcal{O}_K$. This leaves us with a list of all ideals in $\mathcal{O}_K$ with index at most c. This gives a first upper bound for κ.

By algorithm A_{11} we deduce from our list a set of inequivalent ideals together with a multiplication table for J_K.

Algorithm A_{13}

Let K be an algebraic number field, with ring of algebraic integers $\mathcal{O}_K$. Let $\mathbf{a}$, $\mathbf{b}$ be two ideals of $\mathcal{O}_K$. This algorithm finds a number $c \in K$ such that $c\mathbf{b} \subseteq \mathcal{O}_K$ and $c\mathbf{b}$ is coprime to $\mathbf{a}$.

In other words, given an ideal class $\bar{\mathbf{b}}$ of $\mathcal{O}_K$ and an ideal $\mathbf{a}$ we want to find an element of $\bar{\mathbf{b}}$ which is prime to $\mathbf{a}$.

We first split $\mathbf{a}$ by algorithm A_{10} into prime factors:

$$\mathbf{a} = \mathbf{p}_1^{e_1} \cdot \cdots \cdot \mathbf{p}_r^{e_r}$$

Then we determine by algorithm A_{12} an ideal $\mathbf{b}_0$ in the ideal class inverse to the class of $\mathbf{b}$. Again by application of algorithm A_{10} we find:

$$\mathbf{b}_0 = \mathbf{p}_1^{f_1} \cdots \mathbf{p}_r^{f_r} \mathbf{q}_1^{\varepsilon_1} \cdots \mathbf{q}_s^{\varepsilon_s}$$

Here the f_i might be zero.

We then find elements: $\theta_i \in \mathcal{O}_K$ for $i = 1, \ldots, r$ with:

$$\theta_i \in \mathbf{p}^{f_i};\ \theta_i \notin \mathbf{p}^{f_i+1} \qquad \text{for } i = 1, \ldots, r$$

and

$$\eta_i \in \mathcal{O}_K \qquad \text{for } i = 1, \ldots, s$$

with

$$\eta_i \in \mathbf{q}_i^{\varepsilon_i} \qquad \text{for } i = 1, \ldots, s.$$

Then we determine by algorithm A_9 a solution of the congruences:

$$\begin{aligned} z &\equiv \theta_1 \bmod \mathbf{p}_1^{f_1+1} \\ &\vdots \qquad \vdots \\ z &\equiv \theta_r \bmod \mathbf{p}_r^{f_r+1} \\ z &\equiv \eta_1 \bmod \mathbf{q}_1^{\varepsilon_1} \\ &\vdots \qquad \vdots \\ z &\equiv \eta_s \bmod \mathbf{q}_s^{\varepsilon_s} \end{aligned}$$

The ideal $z \cdot \mathcal{O}_K$ is clearly divisible by $\mathbf{b}_0$ hence we find an ideal $\mathbf{b}_1$ such that:

$$z \cdot \mathcal{O}_K = \mathbf{b}_0 \mathbf{b}_1$$

$\mathbf{b}_1$ may be determined by:

$$\mathbf{b}_1 = \{\eta \in \mathcal{O}_K \mid \eta \, \mathbf{b}_0 \subseteq z \cdot \mathcal{O}_K\}.$$

But $\mathbf{b}_1$ then lies in the ideal class of $\mathbf{b}$ and by the choice of our congruences it is prime to $\mathbf{a}$.

Algorithm A_{14}

Let K be an algebraic number field, with ring of algebraic integers $\mathcal{O}_K$. Let $A = (a_{ij})$ be an $n \times m$ matrix with coefficients from $\mathcal{O}_K$ such that:

$$\langle a_{ij} \mid 1 \leq i \leq n;\ 1 \leq j \leq m \rangle = \mathcal{O}_K$$

and

$$\mathrm{rg}_K A \geq 2$$

Algorithm A_{14} determines a vector $\boldsymbol{x} = (x_1, \ldots, x_n)$ with entries in $\mathcal{O}_K$ such that:

$$\boldsymbol{x}A = \boldsymbol{y} = (y_1, \ldots, y_m)$$

with

$$\langle y_1, \ldots, y_m \rangle = \mathcal{O}_K.$$

The rank condition for A allows us to assume that:

$$d = a_{11}a_{22} - a_{21}a_{12}$$

is not zero. We first compute a $\mathbf{Z}$-basis for the ideal $d . \mathcal{O}_K$ and decompose it by algorithm A;

$$d\mathcal{O}_K = \mathbf{p}_1^{\varepsilon_1} \cdots \mathbf{p}_r^{\varepsilon_r}.$$

For each ideal $\mathbf{p}_\nu$ we find an entry $a_{i(\nu),j(\nu)}$ such that:

$$a_{i(\nu),j(\nu)} \notin \mathbf{p}_\nu.$$

By algorithm A_9 we solve the congruences:

$$(11)\qquad x'_\mu \equiv \begin{cases} 1 & \text{if } \mu = i(\nu) \\ 0 & \text{else} \end{cases} \mod \mathbf{p}_\nu$$

for $\mu = 1, \ldots, n$ and $\nu = 1, \ldots, r$. Now put:

$$\boldsymbol{x}' = (x'_1, \ldots, x'_n) \quad \text{and} \quad \boldsymbol{y}' = \boldsymbol{x}'A = (y'_1, \ldots, y'_m).$$

a_{22} and a_{21} not being simultaneously 0 (because of (11)) we may furthermore assume that:

$$y'_2 \neq 0.$$

We apply algorithm A_{10} again to find:

$$y'_2 \mathcal{O}_K = \mathbf{p}_1^{f_1} \cdots \mathbf{p}_r^{f_r} \mathbf{q}_1^{t_1} \cdots \mathbf{q}_s^{t_s}$$

where the f_i might be zero, but where none of the $\mathbf{q}_i$ is a $\mathbf{p}_\nu$. We now find an $a \in \mathcal{O}_K$ with:

$$(12)\qquad \begin{aligned} a &\equiv 1 \mod \mathbf{q}_\nu & \nu &= 1, \ldots, s \\ a &\equiv 0 \mod \mathbf{p}_\nu & \nu &= 1, \ldots, r \end{aligned}$$

It then follows that:

$$\begin{aligned} ad &\not\equiv 0 \mod \mathbf{q}_\nu & \nu &= 1, \ldots, s \\ ad &\equiv 0 \mod \mathbf{p}_\nu & \nu &= 1, \ldots, r. \end{aligned}$$

Then we find a number $b \in \mathcal{O}_K$ such that:

$$y'_1 + abd \not\equiv 0 \mod \mathbf{q}_\nu \qquad \nu = 1, \ldots, s$$

This is possible because of (12).

It is then obvious that the ideal

$$\langle y'_1 + abd, y'_2 \rangle$$

has only prime divisors from the set $\{\mathbf{p}_1, \ldots, \mathbf{p}_r\}$. Now put:

$$\sigma = ba_{22} \quad \text{and} \quad \tau = ba_{21}.$$

We make the further definitions:

$$x_1 = x'_1 + \sigma a, \qquad x_2 = x'_2 + \tau a, \qquad x_\nu = x'_\nu$$

for $\nu = 3, \ldots, n$ and

$$\boldsymbol{y} = \boldsymbol{x}A = (y_1, \ldots, y_m).$$

Because of our choice of a the congruences (11) are still valid for the x_i.

Hence no $\mathbf{p}_\nu$ for $\nu = 1, \ldots, r$ divides (contains) the ideals $\langle y_1, \ldots, y_m \rangle$. On the other hand an easy computation shows:

$$y_1 = y_1' + abd \quad \text{and} \quad y_2 = y_2',$$

so by the above every prime division of $\langle y_1, \ldots, y_m \rangle$ is amongst the $\mathbf{p}_1, \ldots, \mathbf{p}_r$. Thus $\langle y_1, \ldots, y_m \rangle = \mathcal{O}_K$.

Algorithm A_{15}

Let K be an algebraic number field, with ring of algebraic integers $\mathcal{O}_K$. Let $A = (a_{ij})$ be an $n \times m$ matrix with coefficients in $\mathcal{O}_K$ such that

$$\operatorname{rg}_K A \leqslant n - 2.$$

Here we find a vector $\boldsymbol{x} = (x_1, \ldots, x_n)$ with entries in $\mathcal{O}_K$ such that

$$\langle x_1, \ldots, x_n \rangle = \mathcal{O}_K$$

and

$$\boldsymbol{x}A = \boldsymbol{0}.$$

We first find two linearly independent solutions with entries in $\mathcal{O}_K$:

$$\boldsymbol{\alpha} = (\alpha, \ldots, \alpha_n) \qquad \boldsymbol{\beta}' = (\beta_1', \ldots, \beta_n')$$

Put:

$$\langle \boldsymbol{\alpha} \rangle = \langle \alpha_1, \ldots, \alpha_n \rangle \quad \text{and} \quad \langle \boldsymbol{\beta}' \rangle = \langle \beta_1', \ldots, \beta_n' \rangle$$

By algorithm A_{13} we find in the ideal class of $\langle \boldsymbol{\beta}' \rangle$ an ideal $\mathbf{a}$ which is coprime to $\langle \boldsymbol{\alpha} \rangle$. In other words we find a $c \in K$ such that:

$$c\beta_1' =: \beta_1, \ldots, c\beta_n' =: \beta_n \in \mathcal{O}_K$$

and $\langle \boldsymbol{\alpha} \rangle$ is coprime to $\langle \boldsymbol{\beta} \rangle$ where:

$$\boldsymbol{\beta} = (\beta_1, \ldots, \beta_n).$$

By algorithm A_{14} we then find $y_1, y_2 \in \mathcal{O}_K$ such that:

$$(x_1, \ldots, x_n) = (y_1, y_2) \begin{pmatrix} \alpha_1, \ldots, \alpha_n \\ \beta_1, \ldots, \beta_n \end{pmatrix}$$

satisfies: $\langle x_1, \ldots, x_n \rangle = \mathcal{O}_K$.

Algorithm A_{16}

Let K be an algebraic number field with ring of algebraic integers $\mathcal{O}_K$. Let $\boldsymbol{x} = (x_{11}, x_{12}, \ldots, x_{1n})$ be a vector with entries in $\mathcal{O}_K$ such that:

$$\langle x_{11}, \ldots, x_{1n} \rangle = \mathcal{O}_K.$$

Algorithm A_{16} finds a matrix

$$X = \begin{pmatrix} x_{11}, \dots, x_{1n} \\ x_{21}, \dots, x_{2n} \\ \vdots \quad\quad \vdots \\ x_{n1}, \dots, x_{nn} \end{pmatrix}$$

with $\det X = 1$.

We assume we have constructed the matrix X up to the rth row

$$\begin{pmatrix} x_{11}, \dots, x_{1n} \\ \vdots \quad\quad \vdots \\ x_{r1}, \dots, x_{rn} \end{pmatrix}$$

with $r < n-2$ under the hypotheses that:

$$\langle \delta_1, \dots, \delta_s \rangle = \mathcal{O}_K$$

where $\delta_1, \dots, \delta_s$ are the $r \times r$ subdeterminants.

Here $s = \binom{n}{r}$. There is a $n \times \binom{n}{r+1}$ matrix $A(r)$ whose entries are the δ_i with appropriate signs attached, such that the column:

$$(z_1, \dots, z_n) \cdot A(r)$$

has the $(r+1) \times (r+1)$ subdeterminants of

$$\begin{pmatrix} x_{11}, \dots, x_{1n} \\ \vdots \quad\quad \vdots \\ x_{r1}, \dots, x_{rn} \\ z_1, \dots, z_n \end{pmatrix}$$

as entries. The rank of A is $n - r$. As long as $r \leqslant (n-2)$ we may therefore employ algorithm A_{14} to find a $(r+1)$th row such that the $(r+1) \times (r+1)$ subdeterminants still generate the unit ideal.

For the linear algebra involved see [4] Chapter 3.

By this method we find X up to the last row. Let $\delta_1, \dots, \delta_{n+1}$ be the $(n-1) \times (n-1)$ subdeterminants of the so found $(n-1) \times n$ matrix. We know that:

$$\langle \delta_1, \dots, \delta_{n+1} \rangle = \mathcal{O}_K.$$

By writing out a basis for the abelian subgroup generated by $\omega_i \delta_j$ $(i = 1, \dots, m;\ j = 1, \dots, n)$ inside $\mathcal{O}_K$ we find a solution of the equation:

$$x_{n1}\delta_1 + \cdots + x_{nn}\delta_n = 1 \qquad x_{ni} \in \mathcal{O}_K \qquad i = 1, \dots, n$$

Algorithm A_{17}

Let K be an algebraic number field with ring of integers $\mathcal{O}_K$. Let

$\sigma_1, \ldots, \sigma_n \in \mathcal{O}_K^m$ for natural numbers n, m. This algorithm decides whether the $\mathcal{O}_K$-module M generated by the $\sigma_1, \ldots, \sigma_n$ is free. If the answer is "yes" an $\mathcal{O}_K$-module basis is computed in terms of the $\sigma_1, \ldots, \sigma_n$.

Let r be the K-dimension of the vector space generated by the $\sigma_1, \ldots, \sigma_n$. By successive application of the algorithms A_{15} and A_{16} we effectively find a set of generators:

$$\tau_1, \ldots, \tau_{r+1} \qquad \text{for } M$$

in terms of the $\sigma_1, \ldots, \sigma_n$. We then form the matrix:

$$X = \begin{pmatrix} a_{11}, \ldots, a_{1m} \\ \vdots \qquad \vdots \\ a_{r+1,1}, \ldots, a_{r+1,m} \end{pmatrix}$$

whose rows are the $\tau_1, \ldots, \tau_{r+1}$. X has rank r. Let $^*X$ be the left adjuncted matrix to X. Its entries are certain $r \times r$ subdeterminants of X, with appropriate signs attached. $^*X$ has $(r+1)$ columns and many rows and satisfies:

$$^*XX = \boldsymbol{0}$$

X having rank r. X has nonzero entries. For each row $(x'_1, \ldots, x'_{r+1})$ of $^*X$ we test by algorithm A_{11} whether

$$\langle x'_1, \ldots, x'_{r+1} \rangle \qquad \text{is a principal ideal.}$$

Let the answer be "yes" for the row $(x'_1, \ldots, x'_{r+1})$ and put:

$$cx_i = x'_i \qquad \text{for } i = 1, \ldots, r+1$$

for a generator c found by algorithm A_{11}. Then:

$$\langle x_1, \ldots, x_{r+1} \rangle = \mathcal{O}_K$$

and

$$x_1\tau_1 + \cdots + x_{r+1}\tau_{r+1} = 0$$

This follows from the corresponding properties of the x'_i. By algorithm A_{16} we may then effectively find a set of generators for M consisting of r vectors. Then M is free and we have found an $\mathcal{O}_K$-basis in terms of the $\sigma_1, \ldots, \sigma_n$.

Suppose now that no row of $^*X$ generates a principal ideal. We claim that then M will not be free. For this see [19] Theorem 27.

Algorithm A_{18}

Let K be an algebraic number field with ring of algebraic integers $\mathcal{O}_K$. Let B be an explicitly given finitely generated abelian group equipped with an $\mathcal{O}_K$-module structure, which is given on a set of generators of B. Algorithm A_{18} decides whether B is a free $\mathcal{O}_K$-module. If the answer is "yes" an $\mathcal{O}_K$-module basis is computed.

We first test whether B is a free $\mathbf{Z}$-module by Gauss' method. This condition is clearly necessary for B to be a free $\mathcal{O}_K$-module. B being a free $\mathbf{Z}$-module we pick a $\mathbf{Z}$-basis. Then we have:

$$B \simeq \mathbf{Z}^n \subseteq \mathbf{Q}^n = \mathbf{Q}B$$

and $\mathbf{Q}B$ carries a K vector space structure. We pick then in $\mathbf{Q}B$ a K-basis such that:

$$B \subseteq \mathcal{O}_K^r \subseteq K^r = \mathbf{Q}B.$$

Then we express our $\mathbf{Z}$-basis for B as vectors in $\mathcal{O}_K^r$ and use algorithm A_{17}.

Algorithm A_{19}

Let K be an algebraic number field with ring of algebraic integers $\mathcal{O}_K$. Let n be a natural number. This algorithm lists a finite set of generators for $GL_n(\mathcal{O}_K)$.

If for a given n we would have computed a finite set of generators $\gamma_1, \ldots, \gamma_t$ for $SL_n(\mathcal{O}_K)$ we would get a finite set of generators for $GL_n(\mathcal{O}_K)$ by adding matrices

$$\begin{pmatrix} u & & & \\ & 1 & & \\ & & \ddots & \\ & & & 1 \end{pmatrix}$$

where u runs through a set of generators for the unit group of $\mathcal{O}_K$ which is computed by algorithm A_8.

It suffices then to compute a set of generators for $SL_n(\mathcal{O}_K)$:

(1) $n = 2$, $\mathcal{O}_K$ has infinitely many units.

The main result of Wasserstein's paper [25] says that $SL_2(\mathcal{O}_K)$ is then generated by

$$\begin{pmatrix} 0 & -1 \\ 1 & 0 \end{pmatrix}, \begin{pmatrix} 1 & \omega_1 \\ 0 & 1 \end{pmatrix}, \ldots, \begin{pmatrix} 1 & \omega_m \\ 0 & 1 \end{pmatrix}$$

where $\omega_1, \ldots, \omega_m$ is a $\mathbf{Z}$-basis of $\mathcal{O}_K$.

(2) $n = 2$, $\mathcal{O}_K$ is imaginary quadratic.

In this case Swan's paper [21] even gives a presentation for $SL_2(\mathcal{O}_K)$. It can be checked that the constructions of [21] are all effective. See the remarks in section 8 of this paper.

These two cases exhaust SL_2 because of Dirichlet's theorem on units (see [5]).

(3) $n \geq 3$.

By [0] and [15] Corollary 16.3 it follows that $SL_n(\mathcal{O}_K)$ is generated by elementary matrices.

It is quite easy to extract a system of generators for $SL_n(\mathcal{O}_K)$ $n \geq 2$ from the paper [10] of A. Hurwitz. The method used there can also be seen to be effective. A feature of all these methods is that one can give an a priori bound for the number of generators needed for $SL_n(\mathcal{O}_K)$ in terms of n, the discriminant of $\mathcal{O}_K$, the degree of K, and the number of complex valuations of $\mathcal{O}_K$.

References

[0] H. Bass, J. Milnor and J.-P. Serre, Solution of the congruence subgroup problem for $SL_n(n \geq 3)$ and $Sp_{2n}(n \geq 2)$, Publ. Math., IHES 33 (1967).

[1] W.W. Boone, F.B. Cannonito and R.C. Lyndon, Word problems (North-Holland Publishing Comp., Amsterdam, London, 1973).

[2] A. Borel, et al., Seminar on algebraic groups and related finite groups, Lecture Notes in Mathematics 131 (Springer Verlag, Berlin–Heidelberg–New York, 1969).

[3] A. Borel and Harish-Chandra, Arithmetic subgroups of algebraic groups, Annals of Mathematics Vol. 75, No. 3 (1962).

[3a] A. Borel, Arithmetic properties of algebraic groups, Proc. Int. Congr. Math., Stockholm (1962).

[4] N. Bourbaki, Algèbre, Chap. 3 and Chap. 7 (Hermann, Paris, Deuxième Edition, 1958).

[5] Z.I. Borevich and I.R. Shafarevich, Zahlentheorie (Birkhäuser Verlag, Basel u. Stuttgart, 1966).

[6] M. Hall, The theory of finite groups (Macmillan Comp., 1973).

[7] H. Hasse, Zahlentheorie (Akademie-Verlag, Berlin, 1969).

[8] E. Hecke, Vorlesungen über die Theorie der algebraischen Zahlen (Akademische Verlagsgesellschaft, Leipzig, 1923).

[9] G. Hermann, Die Frage der endlich vielen Schritte in der Theorie der Polynomideale, Math. Annalen 95 (1926) 736–788.

[10] A. Hurwitz, Die unimodularen Substitutionen in einem algebraischen Zahlkörper. Nachrichten von der k. Gesellschaft der Wissenschaften zu Göttingen (1895).

[11] R.D. Hurwitz, On the conjugacy problem in a free product with commuting subgroups, Math. Annalen, Vol. 221 (1976).

[12] W. Magnus, Noneuclidian tessalations and their groups (Academic Press, 1974).

[13] W. Magnus, A. Karass and D. Solitar, Combinatorial group theory (Interscience Publishers, 1966).

[14] Charles Miller, III, On group-theoretic decision problems and their classification, Annals of Math. Studies, No. 68, Princeton University Press (1971).

[15] J. Milnor, Introduction to algebraic K-theory, Annals of Math. Studies, No. 72, Princeton University Press (1971).

[16] M. Newman, Integral matrices (Academic Press, 1972).

[17] I. Schur, Über Gruppen linearer Substitutionen mit Koeffizienten aus einem algebraischen Zahlkörper, Math. Annalen, Vol. 71 (1912).

[18] A. Seidenberg, Constructions in algebra, Transactions of the Am. Math. Soc., Vol. 197 (1974).
[19] E. Steinitz, Rechteckige Systeme und Moduln in algebraischen Zahlkörpern I, Math. Annalen, Vol. 71 (1912).
[20] E. Steinitz, Rechteckige Systeme und Moduln in algebraischen Zahlkörpern II, Math. Annalen, Vol. 72 (1912).
[21] R.G. Swan, Generators and relations for certain special linear groups, Advances in Math. 6 (1971) 1–77.
[22] O. Tausky, Matrices of rational integers, Bull. Am. Math. Soc. 66 (1960) 327–345.
[23] B.L. van der Waerden, Eine Bemerkung über die Unzerlegbarkeit von Polynomen, Math. Annalen, Vol. 102 (1930).
[24] B.L. van der Waerden, Moderne algebra I + II, 2nd edition (Springer Verlag, Berlin, 1937).
[25] L.N. Wasserstein, On the group SL_2 over Dedekind domains of arithmetic type (Russian), Mat. Sbornik, Vol. 89 (131) No. 2(10) (1972).
[26] A. Weil, Adèles and algebraic groups, Inst. Adv. Study (1961) (notes polycopies).
[27] M.J. Wicks, Presentations of some classical groups, Bull. Aust. Math. Soc., Vol. 13 (1975).

S.I. Adian, W.W. Boone, G. Higman, eds., Word Problems II

ALGEBRAICALLY CLOSED GROUPS: EMBEDDINGS AND CENTRALIZERS

Kenneth HICKIN* and Angus MACINTYRE**
Michigan State University, East Lansing, MI 48824, USA
Yale University, New Haven, CT 06520, USA

§0. Introduction

Here we present several results on the algebraic structure of a.c. groups. We refer the reader to [2: Chapter IV, §8], [3], and [6] for discussions of the basic properties of a.c. groups.

Theorem 1. *No a.c. group can be embedded into a finitely generated subgroup of itself.*

This suggests the following problem: Is there an ω-homogeneous group (in the sense of Jonsson) which can be embedded into a f.g. subgroup of itself?

If A and B are groups, $A \subset B$ means that A is a subgroup of B.

Theorem 2. *Suppose G is a countable a.c. group. There is a set $\mathcal{U}$ of 2^{ω_1} a.c. groups, each of power ω_1 and ∞-ω-equivalent to G, with the property: each $U \in \mathcal{U}$ has a subgroup $U_0 \cong G$ such that, for all $U \neq V \in \mathcal{U}$ and for all countable B and D with $U_0 \subset B \subset U$ and $V_0 \subset D \subset V$, neither of the centralizers $C_U(B)$ and $C_V(D)$ is embeddable in the other. Hence distinct members of $\mathcal{U}$ are not isomorphic. If the C.H. is assumed, then we can arrange that distinct members of $\mathcal{U}$ are mutually non-embeddable.*

In [5] Shelah and Ziegler give a complete solution to the spectrum problem for a.c. groups using stability theory. Our proof of Theorem 2

* The first author gratefully acknowledges the support and splendid hospitality of the Warwick Symposium on Infinite Groups and Group Rings during the preparation of this paper in May of 1978 at the University of Warwick.
** Both authors were aided in this research by NSF grant MCS77–07731.

shows that, at least in the case of ω_1, extremely elementary techniques involving centralizers suffice to construct the maximum number of ∞-ω-equivalent a.c. groups which are not isomorphic for obvious reasons.

In the remainder of this section G denotes an arbitrary a.c. group. MIN denotes the minimum condition on subgroups.

Theorem 3. *Suppose $A \subset G$ satisfies* MIN *and A is the intersection of finitely many f.g. subgroups of G. Then, for every M with $C_G(A) \subset M \subset G$, there exists $H \subset A$ such that*

$$C_G(H) \subset M \subset N_G(H) \qquad \text{(the normalizer of } H \text{ in } G).$$

In particular, if A is finite, then there are only finitely many subgroups of G containing the centralizer of A.

Corollary. *If $A \subset G$ is finite and characteristically simple, then $N_G(A)$ is a maximal proper subgroup of G.*

Proof. Suppose $N_G(A) \subset M \subset G$. By Theorem 3, $C_G(H) \subset M \subset N_G(H)$ for some $H \subset A$. Since G is a.c., every automorphism of A is induced by an element of $N_G(A)$. Hence, H is characteristic in A and either $H = 1$, $M = G$ or $H = A$, $M = N_G(A)$.

A more complete characterization of the maximal subgroups of countable a.c. groups will be given in a future paper by the first author.

If $P \subset G$ and $\mathcal{P}$ acts on P, we define $N_G^{\mathcal{P}}(P) = \{x \in N_G(P) \mid x$ induces a $\mathcal{P}$-automorphism on $P\}$. $\operatorname{Aut}(P)$ is the automorphism group of P.

Further information on the subgroup lattice between $C_G(A)$ and G is given by

Theorem 4. *Suppose $B_i \subset G$, $1 \leq i \leq n$, are f.g. and $B_1 \cap \cdots \cap B_n$ has* MIN. *Suppose $\mathcal{B}_i \subset \operatorname{Aut}(B_i)$, $1 \leq i \leq n$, and let $K =$ the largest subgroup of $B_1 \cap \cdots \cap B_n$ which is invariant under $\mathcal{B}_1 \cup \cdots \cup \mathcal{B}_n$. Then,*

$$N_G^{\langle \mathcal{B}_1, \ldots, \mathcal{B}_n \rangle}(K) = \langle N_G^{\mathcal{B}_i}(B_i) \mid 1 \leq i \leq n \rangle.$$

In the special case of centralizers Theorem 4 becomes

Lemma 1. *If $B_i \subset G$, $1 \leq i \leq n$, are f.g., then $C_G(B_1 \cap \cdots \cap B_n) = \langle C_G(B_i) \mid 1 \leq i \leq n \rangle$.*

Proof of Theorem 3. Induct on the subgroups of A. Suppose $C_G(A) \subset$

$M \subset G$. If $M \subset N_G(A)$, there is nothing to prove. So, suppose $x \in M - N_G(A)$. We have

$$A_0 = A \cap A^x < A$$

since $A \neq A^x$ and A has MIN. Now, $M \supset \langle C_G(A), X\rangle \supset \langle C_G(A), C_G(A^x)\rangle$. Put $A = D_1 \cap \cdots \cap D_m$ ($D_i \subset G$ f.g.). Thus, $M \supset C_G(D_i)$ and $M \supset C_G(D_i^x)$ for all $1 \leq i \leq m$. Since $A_0 = D_1 \cap D_1^x \cap \cdots \cap D_m \cap D_m^x$, we have by Lemma 1, $M \supset C_G(A_0)$. By induction we now conclude that $C_G(H) \subset M \subset N_G(H)$ for some $H \subset A_0$.

Next we consider the normal structure of normalizers.

Theorem 5. *Suppose $A \subset G$ is f.g. and $x \in N_G(A) - A$. Then $C_G(A) \subset x^{C_G(A)}$. Thus $C_G(A)/C_A(A)$ is simple. (x^C is the subgroup generated by all the $c^{-1}xc$, $c \in C$).*

It is well known that if $A \subset G$ is centerless and f.g., then $C_G(A)$ is a.c. and ∞-ω-equivalent to G. If $C_A(A) \neq 1$, it is in many cases easy to see that $C_G(A)/C_A(A)$ has a pair of isomorphic f.g. subgroups which are not conjugate in it. For example, suppose $C_A(A)$ is not divisible and let $x \in C_A(A)$ have no pth root. Choose $z, y \in C_G(A)$ such that $y^p = x$ and $z^p = 1$, $z \notin C_A(A)$. It is easily checked that $\langle yC_A(A)\rangle$ and $\langle zC_A(A)\rangle$ are not conjugate in $C_G(A)/C_A(A)$ since the former cosets have no elements of order p.

Next we note that Theorem 3 fails if A is infinite cyclic.

Proposition 1. *Suppose $\mathbf{Z} \subset G$ is infinite cyclic. Put $C = \bigcup\{C_G(\mathbf{Z}^n) \mid n \geq 1\}$, $N = \bigcup\{N_G(\mathbf{Z}^n) \mid n \geq 1\}$, and $M = \{x \in G \mid \mathbf{Z} \cap \mathbf{Z}^x \neq 1\}$. Then $C \lhd N \lhd M$, M is maximal in G, C is simple, N/C has order 2, and M/N is free abelian of rank ω.*

Proof. Clearly $M \neq G$ and its maximality follows from Lemma 1 since $x \notin M$ implies $\mathbf{Z} \cap \mathbf{Z}^x = 1$ whence $\langle M, x\rangle \supset \langle C_G(\mathbf{Z}), C_G(\mathbf{Z}^x)\rangle = G$.

The simplicity of C follows from Theorem 5: if $1 \neq x \in C$, there exists $m \geq 1$ such that $x \in C_G(\mathbf{Z}^n) - \mathbf{Z}^n$ for all multiples n of m. Thus, $C_G(\mathbf{Z}^n) \subset x^{C_G(\mathbf{Z}^n)}$ for such n which gives $C \subset x^C$.

Clearly N/C has order 2 and $N \lhd M$.

It remains to consider M/N. For each pair (m, n) of positive integers, there exists $\tau = \tau(m, n) \in M$ such that $\tau^{-1}\mathbf{Z}^m\tau = \mathbf{Z}^n$. We will view τ as an element of M/N. Thus, $\tau(n, n) = 1$, $\tau(n, m)\cdot\tau(m, p) = \tau(n, p)$, and $\tau(nm, np) = \tau(m, p) (\operatorname{mod} N)$ for all n, m, and p. Thus,

M/N is generated by $\{\tau(a,b) \mid a, b$ are relatively prime$\}$ and multiplication in M/N is given by

$$\tau(a,b)\cdot\tau(c,d)=\tau\left(\frac{a\lambda}{b},\frac{d\lambda}{c}\right)$$

where λ is the least common multiple of b and c. We check easily that M/N is also generated by $\{\tau(1,p) \mid p$ is prime$\}$ and that these generators have infinite order, commute, and are independent.

Finally, we will show that a basic construction of group theory can be performed in every a.c. group.

If A is a f.g. group, $W(A)$ denotes the words in some finite generating set of A which are relations of A; $W^-(A)$ denotes the corresponding set of words non-trivial in A. If S and T are (coded) sets of natural numbers, $S \leq_e T$ is the relation "S is enumeration reducible to T" [4: p. 145].

Theorem 6. *Suppose $A, B \subset G$ are f.g. and there exists an f.g. $F \subset G$ such that $W^-(B) \leq_e W(F)$. Then, the restricted wreath product $A \operatorname{wr} B$ is embeddable in G. In particular, this is true if B has a solvable word problem.*

Corollary. *If $A \subset G$ is f.g., there exists a f.g., perfect, centerless group D such that $A \subset D \subset G$.*

Proof. Let $P \neq 1$ be a finite perfect group. Since $P * P$ is SQ-universal [2: Th. 11.3], there is a group $H = \langle P_1, P_2\rangle$ with $P_i \cong P$ such that $A \subset H$. Since G is a.c., we can assume WLOG that $A \subset H \subset G$. Now $P_1 * P_2$ has a solvable word problem; so, by Theorem 6, $D = H \operatorname{wr}(P_1 * P_2)$ is embeddable in G. D is f.g., perfect, and centerless.

Notice that the group D of the corollary cannot always be chosen simple or even subdirectly irreducible. For example, if every f.g. subgroup of G is recursively presented [3: Th. 8] and A has an unsolvable word problem, D cannot be so chosen; and also, if S is a finite non-abelian simple group, then $S \operatorname{wr} A$ is not embeddable in G because $S \operatorname{wr} A$ is subdirectly irreducible. This same reasoning shows that for arbitrary G, the converse to Theorem 6 is also true: namely, if $S \operatorname{wr} B$ is embeddable in G, this group is an adequate choice for F since

$$W^-(B) \leq_e W(S \operatorname{wr} B)$$

since $S \operatorname{wr} B$ is subdirectly irreducible.

§1. Proof of Theorem 1

We will need the

General Higman Embedding Theorem [C.F. Miller III (unpublished) and M. Ziegler [6]]. *Suppose the group K has a presentation $(X, t_n, (n \in \omega)$: $W(A) \cup R)$ where X is a finite generating set of the group A, $R \leq_e W(A)$, and the relations R are consistent over A (and may involve t's and x's). Then K is a subgroup of a f.g. group H which has a similar presentation $(X, s_1, \ldots, s_m : W(A) \cup F)$ where F is finite; furthermore, $\{t_n \mid n \in \omega\}$ is a recursive subset of H.*

And we will also need

Lemma 2. *Suppose $S, T \subset \omega$, $\omega - S \leq_e S$ and T is r.e. in S. Then $T \leq_e S$.*

This is proved by a simple double enumeration argument.

To prove Theorem 1, suppose G is an a.c. group, $A \subset G$ is f.g. and $\varphi : G \to A$ is an embedding. From the inclusions $\varphi(A) \subset \varphi(G) \subset A$ and the fact that G is a simple group it follows that

$$W^-(\varphi(A)) \leq_e W(A) \tag{1}$$

because for all $x, y \in W^-(\varphi(A))$, we have $x \in y^A$.

Let P and R be disjoint subsets of ω which are r.e. in $W(A)$, but such that there is no set $X \subset \omega$ recursive in $W(A)$ with $P \subset X$ and $R \subset \omega - X$. Such sets are obtained easily by relativizing the construction given in [4: p. 94].

Define a group Γ with generators

$$\begin{cases} c_n, u_n, v_n, \quad \text{and} \quad d \ (n \in \omega) \text{ and relations} \\ c_n = 1 \text{ for all } n \in P, \ c_n^{u_n} c_n^{v_n} = d \text{ for all } n \in P. \end{cases} \tag{2}$$

From (1), Lemma 2, and the fact that P and R are r.e. in $W(A)$, it follows that

$$W(\Gamma) \leq_e W(A).$$

So, the General Higman Theorem implies that Γ is a subgroup of an f.g. group H with relations $W(A) \cup F$, F finite, and that the generators (2) form a recursive subset of H.

Since G is a.c. there is a homomorphism $\mu : H \to G$ such that $\mu(d) \neq 1$. From the inclusions $\mu(\Gamma) \subset \mu(H) \subset G \subsetneq A$, the first of which is recursive, we have as in (1) that $W^-(\mu(\Gamma)) \leq_e W(A)$. So,

$$C = \{n \in \omega \mid \mu(c_n) \neq 1\} \leqslant_e W(A),$$

and, trivially, C is r.e. in $W(A)$. Likewise, $W(\mu(\Gamma)) \leqslant_e W(A)$ and $\omega - C$ is r.e. in $W(A)$. Hence C is recursive in $W(A)$.

Since $\mu(d) \neq 1$, we have $R \subset C$ and $P \subset \omega - C$ contrary to the $W(A)$-recursive inseparability of P and R.

§2. Proof of Theorem 2

From Ziegler [6] we need

Lemma 3. *If G is a.c. and $A \subset G$ is f.g., then $A \times A$ is embeddable in G.*

Lemma 4. *Suppose G is a countable a.c. group, $H \subset G$, and $X_n \subset G$, $n \geqslant 1$, are isomorphic to G. Then, there exist embeddings $\varphi : G \to G$ and $\psi : H \to G$ such that*

(1) *$\varphi(G) \oplus \psi(H)$ exists in G and*

(2) *for all $n \geqslant 1$, $C_G(\varphi(X_n)) = \varphi(C_G(X_n)) \oplus \psi(H)$.*

Proof. Let $H = \bigcup\{H_i \mid i \geqslant 1\}$ where $H_i \subset H_{i+1}$ is f.g. and possibly $H = H_n$ for some n. Let $G = \bigcup\{G_i \mid i \geqslant 1\}$ where $G_i \subset G_{i+1}$ is f.g.

We construct φ and ψ inductively. Suppose we have defined $\varphi(G_i)$ and $\psi(H_i)$ so that $\varphi(G_i) \oplus \psi(H_i)$ exists in G. At the next step it is possible

(A) to extend ψ to H_{i+1} so that $S = \varphi(G_i) \oplus \psi(H_{i+1})$ exists in G and

(B) given elements $g_1, \ldots, g_p \in G - S$ and $x_1, \ldots, x_q \in (G_{i+1} - G_i) \cap (\bigcup_{n \geqslant 1} X_n)$, to extend φ to G_{i+1} so that

(a) $\varphi(G_{i+1}) \oplus \psi(H_{i+1})$ exists in G, and

(b) no $\varphi(x_j)$, $1 \leqslant j \leqslant q$, commutes with any g_j, $1 \leqslant j \leqslant p$.

(A) and (a) can be done because $G_{i+1} \oplus H_{i+1}$ is embeddable in G and G is homogeneous, while (b) can be done because we need only force finitely many inequations, which hold in the free amalgamated product $\langle S, x_1, \ldots, x_q\rangle *_S \langle S, g_1, \ldots, g_p\rangle$, to hold in G.

We claim that (A) and (B) suffice to build the desired properties of the embeddings φ and ψ. Note that, by Theorem 1, no X_n is contained in a f.g. subgroup of G, so that every X_n intersects $G_{i+1} - G_i$ for infinitely many values of i. Hence, by choosing the sets $\{g_1, \ldots, g_p\}$ to eventually exhaust $G - (\varphi(G) \oplus \psi(H))$ and the sets $\{x_1, \ldots, x_q\}$ to intersect every X_n for infinitely many values of i, we will guarantee that, for all $n \geqslant 1$,

$$C_G(\varphi(X_n)) \subset \varphi(G) \oplus \psi(H),$$

yielding conclusion (2) of the lemma.

Proposition 2. *Let G be any countable a.c. group and let $H(\alpha)$, $\alpha < \omega_1$, be groups embeddable in G. There exists an a.c. group G^* of power ω_1 which is ∞-ω-equivalent to G and there exists $G_0 \subset G^*$ with $G_0 \cong G$ such that, for all countable S with $G_0 \subset S \subset G^*$, there exists $\beta < \omega_1$ such that*

$$C_{G^*}(S) \cong A \times \Big(\prod_{\beta \leq \alpha < \omega_1} H(\alpha) \Big) \text{ (direct product)}$$

where $A \subset \prod_{0 \leq \alpha < \beta} H(\alpha)$.

If we assume the C.H., then the above conclusion holds for all $G_0 \subset G^*$ such that $G_0 \cong G$.

Proof. We iteratively apply the construction of φ and ψ of Lemma 4 to obtain a chain

$$G_0 < G_1 < \cdots < G_\alpha < \cdots, \qquad (G_\alpha \cong G,\ \alpha < \omega_1)$$

as follows. Let $G_0 \cong G$. Having constructed the chain up to G_α we apply Lemma 4 letting $H = H(\alpha)$ and letting $\{G_\gamma \mid \gamma \leq \alpha\}$ be the collection $\{X_n\}$, thus obtaining embeddings $\varphi : G_\alpha \to G_\alpha$ and $\psi : H(\alpha) \to G_\alpha$ satisfying (1) and (2) of Lemma 4. We now extend G_α to $G_{\alpha+1}$ in such a way that the embeddings $\varphi(G_\alpha) < G_\alpha$ and $G_\alpha < G_{\alpha+1}$ are isomorphic, say by an isomorphism $f : G_\alpha \to G_{\alpha+1}$, and we identify $H(\alpha)$ with $f(\psi(H(\alpha)) < G_{\alpha+1}$. Thus, (1) and (2) become

(i) $G_\alpha \oplus H(\alpha)$ exists in $G_{\alpha+1}$ and

(ii) for all $\gamma \leq \alpha$, $C_{G_{\alpha+1}}(G_\gamma) = C_{G_\alpha}(G_\gamma) \oplus H(\alpha)$.

We impose continuity on the chain $\{G_\alpha\}$ at limit ordinals.

Property (ii) and induction give, for all $\alpha < \beta < \omega_1$, $C_{G_\beta}(G_\alpha) = \bigoplus\{H(\gamma) \mid \alpha \leq \gamma < \beta\}$. So, putting $G^* = \bigcup\{G_\alpha \mid \alpha < \omega_1\}$, we have $C_{G^*}(G_\alpha) = \bigoplus\{H(\gamma) \mid \alpha \leq \gamma < \omega_1\}$, and the first conclusion of the proposition is easily checked.

If the C.H. is assumed, then we can arrange that our lists $\{X_n^\alpha\}$, which we use to construct $G_{\alpha+1}$, form an increasing sequence, i.e., $\alpha < \beta$ implies $\{X_n^\alpha\} \subset \{X_n^\beta\}$, which eventually contains every subgroup $X \subset G^*$ such that $X \cong G$. The second conclusion of the proposition will then follow as above.

Proof of Theorem 2. We have much freedom to specify the groups $H(\alpha)$ in Proposition 2.

If S is any set of primes, let $H(S)$ be a rank 1 torsion-free abelian group such that, for all primes p and for all $1 \neq x \in H(S)$, x is infinitely divisible by p if and only if $p \in S$. Since the additive rationals are embeddable in every a.c. group, so are all the groups $H(S)$.

Let $\mathfrak{A}$ be a collection of infinite sets of primes such that $|\mathfrak{A}| = \omega_1$ and for all $S \neq T \in \mathfrak{A}$, $S \cap T$ is finite. Let $\mathcal{B}$ be a collection of subsets of $\mathfrak{A}$ such that every member of $\mathcal{B}$ is uncountable $|\mathcal{B}| = 2^{\omega_1}$ and for all $Q \neq R \in \mathcal{B}$, $Q \cap R$ is countable.

If $Q \in \mathcal{B}$, let $G^*(Q)$ be the group G^* of Proposition 2 obtained by putting $H(\alpha) = H(S_\alpha)$ where $\{S_\alpha \mid \alpha < \omega_1\}$ is some list of Q.

We define $\mathcal{U} = \{G^*(Q) \mid Q \in \mathcal{B}\}$.

Suppose $U \neq V \in \mathcal{U}$, say $U = G^*(Q)$ and $V = G^*(R)$ where $Q \neq R \in \mathcal{B}$. Let U_0 and V_0 be the subgroups G_0 of Proposition 2 of U and V respectively. Suppose $U_0 \subset B \subset U$ and $V_0 \subset D \subset V$ with D and B countable. By Proposition 2, we have

$$C_1 = C_U(B) \cong A_1 \times \Big(\prod_{\beta \leq \alpha < \omega_1} H(S_\alpha) \Big)$$

and

$$C_2 = C_V(D) \cong A_2 \times \Big(\prod_{\gamma \leq \alpha < \omega_1} H(T_\alpha) \Big)$$

where $Q = \{S_\alpha \mid \alpha < \omega_1\}$, $R = \{T_\alpha \mid \alpha < \omega_1\}$, $\beta, \gamma < \omega_1$, and A_1, A_2 are countable.

We must check that neither of these centralizers is embeddable in the other. Suppose $f: C_1 \to C_2$ were an embedding. Then, for all $\beta \leq \alpha < \omega_1$, $f(H(S_\alpha))$ can have non-trivial projection on $H(T_\delta)$, $\gamma \leq \delta < \omega_1$ only if $S_\alpha \subset T_\delta$; but, since $Q \cap R$ is countable, this is possible for at most countably many values of α, which forces $f(C_1)$ to lie in a countable subgroup of C_2, an impossibility.

If the C.H. is assumed, we use the second part of Proposition 2. Let $U \neq V$ be as above. We must show that U and V are non-embeddable. Suppose $f: U \to V$ were an embedding. Since $G_0 = f(U_0) \cong G$, Proposition 2 implies that

$$C_V(f(U_0)) \cong A_2 \times \Big(\prod_{\gamma \leq \alpha < \omega_1} H(T_\alpha) \Big).$$

But also,

$$C_{f(U)}(f(U_0)) \cong A_1 \times \Big(\prod_{\beta \leq \gamma < \omega} H(S_\alpha) \Big)$$

with the notation as before. Since the latter centralizer is contained in the former, we have a contradiction to the non-embeddability established above.

§3. Proof of Theorem 4 and Lemma 1

We will use the notation of Theorem 4 and we also define

$$H = \langle B_1, \dots, B_n \rangle \subset G, \ A = B_1 \cap \cdots \cap B_n,$$

$$\mathcal{K} = \mathcal{B}_1 * \cdots * \mathcal{B}_n,$$

and if $U \supset H$, then

$$\mathcal{N}_U = \langle N_U^{\mathcal{B}_i}(B_i) \mid 1 \leq i \leq n \rangle.$$

Lemma 5. *Assume the hypotheses of Theorem 4. There exists a group $J \supset H$ such that, for all $\alpha \in \mathcal{K}$, there exists $y \in \mathcal{N}_J$ such that $|y| = \infty$, $\langle y \rangle \cap H = 1$, $H \cap H^y = K$, and y induces α on K (by conjugation).*

Proof. Let J have the presentation $(H, t(i, \alpha)$ where $\alpha \in \mathcal{B}_i$ and $1 \leq i \leq n : W(H)$ and "$t(i, \alpha)$ induces α and B_i by conjugation").

J is a (multiple) HNN extension of H and we will use Britton's Lemma (B.L.).

Put $Q_i = \langle t(i, \alpha) \mid \alpha \in \mathcal{B}_i \rangle \subset J$ and $Q = \langle Q_i \mid 1 \leq i \leq n \rangle$. Note that $Q \subset \mathcal{N}_J$. Q is free on the generators $\{t(i, \alpha)\}$ and $Q \cap H = 1$ by B.L. Also,

$$K = \bigcap \{A^q \mid q \in Q\}. \tag{1}$$

Suppose $w = u_1 \cdots u_k$ is a product such that adjacent factors belong to different Q_i's. Using B.L. in J, we check easily that

$$\begin{cases} \text{for all } h \in H, \ h^w \in H \text{ iff } h^s \in H \text{ for all initial segments} \\ s = u_1 \cdots u_i \ (1 \leq i \leq k) \text{ of } w. \end{cases} \tag{2}$$

Suppose $\alpha \in \mathcal{K}$ is given as in the hypothesis. We will construct y as a product of a sequence of elements $\sigma_1, \dots, \sigma_{k+1}$ of Q to be determined inductively.

We define σ_1 as follows. Let $1 \neq q_i \in Q_i$, $1 \leq i \leq n$ and put $1_i = t(i, 1_{B_i})$. Define $s_1 = q_1$ and inductively $s_{i+1} = s_i 1_{i+1} s_i^{-1} q_{i+1}$, $1 \leq i \leq n$, and define $\sigma_1 = s_n$. We claim

$$H \cap H^{\sigma_1^{\mp 1}} \subset A. \tag{3}$$

To prove this, assume inductively

$$\text{if } h \in H - (B_1 \cap \cdots \cap B_i), \text{ then } h^{s_i} \notin H, \tag{4$_i$}$$

which is obvious if $i = 1$ from B.L. *Suppose*

$$(5) \qquad \begin{cases} h \in H - B_1 \cap \cdots \cap B_{i+1} \text{ and } h^{s_{i+1}} \in H; \text{ this implies } h \notin B_{i+1} \\ \text{or else } (4)_i \text{ is contradicted using (2).} \end{cases}$$

Thus, $h^{s_i} \in H$ by (2). If $h^{s_i} \notin B_{i+1}$, then $h^{s_i 1_{i+1}} \notin H$ by B.L. and hence $h^{s_{i+1}} \notin H$ by (2). So, we have $h^{s_i} \in B_{i+1}$ and hence $h^{s_i l_{i+1}} = h^{s_i}$, whence $h^{s_{i+1}} = h^{s_i s_i^{-1} q_{i+1}} \notin H$ contradicting (5) and proving $(4)_{i+1}$. Thus $(4)_n$ holds and this proves (3).

Suppose $\sigma_1, \ldots, \sigma_i$ have been selected such that the last letter of σ_j and the first of σ_{j+1}, $1 \leq j \leq i$, belong to distinct Q_k's. Put $\pi_i = \sigma_1 \cdots \sigma_i$. Note that

$$(6) \qquad L_i = H \cap H^{\pi_i^{-1}} \subset A \text{ by (3) and (2).}$$

Suppose there exists $a \in L_i - K$. Thus $a^{\pi_i} \notin K$ and by (1) there exists $q \in Q$ such that $a^{\pi_i q} \notin A$, and we can arrange that $a^{\pi_i q} \notin H$ (by replacing q by qr where $1 \neq r \in Q_j$ if $a^{\pi_i q} \in H - B_j$). Putting $\sigma_{i+1} = q$, we have $a \notin L_{i+1}$ (see (6)). So, by (6) and (2) we have

$$A \supset L_1 > \cdots > L_i > L_{i+1} > \cdots \supset K.$$

Since A has MIN, we must have for some k, $L_k = K$. Finally we choose $\sigma_{k+1} \in Q$ so that $y = \pi_k \sigma_{k+1}$ induces α on K (we can begin σ_{k+1} with some 1_i to prevent unwanted cancellation).

An *amalgam* $\mathcal{A} = {}^{B}\underset{A}{\smile}{}^{C}$ is the set-theoretic union of two groups, $\mathcal{A} = B \cup C$, which intersect in a common subgroup $A = B \cap C$. $\mathrm{gp}_*(\mathcal{A})$ is the free product of B and C with amalgamated subgroup A.

Lemma 6. *Suppose $K \subset H \subset J$, $y \in J$ with $y^2 \notin H$, y normalizes K, and $H \cap H^y = K$. Let $\mathcal{A} = {}^{\bar{J}}\underset{H}{\smile}{}^{J}$ be a symmetric amalgam ($- : J \to \bar{J}$ is an isomorphism which fixes H elementwise). Put $\mathfrak{A} = \mathrm{gp}_*(\mathcal{A})$.*

(i) *There exists $t \in \mathcal{N}_{\mathfrak{A}}$ such that $|t| = \infty$, t normalizes K, $\langle t \rangle \cap H = 1$, and*

$$\mathcal{A}' = {}^{\langle t \rangle K}\underset{K}{\smile}{}^{J} \qquad \textit{generates } \mathrm{gp}_*(\mathcal{A}')$$

in $\mathfrak{A}$, and

(ii) *Suppose $\mathcal{K} \subset \mathrm{Aut}(K)$, y induces a $\mathcal{K}$-automorphism on K and for all $\alpha \in \mathcal{K}$, there exists $y_\alpha \in J - H$ which induces α on K. Then, t can be chosen in (i) so that it induces any $\alpha \in \mathcal{K}$ on K.*

Proof. To prove (ii), put $t = \bar{y} y \bar{y}_\beta y \bar{y}^{-1}$ where $\beta \in \mathcal{K}$ is chosen so that t will induce α on K. (To prove (i) we would use $\bar{y}$ in place of $\bar{y}_\beta$.)

Clearly $|t| = \infty$ since $y^2 \notin H$ and $\langle t \rangle \cap H = 1$. We have $\langle t \rangle K \cap J = K$ because every $z = t^i k \in t^i K$ with $i \neq 0$ involves $\bar{y}$ implying $z \notin J$. Hence the amalgam $\mathscr{A}'$ does exist in $\mathrm{gp}_*(\mathscr{A})$.

Let $w = p_0(t^{i_1}k_1)p_1(t^{i_2}k_2)p_2 \cdots (t^{i_n}k_n)p_n$ where $p_j \in J - K$, $i_j \neq 0$, and $k_j \in K$, $1 \leqslant k \leqslant n$ (and possibly p_0 or p_n do not occur) be a reduced product of members of $\mathscr{A}'$. We must show that if $n \geqslant 1$ (i.e., some t occurs), then $w \neq 1$ in $\mathfrak{A}$.

This will be so provided not too much reduction in $\mathfrak{A}$ occurs in segments of the form

$$t^{i_j}k_j p_j t^{i_{j+1}}.$$

To check this we can ignore $k_j \in K$ by consolidating it with p_j and consider subsegments of the possible forms

$$tpt,\ tpt^{-1},\ t^{-1}pt, \quad \text{and} \quad t^{-1}pt^{-1}.$$

All cases being similar, we consider only the first. We have

$$tpt = \bar{y}y\bar{y}_\beta y\bar{y}^{-1}p\bar{y}y\bar{y}_\beta y\bar{y}^{-1}.$$

If $p \in J - H$, this segment is already an $\mathscr{A}$-reduced product. If $p \in H - K$, then $u = \bar{y}^{-1}p\bar{y} \in \bar{J} - H$ since by hypothesis $H \cap H^{\bar{y}^{-1}} = K$; and, making the replacement $u = \bar{y}^{-1}p\bar{y}$ in tpt yields an $\mathscr{A}$-reduced product.

Thus, the middle letter of every t occurring in w survives in the $\mathscr{A}$-reduced form of w, which implies $w \neq 1$ in $\mathfrak{A}$ and finishes the proof of Lemma 6.

Lemma 7. *Suppose $K \subset B \subset G$ where G is a.c. and B is f.g. If $\mathscr{K} \subset \mathrm{Aut}(K)$, then $N_G^{\mathscr{K}}(K)$ is generated by elements of infinite order.*

Proof. Suppose $x \in N_G^{\mathscr{K}}(K)$. Since B is f.g., there exists $c \in G$ with $|c| = \infty$ such that $\langle c \rangle \oplus \langle x, B \rangle$ exists in G (e.g., by Lemma 3). Now x and $c + x$ induce the same automorphism on K and $c + x$ has infinite order; so we only need to show that $C_G(K)$ is generated by elements of infinite order.

Suppose $x \in C_G(K)$. With c as above, we have c and $c + x$ centralize K, have infinite order, and generate x, so we are done.

Lemma 8. *Suppose $\mathscr{A} = {}^{Q}\underset{P}{\smile}{}^{R}$, $M \subset Q$, and $\mathscr{A}_1 = {}^{M}\underset{M \cap P}{\smile}{}^{P}$ generates $\mathrm{gp}_*(\mathscr{A}_1)$ in Q. Then, $\mathscr{A}_2 = {}^{M}\underset{M \cap P}{\smile}{}^{R}$ generates $\mathrm{gp}_*(\mathscr{A}_2)$ in $\mathrm{gp}_*(\mathscr{A})$.*

Proof. A reduced product in $\mathrm{gp}_*(\mathscr{A}_2)$ can be written as $\pi_1 r_1 \cdots \pi_n r_n$ where $r_i \in R - P$ and each π_i is a reduced product in $\mathrm{gp}_*(\mathscr{A}_1)$ (with

π_1, r_n optional). We have $\pi_i \notin P$ for all i, otherwise the product is not reduced. Hence, this equals a reduced product in $\mathrm{gp}_*(\mathscr{A})$.

Proof of Theorem 4. We will use the notation of Lemma 5.

By Lemma 7, $N_G^{\mathscr{K}}(K)$ is generated by elements of infinite order. Let x be such an element. We must show that $x \in \mathscr{N}_G$.

Let $F = \langle \alpha_1, \alpha_2, \alpha_3 \rangle$ be free on $\{\alpha_1, \alpha_2, \alpha_3\}$ and let FK be the semi-direct product such that α_2 and x induce on K the same automorphism and α_1, α_3 centralize K. Put

$$\mathscr{A} = \underset{\langle x \rangle K}{FK \smile \langle x, H \rangle}$$

with $x = \alpha_1 \alpha_2 \alpha_3$.

First, we claim

$$(*) \qquad \begin{cases} \text{the amalgams } \mathscr{A}_i = \underset{K}{\langle \alpha_i \rangle K \smile \langle x, H \rangle} \quad (i = 1, 2, 3) \\ \text{generate } \mathrm{gp}_*(\mathscr{A}_i) \text{ in } \mathrm{gp}_*(\mathscr{A}). \end{cases}$$

To prove this, use Lemma 8 with $M = \langle \alpha_i \rangle K$. Since $\langle \alpha_i \rangle K \cap \langle x \rangle K = K$ in FK, we must show that

$$\mathscr{A}'_i = \underset{K}{\langle \alpha_i \rangle K \smile \langle x \rangle K}$$

generates $\mathrm{gp}_*(\mathscr{A}'_i)$ in FK. Since K is normal, this is so iff α_i and x generate $\langle \alpha_i \rangle * \langle x \rangle$ in F, which is easily checked.

Second, we claim

$$(**) \qquad \begin{cases} \text{there is a group } P \supset \mathrm{gp}_*(\mathscr{A}) \text{ such that } \alpha_i \in \mathscr{N}_P \ (i = 1, 2, 3) \\ \text{and hence } x \in \mathscr{N}_P. \end{cases}$$

To obtain P we first use Lemma 5 to get $J \supset H$ and $y \in \mathscr{N}_J$ such that $|y| = \infty$, $\langle y \rangle \cap H = 1$, $H \cap H^y = K$, and $y = y_\alpha$ can be chosen to induce any $\alpha \in \mathscr{K}$ on K. Now apply Lemma 6 to obtain

$$t_i \in \mathrm{gp}_* \left(\underset{H}{\bar{J} \smile J} \right) = J_i$$

such that $|t_i| = \infty$, $\langle t_i \rangle \cap H = 1$, t_i and α_i induce the same automorphism on K, $t_i \in \mathscr{N}_{J_i}$, and $\underset{K}{\langle t_i \rangle K \smile J}$ generates its free product in J_i. Thus, $\underset{K}{\langle t_i \rangle K \smile H}$ generates its free product in J_i, which is, by (*), isomorphic to the subgroup of $\mathrm{gp}_*(\mathscr{A})$ generated by $\underset{K}{\langle \alpha_i \rangle K \smile H}$ under the map $H \equiv H$ and $t_i \leftrightarrow \alpha_i$. So, we can amalgamate $\mathrm{gp}_*(\mathscr{A})$ with the J_i via these isomorphisms to obtain $P = \langle J_1, J_2, J_3 \rangle \supset \mathrm{gp}_*(\mathscr{A}) = \langle H, F \rangle$.

Finally, by making direct use of the algebraic closedness of G and the existence of P in (**), we can obtain $\bar{P}$ with $\langle H, x\rangle \subset \bar{P} \subset G$ such that $x \in \mathcal{N}_{\bar{P}} \subset \mathcal{N}_G$, as required. To obtain $\bar{P}$, use (**) to express $x = z_1 \cdots z_\varepsilon$ where $z_i \in N_P^{\mathscr{B}_{n(i)}}(B_{n(i)})$. So, the relations $\{x = \bar{z}_1 \cdots \bar{z}_\varepsilon$ and "$\bar{z}_i$ induces the same automorphism on $B_{n(i)}$ as does z_i" $(1 \leq i \leq \varepsilon)\}$ (which can be taken to be a finite set because each B_i is f.g.) are consistent over $\langle H, x\rangle$. So, there are elements $\bar{z}_1, \ldots, \bar{z}_\varepsilon \in G$ which satisfy them and we take

$$\bar{P} = \langle H, x, \bar{z}_1, \ldots, \bar{z}_\varepsilon \rangle.$$

Proof of Lemma 1. In the case of centralizers, in the proof of Theorem 4, we have $\mathscr{B}_i = 1$ $(1 \leq i \leq n)$, $\mathscr{K} = 1$, and hence $K = B_1 \cap \cdots \cap B_n$ and the hypothesis of MIN is not needed in the proof of Lemma 5 in this case, and we obtain Lemma 1.

§4. Proof of Theorem 5

In the notation of Theorem 5, suppose $x \in N_G(A) - A$. Put $C = C_G(A)$.

In the group with presentation $(A, x, \alpha : \alpha$ centralizes $A)$ let $\bar{z} = \alpha^{-1}x\alpha^2x^{-1}\alpha^{-1}$. Then $|\bar{z}| = \infty$, $\bar{z} \in x^{\langle\alpha\rangle}$, and $\langle\bar{z}\rangle \oplus A$ exists. Since G is a.c., there exists $z \in G$ such that $|z| = \infty$, $z \in x^C$, and $\langle z\rangle \oplus A$ exists in G.

We will show that

$$(*) \qquad \begin{cases} C \text{ is generated by elements } w \text{ such that } |w| = \infty \text{ and} \\ (\langle z\rangle * \langle w\rangle) \oplus A \text{ exists in } G. \end{cases}$$

First note that C is generated by elements c such that $|c| = \infty$, $\langle c\rangle \oplus A$ exists in G, $\langle z\rangle \cap \langle A, c\rangle = 1$. To see this, let $u \in C$ and choose v so that $|v| = \infty$, and $\langle v\rangle \oplus \langle A, z, u\rangle$ exists in G. The elements v and $v + u$ satisfy the requirements on c above and generate u. To prove (*), let c be a generator of C mentioned above, let $F = \langle \bar{\alpha}, \bar{\beta}\rangle$ be a free group, and put

$$J = \mathrm{gp}_* \left(\begin{array}{ccc} F \oplus A & & \langle A, c, z\rangle \\ & \searrow \quad \swarrow & \\ & \langle c = \bar{\alpha}\bar{\beta}\rangle \oplus A & \end{array} \right)$$

Since $\langle\bar{\alpha}\rangle$, $\langle\bar{\beta}\rangle$, and $\langle z\rangle$ all intersect the amalgamated subgroup trivially, we see that $\langle\bar{\alpha}\rangle * \langle z\rangle \oplus A$ and $\langle\bar{\beta}\rangle * \langle z\rangle \oplus A$ exist in J. Since G is a.c., there exist $\alpha, \beta \in G$ such that $c = \alpha\beta$ and $(\langle\alpha\rangle * \langle z\rangle) \oplus A$ and $(\langle\beta\rangle * \langle z\rangle) \oplus A$ exist in G (because these groups are embeddable in

G). This proves (*) by taking α and β as values of w, thus generating c and hence all of C.

Now, for every $w \in C$ satisfying (*), there exists $\tau \in C$ such that $\tau^{-1}z\tau = w$, $|\tau| = 2$, and $\tau \in C$. Thus C is generated by elements of the form $z^{\tau} \in x^{C}$. This concludes the proof.

§5. Proof of Theorem 6

We shall deduce Theorem 6 from the following result due essentially to Belegradek [1] who proves it for recursively presented groups.

Proposition 3. *Suppose A and B are f.g. groups with generating sets X and Y. Let $\langle X\rangle$ and $\langle Y\rangle$ be the free groups on X and Y. B is embeddable in every a.c. group which contains A iff $W(B) \leqslant_{e} W(A)$ and there is a function $\mathcal{F} \leqslant_{e} W(A)$ whose domain is $\langle Y\rangle$ and whose range consists of certain sequences in $\langle X\rangle$ (which we denote $\mathcal{F}(y) = (x_y^1, \ldots, x_y^n, \ldots)$) such that, for all $y \in \langle Y\rangle$, $y \in W(B)$ iff $x_y^n \in W(A)$ for all $n \geqslant 1$.*

By $\mathcal{F} \leqslant_{e} W(A)$ we mean that the set of pairs $\{(y, x_y^n) \mid y \in \langle Y\rangle,\ n \geqslant 1\}$ is enumeration reducible to $W(A)$.

The "if" part of Proposition 3 — which we will use — is proved in a manner similar to the proof of B.H. Neumann that every group with a solvable word problem can be embedded into every a.c. group [2: Chapter IV, §8] and the method can also be gleaned from Belegradek's proof for r.p. A and B; but one must use the General Higman Embedding Theorem (§1).

Let us assume the hypothesis of Theorem 6. We can also assume that $A, B \subset F$ and hence that $W(B) \leqslant_{e} W(F)$ as well as $W^{-}(B) \leqslant_{e} W(F)$ because of obvious properties of enumeration reducibility. Let X, P, and Q be finite generating sets of F, A, and B respectively and put $Y = P \cup Q$. So, Y generates $A \operatorname{wr} B$. Since $A, B \subset F$, we can assume $Y \subset X$.

Using Proposition 3 we need only find a function $\mathcal{F} \leqslant_{e} W(F)$ whose domain is $\langle Y\rangle$ and such that, for all $y \in \langle Y\rangle$, $\mathcal{F}(y) = (x_y^1, \ldots, x_y^{m(y)})$ (with $x_y^i \in \langle X\rangle$) and $y \in W(A \operatorname{wr} B)$ iff $x_y^i \in W(F)$ for all $1 \leqslant i \leqslant m(y)$. We will now describe an algorithm for computing $\mathcal{F}$ given an enumeration of $W(F)$.

Suppose $y \in \langle Y\rangle$. Using the fact that $A \operatorname{wr} B = A^{B}B$ is a semidirect product we can collect P's and Q's in y to obtain

$$y = p_1^{w_1} \cdots p_n^{w_n} w \quad \text{where} \quad p_i \in P;\ w, w_i \in \langle Q \rangle.$$

As we enumerate $W(F)$ we can also enumerate $W(B)$ and $W^-(B)$ since these sets are $\leq_e W(F)$. Thus, w will be enumerated either in $W(B)$ or in $W^-(B)$ in finitely many steps. In the latter case, we have $y \notin W(A \operatorname{wr} B)$ and we put $\mathcal{F}(y) = (w)$. In the former case, we likewise determine for all $1 \leq i, j \leq n$ that either $w_i w_j^{-1} \in W(B)$ or $\in W^-(B)$ in finitely many steps. In $A \operatorname{wr} B$, $p_i^{w_i}$ and $p_j^{w_j}$ will commute provided $w_i \neq w_j$. So, the above information allows us to rearrange y as follows:

$$y = p_1^{w_1} \cdots p_n^{w_n} = u_1^{v_1} \cdots u_m^{v_m}$$

where $u_i \in \langle P \rangle$, $v_i \in \langle Q \rangle$, and, if $1 \leq i \neq j \leq m$, then

$v_i \neq v_j$ (each v_i is one of the original w_j).

Since the factors $u_i^{v_i}$, $1 \leq i \leq m$, belong to distinct direct factors of A^B in $A \operatorname{wr} B$, we have $y \in W(A \operatorname{wr} B)$ if and only if $\{u_1, \ldots, u_m\} \subset W(A)$, so we put $\mathcal{F}(y) = (u_1, \ldots, u_m)$.

Note added in proof

The paper "Maximal subgroups of a.c. groups" mentioned in §0 has been submtted for publication. Theorem 3 is generalized in it to effectively embedded subgroups, and applied to study properties of Ziegler's construction [5].

References

[1] O.V. Belegradek, On algebraically closed groups, Algebra and Logic 13 (1974) 135–143.
[2] R. Lyndon and P. Schupp, Combinatorial group theory (Springer-Verlag, 1977).
[3] A. Macintyre, On algebraically closed groups, Annals of Mathematics 96 (1972) 53–97.
[4] H. Rogers, Theory of recursive functions and effective computability (McGraw Hill, 1967).
[5] S. Shelah and M. Ziegler, Algebraically closed groups of large cardinality, to appear.
[6] M. Ziegler, Algebraisch abgeschlossene Gruppen, to appear.

S.I. Adian, W.W. Boone, G. Higman, eds., Word Problems II

SMALL CANCELLATION THEORY OVER GROUPS EQUIPPED WITH AN INTEGER-VALUED LENGTH FUNCTION

Bernard M. HURLEY
University of Zambia, Lusaka, Zambia

§1. Introduction

In this paper, small cancellation theory is developed over a class of groups equipped with an integer-valued length function satisfying certain "natural" axioms. Such groups can also be characterised by the fact that they are equipped with a normal form (for elements) satisfying certain other axioms. Since free groups, free products with amalgamation, and HNN groups all possess a normal form of the required type, our theory includes the "classical" small cancellation theories of Lyndon [13], Schupp [19] and Sacerdote and Schupp [18] over the above mentioned classes of groups. However, the class of groups that we shall consider (we call them NFS groups) is much wider than this and is closed under a fairly large number of constructions, as will be shown in §3.

As with the "classical" theories, there are three "cases" of our theory. The observant reader will notice that we only apply one of the "cases" in §8, whereas we develop the theory of all three in §5. We make no apology for this. We consider the mathematics of §5 to be interesting mathematics in itself.

The applications of §8 have been selected according to two criteria. The first being that the result in question can be proved without too much extra work. The second being that the result is of interest. The applications include various embedding theorems, a characterization of the solubility of the word problem for groups, and proofs of the residual infinite simplicity and the infinite height (in the sense of Pride [16]) of various groups. It is obvious, from the results of §3 and §7, that many of the theorems of §8 could be followed by a corollary, giving a vast list of groups satisfying the theorem (e.g. we could follow Theorem 8.10 with a corollary to the effect that non-abelian free groups, certain HNN groups, etc... are residually infinite simple). Many writers would do this, but we do not see the neccessity for it.

Many interesting applications have been left out of §8, in view of their failure to satisfy our first criterion. Perhaps the most interesting being the use of the theory to prove a version of Higman's Embedding Theorem. In §9 we have given a list of such applications. These, perhaps, should be regarded as "signposts" to things to come. Of course, whether or not one needs signposts depends on who one is. (Anglo-Romany has no word for signpost.)

To the reader unfamiliar with small cancellation theory, we recommend Schupp [20] for an incomplete, but clear, introduction to the "classical" theories. Having read this paper, he/she may be surprised that we do not impose any length restrictions in our C-conditions. Our use of special sequences, in §5, makes this unneccessary.

We have tried to strike a balance between formality and informality. If the reader finds the construction of the diagram, in §5, too informal, he/she should bear in mind that, written out formally, it would involve a four-fold induction.

Notation:

We believe that most of our undefined notation is standard. However, we draw to the reader's attention that, according to context,

$$\square = \begin{cases} \text{proof ends here,} \\ \text{proof omitted,} \\ \text{proof to occur later in text.} \end{cases}$$

It is natural to think of elements of a group that possesses one of our axiomatic normal form structures as "words", by analogy with the words of a free group. We shall often use the word "word" in this loose sense. When we use it in the "strict" sense of a reduced word on a set S of letters, we shall speak of a "word on S", unless the context makes it obvious what we mean.

§2. NFS groups, $\overline{\text{NFS}}$ groups and length functions

In general terms a length function on a group G is a function $G \to \mathbf{R}$, $g \mapsto |g|$ satisfying a "reasonable" set of axioms. Length functions on groups were first studied axiomatically by Lyndon [12]. He imposed five axioms, of which the following two seem to capture the "essence" of the notion of a length function. (The numbering is Lyndon's.):

A2. $|x^{-1}| = |x|$,

A4. $d(x, y) < d(x, z)$ implies $d(y, z) = d(x, y)$,

where $d(x, y) = \frac{1}{2}\{|x| + |y| - |xy^{-1}|\}$. Chiswell [4] and Hoare [8] have studied length functions satisfying these two axioms. A length function is normalised if it satisfies:

A1′. $|1| = 0$.

If $g \mapsto |g|$ is a length function $G \to \mathbf{R}$ satisfying **A2** and **A4**, then the function $g \mapsto \|g\|$, defined by $\|g\| = |g| - 1$, is a normalised length function that still satisfies **A2** and **A4** (see the comment after [8] Proposition 5). Thus there is no loss of generality in considering only normalised length functions.

Geometric small cancellation theory was first developed by Lyndon [13] over free groups and free products. Later Schupp [19] developed the theory over free products with amalgamation, and Sacerdote and Schupp [18] developed it over HNN groups. It is a striking fact that in every case the group under investigation possesses a "natural" length function satisfying **A1′**, **A2** and **A4**. Moreover this length function is always well-based in the sense of Hurley [10]. That is, in addition, it is integer-valued and satisfies the extra axiom:

N1*. $G = \mathrm{gp}\{x \in G : |x| \leq 1\}$.

Intuitively, the function $d(x, y)$ measures the amount of cancellation in the product xy^{-1}. Thus, for instance, we say that *no cancellation occurs* in this product if $d(x, y) = 0$, and that *almost no cancellation occurs* if $d(x, y) \leq 1$. However in order to develop a small cancellation theory we need to do more than merely give a numerical value to the cancellation in a product, and, in each of the above mentioned cases, a central role is played by the appropriate Normal Form Theorem, whereas the length function only appears as a way of simplifying some of the "small cancellation" hypotheses.

Abstract normal form structures (NF structures) on groups were first studied by Hurley [9], however we shall use the axiomatisation of Hurley [10]. We can associate a length function in a natural way with each NF structure on a group. This leads us to the Main Theorem of [10].

Theorem 1.1. *A function $G \to \mathbf{Z}$, $g \mapsto |g|$ on a group is a well-based length function (i.e. it satisfies* **N1***, **A1′**, **A2** *and* **A4**) *if and only if it is the associated length function of some* NF *structure on G.* □

We shall now briefly explain our axiomatisation of the normal form. First we need some definitions in which we shall suppose G is a fixed group, X is a fixed subset of G, satisfying $1 \notin X$, and B is a fixed subgroup of G called the *base group.*

Definition. Let $\boldsymbol{S} = \boldsymbol{S}(G, B, X)$ be the set of all sequences $\sigma = (\sigma_i)_{i=1}^{2n+1}$, where $n \geq 0$, such that $\sigma_{2j+1} \in B$, for $j = 0, \ldots, n$, and $\sigma_{2j} \in X \cup X^{-1}$, for $j = 1, \ldots, n$. We call n the *length* of such a sequence, and denote it by $|\sigma|$. We define the *value* of the sequence to be $\bar{\sigma} = \sigma_1\sigma_2 \cdots \sigma_n$.

If $\sigma = (\sigma_i) \in \boldsymbol{S}$ and for some $1 \leq j \leq n-1$, $\sigma_{2j}\sigma_{2j+1}\sigma_{2j+2} \in B$, then the sequence τ of length $n-2$ defined by:

$$\tau_i = \begin{cases} \sigma_i & \text{if } 1 \leq i \leq 2j-2 \\ \sigma_{2j-1}\sigma_{2j}\sigma_{2j+1}\sigma_{2j+2}\sigma_{2j+3} & \text{if } i = 2j-1 \\ \sigma_{i+4} & \text{if } 2j \leq i \leq 2n-4, \end{cases}$$

clearly lies in $\boldsymbol{S}$ and satisfies $\bar{\tau} = \bar{\sigma}$. We say that τ is obtained from σ by means of a *pinch* between σ_{2j} and σ_{2j+2}.

If $\sigma = (\sigma_i) \in \boldsymbol{S}$ and for some $1 \leq j \leq n$, $\sigma_{2j}\sigma_{2j+1}\sigma_{2j+2} \in B(X \cup X^{-1})B$, then $\sigma_{2j}\sigma_{2j+1}\sigma_{2j+2} = bgc$ for some $g \in X \cup X^{-1}$ and some $b, c \in B$ and the sequence μ of length $n-1$ defined by:

$$\mu_i = \begin{cases} \sigma_i & \text{if } 1 \leq i \leq 2j-2 \\ \sigma_{2j-1}b & \text{if } i = 2j-1 \\ g & \text{if } i = 2j \\ c\sigma_{2j+3} & \text{if } i = 2j+1 \\ \sigma_{i+2} & \text{if } 2j+2 \leq i \leq 2n-2, \end{cases}$$

clearly lies in $\boldsymbol{S}$ and satisfies $\bar{\mu} = \bar{\sigma}$. We say that μ is obtained from σ by means of an *amalgamation* between σ_{2j} and σ_{2j+2}.

A (G, B, X)-sequence σ is *reduced* if no pinch or amalgamation can be performed between any two elements of σ. The set of all such sequences shall be denoted by $\boldsymbol{RS}(G, B, X)$ or just $\boldsymbol{RS}$. Intuitively, $\boldsymbol{RS}$ consists of normal forms for elements of G. If $\sigma \in \boldsymbol{RS}$ and $g = \bar{\sigma}$, then we say that σ *represents* g. Clearly if $\sigma \in \boldsymbol{S}$ then there exists $\tau \in \boldsymbol{RS}$ such that $\bar{\tau} = \bar{\sigma}$. It follows that to ensure that every element $g \in G$ has a normal form (i.e. that every element of G is represented by some member of $\boldsymbol{RS}$), we need merely impose the axiom:

N1. $G = \text{gp}(X, B)$.

We say that $\sigma, \tau \in \boldsymbol{S}$ are parallel, written $\sigma \parallel \tau$, if, either $|\sigma| = |\tau| = 0$ and $\bar{\sigma} = \bar{\tau}$, or $|\sigma| = |\tau| = n > 0$ and there exist $h_i \in B$ for $i = 1, 2, \ldots,, 2n$ such that $\sigma_1 = \tau_1 h_1$, $\sigma_i = h_{i-1}^{-1}\tau_i h_i$ for $2 \leq i \leq 2n$, and

$\sigma_{2n+1} = h_{2n}^{-1}\tau_{2n+1}$. It is easy to see that if $\sigma \parallel \tau$ then $\bar{\sigma} = \bar{\tau}$. The right sort of uniqueness for normal forms turns out to be uniqueness "up to parallelism". This can be obtained by imposing the axiom:

N2. If $\sigma, \tau \in \boldsymbol{RS}(G, B, X)$ and $\bar{\sigma} = \bar{\tau}$, then $\sigma \parallel \tau$.

Definition. A triple (G, B, X), consisting of a group G, a subgroup B, and a subset X, satisfying $1 \notin X$, that satisfies axioms **N1** and **N2** is called an *NFS group* (NFS = normal form structure). Alternatively we say (G, B, X) is an *NF structure* on G.

Given an NFS group (G, B, X), we define the associated length function in the "obvious" way. It easily follows from **N1** and **N2** that any two normal forms for (i.e. sequences in $\boldsymbol{RS}$ representing) an element $g \in G$ have the same length, and so we define $|g| = |\sigma|$ where σ is such a normal form.

An obvious question to ask is "Can distinct NF structures on a group G give rise to the same length function?". The answer is "Yes". Following [10], we call such structures isometric. If (G, B, X) is an NFS group, then it is trivial to check that (G, B, X_1). where $X_1 = B(X \cup X^{-1})B$, is also an NFS group and that these structures are isometric. Clearly these structures are the same if and only if (G, B, X) satisfies:

F. $X = B(X \cup X^{-1})$.

An NFS group satisfying **F** shall be called a *full NFS group* or an $\overline{\text{NFS}}$ *group*, and, correspondingly, we speak of *full NF structures* or $\overline{\text{NF}}$ *structures*. We easily see that $X_1 = \{x \in G : |x| = 1\}$, and it follows that (G, B, X_1) is always full. Moreover, by [10] lemma 2.3, this is the unique $\overline{\text{NFS}}$ group isometric to (G, B, X). Thus **F** is a sort of normalisation axiom. We shall work entirely with $\overline{\text{NFS}}$ groups; by the usual abuse of language we shall speak of the $\overline{\text{NFS}}$ group G. The reader who wishes to reformulate our results in terms of NFS groups will find it a routine, if somewhat messy, matter. It is easy to see that any $\sigma \in \boldsymbol{RS}$, in an $\overline{\text{NFS}}$ group, is parallel to one of the form $(1, x_1, 1, x_2, \ldots, x_n, 1)$ if $n \geq 1$, and is equal to one of the form (h) if $n = 0$. If σ has value $g \in G$, then we say that, according to case, $g = x_1x_2 \cdots x_n$ or $g = h$, *in normal form*, and we abbreviate the sequence to $(x_1, x_2, \ldots, x_n)$ or (h).

Finally, we note that there are alternative axiomatisations of the NFS groups. Consider the following set of axioms:

N3. If $\sigma \in \boldsymbol{RS}$ and $\bar{\sigma} = 1$, then $\sigma = (1)$.

N3*. If $\sigma \in \boldsymbol{S}$ and $\bar{\sigma} = 1$, then either $\sigma = (1)$ or there exists $\tau \in \boldsymbol{S} - \boldsymbol{RS}$ such that $\sigma \parallel \tau$.

N4. If $g, h, gh \in X_1$ but $hk \notin B \cup X_1$, then $ghk \notin \boldsymbol{B} \cup \boldsymbol{X}_1$.

N4*. If $g, h, hk \in X_1$ but $gh \notin B \cup X_1$, then $ghk \notin B \cup X_1$,

where, as before, $X_1 = B(X \cup X^{-1})B$, and so, when **F** is in force, we may drop the suffix 1 in **N4** and **N4***. By [10] Lemma 2.2, **N3** ⇔ **N3***, **N4** ⇔ **N4*** and **N2** ⇔ **N3** & **N4**, giving us various axiomatisations of the NFS groups.

§3. Examples of $\overline{\text{NFS}}$ groups

The purpose of this section is to provide examples of $\overline{\text{NFS}}$ groups. It is to be hoped that these examples will help motivate the remainder of the paper. We shall also show that, together with the appropriate homomorphisms, the $\overline{\text{NFS}}$ groups form a category $\mathcal{NFS}$, in which constructions analogous to free product, free product with amalgamation and HNN extension are possible.

We first show that certain familiar constructions yield $\overline{\text{NFS}}$ groups.

Lemma 3.1. *In the following cases, (G, B, X) is an $\overline{NFS}$ group:*

(i) *G is any group, B is any subgroup of G and $X = G - B$.*

(ii) *G is the free group freely generated by the set Y, $B = 1$ and $X = Y \cup Y^{-1}$.*

(iii) *$G = \langle H * K : B_1 = B_2\rangle$, a free product with amalgamation, $B = B_1$ and $X = (H - B) \cup (K - B)$.*

(iv) *$G = \langle t, B : t^{-1}At = C\rangle$ an HNN extension, and $X = B\{t, t^{-1}\}B$.*

Note on Proof. We feel that the proof of this result may safely be left to the reader. The following remarks may be useful. Parts (ii), (iii) and (iv) are restatements of well known normal form theorems (Britton's Lemma, see [3], in part (iv)). However an alternative way of proving the lemma would be to note that the natural length function satisfies **N1***, **A1′**, **A2** and **A4**, in each case, and then to apply Theorem 1.1. □

Definition. If (G_1, B_1, X_1) and (G_2, B_2, X_2) are $\overline{\text{NFS}}$ groups, then by an *$\overline{NFS}$ homomorphism* $\varphi : (G_1, B_1, X_1) \to (G_2, B_2, X_2)$, we mean a group homomorphism $\varphi : G_1 \to G_2$ satisfying $B_1 = \varphi^{-1}(B_2)$ and $X_1 = \varphi^{-1}(X_2)$.

Our next result, whose proof is routine and therefore omitted, sums up the more trivial properties of $\overline{\text{NFS}}$ homomorphisms.

Lemma 3.2. (i) *The NFS groups together with the NFS homomorphisms form a category, composition being composition of mappings.*

(ii) *Let* (G_2, B_2, X_2) *be an NFS group and let* $\varphi : G_1 \to G_2$ *be a (group) homomorphism. Let* $B_1 = \varphi^{-1}(B_2)$ *and* $X_1 = \varphi^{-1}(X_2)$. *Then* (G_1, B_1, X_1) *is an NFS group if and only if* $G_1 = \mathrm{gp}(X_1, B_1)$. *When this is the case,* φ *is an NFS homomorphism.*

(iii) *Let* (G_1, B_1, X_1) *and* (G_2, B_2, X_2) *be NFS groups. Then a homomorphism* $\varphi : G_1 \to G_2$ *is an NFS homomorphism if and only if* $|g\varphi| = |g|$ *for all* $g \in G$ *(i.e. if and only if* φ *is length preserving).*

(iv) *Let* (G_1, B_1, X_1) *be an NFS group and let* $\varphi : G_1 \to G_2$ *be a (group) epimorphism. Let* $B_2 = \varphi(B_1)$ *and* $X_2 = \varphi(X_1)$. *Then* (G_2, B_2, X_2) *is an NFS group if and only if* $\ker(\varphi) \leqslant B_1$. *In this case* φ *is an NFS homomorphism.* □

Problem 1. Let (G_1, B_1, X_1) be an NFS group and let $\varphi : G_1 \to G_2$ be a (group) homomorphism that is *not* an epimorphism. Under what conditions is it possible to construct an NFS structure on G_2 that makes φ an NFS homomorphism? A necessary condition is $\ker(\varphi) \leqslant B_1$.

Notation. We denote the category of NFS groups and NFS homomorphisms by $\mathcal{NFS}$. We often use the suffix **N** to indicate that we are working in this category. Thus, for example, to indicate that two NFS groups are isomorphic in $\mathcal{NFS}$, we often write $G_1 \cong_{\mathbf{N}} G_2$ instead of $(G_1, B_1, X_1) \cong (G_2, B_2, X_2)$.

Definition. Suppose (G_1, B_1, X_1) and (G_2, B_2, X_2) are NFS groups and $G_1 \leqslant G_2$. Then we say G_1 is a *sub-NFS-group* (a *subgroup*$_{\mathbf{N}}$) of G_2, and write $(G_1, B_1, X_1) \leqslant (G_2, B_2, X_2)$ (or $G_1 \leqslant_{\mathbf{N}} G_2$), if the natural injection $G_1 \to G_2$ is an NFS homomorphism (i.e. if $B_1 = G_1 \cap B_2$ and $X_1 = G_1 \cap X_2$ or, by Lemma 3.2(ii), if the length function on G_2 extends that on G_1). This relation is clearly transitive.

Warning. $\leqslant_{\mathbf{N}}$ is not the same relation as $\preccurlyeq$ of (10).

We now come to the free product in $\mathcal{NFS}$. It is easy to see that this is a co-product in the category theoretic sense.

Lemma 3.3 (Free product for NFS groups). *Let* (G_1, B_1, X_1) *and* (G_2, B_2, X_2) *be NFS groups. Let* $G = G_1 * G_2$, $B = B_1 * B_2 \leqslant G$ *and* $X = B(X_1 \cup X_2)B$, *then* (G, B, X) *is an NFS group. Moreover* $G_i \leqslant_{\mathbf{N}} G$ *for* $i = 1, 2$.

Proof. In this proof we deal with four $\overline{\text{NFS}}$ groups: (G_i, B_i, X_i) for $i = 1, 2$, (G, B, X) and G equipped with the free product (f.p.) $\overline{\text{NF}}$ structure. We shall use $|y|$ to denote either of the G_i length functions (note that these functions agree on $G_1 \cap G_2 = 1$, and so no ambiguity arises from this), and we put $D(x, y) = \frac{1}{2}\{|x| + |y| - |xy^{-1}|\}$. We denote the f.p. length function by $|x|_0$, and we put

$$D_0(x, y) = \tfrac{1}{2}\{|x|_0 + |y|_0 - |xy^{-1}|_0\}.$$

For all $g \in G$ define:

$$\|g\| = \begin{cases} 0 & \text{if } g = 1, \\ \sum_{i=1}^{r} |x_i| & \text{if } g = x_1x_2\cdots x_r \ (r \geq 1) \text{ in f.p. normal form.} \end{cases}$$

It is immediate that $B = \{x \in G : |x| = 0\}$, $X = \{x \in G : |x| = 1\}$ and that the function $g \mapsto |g|$ satisfies **N1***, **A1′** and **A2**. So, by Theorem 2.1 and the remarks following the statement of axiom **F** in §2, (G, B, X) is an $\overline{\text{NFS}}$ group if and only if this length function satisfies **A4**.

We check **A4** in its equivalent form: $d(x, y) \geq m$ and $d(x, z) \geq m$ implies $d(y, z) \geq m$. Where, as usual, $d(x, y) = \frac{1}{2}\{|x| + |y| - |xy^{-1}|\}$, and where m is a real number. Suppose then that we have $m \in \mathbf{R}$ and $x, y, z \in G$ satisfying $d(x, y) \geq m$ and $d(x, z) \geq m$. If $D_0(x, y) < D_0(x, z)$ then, by **A4** applied to the f.p. length function, we see $D_0(y, z) = D_0(x, y)$. If this number is an integer then we see $x = x_1u$, $y = y_1u$ and $z = z_1u$, for some $x_1, y_1, z_1, u \in G$, where no cancellation occurs with respect to the f.p. structure in any of these products, neither does cancellation occur in the products: $y_1z_1^{-1}$ and $x_1y_1^{-1}$ (note that we take the statement "No cancellation occurs in the product xy" to mean that no cancellation or amalgamation occurs in this product; see the remarks following the statement of axiom **N1*** in §2). We now see that $d(y, z) = |u| = d(x, y) \geq m$, as required. If $D_0(y, z)$ is half an odd integer, then we see that $x = x_1x_2u$, $y = y_1y_2u$ and $z = z_1z_2u$ for some $x_1, x_2, y_1, y_2, z_1, z_2, u \in G$, no cancellation occurring with respect to the f.p. structure, where $x_2, y_2, z_2, x_2y_2^{-1}$ and $y_2z_2^{-1}$ are all not equal to 1 and all lie in the same factor of the free product. We now see:

$$\begin{aligned} d(x, y) &= \tfrac{1}{2}\{|x| + |y| - |xy|\} \\ &= \tfrac{1}{2}\{|x_1x_2u| + |y_1y_2u| - |x_1(x_2y_2^{-1})y_1^{-1}|\} \\ &= \tfrac{1}{2}\{|x_1| + \|x_2\| + |u| + |y_1| + \|y_2\| + |u| - |x_1| - \|x_2y_2^{-1}\| - |y_1^{-1}|\} \\ &= |u| + D(x_2, y_2). \end{aligned}$$

Similarly, $d(y,z)=|u|+D(y_2,z_2)$ and $d(x,z)\leqslant|u|+D(x_2,z_2)$, with an inequality in the last case because $x_2z_2^{-1}=1$. Thus we see that $D(x_2,y_2)\geqslant m-|u|$ and $D(x_2,z_2)\geqslant m-|u|$. But we are working with the length function associated with one of the G_i, and this satisfies **A4**. So we see that $D(y_2,z_2)\geqslant m-|u|$, and hence $d(y,z)=|u|+D(y_2,z_2)\geqslant m$, as required. A similar calculation works if $D_0(x,y)>D_0(x,z)$, and so we may suppose $D_0(x,y)=D_0(x,z)$. If this number is an integer, then it is obvious that $d(y,z)\geqslant d(x,y)=d(x,z)\geqslant m$. If $D_0(x,y)$ is half an odd integer, then we can find $x_1,x_2,y_1,y_2,z_1,z_2,u\in G$ such that $x=x_1x_2u$, $y=y_1y_2u$, $z=z_1z_2u$, no cancellation occurring w.r.t. the f.p. structure, such that x_2, y_2 and z_2 all lie in the same free factor of G, and such that $d(x,y)=|u|+D(x_2,y_2)$ and $d(x,z)=|u|+D(x_2,z_2)$. Applying **A4** in this free factor, we see $d(y,z)\geqslant|u|+D(y_2,z_2)\geqslant m$, as required.

It is immediate from our definitions that $G_i\leqslant_{\mathrm{N}}G$ for $i=1,2$. □

Notation. In the situation of Lemma 3.3, we write:

$$(G,B,X)=(G_1,B_1,X_1)*(G_2,B_2,X_2)=G_1*_{\mathrm{N}}G_2.$$

The product, unlike the co-product, of two $\overline{\text{NFS}}$ groups is not always what one might expect it to be. For example:

$$(C_3,1,C_3-1)\times(C_2,1,C_2-1)=(1,1,\emptyset).$$

Moreover the product of two $\overline{\text{NFS}}$ groups does not always exist. We leave it to the reader to verify that $(S_6,1,S_6-1)$ and $(C_2\times C_3,1,C_2\times C_3-1)$ have no product in $\mathcal{NFS}$. We have used C_n and S_n to denote, respectively, the cyclic group of order n and the symmetric group on n letters.

Our next result, which is a trivial consequence of Lemma 3.2(iv), can be used to show that the product of $(H,H,\emptyset)$ with any other $\overline{\text{NFS}}$ group always exists and has the "expected" form.

Lemma 3.4. *If (G,B,X) is an $\overline{\text{NFS}}$ group and H is a group, then $G\times_{\mathrm{N}}H=(G\times H,\ B\times H,\ (B\times H)X(B\times H))$ is an $\overline{\text{NFS}}$ group. Moreover $G\leqslant_{\mathrm{N}}G\times_{\mathrm{N}}H$.* □

Definition. Let (G,B,X) be an NFS group. Then we say that $H\leqslant_{\mathrm{N}}G$ is a *tidy* subgroup$_{\mathrm{N}}$ of G if whenever $x,y\in X$ and $xy\in H\cup X$, then $x,y\in H$ (i.e., H is tidy if it is impossible to amalgamate into it).

Lemma 3.5 (HNN construction for $\overline{\text{NFS}}$ groups). *Let $\varphi:(K,C,Y)\to(L,D,Z)$ be an $\overline{\text{NFS}}$ isomorphism between tidy* *subgroups*$_{\mathbf{N}}$ *of* (G_0, B_0, X_0). *Let* $G = \langle G_0, t : t^{-1}Kt = K\varphi\rangle$, $B = \mathrm{gp}(B_0, T)$ *and* $X = BX_0B$. *Then* (G, B, X) *is an NFS group. Moreover* $G_0 \leqslant_{\mathbf{N}} G$.

Proof. Axioms **N1** and **F** are obviously satisfied by (G, B, X). If $x \in X$ then we can write $x = b\bar{x}c$ where $\bar{x} \in X_0$, and b, c are words in t and the generators of B_0. If $x_1, x_2, \ldots, x_r \in X$ satisfy $r \geqslant 1$ and $x_1x_2 \cdots x_r = 1$ then, to prove that G satisfies **N3***, we must show that this sequence is parallel to a non-reduced sequence. We do this by induction on the number of t^ε that occur in any of the words x_i after as many as possible have been "pinched" out, using Britton's Lemma.

If no t^ε occur in any of the x_i, then $x_i \in X_0$ for all i. Applying **N3*** in G_0, we see that the sequence is non-reduced in G_0 and so a fortiori, it is non-reduced in G.

If t^ε do occur in some of the x_i, then write $x_i = b_i\bar{x}_ic_i$, as above, and consider the equation:

(A) $$b_1\bar{x}_1c_1b_2\bar{x}_2c_2 \cdots b_r\bar{x}_rc_r = 1.$$

Now our calculations are taking place within an HNN group. So, by Britton's Lemma, a "pinch" can be performed between two t-symbols in the word on the left-hand side of (A). But, by hypothesis, no such "pinch" can be performed inside any of the x_i, and this leaves us with two cases to consider.

Case I. For some i, a "pinch" can be performed between some t^ε in c_i and $t^{-\varepsilon}$ in b_{i+1}. Suppose $\varepsilon = 1$ (the other case is similar). We can write $x_i = \bar{x}_itc$ and $x_{i+1} = bt^{-1}\bar{x}_{i+1}$, where $b, c \in B$ and $bc \in L$. Thus $bc \in D$, and since φ is an NFS homomorphism, there exists $d \in C \leqslant B_0$ such that $d = tcbt^{-1}$. So the sequence $(x_1, \ldots, x_{i-1}, x_i, dx_{i+1}, \ldots, x_r)$ has product 1, is parallel to the original sequence, but contains less t-symbols. By induction, this sequence is parallel to a non-reduced sequence, and hence so is the original sequence.

Case II. A "pinch" can be performed around some product of the form $e\bar{x}_ic_ib_{i+1}\bar{x}_{i+1} \cdots b_j\bar{x}_jf$, where we have $c_{i-1}b_i = \bar{e}t^\varepsilon e$ and $c_jb_{j+1} = ft^{-\varepsilon}\bar{f}$, and where, $e, \bar{e}, f, \bar{f} \in B$ and $i < j$ (here we write $c_0 = 1 = b_{r+1}$, if necessary). Suppose $\varepsilon = 1$ (the other case is similar). The word around which we are pinching lies in L and contains no t-symbols. Since $L \leqslant_{\mathbf{N}} G_0$, we may suppose $e = c_i = b_{i+1} = \cdots = c_{r-1} = b_r = f = 1$, and $x_k \in Z$ for $k = i, \ldots, j$. Thus in G:

$$\begin{aligned}(x_1, x_2, \ldots, x_r) &\| (x_1, \ldots, x_{i-2}, x_{i-1}e, tx_i, x_{i+1}, \ldots, x_jt^{-1}, fx_{j+1}, x_{j+2}, \ldots, x_r)\\ &\| (x_1, \ldots, tx_it^{-1}, tx_{i+1}t^{-1}, \ldots, tx_jt^{-1}, \ldots, x_r)\\ &= (x_1, \ldots, (x_i)\varphi^{-1}, (x_{i+1})\varphi^{-1}, \ldots, (x_j)\varphi^{-1}, \ldots, x_r).\end{aligned}$$

Since this last sequence contains less t-symbols than the original, by induction, it and the original are parallel to a non-reduced sequence.

To check **N4**, suppose $g, h, k, gh \in X$ but $hk \notin B \cup X$. Conjugating by an element of B if necessary we may suppose $g = g_1b$ where $g_1 \in X_0$ and $b \in B$. It follows from $gh \in X$ that h can be written $h = b^{-1}h_1c$ where $c \in B$ and $h_1 \in X_0$. Writing $k = dk_1f$ with $d, f \in B$ and $k_1 \in X_0$, we see that $ghk = g_1h_1(cd)k_1f$. If $ghk \in B \cup X$ then it must be possible to eliminate, by pinching round k_1 and g_1h_1 all the t^ε in cd. Note that the assumption that K and L are tidy ensures that, if it is possible to pinch around the product g_1h_1, then it is possible to pinch around g_1 and h_1 individually. In this process, we may have to introduce t-symbols to the left of the product g_1h_1. Eliminating all the t^ε from cd, in this way, we obtain $e_1(g_2h_2)k_2f_1$ where $e_1, f_1 \in B$ and $g_2, h_2, k_2 \in X_0$. At this stage, we have $(g_2h_2)k_2 \in B_0 \cup X_0$. Now if $h_2k_2 \notin B_0 \cup X_0$ then **N4*** applied to (G_0, H_0, X_0) would give $g_2h_2k_2 \notin B_0 \cup X_0$ and hence $h_2k_2 \in B_0 \cup X_0$. But then $hk = b^{-1}h_1cdk_1f = b^{-1}e_1h_2k_2f_1 \in B \cup X$, contrary to assumption. Hence we have $ghk \notin B \cup X$ and **N4** is proved.

It is now easy to see that $G_0 \leqslant_{\mathrm{N}} G$. □

Notation. On the situation of Lemma 3.5, we write:

$$(G, B, X) = \langle (G, B, X), t : t^{-1}(K, C, L)t = (L, D, X)\rangle$$
$$= \mathcal{NFS}\langle G, t : t^{-1}Kt =_{\mathrm{N}} L\rangle.$$

Lemma 3.6 (Free product with amalgamation for $\overline{\text{NFS}}$ groups). *For $i = 1, 2$ suppose (H_i, K_i, Y_i) is a tidy subgroup$_{\mathrm{N}}$ of (G_i, B_i, X_i). Suppose that $H_1 \cong_{\mathrm{N}} H_2$. Let $G = \langle G_1 * G_2 : H_1 = H_2\rangle$, let B be the subgroup of G generated by the B_i, and let $X = B(X_1 \cup X_2)B$. Then (G, B, X) is an $\overline{\text{NFS}}$ group. Moreover $G_i \leqslant_{\mathrm{N}} G$ for $i = 1, 2$.*

Proof. Let $(\bar{G}_2, \bar{B}_2, \bar{X}_2)$ be an $\overline{\text{NFS}}$-isomorphic copy of G_2. Set:

$$(E, C, Z) = \mathcal{NFS}\langle G_1 *_{\mathrm{N}} \bar{G}_2, t : t^{-1}H_1t =_{\mathrm{N}} \bar{H}_2\rangle.$$

Identifying G_2 with $t\bar{G}_2t^{-1}$, we may consider G to be a subgroup of E. It is routine to check that $B = G \cap C$ and $X = G \cap Z$. Now by Lemma 3.2(ii), (G, B, X) is an $\overline{\text{NFS}}$ group. It is easy to see that $G_i \leqslant_{\mathrm{N}} G$ for $i = 1, 2$. □

Notation. In the situation of Lemma 3.6, we write:

$$(G, B, X) = \langle (G_1, B_1, X_1) * (G_2, B_2, X_3) : (H_1, K_1, Y_1) =_{\mathrm{N}} (H_2, K_2, Y_2)\rangle$$
$$= \mathcal{NFS}\langle G_1 * G_2 : H =_{\mathrm{N}} H\rangle.$$

It easily follows from the next result, whose routine proof shall be omitted, that we can iterate the HNN extension and free product with amalgamation for $\overline{\text{NFS}}$ groups to obtain (with an obvious extension of notation):

$$\mathcal{NFS}\langle G, t_\mu\,(\mu \in M) : t_\mu^{-1} K_\mu t_\mu =_{\mathrm{N}} K_\mu \varphi_\mu\,(\mu \in M)\rangle,$$

and:

$$\mathcal{NFS}\left\langle \mathop{*}_{\mu \in M} G : H_\mu =_{\mathrm{N}} H(\mu \in M)\right\rangle .$$

Lemma 3.7. *Let Σ be a non-empty chain (with partial order $\leqslant$). Let $\{(G_\sigma, B_\sigma, X_\sigma)\}_{\sigma\in\Sigma}$ be a family of $\overline{\text{NFS}}$ groups satisfying:*

$$\sigma \leqslant \tau \Rightarrow G_\sigma \leqslant_{\mathrm{N}} G_\tau .$$

Then $\bigcup^{\mathrm{N}}_{\sigma\in\Sigma} G_\sigma = (\bigcup G_\sigma, \bigcup B_\sigma, \bigcup X_\sigma)$ is an $\overline{\text{NFS}}$ group. Moreover:

$$G_\tau \leqslant_{\mathrm{N}} \bigcup_{\sigma\in\Sigma}^{\mathrm{N}} G_\sigma \qquad \text{for all } \tau \in \Sigma. \quad \square$$

Suppose that B is a group generated by a non-empty family $\{B_\mu\}_{\mu\in M}$ of subgroups. Suppose that $\{G_\mu\}_{\mu\in M}$ is a family of groups such that, for each $\mu \in M$, G_μ contains a subgroup $\bar{B}_\mu$ isomorphic to B_μ. We define the *structure-product* of the G_μ over B to be:

$$\mathrm{STR}(G_\mu, B) = \left\langle B * \left(\mathop{*}_{\mu\in M} G_\mu\right) : \bar{B}_\mu = \bar{B}_\mu \text{ for } \mu \in M\right\rangle .$$

If $M = \{1, 2\}$ and $B = B_1 \times B_2$, then the structure product of G_1 and G_2 over B is easily seen to be the *free product with commuting subgroups $\bar{B}_1$ and $\bar{B}_2$*, which is denoted by $\langle G_1 * G_2 : [\bar{B}_1, \bar{B}_2]\rangle$. For the usual definition of this, and the other two products below, see Magnus, Karrass and Solitar [14] pp. 220–222. For our purposes, we could take these products to be defined in terms of the structure product. If H_i $(i = 1, 2)$ are groups containing subgroups C_i $(i = 1, 2)$, and we set $G_1 = H_1 \times C_2$, and $G_2 = H_2 \times C_1$, let $\bar{B}_i$ $(i = 1, 2)$ be the obvious copy of $C_1 \times C_2$, in G_i, and let $B = B_i$ $(i = 1, 2)$, then the structure product of G_1 and G_2 over B is the *free product of H_1 and H_2 with centralised subgroups C_1 and C_2* (in this last example, the structure product we take is, of course, just a free product with amalgamation) and is denoted by $\langle H_1 * H_2 : [H_1, C_2], [H_2, C_1]\rangle$. We define $H \otimes G = \langle H * G : [H, Z(G)], [G, Z(H)]\rangle$, and call it the *free product of H and G with centralised centres.* The properties of this product are studied in [14] Example 36 p. 223. The most important being $H \otimes G \cong G \otimes H$, $K \otimes (H \otimes G) \cong (K \otimes H) \otimes G$, and $Z(H \otimes G) = Z(H) \times Z(G)$. We can clearly generalise this product to the free product with centralised centres of an infinite family $\{G_\mu\}_{\mu\in M}$ of groups. However there are two ways of doing this depending on whether one takes an unrestricted or a restricted direct product of the $Z(G_\mu)$ at the appropriate point in the construction. We choose the restricted product of the $Z(G_\mu)$, and denote the product of the G_μ by $\bigotimes_{\mu\in M} G_\mu$. It is easy to see that $Z(\bigotimes G_\mu) = \times Z(G_\mu)$, where, of course, the product on the right-hand side of this equation is a restricted direct product.

Now observe that all these products have been defined in terms of the free product with amalgamation, and the (restricted) direct product. From Lemmas 3.4 and 3.6, the first of these constructions is always possible in the category $\mathcal{NFS}$, while the direct product is possible (in a reasonable sense) in certain cases. It follows that, in certain cases, these products are also possible in $\mathcal{NFS}$.

We sum up the situation with a series of Lemmas, the proofs of which are easy to construct using the results of this section and are therefore omitted. Note that when working "in $\mathcal{NFS}$", we must replace each group theoretic concept with the corresponding concept$_{\mathrm{N}}$ in $\mathcal{NFS}$.

Lemma 3.8. *The structure product construction works in* $\mathcal{NFS}$. □

As would be expected, we denote the structure product in $\mathcal{NFS}$ by $\mathrm{STR}_{\mathrm{N}}(G_\mu, B)$. It is easy to see that, if we can construct a structure product of a family $\{G_\mu\}_{\mu\in M}$ over B in the category of groups, then, assuming the $\overline{\mathrm{NF}}$ structures $(G_\mu, \bar{B}_\mu, G_\mu - \bar{B}_\mu)$ and $(B, B, \emptyset)$ on the groups concerned, we can make a corresponding construction in $\mathcal{NFS}$. If we work out the resulting $\overline{\mathrm{NF}}$ structure on $\mathrm{STR}(G_\mu, B)$, we obtain the next result.

Lemma 3.9. $(\mathrm{STR}(G_\mu, B), B, B(\bigcup_{\mu\in M}(G_\mu - B_\mu))B)$ *is an* $\overline{\mathit{NFS}}$ *group.* □

We call the $\overline{\mathrm{NF}}$ structure of Lemma 3.9 the *natural* $\overline{\mathrm{NF}}$ structure on the structure product.

The next result is obtained by combining structure product with direct product in $\mathcal{NFS}$. We cannot expect a completely general result because direct products are awkward in $\mathcal{NFS}$.

Lemma 3.10. *Let* G_i $(i = 1, 2)$ *be* $\overline{\mathit{NFS}}$ *groups, and suppose* H_i $(i = 1, 2)$ *has the* $\overline{\mathit{NF}}$ *structure* $(H_i, H_i, \emptyset)$. *If* $H_i \leqslant_{\mathrm{N}} G_i$ $(i = 1, 2)$, *then both the free product of the* G_i, *with the* H_i *commuting, and the free product of the* G_i, *with the* H_i *centralised can be constructed in* $\mathcal{NFS}$. □

Starting with the $\overline{\text{NF}}$ structures $(G_i, H_i, G_i - H_i)$, and working out the resulting structure on the two types of product, we see:

Lemma 3.11. *Suppose that either* $G = \langle G_1 * G_2 : [H_1, H_2]\rangle$, *or* $G = \langle G_1 * G_2 : [H_1, G_2], [H_2, G_1]\rangle$, *then*

$$(G, H_1 \times H_2, (H_1 \times H_2)((G_1 - H_1) \cup (G_2 - H_2))(H_1 \times H_2))$$

is an $\overline{NFS}$ *group.* □

We call the $\overline{\text{NF}}$ structures of Lemma 3.11, the *natural* $\overline{\text{NF}}$ structures on the respective products. We remark that the idea of defining a normal form on a free product with commuting subgroups, that is naturally related to its structure, is not new. For instance, the normal form constructed in a free product with commuting subgroups in [14] Example 35 p. 223 gives rise to an NF structure whose corresponding $\overline{\text{NF}}$ structure is the one given in the lemma. Moreover, a very similar type of normal form has been used by B. Baumslag [1]. Combined with the Conjugacy Theorem (Theorem 4.2), $\overline{\text{NF}}$ structures can be used to tackle the conjugacy problem. Hurley (unpublished) has used this approach to find neccessary and sufficient conditions, on groups G_i $(i = 1, 2)$ and their subgroups H_i $(i = 1, 2)$, for $G = \langle G_1 * G_2 : [H_1, H_2]\rangle$ to have soluble conjugacy problem. The result of Hurwitz [11], which states that if the G_i are free and the H_i are finitely generated then G has soluble conjugacy problem, follows easily from the former result.

Since the free product (of two factors) with centralised centres is a special case of the free product with centralised subgroups, we can apply Lemma 3.10, and then iterate the construction, using Lemma 3.7, to obtain our next result. Since we will use this construction explicitly in §8, we have calculated the resultant $\overline{\text{NF}}$ structure.

Lemma 3.12. *Let* $\{(G_\mu, B_\mu, X_\mu)\}_{\mu \in M}$ *be a family of* $\overline{NFS}$ *groups. Suppose that, for all* $\mu \in M$, $Z(G_\mu) \leqslant B_\mu$, *then the free product of the* G_μ *with centralised centres can be constructed in* $\overline{\mathcal{NFS}}$, *and shall be denoted by* $\bigotimes_{\mu \in M\,(N)} G_\mu$.

Explicitly, we have:

$$\bigotimes_{\mu \in M\,(N)} G_\mu = \left(\bigotimes_{\mu \in M} G_\mu, \bigcup_{\mu \in M} B_\mu, \left(\bigcup_{\mu \in M} B_\mu\right)\left(\bigcup_{\mu \in M} (G_\mu - B_\mu)\right)\left(\bigcup_{\mu \in M} B_\mu\right)\right). \quad \square$$

We close this section by remarking that, although the $\overline{\text{NF}}$ structures of Lemmas 3.9, 3.11 and 3.12 look complicated, this is, in part, the fault of the notation. A little thought reveals that structures are entirely natural, and almost "what one might expect".

§4. $\overline{\text{NFS}}$ groups: The Torsion Theorem, The Conjugacy Theorem and The Centre

In this section (G, B, X) is a fixed NFS-group and $g \mapsto |g|$ shall be its length function. We say that $g \in G$ is *cyclically reduced* (c.r.) if $|g| \leqslant |x^{-1}gx| + 1$ for all $x \in G$ and is *strictly cyclically reduced* (s.c.r.) if $|g| \leqslant |x^{-1}gx|$ for all $x \in G$.

Lemma 4.1. (i) *$g \in G$ is c.r. if and only if either $g \in B$ or g can be written $g = x_1 \cdots x_r\,(r \geqslant 1)$ in normal form where if $r \geqslant 2$ then $|x_r x_1| \neq 0$.*

(ii) *$g \in G$ is s.c.r. if and only if either $g \in B$ or g can be written $g = x_1 \cdots x_r\,(r \geqslant 1)$ in normal form where if $r \geqslant 2$ then $|x_r x_1| = 2$ and if $r = 1$ then $|t^{-1}gt| \geqslant 1$ for all $t \in G$.*

(iii) *If g is c.r. but not s.c.r. then there exists $t \in X$ such that tgt^{-1} is s.c.r.*

Proof. (i) Suppose $g \in G$ is not c.r., then $|g| \geqslant 2$ and there exists $k \in G$ such that $|kgk^{-1}| \leqslant |g| - 2$. By the corollary to [10] lemma 3.3, $k \notin B$. Thus we can write $g = x_1 \cdots x_r\,(r \geqslant 2)$ and $k = c_1 \cdots c_s\,(s \geqslant 1)$ both in normal form. If $|c_s x_1| \neq 0$ then by [10] lemma 2.1 (i) we have $|kg| \geqslant r + s - 1$ and so by [10] lemma 3.3, we have $|kgk^{-1}| \geqslant ||kg| - |k|| = r - 1$ contradicting $|kgk^{-1}| \leqslant r - 2$. Thus $|c_s x_1| = 0$ and similarly $|x_r c_s^{-1}| = 0$. Hence $|x_r x_1| = 0$.

Conversely, if $g = x_1 \cdots x_r\,(r \geqslant 2)$ in normal form and $|x_r x_1| = 0$, then g is clearly not c.r.

(ii) Suppose $g \in G$ is not s.c.r., then $|g| \geqslant 1$ and there exists $k \in G$ such that $|kgk^{-1}| \leqslant |g| - 1$. If $|g| = 1$ then there is nothing to prove, so suppose $|g| \geqslant 2$. If g is not c.r. then from (i), $|x_r x_1| = 0$. If g is c.r. then by (iii) there exists $t \in X$ such that tgt^{-1} is s.c.r. Thus either $|tx_1| = 0$ and $|x_r t^{-1}| = 1$ or $|tx_1| = 1$ and $|x_r t^{-1}| = 0$. In either case $|x_r x_1| = 1$.

Conversely if $g = x_1 \cdots x_r\,(r \geqslant 1)$ in normal form and either $r = 1$ and $|t^{-1}gt| = 0$ for some $t \in X$ or $r \geqslant 2$ and $|x_r x_1| \leqslant 1$, then g is clearly not s.c.r.

(iii) Suppose $g \in G$ is c.r. but not s.c.r., then $|g| \geqslant 1$ and there exists $k \in G$ such that $|kgk^{-1}| = |g| - 1$. Since $|k| \geqslant 1$, we can write $g = x_1 \cdots x_r\,(r \geqslant 1)$ and $k = c_1 \cdots c_s\,(s \geqslant 1)$ both in normal form and consider the reduction of the product $c_1 c_2 \cdots c_s x_1 x_2 \cdots x_r c_s^{-1} \cdots c_2^{-1} c_1^{-1}$ to normal form. First suppose $r = 1$, then $g = x_1 \in X$. If $|c_s g c_s^{-1}| \geqslant 1$, then, by lemma 2.1(i) of [10], we see $|kgk^{-1}| \geqslant 2|k| - 1 \geqslant 1$, contradicting our choice of k. Thus we have $|c_s g c_s^{-1}| = 0 = |g| - 1$ with $c_s \in X$ as required. Now suppose $r \geqslant 2$. If $|c_s x_1| = |x_r c_s^{-1}| = 0$ then $|c_s g c_s^{-1}| = |g| - 2$ contradicting our assumption on g. If either $|c_s x_1| = 2$ or

$|x_r c_s^{-1}| = 2$, then $|kgk^{-1}| \geqslant ||kg| - |k^{-1}|| = g$ contradicting our assumption on k. If $|c_s x_1| = |x_r c_s^{-1}| = 1$, then by [10] lemma 2.1(i) we see $|kgk^{-1}| = 2|k| + |g| - 2 \geqslant |g|$ contradicting our assumptions on k. Thus one of the pair $|c_s x_1|$, $|x_r c_s^{-1}|$ is 0 and the other is 1. Hence $|c_s g c_s^{-1}| = |g| - 1$ and $|c_s g c_s^{-1}|$ is s.c.r. and $c_s \in X$ as required. □

Theorem 4.2 (The Conjugacy Theorem for $\overline{\text{NFS}}$ Groups). *Let (G, B, X) be an NFS group. Suppose $g \in G$ is s.c.r. and suppose $g \sim g'$ where $g' = p_1 p_2 \cdots p_r\ (r \geqslant 2)$ in normal form with $|p_r p_1| = 2$, then g can be obtained from g' by cyclically permuting the elements $p_1, p_2, \ldots, p_r$ and then conjugating by an element of B.*

Proof. From Lemma 4.1, g' is s.c.r. and hence $|g| = |g'| = r$. Since $g \sim g'$, there exists $w \in G$ such that $g = wg'w^{-1}$.

If $|w| = 0$, then $w \in B$ and we are done so suppose $|w| = s \geqslant 1$. We can write $w = c_1 c_2 \cdots c_s$ in normal form. If $|c_s p_1| = |p_r c_s^{-1}| = 1$, then putting $g_1 = p_r c_s^{-1}$, $h_1 = c_s p_1$, $k_1 = p_1^{-1}$, we see $g_1, h_1, k_1 \in X$, $h_1 k_1 = c_s \in X$ but $g_1 h_1 = p_r p_1 \notin B \cup X$. So by **N4***, in the presence of **F**, we conclude $p_r = g_1 h_1 k_1 \notin B \cup X$, contradicting $p_r \in X$. Thus at most one of $|c_s p_1|$ and $|p_r c_s^{-1}|$ is equal to 1. Suppose $|c_s p_1| = 1$. If $|p_r c_s^{-1}| = 0$, then $|c_s g' c_s^{-1}| = |g'| - 1$ contradicting g' being s.c.r. If $|p_r c_s^{-1}| = 2$, then, by [10] lemma 2.1(i), we have $|g| = |wg'w^{-1}| = 2|w| + |g'| - 1 > |g'|$ contradicting $|g| = |g'|$. Thus $|c_s p_1| \neq 1$ and similarly $|p_r c_s^{-1}| \neq 1$. Since $|c_s p_1| = |p_r c_s^{-1}| = 0$ contradicts g' being s.c.r. and $|c_s p_1| = |p_r c_s^{-1}| = 2$ contradicts $|g| = |g'|$, we see that one of the pair $|c_s p_1|$, $|p_r c_s^{-1}|$ is 0 and the other is 2. Suppose $|c_s p_1| = 2$, the other case is similar. Putting $g'' = p_r p_1 \cdots p_{r-1}$ and $w' = wp_r^{-1}$, we see $g = w'g''w'^{-1}$ and $|w'| = |w| - 1$. By induction g can be obtained from g'' by cyclically permuting $p_r, p_1, \ldots, p_{r-1}$ and then conjugating by an element of B. □

Corollary 4.3. *Let $k \in G$ be s.c.r. with $|k| \geqslant 2$ and let $g \in G$ be any conjugate of k, then there exist $w, k' \in G$ such that $g = wk'w^{-1}$ with no cancellation occurring in this product and such that:*

(a) *If $|g| \equiv |k| \pmod 2$ then k' is a s.c.r. conjugate of k and hence can be obtained from k as in Theorem 4.2.*

(b) *If $|g| \not\equiv |k| \pmod 2$ then k' is a c.r. conjugate of k that is not s.c.r. and hence, by Lemma 4.1(iii) can be obtained from some s.c.r. conjugate of k by conjugating by an element of X.*

Proof. Let w be an element of maximal length such that $g = wk'w^{-1}$ for some $k' \in G$ with no cancellation occurring. If k' is not c.r., then by Lemma 4.1(i), and $|k'| \geqslant |k| \geqslant 2$, we see that $k' = x_1 \cdots x_r\ (r \geqslant 2)$ in normal form with $|x_r x_1| = 0$. This contradicts the maximality of the length of $|w|$. Since $k' \sim k$, we see $|k| \leqslant |k'| \leqslant k+1$. But $|k'| = |g| - 2|w| \equiv |g| \pmod 2$. So that if $|g| \equiv |k| \pmod 2$, then $|k| = |k'|$ and k' is s.c.r., while if $|g| \not\equiv |k| \pmod 2$, then $|k| + 1 = |k'|$ and k' is c.r. but not s.c.r. □

The next result is an immediate corollary of the last.

Corollary 4.4. *Let $k \in G$ be s.c.r. with $|k| \geqslant 2$ and let $g \in G$ be any conjugate of k, then there exists $w \in G$ such that $g = wkw^{-1}$ and $|w| \leqslant \frac{1}{2}\{|g| + |k| - 1\}$.* □

No analog of this result holds if $|k| = 0$. Consider an HNN extension of a direct product of a countably infinite number of copies of $\mathbf{Z}$ by an element t that has the effect:

$$t^{-1}(n_1, n_2, n_3, \ldots)t = (0, n_1, n_2, n_3, \ldots).$$

If we equip this group with the usual (Britton's Lemma) $\overline{\text{NFS}}$ structure, then we see that for any choice of $k \neq 1$ with $|k| = 0$, and for any integer N, there exists a conjugate g of k with $|g| = 0$, but such that $wkw^{-1} = g$ implies $|w| \geqslant N$. The situation for $|k| = 1$ is summed up in the next result. Its short proof shall be omitted.

Lemma 4.5. *Let $k \in G$ be s.c.r. with $|k| = 1$ and let $g \in G$ be any conjugate of k, then there exists $w \in G$ wuch that $g = wkw^{-1}$ and $|w| \leqslant \frac{1}{2}\{|g| + 1\}$. Moreover one of the following two cases obtains.*

(a) *$|g|$ is odd and no cancellation occurs in wkw^{-1}.*

(b) *We can write $w = w_1 a$, no cancellation occurring, such that $|a| = 1$, $|ak|$, $|ka^{-1}| \geqslant 1$, $|aka^{-1}| = 1$ or 2 according as $|g|$ is odd or even, and, putting $u = aka^{-1}$, no cancellation occurs in $w_1 u w_1^{-1}$.* □

Theorem 4.6 (The Torsion Theorem for $\overline{\text{NFS}}$ groups). *Let (G, B, X) be an $\overline{\text{NFS}}$ group. Then every element of finite order in G is a conjugate of an element of finite order in $B \cup X$.*

Proof. Let g be an s.c.r. element of G. It follows from Lemma 4.1(ii) that, if $g \notin B \cup X$, then $|g^n| = n|g|$, for all $n \geqslant 1$, and so g must have infinite order. Thus every element of finite order is conjugate to an s.c.r. element, which, having finite order itself, must lie in $B \cup X$. □

Before we study the centre of an $\overline{\text{NFS}}$ group we need a new concept.

Definition. Let B be a group and let $h \in B$. By an *nth root* of the inner automorphism $x \mapsto hxh^{-1}$ of B we mean an automorphism φ of B satisfying:

$$b\varphi = b \quad \text{and} \quad x\varphi^n = bxb^{-1}, \quad \text{for all } x \in B.$$

By a *root inner* automorphism of B we mean an automorphism that is an nth root of some inner automorphism for some $n \geq 1$.

Remarks. Plenty examples of root inner automorphisms can be given. Inner automorphisms and automorphisms of finite order are root inner. If B is the free group freely generated by the set $\{a, b, c\}$, then the automorphism of B that has the effect:

$$a \mapsto bc^{-1}a^{-1}, \; b \mapsto b \quad \text{and} \quad c \mapsto aca^{-1}$$

is root inner (it is a square root of $x \mapsto bxb^{-1}$), but is neither inner nor of finite order.

It should also be noted that, if φ is an nth root of $x \mapsto bxb^{-1}$ and an mth root of $x \mapsto cxc^{-1}$, then it is a $(pn + qm)$th root of $x \mapsto (b^pc^q)x(b^pc^q)^{-1}$. It follows that, if φ is root inner, there exists $n \geq 1$, such that the integral multiples of n are precisely the numbers m for which φ is an mth root. If φ is an nth root of an inner automorphism I, where $n \geq 1$, but is not an mth root for any m satisfying $1 < m < n$, then we call φ a *primitive nth root* of I.

The remainder of this section shall be devoted to the proof of our next result.

Theorem 4.7. *Let (G, B, X) be an $\overline{\text{NFS}}$ group. Then one, and only one, of the following three cases obtains.*

(i) $Z(G) \subseteq B$.

(ii) $Z(G) \not\subseteq B$, *and* $X = G - B$.

(iii) *G is the split extension of B by an infinite cyclic group $\langle t \rangle$, say, such that the automorphism $x \mapsto t^{-1}xt$ of B is root inner, and G has the usual HNN $\overline{\text{NFS}}$ structure $(G, B, B\{t, t^{-1}\}B)$. Moreover, in this case:*

$$Z(G) = \langle t^n b \rangle \times (Z(B) \cap C_B(t)),$$

where $b \in B$, $n \geq 1$ and t is a primitive nth root of $x \mapsto bxb^{-1}$.

Before we start on the proof of Theorem 4.7, we note that if the $\overline{\text{NFS}}$ group (G, B, X) has a factor group$_N$ or an extension$_N$ of the form $(\bar{G}, \bar{B}, \bar{G} - \bar{B})$ or of the form $(\bar{G}, \bar{B}, \bar{B}\{t, t^{-1}\}\bar{B})$, where $\bar{G}$ is a split extension of $\bar{B}$ by $\langle t \rangle$, then G itself has one of these two forms. This implies that taking preimages$_N$ or extensions$_N$ of non-trivial $\overline{\text{NFS}}$ groups preserves the property $Z(G) \leq B$. We prove the theorem via a number of lemmas, in all of which, (G, B, X) is a fixed $\overline{\text{NFS}}$ group.

Lemma 4.8. *If $x, y \in G$ satisfy $xy = yx$, then either*
(i) *there exists $t \in G$ such that*: $|txt^{-1}| = |tyt^{-1}| = 1$, *or*
(ii) *there exist $g, w \in G$, $h, h' \in B$ and $j, k \in \mathbf{Z}$ such that*:

$$x = ghg^{-1}w^{j},$$

$$y = gh'g^{-1}w^{k}$$

and ghg^{-1}, $gh'g^{-1}$ and w commute in pairs.

Proof. We first show:
(*) *If $x, y \in G$ commute, $\varepsilon = \pm 1$ and $\eta = 0$ or ± 1 then the pair (x, y) satisfies* (i) *or* (ii) *if and only is the pair $(x^{\varepsilon}, x^{\eta}y)$ does.*

By the symmetry of the situation and the form of (i) and (ii), it is sufficient to prove (*) only in one direction and only in the case $\varepsilon = \eta = 1$. Suppose (x, y) satisfies (i). Then $|txt^{-1}| = |tyt^{-1}| = 1$, for some $t \in G$. If $|txyt^{-1}| = 0$ then (x, xy) satisfies (ii) while if $|txyt^{-1}| = 1$ then it satisfies (i). Suppose then that $|txyt^{-1}| = |tyxt^{-1}| = 2$. Applying **N3** to the equation $(txt^{-1})(tyt^{-1})(txt^{-1})^{-1}(tyt^{-1})^{-1} = 1$, we see $tyx^{-1}t^{-1} = h \in B$ for some h and $t^{-1}ht = yx^{-1}$ commutes with x. Since $xy = t^{-1}htx^{2}$, we see that (x, xy) satisfies (ii). If (x, y) satisfies (ii) then trivially (x, xy) also satisfies (ii). Thus (*) is proved.

We now prove the lemma by induction on $|x| + |y|$. It is trivial if $|x| + |y| \leq 2$ so suppose $|x| + |y| > 2$. By symmetry we may suppose $|x| \leq |y|$. Again the lemma is trivial if $|x| = 0$. If $|x| = 1$, then, by our assumptions, we can write $y = c_1c_2 \cdots c_s$ $(s \geq 2)$ in normal form. If $|xc_1| = 0$, then $|xy| = |y| - 2$ so by induction (i) or (ii) holds for (x, xy) and thus by (*), (i) or (ii) holds for (x, y). If $|xc_1| = 1$, then $(xc_1)c_2 \cdots c_s$ and $c_1c_2 \cdots (c_sx)$ are both normal forms for xy so by **N3**, $c^{-1}xc_1 \in B$ and hence (ii) holds for (x, y). If $|xc_1| = 2$, then $xc_1c_2 \cdots c_s$ and $c_1'c_2 \cdots c_sx$ are both normal forms for xy and so by **N3**, $|x^{-1}c_1| = 0$. But then (i) or (ii) holds for (x^{-1}, y) and so by (*), (i) or (ii) holds for (x, y). If $|x| \geq 2$, then we can write $x = c_1c_2 \cdots c_r$ $(r \geq 2)$ and $y = d_1d_2 \cdots d_s$ $(s \geq r)$ both in normal form. Since $xyx^{-1}y^{-1} = 1$, either $|c_rd_s^{-1}| = 0$ or else $|c_1^{-1}d_s^{-1}| = 0$. By (*), we may assume $|c_rd_s^{-1}| = 0$. If $|c_rc_1| < 2$, then $|c_rxc_r^{-1}| < x$ and $|c_ryc_r^{-1}| \leq y$, thus by induction (i) or (ii) holds for the pair $(c_rxc_r^{-1}, c_ryc_r^{-1})$ and thus (i) or (ii) holds for (x, y). If $|c_rc_1| = 2$, then no cancellation occurs in either product xy or yx. Comparing normal forms (i.e. using **N2**) in the equation $xy = yx$, we see $|x^{-1}y| = s - r$. By induction (i) or (ii) holds for the pair $(x, x^{-1}y)$ and so by (*) holds for the pair (x, y). □

We define a *pseudo-proper power* (p.p.p.) to be an element of the form: $x^{-1}hxw^k$ where $h \in B$; $x, w \in G$; $k \geqslant 2$ and $x^{-1}hx$ and w commute.

Lemma 4.9. (i) *If* $|x| = 1$, *then either* $\langle x \rangle \subseteq B \cup X$ *or* $|x^n| = |n|$ *for all* $n \in Z$.

(ii) *Suppose* $|x|, |y|, |xy| \geqslant 1$, *but are not all equal to* 1, $xy = yx$ *and* x *is s.c.r., then* y *and* xy *are s.c.r. and there exist* $w \in G$, $h, h' \in B$ *and* $j, k \in Z$ *such that*:

$$x = hw^j, \qquad y = h'w^k,$$

w is s.c.r. with $|w^2| = 2|w|$, *and* h, h' *and* w *commute in pairs.*

(iii) *Let* $x \in X$ *be s.c.r., then either*

$$C_G(x) \subseteq B \cup X,$$

or:

$$C_G(x) = \langle x \rangle \times (B \cap C_G(x)) \quad \text{and} \quad |x^2| = 2.$$

Proof. (i) If $\langle x \rangle \not\subseteq B \cup X$, then there exists $r \geqslant 1$ such that $x^{r+1} \notin B \cup X$. Let r be chosen to be as small as possible. If $x^{r-1} \in B$, then write $b = x^{r-1}$. No cancellation occurs in $(bx)x$, and so no cancellation can occur in xx. Thus $r = 1$. If $x^{r-1} \in X$, then writing $g = x^{-r+1}$, $h = x$ and $k = x^r$ and applying **N4**, we see that $xx = ghk \notin B \cup X$, and again $r = 1$. By the minimality of r, there are no other cases and it is now easy to see that no cancellation occurs in any product of the form $xxx \cdots x$. Thus $|x^n| = |n||x|$ for all $n \in \mathbf{Z}$.

(ii) We first prove:

(**) *Suppose* $|u|, |v|, |uv| \geqslant 1$, *but are not all equal to* 1, *and* $uv = vu$, *then* u *is s.c.r.* $\Leftrightarrow$ v *is s.c.r.* $\Leftrightarrow$ uv *is s.c.r.*

We first note that, by symmetry, we need only prove that if u is s.c.r. then so is uv. Suppose then that u, v and uv satisfy the hypotheses of (**), and that u is s.c.r. If $|uv| \geqslant 2$, then the first and last letters of uv are the same as, respectively, the first and last letters of u. This implies that uv is s.c.r., so suppose $|uv| = 1$. From [10] lemma 2.4 and our assumptions on u and v, the following cases can occur.

Case I. $v = u^{-1}v_1$, where $|v_1| = 1$, and where no cancellation occurs in this product. Since $uv = vu$, we have that $u^{-1}u^{-1}v_1 = u^{-1}v_1u^{-1}$, and no cancellation occurs on either side of this equation because u is s.c.r. Comparing normal forms for $u^{-1}v_1$ and v_1u^{-1}, we easily see that there exists $b \in B$ and $r \geqslant 1$ such that $u = v_1^{-r}b$, $v = v_1^{r+1}b^{-1}$, where $v_1b = bv_1$. We easily see that $uv = v_1$, and that $|v_1^2| = 2$. If uv is not s.c.r., then, by Lemma 4.1(iii), there exists $t \in X$ such that $t^{-1}v_1t \in B$. It follows that $t^{-1}v_1^2t \in B$, from which we conclude that there exist $c, d \in B$ satisfying $v_1 = tc = dt^{-1}$. But now $v_1^2 = dc \in B$, contradicting $|v_1^2| = 2$. Hence uv is s.c.r.

Case II. $u = u_1v^{-1}$, where $|u_1| = 1$, and where no cancellation occurs in this product. This case is similar to Case I.

Case III. $u = u_1z^{-1}$, $v = zv_1$, where no cancellation occurs in these products, and where $|u_1| = |v_1| = |u_1v_1| = 1$. Since we cannot have $|u| = |v| = |uv| = 1$, we conclude that $|z| \geq 1$. Now $uv = vu$, and so Cases I, II and III can occur with the roles of u and v reversed. We may assume Case III obtains, for otherwise we could argue as before to obtain that $uv = vu$ is s.c.r. Now we easily see that there must exist $f, g \in G$ such that $u = u_1fv_1^{-1}$, $v = u_1^{-1}gv_1$, with no cancellation occurring in these products. We now see that $v^{-1}u = uv^{-1}$, with no cancellation occurring because u is s.c.r. We can also see that $|u| = |z| + 1 = |v|$, and so, comparing normal forms, $u = v^{-1}b$ for some $b \in B \cap C_G(v)$. But now $uv = b \in B$, contradicting $|uv| = 1$. Thus this final case cannot occur. Thus (**) is proved.

Now suppose that x and y satisfy the hypotheses of (ii). By (**), x, y and xy are s.c.r., and so, by symmetry, we may suppose that $|x| \geq 2$, and that either $|y| \geq 2$, or $|y| = |xy| = 1$. By Lemma 6.2, there exist $g, w \in G$, $h, h' \in B$ and $j, k \in \mathbf{Z}$, satisfying $x = ghg^{-1}w^j$ and $y = gh'g^{-1}w^k$, where $ghg^{-1}, gh'g^{-1}$ and w commute in pairs. We assert that $w^j \notin B$, for, if not, then we see that $x = g(hg^{-1}w^j) = (w^jgh)g^{-1}$, both products being normal forms, and hence $x = gh''g^{-1}$ for some $h'' \in B$, contradicting x being s.c.r. We also assert $ghg^{-1} \in B$, for, if not, then, since $|x| \geq 2$, we can apply (**) to the pair ghg^{-1} and w^j, to obtain the contradiction that ghg^{-1} is s.c.r., but does not have length 0. It now easily follows from our assumptions on x and (when $|w| = 1$) (i) of the lemma, that w is s.c.r. and satisfies $|w^2| = 2|w|$. Applying a similar argument to y, we see that $w^k \notin B$, and that, if $|y| = 2$, then $gh'g^{-1} \in B$, so that, in this case, we may assume $g = 1$ and (ii) is proved. It remains to prove (ii) when $|y| = |xy| = 1$, and it is clear that it is sufficient to show that $gh'g^{-1} \in B$. Suppose this is not so, then we have $gh'g^{-1}, w^k \in X$, for, if not, we could apply (**) to this pair to obtain the contradiction that $gh'g^{-1}$ is s.c.r. But now we can obtain the same contradiction by observing that $|gh'g^{-1}x| \geq 1$, and then applying (**) to $gh'g^{-1}$ and x. Thus $gh'g^{-1} \in B$, and the proof of (ii) is completed.

(iii) Suppose $x \in X$ is s.c.r. If $C_G(x) \not\subseteq B \cup X$, then x commutes with some element y with $|y| \geq 2$. Since $|xy| = 1$, we can write $x = hw^j$, $y = h'w^k$, as in the conclusion of (ii). Since $|w^2| = 2|w|$ and $|x| = 1$, by (i), $j = \pm 1$. We may clearly suppose $j = 1$. Writing $h'' = h'h^{-k}$, we see that $h'' \in C_G(x) \cap B$ and that $y = x^k h''$. Hence we see $C_G(x) = \langle x \rangle \times (B \cap C_G(x))$. Since $|x^2| = |h^2 w^2| = 2$, (iii) is proved. □

Our next result is an immediate corollary of part (ii) of the lemma.

Corollary 4.10. *If $ghg^{-1}w^j$ is s.c.r. pseudo proper power of length at least 2, then $ghg^{-1} \in B$, so that we may suppose that $g = 1$, and that no cancellation occurs in the product hw^j.* □

Proof of Theorem 4.7. It is easy to see that cases (i), (ii), and (iii) of the theorem are mutually exclusive, so that at most one case obtains. We shall assume that we have an NFS group (G, B, X), for which case (i) does not hold, i.e. for which $Z(G) \not\leq B$, and shall prove that one of the remaining two cases obtains.

Let x be an element of $Z(G) - B$ of smallest possible length. Clearly every element of $Z(G)$ is s.c.r. and so x is s.c.r. If $|x| = 1$, then, by Lemma 4.9(iii), either $G = C_G(x) \subseteq B \cup X$, when clearly $X = G - B$ and (ii) holds, or $G = C_G(x) = \langle x \rangle \times (B \cap C_G(x)) = \langle x \rangle \times B$, and we easily see that $\langle x \rangle$ is infinite cyclic and that $X = B\{x, x^{-1}\}B$. In this case, x induces the identity automorphism on B, which is clearly root inner, and since the centre of G obviously is $\langle x \rangle \times Z(B)$, case (iii) obtains.

Now suppose $|x| \geq 2$. Since $G \neq B, X$ is nonempty, and so we can choose $t \in X$. Clearly $|xt| \geq 1$, so, by Lemma 4.9(ii) and (iii), t is s.c.r., $x \in C_G(t) = \langle t \rangle \times (B \cap C_G(t))$ and $\langle t \rangle$ is infinite cyclic. Thus there exists $b \in B$ such that $x = t^n b$, where $|n| = |x|$. Replacing t by t^{-1}, if necessary, we may assume n is positive. If $s \in X$, then a similar argument shows that $x = s^{\varepsilon n}c$, for some $c \in B$ and $\varepsilon = \pm 1$, in normal form. Comparing these two normal forms for x yields $s = (td)^\varepsilon$, for some $d \in B$. So $G = \mathrm{gp}(t, B)$. Now suppose $e \in B$, then $te \in X$, and so $x = (te)^{\varepsilon n} f$, for some $f \in B$ and $\varepsilon = \pm 1$. If $\varepsilon = -1$, then $te = ht^{-1}$, for some $h \in B$, and so $|x| = |(te)^{-n} f| = |he(te)^{-(n-2)} f| \leq n-2$, contradicting $|x| = n$. Thus $\varepsilon = 1$, and, comparing the two normal forms $(et)^{n-1}ef$ and $t^{n-1}b$ for $t^{-1}x$, we see that $et = th$, for some $h \in B$. But $e \in B$ was chosen arbitrarily, and so G is a normal extension of B by $\langle x \rangle$, and, since $\langle x \rangle$ is free, it is a split extension. It is now easy to see that $X = B\{t, t^{-1}\}B$. Now, $x = t^n b \in Z(G)$, and so for $y \subset B$, we have $t^{-n} y t^n = byb^{-1}$. Since $b \in B \cap C_G(t)$, we have $t^{-1}bt = b$, and so t induces an nth root of $y \mapsto byb^{-1}$. To see that it induces a primitive nth root of this automorphism, suppose $t^{-m} y t^m = cyc^{-1}$ and $t^{-1}ct = c$, for some $c \in B$, some $m \geq 1$, and all $y \in B$, then we see

$t^m c \in Z(G) - B$. By the minimality of the length of $x = t^n b$, $n \leqslant m$, as required. It is now easy to see that the centre of G is of the required form, and so case (iii) obtains. □

§5. Small Cancellation Theory over $\overline{\text{NFS}}$ groups

In this section, we shall assume familiarity with Lyndon [13], and we shall concentrate on the points of difference between Lyndon's theory and ours. For the whole of this section, (G, B, X) shall be a fixed $\overline{\text{NFS}}$ group.

Definitions. A set R of c.r. elements of G is *symmetrised* if whenever $r \in R$ so is r^{-1} and so is any c.r. conjugate of r. (From now on R is a fixed symmetrised set.) An element $p \in G$ is a *piece* (or an R-*piece*) if there exists $r_1 \neq r_2 \in R$ such that $r_1 = ps_1$, $r_2 = ps_2$ with almost no cancellation (see §2) occurring in both products. (Note that we do not require all the elements of R to be s.c.r. and that if $R \neq \emptyset$, then any element of B is a piece.)

We now state our small cancellation conditions, of which all except T_4^2 are restatements, for $\overline{\text{NFS}}$ groups, of corresponding conditions, from [13], for free products.

C(p): No element of R is a product of fewer than p pieces.

C′(λ): If $r \in R$ has the form $r = ab$ with almost no cancellation occurring, where a is a piece, then $|a| < \lambda |r|$.

It is easy to see that C′(λ) with $\lambda \leqslant 1/(p-1)$ implies C(p).

Definition. If $w \in G$ and $w = uxv$, with no cancellation occurring in this product, and $x \in X$, then we say that x is a *letter occurring in w*.

T_3^1: If r_1, r_2 and r_3 are s.c.r. elements of R, then, in at least one of the products r_1r_2, r_2r_3, r_3r_1, no cancellation occurs.

T_3^2: If a_1, a_2 and a_3 are letters occurring in s.c.r. elements of R, then $a_1a_2a_3 \neq 1$.

T_4^1: If $r_1, \ldots, r_5$ are s.c.r. elements of R, with each $r_ir_{i+1} \neq 1$, then there exists a G such that each $r'_i = ar_ia^{-1}$ is in R, and in at least one of the products $r'_ir'_{i+1}$, no cancellation occurs.

T_4^2: If a_1, a_2, a_3, a_4 are letters occurring in s.c.r. elements of R and a_1a_2, a_2a_3, $a_3a_4 \notin B$, then $a_1a_2a_3a_4 \neq 1$.

We now take conditions T_5^1 and T_5^2 to be the obvious analogs of T_3^1 and T_3^2.

We now state the main result of this section. It is an analog, for $\overline{\text{NFS}}$ groups, of Theorems I and IV of [13].

Theorem 5.1. *Let (G, B, X) be an NFS group, R be a symmetrised subset of G, N be the normal closure of R in G, and w be a nontrivial element of N. Under the additional hypothesis*

(i) C(6),

it follows that w contains some r from R with three pieces missing: w and r can be written $w = bac$ and $r = ax_1x_2x_3$ with almost no cancellation occurring in these products, where x_1,x_2 and x_3 are pieces.

Under the hypotheses

(ii) C(4), T_3 and T_3^2,

or

(iii) C(3), T_i^1, T_i^2, $i = 3, 4, 5$,

it follows that w contains some r from R with two pieces missing. □

It is pointed out by Lyndon [13] p. 225 that, in the free product case, the next result is not quite an immediate corollary of the last. This is because, for example, we may have $|x_1x_2x_3| < |x_1| + |x_2| + |x_3|$. However corresponding considerations strengthen the hypothesis $C'(\lambda)$, for free products as opposed to free groups, in a way that more than compensates for this. A similar argument clearly works for general $\overline{\text{NFS}}$ groups.

Corollary 5.2. *Let (G, B, X), R, N and w be as before. If we have*

(i) $C'(\lambda)$ *for some* $\lambda \leq 1/5$,

then we contains a part a of some r in R, with $|a| > (1-3\lambda)|r|$. If we have either

(ii) $C'(\lambda)$, *for some* $\lambda \leq \frac{1}{3}$, T_3^1 *and* T_3^2,

or

(iii) $C'(\lambda)$, *for some* $\lambda \leq \frac{1}{2}$, *and* T_i^1, T_i^2, $i = 3, 4, 5$.

then w contains a part a of some r in R, with $|a| > (1-2\lambda)|r|$. □

To prove Theorem 5.1, we must first construct diagrams over $\overline{\text{NFS}}$ groups, and then show that these diagrams have all the "usual" properties. We turn to this construction now. It is essentially the same as that used by Lyndon [13] for diagrams over ordinary free products, and that used by Schupp [19] for diagrams over free products with amalgamation.

Let R be a symmetrised subset of the NFS group (G, B, X), satisfying (i), (ii) or (iii) of Theorem 5.1. With certain sequences $p_1, p_2, \ldots, p_n$ of conjugates of elements of R we shall associate a *diagram* $M(p_1, p_2, \ldots, p_n)$ which will be a connected, simply-connected, oriented planar map with a distinguished vertex $0 \in M^{\cdot}$, the boundary of M. M will be labelled by a function φ into G satisfying:

(1) If $s_1, \ldots, s_t$ are, in order, the edges in the boundary cycle of M beginning at 0, then, writing $w = p_1 \cdots p_n$, we have $w = \varphi(s_1) \cdots \varphi(s_t)$ with almost no cancellation occurring in this product of labels.

(2) If D is any region of M and $e_1, \ldots, e_j$ are the edges in a boundary cycle δ of D, then $\varphi(e_1) \cdots \varphi(e_j)$ is equal to a c.r. conjugate of one of the p_i, and almost no cancellation occurs in this product.

By a *weak diagram* for a sequence $p_1, \ldots, p_n$ we mean a diagram M satisfying (2), but only a weaker form of (1), namely that the product of the boundary labels, taken in their "correct" order, is equal to $w = p_1 \cdots p_n$. Suppose the (weak) diagram M' can be obtained from the (weak) diagram M by: (a) choosing a new origin $0'$, not necessarily lying on the boundary $M^{\cdot}$ of M, for M', (b) deleting boundary edges ending up with a, possibly disconnected, diagram M'', of which $0'$ is a boundary vertex, and (c) deleting the connected components that do not contain $0'$, *then* we say M' is a subdiagram of M. It is important to notice that, in (b), we not only allow deletion of edges on the boundary of the original diagram M, but we also allow deletion of edges that become boundary edges in virtue of other edges having been deleted. We say a (weak) diagram is *reduced* if the product of the boundary labels (taken in their "correct" order) of any subdiagram is equal to 1 if and only if that subdiagram is a tree.

We say a sequence $p_1, p_2, \ldots, p_n$ of conjugates of elements of R is *minimal* if no shorter such sequence has the same product.

Lemma 5.3. *A (weak) diagram for a minimal sequence is reduced. Here we impose no cancellation hypotheses on R.*

Proof. Let M be a non-reduced (weak) diagram for a minimal sequence. Then M contains a subdiagram M' the product of whose boundary labels is 1, and which is not a tree. We can now divide M into diagrams $\bar{M}'$ and M'' as shown in Figure 1. The product of the boundary labels of M'' is clearly the same as the product w of the boundary labels of M. Since $\bar{M}'$ is not a tree, M'' contains less regions

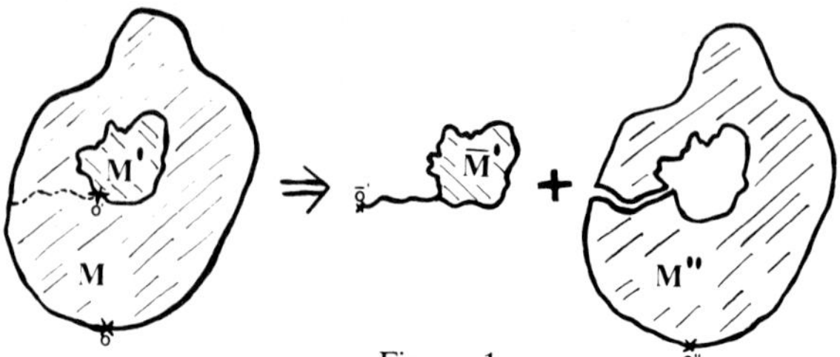

Figure 1.

than M, and so must be a diagram for a shorter sequence. This contradicts M being a diagram for a minimal sequence. □

Exactly as in [13], we may prove the following lemma.

Lemma 5.4. *If M is a reduced (weak) diagram, then the label on an interior edge is a piece, provided the boundary path of every path of every region is a simply connected closed path.* □

We recall the initial construction of the diagram M, over a free product F as described by Lyndon [13]. In this case vertices are divided into two classes, primary and secondary. The labels on every edge belong to a free factor X_i of F, with the labels on edges meeting at primary vertices belonging to different factors X_j, while the labels on edges meeting at secondary vertices belong to the same factor. Moreover in traversing any path through the diagram, one comes across, alternately, primary and secondary vertices. We shall use an analogous initial construction; however, following Schupp [19], we allow 1 to be a label. The precise relationship between the two classes of vertices and the labels on the edges in our initial construction shall be as follows:

(a) The label on any edge has length 0 or 1.

(b) If v_1, v_2, v_3 are vertices of M joined by edges $E_1 = (v_1, v_2)$ and $E_2 = (v_2, v_3)$ and v_1 is primary, then $|\varphi(E_1)\varphi(E_2)| \leq 1$. Moreover if v_1, v_2, v_3 are consecutive vertices of either the boundary path of some region or the boundary path of the whole diagram (starting at 0), then $|\varphi(E_1)\varphi(E_2)| = 1$.

(c) Suppose v_i $(i = 1, \ldots, 5)$ are consecutive vertices of the boundary path of some region, v_1 is primary and $E_i = (v_i, v_{i+1})$, for $i = 1, \ldots, 4$, then $|\varphi(E_1)\varphi(E_2)\varphi(E_3)\varphi(E_4)| = 2$. Unless we are dealing with a weak diagram, we require an analogous condition to obtain when the v_i are consecutive vertices of the boundary path of the whole diagram (starting at 0).

We introduce two ways of adjusting the labels on the edges of a diagram.

(i) Suppose the vertices v_i $(i = 1, \ldots, r)$ are joined to the vertex v by edges $E_i = (v_i, v)$ $(i = 1, \ldots, r)$ with labels $\varphi(E_i)$ $(i = 1, \ldots, r)$. Then we perform an *adjustment of the first kind* if, for each i, we change the label on E_i to $\varphi(E_i)h$, where h is a fixed element of B.

(ii) Suppose the primary vertices v_i $(i = 1, \ldots, r)$ are joined to the secondary vertex v by edges $E_i = (v_i, v)$ $(i = 1, \ldots, r)$ with labels $\varphi(E_i)$ $(i = 1, \ldots, r)$. Then we perform an *adjustment of the second kind* if, for each i, we change the label on E_i to $\varphi(E_i)(\varphi(E_1))^{-1}$.

Figure 2 illustrates an adjustment of the second kind. It is easy to see that adjustments of both kinds preserve properties (a), (b) and (c) of the labeling. Moreover, the precise set of quintuples of boundary points for which the analog of (c) fails remains unchanged by these adjustments. The product w of the labels on the boundary arc is unchanged by any adjustment with $v \neq 0$. If $v = 0$, then an adjustment of the first kind changes w to $h^{-1}wh$, for some $h \in B$, and, since we shall take care to make 0 a primary vertex, adjustments of the second kind will have no effect on w.

Now $R \cap B = \emptyset$, for if $R \neq \emptyset$ then any element of B is a piece, and so, by Lemmas 4.3 and 4.5, any conjugate p of an element of R can be written as $p = wrw^{-1}$ with no cancellation occurring and $r \in R$. Note that, since every element of R is c.r., if $p = w'r'w'^{-1}$ with no cancellation and $r' \in R$, then $|w| = |w'|$. We define $\mathrm{st}(p) = |w|$. We say a sequence $p_1, p_2, \ldots, p_n$ of conjugates of elements of R is *special* if it is minimal, and, for $i = 1, \ldots, n$, $p'_1 p'_2 \cdots p'_i = p_1 p_2 \cdots p_i$, with p'_j a conjugate of something in R for $1 \leq j \leq i$, implies $\mathrm{st}(p_i) \leq \mathrm{st}(p'_i)$.

Our initial construction of a diagram $M(p_1, p_2, \ldots, p_n)$ for a special sequence is as follows. If $n = 0$, then the diagram consists in the

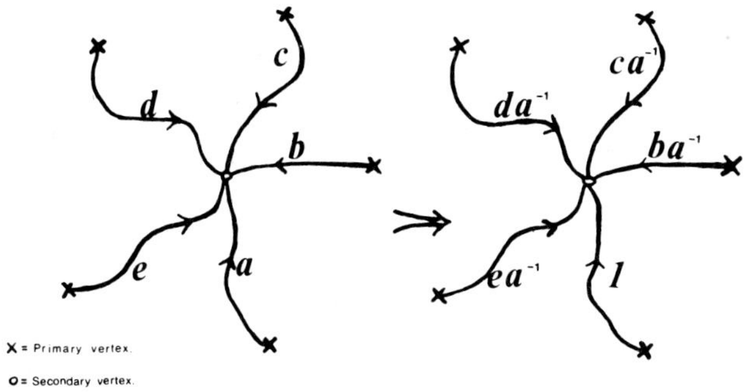

Figure 2.

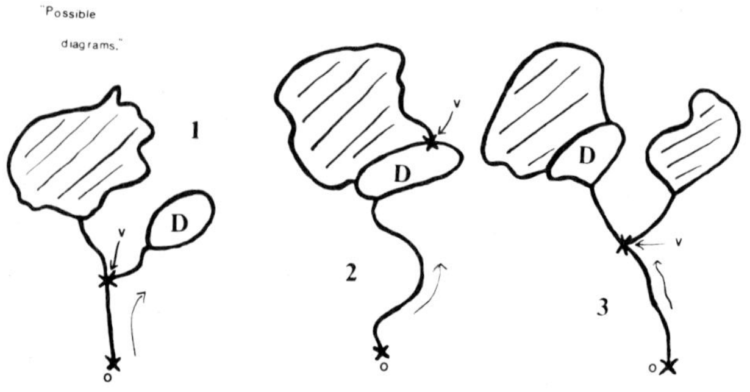

Figure 3.

primary vertex 0. If $n \geq 1$, then $p_1, \ldots, p_{n-1}$ is a special sequence, and so we may assume, inductively, that we have constructed a diagram $M(p_1, \ldots, p_{n-1})$ for it. We also assume, inductively, that the origin is primary, and that, when all vertices of degree 2 have been deleted, the diagram is, according as R satisfies (i), (ii) or (iii) of Theorem 5.1, a (3, 6), (4, 4) or (6, 3) map. Here, by a (p, q) map, we mean one in which each interior vertex has degree at least p and each interior region has degree at least q. We now form the usual 'lollypop' diagram for p_n, making the origin of this diagram primary, and form a weak diagram for $p_1, p_2, \ldots, p_n$ by indentifying the origins of the two diagrams. We now form the diagram $M(p_1, p_2, \ldots, p_n)$ from this diagram by a process of 'cancellation' on the boundary, which we shall describe fully below. Before doing so, we note that, in such a process, only edges on the boundary of the region of the 'lollypop' diagram can become identified with an edge on the boundary of some region of $M(p_1, \ldots, p_{n-1})$, for otherwise we could clearly construct a sequence $p'_1, p'_2, \ldots, p'_n$ of conjugates of elements of R, with $p'_1 p'_2 \cdots p'_n = p_1 p_2 \cdots p_n$ and $\mathrm{st}(p'_n) < \mathrm{st}(p_n)$, contradicting $p_1, p_2, \ldots, p_n$ being special. Informally, this says that the diagram $M(p_1, \ldots, p_n)$ will 'look like' one of the three diagrams of Figure 3, and the same is true of all the intermediate diagrams formed during the cancellation process. In Figure 3, D is the region from the 'lollypop' diagram for p_n, and v is the only vertex, if any, at which our cancellation process can take place.

To see how the cancellation process works, let M^* be an intermediate diagram formed during the process. Then there is precisely one quintuple of consecutive vertices v_i $(i = 1, \ldots, 5)$ of the boundary path joined by edges $E_i = (v_i, v_{i+1})$, for $i = 1, \ldots, 4$, for which

$|\varphi(E_1)\varphi(E_2)\varphi(E_3)\varphi(E_4)| \leq 1$, with v_1 primary. Since M^* 'looks like' one of the diagrams of Figure 3, with $v_3 = v$, we see that $v_2 \neq v_4$. (Our sole reason for using only special sequences in our construction is that it enables us to force this inequality.) We now transform the diagram as follows.

(i) If $|\varphi(E_1)\varphi(E_2)\varphi(E_3)\varphi(E_4)| = 1$, then because $v_2 \neq v_4$, it is possible to force $\varphi(E_2) = \varphi(E_3)^{-1}$, by making adjustments of the first kind. Having made such adjustments, we identify v_2 with v_4 and E_2 with E_3^{-1}, and then we make another adjustment of the first kind, if necessary, to restore the value of the product of the labels on the boundary. Now no further cancellations are possible on the boundary, and $M(p_1, \ldots, p_n)$ has been constructed.

(ii) If $|\varphi(E_1)\varphi(E_2)\varphi(E_3)\varphi(E_4)| = 0$, then we assert $v_1 \neq v_5$. For, if not, then we could construct a reduced diagram whose boundary consisted of a single edge with a label of length 0, and which would be (for reasons which will become clear below), according to case, a (3,6), (4,4) or (6,3) map. Corollary 2.4 of [13] now implies that some element of R is a product of two pieces, a contradiction. Since we also have $v_2 \neq v_4$, it is possible to force $\varphi(E_1) = \varphi(E_4)^{-1}$ and $\varphi(E_2) = \varphi(E_3) = 1$, by means of adjustments of both kinds. Having made such adjustments, we identify v_2 with v_4, E_2 with E_3^{-1}, v_1 with v_5 and E_1 with E_5^{-1}, and again we make a final adjustment of the first kind, if neccessary. We now see that the diagram, so obtained, 'looks like' one of the diagrams of Figure 3, and, if further cancellation is possible on the boundary path, then it takes place at $v_1 = v_5$, which 'looks like' the vertex v of Figure 3.

It is clear that, when we identify two primary vertices in this cancellation process, we obtain a primary vertex. To see that identifying two secondary vertices yields a secondary vertex, consider the situation of Figure 4, where we wish to show, for instance, that $|cd^{-1}| \leq 1$. We know $|ca^{-1}|, |ad^{-1}| \leq 1$, and if either of these is zero, then we are done. Suppose then that $|ca^{-1}| = |ad^{-1}| = 1$, but $|cd^{-1}| = 2$. Then, putting $g = ca^{-1}$, $h = ad^{-1}$ and $k = d$, we see that $g, h, k \in X$ but $gh \notin B \cup X$. So, by **N4***, $c = ghk \notin B \cup X$, which contradicts our assumption that all labels have length 0 or 1. Thus $|cd^{-1}| \leq 1$, as required.

We now wish to show that the cancellation process preserves the property of being, according to case, a (3,6), (4,4) or a (6,3) map, when all vertices of degree 2 have been deleted. We easily see that the T-conditions have the effect of excluding interior vertices of the 'wrong' degrees, except that T_4^2 does not exclude that the diagram should contain an interior vertex P of degree $d(P) = 4$. However

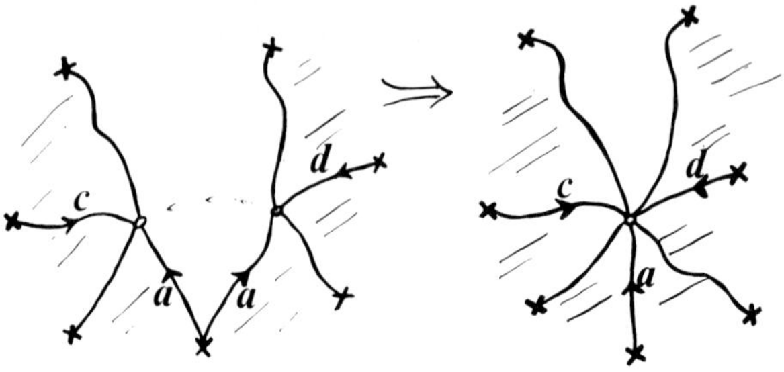

Figure 4.

suppose that in the passage from M^* to M^{**}, the diagram obtained by 'cancelling' at v_3, we have 'created' such a vertex. We wish to use a similar construction to that of Lyndon [13] pp. 224–225 to eliminate this vertex. However, with Lyndon's notation, in our case, T_4^2 only allows us to suppose $a_2a_1 \in B$, which implies $x_1 = hx_3$, for some $h \in B$. However, the vertices P_1 and P_3 must be distinct, for otherwise we should have an impossible subdiagram, which is both a (6,3) map and has label of length 0 on its boundary. Hence it is possible to force $x_1 = x_3$, by means of an adjustment of the first kind, and then to eliminate P as in [13].

We now show that the boundary of any region of our final diagram $M(p_1, \ldots, p_n)$ is a simple closed path. Suppose not, then there exists a region D such that its boundary $D^{\cdot}$ is not a simple closed curve, but that the submap L obtained by taking $D^{\cdot}$ and all of M interior to D contains no other such region. Let l be a loop contained in $D^{\cdot}$, but not the whole of D, such that the subdiagram K obtained by taking l and the whole of M interior to l contains as few regions as possible. We see that at most one vertex v_0, say, of l lies in $D^{\cdot}$. It follows from our T- and C-conditions that every region of K has degree at least p and every interior vertex of K has degree at least q (i.e. K is a $[p, q]$ map), where, according to case, $(p, q) = (3,6)$, (4,4) or (6,3). K contains more than one region, for otherwise C(p) is contradicted, and by [13] corollary 2.4, must therefore, contain more than one vertex. Then, by [13] corollary 2.2, $\Sigma^{\cdot}(p/q + 2 - d(v)) \geq p$, where this sum is taken over the boundary vertices of K. But the T-conditions imply that only v_0 can make a positive contribution to this sum, which gives us the contradiction that $\Sigma^{\cdot}(p/q + 2 - d(v)) < p$.

All the hard work in the proof of Theorem 5.1 is now over. We merely now need to remark that it is obvious that every w in N, the normal closure of R, can be written as a product of a special sequence, and the theorem now follows in the same manner as Theorem I of Lyndon [13]. □

It is also possible to use corollary 2.4 of [13], and our construction of a diagram, in a similar way to prove our next result.

Lemma 5.5. *Let (G, B, X), R, N and w be as before. Suppose further that w is not conjugate to an element of R. If we have*

(i) $C'(\lambda)$, *for some* $\lambda \leq 1/5$,

then some s.c.r. conjugate of w contains two disjoint subwords, a_1 and a_2, such that, for $i = 1, 2$, each a_i is a part of some r_i in R, with $|a_i| > (1-3\lambda)|r_i|$.

If we have either

(ii) $C'(\lambda)$, *for some* $\lambda \leq \frac{1}{3}$, T_3^1 *and* T_3^2,

or

(iii) $C'(\lambda)$, *for some* $\lambda \leq \frac{1}{2}$, T_i^1, T_i^2, $i = 3, 4, 5$,

then some s.c.r. conjugate of w contains two disjoint subwords, a_1 and a_2, such that, for $j = 1, 2$, each a_j is a part of some r_j in R, with $|a_j| > (1-2\lambda)|r_j|$. □

There is, of course, a non-metric version of this last lemma, which the interested reader might like to formulate for himself/herself. We end this section with a few remarks on our results. Firstly it is clear that, by making appropriate adjustments of the second kind to our final diagram, the subwords a of w, in Theorem 5.1 and Corollary 5.2, and the two subwords a_i $(i = 1, 2)$ of an s.c.r. conjugate or w, in Lemma 5.5, can be taken to consist of a consecutive sequence of 'letters' from the normal form of w, or, respectively, the s.c.r. conjugate of w. However, we cannot take a (respectively a_i, for $i = 1, 2$) to consist of a consecutive sequence of 'letters' from a normal form for r (respectively r_i, for $i = 1, 2$), without allowing for amalgamations to take place when we express it as a subword of w (respectively an s.c.r. conjugate of w).

Our second remark concerns the strength of the C-conditions. Suppose R satisfies $C'(\lambda)$, and $r \in R$ has the form $r = ab$ with almost no cancellation occurring, where a is a piece. By definition, there exists $r' \in R$, which can be written $r' = ab'$ with almost no cancellation occurring, with $r \neq r'$. This fact can be illustrated by the two region diagram of Figure 5. If r is not s.c.r., then, provided $|a| \neq 0$, we can make an adjustment of the second kind at the vertex v, which, obviously, is secondary, to make r s.c.r., while leaving r' c.r. and

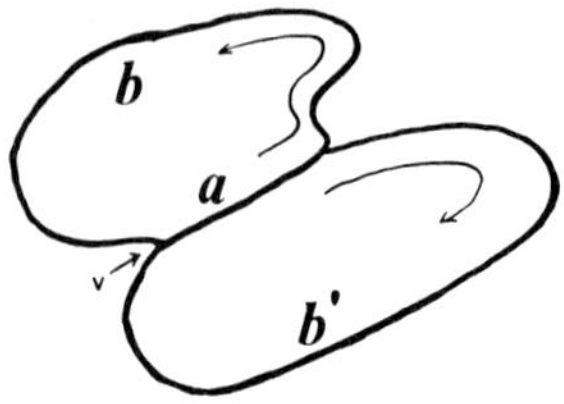

Figure 5.

leaving the length of a constant. We thus see that $C'(\lambda)$ implies that if $r \in R$ and r is *not* s.c.r. and $r = ab$, almost no cancellation occurring, and a is a piece, then $|a| < (|r| - 1)$.

Our third remark concerns the formulation of Corollary 5.2 and Lemma 5.5. For example, in Corollary 5.2(i), to conform with the 'usual' way of formulating such results, we have written $|a| > (1 - 3\lambda)|r|$. But it is clear that a stronger result holds, namely, that we can write $r = ab$, almost no cancellation occurring, with $|b| < 3\lambda|r|$. We shall have occasion to use this stronger form of our results in the next section. The easiest way if doing this, while avoiding undue circumlocutions, is simply to agree that, when we say that a is more than α of r, what we mean is that $r = ab$, for some b, almost no cancellation occurring, where $|b| < (1 - \alpha)|r|$. This convention has the advantage that, if a is more than half of r, then $|b| < |a|$.

Our fourth remark concerns the applications of the results of this section. We shall only apply Case (i) of the various results; we have already given our reasons for including the other cases. The results are so fundamental to the subject, and shall be used so often, that it would become tiresome to refer to them by name at each application. Accordingly, we shall not do so, but we do not anticipate that this will cause the reader undue difficulty. We shall, in fact, be mainly concerned with proving embedding theorems, for which purpose, we shall, for the most part, need Corollary 5.2, or, to be precise, a trivial corollary of it. We leave the reader to judge whether or not, given Corollary 5.2, the next result is worth stating at all. However, if it is to be stated, it must clearly be called a theorem.

Theorem 5.6. *Let (G, B, X) be an $\overline{NFS}$ group, R be a symmetrised subset of G, N be the normal closure of R in G, and w be a non-trivial element of N. If we have $C'(\lambda)$, for some $\lambda \leq 1/5$, and R contains no element of $(B \cup X)^2$, then G/N embeds $B \cup X$.*

Proof. N contains no element of $(B \cup X)^2$. (Note that if $r \in R$ and $|r| \leq 5$, then every R-piece contained in r has length 1.) $\square$

§6. Control over torsion, conjugacy and the centre in 9th and 10th groups

In this section, (G, B, X) is a fixed $\overline{\text{NFS}}$ group, R is a fixed symmetrised subset of G, N is the normal closure of R in G, and F is the factor group G/N.

Lemma 6.1. *Suppose R contains no p.p.p. If $x^m a \in R$, where m, $|x^m a| \geq 2$, x is s.c.r. with $|x| \geq 1$, and almost no cancellation occurs in the product $(x^m)a$, then $ax \neq xa$, and x and x^{m-1} are pieces.*

Proof. Suppose $ax = xa$. Since R contains no p.p.p., $|a| \geq 1$. Applying Lemma 4.9(ii), $x = hw^j$ and $a = h'w^k$, for some $h, h' \in B$, $w \in G$ and $j, k \in \mathbf{Z} - \{0\}$, where w is s.c.r., $|w^2| = 2|w|$, and h, h' and w commute in pairs. Now $x^m a = (h^{mj}h'^k)w^{mj+k}$ is not a p.p.p., and so $mj + k = \pm 1$. Obviously, $|j|, |k|, |w| \geq 1$, and so

$$d(x^m, a^{-1}) = \tfrac{1}{2}\{m\,|j|\,|w| + |k|\,|w| - |mj + k|\,|w|\} \geq 1,$$

and so cancellation occurs in $(x^m)a$, contrary to hypothesis. Thus $ax \neq xa$, and so $x^{m-1}(xa) \neq x^{m-1}(ax) \in R$ and $x(x^{m-1}a) \neq x(x^{m-2}ax) \in R$, with almost no cancellation occurring in any of these products. Hence x and x^{m-1} are pieces. □

Corollary 6.2. *Suppose R satisfies C′(1/5), and contains no element of $(B \cup X)^2$ and no p.p.p. Suppose $x \in X$, $b \in B$, $m \geq 1$ and $|x^2| = 2$, then $x^m b \neq 1$ in F.*

Proof. Since F embeds $B \cup X$, we may assume $m \geq 2$. Since $b \in B$, it is a piece. If $x^m b \in R$, then, by the lemma, it is a product of three pieces, contradicting C′(1/5). Thus, if $x^m b = 1$ in F, then some s.c.r. conjugate of $x^m b$ contains two disjoint subwords, each of which is more than 2/5 of some element of R. From this it easily follows that some element of R has the form $x^n a$, with almost no cancellation occurring, and a being a product of at most three pieces. If $|a| = 0$, then, as above, this element of R is a product of three pieces, contradicting C′(1/5). Thus $|a| \geq 1$, and so, by C′(1/5), $|x^m a| \geq 6$, and so $|x^m| \geq 2$. From the lemma, x and x^{m-1} are pieces, and so $x^m a$ is a product of 5 pieces, contradicting C′(1/5). Hence $x^m b \neq 1$ in F, as required. □

Corollary 6.3. *Suppose $Z(G) \nleq B$, then, if R satisfies C′(1/5) and contains no element of $(B \cup X)^2$ and no p.p.p., then $R = \emptyset$.*

Proof. By Theorem 4.7, if $Z(G) \not\subseteq B$, then either $X = G - B$, when there is nothing to prove, or every element of $G - B$ has the form $x^m b$, where $x \in X$, $b \in B$, $m \geq 1$ and $|x^2| = 2|x|$. Thus, in the latter case, by Corollary 6.2, F embeds G, and so $R = \emptyset$. □

Theorem 6.4 (Torsion theorem for 9th groups). *Let (G, B, X), R, N and F be as above. Suppose R satisfies $C'(1/9)$, and contains no element of $(B \cup X)^2$ and no p.p.p. Then every element of finite order in F is conjugate in F to an element of $B \cup X$. Hence F contains an element of finite order n if and only if G does.*

Proof. Let w have finite order n in F, and let C be the set of all elements of G whose images in F are conjugate, in F, to w. Let $z \in C$ have minimum possible length. If $|z| \geq 2$, then z is s.c.r. and no c.r. conjugate of z can have the form ab, almost no cancellation occurring, with a more than half an element of R. Since R contains no p.p.p., $z^n \not\in R$, and so contains more than 5/9 of some element of R. Replacing z by an s.c.r. conjugate, if necessary, we may suppose $z^n = ub$, no cancellation occurring, where u is more than 6/9 of some element of R. Since u is not a subword of z, by [10] lemma 2.4, $u = z^m t$ and $z = ts$ for some $t, s \in G$, no cancellation occurring in either product. Thus some $r \in R$ has the form $r = uv = (ts)^m tv$, with almost no cancellation occurring in the product uv and no cancellation anywhere else. If $m \geq 2$, then, by Lemma 6.1, $(ts)^{m-1}$ and ts are pieces, and we easily see that t is also a piece, which implies that u is the product of three pieces contradicting its being more than 6/9 of an element of R. If $m = 1$, then $r = tstv$ and t is a piece unless $tstv = tvts$. But, in this case, either $v = sv_1$, no cancellation occurring, when, by Lemma 6.1, ts, and hence t, is a piece, or $s = vs_1$, almost no cancellation occurring, when again t is a piece. Thus t is less than 1/9 of r, and, since tst is more than 6/9 of r, we see that v is less than 3/9 of r. Hence:

$$|z| = |ts| \geq ||tst| - |t|| > \frac{6}{9}|r| - \frac{1}{9}|r| = \frac{5}{9}|r| > |t| + |v| \geq |tv| = |(tv)^{-1}|.$$

But $z = ts = (tv)^{-1}$ in F, which contradicts the minimality of $|z|$.
Hence $|z| \geq 1$, and the theorem is proved. □

Lemma 6.5. *Suppose R satisfies $C'(1/10)$, contains no element of $(B \cup X)^2$, and contains no element that is conjugate to its own inverse. Then for each $g \in G$, there exists $\bar{g} \in G$ such that $g = \bar{g}$ in F, and, for all $s, t \in B \cup X$, if $g^{-1}sg = t$ in F then $\bar{g}^{-1}s\bar{g} = t$ in G.*

Proof. We prove the stronger result (***).

(***) *Suppose R satisfies the hypotheses of Lemma* 6.5. *If* $g \in G$, *then any element* $\bar{g} \in gN$ *of shortest possible length satisfies the conclusion of the lemma.*

Suppose (***) to be false. Let $g \in G$ be an element of smallest possible length such that there exists $\bar{g}$, of smallest possible length in gN, that falsifies (***). Clearly $\bar{g}$ has smallest possible length in $\bar{g}N = gN$, $\bar{g}^{-1}s\bar{g} = t$ in F if and only if $g^{-1}sg = t$ in F, and, by the minimality of the length of g, $|\bar{g}| = |g|$. Thus we may assume $g = \bar{g}$. Note that here we are taking a new choice for g; we do not claim that, by taking $\bar{g}$ to be our original g, the conclusion of the lemma would not hold. Now there exist $s, t \in B \cup X$ such that $g^{-1}sg = t$ in F, but not in G. It easily follows that $|g| \geq 2$. Write $g = g_1 \cdots g_r$ $(r \geq 2)$ in normal form. We assert $|g_1^{-1}sg_1|, |g_rtg_r^{-1}| \geq 2$. Suppose, for instance, that $g_1^{-1}sg_1 = s_1 \in B \cup X$. Then $h = g_2 \cdots g_r$ must be a shortest element of hN, and, by the minimality of g, since $h^{-1}s_1h = t$ in F, this equation also holds in G. But this implies the contradiction that $g^{-1}sg = t$ in G. Hence $|g_1^{-1}sg_1| \geq 2$, and, similarly, $|g_rtg_r^{-1}| \geq 2$.

The word $g^{-1}sgt^{-1}$ must have an s.c.r. conjugate that can be written, in normal form, as $g_r^{-1} \cdots (g_1^{-1}s)g_1 \cdots (g_rt^{-1})$ or as one of the eight similar forms obtained by allowing s to amalgamate with g_1 instead of g_1^{-1}, or by allowing t^{-1} to amalgamate with g_r^{-1} instead of g_r, or by allowing both s to amalgamate with g_1 and t^{-1} to amalgamate with g_r^{-1}, or by allowing less amalgamations.

Call this s.c.r. conjugate of $g^{-1}sgt^{-1}$, w. If $w \in R$, then some c.r. conjugate of w can be written ga, with almost no cancellation occurring, and some c.r. conjugate of w^{-1} can be written gb, with almost no cancellation, but $|g| \geq \frac{1}{4}|w|$, and so, by $C'(1/10)$, $w \sim w^{-1}$, contrary to hypothesis. Thus $w \notin R$, and since $w = 1$ in F, some s.c.r. conjugate of w contains two disjoint subwords each of which is more than 7/10 of some element of R. At least one of these subwords does not "involve" the letter t^{-1}, and so there exists an element $u \in R$, 7/10 of which has the form:

$$v = g_j^{-1} \cdots g_1^{-1}sg_1 \cdots g_k,$$

where, at most, an amalgamation occurs between g_1^{-1} and s or between s and g_1, but not at both places. From the minimality of g, neither $g_1 \cdots g_j$ nor $g_1 \cdots g_k$ is more than half an element of R, and it easily follows that both have length $> 1/10|u|$. By $C'(1/10)$, $u \sim u^{-1}$, contrary to hypothesis. This contradiction proves (***). □

Corollary 6.6. *If R satisfies the hypotheses of Lemma* 6.5, *and contains* *no p.p.p., then F embeds the centraliser of every s.c.r. element of length 1, and, if x is such an element, then* $C_F(x) = C_G(x)$*, with the "obvious" identification.*

Proof. It is immediate from the lemma that if $x \in X$ is s.c.r., then $C_F(x)$ is the image of $C_G(x)$. If $C_G(x) \subseteq B \cup X$, then it is embedded in F, and the result follows. If $C_G(x) \not\subseteq B \cup X$, then, by Lemma 4.9(iii), every element of $C_G(x)$ has the form $x^m b$, where $m \in \mathbf{Z}$ and $b \in B$. Since $|x^2| = 2$, it follows from Corollary 6.2, that F embeds $C_G(x)$, and the result holds. □

The next result is an immediate corollary of Lemma 6.5, but, in view of its content, we label it a theorem.

Theorem 6.7. *Let* (G, B, X)*, R, N and F be as above. Suppose R satisfies* $C'(1/10)$*, and contains no element of* $(B \cup X)^2$ *and no element that is conjugate in G to its own inverse. Then any two elements of* $B \cup X$ *are conjugate in F if and only if they are conjugate in G.* □

Theorem 6.8. *Let* (G, B, X)*, R, N and F be as above. Suppose R satisfies* $C'(1/10)$*, and contains no element of* $(B \cup X)^2$*, no p.p.p., and no element that is conjugate in G to its own inverse. Then* $Z(G)$ *is embedded in F, and, with the "obvious" identification,* $Z(G) = Z(F)$*.*

Proof. If $R = \emptyset$, then the result is trivial, so suppose $R \neq \emptyset$. By Corollary 6.3, $Z(G) \subseteq B$, and so is embedded in F. But $z \in Z(F)$ if and only if $z^{-1}sz = s$, for all $s \in B \cup X$, and so, by Lemma 6.5, $Z(F)$ must be the image in F of $Z(G)$, and the theorem is proved. □

§7. SSC groups

In this section, we consider a class of $\overline{\text{NFS}}$ groups, each member of which has many "nice" small cancellation quotients. In the next section, we shall be concerned mainly, but not exclusively, with quotients of groups from this class. We start with some definitions.

Definitions. Let R be a symmetrised subset of the $\overline{\text{NFS}}$ group (G, B, X). By the *basis number* $b(R)$ of R we mean the number of equivalence classes in R under the equivalence relation "r is conjugate to s or s^{-1}". A *basis* for R is a set of representatives for these classes.

If S is a basis for R, then $\mathrm{Card}(S) = b(R) \leqslant \mathrm{Card}(R)$, but, in general, we need not have $b(R) = \mathrm{Card}(R)$.

Definition. Let κ be an infinite cardinal. Then an $\overline{\text{NFS}}$ group (G, B, X) is an *SSC-κ group*, if $|G| = \kappa$ and it contains a symmetrised set R satisfying $C'(1/6)$, $b(R) = \kappa$, and the centraliser condition (C.C.) below.

C.C. Every element $r \in R$ has an s.c.r. conjugate r' satisfying

$$C_G(r') \cap B = Z(G).$$

An *SSC group* is defined to be an $\overline{\text{NFS}}$ group that is an SSC-κ group for some κ.

Before we give examples of SSC groups, we need a concept introduced by Schupp [19].

Definition. Let A be a subgroup of the group H. Let $\{x_1, x_2\}$ be a pair of distinct elements of H, neither of which are in A. We say that $\{x_1, x_2\}$ is a *blocking pair for A in H* if the following two conditions are satisfied:

(i) $x_i^\varepsilon x_j^\delta \notin A$, $1 \leq i, j \leq 2$, $\varepsilon = \pm 1$, $\delta = \pm 1$, unless $x_i^\varepsilon x_j^\delta = 1$,

(ii) if $a \in A$, $a \neq 1$, then $x_i^\varepsilon a x_j^\delta \notin A$, $1 \leq i, j \leq 2$, $\varepsilon = \pm 1$, $\delta = \pm 1$.

Theorem 7.1. (i) *A non-abelian free group of rank r, with the "usual" NFS structure, is an SSC-κ group, where* $\kappa = \max(r, \aleph_0)$.

(ii) *A free product of two or more non-trivial groups is an SSC-$\aleph_0$ group, with the single exception of the group $C_2 * C_2$, provided it has order $\aleph_0$.*

(iii) *A free product with amalgamation $\langle A * B : H = K\rangle$, where $H \leq A$, $K \leq B$, $H \cong K$, $A \neq H$ and B contains a blocking pair over K, is an SSC-$\aleph_0$ group, provided it has order $\aleph_0$.*

(iv) *An HNN group $\langle H, t : t^{-1}At = A\psi\rangle$, where $\psi : A \to B$ is an isomorphism between subgroups of H and $|H| = \aleph_0$, is an SSC-$\aleph_0$ group under any of the following conditions:*

(a) *There exists $x \in H$, $x \notin A$, $x \notin B$ such that $x^{-1}Bx \cap A = 1$.*

(b) *There exist $x, y \in H$ such that $x^{-1}Ax \cap A = y^{-1}By \cap B = 1$.*

(c) *There exists $m \geq 1$ such that $C_m = D_m = 1$, where $C_0 = A$, $D_0 = B$, and, for $n \geq 0$, $C_{n+1} = A \cap \psi(C_n)$ and $D_{n+1} = B \cap \psi^{-1}(D_n)$.*

(v) *A group that can be presented with at least three generators and only one relator can be equipped with an NFS structure in such a way that it becomes an SSC-$\aleph_0$ group.*

In all the above cases, the SSC groups have a trivial centre.

Proof. These are the "classical" cases. The existence of the appropriate symmetrised sets follows from the results of [13], [18] and [19]. The fact that these groups have trivial centre follows easily from the construction used in each case. Moreover C.C., which now has the form: "Every element $r \in R$ has an s.c.r. conjugate r' satisfying $C_G(r') \cap B = 1$", is easy to check. For example, in case (iii), if $k \in K$, $k \neq 1$, then k cannot commute with either element of the blocking pair $\{x_1, x_2\}$ in B over K, and so the group has trivial centre. If R is the symmetrised set constructed in [19] (to be precise, R is the symmetrised set of [19] §4 with $C = 1$), then for $r \in R$, let r' be an s.c.r. conjugate of r whose first letter in its normal form is $x_1^{\pm 1}$. If r' commutes with $k \in K$, then cancellation takes place in $r'kr'^{-1}$, which implies that $x_1^{\varepsilon} k x_1^{\eta} \in K$, for some $\varepsilon = \pm 1$, $\eta = \pm 1$. From the definition of a blocking pair, we now see $k = 1$, and so C.C. holds.

We remark that Murasugi [15] first noticed that the one relator groups of (v) have trivial centre, however, Sacerdote and Schupp [18] show that they are all IINN groups of type (iv)(a), and, in the present context, this is the easiest way of seeing that they have trivial centre. □

Lemma 7.2. *Let (G, B, X) be an SSC-κ group. Let real numbers $\lambda, n > 0$ be given. Then G contains a symmetrised set R satisfying $C'(\lambda)$, $b(R) = \kappa$, C.C., $|r| > n$ for all $r \in R$, and containing no p.p.p. and no element conjugate to its own inverse.*

Proof. By definition, G contains a symmetrised set R_1 satisfying $C'(1/6)$, $b(R) = \kappa$, and C.C. Partition a basis S_1 for R_1 into pairwise disjoint triples. To each such triple $U = (s_1, s_2, s_3)$, say, we associate a word $W(U)$, which we define to be an s.c.r. conjugate of:

$$\prod_{i=1}^{M} \{s_1 s_2 (s_1 s_3)^i\},$$

where M is some large number. We now take the set of all $W(U)$ to be a basis for a symmetrised set R. Now in each $W(U)$, less than 1/6 of each s_i is lost through cancellation either at the beginning or at the end of this s_i, which leaves at least $\frac{2}{3}$ as a subword of $W(U)$. But since each s_i can be identified by as much as 1/6 of it, it is clear that we can force R to satisfy all the required conditions, except, possibly, C.C., merely by making a large enough choice for M. To see that we can force R to satisfy C.C., consider how cancellation can occur on the left-hand side of the equation $W(U)^{-1} h W(U) = h$, which we shall assume holds for some $h \in B$. Lemma 2.1(i) of [10] tells us that, as soon as an amalgamation takes place, the left-hand side becomes reduced, which implies that no amalgamations take place. But this implies that some $a \in G$ exists such that when we write $W(U) = uav$

and $r = ab$, no cancellation occurring in either product, with a more than 1/6 of $s_i \in U$, and r an s.c.r. conjugate of s_i, then an equation of the form $k_1 a = ak_2$, with $k_1, k_2 \in B$, and k_1 a conjugate of h, must hold. Replacing s_i by an s.c.r. conjugate, if necessary, in the definition of $W(U)$, we can write $W(U)$ in the above form where r satisfies $C_G(r) \cap B = Z(G)$. Since a is not a piece and $k_1 a = ak_2$, we see that k_1 must commute with r. Hence $k_1 \in Z(G)$, and, since h is conjugate to k_1, $h \in Z(G)$. □

Remark. By a similar argument to that used above, we see that if R_1 satisfies C.C. and contains no element of X, then *any* s.c.r. element $r \in R_1$ satisfies $C_G(r) \cap B = Z(G)$, and so no special choice of a c.r. conjugate for s_i in the definition of $W(U)$ is needed, in this case, for the conclusion of the lemma to hold.

The next result is easy to see and its proof shall be omitted.

Lemma 7.3. *Let R be a symmetrised set, in the $\overline{NFS}$ group (G, B, X), satisfying $C'(1/6)$, C.C., $|r| \geq 2$ for all $r \in R$, and containing no p.p.p. and no element conjugate to its own inverse. Then, for all $r \in R$, $C_G(r) \cap (B \cup X) = Z(G)$.* □

Corollary 7.4. *If M is a normal subgroup of the* SSC *group (G, B, X) and $M \leq B$, then $M \leq Z(G)$.*

Proof. By Lemma 7.2, G contains a symmetrised set R satisfying the hypotheses of Lemma 7.3. Let $r \in R$ and $m \in M$. Then $r^{-1}mr = m_1 \in M$. Since r cannot be an R-piece and $mrm^{-1} = rm_1m^{-1} \in R$, we see $m = m_1$, and so $m \in C_G(r) \cap B = Z(G)$. □

It is, perhaps, worth remarking that the last result can be strengthened to the statement that any bounded normal subgroup of an SSC group lies inside the centre, where we say $S \subseteq G$ is *bounded* if $S \subseteq (B \cup X)^n$, for some n.

Lemma 7.5. *If (G, B, X) is an SSC group, then for any subgroup $M \leq Z(G)$, G/M is an SSC group and $Z(G/M) = Z(G)/M$.* In particular, *$G/Z(G)$ is an SSC group with trivial centre.*

Proof. Let us write a bar over symbols to denote image in $\bar{G} = G/M$. It is obvious, from Lemma 7.2, that $X \neq G - B$, and that we do not have $X = B\{t, t^{-1}\}B$, with G a split extension of B by an infinite cycle

$\langle t \rangle$. It follows that $(\bar{G}, \bar{B}, \bar{X})$ does not have either of these two forms, and so, by Theorem 4.7, $Z(\bar{G}) \leqslant \bar{B}$. Let R be the symmetrised subset of G constructed in the proof of Lemma 7.2. Let $p \in G$, and suppose that $\bar{p}$ is an $\bar{R}$-piece. (Note that, since the map $G \to \bar{G}$ is length preserving, $\bar{R}$ is a symmetrised subset of $\bar{G}$.) Then there exist $a, b \in G$ and $r_1 \neq r_2 \in R$, such that $r_1 \equiv pa \pmod{Z(G)}$ and $r_2 \equiv pb \pmod{Z(G)}$, and it follows that p is an R-piece. Thus $\bar{R}$ satisfies C′(1/6) if R does.

Now suppose $r \in R$ and $h \in B$. If $h \in C_{\bar{G}}(\bar{r}) \cap \bar{B}$, then $r^{-1}hr = hz$, for some $z \in Z(G)$. If R satisfies C′(1/6), then $z = 1$. Since R was constructed as in the proof of Lemma 7.2, we may assume it satisfies the hypotheses of Lemma 7.3. Thus, $h \in Z(G)$ and $\bar{R}$ satisfies C.C. Thus G/M is an SSC group. Since $Z(G/M) \subseteq \bar{B}$, the inverse image, in G, of $Z(G/M)$ lies in B, and hence, by Corollary 7.4, lies in $Z(G)$. Hence $Z(G/M) = Z(G)/M$. □

Lemma 7.6. *Let (G, B, X), λ, n be as in Lemma 7.2, let R_1 be a symmetrised subset of G satisfying C′(1/6) and C.C., and suppose T is a finite subset of $G - 1$. Then there exist symmetrised subsets R_2 and R_3 of G, both satisfying the conclusion of Lemma 7.2, such that* (i) *every subword a or $r \in R_2$, satisfying $|a| \geqslant \lambda |r|$, contains every element of T as a subword,* (ii) *$R_2 \subseteq \mathrm{gp}(R_1, T)$ and* (iii) *$R_3 \subseteq \mathrm{gp}(R_1, T) \cap (\bigcap_{t \in T} \langle t \rangle^G)$.*

Proof. Let $T = \{t_1, t_2, \ldots, t_s\}$. By Lemma 7.2, there exists a symmetrised subset R^* of G satisfying C′(1/20), $b(R^*) = \kappa$, C.C., $|r| > 20|t_i|$ for all $r \in R^*$ and all $t_i \in T$, and containing no p.p.p. and no element conjugate to its own inverse. From the form of the construction of R^*, we see $R^* \in \mathrm{gp}(R_1)$. It follows from Lemma 6.1, that there exists, for each $i = 1, \ldots, s$ and each $\varepsilon = \pm 1$, $m(i, \varepsilon) \geqslant 1$, such that, for all $r \in R^*$, $r(t_i^{\varepsilon})^{m(i,\varepsilon)}r$ contains t_i^{ε} as a subword, but

$$2|r| \leqslant |r(t_i^{\varepsilon})^{m(i,\varepsilon)}r| \leqslant \frac{46}{20}|r|.$$

Now, we construct R_2 from R^*, by first partitioning a basis S^* for R^* into pairwise disjoint triples. If $U = (s_1, s_2, s_3)$ is such a triple, we first form the modified triple $U' = (s_1', s_2, s_3)$, where

$$s_1' = s_1 t_1^{m(1,1)} s_1 t_2^{m(2,1)} s_1 \cdots t_s^{m(s,1)} s_1 t_1^{-m(1,-1)} s_1 \cdots t_s^{-m(s,-1)} s_1.$$

We now construct R_2, by a similar construction to that of Lemma 7.2, but using modified triples U' instead of U. It is clear that we can make R_2 satisfy (i) and (ii).

We illustrate the construction of R_3 in the case $T = \{t\}$. The general case follows from an obvious induction argument. The construction is similar to the construction of R_2, but we take our modified triples to be $U'' = (s''_1, s''_2, s''_3)$, where $s''_i = s_i^{-1} t s_i$. Since R^* contains no element conjugate to its own inverse, we see that this works. Obviously $R_3 \subseteq \mathrm{gp}(R_1, t) \cap \langle t \rangle^G$. $\square$

We now come to our most important "New symmetrised sets for old" construction.

Lemma 7.7. *Let (G, B, X) be an NFS group, and suppose λ, μ are real numbers satisfying $0 < 3\lambda < \mu < \frac{1}{2}$. Let R_1 be a symmetrised subset of G, which satisfies $C'(\lambda)$, and which contains no element of length less than $2 + 2/(\mu - 3\lambda)$, no element conjugate to its own inverse, and no p.p.p. Suppose S_1 is a basis for R_1. Let $\varphi : S_1 \to B \cup X$ be a function such that, for all $s \in S_1$, $(s\varphi)s$ is c.r. and $C_G(s) \cap (B \cup X) \subseteq C_G(s\varphi)$. Let $S = \{(s\varphi)s : s \in S_1\}$, and let R be the symmetrised closure of S. Then R satisfies $C'(\mu)$, and contains no element of length less than $2/(\mu - 3\lambda)$, no element conjugate to its own inverse, and no p.p.p.*

Proof. Since the length of an element of G is decreased, at most, by 2 when it is premultiplied by an element of $B \cup X$, it is clear that R contains no element of length less than $v = 2/(\mu - 3\lambda)$. Now suppose we can write $r_1 = pa$, $r_2 = pb$, almost no cancellation occurring, with $r_1 \neq r_2 \in R$. By the comments following Corollary 5.2, we may suppose r_1 to be s.c.r. Suppose $|p| \geq 3\lambda |r_1| + 2$, then it is clear from the construction of R that $p = q_1 f_1 q_2 f_2 q_3$, with no cancellation occurring, with $f_1, f_2 \in B \cup X$, and with q_1, q_2 and q_3 being subwords of r_1 and r_2 that were not "disturbed" during the construction of R from R_1. Clearly at least one of the q_i is not an R_1-piece. This q_i identifies an element $s \in S_1$, from which r_1 and r_2 were both constructed, and it is clear from the fact that R_1 contains no element that is conjugate to its own inverse that $s\varphi$ occurs in r_1 and r_2 to the same power. Thus taking inverses of both elements, if necessary, $r_1 = s_1(s\varphi)s_2$ and $r_2 = s_3(s\varphi)s_4$, where $s_1 s_2 = s_3 s_4$ and $s_2 s_1 = s_4 s_3 = s$. It follows from these equations that $s_3^{-1} s_1$ commutes with s. Write $h = s_3^{-1} s_1$. There exists $x \in X$ such that $x^{-1} s x$ is s.c.r., and so, from Lemma 4.9(ii) and the fact that R_1 contains no p.p.p., we see that $x^{-1} h x \in B$. Thus $|h| \geq 2$. If $|h| = 2$, then from $hs = sh$, we see that $s = xux^{-1}$, with no cancellation, and is not c.r., contradicting R_1 being symmetrised. Thus $h \in C_G(s) \cap (B \cup X) \subseteq C_G(s\varphi)$. Thus $r_1 = s_1(s\varphi)s_2 = s_3 h (s\varphi) s_2 = s_3(s\varphi) h s_2 = s_3(s\varphi)s_4 = r_2$. Thus if $r_1 \neq r_2$, then we must have:

$$|p| < 3\lambda |r_1| + 2 = \left(3\lambda + \frac{2}{|r_1|}\right) r_1 \leq \left(3\lambda + \frac{2}{2/(\mu - 3\lambda)}\right) |r_1| = \mu |r_1|.$$

Thus R satisfies $C'(\mu)$.

Suppose R contains some element conjugate to its own inverse, then we easily see that this element has two subwords that are mutually inverse, have not been disturbed in the construction of R from R_1, and are too long to be R_1-pieces. Thus R_1 contains an element that is conjugate to its own inverse, contrary to hypothesis. Thus no element of R is conjugate to its own inverse.

Suppose R contained a p.p.p. Then S_1 would contain an element of the form bx^m, where $b \in B \cup X$, $m \geqslant 2$, $|bx^m| \geqslant 3$, x is s.c.r. and $|x| \geqslant 1$. If almost no cancellation occurs in $b(x^m)$, then, by Lemma 6.1, x^{m-1} is an R_1-piece and $C'(1/6)$ fails for R_1. If cancellation occurs, then either $m \geqslant 3$, x^{m-2} is an R_1-piece and $C'(1/6)$ fails for R_1, or $m = 2$, and $b(x^2) = x_2' \cdots x_r x_1 x_2 \cdots x_r$ in normal form, where $x = x_1 \cdots x_r$ and $x_2' x_2^{-1} \in B$, and again $C'(1/6)$ fails for R_1. But this contradicts $\lambda < 1/6$. Thus R contains no p.p.p., and the lemma is proved. □

Remarks. When applying Lemma 7.7, it is usually easiest not to compute exact values for λ and μ, but to think of the lemma as showing that if we wish to construct R, satisfying "strong enough" cancellation conditions, then it is merely necessary to impose "strong enough" conditions. However, we have also imposed conditions on the mapping φ. The condition that $(s\varphi)s$ be c.r., for all $s \in S_1$, is nearly redundant, and one could do without it altogether by insisting that μ and λ be small enough. In any case it does not seem to lead to any difficulties in practice. The condition that $C_G(s) \cap (B \cup X) \subseteq C_G(s\varphi)$, is, by Lemma 7.3, automatically satisfied if R satisfies C.C. and G is an SSC group. However, if G is not an SSC group, then it requires careful checking.

§8. Applications

Application I. Simultaneous quotient groups

Definition. Let $\mathscr{L} = \{L_j\}_{j \in J}$ be a family of groups, then, by a *simultaneous quotient group* of $\mathscr{L}$, we mean a group that is a homomorphic image of each L_j, if $J \neq \emptyset$, while, if $J = \emptyset$, we allow any group to be a simultaneous quotient group of $\mathscr{L}$.

Theorem 8.1(A). *Let κ be an infinite cardinal. Let $\mathscr{L} = \{L_j\}_{j \in J}$ be a family of SSC-κ groups, with $|J| \leqslant \kappa$. Suppose G is any group satisfying $|G| \leqslant \kappa$. Then G can be embedded in a simultaneous quotient group Q of $\mathscr{L}$.* □

Before we prove Theorem 8.1(A), we prove a technical lemma. Before stating the lemma, we will define some notation that will be of use throughout this section.

Definition. We say that a symmetrised set R, in an $\overline{\text{NFS}}$ group satisfies $[\lambda, n]'$, for λ, $n > 0$, if it satisfies $C'(\lambda)$, and contains no p.p.p., no element conjugate to its own inverse, and no element of length less than n. We say it satisfies $[\lambda, n]$, if it satisfies $[\lambda, n]'$ and C.C., and we say it satisfies $[\lambda, n, \kappa]$, if it satisfies $[\lambda, n]$ and $b(R) = \kappa$.

Lemma 8.2. *Let J be a non-empty set, $\{\kappa_j\}_{j\in J}$ be a family of infinite cardinals, let $L_j = (L_j, B_j, X_j)$ be an SSC-κ_j group, for each $j \in J$, and let R_j be a symmetrised subset of L_j, with basis S_j, and satisfying $[\lambda, n, \kappa_j]$, for each $j \in J$, where $\lambda \leqslant 1/6$ and $n > 12$. Let*

$$F = \bigotimes_{j\in J}{}_{(\mathrm{N})}\, L_j,$$

the free product with centralised centres of the L_j, with the $\overline{\text{NFS}}$ structure induced on it by the L_j. Let R be the symmetrised closure of $\bigcup_j R_j$ in F, and let $S = \bigcup_j S_j$.

Then S is a basis for R, and R satisfies $[\lambda, n, \Sigma_j \kappa_j]$ in F.

Proof. We first prove the lemma in the case $Z(L_j) = 1$, for all $j \in J$. In this case, F is simply the free product$_{\mathrm{N}}$ of the SSC groups L_j. The base group or F is simply $B = * B_j$. It is clear from Corollary 4.3 that any element of R can be obtained from one in $\bigcup R_j$ by conjugating by an element of B. Let p be an R-piece, then there exist $pu \neq pv \in R$, with almost no cancellation occurring in these products. Let $pu = b_1^{-1} r_1 b_1$ and $pv = b_2^{-1} r_2 b_2$ where $b_1, b_2 \in B$, $r_1 \in L_{j(1)}$ and $r_2 \in L_{j(2)}$, for some $j(1), j(2) \in J$. It is clear that we may assume that when b_i is written in *free product* normal form, it does not end in a letter from $L_{j(i)}$. Now let a_i be the first letter in the $(L_{j(i)}, B_{j(i)}, X_{j(i)})$-normal form for r_i. If $|p| \geqslant 2$, in F, then $a_1^{-1} b_1 b_2^{-1} a_2 \in B$, and from the free product normal form for this element, and the fact that $a_i \notin B_{j(i)}$, we see that $b_1 = b_2$ and $j(1) = j(2) = j$, say. Thus premultiplying p by an element of B, we may assume, if $|p| \geqslant 2$, that $pu = r_1$ and $pv = r_2$ where $r_1, r_2 \in R_j$. A similar argument applied to the products up and vp, shows that, postmultiplying by an element of B, we may assume that $p \in L_j$. It is now clear that R satisfies $C'(\lambda)$, at least as far as pieces of length at least 2 are concerned. But our assumption $n > 12$ ensures that shorter pieces cannot give us any trouble.

It follows from the above argument that $p \in F$, with $|p| \geqslant 2$, is an

R-piece if and only if there exist $b, c \in B$, $u, v \in F$, $u', v' \in L_j$, for some $j \in J$, and an R_j-piece p' such that $p'u' \neq p'v' \in R_j$, almost no cancellation occurring, and $p = b^{-1}p'c$, $u = c^{-1}u'b$ and $v = c^{-1}v'b$. Using this, it is easy to see that R contains no p.p.p., and no element conjugate to its own inverse. Clearly S is a basis for R, and the remainder of $[\lambda, n, \Sigma\, \kappa_j]$ is easy to check.

The general case is proved as follows. We write $\bar{L}_j = L_j/Z(L_j)$, and $\bar{F} = *_{j\in J\,(\mathrm{N})}\, \bar{L}_j$. The homomorphisms $L_j \to \bar{L}_j$, induce a unique homomorphism $F \to \bar{F}$, which is clearly length preserving, and hence, an $\mathcal{NFS}$-homomorphism. We write $\bar{Y}$ for the image of Y under this homomorphism, for any Y. As in the proof of Lemma 7.5, $\bar{R}_j$ satisfies $[\lambda, n, \kappa_j]$, and clearly has basis $\bar{S}_j$. From the $Z(L_j) = 1$ case, it is clear that $\bar{R}$ satisfies $[\lambda, n, \Sigma\, \kappa_j]$, and has basis $\bar{S}$. Since R is the inverse image, in F, of $\bar{R}$, it clearly must have all the desired properties, except, perhaps, C.C. But C.C. follows from the fact that every element of R is conjugate to an element of R_j, for some $j \in J$. □

Proof of Theorem 8.1(A). If $J = \emptyset$, then the result is trivial, so suppose $J \neq \emptyset$. Let $H = \langle G *_{\mathrm{N}} F : [G, Z(F)] = 1\rangle$, where G has the NFS structure $(G, 1, G-1)$, and F is as in Lemma 8.2. We pick a sufficiently small $\lambda > 0$, and a sufficiently large $n > 0$, and we let S_j be a basis for a symmetrised set R_j satisfying $[\lambda, n, \kappa]$ in each L_j. By Lemma 8.2, $s = \bigcup S_j$ is a basis for a symmetrised set R in F satisfying $[\lambda, n, \kappa]$. Clearly R is also symmetrised in H and satisfies the same condition. Now, for all $j \in J$, let $T_j = \bigcup_{k\neq j\in J} (B_k \cup X_k \cup G)$, where B_k, X_k are as in Lemma 8.2. Then $|T_j| \leqslant \kappa = |S_j|$, for all $j \in J$, and so there is an onto map $\varphi_j : S_j \to T_j$. Let $\varphi : S \to F$ be the map whose restriction to S_j is φ_j, for all j. Since R satisfies C.C., and $(s\varphi)s$ is clearly c.r. for all $s \in S$, we see from Lemma 7.7, that the set $S^* = \{(s\varphi)s : s \in S\}$, is a basis for a symmetrised set R^* in H, satisfying $[\mu, m, \kappa]$, for some convenient μ, m, provided only we choose λ, n "correctly". If we choose them so that $\mu \leqslant 1/6$, and $m \geqslant 6$, then letting N^* be the normal closure of R^* in H, H/N^* embeds everything in H of length 0 or 1. Hence H/N^* embeds G. However, it is clear, from the definition of S^*, that given the obvious presentation for H/N^*, we can remove from it, by means of Tietze transformations, all generators the generators of L_j, for some fixed, but arbitrary, $j \in J$. It follows that H/N^* is a simultaneous quotient group of $\mathcal{L}$, and so the theorem is proved with $Q = H/N^*$. □

Before we turn to other versions of Theorem 8.1, we note the following corollary.

Corollary 8.3. *Any countable group G can be embedded in a countable group Q with the property that, for any word $w(a, b, c)$ in $\langle a, b, c\rangle$, the free group on $\{a, b, c\}$, there exists a generating set $\{x_w, y_w, z_w\}$ of Q such that $w(x_w, y_w, z_w) = 1$, in Q.*

Proof. By Theorem 7.1 (v), the three generator one relator groups are SSC-$\aleph_0$ groups. There are clearly $\aleph_0$ of them, and so we can apply the theorem to embed G in a simultaneous quotient Q of them. This group clearly satisfies the conclusion of the corollary. □

It is well known that any group of order κ, where κ is an infinite cardinal, can be embedded in a simple group of order κ. We vary the proof of Theorem 8.1(A) as follows.

(a) Replace the family κ, of SSC groups, by $\bar{\mathscr{L}} = \mathscr{L} \cup F_\kappa$, where F_κ is the free group of rank κ.

(b) Replace the group G by $\bar{G}$, a simple group of order κ containing G.

(c) Add to S^* all elements of the form:

$$\left\{\prod_{i=1}^{M} (t^i g)\right\} t^{-(M^2+M-2)/2} g,$$

where g is some fixed element of $\bar{G}$, M is some "large" number, and t is any element of some basis of F_κ, to form the set S^{**}.

(d) Let R^{**} be the symmetrised closure of S^{**} in H, and let N^{**} be the normal closure of R^{**} in H, and put $Q^{**} = H/N^{**}$.

(e) Let N be a normal subgroup of Q^{**} that is maximal with respect to the property that $g \notin N$, where g is the element used in (c), and let $Q = Q^{**}/N$.

Then we see that, by choosing M large enough, we can make R^{**} satisfy any condition $[\mu, m, \kappa]$ that R^* satisfies. By requiring $\mu \leqslant 1/6$ and $|m| > 6$, we can ensure that Q^{**} embeds $\bar{G}$, and since $N^{**} \geqslant N^*$, where N^* is constructed as in the proof of Theorem 8.1(A), Q^{**} is a simultaneous quotient of the family $\bar{\mathscr{L}}$. Now Q embeds $\bar{G}$, for, if not, then $N \cap \bar{G} \neq 1$, and since $\bar{G}$ is simple $g \in \bar{G} \cap N$, contradicting the definition of N. Finally, Q is simple. For, let P be a non-trivial normal subgroup of Q, then the inverse image P^{**} of P in Q^{**} contains g, and since N must contain all the elements of H introduced in (c), we see that $t \in P^{**}$, for every generator t of F_κ, and since P^{**} is a quotient of F_κ, $P^{**} = Q^{**}$, and so $P = Q$. Thus we have proved the following version of Theorem 8.1.

Theorem 8.1(B). *In Theorem 8.1(A), we may assume Q to be simple.* □

If we let $\kappa = \aleph_0$, and we suppose a two generator group to occur among the L_j, we obtain the following result, which has also been proved by Schupp [21], Goryushkin [6], and Hurley [9].

Corollary 8.4. *Every countable group can be embedded in a 2 generator simple group.* □

In the proof of Theorem 8.1(A), we can replace G by any generating set for G in the definition of the sets T_j, and the conclusion still holds. But note that, if this is done, then no use has been made of the relations between these generators. It follows that, if $M \lhd G$, then $M^Q \cap G = M$, and so G/M is embedded in $Q/(M^Q)$. We express this property by saying that G is an *E-subgroup* of Q. If we ensure $\mu \leqslant 1/10$, and $|m| \geqslant 3$, then since the embedding of G in H is Frattini, the embedding of G in Q is also Frattini, by Lemma 6.5.

From the constructions of §3, we see that the group H constructed in the proof of Theorem 8.1(A), can be given the additional $\overline{\text{NFS}}$ structure (H, Z, Y), where $Y = Z((G-1) \cup (\bigcup_{j \in J} (L_j - Z(L_j))))Z$ and Z is the (restricted) direct product $Z = \times_{j \in J} Z(L_j)$. It follows from Theorem 4.7 that, if $J \neq \emptyset$, then $Z(H) = Z$. From Theorem 4.6, it follows that every element of H of finite order is conjugate to one of the form gz, where $g \in L_j$, for some $j \in J$, and $z \in Z$, and both have finite order. If we ensure that $\mu \leqslant 1/10$, and $|m| > 3$, we can apply Theorems 6.4 and 6.8 to the construction of Q from H to obtain the following version of Theorem 8.1.

Theorem 8.1(C). *In Theorem* 8.1(*A*), *we can assume that G is an E-subgroup of Q, and that the embedding of G in Q is Frattini. Moreover, if $J \neq \emptyset$, we may assume that $Z(Q) = \times_{j \in J} Z(L_j)$, the restricted direct product of the $Z(L_j)$, and that any element of Q of finite order is conjugate, in Q, to an element of the form gz, where $g \in L_j$, for some $j \in J$, and $z \in Z(Q)$.* □

If, in the proof of Theorem 8.1(A), we assume $Z(L_j) = 1$, for all $j \in J$, and we replace H by $H' = H \times_{\mathrm{N}} A$, where A is an abelian group satisfying $|A| \leqslant \kappa$, and T_j by $T'_j = T_j \cup A$, then $Z(H') = A$, and Q is still a simultaneous quotient of $\mathscr{L}$ that embeds G. If we ensure that $\mu < 1/10$, and $|m| \leqslant 3$, we see, from Theorem 6.8, that $Z(Q) = A$. If we do not have $Z(L_j) = 1$, for all $j \in J$, then, by Lemma 7.5, $L_j/Z(L_j)$ is an SSC group with trivial centre, and since any simultaneous quotient of these groups is also a simultaneous quotient of the L_j, we obtain the following version of Theorem 8.1.

Theorem 8.1(D). *In Theorem* 8.1(*A*), *we can assume that* $Z(Q)=A$, *where* A *is any abelian group satisfying* $|A|\leqslant\kappa$. □

The following corollary is immediate.

Corollary 8.5. *Every countable abelian group is the centre of a two generator group.* □

Application II. Embeddings into the join of given groups.

For this application, it is convenient to work with countable groups. However, the results can clearly be generalised so that they work for groups of higher cardinality.

Theorem 8.7. *Let* $\{G_\mu\}_{\mu\in M}$ *be a family of at least two groups, and let* G *be any group. Suppose* $|M|,|G|\leqslant\aleph_0$, *and* $|G_\mu|\leqslant\aleph_0$, *for all* $\mu\in M$. *Suppose each* G_μ *contains a proper subgroup* B_μ, *such that, for all, except perhaps one,* $\mu\in M$, G_μ *contains a blocking pair over* B_μ. *Finally, suppose there exists a group* B, *generated by a family of subgroups* $\{C_\mu\}_{\mu\in M}$, *satisfying* $C_\mu\cong B_\mu$, *for all* $\mu\in M$, *and let* $\mathscr{A}$ *denote the amalgam, obtained from the* G_μ *and* B, *by setting* $B_\mu=C_\mu$, *for all* $\mu\in M$.

Then there exists a group Q, *that embeds the amalgam* $\mathscr{A}$ *and the group* G, *and is generated by any pair of groups* (G_μ,G_ν), *where* $\mu\neq\nu\in M$.

Proof. The proof is very similar to the proof of Theorem 8.1(A), and so we confine ourselves to a few remarks. In the structure product STR (G_μ,B), with its natural $\overline{\text{NFS}}$ structure, for every pair $\mu,\nu\in M$, we can construct a symmetrised set $R_{\mu,\nu}$, satisfying $[\lambda,n,\aleph_0]$, for convenient $\lambda,n>0$, with a basis $S_{\mu,\nu}$ that lies entirely inside $G_\mu\cup G_\nu$. This is possible because at least one of the groups G_μ or G_ν contains a blocking pair over B_μ or B_ν, and the construction is similar to that used in a free product with amalgamation. We now proceed as in the proof of Theorem 8.1(A), but we replace the use of Lemma 8.2 by the construction described above. □

Variants of this theorem can be proved, as in the last application. In fact analogs of Theorems 8.1(B), (C) and (D) hold, where, in case (C), we replace $Z(Q)=\times Z(L_j)$ by $Z(Q)=1$. We leave their formulation and proof to the reader. (Note that, in case (B), a little extra work is needed to ensure that $\mathscr{A}$ is embedded in the simple group Q.) It is also possible to combine Applications I and II.

Application III. Decision problems in group theory.

Theorem 8.8. *A necessary and sufficient condition for a finitely generated, recursively presented, group G to have soluble word problem is that there exists a non-trivial finitely presented group H, such that G can be embedded in every simple factor group of H.*

Proof. Suppose we have a finitely generated group G with soluble word problem. By Theorem I of Boone and Higman [2], we can embed G in a simple group S, which, in turn, can be embedded in a finitely presented group K. As is well known, we may assume K to be generated by two elements, a and b, say. Let $\langle u, v\rangle$ be the free group of rank 2, and form the free product $L = K * \langle u, v\rangle$. Then the set S consisting of the four words:

$$a\prod_{i=1}^{80}(uv^i),\ b\prod_{i=1}^{80}(uv^{80+i}),\ \prod_{i=1}^{80}(su^i)su^{-3239},\ \prod_{i=1}^{80}(sv^i)sv^{-3239},$$

is a basis for a symmetrised subset R of L, equipped with an appropriate NFS structure, where s is some fixed element of $S-1$. We let N be the normal closure of R, and put $H = L/N$. H is visibly finitely presented, and, since R satisfies $C'(1/6)$, embeds K and hence embeds G. Moreover, we easily see that every non-trivial quotient group of H embeds G, and so, in particular, every simple quotient group of H contains a copy of G.

Now suppose we have a finitely generated group G, with presentation $\langle g_1, g_2, \ldots, g_s : K\rangle$, which can be embedded in every simple quotient group of the non-trivial finitely presented group $H = \langle x_1, \ldots, x_r : R\rangle$. We let $v_1, v_2, \ldots, v_s$ be variables. If $L \neq 1$ is a group, then we say $p \neq 1 \in L$ is *consistent in L* if $\langle p\rangle^L \neq L$, and otherwise, we say it is *inconsistent in L.*

We define a, possibly finite, ascending sequence $N_0 \leq N_1 \leq N_2 \cdots$ of finitely generated normal subgroups of H as follows, where we suppose we are given an enumeration U of all s-tuples of words on $\{x_1, \ldots, x_r\}$.

We define $N_0 = 1$. For $i \geq 1$, suppose N_{i-1} has been defined. Let $(w_1, w_2, \ldots, w_s)$ be the ith element in the enumeration U. There are three cases.

(a) If there exists a word $u(v_j)$ such that $u(g_j) = 1$, in G, but $u(w_j)$ is inconsistent in H/N_{i-1}, then define $N_i = N_{i-1}$.

(b) If (a) does not obtain, but there exists a word $u(v_j)$ such that $u(g_j) \neq 1$, in G, but $u(w_j)$ is consistent in H/N_{i-1}, then define N_i to be the normal closure, in H, of N_{i-1} and $u(w_j)$.

(c) If neither (a) nor (b) obtains, then N_k is undefined for $k \geq i$.

Suppose this sequence were infinite, then, since H is finitely generated, and the N_i are proper subgroups of H, there is a maximal normal subgroup M of H containing all the N_i. But H cannot be embedded in the simple quotient group H/M of H, because, for every s-tuple $(w_1, \ldots, w_s)$, of words on $\{x_1, \ldots, x_r\}$, either there exists a word $u(v_j)$ such that $u(g_j) = 1$, in G, but $u(w_j) \neq 1$ in H/M, or there exists a word $u(v_j)$ such that $u(g_j) \neq 1$, in G, but $u(w_j) = 1$, in H/M. This contradicts our assumption that G can be embedded in every simple quotient group of H, and shows that the ascending sequence of normal subgroups of H is finite.

Let N_k be the last member of the sequence $\{N_i\}$. And write $\bar{H} = H/N_k$. From the definition of the sequence, if $(w_1, w_2, \ldots, w_s)$ is the $(k+1)$th element of U, then:

$$\{u(v_j) : u(g_j) \neq 1 \text{ in } G\} = \{u(v_j) : u(w_j) \text{ is inconsistent in } \bar{H}\}.$$

Since $\bar{H}$ is finitely presented, the set on the right-hand side is r.e., by an obvious diagonal enumeration, and hence the set on the left-hand side is r.e. Since G is recursively presented, $\{u(v_j) : u(g_j) = 1 \text{ in } G\}$ is also r.e., and so must be recursive. Hence G has soluble word problem. □

We remark that, using the techniques of Application I, we may assume that H is a simultaneous quotient group of any finite family $\{L_j\}_{j \in J}$ of finitely presented SSC groups.

Problem 2. Can the hypothesis that G be recursively presented be removed from Theorem 8.8?

The proof that G has soluble word problem in Theorem 8.8 is non-constructive, and there seems to be no obvious way of replacing it with a constructive proof. Thus there seems to be no reason why an analog of Theorem III of Boone–Higman [2] should hold, in this case. Indeed, it seems rather unlikely that there should be such an analog. This situation prompts us to ask the next question.

Problem 3. Does there exist a non-trivial finitely presented group H with the property that every finitely generated group G with soluble word problem is embeddable in every simple quotient group of H?

Our Theorem 8.1(B) is a generalisation of Theorem I of Schupp [21]. It is possible to use our theory to obtain a generalisation of his Theorem II. The proof is a simple adaption of Schupp's proof, using methods from the proof of Theorem 8.1. We therefore content ourselves with a statement of this theorem. For the definitions of the terms used in the theorem, we refer the reader to Schupp's paper.

Theorem 8.9. *Let A be a finitely presentable group which has a finitely presentable quotient group L which is an SSC group. Let π be any finite presentation of A, and let P be a Markov property which is possessed by the trivial group. Then the problem of determining P restricted to quotients of π is insoluble. Also the generating problem for $A \times A$ is insoluble.* □

Application IV. Residual simplicity.

Theorem 8.10. *An SSC group with trivial centre is residually infinite simple.*

Proof. We actually prove the following stronger statement.

Let κ be an infinite cardinal. Suppose L is an SSC-κ group, with trivial centre, and let G be a group. Suppose $|G|, |L| \leq \kappa$. Then, if P is any finite set of non-trivial elements of L, there exists a simple quotient group Q of L, containing a copy of G, such that $p \neq 1$, in Q, for all $p \in P$.

Proof of above statement. By Lemma 7.6, L contains a symmetrised set R, satisfying $[\lambda, n, \kappa]$, for some convenient $\lambda, n > 0$, which is contained in $\bigcap_{p \in P} \langle p \rangle^L$. We embed G in a simple group $\bar{G}$, of order κ, and we let $H = \bar{G} * L * F_\kappa$, where F_κ is the free group of rank κ. We proceed, as in the proof of Theorem 8.1(B), to construct a symmetrised set R^*, in H, satisfying $[\mu, m, \kappa]$, for suitable μ, m. We may suppose R^* contains (i) words of the form gr, where $r \in R$ and g is a generator of $\bar{G}$ or F_κ, (ii) words that express the generators of L in terms of those of F_κ, and (iii) words that ensure that all non-trivial quotient groups of $Q^* = H/N^*$, where N^* is the normal closure of R^* in H, contain a copy of $\bar{G}$. We chose μ, m so that $\bar{G}$ is embedded in Q^*, and, as before, construct a simple quotient group Q of Q^*. Now Q is a simple quotient group of L, containing G. If $p = 1$, in Q, for some $p \in P$, then $r = 1$, in Q, for all $r \in R$, and hence $g = 1$, in Q, for all generators of F_κ. But Q is a quotient group of F_κ, and so this would imply $Q = 1$, a contradiction. Hence $p \neq 1$, in Q, for all $p \in P$. □

Application V. The height of SSC groups.

We assume familiarity with Pride [16], and we shall freely use the terminology of Pride's paper.

Theorem 8.11. *Countable SSC groups have infinite height.*

Proof. Suppose G is a countable SSC group. Let $S_0, S_1, \dots$ be an infinite sequence of countable groups. By Theorem 8.9(A), we can construct an infinite group Q that is a simultaneous quotient of the family $\{G\} \cup \{S_i * S_i\}_{i=0}^{\infty}$. For $n = 0, 1, 2, \dots$, define Q_n to be the group whose presentation is obtained from the obvious presentation (i.e., the presentation constructed in the proof of Theorem 8.9(A)) for Q by deleting the generators of $S_i * S_i$, for $i \geqslant n$, and deleting all relators that involve these generators. It is clear that Q_n is a simultaneous quotient of the family $\{G\} \cup \{S_i * S_i\}_{i=0}^{n-1}$, and that Q_{n+1} is a homomorphic image of Q_n, for all n. It is immediate from [16] Theorem 2.1, and the definition of $\preccurlyeq$, which follows [16] corollary 2.1.1, that $G \succcurlyeq Q_0 \succcurlyeq Q_1 \succcurlyeq Q_2 \succcurlyeq \cdots \succcurlyeq Q_n \succcurlyeq \cdots$. The theorem will be established if we can show that, for some choice of the groups S_i, $Q_{n+1} \not\succcurlyeq Q_n$, for all n. We note that the construction of Q can be done in such a way that it does not depend on the defining relations of the S_i, and so, for all i, we can choose S_i to be a countable simple group that is not contained in Q_i. (Note that by Theorem 8.1(B) there are $2^{\aleph_0}$ two generator infinite simple groups, and Q_i can only contain $\aleph_0$ such groups.) Since Q_{n+1} is a homomorphic image of $S_n * S_n$, it is clear that any non-trivial homomorphic image of a subgroup of finite index in Q_{n+1} must contain a copy of S_n, and so cannot be contained in Q_n. By [16], Theorem 2.1, we have $Q_{n+1} \not\succcurlyeq Q_n$, for all n, as required. $\square$

If G is a countable SQ-universal group, then this can usually be established by arguments that use small cancellation theory and the fact that SQ-universality is a large property, in the sense of [16]. This prompts us to ask the following question.

Problem 4. Do all finitely generated SQ-universal groups have infinite height?

We remark that Hurley (unpublished) has constructed a countable SQ-universal group that is minimal, in the sense of Pride [16]. However, a finitely generated SQ-universal group cannot be minimal, because it must have a just infinite quotient group.

Application VI. The rank of certain direct products.

Definition. If G is a finitely generated group, then by the *rank* $r(G)$, of G, we mean the minimum size of a generating set for G.

Theorem 8.12. *If G is a countable SSC group, and C is any countable group, then C can be embedded in a quotient group Q, of G, of rank 2, such that, for all non-trivial finitely generated groups B,*

$$r(Q \times B) = \begin{cases} r(B)+1, & \text{if } B \text{ is free or cyclic,} \\ r(B), & \text{otherwise.} \end{cases}$$

Remark. The theorem says that usually $r(Q \times B) = r(B)$. It is clear that an exception to this rule must occur when B is cyclic. If B is free, then $r(Q \times B) = r(B)$ would imply that $Q \times B$ was free, which contradicts the fact that a free group cannot be decomposed into a non-trivial direct product. Hence an exception must also occur when B is free. Thus the value of $r(Q \times B)$ given by the theorem is always as small as possible.

Proof. Let $v_1, v_2, v_3, \ldots$ be an infinite list of variables, and let U be an enumeration of all pairs $(r, w(v_j))$, where $r \geq 2$ is an integer, and $w(v_j)$ is a reduced word on $\{v_1, v_2, \ldots, v_r\}$ that both begins and ends with $v_1^{\pm 1}$. Note that we do not require $w(v_j)$ to involve all the variables in $v_1, v_2, \ldots, v_r$. Let R be a symmetrised subset of G satisfying $[1/30, 30, \aleph_0]$. Let S be a basis for R. Since $\mathrm{Card}(S) = \aleph_0$, we can write it as a disjoint union

$$S = \bigsqcup_{i=0}^{\infty} S_i,$$

where $\mathrm{Card}(S_0) = \aleph_0$, and, for $i = 1, 2, \ldots, \mathrm{Card}(S_i) = r_i$, where $(r_i, w_i(v_j))$ is the ith element in the enumeration U. We suppose that each S_i is given a standard ordering $(s_1, s_2, \ldots, s_{r_i})$.

For each $i = 1, 2, \ldots,$ we define the set $T_i(v_j)$ of words on $\{v_1, v_2, \ldots, v_{r_i}\}$ to be the set of all words of the form:

$$t_{i,k}(v_j) = \left\{ \prod_{n=1}^{100} (v_2^{100k+n} w_i(v_j)) \right\} v_2^{-10000k-5050} w_i(v_j),$$

for all k larger than $|w_i(v_j)|$. Note that the $t_{i,k}$ are reduced as written. We now write $T_i(v_j)$ as a disjoint union $T_i'(v_j) \sqcup T_i''(v_j)$, where $\mathrm{Card}(T_i') = r_i$, $\mathrm{Card}(T_i'') = \aleph_0$, and we equip both sets with a standard ordering.

We now suppose that $c_1, c_2, c_3, \ldots$ is a generating set for C, and that $g_1, g_2, g_3, \ldots$ is a generating set for G consisting of elements of length 0 and 1. We set

$$H = C * G * \left(\mathop{*}_{i=1}^{\infty} K(i) \right),$$

where $K(i)$ is a free group with basis $\{u_{i,1}, u_{i,2}, \ldots u_{i,r_i}\}$.

We now let R^* be the symmetrised closure, in H, of all words of the forms:

(a) $c_q^{-1}z_q$, where z_q is the qth word in the standard ordering of S_0,

(b) $u_{i,q}^{-1}z_q$, where z_q is the qth word in the standard ordering of S_i,

(c) $u_{i,q}^{-1}t_q$, where t_q is the qth word in the standard ordering of $T_i'(u_{i,j})$, and

(d) $g_q^{-1}t_q$, where t_q is the qth word in the standard ordering of $T_i''(u_{i,j})$.

By an argument similar to that used in the proof of Theorem 8.1, we see that R^* satisfies $[1/10, 10, \aleph_0]$, in H. Thus, if N^* is the normal closure of R^* in H, then $Q = H/N^*$ embeds C. As before, Q is a quotient group of G.

We must now show that Q satisfies the conclusion of the theorem. We first note that, from the construction, Q is a simultaneous quotient group of the family $\{P_i\}_{i=1}^{\infty}$, of groups, presented as follows:

$$P_i = \langle v_1, v_2, \ldots, v_{r_i} : v_q^{-1}t_q \ (t_q \text{ is the } q\text{th word in the standard ordering of } T_i'(v_j),\ 1 \leq q \leq r_i)\rangle.$$

Let us fix some $i \geq 1$, and write $(r, w(v_j)) = (r_i, w_i(v_j))$. Let E be the one relator group with presentation

$$E = \langle x_1, x_2, \ldots, x_r ; w(x_j)\rangle.$$

Let Y be the split extension of E by the free group with basis $\{v_1, v_2, \ldots, v_r\}$, with the v_j acting as follows: $v_j^{-1}x_iv_j = x_j^{-1}x_ix_j$, for all $i, j = 1, \ldots, r$. Let $J = E\{v_1^{\pm 1}, \ldots, v_r^{\pm 1}\}E$. Then, by Lemma 3.2(ii), (Y, E, J) is an $\overline{\text{NFS}}$ group. Note, however, that it need not be an SSC group. Let R^{**} be the symmetrised closure, in Y, of all words of the form $v_q^{-1}t_qx_q$, where, for the fixed i, and for $q = 1, \ldots, r$, the qth word in the standard ordering of $T_i'(v_j)$ is t_q.

We leave it to the reader to check that R^{**} satisfies C′(1/10), in Y. Note that, as well as doing the usual calculations, one must check that the elements $r \in R^{**}$ are not, themselves, R^{**}-pieces. This amounts to showing that, if $b, c \in E$ and $r \in R^{**}$, then $br = rc$ implies $b = c$. This is very easy to do, but since, for instance, the symmetrised closure of $\{t_1x_1\}$ does *not* satisfy this condition, it is non-trivial.

Let N^{**} be the normal closure of R^{**} in Y, and set $D = Y/N^{**}$. Since the t_q are words in the v_j, we can eliminate the x_j from the obvious presentation for D, by means of Tietze transformations, and hence, we see, $r(D) \leq r$. Let P' be the normal closure, in D, of $w(v_j)$, and let $D' = D/P'$. From their definitions, we see, $t_q \in P'$, in D, for $q = 1, \ldots, r$. It follows that $v_q = x_q$, in D', that $D' \cong E$, and that $P' \cap E = \emptyset$. Where, since R^{**} satisfies C′(1/10), E is a subgroup of D. But note that $E \lhd D$, and, since $t_q \in P'$, for all q, $D = \mathrm{gp}(P', E)$. It follows that $D = P' \times E$. Setting $x_q = 1$, in the presentation for D, and deleting the x_q, we obtain the presentation which we used to define P_i, for our fixed i. Thus $D \cong P_i \times E$.

We now let i vary, and accordingly add the suffix i to E defined above. We have shown $r(P_i \times E_i) \leq r_i$, for all $i = 1, 2, \ldots$. Now let B be any non-free group of finite rank $r \geq 2$. For some i, B is a quotient group of E_i, and $r_i = r$. Since Q is a quotient group of P_i, we see that $Q \times B$ is a quotient group of $P_i \times E_i$. Hence $r(Q \times B) \leq r(P_i \times E_i) \leq r_i = r(B)$. Now suppose B is cyclic or free, and let it have rank r. For some i, B is a quotient group of E_i, with $w(v_j) = v_1$, and $r_i = r + 1$, and we conclude $r(Q \times B) \leq r(B) + 1$. Since the value of $r(Q \times B)$, given in the statement of the theorem is as small as possible, the above inequalities can be strengthened to equalities. To see that $r(Q) = 2$, we merely need to note that it is a homomorphic image of the two generator group $Q \times \langle x, y : x^2 \rangle$, that $Q \neq 1$, for it contains a copy of C, and that Q is not cyclic, for cyclic groups do not satisfy the conclusion of the theorem. □

We remark that, as with Theorem 8.1, one can prove variants of Theorem 8.12. In particular, a version of the theorem holds in which Q is simple. The next result is a corollary of this version of the theorem.

Proposition 8.13. *There exists a family $\mathcal{S}$ of simple groups satisfying:*

(i) *Every countable group C can be embedded in some member of $\mathcal{S}$, and*

(ii) *if $S_1, S_2, \ldots, S_n \in \mathcal{S}$, where $n \geq 1$ is finite, then $S_1 \times S_2 \times \cdots \times S_n$ is a two generator group.*

§9. Concluding remarks

The theory has many applications which, for reasons of space, we have been unable to include in §8. We shall mention a few of these here, without going into details.

One construction we have hardly used is the HNN construction in the category $\mathcal{NFS}$. Indeed, the only reason we included it in §3 is that it provides the quickest way we know of proving the results we need about structure products. One of the difficulties with this construction is that it does not, in general, preserve the property of being an SSC group. However, it can be used, for instance, to prove a version of Theorem 8.1, in which all elements of Q of the same finite order k are conjugate to one another. Moreover, it is possible to exploit the pathologies that can occur when using the HNN construction in $\mathcal{NFS}$. For instance, observe that, if R is a symmetrised set in an SSC group G, and R^* is its symmetrised closure in an $\mathcal{NFS}$ HNN extension G^*, then there is no obvious reason why R and R^* should not satisfy the same C- and T-conditions, and yet also satisfy $b(R^*) < b(R)$. This observation has lead us to a new proof of the well-known Embedding Theorem of Higman [7]. The construction is rather nice and allows us to prove results such as the following.

Theorem 9.1. *There exists a finitely presented group G, with soluble word, power and order problems, with a subgroup F, which is free of rank 2, and a recursive functional Φ from the natural numbers to words on the generators of G, such that*:

(i) *if R_e is the r.e. subset of F with r.e. index* e, *then, in G, $F \cap \Phi(\mathrm{e})^G = R_e^G$, and so $\langle G : \Phi(\mathrm{e})\rangle$ embeds $\langle F : R_e\rangle$, and*

(ii) *the embedding of $\langle F : R_e\rangle$ in $\langle G : \Phi(\mathrm{e})\rangle$ is Frattini, and preserves the Turing degrees of the word, power and order problems.* □

Theorem 9.2. *Every recursively enumerable c-degree contains the word problem of some finitely presented group.* □

Theorem 9.3. *A necessary and sufficient condition for an abelian group A to be the centre of some finitely presented group is that it should be recursively presentable.* □

Remarks. We refer the reader to Rogers [17] for the definitions of r.e. index and c-reducibility, and to Collins [5] for the definitions of the power and order problems. For the definition of r.e. index of a subset of the free group F, of rank 2, to make sense, we, of course, assume some Gödel numbering of F into $\mathbf{N}$ to be given. In Theorem 9.3, by recursively presentable we mean, of course, possessing a presentation with an infinite, but recursive, set of generators $a_1, a_2, \ldots$, and an r.e. set $r_1, r_2, \ldots$ of relators on these generators.

A topic we have not mentioned is the study of symmetrised sets, satisfying small cancellation conditions, that are fixed, setwise, by some group of automorphisms of an $\overline{\text{NFS}}$ group. A typical example of a result obtainable by such study is the following.

Theorem 9.4. *Let H, K be countable groups, neither of which can be decomposed into a non-trivial free product. Suppose further that* $|H| \geq 2$, $|K| \geq 3$, *and that K is not an infinite cyclic group. Then all normal extensions of* $H * K$ *are SQ-universal.* □

We remark that P. Hall (unpublished) has constructed an example of a countable SQ-universal group G, that has a normal extension (actually a split extension by an infinite cyclic group) that is not SQ-universal. The reader will notice that Theorem 9.4 gives us no information about what happens when both H and K are infinite cyclic groups, and so we ask the following question.

Problem 5. Are all normal extensions of a free group of rank 2 SQ-universal?

Another topic we have not mentioned, is that of small cancellation towers. That is, possibly infinite, towers $G_1 \leq G_2 \leq \cdots$ of groups, where G_i, for $i \geq 2$, embeds G_{i-1}, by a small cancellation theory argument. We remark that a group with the same property as the group of P. Hall, mentioned above, can be constructed by means of such a tower, that the countable, minimal (in the sense of Pride [16]), SQ-universal group, mentioned after the proof of Theorem 8.11, was constructed by such a tower, and that Problem 7 of Pride [16] has been settled, in the negative, by a small cancellation tower argument. Finally, a small cancellation tower construction can be used to prove the following.

Theorem 9.5. *Every countable group C can be embedded in a non-simple countable group G that is isomorphic to all its non-trivial quotient groups.* □

We shall say a word about the future of small cancellation theory. It is widely believed that it should be possible to iterate small cancellation arguments. That is to "do" small cancellation theory over small cancellation groups. We believe that this should be possible, in the near future. It is possible that such a development would have some relevance to the question of whether or not every group with soluble word problem can be embedded in a finitely presented simple group, the answer to which we believe to be "No". The reader who thinks of using Theorem 8.8, in some way, to obtain the answer "Yes" to this question had better be warned that one can prove a version of this theorem, in which every non-trivial quotient group of H has insoluble word problem, in which case, it can have no recursively presented simple homomorphic image. Returning to the non-iterated theory, we have a feeling that constructions of the type used in the proof of Theorem 8.12 might have some relevance to disproving a famous conjecture in Topology.

And now a word about the history of the results in this paper. The idea of doing the "classical" cases of small cancellation theory in a uniform way has its origins in my (for the remainder of this section, for the sake of naturalness, the pronoun "I" shall be used instead of the conventional mathematical "we") M.Sc. dissertation [9]. This was conceived, written and typed within the space of three weeks, and so contains many errors. However, it does contain a correct proof (The first, I believe, but then, what does it matter who proves things first?) of the fact that every countable group can be embedded in a two generator simple group. The theory remained dormant, for some time, mainly because I got bored with it. My interest revived, when, at the Oxford meeting, I learned of the existence of the axiomatic length-function theory, and it seemed to me that there might be some connection between this theory and my theory of normal forms in groups. As to the value of this work, I am unsure. Dividing things, roughly, into "reality" and "waxworks", most Mathematics falls within the category of "waxworks", and if one thinks *that* then, presumably (apologics to Lewis Carroll) one ought to pay. Perhaps one can do no better than to quote Wittengenstein "Wenn es einen Wert gibt, der Wert hat, so muss er ausserhalb alles Geschehens und So-Seins liegen".

§10. Acknowledgements

Knowledge is not gained in isolation, and my ideas on this subject have benefited from discussion with many people, and I would find it impossible to compile a complete list. However certain people need special mention. The idea of doing small cancellation theory over NFS groups originated in my M.Sc. dissertation, and I must thank my (long suffering) supervisor Professor G. Higman. Incidentally, it was he who started me thinking about small cancellation theory by showing me a paper of Schupp. I thank Professor R. Lyndon, who read an earlier draft of this paper and made many detailed suggestions as to how it might be improved. I must thank Professor W.W. Boone, without whose encouragement, this paper might never have been written.

Finally, I must apologise to the other contributors to this volume for the late appearance of the final version of this paper.

References

[1] B. Baumslag, Residually free groups, Proc. London Math. Soc. 17 (1967) 402–418.

[2] W.W. Boone and G. Higman, An algebraic characterization of groups with soluble word problem, J. Austral. Math. Soc. 18 (1974) 41–53.

[3] J.L. Britton, The word problem, Ann. of Math. 77 (1963) 16–32.

[4] I.M. Chiswell, Abstract length functions in groups, Math. Proc. Camb. Phil. Soc. 80 (1976) 451–463.

[5] D.J. Collins, The word, power, and order problems in finitely presented groups, In: Word problems (North-Holland Publishing Co., Amsterdam, 1973) pp. 401–420.

[6] A.P. Goryushkin, Imbedding of countable groups in 2-generator groups, Mat. Zametki. 16 (1974) 231–275.

[7] G. Higman, Subgroups of finitely presented groups, Proc. Royal Soc. London, Ser. A 262 (1961) 455–475.

[8] A.H.M. Hoare, On length functions and Nielsen methods in free groups, J. London Math. Soc. 14 (1976) 88–92.

[9] B.M. Hurley, Embedding theorems for groups, M.Sc. dissertation (Oxford, 1972).

[10] B.M. Hurley, On length functions and normal forms in groups, Math. Proc. Camb. Phil. Soc. (to appear).

[11] R.D. Hurwitz, On the conjugacy problem in a free product with commuting subgroups, Math. Ann. 221 (1976) 1–8.

[12] R.C. Lyndon, Length functions in groups, Math. Scand. 12 (1963) 209–234.

[13] R.C. Lyndon, On Dehn's algorithm, Math. Ann. 166 (1966) 208–228.

[14] W. Magnus, A. Karrass and D. Solitar, Combinatorial group theory (Wiley, New York, 1966).

[15] K. Murasugi, The center of a group with a single defining relation, Math. Ann. 155 (1964) 246–251.

[16] S.J. Pride, The concept of "largeness" in group theory, in this volume, pp. 299–335.

[17] H. Rogers, Jr., Theory of recursive functions and effective computability (McGraw-Hill, New York, 1967).

[18] G.S. Sacerdote and P.E. Schupp, SQ-universality of HNN and 1-relator groups, J. London Math. Soc. 7 (1974) 733–740.

[19] P.E. Schupp, Small cancellation theory over free products with amalgamation, Math. Ann. 193 (1971) 244–264.

[20] P.E. Schupp, A survey of small cancellation theory, In: Word Problems (North-Holland Publishing Co., Amsterdam, 1973) pp. 569–589.

[21] P.E. Schupp, Embeddings into simple groups, J. London Math. Soc. 13 (1976) 90–94.

S.I. Adian, W.W. Boone, G. Higman, eds., Word Problems II
© North-Holland Publishing Company (1980) 215–245

ON ISOMORPHISMS OF DIRECT POWERS

J.M. Tyrer JONES
Department of Pure Mathematics and Mathematical Statistics, Cambridge University

§1. Introduction

In [2] Corner shows that, given any positive integer n, there exists a countable abelian group H such that $H^r \cong H^s$ if and only if r is congruent to s modulo n. (Where H^r denotes the direct sum of r isomorphic copies of H.) In this paper, we show that similar results can be obtained for finitely generated non-abelian groups. For the case $n = 1$ it is sufficient to construct a non-trivial finitely generated group isomorphic to its own direct square. This was done in [3], and the method of construction used there can easily be adapted to the needs of the general case. For given $n > 0$ we wish to construct a group G such that

(i) $G \cong G^{n+1}$
(ii) $G \not\cong G^r$ for $1 < r < n + 1$.

The fact that $G^r \cong G^s$ if and only if r is congruent to s modulo n follows easily from (i) and (ii). For ease of notation, we shall take the given integer to be $n - 1$, so that we need to construct a group G satisfying

(i)′ $G \cong G^n$
(ii)′ $G \not\cong G^r$ for $1 < r < n$.

The 'building blocks' of our construction are the simple groups constructed by Camm in [1]. We give a brief description of these groups at the beginning of §2, but will assume a general familiarity with the notation and methods of calculation used by Camm. We will make frequent use of the structure theorems for amalgamated free products and HNN extensions. For the terminology of amalgamated free products we will follow [4], and for that of HNN extensions [5]. General structural results to be found in either of these two sources will be utilised without further comment.

§2. The construction

$A = \langle a, p \rangle$ and $B = \langle b, q \rangle$ are two-generator free groups. I is the set

$\{\pm 1, \pm 2, \pm 3, \ldots\}$ and ρ, σ, τ are permutations of I. Let U be the subgroup of A (freely) generated by the set $\{a^i p^{\rho(i)} : i \in I\}$ and V be the subgroup of B generated by the set $\{b^i q^{\sigma(i)} : i \in I\}$. Set $g_i = a^i p^{\rho(i)}$ and $h_i = b^i q^{\sigma(i)}$, and form the free product R of A and B amalgamating U with V under the isomorphism $g_i \mapsto h_{\tau(i)}$, $i = \pm 1, \pm 2, \pm 3, \ldots$.

In [1], Camm shows that if ρ, σ and τ are suitably chosen, then the group R is simple. Her definitions specify the effect of ρ, σ and τ on some of the positive integers. The definitions elsewhere can be made arbitrarily, subject to one technical condition, which states essentially that $|\rho(i)|$, $|\sigma(i)|$ and $|\tau(i)|$ must not be very much bigger than $|i|$. It is easy to see that if, for a given integer t (however large), the negative integers are divided into 'blocks' $B_1 = \{-1, -2, -3, \ldots -t\}$, $B_2 = \{-(t+1), -(t+2), \ldots -2t\}$, $B_3 = \{-(2t+1), -(2t+2), \ldots -3t\}$ etc., and ρ, σ and τ are so defined that for each $r = 1, 2, 3, \ldots$ $\rho(-rt) = \sigma(-rt) = \tau(-rt) = -rt$ and ρ, σ and τ fix each B_n setwise, then Camm's conditions are satisfied, and a simple group R results.

We now proceed to the details of our construction. We are given an integer $n \geqslant 3$, and wish to construct a group G satisfying conditions (i)′ and (ii)′ of §1. We divide the negative integers into blocks of size $9n$, and define permutations ρ, σ and τ of the negative integers by

$$\rho(-9nt + r) = -9nt + \rho_1(r)$$

$$\sigma(-9nt + r) = -9nt + \sigma_1(r)$$

$$\tau(-9nt + r) = -9nt + \tau_1(r) \qquad 0 \leqslant r \leqslant 9n - 1,\ t = 1, 2, 3, \ldots$$

where ρ_1, σ_1, τ_1 are those permutations of the set $\{0, 1, \ldots 9n - 1\}$ defined by $\rho_1 = (13, 14)$, $\sigma_1 = (5, 6)$, $\tau_1 = (9n - 10, 9n - 9)$. By using Camm's definitions on the positive integers, we obtain a simple group $R = A *_{U=V} B$. The subgroup $A = \langle a, p \rangle$ of R is free, and so we may form an HNN extension H of R by adding a generator c and relations $c^{-1}ac = a$, $c^{-1}pc = p^n$, viz.

$$H = \langle a, p, b, q, c : a^i p^{\rho(i)} = b^{\tau(i)} q^{\sigma\tau(i)},$$

$$i = \pm 1, \pm 2, \pm 3, \ldots, c^{-1}ac = a, c^{-1}pc = p^n \rangle.$$

We next construct a group $T = \langle d, e, f : d^{-1}fd = f^2,\ e^{-1}de = d^2 \rangle$ as follows:

Let $\langle f \rangle$ be an infinite cyclic group, and form an HNN extension $\langle d, f : d^{-1}fd = f^2 \rangle$ of $\langle f \rangle$. The element d in this group has infinite order, and so we may make a further HNN extension by adding a generator e and the relation $e^{-1}de = d^2$. The resulting group we call T.

Britton's Lemma shows that the subgroups $\langle b^{-1}a, c\rangle$ of H and $\langle e, f\rangle$ of T are both free groups of rank two, and so we may form the free product of H and T amalgamating $\langle b^{-1}a, c\rangle$ with $\langle e, f\rangle$ according to the relations

$$b^{-1}a = e \quad \text{and} \quad c = f.$$

The resulting group S has presentation

$$S = \langle a, p, b, q, c, d : a^i p^{\rho(i)} = b^{\tau(i)} q^{\sigma\tau(i)},\ i = \pm 1, \pm 2, \pm 3, \ldots, c^{-1}ac = a,$$
$$c^{-1}pc = p^n,\ d^{-1}cd = c^2,\ (b^{-1}a)^{-1}d(b^{-1}a) = d^2\rangle.$$

We now form the cartesian product $C = \Pi^c_{i \in N} S_i$ of copies of S indexed by $N = \{1, 2, 3, \ldots\}$. Elements of C will be written as infinite vectors. The corresponding direct product $D = \Pi_{i \in N} S_i$ is the subgroup of C consisting of all those elements whose projection on S_i is the identity for all but finitely many $i \in N$. We shall denote by H_i, T_i, A_i, etc. the subgroups of S_i corresponding to the subgroups H, T, A, etc. of S.

G is defined to be the subgroup of C generated by the elements

$$\boldsymbol{x} = (b^{-1}a, b^{-1}a, b^{-1}a, \ldots),$$
$$\boldsymbol{y} = (p, p, p, \ldots),$$
$$\boldsymbol{z} = (p^9ap^{-8}, p^{18}ap^{-17}, p^{27}ap^{-26}, \ldots),$$
$$\boldsymbol{u} = (c, c, c, \ldots),$$
$$\boldsymbol{v} = (d, d, d, \ldots).$$

We shall show that G satisfies conditions (i)′ and (ii)′ of §1.

§3. The isomorphism

In this section we prove that the group G defined above satisfies condition (i)′ of §1.

Theorem 3.1. *G is isomorphic to G^n.*

Proof. It is easy to check (by using the definitions $\rho(1) = \sigma(1) = \tau(1) = 1$, specified by Camm, and the definitions of ρ, σ and τ on the negative integers given in §1) that the following equations are consequences of the amalgamation relations of R, and hence hold in S.

(1) $b^{-1}a(p^{9nt-9k}ap^{-9nt+9k+1})a^{-1}b = p^{9nt-9k}ap^{-9nt+9k+1}$ for all $k = 0, 1, \ldots n-2$, and all $t \geq 1$.

(2) $b^{-1}a(p^{9nt-9(n-1)}ap^{-9nt+9(n-1)+1})a^{-1}b = p^{9nt-9(n-1)+1}a^2p^{-9nt+9(n-1)+1}$ for all $t \geqslant 1$.

(3) $b^{-1}a(p^{9nt-14}ap^{-9nt+15})a^{-1}b = p^{9nt-13}ap^{-9nt+15}$ for all $t \geqslant 1$.

(4) $b^{-1}a(p^{9nt-3}ap^{-9nt+4})a^{-1}b = p^{9nt-3}ap^{-9nt+4}q$ for all $t \geqslant 1$.

Using equations (1) and (2) we deduce that

$$\begin{aligned}[\boldsymbol{x}^{-1}, \boldsymbol{z}^{-1}] &= (p^{10}ap^{-9}, 1, 1, \ldots 1, p^{9n+10}ap^{-9n-9}, 1, 1, \ldots 1, p^{18n+10}ap^{-18n-9}, 1, \ldots) \\ &= \boldsymbol{z}_1 \text{ say.}\end{aligned}$$

Equation (3) gives

$$[\boldsymbol{x}^{-1}, \boldsymbol{y}^{9n-24}\boldsymbol{z}_1^{-1}\boldsymbol{y}^{9n+24}] = (p, 1, 1, \ldots 1, p, 1, 1, \ldots 1, p, 1, \ldots) = \boldsymbol{y}_1 \text{ say}$$

and equation (4) gives

$$[\boldsymbol{y}^{9n-13}\boldsymbol{z}_1^{-1}\boldsymbol{y}^{9n+13}, \boldsymbol{x}^{-1}] = (q, 1, 1, \ldots 1, q, 1, 1, \ldots 1, q, 1, \ldots).$$

Since $b^{-1}a = qp^{-1}$, we deduce that G also contains

$$\boldsymbol{x}_1 = (b^{-1}a, 1, 1, \ldots 1, b^{-1}a, 1, 1, \ldots 1, b^{-1}a, 1, \ldots).$$

The relations $[d, b^{-1}a] = d$ and $[c, d] = c$ of S show that the elements

$$\boldsymbol{v}_1 = [\boldsymbol{v}, \boldsymbol{x}_1] = (d, 1, 1, \ldots 1, d, 1, 1, \ldots 1, d, 1, \ldots)$$

and

$$\boldsymbol{u}_1 = [\boldsymbol{u}, \boldsymbol{v}_1] = (c, 1, 1, \ldots 1, c, 1, 1, \ldots 1, c, 1, \ldots)$$

also lie in G.

Let G_1 be the subgroup of G generated by $\boldsymbol{x}_1$, $\boldsymbol{y}_1$, $\boldsymbol{z}_1$, $\boldsymbol{u}_1$ and $\boldsymbol{v}_1$. Then G_1 is the projection of G on the subgroup C_1 of C consisting of all those elements of C whose projection on S_i is trivial for all $i \not\equiv 1 \bmod n$.

By considering the commutator $[\boldsymbol{x}^{-1}, \boldsymbol{y}^{9n-9}\boldsymbol{z}_1^{-1}\boldsymbol{y}^{-9n+9}]$ and proceeding as above, we deduce that G also contains its projection G_2 on C_2 (the set of all elements of C whose projection on S_i is trivial for all $i \not\equiv 2 \bmod n$), and similarly for each i, $1 \leqslant i \leqslant n$. Clearly, $G = G_1 \times G_2 \times \cdots \times G_n$.

The groups G_i, $1 \leqslant i \leqslant n$, are all isomorphic, and so it only remains to prove that $G_1 \cong G$. Now

$$\begin{aligned}G_1 &= \langle \boldsymbol{x}_1, \boldsymbol{y}_1, \boldsymbol{z}_1, \boldsymbol{u}_1, \boldsymbol{v}_1 \rangle \\ &= \langle \boldsymbol{x}_1, \boldsymbol{y}_1, \boldsymbol{y}_1^{9n-10}\boldsymbol{z}_1\boldsymbol{y}_1^{-9n+9}, \boldsymbol{u}_1, \boldsymbol{v}_1 \rangle \\ &= \langle \boldsymbol{x}_1, \boldsymbol{y}_1, \boldsymbol{u}_1\boldsymbol{y}_1^{9n-10}\boldsymbol{z}_1\boldsymbol{y}_1^{-9n+9}\boldsymbol{u}_1^{-1}\boldsymbol{y}_1, \boldsymbol{u}_1, \boldsymbol{v}_1 \rangle.\end{aligned}$$

But

$$\boldsymbol{y}_1^{9n-10}\boldsymbol{z}_1\boldsymbol{y}_1^{-9n+9} = (p^{9n}ap^{-9n}, 1, 1, \ldots 1, p^{18n}ap^{-18n}, 1, 1, \ldots 1, p^{27n}ap^{-27n}, 1, \ldots)$$

so

$$u_1 y_1^{9n-10} z_1 y_1^{-9n+9} u_1^{-1}$$
$$= (p^9 a p^{-9}, 1, 1, \ldots 1, p^{18} a p^{-18}, 1, 1, \ldots 1, p^{27} a p^{-27}, 1, \ldots)$$

and

$$u_1 y_1^{9n-10} z_1 y_1^{-9n+9} u_1^{-1} y_1$$
$$= (p^9 a p^{-8}, 1, 1, \ldots 1, p^{18} a p^{-17}, 1, 1, \ldots 1, p^{27} a p^{-26}, 1, \ldots).$$

The isomorphism betwen G and G_1 is now clear. This completes the proof of Theorem 3.1.

§4. Some preliminary lemmas

We wish to show that $G \not\cong G'$ for $1 < r < n$. Since $G \cong G''$, it is clear that each of G and G' is both a subgroup and a homomorphic image of the other. Consequently many of the standard methods of demonstrating that two groups are not isomorphic are not applicable in our case. For this reason we must proceed by direct calculation. We first prove

Lemma 4.1. *G contains the direct product* $D = \Pi_{i \in N} S_i$.

Proof. As in §3, we see that the following relations hold in S.

(5) $b^{-1} a (p^{9nt-(9k-8)} a p^{-9nt+(9k-8)+1}) a^{-1} b = p^{9nt-(9k-8)} a p^{-9nt+(9k-8)+1}$ for all $t \geq 1$ and $0 \leq k \leq n$.

(6) $b^{-1} a (p^{-1} a p^2) a^{-1} b = p^{-3} a^3 p^6 q^{-5}$.

(To prove (6), we have to use some of Camm's definitions for ρ, σ and τ on the positive integers, namely,

$$\rho(1) = \sigma(1) = \tau(1) = 1, \qquad \rho(2) = \tau(2) = 2,\ \sigma(2) = 3$$
$$\rho(3) = 3,\ \sigma(3) = \tau(3) = 4, \qquad \rho(4) = 5,\ \sigma(4) = 2,\ \tau(4) = 3$$
$$\rho(5) = \sigma(5) = \tau(5) = 5, \qquad \rho(6) = \sigma(6) = \tau(6) = 6.)$$

From (5) and (6) it follows that

$$[x^{-1}, y^{-10} z^{-1} y^{10}] = (p^{-3} a^3 p^6 q^{-5} p^{-2} a^{-1} p, 1, 1, \ldots 1, \ldots).$$

The first entry is a non-trivial element of the subgroup R_1 of S_1. But the projection of G on S_1 is the whole of S_1, and R_1 is simple, so G contains elements $(g, 1, 1, \ldots 1, 1, \ldots)$ for each $g \in R$. In particular, G contains the element $h = (b^{-1} a, 1, 1, \ldots 1, 1, \ldots)$, and hence the elements $[v, h] = (d, 1, 1, \ldots 1, 1, \ldots)$ and $[u, [v, h]] = (c, 1, 1, \ldots 1, 1, \ldots)$ also lie in G. Thus G contains the whole of S_1. Similarly, by considering $[x^{-1}, y^{-19} z^{-1} y^{19}]$, we see that G contains S_2. Repetition of the argument shows that G contains S_i for all $i \geq 1$, and hence that G contains D. □

Lemma 4.2. *S is centreless.*

Proof. By the amalgamated free product structure of S, we have

$$Z(S) \subseteq Z(\langle b^{-1}a, c\rangle).$$

But $\langle b^{-1}a, c\rangle$ is a two-generator free group, and so has trivial centre. □

Lemma 4.3. *If N_1 and N_2 are normal subgroups of S which intersect trivially, then one of N_1 and N_2 is trivial.*

Proof. Suppose that neither N_1 nor N_2 is trivial. We first show that one of them lies in the amalgamated subgroup $K = \langle b^{-1}a, c\rangle$ of S. Suppose $N_1 \not\subseteq K$. Then N_1 must contain a cyclically reduced element of S of normal form length greater than one. For suppose not. If N_1 contains a cyclically reduced element g, say, of length one, then g lies in one of the factors H, T of S, but not in K. Let x be any element of the other factor not lying in K. Then the commutator $[x, g]$ is a cyclically reduced element of length four, lying in N_1. So suppose that every cyclically reduced element of N_1 lies in K. $N_1 \not\subseteq K$, so there is an element $ghg^{-1}(g \in S,\ h \in K)$, of N_1 which does not lie in K. By taking a suitable conjugate of this, we find that N_1 contains an element which lies in a factor, but not in K, and the result then follows as above.

Let $s_1s_2---s_m$ be a cyclically reduced element of N_1, written in normal form with $m > 1$. Without loss of generality, we may assume $s_1 \in H$ and $s_m \in T$. Since $|H : K| \neq 2$, we may find an element $g \in H\backslash K$ such that $gs_1 \notin K$. Thus $gs_1s_2---s_mg^{-1} \in N_1$ and is not cyclically reduced. Consequently N_1 contains both cyclically reduced and non-cyclically reduced elements.

Let x be any element of N_2. Since N_1 and N_2 intersect trivially they generate their direct product, so x commutes with both a cyclically reduced and a non-cyclically reduced element, and thus, by a length argument, $x \in K$. Thus $N_2 \subseteq K$, as required.

Restricting our attention to H, we see that H has a non-trivial normal subgroup N_2 lying entirely within $K = \langle b^{-1}a, c\rangle$. We shall show that this cannot happen. Let

$$g = (b^{-1}a)^{\alpha_1}c^{\beta_1}(b^{-1}a)^{\alpha_2}c^{\beta_2}---(b^{-1}a)^{\alpha_r}c^{\beta_r} \in N_2.$$

Then bgb^{-1} also lies in N_2, and we have an equation of the form

$$b(b^{-1}a)^{\alpha_1}c^{\beta_1}---(b^{-1}a)^{\alpha_r}c^{\beta_r}b^{-1} = (b^{-1}a)^{\gamma_1}c^{\delta_1}(b^{-1}a)^{\gamma_2}c^{\delta_2}---(b^{-1}a)^{\gamma_s}c^{\delta_s}.$$

There are, without loss of generality, two cases to consider:

(i) $\beta_r \neq 0$ and
(ii) $g = (b^{-1}a)^{\alpha_1}$.

In case (i), an application of Britton's lemma to the HNN extension H of R shows that one of b^{-1} and $b^{-1}(b^{-1}a)^{-\gamma_s}$ lies in A, and the normal form theorem for R shows that neither case is possible. In case (ii), Britton's lemma shows that $b(b^{-1}a)^{\alpha_1}b^{-1} = (b^{-1}a)^{\gamma_1}$, which again is impossible by the normal form theorem in R. Thus $N_2 = 1$, as required. □

We are now ready to prove the important

Proposition 4.4. *If $G = A \times B$, then there is a partition $\{P_1, P_2\}$ of N such that $A = G_{P_1}$, $B = G_{P_2}$, where G_P denotes the set of all $g \in G$ such that the projection of g on S_i is the identity for all $i \notin P$.*

Proof. Suppose there exists an $i \in N$ such that A and B both have non-trivial projection on S_i. Then $A \ni \boldsymbol{a} = (a_1, a_2, \dots a_i, \dots)$ with $a_i \neq 1$. By Lemmas 4.1 and 4.2, there exists an element $g_i \in S$ such that $[g_i, a_i] \neq 1$, and $\boldsymbol{g} = (1, 1, \dots 1, g_i, 1, 1, \dots) \in G$. Now $1 \neq [\boldsymbol{g}, \boldsymbol{a}] = (1, 1, \dots 1, [g_i, a_i], 1, \dots) \in A$ since A is normal in G. Thus A has a non-trivial intersection with S_i, $A \cap S_i = N_1$, say. Similarly, B has a non-trivial intersection with S_i, $B \cap S_i = N_2$ say. But then N_1 and N_2 are non-trivial normal subgroups of S_i, which intersect trivially, and this contradicts Lemma 4.3.

Thus there are disjoint subsets P_1 and P_2 of N such that A has non-trivial projection on S_i if and only if $i \in P_1$ and B has non-trivial projection on S_i if and only if $i \in P_2$. Since $S_i \subseteq G$ for each i, and since $G = A \times B$, we see that $\{P_1, P_2\}$ is a partition of N. Now $A \subseteq G_{P_1}$, $B \subseteq G_{P_2}$ and every element g of G can be written in the form $g = ab$ with $a \in A$ and $b \in B$. Hence $A = G_{P_1}$, $B = G_{P_2}$ as required. □

§5. The admissible partitions $\{P_1, P_2\}$

Since $G \supseteq D$, several decompositions of G as a direct product of the form $G \cong S' \times G$ suggest themselves. Other direct decompositions were obtained in §3. In this section, we prove that the only decompositions of G as $G_{P_1} \times G_{P_2}$ can be obtained by making repeated use of these two methods of decomposition. In particular, we prove

Proposition 5.1. *Let P be a subset of N. Then $G = G_P \times G_{N \setminus P}$ if and only if either*

(i) *P is finite or*

(ii) *There exist integers* k, m *and* $t, t \leqslant n^k$, *and congruence classes* $C_1, C_2, \ldots C_t \bmod n^k$ *such that* $P = X \cup C_1 \cup C_2 \cup \cdots \cup C_t$, *where* X *is a subset of* $\{1, 2, \ldots m\}$.

The methods used are those of direct calculation, using the normal form theorems for amalgamated free products and HNN extensions.

We begin with a trivial observation.

Lemma 5.2. *The subgroup of* G *generated by* $\boldsymbol{x}$, $\boldsymbol{u}$ *and* $\boldsymbol{v}$ *is isomorphic to* T *under the map* $\boldsymbol{x} \to e$, $\boldsymbol{u} \to f$, $\boldsymbol{v} \to d$. □

We now attempt to derive similar descriptions of other subgroups of G, in particular, of the subgroup generated by $\boldsymbol{x}$, $\boldsymbol{y}$, $\boldsymbol{z}$ and $\boldsymbol{u}$. To this end, we introduce new elements of C as follows:

For any $\boldsymbol{g} \in C$, let g_i denote the projection of $\boldsymbol{g}$ on S_i.

For each positive integer k, and each integer l, $1 \leqslant l \leqslant n^k$, define new elements $\boldsymbol{x}(l, k)$, $\boldsymbol{y}(l, k)$, $\boldsymbol{u}(l, k)$ and $\boldsymbol{v}(l, k)$ of C by

$$\boldsymbol{x}(l, k)_i = \boldsymbol{y}(l, k)_i = \boldsymbol{u}(l, k)_i = \boldsymbol{v}(l, k)_i = 1 \quad \text{if } i \not\equiv l \bmod n^k.$$

$$\boldsymbol{x}(l, k)_i = b^{-1}a,\ \boldsymbol{y}(l, k)_i = p,\ \boldsymbol{u}(l, k)_i = c,\ \boldsymbol{v}(l, k)_i = d \quad \text{if } i \equiv l \bmod n^k.$$

For each k, l as above, and each integer $s \geqslant 1$, define an element $\boldsymbol{z}(l, k, s)$ of C by

$$\boldsymbol{z}(l, k, s)_i = 1 \qquad \text{if } i \not\equiv l \bmod n^k$$

$$\boldsymbol{z}(l, k, s)_i = p^{9n^s t} a p^{-9n^s t+1} \quad \text{if } i = n^k(t-1) + l.$$

The proof of Theorem 3.1 shows that G contains the elements $\boldsymbol{x}(l, k)$, $\boldsymbol{y}(l, k)$, $\boldsymbol{u}(l, k)$, $\boldsymbol{v}(l, k)$ and $\boldsymbol{z}(l, k, s)$ for all l, k, s as above.

Let $C_{l,k}$ be the subgroup of C consisting of all those elements of C whose projection on S_i is trivial for all $i \not\equiv l \bmod n^k$, and let $D_{l,k}$ be the corresponding direct product.

The proof of Lemma 4.1 can easily be adapted to show that for each l, k, s the group $L_{l,k,s} = \langle \boldsymbol{x}(l, k), \boldsymbol{y}(l, k), \boldsymbol{z}(l, k, s) \rangle$ contains the direct product $D_{l,k}$. We will use bars to denote cosets of $D_{l,k}$ in $L_{l,k,s}$.

Lemma 5.3. *The group* $L_{l,k,s}/D_{l,k}$ *is a free product of free groups* $\bar{A}_{l,k,s} = \langle \bar{\boldsymbol{y}}(l, k), \bar{\boldsymbol{z}}(l, k, s) \rangle$ *and* $\bar{B}_{l,k,s} = \langle \bar{\boldsymbol{x}}(l, k)\bar{\boldsymbol{y}}(l, k), \bar{\boldsymbol{z}}(l, k, s) \rangle$ *with the subgroups* $\bar{U}_{l,k,s} = \langle \bar{\boldsymbol{y}}(l, k)^{-i} \bar{\boldsymbol{z}}(l, k, s) \bar{\boldsymbol{y}}(l, k)^i$, $i \not\equiv 12, 13, 14 \bmod 9n$, $\bar{\boldsymbol{y}}(l, k)^{-12+9nt} \bar{\boldsymbol{z}}(l, k, s) \bar{\boldsymbol{y}}(l, k)^{13-9nt}$, $\bar{\boldsymbol{y}}(l, k)^{-13+9nt} \bar{\boldsymbol{z}}(l, k, s) \bar{\boldsymbol{y}}(l, k)^{14-9nt}$, $\bar{\boldsymbol{y}}(l, k)^{-14+9nt} \bar{\boldsymbol{z}}(l, k, s) \bar{\boldsymbol{y}}(l, k)^{12-9nt}$, $t \in Z \rangle$, *and* $\bar{V}_{l,k,s} = \langle (\bar{\boldsymbol{x}}(l, k)\bar{\boldsymbol{y}}(l, k))^{-i} \bar{\boldsymbol{z}}(l, k, s) (\bar{\boldsymbol{x}}(l, k)\bar{\boldsymbol{y}}(l, k))^i$, $i \not\equiv 4, 5, 6 \bmod 9n$, $(\bar{\boldsymbol{x}}(l, k)\bar{\boldsymbol{y}}(l, k))^{-4+9nt} \bar{\boldsymbol{z}}(l, k, s) (\bar{\boldsymbol{x}}(l, k)\bar{\boldsymbol{y}}(l, k))^{5-9nt}$,

$(\bar{x}(l,k)\bar{y}(l,k))^{-5+9nt}\bar{z}(l,k,s)(\bar{x}(l,k)\bar{y}(l,k))^{6-9nt}$,
$(\bar{x}(l,k)\bar{y}(l,k))^{-6+9nt}\bar{z}(l,k,s)(\bar{x}(l,k)\bar{y}(l,k))^{4-9nt}$, $t \in Z\rangle$ *amalgamated under the isomorphism*

$$\bar{y}(l,k)^{-i}\bar{z}(l,k,s)\bar{y}(l,k)^{i} = (\bar{x}(l,k)\bar{y}(l,k))^{-i}\bar{z}(l,k,s)(\bar{x}(l,k)\bar{y}(l,k))^{i}$$

$$\textit{for all } i \not\equiv 4,5,6,12,13,14,9n-11,9n-10,9n-9 \bmod 9n$$

$$\bar{y}(l,k)^{-4+9nt}\bar{z}(l,k,s)\bar{y}(l,k)^{4-9nt} = (\bar{x}(l,k)\bar{y}(l,k))^{-4+9nt}\bar{z}(l,k,s)(\bar{x}(l,k)\bar{y}(l,k))^{5-9nt}$$

$$\bar{y}(l,k)^{-5+9nt}\bar{z}(l,k,s)\bar{y}(l,k)^{5-9nt} = (\bar{x}(l,k)\bar{y}(l,k))^{-6+9nt}\bar{z}(l,k,s)(\bar{x}(l,k)\bar{y}(l,k))^{4-9nt}$$

$$\bar{y}(l,k)^{-6+9nt}\bar{z}(l,k,s)\bar{y}(l,k)^{6-9nt} = (\bar{x}(l,k)\bar{y}(l,k))^{-5+9nt}\bar{z}(l,k,s)(\bar{x}(l,k)\bar{y}(l,k))^{6-9nt}$$

$$\bar{y}(l,k)^{-12+9nt}\bar{z}(l,k,s)\bar{y}(l,k)^{13-9nt} = (\bar{x}(l,k)\bar{y}(l,k))^{-12+9nt}\bar{z}(l,k,s)(\bar{x}(l,k)\bar{y}(l,k))^{12-9nt}$$

$$\bar{y}(l,k)^{-13+9nt}\bar{z}(l,k,s)\bar{y}(l,k)^{14-9nt} = (\bar{x}(l,k)\bar{y}(l,k))^{-14+9nt}\bar{z}(l,k,s)(\bar{x}(l,k)\bar{y}(l,k))^{14-9nt}$$

$$\bar{y}(l,k)^{-14+9nt}\bar{z}(l,k,s)\bar{y}(l,k)^{12-9nt} = (\bar{x}(l,k)\bar{y}(l,k))^{-13+9nt}\bar{z}(l,k,s)(\bar{x}(l,k)\bar{y}(l,k))^{13-9nt}$$

$$\bar{y}(l,k)^{-(9n-11)+9nt}\bar{z}(l,k,s)\bar{y}(l,k)^{9n-11-9nt} = (\bar{x}(l,k)\bar{y}(l,k))^{-(9n-11)+9nt}\bar{z}(l,k,s)\cdot (\bar{x}(l,k)\bar{y}(l,k))^{-1}\bar{z}(l,k,s)(\bar{x}(l,k)\bar{y}(l,k))^{9n-10-9nt}$$

$$\bar{y}(l,k)^{-(9n-10)+9nt}\bar{z}(l,k,s)\bar{y}(l,k)^{9n-10-9nt} = (\bar{x}(l,k)\bar{y}(l,k))^{-(9n-10)+9nt}\bar{z}(l,k,s)^{-1}\cdot (\bar{x}(l,k)\bar{y}(l,k))^{9n-10-9nt}$$

$$\bar{y}(l,k)^{-(9n-9)+9nt}\bar{z}(l,k,s)\bar{y}(l,k)^{9n-9-9nt} = (\bar{x}(l,k)\bar{y}(l,k))^{-(9n-10)+9nt}\bar{z}(l,k,s)\cdot (\bar{x}(l,k)\bar{y}(l,k))^{-1}\bar{z}(l,k,s)(\bar{x}(l,k)\bar{y}(l,k))^{9n-9-9nt}$$

Proof. An equation $w(\bar{x}(l,k),\bar{y}(l,k),\bar{z}(l,k,s)) = 1$ holds in $\bar{L}_{l,k,s}$ if and only if the projection of the corresponding word $w(x(l,k),y(l,k),z(l,k,s))$ on S_i is trivial for all but finitely many $i \in N$. Thus it is easy to check that the listed equations hold in $\bar{L}_{l,k,s}$.

To show that the subgroups $\bar{A}_{l,k,s}$ and $\bar{B}_{l,k,s}$ are free, we need only note that for any $i \equiv l \bmod n^k$ the projections of $A_{l,k,s}$ and $B_{l,k,s}$ on S_i are the free subgroups A_i and B_i of S_i. Hence $\bar{U}_{l,k,s}$ and $\bar{V}_{l,k,s}$ are free on the listed generators, and the given equations represent an isomorphism between $\bar{U}_{l,k,s}$ and $\bar{V}_{l,k,s}$. Thus $\bar{L}_{l,k,s}$ is a homomorphic image of the required amalgamated free product.

Let $\bar{g} = \bar{h}\bar{s}_1\bar{s}_2---\bar{s}_r$ be an element of $\bar{L}_{l,k,s}$ written in normal form with respect to the relations of the amalgamated free product, so that $\bar{h}$ is a word on the generators of $\bar{U}_{l,k,s}$ and the $\bar{s}_i$ are powers of $\bar{\boldsymbol{y}}(l,k)$ and $\bar{\boldsymbol{x}}(l,k)\bar{\boldsymbol{y}}(l,k)$ taken alternately. If we can prove that $\bar{g} \neq 1$ unless $r = 0$ and $\bar{h} = 1$, then the result will be established.

Let $\bar{\boldsymbol{y}}(l,k)^{m_1}\bar{\boldsymbol{z}}(l,k,s)\bar{\boldsymbol{y}}(l,k)^{m_2}$ be any generator of $\bar{U}_{l,k,s}$ and consider the corresponding word $w = \boldsymbol{y}(l,k)^{m_1}\boldsymbol{z}(l,k,s)\boldsymbol{y}(l,k)^{m_2}$ of $L_{l,k,s}$. Now w_i lies in the subgroup R_i of S_i, and it is easy to check (by taking each generator in turn) that w_i also lies in the amalgamated subgroup U_i of R_i for all sufficiently large $i \equiv l \bmod n^k$.

Now $\bar{h}$ involves only finitely many generators of $\bar{U}_{l,k,s}$ and consequently the projection h_i of h on S_i lies in U_i for all sufficiently large $i \equiv l \bmod n^k$. It follows that, for all sufficiently large $i \equiv l \bmod n^k$, g_i is a word of R_i of normal form length r. Thus $\bar{g} = 1$ in $\bar{L}_{l,k,s}$ if and only if $r = 0$ and $\bar{h} = 1$, as required. □

We next consider the subgroup of G generated by the elements $\boldsymbol{x}(l,k)$, $\boldsymbol{y}(l,k)$ and $\boldsymbol{z}(l,k,s)$ when s is allowed to vary through a finite set. We prove

Lemma 5.4. *Let α and β be fixed positive integers. Then the groups $\bar{L}_{l,k,s}$, $0 \leqslant \alpha \leqslant s \leqslant \beta$ generate their free product amalgamating the subgroup $\langle \bar{\boldsymbol{x}}(l,k), \bar{\boldsymbol{y}}(l,k)\rangle$.*

Proof. The group $\bar{M}_{l,k,\alpha,\beta}$ generated by the $\bar{L}_{l,k,s}$ is clearly a homomorphic image of the required amalgamated free product. We note that any element $\bar{g}$ of $\bar{M}_{l,k,\alpha,\beta}$ may be written in the form

$$\bar{g} = w(\bar{\boldsymbol{x}}(l,k), \bar{\boldsymbol{y}}(l,k))\bar{u}_1\bar{u}_2---\bar{u}_r$$

where each $\bar{u}_i$ is a non-trivial word on the generators of $\bar{U}_{l,k,s}$, for some $s = s(i)$ and where $s(i+1) \neq s(i)$ for any $i = 1, 2, \ldots r-1$. We need only show that $\bar{g} = 1$ if and only if $r = 0$ and $w(\bar{\boldsymbol{x}}(l,k), \bar{\boldsymbol{y}}(l,k))$ is the trivial word.

As in the proof of Lemma 5.3, the projection of $u_1u_2---u_r$ on S_i lies in the amalgamated subgroup U_i of R_i for all sufficiently large $i \equiv l \bmod n^k$. A length argument in R_i then shows that if $\bar{g} = 1$, w must be the trivial word. Thus it is sufficient to consider words of the form $\bar{u}_1\bar{u}_2---\bar{u}_r$.

Suppose $\bar{u}_1\bar{u}_2---\bar{u}_r = 1$ with $r > 1$, and set $i = n^k(t-1)+l$. The projection of u_j on S_i is a word in finitely many elements from among $p^{-m}(p^{9n^st}ap^{-9n^st+1})p^m$, $m \neq 12, 13, 14 \bmod 9n$, $p^{-12+9nm}(p^{9n^st}ap^{-9n^st+1})p^{13-9nm}$, $p^{-13+9nm}(p^{9n^st}ap^{-9n^st+1})p^{14-9nm}$,

$p^{-14+9nm}(p^{9n^st}ap^{-9n^st+1})p^{12-9nm}$, $m \in Z$. Now $u_1u_2---u_r \in D$, so there must exist some j, $1 \leq j \leq r-1$, such that for infinitely many values of $i \equiv l \bmod n^k$, all adjacent p-symbols in the projection of u_ju_{j+1} on S_i cancel. Suppose that $\bar{u}_j$, written as a word on the generators of $\bar{U}_{l,k,s(j)}$ ends in $\bar{y}(l,k)^\gamma \bar{z}(l,k,s)^\varepsilon \bar{y}(l,k)^\delta$, $\gamma, \delta \in Z$, $\varepsilon = \pm 1$, and $s = s(j)$, and $\bar{u}_{j+1}$ begins in $\bar{y}(l,k)^{\gamma'} \bar{z}(l,k,s')^{\varepsilon'} \bar{y}(l,k)^{\delta'}$, $\gamma', \delta' \in Z$, $\varepsilon' = \pm 1$, and $s' = s(j+1) \neq s$. The projections of these segments on S_i, $i = n^k(t-1)+l$, are $p^\gamma(p^{9n^st}ap^{-9n^st+1})^\varepsilon p^\delta$ and $p^{\gamma'}(p^{9n^{s'}t}ap^{-9n^{s'}t+1})^{\varepsilon'}p^{\delta'}$. Thus one of the following must hold for infinitely many values of t:

(i) $-9n^st+1+\delta+\gamma'+9n^{s'}t=0$
(ii) $-9n^st+1+\delta+\gamma'+9n^{s'}t-1=0$
(iii) $-9n^st+\delta+\gamma'+9n^{s'}t=0$
(iv) $-9n^st+\delta+\gamma+9n^{s'}t-1=0$.

Rewriting these, we see that one of the following must hold for infinitely many values of t:

(i)′ $9t(n^{s'}-n^s)+1+\delta+\gamma'=0$
(ii)′ $9t(n^{s'}-n^s)+\delta+\gamma'=0$
(iii)′ $9t(n^{s'}-n^s)+\delta+\gamma'-1=0$.

But δ, γ', s and s' are fixed with $s \neq s'$, so each of these equations can hold for at most one value of t. Thus $\bar{u}_1\bar{u}_2---\bar{u}_r \neq 1$. Since $\bar{U}_{l,k,s}$ is free, the case $r=1$ is easily dealt with, and so the structure of $\bar{M}_{l,k,\alpha,\beta}$ is established. □

We are now in a position to investigate the structure of the subgroup $\langle \boldsymbol{x}, \boldsymbol{y}, \boldsymbol{z}, \boldsymbol{u} \rangle$ of G. We prove

Lemma 5.5. *Suppose w is an element of $\langle \boldsymbol{x}, \boldsymbol{y}, \boldsymbol{z}, \boldsymbol{u} \rangle$ written in the form*

$$w = \boldsymbol{u}^{\alpha_1}\boldsymbol{g}_1\boldsymbol{u}^{\alpha_2}\boldsymbol{g}_2---\boldsymbol{u}^{\alpha_r}\boldsymbol{g}_r$$

where each $\boldsymbol{g}_i \in \langle \boldsymbol{x}, \boldsymbol{y}, \boldsymbol{z} \rangle$. Set $k = \Sigma_{i=1}^r |\alpha_i| + 1$. Then there exists an integer m, and congruence classes $C_1, C_2, \ldots C_t \bmod n^k$ such that the projection of w on S_i is trivial if $i > m$ and $i \notin C_1 \cup C_2 \cup \cdots \cup C_t$, and non-trivial if $i > m$ and $i \in C_1 \cup C_2 \cup \cdots \cup C_t$.

Proof. The projection w_i of w on S_i lies in H_i, and H_i is an HNN extension of R_i. It follows that if $\Sigma_{i=1}^r \alpha_i \neq 0$, then $w_i \neq 1$ for all $i \in N$, and the result is proved. Thus we may assume $\Sigma_{i=1}^r \alpha_i = 0$.

It is clear that there exists a word

$$\hat{w} = \hat{w}(\boldsymbol{x}(l,k), \boldsymbol{y}(l,k), \boldsymbol{z}(l,k,k), \boldsymbol{u}(l,k))$$

such that $\hat{w}_i = w_i$ for each $i \equiv l \bmod n^k$. Thus it is sufficient to prove that for each $l = 1, 2, \ldots, n^k$, there is a positive integer m_l such that if $\hat{w}_i \neq 1$ for some $i > m_l$, then $\hat{w}_i \neq 1$ for every $i > m_l$ such that $i \equiv l \bmod n^k$.

We may write $\hat{w}$ in the form

$$\hat{w} = \boldsymbol{u}(l, k)^{\alpha_1}\hat{\boldsymbol{g}}_1\boldsymbol{u}(l, k)^{\alpha_2}\hat{\boldsymbol{g}}_2 --- \boldsymbol{u}(l, k)^{\alpha_r}\hat{\boldsymbol{g}}_r$$

where each $\hat{\boldsymbol{g}}_r$ is a word in $\boldsymbol{x}(l, k), \boldsymbol{y}(l, k)$ and $\boldsymbol{z}(l, k, k)$. Now the following relations clearly hold in G:

(1) $\boldsymbol{u}(l, k)^{-r}\boldsymbol{z}(l, k, s)\boldsymbol{y}(l, k)^{-1}\boldsymbol{u}(l, k)^{r} = \boldsymbol{z}(l, k, s + r)\boldsymbol{y}(l, k)^{-1}$ for all $r \geq 0$.

(2) $\boldsymbol{u}(l, k)^{r}\boldsymbol{z}(l, k, s)\boldsymbol{y}(l, k)^{-1}\boldsymbol{u}(l, k)^{-r} = \boldsymbol{z}(l, k, s - r)\boldsymbol{y}(l, k)^{-1}$ for all $0 < r < s - 1$.

(3) $\boldsymbol{u}(l, k)^{-1}\boldsymbol{y}(l, k)\boldsymbol{u}(l, k) = \boldsymbol{y}(l, k)^{n}$.

We will call a word in $\bar{M}_{l,k,1,2k}$ *reducible* if it contains a subword of the type

(i) $\bar{\boldsymbol{u}}(l, k)^{-1}\bar{\boldsymbol{g}}\bar{\boldsymbol{u}}(l, k)$ with $\bar{\boldsymbol{g}} \in \bar{M}_{l,k,1,2k-1}$ *or*

(ii) $\bar{\boldsymbol{u}}(l, k)\bar{\boldsymbol{g}}\bar{\boldsymbol{u}}(l, k)^{-1}$ with $\bar{\boldsymbol{g}} \in \bar{N}_{l,k,2,2k} = \langle \bar{\boldsymbol{z}}(l, k, s)\bar{\boldsymbol{y}}(l, k)^{-1}, \bar{\boldsymbol{y}}(l, k)^{n}$ $2 \leq s \leq 2k\rangle$.

Otherwise the word is called *irreducible*. Lemma 5.4 shows that we can always tell of a given word of $\bar{M}_{l,k,1,2k}$ whether or not it lies in $\bar{M}_{l,k,1,2k-1}$ or $\bar{N}_{l,k,2,2k}$.

By using the images of relations (1), (2) and (3) in G/D we see that any reducible word can be replaced by a word equal to it, and involving fewer appearances of $\bar{\boldsymbol{u}}(l, k)$. Thus any word can be replaced in a finite number of steps, by an equal irreducible word.

We apply this process to $\bar{\hat{w}}$. The choice of k ensures that the resulting reduced word contains no subword of the form $\bar{\boldsymbol{u}}(l, k)^{-1}\bar{\boldsymbol{g}}\bar{\boldsymbol{u}}(l, k)$ with $\bar{\boldsymbol{g}} \in \bar{M}_{l,k,1,2k}$ or of the form $\bar{\boldsymbol{u}}(l, k)\bar{\boldsymbol{g}}\bar{\boldsymbol{u}}(l, k)^{-1}$ with $\bar{\boldsymbol{g}} \in \bar{N}_{l,k;1,2k}$. Let $\bar{v}$ be the reduced word thus obtained. Suppose that $\bar{v}$ still involves an appearance of $\bar{\boldsymbol{u}}(l, k)$, but that the projection of v on S_i is trivial for infinitely many $i \equiv l \bmod n^k$. It follows from the structure theorems of H_i that v contains a subword of the type

(i) $\boldsymbol{u}(l, k)^{-1}\boldsymbol{g}\boldsymbol{u}(l, k)$ with g_i lying in A_i for infinitely many $i \equiv l \bmod n^k$ or

(ii) $\boldsymbol{u}(l, k)\boldsymbol{g}\boldsymbol{u}(l, k)^{-1}$ with g_i lying in $\langle a, p^n\rangle$ for infinitely many $i \equiv l \bmod n^k$.

By Lemma 5.4, $\bar{\boldsymbol{g}}$ may be written in reduced from as $w(\bar{\boldsymbol{x}}(l, k), \bar{\boldsymbol{y}}(l, k))\bar{u}_1\bar{u}_2 --- \bar{u}_r$, and for sufficiently large $i \equiv l \bmod n^k$, the projection of $\boldsymbol{g}$ on S_i is equal to the projection of $w(\boldsymbol{x}(l, k), \boldsymbol{y}(l, k))u_1u_2 --- u_r$ on S_i. The projection of each u_j on S_i lies in the amalgamated subgroup U_i of R_i and so it follows from the normal form theorem for R_i that $w(\boldsymbol{x}(l, k), \boldsymbol{y}(l, k)) = \boldsymbol{y}(l, k)^{s}$ for some integer s. Thus $\bar{\boldsymbol{g}} \in \bar{M}_{l,k,1,2k-1}$ and so case (i) leads to a contradiction.

Case (ii) therefore holds, and the projection of $\boldsymbol{y}(l,k)^s u_1 u_2 --- u_r$ on S_i lies in $\langle a, p^n \rangle$ for infinitely many $i \equiv l \bmod n^k$.

Now the projection of $\boldsymbol{z}(l,k,s)\boldsymbol{y}(l,k)^{-1}$ $(1 \leq s \leq 2k)$ on S_i lies in $\langle a, p^n \rangle$ for all i, and so we see that, by writing $\bar{\boldsymbol{g}}$ as a word in $\bar{\boldsymbol{y}}(l,k)$ and $\bar{\boldsymbol{z}}(l,k,s)\boldsymbol{y}(l,k)^{-1}$, $1 \leq s \leq 2k$, we may conclude that $\bar{\boldsymbol{g}}$ lies in $\bar{N}_{l,k,2,2k}$ contradicting the fact that $\bar{v}$ is irreducible. Thus if $\bar{v}$ contains an appearance of $\bar{\boldsymbol{u}}(l,k)$, then v_i is non-trivial for all but finitely many $i \equiv l \bmod n^k$.

If, on the other hand, $\bar{v}$ contains no appearance of $\bar{\boldsymbol{u}}(l,k)$, we may use Lemma 5.4 to write $\bar{v}$ in normal form, and hence we may deduce that there is an integer m_l such that, if $v_i \neq 1$ for some $i > m_l$ then $v_i \neq 1$ for all $i > m_l$ such that $i \equiv l \bmod n^k$.

This completes the proof of Lemma 5.5. □

Lemma 5.6. *Let $w \in \langle \boldsymbol{x}, \boldsymbol{y}, \boldsymbol{z}, \boldsymbol{u} \rangle$ be written in the form $w = \boldsymbol{u}^{\alpha_1}\boldsymbol{g}_1\boldsymbol{u}^{\alpha_2}\boldsymbol{g}_2 --- \boldsymbol{u}^{\alpha_r}\boldsymbol{g}_r$ where each $\boldsymbol{g}_j \in \langle \boldsymbol{x}, \boldsymbol{y}, \boldsymbol{z} \rangle$, and let $k = \Sigma_{i=1}^{r} |\alpha_i| + 1$. Let $\hat{w}$ be the corresponding word of $\langle \boldsymbol{x}(l,k), \boldsymbol{y}(l,k), \boldsymbol{z}(l,k,k), \boldsymbol{u}(l,k) \rangle$, and let $\bar{v} = \bar{\boldsymbol{h}}_0\bar{\boldsymbol{u}}(l,k)^{\varepsilon_1}\bar{\boldsymbol{h}}_1\bar{\boldsymbol{u}}(l,k)^{\varepsilon_2} --- \bar{\boldsymbol{u}}(l,k)^{\varepsilon_m}\bar{\boldsymbol{h}}_m$ $(\varepsilon_j = \pm 1, \bar{\boldsymbol{h}}_j \in \bar{M}_{l,k,1,2k})$ be the reduced form of $\bar{\hat{w}}$. Then the projection v_i of v on S_i lies in $\langle b^{-1}a, c \rangle$ for infinitely many $i \equiv l \bmod n^k$ if and only if there is an element $\xi \in D$, and a word $g = g(\boldsymbol{u}(l,k), \boldsymbol{x}(l,k))$ such that $v = \xi g(\boldsymbol{u}(l,k), \boldsymbol{x}(l,k))$.*

Proof. We proceed by induction on m. If $m = 0$, then $\bar{v} \in \bar{M}_{l,k,1,2k}$ and the result follows from Lemma 5.4, and the structure theorems of H_i.

Suppose $m > 0$. A slight adaptation of Lemma 5.4 shows that we may write $\bar{\boldsymbol{h}}_m$ in the form $\bar{\boldsymbol{h}}_m = \bar{u}_1\bar{u}_2 --- \bar{u}_r w(\bar{\boldsymbol{x}}(l,k), \bar{\boldsymbol{y}}(l,k))$ where each $\bar{u}_j$ is a word on the generators of $\bar{U}_{l,k,s}$ for some $s = s(j)$, and where $s(j+1) \neq s(j)$ for each $j = 1, 2, \dots r-1$. Now the projection of v on S_i lies in $\langle b^{-1}a, c \rangle$ for some suitably large $i \equiv l \bmod n^k$. An application of Britton's lemma in H_i then shows that $\bar{\boldsymbol{h}}_m = \bar{u}_1\bar{u}_2 --- \bar{u}_r\bar{\boldsymbol{y}}(l,k)^{\beta}\bar{\boldsymbol{x}}(l,k)^{\gamma}$ for some β, γ, and that, if $\varepsilon_m = +1$, the projection of $u_1 u_2 --- u_r \boldsymbol{y}(l,k)^{\beta}$ on S_i lies in $\langle a, p^n \rangle$. As in the proof of Lemma 5.5, we see that $\bar{u}_1\bar{u}_2 --- \bar{u}_r\bar{\boldsymbol{y}}(l,k)^{\beta} \in \bar{M}_{l,k,1,2k-1}$ if $\varepsilon_m = -1$, and $\bar{u}_1\bar{u}_2 --- \bar{u}_r\bar{\boldsymbol{y}}(l,k)^{\beta} \in \bar{N}_{l,k,2,2k}$ if $\varepsilon_m = +1$. Hence $\bar{\boldsymbol{u}}(l,k)^{\varepsilon_m}\bar{\boldsymbol{h}}_m$ may be rewritten in the form $\bar{\boldsymbol{g}}\bar{\boldsymbol{u}}(l,k)^{\varepsilon_m}\bar{\boldsymbol{x}}(l,k)^{\gamma}$, where $\bar{\boldsymbol{g}} \in \bar{M}_{l,k,1,2k}$. We may, therefore, rewrite $\bar{v}$ in the form

$$\bar{v} = \bar{\hat{\boldsymbol{h}}}_0\bar{\boldsymbol{u}}(l,k)^{\varepsilon_1}\bar{\hat{\boldsymbol{h}}}_1\bar{\boldsymbol{u}}(l,k)^{\varepsilon_2} --- \bar{\hat{\boldsymbol{h}}}_{m-1}\bar{\boldsymbol{u}}(l,k)^{\varepsilon_m}\bar{\boldsymbol{x}}(l,k)^{\gamma}.$$

The projection of v on S_i then lies in $\langle b^{-1}a, c \rangle$ if and only if the same is true of $\hat{v} = \hat{\boldsymbol{h}}_0\boldsymbol{u}(l,k)^{\varepsilon_1}\hat{\boldsymbol{h}}_1\boldsymbol{u}(l,k)^{\varepsilon_2} --- \hat{\boldsymbol{h}}_{m-1}$, and the result follows by induction. □

We now take a general word in $\langle \boldsymbol{x}, \boldsymbol{y}, \boldsymbol{z}, \boldsymbol{u}, \boldsymbol{v} \rangle$. G is clearly a homomorphic image of the free product of the groups $\langle \boldsymbol{x}, \boldsymbol{y}, \boldsymbol{z}, \boldsymbol{u} \rangle$ and $\langle \boldsymbol{x}, \boldsymbol{u}, \boldsymbol{v} \rangle$ with the subgroup $\langle \boldsymbol{x}, \boldsymbol{u} \rangle$ amalgamated. Any element of G can be written in the form $w = \boldsymbol{g}_1\boldsymbol{h}_1\boldsymbol{g}_2\boldsymbol{h}_2 --- \boldsymbol{g}_r\boldsymbol{h}_r$ where each $\boldsymbol{g}_j \in \langle \boldsymbol{x}, \boldsymbol{y}, \boldsymbol{z}, \boldsymbol{u} \rangle$ and each $\boldsymbol{h}_j \in \langle \boldsymbol{x}, \boldsymbol{u}, \boldsymbol{v} \rangle \backslash \langle \boldsymbol{x}, \boldsymbol{u} \rangle$. By Lemma 5.2, the projection of $\boldsymbol{h}_j$ on S_i does not lie in $\langle b^{-1}a, c \rangle$ for any $j = 1, 2, \dots r$. If $r = 1$, and $w = \boldsymbol{g}_1$, then the result of Lemma 5.5 applies. Otherwise the normal form theorem in S_i shows that if $w_i = 1$ for infinitely many values of i, then there is some j such that the projection of $\boldsymbol{g}_j$ on S_i lies in $\langle b^{-1}a, c \rangle$ for infinitely many values of i, and so the result of Lemma 5.6 applies. We are now ready to prove

Proposition 5.1. *Let P be a subset of N. Then $G = G_P \times G_{N \backslash P}$ if and only if either*

(i) *P is finite or*

(ii) *there exist integers k, m and $t \leq n^k$, and congruence classes $C_1, C_2, \dots C_t$ mod n^k such that $P = X \cup C_1 \cup C_2 \cup \cdots \cup C_t$ where X is a subset of $\{1, 2, \dots m\}$.*

Proof. Suppose $G = G_P \times G_{N \backslash P}$. Then G_P is a homomorphic image of G, and, as such, is finitely generated. Each of the generators of G_P lies in G, and thus may be written as a word on the generators $\boldsymbol{x}$, $\boldsymbol{y}$, $\boldsymbol{z}$, $\boldsymbol{u}$, $\boldsymbol{v}$ of G. We have seen that any such word may be written in the form $\boldsymbol{g}_1\boldsymbol{h}_1\boldsymbol{g}_2\boldsymbol{h}_2 --- \boldsymbol{g}_r\boldsymbol{h}_r$ where each $\boldsymbol{g}_j \in \langle \boldsymbol{x}, \boldsymbol{y}, \boldsymbol{z}, \boldsymbol{u} \rangle$ and each $\boldsymbol{h}_j \in \langle \boldsymbol{x}, \boldsymbol{u}, \boldsymbol{v} \rangle \backslash \langle \boldsymbol{x}, \boldsymbol{u} \rangle$. Each $\boldsymbol{g}_j$ can be written in the form $\boldsymbol{u}^{\alpha_1}\boldsymbol{w}_1\boldsymbol{u}^{\alpha_2}\boldsymbol{w}_2 --- \boldsymbol{u}^{\alpha_r}\boldsymbol{w}_r$ with each $\boldsymbol{w}_j \in \langle \boldsymbol{x}, \boldsymbol{y}, \boldsymbol{z} \rangle$. We set $k_j = \Sigma_{i=1}^{r} |\alpha_i| + 1$ and for each of the finitely many generators $\boldsymbol{g}$ of G_P, we set $k_g = \max k_j$. Let $k = \max k_g$, where the maximum is taken over our set of generators for G_P. We now split each $\boldsymbol{g}_1\boldsymbol{h}_1\boldsymbol{g}_2\boldsymbol{h}_2 --- \boldsymbol{g}_r\boldsymbol{h}_r$ into a product of n^k commuting words on the generators $\boldsymbol{x}(l, k)$, $\boldsymbol{y}(l, k)$, $\boldsymbol{z}(l, k, k)$, $\boldsymbol{u}(l, k)$, $\boldsymbol{v}(l, k)$, $1 \leq l \leq n^k$. Let $w = \hat{\boldsymbol{g}}_1\hat{\boldsymbol{h}}_1\hat{\boldsymbol{g}}_2\hat{\boldsymbol{h}}_2 --- \hat{\boldsymbol{g}}_r\hat{\boldsymbol{h}}_r$ be any such word, and note that $\hat{\boldsymbol{h}}_j \in \langle \boldsymbol{x}(l, k), \boldsymbol{u}(l, k), \boldsymbol{v}(l, k) \rangle \backslash \langle \boldsymbol{x}(l, k), \boldsymbol{u}(l, k) \rangle$. Lemma 5.6 shows that either the projection w_i of w on S_i is non-trivial for all sufficiently large $i \equiv l \bmod n^k$, or some $\boldsymbol{g}_j$ can be written in the form $\boldsymbol{g}_j = \xi g(\boldsymbol{x}(l, k), \boldsymbol{u}(l, k))$ where $\xi \in D$. But if this be the case, $\bar{w}$ may be rewritten in the form $\bar{\boldsymbol{g}}'_1\bar{\boldsymbol{h}}'_1\bar{\boldsymbol{g}}'_2\bar{\boldsymbol{h}}'_2 --- \bar{\boldsymbol{g}}'_m\bar{\boldsymbol{h}}'_m$ with conditions as above, and with $m < r$. Repeated application of the above enables us to conclude that there is an integer m such that, if $w_i \neq 1$ for some $i > m$, then $w_i \neq 1$ for all $i > m$ such that $i \equiv l \bmod n^k$.

We deal thus with each generator of G_P. Since P is equal to the set of all those $i \in N$ such that the projection of $\boldsymbol{g}$ on S_i is non-trivial for some generator $\boldsymbol{g}$ of G_P, the required result follows. □

§6. Equations in S

Suppose $G \cong G^r$. Proposition 4.4 shows that there is a partition $\{P_1, P_2, \dots P_r\}$ of N such that each G_{P_j} is isomorphic to G, and $G = G_{P_1} \times \cdots \times G_{P_r}$. Let $\varphi : G \to G_{P_j}$ be an isomorphism. Then $\varphi(\boldsymbol{x})$, $\varphi(\boldsymbol{y})$, $\varphi(\boldsymbol{z})$, $\varphi(\boldsymbol{u})$, $\varphi(\boldsymbol{v})$ generate G_{P_j} and satisfy any relations satisfied by $\boldsymbol{x}$, $\boldsymbol{y}$, $\boldsymbol{z}$, $\boldsymbol{u}$, $\boldsymbol{v}$. If $i \in P_j$ then the projections $\varphi(\boldsymbol{x})_i$, $\varphi(\boldsymbol{y})_i$, $\varphi(\boldsymbol{z})_i$, $\varphi(\boldsymbol{u})_i$, $\varphi(\boldsymbol{v})_i$ of $\varphi(\boldsymbol{x})$, $\varphi(\boldsymbol{y})$, $\varphi(\boldsymbol{z})$, $\varphi(\boldsymbol{u})$, $\varphi(\boldsymbol{v})$ on S_i must generate S_i and must satisfy any relations satisfied by $\boldsymbol{x}$, $\boldsymbol{y}$, $\boldsymbol{z}$, $\boldsymbol{u}$ and $\boldsymbol{v}$.

We will use the structure theorems of S to establish the possible values of $\varphi(\boldsymbol{x})_i$, $\varphi(\boldsymbol{y})_i$, $\varphi(\boldsymbol{z})_i$, $\varphi(\boldsymbol{u})_i$ and $\varphi(\boldsymbol{v})_i$ and will then use the results of §5 to reconstruct the elements $\varphi(\boldsymbol{x})$, $\varphi(\boldsymbol{y})$, $\varphi(\boldsymbol{z})$, $\varphi(\boldsymbol{u})$ and $\varphi(\boldsymbol{v})$ of G_{P_j}. We will then know which maps from G to G_{P_j} can be isomorphisms, and can use this information to deduce that $G \cong G_{P_j}$ if and only if the number t of congruence classes mod n^k given in Proposition 5.1 is congruent to 1 mod $n-1$. This shows that $G \not\cong G^r$ if $1 < r < n$.

In this section we will investigate which elements of S can satisfy certain relations which hold between the generators $\boldsymbol{x}$, $\boldsymbol{y}$, $\boldsymbol{z}$, $\boldsymbol{u}$, $\boldsymbol{v}$ of G. In §7 we will use this information to reconstruct $\varphi(\boldsymbol{x})$, $\varphi(\boldsymbol{y})$, $\varphi(\boldsymbol{z})$, $\varphi(\boldsymbol{u})$ and $\varphi(\boldsymbol{v})$. The final deduction will be made in §8.

We will make use of the following notation:

$g \sim_G h$ means that g and h are conjugate in the group G,

$g \not\sim_G h$ means that g and h are not conjugate in G,

$\sigma_x(w)$ denotes the exponent sum of x in w, viz. if $w = x^{\alpha_1} w_1 x^{\alpha_2} w_2 --- x^{\alpha_r} w_r$ where each w_i involves no appearance of x, then $\sigma_x(w) = \sum_{i=1}^r \alpha_i$.

Lemma 6.1. *If* $1 \neq w \in K = \langle b^{-1}a, c\rangle$, *then* $w \not\sim_H w^m$ *for any* $m \neq \pm 1$.

Proof. Suppose $1 \neq w \in K$, and suppose $w \sim_H w^m$, $m \neq \pm 1$. Without loss of generality, w may be taken to be a cyclically reduced element of the (free) group K. Since H is an HNN extension of R by c, a consideration of c-length shows that w is c-free, that is $w = (b^{-1}a)^\alpha$ for some $\alpha \neq 0$. Thus $w \in R$, and w is a cyclically reduced element of normal form length 2α in the amalgamated free product R. Thus w is not conjugate in R to an element of $A = \langle a, p\rangle$. It follows that the conjugacy $w \sim w^m$ is achieved within R. But this is clearly impossible, by a length argument. □

Lemma 6.2. *Suppose that $w \neq 1$ is a cyclically reduced element of the free group $\langle e, f\rangle$ and $w \sim_T w^m$ for some $m \neq \pm 1$. Then $w = f^\alpha$ for some α, and if $g^{-1}wg = w^m$ then either $g = d^\beta$ for some $\beta > 0$, or g may be written in the form $d^\beta f^\gamma d^\delta$ for some integers β, γ, δ satisfying $\beta > 0$, $\delta \leq 0$, and either $\delta = 0$ or γ is odd, and $\beta > |\delta|$. Moreover, $m = 2^\beta$ in the first case and $2^{\beta+\delta}$ in the second.*

Proof. As T is an HNN extension of $T_0 = \langle f, d\rangle$ by e, a consideration of e-length yields $w = f^\alpha$ for some $\alpha \neq 0$. Now T_0 is an HNN extension of $\langle f\rangle$ by d, and so a d-length argument shows that w is not conjugate in T_0 to a power of d. It follows that the conjugacy $w \sim w^m$ is achieved in T_0. Now T_0 has presentation $\langle d, f : d^{-1}fd = f^2\rangle$. The conjugates $d^r f d^{-r}$, $r \geq 0$, of f generate a locally cyclic group which is the normal closure of f in T_0. Thus it is easy to see that any element of T_0 may be written in the form $d^\beta f^\gamma d^\delta$ with $\beta \geq 0$, and so, making careful use of the relation $d^{-1}fd = f^2$, we may write g in one of the forms (i) $g = d^\beta$, $\beta \neq 0$ or (ii) $d^\beta f^\gamma d^\delta$ with $\beta \geq 0$, $\delta \leq 0$, and either $\delta = 0$ or γ odd. In case (i), $g^{-1}wg = d^{-\beta}f^\alpha d^\beta$, and it is clear that this is a proper power of w only if $\beta > 0$, in which case $g^{-1}wg = f^{2^\beta \alpha} = w^{2^\beta}$. In case (ii), $g^{-1}wg = d^{-\delta}f^{-\gamma}d^{-\beta}f^\alpha d^\beta f^\gamma d^\delta$. Since $\beta \geq 0$, this is $d^{-\delta}f^{2^\beta\alpha}d^\delta$. Now $\delta \leq 0$, so the result is a proper power of w if and only if $\beta > |\delta|$. In this case $d^{-\delta}f^{2^\beta\alpha}d^\delta = f^{2^{\beta-|\delta|}\cdot\alpha}$. This completes the proof. □

Lemma 6.3. *Suppose $1 \neq w \in T_0$, and $w \not\sim_T f^\alpha$ for any α. Suppose further that $w \sim_T w^m$ with $m \neq \pm 1$. Then $w \sim_T d^\alpha$ for some $\alpha \neq 0$. Moreover, if $g^{-1}d^\alpha g = d^{\alpha m}$, $g \in T$, then either $g = e^\beta$ for some $\beta > 0$, or $g = e^\beta d^\gamma e^\delta$ for integers β, γ, δ satisfying $\beta > 0$, $\delta \leq 0$, and either $\delta = 0$ or γ is odd and $\beta > |\delta|$. Moreover, $m = 2^\beta$ in the first case, and $2^{\beta-|\delta|}$ in the second.*

Proof. As in Lemma 6.2, w may be written in the form $d^\alpha f^\beta d^\gamma$ with $\alpha + \gamma \neq 0$. A consideration of d-length shows that $w \not\sim_{T_0} w^m$. But $w \sim_T w^m$, and so we must have $w \sim_{T_0} d^\alpha$ for some α.

Suppose $g \in T$ satisfies $g^{-1}d^\alpha g = d^{\alpha m}$, $m \neq \pm 1$, and g is written in e-reduced form as $w_0 e^{\alpha_1} w_1 e^{\alpha_2} w_2 --- e^{\alpha_r} w_r$ where each $w_i \in T_0$. Clearly $r \neq 0$, and so $w_0^{-1} d^\alpha w_0 \in \langle d\rangle$. Suppose $w_0 = d^\beta f^\gamma d^\delta$ with $\gamma \neq 0$. We must have $f^{-\gamma}d^\alpha f^\gamma \in \langle d\rangle$, and so it follows by a consideration of d-length in T_0 that $f^{-\gamma}d^\alpha f^\gamma = d^\alpha$, that is, $d^\alpha f^\gamma d^{-\alpha} = f^\gamma$, and this relation clearly does not hold in T_0. Hence $w_0 \in \langle d\rangle$, and repetition of the argument shows that $w_i \in \langle d\rangle$ for each $i = 1, 2, \ldots r$. Hence $g \in \langle e, d\rangle$ and, since the relation $e^{-1}de = d^2$ holds in $\langle e, d\rangle$, we may use the method of Lemma 6.2 to write g in one of the forms (i) e^β, $\beta \neq 0$, or (ii) $e^\beta d^\gamma e^\delta$

with $\beta \geqslant 0$, $\delta \leqslant 0$, and either $\delta = 0$ or γ odd. The remainder of the proof is identical to the corresponding part of Lemma 6.2. □

Lemma 6.4. *Let $w = d^\alpha f^\beta d^\gamma$ with $\alpha + \gamma \neq 0$. Then w is not conjugate in T to an element of $\langle e, f\rangle$.*

Proof. Suppose w is conjugate in T to a cyclically reduced element g of $\langle e, f\rangle$. A consideration of e-length shows that $g = f^\delta$ for some $\delta \neq 0$. Let $h^{-1}wh = f^\delta$ and suppose that h is not e-free. By considering the last e-reduction in the word $h^{-1}wh$, we see that $f^\delta \sim_{T_0} d^\lambda$ for some $\lambda \neq 0$. But a consideration of d-length in T_0 shows that this is impossible. Hence h is e-free, and $d^\alpha f^\beta d^\gamma \sim_{T_0} f^\delta$, and a consideration of d-length again yields a contradiction. □

Lemma 6.5. *Suppose $w \in \langle e, f\rangle$ and $\sigma_e(w) \neq 0$. Let g be an element of T such that $g^{-1}wg \in \langle e, f\rangle$. Then $g \in \langle e, f\rangle$.*

Proof. Without loss of generality, we may take w to be a cyclically reduced element of the free group $\langle e, f\rangle$. We first show that g cannot be a power of d.

We may write w in e-reduced form as $w = e^{\varepsilon_1} f^{\alpha_1} e^{\varepsilon_2} f^{\alpha_2} --- e^{\varepsilon_r} f^{\alpha_r}$, where each $\varepsilon_i = \pm 1$. (Here the α_i are permitted to take the value zero, but if $\alpha_i = 0$, then $\varepsilon_{i+1} \neq -\varepsilon_i$.) If $d^{-\beta} w d^\beta \in \langle e, f\rangle$, an application of Collins' Lemma shows that we have an equation of the form

$$d^{-\beta} e^{\varepsilon_1} f^{\alpha_1} --- e^{\varepsilon_r} f^{\alpha_r} d^\beta = e^{\varepsilon_1} f^{\gamma_1} --- e^{\varepsilon_r} f^{\gamma_r}$$

that is,

$$d^{-\beta} e^{\varepsilon_1} f^{\alpha_1} --- e^{\varepsilon_r} f^{\alpha_r} d^\beta f^{-\gamma_r} e^{-\varepsilon_r} --- f^{-\gamma_1} e^{-\varepsilon_1} = 1.$$

Now $f^\alpha d^\beta f^\gamma$ is equal in T_0 to a power of d if and only if it is equal to d^β (by d-length in T_0). Moreover, $e^{-\varepsilon} d^\beta e^\varepsilon$ is equal to a power of d if and only if it is equal to $d^{2^\varepsilon \beta}$ (where, if $\varepsilon = -1$, this should be interpreted to mean that β is even). Consequently our equation is possible if and only if it results in $d^{-\beta} d^{2^\nu \beta} = 1$ where $\nu = \Sigma_{i=1}^r \varepsilon_i$. But this is $d^{\beta(2^\nu - 1)} = 1$, which is possible only if $2^{\sigma_e(w)} = 1$. Since $\sigma_e(w) \neq 0$, this cannot occur.

An application of Collins' Lemma now shows that the only cyclically reduced conjugates of w lying in $\langle e, f\rangle$ are those achieved by cyclically permuting w. Thus if $g^{-1}wg \in \langle e, f\rangle$ there is an element $h \in \langle e, f\rangle$ such that $g^{-1}wg = h^{-1}wh$. It remains to show that if g commutes with w then $g \in \langle e, f\rangle$.

Suppose g is written in e-reduced form as $g = g_0 e^{\varepsilon_1} g_1 e^{\varepsilon_2} g_2 --- e^{\varepsilon_r} g_r$, where each $\varepsilon_i = \pm 1$ and each $g_i \in T_0$. We will assume that as large as possible an initial segment of g of the form $g_0 e^{\varepsilon_1} g_1 e^{\varepsilon_2} --- g_m e^{\varepsilon_m}$ lies in $\langle e, f\rangle$, viz. $g_0, g_1, \dots g_m$ are powers of f, g_{m+1} is not, and if g can also be written in reduced form as $\hat{g}_0 e^{\varepsilon_1} \hat{g}_1 e^{\varepsilon_2} --- e^{\varepsilon_r} \hat{g}_r$, then at least one of $\hat{g}_0, \hat{g}_1, \dots \hat{g}_{m+1}$ is not equal in T_0 to a power of f. If $g \in \langle e, f\rangle$, we are finished, so assume not. We have $g = hd^{\alpha} f^{\beta} d^{\gamma} k$ where

$$h = g_0 e^{\varepsilon_1} g_1 e^{\varepsilon_2} --- g_m e^{\varepsilon_{m+1}} \in \langle e, f\rangle$$

$$g_{m+1} = d^{\alpha} f^{\beta} d^{\gamma} \notin \langle f\rangle$$

$$k = e^{\varepsilon_{m+2}} g_{m+2} e^{\varepsilon_{m+3}} --- e^{\varepsilon_r} g_r.$$

Case (i). $k \in \langle e, f\rangle$.

Let w_1 and w_2 be the reduced forms of $h^{-1} wh$ and kwk^{-1} in the free group $\langle e, f\rangle$. Then $(d^{\alpha} f^{\beta} d^{\gamma})^{-1} w_1 (d^{\alpha} f^{\beta} d^{\gamma}) = w_2$. We have already established that conjugation by a power of d cannot transform a non-trivial element w of $\langle e, f\rangle$ with $\sigma_e(w) \neq 0$ to another element of $\langle e, f\rangle$, and so, without loss of generality, we may take $\alpha > 0$, $\gamma < 0$ and β odd. Let $w_1 = f^{\alpha_0} e^{\beta_1} f^{\alpha_1} --- e^{\beta_n} f^{\alpha_n}$ and $w_2 = f^{\gamma_0} e^{\delta_1} f^{\gamma_1} --- e^{\delta_t} f^{\gamma_t}$ where each β_i and each $\delta_i = \pm 1$. We have

$$(d^{\alpha} f^{\beta} d^{\gamma})^{-1} (f^{\alpha_0} e^{\beta_1} f^{\alpha_1} --- e^{\beta_n} f^{\alpha_n}) (d^{\alpha} f^{\beta} d^{\gamma}) (f^{-\gamma_t} e^{-\delta_t} --- e^{-\delta_1} f^{-\gamma_0}) = 1.$$

An application of Britton's Lemma yields that $\beta_n = \delta_t$ and that $f^{\alpha_n} d^{\alpha} f^{\beta} d^{\gamma} f^{-\gamma_t}$ lies in $\langle d\rangle$ if $\beta_n = -1$, or in $\langle d^2\rangle$ if $\beta_n = +1$. Since $\alpha > 0$ and $\gamma < 0$, we have $d^{\alpha} f^{2^{\alpha}\alpha_n} f^{\beta} f^{-2^{|\gamma|}\gamma_t} d^{\gamma} \in \langle d\rangle$. But this can happen only if $\beta + 2^{\alpha}\alpha_n - 2^{|\gamma|}\gamma_t = 0$, and this is clearly impossible, as β is odd, and neither α nor γ is zero.

Case (ii). $k \notin \langle e, f\rangle$.

We now assume that as large as possible an end segment of k of the form $e^{\varepsilon_{s+2}} g_{s+2} --- e^{\varepsilon_r} g_r$ lies in $\langle e, f\rangle$. We then have $k = k_1 d^{\lambda} f^{\mu} d^{\upsilon} k_2$ where

$$k_1 = e^{\varepsilon_{m+2}} g_{m+2} --- g_s e^{\varepsilon_{s+1}}$$

$$g_{s+1} = d^{\lambda} f^{\mu} d^{\upsilon} \notin \langle f\rangle$$

$$k_2 = e^{\varepsilon_{s+2}} g_{s+2} --- e^{\varepsilon_r} g_r \in \langle e, f\rangle.$$

If k_1 contains no occurrence of e, then this case reduces to case (i), so we may assume that k_1 involves e. Let w_1, w_2 be the reduced forms of $h^{-1} wh$ and $k_2 w k_2^{-1}$ in $\langle e, f\rangle$. We then have

$$(d^{\lambda} f^{\mu} d^{\upsilon})^{-1} k_1^{-1} (d^{\alpha} f^{\beta} d^{\gamma})^{-1} w_1 (d^{\alpha} f^{\beta} d^{\gamma}) k_1 (d^{\lambda} f^{\mu} d^{\upsilon}) = w_2,$$

so that, when w_1 and w_2 are written as words in $\langle e, f\rangle$, as in case (i), we have

$$(d^{\lambda} f^{\mu} d^{\upsilon})^{-1} k_1^{-1} (d^{\alpha} f^{\beta} d^{\gamma})^{-1} f^{\alpha_0} e^{\beta_1} --- e^{\beta_n} f^{\alpha_n} (d^{\alpha} f^{\beta} d^{\gamma}) k_1 (d^{\lambda} f^{\mu} d^{\upsilon}) f^{-\gamma_t} e^{-\delta_t} --- e^{-\delta_1} f^{-\gamma_0} = 1.$$

An application of Britton's Lemma shows that e-reduction must take place in one of the subwords

(i) $e^{\beta_n}f^{\alpha_n}(d^\alpha f^\beta d^\gamma)e^{\varepsilon_{m+2}}$ or

(ii) $e^{\varepsilon_{s+1}}(d^\lambda f^\mu d^\upsilon)f^{-\gamma_t}e^{-\delta_t}$.

If e-reduction occurs in (i), we have $\beta_n = -\varepsilon_{m+2}$ and $f^{\alpha_n}(d^\alpha f^\beta d^\gamma)$ lies in $\langle d\rangle$ if $\varepsilon_{m+2} = +1$ or in $\langle d^2\rangle$ if $\varepsilon_{m+2} = -1$. Now the assumptions on the form of g show that we have $\alpha \geqslant 0$, $\gamma \leqslant 0$, and *either* $\alpha = 0$, $\varepsilon_{m+2} = -1$ and γ is odd, *or* $\alpha > 0$, and either 2^α does not divide β or $\varepsilon_{m+2} = -1$ and $\alpha + \gamma$ is odd. If $\varepsilon_{m+2} = -1$, then $f^{\alpha_n}(d^\alpha f^\beta d^\gamma) \in \langle d^2\rangle$, so we have $d^\alpha f^{2^\alpha \alpha_n} f^\beta d^\gamma \in \langle d^2\rangle$. This is possible only if $2^\alpha \alpha_n + \beta = 0$ and $\alpha + \gamma$ is even. Since either β is not divisible by 2^α or $\alpha + \gamma$ is odd, we see that this case is impossible. If $\varepsilon_{m+2} = +1$, then $f^{\alpha_n} d^\alpha f^\beta d^\gamma \in \langle d\rangle$, so $d^\alpha f^{2^\alpha \alpha_n + \beta} d^\gamma \in \langle d\rangle$, and this happens only if $2^\alpha \alpha_n + \beta = 0$. But, since $\varepsilon_{m+2} = +1$, 2^α does not divide β, so this case too is impossible. Thus cancellation occurs in (ii). As above, we must have $\varepsilon_{s+1} = \delta_t$ and $(d^\lambda f^\mu d^\upsilon)f^{-\gamma_t}$ lies in $\langle d\rangle$ if $\varepsilon_{s+1} = -1$ or in $\langle d^2\rangle$ if $\varepsilon_{s+1} = +1$. The assumptions on the form of k show that *either* $\varepsilon_{s+1} = -1$, $\lambda \geqslant 0$, $\upsilon < 0$, and $2^{|\upsilon|}$ does not divide μ, *or* $\varepsilon_{s+1} = +1$ and either $\upsilon = 0$ and λ is odd, or $\lambda \geqslant 0$, $\upsilon < 0$, and either $2^{|\upsilon|}$ does not divide μ or $\lambda + \upsilon$ is odd. If $\varepsilon_{s+1} = -1$, we have $(d^\lambda f^\mu d^\upsilon)f^{-\gamma_t} \in \langle d\rangle$, that is $d^\lambda f^{\mu - 2^{|\upsilon|}\gamma_t} d^\upsilon \in \langle d\rangle$, which can happen only if $\mu - 2^{|\upsilon|}\gamma = 0$. since $\upsilon \neq 0$ and $2^{|\upsilon|}$ does not divide μ, this is impossible. Thus $\varepsilon_{s+1} = +1$, and we have $(d^\lambda f^\mu d^\upsilon)f^{-\gamma_t} \in \langle d^2\rangle$, that is $d^\lambda f^{\mu - 2^{|\upsilon|}\gamma_t} d^\upsilon \in \langle d^2\rangle$. This forces $\mu - 2^{|\upsilon|}\gamma_t = 0$, and $\lambda + \upsilon$ even, contradicting the conditions on λ, μ and υ.

Thus the assumption that $g \notin \langle e, f\rangle$ leads to a contradiction, and so the result is established. □

Corollary 6.6. *If* $w = (b^{-1}a)^\alpha d^\beta (b^{-1}a)^\gamma$ *with* $\alpha + \gamma \neq 0$, *then* $w \not\sim_S w^m$ *for any* $m \neq \pm 1$.

Proof. Since $b^{-1}a = e$, a consideration of $b^{-1}a$-length shows that $w \not\sim_T w^m$. Suppose $g = g_1 g_2 --- g_r$ is an element of S, written in normal form with respect to the amalgamated free product structure of S, and suppose that g satisfies $g^{-1}wg = w^m$, $m \neq \pm 1$. If $r = 1$, then $g = g_1 \in H \setminus K$, and $(b^{-1}a)^\alpha d^\beta (b^{-1}a)^\gamma$ lies in K. An application of Britton's Lemma in T shows that $\beta = 0$. Since $\alpha + \gamma \neq 0$, a consideration of normal form length in R shows that $(b^{-1}a)^{\alpha+\gamma}$ is not conjugate in R to an element of A. Thus, if $w \sim_H w^m$, then the conjugacy is achieved in R. But a length argument in R shows that this is not the case.

Thus $r \neq 1$, and so w is conjugate in T to an element of K. Let w_1 be a cyclically reduced conjugate of w lying in K. Collins' Lemma shows that w_1 can be obtained from w by a cyclic permutation of w, followed by a conjugation by a power of d. Since this process cannot introduce any c-symbols, it follows that $w_1 = (b^{-1}a)^{\alpha+\gamma}$. Now $w_1 \sim_S w_1^m$, and we have already seen that this conjugation cannot be achieved by an element of normal form length 0 or 1. Suppose $h = h_1h_2 --- h_s$ is an element of S in normal form such that $h^{-1}w_1h = w_1^m$. If h_1 lies in T, then an application of Lemma 6.5 shows that $h_1 \in K$, contradicting the assumption that h is in normal form. Thus $h_1 \in H$, and a repetition of the argument used in the case $r = 1$ shows that $\sigma_{b^{-1}a}(h_1^{-1}w_1h_1) = \pm(\alpha+\gamma)$. A further application of Lemma 6.5 now shows that $h_2 \in K$, and this contradiction completes the proof. □

Suppose we have a set of elements x, y, z, u, v of S which together generate S, and which satisfy the following relations:

(i) $u^{-1}yu = y^n$
(ii) $v^{-1}uv = u^2$
(iii) $x^{-1}vx = v^2$
(iv) $x^{-1}zx = z$
(v) $x(y^{-1}zy)x^{-1} = y^{-1}zy$
(vi) $x(y^{-14}zy^{14})x^{-1} = y^{-13}zy^{14}$
(vii) $y^{-6}zy^6 = (xy)^{-5}z(xy)^6$.

Lemma 6.7. *x, y, z, u, v are all non-trivial.*

Proof. From (iii), $x = 1$ implies $v = 1$; from (ii), $v = 1$ implies $u = 1$; from (i) $u = 1$ implies $y^{n-1} = 1$. The structure theorems for amalgamated free products and HNN extensions show that S is torsion free, and so $y^{n-1} = 1$ implies $y = 1$. From (vi), $z = 1$ implies $y = 1$.

Thus if any of x, z, u, v is trivial, then y is trivial, so we need only show that $y \neq 1$. Suppose $y = 1$. Equation (vii) then gives $x^{-5}zx^6 = z$. But x commutes with z by (iv), and so $x = 1$. But we have already shown that $x = 1 \Rightarrow v = 1 \Rightarrow u = 1$, and so $\langle x, y, z, u, v\rangle = \langle z\rangle$. But S is not cyclic, and so we have a contradiction. □

Lemma 6.8. *Not all of y, u, v lie in H.*

Proof. Suppose y, u, v all lie in H. Modulo an inner automorphism by an element of H, we may assume that y is c-cyclically reduced, and since $y \sim_H y^n$ it follows that $y \in R$. Now $u \sim_H u^2$, and so u is conjugate in H to an element of R. Suppose u is not c-free. Then u may be written in reduced form as $g^{-1}wg$ where $w \in R$, and g begins in a power of c. Now $w^{-1}(gyg^{-1})w = (gyg^{-1})^n$, and an application of Britton's Lemma shows that $gyg^{-1} \in R$. Thus, modulo an inner automorphism, we may assume that both y and u lie in R. Now $y \sim_R y^n$ and so a length argument in R shows that y lies in a conjugate of a factor (A or B) of R. But A and B are free, and no non-trivial element of a free group is conjugate in that free goup to a proper power of itself. Thus, taking, if necessary, an inner automorphism by an element of R, we may assume that y lies in the amalgamated subgroup U of R. Now u cannot lie in a factor, but we have $v^{-1}uv = u^2$, and if v is not c-free, this forces u to lie in a conjugate of $A = \langle a, p \rangle$. Thus if v is not c-free, we may write u in reduced form (with respect to the structure of R) as $g^{-1}tg$ where t lies in a factor but not in U, and $1 \neq g = g_1 g_2 --- g_r$ where g_1 lies in a different factor from t. Putting this into the equation $u^{-1}yu = y^n$, we obtain $t^{-1}(gyg^{-1})t = (gyg^{-1})^n$. This is possible only if gyg^{-1} lies in U. But then gyg^{-1} and t lie in the same factor, contradicting the fact that the factors are free. Thus v is c-free. But then $u \sim_R u^2$, so u lies in a conjugate of a factor of R, and the same contradiction goes through. □

Lemma 6.9. *Modulo an inner automorphism of S, we have $y \in H \setminus K$, $x, z \in H$, $u \in K$ and $v \in T$.*

Proof. By relation (i) $y \sim_S y^n$. Thus, by a length argument, y lies in a conjugate of a factor (H or T) of S, so, modulo an inner automorphism of S, we may assume that y lies in a factor. By relation (ii), $u \sim_S u^2$, so u also lies in a conjugate of a factor. Suppose u does not lie in a factor. Then we may write u in the form $g^{-1}tg$ where t lies in a factor, but not in K, and $g = g_1 g_2 --- g_r$ in normal form, with g_1 in a different factor from t. By relation (i), $t(gyg^{-1})t^{-1} = (gyg^{-1})^n$, and so a length argument shows that gyg^{-1} lies in K. Lemmas 6.1 and 6.2 show that modulo an inner automorphism we may take $y = c^\alpha$ for some α, and $u = t = d^\beta c^\gamma d^\delta$ for some β, γ, δ with $\beta + \delta \neq 0$. By Lemma 6.4, u does not lie in a conjugate of K, but relation (ii) says $v^{-1}uv = u^2$, and so a length argument shows that $v \in T$. Lemma 6.3 may then be applied to deduce that $v \sim_T (b^{-1}a)^\lambda d^\mu (b^{-1}a)^\nu$ with $\lambda + \mu \neq 0$. But relation (iii) gives $v \sim_S v^2$, and this contradicts Corollary 6.6.

Thus u lies in a factor. If y lies in a conjugate of K, the same contradiction results, so y does not lie in a conjugate of K, and so u must lie in the same factor as y. Suppose that factor is T. Without loss of generality, y may be assumed cyclically reduced, and so the equation $y \sim_T y^n$ implies by a length argument in T, that $y \in T_0$. Now y does not lie in a conjugate of K, and so Lemma 6.3 shows that without loss of generality we may take $y = d^\alpha$ for some α, and $u =$

$(b^{-1}a)^{\beta}d^{\gamma}(b^{-1}a)^{\delta}$ for some β, γ, δ with $\beta+\delta\neq 0$. But $v^{-1}uv=u^2$, and so we have again contradicted Corollary 6.6. Thus we may assume without loss of generality that y and u lie in H, and y does not lie in a conjugate of K.

Suppose that z is not cyclically reduced. Then, modulo an inner automorphism by an element of H, we may assume that z begins and ends in an element of T Now relation (vi) shows that $z\sim_S zy$, and so a length argument yields an immediate contradiction. Exactly the same argument shows that $z\notin T\setminus K$, and so either $z\in H$ or z may, without loss of generality, be written in reduced form as $z=s_1s_2---s_n$ with $s_n\in H$ and $s_1\in T$. Suppose that $z\notin H$. Now $z\sim_S zy$, and so a length argument shows that $s_ny\notin K$. Since $y\notin K$, it follows that $y^{-1}zy$ is reduced but not cyclically reduced. By relations (iv) and (v), x commutes with both a cyclically reduced and a non-cyclically reduced element of S. Hence, by a length argument $x\in K$. Now relation (iii) gives $v\sim_S v^2$, so v lies in a conjugate of a factor. Suppose v does not lie in a factor. Then we may write v in the form $v=g^{-1}tg$ where t lies in a factor, but not in K, and $g=g_1g_2---g_r$ in normal form, where g_1 lies in a different factor from t. We then have $t^{-1}(gug^{-1})t=(gug^{-1})^2$, with $u\in H$. As in previous cases it follows that gug^{-1} lies in K, and we may use Lemmas 6.1, 6.2 and 6.3 to deduce that $u\sim_S c^r$, $v\sim_S d^s$ and $x\sim_S(b^{-1}a)^{\alpha}d^{\beta}(b^{-1}a)^{\gamma}$ with $\alpha+\gamma\neq 0$. But $x\in K$, and so, as in the proof of Corollary 6.6, we have $x\sim_K(b^{-1}a)^{\alpha+\gamma}$ with $\alpha+\gamma\neq 0$. In particular $\sigma_{b^{-1}a}(x)\neq 0$. But $z^{-1}xz=x$, and so $s_1^{-1}xs_1\in K$. But $s_1\in T$, so by Lemma 6.5, $s_1\in K$, a contradiction. Thus if $z\notin H$, then $g=1$. Moreover, if u lies in a conjugate of K, the same contradiction results. It follows that v lies in the same factor as u, that is $v\in H$. Hence y, u, v, x all lie in H, contradicting Lemma 6.8. Thus $z\subset H$.

We next consider x. If x is not cyclically reduced we may suppose, without loss of generality, that x begins and ends in an element of T. Since z commutes with x, a length argument forces $z\in K$. By relation (vii) $z\sim_S zxy$ and, as $y\notin K$, a length argument gives a contradiction. The same contradiction results if $x\in T\setminus K$. Suppose $x\notin H$. We may then write x in normal form as $x=s_1s_2---s_n$ where, without loss of generality, $s_n\in H$ and $s_1\in T$. Now relation (iii) shows that v lies in a conjugate of a factor. Suppose as before that v is written in reduced form as $v=g^{-1}tg$. Assume first that $g\neq 1$. As in previous cases we deduce that $u\sim c^r$, $v\sim d^s$ and $x\sim(b^{-1}a)^{\alpha}d^{\beta}(b^{-1}a)^{\gamma}$ with $\alpha+\gamma\neq 0$. Thus x is conjugate to an element of T contradicting the fact that x is cyclically reduced of length greater than one. Thus v lies in a factor. If u lies in a conjugate of K, the same contradiction results. Thus u does not lie in a conjugate of K, and so v must lie in H. We now have all of y, u, v lying in H, and this contradicts Lemma 6.8. Hence x must lie in H.

We now have all of x, y, z, u lying in H. If v lies in a factor, but u does not lie in a conjugate of K, we are forced to conclude that v lies in H, contradicting the fact that x, y, z, u, v generate S. Thus if v lies in a factor, then that factor is T, so u must lie in K, and we are finished. Suppose therefore that v does not lie in a factor. As usual, v may be written in the form $v = g^{-1}tg$, where t lies in a factor, but not in K, and $g = g_1 --- g_r$ in normal form, with g_1 in a different factor from t. We may further assume, by taking an inner automorphism by an element of H if necessary, that $g_r \in T$. Repeating the argument we have used before, we now obtain $gug^{-1} \sim_K c^r$, $gvg^{-1} \sim_T d^s$, $gxg^{-1} \sim_T (b^{-1}a)^\alpha d^\beta (b^{-1}a)^\gamma$ where $\alpha + \gamma \neq 0$. We have, in particular, $x = g^{-1}lg$ where $l \in T$, and $\sigma_{b^{-1}a}(l) \neq 0$. Since d^s is not conjugate in T to an element of K (Lemma 6.4), we also have $t \in T$, and $g_1 \in H$. The equation $x = g^{-1}lg$ when written out in full yields

$$g_r^{-1} g_{r-1}^{-1} --- g_1^{-1} l g_1 g_2 --- g_r = x.$$

Since $g_r \in T$, and $x \in H$, we conclude that $x \in K$. Also $g_1 \in H$, and $l \in T$, so $l \in K$, and, as in the proof of Corollary 6.6, we deduce that $l = (b^{-1}a)^{\alpha+\gamma}$ with $\alpha + \gamma \neq 0$. Now $g_1^{-1}lg_1$ lies in K, and a repetition of the argument used in the proof of Corollary 6.6 shows that $\sigma_{b^{-1}a}(g_1^{-1}lg_1) \neq 0$. But then Lemma 6.5 shows that $g_2 \in K$, contradicting the fact that g is in normal form. This completes the proof of Lemma 6.9. □

Lemma 6.10. *Modulo an inner automorphism of S, $x = b^{-1}a$, $u = c$, $v = d$, $y = a^\alpha p^\beta a^{-\alpha}$ for some α, β and $z \in U$.*

Proof. By Lemma 6.9 we may take $y \in H \setminus K$, $x, z \in H$, $u \in K$ and $v \in T$. An application of Lemma 6.2 shows that, without loss of generality, $u = c^r$ and $v = d^\alpha c^\beta d^\gamma$ for integers r, α, β, γ with $\alpha + \gamma = 1$. Lemmas 6.3 and 6.4 then show that $v \sim_T d$ and $x \sim_T (b^{-1}a)^\lambda d^\mu (b^{-1}a)^\upsilon$ for integers λ, μ, υ with $\lambda + \upsilon = 1$. Since $x \in H$, x must lie in K, and hence, by the argument of Corollary 6.6, $x = b^{-1}a$. Now $v = d^\alpha c^\beta d^\gamma$ and $(b^{-1}a)^{-1}v(b^{-1}a) = v^2$, so an application of Britton's Lemma in T shows that $\beta = 0$, and so $v = d$.

Next consider z. We have $z^{-1}xz = x$, and $z \in H$. Since $b^{-1}a$ is not conjugate in R to an element of A, we must have $z \in R$. The structure of R as an amalgamated free product then shows that $z = g(b^{-1}a)^k$ for some integer k and some element g of U such that g commutes with $b^{-1}a$. Now $y \in H$ and $y \sim_H y^n$, so we may write y in reduced form as $h^{-1}wh$ where w is an element of R, and either $h = 1$ or h begins in a power of c. Suppose $h \neq 1$. By relation (vi), we have $z \sim_H zy$, that is $g(b^{-1}a)^k \sim_H g(b^{-1}a)^k h^{-1}wh \sim_H hg(b^{-1}a)^k h^{-1}w$. By a c-length argument, we deduce that $g(b^{-1}a)^k \in A$, and so, by length in R, $k = 0$. But relation (vii) shows that we also have $z \sim_H zxy$, and applying the above argument to this equation yields a contradiction. Thus we must have $y \in R$. Since $c^{-r}yc^r = y^n$, we further deduce that $y \in A$, and hence y can be written in the form $y = a^{\alpha_1}p^{\beta_1}a^{\alpha_2}p^{\beta_2}---a^{\alpha_s}p^{\beta_s}$. The equation $c^{-r}yc^r = y^n$ then yields

$$a^{\alpha_1}p^{\beta_1 n^r}a^{\alpha_2}p^{\beta_2 n^r}---a^{\alpha_s}p^{\beta_s n^r} = (a^{\alpha_1}p^{\beta_1}a^{\alpha_2}p^{\beta_2}---a^{\alpha_s}p^{\beta_s})^n$$

where, in the case $r < 0$, each β_i must be divisible by $n^{|r|}$. Since A is free, and $r \neq 0$, this equation is possible only if $r = 1$ and $y = a^{-\alpha}p^{\beta}a^{\alpha}$ for some integers α and β.

We now have $x = b^{-1}a$, $y = a^{-\alpha}p^{\beta}a^{\alpha}$, $z = g(b^{-1}a)^k$ ($g \in U$), $u = c$ and $v = d$. It remains to prove that $k = 0$. By relations (vi) and (vii) $z \sim_R zy$ and $z \sim_R zxy$, which yield

$$g(b^{-1}a)^k \sim_R g(b^{-1}a)^k a^{-\alpha}p^{\beta}a^{\alpha} \sim_R g(b^{-1}a)^{k+1}a^{-\alpha}p^{\beta}a^{\alpha}.$$

A length argument in R proves that this is not possible unless $k = 0$, and the result then follows. □

Lemma 6.11. *If* $\alpha = 0$, *then* $\beta = 1$.

Proof. The relation $z \sim_R zxy$ gives $g \sim_R gb^{-1}ap^{\beta}$. Since $g \in U$, a length argument in R shows that $ap^{\beta} \in U$, that is $\beta = 1$. □

Lemma 6.12. *Suppose that the elements* $x = b^{-1}a$, $y = p$, $u = c$, $v = d$ *and* $z = p^{\alpha_1}a^{\beta_1}p^{\alpha_2}a^{\beta_2}---p^{\alpha_m}a^{\beta_m}p^{\alpha_{m+1}} \in U$ *generate* S. *Suppose also that for each* $i = 1, 2, \ldots m$, $\alpha_i \neq 0$, $\beta_i \neq 0$ *and* $\alpha_i > \max(18n, \beta_i)$, *and that the following relations hold between* x, y *and* z:

(i) $y^{-i}zy^i = (xy)^{-i}z(xy)^i$ *for* $0 \leq i \leq 9n-1$, $i \neq 4, 5, 6, 12, 13, 14, 9n-11, 9n-10, 9n-9$.

(ii) $y^{-4}zy^4 = (xy)^{-4}z(xy)^5$.

(iii) $y^{-5}zy^5 = (xy)^{-6}z(xy)^4$.

(iv) $y^{-6}zy^6 = (xy)^{-5}z(xy)^6$.

(v) $y^{-12}zy^{13} = (xy)^{-12}z(xy)^{12}$.

(vi) $y^{-13}zy^{14} = (xy)^{-14}z(xy)^{14}$.

(vii) $y^{-14}zy^{12} = (xy)^{-13}z(xy)^{13}$.

(viii) $y^{-(9n-11)}zy^{9n-11} = (xy)^{-(9n-11)}z(xy)^{-1}z(xy)^{9n-10}$.

(ix) $y^{-(9n-10)}zy^{9n-10} = (xy)^{-(9n-10)}z^{-1}(xy)^{9n-10}$.

(x) $y^{-(9n-9)}zy^{9n-9} = (xy)^{-(9n-10)}z(xy)^{-1}z(xy)^{9n-9}$.

Then m is odd, and

$$z = B_1B_2 --- B_{\frac{1}{2}(m-1)}(p^{9nt}ap^{-9nt+1})p^{-1}(B_1B_2 --- B_{\frac{1}{2}(m-1)})^{-1}p$$

where each $B_i = p^{9nt_i}a^{9nk_i}p^{-9nt_i+9nk_i}$ *for some* $t_i > \max(2, k_i)$.

Proof. We first note that for each pair of integers (i, j) there exists a unique integer $k = k(i, j)$ such that $p^ia^jp^k$ lies in U. Moreover,

$$\begin{aligned} p^ia^jp^k &= (a^{\rho^{-1}(-i)}p^{-i})^{-1}(a^{j-\rho^{-1}(-i)}p^{\rho(j-\rho^{-1}(-i))}) \\ &= (b^{\tau(\rho^{-1}(-i))}q^{\sigma\tau(\rho^{-1}(-i))})^{-1}(b^{\tau(j-\rho^{-1}(-i))}q^{\sigma\tau(j-\rho^{-1}(-i))}) \\ &= q^{i'}b^{j'}q^{k'} \end{aligned}$$

for some integers i', j', k'. We set $B_1 = p^{\alpha_1}a^{\beta_1}p^{k(\alpha_1,\beta_1)}$, $B_2 = p^{\alpha_2-k(\alpha_1,\beta_1)}a^{\beta_2}p^{k(\alpha_2-k(\alpha_1,\beta_1),\beta_2)}$, etc., so that $z = B_1B_2 --- B_m$, and we call each B_i a block of z.

Now for each integer r, there exists a unique integer s, and blocks $B'_1, B'_2, \ldots B'_m$ such that $y^{-r}B_1B_2 --- B_m = B'_1B'_2 --- B'_my^s$. (We have $B'_1 = p^{\alpha_1-r}a^{\beta_1}p^{k(\alpha_1-r,\beta_1)}$, etc.). Similarly, using the relations $a^ip^{\rho(i)} = b^{\tau(i)}q^{\sigma\tau(i)}$, z may be written as a product of m blocks $\hat{B}_1, \hat{B}_2, \ldots \hat{B}_m$, say, each of type $q^{i'}b^{j'}q^{k'}$, and for each integer r there exists a unique integer s and blocks $\hat{B}'_1, \hat{B}'_2, \ldots \hat{B}'_m$ such that $(xy)^{-r}\hat{B}_1\hat{B}_2 --- \hat{B}_m = \hat{B}'_1\hat{B}'_2 --- \hat{B}'_m(xy)^s$. It follows that an equation of the form $y^{-r}zy^{r'} = (xy)^{-s}z(xy)^{s'}$ can only hold if $y^{-r}B_1 = (xy)^{-s}B_1(xy)^ty^u$ for some integers t and u.

Let $\alpha_1 = 9nt - k$, where $0 \leqslant k < 9n$. The restrictions on α_i and β_i ensure that, in calculating $y^{-r}B_1$ for any $0 \leqslant r < 9n$, the only values of ρ, σ and τ used are those on the negative integers, that is, those for which definitions were made in §1. An inspection of the relations (i) to (x) made in the light of the above comments, shows that $k = 0$ is the only possibility.

Now relations (viii) and (ix) yield

$$\begin{aligned} x(y^{-(9n-11)}zy^{9n-11})x^{-1} &= (xy)(y^{-(9n-10)}zy^{9n-10})(xy)^{-1} \\ &= (xy)^{-(9n-11)}z^{-1}(xy)^{9n-11} \\ &= (y^{-(9n-11)}zy^{9n-11}\,.\,y^{-(9n-10)}zy^{9n-10})^{-1} \\ &= y^{-(9n-10)}z^{-1}yz^{-1}y^{9n-11}, \end{aligned}$$

and, similarly, relations (i), (ix) and (x) yield

$$\begin{aligned} x(y^{-(9n-9)}zy^{9n-9})x^{-1} &= (xy)(y^{-(9n-8)}zy^{9n-8})(xy)^{-1} \\ &= (xy)^{-(9n-9)}z(xy)^{9n-9} \end{aligned}$$

$$= ((y^{-(9n-9)}zy^{9n-9})^{-1}(y^{-(9n-10)}zy^{9n-10})^{-1})^{-1}$$
$$= y^{-(9n-10)}zy^{-1}zy^{9n-9}.$$

The left-hand side of each of these equations is a product of m blocks, whereas the right-hand side of the second equation is $p^{-(9n-10)}B_1B_2---B_m\ p^{-1}B_1B_2---B_mp^{9n-9}$. Thus some cancellation between blocks must take place, and we obtain a series of equations of the form $B_mp^{-1}B_1 = p^{r_1}$ for some integer r_1, $B_{m-1}p^{r_1}B_2 = p^{r_2}$ for some integer r_2, etc., the cancellation continuing until we have obtained a product of m blocks. Suppose $m > 1$. After cancellation, we obtain an expression beginning with a block of the form $p^{-9n+10+\alpha_1}a^{\beta_1}p^{k(-9n+10+\alpha_1,\beta_1)}$, and so it follows that $xy^{-(9n-9)}B_1$ must take the form $p^{-9n+10+\alpha_1}a^{\beta_1}p^{k(-9n+10+\alpha_1,\beta_1)}p^rq^s$ for some integers r and s. Now $\alpha_1 = 9nt$, and the expression $xy^{(9n-9)}B_1$ can be evaluated for each possible congruence class of $\beta_1 \bmod 9n$. The only congruence classes for β_1 which give an answer in the correct form are $\beta_1 \equiv 0$ or $-1 \bmod 9n$. Suppose $\beta_1 \equiv -1 \bmod 9n$, and consider the equation

$$x(y^{-(9n-11)}zy^{9n-11})x^{-1} = y^{-(9n-10)}z^{-1}yz^{-1}y^{9n-11}.$$

We have already noted that $B_mp^{-1}B_1 = p^{r_1}$ for some integer r_1, so $B_m^{-1} = p^{-1}B_1p^{-r_1}$, and the left-hand side of our equation must begin in a block $p^{-9n+9+\alpha_1}a^{\beta_1}p^{k(-9n+9+\alpha_1,\beta_1)}$ and it is easy to check that for $\beta_1 \equiv -1 \bmod 9n$, this is not the case.

Thus there are integers t_1 and k_1, $t_1 > \max(2, k_1)$ such that $B_1 = p^{9nt_1}a^{9nk_1}p^{-9nt_1+9nk_1}$. We next consider B_2. Arguments similar to those used above show that, if $m > 3$, there are integers $t_2 > 2 + t_1 - k_1$ and $k_2 < t_2 - t_1 + k_1$ such that $B_2 = p^{9nt_2}a^{9nk_2}p^{-9nt_2+9nk_2}$. We continue in this way for as many blocks as possible, and note that we also have equations of the form $B_mp^{-1}B_1 = p^{r_1}$, $B_{m-1}p^{r_1}B_2 = p^{r_2}$, etc. The form of B_1, B_2, etc. shows that $r_1 = r_2 = \cdots = -1$. Thus we have proved that if $m > 1$, then either (i) m is even and $z = B_1B_2---B_{\frac{1}{2}m}p^{-1}(B_1B_2---B_{\frac{1}{2}m})^{-1}p$, where for each $i = 1, 2, \ldots, \frac{1}{2}m$ $B_i = p^{9nt_i}a^{9nk_i}p^{-9nt_i+9nk_i}$ for some integers $t_i > 2$ and k_i, or (ii) m is odd and $z = B_1B_2---B_{\frac{1}{2}(m-1)}B_{\frac{1}{2}(m+1)}p^{-1}(B_1B_2---B_{\frac{1}{2}(m-1)})^{-1}p$ where for each $i = 1, 2, \ldots \frac{1}{2}(m-1)$, $B_i = p^{9nt_i}a^{9nk_i}p^{-9nt_i+9nk_i}$ for some integers $t_i > 2$ and k_i, and $B_{\frac{1}{2}(m+1)} = p^{9nt}a^rp^s$ for some integers r, s, t.

In case (i) an easy calculation shows that $y^{-4}zy^4 = (xy)^{-4}z(xy)^4$, and since $xy = q \neq 1$, relation (ii) fails to hold. Thus m is odd, and we have case (ii).

Again we consider the equation $xy^{-(9n-9)}zy^{9n-9}x^{-1} = y^{-(9n-10)}zy^{-1}zy^{9n-9}$. The right-hand side of this equation is

$$p^{-(9n-9)}B_1B_2---B_{\frac{1}{2}(m-1)}B_{\frac{1}{2}(m+1)}p^{-1}B_{\frac{1}{2}(m+1)}p^{-1}(B_1B_2---B_{\frac{1}{2}(m-1)})^{-1}p^{9n-8}$$

and this must be a product of m blocks. It follows that $B_{\frac{1}{2}(m+1)}p^{-1}B_{\frac{1}{2}(m+1)}p^{k}$ is a block for some integer k, that is $p^{9nt}a^rp^{s-1+9nt}a^rp^{s+k}$ is a block. This is possible only if $s = -9nt+1$, and this can occur only if $r = 1$. Thus $B_{\frac{1}{2}(m+1)} = p^{9nt}ap^{-9nt+1}$, as required. The case $m = 1$ is easily dealt with, by similar methods, and results in $z = p^{9nt}ap^{-9nt+1}$ for some $t > 2$. □

§7. The possible isomorphisms between G and G_P

Let $\hat{z} = u^{-1}zy^{-1}uy = (p^{9n}ap^{-9n+1}, p^{18n}ap^{-18n+1}, \ldots, p^{9nt}ap^{-9nt+1}, \ldots)$. Then x, y, $\hat{z}$, u, v generate G, and, by projecting onto each S_i $(i \in N)$, it is easy to check that the following relations hold in G:

(i) $u^{-1}yu = y^n$
(ii) $v^{-1}uv = u^2$
(iii) $x^{-1}vx = v^2$
(iv) $x^{-1}\hat{z}x = \hat{z}$
(v) $x(y^{-1}\hat{z}y)x^{-1} = y^{-1}\hat{z}y$
(vi) $x(y^{-14}\hat{z}y^{14})x^{-1} = y^{-13}\hat{z}y^{14}$
(vii) $y^{-6}\hat{z}y^{6} = (xy)^{-5}\hat{z}(xy)^{6}$.

Suppose $P \subseteq N$ is such that $G = G_P \times G_{N\setminus P}$, and $\varphi : G \to G_P$ is an isomorphism. $\varphi(x)$, $\varphi(y)$, $\varphi(\hat{z})$, $\varphi(u)$, $\varphi(v)$ generate G_P and satisfy the above equations. It follows that for each $i \in P$, $\varphi(x)_i$, $\varphi(y)_i$, $\varphi(\hat{z})_i$, $\varphi(u)_i$ and $\varphi(v)_i$ generate S_i and satisfy the above equations. Their values are, therefore established, within an inner automorphism of S_i, by Lemma 6.10.

Let $C_1, C_2, \ldots C_t$ be the congruence classes of n^k found in Proposition 5.1, and suppose $t > 0$. Let C_i be the congruence class of $l_i \bmod n^k$. For each of the listed generators g of G, $\varphi(g)$ is equal modulo D to a product of commuting words $\varphi_{l_i}(g)$ on the elements $x(l_i, k)$, $y(l_i, k)$, $z(l_i, k, k)$, $u(l_i, k)$ and $v(l_i, k)$. We restrict our attention to one of these words, with $l_i = l$, say. Now the results of §5 show that, provided k is chosen sufficiently large, a necessary and sufficient condition for $\varphi_l(g)_i$ to lie in T_i for all but finitely many $i \equiv l \bmod n^k$ is that there is an element $\xi \in D$, and a word w on the generators $x(l, k)$, $u(l, k)$ and $v(l, k)$ such that $\varphi_l(g) = \xi w$. The results of §6 then show that there is a word g_l on $x(l, k)$, $y(l, k)$, $z(l, k, k)$, $u(l, k)$ and $v(l, k)$ such that

$$\varphi_l(x) = \xi_1 g_l^{-1} x(l, k) g_l$$

$$\varphi_l(u) = \xi_2 g_l^{-1} u(l, k) g_l$$

$$\varphi_l(\boldsymbol{v}) = \xi_3 \boldsymbol{g}_l^{-1}\boldsymbol{v}(l, k)\boldsymbol{g}_l$$

where ξ_1, ξ_2, $\xi_3 \in D$.

We next consider the word $\boldsymbol{g}_l\varphi_l(\boldsymbol{y})\boldsymbol{g}_l^{-1}$. By the results of §6, the projection of this element on S_i is equal to $a^{-\alpha}p^{\beta}a^{\alpha}$ (some α, β) for all sufficiently large $i \equiv l \bmod n^k$. The results of §5 force $\boldsymbol{g}_l\varphi_l(\boldsymbol{y})\boldsymbol{g}_l^{-1} = \xi_4\boldsymbol{y}(l, k)^{\beta}$ for some $\xi_4 \in D$. It then follows by Lemma 6.11 that $\beta = 1$.

Now consider $\boldsymbol{g}_l\varphi_l(\hat{\boldsymbol{z}})\boldsymbol{g}_l^{-1}$. Lemma 6.10 shows that the projection of this element on S_i must lie in U_i for all sufficiently large $i \equiv l \bmod n^k$. We conclude, from the results of §5 that $\boldsymbol{g}_l\varphi_l(\hat{\boldsymbol{z}})\boldsymbol{g}_l^{-1} = \xi_5\boldsymbol{u}_1\boldsymbol{u}_2 --- \boldsymbol{u}_r$ where $\xi_5 \in D$ and each $\boldsymbol{u}_j$ is a word on finitely many of the generators of U_{l,k,s_j}, and where $s_{j+1} \neq s_j$ for each $j = 1, 2, \ldots r - 1$. We now project $\xi_5\boldsymbol{u}_1\boldsymbol{u}_2 --- \boldsymbol{u}_r$ onto S_i where i is a very large integer congruent to $l \bmod n^k$, to obtain a word of the form $p^{\alpha_1}a^{\beta_1}p^{\alpha_2}a^{\beta_2} -- p^{\alpha_m}a^{\beta_m}p^{\alpha_{m+1}}$ where the α_i and β_i satisfy the conditions of Lemma 6.12. It can easily be checked (by projection on each S_i, $i \in N$) that the elements $\boldsymbol{x}$, $\boldsymbol{y}$, $\boldsymbol{z}$ of G satisfy equations (i) to (x) of Lemma 6.12, and hence so also do $\varphi_l(\boldsymbol{x})_i$, $\varphi_l(\boldsymbol{y})_i$, $\varphi_l(\hat{\boldsymbol{z}})_i$ for each $i \equiv l \bmod n^k$. We may, therefore, use Lemma 6.12 to obtain information about the projection of $\xi_5\boldsymbol{u}_1\boldsymbol{u}_2 --- \boldsymbol{u}_r$ on S_i for all sufficiently large $i \equiv l \bmod n^k$. We see that $\boldsymbol{g}_l\varphi_l(\hat{\boldsymbol{z}})\boldsymbol{g}_l^{-1}$ can be written in the form

$$\boldsymbol{g}_l\varphi_l(\hat{\boldsymbol{z}})\boldsymbol{g}_l^{-1} =$$

$$= \xi_6(\boldsymbol{w}_1\boldsymbol{w}_2 --- \boldsymbol{w}_m)\boldsymbol{y}(l, k)^{9nt}\boldsymbol{z}(l, k, s)\boldsymbol{y}(l, k)^{-9nt}\boldsymbol{y}(l, k)^{-1}(\boldsymbol{w}_1\boldsymbol{w}_2 \cdots \boldsymbol{w}_m)^{-1}\boldsymbol{y}(l, k)$$

where $\xi_6 \subset D$, and each $\boldsymbol{w}_i$ is a word of the form $\boldsymbol{y}(l, k)^{9nt_i}(\boldsymbol{z}(l, k, s_i)\boldsymbol{y}(l, k)^{-1})^{9nk_i}\boldsymbol{y}(l, k)^{-9nt_i+9nk_i}$ for some integers s, t, k_i, s_i, t_i, with, for each $i = 1, 2, \ldots m - 1$, either $s_{i+1} \neq s_i$ or $s_{i+1} = s_i$ and $t_{i+1} \neq t_i - k_i$.

Set $\boldsymbol{g}_l\varphi_l(\hat{\boldsymbol{z}})\boldsymbol{g}^{-1} = \boldsymbol{h}$. Now $\boldsymbol{x}(l, k), \boldsymbol{y}(l, k), \boldsymbol{u}(l, k), \boldsymbol{v}(l, k)$ and $\boldsymbol{h}$ generate G_{C_l}, and so there is a word w on these generators such that $\boldsymbol{z}(l, k, k) = w(\boldsymbol{x}(l, k), \boldsymbol{y}(l, k), \boldsymbol{u}(l, k), \boldsymbol{v}(l, k), \boldsymbol{h})$. For all suitable t, let $\boldsymbol{h}^{(t)}$ be the element obtained from $\boldsymbol{h}$ by replacing each occurrence of $\boldsymbol{z}(l, k, r)$ (any r) in $\boldsymbol{h}$ by $\boldsymbol{z}(l, k, r + t)$. The analysis of §5 can now be applied to the group $\langle \boldsymbol{x}(l, k), \boldsymbol{y}(l, k), \boldsymbol{u}(l, k), \boldsymbol{v}(l, k), \boldsymbol{h} \rangle$. Analogues of Lemmas 5.3 to 5.6 with $\boldsymbol{h}$ taking the place of $\boldsymbol{z}(l, k, k)$ and $\boldsymbol{h}^{(t)}$ taking the place of $\boldsymbol{z}(l, k, k + t)$ can be obtained (a certain amount of care being necessary about the range of values that t is allowed to take). It thus becomes clear that the equation

$$\boldsymbol{z}(l, k, k) = w(\boldsymbol{x}(l, k), \boldsymbol{y}(l, k), \boldsymbol{u}(l, k), \boldsymbol{v}(l, k), \boldsymbol{h})$$

is possible only if $\boldsymbol{h} = \xi_6\boldsymbol{y}(l, k)^{9nt}\boldsymbol{z}(l, k, s)\boldsymbol{y}(l, k)^{-9nt}$ for some $\xi_6 \in D$, and some integers s, t.

We now put together the results we have achieved so far to obtain

Proposition 7.1. *Suppose P is an infinite subset of N such that $G = G_P \times G_{N\setminus P}$ and suppose $\varphi : G \to G_P$ is an isomorphism. Then there exist integers k, m, and $t \leq n^k$ and congruence classes $C_1, C_2, \dots C_t$ mod n^k such that $P = X \cup C_1 \cup C_2 \cup \cdots \cup C_t$ where $X \subseteq \{1, 2, \dots m\}$, and, if C_i is the congruence class of l_i mod n^k, there exist elements $\mathbf{g}_{l_i}$ of G_{C_i}, integers s_i, t_i and elements $\xi_1, \xi_2, \xi_3, \xi_4, \xi_5$ of D such that*

$$\varphi(\mathbf{x}) = \xi_1 \prod_{i=1}^{t} \mathbf{g}_{l_i}(\mathbf{x}(l_i, k))\mathbf{g}_{l_i}^{-1}$$

$$\varphi(\mathbf{y}) = \xi_2 \prod_{i=1}^{t} \mathbf{g}_{l_i}(\mathbf{y}(l_i, k))\mathbf{g}_{l_i}^{-1}$$

$$\varphi(\hat{\mathbf{z}}) = \xi_3 \prod_{i=1}^{t} \mathbf{g}_{l_i}(\mathbf{y}(l_i, k)^{9nt_i}\mathbf{z}(l_i, k, s_i)\mathbf{y}(l_i, k)^{-9nt_i})\mathbf{g}_{l_i}^{-1}$$

$$\varphi(\mathbf{u}) = \xi_4 \prod_{i=1}^{t} \mathbf{g}_{l_i}(\mathbf{u}(l_i, k))\mathbf{g}_{l_i}^{-1}$$

$$\varphi(\mathbf{v}) = \xi_5 \prod_{i=1}^{t} \mathbf{g}_{l_i}(\mathbf{v}(l_i, k))\mathbf{g}_{l_i}^{-1}.$$

Moreover, each s_i is greater than or equal to two.

Proof. Only the inequality for s_i remains to be proved. Let $s_j = \min s_i$ and suppose that $s_j = 1$. The equation $9nt_i - 9n^{s_i}r = 9nt_j - 9n^{s_j}r_1$ may be rewritten as $t_i - t_j = n^{s_i-1}r - r_1$, and so it has a solution for the pair (r, r_1). Moreover, if (r, r_1) is one solution, then $(r + r', r_1 + r'n^{s_i-s_j})$ is another.

Now $G_{C_i} \subseteq G$, for each $i = 1, 2, \dots t$, and consequently (ignoring a few terms of the direct product) we have $G_{C_i} \subseteq G_P$. There is therefore a word w on $\varphi(\mathbf{x})$, $\varphi(\mathbf{y})$, $\varphi(\hat{\mathbf{z}})$, $\varphi(\mathbf{u})$ and $\varphi(\mathbf{v})$ whose projection on S_i is trivial for all sufficiently large $i \notin C_i$, but non-trivial for infinitely many $i \in C_i$. But a consideration of the equation $9nt_i - 9n^{s_i}r = 9nt_j - 9n^{s_j}r_1$ shows that the projection of w on the rth term of C_i is a conjugate of the projection of w on the r_1th term of C_j, and this pattern is repeated for all sufficiently large r. Thus the projection of w on S_i is trivial for all but finitely many $i \in C_i$, and we have our contradiction. □

This establishes the form of all possible isomorphisms between G and G_P. We will use this information in the next section to show that $G \not\cong G'$ for any $1 < r < n$.

§8. The non-isomorphisms

We are now ready to prove the final theorem.

Theorem 8.1. *$G \not\cong G^r$ for any r such that $1 < r < n$.*

Proof. Suppose that $G = G_P \times G_{N \setminus P}$, and that $G \cong G_P$. We first show that P is infinite. Suppose not. An easy adaptation of Proposition 4.4 shows that given any finite integer k, the only possible non-trivial decomposition of S^k as a direct product is of the form $S^k = S^r \times S^{k-r}$ for some r, $1 \leqslant r < k$. It follows that S^k can be decomposed into a direct product in only finitely many different ways. But Lemma 4.1 shows that G can be factored as a direct product with an arbitrarily large number of factors. Thus $G \not\cong S^k$ for any k. Hence P is infinite, and so the result of Proposition 7.1 holds. We will prove that the number t of congruence classes mod n^k given in Proposition 7.1 is congruent to 1 mod $n-1$. We proceed by induction on t. If $t = 1$ the result is proved, so assume $t > 1$.

Now the proof of Theorem 3.1 shows that the normal closure in G of the commutator $[\boldsymbol{x}^{-1}, \boldsymbol{z}^{-1}]$ is a subgroup of G isomorphic to G. φ induces an isomorphism between this subgroup and some subgroup of G_P. We will consider the form of this induced isomorphism, and hence establish the basis of an inductive proof.

Now $\boldsymbol{z} = \boldsymbol{u}\hat{\boldsymbol{z}}\boldsymbol{y}^{-1}\boldsymbol{u}^{-1}\boldsymbol{y}$, and so we have

$$\varphi(\boldsymbol{z}) = \xi_6 \prod_{i=1}^{t} g_{l_i}(\boldsymbol{u}(l_i, k)\boldsymbol{y}(l_i, k)^{9nt_i}\boldsymbol{z}(l_i, k, s_i)\boldsymbol{y}(l_i, k)^{-9nt_i}\boldsymbol{y}(l_i, k)^{-1}\boldsymbol{u}(l_i, k)^{-1}\boldsymbol{y}(l_i, k))g_{l_i}^{-1}.$$

Since $s_i \geqslant 2$ for each i, this is $\xi_6 \prod_{i=1}^{t} g_{l_i}(\boldsymbol{y}(l_i, k)^{9t_i}\boldsymbol{z}(l_i, k, s_{i-1})\boldsymbol{y}(l_i, k)^{9t_i})g_{l_i}^{-1}$. We now consider the projection of $\varphi([\boldsymbol{x}^{-1}, \boldsymbol{z}^{-1}])$ on S_i for large $i \equiv l_i \bmod n^k$. If t_i is not congruent to one modulo n, $\varphi([\boldsymbol{x}^{-1}, \boldsymbol{z}^{-1}])_i = 1$. Consequently, if each of the t_i satisfies $t_i \not\equiv 1 \bmod n$, then $\varphi([\boldsymbol{x}^{-1}, \boldsymbol{z}^{-1}])$ lies in D, and so φ induces an isomorphism between G and S^k for some k. We have already seen that no such isomorphism exists, and so there are some integers i, $1 \leqslant i \leqslant t$, such that $t_i \equiv 1 \bmod n$. Set $R = \bigcup_{t_i \equiv 1(n)} C_i$. Then, if we ignore a few terms of the direct product, φ induces an isomorphism between G and G_R. We investigate the form of this isomorphism.

The calculations made in the proof of Theorem 3.1 show that if $\hat{\varphi}$ is the induced isomorphism, then there exist elements $\eta_1, \eta_2, \eta_3, \eta_4, \eta_5$ fo D such that

$$\hat{\varphi}(\boldsymbol{x}) = \eta_1 \prod_{C_i \in R} g_{l_i}(\boldsymbol{x}(l_i, k))g_{l_i}^{-1}$$

$$\hat{\varphi}(y) = \eta_2 \prod_{C_i \in R} g_{l_i}(y(l_i, k))g_{l_i}^{-1}$$

$$\hat{\varphi}(z) = \eta_3 \prod_{C_i \in R} g_{l_i}(y(l_i, k)^{9nt'_i}z(l_i, k, s_i)y(l_i, k)^{9nt'_i})g_{l_i}^{-1}$$

$$\hat{\varphi}(u) = \eta_4 \prod_{C_i \in R} g_{l_i}(u(l_i, k))g_{l_i}^{-1}$$

$$\hat{\varphi}(v) = \eta_5 \prod_{C_i \in R} g_{l_i}(v(l_i, k))g_{l_i}^{-1}.$$

Similarly, (as in Theorem 3.1) the normal closure of $[x^{-1}, (y^{9n-9}zy^{-(9n-9)})^{-1}]$ in G is another subgroup isomorphic to G. If we apply the above arguments to this subgroup, we obtain similar results for those congruence classes C_i for which $t_i \equiv 2 \bmod n$, and, continuing in this way, we derive similar results for those congruence classes C_i for which $t_i \equiv r \bmod n$, for each r, $1 \leqslant r \leqslant n$. Our inductive hypothesis allows us to conclude that the classes C_i can be divided into n sets, each containing a number of classes congruent to $1 \bmod n-1$. Thus t is congruent to $(n \times 1) \bmod n-1$, that is, $t \equiv 1 \bmod n-1$.

Now suppose that $G \cong G^r$ with $1 < r < n$. Then there is a partition $\{P_1, P_2, \ldots P_r\}$ of N such that $G = G_{P_1} \times G_{P_2} \times \cdots \times G_{P_r}$, and each $G_{P_i} \cong G$. By the above reasoning, each set P_i consists of a subset of D, and a number t_i of congruence classes modulo n^k (where k is taken sufficiently large to be the same for each G_{P_i}), such that $t_i \equiv 1 \bmod n-1$. Thus the total number of congruence classes in $N = P_1 \cup P_2 \cup \cdots \cup P_r$ is congruent to $r \times 1 = r \bmod n-1$. But the total number is n^k, which is congruent to $1 \bmod n-1$. Thus $r \equiv 1 \bmod n-1$, contradicting $1 < r < n$.

Thus, $G \not\cong G^r$ for any r such that $1 < r < n$, and the result is established.

References

[1] R. Camm, Simple free products, J. London Math. Soc. 28 (1953) 66–76.

[2] A.L.S. Corner, On a conjecture of Pierce concerning direct decompositions of Abelian groups, Proc. Colloq. Abelian Groups (Tihany, 1963) (Akademiai Kiado, Budapest, 1964) pp. 43–48.

[3] J.M. Tyrer Jones, Direct products and the Hopf property, J. Australian Math. Soc. Vol. 17, Part 2 (1974) 174–196.

[4] W. Magnus, A. Karrass and D. Solitar, Combinatorial group theory, Pure and Applied Mathematics, Vol. 13 (Interscience Publishers, 1966).

[5] C.F. Miller, III, On group-theoretic decision problems and their classification, Annals of Maths. Studies, No. 68 (Princeton University Press, 1971).

S.I. Adian, W.W. Boone, G. Higman, Word Problems II
© North-Holland Publishing Company (1980) 247–254

CANCELLATION THEORY IN FREE PRODUCTS WITH AMALGAMATION

Roger C. LYNDON*
University of Michigan, Ann Arbor, Michigan

The technical details of the original talk appear elsewhere [27], and need not be repeated here. Instead, we first discuss the general context of the problem under consideration, and then give a brief summary of the specific results obtained.

§1. Cancellation theory in group theory

There are two principal methods, admittedly related, in the study of free groups, free products, free products with amalgamation, HNN extensions, and similar group constructions. One is the method of *cancellation arguments*, already used extensively by Nielsen [31, 32, 33]. The second, equally old but less systematically used until recently, derives from topology, and is often described as using *covering space arguments*. One could say that cancellation arguments are based on nothing more than the sheer group axioms, while covering space arguments employ elaborations of Cayley's observation that every abstract group can be realized as a group of transformations of a suitable object.

For general subgroup theorems, covering space arguments give by far the shortest and most transparent proofs. The most elegant theory at present seems to be that of *graphs of groups*, or *groups acting on trees*, introduced by Serre and Bass [43]. The fundamental theorem of this theory can be developed without topology, as is done by Serre and Bass, although a very simple proof can be given, using only a minimum of the most elementary topology, following the ideas of Tretkoff [44]. Once the fundamental theorem is known, no further topology is needed to obtain immediately a subgroup theorem for *graph products* of groups, which contains all the main classical subgroup theorems.

* The author gratefully acknowledges support of the National Science Foundation.

Chiswell [4] has used this theory to obtain a fairly direct and transparent proof of the Grushko–Neumann Theorem, which is comparable in its simplicity (and presumably related) to the topological proof by Stallings [45]. A number of the more technically specialized theorems concerning subgroups of groups of the sorts under consideration have been given improved statements and proofs by Cohen [7, 8], exploiting the implicit interpretation of the Serre–Bass theory in terms of graphs of cosets. The theory has other applications, as noted by Serre, notably to the structure of linear groups, especially PSL_2's, where it is closely related to a fruitful method of Behr [1, 2].

There remains, nonetheless, an area where cancellation arguments appear indispensable. Cancellation arguments themselves can be divided into two kinds. There are those, exemplified historically by the work of Dehn [9], that are concerned typically with the question of membership in the normal subgroup defined by a given set of elements; of this theory, which contains most of *small cancellation theory*, we shall say no more here. The remaining area is exemplified by the problem of characterizing the elements of a subgroup generated by given elements.

A first example is Nielsen's proof of his subgroup theorem. For this limited purpose his method is hardly preferable to that of Schreier [40] (which can be interpreted topologically), and is certainly inferior to the standard simple covering space argument; but it is very fruitful for other purposes. First, it gives immediately a set of generators for the automorphism group of a finitely generated free group (Nielsen [31, 32, 33]), and so also for $GL(n, \mathbf{Z})$. A most important direct outgrowth of this method is the theorem of Whitehead ([46, 47]; see also Rapaport [36], Higgins and Lyndon [17]), giving an effective criterion for two finite sequences of elements from a free group to be equivalent under automorphism. From this has grown in turn McCool's [28, 29] recovery, in simple form, of Nielsen's finite presentation of the automorphism group of a finitely generated free group (and with it of $GL(n, \mathbf{Z})$), as well as McCool's [30] finite presentations for stabilizers in this group, and, consequently, for the classical mapping-class groups. In another direction, Nielsen transformations and their generalizations play an important role in the study of low-dimensional topology.

In the original setting of free groups, the main role of cancellation theory lies in transforming a given finite sequence of elements into one that is *Nielsen reduced.* A Nielsen reduced sequence is then a basis for the subgroup it generates. (An elegant refinement of the Nielsen reduction process was presented at this conference by Hoare [18].) This cancellation argument was formulated axiomatically by Lyndon [22], using *length functions*, to obtain a uniform and sharper form of the Nielsen–Schreier and Kurosh subgroup theorems, as well as a very down-to-earth proof of the Grushko–Neumann Theorem ([23]; see also Cohen [6]). Chiswell [5] has recently shown a close connection between the theory of length functions and the Serre–Bass theory.

Cancellation theory has long been applied to free products, free products with amalgamation, and HNN extensions, to the extent of providing normal form theorems for such groups (Britton's Lemma, in the case of HNN groups), and relative solutions of the word and conjugacy problems. But the role of Nielsen transformations and the status of Nielsen reduced sets had received only small, though important, consideration. In 1970 Zieschang [54] initiated an extension of the full theory, with the necessary modifications, to free products with amalgamation. The essential difficulty in such an extension is that a Nielsen reduced set, even with any reasonable modification of the definition, cannot be expected to be a basis for a free group. However, Zieschang managed to pinpoint the special configurations that must occur in the exceptional cases. By these means he, later together with Peczynski and Rosenberger [35], managed to determine the ranks of all Fuchsian groups. This method was used also by Rosenberger [37] to analyze the situation in which an analog of the Grushko–Neumann Theorem fails for free products with amalgamation.

The work to be described here uses Zieschang's formalism to obtain a proof of a version of the theorem of Karrass and Solitar [19] on subgroups of a free product with amalgamation. Although the proof is admittedly lengthy, we believe that the detailed information obtained is instructive and should be of use in other applications. Indeed, the result as obtained contains the main content of Zieschang's theorem.

We mention only one application that we have immediately in mind. Recent work of Edmunds and others [3, 10, 11, 12, 13, 14, 15] refines earlier work on cancellation theory in free products to extend significantly work of Lyndon, McDonough, Newman, Rosenberger, and Zieschang [21, 24, 25, 26, 38, 39, 51, 52] on solutions of quadratic equations in free products, as well as work of Schupp [41, 42] and Wicks [48, 49, 50] on this and on the closely related *endomorphism problem*: given two elements w and w' in a free group F, when is there a map from F into itself carrying w into w'? A suitable analogous result for free products with amalgamation should put in a more general setting the result of Nielsen ([34]; see also Zieschang [53]) on lifting automorphisms of surface groups. The theory under discussion already gives some promise of revealing to what extent Edmunds' work carries over to free products with amalgamation.

§2. Cancellation arguments

We sketch below, omitting details, the derivation of a form of the Karrass–Solitar Subgroup Theorem for free products with amalgamation, using the method of Zieschang.

Let $G = *_A \{G_\lambda : \lambda \in \Lambda\}$, the free product of groups G_λ with a common subgroup A amalgamated. Every element of G either belongs to A or can be written in the form $w = u_1 \cdots u_n$, $n \geq 1$, where each u_i is in some G_λ, no u_i is in A, and no successive u_i, u_{i+1} are in the same G_λ. We define the *length* of an element w in A to be $|w| = 0$; otherwise w determines the number n uniquely, and we define $|w| = n$. We write $u_1 \cdots u_m \equiv v_1 \cdots v_n$ to mean that equality holds and that the right member is reduced in the sense that $|v_1 \cdots v_n| = |v_1| + \cdots + |v_n|$.

Following Zieschang, we make constant use of the fact that every element of G can be written in the form

$$u \equiv phq^{-1}, \; |p| = |q|, \; |h| \leq 1.$$

Here u uniquely determines pA, qA, and AhA. If $|h| = 0$ we may choose $h = 1$. If $pA = qA$ we may refactor, writing $u \equiv ph_1p^{-1}$, $|h_1| = 1$. Paralleling the usual development of the Nielsen theory for free groups, we define a well-ordering of the cosets Ap such that

(1) *if* $|p| < |q|$ *then* $pA < qA$,

(2) *if* $p \equiv p_1p_2$, $q \equiv q_1q_2$, $|p_1| = |q_1|$, $|p_2| = |q_2|$, *and* $p_1A < q_1A$, *then* $pA < qA$.

As in [22] we define the set U of *non-Archimedean elements* to be

$$U = \{u \equiv php^{-1} : |h| = 1\}.$$

Thus

$$U = \bigcup \{G_\lambda^g : \lambda \in \Lambda, g \in G\}.$$

We write

$$\mathscr{C} = \{G_\lambda^g : \lambda \in \Lambda, g \in G\}.$$

Making the obvious generalization of the concept of *tree product* introduced by Karrass and Solitar [19], we show that the set U is the *tree union* of a graph Γ whose vertices are the sets in the family $\mathscr{C} \cup \{A\}$. In fact, if $C = G_{\lambda_0}^g$ for $g \equiv h_1 \cdots h_n$, $n \geq 1$, all $|h_i| = 1$, and $h_1 \notin G_{\lambda_0}$, we define $C^0 = A^g$ and $C' = G_{\lambda_1}^{h_2 \cdots h_n}$. If $C = G_\lambda$, we define $C^0 = C' = A$. Then we complete the definition of the graph Γ by joining each pair of vertices C and C' by an edge which we take to be (a replica of) C^0. It is easy to see that Γ is in fact a tree, and that U

is essentially the disjoint union of the vertex sets C with the edge sets C^0 amalgamated.

It is now not difficult to show that G is the quotient of the tree product of Γ (now in the category of graphs of groups rather than of sets) modulo a set of *conjugation relations* $u^v = w$, for u, v, w in U.

We are now ready to relativize these ideas to a subgroup G^* of G. We define $\mathscr{C}^*$ to be the set of $C^* = C \cap G^*$ for $C \in \mathscr{C}$, and we define $U^* = \bigcup \mathscr{C}^*$ and $N = \operatorname{Gp} U^*$. The map $\mathscr{C} \to \mathscr{C}^*$ induces a map $\Gamma \to \Gamma^*$, where Γ^* is a tree with vertex sets C^* and edge sets C^{0*}. We have, as before,

(3) *U^* is the tree union of Γ^*,*

(4) *N is the quotient of the tree product of Γ^* modulo the conjugation relations.*

Further, let $\mathscr{D} \subseteq \mathscr{C}^*$ be the set of all $C^* = G_\lambda^{p^{-1}} \cap G^*$ for which Ap is minimum under conjugation of C^* by elements of N. Then $\mathscr{D}$ spans a subtree Δ of Γ^*, and

(5) *N is the tree product of Δ.*

To find a complement F of the normal subgroup N of G^* we follow Federer and Jónsson [16]. We define an order $g_1 < g_2$ on elements of G^* to hold if $|g_1| < |g_2|$ or if $|g_1| = |g_2|$ with $g_1^{\pm 1} \equiv p_1 h q_1^{-1}$, $g_2^{\pm 1} \equiv p_2 h_2 q_2^{-1}$, $|p_1| = |p_2| = |q_1| = |q_2|$, $|h_1| = |h_2| \leq 1$, $p_1 A \leq q_1 A$, $p_2 A \leq q_2 A$, and either $p_1 A < p_2 A$ or else $p_1 A = p_2 A$ and $q_1 A < q_2 A$. Now we define

$$S = \{g : g \notin \operatorname{Gp}(N \cup \{h : h < g\})\}.$$

We find then that

(6) *S is a basis for a free group F,*

(7) *$G^* = FN$,*

(8) *$F \cap N = 1$.*

In short, G^* is a split extension of N by the free group F. In other words, G^* has a presentation with generating set $U \cup S$ and with defining relations a set of relations among the elements of U sufficient to define N, together with a set of relations $u^v = w$, for $u, w \in N$ and $v \in S$, sufficient to define the action by conjugation of F on N.

The details of the proof hinge on a series of unfortunately rather complicated lemmas, which can all be combined into one. In this lemma we consider a finite sequence $\sigma = (u_1, \ldots, u_n)$ of elements of $U \cup S \cup S^{-1}$. We show, roughly, that if the product is trivial, $u_1 \cdots u_n = 1$, then the sequence σ can be reduced to the empty sequence by a succession of steps of two kinds: first, elementary Nielsen transformations (associated in the usual way with a pair or triple of consecutive terms of the sequence), including deletion of a term $u_i = 1$; second, application of the permissible defining relations mentioned above to replace a pair or triple of adjacent terms by another with the same product. As noted, full details are given in [27].

References

[1] H. Behr, Über die endliche Definierbarkeit von Gruppen, J. Reine Angew. Math. 211 (1962) 116–122.

[2] H. Behr, Über die endliche Definierbarkeit verallgemeinerte Einheitengruppen, J. Reine Angew. Math. 211 (1962) 123–135.

[3] R.G. Burns, C.C. Edmunds and E. Formanek, The equation $s^{-1}t^{-1}st = u^{-1}v^{-1}uv$ in a free product of groups, Math. Z. 153 (1977) 83–88.

[4] I.M. Chiswell, The Grushko–Neumann theorem, Proc. London Math. Soc. 33 (1976) 385–400.

[5] I.M. Chiswell, Abstract length functions in groups, Math. Proc. Cambridge Philos. Soc. 80 (1976) 451–463.

[6] D.E. Cohen, Groups of cohomological dimension one, Springer Lecture Notes 245 (1972).

[7] D.E. Cohen, Subgroups of HNN groups, J. Austral. Math. Soc. 17 (1974) 394–405.

[8] D.E. Cohen, Finitely generated subgroups of amalgamated free products and HNN groups, J. Austral. Math. Soc. 22 (1976) 274–281.

[9] M. Dehn, Über unendliche diskontinulerliche Gruppen, Math. Ann. 72 (1912) 116–144.

[10] C.C. Edmunds, On the endomorphism problem for free groups, Comm. Algebra 3 (1975) 7–20.

[11] C.C. Edmunds, Some properties of quadratic words in free groups, Proc. Amer. Math. Soc. 50 (1975) 20–22.

[12] C.C. Edmunds, Products of commutators as products of squares, Canad. J. Math. 27 (1975) 1329–1338.

[13] C.C. Edmunds, A short combinatorial proof of the Vaught conjecture, Canad. Bull. Math. 18 (1975) 607–608.

[14] C.C. Edmunds, On the endomorphism problem for free groups II, Proc. London Math. Soc. 38 (1979) 153–168.

[15] C.C. Edmunds, On words of minimal length under endomorphisms of a free group, Math. Proc. Camb. Phil. Soc. 83 (1978) 191–194.

[16] H. Federer and B. Jónsson, Some properties of free groups, Trans. Amer. Math. Soc. 68 (1950) 1–27.

[17] P.J. Higgins and R.C. Lyndon, Equivalence of elements under automorphisms of a free group, J. London Math. Soc. 8 (1974) 254–258.

[18] A.H.M. Hoare, On Nielsen methods in free groups.

[19] A. Karrass and D. Solitar, The subgroups of a free product of two groups with an amalgamated subgroup, Trans. Amer. Math. Soc. 150 (1970) 227–255.

[20] A. Karrass and D. Solitar, Subgroups of HNN groups and groups with one defining relation, Canad. J. Math. 23 (1971) 933–959.

[21] R.C. Lyndon, The equation $a^2b^2 = c^2$ in free groups, Michigan Math. J. 6 (1959) 155–164.

[22] R.C. Lyndon, Length functions in groups, Math. Scand. 12 (1963) 209–234.

[23] R.C. Lyndon, Grushko's theorem, Proc. Amer. Math. Soc. 16 (1965) 822–826.

[24] R.C. Lyndon, On products of powers in groups, Comm. Pure Appl. Math. 26 (1973) 781–784.

[25] R.C. Lyndon, T. McDonough and M. Newman, On powers of products in groups, Proc. Amer. Math. Soc. 40 (1973) 419–420.

[26] R.C. Lyndon and M. Newman, Commutators as products of squares, Proc. Amer. Math. Soc. 39 (1973) 267–272.

[27] R.C. Lyndon and P.E. Schupp, Combinatorial Group Theory, Ergebnisse der Mathematik, Bd. 89 (Springer, Berlin-Heidelberg-New York, 1977).

[28] J. McCool, A presentation for the automorphism group of a free group of finite rank, J. London Math. Soc. 8 (1974) 259–266.

[29] J. McCool, On Nielsen's presentation of the automorphism group of a free group, J. London Math. Soc. 10 (1975) 265–270.

[30] J. McCool, Some finitely presented subgroups of the automorphism group of a free group, J. Algebra 35 (1975) 205–213.

[31] J. Nielsen, Die Isomorphismen der allgemeinen unendlichen Gruppe mit zwei Erzeugenden, Math. Ann. 78 (1918) 385–397.

[32] J. Nielsen, Über die Isomorphismen unendlicher Gruppen ohne Relation, Math. Ann. 79 (1919) 269–272.

[33] J. Nielsen, Die Isomorphismengruppe der freien Gruppen, Math. Ann. 91 (1924) 169–209.

[34] J. Nielsen, Untersuchungen zur Topologie der geschlossen zweiseitigen Flächen, Acta Math. 50 (1927) 189–358.

[35] N. Peczynski, G. Rosenberger and H. Zieschang, Über Erzeugende ebener diskontinuierlicher Gruppen, Invent. Math. 29 (1975) 161–180.

[36] E.S. Rapaport, On free groups and their automorphisms, Acta Math. 99 (1958) 139–163.

[37] G. Rosenberger, Zum Rang- und Isomorphieproblem für freie Produkte mit Amalgam (Habilitationschrift, Hamburg, 1974).

[38] G. Rosenberger, Anwendung der Nielsenschen Kürzungsmethode in Gruppen mit einer definierenden Relation, Mh. Math. 84 (1977) 55–68.

[39] G. Rosenberger, Produkte von Potenzen und Kommutatoren in freien Gruppen, J. Algebra 53 (1978) 416–422.

[40] O. Schreier, Die Untergruppen der freien Gruppen, Abh. Math. Sem. Univ. Hamburg 5 (1927) 161–183.

[41] P.E. Schupp, On the substitution problem for free groups, Proc. Amer. Math. Soc. 23 (1969) 421–423.

[42] P.E. Schupp, Quadratic equations in groups and cancellation diagrams on compact surfaces, in this Volume.

[43] J.-P. Serre, Arbres, amalgames, SL_2, Astérisque 46 (Soc. Math. de France, 1977).

[44] M. Tretkoff, A topological approach to HNN extensions and the theory of groups acting on trees, preprint.

[46] J.R. Stallings, A topological proof of Grushko's theorem on free products, Math. Z. 90 (1965) 1–8.

[46] J.H.C. Whitehead, On certain sets of elements in a free group, Proc. London Math. Soc. 41 (1936) 48–56.

[47] J.H.C. Whitehead, On equivalent sets of elements in a free group, Ann. of Math. 37 (1936) 782–800.

[48] M.J. Wicks, Commutators in free products, J. London Math. Soc. 37 (1962) 433–444.

[49] M.J. Wicks, A general solution of binary homogeneous equations over free groups, Pacific J. Math. 41 (1972) 543–561.

[50] M.J. Wicks, A relation in free products, Proc. Conf. Canberra 1973. Springer Lecture Notes 372 (1974) 709–716.

[51] H. Zieschang, Über Worte $S_1^{a_1}S_2^{a_2}\cdots S_p^{a_p}$ in einer freien Gruppen mit p freien Erzeugenden, Math. Ann. 147 (1962) 143–153.

[52] H. Zieschang, Alternierende Produkte in freien Gruppen I, II, Abh. Math. Sem. Univ. Hamburg 27 (1964) 13–31; 28 (1965) 219–233.

[53] H. Zieschang, Über Automorphismen ebener diskontinuierlicher Gruppen, Math. Ann. 166 (1966) 148–167.

[54] H. Zieschang, Über die Nielsensche Kürzungsmethode in freien Produkten mit Amalgam, Invent. Math. 10 (1970) 4–37.

S.I. Adian, W.W. Boone, G. Higman, eds., Word Problems II
© North-Holland Publishing Company (1980) 255–259

REPRESENTATIONS OF AUTOMORPHISM GROUPS OF FREE GROUPS

W. MAGNUS and C. TRETKOFF
Polytechnic Institute of New York, Couvart Institute of Mathematics, New York

Let F_n denote the free group of (finite) rank n, let A_n denote its automorphism group and A_n^* its group of automorphism classes, i.e., the quotient group A_n/I_n, where I_n is the group of inner automorphisms.

A finite-dimensional faithful linear representation of A_2^* over the complex numbers **C** is well known. In fact, $A_2^* = \mathrm{GL}(2, \mathbf{Z})$, the general linear group of degree 2 over the integers. No finite-dimensional faithful linear representations over any field are known for A_n^* if $n > 2$ or for A_2. We conjecture that they do not exist, but we have not been able to prove this. However, we shall contribute to the problem and we shall try to explain why it may deserve some interest.

We shall show first that it would suffice to prove our conjecture for A_2. We have

Theorem 1. *A_2 is isomorphic with a subgroup of A_n^* for all $n > 2$.*

Since $A_{n+1}^* \supset A_n^*$, it suffices to prove this for $n = 3$. Let a, b, c be free generators of F_3. Let α be an automorphism of F_2 with free generators a, b. Then α also acts on A_3 as an automorphism by defining $\alpha(c) = c$. But unless α is the identity automorphism, its action on A_3 is never that of an inner automorphism.

Next, we observe that the obvious methods for proving our conjecture do not apply. The groups A_n are residually finite according to a theorem of Baumslag. See [1]. The groups A_n^* are residually finite according to E. Grossman [2]. Therefore, Malcev's Theorem (see [4]) according to which finitely generated linear groups over a field are residually finite, cannot be used to prove our conjecture. The same remark applies to Selberg's Theorem [5] according to which a finitely generated finite-dimensional linear group over **C** has a torsion free subgroup of finite index. Indeed, this is most easily seen to be satisfied by A_2 which has a subgroup S of finite index with the following property: S is the extension of a free group I_2 of rank two (the group of inner automorphisms of F_2) by another free group of rank 2, namely the group generated by the elements represented by the matrices

$$\begin{pmatrix} 1 & 2 \\ 0 & 1 \end{pmatrix}, \quad \begin{pmatrix} 1 & 0 \\ 2 & 1 \end{pmatrix}$$

of $\mathrm{GL}(2, \mathbf{Z})$. This remark also shows that A_2 cannot contain "large" abelian subgroups the existence of which might contradict the existence of a linear representation. We now prove

Theorem 2. *If A_2 has a finite-dimensional faithful linear representation R over $\mathbf{C}$, then at least one of the irreducible components of R represents A_2 faithfully.*

Proof. Let R_λ, $\lambda = 1, \ldots, l$, be the irreducible components of R. (Of course, R need not be fully reducible, i.e., R need not be the direct sum of the R_λ.) Assume first that none of the R_λ represents I_2 faithfully, and let K_λ be the normal subgroup of I_2 represented by the identity in R_λ. Let (K_λ, K_μ) denote the normal subgroup generated by commutators of elements of K_λ with elements of K_μ. Then $(K_\lambda, K_\mu) \subset K_\lambda \cap K_\mu$. Since I_2 is free of rank 2, it follows that the intersection K of all of the K_λ is free of rank $\geqslant 2$. On the other hand, K would be represented in R by supertriangular matrices which would form a solvable group. Therefore R itself could not represent I_2 faithfully.

Suppose now that, in R_λ, an automorphism $\alpha \neq 1$ would be represented by the identity. Let $I(w)$ denote the inner automorphism which maps any element f in F_2 onto $w^{-1}fw$, where $w \in F_2$. Since

$$\alpha^{-1} I(w) \alpha = I(\alpha w)$$

where αw is the image of w in F_2 under the action of α, we would have that, in R_λ, the inner automorphism

$$I(\alpha w) I^{-1}(w) = I((\alpha w) w^{-1})$$

would be represented by the identity. This can happen only if I_2 is not represented faithfully in R_λ since there does not exist any automorphism $\alpha \neq 1$ which maps every $w \in F_2$ onto itself, and since the center of F_2 is trivial.

We shall now analyze the possibilities for unitary representations over $\mathbf{C}$ of A_2. We note that there exist such representations of finite quotient groups in which both the image of I_2 and of its quotient group are non-solvable. See Stork [6].

A presentation of A_2 can be given as follows:

Let x, y be free generators of the free group F_2. We present the group A_2 of its automorphisms as follows:

Generators. P_1, σ_1, σ_2, U, V, U^*, V^*, defined as:

$$P: x \to y,\ y \to x, \qquad \sigma_1: x \to x^{-1},\ y \to y,\ \sigma_2: x \to x,\ y \to y^{-1}.$$

$$U: x \to xy,\ y \to y, \qquad V: x \to yx,\ y \to y.$$

$$U^*: x \to x,\ y \to yx, \qquad V^*: x \to x,\ y \to xy.$$

If $w \in F_2$ is any word in x, y, the inner automorphism $I(w)$ is defined by

$$I(w): x \to w^{-1}xw,\ y \to w^{-1}yw.$$

We denote $I(x)$, $I(y)$ respectively by X, Y and we have

$$X = V^{*-1}U^*,\ Y = V^{-1}U. \tag{1}$$

For any $\alpha \in A_2$, we have

$$\alpha^{-1}I(w)\alpha = I(\alpha(w)) \tag{2}$$

where $\alpha(w)$ is the image of w under the action of α.

The defining relations for A_2 can be put into the form [3, p. 162]

$$P^2 = \sigma_1^2 = \sigma_2^2 = 1,\ \sigma_1\sigma_2 = \sigma_2\sigma_1,\ P\sigma_1P = \sigma_2 \tag{3}$$

$$PUP = U^*,\ PVP = V^* \tag{4}$$

$$\sigma_1U\sigma_1 = V^{-1},\ \sigma_2U^*\sigma_2 = V^{*-1} \tag{5}$$

$$\sigma_2U\sigma_2 = U^{-1},\ \sigma_1U^*\sigma_1 = U^{*-1} \tag{6}$$

$$\sigma_2V\sigma_2 = V^{-1},\ \sigma_1V^*\sigma_1 = V^{*-1} \tag{7}$$

$$U^{-1}U^*V^{-1} = \sigma_1P,\ UV^{*-1}V = \sigma_2P \tag{8}$$

$$UV = VU,\ U^*V^* = V^*U^*. \tag{9}$$

As an easy consequence of (1), (4), (8), we find

$$U^{-1}XU = XY, \tag{10}$$

a relation which also would be derived from (2) and from the definition of U.

To build up a unitary representation of A_2, we start with the maximal abelain subgroup generated by U and V. We can diagonalize U and V simultaneously and we may assume that U (which, according to (10), is conjugate with U^{-1}) has in its main diagonal successively in certain multiplicities the distinct eigenvalues

$$+1, -1, \lambda_1, \lambda_1^{-1}, \ldots, \lambda_r, \lambda_r^{-1}.$$

We call any matrix commuting with U an ω-matrix. An ω-matrix consists of blocks whose sizes equal the multiplicities of the respective eigenvalues. We call blocks belonging to eigenvalues λ_ζ and λ_ζ^{-1} ($\zeta = 1, \ldots, r$) "conjugate blocks."

By using the proof of Clifford's theorem on page 5 in [7], we find

Lemma 1. *The subgroup of* A_2 *generated by* U, V, σ_1, σ_2 *has unitary representations which can be put into monomial form, with* U, V, *in diagonal form. The permutation associated with the monomial matrix* σ_2 *exchanges conjugate blocks in any* ω*-matrix.*

Relations (10), (6), (7) show that

(11) $$X^{-1}UX = V = \sigma_1 U^{-1}\sigma_1 = \sigma_1\sigma_2 U \sigma_2^{-1}\sigma_1^{-1}.$$

Therefore

(12) $$X\sigma_1\sigma_2 = \Omega$$

is an ω-matrix, and by using (1), (5), (6) we find

(13) $$(X\sigma_1)^2 = (\Omega\sigma_2)^2 = \Omega^2 = 1.$$

These remarks prove

Lemma 2. *If* U *has simple eigenvalues in a unitary representation of* A_2, *then* X^2 *commutes with* U *(since* Ω *is diagonal) and therefore* (10) *shows that* $YXY = X$ *and that the representation cannot be faithful.*

We can sharpen Lemma 2. Let $\bar{\sigma}_1$ and $\bar{\sigma}_2$ be the permutations associated with the monomial matrices representing σ_1 and σ_2. Then we have

Theorem 3. *Let* Π *be the permutation group generated by* $\bar{\sigma}_1$, $\bar{\sigma}_2$ *and by the permutations* π *which exchange only eigenvalues of* U *which have the same value. If* Π *is imprimitive with the eigenspaces of* U *as a system of imprimitivity, then the unitary representation of* A_2 *is not faithful.*

It should be noted that the permutations π together with $\bar{\sigma}_2$ certainly generate an imprimitive group which satisfies the conditions of Theorem 3 and that $\bar{\sigma}_1$ commutes with $\bar{\sigma}_2$. That is, $\bar{\sigma}_2$ is given and $\bar{\sigma}_1$ is not entirely arbitrary.

Proof. We show that a system of imprimitivity of Π is also a system of imprimitivity for the group generated by X and Y. To see this, we observe that Ω is of order 2. Therefore the group ring generated by the unitary matrices σ_1, σ_2, Ω can also be generated by diagonal matrices and the matrices in Π. Therefore X is imprimitive if and only if Π has this property. But if a power of X commutes with U, we have, as in Lemma 2, a relation

$$X^m = (XY)^m$$

which cannot hold in a faithful representation since, in A_2, X and Y freely generate a free group.

Acknowledgment

Work on this paper was supported in part by a grant of the U.S. National Science Foundation.

References

[1] G. Baumslag, Automorphism groups of residually finite groups, Proc. London Math. Soc. 38 (1963) 117–118.
[2] E. Grossman, On the residual finiteness of certain mapping class groups, J. London Math. Soc. (2) 9 (1974) 160–164.
[3] W. Magnus, A. Karrass and D. Solitar, Combinatorial group theory (Dover Publications, 1976) pp. 162–165.
[4] A.I. Malcev, On the faithful representation of infinite groups by matrices, Amer. Math. Soc. Translations, Ser. 2, Vol. 45 (1965) 1–18.
[5] A. Selberg, On discontinuous groups in higher dimensional symmetric spaces, Int. Colloq. Function Theory, Tata Inst. Fundamental Res., Bombay (1964) pp. 147–164.
[6] D. Stork, Structure and applications of Schreier coset graphs, Comm. Pure Appl. Mat. 24 (1971) 797–805.
[7] B.A.F. Wehrfritz, Infinite linear groups (Springer Verlag, New York, 1973).

S.I. Adian, W.W. Boone, G. Higman, eds., Word Problems II

ON REDUCIBLE BRAIDS

James McCOOL*

Dept. of Mathematics, University of Toronto, Toronto, Canada

§I. Introduction

The Braid Group B_n ($n \geq 1$) may be defined as the abstract group on the generators $\sigma_1, \sigma_2, \ldots, \sigma_{n-1}$ with defining relations

$$\sigma_i\sigma_j = \sigma_j\sigma_i \qquad \text{if } |i-j| \geq 2,\ 1 \leq i, j \leq n-1 \tag{1.1}$$

and

$$\sigma_i\sigma_{i+1}\sigma_i = \sigma_{i+1}\sigma_i\sigma_{i+1}, \qquad 1 \leq i \leq n-2. \tag{1.2}$$

We denote by $\mathcal{B}$ the set of all ordered pairs (β, r), where r is a positive integer and β is a word on the generators $\sigma_1, \sigma_2, \ldots, \sigma_{r-1}$ and their inverses, and we call $\mathcal{B}$ the set of (algebraic) *braids.*

In [1] J. Birman has defined a braid (β, r) to be *reducible* if β is conjugate in B_r to an element of the form $\gamma\sigma_{r-1}^{\pm 1}$, where γ is a word on $\sigma_1^{\pm 1}, \ldots, \sigma_{r-2}^{\pm 1}$, and has asked how one can recognise, given a braid (β, r), whether or not it is reducible.

The interest of this question stems from a result of Markov, which says that in order to provide an algorithm to determine, given any two links, whether or not they are combinatorially equivalent, it is sufficient to describe an algorithm to determine, given any two algebraic braids, whether or not they are combinatorially equivalent; here braids (β, r) and (β', r') are said to be *combinatorially equivalent* if there is a sequence of braids $(\beta, r) = (\beta_1, r_1), (\beta_2, r_2), \ldots, (\beta_s, r_s) = (\beta', r')$, such that each braid in the sequence can be obtained from its predecessor by applying one of the following operations:

$\mathcal{M}_1$ replace (β, r) by (γ, r) if β and γ represent conjugate elements of B_r,

$\mathcal{M}_2$ replace (β, r) by $(\beta\sigma_r^{\pm 1}, r+1)$, or, if $\beta = \mu\sigma_{r-1}^{\pm 1}$ in B_r, where μ is a word on $\sigma_1^{\pm 1}, \ldots, \sigma_{r-2}^{\pm 1}$, replace (β, r) by $(\mu, r-1)$.

* Research supported by a grant from the National Research Council of Canada.

A full account of Markov's result is given in [1]. The restricted question of finding an algorithm to determine when two given braids (β, r) and (γ, r) are equivalent under $\mathcal{M}_1$ operations, i.e. the conjugacy problem for B_r, has been solved by Garside [3]. The investigation of reducible braids would seem to be a natural next step in the study of the general problem of combinatorial equivalence of braids, since to say a braid (β, r) is reducible is to say that it is joined to a braid $(\gamma, r-1)$ by a single application of operation $\mathcal{M}_2$ (preceded by an application of $\mathcal{M}_1$).

The aim of this paper is to describe an algorithm to determine, given a braid (β, r), whether or not (β, r) is reducible. In addition, we shall show that if (β, r) is reducible to $(\gamma, r-1)$, i.e. if $\beta' = \gamma\sigma_{r-1}^{\pm 1}$ in B_r, for some conjugate β' of β, then γ must belong to a determinable, finite set of conjugacy classes of B_{r-1}.

§II. Statement of results

In order to state our results precisely, we begin with a brief description of some of the results obtained by Garside [3].

A word W on $\sigma_1^{\pm 1}, \ldots, \sigma_{n-1}^{\pm 1}$ is said to be *positive* if it is a word on $\sigma_1, \ldots, \sigma_{n-1}$ only, i.e. no inverse of any generator occurs in W. Of particular interest are the positive words

$$A_i \equiv \sigma_1\sigma_2 \cdots \sigma_i$$

and

$$\Delta_s \equiv A_{s-1}A_{s-2} \cdots A_1,$$

(where $\equiv$ denotes equality of words). When we are considering B_n, the words A_{n-1} and Δ_n will usually be denoted by A and Δ, respectively. A positive word P is said to be *prime* to Δ if there does not exist a positive word Q such that $P = \Delta Q$ in B_n. Garside showed that each element γ of B_n has an expression of the form $\gamma = \Delta^k P$ for some integer k and positive word P prime to Δ. Moreover, if $\Delta^{k_1}P_1$ is another such expression for γ, then $k = k_1$, and so $P = P_1$. The integer k is called the *power* of γ, and such an expression is called a *standard form* for γ.

For $\gamma \in B_n$ we denote by $\mathscr{C}_i(\gamma)$ the set of conjugates of γ of power i. Garside proved that $\mathscr{C}_i(\gamma)$ is finite for each i, that there is a maximum value of i, called the *summit power* of γ, such that $\mathscr{C}_i(\gamma)$ is non-empty, and that elements β, γ of B_n are conjugate if, and only if, they have the same summit power t and $\mathscr{C}_t(\gamma) = \mathscr{C}_t(\beta)$. Garside also provided an algorithm to determine, given $\gamma \in B_n$, the *summit set* $\mathscr{C}_t(\gamma)$ of γ.

We now observe that if r, s are integers such that $1 \leq r \leq s \leq n-1$ and $B_{r,s}$ is the subgroup of B_n generated by the set $\{\sigma_r, \sigma_{r+1}, \ldots, \sigma_s\}$, then it follows easily from the usual geometric definition of B_n that the map $\sigma_1 \to \sigma_r, \sigma_2 \to \sigma_{r+1}, \ldots, \sigma_{s-r+1} \to \sigma_s$ extends to an isomorphism from B_{s-r+2} to $B_{r,s}$ (this may also be established algebraically by noting that the case for $B_{1,n-2}$ was proved by Chow [2], and then using Garside's automorphism $\mathcal{R}$ of B_n, defined in III below, to derive the general case from this). This observation enables us to identify the groups $B_2, \ldots, B_{n-2}$ with the subgroups $B_{1,1}, \ldots, B_{1,n-2}$ of B_n, respectively.

We say that an element γ of B_n is *positively reducible* to $\gamma'\sigma_{n-1}$ if there is a conjugate γ' of γ such that $\gamma'\sigma_{n-1} \in B_{n-1}$. Our main result is

Theorem A. *Let $\gamma \in B_n$ be positively reducible to $\gamma'\sigma_{n-1}$, and let γ have summit power t. Then $t \leq -1$ and there is $\gamma_1 \in \mathcal{C}_{t-2}(\gamma) \cup \mathcal{C}_{t-1}(\gamma) \cup C_t(\gamma)$ such that $\gamma_1\sigma_{n-1} \in B_{n-1}$, and $\gamma_1\sigma_{n-1}$ is conjugate in B_{n-1} to $\gamma'\sigma_{n-1}$.*

Now given $\gamma \in B_n$ it is easy to see, by using Garside's results and Theorem 2–7 of [1], that the finite set $\mathcal{C}_{t-2}(\gamma) \cup \mathcal{C}_{t-1}(\gamma) \cup \mathcal{C}_t(\gamma)$ can be computed, and that it can be determined if any element γ_1 of this set is such that $\gamma_1\sigma_{n-1} \in B_{n-1}$. Thus, given $\gamma \in B_n$, it can be determined if γ is positively reducible; moreover, there is only a finite set of conjugacy classes of B_{n-1} containing an element of the form $\gamma'\sigma_{n-1}$, where γ' is a conjugate of γ, and this set can be determined.

If $\gamma \in B_n$ is such that $\gamma'\sigma_{n-1}^{-1} \in B_{n-1}$, for some conjugate $\gamma' = \beta\gamma\beta^{-1}$ of γ, we say that γ is *negatively reducible* to $\gamma'\sigma_{n-1}^{-1}$. Now $\beta\gamma\beta^{-1}\sigma_{n-1}^{-1} \in B_{n-1}$ if, and only if, $(\sigma_{n-1}\beta)\gamma^{-1}(\sigma_{n-1}\beta)^{-1}\sigma_{n-1} \in B_{n-1}$, i.e. γ is negatively reducible to $\gamma'\sigma_{n-1}^{-1}$ if, and only if, γ^{-1} is positively reducible to $(\gamma'\sigma_{n-1}^{-1})^{-1}$. Now obviously γ is reducible if, and only if, γ is either positively reducible or negatively reducible. We thus have

Corollary B. *Let $\gamma \in B_n$. Then it can be determined if γ is reducible. If γ is reducible and $\mathcal{C}$ is the set of conjugacy classes in B_{n-1} which contain elements to which γ is reducible, then $\mathcal{C}$ is finite, and can be determined.*

§III. Notation and preliminary results

Let U, V be words on $\sigma_1^{\pm 1}, \ldots, \sigma_{n-1}^{\pm 1}$. We write $U \equiv V$ if U and V are equal as words, $U = V$ if U and V represent the same element of B_n, $U \sim V$ if U and V represent conjugate elements of B_n.

If $P \equiv X_1X_2 \cdots X_t$ is any word, where each X_i is a generator or the inverse of a generator, then by the *reverse* of P, rev P, is meant the word $X_t X_{t-1} \cdots X_1$. We have rev $QP \equiv$ rev P rev Q.

We note that the mapping $\sigma_i \to \sigma_{n+1-i}$, $(1 \leqslant i \leqslant n-1)$, extends to an automorphism $\mathcal{R}$ of B_n of order two. We shall write $\hat{X}$ for $\mathcal{R}X$ when this notation is more convenient.

Let S_n be the abstract semigroup on $\sigma_1, \sigma_2, \ldots, \sigma_{n-1}$ with defining relations (1.1) and (1.2). We write $X \doteqdot Y$ to mean X and Y are positive words which represent the same element of S_n. We note that if $X \doteqdot Y$ then rev $X \doteqdot$ rev Y. If $X \doteqdot UV$ we say that X *begins* with the positive word U, and *ends* with the positive word V.

The *diagram* $D(W)$ of the positive word W is defined to be the set of positive words which can be obtained from W by a succession of applications of the operations

(3.1) replace a subword $\sigma_i\sigma_j$ by $\sigma_j\sigma_i$, if $|i-j| \geqslant 2$,

(3.2) replace a subword $\sigma_i\sigma_j\sigma_i$ by $\sigma_j\sigma_i\sigma_j$, if $|i-j| = 1$.

We note that $D(W)$ is finite, and consists of all positive words which are equal to W in S_n.

We have the following results, due to Garside [3].

Theorem 1. *S_n is embedded in B_n under the identity map on the generating set $\sigma_1, \ldots, \sigma_{n-1}$.*

Thus, for positive words X and Y, we have $X = Y$ if, and only if, $X \doteqdot Y$.

Lemma 2. *Let X, Y be positive words in B_n. If $\sigma_i X \doteqdot \sigma_k Y$, then*
(a) $X \doteqdot Y$ *if* $k = i$.
(b) $X \doteqdot \sigma_k Z$, $Y \doteqdot \sigma_i Z$, *for some* Z, *if* $|k-i| \geqslant 2$.
(c) $X \doteqdot \sigma_k\sigma_i Z$, $Y \doteqdot \sigma_i\sigma_k Z$, *for some* Z, *if* $|k-i| = 1$.
If $X\sigma_i \doteqdot Y\sigma_k$, *then*
(d) $X \doteqdot Y$ *if* $k = i$.
(e) $X \doteqdot Z\sigma_k$, $Y \doteqdot Z\sigma_i$, *for some* Z, *if* $|k-i| \geqslant 2$.
(f) $X \doteqdot Z\sigma_i\sigma_k$, $Y \doteqdot Z\sigma_k\sigma_i$, *for some* Z, *if* $|k-i| = 1$.

Lemma 3. *In* B_n,

$$\sigma_s A_t \doteqdot A_t \sigma_{s-1} \quad \text{if } 1 < s \leqslant t \leqslant n-1,$$

$$\sigma_s \hat{A}_t \doteqdot \hat{A}_t \sigma_{s+1} \quad \text{if } 1 \leqslant s < t \leqslant n-1.$$

Lemma 4. *Let $X_1, X_2, \ldots, X_t$ be generators of B_n which commute with σ_i, and such that no X_j is σ_i. We have*

(a) *If* $\sigma_i P \doteq X_1X_2\cdots X_tQ$, *then* Q *begins with* σ_i.
(b) *If* $P\sigma_i \doteq QX_1X_2\cdots X_t$, *then* Q *ends with* σ_i.

Lemma 5.
(a) *If* $\sigma_{i+1}P \doteq A_iQ$ *in* B_n, *then* Q *begins with* $\sigma_{i+1}\sigma_i$.
(b) *If* $P\sigma_{i+1} \doteq Q(\text{rev } A_i)$, *then* Q *ends with* $\sigma_i\sigma_{i+1}$.

Lemma 6. *In* B_n,
(a) $X\Delta = \Delta\hat{X}$, $\Delta X = \hat{X}\Delta$, *for any word* X.
(b) $\Delta = \hat{\Delta} = \text{rev } \Delta$.
(c) Δ *begins and ends with* σ_i, *for each* $i \in \{1, 2, \ldots, n-1\}$.
(d) *If* $r \leq n-1$ *and* W *is a positive word which begins (ends) with* σ_i, *for each* $i \in \{1, 2, \ldots, r\}$, *then* W *begins (ends) with* Δ_{r+1}.
(e) *If* $W \doteq \Delta V$ *and* $W \doteq PQ$, *then, for each* $i \in \{1, 2, \ldots, n-1\}$, *either* P *ends with* σ_i *or* Q *begins with* σ_i.
(f) *If* $\Delta \doteq IF$, *then for each* $i \in \{1, 2, \ldots, n-1\}$, *either* I *ends with* σ_i *or* F *begins with* σ_i, *but not both.*

The next result, due to Birman [1], is of great importance for our work.

Theorem 7. *Let* $\beta \equiv \Delta^m P$ *be in standard form in* B_n. *If* β *is not in summit form (i.e.* m *is less than the summit power of* β*) then there are positive words* I, F, R *with* $\Delta \doteq IF$, *such that*
(a) $P \doteq FRI$ *if* m *is even,*
(b) $P \doteq FR\hat{I}$ *if* m *is odd.*

We shall also need the following result from [1].

Lemma 8. *Let* $\Delta \doteq IF$. *Then* $\Delta \doteq F\hat{I} \doteq \hat{I}\hat{F} \doteq \hat{F}I$.

We now introduce two notational conventions which facilitate the statements of the results to follow.

Let i, j be non-negative integers. We define $\alpha(i;j)$ to be the product $\sigma_i\sigma_{i+1}\cdots\sigma_j$ if $1 \leq i \leq j \leq n-1$, and to be the identity element of B_n otherwise; $\beta(j;i)$ is defined to be the product $\sigma_j\sigma_{j-1}\cdots\sigma_i$ if $1 \leq i \leq j \leq n-1$, and to be the identity element otherwise.

We shall write $Q \equiv Q(r, s)$ to indicate that the word Q involves (at most) the generators $\sigma_r, \sigma_{r+1}, \ldots, \sigma_s$, where $1 \leq r \leq s \leq n-1$. In a context where we have established that $Q \equiv Q(r, s)$, and i is a positive integer such that $i + s - r \leq n-1$, we shall denote by $Q(i, i+s-r)$ the word obtained from Q by replacing $\sigma_r, \sigma_{r+1}, \ldots, \sigma_s$ by $\sigma_i, \sigma_{i+1}, \ldots, \sigma_{i+s-r}$

respectively, and by $Q(i+s-r, i)$ the word obtained from Q by replacing $\sigma_r, \sigma_{r+1}, \ldots, \sigma_s$ by $\sigma_{i+s-r}, \sigma_{i+s-r-1}, \ldots, \sigma_i$ respectively. For example, if $Q \equiv Q(r, s)$ then $\hat{Q}$ may be written as $Q(n-r, n-s)$, and if $s < n-1$ then we may write $AQ(r, s) = Q(r+1, s+1)A$.

Finally, in this section, we note that, in view of the isomorphism exhibited earlier from B_{s-r+2} to $B_{r,s}$, the results listed above may be applied to the subgroup $B_{r,s}$. To give just one example, we have $\Delta_{n-2} \equiv \Delta_{n-2}(1, n-3)$, and from (a) of Lemma 6 we have
$\sigma_i \Delta_{n-3}(2, n-3) \doteq \Delta_{n-3}(2, n-3)\sigma_{n-i-1}$, if $2 \leqslant i \leqslant n-3$.

§IV. Further preliminary results

We now obtain a number of results which are required for the proof of Theorem A.

Lemma 9. *Let X, Y be positive words in B_n with $X \doteq Y$. Then a generator σ_i occurs in X if, and only if, it occurs in Y.*

Proof. This follows immediately from the definition of $D(X)$.

Lemma 10. *Let i, r be integers with $1 \leqslant i \leqslant r \leqslant n-2$. We have*

(a) *If $P\alpha(i; r) \doteq Q\sigma_{r+1}$ in B_n, then $P \doteq Z\alpha(i; r+1)$, for some Z.*
(b) *If $\beta(r; i)P \doteq \sigma_{r+1}Q$ in B_n, then $P \doteq \beta(r+1; i)Z$, for some Z.*
(c) *If $P\beta(r+1; i+1) \doteq Q\sigma_i$ in B_n, then $P \doteq Z\beta(r+1; i)$, for some Z.*
(d) *If $\alpha(i+1; r+1)P \doteq \sigma_i Q$ in B_n, then $P \doteq \alpha(i, r+1)Z$, for some Z.*

Proof. We note that (b), (d) follows from (a), (c) respectively using the fact that $X \doteq Y$ implies rev $X \doteq$ rev Y, while (c) follows from (a) by applying the automorphism $\mathcal{R}$. Thus it is only necessary to prove (a).

We note that (a) is true if $r = i$, by part (f) of Lemma 2. We suppose that (a) holds for i, r as stated, with $r \leqslant n-3$, and that $P_1\alpha(i; r+1) \doteq Q_1\sigma_{r+2}$. Applying (f) of Lemma 2 again, we see that $P_1\alpha(i; r) \doteq Q_2\sigma_{r+1}\sigma_{r+2}$ and $Q_1 \doteq Q_2\sigma_{r+2}\sigma_{r+1}$, for some Q_2. Hence, by (b) of Lemma 4, we have $P_1 \doteq P_2\sigma_{r+2}$ for some P_2, and we then see that $P_2\alpha(i; r) \doteq Q_2\sigma_{r+1}$. It now follows, from our assumption that the result holds for i, r, that $P_2 \doteq Z\alpha(i, r+1)$ for some Z, so that
$P_1 \doteq Z\alpha(i; r+2)$, as required.

Lemma 11. *Let i, j, r be integers with $1 \leqslant i \leqslant j \leqslant r \leqslant n-1$.*

(a) *If $P\alpha(i; r) \doteq Q\sigma_j$, and $j < r$, then P ends in σ_{j+1}.*
(b) *If $P\beta(r; i) \doteq Q\sigma_j$, and $j > i$, then P ends in σ_{j-1}.*

(c) *If* $\alpha(i;r)P \doteq \sigma_j Q$, *and* $j > i$, *then* P *begins with* σ_{j-1}.
(d) *If* $\beta(r;i)P \doteq \sigma_j Q$, *and* $j < r$, *then* P *begins with* σ_{j+1}.

Proof. As in Lemma 10, we need only prove part (a). By Lemma 4, we have $Q \doteq Q_1\alpha(j+2;r)$ for some Q_1, so that $P\alpha(i;j+1) \doteq Q_1\sigma_j$. Hence, by Lemma 2, $P\alpha(i;j) \doteq P_1\sigma_{j+1}\sigma_j$ for some P_1, and so $P\alpha(i;j-1) \doteq P_1\sigma_{j+1}$. Applying Lemma 4 again, we see that P ends in σ_{j+1}, as required.

Corollary 12. *Let* W *be a positive word and* r *a non-negative integer.*
(a) *If* $WA\{\hat{A}A\}^r$ *ends in* σ_i *and* $1 \leq i < n-1$, *then* W *ends in* σ_{i+1}.
(b) *If* $W\{\hat{A}A\}^r$ *ends in* σ_i *and* $1 \leq i < n-1$, *then* W *ends in* σ_i.

Proof. These are immediate consequences of Lemma 11.

We note, comparing with Lemma 10, that each part of Corollary 12 has three variants obtained using the operations rev and $\mathcal{R}$. We leave it to the reader to state these variants.

Lemma 13. *Let* U, V, W *be positive words with* $W \doteq UV$. *Suppose that* U *ends only in* σ_{n-1}, $V \equiv V(1, n-2)$ *and* W *ends in* σ_i, *for some* $i \in \{1, 2, \ldots, n-2\}$. *Then* V *ends in* σ_i.

Proof. We must clearly have $L(V) \geq 1$, where $L(V)$ is the length of the word V. Now if each generator in V is distinct from, and commutes with the generator σ_i, then by Lemma 4, U ends in σ_i. Since this is not the case, we must have either V ends in σ_i, or $V \equiv V_1\sigma_{i+\varepsilon}V_2$, where $\varepsilon = \pm 1$ and each generator in V_2 is distinct from and commutes with σ_i.

In the latter case, we have $W \doteq UV_1\sigma_{i+\varepsilon}V_2 \doteq K\sigma_i$ say, and by Lemma 4 we see that $K \doteq K_1V_2$ for some K_1, so that $UV_1\sigma_{1+\varepsilon} \doteq K_1\sigma_i$. We then have, by Lemma 2, that $UV_1 \doteq K_2\sigma_{1+\varepsilon}\sigma_i$, for some K_2. Now if $L(V) = 1$, then $V_1 = 1$ and U must end in σ_i, which is a contradiction. Hence $L(V) > 1$ and we have, inductively, that V_1 ends in σ_i, $V_1 \doteq V_3\sigma_i$ say.

We now have $UV_3 \doteq K_2\sigma_{i+\varepsilon}$, and $i + \varepsilon \neq n-1$, since $\sigma_{i+\varepsilon}$ occurs in V. Hence, inductively, V_3 must end in $\sigma_{i+\varepsilon}$, $V_3 \doteq V_4\sigma_{i+\varepsilon}$ say. We then have $V \equiv V_1\sigma_{i+\varepsilon}V_2 \doteq V_4\sigma_{i+\varepsilon}\sigma_i\sigma_{i+\varepsilon}V_2 \doteq V_4\sigma_i\sigma_{i+\varepsilon}V_2\sigma_i$, as required.

We leave it to the reader to state the three variants of Lemma 13 obtained using rev and $\mathcal{R}$.

Lemma 14. *Let W be a subword of $\{A\hat{A}\}^m$, $m > 0$. Then $D(W) = W$.*

Proof. This follows immediately from the definition of $D(W)$.

As a consequence of Lemma 14, we note that $A\{\hat{A}A\}^r$ $(r \geqslant 0)$ begins only with σ_1 and ends only with σ_{n-1}.

Lemma 15. *Let X, Y be positive words in B_n.*

(a) *If $XY \doteq \alpha(2; n-1)\alpha(1; n-2)$, then for some k, j with $0 \leqslant j \leqslant n-2$, $1 \leqslant k \leqslant n-1$ and $k - j \geqslant 1$, we have*

$$X \doteq \alpha(2; k)\alpha(1; j), \qquad Y \doteq \alpha(k+1; n-1)\alpha(j+1; n-2).$$

(b) *If $XY \doteq \beta(n-2; 1)\beta(n-1; 2)$, then for some k, j with $2 \leqslant k \leqslant n$, $1 \leqslant j \leqslant n-1$ and $k - j \geqslant 1$, we have*

$$X \doteq \beta(n-2; j)\beta(n-1; k), \qquad Y \doteq \beta(j-1; 1)\beta(k-1; 2).$$

Proof. We need only prove part (a). We let $\mathcal{D}$ be the set of words of the form $U_1V_1U_2V_2 \cdots U_sV_s$, where $s \leqslant n-2$ and

$$U_1U_2 \cdots U_s \equiv \alpha(2; n-1), \qquad V_1V_2 \cdots V_s \equiv \alpha(1; n-2),$$

$$U_i \equiv \alpha(\lambda_i; \lambda_{i+1} - 1), \qquad V_j \equiv \alpha(\mu_j; \mu_{j+1} - 1),$$

for $1 \leqslant i \leqslant s$, with $2 = \lambda_1 < \lambda_2 < \cdots < \lambda_{s+1} = n$, $1 = \mu_1 < \mu_2 < \cdots < \mu_{s+1} = n-1$, and

$$\lambda_{i+1} - (\mu_{i+1} - 1) \geqslant 2 \qquad (i = 1, 2, \ldots, s). \tag{4.1}$$

We claim that $\mathcal{D}$ is the diagram of $W \equiv \alpha(2; n-1)\alpha(1; n-2)$. We note firstly, from (4.1), that $U_iV_j \doteq V_jU_i$ whenever $1 \leqslant j \leqslant i-1$. Thus, if $U_1V_1 \cdots U_sV_s$ is in $\mathcal{D}$, then

$$U_1V_1 \cdots U_sV_s \doteq U_1U_2 \cdots U_sV_1V_2 \cdots V_s \equiv W,$$

so that $\mathcal{D} \subset D(W)$. Now if $Z \in \mathcal{D}$ it clear that no operation of type (3.1) can be applied to Z, while any application of (3.2) to Z will result in an element of $\mathcal{D}$. It follows that $\mathcal{D} = D(W)$.

Hence if $W \doteq XY$, then there is an element $U_1V_1 \cdots U_sV_s$ of $\mathcal{D}$ such that $XY \equiv U_1V_1 \cdots U_sV_s$, and the result follows easily from this.

Lemma 16. *Let P be a positive word in B_n, with P prime to Δ. Then $P\sigma_{n-1}$ has power zero or one, and the latter occurs if, and only if, P ends in $\alpha(2; n-1)\Delta_{n-1}$.*

Proof. Suppose $P\sigma_{n-1}$ has power at least one, $P\sigma_{n-1} \doteq S\Delta$ say. Then, by

(e) of Lemma 6, P ends in each of $\sigma_1, \sigma_2, \ldots, \sigma_{n-2}$, so that by (d) of Lemma 6, P ends in Δ_{n-1}, $P \doteq Q\Delta_{n-1}$ say. Thus $Q\Delta_{n-1}\sigma_{n-1} \doteq S\Delta$, and using Lemma 8, we have $Q\Delta_{n-1}\sigma_{n-1} \doteq S\alpha(2; n-1)\Delta_{n-1}\sigma_{n-1}$, so that $Q \doteq S\alpha(2; n-1)$. Hence P ends in $\alpha(2; n-1)\Delta_{n-1}$, as required.

Conversly, if $P \doteq Z\alpha(2; n-1)\Delta_{n-1}$ then $P\sigma_{n-1} \doteq Z\Delta$. Now Z cannot contain Δ, since P is prime to Δ, and therefore $P\sigma_{n-1}$ has power one. This proves the Lemma.

Lemma 17. *Let Q be a positive word, and r a non-negative integer. We have:*

(a) *$\{A\hat{A}\}^r AQ$ contains Δ if, and only if, Q begins with Δ_{n-1}.*
(b) *$\{\hat{A}A\}^r \hat{A}Q$ contains Δ if, and only if, Q begins with $\hat{\Delta}_{n-1}$.*

Proof. Part (b) follows easily from (a) and the observation that a positive word P contains Δ if, and only if, $\hat{P}$ contains Δ.

To prove (a), we observe firstly that if Q begins with Δ_{n-1} then $Q \doteq \Delta_{n-1}Q_1$ say, and $\Delta = A\Delta_{n-1}$, so that $\{A\hat{A}\}^r AQ$ contains Δ.

Conversely, suppose that $W \equiv \{A\hat{A}\}^r AQ$ contains Δ, so that W begins with each of $\sigma_2, \sigma_3, \ldots, \sigma_{n-1}$. Using (a variant of) Corollary 12, we see that Q must begin with each of $\sigma_1, \sigma_2, \ldots, \sigma_{n-2}$, and so Q begins with Δ_{n-1}.

Lemma 18. *Let V be a positive word such that some generator σ_i does not occur in V. Then $\Delta^r V$ has summit power r, for each integer r.*

Proof. We know, by Lemma 9, that V cannot contain Δ, so that $\Delta^r V$ is in standard form. Suppose that $\Delta^r V$ has summit power greater than r. Then, by Theorem 7 there exist positive words I, F, Y with $\Delta \doteq IF$ and $V \doteq FYI^*$, where $I^* \equiv I$ if r is even, $I^* \equiv \hat{I}$ if r is odd. Since σ_i does not occur in V, it does not occur in F or I^*. However, we have $\Delta \doteq I^*F$ if r is even, and, by Lemma 8, $\Delta \doteq FI^*$ if r is odd. Since σ_i occurs in Δ, we obtain a contradiction from Lemma 9.

Lemma 19. *Suppose that $WV(2, n-1) \doteq U\beta(s; 1)$ in B_n, where $0 \leq s \leq n-1$, and let r be the greatest integer such that W ends in $\beta(r; 1)$, $W \doteq W_1\beta(r; 1)$ say. Then there exists $l \geq 0$, with $s + l \leq r$, and positive words $H_i \equiv H_i(2, s+i-1)$, $K_i \equiv K_i(s+i+1, n-1)$, $1 \leq i \leq l+1$, such that*

$$V \doteq H_{l+1}K_{l+1}\sigma_{s+l}H_lK_l\sigma_{s+l-1} \cdots H_2K_2\sigma_{s+1}H_1K_1$$

and

$$U \doteq W_1\beta(r; s+l+1)H'_{l+1}K_{l+1}\sigma_{s+l-1}H'_lK_l\sigma_{s+l-2}\sigma_{s+l-1} \cdots H'_2K_2\sigma_s\sigma_{s+1}H'_1K_1,$$

where $H'_i \equiv H_i(1, s+i-2)$, and $H_i = 1$ if $2 > s+i-1$.

Proof. If $s = 0$ then we may take $l = 0$, $H_1 = 1$ and $K_1 \equiv V$. Thus we may assume that $s \geqslant 1$.

We consider firstly the case that some word in $D(V)$ is of the form $H_1(2, s)K_1(s+2, n-1)$. It then follows from Lemma 4 that $U \mathrel{\dot{=}} U_1K_1$ for some U_1, so that $WH_1 \mathrel{\dot{=}} U_1\beta(s;1)$. Now applying Lemma 11(b), we see that $U_1 \mathrel{\dot{=}} TH_1(1, s-1)$, for some T. Hence $W \mathrel{\dot{=}} T\beta(s;1)$, and the result holds with $l = 0$.

We now suppose that no element of $D(V)$ is of the form H_1K_1, with H_1K_1 as above. It follows that there must be a word in $D(V)$ of the form $V_1(2, n-1)\sigma_{s+1}H_1(2, s)K_1(s+2, n-1)$. As in the previous case, we then see that $U \mathrel{\dot{=}} U_1H_1'K_1$, for some U_1, so that $WV_1\sigma_{s+1} \mathrel{\dot{=}} U_1\beta(s;1)$. From Lemma 5(b) we now obtain $U_1 \mathrel{\dot{=}} U_2\sigma_s\sigma_{s+1}$, for some U_2, so that $U_1\beta(s;1) \mathrel{\dot{=}} U_2\sigma_s\sigma_{s+1}\beta(s;1) \mathrel{\dot{=}} U_2\beta(s+1;1)\sigma_{s+1}$, and therefore $WV_1 \mathrel{\dot{=}} U_1\beta(s+1;1)$. Since $L(V_1) < L(V)$ an inductive argument now completes the proof of the Lemma.

Corollary 20. *Suppose that $\beta(r;1)V(2, n-1) \mathrel{\dot{=}} U\beta(s;1)$, where $1 \leqslant r$, $s \leqslant n-1$. Then $s \leqslant r$ and $\Delta^{-1}U$ has summit power -1.*

Proof. From the Lemma we have $s + l \leqslant r$ and

$$
\begin{aligned}
U &\mathrel{\dot{=}} \beta(r; s+l+1)H_{l+1}'K_{l+1}\sigma_{s+l-1}\sigma_{s+l}\cdots H_2'K_2\sigma_s\sigma_{s+1}H_1'K_1 \\
&\mathrel{\dot{=}} \beta(r; s+l+1)H_{l+1}'\sigma_{s+l-1}\sigma_{s+l}H_l'\cdots H_2'\sigma_s\sigma_{s+1}H_1'K_{l+1}K_l\cdots K_1 \\
&\mathrel{\dot{=}} H_{l+1}'\sigma_{s+l-1}H_l'\sigma_{s+l-2}\cdots H_2'\sigma_sH_1'\beta(r; s+1)K_{l+1}K_l\cdots K_1.
\end{aligned}
$$

Now writing $Z_1 \equiv H_{l+1}'\sigma_{s+l-1}H_l'\sigma_{s+l-2}\cdots H_2'\sigma_sH_1'$, and $Z_2 \equiv \beta(r; s+1)K_{l+1}K_l\cdots K_1$, we have $U \mathrel{\dot{=}} Z_1Z_2$. Noting that $Z_1 = Z_1(1, n-2)$, $Z_2 = Z_2(2, n-1)$, since $1 \leqslant r$, $s \leqslant n-1$ and $s + l \leqslant r$, we see that $Z_2\hat{Z}_1$ is a positive word on $\sigma_2, \ldots, \sigma_{n-1}$. Since $\Delta^{-1}Z_2\hat{Z}_1$ is conjugate to $\Delta^{-1}U$, it follows from Lemma 18 that $\Delta^{-1}U$ has summit power -1.

We pause to observe that B_n is the trivial group if $n = 1$, and is infinite cyclic if $n = 2$. From this, it is easy to see directly that Theorem A holds if $n = 2$. We shall therefore assume, in what follows, that $n \geqslant 3$.

Lemma 21. *Let r be a positive integer. Then*

(a) *Δ_{n-1}^{r} is in standard form in B_n.*
(b) *$\Delta^{-2r+1}\{A\hat{A}\}^{r-1}A$ is the standard form of Δ_{n-1}^{-2r+1} in B_n.*
(c) *$\Delta^{-2r}\{\hat{A}A\}^{r}$ is the standard form of Δ_{n-1}^{-2r} in B_n.*

Proof. Part (a) follows immediately from Lemma 9. Now if k is a positive integer, it is easy to prove, by induction on k, that

$$\Delta^k \doteq \left\{\prod_{i=k-1}^{0} \mathcal{R}^i(A)\right\} \Delta_{n-1}^k,$$

and therefore

$$\Delta_{n-1}^{-k} = \Delta^{-k}\left\{\prod_{i=k-1}^{0} \mathcal{R}^i(A)\right\}.$$

Now $\Pi_{i=k-1}^{0} \mathcal{R}^i(A)$ is prime to Δ, by Lemma 17, and this proves the result.

Lemma 22. *Let P be a positive word in B_n which is prime to Δ, and let r be a positive integer. Then:*

(a) *$P \in B_{n-1}$ if, and only if, σ_{n-1} does not occur in P.*

(b) *$\Delta^r P$ does not belong to B_{n-1}.*

(c) *$\Delta^{-2r} P \in B_{n-1}$ if, and only if, $P \doteq \{A\hat{A}\}^r Q$, where Q is a positive word in B_{n-1} which is prime to Δ_{n-1}. Moreover, if P has this form, then $\Delta_{n-1}^{-2r} Q$ is a standard form of $\Delta^{-2r} P$ in B_{n-1}.*

(d) *$\Delta^{-2r+1} P \in B_{n-1}$ if, and only if, $P \doteq \{A\hat{A}\}^{r-1} AQ$, where Q is as in (c). Moreover, if P has this form then $\Delta_{n-1}^{-2r+1} Q$ is a standard form of $\Delta^{-2r+1} P$ in B_{n-1}.*

Proof. Suppose that, for some integers k and s, we have $\Delta^k P = \Delta_{n-1}^s Q$, where Q is as in (c). If not both $k < 0$ and $s < 0$ hold, then it is easy to obtain a contradiction, using Lemma 9 and the fact that P is prime to Δ. In particular, this establishes (a) and (b).

Now suppose that $\Delta^k P = \Delta_{n-1}^s Q$, with $k, s < 0$. Then $\Delta^k P = \Delta^s\{\Pi_{i=-s-1}^{0} \mathcal{R}^i(A)\}Q$, and from Lemma 17 it follows that the right-side of this equality is in standard form. Hence we must have $P \doteq \{\Pi_{i=-s-1}^{0} \mathcal{R}^i(A)\}Q$, as required. Conversely, if P has this form then $\Delta^s P = \Delta_{n-1}^s Q$. This proves the Lemma.

§V. Proof of Theorem A

The theorem is an immediate consequence of the following two Lemmas.

Lemma 23. *Suppose that $\Delta^{-2r-1} M$ is in standard form in B_n ($r \geq 0$), and $\Delta^{-2r-1} M\sigma_{n-1} \in B_{n-1}$. Let t be the summit power of $\Delta^{-2r-1} M$. We have:*

(a) *$t = -1$ if $r = 0$.*

(b) *If* $r \geq 1$ *then either* $t \leq -2r+1$, *or there is a conjugate* $\Delta^{-2r}M_1$ *of* $\Delta^{-2r-1}M$ *such that* $\Delta^{-2r}M_1$ *is in standard form,* $\Delta^{-2r}M_1\sigma_{n-1} \in B_{n-1}$ *and* $\Delta^{-2r}M_1\sigma_{n-1}$ *is conjugate to* $\Delta^{-2r-1}M\sigma_{n-1}$ *in* B_{n-1}.

Lemma 24. *Suppose that* $\Delta^{-2r}M$ *is in standard form in* B_n $(r \geq 1)$, *and* $\Delta^{-2r}M\sigma_{n-1} \in B_{n-1}$. *Let t be the summit power of* $\Delta^{-2r}M$. *We have*:

(a) $t \leq -1$ *if* $r = 1$.

(b) *If* $r \geq 2$ *then either* $t \leq -2r+2$, *or there is a conjugate* $\Delta^{-2r+1}M_1$ *of* $\Delta^{-2r}M$ *such that* $\Delta^{-2r+1}M_1$ *is in standard form,* $\Delta^{-2r+1}M_1\sigma_{n-1} \in B_{n-1}$ *and* $\Delta^{-2r+1}M_1\sigma_{n-1}$ *is conjugate to* $\Delta^{-2r}M\sigma_{n-1}$ *in* B_{n-1}.

In order to prove Lemma 23, we shall require the following two results.

Lemma 25. *Let* $\mu \equiv \Delta^{-2r}\hat{A}\{A\hat{A}\}^{r-1}V(2, n-1)$ *be in standard form in* B_n $(r \geq 1)$, *and suppose that* μ *has summit power* $t > -2r$. *Then*

(a) $t = -1$ *if* $r = 1$.

(b) *If* $r \geq 2$ *we have* $V(2, n-1) \doteq X(3, n-1)V_1(2, n-1)Y(2, n-2)$ *for some* X, Y, V_1 *with* $Y(2, n-2)X(2, n-2) \doteq \Delta_{n-2}(2, n-2)$. *Also,* $\mu \sim \Delta^{-2r+1}\hat{A}\{A\hat{A}\}^{r-2}\sigma_1 V_1(2, n-1)$, *and the latter word has power* $-2r+1$.

Lemma 26. *Let* $\phi \equiv \Delta^{-2r+1}\hat{A}\{A\hat{A}\}^{r-2}\sigma_1 V_1(2, n-1)$ *be in standard form in* B_n $(r \geq 2)$, *and suppose that* ϕ *has summit power* $t > -2r+1$. *Then* $V_1(2, n-1)$ *ends with* $\alpha(2, n-1)$.

The proofs of Lemmas 25 and 26 will be given after that of Lemma 23. Similarly, the following two results will be required for the proof of Lemma 24, and their proofs will be given after that of Lemma 24.

Lemma 27. *Let* $\mu \equiv \Delta^{-2r+1}\{A\hat{A}\}^{r-1}V(2, n-1)$ *be in standard form in* B_n $(r \geq 2)$, *and suppose that* μ *has summit power* $t > -2r+1$. *Then* $V(2, n-1) \doteq X(2, n-2)V_1(2, n-1)Y(2, n-2)$ *for some* X, Y, V_1 *with* $\hat{Y}X \doteq \Delta_{n-2}(2, n-2)$. *Also,* $\mu \sim \Delta^{-2r+2}\{\hat{A}A\}^{r-2}\sigma_{n-1}V_1(1, n-2)$, *and the latter word has power* $-2r+2$.

Lemma 28. *Let* $\phi \equiv \Delta^{-2r+2}\{\hat{A}A\}^{r-2}\sigma_{n-1}V_1(1, n-2)$ *be in standard form in* B_n $(r \geq 2)$, *and suppose that* ϕ *has summit power* $t > -2r+2$. *Then* $V_1(1, n-2)$ *ends with* $\alpha(1; n-2)$, *and* $t = -1$ *if* $r = 2$.

We now give the proofs of these Lemmas.

Proof of Lemma 23. Suppose that $\Delta^{-2r-1}M$ is in standard form in B_n ($r \geq 0$), and that $\Delta^{-2r-1}M\sigma_{n-1} \in B_{n-1}$. We suppose, moreover, that $\Delta^{-2r-1}M$ has summit power $t > -2r-1$.

The plan of the proof is as follows. We begin by establishing that $\Delta^{-2r-1}M\sigma_{n-1}$ has power $-2r-1$. We then have, by Lemma 22, $M\sigma_{n-1} \doteq \{A\hat{A}\}^r AQ(1, n-2)$, for some Q which is prime to Δ_{n-1}. Since $t > -2r-1$ we also have, by Theorem 7, $M \doteq FR\hat{I}$ for some F, R, I with $IF \doteq \Delta$, so that $FR\hat{I}\sigma_{n-1} \doteq \{A\hat{A}\}^r AQ(1, n-2)$. We are then able, using the results of the previous sections, to analyse the contributions that $Q(1, n-2)$ makes to F and $\hat{I}$ respectively, and this in turn gives us a description of R. Now $\Delta^{-2r-1}M = \Delta^{-2r-1}FR\hat{I} \sim \Delta^{-2r}R$, and the description obtained for R enables us to complete the proof.

As was noted above, since $t > -2r-1$ we have $M \doteq FR\hat{I}$, where $IF \doteq \Delta$. Also, $\Delta^{-2r-1}FR\hat{I} \sim \Delta^{-2r}R$, and $\Delta^{-2r}R$ has power $-2r$, since R is prime to Δ. We note, by Lemma 16, that $\Delta^{-2r-1}M\sigma_{n-1}$ has power $-2r-1$ or $-2r$. We suppose that its power is $-2r$, and consider firstly the case $r > 0$. Since $\Delta^{-2r-1}M\sigma_{n-1} \in B_{n-1}$, we then have, by Lemma 22, that $FR\hat{I}\sigma_{n-1} \doteq \Delta\{\hat{A}A\}^r Q(1, n-2)$, where Q is prime to Δ_{n-1}. Hence, by Lemma 3, $FR\hat{I}\sigma_{n-1} \doteq \Delta Q(1, n-2)\{\hat{A}A\}^r$. However, since A ends in σ_{n-1}, this would imply that $FR\hat{I}$ contains Δ, which is not the case. Thus $\Delta^{-2r-1}M\sigma_{n-1}$ has power $-2r-1$ if $r > 0$. Now suppose $r = 0$ and $\Delta^{-1}FR\hat{I}\sigma_{n-1}$ has power zero. From Lemma 16 it follows that $FR\hat{I} \doteq S\alpha(2; n-1)\Delta_{n-1}$, so that, in particular, $FR\hat{I}$ ends with each of $\sigma_1, \sigma_2, \ldots, \sigma_{n-2}$. It follows that $\hat{I}$ cannot end with σ_{n-1}, since otherwise, by Lemma 6, $FR\hat{I}$ would contain Δ. Now $\Delta \doteq IF$, so that, by Lemma 6, F must begin with σ_1. We have $\Delta^{-1}FR\hat{I}\sigma_{n-1} = Q(1, n-2)$, where Q is a positive word, and therefore

$$\begin{aligned}
FR\hat{I}\sigma_{n-1} &\doteq \Delta Q(1, n-2) \doteq \alpha(1; n-1)\Delta_{n-1}Q(1; n-2) \\
&\doteq \hat{\Delta}_{n-1}\alpha(1; n-1)Q(1, n-2) \\
&\doteq \hat{\Delta}_{n-1}Q(2, n-1)\alpha(1; n-1),
\end{aligned}$$

so that $FR\hat{I} \doteq \hat{\Delta}_{n-1}Q(2, n-1)\alpha(1; n-2)$. Now $\hat{\Delta}_{n-1}$ begins with each of $\sigma_2, \sigma_3, \ldots, \sigma_{n-1}$, so that $FR\hat{I}$ begins with each of $\sigma_1, \sigma_2, \ldots, \sigma_{n-1}$ and hence contains Δ. This contradicts the fact that M is prime to Δ. Thus we have established that $\Delta^{-2r-1}M\sigma_{n-1}$ has power $-2r-1$.

Since $\Delta^{-2r-1}FR\hat{I}\sigma_{n-1} \in B_{n-1}$ and has power $-2r-1$, we have, by Lemma 22, that $FR\hat{I}\sigma_{n-1} \doteq \{A\hat{A}\}^r AQ(1, n-2)$, where Q is prime to Δ_{n-1}. Hence $FR\hat{I}\sigma_{n-1} \doteq \{A\hat{A}\}^r Q(2, n-1)A$, so that

(5.1) $$FR\hat{I} \doteq \{A\hat{A}\}^r Q(2, n-1)\alpha(1; n-2).$$

We now observe that if $FR\hat{I}$ begins with some σ_i ($i > 1$), then, by (a variant of) Corollary 12, $Q(2, n-1)\alpha(1; n-2)$ must begin with σ_i, and hence, by (a variant of) Lemma 13, $Q(2, n-1)$ must begin with σ_i. Also, if $FR\hat{I}$ ends with some σ_i ($i < n-2$) then, by Lemma 11, $\{A\hat{A}\}'$ must end with σ_{i+1}, so that, by Lemma 13, $Q(2, n-1)$ must end with σ_{i+1}.

We now write $F \doteq F_1F_2$, where $F_1 \equiv F_1(2, n-1)$ and F_2 does not begin with any of $\sigma_2, \sigma_3, \ldots, \sigma_{n-1}$. We also write $I \doteq I_1I_2$, where $I_2 \equiv I_2(3, n-1)$ and I_1 does not end with any of $\sigma_3, \sigma_4, \ldots, \sigma_{n-1}$. From the observations of the preceding paragraph we see, firstly, that $Q(2, n-1) \doteq F_1Q_1(2, n-1)$ for some $Q_1 \equiv Q_1(2, n-1)$, and secondly, since $\hat{I}_2 \doteq I_2(n-3, 1)$, that $Q_1 \doteq Q_2(2, n-1)I_2(n-2, 2)$ for some $Q_2 \equiv Q_2(2, n-1)$. Thus we have

$$Q(2, n-1) \doteq F_1(2, n-1)Q_2(2, n-1)I_2(n-2, 2).$$

We can now write (5.1) as

$$F_2R\hat{I}_1 \doteq \{A\hat{A}\}'Q_2(2, n-1)\alpha(1; n-2). \tag{5.2}$$

In order to 'solve' this equation for R, we seek descriptions of F_2 and I_1. We begin with F_2.

We have

$$\Delta \doteq IF_1F_2 \doteq \hat{I}\hat{F}_1\hat{F}_2 \doteq U\Delta_{n-1}\hat{F}_2$$

for some U, since $\hat{I}\hat{F}_1$ ends with each of $\sigma_1, \sigma_2, \ldots, \sigma_{n-2}$, and therefore ends with Δ_{n-1}. Hence

$$\Delta \doteq \Delta_{n-1}\hat{F}_2\hat{U} \doteq \Delta_{n-1}\beta(n-1; 1),$$

so that $\hat{F}_2\hat{U} \doteq \beta(n-1; 1)$, and therefore we have $F_2 \doteq \alpha(1; l)$ and $U \doteq \alpha(l+1; n-1)$, for some l with $0 \leq l \leq n-1$.

We now consider I_1. Since I_1 does not end with any of $\sigma_3, \sigma_4, \ldots, \sigma_{n-1}$, we know that either (a) $\hat{I}_1$ ends with both σ_{n-2} and σ_{n-1}, or (b) $\hat{I}_1$ ends only with σ_{n-1}, or (c) $I_1 = 1$, or (d) $\hat{I}_1$ ends only with σ_{n-2}. We shall consider each of these four cases separately, and show that the Lemma holds in each case.

Case (*a*). $\hat{I}_1$ ends with both σ_{n-2} and σ_{n-1}. We have

$$\Delta \doteq I_1I_2F \doteq \hat{I}_1\hat{I}_2\hat{F} \doteq \hat{I}_1\Delta_{n-2}X$$

for some X, since $\hat{I}_2\hat{F}$ begins with each of $\sigma_1, \sigma_2, \ldots, \sigma_{n-3}$. Hence

$$\Delta \doteq \hat{X}\hat{I}_1\Delta_{n-2} \doteq \alpha(1; n-1)\alpha(1; n-2)\Delta_{n-2},$$

so that $\hat{X}\hat{I}_1 \doteq \alpha(1; n-1)\alpha(1; n-2)$. Since $\hat{I}_1$ ends in both σ_{n-1} and σ_{n-2}, we have $\hat{I}_1 = V\sigma_{n-2}\sigma_{n-1}\sigma_{n-2}$ for some V, so that

$$\hat{X}\hat{I}_1 \doteq \hat{X}V\sigma_{n-2}\sigma_{n-1}\sigma_{n-2} \doteq \alpha(1; n-1)\alpha(1; n-2)$$
$$\doteq \alpha(2; n-2)\alpha(1; n-2)\sigma_{n-2},$$

and therefore $\hat{X}V \doteq \alpha(2; n-2)\alpha(1; n-3)$. Applying Lemma 15(a) (with $n-1$ in place of n) we obtain $\hat{X} \doteq \alpha(2; k)\alpha(1; j)$ and $V \doteq \alpha(k+1; n-2)\alpha(j+1; n-3)$ for some k, j with $0 \leqslant j \leqslant n-3$, $1 \leqslant k \leqslant n-2$ and $k - j \geqslant 1$. Hence $\hat{I}_1 \doteq \alpha(k+1; n-2)\alpha(j+1; n-1)\sigma_{n-2}$.

Before using the descriptions obtained for F_2 and I_1 to study (5.2), we obtain a description of $I_2(3, n-1)F_1(2, n-1)$. This will be used firstly to show that $l = j$, and then will be used again later in the proof of the Lemma for case (a). We have

$$\Delta \doteq I_2F_1F_2\hat{I}_1 \doteq \hat{X}\hat{I}_1\Delta_{n-2} \doteq \hat{\Delta}_{n-2}\alpha(2; k)\alpha(1; j)\hat{I}_1,$$

so that

$$(5.3) \qquad I_2(3, n-1)F_1(2, n-1)\alpha(1; l) \doteq \Delta_{n-2}(3, n-1)\alpha(2; k)\alpha(1; j),$$

since $\hat{\Delta}_{n-2} \doteq \Delta_{n-2}(n-1, 3) \doteq \Delta_{n-2}(3, n-1)$. We wish to show that $l = j$ and that

$$(5.4) \qquad I_2(3, n-1)F_1(2, n-1) \doteq \Delta_{n-2}(3, n-1)\alpha(2; k).$$

Suppose, firstly, that $l = 0$. Then σ_1 does not occur in the left side of (5.3), and hence cannot occur on the right, so that $j = 0$. Now suppose that $l \geqslant 1$. Then σ_1 occurs on the left side of (5.3), so it must occur on the right, and therefore $j \geqslant 1$. We now apply (a variant of) Lemma 13 to (5.3) as follows. The word $\alpha(1; l)$ on the left begins only with σ_1, while the word $\Delta_{n-2}(3, n-1)\alpha(2; k)$ on the right does not involve σ_1; it now follows, from Lemma 13, that $\Delta_{n-1}(3, n-1)\alpha(2; k)$ is a beginning subword of $I_2(3, n-1)F_1(2, n-1)$, $I_2(3, n-1)F_1(2, n-1) \doteq \Delta_{n-2}(3, n-1)\alpha(2; k)\ X$ say. Similarly, since $\alpha(1; j)$ on the right begins only with σ_1, it follows that $\Delta_{n-2}(3, n-1)\alpha(2; k) \doteq I_2(3, n-1)F_1(2, n-1)Y$, for some Y. Hence $YX = 1$, and since YX is a positive word we have $Y \equiv 1$, $X \equiv 1$. This establishes (5.4), and $l = j$ follows.

We may now rewrite (5.2) as

$$(5.5) \qquad \alpha(1; j)R\alpha(k+1; n-2)\alpha(j+1; n-1)$$
$$\doteq \{A\hat{A}\}^r Q_2(2, n-1)\alpha(1; n-3).$$

Now, since $j \leqslant n-3$, the right side of (5.5) must end in σ_{n-1}, so that, by Lemma 4, $\{A\hat{A}\}^r Q_2(2, n-1)$ must end in σ_{n-1}. Since $A\hat{A}$ ends only in σ_1, it follows, using Lemma 13, that $Q_2(2, n-1)$ ends in σ_{n-1}, $Q_2(2, n-1) \doteq Q_3(2, n-1)\sigma_{n-1}$ say. We then have

(5.6) $$\alpha(1;j)R\alpha(k+1;n-2)\alpha(j+1;n-2)$$
$$\mp\{A\hat{A}\}^r Q_3(2,n-1)\alpha(1;n-3).$$

Since the right side of (5.6) must end in σ_{n-2}, we see, using Lemma 10, that $\{A\hat{A}\}^r Q_3(2,n-1)$ must end in $\alpha(1;n-2)$. Now if $r=0$ this is impossible, so we must have $r\geqslant 1$. Since $\{A\hat{A}\}^r Q_3(2,n-1)$ must end in $\alpha(2;n-2)$ we see, using Lemma 13, that $Q_3(2,n-1)$ ends in $\alpha(2;n-2)$, $Q_3(2,n-1)\mp Q_4(2,n-1)\alpha(2;n-2)$ say. We then have

$$\{A\hat{A}\}^r Q_4(2,n-1)\alpha(2;n-2)$$
$$\mp\{A\hat{A}\}^{r-1}AQ_4(1,n-2)\beta(n-1;2)\alpha(1;n-2),$$

and (5.6) yields

$$R\alpha(k+1;n-2)$$
$$\mp\alpha(j+1;n-1)\{\hat{A}A\}^{r-1}Q_4(1,n-2)\beta(n-2;2)\alpha(2;n-2)\alpha(1;j).$$

Since $j\leqslant k-1$ we have

$$\alpha(2;n-2)\alpha(1;j)\mp\alpha(2;k)\alpha(k+1;n-2)\alpha(1;j)$$
$$\mp\alpha(2;k)\alpha(1;j)\alpha(k+1;n-2),$$

so that

$$R\mp\alpha(j+1;n-1)\{\hat{A}A\}^{r-1}Q_4(1,n-2)\beta(n-1;2)\alpha(2;k)\alpha(1;j).$$

We conclude the proof of the Lemma for case (a) by finding a conjugate $\Delta^{-2r}M_1$ of $\Delta^{-2r}R$ which has the required properties. We have

$$\Delta^{-2r}R\sim\Delta^{-2r}A\{\hat{A}A\}^{r-1}Q_4(1,n-2)\beta(n-1;2)\alpha(2;k)$$
$$\sim\Delta^{-2r}\hat{A}\{A\hat{A}\}^{r-1}\beta(n-1;n-k+1)Q_4(n-1,2)\alpha(1;n-2)$$
$$\equiv\Delta^{-2r}M_1$$

say. Now $\Delta^{-2r}M_1\sigma_{n-1}=\Delta^{-2r}\{\hat{A}A\}^r\beta(n-2;n-k)Q_4(n-2,1)=\Delta_{n-1}^{-2r}\beta(n-2;n-k)Q_4(n-2,1)$, so that $\Delta^{-2r}M_1\sigma_{n-1}\in B_{n-1}$.

Next, we check that $\Delta^{-2r-1}M\sigma_{n-1}$ is conjugate in B_{n-1} to $\Delta^{-2r}M_1\sigma_{n-1}$. We have

$$\Delta^{-2r-1}M\sigma_{n-1}=\Delta_{n-1}^{-2r-1}Q(1,n-2)$$
$$=\Delta_{n-1}^{-2r-1}F_1(1,n-2)Q_4(1,n-2)\alpha(1;n-2)I_2(n-3,1)$$
$$\sim\Delta_{n-1}^{-2r-1}\beta(n-2;1)I_2(2,n-2)F_1(1,n-2)Q_4(1,n-2)$$
$$=\Delta_{n-1}^{-2r-1}\beta(n-2;1)\Delta_{n-2}(2,n-2)\alpha(1;k-1)Q_4(1,n-2)$$

(using (5.4))

$$= \Delta_{n-1}^{-2r}\alpha(1; k-1)Q_4(1, n-2)$$

$$\sim \Delta_{n-1}^{-2r}\beta(n-2; n-k)Q_4(1, n-2)$$

$$= \Delta^{-2r}M_1\sigma_{n-1},$$

and the two conjugacy relations above hold in B_{n-1}.

Finally we must show that $\Delta^{-2r}M$ has power $-2r$. Suppose not. Then M_1 must contain Δ, so that, by Lemma 17, $\beta(n-1; n-k+1)Q_4(n-1, 2)\alpha(1; n-2)$ must begin with $\Delta_{n-1}(n-1, 2)$. Applying Lemma 13, we then have that $\beta(n-1; n-k+1)Q_4(n-1, 2)$ begins with $\Delta_{n-1}(n-1, 2)$, and so $\beta(n-2; n-k)Q_4(n-2, 1)$ must contain Δ_{n-1}. This implies that $\alpha(1; k-1)Q_4(1, n-2)$ contains Δ_{n-1}. However, we have $Q(2, n-1) \doteqdot F_1(2, n-1)Q_4(2, n-1)\alpha(2; n-1)I_2(n-2, 2)$, and applying Lemma 13 to (5.4), we see that $F_1(2, n-1) \doteqdot X\alpha(2; k)$ for some $X \equiv X(2, n-1)$, so that

$$Q(1, n-2) \doteqdot X(1, n-2)\alpha(1; k-1)Q_4(1, n-2)\alpha(1; n-2)I_2(n-3, 1).$$

Since $Q(1, n-2)$ is prime to Δ_{n-1}, so therefore must be $\alpha(1; k-1)Q_4(1, n-2)$. This contradiction proves the Lemma for case (a).

Case (*b*). $\hat{I}_1$ ends only with σ_{n-1}. We have $\Delta \doteqdot \hat{I}_1\hat{I}_2\hat{F} \doteqdot \hat{I}_1\Delta_{n-1}Y$, for some Y, so that $\Delta \doteqdot \hat{Y}\hat{I}_1\Delta_{n-1} \doteqdot \alpha(1; n-1)\Delta_{n-1}$, and therefore $\hat{Y} \doteqdot \alpha(1; s)$, $\hat{I}_1 = \alpha(s+1; n-1)$, for some s with $0 \leqslant s \leqslant n-2$.

Since $\Delta \doteqdot I_2F_1F_2\hat{I}_1 \doteqdot \hat{\Delta}_{n-1}\alpha(1; n-1)$, we now have

$$I_2(3, n-1)F_1(2, n-1)\alpha(1; l) \doteqdot \Delta_{n-1}(2, n-1)\alpha(1; s).$$

As in the previous case we now see, using Lemma 13, that $l = s$ and

$$I_2(3, n-1)F_1(2, n-1) \doteqdot \Delta_{n-1}(2, n-1) \doteqdot \Delta_{n-2}(3, n-1)\alpha(2; n-1), \tag{5.7}$$

and applying Lemma 13 again, we have

$$F_1(2, n-1) \doteqdot W\alpha(2; n-1) \tag{5.8}$$

for some $W \equiv W(3, n-1)$.

We now consider (5.2), which may be written

$$\alpha(1; s)R\alpha(s+1; n-1) \doteqdot \{A\hat{A}\}^r Q_2(2, n-1)\alpha(1; n-2).$$

Now $s \leqslant n-2$, so the left side above ends with σ_{n-1}, and from Lemma 10 it follows that $\{A\hat{A}\}^r Q_2(2, n-1)$ ends with $\alpha(1; n-1)$. This is impossible if $r=0$, so we must have $r\geq 1$. We then see that $Q_2(2,n-1)\doteq Q_3(2,n-1)\alpha(2;n-1)$, and then we have

$$R=\alpha(s+1;n-1)\{\hat{A}A\}^{r-1}Q_3(1,n-2)\beta(n-1;2)\alpha(2;n-1)\alpha(1;s).$$

We now find a conjugate $\Delta^{-2r}M_1$ of $\Delta^{-2r}R$ which has the required properties. We have

$$\begin{aligned}\Delta^{-2r}R &\sim \Delta^{-2r}\alpha(2;n-1)A\{\hat{A}A\}^{r-1}Q_3(1,n-2)\beta(n-1;2)\\ &= \Delta^{-2r}A\{\hat{A}A\}^{r-1}\alpha(1;n-2)Q_3(1,n-2)\beta(n-1;2)\\ &\sim \Delta^{-2r}\hat{A}\{A\hat{A}\}^{r-1}\beta(n-1;2)Q_3(n-1,2)\alpha(1;n-2)\\ &\equiv \Delta^{-2r}M_1\end{aligned}$$

say, and $\Delta^{-2r}M_1\sigma_{n-1}=\Delta_{n-1}^{-2r}\beta(n-2;1)Q_3(n-2,1)$.

We have, using (5.7),

$$\begin{aligned}\Delta^{-2r-1}M\sigma_{n-1} &= \Delta_{n-1}^{-2r-1}Q(1,n-2)\\ &= \Delta_{n-1}^{-2r-1}F_1(1,n-2)Q_3(1,n-2)\alpha(1;n-2)I_2(n-3,1)\\ &\sim \Delta_{n-1}^{-2r-1}\beta(n-2;1)I_2(2,n-2)F_1(1,n-2)Q_3(1,n-2)\\ &= \Delta_{n-1}^{-2r}\alpha(1;n-2)Q_3(1,n-2)\\ &\sim \Delta_{n-1}^{-2r}\beta(n-2;1)Q_3(n-2,1),\end{aligned}$$

where the conjugation relations hold in B_{n-1}. Hence $\Delta^{-2r-1}M\sigma_{n-1}$ is conjugate to $\Delta^{-2r}M_1\sigma_{n-1}$ in B_{n-1}.

To complete the proof of the Lemma for this case, we need to show that $\Delta^{-2r}M_1$ has power $-2r$. If this is not so, then M_1 must contain Δ, so that $\beta(n-1;2)Q_3(n-1,2)\alpha(1;n-2)$ must begin with $\Delta_{n-1}(2,n-1)$, and therefore $\beta(n-1;2)Q_3(n-1,2)$ must begin with $\Delta_{n-1}(2,n-1)$. This implies that $\alpha(1;n-2)Q_3(1,n-2)$ contains Δ_{n-1}. However,

$$\begin{aligned}Q(1,n-2) &\doteq F_1(1,n-2)Q_3(1,n-2)\alpha(1;n-2)I_2(n-3,1)\\ &\doteq W(2,n-2)\alpha(1;n-2)Q_3(1,n-2)\alpha(1;n-2)I_2(n-3,1),\end{aligned}$$

and $Q(1,n-2)$ is prime to Δ_{n-1}, so that $\alpha(1;n-2)Q_3(1,n-2)$ must be prime to Δ_{n-1}. This proves the Lemma for case (b).

Case (*c*). $I_1=1$. We have

$$\begin{aligned}\Delta &\doteq I_2(3,n-1)F_1(2,n-1)F_2\doteq \hat{\Delta}_{n-1}\alpha(1;n-1)\\ &\doteq \beta(n-l-1;1)\Delta_{n-1}(2,n-1)\alpha(1;l),\end{aligned}$$

so that

$$I_2(3, n-1)F_1(2, n-1) \mathrel{\dot=} \beta(n-l-1; 1)\Delta_{n-1}(2, n-1).$$

Since σ_1 does not appear on the left side of the above, we must have $l = n-1$, and so $I_2(3, n-1)F_1(2, n-1) \mathrel{\dot=} \Delta_{n-1}(2, n-1)$.

We now have, from (5.2),

$$\alpha(1; n-1)R \mathrel{\dot=} \{A\hat{A}\}^r Q_2(2, n-1)\alpha(1; n-2).$$

If $r = 0$ then, by using 'rev' of Corollary 20, we obtain a contradiction. Hence we must have $r \geqslant 1$, so that

$$R \mathrel{\dot=} \hat{A}\{A\hat{A}\}^{r-1}Q_2(2, n-1)\alpha(1; n-2),$$

and $\Delta^{-2r}R\sigma_{n-1} = \Delta_{n-1}^{-2r}Q_2(1, n-2)$.

Now

$$\begin{aligned}\Delta^{-2r-1}M\sigma_{n-1} &= \Delta_{n-1}^{-2r-1}Q(1, n-2)\\ &= \Delta_{n-1}^{-2r-1}F_1(1, n-2)Q_2(1, n-2)I_2(n-3, 1)\\ &\sim \Delta_{n-1}^{-2r-1}I_2(2, n-2)F_1(1, n-2)Q_2(1, n-2)\\ &= \Delta_{n-1}^{-2r}Q_2(1, n-2).\end{aligned}$$

Since $\Delta^{-2r}R$ has power $-2r$ and is conjugate to $\Delta^{-2r-1}M$, this proves the Lemma for case (c).

Finally we consider

Case (*d*). $\hat{I}_1$ ends only with σ_{n-2}. We obtain, as before, a description of I_1. We have

$$\Delta \mathrel{\dot=} \hat{I}_1\hat{I}_2\hat{F} \mathrel{\dot=} \hat{I}_1\Delta_{n-2}\sigma_{n-1}H,$$

for some H, so that

$$\Delta \mathrel{\dot=} \Delta_{n-2}\sigma_{n-1}HI_1 \mathrel{\dot=} \Delta_{n-2}\beta(n-1; 1)\beta(n-1; 2),$$

and therefore $HI_1 \mathrel{\dot=} \beta(n-2; 1)\beta(n-1; 2)$. Hence by Lemma 15, $H \mathrel{\dot=} \beta(n-2; a)\beta(n-1; b)$, $I_1 \mathrel{\dot=} \beta(a-1; 1)\beta(b-1; 2)$ for some a, b with $1 \leqslant a \leqslant n-1$, $3 \leqslant b \leqslant n$ and $b - a \geqslant 1$.

Using $\Delta \mathrel{\dot=} \Delta_{n-2}\beta(n-1; a)\beta(n-1; b)I_1 \mathrel{\dot=} \hat{I}_2\hat{F}_1\hat{F}_2I_1$, we obtain

$$\begin{aligned}I_2(3, n-1)F_1(2, n-1)\alpha(1; l) &\mathrel{\dot=} \Delta_{n-2}(3, n-1)\alpha(1; n-a)\alpha(1; n-b)\\ &\mathrel{\dot=} \Delta_{n-2}(3, n-1)\alpha(2; n-b+1)\alpha(1; n-a),\end{aligned}$$

since $b - a \geqslant 1$. As in the previous cases, we see that $l = n - a$ and that, for some $W \equiv W(3, n-1)$,

$$I_2(3, n-1)W \mathrel{\dot=} \Delta_{n-2}(3, n-1), \quad F_1(2, n-1) \mathrel{\dot=} W\alpha(2; n-b+1). \tag{5.9}$$

We may now rewrite (5.2) as

$$\alpha(1; n-a)R\alpha(n-a+1; n-1)\alpha(n-b+1; 2)$$
$$\mp \{A\hat{A}\}^r Q_2(2, n-1)\alpha(1; n-2),$$

so that

$$\alpha(1; n-a)R\alpha(n-a+1; n-1) \div \{A\hat{A}\}^r Q_2(2, n-1)\alpha(1; n-b).$$

If now follows, since $(n-a+1)-(n-b) \geqslant 2$, that $\{A\hat{A}\}^r Q_2(2, n-1)$ ends with $\alpha(n-a+1; n-1)$, and this implies that $Q_2(2, n-1) \mp Q_3(2, n-1)\alpha(n-a+1; n-1)$, for some Q_3. We then have

$$\alpha(1; n-a)R \mp \{A\hat{A}\}^r Q_3(2, n-1)\alpha(1; n-b).$$

Now if $r = 0$ we conclude from Lemma 19 that $n-b \geqslant n-a$, which contradicts the fact that $b-a \geqslant 1$. Hence we must have $r \geqslant 1$, and

$$R \div \alpha(n-a+1; n-1)\hat{A}\{A\hat{A}\}^{r-1} Q_3(2, n-1)\alpha(1; n-b).$$

We now observe that

$$\Delta^{-2r}R \sim \Delta^{-2r}\hat{A}\{A\hat{A}\}^{r-1}\alpha(2; n-b+1)Q_3(2, n-1)\alpha(n-a+1; n-1)$$
$$\equiv \Delta^{-2r}\hat{A}\{A\hat{A}\}^{r-1}V(2, n-1)$$

say. We show that this latter word has power $-2r$. To see this, note that, by (5.9),

$$Q(2, n-1) \mp F_1(2, n-1)Q_2(2, n-1)I_2(n-2, 2)$$
$$\mp W(3, n-1)\alpha(2; n-b+1)Q_3(2, n-1)\alpha(n-a+1; n-1)I_2(n-2, 2),$$

and the desired conclusion follows easily from the fact that $Q(1, n-2)$ is prime to Δ_{n-1}.

Thus we have shown that $\Delta^{-2r-1}M$ is conjugate to $\Delta^{-2r}\hat{A}\{A\hat{A}\}^{r-1}V(2, n-1)$, and that the latter word has power $-2r$. Now from Lemma 25 we see that if $r = 1$ then $\Delta^{-2r-1}M$ has summit power $t = -2$ or $t = -1$. Thus we may suppose that $r \geqslant 2$. Now if $t \leqslant -2r+1$ there is nothing to prove, so we suppose that $t > -2r+1$.

Applying Lemmas 25 and 26 we obtain

$$V(2, n-1) \mp X(3, n-1)V_1(2, n-1)Y(2, n-2)$$
$$\mp X(3, n-1)V_2(2, n-1)\alpha(2; n-1)Y(2, n-2)$$

(for some V_2)

$$\mp X(3, n-1)V_2(2, n-1)Y(3, n-1)\alpha(2; n-1)$$
$$\mp V_3(2, n-1)\alpha(2; n-1)$$

say, where $Y(2, n-2)X(2, n-2) \div \Delta_{n-2}(2, n-2)$.

We now obtain the desired $\Delta^{-2r}M_1$. We have

$$\begin{aligned}\Delta^{-2r-1}M &\sim \Delta^{-2r}A\{A\hat{A}\}^{r-1}V(2, n-1)\\ &= \Delta^{-2r}\{\hat{A}A\}^{r-1}\hat{A}V_3(2, n-1)\alpha(2; n-1)\\ &= \Delta^{-2r}\{\hat{A}A\}^{r-1}V_3(1, n-2)\hat{A}\alpha(2; n-1)\\ &\sim \Delta^{-2r}A\{\hat{A}A\}^{r-1}V_3(1, n-2)\beta(n-1; 2)\\ &\sim \Delta^{-2r}\hat{A}\{A\hat{A}\}^{r-1}V_3(n-1, 2)\alpha(1, n-2)\\ &\equiv \Delta^{-2r}M_1\end{aligned}$$

say, and $\Delta^{-2r}M_1\sigma_{n-1} = \Delta_{n-1}^{-2r}V_3(n-2, 1)$.

We check that $\Delta^{-2r}M_1$ has power $-2r$. If not, then $V_3(n-1, 2)\alpha(1, n-2)$ must begin with $\Delta_{n-1}(2, n-1)$, so that $V_3(n-1, 2)$ must begin with $\Delta_{n-1}(2, n-1)$, and so therefore must $V_3(2, n-1)$. This contradicts the fact that $\Delta^{-2r}\hat{A}\{A\hat{A}\}^{r-1}V(2, n-1)$ has power $-2r$. Hence $\Delta^{-2r}M_1$ has power $-2r$.

To complete the proof of this case, we show that $\Delta^{-2r}M_1\sigma_{n-1}$ is conjugate to $\Delta^{-2r-1}M\sigma_{n-1}$ in B_{n-1}. We have

$$\begin{aligned}\Delta^{-2r-1}M\sigma_{n-1} &= \Delta_{n-1}^{-2r-1}Q(1, n-2)\\ &= \Delta_{n-1}^{-2r-1}F_1(1, n-2)Q_3(1, n-2)\alpha(n-a; n-2)I_2(n-3, 1)\\ &\sim \Delta_{n-1}^{-2r-1}I_2(2, n-2)F_1(1, n-2)Q_3(1, n-2)\alpha(n-a; n-2)\\ &= \Delta_{n-1}^{-2r-1}\Delta_{n-2}(2, n-2)\alpha(1; n-b)Q_3(1, n-2)\alpha(n-a; n-2)\\ &= \Delta_{n-1}^{-2r-1}\Delta_{n-2}(2, n-2)V(1, n-2)\\ &= \Delta_{n-1}^{-2r-1}\Delta_{n-2}(2, n-2)V_3(1, n-2)\alpha(1; n-2)\\ &\sim \Delta_{n-1}^{-2r}V_3(1, n-2)\\ &\sim \Delta_{n-1}^{-2r}V_3(n-2, 1),\end{aligned}$$

as required. This concludes the treatment of case (d).

In the consideration of the above cases, we have shown that if $r = 0$ then $t = -1$, and that if $r \geqslant 1$ then (b) of the Lemma holds. Thus we have established that the Lemma follows from Lemmas 25 and 26.

Proof of Lemma 25. We have $\mu \equiv \Delta^{-2r}\hat{A}\{A\hat{A}\}^{r-1}V(2, n-1)$ is in standard form, $r \geqslant 1$ and μ has summit power $t > -2r$. We thus have $\hat{A}\{A\hat{A}\}^{r-1}V(2, n-1) \mathrel{\overline{\overline{\cdot}}} FUI$ for some F, U, I with $IF \mathrel{\overline{\overline{\cdot}}} \Delta$. We write $F \mathrel{\overline{\overline{\cdot}}} F_1F_2$ where $F_1 \equiv F_1(1, n-2)$ and F_2 does not begin with any of $\sigma_1, \ldots, \sigma_{n-2}$. We also write $I \mathrel{\overline{\overline{\cdot}}} I_1I_2$, where $I_2 \equiv I_2(2, n-1)$ and I_1 does not end with any of $\sigma_2, \ldots, \sigma_{n-1}$. It is then easy to see that $V(2, n-1) \doteq F_1(2, n-1)V_2(2, n-1)I_2(2, n-1)$ for some V_2.

We now obtain descriptions of F_2 and I_1. We have $\Delta \doteq I_1I_2F \doteq I_1\Delta_{n-1}(2, n-1)W$ for some W, so that

$$\Delta \doteq \Delta_{n-1}(2, n-1)W\hat{I}_1 \doteq \Delta_{n-1}(2, n-1)\alpha(1; n-1),$$

so that $\hat{I}_1 = \alpha(j; n-1)$ for some j with $1 \leqslant j \leqslant n$. Also, $\Delta \doteq IF_1F_2 \doteq W_1\Delta_{n-1}F_2$ for some W_1, so that

$$\Delta \doteq \Delta_{n-1}F_2\hat{W}_1 = \Delta_{n-1}\beta(n-1; 1),$$

and therefore $F_2 \doteq \beta(n-1; k)$ for some k with $1 \leqslant k \leqslant n$.

We note that not both $F_2 = 1$ and $I_1 = 1$ can hold, since otherwise we would have $\Delta \doteq I_2(2, n-1)F_1(1, n-2) \doteq F_1(1, n-2)I_2(n-2, 1)$, which would imply that σ_{n-1} does not occur in Δ. We consider separately the cases (a) $F_2 \neq 1$ and $I_1 \neq 1$, (b) $F_2 = 1$, $I_1 \neq 1$, (c) $F_2 \neq 1$, $I_1 = 1$.

Case (*a*). $F_2 \neq 1$ and $I_1 \neq 1$. We have $j \leqslant n-1$, $k \leqslant n-1$ and

$$\Delta \doteq F_2\hat{I}_1\hat{I}_2\hat{F}_1 \doteq \beta(n-1; k)\alpha(j; n-1)\hat{I}_2\hat{F}_1.$$

From Lemma 6 it follows that $k \neq j$. We consider separately the subcases $j > k$, $j < k$.

Subcase (1). $j > k$. We note that

$$\begin{aligned}\Delta &\doteq \Delta_{n-2}(2, n-2)\hat{A}\alpha(2; n-1)\\ &\doteq \Delta_{n-2}(2, n-2)\beta(n-1; k)\beta(k-1; 1)\alpha(2; j-1)\alpha(j; n-1)\\ &\doteq \Delta_{n-2}(2, n-2)\alpha(1; j-2)\beta(n-1; k)\alpha(j; n-1)\beta(k-1; 1)\\ &\doteq \alpha(n-k+1; n-1)\Delta_{n-2}(2, n-2)\alpha(1; j-2)\beta(n-1; k)\alpha(j; n-1),\end{aligned}$$

so that

$$I_2(2, n-1)F_1(1, n-2) \doteq \alpha(n-k+1; n-1)\Delta_{n-2}(2, n-2)\alpha(1; j-2).$$

Using Lemma 13, we now see that

$$I_2(2, n-1) \doteq \alpha(n-k+1; n-1)Y,$$

$$F_1(1, n-2) \doteq X\alpha(1; j-2),$$

for some $X(2, n-2)$ and $Y(2, n-2)$ with $YX \doteq \Delta_{n-2}(2, n-2)$.

We now observe that

$$\begin{aligned}&V(2, n-1)\\ &\quad\doteq X(3, n-1)\alpha(2; j-1)V_2(2, n-1)\alpha(n-k+1; n-1)Y(2, n-2)\end{aligned}$$

is a description of $V(2, n-1)$ of the required form, with $V_1(2, n-1) \equiv \alpha(2; j-1)V_2(2, n-1)\alpha(n-k+1; n-1)$.

Now if $r \geqslant 2$ we have

$$\begin{aligned}
&\Delta^{-2r}\hat{A}\{A\hat{A}\}^{r-1}V(2, n-1) \\
&\quad = \Delta^{-2r}\hat{A}\{A\hat{A}\}^{r-1}X(3, n-1)V_1(2, n-1)Y(2, n-2) \\
&\quad \sim \Delta^{-2r}Y(2, n-2)X(2, n-2)\hat{A}\{A\hat{A}\}^{r-1}V_1(2, n-1) \\
&\quad = \Delta^{-2r}\Delta_{n-2}(2, n-2)\hat{A}V_1(2, n-1)\{A\hat{A}\}^{r-1} \\
&\quad \sim \Delta^{-2r}A\{\hat{A}A\}^{r-2}\hat{A}\Delta_{n-2}(2, n-2)\hat{A}V_1(2, n-1) \\
&\quad = \Delta^{-2r}A\{\hat{A}A\}^{r-2}\Delta\sigma_1 V_1(2, n-1) \\
&\quad = \Delta^{-2r+1}\hat{A}\{A\hat{A}\}^{r-2}\sigma_1 V_1(2, n-1).
\end{aligned}$$

Thus to establish the Lemma in subcase (1), when $r \geqslant 2$, we need only check that this last word has power $-2r+1$. If this is not so, then, since $\hat{A}\{A\hat{A}\}^{r-2}\sigma_1$ ends only in σ_1, $V_1(2, n-1)$ must begin with $\Delta_{n-1}(2, n-1)$. This implies that $V(2, n-1)$ contains $\Delta_{n-1}(2, n-1)$, which contradicts the fact that μ has power $-2r$.

We now suppose that $r = 1$. We then have $\hat{A}V(2, n-1) = FUI$, so that $\hat{A}V_2(2, n-1) \doteq \alpha(n-1; k)U\beta(n-j; 1)$, and therefore $\beta(k-1; 1)V_2(2, n-1) \doteq U\beta(n-j; 1)$, where $1 \leqslant k \leqslant n-2$, $2 \leqslant j \leqslant n-1$ and $k < j$. Now if $k = 1$ we obtain a contradiction, since σ_1 would then occur in $U\beta(n-j; 1)$ but not in $\beta(k-1; 1)V_2(2, n-2)$. Hence $k \geqslant 2$, and it now follows from Corollary 20 that $\Delta^{-1}U$ has summit power -1. Since $\mu \sim \Delta^{-1}U$, this concludes the proof of the Lemma for Subcase (1).

Subcase (II). $k > j$. We have

$$\begin{aligned}
\Delta &\doteq A\Delta_{n-1} \\
&\doteq \alpha(1; j-1)\alpha(j; n-1)\beta(n-2; k-1)\beta(k-2; 1)\Delta_{n-2}(2, n-2) \\
&\doteq \beta(n-1; k)\alpha(1; j-1)\alpha(j; n-1)\beta(k-2; 1)\Delta_{n-2}(2, n-2) \\
&\doteq \alpha(1; j-1)\beta(n-1; k)\alpha(j; n-1)\beta(k-2; 1)\Delta_{n-2}(2, n-2) \\
&\doteq \beta(n-1; k)\alpha(j; n-1)\beta(k-2; 1)\Delta_{n-2}(2, n-2)\beta(n-1; n-j+1),
\end{aligned}$$

so that

$$\hat{I}_2\hat{F}_1 \doteq \beta(k-2; 1)\Delta_{n-2}(2, n-2)\beta(n-1; n-j+1).$$

We then obtain $F_1(1, n-1) \doteq X\alpha(1; j-1)$, $I_2(2, n-1) \doteq \alpha(n-k+2; n-1)Y$ for some X, Y with $YX \doteq \Delta_{n-2}(2, n-2)$. If $r \geqslant 2$

the result then follows as in Subcase (1). If $r = 1$ then we have $\beta(k-1;1)V_2(2,n-1) \doteq U\beta(n-j;1)$, as in Subcase (I), where $1 \leqslant j \leqslant n-2$ and $2 \leqslant k \leqslant n-1$; an application of Corollary 20 now shows that $t = -1$.

Case (*b*). $F_2 = 1$, $I_1 \neq 1$. We have

$$\Delta = I_1 I_2 F_1 \doteq \beta(n-j;1) I_2 F_1 \doteq \beta(n-j;1)\Delta_{n-1}(2,n-1)\alpha(1;j-1),$$

so that

$$\begin{aligned} I_2(2,n-1)F_1(1,n-2) &\doteq \Delta_{n-1}(2,n-1)\alpha(1;j-1) \\ &\doteq \alpha(2;n-1)\Delta_{n-2}(2,n-2)\alpha(1;j-1), \end{aligned}$$

and if $r \geqslant 2$ this gives the desired result, as in the previous case.
If $r = 1$ then we have $\hat{A}V_2(2,n-1) \doteq U\beta(n-j;1)$, so that

$$V_2(1,n-2)\beta(n-1;n-j+1) \doteq U.$$

Hence $\Delta^{-1}U \sim \Delta^{-1}\alpha(1;j-1)V_2(1,n-2)$, and $j \leqslant n-1$ since $I_1 \neq 1$, so that, by Lemma 18, $\Delta^{-1}U$ has summit power -1, as required.

Case (*c*). $F_2 \neq 1$, $I_1 = 1$. We have

$$\begin{aligned} \Delta \doteq I_2 F_1 F_2 &\doteq I_2 F_1 \beta(n-2;k) \\ &\doteq \alpha(n-k+1;n-1)\Delta_{n-1}\beta(n-2;k), \end{aligned}$$

so that

$$\begin{aligned} I_2(2,n-1)F_1(1,n-2) &\doteq \alpha(n-k+1;n-1)\Delta_{n-1} \\ &\doteq \alpha(n-k+1;n-1)\Delta_{n-2}(2,n-2)\alpha(1;n-2). \end{aligned}$$

As before, this establishes the result if $r \geqslant 2$.
If $r = 1$ we have $\hat{A}V_2(2,n-1) \doteq \beta(n-1;k)U$, so that $U \doteq \beta(k-1;1)V_2(2,n-1)$ and $\Delta^{-1}U \sim \Delta^{-1}V_2(2,n-1)\alpha(n-k+1;n-1)$. Now $k \leqslant n-1$ since $F_2 \neq 1$, and the result follows from Lemma 18.
This concludes the proof of Lemma 25.

Proof of Lemma 26. We have $\phi \equiv \Delta^{-2r+1}\hat{A}\{A\hat{A}\}^{r-2}\sigma_1 V_1(2,n-1)$ is in standard form, $r \geqslant 2$ and ϕ has summit power $t > -2r+1$. We therefore have

$$\hat{A}\{A\hat{A}\}^{r-2}\sigma_1 V_1(2,n-1) \doteq FW\hat{I},$$

for some F, W, I with $\Delta \doteq IF$.
We write $F \doteq F_1F_2$, where $F_1 \equiv F_1(2,n-2)$ and F_2 does not begin

with any of $\sigma_1, \sigma_2, \ldots, \sigma_{n-2}$. Now $\sigma_1 V_1(2, n-1)$ must begin with $F_1(3, n-1)$, $V_1(2, n-1) \doteq F_1(3, n-1)V_2(2, n-1)$ say, so that $\hat{A}\{A\hat{A}\}^{r-2}\sigma_1 V_2(2, n-1) \doteq F_2 W\hat{I}$. Now if F_2 begins with σ_1, then $\sigma_1 V_2(2, n-1)$ must begin with σ_2. However, this would imply that $V_2(2, n-1)$ begins with $\sigma_2\sigma_1$, which is impossible. Hence either $F_2 = 1$, or F_2 begins only with σ_{n-1}.

We also write $I \doteq I_1 I_2$, where $I_2 \equiv I_2(1, n-2)$ and I_1 does not end with any of $\sigma_1, \sigma_2, \ldots, \sigma_{n-2}$. We then have $V_2(2, n-1) \doteq V_3(2, n-1)\hat{I}_2$, for some V_3.

We now find descriptions of F_2 and I_1. We have $\Delta \doteq IF_1F_2 \doteq U\Delta_{n-1}F_2$ for some U, so that $\Delta_{n-1}\hat{A} = \Delta_{n-1}F_2\hat{U}$, and $F_2 \doteq \beta(n-1; j)$ for some j with $1 \leqslant j \leqslant n$. Also, $\Delta \doteq I_1I_2F \doteq I_1\Delta_{n-1}H$ for some H, so that $H\hat{I}_1 \doteq \hat{A}$ and $\hat{I}_1 \doteq \beta(k; 1)$ for some k with $0 \leqslant k \leqslant n-1$.

We note that not both $I_1 = 1$ and $F_2 = 1$ can hold, since otherwise we would have $\Delta \doteq I_2(1, n-2)F_1(2, n-2)$, which is impossible. We consider separately the cases (a) $I_1 \neq 1$ and $F_2 \neq 1$, (b) $F_2 \neq 1$, $I_1 = 1$, (c) $F_2 = 1$, $I_1 \neq 1$.

Case (a). $I_1 \neq 1$, $F_2 \neq 1$. We have $1 \leqslant j, k \leqslant n-1$. Now

$$\Delta \doteq I_2F_1F_2\hat{I}_1 \doteq I_2F_1\beta(n-1; j)\beta(k; 1),$$

so that $j \neq k$. If $j < k$ then Δ has a subword

$$\beta(n-1; j)\beta(k; j+1)\beta(j; 1) \doteq \beta(k-1; j)\beta(n-1; j)\beta(j; 1),$$

which is impossible. Hence $k < j$. Now if $j > k+1$ then $j > 1$ and

$$\begin{aligned}\Delta &\doteq \Delta_{n-2}\beta(n-2; k+1)\beta(k; 1)\beta(n-1; j)\beta(j-1; 1)\\ &\doteq \alpha(n-j+1; n-1)\Delta_{n-2}\beta(n-2; k+1)\beta(n-1; j)\beta(k; 1)\\ &\doteq \alpha(n-j+1; n-1)\Delta_{n-2}\beta(n-2; k+1)F_2\hat{I}_1,\end{aligned}$$

so that

$$I_2(1, n-2)F_1(2, n-2) \doteq \alpha(n-j+1; n-1)\Delta_{n-2}\beta(n-2; k+1).$$

However, σ_{n-1} occurs on the right side above, but not the left, which is impossible. Hence we must have $j = k+1$.

Since $j = k+1$ we have $\Delta \doteq I_2F_1\hat{A}$, and therefore

$$I_2(1, n-2)F_1(2, n-2) \doteq \Delta_{n-1} = \beta(n-2; 1)\Delta_{n-2}(2, n-2).$$

Applying Lemma 13, we see that $I_2(1, n-2) \doteq \beta(n-2; 1)Z$, for some $Z \equiv Z(2, n-2)$, so that $\hat{I}_2 = \alpha(2; n-1)Z(n-2, 2) \doteq Z(n-1, 3)\alpha(2; n-1)$. Since $V_1(2, n-1)$ ends with $\hat{I}_2$, this proves the required result.

Case (*b*). $I_1 = 1$, $F_2 \neq 1$. We have $k = 0$, $1 \leqslant j \leqslant n-1$ and

$$I_2(1, n-2)F_1(2, n-2) \doteq U\Delta_{n-1} \doteq \alpha(n-j+1; n-1)\Delta_{n-1}.$$

Now σ_{n-1} does not occur in I_2F_1, and so we must have $j = 1$ and hence $I_2F_1 \doteq \Delta_{n-1}$, which yields the result as in Case (a).

Case (*c*). $I_1 \neq 1$, $F_2 = 1$. We have $1 \leqslant k \leqslant n-1$, $j = n$ and

$$I_2(1, n-2)F_1(2, n-2) \doteq \Delta_{n-1}H \doteq \Delta_{n-1}\beta(n-1; k+1),$$

which is impossible unless $k = n-1$. Thus $I_2F_1 \doteq \Delta_{n-1}$, and the result follows.

This concludes the proof of Lemma 26.

Proof of Lemma 24. Suppose that $\Delta^{-2r}M$ is in standard form, $r \geqslant 1$, and $\Delta^{-2r}M$ has summit power $t > -2r$. We then have $M \doteq FRI$ for some F, R, I with $\Delta \doteq IF$. We note that $\Delta^{-2r}FRI \sim \Delta^{-2r+1}R$, and that $\Delta^{-2r+1}R$ has power $-2r+1$.

We show, firstly, that $\Delta^{-2r}M\sigma_{n-1}$ has power $-2r$. If this is not the case then, by Lemma 16, it has power $-2r+1$, and by Lemma 22 we have $FRI\sigma_{n-1} \doteq \Delta\{A\hat{A}\}^{r-1}AQ$, where $Q \equiv Q(1, n-2)$ and Q is prime to Δ_{n-1}. We then have $FRI\sigma_{n-1} \doteq \Delta\{A\hat{A}\}^{r-1}Q(2, n-1)A$, so that FRI contains Δ. This is a contradiction, and so $\Delta^{-2r}M\sigma_{n-1}$ must have power $-2r$.

We now have, by Lemma 22, that $FRI\sigma_{n-1} = \{\hat{A}A\}^rQ(1, n-2)$, where Q is prime to Δ_{n-1}. Hence

$$FRI \doteq \hat{A}\{A\hat{A}\}^{r-1}Q(2, n-1)\alpha(1; n-2).$$

We write $F \doteq F_1(1, n-2)F_2$, where F_2 does not begin with any of $\sigma_1, \ldots, \sigma_{n-2}$, and $I \doteq I_1I_2(1, n-3)$, where I_1 does not end with any of $\sigma_1, \ldots, \sigma_{n-3}$. We then have $Q(2, n-1) =$ $F_1(2, n-1)Q_1(2, n-1)I_2(2, n-2)$ for some Q_1, so that

$$F_2RI_1 \doteq \hat{A}\{A\hat{A}\}^{r-1}Q_1(2, n-1)\alpha(1; n-2). \tag{5.10}$$

We now obtain a description of F_2. We have $\Delta \doteq IF_1F_2 \doteq U\Delta_{n-1}F_2$ for some U, so that $\Delta \doteq \Delta_{n-1}F_2\hat{U} \doteq \Delta_{n-1}\beta(n-1; 1)$. Hence $F_2 \doteq$ $\beta(n-1; l)$ for some l with $1 \leqslant l \leqslant n$.

We now consider separately the four possibilities for I_1: (a) I_1 ends in both σ_{n-1} and σ_{n-2}, (b) I_1 ends only in σ_{n-1}, (c) $I_1 = 1$, (d) I_1 ends only in σ_{n-2}.

Case (*a*). I_1 ends in both σ_{n-1} and σ_{n-2}. We have $\Delta \doteq I_1I_2F \doteq I_1\Delta_{n-2}H$, for some H, so that $\Delta \doteq \hat{H}I_1\Delta_{n-2} \doteq \alpha(1; n-1)\alpha(1; n-2)\Delta_{n-2}$, and therefore $\hat{H}I_1 \doteq \alpha(1; n-1)\alpha(1; n-2) \doteq \alpha(2; n-2)\alpha(1; n-1)\sigma_{n-2}$. Now $I_1 \doteq W\sigma_{n-2}\sigma_{n-1}\sigma_{n-2}$ say, so that $\hat{H}W \doteq \alpha(2; n-2)\alpha(1; n-3)$. Applying Lemma 15 we obtain $\hat{H} \doteq \alpha(2; k)\alpha(1; j)$ and

$$W \doteq \alpha(k+1; n-2)\alpha(j+1; n-3),$$

for some k, j with $0 \leqslant j \leqslant n-3$, $1 \leqslant k \leqslant n-2$ and $k-j \geqslant 1$, so that $I_1 \doteq \alpha(k+1; n-2)\alpha(j+1; n-1)\sigma_{n-2}$.

We now obtain a description of $I_2(1, n-3)F_1(1, n-2)$. We have

$$\begin{aligned}\Delta &\doteq I_1 I_2 F_1 F_2 \\ &\doteq \alpha(k+1; n-2)\alpha(j+1; n-1)\sigma_{n-2}\Delta_{n-2}\beta(n-2; n-k)\beta(n-1; n-j),\end{aligned}$$

so that

$$I_2(1, n-3)F_1(1, n-2)\beta(n-1; l) \doteq \Delta_{n-2}\beta(n-2; n-k)\beta(n-1; n-j).$$

Using Lemma 13 we see tht $l = n - j$, so that

$$I_2(1, n-3)F_1(1, n-2) \doteq \Delta_{n-2}\beta(n-2; n-k),$$

and, using Lemma 13 again, we have

$$F_1(1, n-2) \doteq Z(1, n-3)\beta(n-2; n-k),$$

for some Z.

We now have, from (5.10), that

$$\begin{aligned}&\beta(n-1; n-j)R\alpha(k+1; n-2)\alpha(j+1; n-1) \\ &\quad \doteq \hat{A}\{A\hat{A}\}^{r-1}Q_1(2, n-1)\alpha(1; n-3).\end{aligned}$$

Since the left side of this ends in σ_{n-1}, we have $Q_1(2, n-1) \doteq Q_2(2, n-1)\sigma_{n-1}$ say, and

$$\begin{aligned}&\beta(n-1; n-j)R\alpha(k+1; n-2)\alpha(j+1; n-2) \\ &\quad \doteq \hat{A}\{A\hat{A}\}^{r-1}Q_2(2, n-1)\alpha(1; n-3).\end{aligned}$$

Since the left side of this ends with σ_{n-2}, we have $Q_2(2, n-1) \doteq Q_3(2, n-1)\alpha(2; n-2)$ say, and

$$\begin{aligned}&\beta(n-1; n-j)R\alpha(k+1; n-2) \\ &\quad \doteq \{\hat{A}A\}^{r-1}Q_3(1, n-2)\beta(n-1; 2)\alpha(2; n-2)\alpha(1; j) \\ &\quad \doteq \{\hat{A}A\}^{r-1}Q_3(1, n-2)\beta(n-1; 2)\alpha(2; k)\alpha(1; j)\alpha(k+1; n-2),\end{aligned}$$

so that

$$\beta(n-1; n-j)R \doteq \{\hat{A}A\}^{r-1}Q_3(1, n-2)\beta(n-1; 2)\alpha(2; k)\alpha(1; j).$$

This equation may be solved directly for R if $r \geqslant 2$, while if $r = 1$ a solution may be obtained using Lemma 19. However, in order to avoid separate consideration of these two cases, we proceed somewhat differently.

We have

$$\Delta^{-2r}M = \Delta^{-2r}FRI = \Delta^{-2r}F_1\beta(n-1; n-j)RI_1I_2$$
$$= \Delta^{-2r}F_1\{\hat{A}A\}^{r-1}Q_3(1, n-2)\beta(n-1;2)\alpha(2;k)\alpha(1;j)\alpha(k+1;n-2)$$
$$\alpha(j+1;n-1)\sigma_{n-2}I_2$$
$$\sim \Delta^{-2r}I_2F_1\{\hat{A}A\}^{r-1}Q_3(1, n-2)\beta(n-1;2)\alpha(2;n-2)\alpha(1;n-1)\sigma_{n-2}$$
$$\sim \Delta^{-2r}\alpha(1;n-1)\alpha(1;n-2)I_2F_1\{\hat{A}A\}^{r-1}Q_3(1,n-2)\beta(n-1;2),$$

and substituting the expression obtained for I_2F_1, we have

$$\Delta^{-2r}M \sim \Delta^{-2r}\alpha(1;n-1)\alpha(1;n-2)\Delta_{n-2}\beta(n-2;n-k)\{\hat{A}A\}^{r-1}$$
$$Q_3(1,n-2)\beta(n-1;2)$$
$$= \Delta^{-2r+1}\{\hat{A}A\}^{r-1}\beta(n-2;n-k)Q_3(1,n-2)\beta(n-1;2)$$
$$\sim \Delta^{-2r+1}\{A\hat{A}\}^{r-1}\alpha(2;k)Q_3(n-1,2)\alpha(1;n-2)$$
$$\equiv \Delta^{-2r+1}M_1$$

say, and $\Delta^{-2r+1}M_1\sigma_{n-1} = \Delta_{n-1}^{-2r+1}\alpha(1;k-1)Q_3(n-2,1)$.

We now show that $\Delta^{-2r}M\sigma_{n-1}$ and $\Delta^{-2r+1}M_1\sigma_{n-1}$ are conjugate in B_{n-1}. We have

$$\Delta^{-2r}M\sigma_{n-1} = \Delta_{n-1}^{-2r}Q(1,n-2)$$
$$= \Delta_{n-1}^{-2r}F_1(1,n-2)Q_3(1,n-2)\alpha(1;n-2)I_2(1,n-3)$$
$$\sim \Delta_{n-1}^{-2r}\alpha(1;n-2)I_2(1,n-3)F_1(1,n-2)Q_3(1,n-2)$$
$$= \Delta_{n-1}^{-2r+1}\beta(n-2;n-k)Q_3(1,n-2)$$
$$\sim \Delta_{n-1}^{-2r+1}\alpha(1;k-1)Q_3(n-2,1),$$

as required.

Next we check that $\Delta^{-2r+1}M_1$ has power $-2r+1$. If this is not the case, then M_1 contains Δ, so that $\alpha(2;k)Q_3(n-1,2)(1;n-2)$ begins with $\Delta_{n-1}(2,n-1)$, and therefore $\alpha(2;k)Q_3(n-1,2)$ also begins with $\Delta_{n-1}(2,n-1)$. However, this would imply that $Q_1(1,n-2)$ contains Δ_{n-1}, since

$$Q_1(1,n-2) \mathrel{\dot{=}} F_1(1,n-2)Q_3(1,n-2)\alpha(1;n-2)I_2(1,n-3)$$
$$\mathrel{\dot{=}} Z(1,n-3)\beta(n-2;n-k)Q_3(1,n-2)\alpha(1;n-2)I_2(1,n-3).$$

This contradiction shows that $\Delta^{-2r+1}M_1$ has power $-2r+1$.

It remains to show, in Case (a), that $t = -1$ if $r = 1$. Now when $r = 1$ we have

$$\Delta^{-1}M_1 \equiv \Delta^{-1}\alpha(2;k)Q_3(n-1,2)\alpha(1;n-2)$$
$$\sim \Delta^{-1}\beta(n-1;2)\alpha(2;k)Q_3(n-1,2),$$

so that $\Delta^{-1}M_1$ has summit power -1, as required.

Case (*b*). I_1 ends only in σ_{n-1}. We then have $\Delta \mathrel{\overline{\overline{\cdot}}} I_1I_2F \mathrel{\overline{\overline{\cdot}}} I_1\Delta_{n-1}H$ for some H, so that $\hat{H}I_1 \mathrel{\overline{\overline{\cdot}}} A$, and therefore $I_1 \mathrel{\overline{\overline{\cdot}}} \alpha(s;n-1)$ for some s with $1 \leqslant s \leqslant n-1$.

Now $\Delta \mathrel{\overline{\overline{\cdot}}} I_1I_2F_1F_2 \mathrel{\overline{\overline{\cdot}}} I_1\Delta_{n-1}\beta(n-1;n-s+1)$, so that

$$I_2(1,n-3)F_1(1,n-2)\beta(n-1;l) \mathrel{\overline{\overline{\cdot}}} \Delta_{n-1}\beta(n-1;n-s+1).$$

From this we conclude that $l = n-s+1$, so that

$$I_2(1,n-3)F_1(1,n-2) \mathrel{\overline{\overline{\cdot}}} \Delta_{n-1} \mathrel{\overline{\overline{\cdot}}} \Delta_{n-2}\beta(n-2;1),$$

and therefore $F_1(1,n-2) \mathrel{\overline{\overline{\cdot}}} J(1,n-3)\beta(n-2;1)$, for some J.

We now see, from (5.10), that

$$\beta(n-1;n-s+1)R\alpha(s;n-1) \mathrel{\overline{\overline{\cdot}}} \hat{A}\{A\hat{A}\}^{r-1}Q_1(2,n-1)\alpha(1;n-2).$$

Since the left side of the above ends in σ_{n-1}, we have $Q_1(2,n-1) \mathrel{\overline{\overline{\cdot}}} Q_2(2,n-1)\alpha(2;n-1)$ say, and then

$$\beta(n-1;n-s+1)R$$
$$\mathrel{\overline{\overline{\cdot}}} \{\hat{A}A\}^{r-1}Q_2(1,n-2)\beta(n-1;2)\alpha(2;n-1)\alpha(1;s-1).$$

We now observe that

$$\Delta^{-2r}M = \Delta^{-2r}FRI = \Delta^{-2r}F_1\beta(n-1;n-s+1)RI_1I_2$$
$$= \Delta^{-2r}F_1\{\hat{A}A\}^{r-1}Q_2(1,n-2)\beta(n-1;2)\alpha(2;n-1)\alpha(1;s-1)\alpha(s;n-1)I_2$$
$$\sim \Delta^{-2r}\alpha(1;n-1)I_2F_1\{\hat{A}A\}^{r-1}Q_2(1,n-2)\beta(n-1;2)\alpha(2;n-1)$$
$$= \Delta^{-2r+1}\{\hat{A}A\}^{r-1}Q_2(1,n-2)\beta(n-1;2)\alpha(2;n-1)$$
$$\sim \Delta^{-2r+1}\{A\hat{A}\}^{r-1}\alpha(2;n-1)Q_2(n-1,2)\alpha(1;n-2)$$
$$\equiv \Delta^{-2r+1}M_1$$

say, and $\Delta^{-2r+1}M_1\sigma_{n-1} = \Delta_{n-1}^{-2r+1}\alpha(1;n-2)Q_2(n-2,1)$.

Now

$$\Delta_{n-1}^{-2r}Q(1,n-2) = \Delta_{n-1}^{-2r}F_1Q_2(1,n-2)\alpha(1;n-2)I_2$$
$$\sim \Delta_{n-1}^{-2r+1}\beta(n-2;1)Q_2(1,n-2)$$
$$\sim \Delta_{n-1}^{-2r+1}\alpha(1;n-2)Q_2(n-2,1),$$

so that $\Delta^{-2r}M\sigma_{n-1}$ is conjugate in B_{n-1} to $\Delta^{-2r+1}M_1\sigma_{n-1}$.

Now it is easy to see that $\Delta^{-2r+1}M_1$ has power $-2r+1$, so to complete the proof of the Lemma in Case (b) we only have to examine what happens when $r = 1$. In that situation, we have $\Delta^{-1}M_1 \sim \Delta^{-1}\beta(n-1;2)\alpha(2;n-1)Q_2(n-1,2)$, so that $t = -1$, as required.

Case (*c*). $I_1 = 1$. We then have

$$I_2(1,n-3)F_1(1,n-2)\beta(n-1;l) \mathrel{\dot{=}} \Delta \mathrel{\dot{=}} \alpha(n-l+1;n-1)\Delta_{n-1}\beta(n-1;l),$$

so that

$$I_2(1,n-3)F_1(1,n-2) \mathrel{\dot{=}} \alpha(n-l+1;n-1)\Delta_{n-2},$$

and therefore $l = 1$.

We may now rewrite (5.10) as

$$R \mathrel{\dot{=}} \{A\hat{A}\}^{r-1}Q_1(2,n-1)\alpha(1;n-2).$$

Hence $\Delta^{-2r+1}R\sigma_{n-1} = \Delta_{n-1}^{-2r+1}Q_1(1,n-2)$.

Now

$$\Delta^{-2r}M\sigma_{n-1} = \Delta_{n-1}^{-2r}Q(1,n-2)$$

$$= \Delta_{n-1}^{-2r}F_1Q_1(1,n-2)I_2 \sim \Delta_{n-1}^{-2r+1}Q_1(1,n-2).$$

Noting that if $r = 1$ then $\Delta^{-1}R$ has summit power -1, we see that the result is established for Case (c).

Case (*d*). I_1 ends only in σ_{n-2}. We then have $\Delta \mathrel{\dot{=}} I_1I_2F \mathrel{\dot{=}} I_1\Delta_{n-2}\sigma_{n-1}H$, for some H, so that $\Delta \mathrel{\dot{=}} \hat{H}I_1\Delta_{n-2}\sigma_{n-1} \mathrel{\dot{=}} \alpha(2;n-1)\alpha(1;n-2)\Delta_{n-2}\sigma_{n-1}$, and therefore $\hat{I}\hat{I}I_1 \mathrel{\dot{=}} \alpha(2;n-1)\alpha(1;n-2)$. From Lemma 15 it follows that $I_1 \mathrel{\dot{=}} \alpha(a+1;n-1)\alpha(b+1;n-2)$ and $\hat{H} \mathrel{\dot{=}} \alpha(2;a)\alpha(1;b)$, for some a, b with $1 \leqslant a \leqslant n-1$, $0 \leqslant b \leqslant n-3$ and $a - b \geqslant 1$.

Hence $\Delta \mathrel{\dot{=}} I_1\Delta_{n-2}\sigma_{n-1}H \mathrel{\dot{=}} I_1I_2F_1F_2$, so that

$$I_2(1,n-3)F_1(1,n-2)\beta(n-1;l)$$

$$\mathrel{\dot{=}} \Delta_{n-2}\beta(n-1;n-a)\beta(n-1;n-b)$$

$$= \Delta_{n-2}\beta(n-2;n-b-1)\beta(n-1;n-a),$$

since $a - b \geqslant 1$. It then follows that $l = n - a$, so that

$$I_2(1,n-3)F_1(1,n-2) \mathrel{\dot{=}} \Delta_{n-2}\beta(n-2;n-b-1),$$

and therefore $F_1(1,n-2) \mathrel{\dot{=}} K(1,n-3)\beta(n-2;n-b-1)$ and $I_2(1,n-3)K(1,n-3) \mathrel{\dot{=}} \Delta_{n-2}$, for some K.

We may now write (5.10) as

$$\beta(n-1;n-a)R\alpha(a+1;n-1)\alpha(b+1;n-2)$$

$$\mathrel{\dot{=}} \hat{A}\{A\hat{A}\}^{r-1}Q_1(2,n-1)\alpha(1;n-2),$$

so that

$$\beta(n-1;n-a)R\alpha(a+1;n-1) \doteq \hat{A}\{A\hat{A}\}^{r-1}Q_1(2,n-1)\alpha(1;b).$$

Since $a-b \geqslant 1$, it then follows that

$$Q_1(2,n-1) \doteq Q_2(2,n-1)\alpha(a+1;n-1)$$

say, and

$$R \doteq \beta(n-a-1;1)\{A\hat{A}\}^{r-1}Q_2(2,n-1)\alpha(1;b).$$

We then have

$$\begin{aligned}\Delta^{-2r+1}R &\sim \Delta^{-2r+1}\beta(n-1;n-b)\{A\hat{A}\}^{r-1}Q_2(2,n-1)\alpha(a+1;n-1)\\ &= \Delta^{-2r+1}\{A\hat{A}\}^{r-1}\beta(n-1;n-b)Q_2(2,n-1)\alpha(a+1;n-1)\\ &\equiv \Delta^{-2r+1}\{A\hat{A}\}^{r-1}V(2,n-1)\end{aligned}$$

say.

We note that

$$\begin{aligned}&Q(1,n-2)\\ &\doteq K(1,n-3)\beta(n-2;n-b-1)Q_2(1,n-2)\alpha(a;n-2)I_2(1,n-3)\end{aligned}$$

and that $Q(1,n-2)$ is prime to Δ_{n-1}. From this it follows easily that $\Delta^{-2r+1}\{A\hat{A}\}^{r-1}V(2,n-1)$ has power $-2r+1$.

Now if $r=1$ then $\Delta^{-1}V(2,n-1)$ has summit power -1. Hence we may assume that $r \geqslant 2$, and $t > -2r+2$.

Applying Lemmas 27 and 28, we obtain

$$\begin{aligned}V(2,n-1) &\doteq X(2,n-2)V_1(2,n-1)Y(2,n-2)\\ &\doteq X(2,n-2)V_2(2,n-1)\alpha(2;n-1)Y(2,n-2)\\ &\doteq X(2,n-2)V_2(2,n-1)Y(3,n-1)\alpha(2;n-1)\\ &\equiv V_3(2,n-1)\alpha(2;n-1)\end{aligned}$$

say, and $\hat{Y}X \doteq \Delta_{n-2}(2,n-2)$.

We now obtain the desired $\Delta^{-2r+1}M_1$. We have

$$\begin{aligned}\Delta^{-2r+1}\{A\hat{A}\}^{r-1}V(2,n-1) &= \Delta^{-2r+1}\{A\hat{A}\}^{r-1}V_3(2,n-1)\alpha(2;n-1)\\ &= \Delta^{-2r+1}A\{\hat{A}A\}^{r-2}V_3(1,n-2)\hat{A}\alpha(2;n-1)\\ &\sim \Delta^{-2r+1}\{\hat{A}A\}^{r-1}V_3(1,n-2)\beta(n-1;2)\\ &\sim \Delta^{-2r+1}\{A\hat{A}\}^{r-1}V_3(n-1,2)\alpha(1;n-2)\\ &\equiv \Delta^{-2r+1}M_1\end{aligned}$$

say, and $\Delta^{-2r+1}M_1\sigma_{n-1} = \Delta_{n-1}^{-2r+1}V_3(n-2,1)$.

Now

$$\begin{aligned}\Delta^{-2r}M\sigma_{n-1} &= \Delta_{n-1}^{-2r}Q(1, n-2)\\ &= \Delta_{n-1}^{-2r}K(1, n-3)V(1, n-2)I_2(1, n-3)\\ &\sim \Delta_{n-1}^{-2r}I_2(1, n-3)K(1, n-3)V(1, n-2)\\ &= \Delta_{n-1}^{-2r}\Delta_{n-2}V_3(1, n-2)\alpha(1; n-2)\\ &\sim \Delta_{n-1}^{-2r+1}V_3(1, n-2),\end{aligned}$$

so that $\Delta^{-2r}M\sigma_{n-1}$ is conjugate to $\Delta^{-2r+1}M_1\sigma_{n-1}$ in B_{n-1}.

It remains to establish that $\Delta^{-2r+1}M_1$ has power $-2r+1$. If this is not the case, then $V_3(n-1, 2)\alpha(1; n-2)$ must begin with $\Delta_{n-1}(2, n-1)$, and so therefore must $V_3(n-1, 2)$. However, this would imply that $\Delta^{-2r}M\sigma_{n-1}$ has power greater than $-2r$ in B_{n-1}. Hence $\Delta^{-2r+1}M_1$ has power $-2r+1$.

The concludes the proof of Case (d) and thereby establishes the Lemma.

Proof of Lemma 27. We have $\mu \equiv \Delta^{-2r+1}\{A\hat{A}\}^{r-1}V(2, n-1)$ is in standard form, $r \geq 2$ and μ has summit power $t > -2r+1$. We then have $\{A\hat{A}\}^{r-1}V(2, n-1) \doteq FW\hat{I}$ for some F, W, I with $\Delta \doteq IF$. We write $F \doteq F_1(2, n-1)F_2$, $I \doteq I_1I_2(1, n-2)$, where F_2 does not begin with any of $\sigma_2, \ldots, \sigma_{n-1}$ and I_1 does not end with any of $\sigma_1, \ldots, \sigma_{n-2}$. It is then easy to see that $V(2, n-1) \doteq F_1(2, n-1)V_2(2, n-1)I_2(n-1, 2)$, for some V_2.

We obtain descriptions of I_1 and F_2. We have $\Delta \doteq I_1I_2F \doteq I_1\Delta_{n-1}U$ for some U, so that $\Delta_{n-1}U\hat{I}_1 \doteq \Delta$, and therefore $\hat{I}_1 = \beta(k; 1)$, for some k with $0 \leq k \leq n-1$. Also, $\Delta \doteq IF_1F_2 \doteq H\Delta_{n-1}(2, n-1)F_2$ for some H, so that $F_2\hat{H} \doteq A$ and $F_2 \doteq \alpha(1; j)$, for some j with $0 \leq j \leq n-1$.

We note that not both $I_1 = 1$ and $F_2 = 1$ can hold, since otherwise $\Delta \doteq F_1(2, n-1)I_2(n-1, 2)$, which is impossible. We consider separately the cases (a) $F_2 \neq 1$ and $I_1 \neq 1$, (b) $I_1 \neq 1$, $F_2 = 1$, (c) $I_1 = 1$, $F_2 \neq 1$.

Case (*a*). We have $\Delta \doteq I_2F_1F_2\hat{I}_1 \doteq I_2F_1\alpha(1; j)\beta(k; 1)$, so that $j \neq k$. We consider separately the subcases (I) $j > k$, (II) $j < k$.

Subcase (*I*). $j > k$. Then

$$\Delta \doteq \beta(n-j-1; 1)\Delta_{n-2}(2, n-2)\beta(n-1; k+2)\alpha(1; j)\beta(k; 1),$$

so that

$$I_2(1, n-2)F_1(2, n-1) \doteq \beta(n-j-1; 1)\Delta_{n-2}(2, n-2)\beta(n-1; k+2).$$

It now follows that there exist $X(2, n-2)$, $Y(2, n-2)$ with $I_2(1, n-2) \doteqdot \beta(n-j-1; 1)Y(n-2, 2)$, $F_1(2, n-1) \doteqdot X(2, n-2)\beta(n-1; k+2)$ and $Y(n-2, 2)X(2, n-2) \doteqdot \Delta_{n-2}(2, n-2)$, and therefore

$$V(2, n-1) \doteqdot X(2, n-2)V_1(2, n-1)Y(2, n-2),$$

where $V_1(2, n-1) \doteqdot \beta(n-1; k+2)V_2(2, n-1)\alpha(j+1; n-1)$.

To establish the Lemma for the subcase under consideration, we need to show that $\mu \sim \Delta^{-2r+2}\{\hat{A}A\}^{r-2}\sigma_{n-1}V_1(1, n-2)$, and that this latter word has power $-2r+2$. We have

$$\begin{aligned}\mu &= \Delta^{-2r+1}\{A\hat{A}\}^{r-1}X(2, n-2)V_1(2, n-1)Y(2, n-2)\\ &= \Delta^{-2r+1}XA\{\hat{A}A\}^{r-2}V_1(1, n-2)\hat{A}Y(2, n-2)\\ &\sim \Delta^{-2r+1}AY(n-2, 2)XA\{\hat{A}A\}^{r-2}V_1(1, n-2)\\ &= \Delta^{-2r+1}\Delta\sigma_{n-1}V_1(1, n-2)\{\hat{A}A\}^{r-2}\\ &\sim \Delta^{-2r+2}\{\hat{A}A\}^{r-2}\sigma_{n-1}V_1(1, n-2).\end{aligned}$$

Now if this last word has power greater then $-2r+2$, then $V_1(1, n-2)$ must contain Δ_{n-1}, which would imply that μ does not have power $-2r+1$. Hence $\Delta^{-2r+2}\{\hat{A}A\}^{r-2}\sigma_{n-1}V_1(1, n-2)$ has power $-2r+2$, as required.

Subcase (*II*). $j < k$. Then

$$\Delta \doteqdot \beta(n-j-2; 1)\Delta_{n-2}(2, n-2)\beta(n-1; k+1)\alpha(1; j)\beta(k; 1),$$

so that

$$I_2F_1 \doteqdot \beta(n-j-2; 1)\Delta_{n-2}(2, n-2)\beta(n-1; k+1),$$

and the result follows as in the previous subcase.

Case (*b*). $I_1 \neq 1$, $F_2 = 1$. We have

$$\begin{aligned}I_2F_1 &\doteqdot \Delta_{n-1}U \doteqdot \Delta_{n-1}\beta(n-1; k+1)\\ &\doteqdot \alpha(1; n-2)\Delta_{n-2}(2, n-2)\beta(n-1; k+1),\end{aligned}$$

and the result follows as above.

Case (*c*). $I_1 = 1$, $F_2 \neq 1$. Then

$$\begin{aligned}I_2F_1 &\doteqdot H\Delta_{n-1}(2, n-1)\\ &\doteqdot \beta(n-j-1; 1)\Delta_{n-2}(2, n-2)\beta(n-1; 2),\end{aligned}$$

and the result follows.

This concludes the proof of Lemma 27. Finally, we have

Proof of Lemma 28. We have $\phi \equiv \Delta^{-2r+2}\{\hat{A}A\}^{r-2}\sigma_{n-1}V_1(1, n-2)$ is in standard form, $r \geqslant 2$ and ϕ has summit power $t > -2r+2$. We therefore have $\{\hat{A}A\}^{r-2}\sigma_{n-1}V_1(1, n-2) \mp FWI$, for some F, W, I with $\Delta \mp IF$.

We write $F \mp F_1(1, n-3)F_2$, where F_2 does not begin with any of $\sigma_1, \ldots, \sigma_{n-3}$. We then have $V_1(1, n-2) \mp F_1(1, n-3)V_2(1, n-2)$ for some V_2, so that $\{\hat{A}A\}^{r-2}\sigma_{n-1}V_2(1, n-2) \mp F_2WI$. Now if F_2 begins with σ_{n-2} then $\sigma_{n-1}V_2(1, n-2)$ begins with σ_{n-2}, so that V_2 begins with $\sigma_{n-2}\sigma_{n-1}$, which is impossible. Hence either $F_2 = 1$ or F_2 begins only with σ_{n-1}.

We also write $I \mp I_1I_2(1, n-2)$, where I_1 does not end with any of $\sigma_1, \ldots, \sigma_{n-2}$. We then have $V_2(1, n-2) \mp V_3(1, n-2)I_2(1, n-2)$, for some V_3.

We now describe I_1 and F_2. We have $\Delta \mp I_1I_2F \mp I_1\Delta_{n-1}U$, for some U, so that $U\hat{I}_1 = \hat{A}$ and $\hat{I}_1 \mp \beta(j, 1)$ for some j with $0 \leqslant j \leqslant n-1$. Also, $\Delta = IF_1F_2 \mp H\Delta_{n-1}F_2$, for some H, so that $F_2\hat{H} = \hat{A}$ and $F_2 \mp \beta(n-1; k)$ for some k with $1 \leqslant k \leqslant n$.

We note that not both $I_1 = 1$ and $F_2 = 1$ can hold. We consider separately the cases (a) $I_1 \neq 1$, $F_2 \neq 1$, (b) $I_1 = 1$, $F_2 \neq 1$, (c) $I_1 \neq 1$, $F_2 = 1$.

Case (*a*). $I_1 \neq 1$, $F_2 \neq 1$. We have $1 \leqslant j \leqslant n-1$, $1 \leqslant k \leqslant n-1$ and

$$\Delta \mp I_2F_1F_2\hat{I}_1 \mp I_2F_1\beta(n-1; k)\beta(j; 1),$$

so that $k \neq j$. If $j > k$ then we obtain a contradiction as in Lemma 26. If $k > j+1$ then

$$\Delta \mp \Delta_{n-2}\beta(n-2; j+1)\beta(n-1; k)\beta(j; 1)\beta(k-1; 1),$$

so that

$$I_2(1, n-2)F_1(1, n-3) \mp \alpha(n-k+1; n-1)\Delta_{n-2}\beta(n-2; j+1).$$

This, however, is impossible unless $k = 1$, but since $k > j+1$ we cannot have $k = 1$. Hence $k = j+1$.

We now have $\Delta = I_2F_1\hat{A}$, so that

$$I_2(1, n-2)F_1(1, n-3) \mp \alpha(1; n-2)\Delta_{n-2},$$

and therefore

$$I_2(1, n-2) \mp \alpha(1; n-2)X(1, n-3) \mp X(2, n-2)\alpha(1; n-2),$$

for some X. This shows that $V_1(1, n-2)$ ends with $\alpha(1; n-2)$.

To complete the proof of this case, we note that when $r = 2$ we have $\sigma_{n-1}V_3(1, n-2) \doteqdot F_2WI_1 \doteqdot \beta(n-1;k)W\alpha(n-j;n-1)$, so that $V_3(1, n-2) \doteqdot \beta(n-2;k)W\alpha(n-j;n-1)$, which is impossible. Hence Case (a) cannot occur when $r = 2$.

Case (*b*). $I_1 = 1$, $F_2 \neq 1$. We have $j = 0$ and $1 \leqslant k \leqslant n-1$. Now

$$I_2(1, n-2)F_1(1, n-3) \doteqdot H\Delta_{n-1} \doteqdot \alpha(n-k+1; n-1)\Delta_{n-1},$$

so that we must have $k = 1$, and $I_2F_1 \doteqdot \Delta_{n-1}$. If $r \geqslant 3$ then this proves the result, as in the previous case. If $r = 2$ we have

$$\sigma_{n-1}V_3(1, n-2) \doteqdot F_2W \doteqdot \hat{A}W,$$

so that $V_3(1, n-2) \doteqdot \beta(n-2;1)W$, and therefore $W \equiv W(1, n-2)$. Now $\Delta^{-2}\sigma_{n-1}V_1(1, n-2) \sim \Delta^{-1}W$, and $\Delta^{-1}W$ has summit power -1, as required.

Case (*c*). $I_1 \neq 1$, $F_2 = 1$. We have $1 \leqslant j \leqslant n-1$ and $k = 0$. Now

$$I_2(1, n-2)F_1(1, n-3) \doteqdot \Delta_{n-1}U \doteqdot \Delta_{n-1}\beta(n-1; j+1),$$

so that we must have $j = n-1$ and $I_2F_1 \doteqdot \Delta_{n-1}$. If $r \geqslant 3$ this establishes the result. If $r = 2$ then we have $\sigma_{n-1}V_2(1, n-2) \doteqdot WA$, so that $\sigma_1V_2(n-1, 2) \doteqdot \hat{W}\hat{A}$. However, from Corollary 20 we see that this is impossible.

This concludes the proof of the Lemma.

References

[1] J.S. Birman, Braids, links and mapping class groups (Princeton University Press, 1975).

[2] W.L. Chow, On the algebraic braid group, Ann. of Math. 49 (1948) 654–658.

[3] F.A. Garside, The braid group and other groups, Quart. J. Math. Oxford 20 (1969) 235–254.

S.I. Adian, W.W. Boone, G. Higman, eds., Word Problems II

ON SOME GROUP PRESENTATIONS*

B.H. NEUMANN
Institute of Advanced Studies, The Australian National University, Canberra

Let p, q, r, s, t, u be integers, and denote by $G(p,q,r,s,t,u)$, or G for short, the group with three generators a, b, c and defining relations

$$a^p b = b a^s,$$

$$b^q c = c b^t,$$

$$c^r a = a c^u.$$

It is known that $G(1,1,1,-1,-1,-1)$ is infinite [2, §2] and that $G(1,1,1,2,2,2)$ is trivial (Higman [1], see also [2, §23]). If

$$(*) \qquad 2 \leqslant p \leqslant |s|, \qquad 2 \leqslant q \leqslant |t|, \qquad 2 \leqslant r \leqslant |u|,$$

then it can be shown that G is infinite. The method consists of constructing a "normal form" for the elements of G. Though the idea is simple, the technical details are complicated.

The groups $G(p,q,r,p+1,q+1,r+1)$ have no proper subgroups of finite index, and thus no non-trivial finite epimorphic images. The proof follows one of Higman [1] (see also [2], §23). On the other hand, if one of $|s-p|$, $|t-q|$, $|u-r|$ is different from 1, the group is easily seen to have non-trivial finite factor groups.

All the presentations considered have solvable word problem; this is an immediate consequence of the fact that there is a normal form, which is readily computable, for the elements of the groups presented.

The question with which the investigation started is, whether $G(2,2,2,3,3,3)$ is finite (and then necessarily trivial) or infinite; and the author is indebted to Dr A.M. Brunner for reminding him of it. This group is infinite. By contrast it follows from recent, more general results of Post [3] that $G(2,2,1,3,3,3)$ is finite, and $G(2,2,1,3,3,2)$ is

* Most of this work was carried out at the Conference, but not formally presented there; it was only shown privately to a few interested participants. It was reported to the *Conference on finite groups and permutation groups* at the Mathematisches Forschungsinstitut Oberwolfach, Germany, in August 1976.

trivial. The author is grateful to Dr Michael J. Post for permitting him to quote his unpublished results.

A more detailed account is to be published in the *Canadian Journal of Mathematics.*

References

[1] Graham Higman, A finitely generated infinite simple group, J. London Math. Soc. 26 (1951) 61–64.

[2] B.H. Neumann, An essay on free products of groups with amalgamations, Phil. Trans. Roy. Soc. London, Ser. A 246 (1954), 503–554.

[3] Michael J. Post, A note on finite three-generator groups with zero deficiency, to be published.

S.I. Adian, W.W. Boone, G. Higman, eds., Word Problems II

THE CONCEPT OF "LARGENESS" IN GROUP THEORY

Stephen J. PRIDE*
Open University, Milton Keynes

§1. Introduction

§1.1. Summary of results

There are many group-theoretic properties which are traditionally thought of as measuring the "largeness" of a group — for example, having cardinality greater than or equal to κ for some infinite cardinal κ, being SQ-universal, having a free subgroup of rank 2, having a properly ascending chain of normal subgroups. There are also many groups which are traditionally thought of as being "large" — non-abelian free groups and Fuchsian groups for example. At the other end of the scale there are groups, which although infinite, are still considered to be rather "small" — infinite groups in which every non-trivial normal subgroup has finite index for instance. The aim of this paper is to develop a theory which gives precision to these vague notions of "largeness". This theory provides a framework in which to discuss several well-known, but until now, unrelated ideas. It also gives a different viewpoint, which leads to new results.

By examining several properties $\mathcal{P}$ which are traditionally thought of as indicating the "largeness" of a group, one finds that they all satisfy three basic conditions, and moreover, it is these conditions which account for the fact that the property is a measure of "largeness".

(LP 1) If G has $\mathcal{P}$ and K maps onto G then K has $\mathcal{P}$.

(LP 2) If $H \leqslant G$ with H of finite index in G then G has $\mathcal{P}$ if and only if H has $\mathcal{P}$.

(LP 3) The trivial group 1 does not have $\mathcal{P}$.

A group-theoretic property satisfying (LP 1)–(LP 3) will be called a *large property*.

In §2.1, partly for illustration, and partly for use in later discussion, several well-known large properties are listed. In §2.2 it is shown how to associate with any infinite group A a large property $\mathcal{L}(A)$ called the *large property generated by* A. This notion enables one to compare two infinite groups G, H. Thus G is said to be *larger than* H (written

* Present address: University of Glasgow.

$H \leqslant G$) if G has $\mathscr{L}(H)$; G and H are said to be *equally large* if G has $\mathscr{L}(H)$ and H has $\mathscr{L}(G)$; and G is said to be *strictly larger* than H if G is larger than H, but G and H are not equally large. If G is larger than H then any large property enjoyed by H is also enjoyed by G; and if G and H are equally large then they have the same large properties.

The relation of *larger than* is a quasi-order, and one would hope that groups traditionally thought of as being "large" would be "high up" in this quasi-order, and groups traditionally thought of as being "small" would be "low down". These two extremes are examined in Sections 3 and 4 respectively.

If G is a finitely generated group then it is easily shown that F_2, the free group of rank 2, is larger than G. Thus G is "as large as it can possibly be" if it is equally as large as F_2. In §3.2 it is shown that many finitely generated groups which are traditionally thought of as being "large" are actually equally as large as F_2. In particular, this is verified for:

(i) Fuchsian groups (Theorem 3.2);

(ii) one-relator groups with torsion on at least two generators (Theorem 3.3);

(iii) certain arithmetically defined linear groups

$$\mathrm{PSL}(2, \quad), \mathrm{SL}(2, \quad), \mathrm{GL}(2, \quad).$$

Some remarks are also made concerning small cancellation groups.

The verification that one-relator groups with torsion on at least two generators have $\mathscr{L}(F_2)$ provides a new and straightforward proof that these groups are SQ-universal.

Also in §3.2, an example is given of a finitely generated one-relator group B which, although having several well-known large properties, nevertheless is not equally as large as F_2. To be precise, it is shown that *if* $B = \langle a, t; t^{-1}a^2t = a^3\rangle$ *then no subgroup of finite index in B maps onto a free group of rank greater than 1* (Theorem 3.4).

In §3.3 the question of which free products have $\mathscr{L}(F_2)$ is discussed. Let $G = H * K$ with $H, K \neq 1$. If $|H| = |K| = 2$ then G is cyclic-by-finite and is "small". On the other hand, if $\max\{|H|, |K|\} > 2$ then G has many well-known large properties. However, it is often quite a complicated affair to establish that G has such properties, and this leads one to think that perhaps G need not necessarily be "naturally large" in the sense of having $\mathscr{L}(F_2)$. This turns out to be the situation. It is shown in §3.3 that *G has* $\mathscr{L}(F_2)$ *if and only if either*: (*i*) *one of H, K has* $\mathscr{L}(F_2)$; *or* (*ii*) *both H and K have non-trivial finite homomorphic images* $\bar{H}$, $\bar{K}$, *with* $\max\{|\bar{H}|, |\bar{K}|\} > 2$ (Theorem 3.7).

Section 4 turns to "small" groups. Firstly, in §4.1, several concepts of "smallness" are discussed. Thus, an infinite group G is said to have height m if whenever one has groups $G_1, \dots, G_r$ with $G_r = G$ and G_{i+1} strictly larger than G_i for $i = 1, \dots, r-1$, then $r \leq m$. Also, G is said to satisfy Max-$\preccurlyeq$ (Min-$\preccurlyeq$) if there is no infinite sequence of groups $G_1, G_2, \dots$ with G larger than G_i and G_{i+1} strictly larger than G_i (G_i strictly larger than G_{i+1}) for $i = 1, 2, \dots$. Related to these two latter properties are chain conditions on certain subgroups of G (see Theorem 4.1).

In §§4.2, 4.3, 4.4 consideration is given to a class of infinite groups which are traditionally thought of as being "small" — namely, infinite groups in which every non-trivial normal subgroup has finite index (the so-called just-infinite groups). Let $\mathcal{M}$ denote the class of minimal groups with respect to the quasi-order relation of *larger than.* It is easy to show that any infinite group in which every non-trivial *subnormal* subgroup has finite index lies in $\mathcal{M}$. However, just-infinite groups which have non-trivial subnormal subgroups of infinite index need not be minimal. Nevertheless, if *G is a just-infinite group satisfying the maximal condition on subnormal subgroups then G has finite height* (see Theorem 4.2). For just-infinite groups not satisfying the maximal condition on subnormal subgroups, one finds that *such a group is either minimal or does not satisfy* Min-$\preccurlyeq$ (see Theorem 4.3). An example is given in §4.4 of a just-infinite group lying in $\mathcal{M}$ but not satisfying the maximal condition on subnormal subgroups.

In §4.5 questions concerning extensions are raised. In particular, are the properties "having finite height", Max-$\preccurlyeq$, Min-$\preccurlyeq$ extension closed? The main result (Theorem 4.4) is that the answer is negative for the first two properties (it remains unresolved for the third). In fact, it is shown that *there is a split extension of one minimal group by another which does not satisfy* Max-$\preccurlyeq$. In contrast to this result it is also shown that *if $M_1, \dots, M_n$ are minimal groups then $M_1 \times \cdots \times M_n$ has height less than or equal to n* (see Theorem 4.5).

Although poly-minimal groups do not in general have finite height, it can be shown that for certain classes $\mathcal{Y}$ of minimal groups, poly-$\mathcal{Y}$ groups do have finite height. In particular, poly-cyclic groups, and groups with a composition series, have finite height. These results will be obtained in a general setting in a sequel to the present paper.*

The work presented in this paper raises many questions, some of which are stated in the text below.

* "Groups of finite height", J. Austral. Math. Soc. (Series A) 28 (1979) 87–99.

§1.2. Notes to the reader

The reader who wishes to get the main results and ideas of the paper, but is not interested in details should read as follows: §2.1, §2.2, §3.2, §3.3 (up to the end of the statement of Theorem 3.7), §4.1, §4.2 (up to Problem 6), §4.5 (up to Problem 7).

The casual reader should note that $\simeq$ does *not* signify isomorphism.

§1.3. Acknowledgements

This paper has benefited from conversations with D. Goldrei, A.J. Wilkie, and most especially with I.M.S. Dey. Visits to New York University and the University of Illinois at Urbana in Spring 1976 were also very beneficial. I thank these universities for their hospitality, and the Overseas Research Committee of the Open University for financial support. Some of the work in this paper was carried out while I was attending the Conference on Word and Decision Problems in Group Theory and Algebra, Oxford, 1976. The work of the organizers and the financial support of the SRC is gratefully acknowledged.

§1.4. Notation

Throughout the paper the text book [14] by Magnus, Karrass and Solitar will be used for matters relating to combinatorial group theory. In particular, the techniques of the Reidemeister–Schreier method as described in [14, §2.3] will be used in several places, and in such computations the notation of [14, §2.3] will be employed.

Additional notation and background material will be needed as follows.

Let G be a group. If A is a subset of G then sgp A will denote the subgroup of G generated by A. If $\{H_i : i \in I\}$ is a set of subgroups of G then $\text{sgp}\{H_i : i \in I\}$ will denote the subgroup of G generated by the elements of the H_i. Let H be a subgroup of G and let $g \in G$. The normalizer of H in G will be denoted by $N_G(H)$. The conjugate subgroup $\{g^{-1}hg : h \in H\}$ of H by g will be denoted by H^g. The intersection of all the conjugates of H in G will be called the *core* of H (in G) and will be denoted by $\text{Cor}(H)$. Clearly $\text{Cor}(H) \trianglelefteq G$. The index of H in G will be denoted by $|G : H|$. If $|G : H| < \infty$ then, as is well-known (and easily established), H has only finitely many distinct conjugates under G and so $|G : \text{Cor}(H)| < \infty$. Thus, *a group has a proper subgroup of finite index if and only if it has a proper normal subgroup of finite index.* This result will be used frequently and without mention in the sequel. The notation $H \trianglelefteq^2 G$ will signify that there is a subgroup K of G with $H \trianglelefteq K \trianglelefteq G$. For $g_1, g_2 \in G$, the commutator $g_1^{-1}g_2^{-1}g_1g_2$ will be denoted by $[g_1, g_2]$.

If $\mathscr{P}$ is a group-theoretic property then $\neg\mathscr{P}$ will denote the negation of $\mathscr{P}$ The properties of satisfying the maximal (minimal) condition for subgroups, normal subgroups, subnormal subgroups will be denoted by Max, Max-n, Max-sn respectively (Min, Min-n, Min-sn respectively).

The integers will be denoted by **Z**, and the rationals by **Q**. The cyclic group of order 2 will be denoted by $\mathbf{Z}_2$.

§2. Large properties

§2.1. Well-known examples of large properties

For illustration, and also for use in later discussions, several well-known large properties of groups will now be listed. For all of these examples it is an easy matter to verify that (LP 1) and (LP 3) hold. However, it is not always straightforward to verify (LP 2), and for several of the examples information will be given relevant to the verification of (LP 2).

Many large properties arise as negations of well-known properties. It is not difficult to see that if $\mathscr{Q}$ is a group-theoretic property which is

(*) closed under taking homomorphic images, normal subgroups of finite index, extensions by finite groups,

then $\neg\mathscr{Q}$ is a large property. (Conversely, if $\mathscr{P}$ is a large property then $\neg\mathscr{P}$ satisfies (*).) To see that (LP 2) holds let G be a group with a subgroup H of finite index. If G has $\neg\mathscr{Q}$ then $\mathrm{Cor}(H)$ has $\neg\mathscr{Q}$ since $G/\mathrm{Cor}(H)$ is finite. Thus H has $\neg\mathscr{Q}$ since $\mathrm{Cor}(H)\trianglelefteq H$. Conversely if H has $\neg\mathscr{Q}$ then $\mathrm{Cor}(H)$ has $\neg\mathscr{Q}$ (by what has just been shown), and so G has $\neg\mathscr{Q}$ since $\mathrm{Cor}(H)$ is normal and of finite index in G.

It follows immediately from the above that if $\mathscr{Q}$ is a group-theoretic property such that:

(**) finite groups have $\mathscr{Q}$; $\mathscr{Q}$ is closed under taking subgroups, homomorphic images, extensions;

then $\neg\mathscr{Q}$ is a large property. Many interesting large properties arise this way.

It is perhaps worth commenting that *if $\mathscr{P}$ is any large property then no finite group can have $\mathscr{P}$*. This is a trivial consequence of (LP 2) and (LP 3).

Example 2.1. The property $\mathscr{C}(\kappa)$ of having cardinality greater than or equal to κ, where κ is an infinite cardinal.

Example 2.2. The property $\mathscr{G}(\kappa)$ of not being generated by less than κ elements, where κ is an infinite cardinal.

This is the same property as $\mathscr{C}(\kappa)$ except when κ is $\aleph_0$.

To verify that (LP 2) holds, let G be a group with subgroup H of finite index. Obviously, if H can be generated by less than κ elements then so can G, since a generating set for H together with the elements of a transversal of H in G constitutes a generating set for G. On the other hand, if G has a generating set of cardinality less than κ, then so does H [14, Theorem 2.7].

Example 2.3. SQ-universality.

A group G is said to be SQ-universal if every countable group is embeddable in a quotient of G. For a verification of (LP 2) see [17] or [7, Lemma 9].

Example 2.4. The property $\mathscr{F}(\kappa)$ of having a free subgroup of rank κ, where κ is a non-zero cardinal.

Notice that, since a free group of rank 2 has free subgroups of every countable rank $\mathscr{F}(2), \mathscr{F}(3), \ldots, \mathscr{F}(\aleph_0)$ are all the same property.

Example 2.5. Having a free subsemigroup of rank κ, where κ is a non-zero cardinal.

Example 2.6. Satisfying no non-trivial law (i.e. generating the variety $\mathcal{O}$ of all groups).

Example 2.7. Non-amenability.

A group G is said to be amenable if there is a finitely additive translation-invariant measure μ on the set of all subsets of G such that $\mu(G) = 1$. The property of amenability satisfies the conditions (**) — see Theorems 1.2.4–1.2.6 of [6].

Example 2.8. Having exponential growth.

The concept of a group having exponential growth has been defined in the literature for finitely generated groups (see [15]). In order to ensure that (LP 1) holds it is necessary to extend the definition to infinitely generated groups by local considerations. Thus, a group G

will be said to have exponential growth if there is a finite subset Γ of elements of G such that the following holds: if $\gamma_\Gamma(r)$ $(r \geq 0)$ denotes the number of distinct elements of G which can be expressed as words of length less than or equal to r in the elements of Γ, then there are constants α, ρ with $\alpha > 0$, $\rho > 1$ such that $\gamma_\Gamma(r) \geq \alpha\rho^r$ for $r = 0, 1, 2, \ldots$ (i.e. γ_Γ grows exponentially).

Suppose G is a group with a subgroup H of finite index. Obviously if H has exponential growth then so does G. Conversely, suppose there is a finite subset Γ of G such that γ_Γ grows exponentially. Let $g \mapsto \bar{g}$ be a right coset representative function for $G \bmod H$, and let Λ be the subset of H consisting of all elements

$$Ua\,.\,\overline{Ua}^{-1},$$

where U is an arbitrary representative and $a \in \Gamma$. Then it follows from [14, pp. 89–90] that if g is an element of G expressible as a word of length less than or equal to r in the elements of Γ, then $g = h\bar{g}$, where h is an element of H expressible as a word of length less than or equal to r in the elements of Λ. This implies that $\gamma_\Gamma(r) \leq |G:H|\,\gamma_\Lambda(r)$, so that H has exponential growth.

Example 2.9. Let $\mathcal{Q}$ be a group-theoretic property which is closed under taking homomorphic images; then the property of not being locally $\mathcal{Q}$-by-finite is a large property.

To verify that (LP 2) holds, suppose H is a subgroup of finite index in a group G. Obviously if G is locally $\mathcal{Q}$-by-finite then so is H. Conversely, suppose H is locally $\mathcal{Q}$-by-finite, and let Γ be a finite subset of G. Let Λ be as constructed in Example 2.8. Then sgp Λ has finite index in sgp Γ. Since sgp Λ is $\mathcal{Q}$-by-finite, so it sgp Γ. Thus G is locally $\mathcal{Q}$-by-finite.

Example 2.10. The properties $\neg$Max, $\neg$Min, $\neg$Max-n, $\neg$Min-n, $\neg$Max-sn, $\neg$Min-sn.

The properties Max, Min satisfy the conditions (**). (See [11, Lemma 1.E.1] and [19, Lemma 1.48, Corollary] in this connection.)

The properties Max-n, Min-n, Max-sn, Min-sn satisfy the conditions (*). (See [19, Lemma 1.48, Corollary] and [26] in this connection.)

There are several group-theoretic properties which are not known to be large properties, although they "ought to be". Two of these are mentioned here.

In [25] Wiegold discusses the class $\mathcal{X}$ of groups G with the property that whenever G acts transitively on a set Ω, there is some element of G displacing every element of Ω.

Problem 1. Is the property of not lying in $\mathscr{X}$ a large property?*

In [2] Chiswell discusses the concept of length functions on groups. One can define a length function on any group by setting the length of every element equal to 0, or by setting the length of the identity equal to zero and the length of every other element equal to 1. However, there are various meanings one can attach to a "non-trivial" length function. For example, one can require the existence of at least one element g such that the length of g^2 is greater than the length of g.

Problem 2. With some interpretation of "non-trivial", is the property of having a "non-trivial" length function a large property?

§2.2. Large properties generated by groups

Let A be an infinite group. Then one can associate with A a large property $\mathscr{L}(A)$, called *the large property generated by* A, defined as follows. A group G has $\mathscr{L}(A)$ if and only if there is a chain of groups $G_0, G_1, \ldots, G_n$ with $G_0 = A$, $G_n = G$, and where for $i = 1, \ldots, n$ *either*

(2.1) G_i is a subgroup of finite index in G_{i-1},

or

(2.2) G_{i-1} is a subgroup of finite index in G_i,

or

(2.3) G_i maps onto G_{i-1}.

It is clear that $\mathscr{L}(A)$ actually is a large property.

Theorem 2.1. *Let A be an infinite group.*

(i) *A group G has $\mathscr{L}(A)$ if and only if there are groups B, C with B of finite index in A, C of finite index in G, and C mapping onto B.*

(ii) *It can be assumed in* (i) *that either $B \trianglelefteq A$ or $C \trianglelefteq G$.*

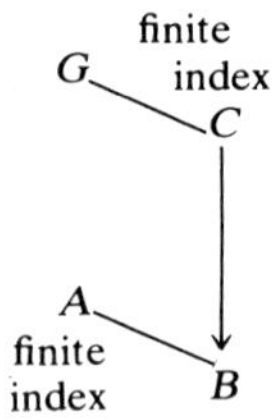

* *Added in proof.* The answer is "No" (P.M. Neumann).

Proof. First consider (i).

Obviously if the conditions are satisfied then G has $\mathscr{L}(A)$.

Conversely, if G has $\mathscr{L}(A)$ then there is a chain of groups $G_0, G_1, \ldots, G_n$ with $G_0 = A$, $G_n = G$, and where for $i = 1, \ldots, n$ one of (2.1)–(2.3) holds. It will be shown by induction on n that the conditions stated in (i) are satisfied.

The result is trivial if $n = 0$.

Suppose $n > 0$. Since G_{n-1} has $\mathscr{L}(A)$ the inductive hypothesis guarantees that there are groups B_1, C_1 with B_1 of finite index in A, C_1 of finite index in G_{n-1} and C_1 mapping onto B_1 by a homomorphism θ say.

Case (i). G_n is of finite index in G_{n-1}.

Let $C = C_1 \cap G_n$. Then C has finite index in both C_1 and G_n. Let $B = \theta(C)$. The fact that C has finite index in C_1 implies that B has finite index in B_1. Thus B also has finite index in A.

Case (ii). G_{n-1} is of finite index in G_n.

Simply take $B = B_1$ and $C = C_1$.

Case (iii). G_n maps onto G_{n-1}.

Suppose $\psi : G_n \to G_{n-1}$ is the homomorphism. Let $C = \psi^{-1}(C_1)$. Then C is of finite index in G_n. Let $B = B_1$. Then $\theta\psi$ maps C onto B.

Now consider (ii). If C is not normal in G one can replace C by $\mathrm{Cor}(C)$ and replace B by the image of $\mathrm{Cor}(C)$ under the homomorphism $C \to B$. On the other hand, if B is not normal in A one can replace B by $\mathrm{Cor}(B)$ and replace C by the inverse image of $\mathrm{Cor}(B)$ under the homomorphism $C \to B$.

This completes the proof of the theorem.

Considerable use will be made of Theorem 2.1 in the sequel. For the present, the following simple corollary is noted.

Corollary 2.1.1. *Let G and A be infinite groups and suppose G has no proper subgroups of finite index. If G has $\mathscr{L}(A)$ then A has a (necessarily normal) subgroup $\bar{G}$ of finite index, where $\bar{G}$ is a homomorphic image of G. In particular A has a subgroup of finite index which has no proper subgroups of finite index.*

The first part of this result is an immediate consequence of Theorem 2.1 (i). The second part follows from the fact that no homomorphic image of G can have a proper subgroup of finite index.

The concept of the large property generated by a group is useful in that it gives a way of comparing two groups. Let G and H be infinite groups. It will be said that G is *larger than* H (written $H \preccurlyeq G$) if G has $\mathscr{L}(H)$; G and H will be said to be *equally large* (written $G \simeq H$) if $H \preccurlyeq G$ and $G \preccurlyeq H$; and it will be said that G is *strictly larger than* H (written $H < G$) if $H \preccurlyeq G$ but H is not larger than G.

It is easy to see that $H \preccurlyeq G$ if and only if $\mathscr{L}(G)$ implies $\mathscr{L}(H)$. Obviously the relation of *larger than* is a quasi-order and the relation of *equally large* is the induced equivalence relation. Another trivial but important fact is that if $\mathscr{P}$ is any large property, and if H has $\mathscr{P}$, then every group larger than H also has $\mathscr{P}$. Thus two groups which are equally large have the same large properties.

The referee has pointed out that an alternative way of viewing the relation $\preccurlyeq$ might be profitable for future work. Define two groups to be equivalent if one is a subgroup of finite index in the other, and let $\lfloor G \rfloor$ denote the equivalence class of G. Then $G \preccurlyeq H$ if and only if some H_0 in $\lfloor H \rfloor$ is a pre-image of some G_0 in $\lfloor G \rfloor$.

§3. "Large" groups

§3.1. Large properties of non-abelian free groups

Theorem 3.1. *Let F and $\bar{F}$ be free groups of ranks r, s respectively with* $2 \leqslant r < s$.

(i) *If s is infinite then $\bar{F} < F$.*

(ii) *If s is finite then $\bar{F} \simeq F$.*

Proof. First consider (i). Since there is a homomorphism of F onto $\bar{F}$ it follows that $\bar{F} \preccurlyeq F$. To show that $\bar{F} < F$ it suffices to find a large property enjoyed by F but not by $\bar{F}$. Clearly $\mathscr{G}(s)$ (Example 2.2) is such a property.

To prove (ii), let F_2 denote the free group of rank 2 freely generated by x, y. The normal closure in F_2 of $\{x^n, y\}$ $(n \geqslant 1)$ has finite index and is free of rank $n+1$ by Schreier's formula [14, Theorem 2.10]. Thus F_2 has subgroups of finite index isomorphic to $\bar{F}$ and F, so $F_2 \simeq \bar{F} \simeq F$, as required.

This proves the theorem.

It is now easy to describe the large properties of non-abelian free groups.

Corollary 3.1.1. *Let F be a free group of rank $r \geqslant 2$, and let $\mathcal{P}$ be a large property.*

(i) *If r is infinite then F has $\mathcal{P}$ if and only if there is an r-generator group with $\mathcal{P}$.*

(ii) *If r is finite then F has $\mathcal{P}$ if and only if there is a finitely generated group with $\mathcal{P}$.*

Proof. (i) is straightforward.

For (ii), note that if there is a finitely generated group G with $\mathcal{P}$ then there is a free group $\bar{F}$ of rank greater than or equal to 2 mapping onto G and therefore having $\mathcal{P}$. Thus if r is finite then F has $\mathcal{P}$ since $F \simeq \bar{F}$.

Taking $\mathcal{P}$ to be $\mathcal{L}(A)$ in the above result one obtains:

Corollary 3.1.2. *Let F be a free group of rank $r \geqslant 2$.*

(i) *If r is infinite then F is larger than every r-generator group.*

(ii) *If r is finite then F is larger than every finitely generated group.*

§3.2. Groups which are equally as large as F_2

It was seen in §3.1 that F_2, the free group of rank 2, is larger than every finitely generated group. Consequently, a finitely generated group is as large as it can possibly be if it is equally as large as F_2. The aim of this section is to show that many groups traditionally thought of as being "very large" are actually equally as large as F_2.

It is clear that any group which has a non-abelian free subgroup of finite index has $\mathcal{L}(F_2)$. The structure of such groups has been determined [3], [10], [22]. For future reference it should be noted that the class includes all free products $A * B$ with A, B finite and $|A| \geqslant 2$, $|B| \geqslant 3$. It also includes all HNN groups, where the base H is finite and the associated subgroups K_{-1}, K_1 are properly contained in H.

1. *Fuchsian groups*

Theorem 3.2. *All finitely generated Fuchsian groups are equally large as F_2.*

Proof. The following argument is adapted from [17].

A finitely generated Fuchsian group G has a presentation with generators

$$a_1, \ldots, a_p, \; b_1, \ldots, b_p, \; c_1, \ldots, c_q, \; e_1, \ldots, e_r,$$

and defining relations

$$e_i^{n_i} = 1 \qquad i = 1, \ldots, r,$$

$$[a_1, b_1] \cdots [a_p, b_p] c_1 \cdots c_q e_1 \cdots e_r = 1,$$

where $n_i \geqslant 2$ for $i = 1, \ldots, r$, and where

$$2p - 2 + q + \sum_1^r (1 - n_i^{-1}) > 0.$$

By a theorem of Nielsen, Bundgaard and Fox [8, p. 68], G has a subgroup H of finite index which can be presented with generators

$$u_1, \ldots, u_m, v_1, \ldots, v_m, x_1, \ldots, x_l,$$

and defining relator

$$[u_1, v_1] \cdots [u_m, v_m] x_1 \cdots x_l = 1.$$

Here $(m, l) \neq (0,0), (0,1), (0,2), (1,0)$. If $l > 0$ then H is free of rank greater than 1, while if $l = 0$ then H maps onto F_2 (put $u_1 = \cdots = u_m = v_3 = \cdots = v_m = 1$). Thus in either case H, and therefore G, has $\mathscr{L}(F_2)$.

2. *One-relator groups*

There are two well-known heuristic principles in the theory of one-relator groups: (i) one-relator groups which do not satisfy a non-trivial law behave "like" free groups; (ii) one-relator groups with torsion which do not satisfy a non-trivial law behave "more like" free groups (G. Baumslag). The following two theorems further illustrate, and in fact give a certain substance, to these two principles.

Theorem 3.3. *Every one-relator group with torsion which does not satisfy a non-trivial law has* $\mathscr{L}(F_2)$.

Theorem 3.4. *There is a two-generator torsion-free one-relator group* B *which does not satisfy a non-trivial law but which is such that* $B < F_2$.

It follows immediately from Theorem 3.3 that if G is a one-relator group with torsion which does not satisfy a non-trivial law then G has every large property enjoyed by F_2. In particular, G is SQ-universal. The SQ-universality of one-relator groups has been investigated by Sacerdote and Schupp in [20]. They obtain results for torsion-free groups as well as groups with torsion, but their methods (small cancellation theory over HNN groups) are much more complicated than those needed to prove Theorem 3.3.

As well as the two heuristic principles mentioned above, there is a third principle, namely that one-relator groups on at least three generators behave "more like" free groups. One is led to ask, therefore, whether such groups actually have $\mathcal{L}(F_2)$. Or to state the question in an alternative form:

Problem 3. Does every one-relator group on at least three generators have a subgroup of finite index mapping onto F_2?

In this connection it is worth remarking that Stallings [23] has shown that for any positive integer n there is an n-generator one-relator group which does not map onto F_2.

A question related to the above has been raised by A.M. Macbeath (private communication): is there an integer $d > 0$ such that whenever a group G can be presented with $r + d$ generators and r relations, then G has $\mathcal{L}(F_2)$?* (See [17, p. 5] for a similar question concerning SQ-universality.)

Proof of Theorem 3.3. Let $G = \langle t, a, b, \ldots; R^n \rangle$ $(n > 1)$. Then G does not satisfy a non-trivial law provided G has at least two generators [9].

Now by [20, Lemma 4.1] it can be assumed that $\sigma_t(R) = 0$. Let $a_i = t^{-i}at^i$, $b_i = t^{-i}bt^i, \ldots$ $(i \in \mathbf{Z})$. Then R can be rewritten as a word P in the $a_i, b_i, \ldots$. There is an integer $m \geq 0$ such that if a_i occurs in P then $|i| \leq m$. Now it is easy to see that G has presentation with generators

$$t, a_{-m}, \ldots, a_m, b_i \ (i \in \mathbf{Z}), \ldots,$$

and defining relations

$$P^n, t^{-1}a_it = a_{i+1} \qquad (i = -m, \ldots, m-1),$$

$$t^{-1}b_it = b_{i+1} \ (i \in \mathbf{Z}), \ldots.$$

The result will therefore follow from the

Lemma 3.1. *Let H be a group which has a presentation with generators*

$$t, a_{-m}, \ldots, a_m, b_i \ (i \in \mathbf{Z}), \ldots$$

and defining relations

* This question has now been answered affirmatively (with $d = 2$). See "Groups with two more generators than relators" by Benjamin Baumslag and Stephen J. Pride, J. London Math. Soc. 17(2) (1978) 425–426.

$$V, W, \ldots, t^{-1}a_it = a_{i+1} \qquad (i = -m, \ldots, m-1),$$

$$t^{-1}b_it = b_{i+1}\ (i \in \mathbf{Z}), \ldots,$$

where $m \geq 0$, and where $V, W, \ldots$ are t-free words. Suppose that there is an integer $n > 1$ such that for $|i| \leq m$ each of $\sigma_{a_i}(V), \sigma_{a_i}(W), \ldots$ is divisible by n. Then H has $\mathscr{L}(F_2)$.

To prove this lemma consider the factor group K of H obtained by imposing the additional relations:

$$a_i^n = 1 \qquad (|i| \leq m),$$

$$b_i = 1\ (i \in \mathbf{Z}), \ldots,$$

$$[a_i, a_j] = 1 \qquad (|i|, |j| \leq m).$$

Then $V, W, \ldots$ are superfluous as defining relators in K, and so K is an HNN group with base the direct product of the finite cyclic groups $\text{sgp}\{a_{-m}\}, \ldots, \text{sgp}\{a_m\}$, associated subgroups

$$\text{sgp}\{a_{-m}, \ldots, a_{m-1}\},$$

$$\text{sgp}\{a_{-m+1}, \ldots, a_m\},$$

and stable letter t. Thus K has a non-abelian free subgroup of finite index (see above) and therefore has $\mathscr{L}(F_2)$. Consequently, H has $\mathscr{L}(F_2)$, as required.

This proves the lemma, and Theorem 3.3 follows.

Before going on to prove Theorem 3.4 it is worth remarking that Lemma 3.1 can be used to show many groups with more than one relator have $\mathscr{L}(F_2)$. For example:

Theorem 3.5.* *Let G be a group with presentation of the form*

$$\langle t, a, b, \ldots; R^n, S^n, \ldots \rangle,$$

where $n > 1$. Suppose that $\sigma_t(R) = \sigma_t(S) = \cdots = 0$, and furthermore there is an integer $\kappa \geq 0$ such that the number of t-symbols in each of $R^n, S^n, \ldots$ does not exceed κ. Then G has $\mathscr{L}(F_2)$.

The requirement in this theorem that there be a bound on the number of t-symbols in the relators $R^n, S^n, \ldots$ cannot be dispensed with in general. For consider the group G_0 with generators a, t and

* I thank A.H.M. Hoare for pointing out a mistake in my original formulation of this theorem.

defining relators $[W_1, W_2]^n$, where W_1, W_2 range over all words in a, t. Then all the conditions of Theorem 3.5 are satisfied except that there is no bound on the number of t-symbols in the relators. Moreover, it is clear that G_0 does not have the large property $\mathcal{F}(2)$, and therefore certainly cannot have $\mathcal{L}(F_2)$.

Lemma 3.1 can also be used to show that many torsion-free one-relator groups have $\mathcal{L}(F_2)$. For example, it is easily shown that if $G = \langle a, t; a^{\alpha_1}t^{\tau_1}\cdots a^{\alpha_r}t^{\tau_r}\rangle$ where $\Sigma\,\tau_i = 0$ and where the α_i have a common factor greater than 1, then G has $\mathcal{L}(F_2)$. (On the other hand, if the α_i do not have a common factor greater than 1 then G need not have $\mathcal{L}(F_2)$, as the group B in Theorem 3.4 shows.)

Proof of Theorem 3.4. Let $B = \langle a, t; t^{-1}a^2t = a^3\rangle$. It will be shown that $B < F_2$. By Theorem 2.1 it must be shown that no normal subgroup of finite index in B can map onto a subgroup of finite index in F_2.

Suppose $N \trianglelefteq B$, $|B:N|$ finite. Since t and a have infinite order in B, some positive power of t and some positive power of a must belong to N, otherwise $|B:N|$ would be infinite. Suppose t^n, a^p $(n, p > 0)$ belong to N, and assume p is the smallest integer i such that $a^i \in N$. Let M be the normal closure of $\{t^n, a^p\}$, so that $M \leqslant N$. Let $\bar{B} = B/M$. Then

$$\bar{B} = \langle a, t; t^{-1}a^2t = a^3, t^n, a^p\rangle.$$

Now the minimality of p guarantees that $(2, p) = (3, p) = 1$. For example, if $p = 2q$ then $a^q = a^{-2q}t^{-1}a^{2q}t \in N$, and $0 < q < p$. It now follows that $\mathrm{sgp}\{a\}$ is normal in $\bar{B}$. Moreover, the minimality of p guarantees that a has order exactly p in $\bar{B}$. Thus every element of $\bar{B}$ can be expressed uniquely in the form

$$t^ia^j \qquad (0 \leqslant i < n,\ 0 \leqslant j < p). \tag{3.1}$$

In particular, M has finite index in B. Thus in order to show N does not map onto a subgroup of finite index in F_2 it suffices to show that M does not map onto a subgroup of finite index in F_2. Now a subgroup of finite index in F_2 is free of rank greater than 1 and therefore maps onto F_2. Consequently, it is enough to show M does not map onto F_2.

The elements in (3.1) constitute a Schreier system for M in B, and so M is generated by the elements

$$t^ia^ja\,.\,\overline{t^ia^ja}^{-1}, \tag{3.2}$$

$$t^ia^jt\,.\,\overline{t^ia^jt}^{-1}, \tag{3.3}$$

where $0 \leq i < n$, $0 \leq j < p$. An element (3.2) is freely equal to 1 unless $j = p-1$. Let a_i denote the element $t^i a^{p-1} a . \overline{t^i a^{p-1} a}^{-1}$ $(= t^i a^p t^{-i})$, and let y denote the element t^n. Then it is easily shown that the following relations hold:

$$a_0^2 = a_1^3, \ldots, a_{n-2}^2 = a_{n-1}^3, \tag{3.4}$$

$$y^{-1} a_0^{2^n} y = a_0^{3^n}. \tag{3.5}$$

Suppose M maps onto a free group F. Then the relation (3.5) holds in F and so, in F, y and a_0 commute. Thus, in F, a_0 has finite order and must therefore define the identity. Consequently, by (3.4), all the a_i define the identity in F. It follows that the factor group $\hat{M}$ of M obtained by putting all the a_i equal to 1 still maps onto F.

Let $s(i, j)$ denote the generator (3.3) of M. Now the defining relators of M are obtained by rewriting the relators

$$t^\tau a^\alpha t a^3 t^{-1} a^{-2} a^{-\alpha} t^{-\tau}$$

$(0 \leq \tau < n, 0 \leq \alpha < p)$ of B in terms of the $s(i, j)$ and the a_i. Thus the defining relations of $\hat{M}$ on the generators $s(i, j)$ are

$$s(\tau, \alpha) s^{-1}(\tau, \alpha + 2) = 1,$$

where $0 \leq \tau < n$, $0 \leq \alpha < p$, and where $\alpha + 2$ is reduced modulo n to lie between 0 and $n-1$. Since $(2, p) = 1$ it follows easily that for $\tau = 0, \ldots, n-1$

$$s(\tau, 0) = s(\tau, 1) = \cdots = s(\tau, p-1).$$

But $t^\tau t . \overline{t^\tau t}^{-1}$ is freely equal to 1 unless $\tau = n - 1$. Consequently, $\hat{M}$ is infinite cyclic generated by $s(n-1, 0)$ $(= y)$, and so F is of rank less than 2.

This completes the proof of Theorem 3.4.

3. *Arithmetically defined linear groups*

Let d be a positive square-free integer, and let I_d be the ring of integers in the quadratic field $\mathbf{Q}(\sqrt{-d})$. Fine and Tretkoff [5] have investigated the SQ-universality of the groups $\mathrm{PSL}(2, I_d)$, $\mathrm{SL}(2, I_d)$, $\mathrm{GL}(2, I_d)$ in case I_d is a Euclidean domain — that is, when $d = 1, 2, 3, 7, 11$. Their work carries over to show that these groups have $\mathscr{L}(F_2)$.

Since $\mathrm{SL}(2, I_d)$ maps onto $\mathrm{PSL}(2, I_d)$, and since, for the values of d under consideration, $\mathrm{SL}(2, I_d)$ has finite index in $\mathrm{GL}(2, I_d)$, it suffices to show $\mathrm{PSL}(2, I_d)$ has $\mathscr{L}(F_2)$.

For $d = 1, 2, 3, 11$ the arguments of Lemmas 1, 2, 4 of [5] can easily be modified. Consider the case $d = 7$. It is shown in Lemma 3 of [5] that $\mathrm{PSL}(2, I_7)$ has a subgroup G of finite index with presentation

$$\langle x, r, s, w\,;\, x^3 = r^3 = s^3 = 1,\, w^{-1}[s^{-1}, r]w = [s^{-1}, r],$$
$$[r^{-1}, x^{-1}] = [s^{-1}, r],\, w^{-1}sw = x^{-1}\rangle.$$

Setting $s = x = 1$ in G gives the group $\bar{G}$ with presentation

$$\langle r, w\,;\, r^3 = 1\rangle.$$

Since $\bar{G}$ has $\mathscr{L}(F_2)$ it follows that $\mathrm{PSL}(2, I_7)$ has $\mathscr{L}(F_2)$.

Fine and Tretkoff also show that for all d, the subgroup $E(2, I_d)$ of $\mathrm{SL}(2, I_d)$ generated by the transvections is SQ-universal [5, Theorem C]. Their argument is easily modified to show that $E(2, I_d)$ has $\mathscr{L}(F_2)$.

R. Zimmert [28] has shown that for many values of d, $\mathrm{SL}(2, I_d)$ has F_2 as a homomorphic image. For such values of d it is obvious that $\mathrm{SL}(2, I_d)$ has $\mathscr{L}(F_2)$.

It follows from [1], [16] that for $n \geq 3$, $\mathrm{SL}(n, I_d)$ does not have $\mathscr{L}(F_2)$.

4. *Small cancellation groups*

Let F be a free group and let $\boldsymbol{r}$ be a symmetrized subset of F which satisfies the small cancellation conditions $C(p)$, $T(q)$ for (p, q) one of $(6, 3)$, $(4, 4)$, $(3, 6)$. Let G be the quotient of F by the normal closure of $\boldsymbol{r}$. Then G is called a small cancellation group. The reader unfamiliar with small cancellation theory should consult [21].

Small cancellation groups tend to be "quite large". For example, it has been shown by Collins [4] that if $\boldsymbol{r}$ satisfies $C(4)$ and $T(4)$ then, with a few trivial exceptions, G has the large property $\mathscr{F}(2)$. Recently it has been shown by M. al-Janabi in his PhD thesis at London University that if $\boldsymbol{r}$ is finite and satifies $C(6)$, then again, apart from a few trivial exceptions, G has $\mathscr{F}(2)$. Al-Janabi has also established that if $\boldsymbol{r}$ is finite and satisfies $C(7)$ then G is actually SQ-universal whenever it has $\mathscr{F}(2)$.

One is led to ask the following question.

Problem 4. Do "most" finitely presented small cancellation groups have $\mathscr{L}(F_2)$?

I suspect that the answer is negative (see the comments in the second paragraph of §3.3 in this regard).

It should be remarked that many small cancellation groups can be shown to have $\mathscr{L}(F_2)$ using Lemma 3.1. The following lemma is also useful.

Lemma 3.2. *Let* $G = \langle a, b, x, y, \ldots; R, S, \ldots \rangle$. *Suppose there are integers* p, q *greater than* 1 *and not both* 2 *such that all the* a*-exponents in* $R, S, \ldots$ *are divisible by* p *and all the numbers* $\sigma_b(R), \sigma_b(S), \ldots$ *are divisible by* q. *Then* G *has* $\mathscr{L}(F_2)$.

Proof. Let $\bar{G}$ be the image of G obtained by putting $a^p = b^q = 1$, and setting $x, y, \ldots$ equal to 1. Then $\bar{G} = \langle a, b; a^p, b^q \rangle$, so that $\bar{G}$ has $\mathscr{L}(F_2)$. Consequently G has $\mathscr{L}(F_2)$.

Finitely generated infinitely related small cancellation groups need not have $\mathscr{L}(F_2)$, even though they can be "quite large". Roughly speaking, this is because there is considerable scope to "impose relations which destroy largeness".

Theorem 3.6. *Let* ν *be a number greater than or equal to* 5, *and let* F *be the free group on* a, b. *There is an infinite symmetrized subset* $\boldsymbol{r}$ *of* F *satisfying* $C'(1/\nu)$ *such that the factor group* G *of* F *by the normal closure* N *of* $\boldsymbol{r}$ *is such that* $G < F_2$. *The group* G *is SQ-universal.*

Proof. The construction of G is similar to the construction given in [18, §2].

Let $n > 2\nu$ and let $\alpha_1, \ldots, \alpha_n$ be numbers satisfying $|\alpha_i| > 1$, $\Sigma \alpha_i = 1$, $|\alpha_i| \neq |\alpha_j|$ for $i \neq j$. Let $\alpha = \max\{|\alpha_i| : i = 1, \ldots, n\}$, and suppose $2\alpha/\Sigma|\alpha_i| < 1/\nu$. Let $\boldsymbol{r}$ be the symmetrized closure of the following elements of F;

$$(3.6) \qquad ab^{\alpha_1}ab^{\alpha_2}\cdots ab^{\alpha_n},$$

$$(3.7) \qquad a^{\alpha_1}b^pa^{\alpha_2}b^p\cdots a^{\alpha_n}b^p, p = \alpha + 3, \alpha + 4, \ldots .$$

Then it is easily shown that pieces relative to $\boldsymbol{r}$ are subwords of $(b^{\alpha_i}ab^{\alpha_{i+1}})^{\pm 1}$, $(a^{\alpha_i}b^pa^{\alpha_{i+1}})^{\pm 1}$, $(b^pa^{\alpha_i}b^p)^{\pm 1}$ for $i = 1, \ldots, n$ (where subscripts are calculated modulo n), and it thus follows that $\boldsymbol{r}$ satisfies $C'(1/\nu)$.

Now G has no non-trivial finite homomorphic image. For if G maps onto $\bar{G}$ with $\bar{G}$ finite, then in $\bar{G}$, $b^p = 1$ for some $p \geqslant \alpha + 3$, and so it follows from the relators (3, 6), (3, 7) (which of course hold in $\bar{G}$), that $a = b = 1$. Thus $\bar{G}$ is trivial.

Now since F_2 does not have a subgroup of finite index which has no proper subgroups of finite index, it follows from Corollary 2.1.1 that $G < F_2$.

To show that G is SQ-universal it suffices to show that any two-generator group C can be embedded in a quotient of G. Suppose C is generated by h, k and let $L = \langle a \rangle * \langle b \rangle * C$. Let $\boldsymbol{s}$ be the symmetrized closure *in* L of the elements (3.6), (3.7) together with

$$ha^{\alpha_1}b^{\alpha+1}a^{\alpha_2}b^{\alpha+1}\cdots a^{\alpha_n}b^{\alpha+1},$$

$$ka^{\alpha_1}b^{\alpha+2}a^{\alpha_2}b^{\alpha+2}\cdots a^{\alpha_n}b^{\alpha+2}.$$

Then it is easily shown that s satisfies $C'(1/\nu)$, so the quotient of L by the normal closure K of s is a small cancellation product of $\langle a\rangle$, $\langle b\rangle$, C. In particular, C is embedded in L/K. It is easy to see that L/K is a quotient of G.

This completes the proof.

§3.3. Free products

Let $G = H * K$ with $|H|, |K| \neq 1$. If $|H| = |K| = 2$ then G is a finite extension of the infinite cyclic group, and is therefore a minimal group. On the other hand, if $\max\{|H|, |K|\} > 2$ then G has several well-known large properties, and is usually thought of as being "quite large". For example, it has been known for a long time that G has $\mathcal{F}(2)$. More recently, it has been shown that G is SQ-universal ([21, Theorem 5] [7, Corollary 9.2]).

Now verifying that G has large properties is not always easy — see for example, the two proofs of SQ-universality. This leads one to think that although G tends to have large properties, perhaps it is not always the case that G is "naturally large" in the sense of having $\mathcal{L}(F_2)$. This turns out to be so.

Theorem 3.7. *Let $G = H * K$ with $|H|, |K| \neq 1$. Then G has $\mathcal{L}(F_2)$ if and only if one of the following holds*:

(3.8) *either H or K has $\mathcal{L}(F_2)$;*

(3.9) *H, K have non-trivial finite homomorphic images $\bar{H}$, $\bar{K}$ respectively, with $\max\{|\bar{H}|, |\bar{K}|\} > 2$.*

Obviously (3.8) is a sufficient condition for G to have $\mathcal{L}(F_2)$. To see that (3.9) is a sufficient condition, note that G maps onto $\bar{H} * \bar{K}$, and $\bar{H} * \bar{K}$ has $\mathcal{L}(F_2)$, since it has a non-abelian free subgroup of finite index.

In order to establish the necessity of the conditions (3.8), (3.9), it is just as easy to work in a more general situation.

Theorem 3.8. *Let G be a group generated by two subgroups H, K. Let A be an infinite group with the following properties*:

(3.10) *if $B \leqslant A$, $B \neq 1$, then B has proper subgroups of finite index*;

(3.11) *if* $B \leq A$ *with* $|A:B|$ *finite then* B *is not a homomorphic image of a subgroup of* $\mathbf{Z}_2 * \mathbf{Z}_2$.

Then G *has* $\mathcal{L}(A)$ *only if either* H *or* K *has* $\mathcal{L}(A)$, *or* H, K *have non-trivial finite homomorphic images* $\bar{H}$, $\bar{K}$ *respectively with* $\max\{|\bar{H}|,|\bar{K}|\} > 2$.

The necessity of the conditions (3.8), (3.9) obviously follows from Theorem 3.8, taking $A = F_2$.

The rest of this section is devoted to proving Theorem 3.8. The proof proceeds by a number of lemmas. All groups referred to in these lemmas will be as in the statement of Theorem 3.8.

Lemma 3.3. *Suppose* H *has no proper subgroups of finite index. Let* C *be a subgroup of* G *with* $|G:C|$ *finite. Then* $C = \mathrm{sgp}\{N, K_1\}$, *where* N *has no proper subgroups of finite index, and* $K_1 \leq K$ *with* $|K:K_1|$ *finite.*

Proof. If $g \in G$ then $H^g \cap C$ is of finite index in H^g and is therefore equal to H^g. Thus $H^g \leq C$, and so C contains the normal subgroup N of G generated by H. Now N has no proper subgroups of finite index. For suppose $L \leq N$, $|N:L|$ finite. For $g \in G$, $L \cap H^g$ is of finite index in H^g, and so is equal to H^g. Thus $H^g \leq L$ for all $g \in G$, and so $N \leq L$. Consequently $N \doteq L$.

Now let $K_1 = C \cap K$. Then K_1 is of finite index in K, and it is easily shown that $C = \mathrm{sgp}\{N, K_1\}$.

Lemma 3.4. *If* H *has no proper subgroups of finite index and* K *does not have* $\mathcal{L}(A)$ *then* G *does not have* $\mathcal{L}(A)$.

Proof. Assume, by way of contradiction, that G has $\mathcal{L}(A)$. By Theorem 2.1, G has a subgroup C of finite index, with C mapping onto a subgroup B of finite index in A. Now by Lemma 3.3, $C = \mathrm{sgp}\{N, K_1\}$ with N having no proper subgroups of finite index, and $K_1 \leq K$, $|K:K_1|$ finite. The homomorphism of C onto B carries N, K_1 to subgroups $\bar{N}$, $\bar{K}_1$ respectively, and $B = \mathrm{sgp}\{\bar{N}, \bar{K}_1\}$. Since $\bar{N}$ has no proper subgroups of finite index, it follows from (3.10) that $\bar{N} = 1$. But then $B = \bar{K}_1$, which implies $\bar{K}_1$, and therefore K, has $\mathcal{L}(A)$ — a contradiction.

Lemma 3.5. *Suppose* H, K *have subgroups* N_H, N_K *respectively each of index 2, and that* H, K *have no proper subgroups of any other finite index. Let* N *be the normal subgroup of* G *generated by* N_H, N_K. *Then* N

has no proper subgroups of finite index. Any subgroup C of finite index in G contains N, and C/N is a homomorphic image of a subgroup of $\mathbf{Z}_2 * \mathbf{Z}_2$.

Proof. First note that N_H, N_K are the unique proper subgroups of finite index in H, K respectively.

To see that N has no proper subgroups of finite index suppose $L \leqslant N$ with $|N : L|$ finite. Then for $g \in G$, $L \cap N_H^g$ is of finite index in N_H^g and is therefore equal to N_H^g. Thus $N_H^g \leqslant L$. Similarly $N_K^g \leqslant L$. It now follows that $N \leqslant L$, so $N = L$.

Now suppose C is a subgroup of G of finite index. Then for $g \in G$, $C \cap N_H^g$ is of finite index in N_H^g, and so $N_H^g \leqslant C$. Similarly $N_K^g \leqslant C$. Thus $N \leqslant C$. Now G/N is a homomorphic image of $\mathbf{Z}_2 * \mathbf{Z}_2$, and so C/N is a homomorphic image of a subgroup of $\mathbf{Z}_2 * \mathbf{Z}_2$.

Lemma 3.6. *Suppose H, K have subgroups N_H, N_K respectively each of index 2, but have no proper subgroups of any other finite index. Then G does not have $\mathscr{L}(A)$.*

Proof. Assume, by way of contradiction, that G has $\mathscr{L}(A)$. By Theorem 2.1, G has a subgroup C of finite index, with C mapping onto a subgroup B of finite index in A. Let N be the normal subgroup of G generated by N_H and N_K. Then $N \leqslant C$ by Lemma 3.5. The homomorphism of C onto B carries N to a normal subgroup $\bar{N}$, and there is an induced homomorphism of C/N onto $B/\bar{N}$. Now since N has no proper subgroup of finite index (by Lemma 3.5), neither does $\bar{N}$. It therefore follows from (3.10) that $\bar{N} = 1$. Thus B is a homomorphic image of a subgroup of $\mathbf{Z}_2 * \mathbf{Z}_2$ (again using Lemma 3.5), and this contradicts (3.11).

This proves the lemma.

It is now an easy matter to prove Theorem 3.8.

Suppose G has $\mathscr{L}(A)$. If, say H, does not have a non-trivial finite homomorphic image then it follows from Lemma 3.4 that K has $\mathscr{L}(A)$. If both H and K have non-trivial finite homomorphic images $\bar{H}$, $\bar{K}$ then it follows from Lemma 3.6 that not both of $|\bar{H}|$, $|\bar{K}|$ can be 2.

§4. "Small" groups

§4.1. Concepts of "smallness"

Throughout this subsection G will denote an infinite group.

The *height* of G is defined to be

$$\sup\{r : r \text{ is a non-negative integer, there are groups } G = G_1, \ldots, G_r \text{ with } G_r < \cdots < G_1\}.$$

As will be seen, groups of finite height tend to be "small". Notice that G is a minimal group (that is, lies in $\mathcal{M}$) if and only if it has height one. Notice also that the property of having height greater than or equal to m (where m may be ∞) is a large property. It is consistent with the above definition to define the height of a finite group to be zero.

Example 4.1. Let $A(n)$ be a free abelian group of rank $n \geq 0$. Then $A(n)$ has height n. This is trivial if $n = 0$. Assume $n > 0$. Using Theorem 2.1 together with the general theory of abelian groups, it is easily established that if $H \leq A(n)$ then $H \simeq A(m)$ for some m with $0 < m \leq n$. Clearly, $A(1) \leq A(2) \leq \cdots \leq A(n)$. It will be shown in fact that if $0 < s < r \leq n$ then $A(s) < A(r)$.

If, on the contrary, $A(r) \leq A(s)$ then by Theorem 2.1 and general results on abelian groups, $A(r)$ would have a subgroup D of finite index, with D free abelian of rank less than r. As is well-known, this is impossible. A proof can be given as follows.

Let $A(r) = C_1 \times \cdots \times C_r$, where each C_i is infinite cyclic generated by x_i say. Let $B_i = \operatorname{sgp}\{C_j : j < i\}$, and let

$$E_i = \{p : p > 0, \text{ there exists } u \in B_i \text{ such that } ux_i^p \in D\}.$$

Since $C_i \cap D$ has finite index in C_i, E_i is non-empty. Let $p_i = \min E_i$. Then there exists $u_i \in B_i$ such that $u_i x_i^{p_i} \in D$. Now the $u_i x_i^{p_i}$ obviously freely generate a subgroup. It will be shown that they generate D, so D has rank r, contrary to assumption.

Suppose $h \in D$. Then $h = wx_r^{m_r}$ where $w \in B_r$. Now p_r divides m_r. For if $d = (p_r, m_r)$ then $d = \alpha p_r + \beta m_r$ for certain integers α, β, and so $(w^\beta x_r^{\beta m_r})(u_r^\alpha x_r^{\alpha p_r}) \in D$ — that is, $w^\beta u_r^\alpha x_r^d \in D$. Thus $d = p_r$ by minimality. It now follows that $wx_r^{m_r} = w'(u_r x_r^{p_r})^{l_r}$ for some $w' \in B_r$ and some integer l_r. Now $w' = vx_{r-1}^{m_{r-1}}$ with $v \in B_{r-1}$, and a similar argument shows that $vx_{r-1}^{m_{r-1}} = v'(u_{r-1}x_{r-1}^{p_{r-1}})^{l_{r-1}}$ where $v' \in B_{r-1}$. Continuing in this way one can express h as a product of the $u_i x_i^{p_i}$.

Example 4.2. If $A(\aleph_0)$ is a free abelian group of countably infinite rank then $A(\aleph_0)$ maps onto $A(n)$ for all $n > 0$, so $A(\aleph_0)$ has infinite height.

The group G is said to satisfy Max-$\leq$ (Min-$\leq$) if there is no infinite sequence of groups $G_0, G_1, G_2, \ldots$ with $G_i \leq G$ and $G_i < G_{i+1}$ ($G_{i+1} < G_i$) for $i = 0, 1, 2, \ldots$. Related to these two properties are chain conditions on certain subgroups of G, defined as follows.

A subgroup A of G is said to be *almost normal* if it is normal in some subgroup of finite index in G. Thus A is almost normal if and only if $|G : N_G(A)| < \infty$. If A is almost normal then $G(A)$ will denote the group $N_G(A)/A$. The maximal and minimal conditions on almost normal subgroups will be denoted by Max-an and Min-an respectively.

Note that $\neg$Max-$\leq$, $\neg$Min-$\leq$, $\neg$Max-an, $\neg$Min-an are all large properties.

Theorem 4.1. *If G satisfies* Max-an *then G satisfies* Min-$\leq$.

Proof. Suppose $\cdots G_{r+1} < G_r < \cdots < G_2 < G_1 = G$, and that almost normal subgroups $N_1 < N_2 < \cdots < N_r$ have been found with $G(N_i) \simeq G_i$ for $i = 1, \ldots, r$. Since $G_{r+1} < G(N_r)$ there is a subgroup H/N_r of finite index in $G(N_r)$ mapping onto a subgroup A of finite index in G_{r+1}. Thus there is a normal subgroup N_{r+1} of H with $N_r < N_{r+1}$ and H/N_{r+1} isomorphic to A. Thus $G(N_{r+1}) \simeq G_{r+1}$.

It is worth pointing out that *if A, B are almost normal subgroups of G with B properly contained in A and $|G : A| = \infty$, then $G(A) \leq G(B)$.* One cannot conclude in gèneral that $G(A) < G(B)$, for otherwise the converse of Theorem 4.1 would be true. However, as the following example shows this is not the case.

Example 4.3. Let S be a non-trivial finite non-abelian simple group and let I be a countably infinite set. For $i \in I$ let S_i be a copy of S, and let C be the restricted direct product of the S_i. It will be shown that if $L \leq C$ then L has a subgroup of finite index isomorphic to C; consequently $L \simeq C$, and so C is a minimal group. However, C satisfies neither Max-an nor Min-an (in fact, it does not satisfy either Max-n or Min-n).

Let N be a normal subgroup of C and let $z \in N$. Suppose the ith coordinate s of z is non-trivial, and let $x \in S_i$. Then $[z, x] \in N$ and $[z, x] = [s, x]$. Since $[s, x] \neq 1$ for at least one x, it follows that $S_i \cap N \neq 1$. Thus $S_i \cap N = S_i$, or in other words $S_i \leq N$. It is now easy to see that if J is the subset of I consisting of all those i for which some non-trivial element of S_i occurs as the ith coordinate of an element of N, then $N = \mathrm{sgp}\{S_i : i \in J\}$.

Now suppose $L \preccurlyeq C$. By Theorem 2.1, C has subgroups M, H with $M \trianglelefteq H \trianglelefteq C$, $|C:H|$ finite and H/M isomorphic to a subgroup of finite index in L. Using the result of the previous paragraph, it is easy to show that both H and H/M are isomorphic to C.

§4.2. Just-infinite groups

As mentioned in §1.1, a group is said to be *just-infinite* if it is infinite but has every proper quotient finite. Just-infinite groups have been investigated by several authors [12, 13, 24, 27]. One has the feeling that such groups should be "quite small", and the aim of the next three subsections is to examine these groups in terms of the notions introduced in §4.1.

Following Wilson [27], let $\mathcal{D}_2$ denote the class of groups in which every non-trivial subnormal subgroup is of finite index. It is easy to see that *an infinite $\mathcal{D}_2$-group G is a minimal group.* For suppose $H \preccurlyeq G$. By Theorem 2.1 there are groups B, C with B of finite index in H, C normal and of finite index in G, and C mapping onto B by a homomorphism θ say. Let K be the kernel of θ. Then K is subnormal in G and therefore must be trivial since $|G:K| = \infty$. Consequently, θ is $1:1$, and so H has a subgroup of finite index mapping onto a subgroup of finite index in G. Thus $G \preccurlyeq H$.

A just-infinite group G which lies outside $\mathcal{D}_2$ need not be minimal. Nevertheless if G satisfies the maximal condition on subnormal subgroups then G still has finite height. To be more precise:

Theorem 4.2. *Let G be a just-infinite group which satisfies* Max-sn. *Then G has a subgroup of finite index which is a direct product $M_1 \times \cdots \times M_n$, where the M_i are pairwise isomorphic subnormal subgroups of G. The M_i are $\mathcal{D}_2$-groups and are therefore minimal. If $H \preccurlyeq G$ then $H \simeq M_1 \times \cdots \times M_r$ for some $1 \leqslant r \leqslant n$. Moreover*

$$M_1 < M_1 \times M_2 < \cdots < M_1 \times \cdots \times M_n.$$

Thus G has height n.

For just-infinite groups not satisfying Max-sn the following theorem applies.

Theorem 4.3. *Let G be a just-infinite group not satisfying* Max-sn. *Then either G lies in $\mathcal{M}$ or G does not satisfy* Min-$\preccurlyeq$.

An example will be given in §4.4 of a just-infinite group not satisfying Max-sn which is minimal. I do not have an example of a just-infinite group not satisfying Max-sn which also does not satisfy Min-$\preccurlyeq$. Probably an infinite wreath product $\mathrm{Wr}_{Z^-} S_{-n}$, where the S_{-n} are non-isomorphic finite perfect simple groups, would provide such an example, but I have been unable to verify this.

The proofs of Theorems 4.2, 4.3 will rely heavily on results on the structure of just-infinite groups obtained by Wilson in [27]. In particular, frequent use *without explicit mention* will be made of Wilson's result [27, Proposition 3], that a just-infinite group has no non-trivial finite subnormal subgroups.

Before discussing the proofs of Theorems 4.2, 4.3, some consequences will be noted.

Corollary. *Let G be a just-infinite group. Then G lies in $\mathcal{M}$ if and only if either G lies in $\mathcal{D}_2$ or G does not satisfy* Max-sn.

Proof. If G satisfies Max-sn and lies in $\mathcal{M}$ then it follows from Theorem 4.2 that G has a $\mathcal{D}_2$-subgroup H of finite index. This implies that G itself is a $\mathcal{D}_2$-group. For let K be a non-trivial subnormal subgroup of G. Then $K \cap H$ is subnormal in H. Now since $|K : K \cap H| < \infty$, $K \cap H$ cannot be trivial, else K would be finite. Thus $|H : K \cap H| < \infty$, and so $|G : K| < \infty$, as required.

If G does not satisfy Max-sn then Theorem 4.3 applies.

Corollary. *If $\mathcal{Y}$ is a class of groups which is closed under taking infinite homomorphic images, and if each infinite group in $\mathcal{Y}$ has a just-infinite quotient, then every group in $\mathcal{Y} \cap \mathcal{M}$ is equally as large as some just-infinite $\mathcal{Y}$-group which either lies in $\mathcal{D}_2$ or does not satisfy* Max-sn.

For if K lies in $\mathcal{Y} \cap \mathcal{M}$ then K has a just-infinite quotient G with $K \simeq G$, and the result then follows from the previous corollary.

The last corollary applies, for example, if $\mathcal{Y}$ is taken to be the class of groups satisfying Max-n. It also applies if $\mathcal{Y}$ is taken to be the class of finitely generated groups [19, Lemma 6.17]. In this connection the following question naturally arises.

Problem 5. Do there exist *finitely generated* just-infinite groups not satisfying Max-sn?

The last corollary also suggests the following, admittedly rather vague, question.

Problem 6. What finiteness conditions on an infinite group G ensure that G has a just-infinite quotient?

It is worth pointing out that not every minimal group is equally as large as some just-infinite group. For instance, let C be the group in Example 4.3. Then any group $L \simeq C$ has a subgroup of finite index isomorphic to C. Thus L cannot satisfy Max-n (since subgroups of finite index in groups with Max-n also have Max-n [26]), and so L certainly cannot be just-infinite.

Some aspects of the proofs of Theorems 4.2, 4.3 will now be discussed. Other parts of the proof of Theorem 4.2 will be given in §4.3, and the majority of the proof of Theorem 4.3 will be given in §4.4.

As Wilson remarks [27, p. 374] the structure of a just-infinite group G depends very strongly on its Baer radical. (Recall that the Baer radical of a group is the subgroup generated by the cyclic subnormal subgroups.) If G has non-trivial Baer radical then [27, Theorem 2] G is a finite extension of a free abelian group A of finite rank. (Thus G satisfies Max, and therefore certainly Max-sn.) In this case one takes the M_i in Theorem 4.2 to be the cyclic factors in a decomposition of A. The argument given above in Example 4.1 shows that all the required conditions are satisfied.

For groups satisfying Max-sn which have trivial Baer radical the argument is not quite so straightforward, and some preliminary results are needed. These results also apply to groups not satisfying Max-sn, and will be required in the proof of Theorem 4.3. So for the rest of this section G_0 will denote an arbitrary just-infinite group with trivial Baer radical.

Now it is shown in [27, Theorem 3B] that every subnormal subgroup K of G_0 has a near-complement C. (Recall that C is a near-complement to K in G_0 if C is subnormal, $\mathrm{sgp}\{K, C\} = K \times C$, $|G_0 : K \times C| < \infty$.) As the following lemma shows, this implies that in discussing those groups H with $H \preccurlyeq G_0$ it suffices to concentrate on subnormal subgroups of G_0.

Lemma 4.2. (i) *If $H \preccurlyeq G_0$ then H is equally as large as some subnormal subgroup of G_0.*

(ii) *If L, M are non-trivial subnormal subgroups of G_0 with $L \leq M$ then $L \preccurlyeq M$.*

Proof. (i) If $H \preccurlyeq G_0$ then, by Theorem 2.1, there is a normal subgroup A of finite index in G_0 and a homomorphism θ of A onto a subgroup

B of finite index in H. Let K be the kernel of θ. Then K is subnormal in G_0 and so K has a near-complement C in G_0. Since $|G_0 : K \times C| < \infty$, $|A : K \times (C \cap A)| < \infty$, and so A/K has a subgroup of finite index isomorphic to $C \cap A$. Thus $H \simeq C \cap A$.

(ii) Let D be a near-complement for L in G_0. Then $M \cap (L \times D) = L \times (M \cap D)$, and $|M : L \times (M \cap D)| < \infty$. Since $L \times (M \cap D)$ maps onto L, it follows that $L \preccurlyeq M$.

Now in [27, §4.2] Wilson defines a congruence $\sim$ on the lattice of subnormal subgroups of G_0 as follows: for K, L subnormal in G_0, $K \sim L$ if and only if $K \cap L$ has finite index in both K and L. The quotient of the lattice of subnormal subgroups of G_0 by $\sim$ is called the *structure lattice* of G_0. Its elements are congruence classes $[K]$ of subnormal subgroups of G_0.

Lemma 4.3. *Let K, L be non-trivial subnormal subgroups of G_0. If $[K] = [L]$ then $K \simeq L$.*

This is a trivial consequence of the definition of $\sim$.

It is shown in [27, §4.2] that the structure lattice is Boolean. If G_0 satisfies Max-sn then the structure lattice is finite [27, Theorem 4]. If G_0 does not satisfy Max-sn then the structure lattice is infinite, isomorphic to the lattice of all closed-and-open subsets of Cantor's ternary set [27, Theorem 6].

Now to return to the proof of Theorem 4.2. Suppose G is a just-infinite group satisfying Max-sn, and assume G has trivial Baer radical. Since the structure lattice of G is finite it must be isomorphic to the lattice of all subsets of a set of n elements for some positive integer n. By investigating the significance of the integer n, Wilson obtains the following description of G [27, Proposition 7]. The group G has a subnormal $\mathcal{D}_2$-subgroup $M \trianglelefteq^2 G$ such that the normal closure of M in G is the direct product $M_1 \times \cdots \times M_n$ of the distinct conjugates of M under G. If K is subnormal in G then $K \sim M_{i_1} \times \cdots \times M_{i_r}$ for some subset $\{i_1, \ldots, i_r\}$ of $\{1, \ldots, n\}$ (and so the mapping $\{i_1, \ldots, i_r\} \to [M_{i_1} \times \cdots \times M_{i_r}]$ is an isomorphism from the lattice of subsets of $\{1, \ldots, n\}$ onto the structure lattice of G). Now using the above result together with Lemma 4.3, it is easily seen that if K is a non-trivial subnormal subgroup of G_0 then $K \simeq M_1 \times \cdots \times M_r$ for some $1 \leqslant r \leqslant n$. Taking account of Lemma 4.2 (i), it thus follows that the proof of Theorem 4.2 will be completed once the following lemma has been established.

Lemma 4.4. *If $1 \leqslant p < q \leqslant n$ then $M_1 \times \cdots \times M_p < M_1 \times \cdots \times M_q$.*

This lemma will be proved in §4.3.

It is interesting to note that the results described in the next-to-last paragraph can be summarized as follows: *if K, L are non-trivial subnormal subgroups of G, then $K \simeq L$ if and only if $[K]$, $[L]$ have the same height in the structure lattice of G.* Thus the $\preccurlyeq$ relation is intimately connected with the order relation in the structure lattice.

§4.3. Proof of Lemma 4.4

Let $H = M_1 \times \cdots \times M_p$, $L = M_1 \times \cdots \times M_q$, and suppose by way of contradiction that $H \simeq L$. Then by Theorem 2.1 there would be a subgroup A of finite index in H and a homomorphism θ of A onto a subgroup B of finite index in L. Let $A_i = A \cap M_i$ $(i = 1, \ldots, p)$. Then $A_1 \times \cdots \times A_r \leqslant A$. Moreover, since for each i, $|M_i : A_i| < \infty$, $A_1 \times \cdots \times A_p$ is of finite index in H. Let B_i $(i = 1, \ldots, p)$ be the image of A_i under θ. Then $\mathrm{sgp}\{B_1, \ldots, B_p\}$ is of finite index in B. Note that for $i \neq j$, each element of B_i commutes with each element of B_j (and so in particular $B_i \trianglelefteq \mathrm{sgp}\{B_1, \ldots, B_p\}$ for $i = 1, \ldots, p$).

Now by [24, Theorem 2], A_i $(i = 1, \ldots, p)$ lies in $\mathscr{D}_2$. Consequently either B_i is finite or the restriction of θ to A_i is an isomorphism onto B_i. By relabelling, if necessary, it can be supposed that B_i is infinite for $i \leqslant r$, and B_i is finite for $i > r$. Then $\mathrm{sgp}\{B_1, \ldots, B_r\}$ has finite index in $\mathrm{sgp}\{B_1, \ldots, B_p\}$, and so has finite index in L.

Let C be the core of $\mathrm{sgp}\{B_1, \ldots, B_r\}$ in L. Then $|L : C| < \infty$. Let $C_i = C \cap B_i$ $(i = 1, \ldots, r)$. Then $|B_i : C_i| < \infty$ so that $\mathrm{sgp}\{C_1, \ldots, C_r\}$ is of finite index in L. Moreover, since $B_i \trianglelefteq \mathrm{sgp}\{B_1, \ldots, B_r\}$, $C_i \trianglelefteq C$, so that C_i is subnormal in L and therefore also in G. Note that each C_i lies in $\mathscr{D}_2$, by [24, Theorem 2].

Now for $1 \leqslant i < j \leqslant r$, $C_i \cap C_j$ is abelian, and normal in C_i. Consequently, $C_i \cap C_j$ is an abelian subnormal subgroup of G, and so $C_i \cap C_j = 1$, since G has trivial Baer radical. Thus $\mathrm{sgp}\{C_1, \ldots, C_r\} = C_1 \times \cdots \times C_r$.

For each M_j $(1 \leqslant j \leqslant q)$ there is a $C_{i(j)}$ such that $M_j \cap C_{i(j)} \neq 1$. For if $M_j \cap C_i = 1$ for all $1 \leqslant i \leqslant r$ then $M_j \cap \mathrm{sgp}\{C_1, \ldots, C_r\} = 1$ by [27, Lemma 14(b)], contradicting the fact that $\mathrm{sgp}\{C_1, \ldots, C_r\}$ has finite index in L. Now if $j \neq l$ then $C_{i(j)} \neq C_{i(l)}$. For if $C_{i(j)} = C_{i(l)}$ then $|C_{i(j)} : M_j \cap C_{i(j)}|\ |C_{i(j)} : M_l \cap C_{i(j)}| < \infty$ since $C_{i(j)}$ is a $\mathscr{D}_2$-group, and so $(M_j \cap C_{i(j)}) \cap (M_l \cap C_{i(j)})$ would be of finite index in $C_{i(j)}$. But $(M_j \cap C_{i(j)}) \cap (M_l \cap C_{i(j)}) = 1$, so that $C_{i(j)}$ would be finite, a contradiction. It now follows that the mapping $j \mapsto i(j)$ is 1 : 1, which is impossible since $r < q$. This contradiction shows that $H < L$, as required.

§4.4. Proof of Theorem 4.3, and an example

The aims of this subsection are firstly to provide a proof of Theorem 4.3, and secondly to give an example of a just-infinite minimal group not satisfying Max-sn.

Proof of Theorem 4.3. Throughout the proof implicit use will be made of the fact that every subnormal subgroup of a just-infinite group has only finitely many distinct conjugates (by [27, Theorem 3]).

Let G be a just-infinite group not satisfying Max-sn and suppose there is a minimal group $M \preccurlyeq G$. It will be shown that $M \simeq G$.

By Lemma 4.2 (i) it can be assumed that M is a subnormal subgroup of G. Moreover, by [27, Lemma 16] it can be supposed that there is no subnormal subgroup L of G with $M \leqslant L$ and $1 < |L : M| < \infty$. Let $M_1, \ldots, M_n$ be the distinct conjugates of M under G.

Now M cannot lie in $\mathcal{D}_2$. For if M lay in $\mathcal{D}_2$ and $g, g' \in G$ with $M^g \cap M^{g'} \neq 1$, then $|M^g : M^g \cap M^{g'}|\, |M^{g'} : M^g \cap M^{g'}| < \infty$, and so $M^g = M^{g'}$ by [27, Lemma 16]. Consequently, $M_1, \ldots, M_n$ would intersect trivially in pairs, and so $\operatorname{sgp}\{M_1, \ldots, M_n\} = M_1 \times \cdots \times M_n$ by [27, Lemma 14]. But this would imply that G satisfied Max-sn by [27, Theorem 4].

Now suppose, by way of contradiction, that G is not a minimal group. Then it will be shown that there is a non-trivial subnormal subgroup D of G such that $D \cap M_i = 1$ for $i = 1, \ldots, n$. This implies (using [27, Lemma 14 (b)]) that $D \cap \operatorname{sgp}\{M_1, \ldots, M_n\} = 1$, and so $\operatorname{sgp}\{M_1, \ldots, M_n\}$ has infinite index in G. But since $\operatorname{sgp}\{M_1, \ldots, M_n\}$ is normal, this contradicts the fact that G is just-infinite.

To obtain D, a sequence of subnormal subgroups $D_1, \ldots, D_n$ of G will be constructed satisfying the following: for $m = 1, \ldots, n$

(i) D_m is non-trivial;

(ii) $M_i \cap D_m = 1$ for $i = 1, \ldots, m$;

(iii) there is a subnormal subgroup B_m of G with $B_m \simeq M$,

$$B_m \cap D_m = 1,\ |G : \operatorname{sgp}\{B_m, D_m\}| < \infty.$$

One then takes D to be D_n.

The following fact will be required: *if A, B are two groups with $A \simeq M$, $B \simeq M$ then $A \times B \simeq M$.* To prove this, first note that since M is not a $\mathcal{D}_2$-group, M has a non-trivial subnormal subgroup K of infinite index. Let C be a near-complement for K in G. Then $|G : K \times C| < \infty$, so $|M : K \times (C \cap M)| < \infty$. Note that since $|M : K| = \infty$, $C \cap M$ is infinite. Now it follows from Lemma 4.2(ii) that $K \preccurlyeq M$ and $C \cap M \preccurlyeq M$. Consequently, $K \simeq C \cap M \simeq M$, since M is minimal.

Now it is clear that $A \times B \simeq K \times (C \cap M)$, and since $K \times (C \cap M)$ has finite index in M, it follows that $A \times B \simeq M$, as required.

The groups $D_1, \ldots, D_n$ are obtained as follows. For D_1 choose any near-complement of M_1 in G. Suppose $1 \leq m < n$ and that $D_1, \ldots, D_m$ have been obtained. Let L be a near-complement of $M_{m+1} \cap D_m$ in G. Then $|G : (M_{m+1} \cap D_m) \times L| < \infty$, and so $|D_m : (M_{m+1} \cap D_m) \times (L \cap D_m)| < \infty$. Let $D_{m+1} = L \cap D_m$. Now D_{m+1} is non-trivial. For suppose not. Then $M_{m+1} \cap D_m$ would be of finite index in D_m, so that $M_{m+1} \cap D_m \simeq D_m$. Consequently, $D_m \simeq M_{m+1}$ (since $M_{m+1} \cap D_m \leq M_{m+1}$ by Lemma 4.2(ii) and M_{m+1} is minimal). However, if B_m is as in (iii) then $\mathrm{sgp}\{B_m, D_m\} = B_m \times D_m$ (using [27, Lemma 14(a)]) and so, by what was shown in the previous paragraph, $B_m \times D_m \simeq M$. However, $B_m \times D_m \simeq G$. This contradicts the assumption that G is not minimal. Consequently, D_{m+1} is non trivial, and so (i) holds. Obviously (ii) holds. To see that (iii) holds let $B_{m+1} = \mathrm{sgp}\{B_m, M_{m+1} \cap D_m\}$. Since B_m, $M_{m+1} \cap D_m$, D_{m+1} intersect trivially in pairs, it follows from [27, Lemma 14(a)] that $\mathrm{sgp}\{B_{m+1}, D_{m+1}\} = B_m \times (M_{m+1} \cap D_m) \times D_{m+1}$, and so, since $\mathrm{sgp}\{B_m, D_m\} = B_m \times D_m$, $\mathrm{sgp}\{B_{m+1}, D_{m+1}\}$ has finite index in G. Moreover, since $B_{m+1} = B_m \times (M_{m+1} \cap D_m)$, and since $M_{m+1} \cap D_m$ is either trivial or equally as large as M_{m+1} (using Lemma 4.2 (ii) and the fact that M_{m+1} is minimal), it follows from the previous paragraph that $B_{m+1} \simeq M$.

This completes the proof.

Example 4.4. Let S be a non-trivial finite perfect group and for $i = -1, -2, \ldots$, let S_i be a copy of S. Let $G = \mathrm{Wr}_{i<-1} S_i$. Then it is shown in [27] that G is just-infinite (see pp. 376–377) but G does not satisfy Max-sn (see pp. 378–379). It will be shown here that G lies in $\mathcal{M}$.

Suppose $H \dot{\leq} G$. By Theorem 2.1 there is a subgroup A of finite index in G mapping, under a homomorphism θ say, onto a subgroup of finite index in H. Now A contains the base group of some segmentation of G. To be more precise, there is an integer $m > 0$ such that $G = G_1 \wr G_2$, where

$$G_1 = \mathrm{Wr}_{i<-m} S_i,$$

$$G_2 = \mathrm{Wr}_{-m \leq i < 0} S_i,$$

and where A contains the base group D of $G_1 \wr G_2$. Note that G_1 is isomorphic to G and so D is a finite direct product of isomorphic copies of G.

Let K be the kernel of the restriction of θ to D. Note that K is subnormal in G. Since $|D:K|=\infty$, K must intersect at least one of the factors of D trivially. Thus $D = G_1 \times L$ with $K \cap G_1 = 1$. By [27, Lemma 14(b)], $\mathrm{sgp}\{L, K\} \cap G_1 = 1$, and so D/K maps onto G_1. Thus $G \simeq G_1 \preccurlyeq D/K \simeq H$. Consequently, $H \simeq G$, and so G is minimal.

§4.5. Extensions

It is not difficult to see that if A is an almost normal subgroup of a group G, and if θ is a homomorphism of G, then $\theta(A)$ is almost normal in $\theta(G)$. In addition if $H \leqslant G$ then $H \cap A$ is almost normal in H. It thus follows from [19, Lemma 1.48] that *the properties* Max-an *and* Min-an *are extension closed.* Moreover, *suppose a group G has a normal subgroup N such that every properly ascending chain of almost normal subgroups in N has length at most r, and every properly ascending chain of almost normal subgroups in G/N has length at most s; then every properly ascending chain of almost normal subgroups in G has length at most rs.*

To prove this latter result* consider a chain $A_1 \leqslant A_2 \leqslant \cdots \leqslant A_{rs+1}$ of almost normal subgroups of G. Then

$$A_1N/N \leqslant A_2N/N \leqslant \cdots \leqslant A_{rs+1}N/N,$$

and by the condition imposed on G/N, $A_iN/N = \cdots = A_{i+r}N/N$ for some i. Also, since $A_i \cap N \leqslant \cdots \leqslant A_{i+r} \cap N$, there exists $i \leqslant j < l \leqslant i+r$ such that $A_j \cap N = A_l \cap N$, by the condition imposed on N. Since $A_jN = A_lN$ and $A_j \subseteq A_l$ one now has:

$$\begin{aligned} A_j &= A_j \cap A_jN \\ &= A_j \cap A_lN \\ &= A_l(A_j \cap N) \\ &= A_l(A_l \cap N) \\ &= A_l. \end{aligned}$$

Now it was shown in §4.1 that there is a relationship between the almost normal subgroups of an infinite group G and the groups H with $H \preccurlyeq G$. It is, therefore, natural to ask whether results analogous to those stated above apply for the relation $\preccurlyeq$. For example are Max-$\preccurlyeq$ and Min-$\preccurlyeq$ extension closed? Is the property of having finite height extension closed? The main aim of this subsection is to show

* I thank B.A.F. Wehrfritz for supplying me with this argument.

Theorem 4.4. *The properties* Max-$\leqslant$ *and "having finite height" are not extension closed. In fact, there is a split extension of one minimal group by another which does not satisfy* Max-$\leqslant$.

In contrast to Theorem 4.4 the following result will also be proved in this subsection.

Theorem 4.5. *Let $M_1, \ldots, M_n$ be minimal groups, and let $G = M_1 \times \cdots \times M_n$. Let $H \leqslant G$. Then $H \simeq M_{i_1} \times \cdots \times M_{i_r}$ where $\{i_1, \ldots, i_r\} \subseteq \{1, \ldots, n\}$. In particular G has height less than or equal to n.*

It should be mentioned that the height of G in Theorem 4.5 can be less than n. For example, if M is a minimal just-infinite group not satisfying Max-sn then $M \times M \simeq M$, as can be seen from the proof of Theorem 4.3.

The following question remains open.

Problem 7. Is Min-$\leqslant$ extension closed?*

The rest of this subsection is devoted to the proofs of Theorems 4.4 and 4.5.

For Theorem 4.4 the following construction is required.

Let I be a non-empty set and for $i \in I$ choose a non-trivial group A_i. For $(i, n) \in I \times \mathbf{Z}$ let $A(i, n)$ be a copy of A_i, and let B be the restricted direct product $\Pi^D_{(i,n)} A(i, n)$ of the $A(i, n)$. Then $B = \Pi^D_{i \in I} B_i$, where $B_i = \Pi^D_{n \in \mathbf{Z}} A(i, n)$. Now for each i there is an automorphism θ_i of B_i obtained by permuting the factors according to the permutation of $\mathbf{Z}$ defined by $n \mapsto n+1$. Let θ be the unique automorphism of B whose restriction to B_i is θ_i for $i \in I$, and form the split extension of B by an infinite cyclic group $\langle t \rangle$. If G is (isomorphic to) the resulting group it will be convenient to write $G = [A_i (i \in I), t]$. Define the *rank* of G to be the cardinality of I.

Lemma 4.5. *Assume each A_i is perfect. Let $N \trianglelefteq G$ and suppose $bt^p \in N$ with $b \in B$ and $p \neq 0$. Then $B \leqslant N$.*

Proof. For each i there exixts n_0 such that the (i, n_0) coordinate of b is 1. Let $a_1, a_2 \in A(i, n_0)$. Then $t^{-p}b^{-1}a_1bt^p = t^{-p}a_1t^p \in A(i, n_0 + p)$, and so $[[bt^p, a_1], a_2] = [a_1, a_2]$. But $[[bt^p, a_1], a_2] \in N$, and since a_1, a_2 are arbitrary it follows that N contains the derived group of $A(i, n_0)$, and

* *Added in proof.* The answer is "No" (B. Hurley).

therefore the whole of $A(i, n_0)$ since A_i is perfect. Conjugating $A(i, n_0)$ by powers of t then establishes that $A(i, n) \leqslant N$ for all $n \in \mathbf{Z}$. Thus $B_i \leqslant N$, and since i was arbitrary, $B \leqslant N$ as required.

Lemma 4.6. *Suppose each A_i is perfect and let H be a subgroup of finite index in G. Then $H = \mathrm{sgp}\{B, t^q\}$ for some $q > 0$. Moreover $H = [C_i\,(i \in I), s]$ where $C_i = A_i^q$. In particular, the rank of H is the same as the rank of G.*

Proof. Now there is a normal subgroup N of finite index in G containing H. In particular, $t^p \in N$ for some $p \neq 0$, and so it follows from the previous lemma that $B \leqslant N \leqslant H$. Thus $H = \mathrm{sgp}\{B, t^q\}$ for some $q > 0$.

Now let $s = t^q$, and for $(i, n) \in I \times \mathbf{Z}$ let $C(i, n) = A(i, nq) \times A(i, nq+1) \times \cdots \times A(i, nq+q-1)$. Then for all $n \in \mathbf{Z}$, $C(i, n)$ is isomorphic to A_i^q, and it is readily seen that $H = [C_i\,(i \in I), s]$.

Lemma 4.7. *Suppose $A_i = \Pi^D_{\Lambda_i} S_\lambda(i)\ (i \in I)$, where each $S_\lambda(i)$ is a non-abelian simple group. Let $\bar{G}$ be an infinite homomorphic image of G. Then $\bar{G} = [\Pi^D_{\Gamma_j} S_\gamma(j)\ (j \in J), t]$, where $J \subseteq I$ and where for each $j \in J$, Γ_j is a non-empty subset of Λ_j. In particular, the rank of $\bar{G}$ is less than or equal to the rank of G.*

Proof. In the copy $A(i, n)$ of A_i, the copy of $S_\lambda(i)$ will be denoted by $S_\lambda(i, n)$, so that $A(i, n) = \Pi^D_{\Lambda_i} S_\lambda(i, n)$.

Some of the following calculations are similar to those in Example 4.3 but are repeated in detail here for convenience.

Let N be the kernel of the homomorphism $G \to \bar{G}$. It follows from Lemma 4.5 that $N \leqslant B$. Consider the subgroups $N \cap A(i, n)$. It will be shown that these generate N.

Let b be an element of B belonging to N, and suppose that the (i, n) coordinate, a say, of b is non-trivial. Now $A(i, n) = \Pi^D_{\Lambda_i} S_\lambda(i, n)$. Suppose the λth coordinate, s say, of a is non-trivial. Let $z \in S_\lambda(i, n)$. Then $[b, z] \in N$ and $[b, z] = [s, z]$. Since $[s, z] \neq 1$ for at least one z, it follows that $S_\lambda(i, n) \leqslant N$. Consequently, $a \in N$, and so $b \in \mathrm{sgp}\{N \cap A(i, n) : (i, n) \in I \times \mathbf{Z}\}$, as required.

Now similar calculations to those in the previous paragraph show that $N \cap A(i, n)$ is the subgroup generated by $S_\lambda(i, n)$ with λ ranging over some subset Θ_i of Λ_i. This subset Θ_i depends only on i, and not on n. For if $S_\lambda(i; n) \leqslant N \cap A(i, n)$, then conjugating by t^p shows that $S_\lambda(i, n+p) \leqslant N \cap A(i, n+p)$.

It is now not difficult to see that one can take J to be the subset of I consisting of those elements i for which $\Theta_i \neq \Lambda_i$, and then put $\Gamma_j = \Lambda_j \backslash \Theta_j$ for $j \in J$.

This proves the lemma.

Proof of Theorem 4.4. In the above construction take $I = \{1, 2, \ldots\}$, and take all the A_i to be isomorphic copies of some finite non-abelian simple group. Then B is minimal (see Example 4.3), and G is a split extension of B by the minimal group $\langle t \rangle$. It will be shown that G does not have Max-$\preccurlyeq$.

For $p = 1, 2, \ldots$ let $G_p = [A_i\,(i = 1, \ldots, p), t]$. Then $G_1 \preccurlyeq G_2 \preccurlyeq \cdots \preccurlyeq G$. It will be shown that $G_p < G_{p+1}$. Suppose, by way of contradiction, that $G_{p+1} \preccurlyeq G_p$. Then by Theorem 2.1, G_p would have a subgroup H_p of finite index mapping onto a subgroup H_{p+1} of finite index in G_{p+1}. Now the rank of H_p would be p, by Lemma 4.6. Moreover, $H_p = [A_i^q(i = 1, \ldots, p), t]$ for some q. Consequently, by Lemma 4.7, H_{p+1} would have rank less than or equal to p. On the other hand, H_{p+1} would have rank $p + 1$, by Lemma 4.6. This contradiction shows $G_p < G_{p+1}$, as required.

Proof of Theorem 4.5. The proof is by induction on n.

If $n = 1$ the result is trivial.

Suppose $n > 1$, and let $H \preccurlyeq G$. By Theorem 2.1 there is a subgroup A of finite index in G mapping, by a homomorphism θ say, onto a subgroup of finite index in H. Let $A_i = A \cap M_i$ for $i = 1, \ldots, n$. Then $|M_i : A_i| < \infty$ and so $|G : A_1 \times \cdots \times A_n| < \infty$. Notice that $\theta(A_1 \times \cdots \times A_n)$ has finite index in H. Let N be the kernel of the restriction of θ to $A_1 \times \cdots \times A_n$. For $i = 1, \ldots, n$ let

$$N_i = \{a : a \in A_i, \text{ there exists } u \in A_1 \times \cdots \times A_{i-1} \times A_{i+1} \times \cdots \times A_n \text{ such that } au \in N\}.$$

Then $N_i \trianglelefteq A_i$.

Case 1. For some i, $|A_i : N_i| < \infty$.

Assume for definiteness that $|A_1 : N_1| < \infty$. Then $(A_2 \times \cdots \times A_n)N/N$ has finite index in $(A_1 \times \cdots \times A_n)/N$. For let $z_1, \ldots, z_p$ be coset representatives of N_1 in A_1, and let $av \in A_1 \times \cdots \times A_n$ with $a \in A_1$, $v \in A_2 \times \cdots \times A_n$. Then $a = z_j a'$ for some z_j and some $a' \in N_1$. Moreover, since $a' \in N_1$, there exists $u \in A_2 \times \cdots \times A_n$ such that $a'u \in N$. Thus $au = z_j(a'u)(u^{-1}v)$ and so $auN = z_j(u^{-1}v)N$. Consequently $(A_1 \times \cdots \times A_n)/N = \bigcup_1^p (z_j N)((A_2 \times \cdots \times A_n)N/N)$.

It now follows that

$$(A_1 \times \cdots \times A_n)/N \simeq (A_2 \times \cdots \times A_n)/N \cap (A_2 \times \cdots \times A_n).$$

Since

$$(A_2 \times \cdots \times A_n)/N \cap (A_2 \times \cdots \times A_n) \leqslant M_2 \times \cdots \times M_n,$$

the inductive hypothesis now applies to give the required result.

Case 2. For all i, $|A_i : N_i| = \infty$.

Now $N \leqslant \text{sgp}\{N_1, N_2, \ldots, N_n\}$. Thus $(A_1 \times \cdots \times A_n)/\text{sgp}\{N_1, \ldots, N_n\} \leqslant (A_1 \times \cdots \times A_n)/N$. But $(A_1 \times \cdots \times A_n)/\text{sgp}\{N_1, \ldots, N_n\}$ is isomorphic to $A_1/N_1 \times \cdots \times A_n/N_n$, and since for each i, $A_i/N_i \simeq M_i$, it follows that $A_1/N_1 \times \cdots \times A_n/N_n \simeq G$. Thus $H \simeq G$.

This completes the proof.

§5. A final question

Let $\mathcal{P}$ be a large property and let $\mathcal{Y}$ be a class of groups. Say that *$\mathcal{P}$ is large for $\mathcal{Y}$* if every $\mathcal{Y}$-group with $\mathcal{P}$ has infinite height.

With the possible exception of SQ-universality, none of the properties listed in §2.1 is large for finitely presented groups. In fact, for all the properties except SQ-universality there are finitely presented minimal groups with the property. On the other hand, finitely generated SQ-universal groups cannot be minimal (since finitely generated groups have just-infinite quotients).

Now SQ-universality is generally agreed to be quite a good measure of largeness for countable groups. Can this be made more precise?

Problem 8. Is SQ-universality large for finitely presented, finitely generated, or even countable groups?*

Of course, SQ-universality is not large for all groups since there are simple (and hence minimal) SQ-universal groups.

References

[1] H. Bass, J. Milnor and J.-P. Serre, Solution of the congruence subgroup problem for SL_n $(n \geqslant 3)$ and Sp_{2n} $(n \geqslant 2)$, Inst. Haute Études Sci. Publ. Math. 33 (1967) 59–137.

[2] I.M. Chiswell, Abstract length functions on groups, Math. Proc. Camb. Phil. Soc. 80 (1976) 451–463.

* *Added in proof.* B. Hurley has constructed a countable SQ-universal minimal group.

[3] D.E. Cohen, Groups with free subgroups of finite index, Conference on Group Theory, Springer Lecture Notes No. 319, 26–44.
[4] D.J. Collins, Free subgroups of small cancellation groups, Proc. London Math. Soc. (2) 26 (1973) 193–206.
[5] B. Fine and M. Tretkoff, The SQ-universality of certain arithmetically defined linear groups, J. London Math. Soc. (2) 13 (1976) 65–68.
[6] F.P. Greenleaf, Invariant means on topological groups, Van Nostrand Mathematical Studies No. 16 (Van Nostrand–Reinhold Company, New York, Toronto, London, Melbourne, 1969).
[7] P. Hall, On embedding a group into the join of given groups, J. Austral. Math. Soc. 17 (1974) 434–495.
[8] A.H.M. Hoare, A. Karrass and D. Solitar, Subgroups of infinite index in Fuchsian groups, Math. Z. 125 (1972) 59–69.
[9] A. Karrass and D. Solitar, Subgroups of HNN groups and groups with one defining relation, Can. J. Math. 23 (1971) 627–643.
[10] A. Karrass, A. Pietrowski and D. Solitar, Finite and infinite cyclic extensions of free groups, J. Austral. Math. Soc. 26 (1973) 458–466.
[11] O.H. Kegel and B.A.F. Wehrfritz, Locally finite groups, North-Holland Mathematical Library, Vol. 3 (North-Holland, Amsterdam, London, New York, 1973).
[12] D. McCarthy, Infinite groups whose proper quotient groups are finite I, Comm. Pure Appl. Math. 21 (1968) 545–562.
[13] D. McCarthy, Infinite groups whose proper quotient groups are finite II, Comm. Pure Appl. Math. 23 (1970) 767–790.
[14] W. Magnus, A. Karrass and D. Solitar, Combinatorial group theory: Presentations of groups in terms of generators and defining relations (Interscience Publishers, New York, London, Sydney, 1966).
[15] J. Milnor, A note on curvature and fundamental group, J. Differential Geometry 2 (1968) 1–7.
[16] J.L. Mennicke, Finite factor groups of the unimodular group, Ann. of Math. (2) 81 (1965) 31–37.
[17] P. Neumann, The SQ-universality of some finitely presented groups, J. Austral. Math. Soc. 16 (1973) 1–6.
[18] S.J. Pride, On quotients of certain countable groups, Bull Austral. Math. Soc., 16 (1977) 225–228.
[19] D.J.S. Robinson, Finiteness conditions and generalized soluble groups, Parts 1 and 2, Ergebnisse der Mathematik und ihrer Grenzgebiete, Bands 62 and 63 (Springer-Verlag, New York, Berlin, 1972).
[20] G. Sacerdote and P.E. Schupp, SQ-universality in HNN groups and one relator groups, J. London Math. Soc. (2) 7 (1974) 733–740.
[21] P.E. Schupp, A survey of small cancellation theory, in Word Problems (North-Holland Publishing Company, Amsterdam, London, 1973).
[22] G.P. Scott, An embedding theorem for groups with a free subgroup of finite index, Bull. London Math. Soc. 6 (1974) 304–306.
[23] J.R. Stallings, Quotients of the powers of the augmentation ideal in a group ring, in Knots, Groups and 3-Manifolds, Annals of Mathematics Studies No. 84 (Princeton University Press, Princeton, 1975).
[24] C. Tretkoff, Some remarks on just-infinite groups, Commun. Algebra 4 (1976) 483–489.

[25] J. Wiegold, Transitive groups with fixed-point free permutations, Arch. Math. 27 (1976) 473–475.

[26] J.S. Wilson, Some properties of groups inherited by normal subgroups of finite index, Math. Z. 114 (1970) 19–21.

[27] J.S. Wilson, Groups with every proper quotient finite, Proc. Cambridge Philos. Soc. 69 (1971) 373–391.

[28] R. Zimmert, Zur SL_2 der ganzen Zahlen eines imaginär-quadratischen Zahlkorpers, Inventiónes Math. 19 (1973) 73–81.

S.I. Adian, W.W. Boone, G. Higman, eds., Word Problems II
© North-Holland Publishing Company (1980) 337–346

ALGORITHMIC PROBLEMS FOR SOLVABLE GROUPS

V.N. REMESLENNIKOV and N.S. ROMANOVSKII
Institute of Mathematics, Novosibirsk

§1. Introduction

Classical algorithmic problems — the word problem, conjugacy problem, and isomorphism problem — arose in the theory of groups from topolocal considerations and were formulated for the first time at the beginning of this century by Dehn. In the middle fifties it was shown that these problems have negative solutions in the class of all groups. However, for important classes of groups such as nilpotent and solvable groups, these problems remained unsolved. At the present moment a number of interesting results have been obtained in this field, and this paper is intended to survey them.

Let us recall the main definitions and the formulation of the classical algorithmic problems for the class of all groups.

We call the pair $\langle X, R\rangle$ the presentation of group G, where X is a non-empty set and R is a set of the words in the alphabet $X \cup X^{-1}$. The group G is a factor group of the free group with the base X by the normal subgroup, generated by the set R. With this understanding we shall write $G = \langle X, R\rangle$; further, X is called the set of the generators of group G, and R — the set of defining relators. If the sets X and R are finite, we say that group G is finitely presented. We shall also consider the case when X is finite and R is recursively enumerable. In this case G is called a recursively presented group.

Let G be a given finitely presented (recursively presented) group. The word problem, conjugacy problem and membership problem are the problems of establishing the existence of algorithms to decide respectively

(i) whether or not an arbitrary element (word) of group G equals 1;

(ii) whether or not two arbitrary elements from G are conjugate in G;

(iii) for a given arbitrary finite set $\{u, v_1, \ldots, v_n\}$ of elements of G

whether or not the element u belongs to the subgroup generated by $v_1, \ldots, v_n$.

Finally, let $\phi = \{G_i \mid i \in N\}$ be a recursive class of finitely presented groups. The isomorphism problem for the class ϕ consists in establishing the existence of an algorithm to decide for arbitrary i, j whether or not the groups G_i and G_j are isomorphic.

P.S. Novikov [10] and W.W. Boone [27] constructed examples of finitely presented groups, for which the word problem was solved negatively. This implied the negative solution of the conjugacy and membership problems. Aided by this result, S.I. Adian [1] proved that the isomorphism problem in the class of all groups also has a negative solution. In addition, algorithmic unsolvability was proved for a number of other problems, such as the recognition of the following properties: nilpotency, finiteness, simplicity or unity of a given group presentation.

Let H be a subgroup of the finitely presented group G, generated by the elements $u_1, \ldots, u_n$. The set of all the words from the u_i is recursively enumerable, as is the set of all the words from G equal to 1. The intersection of these two sets forms the recursively enumerable set of the presenting relations of group H in the generators $u_1, \ldots, u_n$. Therefore, the finitely generated subgroup of the finitely presented group is recursively presented. Higman [30] showed that the converse statement is also correct; i.e. every recursively presented group is embeddable in some finitely presented group.

§2. The setting of the problems

Thus we see that the majority of algorithmic problems has a negative solution in the class of all groups. Therefore, it is natural to study algorithmical problems with additional restrictions on the groups considered. In a number of papers, such restrictions were on the form of the defining relations, e.g., Magnus' theorem [32], proved in 1932, and which deals with the solvability of the word problem for groups with one defining relation. However, we shall consider restrictions having a natural group-theoretic character, such as nilpotency, polycyclicity and solvability.

Here, two approaches to such problems are possible. The first approach consists in the algorithmic problems being considered for a finitely presented group (or a set of groups) under the assumption that such group turns out to be, say, solvable of given steps of solvability;

i.e. it is assumed that the condition of solvability results from the defining relators.

In the second approach, groups which are finitely presented in a given variety are studied. This means the following:

Let V be a variety given by a finite set of identities. We say that a group G is given in the variety V by generators X and relations R, if it is a factor group of the free group of the variety V with the base X by the normal subgroup, generated by the set R. Finitely presented group and recursively presented group in the variety V are defined in the obvious way.

Let us introduce the corresponding designations FP, RP, FPV, RPV for the classes: finitely presented, recursively presented, finitely presented in the variety V, recursively presented in the variety V. In the language of these classes the first of the formulated approaches leads to the study of groups from $\mathrm{FP} \cap V$, if the additional condition consists of membership in the variety V. In the second approach groups from FPV are studied. Evident inclusions take place:

$$\mathrm{FP} \cap V \subseteq \mathrm{FPV} \subseteq \mathrm{RP} \cap V = \mathrm{RPV}.$$

For some varieties these relations may be made more exact. If V is the variety of groups of nilpotency class c, then it is well known that

$$\mathrm{FP} \cap V = \mathrm{FPV} = \mathrm{RPV}.$$

For the variety of l-step solvable groups, denoted by $\mathcal{A}^l$, where $l \geqslant 2$ strict inclusion takes place:

$$\mathrm{FP} \cap V < \mathrm{FPV}.$$

For $l = 2$, this was obtained by G. Baumslag [24], who showed that the wreath product of two infinite cyclic groups lies in $\mathrm{FPV} \setminus \mathrm{FP}$, and for other l from the result obtained by A.L. Shmel'kin [23], who had proved the corresponding statement for the free solvable group. It should also be noted that at $l = 2$ $\mathrm{FPV} = \mathrm{RPV}$, which follows from the maximal condition for normal subgroups in finitely generated metabelian groups, and at $l > 3$ the inclusion is strict $\mathrm{FPV} < \mathrm{RPV}$, as it was shown by A.L. Shmelkin [23], who proved that the free metabelian group is not finitely presented in $\mathcal{A}^l$.

Recalling Higman's theorem about the embedding of recursively presented groups into finitely presented ones, we may formulate a few problems for the varieties $\mathcal{A}^l$, which acquire an important meaning, taking into account V.N. Remeslennikov's theorem, which we shall deal with below.

Problem 1. Can any RP$\mathscr{A}^l$-group, where $l > 3$, be embedded into an FP$\mathscr{A}^m$-group for suitable m?

Problem 2. Can any FP$\mathscr{A}^l$-group, where $l > 3$, be embedded into an FP $\cap\, \mathscr{A}^m$-group for suitable m?

Problem 3. Can any RP$\mathscr{A}^l$-group, where $l > 3$, be embedded into an FP $\cap\, \mathscr{M}^m$-group for suitable m?

For $l = 2$ these problems have been solved positively, since G. Baumslag [25] and V.N. Remeslennikov [13, 15] have shown that any finitely generated metabelian group can be embedded into a finitely presented metabelian group.

§3. Classical algorithmic problems for solvable groups

Before supplying the formulations of the main results obtained, we shall take note of the connection of the algorithmic problems with the finite approximatability of the groups. Let τ be some group-theoretic predicate. We say that the group G is finitely approximated with respect to the predicate τ, if for any collection of elements which are not related under τ, there exists a homomorphism of group G to a finite group H such that the images of the elements considered are not related under τ in H. Let us consider, for instance, the predicate: to be equal to the element 1. Groups which are finitely approximated with respect to this predicate are called residually finite.

Let G be a group finitely presented in the variety V. Let the variety V be given by a finite set of identities. If G is residually finite, then the word problem can be positively solved in G. I.e., the set of words representing 1 is recursive. It is evident that this set is recursively enumerable. Therefore, it is enough to show that its complement is also recursively enumerable. Actually, because of the residual finiteness the complement may be enumerated by searching through all possible homomorphisms of group G to finite groups. Similarly, if the group G is residually finite with respect to conjugacy or membership, then in it the problems of conjugacy and membership are solved positively.

Let us consider now the word problem for groups in $\mathscr{A}^l$. By Hall's theorem [29] finitely generated metabelian groups are residually finite, therefore, the word problem for groups finitely presented in the variety $\mathscr{A}^2$, is solved positively. On the other hand, V.N. Remeslennikov's theorem [14] states that for $l > 5$ there exists a group finitely presented in the variety $\mathscr{A}^l$, for which the word problem is solved negatively. To be more precise, for each l a specific representation of this group can be obtained. Since $\mathrm{FP} \cap \mathscr{A}^l < \mathrm{FP}\mathscr{A}^l$ for $l > 3$, we are led to the following question:

Problem 4. Does there exist a solvable finitely presented group with unsolvable word problem?

Let us note that a similar question was formulated by S.I. Adian, who asked if there exists a group with unsolvable word problem which satisfies some nontrivial identity. It is clear that an affirmative answer to problem 2 and 3 gives an affirmative answer to problem 4.

The cases $l = 3, 4$ are not covered by V.N. Remeslennikov's theorem. Hence, we have the following question:

Problem 5. Is the word problem solvable for groups from $\mathrm{FP}\mathscr{A}^3$ or $\mathrm{FP}\mathscr{A}^4$?

As for the conjugacy problem, we know still less about it. It follows from V.N. Remeslennikov's theorem that for $l > 5$ there exist examples of groups finitely presented in the variety $\mathscr{A}^l$, for which the conjugacy problem has negative solution. However, this problem remains uninvestigated for solvable groups of 2, 3 and 4 steps. It should be noted that it cannot be solved by using the finite approximation method, because M.I. Kargapolov and E.I. Timoshenko [5], and Wehrfritz [35], have constructed examples of finitely generated metabelian groups which are not residually finite with respect to conjugacy.

As for the membership problem, there exist two main results. On the one hand, N.S. Romanovskii [18] proved that it is solved positively for metabelian groups. On the other hand V.N. Remeslennikov [14], for $l \geqslant 4$, has constructed an example of a group which is finitely presented in the variety $\mathscr{A}^l$, and with a finitely generated subgroup for which the membership problem is solved negatively. Hence, we have the following question:

Problem 6. Is the membership problem solvable for groups in $\mathrm{FP}\mathscr{A}^3$?

By using V.N. Remeslennikov's theorem, for each $l \geqslant 7$, there was constructed in [6] a group G finitely presented in $\mathscr{A}^l$, for which there exists no algorithm, deciding for any group H finitely presented in $\mathcal{A}^l$ whether or not it is isomorphic to G. By this example the isomorphism problem for FP$\mathcal{A}^l$ for $l \geqslant 7$ is solved negatively. Hence, we have the following

Problem 7. Is the isomorphism problem solvable for metabelian groups?

We recall that in the class of all groups the isomorphism problem for a unit group is solved negatively. The analogous statement is wrong for the variety $\mathcal{A}^l$, because there $G \neq 1$ if and only if $G/G' \neq 1$. Therefore, the problem is reduced to the same problem for abelian groups, where, as is well known, it has a positive solution.

We may also remark that for groups from FP$\mathcal{A}^l$ there exists an algorithm to decide whether a given group is finite or not, and in the positive case to find its multiplication table. This can be proved by induction on the solvability step of the group.

It should be noted that, for solvable groups, there does not exist a general theorem on the algorithmic undecidability of group-theoretic properties, similar to the theorem of Adian–Rabin. Perhaps, we can prove such a theorem if we can solve the following:

Problem 8. Is there an algorithm which decides if groups in $\mathcal{A}^l, l > 2$, are nilpotent?

Now a few words about the methods of proof of the majority of theorems of this kind. They use the so-called Magnus embedding of a free solvable group, the essence of which lies in the following.

Let F_l be a free solvable group of step l and rank n and T the left free module of rank n over the ring $\mathbf{Z}[F_l]$. Then the free solvable group F_{l+1} of the step $l+1$ and rank n can be embedded into the group of matrices M of the type $\begin{pmatrix} f & t \\ 0 & 1 \end{pmatrix}$, where $f \in F_l$ and $t \in T$. We may consider the group M as the wreath product of the free abelian group of rank n with F_l. The Magnus embedding turns out to be convenient, for instance, in the case that N is a normal subgroup of F_{l+1}; for in this case the embedding may be extended to the normal subgroup $\bar{N}$ of group M, which represents the semidirect product of the subgroups consisting of unitriangular and diagonal matrices such that $\bar{N} \cap F_{l+1} = N$[18].

Thanks to the Magnus embedding many questions concerning solvable groups can be replaced by corresponding questions about modules over group rings of lesser solvability step. In particular, a number of algebraic problems for two-step solvable groups become problems for free modules over the ring $\mathbf{Z}[\mathscr{X}_1, \ldots, \mathscr{X}_n]$.

§4. Free solvable groups

As has been mentioned above, free solvable groups of finite rank are recursively defined in the class of all groups, and evidently finitely defined in the corresponding variety $\mathfrak{A}^l$. By the use of the Magnus embedding for a free solvable group, the positive solution of the word problem is easily established.

Matteus [33] showed that in the wreath product of groups A and B the conjugacy problem is solved positively, if it is solved positively in A and B, and additionally, the membership problem for cyclic subgroups is positively solvable in B. Making use of this fact and of the Magnus embedding, M.I. Kargapolov and V.N. Remeslennikov [3] positively solved the conjugacy problem for free solvable groups by induction on the solvability step. Later on, V.N. Remeslennikov and V.S. Sokolov [16] established the finite approximatability of those groups with respect to conjugacy. R.A. Sarkisjan [19] proved that the conjugacy problem is positively solved for free polynilpotent groups. The next problem is still open.

Problem 9. Is the membership problem solvable for free solvable groups?

This problem is closed connected with the following.

Problem 10. Is there an algorithm for solving finite systems of linear equations over $\mathbf{Z}[F_e]$?

Here, F_e is a free solvable group with solvability length l.

Let us also note that in an absolutely free group there exist algorithms (for instance, Nilsen's method), to decide if a given finite set is a basis. A.F. Krasnikov [7] has found a similar algorithm for free solvable groups.

The class of groups with one defining relation in the variety $\mathfrak{A}^l$ is the closest to free solvable groups. We know little about these groups so far. Let us still note that N.S. Romanovskii [17] proved the analog of Magnus' Freiheitssatz for a group with one relation in the variety $\mathfrak{A}^l$, and the word problem with some restrictions on the single relation has been solved [18]. However, the general case remains open:

Problem 11. Is the word problem solvable for groups with one defining relation in the variety $\mathfrak{A}^l, l \geqslant 3$?

§5. Algorithmic problems for nilpotent groups

In 1955 A.I. Mal'cev [8] showed that the word problem can be solved positively for nilpotent groups. He also showed [9], that finitely generated nilpotent groups are residually finite with respect to membership, hence the membership problem is solvable. Blackburn [26] has positively solved the conjugacy problem for nilpotent groups by the same method. M.I. Kargapolov and his students [4] raised and solved the following algorithmic problems for $\mathfrak{O}$-power groups over a "good" ring $\mathfrak{O}$: those of word, conjugacy, membership, separating of $\mathfrak{O}$-periodical part, intersection, the description of subgroups in the terms of relations.

Thus, we see that in nilpotent groups the picture is diametrically opposed to that in the class of all groups we have the following:

Problem 12. Is the isomorphism problem solvable for nilpotent groups?

This problem cannot be solved by the method of finite approximation, for at present we know many examples of non-isomorphic finitely generated nilpotent groups with the same families of finite homomorphic images. Concerning this we should note Pickel's theorem [34]. He showed that there can only exist a finite number of groups with the same family of finite homomorphic images in the class of finitely generated nilpotent groups.

It is highly probable that problem 12 will be answered negatively, hence, we have another interesting problem:

Problem 13. Is the isomorphism problem solvable for groups with one defining relation in the variety of nilpotent groups with given nilpotency class?

Such an algorithm exists for class 2-nilpotent groups [20].

§6. Algorithmic problems for polycyclic groups

It should be noted at once that any polycyclic group is finitely presented, so it is possible to discuss algorithmic problems for polycyclic groups. All results known to us here were obtained by means of finite approximatability.

Initially, Hirsch [31] showed that polycyclic groups are residually finite. Then A.I. Mal'cev [9] showed that they are finitely approximated with respect to membership. Finally, V.N. Remeslennikov [12] and Formanek [28] proved the finite approximatability of polycyclic groups with respect to conjugacy. The isomorphism problem for polycyclic groups is still unsolved.

References

[1] S.I. Adjan, Insolvability of some algorithmic problems of group theory, Trudy Moskovoskogo Matem. ob–va 6 (1957) 213–298 (Russian).

[2] M.I. Kargapolov, Finite approximatability of supersolvable groups with respect to conjugacy, Algebra i logika 6, No. 1 (1967) 63–68 (Russian).

[3] M.I. Kargapolov and V.N. Remeslennikov, Conjugacy in free solvable groups, Algebra i logika 5, No. 6 (1966) 15–25 (Russian).

[4] M.I. Kargapolov, V.N. Remeslennikov, N.S. Romanovskii V.A. Roman'kov and V.A. Churkin, Algorithmic problems for $\mathcal{O}$ power groups, Algebra i logika 8, No. 6 (1969) 643–659 (Russian).

[5] M.I. Kargapolov and E.I. Timoshenko, On the problem of finite approximatability with respect to conjugacy of metabelian groups, 4 Vsesoyuznij simpozium po teorü grupp (Tezisy dokladov, Novosibirsk 1973) (Russian).

[6] A.S. Kirkinskii and V.N. Remeslennikov, The isomorphism problem for solvable groups, Matematiceskie zametki 18, 3 (1975) 437–443 (Russian).

[7] A.F. Krasnikov, On the bases of free solvable groups, to appear (Russian).

[8] A.I. Mal'cev, Two remarks on nilpotent groups, Matematiceskij sbornik 37 (1955) 567–572 (Russian).

[9] A.I. Mal'cev, On homomorphisms to finite groups, Ucenye zapiski Iranovskogo ped. instituta 18 (1958) 49–60 (Russian).

[10] P.S. Novikov, On the algorithmic unsolvability of the word problem in the theory of groups, Trudy matematiceskogo instituta AN SSSR 44 (1955) 1–144 (Russian).

[11] V.N. Remeslennikov, Conjugacy of subgroups in nilpotent groups, Algebra i logika 6, No. 2 (1967) 61–76 (Russian).

[12] V.N. Remeslennikov, Conjugacy in polycyclic groups, Algebra i logika 8, No. 6 (1969) 712–725 (Russian).

[13] V.N. Remeslennikov, On finitely presented groups, 4 Usesoyuznyj simpozium po teorü grupp, Novosibirsk 1973, pp. 164–169 (Russian).

[14] V.N. Remeslennikov, An example of a group, finitely presented in the variety $\mathfrak{A}^5$, with the unsolvable word problem, Algebra i logika 12, No. 5 (1973) 577–602 (Russian).

[15] V.N. Remeslennikov, Investigations of infinite solvable and finitely-approximated groups, Doctoral dissertation, Novosibirsk, 1974 (Russian).

[16] V.N. Remeslennikov and V.G. Sokolov, Some properties of Magnus' imbedding, Algebra i logika 9, No. 5 (1970) 566–578 (Russian).

[17] N.S. Romanovskii, The freedom theorem for groups with one defining relation in

the varieties of solvable and nilpotent groups of given steps, Matematiceskij sbornik 89, No. 1 (1972) 93–99 (Russian).
[18] N.S. Romanovskii, On some algorithmic problems for solvable groups, Algebra i logika 13, No. 1 (1974) 26–34 (Russian).
[19] R.A. Sarkisjan, Conjugacy in free polynilpotent groups, Algebra i logika 11, No. 6 (1972) 694–710 (Russian).
[20] N.F. Sesekin, On the classification of metabelian (two-step nilpotent) torsion free groups, Ucenye zapiski Ural'skogo universiteta 19 (1965) 27–41 (Russian).
[21] V.G. Sokolov, An algorithm for the word problem for a class of solvable groups, Sibirskij matematiceskij žurnal 12, No. 6 (1971) 1405–1410 (Russian).
[22] E.I. Timoshenko, Some algorithmic problems for metabelian groups, Algebra i logika 12, No. 2 (1973) 232–240 (Russian).
[23] A.L. Shmel'kin, Wreath products and varieties of groups, Izv. AN SSSR, ser. mat. 29 (1965) 149–170 (Russian).
[24] G. Baumslag, Wreath products and finitely presented groups, Math. Z. 75 (1961) 22–28.
[25] G. Baumslag, Subgroups of finitely presented metabelian groups, J. Austral. Math. Soc. 16 (1973) 98–110.
[26] N. Blackburn, Conjugacy in nilpotent groups, Proc. Amer. Math. Soc. 16 (1965) 143–148.
[27] W. Boone, The word problem, Ann. Math. 70, No. 2 (1959) 207–265.
[28] E. Formanek, Conjugate separability in polycyclic groups, J. Algebra 42, No. 1 (1976) 1–10.
[29] P. Hall, On the finiteness of certain solvable groups, Proc. London Math. Soc. 9 (1959) 595–622.
[30] G. Higman, Subgroups on finitely presented groups, Proc. Roy. Soc. London A262 (1961) 455–475.
[31] K.A. Hirsch, On infinite solvable groups, IV, J. London Math. Soc. 27 (1952) 81–85.
[32] W. Magnus, Das Identitäts problem für Gruppen mit einer definierenden Relation, Math. Ann. 106 (1932) 295–307.
[33] J. Matteus, The conjugacy problem in wreath products and free metabelian groups, Trans. Amer. Soc. 121 (1966) 329–339.
[34] P.F. Pickel, Finitely generated nilpotent groups with isomorphic finite quotients, Trans. Amer. Math. Soc. 160 (1971) 327–341.
[35] Wehrfritz, Two examples of solvable groups that are not conjugacy separable, J. London Math. Soc. (2), 7 (1973) 312–316.

S.I. Adian, W.W. Boone, G. Higman, eds., Word Problems II

QUADRATIC EQUATIONS IN GROUPS, CANCELLATION DIAGRAMS ON COMPACT SURFACES, AND AUTOMORPHISMS OF SURFACE GROUPS

Paul E. SCHUPP*

The University of Illinois at Urbana-Champaign

§1. Introduction

In recent years cancellation diagrams have become a fundamental tool of combinatorial group theory, and we assume familiarity with the basic facts about such diagrams. (See, for example, [9], [10], or [15].) The basic inspiration for this paper is a remark of Roger Lyndon who once stated that "There is an obvious intuitive connection between the question of commuting elements and cancellation diagrams on the torus, which has yet to be made precise." It turns out that the connection can indeed be made precise, not only for the basic commutator, but for any quadratic word. In terms to be defined precisely below, we show that a "non-trivial" solution of a "quadratic equation" $W = 1$ in a group $G = \langle X; R \rangle$ induces a "non-trivial" cancellation diagram on a compact surface S defined by an endomorphic image of W. If we assume that R satisfies a suitable small cancellation hypothesis, such a diagram cannot exist, and we can thus conclude that all solutions of $W = 1$ in G are "trivial". Consequences of this result are discussed below. It turns out that the present methods also yield a very simple proof of the important theorem of Nielsen [14] that if G is the fundamental group of a compact surface then all the automorphisms of G are induced by automorphisms of the corresponding free group. It is a pleasure to acknowledge many helpful conversations with C.C. Edmunds during the research leading to this paper.

We now turn to definitions and precise statements of results. Let $\Phi = \langle \alpha_1, \alpha_2, \dots \rangle$ be a free group of countably infinite rank. We shall use the letters α, β, γ, etc. to denote generators or inverses of generators of Φ. A word $W \in \Phi$ is *quadratic* if every generator of Φ

* This research was supported by the U.S. National Science Foundation and the National Research Council of Canada.

which occurs in W occurs exactly twice. Each quadratic word W defines a closed compact surface as the quotient space of a polygon whose sides are labelled, in counterclockwise order, by W. (We assume that the reader is familiar with the proof of the classification theorem for compact 2-manifolds; see, for example, Massey [12].) It is well-known that if W is a quadratic word, then there is an automorphism of Φ sending W to one of the *canonical forms* $[\alpha_1, \beta_1]\cdots[\alpha_g, \beta_g]$ or $\alpha_1^2\cdots\alpha_g^2$. (The proof of the classification theorem tells one how to construct the automorphism.)

We say that W is *orientable* (*non-orientable*) if the surface defined by W is orientable (non-orientable). It is well-known that W is orientable if and only if for every generator α_i which occurs in W, the two occurrences of α_i have opposite signs. We define the *Euler characteristic of* W, written $\chi(W)$, to be the Euler characteristic of the surface defined by W. To calculate the Euler characteristic of W, we write W counterclockwise around the boundary of a polygon in the plane, and then count the numbers V, E, and F of vertices, edges, and faces *after* identifying each pair of edges labelled by the same generator, and set $\chi(W) = V - E + F$. If W contains n generators, then there are n edges after identification. If W is a canonical form it is easy to verify that there is only one vertex. Since there is exactly one face, we have $\chi(W) = 2 - n$ for W a canonical form containing n generators. We shall often use this observation.

Let $F = \langle X \rangle$ be a free group, and let $G = \langle X; R \rangle$ be a quotient of F. We shall always assume that the set R of defining relators for G is *symmetrized*, that is, all elements of R are cyclically reduced and R is closed under taking cyclic permutations and inverses. Let N be the normal closure of R in F, so that $G = F/N$, and let $\pi : F \to G$ be the natural map. We want to investigate solutions of quadratic equations in G. Within the set of all solutions we distinguish those solutions which arise in an obvious manner from solutions in the free group F.

Definition. Let $W(\alpha_1, \ldots, \alpha_n) \in \Phi$. A *solution* of the equation $W = 1$ in G is an n-tuple of words $(a_1, \ldots, a_n)$ on $X^{\pm 1}$ such that $W(a_1, \ldots, a_n) = 1$ in G. We say that the equation is *quadratic* if W is quadratic. We say that the solution $(a_1, \ldots, a_n)$ is *free* if there exist words $b_1, \ldots, b_n$ in F such that $\pi(b_i) = a_i$ for $i = 1, \ldots, n$, and $W(b_1, \ldots, b_n) = 1$ in the free group F. (Note in which groups the equations hold.)

For example, since two elements of a free group commute if and only if they are powers of a common element, a non-free solution of $\alpha_1\alpha_2\alpha_1^{-1}\alpha_2^{-1} = 1$ in G is a pair (a_1, a_2) representing elements of G which commute but which are not powers of a common element.

For complicated quadratic equations, exact descriptions of all possible solutions are not known even in the free group F. There is, however, one general result which we shall find very useful. This is the "rank formula" of Lyndon [10] which states that if $W(\alpha_1, \ldots, \alpha_n)$ is a canonical form involving n generators and $(a_1, \ldots, a_n)$ is a solution of $W = 1$ in F, then the rank of the subgroup $H = \mathrm{Gp}\{a_1, \ldots, a_n\}$ generated by the entries in the solution must satisfy the bound $\mathrm{rank}(H) \leq [n/2]$ (where, as usual, $[m]$ denotes the greatest integer not exceeding m). We shall give a simple proof of the rank formula in the next section.

In studying solutions of a particular equation $W = 1$ it turns out that we must consider a larger class of equations. We shall denote by $\mathscr{E}(W)$ the set of all quadratic words of Φ which are endomorphic images of W. (If W is orientable then $\mathscr{E}(W)$ consists of all orientable quadratic words which have Euler characteristic greater than or equal to $\chi(W)$. If W is non-orientable, $\mathscr{E}(W)$ consists of all non-orientable quadratic words of characteristic greater than or equal to $\chi(W)$, and all orientable quadratic words with Euler characteristic strictly greater than $\chi(W)$.)

We now turn to the definition of a cancellation diagram M on a compact surface S. First of all, M is a tessellation of S and there is a function ϕ assigning to each oriented edge e of M a *label* $\phi(e)$ in the free group F such that $\phi(e) \neq 1$ and $\phi(e^{-1}) = \phi(e)^{-1}$.

Let e be an unoriented or "geometric" edge of M. If e is on the boundary of two distinct regions D_1 and D_2, we say that e occurs with *multiplicity one* on the boundaries of D_1 and D_2. If e occurs only on the boundary of a single region D, we say that e occurs with *multiplicity two* in the boundary of D. If D is any region of M, the *degree of D*, written $d(D)$, is the number of unoriented edges, counted with multiplicity, in the boundary of D.

Let R be a symmetrized subset of F. We say that M is an *R-diagram* if for every region D of M there is a closed path δ with the following properties. All the edges in δ lie in ∂D, and for each pair $\{e, e^{-1}\}$ of oriented edges lying in the boundary of D, the total number of occurrences of either e or e^{-1} in δ is equal to the multiplicity with which the geometric edge e occurs in ∂D. Further, if $\delta = e_1 \cdots e_n$ say, and $\phi(e_i) = c_i \in F$, then the product $r = c_1 \cdots c_n$ is cyclically reduced without cancellation and is an element of R. If we are given one such δ then, since R is symmetrized, any path which is a cyclic permutation of δ or δ^{-1} also has the same properties. We shall assume then that, when we have an R-diagram M, there is specified for each region D of M a class of paths, called *distinguished boundary cycles of D*, such that each path has the properties of δ above and the class is closed under cyclic permutations and inverses.

We now recall the basic "non-triviality" condition on R-diagrams. If there are elements $r_1 \equiv cb_1$ and $r_2 \equiv cb_2$ of R with $r_2 \neq r_1$ then c is called a *piece*. In the plane, we say that an R-diagram is *reduced* if the label on every interior edge is a piece. If M is an R-diagram which tessellates a compact surface S, we say that M is reduced if the label on every edge is a piece. Geometrically, this means that if e is an edge on the boundaries of regions D_1 and D_2 (not necessarily distinct) and if δ_i is the boundary cycle of D_i beginning with e, then $\phi(\delta_1) \neq \phi(\delta_2)$. (In the case that $D_2 = D_1$, δ_1 and δ_2 are boundary cycles of D_1 beginning with distinct occurrences of e.)

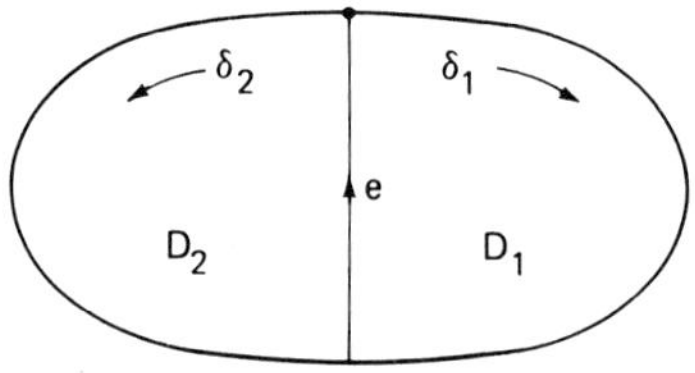

Figure 1.

The basic connection between non-free solutions of quadratic equations and reduced diagrams is given by the following.

Theorem 1. *Let $W \in \Phi$ be quadratic, and let $G = \langle X; R\rangle$. If W is non-orientable, assume that R contains no proper powers. If G admits a non-free solution of the equation $W = 1$, then there is a reduced R-diagram on a surface S defined by some $U \in \mathscr{E}(W)$.*

The above theorem requires no hypothesis on R except the exclusion of proper powers in the case where W is non-orientable. In this generality, we cannot hope to say much about whether or not all solutions of specific equations are free. In recent years, small cancellation theory has become an important part of combinatorial group theory, and it turns out to be precisely the tool needed here in order to obtain sharp results. We now assume that the reader is familiar with the basic notation and hypotheses of small cancellation theory. (See, for example, [9], [10], or [16].) We need here mainly an understanding of the hypotheses, for we shall actually use very few results.

Theorem 2. *Let $W \in \Phi$ be a quadratic word with $\chi = \chi(W) \leq 0$. Let $G = \langle X; R \rangle$, and assume that if W is non-orientable then R contains no proper powers. Suppose that R satisfies any one of the small cancellation hypotheses* $C(7-6\chi)$, *or* $C(5-4\chi)$ *and* $T(4)$, *or* $C(4-3\chi)$ *and* $T(6)$. *Then all solutions of $W = 1$ in G are free.*

We turn to a consideration of some of the consequences of the theorem. Solutions of quadratic equations $W = 1$ where the Euler characteristic of W is non-negative have previously been investigated by a variety of ad hoc methods.

Remark 1. Let W be α^2, which defines the projective plane. Since, of course, $\chi(W) = 1$, the statement of the theorem does not apply. We shall see from the proof however, that if we assume that R contains no proper powers and satisfies C(6), or C(4) and T(4), we can conclude that G has no elements of even order. It is fairly well known that if R contains no proper powers and satisfies one of the stronger metric hypotheses, either $C'(\frac{1}{6})$ or $C'(\frac{1}{4})$ and T(4), then G is, in fact, torsion-free. These results were established by Greendlinger [5] and Soldatova [18]. It has been strongly conjectured that the torsion result is still true assuming only C(6), or C(4) and T(4), but the methods here get only "half way" towards this goal. Seymour [17] has shown that if R is finite, contains no proper powers, satisfies C(4) and T(4), and no piece has length greater than one, then G is torsion-free. Chris Chalk [1] has recently proven that if R contains no proper powers and satisfies C(7), or C(5) and T(4), then G is torsion-free.

Remark 2. Let W be $\alpha\beta\alpha^{-1}\beta^{-1}$, which defines the torus. If we assume that R satisfies C(7), or C(5) and T(4), we conclude that two elements of G commute only if they are powers of a common element. This result was established by Greendlinger for R satisfying $C'(\frac{1}{8})$ [6], and subsequently [7] strengthened to $C'(\frac{1}{6})$. Comerford has extended these results to small cancellation quotients of free products.

Remark 3. Let W be either $\alpha\beta\alpha\beta^{-1}$ or $\alpha^2\beta^2$, which define the Klein bottle. We call an element of G *real* if it is conjugate to its own inverse. Since the only real element in a free group is the identity, if we assume that R contains no proper powers and satisfies C(7), or C(5) and T(4), then we conclude that G has no real elements except the identity. Equivalently, we conclude that whenever square roots exist in G, they are unique. Comerford [2] established that if R contains no even powers and satisfies $C'(\frac{1}{6})$, or $C'(\frac{1}{4})$ and T(4), then G

has no non-trivial real elements. Earlier, Gowdy [4] had proved that if R contains no proper powers and satisfies $C'(\frac{1}{8})$, then G has no real elements.

Remark 4. Let W be $\alpha^2\beta^2\gamma^2$, which defines the non-orientable surface with Euler characteristic -1. It is a well-known result of Lyndon [8] (and an immediate consequence of his rank formula), that if $a^2b^2c^2 = 1$ in the free group F then a, b, and c are all powers of a common element. Thus if we assume that R contains no proper powers and satisfies either C(13), or C(9) and T(4), the same result holds for $G = \langle X; R\rangle$.

For more complicated quadratic equations $W = 1$ we lack explicit descriptions of the solutions even in the free group F. We do, however, transfer the rank formula to all those groups $G = \langle X; R\rangle$ for which we can prove that all solutions of $W = 1$ are free.

Remark 5. Another interesting consequence of the theory is the following result. Let $W(\alpha_1, \ldots, \alpha_n)$ be a canonical form involving n generators, and let S be the surface defined by W. The standard presentation of the fundamental group G of S is $G = \langle x_1, \ldots, x_n; W(x_1, \ldots, x_n)\rangle$. Let V be any quadratic word involving k generators where $k < n$. Then all solutions of $V = 1$ in G are free.

It is tempting, in view of the known results on torsion elements and real elements, to attempt to weaken the hypothesis that R contains no proper powers to assuming only that R contains no even powers. The following example, due to Comerford, shows that this cannot be done in general, regardless of how good a small cancellation condition is assumed. Let

$$G = \langle x_1, \ldots, x_{g-1}; (x_1^2 \cdots x_{g-1}^2)^{2k+1}\rangle$$

where $g > 2$. Let W be $\alpha_1^2 \cdots \alpha_g^2$. Then $(x_1, \ldots, x_{g-1}, (x_1^2 \cdots x_{g-1}^2)^k)$ is a solution of $W = 1$ in G. The subgroup generated by the entries in the solution is all of G, and has rank $g - 1$. Thus the solution is non-free by the rank formula. The above presentation satisfies an arbitrarily prescribed cancellation condition $C(m)$ if k is chosen large enough.

It is an important theorem of Nielsen [14] that if G is the fundamental group of a compact surface S, say $G = \langle X; r\rangle$ where r is one the canonical relators, then every automorphism of G is induced by an automorphism of the free group $F = \langle X\rangle$. (See also Zieschang, Coldewey, and Vogt [19].) Let $r = W(x_1, \ldots, x_n)$. If $\theta : G \to G$ is any endomorphism of G, then, of course, the n-tuple $(\theta(x_1), \ldots, \theta(x_n))$ is a solution of $W(\alpha_1, \ldots, \alpha_n) = 1$ in G. Assuming that θ is one-to-one, the rank of the subgroup generated by $(\theta(x_1), \ldots, \theta(x_n))$ is n, the rank of G, and we thus have a non-free solution. Let R be the symmetrized subset of F generated by r. It turns out that if $\chi(S) < 0$, then the possible tessellations of S by reduced R-diagrams are severely limited; indeed, such a tessellation must have only one region. We shall use this fact to deduce that the n-tuple $(\theta(x_1), \ldots, \theta(x_n))$ is obtained from $(x_1, \ldots, x_n)$ by Nielsen transformations, and thus θ is induced by an automorphism of F.

§2. Quadratic words and equations

In this section we collect the results which we need about quadratic words and equations in free groups. We assume that the reader is familiar with Nielsen transformations and the fact that they generate the automorphism group of a free group of finite rank. (See [10] or [11].) Let $\Phi = \langle \alpha_1, \alpha_2, \ldots \rangle$, and let $W(\alpha_1, \ldots, \alpha_n) \in \Phi$ be quadratic. Let $F = \langle X \rangle$ be a free group, and let $\sigma = (a_1, \ldots, a_n)$ be an n-tuple of elements of F. If we substitute a_i for α_i in W, we obtain the element $W(a_1, \ldots, a_n) = w \in F$. Thus $(a_1, \ldots, a_n)$ is a solution of the equation $W(\alpha_1, \ldots, \alpha_n) = w$ in F. We need to consider the process of performing certain *attached transformations*, which will be defined by the list below, to the triple W, w, and σ. The transformations will, in each case, consist of applying an endomorphism of Φ to W to obtain a quadratic word $U(\beta_1, \ldots, \beta_k)$, applying an inner automorphism of F to w to obtain u, and replacing the n-tuple $\sigma = (a_1, \ldots, a_n)$ by a k-tuple $\tau = (b_1, \ldots, b_k)$ such that $U(b_1, \ldots, b_k) = u$.

For ease of notation we adopt the following convention. We use $\alpha, \beta, \gamma, \ldots$ to denote a *letter* of Φ, that is, a generator of Φ or its inverse. If we are considering a particular transformation, we shall write $W(\ldots, \alpha, \ldots, \beta, \ldots)$ displaying only the generators which are involved in the transformation. In defining an endormorphism of Φ, the endomorphism is understood to fix all generators not explicitly mentioned in the definition. Given a tuple $(\ldots, a, \ldots, b, \ldots)$ it is understood that the element of F denoted by a Roman letter is substituted for the corresponding Greek letter. If we replace the tuple $(\ldots, a, \ldots, b, \ldots)$ by a new tuple $(z, \ldots, a, \ldots, b, \ldots)$ it is understood that all entries not explicitly mentioned are the same in the new tuple as in the old, and that new letters denote new entries in the tuple. We write $a \equiv bc$ to mean that a is freely reduced as written, that is, there is no cancellation between b and c.

Given a quadratic $W(\alpha_1, \ldots, \alpha_n)$ and a tuple $\sigma = (a_1, \ldots, a_n)$ with $W(a_1, \ldots, a_n) = w$, a transformation of any of the following types is said to be *attached* to the triple (W, w, σ).

(1) Suppose that $\alpha\beta$ occurs in $W(\ldots, \alpha, \ldots, \beta, \ldots)$ and that $a \equiv a_1 z$, $b \equiv z^{-1} b_1$ where $z \neq 1$. Obtain $U(\zeta, \ldots, \alpha, \ldots, \beta, \ldots)$ from W by applying the automorphism of Φ defined by $\alpha \to \alpha\rho$, $\beta \to \rho^{-1}\beta$ where ζ does not occur in W. Replace the n-tuple $(\ldots, a, \ldots, b, \ldots)$ by the $(n+1)$-tuple $(z, \ldots, a_1, \ldots, b_1, \ldots)$. It is clear that U is quadratic and that $U(z, \ldots, a_1, \ldots, b_1, \ldots) = w$. Leave w unchanged.

(2) Suppose that $\alpha\beta$ or $\beta^{-1}\alpha^{-1}$ occurs in W. Obtain $U(\ldots, \alpha, \ldots, \beta, \ldots)$ from W by applying the automorphism of Φ defined by $\alpha \to \alpha\beta^{-1}$, and replace the tuple $(\ldots, a, \ldots, b, \ldots)$ by the tuple $(\ldots, a_1, \ldots, b, \ldots)$ where $a_1 = ab$. Note that the new tuple is obtained from the old by a Nielsen transformation.

(3) Suppose that α occurs in W and that $a \equiv a_1 z$. Obtain $U(\zeta, \ldots, \alpha, \ldots)$ from W by applying the automorphism of Φ defined by $\alpha \to \alpha\zeta$ where ζ does not occur in W. Replace the n-tuple $(\ldots, a, \ldots)$ by the $(n+1)$-tuple $(z, \ldots, a_1, \ldots)$. Leave w unchanged.

(4) Suppose that W begins with α. Obtain U from W by applying the conjugation $W \to \alpha^{-1} W \alpha$, and do not change the tuple $(\ldots, a, \ldots)$. Replace w by $a^{-1} w a$.

(5) Suppose that α occurs in $W(\ldots, \alpha, \ldots, \beta, \ldots)$ and that $a = 1$. Obtain U from W by the endomorphism of Φ defined by $\alpha \to 1$. Replace the n-tuple $(\ldots, a, \ldots, b, \ldots)$ by the $(n-1)$-tuple $(\ldots, b, \ldots)$. Leave w unchanged. We call a transformation of type (5) a *singular* transformation.

Suppose that we are given a quadratic word W and a solution $\sigma = (a_1, \ldots, a_n)$ of $W(\alpha_1, \ldots, \alpha_n) = w$ in F. We say that the equation $U(\beta_1, \ldots, \beta_k) = u$ and the solution $\tau = (b_1, \ldots, b_k)$ are *derived from W, w and σ by a sequence of attached transformation* if there is a sequence

$$(W, w, \sigma) = (W_0, w_0, \sigma_0) \to \cdots \to (W_n, w_n, \sigma_n) = (U, u, \tau)$$

where each $(W_{i+1}, w_{i+1}, \sigma_{i+1})$ is obtained from (W_i, w_i, σ_i) by a transformation attached to (W_i, w_i, σ_i).

If $a \in F$, then $|a|$ will denote the length of a relative to the fixed basis X of F. We define the length of an n-tuple by adding the lengths of the entries, $|(a_1, \ldots, a_n)| = \Sigma_{i=1}^n |a_i|$. Note that if we derive the tuple $(b_1, \ldots, b_k)$ from the tuple $(a_1, \ldots, a_n)$ by an attached transformation of type (1), then $|(b_1, \ldots, b_k)| < |(a_1, \ldots, a_n)|$.

Let $W \in \Phi$, say $W \equiv \alpha_{i_1} \cdots \alpha_{i_m}$. We say that the n-tuple $(a_1, \ldots, a_n)$ (of elements of the free group F) is *cancellation-free* in W if no $a_i = 1$, and if $w = W(a_1, \ldots, a_n) \equiv a_{i_1} \cdots a_{i_n}$ is cyclically reduced as written. In other words, no cancellation occurs, even cyclically, between any of the a_i. Thus (xyx, yxy) is cancellation-free in $\alpha^2\beta^2$, while (xy^{-1}, yx) is not cancellation-free in $\alpha^2\beta^2$.

Lemma 1. *Let $W(\alpha_1, \ldots, \alpha_n) \in \Phi$, let $(a_1, \ldots, a_n)$ be an n-tuple of elements of F, and let $W(a_1, \ldots, a_n) = w$. Then there is a triple $(U(\beta_1, \ldots, \beta_k), (b_1, \ldots, b_k), u)$ derived from $(W, (a_1, \ldots, a_n), w)$ by a sequence of attached transformations such that u is a cyclically reduced conjugate of w and $(b_1, \ldots, b_k)$ is cancellation-free in U.*

Proof. Suppose that $\alpha_i\alpha_j$ occurs in W while $a_i \equiv a'_i z$ and $a_j \equiv z^{-1}a'_j$ with $z \neq 1$. Then apply the transformation of type (1) where U is obtained by applying the automorphism $\alpha_i \to \alpha_i\zeta$ and $\alpha_j \to \zeta^{-1}\alpha_j$ and the tuple $(\ldots, a_i, \ldots, a_j, \ldots)$ is replaced by the tuple $(z, \ldots, a'_i, \ldots, a'_j, \ldots)$. In this case the length of the new tuple is less than the length of the old tuple. If any of the entries $a_k = 1$, apply the appropriate singular transformation sending $\alpha_k \to 1$. If $W(a_1, \ldots, a_n)$ is not cyclically reduced, a conjugation of type (4) brings us to the case considered above. Since each transformation of type (1) produces a tuple of shorter length, a finite number of transformations must lead to a U and $(b_1, \ldots, b_k)$ which is cancellation-free in U. □

Lemma 2. *Let W be a quadratic word of Φ, and let $V \in \Phi$ be any quadratic word which is an endomorphic image of W. Then a cyclically reduced conjugate of V is obtainable from W by a sequence of attached transformations.*

Proof. By assumption, there are words $Y_1, \ldots, Y_n$ of Φ, not necessarily quadratic, such that $V = W(Y_1, \ldots, Y_n)$. By Lemma 1, some cyclically reduced conjugate V^* of V is obtainable by a cancellation-free substitution $(Z_1, \ldots, Z_k)$ into $U(\beta_1, \ldots, \beta_k)$ where U is derived from W by a sequence of attached transformations. Since both U and V are quadratic and the substitution is cancellation-free, a generator which occurs in some Z_i can occur only in that Z_i. By transformations of type (3) we can "subdivide" each β_i into a product of $|Z_i|$ generators. If the result is $U^*(\gamma_1, \ldots, \gamma_m)$ then V^* is obtainable from U^* by a letter for letter substitution and thus differs from U^* only by a permutation of the generators and their inverses. Such a permutation is obtainable by a sequence of attached transformations. □

The following lemma is well-known.

Lemma 3. *Let $W \in \Phi$ be a quadratic word. If U is obtained from W by an attached transformation which is an automorphism of Φ, then $\chi(U) = \chi(W)$. If U is obtained from W by applying one singular transformation then $\chi(W) \leqslant \chi(U) \leqslant \chi(W) + 2$.*

In view of Lemmas 1 through 3 we have the

Corollary. *If W is quadratic and U is a quadratic endomorphic image of W, then $\chi(U) \geqslant \chi(W)$.*

Let F be a free group. Recall that a sequence $y_1, \ldots, y_m$ of elements of F is said to be *Nielsen-reduced* if the following three conditions hold.

(N1) Each $y_i \neq 1$.

(N2) More than half of y_i does not cancel in either of the products $y_{i-1}y_i$ or $y_i y_{i+1}$.

(N3) No y_i cancels exactly half in both products $y_{i-1}y_i$ and $y_i y_{i+1}$.

A set S of elements of F is said to be *Nielsen-reduced* if every sequence $y_1, \ldots, y_m$ of elements $y_i \in S^{\pm 1}$ such that no $y_{i+1} = y_i^{-1}$ is Nielsen reduced. If T is a finite subset of F, then a finite number of Nielsen transformations lead from T to a set S which is Nielsen reduced. (For a fuller discussion see [10].)

We shall need the following relativization of the concept of being Nielsen reduced. Let $W(\alpha_1, \ldots, \alpha_n) \in \Phi$, say $W \equiv \alpha_{i_1}^{\varepsilon_1} \cdots \alpha_{i_m}^{\varepsilon_n}$ where each $\varepsilon_i = \pm 1$. Let $(a_1, \ldots, a_n)$ be an n-tuple of elements of F. We say that $(a_1, \ldots, a_n)$ is *Nielsen-reduced relative to W* if the particular sequence $a_{i_1}^{\varepsilon_1}, \ldots, a_{i_m}^{\varepsilon_m}$ satisfies conditions (N1) through (N3). In short, we consider only the products which result from substituting the a_i into W.

Transformations of types (2) and (5) effect Nielsen transformations on the tuples involved. It is easy to see that given any $W(\alpha_1, \alpha_n) \in \Phi$ and any n-tuple $(a_1, \ldots, a_n)$ we can, by a sequence of attached transformations, of types (2) and (5), obtain $U(\beta_1, \ldots, \beta_k)$ and tuple $(b_1, \ldots, b_k)$ which is Nielsen-reduced relative to U.

Lemma 4 (Lyndon's Rank Formula). *Let $W \in \Phi$ be a quadratic word which involves n generators and which is of minimal length among its images under automorphisms of Φ. Let F be a free group, and let $(a_1, \ldots, a_n)$ be any n-tuple of elements of F such that $W(a_1, \ldots, a_n) = 1$. Then the rank of the subgroup H generated by $\{a_1, \ldots, a_n\}$ is less than or equal to $[n/2]$.*

Proof. It is well-known that any canonical form has minimal length among its automorphic images. Let W^* be the canonical form which is an image of W under an automorphism of Φ. Since W is of minimal length under automorphism, $|W^*| = |W|$, and thus W^* involves n generators. Hence, $\chi(W) = \chi(W^*) = 2 - n$.

There is a sequence of attached transformations of types (2) and (5) leading from W and $(a_1, \ldots, a_n)$ to $U(\beta_1, \ldots, \beta_k)$ and a tuple $(b_1, \ldots, b_k)$ which is Nielsen reduced relative to U and with $U(b_1, \ldots, b_k) = 1$. Now the product of elements in a Nielsen reduced sequence $y_1, \ldots, y_m$ with $m \geqslant 1$ cannot be equal to the identity. We conclude that $U \equiv 1$. Let d be the number of singular transformations applied in obtaining U from W. Since a singular transformation is applied only when an entry in the tuple is the identity, it is clear that $\operatorname{rank}(H) \leqslant (n - d)$. Since $\chi(W) = 2 - n$, and $\chi(1) = +2$, in going from W to U the Euler characteristic is raised by n. According to Lemma 3, each automorphism preserves the Euler characteristic, while one singular transformation can increase the Euler characteristic by at most two. Thus the number d of singular transformations must be at least $n/2$ if n is even, and at least $(n+1)/2$ if n is odd. Hence, $\operatorname{rank}(H) \leqslant (n - d) \leqslant [n/2]$. □

As usual, let $F = \langle X \rangle$ be a free group, and let $G = \langle X; R \rangle$ be a quotient group of F. Let $W(\alpha_1, \ldots, \alpha_n) \in \Phi$, and let $(a_1, \ldots, a_n)$ be a non-free solution of $W = 1$ in G. In the next section we shall transform given equations and solutions, and we shall need to know that we preserve the non-freeness of the solutions. All the situations which will be encountered are covered by the following lemma.

Lemma 5. *Suppose that $(a_1, \ldots, a_n)$ is a non-free solution of $W(\alpha_1, \ldots, \alpha_n) = 1$ in G. Suppose that there are words $Z_i(\beta_1, \ldots, \beta_k)$ of Φ, and a k-tuple of $(b_1, \ldots, b_k)$ of words of F such that $a_i = Z_i(b_1, \ldots, b_k)$ in G for $i = 1, \ldots, n$, and $U(\beta_1, \ldots, \beta_k) = W(Z_1, \ldots, Z_n)$ in Φ. Then $(b_1, \ldots, b_k)$ is a non-free solution of $U = 1$ in G.*

Proof. If the solution $(b_1, \ldots, b_k)$ of $U = 1$ in G were free, there would be words $b_1^*, \ldots, b_k^*$ such that each $b_j^* = b_j$ in G and $U(b_1^*, \ldots, b_k^*) = 1$ in F. But $Z_i(b_1^*, \ldots, b_k^*) = a_i$ in G and

$$W(Z_1(b_1^*, \ldots, b_k^*), \ldots, Z_n(b_1^*, \ldots, b_k^*)) = U(b_1^*, \ldots, b_k^*) = 1$$

in F. This contradicts $(a_1, \ldots, a_n)$ being a non-free solution of $W = 1$. □

§3. Cancellation diagrams on compact surfaces

We now assume that the reader is familiar with the basic facts about cancellation diagrams in the plane. (See Chapter V of [10].) Let $F = \langle X \rangle$ be a free group, let R be a symmetrized subset of F, and let $G = \langle X; R \rangle$. Let N be the normal closure of R in F, so that $G = F/N$, and let $\pi : F \to G$ be the natural map. Let $W(\alpha_1, \ldots, \alpha_n) \in \Phi$ be a quadratic word, and suppose that there is a non-free solution $(a_1, \ldots, a_n)$ of $W = 1$ in G. Note that $W(a_1, \ldots, a_n)$ is a non-trivial element of N. We consider the following

Choice. Among all $U \in \mathscr{E}(W)$ and all tuples of words $(b_1, \ldots, b_k)$ which are non-free solutions of $U = 1$ in G, pick a pair U and $(b_1, \ldots, b_k)$ such that

(1) The number, m, of regions in the minimal connected simply connected R-diagram M in the plane with boundary label $U(b_1, \ldots, b_k)$ is as small as possible.

(2) Subject to (1), the length of the free group element $U(b_1, \ldots, b_k)$ is as small as possible.

(3) Subject to (1) and (2), the length $|(b_1, \ldots, b_k)|$ of the solution tuple is as small as possible.

In the next sequence of lemmas, U and $(b_1, \ldots, b_k)$ refer to the pair chosen above, and M is a minimal connected simply connected R-diagram in the plane with boundary label $U(b_1, \ldots, b_k)$.

Lemma 6. *The tuple $(b_1, \ldots, b_k)$ is cancellation-free in U.*

Proof. If cancellation occurs we can, by an attached transformation as in Lemma 1, obtain $V(\gamma_1, \ldots, \gamma_m)$ and a shorter tuple $(c_1, \ldots, c_n)$. Since the free group element $v = V(c_1, \ldots, c_m)$ is a conjugate of $u = U(b_1, \ldots, b_k)$, the minimal R-diagram with boundary label v still has only m regions. This contradicts our minimal choice. □

By using transformations of type (3) we can "subdivide" the variables so $U(\beta_1, \ldots, \beta_k)$ is such that each entry b_i in $(b_1, \ldots, b_k)$ is a generator or the inverse of a generator of F. We now assume that this has been done.

Lemma 7. *The boundary cycle of M is a simple closed path.*

Proof. Suppose that M is not bounded by a simple closed path and let K be an extremal disk of M. (See [10] or [13].) Both K and $M \setminus K$

contain regions. Since each letter of U is replaced by a letter from $X^{\pm 1}$, the label on the boundary of K is a substitution instance of $V(\beta_{i_1}, \ldots, \beta_{i_l})$ where some cyclic permutation of U has the form VZ.

First suppose that V is quadratic, so that for each β_i which occurs in V, both of the occurrences of β_i are in V. Then both V and Z are quadratic. Substituting the appropriate b_i into V and Z yields solutions of the quadratic equations $V = 1$ and $Z = 1$ in G. If both of these solutions were free, then $(b_1, \ldots, b_k)$ would be a free solution of $U = 1$ in G, which is not the case. On the other hand, if at least one solution is non-free, say that of $V = 1$, then there is an R-diagram, namely K, with fewer than m regions verifying that $V(b_{i_1}, \ldots, b_{i_n}) = 1$ in G. This contradicts the minimality of our choice.

We are left with the possibility that some generator β occurs exactly once in V. Write $V = V_1 \beta V_2$. Since $V(b_{i_1}, \ldots, b_{i_l})$ is the boundary label of an R-diagram, it follows that $V(b_{i_1}, \ldots, b_{i_l}) = 1$ in G. Let $v_1 = V_2(b_{i_1}, \ldots, b_{i_l})$, and $v_2 = V_2(b_{i_1}, \ldots, b_{i_l})$. Solving for b we have $b = v_1^{-1} v_2^{-1}$ in G. Obtain U^* from U by replacing β by $V_1^{-1} V_2^{-1}$ and replace $(\ldots, b, \ldots)$ by $(\ldots, v_1^{-1} v_2^{-1}, \ldots)$. Obtain the R-diagram M_1 from M by removing the extremal disk K and reattaching K by sewing, in the appropriate orientation, the edge labelled by β in K to the edge labelled by β in $M \backslash K$.

Now M_2 has the same number of regions as M_1, and a boundary label of M_1 is $u^* = U^*(\ldots, v_1^{-1} v_2^{-1}, \ldots)$. But u^* is shorter than u. This contradicts the minimality of our choice, so we must conclude that M is bounded by a simple closed path. □

Since the label on the boundary of M is a cancellation-free substitution instance of U, we can regard ∂M as a polygon whose boundary "has the form U". We can then identify the edges in ∂M to

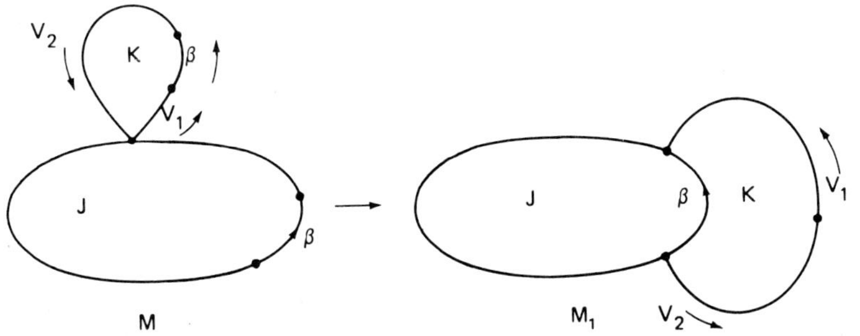

Figure 2.

obtain an R-diagram, which we also call M, on the surface S defined by U. Let D be a region of the diagram M in the plane, and let $\delta = e_1 \cdots e_k$ be a boundary cycle of D. Considering D as a region of the diagram M on the surface S, a distinguished boundary cycle of D will be the sequence $e_1 \cdots e_k$ after identification.

Lemma 8. *The diagram M is still reduced on the surface S provided that, if W is non-orientable, we make the additional assumption that R contains no proper powers.*

Proof. Recall that M is reduced if, for any edge e on the common boundary of regions D_1 and D_2 (which may coincide), the labels $\phi(\delta_1)$ and $\phi(\delta_2)$ are not the same, where δ_i is the boundary cycle of D_i which begins with e.

Since the diagram M was reduced in the plane, we need only consider the edges identified according to U. Suppose that the identification of two edges e_1 and e_2 on the boundaries of two distinct regions makes the diagram not reduced. (See Figure 3 which pictures the orientable case.)

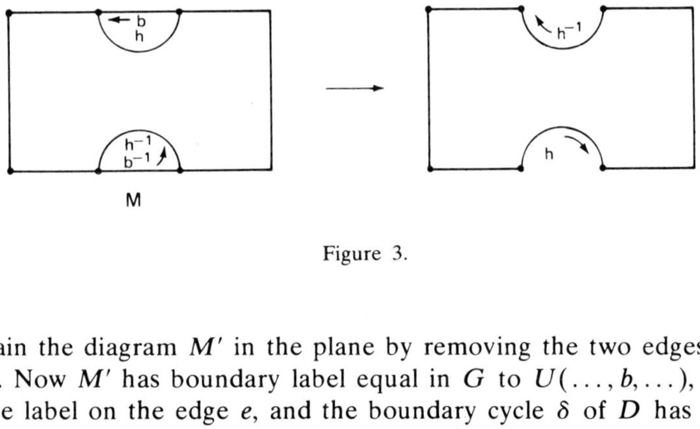

Figure 3.

Obtain the diagram M' in the plane by removing the two edges e_1 and e_2. Now M' has boundary label equal in G to $U(\ldots, b, \ldots)$, for if b is the label on the edge e, and the boundary cycle δ of D has label $\phi(\delta) = bh \in R$, then we have replaced b by h^{-1}. The diagram M' has fewer regions than M, contradicting the minimal choice.

It is conceivable that two edges of the same region D are identified in such a way that the diagram becomes not reduced on the surface S. If the identification of the two edges is an orientable identification (in the obvious sense that the edges are labelled by b and b^{-1}) then the diagram being non-reduced means that the label r on D is conjugate to r^{-1} in the free group F, which is impossible.

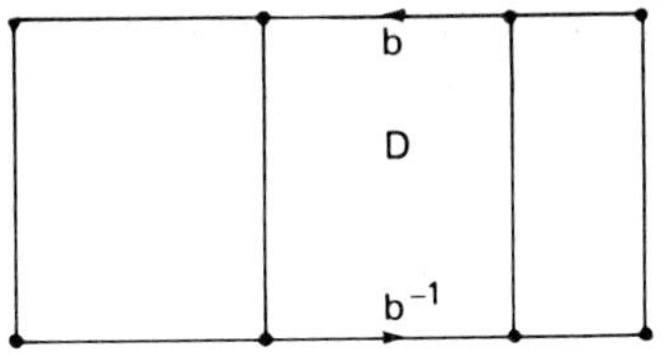

Figure 4.

There remains the possibility of a non-orientable identification making the diagram not reduced. (See Figure 5.)

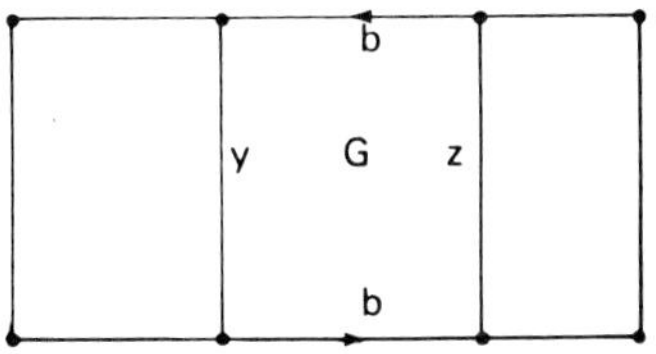

Figure 5.

Let D have boundary cycle $e_1\eta_1e_2\eta_2$ where $\phi(e_1)=b=\phi(e_2)$, $\phi(\eta_1)=y$, and $\phi(\eta_2)=z$. The diagram being non-reduced on S means that $bybz = bzby$ in the free group F. Thus $ybzy^{-1}b^{-1}z^{-1}$, which is equal to the commutator $(yb)(zb)(yb)^{-1}(zb)^{-1}$, is equal to 1 in F. Since this implies that yb and zb are powers of a common element, the label $r = bybz$ must be a proper power, but we have assumed that this is not the case. □

We have completed the proof of Theorem 1 and now consider small cancellation theory. In our constructions so far, it has been convenient to assume that edges are labelled by generators or their inverses. We now want to do the opposite, eliminating as many unnecessary vertices as possible. If v is a vertex of a diagram M, either in the plane or on a surface, we use $d(v)$ to denote the *degree* of v, that is, the number of edges incident at v, where, if both endpoints of an edge are at v, we count the edge twice.

Lemma 9. *Let M be an R-diagram on a compact surface S, where M is obtained by identifying the boundary of an R-diagram in the plane as in the proof of Theorem 1. (Thus S is not the sphere.) We can modify M so* *that M has no vertices of degree less than three unless S is the projective plane. If S is the projective plane, we may assume that M has at most one vertex of degree two.*

Proof. Consider the diagram M in the plane before identification. Since M is an R-diagram with cyclically reduced boundary label, M has no vertices of degree one. If v is an interior vertex of degree two, say v separates edges e_1 and e_2, we can simply delete v and combine e_1 and e_2 into a single edge e with label $\phi(e) = \phi(e_1)\phi(e_2)$.

Suppose that there are successive edges e_1 and e_2 in ∂M separated by a vertex v which has degree two in the plane, and where the labels on e_1 and e_2 correspond to successive occurrences of α and β in U with $\beta \neq \alpha^{\pm 1}$. Now v will have degree at lest three after identifying the boundary edges of M unless the edges e_3 and e_4 corresponding to the two other occurrences of α and β in U are situated so that the end of e_3 is the beginning of e_4. This means that in U (or a cyclic permutation of U) the occurrences of α and β are in two subwords of the form $(\alpha\beta)^{\pm 1}$. We can replace these occurrences of $(\alpha\beta)^{\pm 1}$ by $\gamma^{\pm 1}$ where γ is a new variable not occurring in U. Delete the vertex v, combining e_1 and e_2 into a single edge e with label $\phi(e) = \phi(e_1)\phi(e_2)$. Similarly, combine the two edges corresponding to the other occurrence of $(\alpha\beta)^{\pm 1}$ into a single edge. (In short, all that we have done is to eliminate an unnecessary subdivision.)

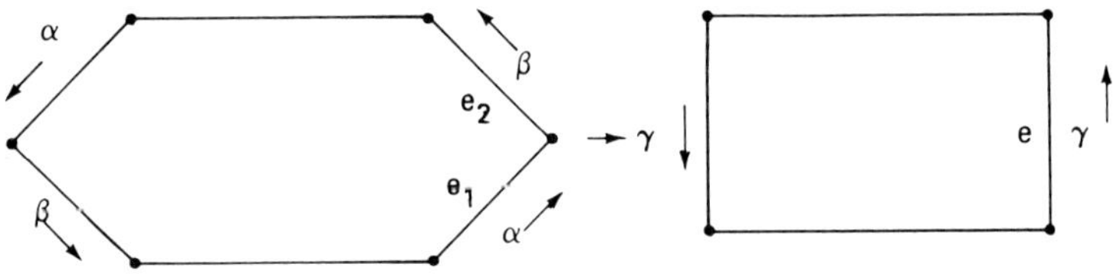

Figure 6.

Iterate the above process, eliminating as many vertices of degree two as possible. The only situation not covered is that of a vertex v separating edges e_1 and e_2 corresponding to successive occurrences of a letter α in U. Now v will certainly have degree at least three after the identification of ∂M unless e_1 and e_2 are all of ∂M. In this case, U is α^2, the surface S is the projective plane, and v is the only exceptional vertex. □

From now on, when we consider a reduced R-diagram M tessellating a compact surface S, we assume that M has no vertices of degree less than three; except for the possibility of one exceptional vertex in the case of the projective plane. Since M is reduced, the label on every edge is a piece and the small cancellation hypotheses have their usual geometric meanings. (See [9] or [10].) If R satisfies the condition C(k), then no element of R is a product of fewer than k pieces, and thus $d(D) \geqslant k$ for every region D of M. If R satisfies the condition T(j) and v is a vertex of degree at least three, then, in fact, $d(v) \geqslant j$. Thus every vertex of M has degree at least j, except possibly the one exceptional vertex in the case that S is the projective plane.

The basic tool of small cancellation theory is the summation formula given below. We use the following convention on summation signs: if M is a fixed diagram, $\Sigma_M [p - d(D)]$ denotes the sum of $[p - d(D)]$ for all regions D of M, while $\Sigma_M [q - d(v)]$ denotes $[q - d(v)]$ summed over all vertices v of M. We shall usually omit the subscript naming the diagram.

Lemma 10 (The summation formula). *Let M be a tessellation of a compact surface S. Let p and q be positive integers with* $1/p + 1/q = 1/2$. *Then*

$$p\chi(S) = \sum_M [p - d(D)] + \frac{p}{q} \sum_M [q - d(v)].$$

Proof. Let M have V vertices, E edges, and F regions. (This is our only departure from using F to denote a free group.) Euler's formula is

(1) $$\chi(S) = V - E + F.$$

Since we have counted degrees with the appropriate multiplicity,

(2) $$2E = \sum d(v) = \sum d(D).$$

Let n be a positive real number. We have

(3) $$2(n+1)\chi(S) = 2(n+1)V - 2(n+1)E + 2(n+1)F.$$

Using (2), we can eliminate E from (3),

(4) $$2(n+1)\chi(S) = 2(n+1)F - \sum d(D) + 2(n+1)V - n \sum d(D).$$

Since V is the number of vertices and F is the number of regions,

(5) $$2(n+1)\chi(S) = \sum [2(n+1) - d(D)] + n \sum \left[\frac{2(n+1)}{n} - d(v)\right].$$

Let $p = 2(n+1)$ and $q = 2(n+1)/n$. Then $n = p/q$ and $1/p + 1/q = 1/2$. Substitution in (5) yields

$$\text{(6)} \qquad p\chi(S) = \sum [p - d(D)] + \frac{p}{q}\sum [q - d(v)]$$

which is the desired formula. □

We can now prove Theorem II. Suppose that we start with a quadratic equation $W = 1$ where $\chi = \chi(W)$ is not positive; and a non-free solution of $W = 1$ in the group $G = \langle X; R\rangle$. If W is non-orientable we assume that R contains no proper powers. Then there is a reduced R-diagram M on a surface S defined by an endomorphic image U of W. Thus $\chi(S) = \chi(U) \geqslant \chi(W)$. Consider the summation formula with $(p, q) = (6, 3)$. We have

$$(*) \qquad 6\chi(W) \leqslant 6\chi(S) = \sum_M [6 - d(D)] + 2\sum_M [3 - d(v)].$$

The basic idea is simply to assume a good enough small cancellation condition to force the right-hand side to be less than p times $\chi(W)$. Supposing that S is not the projective plane, all vertices of M have degree at least three. Since M has at least one region, the equation $(*)$ is impossible if R satisfies the small cancellation condition $C(7 - 6\chi)$. If S is the projective plane, $\chi(S) = +1$, and we have

$$(**) \qquad 6 = \sum_M [6 - d(D)] + 2\sum_M [3 - d(v)].$$

Since there is at most one vertex of degree two, this equation is impossible as long as R satisfies C(6). In summary, if R satisfies $C(7 - 6\chi)$ then the required diagram M cannot exist. We conclude that there cannot be a non-free solution of $W = 1$ in G. By letting $(p, q) = (4, 4)$, we see that it is sufficient to assume that R satisfies $C(5 - 4\chi)$ and T(4). If we set $(p, q) = (3, 6)$, we see also that it suffices to assume that R satisfies $C(4 - 3\chi)$ and T(6).

§4. Automorphisms of surface groups

Let $W(\alpha_1, \ldots, \alpha_n)$ be one of the canonical forms $[\alpha_1, \alpha_2] \cdots [\alpha_{n-1}, \alpha_n]$ or $\alpha_1^2 \cdots \alpha_n^2$. Let F be the free group on $X = \{x_1, \ldots, x_n\}$, let $r = W(x_1, \ldots, x_n)$, and let R be the symmetrized closure of r in F. We say that $\langle X; R\rangle$ is the *standard presentation* of the fundamental group G of the surface S defined by W. We first observe some facts about the standard presentations.

Lemma 11. *Let $\langle X; R\rangle$ be the standard presentation of the group of the surface S defined by $W(\alpha_1, \ldots, \alpha_n)$. Then R satisfies both of the cancellation conditions* C(2n) *and* T(2n).

Proof. We prove the lemma in the case where R is the symmetrized closure of $x_1^2 \cdots x_n^2$; the orientable use is analogous. To verify C(2n) it suffices to observe that any two-letter word, of the form x_i^2 or $x_i x_{i+1}$, has at most one ocurrence in any element of R. Thus a piece consists of only one letter.

To verify T(2n) our assumption is that we have elements $r_1, \ldots, r_n$ of R with each $r_{i+1} \neq r_i^{-1}$, $r_h \neq r_1^{-1}$, and that there is cancellation in each of the products $r_1r_2, r_2r_3, \ldots, r_{h-1}r_h, r_hr_1$. Now $h > 2$ and one of r_1 or r_2 must be of the form $(x_i^2 \cdots x_n^2 x_1^2 \cdots x_{i-1}^2)^{\pm 1}$ and the other of the form $(x_j x_{j+1}^2 \cdots x_{j-1}^2 x_j)^{\mp 1}$. By symmetry, we may suppose that $r_1 = x_1^2 \cdots x_n^2$. Then we must have $r_2 = x_n^{-1} x_{n-2}^{-2} \cdots x_1^{-2} x_n^{-1}$. Consequently, $r_3 = x_n^2 x_1^2 \cdots x_{n-1}^2$. Continuing thus, we see that it takes at least $2n$ steps to obtain an r_h which can cancel against r_1. Thus $h \geq 2n$. □

Lemma 12. *Let $G = \langle X; R\rangle$ be given by the standard presentation of the fundamental group of the surface S defined by a canonical form $W(\alpha_1, \ldots, \alpha_n)$ where W involves $n \geq 2$ generators. Let $V(\beta_1, \ldots, \beta_k)$ be a quadratic word involving k generators where $k < n$. Then all solutions of $V = 1$ in G are free.*

Proof. The canonical form V^* to which V is equivalent under an automorphism of Φ involves at most $(n-1)$ generators. Thus $\chi(V) \geq 2-(n-1) = 3-n$. If G admits a non-free solution of $V = 1$, then there is a reduced R-diagram M on a surface S^* defined by an endomorphic image of V^*. Using the summation formula with $(p, q) = (4, 4)$ we have

$$(*) \qquad 4(3-n) \leq 4\chi(S^*) = \sum_M [4 - d(D)] + \sum_M [4 - d(v)].$$

First assume that S^* is not the projective plane. Since R satisfies C(2n) and T(2n) the degree of every region and every vertex is at least $2n$, so every term in the right-hand side of (*) is non-positive. Since M has at least one region and one vertex equation (*) implies that

$$4(3-n) \leq (4-2n) + (4-2n),$$

which says that $(12-4n) \leq (8-4n)$, a contradiction. If S^* is the projective plane, then $4\chi(S^*) = 4$ and there is at most one vertex of degree two, so the equation $(*)$ clearly cannot hold. Thus assuming the existence of a non-free solution of $V=1$ yields a contradiction. □

Lemma 13. *Let S be a surface defined by a canonical form $W(\alpha_1,\ldots,\alpha_n)$ where $n \geqslant 3$. Let $\langle X; R\rangle$ be the standard presentation for the group G of S. If M is a reduced R-diagram which tessellates S, then M has only one region.*

Proof. Since W is a canonical form, $\chi(S)=\chi(W)=2-n$. The summation formula with $(p,q)=(4,4)$ says that

$$4(2-n)=\sum_M (4-d(D))+\sum_M (4-d(v)).$$

Let k be the number of regions of M. Since R satisfies C($2n$) and T($2n$) and M has at least one vertex, we have

$$4(2-n)\leqslant k(4-2n)+(4-2n),$$

or

$$0\leqslant (k-1)(4-2n).$$

Since $n\geqslant 3$, this implies that $(k-1)\leqslant 0$. □

We note that in the case $n=2$ where the surface is the torus or the Klein bottle, there are reduced R-diagrams with arbitrarily many regions tessellating the appropriate surface. In the case of the torus, when R is the symmetrized closure of $xyx^{-1}y^{-1}$, the minimal R-diagram with boundary $xy^kx^{-1}y^{-k}$ has k regions, and $xy^kx^{-1}y^{-k}$ is the result of a cancellation-free substitution into $\alpha\beta\alpha^{-1}\beta^{-1}$.

We now turn to a proof of Nielsen's theorem on automorphisms of surface groups. Let S be a surface defined by a canonical form $W(\alpha_1,\ldots,\alpha_n)$ which involves n generators. Let $G=\langle X; R\rangle$ be the standard presentation of the fundamental group of S. If $n=1$, the theorem is trivial. If $n=2$ and S is orientable, then G is the free abelian group on two generators, and the theorem is easy to prove. (See [11].) The proof which we give is valid for n at least three, which we now assume. (Whether S is orientable or non-orientable makes no difference.) Let $\theta: G\to G$ be an automorphism of G. The rank of the group G is n, so the n-tuple $(\theta(x_1),\ldots,\theta(x_n))$ is a non-free solution of $W=1$ in G.

Let F be the free group on X. In discussing Nielsen transformations on tuples of elements of F one fixes a well-ordering $<$ of the words of F which is compatible with length; if $|u|<|v|$ then $u<v$. (See [10].) The ordering $<$, induces a lexicographical well-ordering, which we also denote by $<$, on n-tuples of elements of F. This ordering is used to decide whether or not to perform Nielsen transformations which leave the lengths of the entries in an n-tuple fixed.

Suppose that we are given a quadratic word $U(\beta_1, \ldots, \beta_n) \in \Phi$ and an n-tuple $\tau = (b_1, \ldots, b_n)$ of elements of F. Note that an attached transformation of type (4) does not affect the entries in τ, but only cyclically permutes U. We say that $(b_1, \ldots, b_n)$ is *cyclically Nielsen reduced* relative to U if $(b_1, \ldots, b_n)$ is Nielsen reduced relative to all cyclic permutations of U.

In studying the authomorphism θ we shall find it convenient to work with all automorphisms θ' which are equal to θ followed by an inner automorphism.

Let $\mathcal{N}_1(W, \theta)$ consist of all pairs (W, σ) where $\sigma = (a_1, \ldots, a_n)$ is an n-tuple of words of F, and there is an automorphism θ' of G differing from θ by an inner automorphism such that $a_i = \theta'(x_i)$ in G for $i = 1, \ldots, n$. Let $\mathcal{N}(W, \theta)$ be the set of all pairs (U, τ) such that there is a sequence

$$(W_1, \sigma_1) \to \cdots \to (W_k, \sigma_k) = (U, \tau)$$

where $(W_1, \sigma_1) \in \mathcal{N}_1(W, \theta)$ and each (W_{i+1}, σ_{i+1}) is obtained from (W_i, σ_i) by an attached transformation of type (2) or (4).

Note that in the above definition if a pair (U, τ) is in $\mathcal{N}(W, \theta)$, the tuple τ is derived from the tuple σ of a pair in $\mathcal{N}_1(W, \theta)$ solely by Nielsen transformations in the free group F. We have, however, the following

Observation. Suppose that $(U, \tau) \in \mathcal{N}(W, \theta)$ with $\tau = (b_1, \ldots, b_n)$. If $\tau' = (b'_1, \ldots, b'_n)$ where $b'_i = b_i$ in G, $i = 1, \ldots, n$, then $(U, \tau') \in \mathcal{N}(W, \theta)$.

To prove the observation, suppose that (U, τ) is derived from an element (W, σ) in $\mathcal{N}_1(W, \theta)$ by a sequence of transformations $N_1, \ldots, N_k$. We shall write transformations on the right, so $(U, \tau) = (W, \sigma)N_1 \cdots N_k$. Now $(U, \tau')N_k^{-1} \cdots N_1^{-1}$ is a member (W, σ') of $\mathcal{N}_1(W, \theta)$. So $(W, \sigma')N_1 \cdots N_k = (U, \tau')$, verifying that $(U, \tau') \in \mathcal{N}(W, \theta)$.

We now make essentially the same minimal choice as in the proof of Theorem 1, except that we use the ordering $<$ in the third condition.

Choice. Among all elements of $\mathcal{N}(W, \theta)$ pick a pair U and $(b_1, \ldots, b_n)$ such that:

(1) The number of regions in the minimal connected simply connected R-diagram M in the plane with boundary label $U(b_1, \ldots, b_n)$ is as small as possible.

(2) Subject to (1), the length of the free group element $U(b_1, \ldots, b_n)$ is as small as possible.

(3) Subject to (1) and (2), the n-tuple $(b_1, \ldots, b_n)$ is as small as possible in the ordering $<$.

For the remainder of this section, we assume that U and $(b_1, \ldots, b_n)$ are chosen as above, and that M is a minimal connected simply connected R-diagram in the plane with boundary label $U(b_1, \ldots, b_n)$.

If $\sigma = (a_1, \ldots, a_n)$ is the tuple in a pair $(W_1, \sigma) \in \mathcal{N}_1(W, \theta)$, then the rank of the subgroup of F generated by $\{a_1, \ldots, a_n\}$ is n. Since $(b_1, \ldots, b_n)$ is obtained from such a tuple by a sequence of Nielsen tranformations, the rank of the subgroup generated by $\{b_1, \ldots, b_n\}$ is also n. In particular, no $b_i = 1$. Also, applying a fixed inner automorphism of F to each b_i cannot yield a tuple of shorter length, for this would violate our minimal choice. Exactly similar to Lemma 6 we have

Lemma 14. *The tuple* $(b_1, \ldots, b_n)$ *is cyclically Nielsen reduced relative to U.*

Let $U \equiv \beta_{i_1}, \ldots, \beta_{i_{2n}}$ in Φ. It follows that the sequence $b_{i_1}, \ldots, b_{i_{2n}}$ satisfies the Nielsen conditions (N1) through (N3). In particular, there will be a "middle part" of each b_i which is not cancelled from either occurrence of $b_i^{\pm 1}$ when freely cyclically reducing $U(b_1, \ldots, b_n)$. (See [10] or [11].) We thus write each $b_i \equiv c_i b_i^* d_i$ where $b_i^* \neq 1$, no letter from b_i^* is cancelled from either occurrence of $b_i^{\pm 1}$ when freely reducing $U(b_1, \ldots, b_n)$, and each letter of c_i or d_i is cancelled in one of the occurrences of $b_i^{\pm 1}$. If all the c_i and d_i are empty, the tuple $(b_1, \ldots, b_n)$ is cancellation-free in U, but we now have to take care of the situation where some cancellation occurs.

We call the generators β_i which occur in U *primary variables.* We introduce, by successive transformations of type (1), new *auxiliary variables* ζ, η, etc. in one-to-one correspondence with the letters cancelled in the c_i and d_i. When the elements substituted for two auxiliary variables cancel, say in a product $\zeta\eta$ where some y is substituted for ζ and y^{-1} is substituted for η, we perform the transformation $\eta \to \zeta^{-1}$. Such a transformation affects only the auxiliary variables. If the letter substituted for ρ cancels in the product $\zeta\beta$, we perform the substitution $\beta \to \rho^{-1}\beta$. We thus arrive at a quadratic word $U^*(\beta_1, \ldots, \beta_n, \zeta_1, \ldots, \zeta_i)$ and a tuple $\tau^* = (b_1^*, \ldots, b_n^*, y_1, \ldots, y_j)$ where

(i) U^* is obtained from U by an automorphism Δ of Φ of the form $\beta_i \to C_i\beta_i D_i$ where each C_i and D_i is a word on the auxiliary variables,

(ii) the b_i^* are those in the decomposition $b_i = c_i b_i^* d_i$, and each y_l is a generator of F or its inverse,

(iii) the tuple τ^* is cancellation-free in U^* and $U^*(b_1^*, \ldots, b_n^*, y_1, \ldots, y_j) = U(b_1, \ldots, b_n)$ in F.

Note that U is obtainable from U^* by deleting all the auxiliary variables.

The following lemma is easily proved by induction on the number of transformations needed to obtain U^* from U.

Lemma 15. *Let U^* be obtained from U as described above. Let $V^*(\beta_{i_1}, \ldots, \beta_{i_t}, \zeta_{j_1}, \ldots, \zeta_{j_l})$ be a quadratic subword of a cyclic permutation of U^*, and suppose that $V^*(b_{i_1}^*, \ldots, b_{i_t}^*, y_{j_1}, \ldots, y_{j_l}) = 1$ in G. Let V be (the subword of a cyclic permutation of U) obtained from V^* by deleting all the auxiliary variables. Then, substituting the original b_i for the primary variables in V, we have $V(b_{i_1}, \ldots, b_{i_t}) = 1$ in G. Further, if Z^* contains all the primary variables in U^*, then Z^* is U^*.*

We turn to the analogue of Lemma 7.

Lemma 16. *Any boundary cycle of M is a simple closed path.*

Proof. If the boundary of M is not a simple closed path let K be an extremal disk of M. Let K have boundary label u_1 where u_1u_2 is a cyclic permutation of the boundary label u of M. First suppose that $u_1 = Z^*(b_{i_1}^*, \ldots, b_{i_t}^*, y_{j_1}, \ldots, y_{j_l})$ where $Z^*(\beta_{i_1}, \ldots, \beta_{i_t}, \zeta_{i_1}, \ldots, \zeta_{j_l})$ is a proper quadratic subword of a cyclic permutation of U^*. Since u_1 is the boundary label of a simply-connected R-diagram in the plane, $u_1 = 1$ in G. By Lemma 15, $Z(b_{i_1}, \ldots, b_{i_t}) = 1$ in G, where Z is obtained from Z^* by deleting the auxiliary variables. Since Z involves t primary variables, and the rank of the subgroup generated by $\{b_{i_1}, \ldots, b_{i_t}\}$ must be t, $(b_{i_1}, \ldots, b_{i_t})$ is certainly a non-free solution of $Z = 1$ in G. But since $t < n$, this is impossible by Lemma 12.

Since the above situation cannot occur, there is some variable γ (either primary or auxiliary) so that part of the result of substituting the entry in the tuple τ^* corresponding to γ appears in u_1 and part appears in u_2. Then, exactly as in the proof of Lemma 7, we may remove and reattach K, obtaining an R-diagram with the same number of regions but with a shorter boundary label u'. We have replaced one entry in the tuple τ^* by a word representing the same element of G. Calculating the corresponding change in τ, we replace τ by $\tau' = (b_1', \ldots, b_n')$ with each $b_i' = b_i$ in G. By our previous observation,

$(U, \tau') \in \mathcal{N}(W, \theta)$ and $U(b'_1, \ldots, b'_n) = u'$. But this contradicts our minimal choice. $\square$

We now know that the boundary of M is a simple closed path labelled by a cancellation-free substitution instance of $U^*(\beta_1, \ldots, \beta_n, \zeta_1, \ldots, \zeta_j)$. Since U^* is the image of U under an automorphism of Φ, the surface defined by U^* is the surface S defined by U. Identifying the edges in the boundary of M according to U^*, we obtain an R-diagram M on the surface S. Exactly as in the proof of Lemma 8 we have

Lemma 17. *The diagram M is reduced on S.*

Since R is thc standard presentation of the fundamental group of the surface S defined by the canonical form W on $n \geqslant 3$ generators, the diagram M can have only one region D by Lemma 13. The boundary label r of D is a cyclic permutation of $W(x_1, \ldots, x_n)^{\pm 1}$.

Since $r = U^*(b_1^*, \ldots, b_n^*, y_1, \ldots, y_j)$, no cancellation occurs, and each $b_i^* \neq 1$, we conclude that U^* contains no auxiliary variables. Thus $U^* = U$. Further, each b_i is some $x_{t_i}^{\pm 1}$, and up to a possible relabelling of the β_i and their inverses, U is a cyclic permutation of $W^{\pm 1}$. We next want to conclude that each c_i and d_i is the identity. To illustrate this, we do an example. (Although we are assuming that $n \geqslant 3$, our example is on two generators.) Suppose that U is $\beta_1\beta_2\beta_1^{-1}\beta_2^{-1}$ and that $d_1 \neq 1$. Suppose $b_1^* = x_1$ and $b_2^* = x_2$. Substituting b_1 and b_2 into U, we have that the product

$$(c_1x_1d_1)(c_2x_2d_2)(d_1^{-1}x_1^{-1}c_1^{-1})(d_2^{-1}x_2^{-1}c_2^{-1})$$

cyclically reduces to $x_1x_2x_1^{-1}x_2^{-1}$ and the indicated occurrences of x_1 and x_2 are not cancelled. It follows that $c_2 = d_1^{-1}$, $d_2 = d_1$, and $c_1 = d_2$. Thus each b_i is of the form $d_1^{-1}x_id_1$ with $d_1 \neq 1$. In the general case, we see that assuming some c_i or d_i is not the identity forces each b_i to have the form $zx_{t_i}^{\pm 1}z^{-1}$ with $z \neq 1$. But this violates our minimal choice. We conclude that each b_i is some $x_{t_i}^{\pm 1}$.

Now $(b_1, \ldots, b_n)$ is obtained by a sequence of Nielsen transformations from a tuple $(a_1, \ldots, a_n)$ where $a_i = \theta'(x_i)$ in G for some automorphism θ' of G differing from the given θ by an inner automorphism. Hence there is an automorphism ψ' of the free group F sending x_i to a_i. Correcting by the inverse of inner automorphism we see that there is an automorphism ψ of F with $\psi(x_i) = \theta(x_i)$ in G, that is, θ is induced by an automorphism of F. Tracing through the effect of ψ on W, we also see that ψ sends W to a conjugate of $W^{\pm 1}$

References

[1] C. Chalk, Ph.D. thesis, University of Nottingham, 1977.

[2] L.P. Comerford, Real elements in small cancellation groups, Math. Annalen 208 (1974) 279–293.

[3] C.C. Edmunds, On the endomorphism problem for free groups, Comm. Algebra 3 (1975) 1–20.

[4] S.O. Gowdy, On Greendlinger's eight-groups, Ph.D. thesis, Temple University, Philadelphia, 1971.

[5] M. Greendlinger, On Dehn's algorithms for the word and conjugacy problems with applications, Comm. Pure Appl. Math. 13 (1960) 641–677.

[6] M. Greendlinger, A class of groups all of whose elements have trivial centralizers, Math. Zeit. 78 (1962) 91–96.

[7] M. Greendlinger, Problem of conjugacy and coincidence with anticenter in group theory, Siberian Math. Journal 7 (1966) 626–640.

[8] R.C. Lyndon, On the equation $a^2b^2 = c^2$ in free groups, Michigan Math. J. 6 (1959) 89–92.

[9] R.C. Lyndon, On Dehn's Algorithm, Math. Ann. 166 (1966) 208–228.

[10] R.C. Lyndon and P.E. Schupp, Combinatorial group theory (Springer-Verlag, Heidelburg, 1977).

[11] W. Magnus, A. Karrass and D. Solitar, Combinatorial group theory (Wiley, New York, 1966).

[12] W. Massey, Algebraic topology, an introduction (Harcourt, Brace and World, New York, 1967).

[13] C.F. Miller and P.E. Schupp, The geometry of HNN extensions, Comm. Pure Appl. Math. 26 (1973) 787–802.

[14] J. Nielsen, Untersuchungen zur Topologie der Geschlossenen Zweiseitigen Flächen, I, II, III, Acta Math. 50 (1927) 189–358; 53 (1929) 1–76; 58 (1931) 87–167.

[15] P.E. Schupp, On Dehn's Algorithm and the conjugacy problem, Math. Ann. 178 (1968) 119–130.

[16] P.E. Schupp, A survey of small cancellation theory, in Word Problems, edited by Boone, Cannonito and Lyndon (North-Holland Publishing Company, Amsterdam, 1973).

[17] J.K. Seymour, On conjugate powers in small cancellation groups, Ph.D. thesis, University of Illinois, Urbana, 1974.

[18] V.V. Soldatova, On groups with a δ-basis, for $\delta < 1/4$, and a single additional condition, Siberian Math. J. 7 (1966) 504–511.

[19] H. Zieschang, E. Vogt and H.-D. Coldewey, Flächen und ebene diskontinuierliche Gruppen, Springer Lecture Notes, 122 (1970).

S.I. Adian, W.W. Boone, G. Higman, eds., Word Problems II

ON A PROBLEM OF KUROSH, JONSSON GROUPS, AND APPLICATIONS

Saharon SHELAH*
Institute of Mathematics, The Hebrew University, Jerusalem, and University of Wisconsin, Madison

Abstract. We prove some results in group theory in a model theoretic spirit.

(i) We construct Jonsson groups of cardinality $\aleph_1$ and other cardinalities as well. This answers an old question of Kurosh.

(ii) Our group is simple with no maximal subgroup; so it follows that taking Frattini subgroups does not commute with direct products.

(ii) Assuming the continuum hypothesis, our group is not a topological group, except with the trivial topologies. This answers a quite old question of A.A. Markov.

In the construction we use small cancellation theory. We try to make the paper intelligible to both group theorists and model theorists. Only a knowledge of naive set theory and group theory is needed.

§0. Introduction

We first give the background, state the results, and then explain the proof. Schmidt asked whether infinite groups with no infinite proper subgroups exist; there has been much work in Schmidt groups, see e.g. [16]. Kurosh generalized this question to the following: Does there exist a group of cardinality $\aleph_1$ which has no proper subgroup of the same cardinality? Later Jonsson asked the same question for any algebra; so now an algebra with no proper subalgebra of the same cardinality is called a Jonsson algebra. Chang and Keisler [5] in their list of open problems, repeat Kurosh's question in this terminology: is there a Jonsson group of cardinality $\aleph_1$? McKenzie [11] proved that, for almost any cardinal λ, every Jonsson semi-group of cardinality λ is a group. Much work was done on the following question: for which λ

* The author would like to thank the United States–Israel Binational Science Foundation for partially supporting his research, by Grant 1110, and the U.S. National Science Foundation for similar support under Grant 144-H 747.

is there a Jonsson algebra of cardinality λ (with countably many operations, of course). See e.g. [5]. Magidor and Malitz showed, from a general theorem, that if there is a Jonsson group in some regular cardinal, and $V = L$ (or even $\diamondsuit_{\aleph_1}$) holds, then there is a Jonsson group of cardinality $\aleph_1$.

The main body of the paper is a proof of the following result:

Theorem A. *There is a Jonsson group of cardinality* $\aleph_1$ *and also of cardinality* λ^+ *when* $\lambda^+ = 2^\lambda$.

The groups we construct can serve as counterexamples for some problems; more properties of these groups are stated in Theorem 1, and more hold by the construction.

It has been asked whether the operation of taking the Frattini subgroup commutes with direct products. Now $\tau(G)$, the Frattini subgroup of G, is the intersection of all proper maximal subgroups. It was well known that any simple group G with no maximal subgroup will provide a counterexample (because $\tau(G) = G$, but $\tau(G \times G) =$ the diagonal subgroup $= \{\langle a, a\rangle : a \in G\}$). Our groups serve as examples.

Theorem B. (1) *There is a simple group* (*of power* $\aleph_1$) *with no maximal subgroup.*

(2) *Taking Frattini subgroups does not commute with direct products.*

Problem. Does Theorem B hold for countable groups?

A.A. Markov [18] asked about the existence of an untopologizable group; i.e., a group which admits only the discrete topology. A.A. Markov [19] and Podewski [12] reported this question and proved that for any Hausdorff indiscrete topologizable group, any finite set of inequations which has at least one solution has at least two; and that for countable groups this condition on the group is necessary and sufficient for the existence of a Hausdorff indiscrete topology for the group. (The demand of "Hausdorff" is quite natural.) It is still unknown whether countable groups not satisfying this condition exist. Podowski [12] also gives a sufficient condition on a not necessarily countable group G (any system of less than $|G|$ inequations which has at least one solution has at least two) for the existence of such a topology. He also deals with other algebras. Previously Hanson [7] gave an untopologizable groupoid and Arnautov [2], [3] proved results on rings similar to those of Podewski. Kertesz and Szele [8] showed that for abelian groups a nontrivial topology always exists.

Theorem C. *Assume CH (i.e.* $2^{\aleph_0} = \aleph_1$*). Then there is an untopologizable group of cardinality* $\aleph_1$.

In fact, every countable subgroup of this group is topologized, thus answering negatively a question of Makowski. Of course we can replace $\aleph_1$ by any $\lambda^+ = 2^\lambda$.

Bokut [4] asked whether every algebra M over a field K (M not necessarily associative) of infinite dimension can be represented as $\bigcup_{n<\omega} M_n$, M_n a subalgebra over K, $\dim(M_n) = \dim(M_{n+1}, M_n) = \lambda$ for every n.

Theorem D. *There is a group G of cardinality* $\aleph_1$ *such that for every field K, the group-ring K[G] is not the union of a strictly increasing chain of length* ω.

Note that Sabbagh [13] had proved the result for modules and groups; but they were of cardinality $\lambda = \lambda^{\aleph_0}$; but his group can serve as well, and we can easily change it to cardinality $\aleph_1$.

Koppelberg and Tits [9] have shown that no complete Boolean algebra is the union of a strictly ascending chain of subalgebra of length ω.

I would like to thank G. Hesse wholeheartedly for pointing out the incorrectness of 2.11 as it was stated (it was needed for Theorem 2.9) and suggesting a proof of 2.9 avoiding 2.11. The error was that if $K \setminus H$ contains torsion elements we cannot get $L <_{md} L^{**}$ so we added in 2.11 the hypothesis "all groups are torsion-free" and added a proof to 2.11 (which was left to the reader in the first version). Hesse's proof is added too. (Note that by his method in 2.9 for any uncountable set of elements I of the group, and element a, a belongs to the subgroup generated by three elements instead of two, but the length of the word is shorter.)

We shall first present small cancellation theory. We prove everything except the main theorem. We also slightly improve an application from [14]. We shall prove (in Theorem 2.1) that for $\lambda^+ = 2^\lambda$, $\lambda > \aleph_0$, there is a Jonsson group of cardinality λ^+ satisfying some other conditions. Then we show that with small changes our proof works for $\lambda = \aleph_0$. Next with less details (Theorem 2.9) we prove there is a Jonsson group of cardinality $\aleph_1$ (without assuming CH). Now Theorems A, B, follow immediately from 2.1, 2.9; we then give the (short) proof of theorems C, D, and we finish the paper by making a few remarks.

I would like to thank Paul Schupp wholeheartedly for explaining small cancellation theory to me, and for checking the proof.

Let me try to explain the proof of Theorem 1. We construct the group M as the union of an ascending chain of length λ^+, of groups of cardinality λ, say $M_\alpha\,(\alpha < \lambda^+)$. For definiteness we assume that the set of elements of M_α is $\lambda(1+\alpha)$ (= the set of ordinals $< \lambda(1+\alpha)$). We try to prevent the existence of large proper subgroups G. In stage α M_α is already defined, and we are defining $M_{\alpha+1}$: we have a list of proper subgroups of M_α of cardinality λ $\{S_\beta : \beta \leq \alpha\}$, we look at them as approximations in some $\alpha(0) \leq \alpha$ to a G (i.e. as $G \cap M_{\alpha(0)}$) and try not to let them "grow". More specifically, we want that for every $a \in M_{\alpha+1} - M_\alpha$, and $\beta \leq \alpha$, the subgroup of $M_{\alpha+1}$ generated by S_β and a includes M_α. This means that if G is a proper subgroup of $M, M_{\alpha(0)} \not\subseteq G$, $S_\beta = G \cap M_{\alpha(0)}$ then G is disjoint to $M_{\alpha+1} - M_\alpha$. If we choose S_β $(\beta < \lambda^+)$ so that every subgroup of M of cardinality λ appears (and this can be done by $2^\lambda = \lambda^+$) this scheme works, provided that we can define $M_{\alpha+1}$ from M_α. We construct $M_{\alpha+1}$ by a series of approximations of smaller cardinality $L_\beta\,(\beta < \lambda)$ (L_β ascending and continuous, of course) and let $H_\beta = L_\beta \cap M_\beta$ (of course $\bigcup_\beta H_\beta = M_\alpha$, $\bigcup_\beta L_\beta = M_{\alpha+1}$). So we have to amalgamate L_β, $H_{\beta+1}$ over H_β, faithfully. The free product of L_β, $H_{\beta+1}$ with amalgamation over H_β satisfies this; but we have tasks to fulfil. To ensure $\bigcup_{\beta<\lambda} H_\beta = M_\alpha$ is easy; but we also have to ensure that each $b \in M_\alpha$ belongs to $\langle a, S_\gamma \rangle$ for $a \in L_\beta - H_\beta$, $\gamma \leq \alpha$. There are λ such tasks, so in each amalgamation we can deal with one such task only. We can choose $H_{\beta+1}$ such that $b \in H_{\beta+1}$, and $S_\gamma \cap H_{\beta+1}$ is "quite" large. But how to do this? We want something like free amalgamation, with an extra relation, saying that a word in a and some $x \in S_\gamma$ is equal to b.

Small cancellation theory is just the right theory. However one needs some hypothesis on a and x. For this we make the induction assumption that H_β is a malnormal subgroup of L_β (see "Notation", just below, for a definition), and we use the fact that $|H_\beta| < \lambda \doteq |S'_\gamma|$ to find suitable $x, y \in S_\gamma \cap H_{\beta+1}$. Now a, x, y satisfy a variant of the blocking pair condition, so small cancellation theory works.

For $\lambda = \aleph_0$ (see 2.7) we should replace usually "of cardinaltiy $< \lambda$" by "finitely generated". The main point is that a set $S \subseteq M_\alpha$ which is not included in a finitely generated subgroup of M_α may be included in a finitely generated subgroup of some M_β, $\beta \geq \alpha$. However our construction prevents this possibility, as shown in fact by 2.8, which is useful also in replacing $\diamondsuit_{\aleph_1}$ by CH in Macintyre [10] for algebraically closed groups (see [17]).

Theorem 2.9, which says that in power $\aleph_1$ Jonsson groups always exist, demands more changes, but we give fewer details and the ideas are essentially the same.

Notation. G, H, K, L, M will be groups. $G \leqslant H$ means G is a subgroup of H. If $G \leqslant H$, $x \in H$, then we call x *malnormal* over G (relative to H, of course) if G, G^x are disjoint, except for the unit element which we ignore where $G^x = \{xgx^{-1} : g \in G\}$. If $G \leqslant H$ and every x in $H - G$ is malnormal over G, then H is a *malnormal extension* of G, and G a *malnormal subgroup* H and we write $G \leqslant_m H$. If $G \leqslant H$, $x \in H$ then the *right, left, double* coset of x over G in H is xG, Gx, GxG resp; and belonging to the same right (or left, or double) coset, is an equivalence relation; and inequivalent elements have disjoint right (left or double) cosets.

We do not distinguish strictly between a group and its set of elements. $|A|$ is the number of elements of A, i.e., its cardinality.

For $X \subseteq G$, $\langle X \rangle$ is the subgroup of G generated by X. We call $x, y \in H$ *good fellows* over G if $x, y \in G - H$ with $x^{\pm 1} \notin Gy^{\pm 1}G$. Note that among any three elements of $G - H$ with distinct double cosets at least two are good fellows over G. Note also that for good fellows x, y $(Gx^{\pm 1}G) \cap (Gy^{\pm 1}G) = \emptyset$; and that G itself is a double coset. The relation of not being good fellows is an equivalence relation.

§1. Free products with amalgamation

Definition 1.1. Suppose H, K, L are groups, $K \cap L = H$ (for notational simplicity only). We now define the free product with amalgamation of K, L over H, denoted by $L^* = K *_H L$ as follows:

i) Let F_1 be the free group generated by the elements $K \cup L$.

ii) Let N_1 be the normal subgroup of F_1 generated by $\{g_1g_2g_3 : g_1, g_2, g_3 \in K,\ g_1g_2 = g_3^{-1}$ *or* $g_1, g_2, g_3 \in L,\ g_1g_2 = g_3^{-1}\}$.

iii) Let $L^* = F_1/N_1$. Now K, L, H have natural homomorphisms into $L^* : g \mapsto g/N_1$.

Fact 1.2. These homomorphisms are embeddings, and the intersection of the images of K and L is the image of their intersection, H (see e.g. [4]).

We shall not from now on distinguish between g and g/N_1, and we shall call an element of F_1 a word, and of $K \cup L$ a letter. It follows that every element of L^* which is not in H is equal to a product of the form $g_1 \cdots g_n$ such that for each l, $g_l \in L \cup K - H$, and $g_l \in L$ iff

$g_{l+1} \in K$. Such a product will be called a *canonical representation*. For $g \in H$, g itself is the canonical representation. A subword of (a canonical representation) $g_1 \cdots g_n$ is $g_l \cdots g_m$, $1 \leq l \leq m \leq n$. In general canonical representation is not unique but

Fact 1.3. If $g \in L^*$ has the canonical representations $g_1 \cdots g_n$, $g_1^1 \cdots g_m^1$ then:

(i) $n = m$.

(ii) $g_l \in K$ iff $g_l^1 \in K$.

(iii) There are $h_1, \ldots, h_{n-1} \in H$ such that letting $h_0 = h_n = e$, for every l, $g_l^1 = h_l g_l h_{l+1}^{-1}$.

Definition 1.4. If $g \in L^*$ has a canonical representation $g_1 \cdots g_n$, n will be called the length of g and denoted by $|g|$.

Definition 1.5. The canonical representation $g_1 \cdots g_n$ is called *weakly cyclically reduced* if n is even, or $n = 1$ or $g_n g_1 \notin H$ (equivalently, $g_1 \cdots g_n$ has no conjugate of length $< n - 1$). Notice that this is a property of the element.

Small cancellation theory

The aim of this theory in this context, is as follows: We have in $L^* = L *_H K$, a set R of words which are "long and complicated", which we want to make equal to the identity without "hurting" L, K, and short words in general. More accurately, we want to divide L^* by the normal subgroup N of L^* generated by R, and want that N will be disjoint to K, L and moreover will not have "short" elements.

For simplicity R will always be a set of weakly cyclically reduced elements.

Definition 1.6. (1) The symmetrized closure of R is obtained from R by the following operations:

(i) Add the inverses of the elements in R.

(ii) Add the conjugates (in L^*) which are weakly cyclically reduced.

(2) R is symmetrized if it is equal to its symmetrized closure.

(3) A part of a cyclically reduced word is a subword of a weakly cyclically reduced conjugate of it. A part of R is a part of one of its elements.

Claim 1.7. If $R = \{g_1 \cdots g_n\}$, n even, $g_1 \cdots g_n$ a canonical representation, the symmetrized closure of R consists of the following elements: for each $1 \leq l \leq n$, $g_l = g_l^1 g_l^2$, $g_l^i \in K \Leftrightarrow g_l \in K$, the words:

$g_l^2 g_{l+1} \cdots g_n g_1 \cdots g_{l-1} g_l^1$ and $(g_l^1)^{-1} g_{l-1}^{-1} \cdots g_1^{-1} g_n^{-1} \cdots g_{l+1}^{-1} (g_l^2)^{-1}$. (Note that we write the elements in canonical form except that maybe $g_l^\delta \in H$ and then we multiply it with its neighbor.)

Definition 1.8. A symmetrized R satisfies the condition $C'(\theta)$ (θ a real positive number < 1) if whenever $g^* = g^m \cdots g^1$, $g_* = g_1 \cdots g_n$ are canonical representations of elements of R, $g^* \neq g_*^{-1}$ and $g^{l(0)} \cdots g^1 g_1 \cdots g_{l(0)} \in H$ (hence this hold for any $l \leq l(0)$) *then* $l(0) < \theta n$, $l(0) < \theta m$ and $n, m > (1/\theta)$ (this means $g^*, (g_*)^{-1}$ have no common segment of this length. Clearly $l(0)$ depends on g^* and g_* and not on the representation).

Main Theorem 1.9. *If $L^* = K *_H L$, $R \subseteq L^*$ symmetrized and satisfies $C'(1/k)$, $k \geq 6$, N the normal subgroup of L^* that R generates, $w = g_1 \cdots g_n \in N$ in a weakly cyclically reduced canonical form, then w has a part w_0 which is part of some $w_1 \in R$, and $|w_0| \geq [(k-3)/k] |w_1|$.*

Now we have to find suitable R. Schupp [14], [15] suggests, as a nice sufficient condition for existence, that L (or K) contains a blocking pair $\{x, y\}$ over H, which means a pair of malnormal elements over H which are good fellows except that possibly $x = y^{-1}$. Then for a $a \in L \setminus H$ the symmetrized closure of $\{axayax(ay)^2ax(ay)^3 \cdots ax(ay)^{80}\}$ satisfies $C'(1/10)$. We notice two weaker conditions:

(1) there is a malnormal $a \in L$ over H, and two good fellows $x, y \in K - H$;

(2) there is a malnormal $a \in L$, and $x \neq y \in K - H$ (this is weaker than (1) but the word contains inverses). So we can somewhat improve Theorem 10, p. 582 of Schupp [14] (see [15]).

Theorem 1.10. *Let $L^* = L *_H K$ be a free product with amalgamation where $L \neq H$, $K \neq H$, and in at least one of them there is a malnormal element over H. Then L^* is SQ-universal except when L, K, H are cyclic groups of order* 2, 2, 1 *resp. (SQ-universal means every countable group can be embedded in a quotient group of K).*

Now we present this more accurately. We denote by $w(\bar{x}) = w(x_1, \ldots, x_r)$ a sequence composed of the letters $x_1, \ldots, x_r$. For every group (or semigroup) G and $a_1, \ldots, a_r \in G$ the meaning of $w(a_1, \ldots, a_r)$ is clear.

Definition 1.11. $w(\bar{x}) = w(x_1, \ldots, x_r) = x^1 \cdot \cdots \cdot x^k$, where $x^l \in \{x_1, \ldots, x_r\}$ and we stipulate $x^j = x^i$ when $i = j \bmod k$ (for latter use).

(1) We call $w(\bar{x})$ n-random if

(i) whenever $1 \leqslant p$, $q \leqslant k$, and $(\forall i)$ $(1 \leqslant i \leqslant k/n \rightarrow x^{p+i} = x^{q+i})$ then $p = q$,

(ii) for every p, $1 \leqslant p$, $q \leqslant k$, for some i, $1 \leqslant i \leqslant k/n$ and $x^{p+i} = x^{q-i}$.

(2) We call $w(\bar{x})$ strongly *n-random* if

(iii) if $1 \leqslant p$, $q \leqslant k$, $v_1 \cdots v_n$, $u_1 \cdots u_n$ sequences of x_i's, $\varepsilon, \delta \in \{1, -1\}$ *then* for some l, $1 \leqslant l < k/n - n$, $x^{p+\delta(l+i)} = u_i$, $x^{q+\varepsilon(l+i)} = v_i$ for every i, $1 \leqslant i \leqslant n$, except when an apparent contradiction arises (that is $\delta = \varepsilon$, and for some i, j, $1 \leqslant j \leqslant n$, $p + \delta i = q + \varepsilon j$, $u_i \neq v'_j$ (so $|p - q| < n$).

Remark. It is easy to check that a strongly n-random sequence is an n-random sequence.

Claim 1.12. For every n, r for every big enough k, there is an n-random word $w^r_n(\bar{x}) = w^r_n(x_1, \ldots, x_r)$ which is even strongly n-random.

Proof. For every large enough k, compute the number of sequences, and number of non-strongly n-random sequences.

Claim 1.13. (1) Suppose $L^* = L *_H K$, $z \in L \cup K$, $a \in L$ is malnormal over H, and $x, y \in K$ are good fellows over H. If $w(x_1, x_2) = x^1 \cdots x^k$ is $4/\theta$-random *then* the symmetrized closure R of $\{zw(ax, ay)\}$ satisfies $C'(\theta)$

(2) Suppose $L^* = L *_H K$, $z \in L \cup K$, $a \in L$ is malnormal over H, and $x, y \in K - H$, $x \neq y$. If $w(x_1, x_2, x_3, x_4)$ is strongly $(4/\theta)$-random *then* the symmetrized closure of $\{zw(ax, ay, a^{-1}x, a^{-1}y)\}$ satisfies $C'(\theta)$.

Proof. (1) The length of every word in R is $2k$ or $2k + 1$ (note that $w(ax, ay)$ is already in canonical form, and of even length $2k$). Also if $g = g_1 g_2 \cdots g_m \in R$ (in canonical form) then we can assume for some $\varepsilon \in \{0, 1\}$, $\delta \in \{1, -1\}$ and p the following hold:

$$g_{\varepsilon+2i} = a^{\delta}, \; g_{\varepsilon+2i+1} = (x)^{\delta} \text{ when } x^{p+\delta i} = x_1;$$

$$g_{\varepsilon+2i} = a^{\delta}, \; g_{\varepsilon+2i+1} = (y)^{\delta} \text{ when } x^{p+\delta i} = x_2$$

when the index of g is $< m$ and > 2, except possibly once (because of z). Of course ε, δ and p depends on g, so we shall write $\varepsilon(g)$, $\delta(g)$, and $p(g)$.

Suppose now $g^*, g_*, l(0)$ are as in 1.8, and let $h_l = g^l \cdots g^1$, $g_1 \cdots g_l \in H$ for $l \leqslant l(0)$; so $h_{l+1} = g^{l+1} h_l g_{l+1}$, $h_0 = e$; and note $g^l \in K \Leftrightarrow g_l \in K$ (otherwise $l(0) = 0$). Except for at most three l's (1, and one exception for g_*, and one for g^*) $g^l \in L \Rightarrow [g^l, g_l = a^{\pm 1}]$ and $g^l \in K \Rightarrow [g_l, g^l \in \{x^{\pm 1}, y^{\pm 1}\}]$. There are $1 < l(1) < l(2) \leqslant l(0)$, $l(2) - l(1) \geqslant l(0)/3$, such that no l, $l(1) < l \leqslant l(2)$ is exceptional. So for every such l, if $g^l \in K$, (as x, y are good fellows and $g^l h_{l-1} g_l \in H$), then $g_l = x^{\pm 1}$ iff $g^l = x^{\pm 1}$. This means for $l(1)/2 < i < l(2)/2$, $x^{l(0)-[p(g^*)+\delta(g^*)i]} = x^{[p(g_*)+\delta(g_*)i-(\varepsilon(g^*)-\varepsilon(g_*))/2]}$ (note g^* was written in a reverse order).

By the $(4/\theta)$-randomness of $w(x_1, x_2)$ this implies $\delta(g_*) = -\delta(g^*)$ and $g^l = (g_l)^{-1}$ for $1 < l < \min\{m, n\}$. If $g^1 g_1 \neq e$, then for every $l < l(0)$, $h_l \neq e$ (as a conjugate of an element $\neq e$ is $\neq e$) and for some l, $g^l = a^\delta$ so $g_l = a^{-\delta}$ and $h_{l+1} = a^\delta h_l a^{-\delta}$, so by the malnormality of a, $h_{l+1} \notin H$, contradiction. So necessarily $g^1 = g_1^{-1}$, hence $n = m$, $g^n = g_n^{-1}$, so $g^* = g_*^{-1}$. So we finish.

(2) We proved as before and let $v \in \{x, y\}$, $v \neq x^{-1}$. Suppose $\delta(g^*) = \delta(g_*) = 1$ for simplicity. But now by strong $(4/\theta)$-randomness we can find $l, l(1) < l$, $l + 2 < l(2)$ such that $g^l = a$, $g_l = a^{-1}$, $g^{l+1} = x$, $g_{l+1} = v$, $g^{l+2} = a$, $g_{l+2} = a^{-1}$. As $h_l = g^l h_{l-1} g_l \in H$, a malnormal over H, clearly $h_{l-1}, h_l \in H$ so $h_l = h_{l-1} = e$ (otherwise $h_l \notin H$ by a being malnormal over H) so $h_{l+1} = xv \neq e$ so $h_{l+2} = a(xv)a^{-1} \notin H$, contradiction. In the other cases we get similar contradictions except in the desired case.

§2. The theorems

Theorem 2.1. *Suppose λ is an infinite uncountable cardinal and $\lambda^+ = 2^\lambda$.*

(1) *There is a Jonsson group of cardinality λ^+.*

(2) *Moreover this group is a Jonsson semigroup (i.e. has no proper semigroup of the same cardinality), is simple, and there is a natural number n_0 such that for any subset S of the group of cardinality λ^+, any element of the group is equal to the product of n_0 elements of S.*

Proof. We will note some facts on groups, then we describe the construction, and at last prove it works.

Fact 2.2. Suppose H is a subgroup of K and A a subset of K such that either

(i) $3|H|^2 < |A|$, or

(ii) H is included in a finitely generated subgroup of K and A is not included in a finitely generated subgroup of K.

Then there are $x, y \in A$ which are good fellows over H.

Proof. Say $x \approx y$ if x or $x^{-1} \in HyH$. Now $\approx$ is an equivalence relation on $A - H$. Then x, y are *good fellows* over H iff they are not

$\approx$-equivalent. Thus if no $x, y \in K$ are good fellows over H, $A - H$ is contained in the union of at most 2 double cosets: HaH, $Ha^{-1}H$ (a any element of $A - H$); which contradicts (i), and contradicts (ii) as if H is contained in a finitely generated subgroup of K, so is $(HaH) \cup (Ha^{-1}H) \cup H$.

Fact 2.3. Suppose $H = K \cap L$ (so H is a subgroup of K and of L), and $H \leqslant_m L$, and $L^* = K *_H L$ (i.e. L^* is the free product of K and L with amalgamation over H). *Then* $K \leqslant_m L^*$

Proof. Let $g \in K$, $g \neq e$, $p = w_1 w_2 \cdots w_n \in L^* - K$ (a canonical form, the w's are letters; so each w_i belongs to $L - H$ or $K - H$, and successive letters do not belong to the same one). Note that $n = 1 \Rightarrow w_1 \in L - H$ as $p \notin K$. We should prove that $q = pgp^{-1} = w_1 \cdots w_n g w_n^{-1} \cdots w_1^{-1}$ does not belong to K.

(i) If $w_n \in L - H$, $g \in K - H$, q is already written in canonical form (of length $2n + 1 > 1$) hence $q \notin K$.

(ii) If $w_n \in L - H$, $g \in H$, then $w_n g w_n^{-1} \in L - H$ by the malnormality of H in L, hence q has the canonical form $w_1 w_2 \cdots w_{n-1}(w_n^{-1} g w_n) w_{n-1}^{-1} \cdots w_2^{-1} w_1^{-1}$ and $w_n^{-1} g w_n \notin K$. So $q \notin K$.
So we can assume $w_n \in K - H$, so as $p \notin K$, $n > 1$.

(iii) If $w_n g w_n^{-1} \notin H$, then $w_1 \cdots w_{n-1}(w_n g w_n^{-1}) w_{n-1}^{-1} \cdots w_1^{-1}$ is a canonical form of q hence $q \notin K$.

(iv) If $g_1 = w_n g w_n^{-1} \in H$, then clearly $g_1 \neq 1$, and as $n > 1$, we are reduced to case (ii).
We exhaust all possibilities, thus finish.

We shall need the following fact about small cancellation theory over free products with amalgamation.

Fact 2.4. $L^* = K *_H L$ where $H \leqslant_m L$. Suppose that $x, y \in K - H$ are good fellows over H and let $a \in L - H$, $z \in K$.

Let $r = r(a, x, y, z) = z^{-1}xzyaxa(ya)^2xa(ya)^3 \cdots xa(ya)^{80}$, and let R be the symmetrized closure of r. Let N be the normal closure of R in L^*, and let $L^{**} = L^*/N$. Then

(i) the natural map $r : L^* \to L^{**}$ embeds H and K, so that their intersection does not increase,

(ii) $K \leqslant_m L^{**}$.

Remarks. In fact r has to be a long enough random word consisting of instances of xa, ya; then multiplied by z^{-1}; but group theorists like this particular r. "Random" means that no two distinct "large" (e.g. of length at least 1/100 of that of r) segments of r are the same, *even if we allow to inverting the order* (but a segment and its inversion are considered distinct).

We could have replaced "good fellows" by "with distinct double coset representations" but then the random word *should* consist also of instances of ax^{-1}, ay^{-1}, so later we should not get a Jonsson semigroup.

Proof. For (i) see 1.13 (1) and then 1.9.

To see that (ii) holds, let $e \neq k \in K$. Suppose $u \notin K$. We can assume that u does not contain more that half of an element of R. Write $u = u_1 u_2 \cdots u_n$ in reduced form in L^*. If $u^{-1}ku = k' \in K$, we have the equation $u^{-1}ku(k')^{-1} = e$ in L^{**} and thus the left-hand side contains a part of more than 7/10 of an element of R by length. This cannot occur in u^{-1} nor in u (as they do not contain more than half of a generator), so this occurs around k (or $(k')^{-1}$), and at least 2/10 of it lies on each side of k. This means that for some v (initial segment of u) $v^{-1}kv$ is a part of more than 1/10 of a member of R. But no element of R contains a long subword of the form $c^{-1}gc$ where g has length 1. Thus the above equation cannot hold. If the part is around $(k')^{-1}$, the proof is similar.

The construction 2.5 (*for Theorem* 2.1). As we have assumed $2^\lambda = \lambda^+$ the number of subsets of λ^+ (as a set of ordinals) of cardinality exactly λ is $2^\lambda = \lambda^+$, so let $\{S_\alpha : \alpha < \lambda^+\}$ be a list of them.

We now define an increasing sequence of groups M_α $(\alpha < \lambda^+)$ such that the set of elements of M_α is $\lambda(1+\alpha)$. We define them such that

(i) M_α is a malnormal subgroup of $M_{\alpha+1}$.

(ii) For every $\gamma \leqslant \alpha$ and $a \in M_{\alpha+1} - M_\alpha$, if $S_\gamma \subseteq M_\alpha$ then the subgroup $\langle S_\gamma \cup \{a\}\rangle$ includes M_α. In fact, every element of M_α is a product of length n_0 elements from $S_\gamma \cup \{a\}$ (where n_0 is the length of the r in Fact 2.4).

(iii) For limit δ, $M_\delta = \bigcup_{\alpha<\delta} M_\alpha$.

We do the induction step later, and now let us prove that $M = \bigcup_{\alpha<\lambda^+} M_\alpha$ is as desired. Suppose by contradiction that M has a proper sub-semigroup, M^*, of cardinality λ^+. Clearly, for some $\alpha(0) < \lambda^+$, $S = M^* \cap M_{\alpha(0)}$ has cardinality λ, and let $a \in M - M^*$, for some $\alpha(1)$, $a \in M_{\alpha(1)}$. Now S is a subset of λ^+ of cardinality λ, hence for some $\alpha(3)$, $S = S_{\alpha(3)}$. Let $\alpha = \max\{\alpha(0), \alpha(1), \alpha(3)\}$. Since M^* has cardinality λ^+, it is not included in M_α and hence for some $b \in M^* - M_\alpha$. So necessarily for some $\beta \geqslant \alpha$, $b \in M_{\beta+1} - M_\beta$. Thus by (ii) ($\beta, \alpha(3)$ here stands for α, γ there) the subgroup generated by b and $S_{\alpha(3)}$ includes

M_α. Therefore it includes $M_{\alpha(1)}$ and hence a belongs to it. But $b \in M^*$, $S_{\alpha(3)} \subseteq M^*$, hence $a \in M^*$, contradicting its choice.

This finishes the proof of 2.1(1). As for part 2 of Theorem 2.1, M is a Jonsson semi-group as just proved; moreover checking how the group generated by b and $S_{\alpha(3)}$ includes M_β (by (ii)) we see that we have proved that if S is any subset of M of cardinality λ^+, any element of M is equal to the product of n_0 elements of S, here n_0 is the length of the word r from Fact 2.4 and is a fixed natural number. From 2.1(2) only the simplicity remains, but if $a \in M$, a not the unit, for some $\alpha, a \in M_\alpha$, so for every $\beta \geq \alpha$ a has a conjugate in $M_{\beta+1} - M_\beta$ (as $M_{\beta+1}$ is a malnormal extension of M_β, for each $b \in M_{\beta+1} - M_\beta$ we have $bab^{-1} \in M_{\beta+1} - M_\beta$). Hence the set of conjugates of a has power λ^+, so the subgroup they generate is the whole group M. In other words the normal subgroup a generates is M, so M is simple.

The induction step 2.6. So M_α is given and we should define $M_{\alpha+1}$. Let $\{c_i : i < \lambda\}$ be a list of the elements of M_α. Let $\{\langle a_\beta, \gamma_\beta, b_\beta\rangle : \beta < \lambda\}$ be a list of all triples $\langle a, \gamma, b\rangle$, $b \in M_\alpha$, $\gamma \leq \alpha$, $a \in M_{\alpha+1} - M_\alpha$ ($M_{\alpha+1}$ is not yet defined, but $M_{\alpha+1} - M_\alpha$ is $A_\alpha = \{\xi : \lambda(1+\alpha) \leq \xi < \lambda(1+\alpha+1)\}$) and each triple appearing λ times. (This can be done by cardinality considerations.) Now we shall define groups L_β, $H_\beta (\beta < \lambda)$ (more accurately L_β^α, H_β^α) and later let $M_{\alpha+1} = \bigcup_{\beta<\alpha} L_\beta$.

We define them such that:

(a) $|L_\beta| < \lambda$, moreover $|L_\beta| \leq \aleph_0 + |\beta|$.

(b) L_β is a subset of $M_\alpha \cup A_\alpha$; $L_\beta \cap M_\alpha = H_\beta \leq H_{\beta+1} \leq M_\alpha$, and for limit $\delta < \lambda$, $L_\delta = \bigcup_{\beta<\delta} L_\beta$ so $H_\delta = \bigcup_{\alpha<\delta} H_\beta$.

(c) $c_\beta \in H_{\beta+1}$ (so $M_\alpha = \bigcup_{\beta<\lambda} H_\beta$) and $\lambda(1+\alpha)+\beta \in L_{\beta+1}$ (so $M_{\alpha+1}$ will have the appropriate set of elements). (c_β is from the list of elements of M_α.)

(d) If $a_\beta \in L_\beta$, $S_{\gamma_\beta} \subseteq M_\alpha$ then $b_\beta \in \langle S_{\gamma_\beta} \cap H_{\beta+1}, a_\beta\rangle$, in fact it is the product of length n_0 of elements of $(S_{\gamma_\beta} \cap H_{\beta+1}) \cup \{a_\beta\}$.

(e) H_β is a malnormal subgroup of L_β.

We define L_β, H_β by induction on $\beta : H_0$ is the trivial group, L_0 the free group with one generator. For limit β define by (b). Suppose we have defined for β and define for $\beta+1$. Now we can by Fact 2.1(i) find $x, y \in S_{\gamma_\beta}$ which are good fellows over H_β, and let $H_{\beta+1} = \langle H_\beta, x, y, b_\beta, c_\beta\rangle$. Clearly $H_{\beta+1}$ satisfies (c), (b), and we can define $L_{\beta+1}$ by Fact 2.4, so that (d), (e) holds.

It is easy to check that $M_{\alpha+1} = \bigcup_{\beta<\lambda} L_\beta$ is as required: part (i) as $H_\beta \leq_m L_\beta$ (and easy checking) part (ii) as for every $a \in M_{\alpha+1} - M_\alpha$ for some β_0, $a \in L_{\beta_0}$, and for every $\gamma \leq \alpha$, $b \in M_\alpha$, the triple $\langle a, \gamma, b\rangle$ is $\langle a_\beta, \gamma_\beta, b_\beta\rangle$ for many $\beta \geq \beta_0$, (as each triple appears λ times) so we can apply (d). Part (iii) and the condition on the set of elements of $M_{\alpha+1}$ holds by (b) and (c).

Statement 2.7. The proof works for $\lambda = \aleph_0$, too, the only changes being:

(A) In the construction 2.5 in (ii) we have to say "if $S_\gamma \subseteq M_\alpha$ is not included in a finitely generated subgroup of M_α".

(B) In the induction step 2.6 at the end we have to use Fact 2.2(ii) instead of 2.2(i); and in (a) we should assert that L_β, H_β are finitely generated and $\{\xi < \omega(1+\alpha+1): \xi \notin M_\alpha, \xi \notin L_\beta\}$ is infinite.

(C) In the construction 2.5 when we prove the construction works, we have to define $S = M^* \cap M_{\alpha(0)}$ somewhat more carefully. First of all we have to choose it so that it is not included in a finitely generated subgroup of $M_{\alpha(0)}$ which can be done by a Lowenheim–Skolem argument. However, a priori, maybe in M_β this is no longer true; but the following fact closes the gap.

Fact 2.8. Suppose $M_\alpha\,(\alpha < \delta)$ is an increasing continuous chain of groups, and $M_{\alpha+1}$ is defined from M_α as in 2.6 for $\lambda = \aleph_0$, i.e. $M_{\alpha+1} = \bigcup_{\beta<\omega} L^\alpha_\beta$, $L^\alpha_\beta \cap M_\alpha = H^\alpha_\beta$, H^α_β is a finitely generated subgroup of M_α (or even is included in such a subgroup) $M_\alpha = \bigcup_{\beta<\omega} H^\alpha_\beta$. *Then* if $\alpha < \delta$, and G a subgroup of M_α not included in a finitely generated subgroup of M_α, *then* G is not included in any finitely generated subgroup of M_δ (of course, we can replace group by algebra of some fixed kind).

Proof. We prove there is no finitely generated subgroup of $M_\beta\,(\beta \leqslant \delta)$ which includes G, by induction on β. For $\beta \leqslant \alpha$ this is a hypothesis, for β limit it is easy. For $\beta+1$, suppose $a_1, \ldots, a_k$ generates some such subgroup. Then for some n $a_1, \ldots, a_k$ are in L^β_n, hence $G \subseteq \langle a_1, \ldots, a_k \rangle \cap M_\alpha \subseteq L^\beta_n \cap M_\alpha = H_n$, so G is included in a finitely generated subgroup of M_β, contradiction.

Theorem 2.9. (1) *There is a Jonsson group of cardinality* $\aleph_1$.

(2) *This group is simple, and is a Jonsson semigroup.*

Proof. We first we state a definition and a fact.

Definition 2.10. (1) When $H \subseteq L$, $x \in L$ is *made over* H if for n, m natural numbers, $h_1, h_2 \in H$, $h_1 x^n h_2 = x^m$ implies $n = m$, $h_1 = h_2 = e$.

(2) H is a mad subgroup of L, and L is a mad extension of H, if every $x \in L - H$ is mad over H; and we write $H \subseteq_{md} L$.

Fact 2.11. Let $L^* = L *_H K$, and $H \leqslant_{md} L$, all of them countable torsion-free. Let $\{\langle b_n, c_n, z_n \rangle : n < \omega\}$ be a list of all triples $\langle b, c, z \rangle$, $b \in L - H$, $c \in K - H$, and $z \in K$. We can find natural numbers $k(n)$ $(n < \omega)$ such that the following holds.

Let R be the symmetrized closure of $\{r(c_n b_n^{k(2n)}, c_n b_n^{k(2n+1)}) z_n^{-1} : n < \omega\}$ where r is strongly 4000-random and N the normal closure of R, and $L^{**} = L^*/N$. Then

(i) R satisfies the small cancellation condition $C'(1/1000)$,

(ii) the natural maps $L^* \to L^{**}$ embed K and L, and the intersection of their images is the image of H,

(iii) $K \leqslant_{md} L^{**}$,

(iv) L^{**} is torsion-free.

Proof of 2.11. For each n, the classes $Hb_n^k H$ $(0 < k < \omega)$ are distinct (hence disjoint), because H is a mad subgroup of L. A similar assertion holds for $Hb_n^{-k} H$ $(0 < k < \omega)$. Hence we can define by induction on n, $k(n) > 0$ such that $2n + p \neq 2m + q$, n, m natural numbers, $p = 0, 1$, $q = 0, 1$, $h_1, h_2 \in H$ implies $h_1 b_n^{\pm k(2n+p)} h_2 \neq b_m^{\pm k(2m+q)}$ or, equivalently, $b_n^{\pm k(2n+p)} h_2 b_m^{\pm k(2m+q)} \neq h_1$.

Let us check each part:

(i) We use the notation of Definition 1.8, and let $g^m \cdots g^1 g_1 \cdots g_m = h_m \in H$, so $h_0 = e$, $g^{m+1} h_m g_{m+1} = h_{m+1}$, so by the choice of the $k(n)$, for some $r_n = r(c_n b_n^{k(2n)}, c_n h_n^{k(2n+1)}) z_n^{-1}$, g^*, g_* are cyclically reduced conjugations of r_n, r_n^{-1} respectively or of r_n^{-1}, r_n respectively. By the strong 4000-randomness we get the desired contradiction (like 1.13).

(ii) Follows from (i).

(iii) Suppose $x \in L^{**} - K$, $k_1 \in K$, $k_2 \in K$, and n, m are distinct natural nůmbers > 0, and $k_1 x^m k_2 = x^n$ and we shall get a contradiction.

Among the representations of x we choose one $y^{-1} z y$, $y = y_1 \cdots y_p$, $z = z_1 \cdots z_q$ (where $y_1 \cdots z_1 \cdots \in K \cup L$) with smallest $p + 2q$ (p, q natural numbers). So $y_p^{-1} \cdots y_1^{-1} z_1 \cdots z_q y_1 \cdots y_p$ is in canonical form except that we may put together $y_1^{-1} z_1$, $z_q y_1$, and $z_1 \cdots z_q$ is weakly cyclically reduced. [Otherwise $q > 1$ is odd, $z_q z_1 \in H$, so $x = (y_p^{-1} \cdots y_1^{-1} z_q^{-1})((z_q z_1 z_2) z_3 \cdots z_{q-1}(z_q y_1 \cdots y_p)$ so we can let $y' = z_q y_1 \cdots y_p$, $z' = (z_q z_1 z_2) z_3 \cdots z_{q-1})$. (Note $z_q z_1 z_2 \in L \cup K - H$) so $p' = p + 1$, $q' = q - 2$, contradicting the minimality of $p + 2q$).] Similarly $q > 1$ implies q is even; $y_1, \ldots, z_1 \cdots \notin H$.

As $x \in L^{**} - K$ clearly $q \geqslant 1$.

Note:

A) y, y^{-1}, z cannot contain more than half of a word from R. (As then we can decrease p without changing q or vice versa.)

B) $y^{-1}z$, zy cannot contain more than 9/10 of a word from R.

By symmetry suppose $z_{i+1}\cdots z_q y_1\cdots y_j$ is a subword of a word w from R, of length $>9|w|/10$, so w.l.o.g. $w = z_{i+1}\cdots z_q y_1\cdots y_j t$ (t a word $|t|\leq|w|/10$). Clearly

$$\begin{aligned}
x &= y_p^{-1}\cdots y_1^{-1}z_1\cdots z_q y_1\cdots y_p\\
&= (y_p^{-1}\cdots y_{j+1}^{-1})(y_j^{-1}\cdots y_1^{-1})(z_1\cdots z_i)(z_{i+1}\cdots z_q)(y_1\cdots y_j)(y_{j+1}\cdots y_p)\\
&= (y_p^{-1}\cdots y_{j+1}^{-1})[(y_j^{-1}\cdots y_1^{-1})(z_1\cdots z_i)t^{-1}](y_{j+1}\cdots y_p).
\end{aligned}$$

So we get a representation with $y' = y_{j+1}\cdots y_p$, $z' = y_j^{-1}\cdots y_1^{-1}z_1\cdots z_i t^{-1}$. So $p' = p - j$, $q' = j + i + |t^{-1}|$, hence

$$\begin{aligned}
(p+2q)-(p'+2q') &\geq (p+2q)-(p-j+2j+2i+2|t^{-1}|)\\
&= 2(q-i)-j-2|t^{-1}|\\
&\geq 2(q-i)-j-2|w|/10.
\end{aligned}$$

But $p+2q$ was minimal, hence $\leq p'+2q'$, hence $j \geq 2(q-i)-2|w|/10$. But also $j+(q-i)\geq 9|w|/10$, hence

$$3j/2 = j + j/2 \geq j + (q-i) - |w|/10 \geq 9|w|/10 - |w|/10 = 4|w|/5.$$

So $j > |w|(4\cdot 2/5\cdot 3) = |w|(8/15) > |w|/2$, contradiction.

C) zz cannot contain more than 9/10 of a word from R.

So suppose $z_{i+1}\cdots z_q z_1\cdots z_j$ is a subword of a word w from R of length $>9|w|/10$. So w.l.o.g. $w = z_{i+1}\cdots z_q z_1\cdots z_j\, t$ (t a word so $|t|<|w|/10$). Assume first $j<i$.

So

$$\begin{aligned}
x &= y_p^{-1}\cdots y_1^{-1}z_1\cdots z_q y_1\cdots y_p\\
&= (y_p^{-1}\cdots y_1^{-1})(z_q^{-1}\cdots z_{i+1}^{-1})(z_{i+1}\cdots z_q)(z_1\cdots z_j)(z_{j+1}\cdots z_q)(y_1\cdots y_p)\\
&= (y_p^{-1}\cdots y_1^{-1}z_q^{-1}\cdots z_{i+1}^{-1})(t^{-1}z_{j+1}\cdots z_i)(z_{i+1}\cdots z_q y_1\cdots y_p).
\end{aligned}$$

So let $y' = z_{i+1}\cdots z_q y_1\cdots y_p$, $z' = t^{-1}z_j\cdots z_i$. Then $x = (y')^{-1}z'y'$, and $p' \leq p + (q-i)$, $q' \leq |t^{-1}| + i - j \leq |w|/10 + i - j$. Again

$$\begin{aligned}
0 &\geq (p+2q)-(p'+2q')\\
&\geq (p+2q)-(p+(q-i)+2|w|/10+2(i-j))\\
&= q-i+2j-|w|/5.
\end{aligned}$$

So $q-i \leq |w|/5 - 2j$, but by the choice of w, i, j, t clearly $(q-i)+j \geq 9|w|/10$, hence $q-i \geq 9|w|/10 - j$. Those two inequalities imply $|w|/5-2j \geqslant 9|w|/10-j$, which is a contradiction (as $|w| \geqslant 1$, $j \geqslant 0$).

Now we are left with the case $j \geqslant i$, but then by the strong randomness of r, $j-i \leqslant |w|/1000$, so replace j by $i-8$, and repeat the same argument.

D) In B) and C) we can replace $9|w|/10$ by $|w|(9/10-1/1500)$.

We have assumed $n \neq m > 0$, $k_1 x^m k_2 = x^n$. We shall get weakly cyclically reduced forms of word which is e, and using 1.9 and A)–D) get a contradiction.

Case I. $q = 1$.

Notice $z_1 \in K-H \Rightarrow y_1 \in L-H$ by $p+2q$ minimality. Then $x^n = y_p^{-1} \cdots y_1^{-1} z_1^n y_1 \cdots y_p$.

If $k_1 = k_2 = e$ we get $z_1^{n-m} = e$ and as K, L are torsion free, $n = m$.

If $k_1 = e \neq k_2$, $m > n$ we get $y_p^{-1} \cdots y_1^{-1} z_1^{m-n} y_1 \cdots y_p k_2 = e = y_p^{-1} \cdots y_1^{-1} z^{m-n} y_1 \cdots y_{p-1}(y_p k_2)$.

As before, $z_1^{m-n} \neq e$. As $y_1 \cdots z_1 \cdots$ are in $K \cup L - H$, if $k_2 \in H$, $z^{m-n} \notin H$ then the word is in canonical form.

If $k_2 \in H$, $z^{m-n} \in H$, $y_1 \in L-H$, by the madness condition $w = y_p^{-1} \cdots y_2^{-1}(y_1^{-1} z^{m-n} y_1) y_2 \cdots y_{p-1}(y_p k_2)$ is in canonical form ($z^{m-n} \neq e$ as K is torsion free) when $p > 1$, and $(y_1^{-1} z^{m-n} y_1 h_2) \in L-H$ is in canonical form when $p = 1$. When $k_2 \notin H$ we have a similar situation. So in all cases in the word w is not e in L^*. As it is e it should be long, so we can make it weakly cyclically reduced by small changes and we get easy contradiction by the strong 4000-randomness.

The case $k_1, k_2 \neq e$ is similar.

Case II. $q > 1$ hence q is even.

We get that

$$e = k_1 x^m k_2 x^{-n} = k_1 y_p^{-1} \cdots y_1^{-1} z_1 \cdots z_q \cdots z_1 \cdots z_q y_1 \cdots y_p k_2$$
$$y_p^{-1} \cdots y_1^{-1} z_q^{-1} \cdots z_1^{-1} \cdots z_q^{-1} \cdots z_1^{-1} y_1 \cdots y_p =^{\mathrm{df}} w^*.$$

The word is not weakly cyclically reduced only, possibly in $k_1, k_2, y_1^{-1} z_1, z_q y_1, y_1^{-1} z_q^{-1}, z_1^{-1} y_1$. But if $k_1, k_2 \neq e$, the needed changes involve few letters (much less than a hundred) so we ignore them. Let w^* be the weakly cyclically reduced form. If $k_1 = k_2 = e$ we get $e = x^{m-n} = z_1 \cdots z_q \cdots z_1 \cdots z_q$. If $k_1 = e \neq k_2$

$$e = x^{m-n} k_2 = y_p^{-1} \cdots y_1^{-1} z_1 \cdots z_q \cdots z_1 \cdots z_q y_1 \cdots y_p k_2.$$

Both cases are easier, and we leave them to the reader.

So by 1.9 there is $t = t_1 \cdots t_l$ a part of w^* and of a word w from R $|t| \geqslant 997|w|/1000$.

If for some natural number $j > |w|/1000$, $1 < i < i < i + j < q$, t contains $z_i \cdots z_{i+j}$ from two copies of z, we get a contradiction to the strong 4000-randomness of r. Similarly if t contains $z_1 \cdots z_{i+j}$, $z_{i+j}^{-1} \cdots z_i^{-1}$. Also if for some $j > |w|/4000$, $1 < i < i + j < p$, t contains $y_{i+j}^{-1} \cdots y_i^{-1}$, and $y_i \cdots y_{i+j}$ (or two copies from one of them) we get a contradiction.

But t is a part of w^*, so looking at it we can see that if it intersects two among the four copies of y, y^{-1} in w^* with length $> |w|/4000$, we get a contradiction to the above. With the one left its intersection has length $\leqslant |w|/2$ (by A).

Necessarily the sum of its intersection with z^n, z^{-n} is $\geqslant$ $|w|(99/100 - 3/4000 - 1/2) > 496|w|/1000$ so with one of them, e.g. z^m, it is $\geqslant 2|w|/10$.

If the length of z is $< |w|/100$, then for some i, $1 < i < l$, for every j, $i \leqslant j < i + |w|/10$ t_j is equal to t_{j+q} (or t_{j+q-1}) contradicting the strong 4000-randomness of r. So the length of z is $> |w|/100$, hence t cannot contain two copies of z (see above).

So summing our observations we have the following possibilities only:

a) t is contained in $y^{-1}zz$, and is not disjoint to y^{-1}.

So its intersection with the second z has length $< |w|/1000$, so $y^{-1}z$ contains a subword of w of length $> (91/100 - 1/100)|w| = 9|w|/10$, contradiction to (B).

b) t is contained in zzy and is not disjoint to y.

The same contradiction.

c) t is contained in zz, so it is

$$z'_i z_{i+1} \cdots z_q z_1 \cdots z_{j-1} z'_j.$$

We get contradiction to (C).

d) t is contained in $zzyk_2y^{-1}zz$ (or similarly with k_1). We can get similar contradictions.

(iv) Left to the reader.

Proof of Theorem 2.9. The construction is as in 2.5, but the list $\{S_\gamma : \gamma < \lambda^+\}$ is no longer necessary; and we make the changes mentioned in 2.7 and assume all groups are torsion-free. The main point is that in the induction step 2.6 we use Fact 2.11 rather than Fact 2.4. So in 2.5, condition (ii) is replaced by

(ii)′ For every $a \in M_{\alpha+1} - M_\alpha$, for an $S \subseteq M_\alpha$ which is not included in a finitely generated subgroup of M_α, $M_\alpha \leqslant \langle a, S \rangle$. Let us prove that the definition of $M_{\alpha+1}$ (see 2.6) satisfies this.

So let $b \in M_\alpha$, and we should prove $b \in \langle a, S \rangle$. Clearly for big enough n, $a \in L_n$, $b \in H_n$; and we can find $m \geqslant n$ such that

$S \cap (H_{m+1} - H_m) \neq \emptyset$ (as $M_\alpha = \bigcup_{m<\omega} H_m$, but for no m is $S \subseteq H_m$). Now choose $c \in S \cap (H_{m+1} - H_m)$. As we have used Fact 2.11 in L_{n+1}, $b \in \langle a, c \rangle$; so we finish.

Proof of Theorem C. We assume $2^{\aleph_0} = \aleph_1$, and let M be the group from 2.7. Suppose $\underset{\sim}{U}$ is a non-trivial topology which makes M a topological group. Choose a neighborhood $U_0 \neq M$ of the unit, and define inductively neighbourhoods U_n of the unit such that $U_{n+1} \subseteq U_n$, and $x, y \in U_{n+1} \Rightarrow xy \in U_n$.

If U_{n_0} is uncountable, every element of M is the product of n_0 elements of it and hence belongs to U_0, so $U_0 = M$. Contradiction. If U_{n_0} is countable, it is a subset of M_α for some $\alpha < \omega_1$. Choose $x \in M - M_\alpha$; $xU_{n_0}x^{-1}$ is necessarily open, so $U_{n_0} \cap xU_{n_0}x^{-1}$ is a neighbourhood of the unit; but by the malnormality condition ($M_\alpha \leqslant_m M$, see 2.5(i)) this intersection contains the unit alone. So any singleton is an open set, so any subset of M is open, a contradiction.

We can conclude that $\underset{\sim}{U}$ is either $\{M, \emptyset\}$ or the discrete topology.

Proof of Theorem D. Let M be the group of Theorem 2.9. Clearly we cannot find a strictly increasing sequence of sub-semi-groups M_n, $M = \bigcup_{n<\omega} M_n$ (as some M_n is necessarily uncountable, so $M_n = M$). Hence if K is a field, $K(M)$ the group-ring, $K(M) = \bigcup_{n<\omega} A_n$, then $M = \bigcup_{n<\omega} (A_n \cap M)$. Now $A_n \cap M$ is a sub-semi-group of M. Clearly $M \not\subseteq A_n$, so $A_n \cap M$ is strictly increasing and get a contradiction to the previous observation.

Additional information

2.15. Simplicity of Jonsson groups

Macintyre has shown that in fact "almost" any Jonsson group is simple. More exactly, there is no Jonsson abelian group, hence M has centre $Z(M)$ of power $< |M|$. For any $a \in M - Z(M)$, its centralizer again (is by its choice $\neq M$, hence) has cardinality $< |M|$; so the number of conjugates of a is $|M|$, so the normal subgroup it generates is M. So $M/Z(M)$ is a Jonsson group, and is simple.

2.16. Jonsson groups with centre

This naturally raises the question whether there are Jonsson groups with a non-trivial centre. We can repeat the proofs and constructions of 2.1, 7, 9 by starting with an abelian group Z, $|Z| \leqslant \lambda$, and change the definitions and requirements accordingly. So all groups will extend

Z, and Z will be in their centre; $H \leqslant_m L$ means $a \in L - H$, $b \in H - Z \Rightarrow aba^{-1} \notin H$, etc. So the generalization will be easy.

2.17. On torsion Jonsson groups

The groups we constructed are torsion free, and moreover satisfy $x^n = y^n \Rightarrow x = y$ for $n \neq 0$. We may like to build torsion Jonsson groups. Now free products with "good" amalgamation for some torsion groups (i.e. the given groups and the result are torsion) exists (by Adian [1]) but not with small cancellation, so we can only hope.

2.18. Jonsson group in $\aleph_2$

The proof of Theorem 2.9 works also for $\lambda = \aleph_2$ without any *CH* but for any $\aleph_n$, we need more complicated amalgamations, and the situation is not clear.

Appendix

Another proof of Theorem 2.9 avoiding 2.11. This proof is due to G. Hesse.

Lemma. *Let H, K, L be groups such that $K \cap L = H$ and $H \leqslant_m L$, and let Q be a subset of $H \times (K \setminus H) \times (L \setminus H)^2$ satisfying:*

(i) *If $(h, a, b, b') \in Q$, then b, b' are good fellows over H.*

(ii) *If (h_1, a_1, b_1, b_1') and (h_2, a_2, b_2, b_2') are different elements of Q, then at least one of the pairs b_1, b_2 and b_1', b_2' is a pair of good fellows. Suppose $L^* = K *_H L$, $w(x_1, x_2)$ is the word $x_1x_2x_1x_2^2 \cdots x_1x_2^{80}$, $R \subseteq L^*$ is the symmetrized closure of $\{h^{-1}w(ba, b'a) \mid (h, a, b, b') \in Q\}$, N is the normal closure of R in L^* and $L^{**} = L^*/N$. Then:*

(1) *R satisfies $C'(1/10)$, and the natural map $\pi : L^* \to L^{**}$ embeds K and L, so that their intersection does not increase.*

(2) *$K \leqslant_m L^{**}$.*

(3) *If $a \in K \setminus H$, $b \in L \setminus H$ and $0 \leqslant m < n \in \omega$, then $(ab)^m$, $(ab)^n$ are good fellows over K in L^*.*

(4) *If $b_1, b_2 \in L \setminus H$ are good fellows over H, then b_1, b_2 are good fellows over K in L^{**}.*

Proof. (1) Let $g^* = g^m \cdots g^1$, $g_* = g_1 \cdots g_n$ be canonical representations of elements of R such that $g^*g_* \neq e$, and let $g^l \cdots g^1 g_1 \cdots g_l \in H$ for some $l \leqslant \min\{m, n\} =: \mu$. An easy computation shows $m, n \in \{k, k+1\}$, where $k = 6640$. We may assume that there are elements (h_1, a_1, b_1, b'_1) and (h_2, a_2, b_2, b'_2) of Q, canonical representations $h_1^{-1}w(b_1a_1, b'_1a_1) = u_1 \cdots u_k$ and $h_2^{-1}w(b_2a_2, b'_2a_2) = V_1 \cdots V_K$, $p, q \in \{1, \ldots, k\}$ and $\delta, \varepsilon \in \{-1, 1\}$ such that

(a) $g^i = u^{\delta}_{p-\delta i}$, $g_i = V^{\varepsilon}_{q+\varepsilon i}$ $(1 < i < \mu)$,

(b) $g^1 g^m \cdots g^{\mu} = u^{\delta}_{p-\delta} u^{\delta}_{p-\delta k} \cdots u^{\delta}_{p-\delta\mu}$, $g_{\mu} \cdots g_n g_1 = V^{\varepsilon}_{q+\varepsilon\mu} \cdots V^{\varepsilon}_{q+\varepsilon k} V^{\varepsilon}_{q+\varepsilon}$,

where $u_i = u_j$ and $V_i = V_j$ when $i \equiv j \bmod K$.

Case 1. $p \neq q$ or $\varepsilon = \delta$.

Then by (i) and the choice of w we can find $i \in \{2, \ldots, 664\}$ such that $g^i = u^{\delta}_{p-\delta i}$ and $g_i = V^{\varepsilon}_{q+\varepsilon i}$ are good fellows over H. Hence $g^i h g_i \notin H$ for every $h \in H$, and we have $l < i \leqslant 664 \leqslant \mu/10$.

Case 2. $p = q$ and $\varepsilon = -\delta$.

We find $i, j \in \{2, \ldots, 664\}$ such that w.l.o.g. $g^i = u^{-\varepsilon}_{p+\varepsilon i} = b_1^{-\varepsilon}$, $g_i = V^{\varepsilon}_{p+\varepsilon i} = b_2^{\varepsilon}$, $g^j = u^{-\varepsilon}_{p+\varepsilon j} = b_1^{1-\varepsilon}$ and $g_j = V^{\varepsilon}_{p+j} = b_2^{1-\varepsilon}$. If we assume $l \geqslant 664$, then none of the pairs b_1, b_2 and b'_1, b'_2 is a pair of good fellows. By (ii), $(h_1, a_1, b_1, b'_1) = (h_2, a_2, b_2, b'_2)$ and w.l.o.g. $u_i = V_i$ $(i = 1, \ldots, k)$. Choose $v \in \{2, 3\}$ and $b \in L \setminus H$ with $g^{\nu} = b^{-\varepsilon}$, $g_{\nu} = b^{\varepsilon}$. Since by assumption $b^{-\varepsilon}(g^{\nu-1} \cdots g^1 g_1 \cdots g_{\nu-1}) b^{\varepsilon} \in H$, by the malnormality of b over H we have $g^{\nu-1} \cdots g^1 g_1 \cdots g_{\nu-1} = e$. Therefore by (a) and (b):

$$\begin{aligned} g^* g_* &= g^m \cdots g^{\mu} g^{\mu-1} \cdots g^{\nu} g_{\nu} \cdots g_{\mu-1} g_{\mu} \cdots g_n \\ &= g^m \cdots g^{\mu} g_{\mu} \cdots g_n \\ &= (g^{\nu-1} \cdots g^1)^{-1} g^{\nu-1} \cdots g^1 g^m \cdots g^{\mu} g_{\mu} \cdots g_n g_1 \cdots g_{\nu-1} (g_1 \cdots g_{\nu-1})^{-1} \\ &= (g^{\nu-1} \cdots g^1)^{-1} (g_1 \cdots g_{\nu-1})^{-1} = e, \end{aligned}$$

a contradiction.

The embedding property follows now from 1.9.

The proof of (2) is exactly the same as the proof of Fact 2.4(ii).

(3) Suppose $n, n \in \omega$, $m \neq n$, $\varepsilon \in \{-1, 1\}$, $a_1, a_2 \in K$ and $(ab)^m a_1 (ab)^{\varepsilon \cdot n} a_2 = e$ in L^{**}. Let $w = g_1 \cdots g_l$ be a canonical representation of the element $(ab)^m a_1 (ab)^{\varepsilon \cdot n} a_2$ of L^*. Obviously there is at most one $i \in \{1, \ldots, l\}$ such that g_i, b are good fellows over H in L. Since $m \neq n$, we have $l \geqslant 1$. Thus by (1) and the Main Theorem 1.9, $g_1 \cdots g_l$ contains a long subword w_0 which is also a piece of some $w_1 \in R$. It follows from (i) that there are at least two $i \in \{1, \ldots, l\}$ such that g_i, b are good fellows over H in L, a contradiction.

The proof of (4) is left to the reader.

Proof of Theorem 2.9. As before M is constructed as the union of an increasing continuous chain $(M_{\alpha} \mid \alpha < \aleph_1)$ of countable groups, where no M_{α} is finitely generated If M_{α} has already been constructed, we choose a strictly increasing chain $(H_n \mid n \in \omega)$ of finitely generated subgroups such that $H_0 = \{e\}$ and $M_\alpha = \bigcup\{H_n \mid n \in \omega\}$. By induction, we now define a strictly increasing chain $(L_n \mid n < \omega)$ of groups with the following properties:

(a) $|L_n| = \aleph_0$.

(b) $L_n \cap M_\alpha = H <_{n \neq m} L_n$.

(c) If $a \in H_{n+1} \setminus H_n$, $b \in L_n \setminus H_n$, $0 \leq m < n < \omega$, then $(ab)^m$, $(ab)^n$ are good fellows over H_{n+1} in L_{n+1}.

(d) If $b_1, b_2 \in L_n \setminus H_n$ are good fellows over H_n, then b_1, b_2 are good fellows over H_{n+1} in L_{n+1}.

In order to define L_{n+1}, let $((h_i, a_i, a'_i, b'_i) \mid i \in \omega)$ be an enumeration of all (h, a, a', b') such that $h \in H_n$, $a \in H_{n+1} \setminus H_n$, $a' \in H_n \setminus H_m$ and $b' \in L_m \setminus H_m$ for some $m < n$. Using the induction hypothesis and the Lemma above, one can define a sequence $(b_i \mid i \in \omega)$ of elements of $L_n \setminus H_n$ such that:

(1) $b_i \in L_n \setminus H_n$.

(2) b_i is a product of elements of $\{a'_i, b'_i\}$.

(3) b_i, b'_i are good fellows over H.

(4) If $j < i$ then b_i and b_j are good fellows over H.

By induction hypothesis "$H_n \leq_m L_n$" and by the lemma, the symmetrized closure R of $\{h_i^{-1} \cdot w(b_i a_i, b'_i a_i) \mid i \in \omega\}$ satisfies C′(1/10) in $L^*_{n+1} := H_{n+1} *_{H_n} L_n$, and we may define $L_{n+1} := L^*_{n+1}/N$, where N is the normal closure of R in L^*_{n+1} and w.l.o.g. $L_{n+1} \cap M_\alpha = H_{n+1}$. The desired properties of L_{n+1} follows from the lemma. This concludes the main step of our construction, and we put $M_{\alpha+1} = \bigcup\{L_n \mid n \in \omega\}$.

Suppose now that S is an uncountable subset of $M = \bigcup\{M_\alpha \mid \alpha < \aleph_1\}$ and h is an element of M. Then there is an $\alpha < \aleph_1$ such that $S \cap (M_{\alpha+1} \setminus M_\alpha) \neq q$ and $S \cap M_\alpha$ contained in no finitely generated subgroup of M_α.

Choose $m < n < \omega$ and $a, a', b' \in S$ such that $h \in H_n$, $a \in H_{n+1} \setminus H_n$, $a' \in H_n \setminus H_m$ and $b' \in L_m \setminus H_m$, where the groups H_i, L_i are as in the construction of $M_{\alpha+1}$. By construction, h is a product of elements of $\{a, a', b'\}$ in L_{n+1} and hence in M.

References

[1] S.I. Adian, Periodical products of groups, Trudy Mat. Inst. Steklov Vol. 142 (1976) (dedicated to 85th birthday of I.M. Vinogradov).

[2] V.I. Arnautov, Non-discrete topologizability of infinite commutative rings, Soviet Math. Dokl. 11 (1970) 1307–1309.

[3] V.I. Arnautov, Nondiscrete topologizability of countable rings, Soviet Math. Dokl. 11 (1970) 423–426.

[4] L.A. Bokut, Imbeddings in simple algebras, Algebra and Logica, 1976, No. 2.

[5] C.C. Chang and H.J. Keisler, Model Theory (North-Holland Publishing Co., Amsterdam, 1973).
[6] P. Erdos, A. Hajnal and R. Rado, Partition relations for cardinal numbers, Acta Math. Acad. Sci. Hungar. 16 (1965) 93–196.
[7] J. Hanson, An infinite groupoid which admits only trivial topologies, Amer. Math. Monthly 74 (1967) 586–589.
[8] A. Kertsz and T. Szele, On the existence of non-discrete topologies in infinite abelian groups, Publ. Math. Debrecn 3 (1953) 187–189.
[9] S. Koppellberg and J. Tits, Comptes Rendus, 279, serie A, 1974, p. 583.
[10] A. Macintyre, Existentially closed structures and Jensen's principle, Israel J. Math. 25 (1976) 202–210.
[11] R. McKenzie, On semigroups whose proper subsemigroups have lesser power, Algebra Universales 1 (1971) 21–25.
[12] K.P. Podewski, Topologisierung algebraischer strukturen, a preprint.
[13] G. Sabbagh, Sur les groupes qui ne sont réunion d'une suite croissante de sous-groupes proper, C.R. Acad. Sc. Paris Vol. 280, 766–Series A.
[14] P.E. Schupp, A survey of small cancellation theory, in: Word problems, Decision problems and the Burnside problem in group theory (Boone, Cannomito and Lyndon eds. (North-Holland Publ. Co., Amsterdam, 1973) pp. 569–590.
[15] P.E. Schupp, Small cancellation theory over free products with amalgamation, Math. Annal 193 (1971) 255–264.
[16] S.P. Strunkor, Subgroups of periodic groups, Soviet Math. Dold 7 (1968) 1201–1203.
[17] S. Shelah, Essentially closed groups in $\aleph_1$, Submitted to Bull. of the Greek Math. Soc.
[18] A.A. Markov, On free topological groups, C.R. (Doklady), Acad. Sci. USSR, (N.S.) 31 (1941) 299–301. Bull. Acad. Sci. USSR Ser. Math. [Izvestya Akad. Nauk., SSSR] 9 (1945) 3–64 (Russian, English summary). English transl., Amer. Math. Soc. Translation No. 30 (1950) 11–88; reprint Amer. Math. Soc. Transl. (1) 8 (1962) 195–273.
[19] A.A. Markov, On unconditionally closed sets, Matematiceskii zbornik, 18 (60), No. 1 (1946) 3–28 (Russian, English summary).

S.I. Adian, W.W. Boone, G. Higman, eds., Word Problems II
© North-Holland Publishing Company (1980) 395–400

THE WORD AND TORSION PROBLEMS FOR COMMUTATIVE THUE SYSTEMS

H. SIMMONS
Department of Mathematics, University of Aberdeen, Aberdeen

In this note I give a proof of the following result.

Theorem. *There are primitive recursive algorithms WPA, TPA such that for each commutative Thue system $A = (X; R)$ and words U, V on the alphabet X of A,*

(a) *WPA will decide whether or not $U = V$ in A and if so will produce an A-transformation of U to V.*

(b) *TPA will decide whether or not there is an integer $k \geqslant 1$ such that $U^k = \emptyset$ in A (where $\emptyset$ is the empty word) and if so will produce such a k and an A-transformation of U^k to $\emptyset$.*

In more concise but less precise language this shows that the word problem and the torsion problem for finitely presented commutative semigroups are uniformly solvable in a strong sense.

The solvability of this word problem has been known to some people for some time (for instance it follows easily from the residual finiteness of f.p. commutative semigroups), however it has not yet achieved the doubtful status of 'folklore'. In fact the problem has been discussed recently in the Queries column of the Notices AMS, (see [0]). The response by Schein in [0] gives several references to earlier work by Russian authors on the algebraic structure of commutative semigroups and related decision problems. In the late 1950s S. Kochen also found a positive solution to the word problem for commutative semigroups. The method given here (which is essentially the same as the one sketched by Bergman in [0]) was shown to me (around 1964) by J. Shepherdson, and is derived from an argument used in [3]. A similar method is used in [4] to solve the corresponding problem for commutative rings.

I am grateful to W. Boone for suggesting that, because of its simplicity, the method ought to be written up.

Let $A = (X; R)$ be some fixed (but arbitrary) commutative Thue system. We will describe algorithms which solve the word problem and torsion problem for A. By inspection of these algorithms it will be clear that they are primitive recursive and uniform in A, and so we will obtain the above result.

Let

$$X = \{x_1, \dots, x_n\}$$

and let the relations of A be

$$U_1 = V_1, \dots, U_r = V_r$$

(so that $U_1, \dots, U_r, V_1, \dots, V_r$ are words on the alphabet X). We may regard $x_1, \dots, x_n$ not only as the generating letters of A but also as the indeterminates in the polynomial ring $D = Q[x_1, \dots, x_n]$, and hence each word W on X may be construed as a monomial in D. (The empty word $\emptyset$ is construed as the identity 1 of D.) This means we may consider the polynomials

$$f_1 = U_1 - V_1, \dots, f_r = U_r - V_r$$

of D (and the corresponding ideal $\mathscr{A} = (f_1, \dots, f_r)$ of D).

Now let U, V be arbitrary words on X and let $f = U - V$ be the corresponding polynomial of D. The following lemma reduces the word problem for A to a problem concerning polynomials of D.

Reduction lemma. *Let $A, f_1, \dots, f_r, \mathscr{A}, U, V, f$ be as above.*

(a) *The following are equivalent.*

(i) *$U = V$ in A.*

(ii) *$f \in \mathscr{A}$ in D, that is there are polynomials $g_1, \dots, g_r$ of D such that*

(1) $$f = g_1 f_1 + \cdots + g_r f_r$$

holds.

(b) *There is a primitive recursive algorithm which, when given polynomials $g_1, \dots, g_r$ of D such that* (1) *holds, will produce an A-transformation of U to V.*

Proof. In this proof it is convenient to use '$=$' for equality of words in A and '$\equiv$' for equality of polynomials in D.

Since A is a Thue system (not just a semi-Thue system) we may assume that A is symmetric, that is, for each relation $U_i = V_i$ of A, $V_i = U_i$ is also a relation. In other words, for each $i \in \{1, \dots, r\}$ there is some $j \in \{1, \dots r\}$ such that $V_i \equiv U_j$, $U_i \equiv V_j$. This means that $U = V$

in A if and only if there is a sequence $i_1, \dots i_s$ of members of $\{1, \dots, r\}$ and a sequence $W_1, \dots, W_s$ of words on X such that

$$
\begin{aligned}
U &\equiv W_1 U_{i_1} \\
& \qquad W_1 V_{i_1} \equiv W_2 U_{i_2} \\
& \qquad\qquad W_2 V_{i_2} \equiv \\
& \qquad\qquad\qquad \ddots \\
& \qquad\qquad\qquad \equiv W_s U_{i_s} \\
& \qquad\qquad\qquad W_s V_{i_s} \equiv V.
\end{aligned} \tag{2}
$$

Let us first prove (a: (i) $\Rightarrow$ (ii)).

Suppose $U = V$ in A so there is a situation (2) above. Then in D we have

$$
\begin{aligned}
U &\equiv W_1 U_{i_1} \\
&\equiv W_1 f_{i_1} + W_1 V_{i_1} \\
&\equiv W_1 f_{i_1} + W_2 U_{i_2} \\
&\equiv W_1 f_{i_1} + W_2 f_{i_2} + W_2 V_{i_2} \\
&\ \vdots \\
&\equiv W_1 f_{i_1} + \cdots + W_s f_{i_s} + V \\
&\equiv g_1 f_1 + \cdots + g_r f_r + V
\end{aligned}
$$

where $g_1, \dots, g_r$ are suitable polynomials built up from the monomials $W_1, \dots, W_s$. Notice that these polynomials $g_1, \dots, g_r$ have integer coefficients. This verifies (ii).

Now let us prove (a; (ii) $\Rightarrow$ (i)) and (b).

Suppose we are given polynomials $g_1, \dots, g_r$ such that (1) holds. Thus we can find an integer $m \geqslant 0$ and polynomials $h_1, \dots, h_r$ with integer coefficients such that

$$(m + 1)f \equiv h_1 f_1 + \cdots + h_r f_r.$$

This gives us an equality

$$(m + 1)(U - V) \equiv \sum m_j W_j (U_{i_j} - V_{i_j})$$

where $W_1, \dots, W_k$ are monomials (words on X) and $m_1, \dots, m_k$ are integers. Here and below the range of Σ and the range of the index j is $\{1, 2, \dots, k\}$.

Since A is symmetric we may assume that each $m_j \geqslant 0$. Thus we can rewrite this equality as

$$(3) \qquad (m+1)U + \sum m_j W_j V_{i_j} \equiv (m+1)V + \sum m_j W_j U_{i_j}.$$

In the following argument we should remember that the empty word is treated as the identity of D.

Consider the monomial U occurring explicitly on the left of (3). Since all the coefficients are positive U must occur explicitly on the right of (3), so either $U \equiv V$ (in which case we are done) or there is some j (say $j = 1$) such that $U \equiv W_1 U_{i_1}$. But then we have

$$(4) \qquad mU + W_1 V_{i_1} + \sum m'_j W_j V_{i_j} \equiv (m+1)V + \sum m'_j W_j U_{i_j}$$

where

$$m'_j = \begin{cases} m_1 - 1 & \text{if } j = 1 \\ m_j & \text{if } j \neq 1. \end{cases}$$

Now consider the monomial $W_1 V_{i_1}$ occurring explicitly on the left of (4). As above $W_1 V_{i_1}$ must occur explicitly on the right of (4), so either $W_1 V_{i_1} \equiv V$ (and we are done) or there is some j (say $j = 2$) such that $W_1 V_{i_1} \equiv W_2 U_{i_2}$. But then we have

$$mU + W_2 V_{i_2} + \sum m''_j W_j V_{i_j} \equiv (m+1)V + \sum m''_j W_j U_{i_j}$$

for some suitable positive integers $m''_1, \ldots, m''_k$.

Now consider the monomial $W_2 V_{i_2}$ occurring explictly ...

Clearly this procedure can continue for no more than $m_1 + \cdots + m_k$ steps, and when the procedure stops we have built up an A-transformation (2).

This completes the proof of the lemma.

Before we continue with the proof of the Theorem we note that M. Rabin has observed (in a letter to Shepherdson) that the above argument with Hilbert's basis theorem implies that each finitely generated commutative semigroup is finitely presentable. To see this let

$$(x_1, \ldots, x_n; \{U_i = V_i : i \in I\})$$

be a presentation of such a semigroup A (so the index set I may be infinite). As above let D be the polynomial domain $Q[x_1, \ldots, x_n]$ and let $\mathcal{A}$ be the ideal of D generated by $\{U_i - V_i : i \in I\}$. Then as in the lemma, for each two words U, V on $\{x_1, \ldots, x_n\}$

$$U = V \text{ in } A \Leftrightarrow U - V \in \mathcal{A}.$$

But (since D is noetherian) $\mathcal{A}$ is finitely generated and so there is some finite $J \subseteq I$ such that $\{U_i - V_i : i \in J\}$ generates $\mathcal{A}$. Thus we see that

$$(x_1, \dots, x_n; \{U_i = V_i : i \in J\})$$

is a finite presentation of A.

Now that we have the reduction lemma the algorithm *WPA* (of the theorem) is constructed easily using the following proposition of G. Hermann [1]. A more readable proof of this proposition can be found in [2].)

Proposition. There is a primitive recursive function $m(\cdot,\cdot)$ such that for each polynomial $f, f_1, \dots, f_r$ of $D = Q[x_1, \dots, x_n]$ of degrees at most d, if there are polynomials $g_1, \dots, g_r$ satisfying (1) then there are such polynomials of degrees at most $m(d, n)$.

To complete the proof of the theorem we must obtain the algorithm *TPA*. This algorithm is constructed easily using *WPA* and the following lemma.

Lemma. *Let $f, f_1, \dots, f_r$ be polynomials of $D = Q[x_1, \dots, x_n]$ of degrees at most d. Let $\mathcal{A}$ be the ideal of D generated by $f_1, \dots, f_r$ and let $m = m(d+1, n+1)+1$. Then there is an integer $k \geq 1$ such that $f^k \in \mathcal{A}$ if and only if $f^m \in \mathcal{A}$.*

Proof. Suppose there is some integer k with $f^k \in \mathcal{A}$. We introduce a new indeterminate y and consider the polynomials

$$1 - yf, f_1, \dots, f_r$$

of $D[y]$. These polynomials have no common root (since $f^k \in \mathcal{A}$) and so, by the Nullstellensatz, there are polynomials $h, h_1, \dots, h_r$ of $D[y]$ such that

$$1 = h(1 - yf) + h_1 f_1 + \cdots + h_r f_r. \tag{5}$$

The above proposition allows us to assume that each of $h, h_1, \dots, h_r$ has degree at most $m(d+1, n+1) = m - 1$.

We now replace y throughout (5) by y^{-1} and, after multiplying up by y^m, we obtain

$$y^m = h'(y - f) + h'_1 f_1 + \cdots + h'_r f_r$$

where $h', h'_1, \dots, h'_r$ are some suitable polynomials of $D[y]$. The desired result is now achieved by substituting f for y.

This concludes the proof of the theorem.

When I explained the above proof to Boone he suggested that a similar technique might solve the word problem for commutative semi-Thue systems. I have been unable to decide whether or not this is so. However, for such systems there is a corresponding reduction lemma. The crucial observation is that a semi-Thue system may not be symmetric (for otherwise it is a Thue system) and so, in the above proof, we must assume that the integers m_j are positive. This means that the given polynomials $g_1, \ldots, g_r$ must have positive coefficients. Thus a positive solution to the following problem will show that the word problem for commutative semi-Thue systems is solvable.

Problem. Is there an algorithm which, given polynomials $f, f_1, \ldots, f_r$ of $D = Q[x_1, \ldots, x_n]$, will decide whether or not there are polynomials $g_1, \ldots, g_r$ of D, each with positive coefficients, such that (1) holds.

Added 10 October 1977: I am grateful to the referee A.L. Semenov for pointing out that the word problem for commutative semigroups is solved also in [5]. The method used in [5] gives an algorithm which is faster than the algorithm given here.

References

[0] American Math. Soc. Notices 23 (1976) 80, 126, 223.

[1] G. Hermann, Die Frage der Endlich Vielen Schritte der Theorie der Polynomideale, Math. Ann. 95 (1926) 736 and 788.

[2] A. Seidenberg, Constructions in algebra, Americal Math. Soc. Transactions 197 (1974) 273–313.

[3] J.C. Shepherdson, Inverses and zero divisors in matrix rings, London Math. Soc. Proceedings (3) 1 (1951) 71–85.

[4] H. Simmons, The solution of a decision problem for several classes of rings, Pacific J. Math. 34 (1970) 547–557.

[5] E. Cardoza, R. Lipton and A.R. Meyer, Exponential space complete problems for Petri nets and commutative semigroups, 8th Ann. ACM Symp. on Theory of Computing, May 1976, pp. 50–54.

S.I. Adian, W.W. Boone, G. Higman, eds., Word Problems II

EMBEDDINGS INTO FINITELY GENERATED SIMPLE GROUPS WHICH PRESERVE THE WORD PROBLEM

Richard J. THOMPSON
University of California, Berkeley

The main result of this paper is that a finitely generated group has a solvable word problem if and only if there is an embedding of the group (such that two elements not conjugate in the original group will not be conjugate in the embedding group) into a finitely generated simple group which is a subgroup of a finitely presented group. It is known that a finitely generated simple group is a subgroup of a finitely presented group if and only if it has a recursively enumerable set of defining relations, and that it has a recursively enumerable set of defining relations if and only if it has a solvable word problem. Boone and Higman recently obtained a result similar to the given result, but without any reference to conjugacy and with no requirement that the simple group be finitely generated. The construction used was quite different from those used here, the simple group being obtained as an increasing union of groups, making it infinitely generated. It should be noted that the constructions of §2 and §3 can be applied in fact to arbitrary groups or to arbitrary countable groups (or groups which are just isomorphic to permutation groups of countable sets) respectively, so that the fact that these embeddings preserve the solvability of the word problem is only an incidental consequence of their well-behaved character. In §4 the constructions of the previous sections will be put together to obtain the main result and some subsidiary results (including some old ones not concerned with the word problem); outside of §4 the only role recursiveness will play is in our remarking that certain procedures are effective (where we will rely on Church's thesis).

§0. Preliminaries

The notation used will be much as in [6]. Thus the set of all natural numbers is denoted by ω, while every natural number n is considered to be identical with the set $\{0, 1, \ldots, n-1\}$ and (given two sets X and

Y) ${}^YX$ denotes the set of all functions from Y into X. However, here we will be concerned with ω_2 (the set of all infinite binary sequences of length ω) and its subsets, rather than with ${}^\omega\omega$. By ${}^{\underset{\smile}{\omega}}2$ is meant the set of all finite binary sequences; thus it is the union of the collection of all sets ${}^n2$, for $n \in \omega$. The Greek letters ρ, σ, and τ will be used to designate finite binary sequences, and the letters α, β, and γ will be used to designate infinite binary sequences. The *length* of $\sigma \in {}^{\underset{\smile}{\omega}}2$ will be the unique $n \in \omega$ such that $\sigma \in {}^n2$, and for this n we can write $\sigma = \langle\sigma(0), \sigma(1), \ldots, \sigma(n-1)\rangle$ (where no confusion results, this may be written as $\langle\sigma(0)\sigma(1)\cdots\sigma(n-1)\rangle$ or even $\sigma(0)\sigma(1)\cdots\sigma(n-1)$); if τ is a sequence of length m, the concatenation of σ with τ will be the sequence $\langle\sigma(0), \ldots, \sigma(n-1), \tau(0), \ldots, \tau(m-1)\rangle$, which will be designated by $\sigma^\frown\tau$ (or even by $\sigma\tau$, when no confusion results). In fact, for $\mu \in {}^{\underset{\smile}{\omega}}2 \cup {}^\omega 2$ and $\sigma \in {}^{\underset{\smile}{\omega}}2$ of length n the sequence $\sigma^\frown\mu$ will be the function such that $(\sigma^\frown\mu)(i) = \sigma(i)$ for $i < n$ and $(\sigma^\frown\mu)(i) = \mu(i-n)$ for $i \geqslant n$, with $\sigma^\frown\mu \in {}^{\underset{\smile}{\omega}}2$ if $\mu \in {}^{\underset{\smile}{\omega}}2$. For $\mu \in {}^{\underset{\smile}{\omega}}2 \cup {}^\omega 2$ the formula $\sigma \subset \mu$ will be used to assert that for some $\nu \in {}^{\underset{\smile}{\omega}}2 \cup {}^\omega 2$, $\sigma^\frown\nu = \mu$; we will say that σ is an initial part of μ (or μ begins with σ). The notation $\sigma^{(n)}$ will be used for the sequence obtained by concatenating σ with itself n times (σ^n may be used when the context is clear). Thus $\langle 01^3 0^2\rangle$ is $\langle 011100\rangle$.

In the composition of permutations (and, unlike [6], of functions in general) we will take $(fg)(i)$ to be the same as $g(f(i))$. If x and y are two elements of a given group, their commutator is the element $[x, y] = xyx^{-1}y^{-1}$; so $[x, y] = 1$ if and only if x and y commute (here "1" denotes the identity element of the group). The empty set is $\emptyset$.

Definition 0.1. Fr is the set of all non-empty subsets K of ${}^\omega 2$ such that for every finite binary sequence σ and $\alpha \in {}^\omega 2$, $\sigma^\frown\alpha \in K$ if and only if $\alpha \in K$. The elements of Fr will be called the *finitely replaceable* sets.

For $K \in \mathrm{Fr}$, the *interval* in K determined by σ is $\{\alpha \in K : \sigma \subset \alpha\}$; when K is clear from the context this set will be designated by $[\sigma]$.

Definition 0.2. For $K \in \mathrm{Fr}$, $\mathrm{Pa}(K)$ (the *partition group* of K) is the group of permutations of K whose members are the permutations F such that for every $\alpha \in K$ there are $\sigma, \tau \in {}^{\underset{\smile}{\omega}}2$ with $\sigma \subset \alpha$ and, for every $\beta \in K$, $F(\sigma^\frown\beta) = \tau^\frown\beta$.

It is not hard to justify this definition by showing that if F and G satisfy the defining conditions then so do the permutations FG and F^{-1}. Let us say that a set $\Sigma \subseteq {}^{\underset{\smile}{\omega}}2$ is a *partition set* for $K \in \mathrm{Fr}$ provided that every $\alpha \in K$ begins with exactly one element belonging to Σ (in other words, provided the intervals $[\sigma]$, $\sigma \in \Sigma$, form a partition of K). For example, $\{\langle 0\rangle, \langle 1\rangle\}$ is a partition set for every $K \in \mathrm{Fr}$.

Theorem 0.3. *For $K \in \mathrm{Fr}$ let Σ_0, Σ_1, ψ be any triple where Σ_0 and Σ_1 are partition sets for $K \in \mathrm{Fr}$ and ψ is a one-one map from Σ_0 onto Σ_1. Then the formulas $F(\sigma^\frown\beta) = \psi(\sigma)^\frown\beta$ (for $\sigma \in \Sigma_0$ and $\beta \in K$) define a permutation F which belongs to* Pa(K). *Moreover, every member of* Pa(K) *can be put in this form, with the further property that for any $\sigma, \tau \in {}^{\underset{\smile}{\omega}}2$ such that for every $\gamma \in {}^{\omega}2$ $F(\sigma^\frown\gamma) = \tau^\frown\gamma$ there exists some $\rho \subset \sigma$ with $\rho \in \Sigma_0$.*

Proof. The first statement is clear from Definitions 0.1 and 0.2. On the other hand, suppose $F \in \mathrm{Pa}(K)$, where $K \in \mathrm{Fr}$. Then we let $\psi'(\sigma, \tau)$ (for $\sigma, \tau \in {}^{\underset{\smile}{\omega}}2$) mean that $F(\sigma^\frown\beta) = \tau^\frown\beta$ whenever $\beta \in K$. We put

$$\Sigma_0 = \{\sigma\colon \text{For all } \rho, \rho = \sigma \text{ if and only if for some } \tau, \psi'(\rho, \tau)\ \&\ \rho \subset \sigma\}.$$

As ψ' is a function (taking $\psi'(\sigma, \tau)$ and $\psi'(\sigma) = \tau$ to have the same meaning), if we let ψ be the restriction of ψ' to Σ_0, and Σ_1 be the range of ψ, we can see that Σ_0, Σ_1, ψ and F are related as required by the theorem.

Note that ${}^{\omega}2 \in \mathrm{Fr}$. Because of the compactness of the Cantor space ${}^{\omega}2$, we have:

Proposition 0.4. *Every partition set of ${}^{\omega}2$ is finite.*

Proposition 0.5. *For $K \in \mathrm{Fr}$, the finite partition sets of K coincide with the partition sets of ${}^{\omega}2$.*

Proof. First, every partition set of ${}^{\omega}2$ is finite, by Proposition 0.4, and from the definition, every partition set of ${}^{\omega}2$ is a partition set of K. On the other hand, if Σ is a finite partition set of $K \in \mathrm{Fr}$ there will be some $n \in \omega$ such that every element of Σ is of length $\leqslant n$. Given $\alpha \in {}^{\omega}2$ there is some $\tau \in {}^{\underset{\smile}{\omega}}2$ of length n such that $\alpha = \tau^\frown\beta$ for some $\beta \in {}^{\omega}2$. Now pick $\gamma \in K$. As $K \in \mathrm{Fr}$, $\tau^\frown\gamma \in K$ so that for some $\sigma \in \Sigma$, $\sigma \subset \tau^\frown\gamma$. As σ is of length $\leqslant n$ and τ is of length n, $\sigma \subset \tau$ and so $\sigma \subset \tau^\frown\beta = \alpha$. So Σ is also a partition set of ${}^{\omega}2$.

Proposition 0.6. *If Σ is a finite subset of ${}^{\underset{\smile}{\omega}}2$ such that $[\sigma] \cap [\tau] = \emptyset$ whenever $\sigma, \tau \in \Sigma$ and $\sigma \neq \tau$, then Σ can be extended to a finite partition set Σ^* for ${}^{\omega}2$.*

Proof. Given Σ as in the proposition, let $\Sigma^* = \Sigma \cup \{\rho$: For every ρ', if $\rho' \subset \rho$ and for every $\sigma \in \Sigma$, $[\sigma] \cap [\rho'] = \emptyset$, then $\rho' = \rho$, and for every $\sigma \in \Sigma$, $[\sigma] \cap [\rho] = \emptyset\}$. If $\mu, \nu \in \Sigma^*$ and $\mu \neq \nu$, then $[\mu] \cap [\nu] = \emptyset$. This is clear from the hypothesis concerning Σ and the definition of Σ^*, unless $\mu, \nu \notin \Sigma$. But, in that case, if $[\mu] \cap [\nu] \neq \emptyset$ then either $\mu \subset \nu$ or else $\nu \subset \mu$, which requires $\mu = \nu$ by the definition of Σ^*. As Σ is finite there is some $n \in \omega$ such that every element of Σ is of length $\leqslant n$. Now, for every $\rho \in {}^{\underset{\smile}{\omega}}2$ of length n, there is some $\rho' \in \Sigma^*$ such that $\rho' \subset \rho$. (If $[\sigma] \cap [\rho] \neq \emptyset$ for some $\sigma \in \Sigma$ we can choose $\rho' = \sigma$, as every member of Σ has length $\leqslant n$; otherwise we can take ρ' to be that initial part of ρ of smallest length such that $[\sigma] \cap [\rho'] = \emptyset$ for every $\sigma \in \Sigma$.) This (with the earlier result) implies that every element of Σ^* has length $\leqslant n$ so that Σ^* is finite, and also implies that for every $\alpha \in {}^{\omega}2$ there exists $\rho' \in \Sigma^*$ with $\alpha \in [\rho']$ (as $\alpha = \rho^\frown\beta$ for some $\beta \in {}^{\omega}2$ and $\rho \in {}^{\underset{\smile}{\omega}}2$ of length n, and if $\rho' \subset \rho$ then $\alpha \in [\rho']$). Thus Σ^* is a finite partition set.

Proposition 0.7. *If $K \in \mathrm{Fr}$ and $F \in \mathrm{Pa}(K)$ is not the identity, then for some $\sigma, \tau \in {}^{\underset{\smile}{\omega}}2$ such that $[\sigma] \cap [\tau] = \emptyset$ (in K) for all $\alpha \in K$, $F(\sigma^\frown\alpha) = \tau^\frown\alpha$. Further, if Σ_0, Σ_1, ψ is any triple where Σ_0 and Σ_1 are partition sets for K, ψ is a one-one map from Σ_0 onto Σ_1, and $F(\rho^\frown\beta) = \psi(\rho)^\frown\beta$ for every $\rho \in \Sigma_0$ and $\beta \in K$, then σ and τ can be chosen so that $\sigma \in \Sigma_0$, $\tau \in \Sigma_1$, and $\psi(\sigma) = \tau$.*

Proof. In view of Theorem 0.3, it is enough to prove the last statement. If F is not the identity then for some $\sigma' \in \Sigma_0$, $\sigma' \neq \psi(\sigma')$. If, in K, $[\sigma'] \cap [\psi(\sigma')] = \emptyset$, then we can set $\sigma = \sigma'$, $\tau = \psi(\sigma')$. Otherwise, either $\sigma' \subset \psi(\sigma')$ or $\psi(\sigma') \subset \sigma'$ If $\psi(\sigma') \subset \sigma'$, then as $\psi(\sigma') \neq \sigma'$ we have for $\gamma \in K$ that exactly one of $\psi(\sigma')^\frown\langle 0\rangle^\frown\gamma$ and $\psi(\sigma')^\frown\langle 1\rangle^\frown\gamma$ belongs to $[\sigma']$ in K. As Σ_0 is a partition set for K, the other of these belongs to some interval $[\mu]$ in K, where $\mu \in \Sigma_0$ is such that $\psi(\sigma') \subset \mu$, but $\mu \neq \sigma'$. Then we can take $\sigma = \mu$, $\tau = \psi(\mu)$, because $[\psi(\mu)] \cap [\psi(\sigma')] = \emptyset$ in K (as ψ is one-one and Σ_1 is a partition set for K) and $[\mu] \subseteq [\psi(\sigma')]$ in K (as $\psi(\sigma') \subset \mu$) so that $[\mu] \cap [\psi(\mu)] = \emptyset$. If $\sigma' \subset \psi(\sigma')$, the same argument applied to F^{-1} shows that for some $\mu \in \Sigma_1$, $[\mu] \cap [\psi^{-1}(\mu)] = \emptyset$, and we can take $\sigma = \psi^{-1}(\mu)$, $\tau = \mu$.

Proposition 0.8. *If $K \in \mathrm{Fr}$ and η is the mapping with domain $\mathrm{Pa}({}^{\omega}2)$ such that, for $F \in \mathrm{Pa}({}^{\omega}2)$, $\eta(F)$ is the restriction of F to K, then η is an isomorphism from $\mathrm{Pa}({}^{\omega}2)$ into $\mathrm{Pa}(K)$.*

Proof. Given $K \in \mathrm{Fr}$ and η as in the proposition, by Theorem 0.3 and

Proposition 0.5 we see that η maps $\mathrm{Pa}({}^\omega 2)$ into $\mathrm{Pa}(K)$. For $\alpha \in K$ and $F, G \in \mathrm{Pa}({}^\omega 2)$ we have (as $F(\alpha) \in K$ if $\alpha \in K$, since $K \in \mathrm{Fr}$) that $(FG)(\alpha) = G(F(\alpha)) = \eta(G)(F(\alpha)) = \eta(G)(\eta(F)(\alpha)) = (\eta(F)\eta(G))(\alpha)$, so that η is a homomorphism. If $F \in \mathrm{Pa}({}^\omega 2)$ is not the identity then by Proposition 0.7 there are $\sigma, \tau \in {}^{\omega}2$ such that (in ${}^\omega 2$) $[\sigma] \cap [\tau] = \emptyset$ and for every $\beta \in {}^\omega 2$, $F(\sigma^\frown\beta) = \tau^\frown\beta$. By choosing $\gamma \in K$ we have (as $K \in \mathrm{Fr}$) both $\sigma^\frown\gamma \in K$ and $\tau^\frown\gamma \in K$, so that $(\eta(F))(\sigma^\frown\gamma) = F(\sigma^\frown\gamma) = \tau^\frown\gamma$, while $\sigma^\frown\gamma \neq \tau^\frown\gamma$ (or the intervals $[\sigma]$ and $[\tau]$ of ${}^\omega 2$ would not be disjoint), so that $\eta(F)$ is not the identity, and therefore η is an isomorphism.

For $K \in \mathrm{Fr}$, $\mathrm{Ft}(K)$ will designate the set of all mappings belonging to $\mathrm{Pa}(K)$ which correspond to a triple Σ_0, Σ_1, ψ as in Theorem 0.3 such that Σ_0 (and thus Σ_1) is finite. From Theorem 0.3, Proposition 0.5, and Proposition 0.8 it is now apparent that $\mathrm{Ft}(K)$ is a group (with composition of functions as the operation), which will be called the group of *finite table permutations* of K, and that $\mathrm{Ft}(K)$ is isomorphic to $\mathrm{Pa}({}^\omega 2)$. More precisely:

Proposition 0.9. *If* $K \in \mathrm{Fr}$ *and* η *is as in Proposition* 0.8, *then* η *is an isomorphism which maps* $\mathrm{Ft}({}^\omega 2) = \mathrm{Pa}({}^\omega 2)$ *onto* $\mathrm{Ft}(K)$ *in such a way that for* $F \in \mathrm{Pa}({}^\omega 2)$ *corresponding to a triple* Σ_0, Σ_1, ψ *as in Theorem* 0.3 *where* Σ_0 *and* Σ_1 *are partition sets for* ${}^\omega 2$ *(and thus are finite)* $\eta(F)$ *corresponds to the same triple.*

As a consequence of Proposition 0.9, $\mathrm{Ft}(K) \cong \mathrm{Ft}(K')$ for $K, K' \in \mathrm{Fr}$ and we can identify elements of $\mathrm{Ft}(K)$ and $\mathrm{Ft}(K')$ which correspond to the same triple Σ_0, Σ_1, ψ (with Σ_0 and Σ_1 finite). We conclude this section by pointing out some facts concerning permutation groups which will be needed later:

Lemma 0.10. *Suppose that* $M = M_1 \cup M_2$, $M_1 \cap M_2 = \emptyset$, *and* g *and* g' *are permutations of* M *which both map* M_1 *onto* M_1 *and* M_2 *onto* M_2. *Then*:

(i) *If* $g(x) = x$ *for every* $x \in M_1$, *while* $g'(y) = y$ *for every* $y \in M_2$, *then* $gg' = g'g$.

(ii) *If for every* $x \in M_1$, $g(x) \neq x$ *and* $g'(x) \neq x$, *while for every* $y \in M_2$ $g(y) = y$ *and* $g'(y) = y$, *then for every permutation* h *of* M *such that* $h^{-1}gh = g'$, h *also maps* M_1 *onto* M_1 *and* M_2 *onto* M_2.

Proof. (i): This follows by examining the cases $z \in M_1$ and $z \in M_2$ to show that $(gg')(z) = (g'g)(z)$ for every $z \in M$. (ii): Suppose $z \in M_2$ but

$h(z) \in M_1$. Then $(h^{-1}gh)(h(z)) = (gh)(z) = h(g(z)) = h(z)$ (as $g(z) = z$, since $z \in M_2$), but $g'(h(z)) \neq h(z)$ (as $h(z) \in M_1$). On the other hand, suppose $z \in M_1$ but $h(z) \in M_2$. Then $(h^{-1}gh)(h(z)) = (gh)(z) = h(g(z)) \neq h(z)$ (as $g(z) \neq z$, since $z \in M_1$), but $g'(h(z)) = h(z)$ (as $h(z) \in M_2$). So h maps M_2 into M_2 and M_1 into M_1, thus M_1 onto M_1 and M_2 onto M_2.

§1. About table permutations

Throughout this section K will be a fixed element of Fr. A *table* will be a triple Σ_0, Σ_1, ψ as in Theorem 0.3; the table being called "finite" if Σ_0 and Σ_1 are finite. A *line* (which will be called a regular line in §3) will be an object $\sigma \to \tau$ corresponding to an ordered pair $\langle \sigma, \tau \rangle$ where $\sigma, \tau \in {}^{\omega}2$. We will say that the line $\sigma \to \tau$ belongs to the table T just in case $\sigma \in \Sigma_0$, $\tau \in \Sigma_1$ and $\psi(\sigma) = \tau$, T being the triple Σ_0, Σ_1, ψ. If T is a finite table it can be given just by listing all of the lines belonging to it; elements of $\mathrm{Ft}(K)$ will usually be given by listing the lines of a corresponding table. The *left partition set* of a table Σ_0, Σ_1, ψ is Σ_0; the *right partition set* is Σ_1.

As a practical matter, it is useful to be able to multiply members of $\mathrm{Ft}(K)$ by "composing" corresponding finite tables. If $F, G \in \mathrm{Ft}(K)$ have the tables Σ_0, Σ_1, ψ and Σ_1, Σ_2, ψ' corresponding, the table Σ_0, Σ_2, $\psi\psi'$ will evidently correspond to FG.

Definition 1.1. If $\sigma \to \tau$ is a line, then the *direct extracts* of $\sigma \to \tau$ are $\sigma 0 \to \tau 0$ and $\sigma 1 \to \tau 1$.

We immediately have:

Proposition 1.2. *If the table Γ' is obtained from the finite table Γ by replacing a line belonging to Γ by its direct extracts, then Γ and Γ' correspond to the same element of* $\mathrm{Ft}(K)$.

Proposition 1.3. *Suppose that the finite table Σ_0, Σ_1, ψ and $m, n \in \omega$ are such that the lengths of the longest sequences in Σ_0 and Σ_1 are $\leq m$ and $\leq n$ respectively. Let Σ_0' and Σ_1^* be, respectively, the set consisting of all binary sequences of length m and the set consisting of all binary sequences of length n. Then there exist partition sets Σ_1' and Σ_0^* and one-one functions ψ' and ψ^* such that the tables Σ_0', Σ_1', ψ' and Σ_0^*, Σ_1^*, ψ^* correspond to the same element of* $\mathrm{Ft}(K)$ *as* Σ_0, Σ_1, ψ.

Proof. There are only finitely many binary sequences of length less than or equal to m or n; thus by appealing to Proposition 1.2 we can, if $\Sigma_0 \neq \Sigma_0'$, choose $\sigma \in \Sigma_0$ of length $< m$ and replace $\sigma \to \psi(\sigma)$ in Σ_0, Σ_1, ψ by its direct extracts and repeat this process to obtain Σ_0', Σ_1', ψ' — if $\Sigma_1 \neq \Sigma_1^*$ we can similarly start with $\tau \in \Sigma_1$ of length $< n$ and replace $\psi^{-1}(\tau) \to \tau$ by its direct extracts, repeating this process to obtain Σ_0^*, Σ_1^*, ψ^*

A table obtained from another table by an iterated process of replacing a line by its direct extracts will be called a *refinement* of the other table. Proposition 1.3 shows that if the finite tables Σ_0, Σ_1, ψ and Σ_2, Σ_3, θ correspond to $F, G \in \mathrm{Ft}(K)$ we can, by choosing $n \in \omega$ such that every element of $\Sigma_1 \cup \Sigma_2$ is of length $\leq n$, and taking $\Sigma_1' = \Sigma_2'$ to be the set of all sequences of length n, find tables Σ_0', Σ_1', ψ' and Σ_2', Σ_3', θ' which are refinements of Σ_0, Σ_1, ψ and Σ_2, Σ_3, θ respectively, so that Σ_0', Σ_3', $\psi'\theta'$ corresponds to FG. Note that the process described in the proof of Proposition 1.3 is effective, so that the word problem for $\mathrm{Ft}(K)$ is solvable (when the elements are given by finite tables): a finite table Σ_0, Σ_1, ψ corresponds to the identity element if and only if ψ is the identity, while we can effectively find a finite table corresponding to the product of two elements of $\mathrm{Ft}(K)$ given by finite tables. Of course, if the finite table Σ_0, Σ_1, ψ corresponds to $F \in \mathrm{Ft}(K)$, then Σ_1, Σ_0, ψ^{-1} corresponds to F^{-1}.

Theorem 1.4. *For $K \in \mathrm{Fr}$, $\mathrm{Ft}(K)$ is finitely generated, with the elements E (given by the table $0 \to 00$, $10 \to 01$, $11 \to 1$), D (given by the table $0 \to 0$, $10 \to 100$, $110 \to 101$, $111 \to 11$), π_0 (given by the table $0 \to 10$, $10 \to 0$, $11 \to 11$), π_1 (given by the table $0 \to 0$, $10 \to 110$, $110 \to 10$, $111 \to 111$), and π_1^* (given by the table $0 \to 0$, $10 \to 11$, $11 \to 10$) as one set of generators.*

Proof. First we show that E and D generate the subgroup $\mathbb{P}$ of $\mathrm{Ft}(K)$ consisting of all elements of $\mathrm{Ft}(K)$ which are order-preserving, the order in question being the lexicographic order on K (that is, the ordering $\preccurlyeq$ such that, for $\alpha, \beta \in K$, $\alpha \preccurlyeq \beta$ if and only if $\alpha = \beta$ or for some $\rho \in {}^{\omega}2$ we have $\alpha \in [\rho 0]$ and $\beta \in [\rho 1]$, ρ possibly being the empty sequence; thus K is simply ordered by $\preccurlyeq$). Note that whenever Σ_0 and Σ_1 are two finite partition sets of the same cardinality there exists exactly one function ψ such that Σ_0, Σ_1, ψ is a finite table corresponding to an element of $\mathbb{P}$; for $\sigma, \tau \in {}^{\omega}2$ such that $[\sigma] \cap [\tau] = \emptyset$ either $\alpha \preccurlyeq \beta$ for every $\alpha \in [\sigma]$ and $\beta \in [\tau]$ or $\beta \preccurlyeq \alpha$ for every $\alpha \in [\sigma]$ and $\beta \in [\tau]$, so that (indicating the former case by $\sigma \preccurlyeq \tau$ and the latter case by $\tau \preccurlyeq \sigma$) if Σ_0 has as elements $\sigma_0, \ldots, \sigma_{n-1}$ with $\sigma_0 \preccurlyeq \sigma_1 \preccurlyeq \cdots$

$\leqslant \sigma_{n-1}$ and Σ_1 has as elements $\tau_0, \ldots, \tau_{n-1}$ with $\tau_0 \leqslant \tau_1 \leqslant \cdots \leqslant \tau_{n-1}$, then ψ must be the mapping defined by $\psi(\sigma_i) = \tau_i$, for $0 \leqslant i < n$.

Now let λ_0 be $\langle 0 \rangle$ and let λ_n be $\langle 1^{(n)}0 \rangle$ and λ_n^* be $\langle 1^{(n)} \rangle$ for $n \in \omega$ with $n \neq 0$. For $n \in \omega$ let Γ_n be $\{\lambda_0, \ldots, \lambda_n, \lambda_{n+1}^*\}$. It is clear that Γ_n is a finite partition set of cardinality $n+2$. Let $\mathbb{P}^*$ be the subset of $\mathbb{P}$ consisting of all elements of $\mathbb{P}$ corresponding to a finite table Σ_0, Σ_1, ψ where Σ_0 is Γ_n for some $n \in \omega$. (In fact, $\mathbb{P}^*$ is a subsemigroup of $\mathbb{P}$.) From their definitions, E and D belong to $\mathbb{P}^*$ and $\mathbb{P}$. Let $W_0 = E$ and let $W_{m+1} = E^m D E^{-m}$ for $m \in \omega$, so that $W_1 = D$. Now, for $n \geqslant m+1$, W_m corresponds to the finite table Γ_n, Σ, θ where Σ is the range of θ and $\theta(\lambda_k) = \lambda_k$ for $k < m$, $\theta(\lambda_m) = \lambda_m 0$, $\theta(\lambda_{m+1}) = \lambda_m 1$, $\theta(\lambda_{k+1}) = \lambda_k$ for $n > k > m$, and $\theta(\lambda_{n+1}^*) = \lambda_n^*$. This can be shown for E and D by refining the tables which were used to define them, and for W_m with $m \geqslant 2$ by induction on m, as EW_mE^{-1} is easily computed.

For $p \in \mathbb{P}^*$, p belongs to the subgroup of $\mathbb{P}$ generated by E and D. This can be shown by induction: First, there is only one element of $\mathbb{P}^*$, the identity, which corresponds to a finite table whose left partition set is Γ_0. Now let us suppose that $n \geqslant 1$ and that p corresponds to a finite table Γ_n, Σ_1, ψ, while every element of $\mathbb{P}^*$ corresponding to a finite table whose left partition set is Γ_j for some $j < n$ belongs to the group generated by E and D. Let us choose $\sigma \in \Sigma_1$ such that σ is of maximum length. As $n \geqslant 1$, σ is either $\rho 0$ or $\rho 1$ for some $\rho \in {}^{\omega}2$ of length $\geqslant 1$. Further, both $\rho 0$ and $\rho 1$ belong to Σ_1 (since Σ_1 is a partition set and σ is of maximum length). *Case 1:* $\rho 1$ is $\psi(\lambda_{n+1}^*)$. Then, $\rho 0$ must be $\psi(\lambda_n)$, and if we define the function ψ' with domain Γ_{n-1} by setting $\psi'(\lambda_k) = \psi(\lambda_k)$ for $k < n$ and $\psi'(\lambda_n^*) = \rho$, and put Σ_1' equal to the range of ψ', p will correspond to the finite table Γ_{n-1}, Σ_1', ψ' (for replacing $\rho 0$ and $\rho 1$ in Σ_1 by ρ still leaves a finite partition set), and thus belongs to the subgroup generated by E and D. *Case 2:* $\rho 1$ is $\psi(\lambda_{m+1})$ for some $m < n$. Then, $\rho 0$ must be $\psi(\lambda_m)$, and we define the function ψ' with domain Γ_{n-1} by setting $\psi'(\lambda_k) = \psi(\lambda_k)$ for $k < m$, $\psi'(\lambda_m) = \rho$, $\psi'(\lambda_k) = \psi(\lambda_{k+1})$ for $n > k > m$, and $\psi'(\lambda_n^*) = \psi(\lambda_{n+1}^*)$, and put Σ_1' equal to the range of ψ', so that Σ_1' is a finite partition set. If p^* is the element of $\mathbb{P}^*$ corresponding to the finite table Γ_{n-1}, Σ_1', ψ', then p^* must belong to the subgroup generated by E and D. But it is now easy to compute that $p = W_m \cdot p^*$, so that p also belongs to the subgroup generated by E and D. (Replacing the references above to the group generated by E and D by references to the semigroup generated by the W_m, $m \geqslant 0$, we see that this semigroup includes $\mathbb{P}^*$ and so coincides with it.)

Now, every $r \in \mathbb{P}^*$ corresponds to a finite table Σ_0, Σ_1, ψ in which Σ_0 and Σ_1 both contain $n+2$ elements for some $n \in \omega$. Let p be the unique element of $\mathbb{P}$ which corresponds to a finite table Γ_n, Σ_0, ξ and let q be the unique element of $\mathbb{P}$ which corresponds to a finite table Γ_n, Σ_1, η. From $p, q \in \mathbb{P}$ it follows that $p, q \in \mathbb{P}^*$. Further, the element $p^{-1}q$ corresponds to the finite table Σ_0, Σ_1, $\xi^{-1}\eta$ (as p^{-1} corresponds to the finite table Σ_0, Γ_n, ξ^{-1}), and thus must be equal to r, as both $p^{-1}q$ and r belong to $\mathbb{P}$ (so that $\xi^{-1}\eta$ is equal to ψ). As p and q belong to the group generated by E and D, so does $p^{-1}q = r$, and we conclude that $\mathbb{P}$ is generated by E and D.

The definition of π_0, π_1, and π_1^* has been given in the statement of the theorem. For $m > 0$, let $\pi_{m+1} = E\pi_m E^{-1}$ and $\pi_{m+1}^* = E\pi_m^* E^{-1}$. Then for $n > m$, π_m corresponds to the finite table Γ_n, Γ_n, θ' where for $k \neq m$, $m+1$ we have $\theta'(\lambda_k) = \lambda_k$ with $\theta'(\lambda_m) = \lambda_{m+1}$ and $\theta'(\lambda_{m+1}) = \lambda_m$, while π_n^* corresponds to a finite table Γ_n, Γ_n, θ'' where $\theta''(\lambda_k) = \lambda_k$ for $k < n$ with $\theta''(\lambda_n) = \lambda_{n+1}^*$ and $\theta''(\lambda_{n+1}^*) = \lambda_n$. For π_1 this is true as inspection shows: the rest follows by computation and induction.

Now, every $g \in \mathrm{Ft}(K)$ corresponds to a finite table Σ_0, Σ_1, ψ in which Σ_0 and Σ_1 both contain $n+2$ elements and $n > 0$. As before, let p and q be the unique elements of $\mathbb{P}$ corresponding to finite tables Γ_n, Σ_0, ξ and Γ_n, Σ_1, η. Then $\xi\psi\eta^{-1}$ is a permutation of Γ_n so that Γ_n, Γ_n, $\xi\psi\eta^{-1}$ is a finite table corresponding to an element $g' \in \mathrm{Ft}(K)$. Consequently, as the tables involved can be directly multiplied to show that $g = p^{-1}g'q$, to show that g belongs to the group generated by E, D, π_0, π_1, and π_1^* it is enough to show that g' belongs to this group. But $\xi\psi\eta^{-1}$ is a permutation of Γ_n, and is thus equal to a product of transpositions, in fact of transpositions which transpose λ_i and λ_{i+1} for some $i < n$ or transpose λ_n and λ_{n+1}^*. This means, in turn, that g' is a product of the elements π_i, $i < n$, and π_n^*. So g' and consequently g belong to the group generated by E, D, π_0, π_1, and π_1^*, which thus coincides with $\mathrm{Ft}(K)$.

Proposition 1.5. *For* $K \in \mathrm{Fr}$, $\mathrm{Ft}(K)$ *is generated by two elements. Two such elements are* $\pi_2^*\pi_1 D$ *and* $\pi_0\pi_1\pi_2^*$. $\mathrm{Ft}(K)$ *is also generated by the four elements* E, D, π_0, *and* π_1^*, *and by the three elements* E, D, *and* $\pi_0\pi_1^*\pi_0$.

Proof. As E, D, π_0, π_1, and π_1^* are a set of generators by Theorem 1.4, and $\pi_1 = \pi_0\pi_1^*D^{-1}\pi_0 D\pi_1^*\pi_0$, as a computation will show, $\mathrm{Ft}(K)$ is generated by E, D, π_0, and π_1^*. In fact, it is generated by E, D, and $\pi_0\pi_1^*\pi_0$, as $\pi_0 = D^{-1}E(\pi_0\pi_1^*\pi_0)D(\pi_0\pi_1^*\pi_0)D^{-1}E$ and $\pi_1^* = D(\pi_0\pi_1^*\pi_0)D^{-1}E(\pi_0\pi_1^*\pi_0)D$. The last reduction is more lengthy. Let g_1 be $\pi_2^*\pi_1 D$ and let g_2 be $\pi_0\pi_1\pi_2^*$. Put g_3 equal to $(g_2^3 g_1)^3$ and g_4 equal to $g_2^2 g_1 g_2^3 g_1 g_2$, and then set g_5 equal to $g_3 g_4 g_3 g_4^2 g_3$. (So $g_5 = \pi_2^*$.)

Computation then shows that $\pi_1^* = g_2 g_5 g_2^2 g_1$ and $\pi_0 = g_2^2 g_5 g_2^2$, while $D = g_1 \pi_1^* g_1$ and $E = g_2^3 D g_2 D$.

Now we turn to results connected with simple subgroups of $\mathrm{Pa}(K)$.

Proposition 1.6. *For $K \in \mathrm{Fr}$ there is for every non-identity element $g \in \mathrm{Pa}(K)$ some $h \in \mathrm{Ft}(K)$ such that $h^{-1}gh$ corresponds to a table Σ_0^*, Σ_1^*, ψ^* such that $\psi^*(\langle 0\rangle) = \langle 10\rangle$.*

Proof. Let g be a non-identity element of $\mathrm{Pa}(K)$. Then there will be some table Σ_0, Σ_1, ψ corresponding to g; we can assume that $\langle 0\rangle \notin \Sigma_0$ and $\langle 1\rangle \notin \Sigma_0$, since a line $0 \to \rho$ could be replaced by lines $00 \to \rho 0$ and $01 \to \rho 1$, and $1 \to \rho'$ could be replaced by $10 \to \rho' 0$ and $11 \to \rho' 1$ without changing the corresponding element of $\mathrm{Pa}(K)$. By Proposition 0.6 there will then be some finite partition set Σ with $\sigma, \tau \in \Sigma$, where $\sigma \in \Sigma_0$ and $\tau \in \Sigma_1$ have been chosen according to Proposition 0.7 so that $\psi(\sigma) = \tau$ and $[\sigma] \cap [\tau] = \emptyset$. As $\sigma \neq \tau$, Σ has cardinality $\geqslant 2$. In fact, Σ must have cardinality $\geqslant 3$, as if Σ had cardinality equal to 2 then we would have $\Sigma = \{\langle 0\rangle, \langle 1\rangle\}$, and so $\sigma = \langle 0\rangle$ or $\sigma = \langle 1\rangle$. Thus Σ has the same cardinality as some Γ_n, $n \geqslant 1$ (where Γ_n is as in the proof of Theorem 1.4). Because $n \geqslant 1$, $\langle 0\rangle = \lambda_0 \in \Gamma_n$ and $\langle 10\rangle = \lambda_1 \in \Gamma_n$. We can take ψ' to be some one-one mapping of Σ onto Γ_n such that $\psi'(\sigma) = \langle 0\rangle$ and $\psi'(\tau) = \langle 10\rangle$. Then there is $h \in \mathrm{Ft}(K)$ corresponding to the finite table Σ, Γ_n, ψ'. Now, for $\beta \in K$, $(h^{-1}gh)(\langle 0\rangle^\frown\beta) = (gh)(h^{-1}(\langle 0\rangle^\frown\beta)) = (gh)(\sigma^\frown\beta) = h(\tau^\frown\beta) = \langle 10\rangle^\frown\beta$, so by Theorem 0.3 there will be a table Σ_0^*, Σ_1^*, ψ^* corresponding to $h^{-1}gh$ such that for some $\rho \subset \langle 0\rangle$, $\rho \in \Sigma_0^*$. Thus (as $h^{-1}gh$, like g, is not the identity) $\langle 0\rangle = \rho \in \Sigma_0^*$ and we must have $\psi^*(\langle 0\rangle) = \langle 10\rangle$.

Proposition 1.7. *For $K \in \mathrm{Fr}$, if H is a group such that $\mathrm{Ft}(K) \subseteq H \subseteq \mathrm{Pa}(K)$ then every non-trivial normal subgroup of H contains the element of $\mathrm{Ft}(K)$ corresponding to the finite table* $00 \to 000$, $010 \to 001$, $011 \to 01$, $1000 \to 100$, $1001 \to 1010$, $101 \to 1011$, $11 \to 11$.

Proof. Suppose H is as in the proposition, and N is a normal subgroup of H with $g \in N$ and g not equal to the identity. By Proposition 1.6 there will be some $j \in N$ corresponding to a table Σ_0^*, Σ_1^*, ψ^* such that $\langle 0\rangle \in \Sigma_0^*$, $\langle 10\rangle \in \Sigma_1^*$, and $\psi^*(\langle 0\rangle) = \langle 10\rangle$. Let $f \in \mathrm{Ft}(K)$ correspond to the finite table $0 \to 0$, $100 \to 1000$, $1010 \to 1001$, $1011 \to 101$, $11 \to 11$. Then, jfj^{-1} is the element corresponding to the finite table $00 \to 000$, $010 \to 001$, $011 \to 01$, $1 \to 1$. For, given any $\beta \in K$ we have $j(\langle 1\rangle^\frown\beta) \notin [10]$ so that $(jfj^{-1})(\langle 1\rangle^\frown\beta) = j^{-1}(f(j(\langle 1\rangle^\frown\beta))) =$

$j^{-1}(j(\langle 1\rangle^\frown\beta)) = \langle 1\rangle^\frown\beta$. On the other hand, if σ is $\langle 0\rangle$, $\langle 10\rangle$, or $\langle 11\rangle$ and σ^* is $\langle 00\rangle$, $\langle 01\rangle$, or $\langle 1\rangle$ respectively, then $(jfj^{-1})(\langle 0\rangle^\frown\sigma^\frown\beta) = (fj^{-1})(\langle 10\rangle^\frown\sigma^\frown\beta) = j^{-1}(\langle 10\rangle^\frown\sigma^{*\frown}\beta) = \langle 0\rangle^\frown\sigma^{*\frown}\beta$. As $f \in \mathrm{Ft}(K) \subseteq H$, $[j, f] \in N$, and it is easily computed that $[j, f] = (jfj^{-1})f^{-1}$ corresponds to the finite table given in the proposition.

Proposition 1.8. *For* $K \in \mathrm{Fr}$, *if* H *is a group such that* $\mathrm{Ft}(K) \subseteq H \subseteq \mathrm{Pa}(K)$ *then* $\mathrm{Ft}(K)$ *is a subgroup of every non-trivial normal subgroup of* H.

Proof. Let H be as in the proposition. It is enough, in view of Proposition 1.7, to show that $\mathrm{Ft}(K)$ coincides with the normal subgroup N of $\mathrm{Ft}(K)$ generated by the element k of $\mathrm{Ft}(K)$ which is mentioned in Proposition 1.7. Now, let g_1 be $D^{-1}ED^{-1}E^{-1}D$. Then, as $k \in N$, $[k, g_1] = kg_1k^{-1}g_1^{-1} \in N$. Computation shows that $kg_1k^{-1}g_1^{-1} = D^{-2}ED^{-1}EDE^{-2}D^2 = (D^{-2}E)(D^{-1}EDE^{-1})(E^{-1}D^2)$; $D^{-1}EDE^{-1}$ is conjugate to this and so belongs to N. Next we observe that $D^{-1} \in N$ as $D^{-1} = (D\pi_1^*\pi_0E)^{-1}(D^{-1}EDE^{-1})(D\pi_1^*\pi_0E)$, and $E^{-1}D = (\pi_0\pi_1\pi_2^*)^{-1}(D^{-1}EDE^{-1})(\pi_0\pi_1\pi_2^*)$ so that $E^{-1}D \in N$. So $D \in N$ and $E = ((E^{-1}D)D^{-1})^{-1} \in N$. Thus, since $(\pi_0\pi_1^*E)^{-1}E(\pi_0\pi_1^*E) \in N$ there follows $\pi_0\pi_1^* = E(\pi_0\pi_1^*E)^{-1}E(\pi_0\pi_1^*E) \in N$. So, as $\pi_0^{-1}D\pi_0 \in N$, $\pi_0\pi_1^*\pi_0 = E^{-1}(\pi_0\pi_1^*)D^{-1}(\pi_0^{-1}D\pi_0)E^{-1}(\pi_0\pi_1^*)D^{-1} \in N$. Since, by Proposition 1.5, E, D, and $\pi_0\pi_1^*\pi_0$ are generators of $\mathrm{Ft}(K)$, N must coincide with $\mathrm{Ft}(K)$.

Corollary 1.9. *For* $K \in \mathrm{Fr}$, $\mathrm{Ft}(K)$ *is a simple group.*

Proof. Take $H = \mathrm{Ft}(K)$ in Proposition 1.8.

Theorem 1.10. *For* $K \in \mathrm{Fr}$, *is* H *is a group such that* $\mathrm{Ft}(K) \subseteq H \subseteq \mathrm{Pa}(K)$, *then* $\mathrm{Ft}(K)$ *is a subgroup of the commutator group of* H, *and this group is a subgroup of every non-trivial normal subgroup of* H.

Proof. Let H be as in the theorem. As $\mathrm{Ft}(K)$ is a non-Abelian group, so is H. Thus the commutator group of H is a non-trivial normal subgroup, and so has $\mathrm{Ft}(K)$ as a subgroup by Proposition 1.8. Now let N be a non-trivial normal subgroup of H, so that $\mathrm{Ft}(K) \subseteq N$ by Proposition 1.8. Given $f, g \in H$, by Proposition 1.6 there will be $h_0, h_1 \in \mathrm{Ft}(K)$ such that $h_0^{-1}fh_0$ and $h_1^{-1}gh_1$ correspond to tables Σ_0', Σ_1', ψ' and Σ_0^*, Σ_1^*, ψ^* respectively with $\langle 0\rangle \in \Sigma_0'$, $\langle 10\rangle \in \Sigma_1'$, $\langle 0\rangle \in \Sigma_0^*$, $\langle 10\rangle \in \Sigma_1^*$, and $\psi'(\langle 0\rangle) = \langle 10\rangle = \psi^*(\langle 0\rangle)$. Let $x = h_0^{-1}fh_0\pi_0$ and $y^* = h_1^{-1}gh_1\pi_0$. Then, for every $\beta \in K$, the restriction of x to $[\langle 0\rangle]$ is the identity mapping, as $x(\langle 0\rangle^\frown\beta) = \pi_0((h_0^{-1}fh_0)(\langle 0\rangle^\frown\beta)) = \pi_0(\langle 10\rangle^\frown\beta) = \langle 0\rangle^\frown\beta$, while x permutes the elements of $[\langle 1\rangle]$; similarly, the restriction of y^* to $[\langle 0\rangle]$ is the identity map. Note that $\pi_0\pi_1^*E$ corresponds to the finite table $0\to 1$, $1\to 0$. If we set $\pi=\pi_0\pi_1^*E$ we then have, for every $\beta\in K$, $(\pi^{-1}y^*\pi)(\langle 1\rangle^\frown\beta)=(y^*\pi)(\langle 0\rangle^\frown\beta)=\pi(\langle 0\rangle^\frown\beta)=\langle 1\rangle^\frown\beta$, so that the restriction of $\pi^{-1}y^*\pi$ to $[\langle 1\rangle]$ is the identity mapping, while $\pi^{-1}y^*\pi$ permutes the elements of $[\langle 0\rangle]$. If we let $y=\pi^{-1}y^*\pi$, we then have by Lemma 0.10 (i) that $xy=yx$. So $[f,g]=fgf^{-1}g^{-1}=fgy^{-1}x^{-1}yxf^{-1}g^{-1}=(fx^{-1})(x(gy^{-1})x^{-1})(y(xf^{-1})y^{-1})(yg^{-1})\in N$, N being a normal subgroup of H, provided that $(fx^{-1}),(gy^{-1})\in N$ (so that (xf^{-1}), $(yg^{-1})\in N$). But $fx^{-1}=f\pi_0^{-1}h_0^{-1}f^{-1}h_0=(f(\pi_0^{-1}h_0^{-1})f^{-1})h_0\in N$ (since $\pi_0^{-1}h_0^{-1},h_0\in \mathrm{Ft}(K)\subseteq N$) and $gy^{-1}=g\pi^{-1}\pi_0^{-1}h_1^{-1}g^{-1}h_1\pi=(g(\pi^{-1}\pi_0^{-1}h_1^{-1})g^{-1})h_1\pi\in N$ (since $\pi^{-1}\pi_0^{-1}h_1^{-1}$, $h_1\pi\in\mathrm{Ft}(K)\subseteq N$). As f and g were arbitrary elements of H, we conclude that the commutator group of H is a subgroup of N, and the last part of the theorem follows.

As a matter of act, for H as in the last theorem the commutator group of H is simple; this result is not needed later however, the following corollary being sufficient.

Corollary 1.11. *For* $K\in\mathrm{Fr}$, *if* H *is a subgroup of* $\mathrm{Pa}(K)$ *and* H *is equal to its commutator group, then the subgroup of* $\mathrm{Pa}(K)$ *generated by* $H\cup\mathrm{Ft}(K)$ *is simple.*

Proof. Let H be as in the proposition, and let B be the subgroup of $\mathrm{Pa}(K)$ generated by $H\cup\mathrm{Ft}(K)$, so that $\mathrm{Ft}(K)\subseteq B\subseteq\mathrm{Pa}(K)$. Then the commutator group of H is a subgroup of the commutator group of B, so that H is a subgroup of the commutator group of B, and $\mathrm{Ft}(K)$ is a subgroup of the commutator group of B by Theorem 1.10. Thus B is equal to the commutator group of B, and from Theorem 1.10 it now follows that B is simple.

§2. Splinter groups

Definition 2.1. Suppose $K\in\mathrm{Fr}$ and Y is a group of permutations of a set L. Then $\mathrm{Sp}(Y,K)$, the *splinter group* corresponding to Y and K, is the group of permutations of $L\times K$ generated by the set $Y=\{\bar g: g\in Y\}$, where $\bar g(\langle x,\alpha\rangle)=\langle g(x),\alpha\rangle$ for $g\in Y$, $x\in L$, and $\alpha\in[01]$ and where $\bar g(\langle x,\alpha\rangle)=\langle x,\alpha\rangle$ for $g\in Y$, $x\in L$, and $\alpha\notin[01]$, and the set $\mathrm{Ft}(K;L)=\{\ddot F: F\in\mathrm{Ft}(K)\}$, where $\ddot F(\langle x,\alpha\rangle)=\langle x,F(\alpha)\rangle$ for all $x\in L$ and $\alpha\in K$.

Note that both Y and $\mathrm{Ft}(K;L)$ are subgroups of $\mathrm{Sp}(Y,K)$, and that $Y \cong Y$ and $\mathrm{Ft}(K;L) \cong \mathrm{Ft}(K)$. The name "splinter group" refers to the way in which the action of an element of $\mathrm{Sp}(Y,K)$ on a subset of $L \times K$ whose projection on K is contained in a sufficiently small interval in K is determined by a single element of Y; see also Proposition 2.4. Throughout the rest of the section we assume that Y is a group of permutations of a set L and that $K \in \mathrm{Fr}$.

Proposition 2.2. *For every* $g \in Y$, *if* $F_1, F_2 \in \mathrm{Ft}(K)$ *are given by the finite tables* $00 \to 000$, $010 \to 001$, $011 \to 01$, $1 \to 1$ *and* $00 \to 00$, $01 \to 010$, $10 \to 011$, $11 \to 1$ *respectively, then* $[\bar{g}, \ddot{F}_1] = \ddot{F}_2^{-1}\bar{g}\ddot{F}_2$.

Proof. We can show that $([\bar{g}, \ddot{F}_1])(\langle x, \alpha\rangle) = (\ddot{F}_2^{-1}\bar{g}\ddot{F}_2)(\langle x, \alpha\rangle)$ for arbitrary $x \in L$ and $\alpha \in K$ by checking that this holds in the four separate cases of $\alpha \in [00]$, $\alpha \in [010]$, $\alpha \in [011]$, and $\alpha \in [1]$.

Theorem 2.3. $\mathrm{Sp}(Y,K)$ *is equal to its commutator group.*

Proof. This follows from Proposition 2.2, which implies that $\ddot{Y}$ is contained in the commutator group of $\mathrm{Sp}(Y,K)$, and the fact that $\mathrm{Ft}(K;L) \cong \mathrm{Ft}(K)$, which is simple (and so equal to its commutator group, as it is non-Abelian) by Corollary 1.9.

Let us now define a *splinter table* to be a quadruple Σ_0, Σ_1, ψ, ξ such that Σ_0, Σ_1, ψ is a finite table and ξ is a mapping of Σ_0 into Y. By the permutation of $L \times K$ corresponding to the splinter table Σ_0, Σ_1, ψ, ξ is meant that permutation Q of $L \times K$ such that for $\sigma \in \Sigma_0$, $\alpha \in K$, and $x \in L$, $Q(\langle x, \sigma^\frown\alpha\rangle) = \langle(\xi(\sigma))(x), \psi(\sigma)^\frown\alpha\rangle$.

Proposition 2.4. $\mathrm{Sp}(Y,K)$ *is equal to the set of permutations of* $L \times K$ *corresponding to splinter tables.*

Proof. First of all, every splinter table corresponds to an element of $\mathrm{Sp}(Y,K)$. For, given a splinter table Σ_0, Σ_1, ψ, ξ, the corresponding permutation of $L \times K$ is the product of the permutations corresponding to the splinter tables Σ_0, Σ_0, ψ^*, ξ and Σ_0, Σ_1, ψ, ξ^*, where ψ^* is the identity mapping on Σ_0 and ξ^* is the mapping whose domain is Σ_0 and whose range consists of a single element, the identity of Y. The permutation corresponding to the second table evidently belongs to $\mathrm{Ft}(K;L)$. As for the permutation corresponding to the first table, if $\Sigma_0 = \{\sigma_1, \ldots, \sigma_n\}$, take for $1 \leq i \leq n$ the mapping ξ_i to have domain Σ_0

with $\xi_i(\sigma_i) = \xi(\sigma_i)$ but with $\xi_i(\sigma_j)$ being the identity of Y for $j \neq i$. Then this permutation will be equal to the product of permutations corresponding to splinter tables Σ_0, Σ_0, ψ^*, ξ_i for $1 \leq i \leq n$ (of course, by Lemma 0.10 (i) these later permutations will commute), so it will be enough to remark that such permutations are, when Σ_0 has cardinality greater than 1, equal to elements $F_i^{-1}\xi(\sigma_i)F_i$ of $\mathrm{Sp}(Y,K)$ where $\xi(\sigma_i) \in \bar{Y}$ and F_i is an element of $\mathrm{Ft}(K;L)$ which maps $L \times [01]$ onto $L \times [\sigma_i]$. When Σ_0 has cardinality 1, the permutation corresponding to Σ_0, Σ_0, ψ^*, ξ_1 will also corespond to $\{\langle 0\rangle, \langle 1\rangle\}$, $\{\langle 0\rangle, \langle 1\rangle\}$, ψ', ξ_1', where ψ' is the identity on $\{\langle 0\rangle, \langle 1\rangle\}$, and $\xi_1'(\langle 0\rangle)$ and $\xi_1'(\langle 1\rangle)$ are both equal to that element of Y which is the range of ξ_1; this reduces to the previous case.

On the other hand, the elements of $\mathrm{Ft}(K;L)$ correspond to those splinter tables Σ_0, Σ_1, ψ, ξ where Σ_0, Σ_1, ψ is a finite table and the range of ξ is the identity element of Y, while $\bar{g} \in \bar{Y}$ corresponds to the splinter table $\{\langle 00\rangle, \langle 01\rangle, \langle 1\rangle\}$, $\{\langle 00\rangle, \langle 01\rangle, \langle 1\rangle\}$, ψ^*, ξ^* where ψ^* is the identity map and $\xi^*(\langle 01\rangle) = g$ with $\xi^*(\langle 00\rangle)$ and $\xi^*(\langle 1\rangle)$ being equal to the identity of Y. So to show that every element of $\mathrm{Sp}(Y,K)$ corresponds to a splinter table it is enough (with $\bar{Y}$ and $\mathrm{Ft}(K;L)$ being closed under inverses) to show that the product of permutations corresponding to splinter tables also corresponds to a splinter table. Now, if $\sigma \in \Sigma_0$ the splinter tables Σ_0, Σ_1, ψ, ξ and Σ_0', Σ_1', ψ', ξ' correspond to the same permutation when Σ_0', Σ_1', ψ' is obtained from Σ_0, Σ_1, ψ by replacing the line $\sigma \to \psi(\sigma)$ by its direct extracts, and ξ' is obtained by setting $\xi'(\rho) = \xi(\rho)$ for $\rho \neq \sigma 0, \sigma 1$, with $\xi'(\sigma 0) = \xi'(\sigma 1) = \xi(\sigma)$. So splinter tables can be refined, just like finite tables. Thus, by refining the right partition set of one splinter table and the left partition set of another splinter table until they are equal, we can multiply the two splinter tables: for the product of the permutations corresponding to the splinter tables Σ_0, Σ_1, ψ, ξ and Σ_1, Σ_2, ψ', ξ' is the permutation corresponding to the splinter table Σ_0, Σ_2, $\psi\psi'$, ξ^*, where $\xi^*(\rho)$ is, for $\rho \in \Sigma_0$, $\xi(\rho) \cdot (\psi\xi')(\rho)$. (The inverse of the permutation corresponding to Σ_0, Σ_1, ψ, ξ_0 is the permutation corresponding to Σ_1, Σ_0, ψ^{-1}, ξ_1, where $\xi_1(\rho) = (\xi_0(\psi^{-1}(\rho)))^{-1}$ for $\rho \in \Sigma_1$.)

Definition 2.5. An embedding of a group G into a group H is a *Frattini embedding* just in case, whenever $g, g' \in G$ are conjugate in H, they are conjugate in G.

Theorem 2.6. *Suppose that only the identity element of Y has any fixed points. Then the embedding of $\bar{Y}$ into* $\mathrm{Sp}(Y,K)$ *is a Frattini embedding.*

Proof. Suppose $a, b \in Y$ and $g \in \mathrm{Sp}(Y, K)$ are such that $g^{-1} \bar{a} g = b$. If $a = b$, obviously $\bar{a}$ and $\bar{b}$ are conjugate in Y. If $a \neq b$, then both $\bar{a}$ and b are distinct from the identity permutation of $K \times L$ and map $K \times [01]$ onto itself but have no fixed points on this set (because, for $x \in L$, $a(x)$, $b(x) \neq x$), although they are pointwise fixed on the rest of $K \times L$. Thus Lemma 0.10 (ii) applies and g must map $K \times [01]$ onto $K \times [01]$. By Proposition 2.4 there will be some splinter table Σ_0, Σ_1, ψ, ξ corresponding to g. In fact (because we can refine a splinter table if necessary) we can assume that there is some $\sigma \in \Sigma_0$ such that $\langle 01 \rangle \subset \sigma$. As g maps $K \times [01]$ onto $K \times [01]$ it follows that $\langle 01 \rangle \subset \psi(\sigma)$. If we put $h = \xi(\sigma)$ we have for all $x \in L$ and $\beta \in K$ that $(g^{-1} \bar{a} g)(\langle x, \psi(\sigma)^{\frown} \beta \rangle) = (ag)(\langle h^{-1}(x), \sigma^{\frown} \beta \rangle) = g(\langle a(h^{-1}(x)), \sigma^{\frown} \beta \rangle) = \langle h(a(h^{-1}(x))), \psi(\sigma)^{\frown} \beta \rangle$, while $b(\langle x, \psi(\sigma)^{\frown} \beta \rangle) = \langle b(x), \psi(\sigma)^{\frown} \beta \rangle$, so that for all $x \in L$, $b(x) = h(a(h^{-1}(x))) = (h^{-1} a h)(x)$ and consequently $b = h^{-1} a h$. As $h \in Y$, a and b are thus conjugate in Y, so $\bar{a}$ and $\bar{b}$ are conjugate in Y.

Proposition 2.7. *If the word problem for Y is solvable, so is the word problem for $\mathrm{Sp}(Y, K)$.*

Proof. We can appeal to Proposition 2.4 to see that the word problem for $\mathrm{Sp}(Y, K)$ is solvable if we have an effective means of multiplying and inverting splinter tables and determining whether or not a splinter table corresponds to the identity mapping of $K \times L$ onto $K \times L$. This last determination can certainly be made effectively if the word problem for Y is solvable, for a splinter table Σ_0, Σ_1, ψ, ξ corresponds to the identity mapping of $K \times L$ onto $K \times L$ just in case $\Sigma_1 = \Sigma_0$, ψ is the identity mapping of Σ_0 onto Σ_0, and ξ is the mapping whose range consists of the identity element of Y. The last half of the proof of Proposition 2.4 shows that splinter tables can be multiplied and inverted effectively in terms of Y (the word problem being solvable for $\mathrm{Ft}(K; L) \cong \mathrm{Ft}(K)$).

Although no proofs will be given here, it is worth remarking that $\mathrm{Sp}(Y, K)$ is such a well-behaved extension of (an isomorphic image of) Y that it has a finite presentation if Y has a finite presentation. On the other hand, $\mathrm{Sp}(Y, K)$ has the interesting property (which is not hard to prove) that the countable weak direct product of a collection of subgroups of $\mathrm{Sp}(Y, K)$ is always isomorphic to a subgroup of $\mathrm{Sp}(Y, K)$. This property is also possessed by $\mathrm{Ft}(K)$; in the former case Proposition 2.4 can be used, while finite tables are used in the latter case.

§3. The main construction

Throughout this section J will denote the set of all positive integers, and K_0 will denote the subset of ${}^{\omega}2$ consisting of every $\alpha \in {}^{\omega}2$ such that there is, for every $n \in \omega$, some $m > n$ with $\alpha(m) \neq \alpha(n)$. (Thus K_0 consists of every sequence belonging to ${}^{\omega}2$ which is not "eventually" either 0 or 1.) It is easy to see that $K_0 \in \mathrm{Fr}$. Note that every $\beta \in K_0$ is equal to $\langle 1\rangle^{i\frown}\langle 0\rangle^{j\frown}\langle 1\rangle^{\frown}\beta'$ for some unique $i \in \omega$, $j \in J$, and $\beta' \in K_0$; by the *index* of β will be meant j, and by the *parity*, the integer $j - i$.

For the remainder of this section A will be a fixed group of permutations of J, possibly satisfying these conditions:

C1: The word problem for A is solvable.

C2: Given $g \in A$ and $j, k \in J$ it is always effectively decidable whether or not $g(j) = k$.

C3: If $g \in A$ is such that $\{j \in J : g(j) \neq j\}$ is finite, then g is the identity of A.

C4: If $g \in A$ is not the identity of A, then $g(j) \neq j$ for every $j \in J$.

For $g \in A$ let g^* be the function with domain K_0 such that, for $\beta \in K_0$ with parity not equal to 0, $g^*(\beta) = \beta$, while for $\alpha \in K_0$ and $m \in J$,

$$g^*(\langle 1\rangle^{m\frown}\langle 0\rangle^{m\frown}\langle 1\rangle^{\frown}\alpha) = \langle 1\rangle^{g(m)\frown}\langle 0\rangle^{g(m)\frown}\langle 1\rangle^{\frown}\alpha.$$

As g is a permutation of J, g^* is a permutation of K_0 which maps the set of elements of parity 0 onto itself. Further, in view of Definition 0.2, $g^* \in \mathrm{Pa}(K_0)$. If we set $A^* = \{g^* : g \in A\}$ it is evident that (taking the group operation for A^* to be functional composition) we have $A \cong A^*$, with A^* a subgroup of $\mathrm{Pa}(K_0)$.

In order to deal with the subgroup of $\mathrm{Pa}(K_0)$ generated by $A^* \cup \mathrm{Ft}(K_0)$ using objects finitely expressible in terms of A we have devised A-tables. Thus the reader should be careful to note that the constructions to be given in connection with A-tables are effectively obtained, granted that C1 and C2 hold.

Let $\mathrm{Fi}(A)$ be the set of all functions whose domain is a finite, non-empty subset of J and whose range is a subset of A. For $b \in \mathrm{Fi}(A)$ let $\zeta(b) = \{\langle m+1, g\rangle : \langle m, g\rangle \in b\}$; then $\zeta(b) \in \mathrm{Fi}(A)$. For $i \in \omega$, by $\zeta^{i+1}(b)$ will be meant $\zeta(\zeta^{i}(b))$, $\zeta^{0}(b)$ being b.

Definition 3.1. An element b of $\mathrm{Fi}(A)$ will be called *n-bolstered*, for $n \in \omega$, just in case for every $\langle m, g\rangle \in b$ and every $j \in J$ such that $j \geqslant m$ we have $g(j) + n \geqslant m$.

Lemma 3.2. *Suppose that $b \in \mathrm{Fi}(A)$ is n-bolstered. Then*:

(i) *For $n' \geqslant n$, b is n'-bolstered.*

(ii) *For $i \in \omega$, $\zeta^i(b)$ is $(n+i)$-bolstered.*

(iii) *For every $s \in J$ there is some $r \in J$, $r \geqslant s$, such that $\zeta^r(b)$ is $(n+r-s)$-bolstered.*

Proof. We obtain (i) and (ii) directly from Definition 3.1. For (iii), given $s \in J$ let us first set m^* equal to the largest element in the domain of b. As the range of b is finite, and every $g \in A$ is a permutation of J, there must be some $r \geqslant s$ such that for every $x \geqslant r$ we have $g(x) \geqslant m^* + s$ for each g in the range of b. Thus if $\langle m, g' \rangle \in \zeta^r(b)$ we will have $r < m \leqslant m^* + r$ so that, for every $j \geqslant m$, $g'(j) + (n+r-s) \geqslant (m^*+s) + (n+r-s) \geqslant m^* + r \geqslant m$. This yields (iii).

Note that, given s in Lemma 3.2 (iii), r can be obtained effectively when C2 holds: for each g belonging to the range of b we compute in succession $g(1), g(2), \ldots$ until every positive integer less than $m^* + s$ has appeared (which must happen as we are dealing with permutations); then r can be taken to be the smallest integer which has not been used as an argument in our computations.

By a *regular line* is meant what was called a line in §1; in this section a line will be either a regular line or an A-line, defined as follows:

Definition 3.3. An *A-line* is a quadruple σ, b, τ, n such that $\sigma, \tau \in {}^{\omega}2$ and $b \in \mathrm{Fi}(A)$, while $n \in \omega$ is such that b is n-bolstered; it will be written as $\sigma, b \to \tau, n$.

Definition 3.4. (i) The *line function* corresponding to a regular line $\sigma \to \tau$ will be that function x with domain $[\sigma]$ such that $x(\sigma^\frown\beta) = \tau^\frown\beta$ for $\beta \in K_0$.

(ii) The *line function* corresponding to an A-line $\sigma, b \to \tau, n$ is that function x with domain $[\sigma]$ such that for $\beta \in K_0$ with parity not belonging to the domain of b, $x(\sigma^\frown\beta) = \tau^\frown\langle 1\rangle^{n\frown}\beta$, while for $\beta \in K_0$ such that β has parity m (where m belongs to the domain of b) so that $\beta = \langle 1\rangle^{k-m\frown}\langle 0\rangle^{k\frown}\langle 1\rangle^\frown\beta'$ for some $\beta' \in K_0$ and $k \geqslant m$, $x(\sigma^\frown\beta) = \tau^\frown\langle 1\rangle^{(g(k)+n-m)\frown}\langle 0\rangle^{g(k)\frown}\langle 1\rangle^\frown\beta'$, where $g = b(m)$. (Observe that from $k \geqslant m$ and b being n-bolstered it follows that $g(k)+n \geqslant m$.)

The *left* sequence of a line $\sigma \to \tau$ or $\sigma, b \to \tau, n$ will be σ, and the *right* sequence, τ.

Definition 3.5. A *partial table* is a finite set of regular lines and A-

lines such that all of the left sequences of these lines are distinct and the intervals in K_0 they determine are all disjoint.

Definition 3.6. The *left sequence set* of a partial table is the set consisting of all the left sequences of lines belonging to it.

Definition 3.7. An *A-table* is a partial table whose left sequence set is a finite partition set for K_0.

By the function defined by a partial table or A-table will be meant the union of the line functions (which is again a function, as the left sequences of the lines determine disjoint intervals in K_0). For an A-table this corresponding function will have a domain equal to K_0 (the left sequence set being a finite partition set for K_0); as a line function is always a one-one function an A-table will correspond to a one-one function just in case the ranges of the line functions (for the lines belonging to the A-table) are disjoint. Note that, if a regular line appears in a finite table corresponding to an element of $\mathrm{Ft}(K_0)$, this element of $\mathrm{Ft}(K_0)$ will be an extension of the line function corresponding to the regular line, which gives:

Proposition 3.8. *If an A-table and a finite table have the same lines belonging to them (which will thus all be regular lines) then they correspond to the same element of* $\mathrm{Ft}(K_0)$.

Proposition 3.9. *For every A-table having only regular lines and corresponding to an element of* $\mathrm{Pa}(K_0)$, *this element belongs to* $\mathrm{Ft}(K_0)$.

Proof. An A-table has a left sequence set which is a finite partition set; if all its lines are regular it can only define an element of $\mathrm{Pa}(K_0)$ if the set of the right sequences of its lines is a finite partition set of the same cardinality as its left sequence set and the set of its lines. In this case there is a finite table with the same lines as the A-table.

From the relevant definitions we directly obtain:

Proposition 3.10. *For* $g \in A$, *if* $b = \{\langle 1, g\rangle\}$ *then* $b \in \mathrm{Fi}(A)$, *b is* 0-*bolstered, and the A-table with the lines* $\langle 0\rangle \to \langle 0\rangle$ *and* $\langle 1\rangle, b \to \langle 1\rangle, 0$ *corresponds to* $g^* \in A^*$.

Proposition 3.11. *For* $k \in J$ *and* $\sigma, \tau \in {}^{\omega}2$, *if* $b \in \mathrm{Fi}(A)$ *is n-bolstered for* $n \in \omega$ *(and so* $(n+k)$*-bolstered) then* $\sigma, b \to \tau, n+k$ *and* $\sigma, b \to \tau^\frown\langle 1\rangle^k, n$ *determine the same line function.*

The direct extracts of a regular line have already been defined, in Definition 1.1. For A-lines we make the following definition:

Definition 3.12. The *direct extracts* of the A-line $\sigma, b \to \tau, n$ are, where m^* is the largest element in the domain of b, the regular line $\sigma^\frown\langle 0\rangle^{m^*+1} \to \tau^\frown\langle 1\rangle^{n\frown}\langle 0\rangle^{m^*+1}$, and for $0 < m \leq m^*$ the regular line $\sigma^\frown\langle 0\rangle^{m\frown}\langle 1\rangle \to \tau^\frown\langle 1\rangle^{n\frown}\langle 0\rangle^{m\frown}\langle 1\rangle$ (when m does not belong to the domain of b) or the regular line $\sigma^\frown\langle 0\rangle^{m\frown}\langle 1\rangle \to \tau^\frown\langle 1\rangle^{(g(m)+n-m)\frown}\langle 0\rangle^{g(m)\frown}\langle 1\rangle$ (when m belongs to the domain of b and $b(m) = g$) together with the A-line $\sigma^\frown\langle 1\rangle, \zeta(b) \to \tau, n+1$. (Noting that $\zeta(b)$ is $(n+1)$-bolstered by (ii) of Lemma 3.2.)

Definition 3.13. An *extract* of a line is either the line itself or a line obtained from it as the last in a series of direct extracts, starting from the given line.

From Definition 1.1 or Definition 3.12, using Definition 3.5, etc., we obtain:

Proposition 3.14. *The function determined by the partial table consisting of the direct extracts of a line is the line function corresponding to the line.*

Corollary 3.15. *The line function corresponding to a line is an extension of every line function corresponding to an extract of the line.*

Definition 3.16. Suppose $n \in \omega$ and $b, c \in \mathrm{Fi}(A)$. Then the *n-alignment of b and c*, or $\mathrm{al}(n, b, c)$, is the function whose domain is the union of the domains of b and $\zeta^n(c)$, while $(\mathrm{al}(n, b, c))(m) = (b(m)) \cdot ((\zeta^n(c))(m))$ for m belonging to both domains, $(\mathrm{al}(n, b, c))(m) = (\zeta^n(c))(m)$ for m belonging to the domain of $\zeta^n(c)$ only, and $(\mathrm{al}(n, b, c))(m) = b(m)$ for m belonging to the domain of b only. (Thus $\mathrm{al}(n, b, c) \in \mathrm{Fi}(A)$.)

Further consideration of the separate cases of the definition shows:

Proposition 3.17. *If $b, c \in \mathrm{Fi}(A)$, $n, n' \in \omega$, b is n-bolstered, and c is n'-bolstered, then* $\mathrm{al}(n, b, c)$ *is* $(n + n')$*-bolstered.*

Definition 3.18. Suppose $\rho, \sigma, \tau \in {}^{\omega}2$, and $b, c \in \mathrm{Fi}(A)$, with b being n-bolstered and c being n'-bolstered. Then the (symbolic) composition of lines is stipulated to be such that:

(1) $(\sigma \to \tau) \cdot (\tau \to \rho) = (\sigma \to \rho)$.
(2) $(\sigma \to \tau) \cdot (\tau, b \to \rho, n) = (\sigma, b \to \rho, n)$.
(3) $(\sigma, b \to \tau, n) \cdot (\tau \to \rho) = (\sigma, b \to \rho, n)$.
(4) $(\sigma, b \to \tau, n) \cdot (\tau, c \to \rho, n') = (\sigma, \mathrm{al}(n, b, c) \to \rho, n + n')$.

Proposition 3.19. *The line function corresponding to the composition of two lines is the same function as the composition of the two line functions which correspond to the lines.*

Proof. This is clear enough for the cases (1)–(3) of Definition 3.18, using the definition of line function. For (4) we have to consider the effect of the two compositions on $\sigma^\frown\beta$, where $\beta \in K_0$; there are four subcases depending on whether or not the parity m of β belongs to the domains of b or $\zeta^n(c)$, and each is easily checked.

Just as in §1, an A-table (or partial table) obtained from another A-table (or partial table) by an iterated process of replacing a line by its direct extracts will be called a *refinement* of the other table; if, in this process, we also allow the replacement of a line $\sigma, b \to \tau, n + k$ (where $k \in J$) by the line $\sigma, b \to \tau^\frown\langle 1\rangle^k, n$ when b is n-bolstered, we will call the result a *semi-refinement*. Appealing to Proposition 3.14 and Proposition 3.11 we now see that:

Proposition 3.20. *If an A-table (or partial table) is obtained from another A-table (or partial table) as a refinement or semi-refinement, it corresponds to the same function.*

Definition 3.21. $\mathrm{Ta}(A)$ is the subset of $\mathrm{Pa}(K_0)$ consisting of all elements of $\mathrm{Pa}(K_0)$ which are defined by A-tables.

Definition 3.22. If $\sigma \in {}^{\omega}2$ is equal to $\mu^\frown\langle 1\rangle$ for some $\mu \in {}^{\omega}2$ it will be said to be *$\langle 1\rangle$-ending*; a line whose right sequence is $\langle 1\rangle$-ending will also be said to be *$\langle 1\rangle$-ending*.

Proposition 3.23. *Every extract of an A-line with left sequence σ is either a regular line or has a left sequence equal to $\sigma^\frown\langle 1\rangle^k$ for some $k \in \omega$.*

Proof. This follows because, given an A-line with left sequence σ, the only direct extract which is an A-line has $\sigma^\frown\langle 1\rangle$ as its left sequence — while all extracts of regular lines are regular lines.

Lemma 3.24. *Suppose $\sigma, \sigma' \in {}^{\omega}2$ with $\sigma' \subset \sigma$ while $\sigma', b \to \tau, n$ is an A-line. If σ is either $\langle 1\rangle$-ending or else, for some $\mu \in {}^{\omega}2$ of length t, is equal to $\mu^\frown\langle 0\rangle^{m+t}$ for some $m \in J$ which is greater than every element of the domain of b, and $\sigma' \subset \mu$ in the second case, then there exists exactly one line which is an extract of this line and has σ as a left sequence.*

Proof. The intervals in K_0 determined by the left sequences of the direct extracts of a regular line or A-line are all disjoint; as these left sequences are distinct from the left sequence of the line itself (but are extensions of it), it follows that there can be at most one line which is an extract of a given line and has a given left sequence. It remains to show that whenever σ, σ', b, τ, and n are as in the lemma there is some line with σ as its left sequence which is an extract of the A-line $\sigma', b \to \tau, n$. Let σ'' be the element of ${}^{\omega}2$ of maximum length such that $\sigma'' \subset \sigma$ and σ'' is either σ' or is equal to $\sigma'^\frown\langle 1\rangle^s$ for some $s \in J$. Then σ'' is the left sequence of an A-line which is an extract of the A-line $\sigma', b \to \tau, n$, being either this line itself or, for some $s \in J$, the line $\sigma'^\frown\langle 1\rangle^s, \zeta^s(b) \to \tau, n+s$. So if $\sigma'' = \sigma$, the lemma holds. Otherwise, $\sigma''^\frown\langle 0\rangle \subset \sigma$. Then, if σ is $\langle 1\rangle$-ending, there will be a regular line which is a direct extract of the A-line with left sequence σ'' and which has σ as an extension of its left sequence; this regular line will then have an extract which has σ as its left sequence, and the lemma will again hold. Finally, if σ is equal to $\mu^\frown\langle 0\rangle^{m+t}$ for some $\mu \in {}^{\omega}2$ of length t and $m \in J$ which is greater than every element of the domain of b, while $\sigma' \subset \mu$, then $\sigma'' \subset \mu$ (since $\sigma'' \subset \sigma$) so that if σ'' is $\sigma'^\frown\langle 1\rangle^s$ for $s \in J$ then $s \leqslant t$ and thus $m+s \leqslant m+t$ so that $m+t$ is greater than every element of the domain of $\zeta^s(b)$, just as m is greater than every element of the domain of b; consequently, there will be (as $\sigma'' \subset \mu$ and also $\sigma''^\frown\langle 0\rangle \subset \sigma$) a direct extract of the A-line with left sequence σ'' which is a regular line and has σ as an extension of its left sequence, and so has an extract whose left sequence is σ, so that the lemma holds in this case also.

Lemma 3.25. *Suppose Γ_1 is an A-table or partial table. Then, for every $k, m \in J$ there is an A-table or partial table, respectively, which is a semi-refinement of Γ_1 and in which every line has a right sequence of length $\geqslant k$ and is either $\langle 1\rangle$-ending or else is a regular line with a right sequence equal to $\mu^\frown\langle 0\rangle^{m+t}$ for some $t \in J$ and $\mu \in {}^{\omega}2$ with length $\leqslant t$.*

Proof. First we show that there is a semi-refinement Γ_1^* of Γ_1 in which every A-line has length $\geqslant k$ and is $\langle 1\rangle$-ending. Suppose that, for $n \in J$, there are exactly n A-lines in Γ_1 which are either not $\langle 1\rangle$-ending or are of length less than k. Let $\sigma, b \to \tau, j$ be one such A-line. By (iii) of Lemma 3.2 there is some $r \in J$ with $r \geqslant k$ such that $\zeta'(b)$ is $(j+r-k)$-bolstered. For $1 \leqslant m \leqslant r$ let Γ_{m+1} be obtained from Γ_m by replacing the A-line belonging to Γ_m which is an extract of $\sigma, b \to \tau, j$ by its direct extracts. Then Γ_{r+1} has $\sigma^\frown\langle 1\rangle^r, \zeta^r(b) \to \tau, j+r$ as one of its A-lines (with this being an extract of $\sigma, b \to \tau, j$) and has exactly $n-1$ other A-lines which are either not $\langle 1\rangle$-ending or are of length less than k. Now, Γ_{r+1} is a refinement of Γ_1, and if Γ'_{r+1} is the A-table resulting from replacing $\sigma^\frown\langle 1\rangle^r, \zeta^r(b) \to \tau, j+r$ by $\sigma^\frown\langle 1\rangle^r, \zeta^r(b) \to \tau^\frown\langle 1\rangle^k, j+r-k$ then Γ'_{r+1} will be a semi-refinement of Γ_{r+1} and Γ_1. Note that Γ'_{r+1} has only $n-1$ A-lines which are either not $\langle 1\rangle$-ending or are of length less than k. Proceeding from Γ'_{r+1} we can continue to refine the table in the same way until we obtain a semi-refinement Γ_1^* of Γ_1 in which all A-lines are $\langle 1\rangle$-ending and of length $\geqslant k$. (Of course, if there are no A-lines in Γ_1 which are not $\langle 1\rangle$-ending or are of length less than k, we take $\Gamma_1^* = \Gamma_1$.) Now Γ''_1 can be obtained from Γ_1^* by replacing each regular line $\sigma \to \tau$ of Γ_1^* by the 2^k extracts consisting of all the lines $\sigma^\frown\nu \to \tau^\frown\nu$ such that $\nu \in {}^{\omega}2$ is of length k. Then Γ''_1 is a semi-refinement of Γ_1^* and so of Γ_1, while every line of Γ''_1 is of length $\geqslant k$ and is $\langle 1\rangle$-ending if it is an A-line. Finally Γ'_1 is obtained from Γ''_1 by replacing each regular line $\sigma' \to \tau'$ by the regular lines (where t is the length of τ') $\sigma'^\frown\langle 1\rangle \to \tau'^\frown\langle 1\rangle$, $\sigma'^\frown\langle 0\rangle^{m'}{}^\frown\langle 1\rangle \to \tau'^\frown\langle 0\rangle^{m'}{}^\frown\langle 1\rangle$ (for each m' such that $0 < m' < m+t$), and $\sigma'^\frown\langle 0\rangle^{m+t} \to \tau'^\frown\langle 0\rangle^{m+t}$; Γ'_1 will be a semi-refinement of Γ''_1 (and so of Γ_1) with all the required properties.

Theorem 3.26. *The set* Ta(A) *is* (*with functional composition as the operation*) *a subsemigroup of* Pa(K_0).

Proof. Suppose that F and G are elements of Ta(A), with Γ_1 and Γ_2 being A-tables which define F and G respectively. Let k be the least integer greater than the lengths of all left sequences of Γ_2, and let m be the least integer greater than every element belonging to the range of some $b \in \mathrm{Fi}(A)$ occurring in an A-line of Γ_2. By Lemma 3.25 there will be an A-table Γ'_1 which is a semi-refinement of Γ_1 and has only lines, with right sequences of length $\geqslant k$, that are $\langle 1\rangle$-ending or else are regular lines with a right sequence equal to $\mu^\frown\langle 0\rangle^{m+t}$ for some $t \in J$ and $\mu \in {}^{\omega}2$ with length $\leqslant t$. By Proposition 3.20, Γ'_1 also defines F. Now we will define an A-table Γ_3 (as the "composition" of the two A-tables Γ'_1 and Γ_2) as follows: we replace each line $\sigma \to \tau$ or $\sigma, b \to \tau, n$ of Γ'_1 by the composition of this line with an extract of a line of Γ_2 to obtain a line with σ as its left sequence. Given a line of Γ'_1, say with left sequence σ and right sequence τ, it follows that, as the left sequences of Γ_2 are a partition set for K_0, and all of them are of length $< k$, while τ is of length $\geqslant k$, that τ is an extension of some left sequence τ' of Γ_2.

Case 1: τ' is the left sequence of a regular line $\tau' \to \rho$ of Γ_2. Then let $\mu \in {}^{\omega}2$ be such that $\tau = \tau'^\frown \mu$, and replace the line of Γ_1' which has σ as its left sequence and τ as its right sequence with the composition (according to (1) or (3) of Definition 3.18) of this line and the extract $\tau'^\frown \mu \to \rho^\frown \mu$ of the line $\tau' \to \rho$.

Case 2: τ' is the left sequence of an A-line $\tau', c \to \rho, n'$ of Γ_2. By Lemma 3.24 there will exist exactly one line with τ as its left sequence which is an extract of $\tau', c \to \rho, n'$. Let the line of Γ_1' which has σ as its left sequence and τ as its right sequence be replaced by the composition (according to (2) or (4) of Definition 3.18) of this line of Γ_1' with the extract of $\tau', c \to \rho, n'$ which has τ as its left sequence.

Now, we obtain in this way an A-table Γ_3 with the same number of lines as Γ_1' and the same set of left sequences. If H is the function defined by Γ_3 then the restriction of H to an interval $[\sigma]$, where σ is a left sequence of Γ_3 and so of Γ_1', is evidently a line function equal by Proposition 3.19 to the composition of the restriction of F to $[\sigma]$ and a function which is, by Corollary 3.15, a restriction of G (because it is the line function corresponding to a line which is an extract of a line of Γ_2). Thus the restriction of H to an interval $[\sigma]$, σ being a left sequence of Γ_3, is a function of which FG is an extension. It follows that H itself has FG as an extension; as they have the same domain, H is equal to FG, and thus the theorem holds.

Theorem 3.27. *If A satisfies condition* C3, *then an A-table Γ will define the idenity element of* $\mathrm{Pa}(K_0)$ (*that is, the identity permutation of* K_0) *if and only if every right sequence of a regular line belonging to Γ is the same as its left sequence and, for every A-line $\sigma, b \to \tau, n$ of Γ, $\sigma = \tau^\frown\langle 1\rangle^n$ and the range of b consists of only one element, the identity of A.*

Proof. The sufficiency of the requirement concerning Γ is clear from the definitions of the line functions of regular lines and A-lines. The necessity is clear enough, as regards regular lines, since a regular line $\sigma \to \tau$ corresponds to a line function which maps $[\sigma]$ onto $[\tau]$. For an A-line $\sigma, b \to \tau, n$ of an A-table defining the identity element of $\mathrm{Pa}(K_0)$ we must have $\sigma = \tau^\frown\langle 1\rangle^n$ as, for $m \in J$ sufficiently large, $[\sigma^\frown\langle 0\rangle^m]$ will be mapped onto $[\tau^\frown\langle 1\rangle^{n\frown}\langle 0\rangle^m]$ by the line function corresponding to $\sigma, b \to \tau, n$. Then, in view of Definition 3.4, this line function will be the identity mapping on $[\sigma]$ only if every $g \in A$ belonging to the range of b is equal to the identity of A, as if $m \in J$

belonging to the domain of b is such that $g = b(m)$ is not equal to the identity of A then by C3 there will exist $k \geqslant m$ such that $g(k) \neq k$ and thus $[\sigma^\frown\langle 1\rangle^{k-m\frown}\langle 0\rangle^{k\frown}\langle 1\rangle]$ will be mapped onto $[\tau^\frown\langle 1\rangle^{g(k)+n-m\frown}\langle 0\rangle^{g(k)\frown}\langle 1\rangle]$, which must be distinct as $g(k) \neq k$.

From the next result the significance of Theorem 3.26 and Theorem 3.27 becomes apparent.

Theorem 3.28. *The subgroup of* $\mathrm{Pa}(K_0)$ *generated by* $A^* \cup \mathrm{Ft}(K_0)$ *is a subsemigroup of* $\mathrm{Ta}(A)$.

Proof. As every inverse of an element of $A^* \cup \mathrm{Ft}(K_0)$ belongs to this set, the subgroup of $\mathrm{Pa}(K_0)$ generated by $A^* \cup \mathrm{Ft}(K_0)$ is the samc as the subsemigroup of $\mathrm{Pa}(K_0)$ generated by $A^* \cup \mathrm{Ft}(K_0)$, and thus, because of Proposition 3.8 and Proposition 3.10, is by Theorem 3.26 a subsemigroup of $\mathrm{Ta}(A)$.

Theorem 3.29. *Suppose that A satisfies conditions* C1, C2, *and* C3. *Then the word problem for the subgroup of* $\mathrm{Pa}(K_0)$ *generated by* $A^* \cup \mathrm{Ft}(K_0)$ *is solvable (for a presentation appropriately related to the presentation for which A satisfies* C1 *and* C2).

Proof. Given that A satisfies condition C3, Theorem 3.27 will apply, and we will be able to effectively determine whether or not an element of the subgroup of $\mathrm{Pa}(K_0)$ generated by $A^* \cup \mathrm{Ft}(K_0)$ which is given in terms of an A-table is equal to the identity element (of $\mathrm{Pa}(K_0)$ and so of the subgroup) using condition C1. In view of Proposition 3.10 and Proposition 3.8 we can effectively find A-tables which correspond to given elements of $A^* \cup \mathrm{Ft}(K_0)$; as this set is closed under inverses, and the proof of Theorem 3.26 shows that there is an effective procedure (relative to a solution of the word problem for A, and an effective method of determining for $j, k \in J$ and $g \in A$ whether or not $g(j) = k$) which yields an A-table corresponding to the composition of two elements of $\mathrm{Ta}(A)$ given by A-tables, we have a procedure that effectively determines whether or not an element of the subgroup of $\mathrm{Pa}(K_0)$ generated by $A^* \cup \mathrm{Ft}(K_0)$ is equal to the identity element, so that the word problem is solvable.

Theorem 3.30. *Suppose that A satisfies condition* C4. *Then the embedding of* A^* *into the subroup of* $\mathrm{Pa}(K_0)$ *generated by* $A^* \cup \mathrm{Ft}(K_0)$ *is a Frattini embedding.*

Proof. Let B be the subgroup of $\mathrm{Pa}(K_0)$ generated by $A^* \cup \mathrm{Ft}(K_0)$, and let M be the set of all $\beta \in K_0$ with parity equal to 0. Suppose $g, h \in A$ and $f \in B$ are such that $f^{-1}g^*f = h^*$. If $g = h$, obviously g^* and h^* are conjugate in A^*. If $g \neq h$ then both g^* and h^* are distinct from the identity permutation of K_0 so that they both map M onto itself but have no fixed points on this set (by C4 and the definition of g^* and h^*) and are pointwise fixed on the rest of K_0. Thus Lemma 0.10 (ii) applies and f must map M onto M. Now, by Theorem 3.28, f is defined by some A-table Γ_0. Then there is some semi-refinement Γ_1 of Γ_0 (also defining f) which has at least two lines, thus possessing a unique line with (for some $r \in J$) a left sequence $\sigma = \langle 1\rangle^r$, this unique line being $\langle 1\rangle$-ending. (After first obtaining, if necessary, a refinement of Γ_0 with more than one line, the unique line with a left sequence of the form $\langle 1\rangle^s$ for some $s \in J$ is either replaced by its direct extracts if it is a regular line, or if it is an A-line an appeal is first made to Lemma 3.25.) Whether the line with σ as its left sequence is a regular line or an A-line, the corresponding line function will map $[\sigma]$ into $[\tau]$, where τ is the right sequence of the line. If τ is not $\langle 1\rangle^s$ for some $s \in J$, the parity of every element of $[\tau]$ will be the same (as τ is $\langle 1\rangle$-ending), so that f either maps $[\sigma] = [\langle 1\rangle^r]$ into M or maps it into the complement of M in K_0. But this is impossible, as $[\langle 1\rangle^r] \cap M \neq \emptyset$ and $[\langle 1\rangle^r]$ is not contained in M, so that the image of $[\sigma]$ under f cannot lie wholly within either M or its complement. Thus τ is $\langle 1\rangle^s$ for some $s \in J$. If τ is the right sequence of a regular line, then $s = r$, as we can choose $\alpha \in K_0$ such that α has parity equal to r, so that $\sigma^\frown\alpha$ has parity 0 and belongs to M and thus the value of f for $\sigma^\frown\alpha$, which is $\tau^\frown\alpha$ with parity $r - s$, also belongs to M. Further, if τ is the right sequence of an A-line $\sigma, b \to \tau, n$ then $s = r - n$, as we can choose $\alpha \in K_0$ such that α has parity equal to r, so that $\sigma^\frown\alpha$ has parity 0 and belongs to M, and thus the value of f for $\sigma^\frown\alpha$, which has parity equal to $r - (s + n)$ by Definition 3.4, belongs to M.

Now we remark that there is some $u \in A$ such that for every $\alpha \in K_0$, and for every $k \geq r$,

$$f(\langle 1\rangle^{k\frown}\langle 0\rangle^{k\frown}\langle 1\rangle^\frown\alpha) = \langle 1\rangle^{u(k)\frown}\langle 0\rangle^{u(k)\frown}\langle 1\rangle^\frown\alpha.$$

If the line with σ as its left sequence is a regular line (i.e., if it is $\langle 1\rangle^r \to \langle 1\rangle^r$) we can take u to the identity element of A (so that $u(k) = k$ for all $k \in J$), and if σ is the left sequence of an A-line $\sigma, b \to \tau, n$ we can take u (in view of Definition 3.4) to be the identity element of A when r does not belong to the domain of b, and $b(r)$ when r belongs to the domain of b. Then, $u^{-1}gu = h$. For otherwise $u^{-1}guh^{-1}$ will not be the identity permutation and so, by C4 (in fact, by C3 alone), as u, g, and h are all permutations there will be some $m \in J$ such that $(u^{-1}guh^{-1})(m) \neq m$ while for $t = u^{-1}(m)$ (thus $(gu)(t) \neq (uh)(t)$) we have $t \geqslant r$ and $g(t) \geqslant r$. For such an m and corresponding t we would then have, for every $\alpha \in K_0$,

$$\begin{aligned}(f^{-1}g^*f)(\langle 1\rangle^{u(t)\frown}\langle 0\rangle^{u(t)\frown}\langle 1\rangle^\frown\alpha) &= (g^*f)(\langle 1\rangle^{t\frown}\langle 0\rangle^{t\frown}\langle 1\rangle^\frown\alpha)\\ &= f(\langle 1\rangle^{g(t)\frown}\langle 0\rangle^{g(t)\frown}\langle 1\rangle^\frown\alpha)\\ &= 1^{u(g(t))}0^{u(g(t))}1^\frown\alpha\\ &\neq 1^{h(u(t))}0^{h(u(t))}1^\frown\alpha\\ &= h^*(\langle 1\rangle^{u(t)\frown}\langle 0\rangle^{u(t)\frown}\langle 1\rangle^\frown\alpha),\end{aligned}$$

so that $f^{-1}g^*f \neq h^*$, contrary to hypothesis. Thus if g^* is conjugate to h^* in B, g is conjugate to h in A and so, as $A \cong A^*$, g^* is conjugate to h^* in A^*.

The results that are really needed for §4 have now been obtained, but the question naturally arises as to whether or not $\mathrm{Ta}(A)$ is actually a group — in particular, the subgroup of $\mathrm{Pa}(K_0)$ generated by $A^* \cup \mathrm{Ft}(K_0)$. It actually is the case that $\mathrm{Ta}(A)$ is a subgroup of $\mathrm{Pa}(K_0)$, the one generated by $A^* \cup \mathrm{Ft}(K_0)$. This makes both $\mathrm{Ta}(A)$ and A^* appear less arbitrarily chosen, the exact form of the definitions not being so important.

Theorem 3.31. *The subgroup of* $\mathrm{Pa}(K_0)$ *generated by* $A^* \cup \mathrm{Ft}(K_0)$ *is equal to* $\mathrm{Ta}(A)$.

Proof. Let us say that the A-multiplicity of a regular line is 0, the A-multiplicity of an A-line $\sigma, b \to \tau, n$ is equal to the cardinality of the domain of b, and the A-multiplicity of an A-table is the sum of the A-multiplicities of its lines. Let B be the subgroup of $\mathrm{Pa}(K_0)$ generated by $A^* \cup \mathrm{Ft}(K_0)$; the theorem follows (in view of Theorem 3.28) once it is shown that every element of $\mathrm{Ta}(A)$ belongs to B.

Note that if $\rho \in {}^{\omega}2$ is non-empty there will be a finite table Γ_0 with the line $\rho \to \langle 1\rangle$; if $F_1 \in \mathrm{Ft}(K_0)$ is defined by this table then, for $g \in A$, $G = F_1 g^* \in B$ will be defined by the A-table obtained from Γ_0 by replacing the line $\rho \to \langle 1\rangle$ by the line $\rho, \{\langle 1, g\rangle\} \to \langle 1\rangle, 0 = (\rho \to \langle 1\rangle) \cdot (\langle 1\rangle, \{\langle 1, g\rangle\} \to \langle 1\rangle, 0)$.

Now suppose $F \in \mathrm{Pa}(K_0)$ is defined by an A-table Γ_1 with A-multiplicity $\leqslant 1$. Then, if Γ_1 has A-multiplicity 0, $F \in \mathrm{Ft}(K_0) \subseteq B$, by Proposition 3.9; otherwise Γ_1 will have the single A-line:

(1) $\qquad \sigma, \{\langle m, g\rangle\} \to \tau, n.$

If necessary, Γ_1 can be refined to ensure that $\tau \in {}^{\omega}2$ is a non-empty sequence.

Case 1: $n \geqslant m-1$. As $\{\langle m, g\rangle\}$ is $(m-1)$-bolstered, if n is $(m-1)+j$ for $j \in J$ then line (1) can be replaced by the line $\sigma, \{\langle m, g\rangle\} \to \tau^\frown\langle 1\rangle^j$, $m-1$ which will define the same line function. Thus we can assume $n = m-1$. As noted above there will be $G' \in B$ defined by an A-table Γ_2 whose only A-line is

(2) $\qquad \tau, \{\langle 1, g^{-1}\rangle\} \to \langle 1\rangle, 0.$

Since $n = m-1$, the composition of lines (1) and (2) is, by (4) of Definition 3.18:

(3) $\qquad \sigma, \{\langle m, gg^{-1}\rangle\} \to \langle 1\rangle, m-1.$

By refining Γ_1 we can get an A-table Γ_1' of which (1) is still the only A-line while every other line has a right sequence equal to the left sequence of some extract of a line of Γ_2, this extract being a regular line in view of Proposition 3.23 and the fact that (1) is a line of Γ_1' while $F \in \mathrm{Pa}(K_0)$. Composing the A-tables Γ_1' and Γ_2 we obtain an A-table Γ_3 which defines FG' and has (3) as its only A-line. As the same line function corresponds to the regular line $\sigma \to \langle 1\rangle^m$ as to (3) (because gg^{-1} is the identity permutation on J), by replacing (3) with this regular line in Γ_3 we obtain an A-table Γ_3' also defining FG', but with only regular lines. So $FG' \in B$, and $F = (FG')(G')^{-1} \in B$ as $G' \in B$, as required.

Case 2: $n < m-1$. Let Γ_4 be a finite table with one of its lines being $\tau \to \tau^\frown\langle 1\rangle^{(m-1)-n}$. Then, where $G'' \in \mathrm{Ft}(K_0)$ corresponds to Γ_4, FG'' will be defined by an A-table whose only A-line is $\sigma, \{\langle m, g\rangle\} \to \tau^\frown\langle 1\rangle^{(m-1)-n}, n$ (the composition of (1) and $\tau \to \tau^\frown\langle 1\rangle^{(m-1)-n}$ according to (3) of Definition 3.18), which defines the same line function as σ, $\{\langle m, g\rangle\} \to \tau$, $m-1$. So there is an A-table Γ_5 which has this line as its only A-line and which defines $FG'' \in \mathrm{Pa}(K_0)$; by case 1 we have $FG'' \in B$ so that, as $G'' \in B$, $F = (FG'')(G'')^{-1} \in B$. Thus every $F \in \mathrm{Pa}(K_0)$ defined by an A-table with A-multiplicity $\leqslant 1$ belongs to B.

Now let us assume that $p \geqslant 1$ and every element of $\mathrm{Pa}(K_0)$ defined by an A-table of A-multiplicity $\leqslant p$ belongs to B. Let $F \in \mathrm{Pa}(K_0)$ be defined by an A-table Γ_6 of A-multiplicity $p+1$. Then Γ_6 will have an A-line; let

(4) $\qquad \sigma, b \to \tau, n$

be such a line, and choose m to belong to the domain of b. As $g = b(m)$ is a permutation of J there will be some $w \in J$ such that for $k \geqslant w$, $g^{-1}(k) \geqslant m$. Then $X = \{j \in J : j < m + w$ and $g(j) \geqslant m + w\} = \{j \in J : m \leqslant j < m + w$ and $g(j) \geqslant m + w\}$ and the set $Y = \{j \in J : j \geqslant m + w$ and $g(j) < m + w\}$ have the same finite cardinality and there is a one-one mapping θ of X onto Y. For $j \in X$, let $\text{li}(j)$ be

$$\sigma^\frown\langle 1\rangle^{j-m\frown}\langle 0\rangle^{j\frown}\langle 1\rangle \to \sigma^\frown\langle 1\rangle^{\theta(j)-m\frown}\langle 0\rangle^{\theta(j)\frown}\langle 1\rangle,$$

which is a regular line. Then there is a partial table Γ^* whose lines consist of the lines $\text{li}(j)$ for $j \in X$, together with the A-line

(5) $$\sigma^\frown\langle 1\rangle^w, \{\langle m + w, g^{-1}\rangle\} \to \sigma, w.$$

Let Σ be the set of all left sequences of Γ_6 except σ, let Σ^* be the left sequence set of Γ^*, and let $\Sigma_0 = \Sigma \cup \Sigma^*$; as Γ_6 is an A-table and the left sequence of (5) and of every line $\text{li}(j)$ for $j \in X$ is an extension of σ, Proposition 0.6 and Proposition 0.5 apply and there is a finite partition set which is an extension of Σ_0. Note that we can arrange that the added sequences of this partition set Σ' are all left sequences of some extract of line (4) (which will be, by Proposition 3.23, a regular line, as it cannot have $\sigma^\frown\langle 1\rangle^j$ for a left sequence for any $j \in \omega$, since $\sigma^\frown\langle 1\rangle^w$ belongs to the parition set Σ_0). Let Γ_7 be the A-table with left partition set Σ' which is an extension of Σ^* by regular lines with the same left and right sequences. The A-multiplicity of Γ_7 is 1, with (5) the sole A-line; thus the function H defined by Γ_7 belongs to B as it belongs to $\text{Pa}(K_0)$ (as inspection shows that the partial table Σ^* determines a one-one function whose range equals its domain). Composing Γ_7 with Γ_6 yields the A-table Γ_8: First, each line of Γ_7 whose left sequence belongs to Σ is replaced by the line of Γ_6 with the same left sequence. Second, every regular line of Γ_7 with a right sequence σ such that $\sigma \subset \sigma'$ is replaced by the composition of this line, according to (1) of Definition 3.18, with the unique regular line which is an extract of line (4) and has σ' as its left sequence (this extract exists as, for $j \in X$, the line $\text{li}(j)$ has a $\langle 1\rangle$-ending right sequence, and the other regular lines have right sequences equal to their left sequences, chosen to be left sequences of extracts). Third, letting b' be the function with the same domain as $\zeta^w(b)$, and agreeing with it except that $b'(m + w) = g^{-1}g$, the line (5) of Γ_7 is replaced by

(6) $$\sigma^\frown\langle 1\rangle^w, b' \to \tau, n + w.$$

The A-table Γ_8 defines the function HF and has exactly the same A-lines as Γ_6, except that the A-line (5) is replaced by the A-line (6). If $m + w$ is the only element belonging to the domain of b', (6) can be replaced in Γ_8 by the regular line $\sigma^\frown\langle 1\rangle^w \to \tau^\frown\langle 1\rangle^{n+w}$, and otherwise b' can be replaced in (6) by the $b'' \in \text{Fi}(A)$ which is like b' except for not having $m + w$ as an element of its domain. In this way we obtain an A-table Γ_9, also defining HF, which has A-multiplicity less than that of Γ_8 and Γ_6. So $HF \in B$ and $F = (H^{-1})(HF) \in B$ as $H \in B$. Hence every element of $\mathrm{Pa}(K_0)$ defined by an A-table of A-multiplicity $p + 1$ belongs to B. Thus, by induction, every element of $\mathrm{Ta}(A)$ belongs to B, and so B is equal to $\mathrm{Ta}(A)$.

§4. Conclusions

In this section, as in §3, J will be the set of all positive integers. It was shown by Rabin (in [8]) that if a finitely generated group has a word problem which is solvable with respect to one presentation on a finite set of generators then the word problem is solvable with respect to every presentation on a finite set of generators. Thus we can say that the word problem for a finitely generated group is solvable or unsolvable without making reference to a specific presentation (on a finite set of generators).

As only countable groups will be discussed in this section, it will be tacitly assumed that all the presentations referred to are on a finite or countably infinite set of generators. In the case where a presentation is given on a countably infinite set of gernerators of a group G there will be a function λ whose domain is J and whose range is a set of generators of G, with $\lambda(j)$ being, for $j \in J$, the element of G correspodning to the j-th element of an enumeration of the generators of the presentation. Note that λ need not be a one-one function. From the proof of Proposition 4.1 it will be apparent that the word problem for the presentation depends in fact only on G and λ. The ordering of the generators of the presentation (when there are more than finitely many of these) is important, however, so it will be assumed that with every presentation on a countably infinite set of generators there is also "given" an ordering, of the same order type as J, of the generators; when the presentation has only finitely many generators we will assume that a simple ordering of these is also provided, but here we rely on the fact that the specific finite simple ordering assigned does not affect the Turing degree of the word problem (as this is explicated in the proof of Proposition 4.1).

Proposition 4.1. *Given a presentation of a countable group C there exists an isomorphic group C' which is a group of permutations of J such that only the identity element has a fixed point. Further, C' can be construed as given by the same presentation as C in such a way that for $j, k \in J$*

and a word w on the generators of the presentation, with $g \in C'$ *corresponding to w, it can be effectively determined whether or not* $g(j) = k$ *relative to a solution of the word problem for the given presentation (of C and C').*

Proof. It will be convenient to make the obvious adjustments enabling us to speak of recursive functions on J instead of ω. Let F be a free group with the same number of independent elements required to generate it as the number of generators in the presentation of the countable group C. The words on the generators of F (which will include the empty word) form a countably infinite set (even if F is finitely generated), so there is a one-one mapping ξ of this set onto J. The words of length one on F correspond either to the generators or their inverses; let K_1 be the subset of J which is the image under ξ of the set of words corresponding in this way to the generators. Now, ξ can easily be chosen in such a way that K_1 is a recursive subset of J, while ψ and θ are recursive functions, where ψ and θ are the unique binary and unary functions from J into J such that for words u and v on the generators of F we have $\psi(\xi(u), \xi(v)) = \xi(uv)$ and $\theta(\xi(u)) = \xi(u')$ where uv is the concatenation of the words u and v and u' is the inverse of the word u (obtained by reversing the order of u and then replacing generators by their inverses and vice-versa — the empty word being its own inverse, of course).

The generators of the presentation of C can now be identified with the elements of K_1, with the first generator of the presentation identified with the smallest element of K_1, the second generator identified with the second-smallest element of K_1, etc. Words on the generators of the presentation are thus implicitly identified with the image under ξ of corresponding words on the generators of F. Let K_2 be the set of all elements $j \in J$ such that the word on the generators of the presentation with which j is identified corresponds to the identity element of C. Note that K_2 depends only on the choice of generators of C and the ordering given to the generators. We can take the Turing degree of the word problem for the presentation to be the Turing degree of K_2. A recursive permutation of the ordering given the generators will not result in a change in the Turing degree of K_2; in particular, the Turing degree will be independent of the ordering if the presentation has only finitely many generators.

Using K_2, the group C' of permutations of J can be defined. First of all, let us define the equivalence relation $\approx$ on J by setting $j \approx k$ for $j, k \in J$ just in case the two words (on the generators of the presentation) with which they are identified correspond to the same element of C. Then we have $\psi(\theta(j), k) \in K_2$ if and only if $j \approx k$. As ψ and θ are recursive functions, we can determine effectively (relative to K_2) whether or not $j \approx k$ for $j, k \in J$. Note that for every element of C there are infinitely many distinct words on the generators of the presentation, and so elements of J, which correspond to it; thus we can now effectively determine (relative to K_2) the smallest, second-smallest, third-smallest... members of J corresponding to a given element of C (given by specifying a word on the generators of the presentation — and so an element of J — to which it corresponds). We now define the function r by letting $r(j)$ be, for $j \in J$, the unique $n \in J$ such that j is the nth smallest element of the equivalence class it determines. For $g \in C$ we let $\delta(g) \in C'$ be the function with domain J such that, for $j \in J$, $(\delta(g))(j)$ is the unique element $i \in J$ such that $r(i) = r(j)$ and i belongs to the equivalence class determined by $\psi(j, k)$, where k is the smallest element of J corresponding to g. Note that ψ is a congruence relation relative to $\approx$, while for $i, j, k \in J$ we have $\psi(\psi(i, j), k) \approx \psi(i, \psi(j, k))$. For $g, h \in C$ we have for every $j \in J$ (where k_1, k_2, and k_3 are respectively the smallest elements of J corresponding to gh, g, and h) $(\delta(gh))(j) \approx \psi(j, k_1) \approx \psi(j, \psi(k_2, k_3))$ (as $k_1 \approx \psi(k_2, k_3)) \approx \psi(\psi(j, k_2), k_3) \approx \psi((\delta(g))(j), k_3) \approx (\delta(h))((\delta(g))(j))$, while $r((\delta(gh))(j)) = r(j) = r((\delta(g))(j)) = r((\delta(h))((\delta(g))(j)))$. Thus, $(\delta(gh))(j) = (\delta(h))((\delta(g))(j))$ for every $j \in J$ and so C' is a homomorphic image of C. Note that $\delta(g)$ only has a fixed point if g is the identity element of C, as for $j \in J$ (with $k \in J$ being the smallest element of J corresponding to g) $(\delta(g))(j) = j$ if and only if $j \approx \psi(j, k)$, which holds if and only if $k \in K_2$. Thus C' is isomorphic to C and can be given by the same presentation — and as it can be effectively determined, relative to K_2, whether or not for $i, j, k \in J$ we have both $r(i) = r(j)$ and i a member of the equivalence class determined by $\psi(j, k)$, the same applies to the determination of whether or not $g(j) = i$ for $g \in C'$.

Lemma 4.2. *Given a presentation Q of a countable group G there exists a group V with a presentation Q' such that V is equal to its commutator group, G is a subgroup of V, and the embedding of G in V is a Frattini embedding, while Q' is obtained from Q by adjoining* 2 *generators and further relations, with the word problems for them Turing equivalent.*

Proof. Given Q and G, we see by Proposition 4.1 that G is isomorphic to a group Y of permutations of J such that only the identity element of Y has any fixed points; by Theorem 2.6 and Definition 2.1 we have $Y \cong \bar{Y}$ where $\bar{Y}$ is a subgroup of $\mathrm{Sp}(Y, {}^{\omega}2)$

whose embedding into $\mathrm{Sp}(Y, {}^{\omega}2)$ is a Frattini embedding. Further, it appears from the proof of Proposition 2.7 that the word problems for the presentation Q of Y (and G and Y) and the presentation Q' of $\mathrm{Sp}(Y, {}^{\omega}2)$ obtained by adjoining to Q two generators corresponding to the elements $(\pi_2^*\pi_1 D)^{\cdot\cdot}$ and $(\pi_0\pi_1\pi_2^*)^{\cdot\cdot}$ of $\mathrm{Ft}(Y; {}^{\omega}2)$ (these will generate $\mathrm{Ft}(Y; {}^{\omega}2)$, in view of Proposition 1.5 and the fact that $\mathrm{Ft}(Y; {}^{\omega}2) \cong \mathrm{Ft}({}^{\omega}2))$ and all the relations valid in $\mathrm{Sp}(Y, {}^{\omega}2)$ will have the same Turing degree. We now just choose V so that there is an isomorphism of $\mathrm{Sp}(Y, {}^{\omega}2)$ onto V whose restriction to Y is an isomorphism of Y onto G. As $V \cong \mathrm{Sp}(Y, {}^{\omega}2)$, V is equal to its commutator group by Theorem 2.3.

Lemma 4.3. *Given a presentation S of a countable group V equal to its commutator group there exists a simple group W with a presentation S' such that V is a subgroup of W, the embedding of V in W is a Frattini embedding, and S' is obtained from S by adjoining 2 generators and further relations, with the word problems for S and S' being Turing equivalent.*

Proof. Given S and V, we see by Proposition 4.1 that V is isomorphic to a group A of permutations of J satisfying condition C4 of §3 (and so C3) and conditions C1 and C2 relative to a solution of the word problem for the presentation S of V. Let A^* be defined as in §3, and let B be the subgroup of $\mathrm{Pa}(K_0)$ generated by $A^* \cup \mathrm{Ft}(K_0)$. Then $A \cong A^*$ and the embedding of A^* into B is a Frattini embedding by Theorem 3.30. Further, it appears from the proof of Theorem 3.29 that the word problems for the presentation S of A (and V and A^*) and the presentation S' of B obtained by adjoining to S two generators corresponding to the elements $\pi_2^*\pi_1 D$ and $\pi_0\pi_1\pi_2^*$ of $\mathrm{Ft}(K_0)$ (these will generate $\mathrm{Ft}(K_0)$, in view of Proposition 1.5) and all the relations valid in B have the same Turing degree. We choose W so that there is an isomorphism of B onto W whose restriction to A^* is an isomorphism of A^* onto V. As $W \cong B$, W is simple by Corollary 1.11, taking H there to be A^*, equal to its commutator group as $A^* \cong V$.

Theorem 4.4. *Given a presentation Q_1 of a countable group G there exists a simple group H with a presentation Q_2 such that G is a subgroup of H, the embedding of G in H is a Frattini embedding, and Q_2 is obtained from Q_1 by adjoining 4 generators and further relations, with the word problems for Q_1 and Q_2 being Turing equivalent.*

Proof. Given Q_1 and G we obtain Q' and V by Lemma 4.2, adjoining two generators; as V is equal to its commutator group we can apply Lemma 4.3 (with Q' as S) to obtain Q_2 (that is, S') and the simple group H (that is, W), adjoining two more generators. The word problem for Q_1 is Turing equivalent to that for Q', which is Turing equivalent to that for Q_2, so the word problems for Q_1 and Q_2 are Turing equivalent. As the embedding of the subgroup G of V into V is a Frattini embedding, and the embedding of the subgroup V of H into H is also a Frattini embedding, G is a subgroup of H and its embedding into H is a Frattini embedding.

Lemma 4.5. *Given a finitely generated simple group H, the word problem for H will be solvable if and only if there is a presentation of H on a finite set of generators with a recursively enumerable set of defining relations.*

Proof. If the word problem for H is solvable, there will evidently be a recursively enumerable set of defining relations for H: after choosing a finite set of generators for H we can take the set of defining relations to consist of those words on the generators which correspond to the identity element of H; this set is recursive. But on the other hand, if there is a presentation of H on a finite set of generators with a recursively enumerable set of defining relations there must be a recursive enumeration of those words on the generators of the presentation which correspond to the identity element of H. Let us choose a fixed word w_0 on the generators of the presentation which does not correspond to the identity element of H. Then (because the defining relations of the presentation can be recursively enumerated) there is a recursive enumeration of those words on the generators of the presentation such that their (individual) adjunction to the defining relations determines a group in which w_0 corresponds to the identity element. As H is simple, every word on the generators of the presentation will occur in one of these two enumerations, but not both; thus the word problem for H is solvable.

If we start with a countable group which is not finitely generated, it is necessary to supplement Theorem 4.4 in order to obtain an embedding of the group in a finitely generated simple group. Using the Higman–Neumann–Neumann embedding technique we can embed a countable group in a finitely generated group (Rotman's book [9] serves as a reference for the particular proof used here for Proposition 4.6).

Proposition 4.6. *Given a presentation Q of a countable group C on an infinite set of generators, there is a group C' generated by 3 elements such that C is a subgroup of C', the embedding of C in C' is a Frattini embedding, and the word problem for C' is Turing equivalent to the word problem for the presentation Q.*

Proof. Let the generators of the presentation Q be, in order, $g_1, g_2, \ldots, g_n, \ldots$; call the set of these generators Γ. Let F be the free group on the two (independent) generators a and b, and let G_1 be the free product $C * F$ of C and F. A subgroup U of F with infinitely many free generators can be chosen so that there is a recursive set of words on a and b corresponding to the (independent) generators of U: let these words be $u_1, u_2, \ldots, u_n, \ldots$. For $i \in J$ let w_i be the word $g_i u_i$. Let G_1' and G_1'' be, respectively, the factor groups of G_1 obtained by putting all the elements of C and F, respectively, equal to the identity. Let W be the subgroup of G_1 generated by the w_i, $i \in J$; then W is isomorphic to U via the mapping η defined by setting $\eta(w_i) = u_i$ for $i \in J$. (For in G_1' the images of the generators of W are independent free generators of the image of U.) As F is a free group and G_1 is a free product, G_1 has a presentation Q_1 whose generators are, in order, $a, b, g_1, g_2, \ldots, g_n, \ldots$ and whose defining relations are exactly the defining relations of Q. We now let C' be the group given by the presentation Q' obtained by adjoining the generator t and the defining relations $t^{-1} w_i t = u_i$ for $i \in J$ to the presentation Q_1. Note that C' is generated by $\{a, b, t\}$, for in C' we have $t^{-1} g_i u_i t = u_i$ and thus $g_i = t u_i t^{-1} u_i^{-1}$ for $i \in J$.

As η is an isomorphism we can apply Britton's Lemma to conclude that G_1 is a subgroup of C' (that is, words on $\Gamma \cup \{a, b\}$ corresponding to distinct elements of G_1 remain so for C') and that a word w on $\Gamma \cup \{t, a, b\}$ in which t or t^{-1} occurs can only be equal to the identity element of C' if it contains (where v and v' are words on $\Gamma \cup \{a, b\}$) either a subword $t^{-1} v t$ or $t v' t^{-1}$, where v is equal in G_1 to an element of W, and v' to an element of U (so the subword is equal to an element of U or W in C'). Now, given words p and q on Γ not corresponding to the identity element of C, if p and q are conjugate in C' there will be a word s with a minimum number of occurrences of t and t^{-1} such that $s^{-1} p s = q$ in C', and thus $s^{-1} p s q^{-1}$ is the identity element of C'. By Britton's Lemma there will be a subword of $s^{-1} p s q^{-1}$ of the form $t^{-1} v t$ or $t v' t^{-1}$ (with v and v' as above) if s is not a word on $\Gamma \cup \{a, b\}$. But the subword cannot be a subword of s^{-1} or s (as it could be replaced in s^{-1} or s by a word on $\Gamma \cup \{a, b\}$ equal to it in C', and s would not be minimal in terms of number of occurrences of t and t^{-1}), nor can it contain p as a subword and thus be conjugate to p (because an element of U or W distinct from the identity will have, in G_1', an image distinct from the identity, no element of C except the identity element can be conjugate in G_1 to an element of U or W). As these are the only possibilities for a subword, s must be a word on $\Gamma \cup \{a, b\}$ so that elements of C conjugate in C' are conjugate in G_1. And if two elements of C are conjugate in G_1 they are conjugate in C, since if they were conjugate in G_1 they would be conjugate in G_1''. Thus the embedding of C in C' is a Frattini embedding.

By using the normal form for free products (and the fact that F is a free group) we observe that a freely reduced non-empty word on $\Gamma \cup \{a, b\}$ will be equal to the identity in G_1 only if there is some non-empty subword on Γ which is equal to the identity in C. This allows us to reduce the word problem for Q_1 to that for Q, so their Turing degrees are the same. Similarly, Britton's Lemma allows us, relative to a solution of the word problem for Q_1, to either effectively determine that a word on $\Gamma \cup \{t, a, b\}$ is not equal to any word on $\Gamma \cup \{a, b\}$ or else obtain (by replacing subwords $t^{-1}vt$ or $tv't^{-1}$ by words on $\Gamma \cup \{a, b\}$) a word on $\Gamma \cup \{a, b\}$ to which it is equal in C' and thus in G_1 (because we can effectively determine of a word on $\Gamma \cup \{a, b\}$ what element of U, or W, it could be equal to in G_1 by examining the factor group G_1'). So the word problems for Q_1 and Q' have the same Turing degree. Finally, C' has a presentation Q'' on the generators t, a, and b whose defining relations consist of the defining relations of Q with each g_i, for $i \in J$, replaced by the word $tu_it^{-1}u_i^{-1}$. That Q'' is a presentation of C' can be seen from the fact that by defining g_i as $tu_it^{-1}u_i^{-1}$ for $i \in J$ we obtain the relations $t^{-1}w_it = u_i$ for $i \in J$ as well as the relations of Q (and Q_1). Because we can effectively eliminate the generators belonging to Γ from words on $\Gamma \cup \{t, a, b\}$ by using the equality $g_i = tu_it^{-1}u_i^{-1}$ holding in C', it follows that the word problems for Q' and Q'' have the same Turing degree. Thus, so do the word problems for Q and Q''; as Q'' is a presentation of C' on a finite number of generators, the word problem for C' is Turing equivalent to the word problem for the presentation Q.

The construction in the proof of Proposition 4.6 could be continued so as to reduce the number of generators to two, but (for finitely generated groups) it is more convenient here to rely on a result which can, for example, be extracted directly from the main theorem of [7]:

Proposition 4.7. *Every countable group G has a Frattini embedding into* *a two-generator group H, with the Turing degree of the word problem for H being the same as that for G, if G is finitely generated.*

Proposition 4.8. *Given a presentation Q of a countable group C there is a group C′ generated by 2 elements such that C is a subgroup of C′, the embedding of C into C′ is a Frattini embedding, and the word problem for C′ is Turing equivalent to the word problem for the presentation Q.*

Proof. If Q is a presentation of C on finitely many generators, we can use Proposition 4.7. If Q is a presentation of C on infinitely many generators, we can put Proposition 4.6 and Proposition 4.7 together, much as was done with Lemma 4.2 and Lemma 4.3 to obtain Theorem 4.4.

The main theorem of Higman's paper [5] gives a characterization of finitely generated groups with recursively enumerable sets of defining relations. We state it in the following form:

Proposition 4.9. *A finitely generated group can be embedded in a finitely presented group if and only if it has a presentation on a finite set of generators with a recursively enumerable set of defining relations.*

Applying Proposition 4.9 to Lemma 4.5 yields:

Proposition 4.10. *A finitely generated simple group has a solvable word problem if and only if it can be embedded in a finitely presented group.*

From Theorem 4.4 it follows that every finitely generated group can be embedded in a finitely generated simple group (by adjoining at most four extra generators) as was proved originally by Philip Hall; Theorem 4.11 below shows that, as a crude estimate (the best result will be given later), there will always be a Frattini embedding of a countable group into a simple group generated by no more than six elements. (In [4], Hall shows that every countable group can be embedded in a simple group with three generators; A.P. Goryushkin reduced the number to two in [3], and P.E. Schupp in [11] showed that these two generators could be chosen to be elements of order two and order three.)

Theorem 4.11. *Given a presentation Q of a countable group C there is a Frattini embedding of C into a simple group H which is generated by 6 elements and has a word problem with the same Turing degree as the* *word problem for the presentation Q. Further, if the word problem for Q is solvable, there will exist a finitely presented group K such that H is a subgroup of K and K, like H, has a solvable word problem.*

Proof. In Clapham's paper [2] it is shown that when a finitely generated group possesses a presentation on a finite set of generators with a recursively enumerable set of defining relations it can be embedded in a finitely presented group in a way that preserves the Turing degree. So, in view of Lemma 4.5, the last part of the theorem follows from the rest. As for the rest, we put Proposition 4.8 and Theorem 4.4 together (in the same way that Lemma 4.2 and Lemma 4.3 were put together to obtain Theorem 4.4).

Corollary 4.12. *For any Turing degree of unsolvability, not necessarily recursively enumerable, there exists a simple group, generated by* 6 *elements, whose word problem has this degree.*

Proof. For any Turing degree of unsolvability there is a presentation Q of a countable group C which has this degree. Then by Theorem 4.11 the appropriate simple group H exists.

At this point it is easy to show that all the results obtained by Boone and Higman in [1] concerning groups still remain valid when "simple group" is replaced by "finitely generated simple group." For instance, when this replacement is made in Theorem I′ and Theorem IV of [1] we obtain stronger results which are weakened versions of Theorem 4.11 (weakened by failing to specify the number of elements required to generate it and omitting the requirement that the embedding be Frattini). When the "Corollary to Theorem IV" is strengthened by this replacement it becomes a weaker version of Corollary 4.12. The same replacement applied to Theorem III of [1] yields the first sentence of the next theorem:

Theorem 4.13. *A necessary and sufficient condition that any recursively enumerable class Γ of finitely presented groups have a uniformly solvable word problem is that there exist a finitely generated simple group H, and a finitely presented group K, such that for each member G of Γ, G is a subgroup of H, and H is a subgroup of K. Further, it can be required that the embedding of G in H be a Frattini embedding for each member G of Γ, while H is generated by* 6 *elements.*

Proof. As the condition is stronger than that of the condition of

Theorem III of [1], the proof of sufficiency given there (of a constructive form, Theorem III′, in which the replacement of "simple" by "finitely generated and simple" also produces a weaker result) applies here also. As regards necessity, we note as in [1] that if Γ has a uniformly solvable word problem then the obvious presentation of the free product G_Γ of the members of Γ has a solvable word problem, and G_Γ contains each member of Γ as a subgroup. Further, the embedding of each member G of Γ into G_Γ is a Frattini embedding (we examine, as in the proof of Proposition 4.6, the factor groups obtained by putting all the elements of G_Γ not belonging to the given G equal to the identity). Applying Theorem 4.11 to G_Γ and its presentation, we obtain the required H.

Without the use of Proposition 4.8 or Proposition 4.6 we can obtain Theorem 4.14 and (using exactly the same proof) Theorem 4.15. (When "simple group" is replaced by "finitely generated simple group" in Theorem I of [1] the result is Theorem 4.15.)

Theorem 4.14. *A finitely generated group G has a solvable word problem if and only if there is a Frattini embedding of G into a finitely generated simple subgroup of a finitely presented group.*

Proof. When there is an embedding of G into a finitely generated simple subgroup H of a finitely presented group K, H will have a solvable word problem by Proposition 4.10, and as G is a finitely generated subgroup of H, so will G. Since G has a presentation on a finite set of generators, the other part follows from Theorem 4.4 and Proposition 4.10.

Theorem 4.15. *A necessary and sufficient condition that a finitely generated group G have a solvable word problem is that there exist a finitely generated simple group H, and a finitely presented group K, such that G is a subgroup of H, and H is a subgroup of K.*

An algebraic characterization of finitely generated groups with solvable word problems is provided by Theorem 4.15, just as it is provided by Theorem I of [1]. Using only the construction of §3 as a basis we could prove a version of Lemma 4.3 in which V is not required to be equal to its commutator group and W (instead of being required to be simple) is only required to be a group such that every proper factor group is Abelian. This would lead to a proof of the variant of Theorem 4.15 obtained by replacing "finitely generated simple group H" by "finitely generated group H whose proper factor groups are Abelian." Boone and Higman ask in [1] whether or not every finitely generated group with a solvable word problem is embeddable in a finitely presented simple group. If so, the finitely generated subgroups of finitely presented simple groups would consist precisely of those finitely generated goups which have a solvable word problem. The construction of §3 (unlike that of §2) does not preserve finite presentability (because applied to finitely presented groups with unsolvable word problems it yields a finitely generated simple group); something like the piecemeal approach (depending on a genetic characterization of the recursive function which solves the word problem for the group to be embedded) which Higman (in [5]) and Clapham (in [2]) employ is probably needed for a positive answer.

The question also arises as to whether or not a finitely generated simple group which is sufficiently well-behaved to have a solvable word problem must have a solvable conjugacy problem. The answer is given by Proposition 4.16, and follows from the fact that there exist finitely generated groups with solvable word problems and unsolvable conjugacy problems.

Proposition 4.16. *There exists a simple group generated by 6 elements which has a solvable word problem but an unsolvable conjugacy problem.*

Proof. Starting with a finitely generated group G with a solvable word problem but unsolvable conjugacy problem we obtain by Theorem 4.11 a Frattini embedding of G into a simple group H which is generated by 6 elements and has a solvable word problem. Since G is a finitely generated subgroup of H, H cannot have a solvable conjugacy problem, as then we would be able to determine effectively whether or not two elements of G were conjugate in H — and so in G.

Although the proofs cannot be given here, there are some significant observations that can be made regarding the number of generators required for the simple groups referred to in the theorems above. First of all:

Remark 4.17. For $K \in \mathrm{Fr}$ and Y a finitely generated permutation group, $\mathrm{Sp}(Y, K)$ is generated by 2 elements of finite order.

The proof that $\mathrm{Sp}(Y, K)$ can be generated by three elements relies on Proposition 2.4 (further reduction depends on a careful examination of the generators of $\mathrm{Ft}(K)$). Note that Proposition 4.7 follows from Remark 4.17 (and the proof of Lemma 4.2), and Proposition 4.6 is only required when we deal with infinitely generated groups. So the construction of §2 can serve as a partial substitute for the Higman–Neumann–Neumann embedding technique. Consideration of Theorem 3.31 eventually leads to:

Remark 4.18. When A is a group of permutations of J generated by $k \geqslant 2$ elements, two of which are of finite order, then $\dot{\mathrm{T}}\mathrm{a}(A)$ can be generated by k elements, two of them of finite order.

It is now a straightforward matter to show that, using Remark 4.17 and Remark 4.18, we can replace 6 by 2 in Theorem 4.11, Corollary 4.12, Theorem 4.13, and Proposition 4.16 (with these two generators both being elements of finite order); in addition, we can require that the simple group generated by two elements be such that the countable weak direct product of a collection of subgroups is always isomorphic to a subgroup. This last part depends on the following remark:

Remark 4.19. When A is a group of permutations of J, the countable weak direct product of a collection of subgroups of $\mathrm{Ta}(A)$ is always isomorphic to a subgroup of $\mathrm{Ta}(A)$.

George Sacerdote's paper [10] has been included in the references below because it uses Theorem 4.14 to give (among other characterizations) an algebraic characterization of groups with a solvable conjugacy problem.

References

[1] W.W. Boone and G. Higman, An algebraic characterization of groups with solvable word problem, J. Aust. Math. Soc. 18 (1974) 41–53.

[2] C.R.J. Clapham, An embedding theorem for finitely generated groups, Proc. London Math. Soc. (3) 17 (1967) 419–430.

[3] A.P. Goryushkin, Imbedding of countable groups in 2-generated simple groups (in Russian), Mat. Zametki 16 (1974) 231–235. The English translation appears in Math. Notes 16 No. 2 (1975; for 1974) 725–727.

[4] P. Hall, On the embedding of a group in a join of given groups, J. Aust. Math. Soc. 17 (1974) 434–495.

[5] G. Higman, Subgroups of finitely presented groups, Proc. Roy. Soc. London, Ser. A, 262 (1961) 455–475.

[6] Ralph McKenzie and Richard J. Thompson, An elementary construction of unsolvable word problems in group theory, in: Word problems, ed. W.W. Boone,

F.B. Cannonito, R.C. Lyndon, (North-Holland Publishing Co., Amsterdam, 1973) pp. 457–478.

[7] C.F. Miller and P.E. Schupp, Embeddings into Hopfian groups, J. Algebra 17 (1971) 171–176.

[8] M.O. Rabin, Computable algebra, general theory and theory of computable fields, Trans. Amer. Math. Soc. 95 (1960) 341–360.

[9] J.J. Rotman, The theory of groups, an introduction (second edition, Allyn and Bacon, Boston, 1973).

[10] George S. Sacerdote, The Boone-Higman theorem and the conjugacy problem. Preprint version; for a later version see J. Algebra 49 (1977) 212–221.

[11] P.E. Schupp, Embeddings into simple groups, J. London Math. Soc. (2) 13 (1976) 90–94.

S.I. Adian, W.W. Boone, G. Higman, eds., Word Problems II
© North-Holland Publishing Company (1980) 443–448

LAWS IN FINITE ALGEBRAS

M.R. VAUGHAN-LEE
Mathematical Institute, Oxford

In the first part of this talk I shall describe a method which has been used with great success by several authors to show that certain classes of finite algebras have finite bases for their laws. (Here I am using the word 'algebra' in the sense of Universal Algebra.) In the second part of the talk I shall give some examples of finite algebras which do not have finite bases for their laws.

If A is a finite algebra then the variety generated by A, $\operatorname{Var} A$, is a locally finite variety. Any locally finite variety is generated by its critical algebras, and so the critical algebras in $\operatorname{Var} A$ play an important role. (A finite algebra is critical if it is not contained in the variety generated by its proper subalgebras and proper homomorphic images.) A locally finite variety $\boldsymbol{V}$ is Cross if

(a) $\boldsymbol{V}$ has a finite basis for its laws,

(b) $\boldsymbol{V}$ has only finitely many critical algebras.

Finite groups, rings, Lie rings, and finite algebras in varieties all of whose algebras have distributive congruence lattices, all generate Cross varieties. The basic method of proving that a finite algebra A generates a Cross variety is to find a finite set Γ of first order sentences with the following properties.

(1) Every algebra in $\operatorname{Var} A$ satisfies Γ.

(2) Every finitely generated algebra satisfying Γ is finite.

(3) There are only finitely many critical algebras satisfying Γ. Then because $\operatorname{Var} A$ is axiomatized by its laws, it follows from (1) that each sentence in Γ is a consequence of the laws of A. Since Γ is finite this implies that the sentences in Γ are all consequences of a finite set V of laws of A. V determines a finitely based variety $\boldsymbol{V}$ of algebras containing $\operatorname{Var} A$, and (2) and (3) imply that $\boldsymbol{V}$ is Cross. The fact that $\operatorname{Var} A$ is Cross follows from the result proved below that a subvariety of a Cross variety is Cross. In most applications the sentences in Γ are laws, but this is not necessary, and is not the case in the proof that a finite algebra generates a Cross variety if it lies in a variety all of whose algebras have distributive congruence lattices. The power of the

method is that it is not necessary to find an explicit basis for the laws of A, but only necessary to find a finite set of first order sentences which imply the existence of a Cross variety containing A.

The following theorem shows the strength of property (b) of a Cross variety.

Theorem. *If* $\boldsymbol{V}$ *is a locally finite variety then the following conditions are equivalent.*

(b) $\boldsymbol{V}$ *has only finitely many critical algebras.*

(c) $\boldsymbol{V}$ *has only finitely many subvarieties.*

(d) $\boldsymbol{V}$ *satisfies the maximal and minimal conditions on subvarieties.*

The equivalence of (b) and (c) is well known (see L'vov [1]). The maximal condition on subvarieties is equivalent to the condition that every subvariety (including $\boldsymbol{V}$) is generated by a finite algebra. The minimal condition on subvarieties is equivalent to the condition that every subvariety is finitely based *as a subvariety*, that is every subvariety is determined by the laws of $\boldsymbol{V}$ together with a finite set of additional laws. Thus the result that subvarieties of Cross varieties are Cross follows from the fact that (b) implies the minimal condition on subvarieties.

Proof of Theorem. Every subvariety of $\boldsymbol{V}$ is generated by its critical algebras, that is by some subset of the critical algebras of $\boldsymbol{V}$. Thus (c) follows from (b). Trivially (c) implies (d). To show that (d) implies (b) we will assume that $\boldsymbol{V}$ is a locally finite variety which satisfies the minimal condition on subvarieties, but which has infinitely many critical algebras. We will then prove that $\boldsymbol{V}$ fails to satisfy the maximal condition on subvarieties. First some notation: if A is an algebra then $(QS-1)A$ is the set of proper factors (or sections) of A. A is critical if $A \notin \mathrm{Var}(QS-1)A$. We will show that if $\boldsymbol{V}$ has a subvariety $\boldsymbol{U}$ such that $\boldsymbol{V}$ has infinitely many critical algebras A with $\mathrm{Var}(QS-1)A \geqslant \boldsymbol{U}$, then $\boldsymbol{V}$ has a subvariety $\boldsymbol{W}$ with this property which properly contains $\boldsymbol{U}$. By assumption $\boldsymbol{V}$ has infinitely many critical algebras, and if A is any algebra then $\mathrm{Var}(QS-1)A$ contains the trivial variety determined by the law $x = y$. It follows by induction that $\boldsymbol{V}$ has a strictly ascending sequence of subvarieties.

Now let $\boldsymbol{U}, \boldsymbol{W}$ be subvarieties of $\boldsymbol{V}$, and let $\boldsymbol{U}$ be a proper subvariety of $\boldsymbol{W}$. Since the subvarieties of $\boldsymbol{V}$ satisfy the minimal condition, $\boldsymbol{U}$ is determined by the laws of $\boldsymbol{V}$ together with a finite set of additional laws. Let this additional set consist of n-variable laws. Then $\boldsymbol{W}$ must fail to satisfy some n-variable law of $\boldsymbol{U}$. So $\boldsymbol{W}$ contains an n-generator algebra B, say, which does not lie in $\boldsymbol{U}$. Then $\boldsymbol{U} < \boldsymbol{U} \vee \operatorname{Var} B \leq \boldsymbol{W}$. Now there are only finitely many n-generator algebras in $\boldsymbol{V}$, and so this implies that there are only finitely many subvarieties of $\boldsymbol{V}$ which are minimal with respect to strictly containing $\boldsymbol{U}$. Let these be $\boldsymbol{W}_1, \boldsymbol{W}_2, \ldots, \boldsymbol{W}_m$. Now suppose that A is a critical algebra in $\boldsymbol{V}$ and that $\operatorname{Var}(QS-1)A \geq \boldsymbol{U}$, but that $\operatorname{Var}(QS-1)A \not\geq \boldsymbol{W}_i$ for any $i = 1, 2, \ldots, m$. Then $\operatorname{Var}(QS-1)A = \boldsymbol{U}$, which implies that A is n-generator. But $\boldsymbol{V}$ has only finitely many n-generator algebras, and so if $\boldsymbol{V}$ has infinitely many critical algebras A such that $\operatorname{Var}(QS-1)A \geq \boldsymbol{U}$ then for some i, $1 \leq i \leq m$, $\boldsymbol{V}$ has infinitely many critical algebras A such that $\operatorname{Var}(QS-1)A \geq \boldsymbol{W}_i$. This completes the proof of the theorem. Note that the proof actually gives that (d) implies that $\boldsymbol{V}$ has only finitely many S-critical algebras. (A finite algebra is S-critical if it is not contained in the variety generated by its proper subalgebras.)

This theorem, and the success of the method I have just described, suggest that the two properties (a) and (b) of a Cross variety may be closely related. However the examples below show that this is not the case. The first is a finite algebra which generates a variety satisfying (a) but not (b), and the second is a finite algebra which generates a variety satisfying (b) but not (a).

The examples are non-associative algebras over an arbitrary finite field F. (A non-associative algebra over F is a vector space over F with a bilinear product.) From the point of view of Universal Algebra, non-associative algebras are very well behaved. They are unital, that is every algebra contains the unique one element algebra $\{0\}$. They have regular congruences, that is two congruences of an algebra are equal if and only if the corresponding congruence classes of 0 are equal. Most important of all, they have permutable congruences and their congruence lattices are modular. Finite *associative* algebras do generate Cross varieties, but Polin [2] has given examples of finite non-associative algebras which do not have finite bases for their laws. The first of the examples below is a finite algebra A such that $\operatorname{Var} A$ does not satisfy the minimum condition on subvarieties. Thus Polin's examples and this example show that the variety generated by a finite non-associative algebra need not be finitely based, and may have subvarieties which are not finitely based *even as subvarieties*.

First we establish some notation. A left normed convention is used: thus abc denotes $(ab)c$. We define ab^n inductively by $ab^0 = a$, $ab^n = (ab^{n-1})b$. Thus $ab^2 = (ab)b$ and $ab^3 = ((ab)b)b$. F is an arbitrary finite field, and we let $|F| = q$.

The first example is an algebra A with basis a, b, c, d, ab, abc, abd, $abcb$, $abcd$, $abdb$, $abdc$, $abcdb$ over F. The products of basis vectors are all zero, except for those of the form xy, $x \in \{a, ab, abc, abd, abcb, abcd, abdb, abdc, abcdb\}$, $y \in \{b, c, d\}$. These products are given by the following table.

	b	c	d
a	ab	0	0
ab	ab	abc	abd
abc	$abcb$	abc	$abcd$
abd	$abdb$	$abdc$	abd
$abcb$	$abcb$	abc	$abcd$
$abcd$	$abcdb$	$abdc$	$abcd$
$abdb$	$abdb$	$abdc$	abd
$abdc$	$abcdb$	$abdc$	$abcd$
$abcdb$	$abcdb$	$abdc$	$abcd$

It is straightforward to check that the following three laws are a basis for the laws of A (as a non-associative algebra over F).

$$x_1(x_2x_3) = 0,$$

$$x_1x_2x_3x_4x_5 = x_1x_2x_4x_3x_5,$$

$$x_1x_2x_3^qx_4 = x_1x_2x_3x_4.$$

We show that $\operatorname{Var} A$ does not satisfy the minimum condition on subvarieties by finding a finite algebra $B \in \operatorname{Var} A$ which does not have a finite basis for its laws. Furthermore it can be shown that $\operatorname{Var} B$ has only finitely many subvarieties. This implies the existence of a finite algebra $C \in \operatorname{Var} B$ with the following properties.

(1) C does not have a finite basis for its laws.

(2) Every proper subvariety of $\operatorname{Var} C$ is Cross.

(3) $\operatorname{Var} C$ has only finitely many subvarieties and only finitely many critical algebras.

The algebra B has a basis a, b, c, ab, ac, abc, acb, $abcb$ over F. All products of these basis vectors are zero except for those of the form xy, $x \in \{a, ab, ac, abc, acb, abcb\}$, $y \in \{b, c\}$. Products of this form are given by the following table.

	b	c
a	ab	ac
ab	ab	abc
ac	acb	ac
abc	$abcb$	abc
acb	acb	$abc + acb - abcb$
$abcb$	$abcb$	abc

The following laws are a basis for the laws of B.

$$x_1(x_2x_3) = 0,$$

$$x_1x_2x_3x_4x_5 = x_1x_2x_4x_3x_5,$$

$$x_1x_2x_3^qx_4 = x_1x_2x_3x_4,$$

$$u_i = 0, \qquad i = 1, 2, 3, 4, 5,$$

$$w_i = 0, \qquad i = 6, 7, \ldots, \text{ where}$$

$$u_1 := x_1x_2^{q+1} - x_1x_2x_2,$$

$$u_2 := x_1x_2^qx_3^q - x_1x_2x_3^q - x_1x_2^qx_3 + x_1x_2x_3,$$

$$u_3 := x_1x_2^qx_3x_4 - x_1x_2^qx_4x_3 - x_1x_2x_3x_4 + x_1x_2x_4x_3,$$

$$u_4 := x_1x_2x_3x_4 + x_1x_3x_4x_2 + x_1x_4x_2x_3 - x_1x_3x_2x_4 - x_1x_2x_4x_3 - x_1x_4x_3x_2,$$

$$u_5 := x_1x_2x_3x_4x_5 - x_1x_3x_2x_4x_5 - x_1x_2x_3x_5x_4 + x_1x_3x_2x_5x_4, \text{ and}$$

$$w_i := x_1x_2x_3x_6x_7 \cdots x_ix_4x_5 - x_1x_3x_2x_6x_7 \cdots x_ix_4x_5 - x_1x_2x_3x_6x_7 \cdots x_ix_5x_4 + x_1x_3x_2x_6x_7 \cdots x_ix_5x_4,$$

for $i = 6, 7, \ldots$.

Note that the first three laws of this basis form a basis for the laws of A, and so $B \in \operatorname{Var} A$. It is straightforward to check that B satisfies these laws, but it is extremely tedious to check that they do form a basis for the laws of B. However there are no real difficulties. The main step is to notice that it is sufficient to consider laws of the form $u = 0$, where u is a linear combination of terms of the form $x_1x_ix_j \cdots x_k$ with $i, j, \ldots, k \geq 2$.

To show that B does not have a finite basis for its laws we proceed as follows. It is not difficult to show that for $i = 1, 2, 3, 4, 5$ any consequence of $u_i = 0$ is of the form $u + v = 0$, where $u = 0$ is a law of A, and v is a (non-associative) polynomial whose degree is the same as the degree of u_i. Similarly for $i = 6, 7, \ldots$ any consequence of $w_i = 0$ is of the form $u + v = 0$, where $u = 0$ is a law of A and v is a polynomial of degree i. Now if B has a finite basis for its laws, then for some integer n greater than the degree of u_i for $i = 1, 2, 3, 4, 5$, B has a basis consisting of the laws of A together with $u_i = 0$ for $i = 1, 2, 3, 4, 5$ and $w_i = 0$ for $6 \leqslant i < n$. But then $w_n = 0$ must be a consequence of these laws, and so, by the above remarks, w_n can be expressed in the form $u + v$ where $u = 0$ is a law of A and v is a polynomial of degree at most $n - 1$. Clearly we may assume that u and v only involve the variables $x_1, x_2, \ldots, x_n$. Now, for $i = 1, 2, \ldots, n$, let π_i be the endomorphism of the free non-associative algebra over F generated by $x_1, x_2, \ldots, x_n$ which maps x_i to 0 and maps the other generators to themselves. Let μ be the endomorphism $(1 - \pi_1)(1 - \pi_2) \cdots (1 - \pi_n)$. Then if v is any polynomial of degree less than n, $v\mu = 0$. So $w_n = w_n\mu = u\mu + v\mu = u\mu$. This implies that $w_n = 0$ is a law of A. However it is easy to see that $w_i = 0$ is not a law of A for any $i \geqslant 6$, and so B cannot have a finite basis for its laws.

Let $\boldsymbol{V}$ be the subvariety of $\operatorname{Var} A$ determined by the laws $u_5 = 0$, $w_i = 0$ for $i = 6, 7, \ldots$. Then the argument given above shows that $\boldsymbol{V}$ does not have a finite basis for its laws, and hence that $\operatorname{Var} A$ does not satisfy the minimum condition on subvarieties. It is possible to prove that any subvariety of $\boldsymbol{V}$ is determined by 4-variable laws. It follows that $\boldsymbol{V}$ has only finitely many subvarieties, and since $B \in \boldsymbol{V}$ this implies that $\operatorname{Var} B$ has only finitely many subvarieties. However since $\boldsymbol{V}$ has only finitely many subvarieties it follows from the theorem that $\boldsymbol{V}$ is itself generated by a finite algebra. Thus the example B is, in a sense, redundant, but I have included it as it seems more satisfactory to have a specific example of a finite algebra which does not have a finite basis for its laws, rather than just to have proved the existence of one.

References

[1] I.V. L'vov, Varieties of associative rings, Algebra i logika 12 (1973) 269–297.
[2] S.V. Polin, The identities of finite algebras, Sib. Math. J. 17 (1976) 1356–1366.

S.I. Adian, W.W. Boone, G. Higman, eds., Word Problems II

ALGEBRAISCH ABGESCHLOSSENE GRUPPEN

Martin ZIEGLER
Mathematical Insitute, Technical University, Berlin

Introduction

We characterize algebraically closed groups up to partial isomorphism by "recursion-theoretic" invariants and determine their properties by looking at these invariants. In the course of our investigations we obtain most of the known results* about algebraically closed groups (in [21, 22, 14, 15, 2, 3]) from more general theorems. We started from the problems of A. MacIntyre in [14, 15, 17] and solve many of them.

We survey some of our results:

A non-trivial group M is algebraically closed if every finite system of equations with coefficients from M, which is solvable in a supergroup of M, has a solution in M. By the theorem of Higman, Neumann, and Neumann ("every isomorphism of subgroups is extendable to an inner automorphism of a supergroup") one can conclude: Algebraically closed groups are ω-homogeneous, i.e. every isomorphism of finitely generated subgroups is extendable to an automorphism (I, 1.10).

ω-homogeneous groups M are determined up to partial isomorphism (u.t.p.i.) by their skeleton $\mathrm{Sk}(M)$ (the class of all finitely generated groups which are embeddable in M) (I, 2.10). So in the study of properties which are compatible with partial isomorphism, it is enough to study the skeletons of algebraically closed groups.

First we characterize those classes $\mathscr{K}$ of finitely generated groups which occur as skeletons of algebraically closed groups. $\mathscr{K}$ has to satisfy the following conditions (I, 3.8):

(U) If $G \in \mathscr{K}$ and H is a finitely generated group, which is embeddable in G, then $H \in \mathscr{K}$.

* This paper — my "Habilitationsschrift" at the Technische Universtität Berlin — was finished in its original version in June 1976. I here omit the last chapter of that version, which dealt with the construction of uncountable groups, because of the great progress made in this area since then; see e.g. [34] and [35].

(JEP) If $H, G \in \mathcal{K}$, then there is $F \in \mathcal{K}$, in which both H and G are embeddable.

(AA) Every finite system of equations with coefficients from $G \in \mathcal{K}$ which is solvable in a group containing G has a solution in a supergroup of G which belongs to $\mathcal{K}$.

B.H. Neumann showed that we can disregard the finitely generated groups with solvable word problem ([22], cf. [27]): Every finitely generated group with solvable word problem is in the skeleton of every algebraically closed group. MacIntyre proved the converse: If G is in the skeleton of every algebraically closed group, it has solvable word problem. And moreover, if G is in the skeleton of every algebraically closed group which contains the finitely generated group F, the word problem of G is Turing-reducible to the word problem of F ([15]).

It was asked in [14] whether this theorem has a converse. The answer is negative ([3], III, 3.5.3).

We define a new notion of reducibility $\leqslant^*$, stronger than Turing reducibility, and prove: for all finitely generated groups F, G the following are equivalent (III, 1.8.1):

(a) for all algebraically closed M, $F \in \mathrm{Sk}(M) \Rightarrow G \in \mathrm{Sk}(M)$.

(b) $W(G) \leqslant^* W(F)$ ($W(G)$ stands for the word problem of G).

$\leqslant^*$ induces an equivalence relation $\equiv^*$ (on the subsets of the set of natural numbers), which partitions $\mathcal{P}(\omega)$ into $*$-degrees. V, the set of $*$-degrees, is — like the set of Turing degrees — an upper semilattice in a natural way. "(b)$\rightarrow$(a)" of III, 1.8.1 shows that the skeleton of an algebraically closed group M is already determined by $W_*(M) = \{W(G)/{\equiv^*} \mid G \in \mathrm{Sk}(M)\}$. The following characterization of these subsets I of V, which are of the form $W_*(M)$ for an algebraically closed group M, turns problems about algebraically closed groups into recursion theoretic problems. (Note that there is u.t.p.i. at most one M s.t. $I = W_*(M)$ (III, 3.12).) There is an algebraically closed group M s.t. $I = W_*(M)$ iff the following conditions hold:

(i) If $b \in I$, $a \leqslant b$, then $a \in I$.

(ii) If $a, b \in I$, then $\sup(a, b) \in I$.

(iii) If $(A \vee B) \in \mathcal{H}$ for a r.e. horn class $\mathcal{H}$ and $A \in \bigcup I$, then there is $C \in \bigcup I$ s.t. $(A \vee C) \in \mathcal{H}$.

We call $I \subset V$ satisfying (i), (ii), (iii) a closed ideal. ($A \vee B$ is the disjoint union of A and B, $A, B \subset \omega$. R.e. horn classes — our recursion theoretic substitute for finite systems of equations — are defined from r.e. sets $\{\langle n_0^i, \ldots n_{r_i}^i \rangle \mid i \in \omega\}$ of finite sequences of natural numbers by $\mathcal{H} = \{X \subset \omega \mid \forall i\ n_1^i \in X \wedge \cdots \wedge n_{r_i}^i \in X \rightarrow n_0^i \in X\}$. Cf. III, 3.8.) The main result of Chapter II is: For every r.e. horn class $\mathcal{H}$ and every natural number m, there is a finite system $S(\vec{g}, \vec{x})$, which is solvable in a supergroup of a group generated by $g_1, \ldots g_m$ if the word problem of $\langle g_1, \ldots g_m \rangle$ is contained in $\mathcal{H}$ (II, 2.6).

As a first application of (III, 3.12) we give in III, 4.1 a recursion theoretic proof of III, 1.8.1 (a)→(b):

Let $a, b \in V$. If for every closed ideal $I \subset V$, $a \in I \Rightarrow b \in I$, then $b \leqslant a$.

We prove the following three theorems in III, 4 using the equivalence of algebraically closed groups and closed ideals:

1. Let the word problem of F be a complete set, then there is a smallest algebraically closed group M which contains F, i.e. M is embeddable over F in every algebraically closed supergroup of G (cf. III, 2.2). Such an M exists uniquely.

2. M_0, the countable algebraically closed group whose skeleton consists of all finitely generated groups with r.e. word problem, is minimal, i.e., isomorphic to each algebraically closed subgroup.

3. There are 2^{ω_1} algebraically closed groups of power ω_1, which are pairwise not partially isomorphic.

All algebraically closed groups satisfy the same (elementary) $\forall_2$-sentences (i.e sentences of the form $\forall \vec{x}\, \exists \vec{y}\, \varphi(x, y)$, where φ is a quantifier-free formula). In [14] MacIntyre exhibited two algebraically closed groups and a $\forall_4$-sentence which holds only in one of them. One of the problems in [14] was the question whether there is a $\forall_3$-sentence by which one can distinguish algebraically closed groups.

What are the elementary properties of algebraically closed groups in terms of their associated closed ideal? We assign to $W_*(M)$ the ω-model $\omega(M) = (\omega, +, \cdot, \bigcup W_*(M), \in)$. We speak about $\omega(M)$ in the language L^2 — the elementary language of second-order number theory. It is shown in Chapter IV that the properties of $\omega(M)$ which are expressible by L^2-sentences, correspond to the elementary properties of M: For every L^2-sentence ρ there is an elementary sentence φ, which holds in an algebraically closed group M iff ρ holds in $\omega(M)$, and vice versa (IV, 2.4). We have a good control over the mutual dependence of he complexity of ρ and the complexity of φ. E.g., for every r.e. set A there is a $\forall_3$-sentence φ, which is true in an algebraically closed group M iff $A \not\in \bigcup W_*(M)$. φ is false in M_0. If A is not recursive, there are also (by [15]) algebraically closed groups where φ holds. This solves the mentioned problem from [14]. There are in fact 2^{ω}-many algebraically closed groups which satisfy pairwise different $\forall_3$-sentences (IV, 3.5.1). (This was also proved in [40].)

By this method we can answer a further question from [14]. Which properties of algebraically closed groups are definable by elementary formulas? [14] contains some examples of "infinitary notions", which are in algebraically closed groups elementarily expressible. There is, e.g., a $\forall_2$-formula $\varphi(x_0, \ldots x_n)$, which holds in M for $a_1, \ldots a_n$ iff the group generated by $a_1, \ldots a_n$ is simple (cf. IV, 3.1.1).

In all ω-homogeneous M the L^2-properties of $\omega(M)$ correspond canonically to the "arithmetical" properties of M, which are described in III in two ways: As the properties which are obtained from "recursive" properties by quantification, and as the properties which are expressible in L^*, a weak second order logic with "in-built number theory". In algebraically closed groups all arithmetical properties are "elementary". The examples in [14, 2] are easily seen to be arithmetical properties. This characterization was independently given in [33].

The algebraically closed groups which we construct in this paper — e.g., in the proof of I, 3.8 (characterization of the skeletons of algebraically closed groups) or in the proof of III, 1.8.1 — are built up using step-by-step methods, not by "forcing in model theory". On the contrary we used our methods to study generic groups.

In V, 1 we give a simple description of the ∞-generic groups. An algebraically closed group M is ∞-generic iff $\omega(M)$ is an elementary substructure of $(\omega, +, \cdot, \mathcal{P}(\omega), \in)$.

V, 2 gives a new approach to finite generic groups: We define the forcing relation "game theoretically", in a way which clarifies the connection with the step-by-step methods. The usual syntactic definition of forcing is now Lemma V, 2.6. The results of IV ("arithmetical properties are elementary") allow us to prove a simple characterization of the generic groups, in which the forcing relation and elementary sentences are not used. A group M is generic iff every "dense", arithmetical family of finite systems of equations has a member which has a solution in M (V, 3.8).

In Chapter VI we study the properties of $W_*(M)$, for generic M. A family $\mathcal{F}$ of r.e. horn classes is "dense" if $\mathcal{H} \cap \bigcup \mathcal{F} \neq \emptyset$ for all non-empty r.e. horn classes $\mathcal{H}$. $B \subset \omega$ is said to be "subgeneric" if B belongs to the union of every arithmetical dense family of r.e. horn classes. Theorem (VI, 3.3) is: An algebraically closed group M is generic iff $\bigcup W_*(M)$ contains only subgeneric sets.

We list four theorems, which we prove by this characterization:

(VI, 3.3) For every generic group M there is a unique $b \in V$ s.t. $W_*(M) = \{a \in V \mid a \leq b\}$ (the b's which occur in this way can be easily characterized).

(VI, 3.4.4) Countable generic groups are minimal.

(VI, 4.4.2) Every generic group M contains a finitely generated group F s.t. $F * F \notin \mathrm{Sk}(M)$.

(VI, 2.10) A $\forall_3$-sentence, which holds in some algebraically closed group, holds in all generic groups.

The last theorem answers a question from [14]: Is there a $\forall_3$-sentence true in generic groups which does not hold in ∞-generic groups? It is enough to note that every $\forall_3$-sentence which holds in ∞-generic groups, holds in all algebraically closed groups (IV, 3.6.2).

C.F. Miller III proved many of our theorems (e.g. II, 3.10, III, 1.8.1) independently and at about the same time.

I thank Susanne Ziegler and Robert Fittler for their help and encouragement.

Bezeichnungen

Eine Ordinalzahl ist die Menge aller kleineren Ordinalzahlen. ω, die kleinste Limesordinalzahl, ist die Menge der natürlichen Zahlen. $\alpha+1$ ist der Nachfolger der Ordinalzahl α. Wenn κ eine Kardinalzahl ist, ist κ^+ die Nachfolgerkardinalzahl. Statt ω^+ schreiben wir ω_1. Die Kontinuumshypothese (CH) sagt $2^\omega = \omega_1$.

$|A|$ ist die Mächtigkeit der Menge A. A ist abzählbar, wenn $|A| = \omega$. Die Potenzmenge von A bezeichnen wir mit $\mathcal{P}(A)$. Ist κ eine Kardinalzahl, bedeutet $\mathcal{P}_\kappa(A)$ $\{X \subset A \mid |X| < \kappa\}$.

${}^AB$ ist die Menge der Funktionen $f: A \to B$ von A nach B. Für $C \subset A$ ist $f[C] = \{f(x) \mid x \in C\}$. A ist der Vorbereich $\mathrm{Vb}\, f$ von f, $f[A] = \mathrm{Nb}\, f$ der Nachbereich. id_A ist die Funktion $\{(x,x) \mid x \in A\}$. f setzt g fort, wenn $g \subset f$. $f|_C$ bezeichnet die Einschränkung $f \cap (C \times \mathrm{Nb}\, f)$ auf C. Wenn f injektiv ist, ist f^{-1} die Umkehrfunktion von f. Ist der gemeinte Vorbereich klar, schreiben wir $\lambda x \cdots x \cdots$ für die Funktion, die jedem $x \cdots x \cdots$ zuordnet. fg ist die Funktion $\lambda x f(g(x))$.

Eine Funktion f können wir als die Familie $(f(x) \mid x \in \mathrm{Vb}\, f)$ auffassen. Ist α eine Ordinalzahl, nennen wir $(a_\beta \mid \beta < \alpha)$ eine Wohlordnung von $\{a_\beta \mid \beta < \alpha\}$. ${}^{\underline{\alpha}}B := \bigcup\{{}^\beta B \mid \beta < \alpha\}$. Mit $\vec{b}$ meinen wir eine endliche Folge $(b_0, \ldots, b_{n-1})$ aus ${}^{\underline{\omega}}B$. n ist die Länge $l(\vec{b})$ von b. Wir schreiben häufig kürzer $\vec{b} \in B$. Wenn $g \in {}^BC$, meinen wir mit $g(\vec{b})$ die Folge $(g(b_0), \ldots g(b_{n-1}))$. $\vec{b}^\frown\langle c\rangle$ ist die Folge $(b_0, \ldots, b_{n-1}, c)$. Elemente von ${}^\omega B$ bezeichnen wir mit $\vec{b}$.

Ist $\equiv$ eine Äquivalenzrelation auf A, ist $A/{\equiv}$ die Menge der Äquivalenzklassen $a/{\equiv}$, $a \in A$. C trennt A und B, wenn $A \subset C$ und $B \cap C = \emptyset$.

Wir betrachten L-Strukturen $\mathfrak{A}, \mathfrak{B} \ldots$ für eine abzählbare Sprache L. (L ist eine Menge von Konstanten, Funktionszeichen und Relationszeichen. Außer im ersten Kapitel wird L immer die Sprache L^G der "Gruppentheorie" sein: L^G enthält eine Konstante $\boldsymbol{e}$ für das neutrale Element, ein zweistelliges Funktionszeichen $\cdot$ für die

Gruppenmultiplikation und das einstellige Funktionszeichen^{-1}, die Inversenbildung.) Wir unterscheiden vielfach die Struktur nicht von ihren Grundbereich, z. B. in Schreibweisen wie $X \cap \mathfrak{A} = \emptyset$, $x \in \mathfrak{A}$, $\vec{a} \in \mathfrak{A}$, $f[\mathfrak{A}]$. Mit $\mathfrak{A} \subset \mathfrak{B}$ meinen wir aber, daß $\mathfrak{A}$ Unterstruktur von $\mathfrak{B}$ ist. $\mathfrak{A} < \mathfrak{B}$ heißt: $\mathfrak{A}$ ist (isomorph) in $\mathfrak{B}$ einbettbar. Ein Homomorphismus $\nu : \mathfrak{A} \to \mathscr{L}$ ist "über C", wenn ν auf C identisch operiert. Wir schreiben dann $\nu : \mathfrak{A} \to_C \mathfrak{B}$ und $\mathfrak{A} <_C \mathfrak{B}$, wenn es eine Einbettung von $\mathfrak{A}$ in $\mathfrak{B}$ über C gibt. $\mathfrak{A} \cong_C \mathfrak{B}$ sagt, daß es einen Isomorphismus von $\mathfrak{A}$ und $\mathfrak{B}$ über C gibt.

Aut($\mathfrak{A}$) ist die Automorphismengruppe von $\mathfrak{A}$. $\mathrm{id}_{\mathfrak{A}}$ ist der triviale Automorphismus.

Wenn $B \subset \mathfrak{A}$, bezeichnet $\langle B \rangle$ die von B erzeugte Unterstruktur. Entsprechende Bedeutung haben $\langle B, C\rangle$, $\langle \mathfrak{B}, C\rangle$, $\langle \vec{a}\rangle$, $\langle B, \vec{a}\rangle$, $\langle \vec{b}, \vec{a}\rangle$, $\langle a_i \mid i \in I\rangle, \ldots$ usw.

Wir erweitern jedes L durch Hinzufügen einer Menge $C = \{c_i \mid i \in \omega\}$ von neuen Konstanten zu $L(C)$. Wenn $\vec{a} \in \mathfrak{A}$, wird $\mathfrak{A}$ zur $L(c_0, \ldots c_{n-1})$-Struktur $(\mathfrak{A}, \vec{a})$, in der c_i durch a_i interpretiert wird. Für c_i schreiben wir dann $\boldsymbol{a}_i$.

$(\langle \vec{a}\rangle, \vec{a})$ kürzen wir mit $\langle \vec{a}\rangle'$ *ab*. $\nu : \langle \vec{a}\rangle \to \langle \vec{b}\rangle$ ist also genau dann ein Homomorphismus von $\langle \vec{a}\rangle'$ nach $\langle \vec{b}\rangle'$, wenn ν ein Homomorphismus von $\langle \vec{a}\rangle$ nach $\langle \vec{b}\rangle$ ist, und $\nu(\vec{a}) = \vec{b}$. Entsprechend meinen wir mit $\langle B, a\rangle'$ die $L(\vec{c})$-Struktur $(\langle B, \vec{a}\rangle, \vec{a})$ usw. a und b haben den gleichen Typ über C, wenn $\langle a\rangle' \cong_C \langle b\rangle'$ (kurz für $\langle C, a\rangle' \cong_C \langle C, b\rangle'$).

Der Sprache L ($L(C)$) ordnen wir die Menge $L_{\omega,\omega}$ ($L_{\omega,\omega}(C)$) der elementaren L- ($L(C)$-) Formeln zu. Die Formeln bauen sich aus den atomaren Fomeln $t_1 \doteq t_2$ und $R(t_1, \ldots t_n)$ mit $\exists x, \wedge, \neg$ auf (t_i L- ($L(C)$-) Terme). Die Formeln von $L_{\infty,\omega}$ erhält man mit der zusätzlichen Bildungsregel "ist S eine Menge von Formeln, so sind auch $\bigwedge S$ und $\bigvee S$ Formeln". Diese Schreibweise benützen wir, wenn S endlich ist, auch, um $L_{\omega,\omega}$-Formeln zu beschreiben. Statt $\bigwedge\{\varphi_i \mid i \in I\}$ verwenden wir auch $\bigwedge_{i \in I} \varphi_i$. Wenn S leer ist, ist $\bigwedge S = \top$ und $\bigvee S = \bot$ ("wahr" und "falsch"). Wenn man nur höchstens abzählbare Konjunktionen und Disjunktionen zuläßt, gelangt man zu den Formeln von $L_{\omega_1,\omega}$.

Daß in der $L_{\omega,\omega}(C)$-Formel φ höchstens die freien Variablen $x_0, \ldots x_n$ (und die neuen Konstanten $c_0, \ldots c_k$) vorkommen, drücken wir durch $\varphi(x_0, \ldots, x_n)$ ($\varphi(c_0, \ldots c_k, x_0, \ldots x_n)$) aus. Für das Resultat der Ersetzung der x_i durch Terme t_i (und der c_i durch t'_i) schreiben wir $\varphi(t_0, \ldots)$ ($\varphi(t'_0, \ldots t_0, \ldots)$). Entsprechend benützen wir die Schreibweise $S(x_0, \ldots)$ für Formelmengen.

Wenn $\vec{a} \in \mathfrak{A}$, bedeutet $\mathfrak{A} \models \varphi(\vec{\boldsymbol{a}})$, daß $(\mathfrak{A}, \vec{a}) \models \varphi(\vec{\boldsymbol{a}})$ (oder $(\mathfrak{A}, \vec{a}) \models \varphi(\vec{c})$). $t(\vec{a})$, für einen L-Term $t(\vec{x})$, bedeutet genauer $t(\vec{\boldsymbol{a}})^{\mathfrak{A}}$. Ist $\vec{t}(\vec{x})$ eine Folge von L-Termen, ist $\vec{t}(\vec{a})$ die Folge $t_0(\vec{a}), t_1(\vec{a}), \ldots$.

Die Menge $S(\vec{x})$ von Formeln ist in $\mathfrak{A}$ erfüllbar, wenn $\mathfrak{A} \models S(\vec{a})$ für geeignete $\vec{a}$ aus $\mathfrak{A}$. Wenn T eine Menge von Aussagen ist, ist $\{\varphi \mid T \vdash \varphi\}$ die Menge der logischen Folgerungen von T. $\mathfrak{A} \equiv \mathfrak{B}$ heißt, daß $\mathfrak{A}$ und $\mathfrak{B}$ elementar äquivalent sind, $\mathfrak{A} < \mathfrak{B}$, daß $\mathfrak{A}$ elementare Unterstruktur von $\mathfrak{B}$ ist. Eine $\exists_n$-Formel ψ hat in pränexer Normalform die Gestalt $\exists \vec{x}_1 \forall \vec{x}_2 \exists \cdots Q\vec{x}_n \varphi$, φ quantorfrei. Dann ist $\neg\psi$ eine $\forall_n$-Formel. $\mathfrak{A} \equiv_{\exists_n} \mathfrak{B}$ meint: alle $\exists_n$-Aussagen gelten genau dann in $\mathfrak{A}$, wenn sie in $\mathfrak{B}$ gelten.

$\mathfrak{A}$ ist 1-elementare Unterstruktur von $\mathfrak{B}$, wenn $\mathfrak{A} \subset \mathfrak{B}$ und für alle $\vec{a} \in \mathfrak{A}$ jede $\exists_1$-Formel aus $L(\vec{a})$, die in $\mathfrak{B}$ gilt, auch in $\mathfrak{A}$ gilt, $\mathfrak{A} <_1 \mathfrak{B}$.

Es sei nun $L = L^G$. T^G ist die Menge der Gruppenaxiome. Gruppen sind Modelle von T^G. Wir schreiben $\cdots \vdash^G \cdots$ für $\cdots \cup T^G \vdash \cdots$. Eine Gleichung (Ungleichung) ist eine Formel der Form $(\neg)t_1(\vec{x}) \doteq t_2(\vec{x})$, t_i $L(C)$-Terme. Relativ zu T^G ist jede Gleichung äquivalent zu einer Gleichung der Form $t(\vec{x}) \doteq e$. Weiter können wir Terme mit Wörtern identifizieren; das sind endliche Folgen von x_i und x_i^{-1}. Wenn W ein Wort in $x_0, \ldots x_k$ ist und $g_0, \ldots g_m$ Elemente einer Gruppe G sind, bedeutet $W(g_0, \ldots g_m)$ — wenn $k \leq m$ — $W(g_0, \ldots g_k)$, und — wenn $m < k$ — $W(g_0, \ldots g_m, e, e, \ldots)$.

$\mathrm{Gl}(G, \vec{g})$ ist die Menge aller Gleichungen aus $L(\vec{g})$, $\mathrm{Ungl}(G, \vec{g})$ die Menge aller Ungleichungen aus $L(\vec{g})$, die in G gelten.
$\mathrm{Diag}(G, \vec{g}) := \mathrm{Gl}(G, \vec{g}) \cup \mathrm{Ungl}(G, \vec{g})$.

Wenn $q_0, \ldots, q_n$ Aussagenvariable sind, nennen wir die Formel $q_1 \wedge q_2 \wedge \cdots \wedge q_n \rightarrow q_0$ bzw. $q_1 \wedge q_2 \wedge \cdots \wedge q_n \rightarrow$ (das bedeutet $(q_1 \wedge \cdots \wedge q_n \rightarrow \bot)$ eine positive bzw. negative aussagenlogische Implikation). Eine (positive bzw. negative) Implikation bekommt man, wenn man in einer aussagenlogischen Implikation die Aussagenvariablen durch Gleichungen ersetzt.

Vermöge einer Gödelnumerierung ($\ulcorner\varphi\urcorner$ ist die Gödelnumer von φ) übertragen wir rekursionstheoretische Begriffe auf $L_{\omega,\omega}(C)$. z. B. heißt eine Menge von Formeln rekursiv aufzählbar (r.a.), wenn die entsprechende Menge von Gödelnummern r.a. ist. Für Wörter nehmen wir eine besondere Gödelnumerierung. Wir wählen eine rekursive Bijektion von ${}^{\omega}\omega$ und ω. Dadurch ist jede natürliche Zahl s Gödelnummer einer Folge $(s(0), s(1), \ldots s(l(s)-1))$. Dem Wort $W = x_{k_0}^{\varepsilon_0} \cdots x_{k_n}^{\varepsilon_n}$, $\varepsilon_i \in \{1, -1\}$, ordnen wir die Folge $m_0, \ldots m_n$ zu, wobei $m_i = 2k_i$ $(= 2k_i + 1)$, wenn $\varepsilon_i = 1$ $(= -1)$. Die Gödelnummer von W ist die Gödelnummer s der Folge $m_0, \ldots m_n$. Wir schreiben $W = V_s$. Wenn $\vec{g} \in G$, definieren wir $W(G, \vec{g}) = \{i \mid V_i(\vec{g}) = e\}$. Wenn G endlich erzeugt ist, und $\vec{g}$ und $\vec{h}$ zwei Erzeugendensysteme von G sind, sind $W(G, \vec{g})$ und $W(G, \vec{h})$ rekursiv isomorph $(W(G, \vec{g}) \equiv_1 W(G, \vec{h}))$. Wir schreiben dann einfach $W(G)$ für $W(G, \vec{g})$, das Wortproblem von G.

G hat lösbares Wortproblem, wenn $W(G)$ rekursiv ist. G ist rekursiv präsentiert, wenn $W(G)$ rekursiv aufzählbar ist. Für eine Untergruppe U von G definieren wir $W(G \mid U, \vec{g}) := \{i \mid V_i(\vec{g}) \in U\}$.

Mit einer rekursiven Bijektion $n, m \mapsto \langle n, m\rangle$ ($\geqslant n, m$) identifizieren wir ω^2 mit ω. Wir können so eine Teilmenge von ω auch als zweistellige Relation auffassen. $\langle a, b, c, \ldots\rangle$ bedeutet $\langle \cdots \langle\langle a, b\rangle, c\rangle \cdots\rangle$. Die disjunkte Vereinigung $A \vee B$ von A, B ist $2A \cup (2B+1)$ d. h. $\{2x \mid x \in A\} \cup \{2x+1 \mid x \in B\}$. $A \vee B \vee C \vee \cdots$ bedeutet $((\cdots((A \vee B) \vee C) \vee \cdots)$. Wir verwenden Gödelnumerierungen $i \mapsto D_i$, D_i^1, D_i^2 aller endlichen Mengen, aller Mengen mit höchstens einem Element, aller Mengen mit höchstens zwei Elementen.

W_z bezeichnet die z-te r.a. Menge, z ist ein Σ_1^0-Index von W_z. A ist r.a. in B, $A \leqslant_{\mathrm{ra}} B$, wenn für ein $z \in \omega$ $A =$ $\{x \mid \exists u, w \langle x, u, w\rangle \in W_z \wedge D_u \subset B \wedge D_w \subset \omega \setminus B\}$. A ist Turing-reduzierbar auf B, $A \leqslant_T B$, wenn $A \leqslant_{\mathrm{ra}} B$ und $\omega \setminus A \leqslant_{\mathrm{ra}} B$. A ist m-reduzierbar (1-reduzierbar) auf B vermöge f, wenn f eine (injektive) rekursive Funktion ist und $A = \{x \mid f(x) \in B\}$, Schreibweise: $A \leqslant_m B$, $A \leqslant_1 B$.

Eine Σ_n^0-Menge $A \subset \omega^k$ ist eine Menge der Form $\{(x_1, \ldots x_k) \mid \exists v_1 \forall v_2 \exists \cdots Q v_n R(v_1, \ldots x_k)\}$ für eine rekursive Relation R. A ist Π_n^0, wenn $\omega^k \setminus A$ Σ_n^0 ist, und Δ_0^n, wenn A Σ_n^0 und Π_n^0 ist.

A ist arithmetisch, wenn A Σ_n^0 ist für ein $n \in \omega$. $\phi^{(n)}$ ist die vollständige Σ_n^0-Menge aus [24]. $\phi^{\omega} = \{\langle n, k\rangle \mid k \in \phi^{(n)}\}$. Entsprechend definiert man Π_n^0 (Σ_n^0, arithmetische) Teilmengen von $\omega^k \times (\mathcal{P}(\omega))^m$, (in [24] $\Sigma_n^{(s)}$, $\Pi_n^{(s)}$). A ist implizit arithmetisch definierbar in B, wenn $\{A\} =$ $\{Y \subset \omega \mid (Y, B) \in R\}$ für ein arithmetisches $R \subset (\mathcal{P}(\omega))^2$.

Zu jeder Teilmenge $\mathcal{S}$ von $\mathcal{P}(\omega)$ gehört das ω-Modell $(\omega, \mathcal{S}) =$ $(\omega, +, \cdot, \mathcal{S}, \in)$. Wir beschreiben ω-Modelle mit L^2-Aussagen. L^2 hat Variable $v_1, \ldots w_1, \ldots$ für natürliche Zahlen, $X, Y, Z, \ldots$ für Elemente von $\mathcal{S}$ und für jedes $n \in \omega$ eine Konstante. Aus den atomaren Formeln $t_1 \doteq t_2$, $t_1 \in X$ (t_i Zahlterme) baut man die Formeln von L^2 mit $\neg, \wedge, \exists v_i$ und $\exists X_i$ auf.

R ist analytisch, wenn R in $(\omega, \mathcal{P}(\omega))$ mit einer L^2-Formel definiert werden kann. A ist analytisch in B, wenn $A = \{x \mid (B, x) \in R\}$ für ein analytisches R.

Die L^2-Formeln ohne gebundene Mengenvariable beschreiben gerade arithmetische Eigenschaften. Da die Gültigkeit einer solchen Formel φ nicht von $\mathcal{S}$ abhängt, übernehmen wir häufig φ in die Metasprache und schreiben $\varphi(A)$ statt $(\omega, \cdots) \models \varphi(\boldsymbol{A})$. Wir nennen eine solche Formel Σ_n^0-Formel, wenn sie eine Σ_n^0-Menge definiert. Wir denken uns alle arithmetischen Relationen als Relationszeichen in L^2 aufgenommen.

Eine L^2-Formel der Form $\exists \vec{v}_1, \vec{X}_1 \forall \vec{v}_2, \vec{X}_2 \cdots Q\vec{v}_n, \vec{X}_n R$ für ein rekursives R nennen wir eine $\tilde{\Sigma}^1_n$-Formel. Entsprechend definiert man $\tilde{\Pi}^1_n$-Formeln.

Wenn A eine Teilmenge der Gruppe G ist, bezeichnet $\langle A\rangle^N$ den von A erzeugten Normalteiler. G ist genau dann einfach, wenn für alle $a, b \neq e$ $a \in \langle b\rangle^N$. $\mathrm{Fr}(S)$ ist die von (von den Elementen von) S erzeugte freie Gruppe. $\mathrm{Fr}(\vec{b})$ ist $\mathrm{Fr}(\{b_0, \ldots b_{n-1}\})$. G wird von der Menge von Gleichungen $S(\vec{g})$ präsentiert, wenn — falls $S(\vec{g}) = \{W(\vec{g}) \doteq e \mid W \in A\}$ — $(G, \vec{g})$ isomorphes Bild von $(\mathrm{Fr}(\vec{g})/\langle W(\vec{g}) \mid W \in A\rangle^N, \vec{g})$ ist. Insbesondere wird also G von den $\vec{g}$ erzeugt.

Wenn H, F Untergruppen von G sind, ist "$H \cdot F$ direkt", wenn $H \cdot F = H \times F$ (inneres Produkt) ist. Das heißt $H \cap F = E$ (E ist die triviale Gruppe) and $H \subset Z'(F)$ ($Z'(F)$ ist der Zentralisator von F in G).

G sei Untergruppe von H, F. Wir fassen das amalgamierte Produkt $H *_G F$ als Obergruppe von H und F auf. Das amalgamierte der Produkt der Obergruppen F_j von G, $j \in J$ ist $*_G \{F_j \mid j \in J\}$. $\bigoplus \mathcal{K}$ ist die direkte Summe aller Gruppen aus $\mathcal{R}$, wir schreiben auch $\bigoplus_{G \in \mathcal{K}} G$ oder $\times_{i \in n} F_i$. $Z(G)$ ist das Zentrum von G, $[g, h]$ der Kommutator $ghg^{-1}h^{-1}$. $\tau_g = \lambda x\, gxg^{-1}$ ist der zu g gehörende innere Automorphismus von G.

I. Algebraisch abgeschlossene Gruppen als ω-homogene Strukturen

Im ersten Abschnitt zeigen wir, daß sich jede Gruppe in eine algebraisch abgeschlossene (a.a.) Gruppe einbetten läßt (1.3). Da jede 1-elementare Unterstruktur einer a.a. Gruppe wieder a.a. ist (1.5.2), findet man zu jeder abzählbaren Gruppe eine abzählbare a.a. Obergruppe (1.6). Das zeigt, weil es 2^ω nicht-isomorphe endlich erzeugte Gruppen gibt, daß es auch 2^ω nicht-isomorphe abzählbare a.a. Gruppen gibt.

Um die Isomorphietypen der abzählbaren a.a. Gruppen zu bestimmen, beachten wir, daß a.a. Gruppen ω-homogen sind (2.1): Jeder partielle Isomorphismus endlich erzeugter (e.e.) Unterstrukturen läßt sich zu einem Automorphismus fortsetzen (1.9).

Abzählbare ω-homogene L-Strukturen (für eine Sprache L) sind bis auf Isomorphie eindeutig durch ihr Skelett — die Klasse aller einbettbaren e.e. L-Strukturen — bestimmt (2.11.1). Allgemeiner: Zwei ω-homogene Strukturen sind genau dann partiell isomorph (oder $L_{\infty,\omega}$-äquivalent), wenn sie das gleiche Skelett haben (2.10.1). Wir können also (zumindest theoretisch) Eigenschaften ω-homogener Strukturen, die nur vom "partiellen Isomorphietyp" abhängen, am Skelett erkennen. So ist z. B. (wenn L die Sprache der Gruppentheorie ist) eine ω-homogene L-Struktur genau dann eine a.a. Gruppe, wenn ihr Skelett aus Gruppen besteht und algebraisch abgeschlossen ist, d. h. daß jedes über einer Gruppe des Skeletts lösbare Gleichungssystem in einer Obergruppe aus dem Skelett lösbar ist (3.7).

Um das Studium der ω-homogenen Strukturen auf das Studium der Skelette zurückzuführen, müssen wir die Klassen der e.e. Strukturen kennzeichnen, die als Skelett vorkommen. (3.5) sagt: Eine Klasse $\mathcal{K}$ endlich erzeugter Strukturen (in der höchstens ω_1 viele verschiedene Isomorphietypen vorkommen) ist genau dann Skelett einer ω-homogenen Struktur, wenn $\mathcal{K}$ "unterstruktur-abgeschlossen" ist (d. h. mit einer Struktur auch jede in sie einbettbare e.e. Struktur enthält), die "joint embedding property" und die Amalgamierungseigenschaft besitzt.

Dieser Satz liefert uns ein einfaches Verfahren zur Konstruktion a.a. Gruppen. Wir bekommen z. B. eine (dadurch eindeutig bestimmte) abzählbare a.a. Gruppe deren Skelett gerade aus den e.e. Gruppen besteht, deren Wortproblem rekursiv aufzählbar ist (3.9.2).

Im vierten Abschnitt konstruieren wir mit den Methoden von 3 zu jeder abzählbaren a.a. Gruppe eine partiell isomorphe Gruppe der Mächtigkeit ω_1. In 4.6 und 4.7 werden einfache Bedingungen für ω-homogene Strukturen angegeben zu einer Struktur der Mächtigkeit ω_1 partiell isomorph zu sein. Wir zeigen auf drei verschiedene Arten, daß a.a. Gruppen diesen Bedingungen genügen: in 4.3, 4.9, 4.10.

1. Einfache Konstruktionen algebraisch abgeschlossener Gruppen

Ein Körper heißt algebraisch abgeschlossen, wenn für jedes nichtkonstante Polynom $p \in K[X]$ — ein Polynom also, das in einem Oberkörper eine Nullstelle hat — die Gleichung $p(x) = 0$ eine Lösung hat. Hilberts Nullstellensatz zeigt, daß in allen algebraisch abgeschlossenen (a.a.) Körpern sogar jedes endliche System von Gleichungen

$$p_1(x_1, \ldots, x_r) = 0, \ldots, p_n(x_1, \ldots, x_r) = 0 \quad (p_1, \ldots, p_n \in K[X_1, \ldots])$$

das in einem Oberkörper von K eine Lösung besitzt, schon in K lösbar ist. Da man nicht erwarten kann ein ähnliches Resultat für Gruppen zu erhalten, definiert man:

Definition 1.1 (Scott, Neumann). Eine nichttriviale Gruppe G ist algebraisch abgeschlossen, wenn für jede endliche Folge von Wörtern

$W_1(y_0, \ldots, y_r, x_0, \ldots, x_s), \ldots W_n(y_0, \ldots, x_s)$ und Koeffizienten $g_0, \ldots, g_r \in G$ das Gleichungsystem ("mit Koeffizienten aus G")

$$\{W_1(g_0, \ldots, g_r, x_0, \ldots, x_s) \doteq e, \ldots, W_n(g_0, \ldots, x_s) \doteq e\} \quad (=: S(\vec{g}, \vec{x}))$$

in G lösbar ist, wenn es in einer Obergruppe von G lösbar ist.

(E, die triviale Gruppe, hat diese Eigenschaft, gilt aber per definitionem nicht als algebraisch abgeschlossen. Eine Lösung von $S(\vec{g}, \vec{x})$ in G ist eine Folge von Elementen $\vec{f} \in G$, auf die alle Gleichungen von S zutreffen, für die also $G \models \bigwedge S(\vec{g}, \vec{f})$. Statt "a.a. Gruppe" sagen wir auch "a.a.Gr.", und für "in einer Obergruppe von G lösbar" "über G lösbar".)

Wenn F und H Obergruppen von G sind, sind sie über G in das amalgamierte Produkt $F *_G H$ einbettbar. Wir schließen daraus

Bemerkung 1.2. Ein Gleichungssystem mit Koeffizienten aus $G \subset F$ ist über G lösbar gdw. es über F lösbar ist.

In [26] wurde der erste Satz über a.a. Gruppen bewiesen:

Satz 1.3. *Jede Gruppe ist Untergruppe einer algebraisch abgeschlossenen Gruppe.*

Beweis. Sei G eine Gruppe und $(S_\beta \mid \beta \in \alpha \setminus \{0\})$ eine Wohlordnung aller endlichen Gleichungssysteme mit Koeffizienten aus G, die über G lösbar sind. Wir definieren rekursiv eine aufsteigende Folge von Gruppen G_β, $\beta < \alpha$: $G_0 := G$; für $\beta > 0$ sei G_β eine Obergruppe von $\bigcup\{G_\gamma \mid \gamma < \beta\}$, in der S_β eine Lösung hat (vgl. 1.2). Wir bilden $G^+ := \bigcup\{G_\beta \mid \beta < \alpha\}$ und iterieren diese Konstruktion: $G^0 := G$; $G^{n+1} := (G^n)^+$. Die gesuchte Obergruppe von G ist $\bigcup\{G^n \mid n < \omega\}$. □

Folgerung 1.4. *Zu jeder Menge $\mathcal{K}$ von Gruppen, gibt es eine a.a.Gr., in die jedes Element von $\mathcal{K}$ einbettbar ist.*

Beweis. Man wende 1.3 auf $\bigoplus_{G \in \mathcal{K}} G$ an. □

Wir geben noch zwei andere Konstruktionsverfahren für a.a. Gruppen an.

Lemma 1.5. 1. *Die Vereinigung einer aufsteigenden Kette von a.a. Gruppen ist algebraisch abgeschlossen.*

2. *Jede 1-elementare Unterstruktur einer a.a. Gruppe ist algebraisch abgeschlossen.*

Wir werden später sehen, daß sich 2 umkehren läßt: a.a. Untergruppen sind 1-elementare Unterstrukturen. Zum Beweis von 1: Ein endliches Gleichungssystem, das über der Vereinigung einer Kette a.a. Gruppen lösbar ist, besitzt schon eine Lösung in jedem Kettenglied, in dem alle Koeffizienten des Systems liegen. Zu 2: Sei $G <_1 M$ a.a. Wenn $S(\vec{g}, \vec{x})$ über G lösbar ist, ist S auch über M und also in M lösbar. Aus $M \models \exists \vec{x} \wedge S(\vec{g}, \vec{x})$ folgt wegen der Voraussetzung $G \models \exists \vec{x} \wedge S(\vec{g}, \vec{x})$: Es gibt eine Lösung von S in G. □

Folgerung 1.6. 1. *A sei eine Teilmenge der a.a.Gr. M. Dann gibt es eine a.a.Gr.* $A \subset N \subset M$ *mit* $|N| = |A| + \omega$.
2. *Zu jeder Gruppe G und jeder Kardinalzahl* $\kappa \geqslant |G|$ *gibt es eine a.a.Gr.* $M \supset G$, $\kappa = |M|$.

(Aus 4.5.2 wird sich ergeben, daß a.a. Gruppen nicht endlich sind.) 1 bekommt man aus 1.5.2 mit Hilfe des Satzes von Löwenheim Skolem, der sogar ein $A \subset N < M$, $|N| = |A| + \omega$ liefert (siehe auch 2.11.5). Nach 1.3 ist G in beliebig großen Gruppen enthalten, also folgt 2 aus 1. □

In jeder Mächtigkeit gibt es also a.a. Gruppen. Überabzählbare a.a. Körper fester Charakteristik sind durch ihre Mächtigkeit (bis auf Isomorphie) eindeutig bestimmt. Es gibt abzählbar viele abzählbare a.a. Körper. Wieviel a.a. Gruppen gibt es in jeder Mächtigkeit? Im Laufe dieser Untersuchung werden wir zeigen, daß es in jeder überabzählbaren Mächtigkeit 2^{ω_1} a.a. Gruppen gibt. (Tatsächlich gibt es in jeder Mächtigkeit κ genau 2^{κ} nichtisomorphe a.a. Gruppen, siehe [34].)

Satz 1.7 [22]. *Es gibt* 2^{ω} *abzählbare a.a. Gruppen.*

Der Satz folgt aus

Lemma 1.8 [19] (siehe auch III, 3.5.2). *Es gibt* 2^{ω} *von zwei Elementen erzeugte Gruppen.*

Denn jede abzählbare Gruppe enthält nur abzählbar viele von zwei Elementen erzeugte Untergruppen. Jede von zwei Elementen erzeugte Gruppe ist aber in einer abzählbaren a.a.Gr. enthalten Andererseits gibt es überhaupt nur 2^{ω} abzählbare Gruppen. □

Die Lösbarkeit eines endlichen Gleichungssystems S mit Koeffizienten $\vec{g} \in M$ in der a.a.Gr. M hängt nach 1.2 nur von $\langle \vec{g} \rangle$ (bzw. den Obergruppen von $\langle \vec{g} \rangle$) ab. Der nächste Satz zeigt, daß alle

Eigenschaften von $\vec{g}$ in M nur vom Isomorphietyp von $\langle\vec{g}\rangle$ abhängen: M ist "ω-homogen".

Satz 1.9. *In algebraisch abgeschlossenen Gruppen läßt sich jeder Isomorphismus zwischen endlich erzeugten Untergruppen zu einem inneren Automorphismus fortsetzen.*

Zum Beweis verwenden wir

Lemma 1.10 [8]. *Jeder Isomorphismus zwischen zwei Untergruppen einer Gruppe läßt sich zu einem inneren Automorphismus einer geeigneten Obergruppe fortsetzen.*

Sei nun M algebraisch abgeschlossen, $\vec{g} \in M$ und $\mu : \langle\vec{g}\rangle \rightarrow M$ eine Einbettung. In einer Obergruppe von M gibt es einen inneren Automorphismus $\tau_f \supset \mu$. f ist also eine Lösung des Gleichungssystems $\{xg_ix^{-1} = \mu(g_i) \mid i = 0, \ldots, r\}$. Wenn f' eine Lösung in M ist, leistet $\tau_{f'}$ das verlangte. □

Im nächsten Abschnitt untersuchen wir beliebige Strukturen für eine (abzählbare) Sprache L, die ein Analogon von 1.10 erfüllen.

2. ω-homogene Strukturen

Definition 2.1 (siehe [7]). Eine Struktur $\mathfrak{M}$ ist ω-homogen, wenn sich jeder Isomorphismus zwischen endlich erzeugten (e.e.) Unterstrukturen "schrittweise" fortsetzen läßt; d. h. wenn $\mathfrak{A}$ e.e., $\mathfrak{A} \subset \mathfrak{M}$, $\mu : \mathfrak{A} \rightarrow \mathfrak{M}$ eine Einbettung ist, gibt es für jedes $a \in \mathfrak{M}$ eine Fortsetzung $\mu \subset \nu : \langle \mathfrak{A}, a\rangle \rightarrow \mathfrak{M}$.

Bemerkung 2.2. Nach 1.10 sind a.a. Gruppen ω-homogen. Ist $\mathfrak{M}$ ω-homogen und $\vec{a} \in \mathfrak{M}$, so ist auch (die $L(\vec{c})$-Struktur) $(\mathfrak{M}, \vec{a})$ ω-homogen.

Lemma 2.3. 1. *$\mathfrak{M}$ ist genau dann ω-homogen, wenn für jedes e.e. $\mathfrak{A} \subset \mathfrak{M}$ jede endlich erzeugte Oberstruktur von $\mathfrak{A}$, die in $\mathfrak{M}$ einbettbar ist, über $\mathfrak{A}$ in $\mathfrak{M}$ einbettbar ist.*

2. *Die Vereinigung einer aufsteigenden Kette von ω-homogenen Strukturen ist ω-homogen.*

3. *A sei Teilmenge der unendlichen ω-homogenen Struktur $\mathfrak{M}$. Dann gibt es eine ω-homogene Struktur $A \subset \mathfrak{A} \subset \mathfrak{M}$ mit $|\mathfrak{A}| = |A| + \omega$.*

Beweis. 1. Sei $\mathfrak{M}$ ω-homogen, e.e. $\mathfrak{A} \subset \mathfrak{M}$, $\mathfrak{A} \subset \mathfrak{B}$ e.e. und $\mu : \mathfrak{B} \to \mathfrak{M}$ eine Einbettung. Wir setzen den Isomorphismus $\overset{-1}{\mu}_{\mu[\mathfrak{A}]} : \mu[\mathfrak{A}] \to \mathfrak{A}$ fort zu $\nu : \mu[\mathfrak{B}] \to \mathfrak{M}$. Dann ist $\nu\mu : \mathfrak{B} \to_{\mathfrak{A}} \mathfrak{M}$ die gesuchte Einbettung. Sei umgekehrt die Bedingung von 1 erfült und $\mu : \mathfrak{A} \to \mathfrak{M}$ eine isomorphe Einbettung einer e.e. Unterstruktur, $a \in \mathfrak{M}$. Wir wählen eine Oberstruktur $\mu[\mathfrak{A}] \subset \mathfrak{B}$ mit einem Isomorphismus $\mu \subset \nu : \langle \mathfrak{A}, a \rangle \to \mathfrak{B}$. $\mathfrak{B}$ ist vermöge ν^{-1} in $\mathfrak{M}$ einbettbar. Also gibt es eine Einbettung $\pi : \mathfrak{B} \to_{\mu[\mathfrak{A}]} \mathfrak{M}$. $\pi\mu : \langle \mathfrak{A}, a \rangle \to \mathfrak{M}$ ist die gesuchte Fortsetzung von μ.

Wir überlassen dem Leser den Beweis von 2 und 3. □

ω-homogene Strukturen sind bis auf "partielle Isomorphie" durch ihre endlich erzeugten Unterstrukturen eindeutig bestimmt:

Definition 2.4 ([11]). 1. Zwei L-Strukturen $\mathfrak{M}$, $\mathfrak{N}$ sind partiell isomorph — $\mathfrak{M} \cong_p \mathfrak{N}$ —, wenn es eine nichtleere Familie I von Isomorphismen zwischen Unterstrukturen von $\mathfrak{M}$ und $\mathfrak{N}$ gibt, die folgende Eigenschaften hat:

(a) für alle $\pi \in I$, $a \in \mathfrak{M}$ gibt es $\nu \supset \pi$, $\nu \in I$, $a \in \mathrm{Vb}\,\nu$.

(b) Für alle $\pi \in I$, $b \in \mathfrak{M}$ gibt es $\nu \supset \pi$, $\nu \in I$, $b \in \mathrm{Nb}\,\nu$.

2. $\mathfrak{M}$ ist partiell isomorphe Substruktur von $\mathfrak{N}$ — $\mathfrak{M} <_p \mathfrak{N}$ —, wenn $\mathfrak{M} \subset \mathfrak{N}$, und für alle $\vec{a} \in \mathfrak{M}$ $(\mathfrak{M}, \vec{a}) \cong_p (\mathfrak{N}, \vec{a})$.

3. $\mathfrak{M}$ heißt partiell in $\mathfrak{N}$ einbettbar — $\mathfrak{M} <_p \mathfrak{N}$ —, wenn es eine nichtleere Familie I von Isomorphismen von Unterstrukturen von $\mathfrak{M}$ und $\mathfrak{N}$ gibt, die die Eigenschaft (a) von 1 hat.

Natürlich sind isomorphe Strukturen partiell isomorph und einbettbare Strukturen partiell einbettbar.

Beispiel 2.5. Wenn $\mathfrak{M}$ und $\mathfrak{N}$ partiell isomorph sind, so ist mit $\mathfrak{M}$ auch $\mathfrak{N}$ ω-homogen. Denn wenn $\mu : \mathfrak{A} \Rightarrow \mathfrak{B}$ ein Isomorphismus zwischen endlich erzeugten Unterstrukturen von $\mathfrak{N}$ und $a \in \mathfrak{N}$ ist, wählen wir nach 1(b) ein $\pi \in I$ mit $\langle \mathfrak{A}, \mathfrak{B}, a \rangle \subset \mathrm{Nb}\,\pi$. Weil $\mathfrak{M}$ ω-homogen ist, können wir den Isomorphismus $\pi^{-1}\mu\pi \restriction_{\pi^{-1}[\mathfrak{A}]} : \pi^{-1}[\mathfrak{A}] \to \mu^{-1}[\mathfrak{B}]$ zu einer Einbettung $\mu' : \pi^{-1}[\langle \mathfrak{A}, a \rangle] \to \mathfrak{M}$ fortsetzen. Mit (a) wählen wir ein $\pi \subset \nu \in I$ mit $\mu'[\pi^{-1}\langle \mathfrak{A}, a \rangle] \subset \mathrm{Vb}\,\nu$. Die gesuchte Fortsetzung von μ ist $\nu\mu'\nu^{-1} \restriction_{\langle \mathfrak{A}, a \rangle}$.

Die eben eingeführten Beziehungen lassen sich einfach durch infinitäre Sprachen beschreiben:

Satz 2.6 ([11]). 1. $\mathfrak{M} \cong_p \mathfrak{N}$ *gdw.* $\mathfrak{M} \equiv_{\infty, \omega} \mathfrak{N}$.

2. $\mathfrak{M} <_p \mathfrak{N}$ *gdw.* $\mathfrak{M} <_{\infty, \omega} \mathfrak{N}$.

3. $\mathfrak{M} <_p \mathfrak{N}$ *gdw.* $\mathfrak{M} \Rrightarrow_{\exists\infty,\omega} \mathfrak{N}$.
($\mathfrak{M} \Rrightarrow_{\exists\infty,\omega} \mathfrak{N}$ *bedeutet, daß alle Existenzaussagen von* $L_{\infty,\omega}$, *die in* $\mathfrak{M}$ *gelten, auch in* $\mathfrak{N}$ *gelten.*)

Folgerungen 2.7. "$\cong_p$", "$<_p$", "$<_p$" *sind transitive Relationen. Aus* $\mathfrak{M}_1 \cong_p \mathfrak{M}_2 <_p \mathfrak{N}_1 \cong_p \mathfrak{N}_2$ *folgt* $\mathfrak{M}_1 <_p \mathfrak{N}_2$. *Wenn* $\mathfrak{N}$ *Vereinigung der Folge* $(\mathfrak{M}_\alpha \mid \alpha < \gamma)$ *ist, und* $\mathfrak{M}_\alpha <_p \mathfrak{M}_\beta$ *für* $\alpha < \beta$, *ist für alle* α $\mathfrak{M}_\alpha <_p \mathfrak{N}$.

Der nächste Satz ist wohlbekannt.

Satz 2.8. 1. $\mathfrak{M}$ *und* $\mathfrak{N}$ *seien höchstens abzählbar. Dann ist* $\mathfrak{M} \cong_p \mathfrak{N}$ *gdw.* $\mathfrak{M} \cong \mathfrak{N}$.
2. *Wenn* $\mathfrak{M}$ *höchstens abzählbar ist, ist* $\mathfrak{M} \cong_p \mathfrak{N}$ *gdw.* $\mathfrak{M}$ *zu einer partiell isomorphen Substruktur von* $\mathfrak{N}$ *isomorph ist.*
3. *Wenn* $\mathfrak{M}$ *höchstens abzählbar ist, ist* $\mathfrak{M} <_p \mathfrak{N}$ *gdw.* $\mathfrak{M} < \mathfrak{N}$.

Wir deuten einen Beweis von 2 an. Es ist klar, daß aus $\mathfrak{M} <_p \mathfrak{N}$, $\mathfrak{M} \cong_p \mathfrak{N}$ folgt. Sei andererseits $\mathfrak{M} \cong_p \mathfrak{N}$ und $(a_n \mid n \in \omega)$ eine Aufzählung von $\mathfrak{M}$, I eine Familie von partiellen Isomorphismen, die $\mathfrak{M}$ und $\mathfrak{N}$ partiell isomorph macht. Wenn man in jedem Schritt 2.4.1(a) anwendet, gewinnt man eine Folge $\nu_0 \subset \nu_1 \subset \cdots$ von Isomorphismen aus I, $a_n \in \mathrm{Vb}\, \nu_n$. $\nu := \bigcup_{n<\omega} \nu_n$ ist eine isomorphe Einbettung von $\mathfrak{M}$ in $\mathfrak{N}$. Da ν_n aus I ist, ist $(\mathfrak{M}; a_0, \ldots, a_n) \cong_p (\mathfrak{N}; \nu(a_0), \ldots, \nu(a_n))$. □

Definition 2.9 (vgl. [14]). Das Skelett $\mathrm{Sk}(\mathfrak{M})$ einer Struktur ist die Klasse aller endlich erzeugten, in $\mathfrak{M}$ einbettbaren Strukturen. Wenn $\mathcal{K}$ eine Klasse von Strukturen ist, bezeichne $\|\mathcal{K}\| = |\mathcal{K}/_{\cong}|$ die Zahl der verschiedenen Isomorphietypen in $\mathcal{K}$.

Den nächsten Satz kann man als Verallgemeinerung des Satzes über die Isomorphie aller abzählbaren homogenen und $(\mathrm{Sk}(\mathfrak{M})-)$ universellen Strukturen auffassen. Für a.a. Gruppen findet er sich in [14].

Satz 2.10. 1. $\mathfrak{M}$ *und* $\mathfrak{N}$ *seien* ω*-homogen. Dann ist*
(a) $\mathfrak{M} \cong_p \mathfrak{N}$ *gdw.* $\mathrm{Sk}(\mathfrak{M}) = \mathrm{Sk}(\mathfrak{N})$. (*Es ist dann sogar* $(\mathfrak{M}, \vec{a}) \cong_p (\mathfrak{N}, \vec{b})$, *wenn* $\langle \vec{a} \rangle' \cong \langle \vec{b} \rangle'$.)
(b) *Wenn* $\mathfrak{M} \subset \mathfrak{N}$, $\mathfrak{M} <_p \mathfrak{N}$ *gdw.* $\mathrm{Sk}(\mathfrak{M}) = \mathrm{Sk}(\mathfrak{N})$.
2. *Sei* $\mathfrak{A}$ ω*-homogen. Dann ist* $\mathfrak{M} <_p \mathfrak{N}$ *gdw.* $\mathrm{Sk}(\mathfrak{M}) \subset \mathrm{Sk}(\mathfrak{N})$.

Beweis. 2. Sei $\mathfrak{M} <_p \mathfrak{N}$ und $\mathfrak{A} \in \mathrm{Sk}(\mathfrak{M})$. Wenn μ $\mathfrak{A}$ in $\mathfrak{M}$ einbettet, wählen wir ein $\nu \in I$ mit $\mu[\mathfrak{A}] \subset \mathrm{Vb}\, \nu$. Das zeigt, daß $\mathfrak{A} < \mathfrak{N}$. Sei umgekehrt $\mathrm{Sk}(\mathfrak{M}) \subset \mathrm{Sk}(\mathfrak{N})$. Für I nehmen wir die Menge aller

Isomorphismen zwischen e.e. Unterstrukturen von $\mathfrak{M}$ und $\mathfrak{N}$. Aus der ω-Homogenität von $\mathfrak{N}$ folgt 2.4.1(a). Denn sei $\mathfrak{A} \subset \mathfrak{M}$, $\pi : \mathfrak{A} \to \mathfrak{N}$, $\pi \in I$ und $a \in \mathfrak{M}$. Es gibt eine Oberstruktur $\mathfrak{B}$ von $\pi[\mathfrak{A}]$ und eine Fortsetzung $\pi' : \langle \mathfrak{A}, a \rangle \to \mathfrak{B}$ von π. Da $\mathfrak{B} \in \mathrm{Sk}(\mathfrak{M})$, ist nach Voraussetzung $\mathfrak{B} \in \mathrm{Sk}(\mathfrak{N})$. Wir haben also, weil $\mathfrak{N}$ ω-homogen ist, mit 2.3.1 eine Einbettung $\mu : \mathfrak{B} \to_{\pi[\mathfrak{A}]} \mathfrak{M}$. $\nu = \mu\pi'$ ist die gesuchte Fortsetzung von $\pi : \nu \in I$, $a \in \mathrm{Vb}(\nu)$.

1(a). Wenn $\mathfrak{M} \cong_p \mathfrak{N}$, ist $\mathfrak{M} <_p \mathfrak{N}$ und $\mathfrak{M} <_p \mathfrak{N}$, also wegen 2 $\mathrm{Sk}(\mathfrak{M}) = \mathrm{Sk}(\mathfrak{N})$. Wenn $\mathrm{Sk}(\mathfrak{M}) = \mathrm{Sk}(\mathfrak{N})$, so hat das im Beweis von 2 definierte I auch die Eigenschaft 2.4.1(b).

1(b) folgt aus dem Zusatz von 1(a). □

Folgerungen 2.11. 1. *$\mathfrak{M}$ und $\mathfrak{N}$ seien höchsten abzählbar und ω-homogen. Dann ist $\mathfrak{M} \cong \mathfrak{N}$ gdw.* $\mathrm{Sk}(\mathfrak{M}) = \mathrm{Sk}(\mathfrak{N})$.

2. *$\mathfrak{M}$ sei höchstens abzählbar und ω-homogen. Dann läßt sich jeder Isomorphismus zwischen e.e. Unterstrukturen zu einem Automorphismus von $\mathfrak{M}$ fortsetzen.* (1.10 *zeigt, daß man hier für a.a.Gr. die Abzählbarkeit nicht vorauszusetzen muß.*)

3. *$\mathfrak{M}$ sei höchstens abzählbar und $\mathfrak{N}$ ω-homogen. Dann ist $\mathfrak{M} < \mathfrak{N}$ gdw.* $\mathrm{Sk}(\mathfrak{M}) \subset \mathrm{Sk}(\mathfrak{N})$.

4. *$\mathfrak{N}$ sei aufsteigende Vereinigung der Folge $(\mathfrak{M}_\alpha \mid \alpha < \beta)$. $\mathfrak{M}_0$ sei ω-homogen und für alle $\alpha < \beta$ $\mathfrak{M}_\alpha \cong_p \mathfrak{M}_0$. Dann ist $\mathfrak{M}_0 \cong_p \mathfrak{N}$.*

5. *A sei Teilmenge der unendlichen ω-homogenen Struktur $\mathfrak{M}$. Dann gibt es ein $A \subset \mathfrak{N} <_p \mathfrak{M}$ mit $|\mathfrak{N}| = |A| + \|\mathrm{Sk}(\mathfrak{M})\| + \omega$.*

3. Kennzeichnung der Skelette ω-homogener Strukturen

Für die Untersuchung der Eigenschaften ω-homogener Strukturen, die sich auf partiell isomorphe Strukturen übertragen, genügt es nach dem Vorangehenden, die Skelette ω-homogener Strukturen zu betrachten. Nicht jede Klasse endlich erzeugter Strukturen ist Skelett. In 3.2 geben wir zwei notwendige Bedingungen (U, JEP) an, die für abzählbare Klassen auch hinreichend dafür sind, Skelett zu sein. Die Skelette ω-homogener Strukturen haben zusätzlich die Amalgamierungseigenschaft (AE). Hier bekommt man sogar: (3.5) Eine Klasse e.e. Strukturen, von höchstens der Mächtigkeit ω_1, ist genau dann Skelett einer ω-homogenen Strukture, wenn sie (U, JEP, AE) erfüllt. Unter Voraussetzung der Kontinuumshypothese sind dadurch also die Skelette ω-homogener Strukturen vollständig gekennzeichnet. Zum Schluß geben wir eine Anwendung dieser Methode auf a.a.Gr.: Eine ω-homogene Gruppe ist genau dann a.a., wenn ihr Skelett die Eigenschaft (AA) hat.

(Wir betrachten Strukturen für eine abzählbare Sprache L.)

Definition 3.1. Eine Klasse $\mathcal{K}$ endlich erzeugter Strukturen erfüllt

1 die Bedingung (U) — $\mathcal{K}$ ist Unterstruktur-abgeschlossen — wenn $\mathcal{K}$ mit jeder Struktur $\mathfrak{A}$ jede Struktur enthält, die in $\mathfrak{A}$ einbettbar ist.

2 $\mathcal{K}$ erfüllt (JEP) — joint embedding property — wenn es für alle $\mathfrak{A}$, $\mathfrak{B} \in \mathcal{K}$ ein $\mathfrak{C}$ aus $\mathcal{K}$ mit $\mathfrak{A} < \mathfrak{C}$ und $\mathfrak{B} < \mathfrak{C}$ gibt. Weiter soll $\mathcal{K}$ nicht leer sein.

Satz 3.2. 1. *Für jede Struktur* $\mathfrak{M}$ *hat* $\mathrm{Sk}(\mathfrak{M})$ *die Eigenschaften U und JEP.*

2. $\mathcal{K}$ *erfülle (U) und (JEP). Wenn* $\|\mathcal{K}\| \leq \omega$, *gibt es eine Struktur* $\mathfrak{M}$ *mit* $\mathcal{K} = \mathrm{Sk}(\mathfrak{M})$.

Zusatz: *Für alle* $\mathfrak{M}$ *ist* $\|\mathrm{Sk}(\mathfrak{M})\| \leq \min(2^{\omega}, |\mathfrak{M}| + \omega)$. *In* 2 *findet man ein* $\mathfrak{M}$, *das höchstens abzählbar ist.*

Beweis. 1 ist trivial. 2: $(\mathfrak{A}_n \mid n < \omega)$ sei eine Aufzählung von Elementen von $\mathcal{K}$, unter denen alle Isomorphietypen von $\mathcal{K}$ vorkommen. Wir setzen $\mathfrak{B}_0 := \mathfrak{A}_0$ und wählen für $\mathfrak{B}_{n+1} \in \mathcal{K}$ eine Oberstruktur von $\mathfrak{B}_n$, in die $\mathfrak{A}_n$ einbettbar ist; dazu brauchen wir (JEP). Wegen (U) ist $\mathcal{K}$ das Skelett von $\mathfrak{M} := \bigcup\{\mathfrak{B}_n \mid n < \omega\}$. □

$\mathfrak{M}$ ist weder durch $\mathcal{K}$ eindeutig bestimmt, noch kann es im allgemeinen ω-homogen gewählt werden. Wir definieren daher

Definition 3.3. Eine Klasse von endlich erzeugten Strukturen $\mathcal{K}$ hat die Amalgamierungseigenschaft (AE), wenn es zu jeder Einbettung $\nu : \mathfrak{A} \to \mathfrak{B}$ von zwei Strukturen aus $\mathcal{K}$ und jeder Oberstruktur $\mathfrak{A} \subset \mathfrak{A}' \in \mathcal{K}$ eine Fortsetzung $\nu \subset \mu : \mathfrak{A}' \to \mathfrak{B}' \in \mathcal{K}$ gibt.

Bemerkung 3.4. 1. Die Klasse $\mathcal{G}$ aller endlich erzeugten Gruppen erfüllt (AE). Man identifiziert $\mathfrak{A}$ vermöge ν mit einer Untergruppe von $\mathfrak{B}$ und setzt $\mathfrak{B}' = \mathfrak{A}' *_{\mathfrak{A}} \mathfrak{B}$.

2. Wenn $\emptyset \neq \mathcal{K} \subset \mathcal{G}$, folgt (JEP) aus (U) und (AE).

Satz 3.5. 1. *Wenn* $\mathfrak{M}$ ω*-homogen ist, hat* $\mathrm{Sk}(\mathfrak{M})$ *die (AE).*

2. *Wenn* $\|\mathcal{K}\| \leq \omega_1$ *und* $\mathcal{K}$ *die Bedingungen (U), (JEP) und (AE) erfüllt, gibt es ein* ω*-homogenes* $\mathfrak{M}$ *mit* $\mathcal{K} = \mathrm{Sk}(\mathfrak{M})$.

Zusatz. *Aus* 2.11.5 *folgt, daß sich bei 2 ein* $\mathfrak{M}$ *mit* $|\mathfrak{M}| \leq \|\mathcal{K}\| + \omega$ *finden läßt.*

Beweis. 1. $\mathfrak{A} \subset \mathfrak{A}'$ seien aus $\mathrm{Sk}(\mathfrak{M})$ und $\nu : \mathfrak{A} \to \mathfrak{B} \in \mathrm{Sk}(\mathfrak{M})$ eine

Einbettung. Wir können $\mathfrak{A}' \subset \mathfrak{M}$ und $\mathfrak{B} \subset \mathfrak{M}$ annehmen. Da $\mathfrak{M}$ ω-homogen ist, gibt es eine Fortsetzung $\nu \subset \mu : \mathfrak{A}' \to \mathfrak{M}$. Wir wählen für $\mathfrak{B}' := \mu[\mathfrak{A}'] \in \mathrm{Sk}(\mathfrak{M})$ und haben so (AE) nachgewiesen.

Wir fassen beim Beweis von 2 zur Vereinfachung $\emptyset$ als endlich erzeugte Struktur auf, die durch $\emptyset$ in jede Struktur eingebettet ist. (JEP) wird so ein Sonderfall von (AE). Wir brauchen zwei Hilfssätze:

Hilfssatz 1. *Sei* $\mathfrak{N}$ *höchstens abzählbar,* $\mathrm{Sk}(\mathfrak{N}) \subset \mathcal{K}$, $\mathfrak{A}$ *e.e.,* $\mathfrak{A} \subset \mathfrak{N}$, $\nu : \mathfrak{A} \to \mathfrak{B} \in \mathcal{K}$ *eine Einbettung. Dann gibt es* $\mathfrak{N} \subset \mathfrak{N}'$, $|\mathfrak{N}'| \leqslant \omega$, $\mathrm{Sk}(\mathfrak{N}') \subset \mathcal{K}$ *und eine Einbettung* $\mu : \mathfrak{B} \to \mathfrak{N}'$, $\mu\nu = \mathrm{id}_{\mathfrak{A}}$.

Beweis. $\mathfrak{N}$ sei Vereinigung der endlich erzeugten Strukturen $\mathfrak{A} = \mathfrak{A}_0 \subset \mathfrak{A}_1 \subset \cdots$. Wir definieren eine Folge $\mathfrak{B} = \mathfrak{B}_0 \subset \mathfrak{B}_1 \subset \cdots$ von Strukturen aus $\mathcal{K}$ und Enbettungen $\nu = \nu_0 \subset \nu_1 \subset \cdots$, $\nu_i : \mathfrak{A}_i \to \mathfrak{B}_i$, indem wir, um $\mathfrak{B}_{i+1}$ und ν_{i+1} zu erhalten, (AE) auf $\mathfrak{A}_i \subset \mathfrak{A}_{i+1}$ und ν_i anwenden. Dann setzen wir $\mathfrak{N}'' = \bigcup\{\mathfrak{B}_i \mid i < \omega\}$ und $\mu' = \bigcup\{\nu_i \mid i < \omega\}$. Wir setzen nun μ' zu einem Isomorphismus $\mu'' : \mathfrak{N}' \to \mathfrak{N}''$ einer Oberstruktur von $\mathfrak{N}$ fort. $\mu : \mu''^{-1}_{|\mathfrak{B}}$ leistet das verlangte.

$(\mathfrak{B}_\alpha \mid \alpha < \omega_1)$ sei eine Folge von Elementen von $\mathcal{K}$, unter denen alle Isomorphietypen von $\mathcal{K}$ vorkommen.

Hilfssatz 2. *Sei* $\mathfrak{N}$ *höchstens abzählbar,* $\mathrm{Sk}(\mathfrak{N}) \subset \mathcal{K}$, $\beta < \omega_1$. *Dann gibt es ein* $\mathfrak{N}^\beta \supset \mathfrak{N}$, $|\mathfrak{N}^\beta| \leqslant \omega$, $\mathrm{Sk}(\mathfrak{N}^\beta) \subset \mathcal{K}$, *sodaß es für alle Einbettungen* $\nu : \mathfrak{A} \to \mathfrak{B}_\alpha$ *von e.e.* $\mathfrak{A} \subset \mathfrak{N}$ $(\alpha < \beta)$ *eine Einbettung* $\mu : \mathfrak{B}_\alpha \to \mathfrak{N}^\beta$ *mit* $\mu\nu = \mathrm{id}_{\mathfrak{A}}$ *gibt.*

Beweis. $(\nu_n : \mathfrak{A}_n \to \mathfrak{B}_{\alpha_n} \mid n \in \omega)$ sei eine Aufzählung aller dieser Einbettungen. Wir konstruieren eine Kette $\mathfrak{N} = \mathfrak{N}_0 \subset \mathfrak{N}_1 \subset \cdots \mathrm{Sk}(\mathfrak{N}_n) \subset \mathcal{K}$ höchstens abzählbaren Strukturen, indem wir den Hilfssatz 1 auf $\mathfrak{N}_n$ und $\nu_n : \mathfrak{A}_n \to \mathfrak{B}_{\dot{\alpha}_n}$ anwenden, und so $\mathfrak{N}_{n+1}$ konstruieren. Bei diesem Schritt erhält man auch die Abbildung $\mu_n : \mathfrak{B}_{\alpha_n} \to \mathfrak{N}_{n+1} \subset \mathfrak{N}^\beta := \bigcup\{\mathfrak{N}_n \mid n < \omega\}$ mit $\mu_n\nu_n = \mathrm{id}_{\mathfrak{A}_n}$.

Beweis von 3.5.2. Wir definieren $\mathfrak{N}_0 = \emptyset$ (s. Bem. zu Beginn des Beweises) und — für $\alpha < \omega_1$ — $\mathfrak{N}_\alpha = (\bigcup\{\mathfrak{N}_\beta \mid \beta < \alpha\})^\alpha$ wie im zweiten Hilfssatz. $\mathfrak{M} := \bigcup\{\mathfrak{N}_\alpha \mid \alpha < \omega_1\}$ ist nach 2.3.1 ω-homogen. □

Man kann sich leicht überlegen — oder aus dem nächsten Satz folgern —, daß jede Gruppe, die zu einer a.a.Gr. partiell isomorph ist, selbst algebraisch abgeschlossen ist. Es muß also möglich sein, die a.a. Gruppen als ω-homogene Gruppen mit bestimmten Skelett zu charakterisieren. Dazu definieren wir

Definition 3.6. Eine Klasse $\mathcal{K}$ von endlich erzeugten Gruppen ist algebraisch abgeschlossen (erfüllt AA), wenn jedes endliche Gleichungssystem mit Koeffizienten aus $F \in \mathcal{K}$, das über F lösbar ist, in einer Obergruppe von F lösbar ist, die zu $\mathcal{K}$ gehört.

Satz 3.7. *Eine ω-homogene Gruppe ist genau dann algebraisch abgeschlossen, wenn ihr Skelett algebraisch abgeschlossen ist.*

Beweis. Wenn M a.a. ist, folgt (AA) für das Skelett von M sofort aus 1.2. Sei umgekehrt M ω-homogen und erfülle $\mathrm{Sk}(M)$ (AA). Das endliche Gleichungssystem S mit Koeffizienten aus der e.e. Untergruppe $F \subset M$ habe eine Lösung in der e.e. Gruppe $G \supset F$. Wegen (AA) können wir $G \in \mathrm{Sk}(M)$ annehmen. Nach 2.3.1 ist G über F in M einbettbar und also S in M lösbar. M ist also algebraisch abgeschlossen. □

Folgerungen 3.8 (2 ist im wesentlichen Th. 17 aus [14]). 1. *Aus M a.a. und $N \cong_p M$ folgt N a.a.*

2. *$\mathcal{K} \subset \mathcal{G}$ ist genau dann Skelett einer abzählbaren a.a. Gruppe, wenn $\mathcal{K}$ abzählbar ist und (U, JEP, AA) erfüllt. Die Gruppe ist durch $\mathcal{K}$ eindeutig bestimmt.*

3. *$\mathcal{K} \subset \mathcal{G}$ ist genau dann Skelett einer a.a.Gr. von höchstens der Mächtigkeit ω_1, wenn $\mathcal{K}$ höchstens die Mächtigkeit ω_1 hat und (U, JEP, AA) erfüllt.*

4. (CH) *$\mathcal{K} \subset \mathcal{G}$ ist genau dann Skelett einer a.a.Gr., wenn $\mathcal{K}$ (U, JEP, AA) erfüllt.*

Beweis. 1 folgt sofort aus 2.2, 2.5 und 2.10.1. Um für 2, 3 und 4 die Sätze 3.5 und 3.7 anwenden zu können, müssen wir zeigen, daß aus JEP und AA die Amalgamierungseigenschaft folgt. Wir nehmen dazu $G \subset G'$ aus $\mathcal{K}$ und eine Einbettung $\nu : G \to F \in \mathcal{K}$. JEP gestattet es $G' \subset F$ anzunehmen. Wie im Beweis von 1.9 finden wir ein endliches Gleichungssystem S mit Koeffizienten aus F, das f erfült, wenn $\tau_f \supset \nu$. Weil $\mathcal{K}$ algebraisch abgeschlossen ist, ist S in einem $F \subset H' \in \mathcal{K}$ lösbar, die Lösung sei f'. Dann ist $\nu \subset \tau_{f' \restriction F} : F \to H'$ die gesuchte Fortsetzung von ν. □

Zwei Beispiele 3.9. 1. $\mathcal{G}$ — die Klasse der endlich erzeugten Gruppen — hat die Eigenschaften U, JEP und AA. Wenn $\mathrm{Sk}(M) = \mathcal{G}$ — M ist "ω-universell" — und M ω-homogen ist, ist M also algebraisch abgeschlossen. Mit (CH) liefert uns der letzte Satz ω-universelle, homogene Gruppen. Wir brauchen aber weder CH noch den letzten Satz, denn 1.4 verschafft uns eine ω-universelle a.a.Gr., 2.11.5 sogar eine a.a.Gr. der Mächtigkeit 2^{ω}.

2. $\mathcal{K}_0$, die Klasse der endlich erzeugten Gruppen mit rekursiv aufzählbarem Wortproblem, hat die Eigenschaften U, JEP und AA. Denn nach dem Satz von Higman ([9]) besteht $\mathcal{K}_0$ gerade aus den endlich erzeugten Untergruppen endlich präsentierter Gruppen. $\mathcal{K}_0$ erfüllt also U. Wenn F durch das endliche Gleichungssystem $S(\vec{f})$ präsentiert wird und G durch $T(\vec{g})$, wird $F * G$ durch $S(\vec{f}) \cup T(\vec{g})$ präsentiert, also gilt JEP. Um AA zu zeigen, sei $S(\vec{f}, \vec{x})$ ein endliches Gleichungssystem, das über $F \in \mathcal{K}_0$ lösbar ist. Man kann annehmen, daß F — durch $T(\vec{f})$ — endlich präsentiert ist. $S(\vec{f}, \vec{g}) \cup T(\vec{f})$ präsentiert dann eine Obergruppe von F, in der S — von $\vec{g}$ — gelöst wird. Zu $\mathcal{K}_0$ gehört also eine eindeutig bestimmte abzählbare a.a. Gruppe M_0 mit $\mathrm{Sk}(M_0) = \mathcal{K}_0$. M_0 wurde zuerst in [14] konstruiert.

4. ω-homogene Strukturen der Mächtigkeit ω_1

Wir haben zu abzählbaren Skeletten abzählbare ω-homogene Strukturen und zu Skeletten der Mächtigkeit ω_1 ω-homogene Strukturen der Mächtigkeit ω_1 konstruiert. Gibt es überabzählbare ω-homogene mit abzählbaren Skelett? Diese Strukturen wären zu ω-abzählbaren Strukturen partiell isomorph. Nach einem Satz von Kueker ([13]) besäße dann die abzählbare Struktur 2^{ω} viele Automorphismen. Wir untersuchen zunächst die Zahl der Automorphismen abzählbarer ω-homogener Strukturen. 4.2 charakterisiert auf einfache Weise die abzählbaren ω-homogenen Strukturen mit 2^{ω} Automorphismen. In 4.3 zeigen wir, daß abzählbare a.a.Gr. der Bedingung von 4.2 genügen. Die Aussage von 4.3 stellt sich für beliebige abzählbare ω-homogene Strukturen sogar als äquivalent zur Existenz einer partiell isomorphen Erweiterung der Mächtigkeit ω_1 heraus. Im letzten Teil dieses Abschnitts geben wir noch zwei andere Möglichkeiten an, zu abzählbaren a.a.Gr. ω_1-mächtige partiell isomorphe Gruppen zu konstruieren. In [34] wird gezeigt, daß jede a.a. Gruppe zu Gruppen beliebig großer Mächtigkeit partiell isomorph ist.

Der folgende Satz findet sich in ([13]).

Satz 4.1. *Eine abzählbare Struktur $\mathfrak{M}$ besitzt genau dann 2^{ω} viele Automorphismen, wenn es zu jedem endlich erzeugten $\mathfrak{A} \subset \mathfrak{M}$ einen nichttrivialen Automorphismus von $\mathfrak{M}$ über $\mathfrak{A}$ gibt. $\mathfrak{M}$ besitzt sonst nur höchstens abzählbar viele Automorphismen.*

Folgerung 4.2. *Eine abzählbare ω-homogene Struktur $\mathfrak{M}$ besitzt genau* *dann* 2^ω *Automorphismen, wenn es zu jedem* $\mathfrak{A} \in \mathrm{Sk}(\mathfrak{M})$ *ein* $\langle \mathfrak{A}, a, b\rangle \in \mathrm{Sk}(\mathfrak{M})$ *gibt, so daß* $a \neq b$ *und* $\langle \mathfrak{A}, a\rangle' \cong_{\mathfrak{A}} \langle \mathfrak{A}, b\rangle'$.

Algebraisch abgeschlossene Gruppen haben die in 4.2 geforderte Eigenschaft, es gilt sogar:

Satz 4.3. $F \subset G$ *seien e.e. Untergruppen der a.a. Gruppen* M *und* $f \notin F$. *Dann gibt es einen inneren Automorphismus* τ *von* M *über* F *mit* $f \notin \tau[G]$.

Zum Beweis brauchen wir das folgende Lemma

Lemma 4.4. F *sei Untergruppe von* G. *Dann gibt es einen inneren Automorphismus* τ *einer Obergruppe von* G *mit* $\tau[G] \cap G = F$ *und* $\tau|_F = \mathrm{id}_F$.

Beweis. G' sei eine isomorphe Kopie von G über F, $G \cap G' = F$. Wir bilden $H = G *_F G'$ und setzen $\mu : G \cong_F G'$ zu einem inneren Automorphismus τ einer Obergruppe von H fort. □

Seien nun f, F, G, M wie in 4.3. Unser Lemma liefert einen inneren Automorphismus τ_g einer Obergruppe $N \supset M$, mit $\tau_{g|F} = \mathrm{id}_F$ und $f \notin \tau_g[G]$. Nach eine weiteren Anwendung von 4.4 haben wir in einer Obergruppe (o.E. N) einen inneren Automorphismus τ_h über $\tau_g[G]$ mit $\tau_h(f) \neq f$. Wenn $G = \langle g_0, \ldots, g_n\rangle$, $F = \langle f_0, \ldots, f_m\rangle$, gilt in N $gf_0g^{-1} = f_0 \cdots gf_mg^{-1} = f_m$, $h(gg_0g^{-1})h^{-1} = gg_0g^{-1} \cdots h(gg_ng^{-1})h^{-1} = gg_ng^{-1}$ und $hfh^{-1} \neq f$.

Wir benützen nun 1.3.1 des nächsten Kapitels: Weil also das endliche System von Gleichungen und *Ungleichungen*

$$\begin{aligned} S(\vec{f}, \vec{g}, f, x, y) = {} & \{xf_ix^{-1} \doteq f_i \mid i \leq m\} \\ & \cup \{y(xg_ix^{-1})y^{-1} \doteq xg_ix^{-1} \mid i \leq n\} \\ & \cup \{\neg\, yfy^{-1} \doteq f\} \end{aligned}$$

in einer Obergruppe von M (durch g, h) gelöst wird, besitzt es auch eine Lösung g', h' in M. $\tau = \tau_{g'}$ hat die gewünschten Eigenschaften. □

Folgerungen 4.5. 1. $F \subset G$ *seien endlich erzeugte Untergruppen der a.a. Gruppe* M, $S \cap F = \emptyset$ *eine endliche Teilmenge von* M. *Dann existiert ein innerer Automorphismus* τ *über* F *mit* $S \cap \tau[G] = \emptyset$.

2. *Algebraisch abgeschlossene Gruppen sind nicht endlich erzeugt.*

3. *Jede abzählbare a.a. Gruppe besitzt* 2^ω *Automorphismen* ([14]).

Wir beweisen 1 durch Induktion über $|S|$. Dazu nehmen wir ein $f \in S$. Wenn $\langle F, f\rangle \cap (S\setminus\{f\}) \neq \emptyset$, folgt aus $\tau|_F = \mathrm{id}_F$ und $\tau[G] \cap (S\setminus\{f\}) = \emptyset$, daß $\tau[G] \cap S = \emptyset$. In diesem Fall folgt also die Behauptung aus der Induktionsvoraussetzung. Sonst wählen wir einen inneren Automorphismus τ über F mit $f \notin \tau[G]$ und einen inneren Automorphismus π über $\langle F, f\rangle$ mit $\pi[\langle \tau[G], f\rangle] \cap (S\setminus\{f\}) = \emptyset$. Dann ist $\pi\tau[G] \cap S = \emptyset$.

2. Wäre M e.e. müßte es für $f \in M\setminus E$ einen inneren Automorphismus geben mit $f \notin \tau[M]$.

3. Sei F endlich erzeugte Untergruppe der a.a.Gr. M. Da M nicht e.e. ist, gibt es $f \in M\setminus F$. Wähle einen Automorphismus τ über F, $f \notin \tau[\langle F, f\rangle]$. Natürlich ist $\tau \neq \mathrm{id} M$. □

Wir haben ein einfaches Kriterium für die Existenz partiell isomorpher Strukturen der Mächtigkeit ω_1. Die Voraussetzung der ω-Homogenität ist eigentlich nicht nötig, vereinfacht aber Formulierung und Beweis. (a)→(b) folgt aus Lemma 34 ([14]).

Lemma 4.6. *$\mathfrak{M}$ sei abzählbar und ω-homogen. Dann sind äquivalent*
(a) *Es gibt* $\mathfrak{N} \subsetneqq \mathfrak{M}$, $\mathfrak{N} \cong \mathfrak{M}$.
(b) *Es gibt* $\mathfrak{N} \cong_p \mathfrak{M}$, $|\mathfrak{N}| = \omega_1$.

Beweis. (a)→(b) ([14]) Wir definieren eine aufsteigende Folge $\mathfrak{M} = \mathfrak{M}_0 \subsetneqq \mathfrak{M}_1 \subsetneqq \cdots \mathfrak{M}_\alpha \subsetneqq \cdots$ $\alpha \in \omega_1$ von zu $\mathfrak{M}$ isomorphen Strukturen. $\mathfrak{M}_{\alpha+1}$ existiert wegen (a). Für Limeszahlen nehmen wir $\mathfrak{M}_\lambda = \bigcup\{\mathfrak{M}_\alpha \mid \alpha < \lambda\}$. Aus 2.11.4 und 2.8.1 folgt $\mathfrak{M}_\lambda \cong \mathfrak{M}$. $\mathfrak{N} :- \bigcup\{\mathfrak{M}_\alpha \mid \alpha < \omega_1\}$ hat die gewünschten Eigenschaften, wieder wegen 2.11.4. (b)→(a) Man kann wegen 2.8.2 $\mathfrak{M} <_p \mathfrak{N}$ voraussetzen. Sei $a \in \mathfrak{N}\setminus\mathfrak{M}$. 2.11.5 liefert ein abzählbares $\mathfrak{N}'$ mit $\mathfrak{M} \cup \{a\} \subset \mathfrak{N}' <_p \mathfrak{N}$. Also ist $\mathfrak{M} \cong \mathfrak{N}'$ und $\mathfrak{M} \subsetneqq \mathfrak{N}'$. □

Der nächste Satz zeigt, daß die in 4.3 beschriebene Eigenschaft a.a. Gruppen sogar noch stärker als (b) von 4.6 ist.

Satz 4.7. *$\mathfrak{M}$ sei abzählbar und ω-homogen, S eine Teilmenge von $\mathfrak{M}$. Dann sind äquivalent:*
(a) *Für alle e.e. Unterstrukturen $\mathfrak{A} \subset \mathfrak{B}$ von $\mathfrak{M}$ mit $S \cap \mathfrak{A} = \emptyset$ gibt es einen Automorphismus τ von $\mathfrak{M}$ über $\mathfrak{A}$ mit $\tau[\mathfrak{B}] \cap S = \emptyset$.*
(b) *Jede zu S disjunkte e.e. Unterstruktur von $\mathfrak{M}$ ist in einem $\mathfrak{N} \subset \mathfrak{M}$ enthalten mit $\mathfrak{N} \cong \mathfrak{M}$, $\mathfrak{N} \cap S = \emptyset$.*

Beweis. (b)→(a) $\mathfrak{A} \subset \mathfrak{B}$ seien wie in (a). Für $\mathfrak{A}$ wählen wir $\mathfrak{A} \subset \mathfrak{N}$ wie in (b). Es gibt eine Einbettung $\nu : \mathfrak{B} \to \mathfrak{N}$. Weil $\mathfrak{N}$ ω-homogen ist, können wir $\nu_{|\mathfrak{A}} = \mathrm{id}_{\mathfrak{A}}$ annehmen (2.3.1). Für das gesuchte τ nehmen wir eine Fortsetzung von ν (2.11.2).

(a)→(b) $\mathfrak{A}$ sei zu S disjunkte e.e. Unterstruktur von $\mathfrak{M}$. Wir stellen $\mathfrak{M}$ als Vereinigung einer Folge $\mathfrak{A} = \mathfrak{A}_0 \subset \cdots \mathfrak{A}_1 \subset \cdots$ von e.e. Unterstrukturen dar, und definieren eine Folge $\nu_0 \subset \nu_1 \subset \cdots$ von Einbettungen $\nu_i : \mathfrak{A}_i \to \mathfrak{M}$ mit $\nu_i[\mathfrak{A}_i] \cap S = \emptyset$. Für ν_0 nehmen wir die Inklusion von $\mathfrak{A}$ in $\mathfrak{M}$. Sei ν_i definiert und μ eine Fortsetzung auf $\mathfrak{A}_{i+1}$. (a) angewandt auf $\mu[\mathfrak{A}_i] \subset \mu[\mathfrak{A}_{i+1}]$ gibt einen Automorphismus τ von $\mathfrak{M}$ mit $\tau_{|\mu[\mathfrak{A}_i]} = \mathrm{id}_{\mu[\mathfrak{A}_i]}$ und $S \cap \tau[\mu[\mathfrak{A}_{i+1}]] = \emptyset$. Setze $\nu_{i+1} = \tau\mu$. $\nu := \bigcup\{\nu_i \mid i < \omega\}$. $\mathfrak{N} := \nu[\mathfrak{M}]$ erfüllt (b). □

Folgerungen 4.8. 1. *Sei F e.e. Untergruppe der abzählbaren a.a. Gruppe M und S eine endliche zu F disjunkte Teilmenge von M. Dann gibt es $F \subset N \subset M$, $N \cap S = \emptyset$, $N \cong M$. Über keiner endlich erzeugten Gruppe gibt es also eine minimale a.a. Gruppe.*

2. ([14]) *Jede abzählbare a.a. Gruppe ist partiell isomorphe Substruktur einer a.a. Gruppe der Mächtigkeit ω_1.*

3. *Es gibt 2^ω verschiedene a.a. Gruppen der Mächtigkeit ω_1.* (3 *gilt, weil es 2^ω abzählbare a.a.Gr. gibt. Siehe* III, 4.2.)

Bemerkung 4.9. Wir werden später sehen, daß das Skelett einer algebraisch abgeschlossenen Gruppe mit F und G auch $F \times G$ enthält. Also ist, wenn M a.a. und $F \in \mathrm{Sk}(M)$, $\mathrm{Sk}(M \times F) = \mathrm{Sk}(M)$. Ist M abzählbar, kann man daher $M \times F$ isomorph in M einbetten (2.11.3). Auf diese Weise wurde in [14] 4.6 (a) für a.a.Gr. nachgewiesen.

Es gibt eine dritte Möglichkeit in einer abzählbaren a.a. Gruppe eine isomorphe echte Untergruppe zu finden:

Satz 4.10. 1. *Der Zentralisator $Z'(F)$ einer endlich erzeugten Untergruppe F einer a.a.Gr. M hat dieselbe Mächtigkeit wie M.*

2. *Wenn das Zentrum von F trivial ist, ist $Z'(F) \cong_p M$.*

Bemerkungen 4.11. 1. Wenn $Z(F) = E$, ist $Z'(F)$ also algebraisch abgeschlossen, hat dasselbe Skelett wie M und ist, wenn M abzählbar ist, zu M isomorph.

2. Wenn $F \neq E$ und $Z(F) = E$, ist $Z'(F) \subsetneq M$. Da man jede endliche Gruppe in M einbetten kann, gibt es immer solche F in M (siehe II, 1.3.3).

3. Wenn $Z(F) \neq E$, ist $Z(F)$ nicht algebraisch abgeschlossen. Denn

ein $f \in Z(F)\setminus E$ ist auch in $Z'(F)$ und die Ungleichung $\neg xf \doteq fx$ ist zwar in M, nicht aber in $Z'(F)$ lösbar.

(1 beantwortet eine Frage aus [17].)

Wir beweisen zuerst ein Lemma

Lemma 4.12. *F und $G \subset H$ seien e.e. Untergruppen der a.a.Gr. M. Wenn $F \times G \subset M$, gibt es einen inneren Automorphismus τ von M über G, so daß $\langle F, \tau[H]\rangle = F \times \tau[H]$.*

Beweis. Wir werden in III, 1.5.2 beweisen, daß mit F und H auch $F \times H$ in M einbettbar sind. Also betten wir vermöge μ $F \times H$ über $F \times G$ in M ein (M ist ω-homogen) und wählen τ so, daß $\tau_{|G} = \mathrm{id}_G$ und $\tau[H] = \mu[H]$. □

Beweis von 4.10.1. Wir unterscheiden zwei Fälle:

(a) In M gibt es $|M|$ viele Elemente mit verschiedenem Typ über F. d.h. Es gibt $A \subset M$, $|A| = |M|$, für alle $a \neq b \in A$ $\langle a\rangle' \not\cong_F \langle b\rangle'$. Nach 4.12 gibt es eine isomorphe Kopie F' von F, so daß $F \times F' \subset M$. Da M ω-homogen ist, gibt es auch $|M|$ viele Elemente mit verschiedenen Typ über F'; sei $B \subset M$, $|B| = |M|$, für alle $a \neq b \in B$ $\langle a\rangle' \not\cong_{F'} \langle b\rangle'$. Wir wenden nochmal 4.12 an und finden zu jedem $a \in B$ ein $f_a \in M$ mit $\langle f_a\rangle' \cong_{F'} \langle a\rangle'$ und $\langle F, F', f_a\rangle = F \times \langle F', f_a\rangle$. Die f_a, $a \in B$ sind also alle verschieden und aus $Z'(F)$.

(b) Wenn (a) nicht eintritt, gibt es nach dem Schubfachprinzip für alle $\kappa < |M|$ mindestens κ^+ Elemente vom gleichen Typ über F. Sei also für alle $a, b \in A$ $\langle a\rangle' \cong_F \langle b\rangle'$ und $|A| = \kappa^+$. $a \in A$ sei fest gewählt und für jedes $b \in A$ ein innerer Automorphismus τ_{f_b} über F mit $\tau_{f_b}(a) = b$. Die f_b sind alle verschieden und aus $Z'(F)$. Also ist für jedes $\kappa < |M|$ $|Z'(F)| \geq \kappa^+$.

Beweis von 4.10.2. Sei G endlich erzeugte Untergruppe von $Z'(F)$ und $G \subset H \in \mathrm{Sk}(M)$. Wir zeigen, daß H über G in $Z'(F)$ einbettbar ist. Damit ist sowohl nach 2.3.1 die ω-Homogenität von $Z'(F)$ gezeigt, als auch $\mathrm{Sk}(Z'(F)) = \mathrm{Sk}(M)$. Daraus folgt mit 2.10.1 die Behauptung. Weil $Z(F) = E$, ist aber $\langle F, G\rangle = F \times G$; H ist also wegen 4.12 über G in $Z'(F)$ einbettbar. □

II. Auflösbare Gleichungssysteme

Ein Gleichungssystem $S(\vec{c}, \vec{x})$ sei gegeben. Wir betrachten die Klasse $\mathscr{K}$

aller Gruppen G und Folgen von Parametern $\vec{g} \in G$, für die $S(\vec{g}, \vec{x})$ über G lösbar ist.

Im ersten Abschnitt zeigen wir, daß man auf diese Weise gerade die Klassen der Form $\mathcal{K} = \{(G, \vec{g}) \mid G \models I(\vec{g})\}$ — für eine Menge I von positiven Implikationen — erhält.

Die $\mathcal{K}$, die sich durch r.a. Mengen von Implikationen axiomatisieren lassen, gehören auf diese Weise zu endlichen Gleichungssystemen, wie wir im zweiten Abschnitt nachweisen. Das hat zur Folge, daß man r.a. Gleichungssysteme in vieler Hinsicht wie endliche Gleichungssysteme behandeln kann. So ist ein r.a. System von Implikationen in einer algebraisch abgeschlossenen Gruppe genau dann erfüllbar, wenn es in einer Obergruppe erfüllbar ist (2.7).

Der Begriff der "Aufzählungsreduzierbarkeit" gestattet es, die Ergebnisse des zweiten Abschnitts zu relativieren. Wir geben im dritten Kapitel zunächst eine rekursionstheoretische (3.4) dann eine gruppentheoretische Charakterisierung der Aufzählungsreduzierbarkeit (3.10). 3.10 ist eine "Relativierung" des Satzes von Higman, der die Gruppen mit r.a. Wortproblem als die e.e. Untergruppen endlich präsentierter Gruppen beschreibt: Die Gruppen, deren Wortproblem auf das Wortproblem von G aufzählungsreduzierbar ist, sind gerade die e.e. Untergruppen endlich "über G" präsentierter Gruppen. Dann untersuchen wir die Auflösbarkeit von endlichen Gleichungssystemen, bei denen wir einen Teil der Koeffizienten "fest" in einer Gruppe G interpretieren. Wie im zweiten Abschnitt entsprechen dann endliche Gleichungssysteme Mengen von positiven Implikationen, die auf das Wortproblem von G aufzählungsreduzierbar sind (z. B. 3.12).

1. Gleichungssysteme und positive Implikationen

Wir betrachten zwei Beispiele

Beispiel 1.1. $S(\vec{a}, \vec{b}, x) = \{xa_ix^{-1} \doteq b_i \mid i = 0, \ldots, n\}$. Wenn $\vec{a}, \vec{b} \in G$ ist nach I, 1.10 S genau dann über G lösbar, wenn $\langle \vec{a} \rangle' \cong \langle \vec{b} \rangle'$. Das ist äquivalent mit der Gültigkeit der folgenden Menge von Implikationen in $(G; \vec{a}, \vec{b})$

$$I(\vec{a}, \vec{b}) = \{W(\vec{a}) \doteq e \rightarrow W(\vec{b}) \doteq e \mid W \text{ Wort in } x_0, \ldots, x_n\}$$
$$\cup \{W(\vec{b}) \doteq e \rightarrow W(\vec{a}) \doteq e \mid W \text{ Wort in } x_0, \ldots, x_n\}.$$

Beispiel 1.2. Wir betrachten umgekehrt eine Implikation $a \doteq e \rightarrow b \doteq e$. Das nächste Lemma gibt eine Gleichung an, die genau dann in einer Obergruppe lösbar ist, wenn die Implikation gilt.

Lemma ([14]). *Die Gleichung* $\iota_1(\boldsymbol{b}, \boldsymbol{a}, x_0, x_1) = \boldsymbol{b} \doteq [[\boldsymbol{a}, x_0], x_1]$ *ist genau dann über* G *lösbar* $(a, b \in G)$, *wenn* $G \models \boldsymbol{a} \doteq \boldsymbol{e} \rightarrow \boldsymbol{b} \doteq \boldsymbol{e}$.

(*In* [14] *wird die einfachere Gleichung* $\boldsymbol{b} \doteq x_0 \boldsymbol{a} x_0^{-1} x_1 \boldsymbol{a} x_1^{-1}$ *benutzt.*)

Beweis. Wenn die Gleichung in einer Obergruppe lösbar ist, folgt natürlich $b = e$ aus $a = e$. Sei umgekehrt $b = e$ oder $a \neq e$.

1. Fall $a = b$.
Sei $G' = G \times \langle a' \rangle$ für ein a' mit der selben Ordnung wie a. In einer geeigneten Obergruppe wählen wir mit 1.10 ein g_0 mit $g_0 a^{-1} g_0^{-1} = a'$ und ein g_1 mit $g_1(aa')g_1^{-1} = a'$. Dann ist $[a, g_0] = aa'$ und $[[a, g_0], g_1] = aa'(a')^{-1} = a = b$.

2. Fall $a \neq b$.
Sei H beliebig und $g_0 \in H \setminus E$. Weil $a \neq b$ und also $a \neq e$, haben $b^{-1}[a, g_0]$ und $[a, g_0]$ in $G * H$ unendliche Ordnung. Wir finden daher in einer Obergruppe von $G * H$ ein g_1 mit $g_1([a, g_0])g_1^{-1} = b^{-1}[a, g_0]$. Dann ist $[[a, g_0], g_1] = [a, g_0](b^{-1}[a, g_0])^{-1} = b$. □

Folgerungen 1.3. 1. *Jedes endliche System von Gleichungen und Ungleichungen mit Koeffizienten aus einer a.a. Gruppe M, das über M lösbar ist, ist in M lösbar* ([21]).

2. *Algebraisch abgeschlossene Gruppen sind existentiell abgeschlossen; d. h. M ist 1-elementare Unterstruktur jeder Obergruppe.*
3. *Endliche Gruppen sind in alle a.a.Gr. einbettbar* ([26]).
4. *Lokalendliche abzählbare Gruppen sind in alle a.a.Gr. einbettbar.*
5. *Algebraisch abgeschlossene Gruppen sind einfach* ([21]).

Beweis. 1. Sei $\vec{g} \in M$ und

$$S(\vec{g}, \vec{x}) = \{W_i(\vec{g}, \vec{x}) \doteq \boldsymbol{e} \mid i < n\} \cup \{\neg\, U_i(\vec{g}, \vec{x}) \doteq \boldsymbol{e} \mid i < m\}$$

ein System von Gleichungen und Ungleichungen, das in einer Obergruppe H von M lösbar ist. a sei aus $M \setminus E$ und $H \models S(\vec{\boldsymbol{g}}, \vec{\boldsymbol{h}})$ für geeignete $\vec{h} \in H$. Nach dem Lemma gibt es für jedes $i < m$ Elemente $\vec{f}_i$ in einer Obergruppe F von H mit $F \models \iota_1(\boldsymbol{a}, U_i(\vec{\boldsymbol{g}}, \vec{\boldsymbol{h}}), \vec{\boldsymbol{f}}_i)$. Es gibt also auch in M eine Lösung $\vec{h}'$, f'_i des Systems von Gleichungen

$$\{W_i(\vec{\boldsymbol{g}}, \vec{x}) \doteq \boldsymbol{e} \mid i < n\} \cup \{\iota_1(\boldsymbol{a}, U_i(\vec{\boldsymbol{g}}, \vec{x}), \vec{y}_i) \mid i < m\}.$$

Daraus folgt, daß $U_i(\vec{g}, \vec{h}') \neq e$ für alle $i < m$.

2. Sei $M \subset G$, $\varphi(\vec{y})$ eine Existenzformel, $\vec{g} \in M$, $G \models \varphi(\vec{\boldsymbol{g}})$. Jede Existenzformel ist logisch äquivalent zu einer Formel der Form $\exists \vec{x} \vee \{\wedge\, S_i(\vec{y}, \vec{x}) \mid i < n\}$, wobei die S_i endliche Mengen von Gleichungen und Ungleichungen sind. Eines der Gl. & Ungl. systeme $S_i(\vec{\boldsymbol{g}}, \vec{x})$ ist also in G und daher wegen 1 in M lösbar. $\varphi(\vec{\boldsymbol{g}})$ gilt also auch in M.

3. F sei eine endliche Gruppe. Das endliche System $S((x_f \mid f \in F)) = \{\neg x_f \doteq x_g \mid f, g \in F, f \neq g\} \cup \{x_f x_g \doteq x_{fg} \mid f, g \in F\}$ von Gleichungen und Ungleichungen ist in F und also auch in $M \times F$ (über M) lösbar. Wenn $(g_f \mid f \in F)$ eine Lösung in M ist, ist $\lambda f g_f$ eine isomorphe Einbettung von F in M.

4. Wenn G lokalendlich ist, ist nach 3 $\mathrm{Sk}(G) \subset \mathrm{Sk}(M)$ für alle a.a. M. Ist G abzählbar, folgt $G < M$ aus I, 2.11.3.

5. Wenn N ein nichttrivialer Normalteiler der a.a.Gr. M ist, finden wir $a \in M \setminus N$ und $b \in N \setminus E$. Nach dem Lemma gibt es in einer Obergruppe — und also in M selbst — eine Lösung $\vec{g}$ der Gleichung $\iota_1(\boldsymbol{a}, \boldsymbol{b}, \vec{x})$. Dann gilt aber in M/N $\iota_1(aN, bN, \vec{g}N)$. Daher muß, weil $bN = eN$, $aN = eN$ sein — in Widerspruch zu $a \notin N$. □

Wir wollen zeigen, daß sich für jedes Gleichungssystem S die Klasse der Gruppen über denen S lösbar durch eine Menge von positiven Implikationen axiomatisieren läßt. Wir benützen dabei nur — im folgenden Lemma —, daß T^G eine universelle Horntheorie ist, d. h. daß Unterstrukturen direkter Produkte von Gruppen wieder Gruppen sind.

Lemma 1.4. *Sei I eine Menge von Implikationen und $\varphi_0, \ldots, \varphi_n$ eine Folge von Gleichungen. Wenn $I \vdash^G \varphi_0 \vee \cdots \vee \varphi_n$, ist für ein $i \leq n$ $I \vdash^G \varphi_i$.*

Beweis. Sonst gibt es für alle $i \leq n$ eine Gruppe G_i und Interpretationen der Konstanten aus S $\vec{g}_i \in G$ mit $(G_i, \vec{g}_i) \not\models \varphi_i$ und $(G_i, \vec{g}_i) \models I$. Dann ist aber $\times_{i=0}^n (G_i, \vec{g}_i) \models I$ und $\times_{i=0}^n (G_i, \vec{g}_i) \not\models \varphi_0 \vee \cdots \vee \varphi_n$. □

Folgerung 1.5. I sei eine Menge von Implikationen, U eine Menge von Ungleichungen, $\psi_1, \ldots, \psi_n$, $\varphi_1, \ldots, \varphi_m$ $(n, m \in \omega)$ Gleichungen. Wenn $I \cup U \vdash^G \psi_1 \wedge \cdots \wedge \psi_n \rightarrow \varphi_1 \vee \cdots \vee \varphi_m$, gibt es ein $\chi \in U$ mit $I \cup \{\chi\} \vdash^G \psi_1 \wedge \cdots \psi_n \rightarrow$ oder es ist $I \vdash^G \psi_1 \wedge \cdots \wedge \psi_n \rightarrow \varphi_i$ für ein $i \leq m$.

Beweis. Sei o.E. U endlich und $= \{\chi_1, \ldots, \chi_k\}$. Dann ist $I \cup \{\psi_1, \ldots, \psi_n\} \vdash^G \neg \chi_1 \vee \cdots \vee \neg \chi_k \vee \varphi_1 \vee \cdots \vee \varphi_m$. Wenn für ein $j \leq k$ $I \cup \{\psi_1, \ldots, \psi_n\} \vdash^G \neg \chi_j$, ist $I \cup \{\chi_j\} \vdash^G \psi_1 \wedge \cdots \wedge \psi_n \rightarrow$. Wenn für ein $i \leq m$ $I \cup \{\psi_1, \ldots, \psi_n\} \vdash^G \varphi_i$, ist $I \vdash^G \psi_1 \wedge \cdots \wedge \psi_n \rightarrow \varphi_i$. □

Satz 1.6. *Zu jedem System von Gleichungen $S(\vec{c}, \vec{x})$ gibt es eine Menge $I(\vec{c})$ von positiven Implikationen, sodaß für alle $\vec{g} \in G$ $S(\vec{g}, \vec{x})$ genau dann über G lösbar ist, wenn $G \models I(\vec{g})$.*

(Wenn S ein System von Gleichungen und Ungleichungen ist, leistet eine Menge I von Implikationen das gewünschte.)

Bemerkung 1.7. Man kann für I die Menge $\{\varphi \mid \varphi$ positive Implikation aus $L(\vec{c})$, $S(\vec{c}, \vec{d}) \vdash^G \varphi\}$ nehmen.

Beweis. $I(\vec{c})$ sei wie in 1.7.

$S(\vec{g}, \vec{x})$ sei über G nicht lösbar. Dann ist $\text{Diag}(G, \vec{g}) \cup S(\vec{g}, \vec{d})$ nicht erfüllbar, vgl. I, 1.2. Es gibt also eine endliche Menge $J \subset \text{Diag}(G, \vec{g})$, für die $J \cup S(\vec{g}, \vec{d})$ nicht erfüllbar ist. Sei $J = \{\neg\varphi_1, \ldots \neg\varphi_n, \psi_1, \ldots \psi_m\}$ für Gleichungen φ_i, ψ_i. Es ist $S(\vec{g}, \vec{d}) \vdash^G \psi_1 \wedge \cdots \wedge \psi_m \rightarrow \varphi_1 \vee \cdots \vee \varphi_n$. Nach 1.5 ist $S(\vec{g}, \vec{d}) \vdash^G \psi_1 \wedge \cdots \wedge \psi_m \rightarrow \varphi_j$ für ein $j \leq n$. Die positive Implikation $\psi_1 \wedge \cdots \wedge \psi_m \rightarrow \varphi_j$ gehört zu I. Also $G \nvDash I(\vec{g})$. (Wenn S auch Ungleichungen enthält, kann I auch $\psi_1 \wedge \cdots \wedge \psi_m \rightarrow$ enthalten.) □

Der nächste Satz kehrt (1.6) um:

Satz 1.8. *Zu jeder Menge $I(\vec{c})$ von positiven Implikationen gibt es ein Gleichungssystem $S(\vec{c}, \vec{x})$, so daß für alle $\vec{g} \in G$ $S(\vec{g}, \vec{x})$ genau dann über G lösbar ist, wenn $G \vDash I(\vec{g})$.*

Der Satz folgt sofort aus dem nächsten Lemma

Lemma 1.9. 1 ([14]). *Für jedes n kann man eine Gleichung $\iota_n(c_0, \ldots, c_n, \vec{x})$ angeben, so daß für alle $\vec{g} \in G$ $\iota_n(\vec{g}, \vec{x})$ genau dann über G lösbar ist, wenn $G \vDash \boldsymbol{g}_1 \doteq \boldsymbol{e} \wedge \cdots \wedge \boldsymbol{g}_n \doteq \boldsymbol{e} \rightarrow \boldsymbol{g}_0 \doteq \boldsymbol{e}$.*

2. *$\mathcal{F}$ sei eine Familie von Gleichungssystemen mit Koeffizienten aus G. Wenn keine Variable in zwei Gleichungssystemen von $\mathcal{F}$ vorkommt, ist $\bigcup \mathcal{F}$ genau dann über G lösbar, wenn jedes System aus $\mathcal{F}$ über G lösbar ist.*

Beweis. 1. Für $n = 1$ ist 1 die Behauptung von 1.2. Sei $\iota_n(c_0, \ldots, c_n, \vec{x})$ äquivalent zur Gleichung $t(c_0, \ldots, c_n, \vec{x}) \doteq \boldsymbol{e}$. Dann nimmt man für $\iota_{n+1}(c_0, \ldots, c_{n+1}, \vec{x}, \vec{y})$ die Gleichung $\iota_1(t(c_0, \ldots c_n, \vec{x}), c_{n+1}, \vec{y})$. Die so rekursiv konstruierten ι_n haben die geforderte Eigenschaft, weil $\bigwedge_{i=1}^{n} c_i \doteq \boldsymbol{e} \rightarrow c_0 \doteq \boldsymbol{e}$ dasselbe bedeutet wie $c_n \doteq \boldsymbol{e} \rightarrow (c_{n-1} \doteq \boldsymbol{e} \rightarrow (\cdots (c_1 \doteq \boldsymbol{e} \rightarrow c_0 \doteq \boldsymbol{e}) \cdots))$.

(Wenn $\iota_1(c_0, c_1, \vec{x})$ wie in 1.2 die Gleichung $t(c_1, \vec{x}) \doteq c_0$ ist, kann man so die Darstellung von ([14]) für ι_n bekommen: $c_0 \doteq t(c_1, \vec{x}_1) \cdots t(c_n, \vec{x}_n)$, der man die gewünschte Eigenschaft leicht ansieht. Unsere kompliziertere Darstellung zeigt, wie wenig man die

Gruppeneigenschaften braucht, um das Lemma aus 1.2 zu schließen.)

2. Sei $\mathscr{F} = \{S_j(\vec{g}, \vec{x}_j) \mid j \in J\}$. Wenn dann S_j in $F_j \supset G$ gelöst wird, ist $\bigcup \mathscr{F}$ in $*_G\{F_j \mid j \in J\}$ lösbar. □

2. Endliche Gleichungssysteme und rekursiv aufzählbare Mengen von positiven Implikationen

Wir haben gesehen, daß Gleichungssysteme, die in Obergruppen gelöst werden sollen, Mengen von positiven Implikationen entsprechen. In diesem Abschnitt wird gezeigt, daß auf diese Weise *endliche* Gleichungssysteme gerade zu rekursiv aufzählbaren Mengen von positiven Implikationen gehören.

Satz 2.1. *Jedem endlichen Gleichungssystem $S(\vec{c}, \vec{x})$ kann man eine rekursiv aufzählbare Menge von positiven Implikationen $I(\vec{c})$ zuordnen, so daß für alle $\vec{g} \in G$ $S(\vec{g}, \vec{x})$ genau dann über G lösbar ist, wenn $G \vdash I(\vec{g})$.*

Beweis. $\{\varphi \in L_{\omega\omega}(\vec{c}) \mid \vdash^G \varphi\}$ ist r.a. Also ist auch $I(c) = \{\varphi(\vec{c}) \mid \vdash^G \bigwedge S(\vec{c}, \vec{d}) \rightarrow \varphi(\vec{c}),\ \varphi$ positive Implikation$\}$ rekursiv aufzählbar. □

Bemerkung 2.2. Die Zuordnung $S \mapsto I$ ist effektiv: der Gödelnummer von S wird rekursiv ein Σ_1^0-Index von I zugeordnet (genauer: ein Σ_1^0-Index der Menge der Gödelnummern der Elemente von I).

Beim Beweis von Satz 1.8 haben wir jeder positiven Implikation aus I ein eigenes Gleichungssystem zugeordnet. Wenn I unendlich ist, bekommen wir also so ein Gleichungssystem mit unendlich vielen Variablen. Um zunächst diese Schwierigkeit bei der Umkehrung von 2.1 zu überwinden, zitieren wir aus ([8]):

Lemma 2.3. *Es gibt eine Folge von Wörtern $N_i(x, y)$, so daß für alle Folgen $(g_i \mid i < \omega)$ aus einer Gruppe G das Gleichungssystem $\{N_i(x, y) \doteq g_i \mid i < \omega\}$ über G lösbar ist.*

Bemerkung. In ([20]) ist $N_i(x, y) = [[x, y^{2i+1}], x]$.

Folgerungen 2.4. 1 ([8]). *Jede abzählbare Gruppe ist in eine von zwei Elementen erzeugte Gruppe einbettbar.*

2. *Jede endlich erzeugte Untergruppe einer a.a.Gr. ist in einer von zwei Elementen erzeugten Untergruppe enthalten.*

3. *Zu jedem (endlichen, r.a., rekusiven) Gleichungssystem $S(\vec{c}, \vec{x})$ gibt*

es ein (endliches, r.a., rekursives) Gleichungssystem $S'(\vec{c}, x_1, x_2)$ — *mit nur zwei Variablen* — *das genau dann in einer Obergruppe lösbar ist, wenn* S *in einer Obergruppe lösbar ist.*

Beweis. 2. Wenn $\vec{g} \in M$ a.a., ist $\langle \vec{g} \rangle \subset \langle h_1, h_2 \rangle \subset M$; wobei h_1, h_2 eine Lösung von $\{N_i(x_1, x_2) \doteq g_i \mid i < n\}$ ist.

3. Setze einfach $S'(\vec{c}, x_1, x_2) = S(\vec{c}, N_0(x_1, x_2), \ldots, N_n(x_1, x_2), \ldots)$. □

Bevor wir in 2.6 Satz 2.1 umkehren, behandlen wir noch einen Spezialfall: Für jedes n ist

$$\{W(\vec{c}) \doteq e \rightarrow W(\vec{d}) \doteq e \mid W \text{ Wort in } x_0, \ldots, x_n\}$$

eine r.a. Menge von positiven Implikationen, die auf $\vec{a}, \vec{b} \in G$ genau dann zutrifft, wenn $\langle \vec{b} \rangle'$ homomorphes Bild von $\langle \vec{a} \rangle'$ ist. Das nächste Lemma ordnet also dieser Menge ein endliches Gleichungssystem zu.

Lemma 2.5. *Man kann für jedes n ein endliches Gleichungssystem* $H_n(\vec{c}, \vec{d}, x, y)$ *angeben, so daß für alle* $\vec{a}, \vec{b} \in G$ $\langle b_0, \ldots, b_n \rangle'$ *genau dann homomorphes Bild von* $\langle a_0, \ldots, a_n \rangle'$ *ist, wenn* $H_n(\vec{a}, \vec{b}, x, y)$ *über* G *lösbar ist.*

Beweis. Sei $\vec{a}, \vec{b} \in G$ und $\langle a'_0, \ldots, a'_n \rangle'$ eine isomorphe Kopie von $\langle a_0, \ldots, a_n \rangle'$. $\langle b_0, \ldots, b_n \rangle'$ ist genau dann homomorphes Bild von $\langle a_0, \ldots, a_n \rangle'$, wenn in $\langle a'_1, \ldots, a'_n \rangle \times G$ $\langle (a'_0, b_0), \ldots, (a'_n, b_n) \rangle'$ und $\langle a_0, \ldots, a_n \rangle'$ isomorph sind. In diesem Fall finden wir in einer geeigneten Obergruppe H von $\langle a'_0, \ldots, a'_n \rangle \times G$ Elemente f, g mit $ga_0g^{-1} = a'_0, \ldots, ga_ng^{-1} = a'_n$ und $fa_0f^{-1} = ga_0g^{-1}b_0, \ldots, fa_nf^{-1} = ga_ng^{-1}b_n$. Das Gleichungssystem $H_n(\vec{a}, \vec{b}, x, y) := \{xa_ix^{-1} \doteq ya_iy^{-1}b_i \mid i \leq n\} \cup \{ya_iy^{-1}b_j \doteq b_jya_iy^{-1} \mid i, j \leq n\}$ ist also in einer Obergruppe von G lösbar, wenn $\langle b_0, \ldots, b_n \rangle'$ homomorphes Bild von $\langle a_0, \ldots, a_n \rangle'$ ist. Wenn andererseits f, g eine Lösung von $H_n(\vec{a}, \vec{b}, x, y)$ sind, gilt für jedes Wort $W(x_0, \ldots, x_n)$,

$$\begin{aligned} fW(\vec{a})f^{-1} &= W(fa_0f^{-1}, \ldots, fa_nf^{-1}) \\ &= W(ga_0g^{-1}b_0, \ldots, ga_ng^{-1}b_n) \\ &= W(ga_0g^{-1}, \ldots, ga_ng^{-1})W(b_0, \ldots, b_n) \\ &= gW(\vec{a})g^{-1}W(\vec{b}). \end{aligned}$$

Aus $W(\vec{a}) = e$ folgt also $W(\vec{b}) = e$. □

Satz 2.6. *Zu jeder rekursiv aufzählbaren Menge* $I(\vec{c})$ *von positiven Implikationen läßt sich ein endliches Gleichungssystem* $S(\vec{c}, \vec{x})$ *angeben,* *so daß für alle $\vec{g} \in G$ $S(\vec{g}, \vec{x})$ genau dann über G lösbar ist, wenn $G \models I(\vec{g})$.*

Beweis. Mit Hilfe von 1.9 verschaffen wir uns zunächst ein r.a. Gleichungssystem $S'(\vec{c}, \vec{c})$, so daß $S'(\vec{g}, \vec{x})$ genau dann über G lösbar ist, wenn $G \models I(\boldsymbol{g})$. 2.4.3 zeigt, daß wir annehmen können, daß S' nur zwei Variable hat: $S'(\vec{c}, x_1, x_2)$. H sei die Gruppe, die von den Relationen $S'(\vec{\boldsymbol{a}}, \boldsymbol{b}_1, \boldsymbol{b}_2)$ in den Erzeugenden $\vec{a}, b_1, b_2$ präsentiert wird.

Da für ein Wort $W(\vec{y}, x_1, x_2)$

$$W(\vec{a}, b_1, b_2) = e \quad \text{gdw.} \quad S'(\vec{\boldsymbol{a}}, \boldsymbol{b}_1, \boldsymbol{b}_2) \vdash^G W(\vec{\boldsymbol{a}}, \boldsymbol{b}_1, \boldsymbol{b}_2) \doteq \boldsymbol{e}$$

und S' rekursiv aufzählbar ist, ist das Wortproblem von H rekursiv aufzählbar. Nach dem Satz von Higman ([9]) läßt sich H in eine endlich präsentierte Gruppe F einbetten. $\vec{a}, b_1, b_2, \vec{a}'$ seien die Erzeugenden von F und $R(\vec{\boldsymbol{a}}, \boldsymbol{b}_1, \boldsymbol{b}_2, \vec{\boldsymbol{a}}')$ das definierende Gleichungssystem. Sei n die Länge von $\vec{c}$. Das gesuchte Gleichungssystem ist

$$S(\vec{c}, x_1, x_2, \vec{y}, z_1, z_2, \vec{u}, v_1, v_2) :=$$

$$:= R(\vec{y}, z_1, z_2, \vec{u}) \cup H_{n+1}(\vec{y}, z_1, z_2; \vec{c}, x_1, x_2; v_1, v_2).$$

Wenn in einer Obergruppe M von G $M \models S(\vec{\boldsymbol{g}}, \boldsymbol{h}_1, \boldsymbol{h}_2, \vec{\boldsymbol{g}}', \boldsymbol{h}'_1, \boldsymbol{h}'_2, \vec{\boldsymbol{f}}, \boldsymbol{f}'_1, \boldsymbol{f}'_2)$ für $h_1, \ldots, f'_2 \in M$, ist $\langle \vec{g}', h'_1, h'_2, \vec{f} \rangle'$ homomorphes Bild von $(F; \vec{a}, b_1, b_2, \vec{a}')$ und $\langle \vec{g}, h_1, h_2 \rangle'$ homomorphes Bild von $\langle \vec{g}', h'_1, h'_2 \rangle'$. $\langle \vec{g}, h_1, h_2 \rangle'$ ist also homomorphes Bild von $(H; \vec{a}, b_1, b_2)$ und daher gelten die definierenden Relationen von H auch in $\langle \vec{g}, h_1, h_2 \rangle'$. h_1, h_2 sind also eine Lösung von $S'(\vec{\boldsymbol{g}}, x_1, x_2)$, das bedeutet $G \models I(\vec{\boldsymbol{g}})$.

Sei umgekehrt $G \models I(\vec{g})$ und daher $M \models S'(\vec{\boldsymbol{g}}, \boldsymbol{h}_1, \boldsymbol{h}_2)$ für h_1, h_2 aus einer Obergruppe M von G. $\langle \vec{g}, h_1, h_2 \rangle'$ ist also homomorphes Bild von $(H; \vec{a}, b_1, b_2)$. Also gibt es in einer Obergruppe von $M \times F$ eine Lösung f'_1, f'_2 von $H_{n+1}(\vec{\boldsymbol{a}}, \boldsymbol{b}_1, \boldsymbol{b}_2; \vec{\boldsymbol{g}}, \boldsymbol{h}_1, \boldsymbol{h}_2, v_1, v_2)$.

$h_1, h_2, \vec{a}, b_1, b_2, \vec{a}', f'_1, f'_2$ ist dann eine Lösung von $S(\vec{\boldsymbol{g}}, x_1, \ldots, v_2)$. □

Als erste Folgerung aus 2.6 bekommen wir, daß die "bzgl. endlicher Gleichungssysteme" a.a. Gruppen auch bzgl. "r.a. Gleichungssysteme" algebraisch abgeschlossen sind. Wir haben sogar

Satz 2.7. *$I(\vec{g}, \vec{x})$ sei ein rekursiv aufzählbares System von Implikationen mit Koeffizienten $\vec{g}$ aus der algebraisch abgeschlossenen Gruppe M. Wenn $I(\vec{g}, \vec{x})$ in einer Obergruppe (— über M —) erfüllbar ist, ist $I(\vec{g}, \vec{x})$ schon in M erfüllbar.*

Beweis. Wir nehmen $g_0 \neq e$ an und verfahren wie beim Beweis von 1.3.1. Wir ersetzen jede negative Implikation

$$W_1(\vec{g}, \vec{x}) \doteq e \wedge \cdots \wedge W_n(\vec{g}, \vec{x}) \doteq e \rightarrow$$

aus I durch die positive Implikation

$$W_1(\vec{g}, \vec{x}) \doteq e \wedge \cdots \wedge W_n(\vec{g}, \vec{x}) \doteq e \rightarrow g_0 \doteq e.$$

So können wir annehmen, daß I nur aus positiven Implikationen besteht; weiter kommen wir in I wegen 2.3 mit zwei Variablen x_1, x_2 aus. Mit 2.6 wählen wir ein endliches Gleichungssystem $S(\vec{g}, c_1, c_2, \vec{y})$, so daß für alle $\vec{g}, h_1, h_2 \in H$ $S(\vec{g}, h_1, h_2, \vec{y})$ genau dann über H lösbar ist, wenn $H \models I(\vec{g}, h_1, h_2)$.

Wenn also h_1, h_2 aus einer Obergruppe H von M I erfüllen, ist $S(\vec{g}, h_1, h_2, \vec{y})$ in einer Obergruppe von H lösbar. Das Gleichungssystem $S(\vec{g}, x_1, x_2, \vec{y})$ ist daher über M und somit in M lösbar. Wenn $h'_1, h'_2, \vec{f}$ eine Lösung in M ist, erfüllt h'_1, h'_2 das System $I(\vec{g}, x_1, x_2)$. □

Der nächste Satz verallgemeinert 1.3.3: endliche Gruppen lassen sich durch ein endliches System von Gleichungen und Ungleichungen beschreiben. Die Gruppen, die sich vollständig durch eine r.a. Menge von Gleichungen und Ungleichungen beschreiben lassen, deren Wortproblem also — wie das Komplement des Wortproblems — r.a. ist, sind gerade die Gruppen mit rekursiven (— "lösbarem" —) Wortproblem. Wir werden später sehen, daß Gruppen mit nicht-lösbarem Wortproblem sich sogar in folgendem Sinn nicht durch ein r.a. System von Gleichungen und Ungleichungen beschreiben lassen: Es gibt für jede solche Gruppe eine a.a.Gr., in die sie nicht einbettbar ist (III, 1.8.2).

Satz 2.8 ([22]). *Endlich erzeugte Gruppen mit lösbarem Wortproblem sind in jede algebraisch abgeschlossene Gruppe einbettbar.*

Beweis. $G = \langle \vec{g} \rangle$ habe lösbares Wortproblem, M sei algebraisch abgeschlossen. Die beiden Systeme von Gleichungen und Ungleichungen $\{W(\vec{x}) \doteq e \mid W \text{ Wort mit } W(\vec{g}) = e\}$, $\{\neg W(\vec{w}) \doteq e \mid W(\vec{g}) \neq e\}$ sind rekursiv. Ihre Vereinigung wird in $M \times G$ durch $\vec{g}$ gelöst. Nach 2.7 gibt es eine Lösung $\vec{g}'$ in M. Es ist dann $\langle \vec{g}' \rangle' \cong (G, \vec{g})$. □

Bemerkung 2.9 ([22, 27]). Wenn man den Beweis von 2.8 bis zum Beweis von 2.7 zurückverfolgt, erkennt man, daß man für G (die Gruppe mit lösbarem Wortproblem), ein endliches System $T(\vec{x}, \vec{y})$ von Gleichungen und Ungleichungen findet, das lösbar ist und für dessen Lösungen $(H, \vec{a}, \vec{b})$ immer $\langle \vec{a} \rangle' \cong (G, \vec{g})$ gilt. Solche Gruppen heißen absolut endlich (a.e.) präsentiert. Endlich erzeugte Gruppen mit lösbarem Wortproblem sind also a.e. präsentierbar. Umgekehrt has jede a.e. präsentierte Gruppe lösbares Wortproblem. Denn $W(\vec{g}) = e$ gdw. $T(\vec{c}, \vec{d}) \vdash^G W(\vec{c}) \doteq \boldsymbol{e}$ und $W(\vec{g}) \neq e$ gdw. $T(\vec{c}, \vec{d}) \vdash^G \neg W(\vec{c}) \doteq \boldsymbol{e}$. Also ist sowohl das Wortproblem, als auch das Komplement des Wortproblems von G r.a. Das Wortproblem ist rekursiv.

Folgerungen 2.10. 1. *Abzählbare Gruppen mit lokal lösbarem Wortproblem sind in jede a.a. Gruppe einbettbar.* (*"lokal lösbares WP" bedeutet: jede e.e. Untergruppe hat lösbares WP*).

2. *Abzählbare abelsche Gruppen sind in jede a.a. Gruppe einbettbar.*

(1 folgt aus 2.8 und I, 2.11.3. Abelsche Gruppen haben lokal lösbares Wortproblem, denn jede e.e. abelsche Gruppe ist direkte Summe von endlich vielen zyklischen Gruppen.)

Es gibt natürlich nach I, 1.3 a.a. Gruppen, die e.e. Untergruppen mit nicht-lösbaren Wortproblemen enthalten. Darüber hinaus gilt:

Satz 2.11 ([14]). *Jede a.a. Gruppe enthählt eine e.e. Untergruppe mit nicht-lösbarem Wortproblem.*

Beweis. A und B seien zwei disjunkte r.a. Teilmengen von ω, die nicht durch eine rekursive Menge zu trennen sind ([24]). Das Gl. & Ungl.system $S(x, y) = \{N_i(x, y) \doteq \boldsymbol{e} \mid i \in A\} \cup \{\neg N_i(x, y) \doteq \boldsymbol{e} \mid i \in B\}$ ist — weil $A \cap B = \emptyset$ — lösbar nach 2.3 und rekursiv aufzählbar. Wenn a, b eine Lösung von S in der a.a.Gr. M ist, hat $\langle a, b\rangle$ nicht-lösbares Wortproblem, denn $\{i \mid N_i(a, b) = e\}$ trennt A und B. □

Bemerkung 2.12 ([18]). Wenn man den Beweis von 2.11 zurückverfolgt, erhält man ein endliches lösbares System von Gleichungen und Ungleichungen, dessen Lösungen immer eine Gruppe mit nicht-lösbarem Wortproblem erzeugen.

Satz 2.7 gestattet uns eine Verschärfung von I, 4.10.2.

Definition 2.13. F ist *r.a. erzeugte* Untergruppe von M, wenn Elemente $\vec{g} \in M$ und eine r.a. Menge $\mathcal{W}$ von Wörtern existieren, sodaß

$$F = \langle\{W(\vec{g}) \mid W \in \mathcal{W}\}\rangle.$$

Satz 2.14. *F sei eine r.a. erzeugte Untergruppe der a.a. Gruppe M. Wenn F triviales Zentrum hat, ist $M \cong_p Z'(F)$.*

Beweis. Wie mann aus dem Beweis von I, 4.10 sieht, genügt es, folgende Verschärfung von I, 4.12 zu zeigen: "Sind $G \subset H$ endlich erzeugte Untergruppen von M und $F \times G \subset M$, so gibt es einen inneren Automorphismus τ_a über G mit $\langle F, \tau_a[H]\rangle = F \times \tau_a[H]$".

Beweis. Weil $Z(F) = E$, brauchen wir a bloß so zu wählen, daß $\tau_a[H] \subset Z'(F)$. Wenn $F \subset \langle \vec{g}' \rangle \subset M$ und $F = \langle\{W(\vec{g}') \mid W \in \mathcal{W}\}\rangle$ für eine r.a. Menge von Wörtern $\mathcal{W}$, $H = \langle \vec{h} \rangle$ und $G = \langle \vec{g} \rangle$, muß a also gerade das r.a. System

$$\{xg_ix^{-1} \doteq g_i \mid i < n\} \cup \{W(\vec{g}')xh_ix^{-1} \doteq xh_ix^{-1}W(\vec{g}') \mid W \in \mathcal{W}, i < m\}$$

lösen. Da wir aber ein τ mit den gewünschten Eigenschaften in einer Obergruppe von M finden, folgt die Behauptung aus 2.7. □

Damit beenden wir zunächst die Reihe der Folgerungen aus 2.7. Wir geben noch eine Verbesserung von 2.10.2 an:

Satz 2.15 (vgl. [10]). *Jede abzählbare abelsche Gruppe, die nicht endlich erzeugt ist, ist in jede abzählbare a.a. Gruppe als maximal abelsche Gruppe einbettbar.*

Beweis. G sei abzählbare abelsche Gruppe, nicht e.e., M a.a. und abzählbar. $(g_i \mid i < \omega)$ sei eine Folge von Erzeugenden von G mit $g_{i+1} \notin \langle g_0, \ldots, g_i \rangle$; $(m_i \mid i < \omega)$ eine Aufzählung von M. Wir konstruieren eine Folge $(a_i \mid i < \omega)$ aus M, so daß $\langle a_0, \ldots, a_i \rangle' \cong \langle g_0, \ldots, g_i \rangle'$ für alle i. a_0 wählen wir beliebig mit $\langle a_0 \rangle \cong \langle g_0 \rangle$. Seien $a_0, \ldots, a_i$ bereits konstruiert. $\langle g_0, \ldots, g_{i+1} \rangle$ ist in M einbettbar, also gibt es wegen der ω-Homogenität von M ein $a \subset M$, so daß $\langle a_0, \ldots a_i, a \rangle' \cong \langle g_0, \ldots g_{i+1} \rangle'$.

1. Fall $m_i \in \langle a_0, \ldots, a_i \rangle$:
Setze $a_{i+1} := a$.

2. Fall $m_i \notin \langle a_0, \ldots, a_i \rangle$:
Das System $xa_0x^{-1} \doteq a_0, \ldots, xa_ix^{-1} \doteq a_i, \neg\, xax^{-1}m_i \doteq m_ixax^{-1}$ besitzt dann eine Lösung in einer Obergruppe von $M *_{\langle a_0, \ldots, a_i \rangle} \langle a_0, \ldots, a_i, a \rangle$. Wenn f eine Lösung in M ist, setzen wir $a_{i+1} := faf^{-1}$. Es ist dann $\langle g_0, \ldots, g_{i+1} \rangle' \cong \langle a_0, \ldots, a_{i+1} \rangle'$ und $a_{i+1}m_i \neq m_ia_{i+1}$.

Das Erzeugnis $\langle \vec{a} \rangle$ der a_i, $i < \omega$ ist die gesuchte maximal abelsche Untergruppe von M. Denn, wenn $m_i \notin \langle \vec{a} \rangle$, so ist $m_ia_{i+1} \neq a_{i+1}m_i$. □

3. Aufzählungsreduzierbarkeit

Wir untersuchen algebraisch abgeschlossene Gruppen als ω-homogene Strukturen anhand ihrer Skelette. Wir haben gesehen, daß alle endlich erzeugten Gruppen mit lösbarem Wortproblem im Skelett jeder a.a. Gruppe vorkommen. Das beim Beweis dieses Satzes letztlich verwendete Gleichungssystem, das eine Lösung in der a.a. Gruppe haben mußte, hatte keine Koeffizienten. Wenn wir Koeffizienten aus einer endlich erzeugten Untergruppe zulassen, können wir die Existenz von Lösungen "komplizierterer" Systeme von Implikationen im Skelett algebraisch abgeschlossener Gruppen — die die Koeffizientengruppe enthalten — erschließen. Dieser Abschnitt präzisiert den Einfluß vorgeschriebener Koeffizienten auf die "Ausdruckskraft" endlicher Gleichungssysteme. Wie im letzten Abschnitt endliche Gleichungssysteme r.a. Mengen von Implikationen entsprochen haben, entsprechen nun endliche Gleichungssysteme mit fester Interpretation (eines Teils) der Koeffizienten Mengen von Implikationen, die aufzählungsreduzierbar auf das Wortproblem der "Koeffizientengruppe sind.

Definition 3.1 ([24]). A, B seien Teilmengen von ω. A ist aufzählungsreduzierbar auf B — $A \leqslant_e B$ —, wenn es ein $z \in \omega$ gibt, so daß für alle $n \in \omega$, $n \in A$ gdw. $\exists i\,(\langle n, i\rangle \in W_z \wedge D_i \subset B)$. Wir schreiben dann auch $z : A \leqslant_e B$ oder $A = W_z^e[B]$.

Ein erster Zusammenhang mit $\leqslant_{\text{ra}}$ ist: $A \leqslant_{\text{ra}} B$ gdw. $A \leqslant_e B \vee (\omega \setminus B)$. "$i : A \leqslant_e B$" ist eine Π_2^0-Relation.

***Beispiel* 3.2.** *Wenn T* eine Menge von Aussagen einer Sprache $L'_{\omega,\omega}$ ist, ist $\{\varphi \in L'_{\omega,\omega} \mid T \vdash \varphi\} \leqslant_e T$. Denn $T \vdash \varphi$ gdw. $\exists i\,(D_i \vdash \varphi \wedge D_i \subset T)$.

Beispiel 3.3. U sei r.a. erzeugte Untergruppe der e.e. Gruppe G. Dann ist $W(G \mid U) \leqslant_e W(G)$. Denn wenn $G = \langle \vec{g} \rangle$ und (o.E.) $U = \langle W(\vec{g}) \mid W \in \mathscr{W} \rangle$ für eine r.a. Menge von Wörtern, ist $W(\vec{g}) \in U$ gdw. ex. Wörter $W_1, \ldots, W_k \in \mathscr{W}$ und $\tilde{W}(x_1, \ldots, x_k)$ mit

$$W(\vec{g}) = \tilde{W}(W_1(\vec{g}), \ldots, W_k(\vec{g})).$$

Diese Gleichung läßt sich aber durch $W^{-1}\tilde{W}(W_1, \ldots, W_k)(\vec{g}) \in \mathrm{Gl}(G, \vec{g})$ ausdrücken.

Im Gegensatz zu $\leqslant_{\text{ra}}$ ist $\leqslant_e$ transitiv: Aus $A \leqslant_e B$, $B \leqslant_e C$ folgt $A \leqslant_e C$. (Durch $A \equiv_e B :\Leftrightarrow A \leqslant_e B$, $B \leqslant_e B$, erhalten wir also eine Äquivalenzrelation.) Daraus folgt (siehe 3.1) daß $A \leqslant_e B$, $B \leqslant_{\text{ra}} C \Rightarrow A \leqslant_{\text{ra}} C$. Diese Eigenschaft charakterisiert $\leqslant_e$:

Satz 3.4. *$A \leqslant_e B$ gdw. für alle $C \subset \omega$ $B \leqslant_{\text{ra}} C \Rightarrow A \leqslant_{\text{ra}} C$.*

(Ohne Beweis.)

Lemma 3.5. *Für $B \subset \omega$ sind äquivalent:*

(a) *Für alle $A \subset \omega$, $A \leqslant_{\text{ra}} B \Rightarrow A \leqslant_e B$,*

(b) $\omega \setminus B \leqslant_e B$.

Bemerkungen 3.6. 1. Es gibt B mit $\omega \setminus B \not\leqslant_e B$, z. B. wenn B r.a. aber nicht rekusiv ist (siehe auch III, 2.5.2).

2. $\omega \setminus B \leqslant_e B$ gilt zum Beispiel, wenn $B \subset \omega \times \omega$ Funktion ist:

$$\langle x, y\rangle \in \omega \setminus B \Leftrightarrow \exists y\,((\exists u\, D_y = \{\langle x, u\rangle\} \wedge u \neq z) \wedge D_y \subset B)$$

Beweis. (a)→(b) ist klar, weil $\omega \setminus B \leqslant_{\text{ra}} B$.

(b)→(a) Wenn $\omega \setminus B \leqslant_e B$, folgt aus $A \leqslant_{\text{ra}} B$ $A \leqslant_e B \vee (\omega \setminus B) \leqslant_e B \vee B \equiv_m B$. Also ist $A \leqslant_e B$. □

Um die Gruppen zu charakterisieren, deren Wortprobleme aufeinander aufzählungsreduzierbar sind, verallgemeinern wir in der folgenden Definition den Begriff "endlich präsentiert".

Definition 3.7. $G \subset F$ seien endlich erzeugte Gruppen. G werde durch $\vec{g}$, F durch $\vec{g}, \vec{f}$ erzeugt. F ist *endlich präsentiert über* G, wenn es eine endliche Menge $S(\vec{g}, \vec{f})$ von Gleichungen gibt, so daß F durch $\mathrm{Gl}(G, \vec{g}) \cup S(\vec{g}, \vec{f})$ präsentiert ist.

Beispiel 3.8. Wenn H endlich präsentiert ist, ist $G * H$ endlich über G präsentiert. Denn wenn H durch $S(\vec{h})$ präsentiert wird, wird $G * H$ durch $\mathrm{Gl}(G, \vec{g}) \cup S(\vec{h})$ präsentiert.

Lemma 3.9. 1. *Wenn F über G endlich präsentiert ist, ist $W(F) \leqslant_e W(G)$.*

2. *Wenn $F \subset G$ endlich erzeugt sind, ist $W(F) \leqslant_m W(G)$ und also erst recht $W(F) \leqslant_e W(G)$.*

Beweis. 1. Es ist $W(\vec{f}, \vec{g}) = e$ gdw. $\mathrm{Gl}(G, \vec{g}) \vdash^G \wedge S(\vec{g}, \vec{f}) \rightarrow W(\vec{f}, \vec{g}) \doteq e$. Die Behauptung folgt nun aus 3.2. 2. F sei von $\vec{f} = \vec{U}(\vec{g})$ erzeugt; dann ist $W(\vec{f}) = e$ gdw. $W(\vec{U})(\vec{g}) \in \mathrm{Gl}(G, \vec{g})$. □

Satz 3.10. *F und G seien endlich erzeugte Gruppen. Dann ist $W(F) \leqslant_e W(G)$ gdw. sich F in eine über G endlich präsentierte Gruppe einbetten läßt.*

Wenn $G = E$, so sind die endlich über G präsentierten Gruppen gerade die endlich präsentierten Gruppen und $A \leqslant_e W(G)$ gdw. A r.a. ist. So erhält man für $G = E$ aus 3.10 den Satz von Higman ([9]).

Beispiel. G' sei isomorphe Kopie von $G = \langle \vec{g} \rangle$. Dann ist in $G * G'$, $W(\vec{g}, \vec{g}') = e$ gdw. $\mathrm{Gl}(G, \vec{g}) \cup \mathrm{Gl}(G', \vec{g}') \vdash W(\vec{g}, \vec{g}') \doteq e$. $\mathrm{Gl}(G, \vec{g})$ und $\mathrm{Gl}(G', \vec{g}')$ sind rekursiv isomorph, es folgt also $W(G * G') \leqslant_e W(G)$. $G * G'$ muß daher in eine endlich über G präsentierte Gruppe einbettbar sein. Tatsächlich ist $G * G'$ in $G * \mathbf{Z}$ einbettbar.

Beweis von 3.10. Die eine Richtung des Satzes folgt aus 3.9. Für die andere Richtung nehmen wir $z : W(F) \leqslant_e W(G)$ an. F werde von $\vec{f}$, G von $\vec{g}$ erzeugt. Wir haben also für alle i $V_i(\vec{f}) = e$ gdw. $\exists u\, (\langle i, u \rangle \in W_z \wedge D_u \subset W(G, \vec{g}))$. Das bedeutet, daß die r.a. Menge von positiven Implikationen

$$I(\vec{g}, \vec{f}) := \{\wedge \{V_j(\vec{g}) \doteq e \mid j \in D_u\} \to V_i(\vec{f}) \doteq e \mid \langle i, u \rangle \in W_z\}$$

in $G \times F$ gilt. Nach 2.6 findet man für I ein endliches Gleichungssystem $S(\vec{g}, \vec{f}, \vec{x})$, das genau dann in einer Obergruppe lösbar ist, wenn I gilt. Weil $S(\vec{g}, \vec{y}, \vec{x})$ über G lösbar ist, präsentiert $\mathrm{Gl}(G, \vec{g}) \cup S(\vec{g}, \vec{y}, \vec{x})$ eine Obergruppe $\langle \vec{g}, \vec{f}', \vec{h} \rangle$ von G. S ist so gewählt, daß $\langle \vec{g}, \vec{f}' \rangle \vDash I(\vec{g}, \vec{f}')$. Daraus folgt $W(\langle \vec{f} \rangle') \subset W(\langle \vec{f}' \rangle')$. Weil andererseits $\mathrm{Gl}(G, \vec{g}) \cup S(\vec{g}, \vec{f}, \vec{x})$ in einer Obergruppe von $G \times F$ lösbar ist, ist $(F, \vec{f})$ homomorphes Bild von $\langle \vec{f}' \rangle'$. Daraus folgt $W(\langle \vec{f}' \rangle') \subset W(\langle \vec{f} \rangle')$. Das ergibt zusammen $W(\langle \vec{f}' \rangle') = W(\langle \vec{f} \rangle')$, also $\langle \vec{f} \rangle' \cong \langle \vec{f}' \rangle'$. F ist also in die endlich über G präsentierte Gruppe $\langle \vec{g}, \vec{f}', \vec{h} \rangle$ einbettbar. $\square$

Um auch die Ungleichungen der "Koeffizientengruppe" zu behandeln, brauchen wir noch den folgenden Begriff:

Definition 3.11. A ist 1-aufzählungsreduzierbar auf B — $A \leqslant_e^1 B$ —, wenn es ein $z \in \omega$ gibt, so daß für alle $n \in \omega$, $n \in A$ gdw. $\exists j, i (\langle m, j, i \rangle \in W_z \wedge D_j \subset B \wedge D_i^1 \subset \omega \setminus B)$. Wir schreiben dann $z : A \leqslant_e^1 B$ oder $A = W_z^1[B]$; das ist ein Π_2^0-Relation zwischen A, B und z.

Der nächste Satz relativiert 2.7.

Satz 3.12. *$I(\vec{f}, \vec{x})$ bzw. $J(\vec{f}, \vec{x})$ seien Systeme von positiven bzw. negativen Implikationen mit Koeffizienten aus der algebraisch abgeschlossenen Gruppe M. Für $G \in \mathrm{Sk}(M)$ sei $I \leqslant_e W(G)$ und $J \leqslant_e^1 W(G)$. Wenn dann $I(\vec{f}, \vec{x}) \cup J(\vec{f}, \vec{x})$ über M erfüllbar ist, ist $I(\vec{f}, \vec{x}) \cup J(\vec{f}, \vec{x})$ auch in M erfüllbar.*

Beweis. Sei $z : I(\vec{f}, \vec{x}) \leqslant_e W(G, \vec{g})$ und $z' : J(\vec{f}, \vec{x}) \leqslant_e^1 W(G, \vec{g})$. $K(\vec{f}, \vec{g}, \vec{x})$ sei die Vereinigung von

$$\{\wedge \{V_i(\vec{g}) \doteq e \mid i \in D_u\} \to \varphi \mid \langle \overline{\varphi}, u \rangle \in W_z,\ \varphi \in L_{\omega\omega}(\vec{f})\}$$

und

$$\{\wedge\{V_i(\vec{g}) \doteq e \mid i \in D_u\} \wedge \wedge\{\neg V_j(\vec{g}) \doteq e \mid j \in D^1_{u'}\} \rightarrow \varphi \mid \langle \overline{\varphi}, u, u' \rangle \in W_z\}.$$

K ist ein r.a. System von Implikationen, denn, wenn $\varphi_1, \ldots, \varphi_n$ Gleichungen sind, ψ_1 bzw. ψ_2 eine positive bzw. negative Implikation, so sind

$$\varphi_1 \wedge \cdots \wedge \varphi_n \rightarrow \psi_1 \quad \text{und} \quad \varphi_1 \wedge \cdots \wedge \varphi_{n-1} \wedge \neg \varphi_n \rightarrow \psi_2$$

wieder zu Implikationen äquivalent.

Offenbar ist K — in allen Gruppen, die G enthalten — mit $I \cup J$ äquivalent. Wenn also $I \cup J$ über M erfüllbar ist, ist K über M erfüllbar. Nach 2.7 hat K eine Lösung in M, die also auch eine Lösung von $I \cup J$ ist. □

Wenn man den Beweis von 3.12 zurückverfolgt, erhält man eine relativierte Version von 2.6:

Lemma 3.13. *$I(\vec{g}, \vec{c})$ bzw. $J(\vec{g}, \vec{c})$ seien Mengen von positiven bzw. negativen Implikationen und $I \leqslant_e W(G)$, $J \leqslant^1_e W(G)$. Dann gibt es ein endliches System $S(\vec{g}, \vec{h}, \vec{x})$, sodaß für alle $\vec{h}$ aus einer Obergruppe H von G $S(\vec{g}, \boldsymbol{h}, \vec{x})$ genau dann über lösbar ist, wenn $H \models I(\vec{g}, \vec{h}) \cup J(\vec{g}, \vec{h})$. $G \neq E$ oder $J = \emptyset$, genügt für S ein Gleichungssystem, sonst nur* eine *Ungl. in S. Es genügen zwei Variable.)*

Folgerung 3.14. *U sei Untergruppe der endlich erzeugten Gruppe G. G Untergruppe der a.a. Gruppe M, F aus dem Skelett von M, $W(G \mid U) \leqslant_e F$. Dann gibt es für jedes $f \in M \setminus U$ ein $h \in M$ mit $\tau_{h|U} = \mathrm{id}_U$ und $\tau_h(f) \neq f$ (nach* II, 3.3 *ist $W(G \mid U) \leqslant_e W(G)$ für endlich erzeugtes U, in diesem Fall folgt die Behauptung aber auch aus* I, 4.3).

Beweis. Solch ein innerer Automorphismus existiert in einer Obergruppe von M (I, 4.4). Da wir aber die gewünschte Eigenschaft von h durch folgendes Gl. & Ungl.system ausdrücken können

$$\{xV_i(\vec{g})x^{-1} \doteq V_i(\vec{g}) \mid i \in W(G \mid U)\} \cup \{\neg xfx^{-1} \doteq f\},$$

das m-reduzierbar auf $W(G \mid U)$ und daher aufzählungsreduzierbar auf $W(F)$ ist, folgt die Behauptung aus 3.12. □

III. Rekursionstheoretische Kennzeichung algebraisch abgeschlossener Gruppen

Im letzten Kapitel haben wir gesehen, daß jedes System von Implikationen, das über einer a.a. Gruppe erfüllbar ist, und das aufzählungsreduzierbar ist auf das Wortproblem einer Gruppe $G \in \mathrm{Sk}(M)$, auch in M erfüllbar ist. M enthält also alle Gruppen F, die durch solche Systeme beschreibbar sind. Das sind gerade die F, deren Wortproblem auf das Wortproblem von G "$*$-reduzierbar" ist, (1.4). Im ersten Abschnitt zeigen wir, daß auch die Umkehrung gilt: Wenn die e.e. Gruppe F in alle a.a. M mit $G \in \mathrm{Sk}(M)$ einbettbar ist, ist $W(F)$ $*$-reduzierbar auf $W(G)$ (1.7).

Im zweiten Abschnitt grenzen wir den Begriff der $*$-Reduzierbarkeit gegen naheliegende stärkere und schwächere Definitionen ab. Dann "berechnen" wir die "$*$-Grade" einiger e.e. Gruppen.

Nach 1.3 ist klar, daß man das Skelett einer a.a. Gruppe kennt, wenn man weiß, welche $*$-Grade die Wortprobleme der e.e. Untergruppen haben. Da a.a. Gruppen bis auf partielle Isomorphie durch ihr Skelett vollständig bestimmt sind (I, 2.10), entsprechen also die a.a. Gruppen gerade bestimmten Mengen von $*$-Graden. Im dritten Abschnitt charakterisieren wir diese Mengen mit rekursionstheoretischen Begriffen. Wir brauchen dabei, daß jeder $*$-Grad das Wortproblem einer endlich erzeugten Gruppe enthält und ein Äquivalent für endliche Gleichungssysteme: r.a. Hornklassen (3.8) und (3.10). Auf diese Weise wird die Theorie der abzählbaren a.a. Gruppen ein Teil der Rekursionstheorie. Im vierten Abschnitt geben wir einige Beispiele für diese Beschreibung a.a. Gruppen.

1. Gruppen, deren Wortprobleme aufeinander $*$-reduzierbar sind

Definition 1.1 (A und B seien Teilmengen von ω).

1. A ist $*$-reduzierbar auf B — $A \leqslant^* B$ —, wenn $A \leqslant_e B$ und $\omega \setminus A \leqslant_e^1 B$. Wenn $A = W_z^e[B]$ und $\omega \setminus A = W_{z'}^1[B]$, schreiben wir (z, z'): $A \leqslant^* B$.

2. A ist $+$-reduzierbar auf B — $A \leqslant^+ B$ —, wenn es eine rekursive Funktion $f: \omega \to \mathcal{P}_\omega(\omega)$ gibt, so daß für alle n $n \in A$ gdw. $f(n) \subset B$. Wir schreiben dann $f: A \leqslant^+ B$.

1.2. Wir bemerken, daß $A \leqslant_m B \Rightarrow A \leqslant^+ B \Rightarrow A \leqslant^* B \Rightarrow A \leqslant_T B$. Später werden wir sehen, daß sich keiner der Pfeile umkehren läßt (3.5, 2.10, 2.4).

Beispiel 1.3 (siehe II, 3.14). U sei Untergruppe der e.e.Gr. G. G Untergruppe der a.a.Gr. M, $F \in \mathrm{Sk}(M)$, $W(G \mid U) \leqslant^* W(F)$. Dann gibt es ein $h \in M$ mit $U = \{f \in G \mid hf = fh\}$. Denn, wenn

$$I(\vec{g}, x) = \{x V_i(\vec{g}) x^{-1} \doteq V_i(\vec{g}) \mid i \in W(G \mid U)\}$$

und

$$J(\vec{g}, x) = \{\neg xV_i(\vec{g})x^{-1} \doteq V_i(\vec{g}) \mid i \notin W(G \mid U)\},$$

muß h gerade $I \cup J$ erfüllen. Da $I \leqslant_e W(G \mid U)$ und $J \leqslant_e^1 W(G \mid U)$, ist (2.1) $I \leqslant_e W(F)$ und $J \leqslant_e^1 W(F)$. Die Behauptung folgt nun aus II, 3.12 denn nach I, 4.4 ist $I \cup J$ in einer Obergruppe von M erfüllbar.

Der nächste Satz verallgemeinert II, 2.8, denn wenn F lösbares Wortproblem hat, ist $W(F) \leqslant^* W(E)$.

Satz 1.4. *F und G seien endlich erzeugte Gruppen, $W(F) \leqslant^* W(G)$. Dann ist F in jede algebraisch abgeschlossere Gruppe einbettbar, in die G einbettbar ist.*

Beweis. F sei von $\vec{f}$ erzeugt und $I(\vec{x}) = \{W(\vec{x}) \doteq e \mid W(\vec{f}) = e\}$, $J(\vec{x}) = \{\neg W(\vec{x}) \doteq e \mid W(\vec{f}) \neq e\}$. Offenbar ist $I \leqslant_e W(F)$ und $J \leqslant_e^1 W(F)$, daraus folgt $I \leqslant_e W(G)$, $J \leqslant_e^1 W(G)$. Da $I \cup J$ in der Obergruppe $M \times F$ von M lösbar ist, gibt es nach II, 3.12 eine Lösung $\vec{f} \in M$. Natürlich ist $\langle f' \rangle \cong F$. □

Folgerungen 1.5. 1. *Zu jeder e.e. Untergruppe F der abzählbaren Gruppe H gebe es ein G aus dem Skelett der a.a. Gruppe M mit $W(F) \leqslant^* W(G)$. Dann ist H in M einbettbar.* (*Das verallgemeinert* II, 2.10.1.)

2. *Sei M a.a. Wenn $F, G \in \mathrm{Sk}(M)$, ist auch $F \times G \in \mathrm{Sk}(M)$.*

3. *Sei M a.a., G e.e. Wenn $F_1, \ldots, F_n \in \mathrm{Sk}(M)$ und $W(G) \leqslant^* W(F_1 \times \cdots \times F_n)$, ist $G \in \mathrm{Sk}(M)$.*

Wir beweisen 2: Sei $F, G \subset H$ und $H = \langle F, G \rangle$. Es ist $W(F \times G) \leqslant^+ W(H)$. Denn $W(\vec{f}, \vec{g}) \in \mathrm{Gl}(F \times G; \vec{f}, \vec{g})$ gdw. $W(\vec{f}, e) = e$ und $W(e, \vec{g}) = e$ gdw. $\{W(\vec{f}, e), W(e, \vec{g})\} \subset \mathrm{Gl}(H; \vec{f}, \vec{g})$.

Bemerkung 1.6. 1. Wir nennen $F = \langle \vec{f} \rangle$ absolut endlich (a.e.) über $G = \langle \vec{g} \rangle$ präsentiert, wenn es ein endliches Gl. & Ungl.system $S(\vec{g}, \vec{y}, \vec{x})$ gibt, das über G lösbar it und für dessen Lösungen $\langle \vec{g}, \vec{f}', \vec{h} \rangle$ immer $\langle \vec{f}' \rangle' \cong \langle \vec{f} \rangle'$ ist. (Man sieht leicht; wenn $G \neq E$, braucht man für S nur ein Gleichungssystem; F ist über E a.e. präsentierbar, wenn F a.e. präsentierbar ist.) Wenn $G \neq E$ und $W(G)$ r.a., ist F genau dann a.e. über G präsentiert, wenn G und F so in eine endlich präsentierbare H einbettbar sind, daß jeder Homomorphismus auf H, der auf G injektiv ist, auch auf F injektiv ist ([3]). Denn, wenn $S(\vec{g}, \vec{f}, \vec{h})$ H endlich präsentiert, zeigt S, daß F a.e. über G präsentierbar ist. Wenn andererseits F durch S a.e. über G präsentiert wird, und S' endlich eine

Obergruppe von G präsentiert (G hat r.a. Wortproblem), präsentiert $S \cup S'$ eine Gruppe H mit den gewünschten Eigenschaften.

2. Wenn $W(F) \leq^* W(G)$, ist F über G a.e. präsentierbar. Das Gl. & Ungl.system S bekommt man, wenn man auf die Mengen I und J, die im Beweis von 1.4 vorkommen, II, 3.13 statt II, 3.12 anwendet. (Wir haben damit eine Verallgemeinerung von II, 2.9.) Da natürlich, wenn F über G a.e. präsentiert ist, F in jede a.a. Gruppe einbettbar ist, in die G einbettbar ist, erhalten wir so einen anderen Beweis von 1.4.

Umgekehrt ist $W(F) \leq^* W(G)$, wenn F über G a.e. präsentiert ist. Wir lassen den sehr einfachen Beweis weg, weil dieses Resultat aus dem nächsten Satz folgt.

Satz 1.7. *$F_i, G_i, i < \omega$ seien endlich erzeugte Gruppen. Wenn für alle n, m $W(F_n) \not\leq^* W(G_0 \times \cdots \times G_m)$, gibt es eine abzählbare algebraisch abgeschlossene Gruppe, in die alle G_i, aber kein F_i einbettbar ist.*

(Für $F = F_i$, $G = G_i$ mit r.a. Wortproblem, folgt 1.7 aus Th-1.1 in ([3]).)

Folgerungen 1.8. 1. *Für e.e. F, G sind äquivalent*: (a) $W(F) \leq^* W(G)$, (b) *F ist in jede a.a. Gruppe einbettbar, in die G einbettbar ist. (Zum Beispiel ist also $W(F) \leq^* W(G)$, wenn $F \subset G$. Das folgt aber natürlich auch aus* II, 3.9.2.)

2. *Die e.e. Gruppe F hat genau dann lösbares Wortproblem, wenn F in jede a.a. Gruppe einbettbar ist* ([15]).

3. *Wenn $W(F) \not\leq_T W(G)$, gibt es eine a.a.Gr., in die G aber nicht F einbettbar ist* ([15]).

Beweis. (Wir werden in 4.1 noch einen anderen Beweis angeben.) Die G_i seien von $\vec{g}_i$ erzeugt. Wir konstruieren ein (unendliches) Gl. & Ungl.system $S(\vec{g}, \vec{x})$ in Koeffizienten $\vec{g}_0, \vec{g}_1, \ldots, = \vec{g}$, das mit $D = \mathrm{Diag}(\bigoplus_{i<\omega} G_i, \vec{g}) = \bigcup_{n<\omega} \mathrm{Diag}(\bigoplus_{i<n} G_i; \vec{g}_0, \ldots, \vec{g}_{n-1})$ verträglich ist. Die algebraisch abgeschlossene Gruppe M wird dann eine von $\vec{g}$ und einer Lösung $\vec{h}$ von $S \cup D$ erzeugte Gruppe sein.

T_i, $i < \omega$ sei eine Durchzählung aller endlichen Gleichungssystemen mit Koeffizienten $\vec{g}$ und Variablen $\vec{x}$ und $\vec{y}$. $\vec{W}^{(i)} = W_0^{(i)}, \ldots, W_{n_i}^{(i)}$, $i < \omega$ sei eine Durchzählung aller endlichen Folgen von Wörtern $W(\vec{g}, \vec{x})$. Die F_i seien von $\vec{f}_i$ erzeugt. Wir konstruieren S als Vereinigung einer aufsteigenden Folge S_i von endlichen Gl. & Ungl.systemen.

Wir setzen $S_0 = \emptyset$ und unterscheiden 3 Fälle.

(i) $n = 3i$:

(a) Wenn $T_i \cup S_n \cup D$ widerspruchsvoll ist, setze $S_{n+1} = S_n$.

(b) Wenn $T_i(\vec{x}, \vec{y}) \cup S_n \cup D$ widerspruchsfrei, gibt es $x_k, x_{k+1}, \ldots, x_{k+r}$, so daß $T_i(\vec{x}; x_k, \ldots, x_{k+r}) \cup S_n \cup D$ widerspruchsfrei ist. Setze $S_{n+1} = T_i(\vec{x}; x_k, \ldots, x_{k+r}) \cup S_n$.

(ii) $n = 3i + 1$:

Wähle $x_k, \ldots, x_{k+n_i}$ genügend groß, so daß $S_{n+1} = \{W_j^{(i)} \doteq x_{k+j} \mid j \leq n_i\} \cup S_n \cup D$ widerspruchsfrei ist.

(iii) $n = 3i + 2$:

Sei $\langle k, m\rangle = i$ und $\mathrm{Diag}(F_m, \vec{f}_m) = R(\vec{f}_m)$. $s + 1$ sei die die Länge von $\vec{f}_m$. Mit $\vec{x}'$ kürzen wir $x_k, \ldots, x_{k+s}$ ab.

(a) Wenn $S_n \cup D \nvdash^G R(\vec{x}')$, wählen wir ein $\varphi \in R(\vec{x}')$ mit $S_n \cup D \nvdash^G \varphi$ und setzen $S_{n+1} = S_n \cup \{\neg \varphi\}$.

(b) Der Fall $S_n \cup D \vdash^G R(\vec{x}')$ kann nicht eintreten: Wenn höchstens $\vec{g}_0, \ldots, \vec{g}_{r-1}$ in S_n vorkommen, würde $S_n \cup \mathrm{Diag}(\bigoplus_{i<r} G_i; \vec{g}_0, \ldots, \vec{g}_{r-1}) \vdash R(\vec{x}')$ sein. Wir schreiben $\boldsymbol{G}$ für $(\bigoplus_{i<r} G_i; \vec{g}_0, \ldots, \vec{g}_{r-1})$. Für alle W ist $W(\vec{f}_m) \in \mathrm{Gl}(F_m, \vec{f}_m)$ gdw. $\mathrm{Diag}(\boldsymbol{G}) \vdash^G \bigwedge S_n \to W(\vec{x}') \doteq \boldsymbol{e}$. Da $\mathrm{Diag}(\boldsymbol{G}) \nvdash^G \bigwedge S_n \to$, ist also wegen II.1.5 dies äquivalent zu $\mathrm{Gl}(\boldsymbol{G}) \vdash^G \bigwedge S_n \to W(\vec{x}') \doteq \boldsymbol{e}$. Daraus folgt $W(F_m) \leq_e W(\boldsymbol{G})$. Für alle W ist $W(\vec{f}_m) \notin \mathrm{Gl}(F_m, \vec{f}_m)$ gdw. $\mathrm{Diag}(\boldsymbol{G}) \cup S_n \vdash^G \neg W(\vec{x}') = \boldsymbol{e}$. Wegen II.1.5 also gdw. es ein $\chi \in \mathrm{Ungl}(\boldsymbol{G})$ mit $\mathrm{Gl}(\boldsymbol{G}) \cup S_n \cup \{\chi\} \vdash^G \neg W(x') \doteq \boldsymbol{e}$ gibt. Daraus folgt $\omega \setminus W(F_m) \leq_e^1 W(\boldsymbol{G})$. Also zusammen $W(F_m) \leq^* W(\boldsymbol{G})$, in Widerspruch zur Voraussetzung. Damit ist die Konstruktion der S_n abgeschlossen.

$\vec{h}$ sei eine Lösung von $D \cup S$ in der von $\vec{g}, \vec{h}$ erzeugten Gruppe M. Offenbar ist M Obergruppe der direkten Summe der G_i, alle G_i sind also in M einbettbar. Wir zeigen, daß die F_m nicht einbettbar sind.

Sei $\mu : F_m \to M$ eine Einbettung und $\mu(\vec{f}_m) = \vec{W}^{(j)}(\vec{g}, \vec{h})$. Im Konstruktionsschritt $3j + 1$ wurde sichergestellt, daß es $\vec{h}' = h_k, \ldots, h_{k+n_j}$ gibt, mit $\vec{W}^{(j)}(\vec{g}, \vec{h}) = \vec{h}'$. Wenn $i = \langle k, m\rangle$, wurde im Konstruktionsschritt $n = 3i + 2$ ein $\varphi(\vec{x}')$ in S aufgenommen mit $F_m \nvDash \varphi(\vec{f}_m)$. Da also $M \vDash \varphi(\vec{h}')$, kann μ keine Einbettung sein.

Wir weisen noch nach, daß M algebraisch abgeschlossen ist. Sei dazu $T^i(\vec{g}, \vec{h}, \vec{y})$ ein endliches Gleichungssystem, das in einer Obergruppe von M lösbar ist. Dann tritt bei der Konstruktion an der Stelle $3i$ der Fall (b) ein. Mit der dortigen Bezeichung ist dann $h_k, \ldots, h_{k+r}$ eine Lösung von T^i in M. □

2. $*$-Grade

2.1. Aus $A \leq_e^1 B \leq^* C$ folgt $A \leq_e^1 C$; zusammen mit der Transitivität von $\leq_e$ ergibt sich also die Transitivität von $\leq^*$. Wir können deshalb sinnvoll die Äquivalenzrelation $\equiv^*$ einführen: $A \equiv^* B$ gdw. $A \leqslant^* B \leqslant^* A$, "$A$ und B haben denselben $*$-Grad". $V := \mathcal{P}(\omega)/\equiv^*$ ist die Menge der $*$-Grade. Da jeder $*$-Grad abzählbar ist, ist $|V| = 2^\omega$. Wir übertragen $\leqslant^*$ auf $V: A/\equiv^* \leqslant B/\equiv^*$ gdw. $A \leqslant^* B$. $(V, \leqslant)$ ist ein Halbverband mit kleinstem Element $\phi/\equiv^*$. Es ist nämlich, wie man leicht überlegt, $\sup(A/\equiv^*, B/\equiv^*) = (A \vee B)/\equiv^*$; $\phi/\equiv^*$ besteht gerade aus den rekursiven Mengen.

Aus $A \equiv^* B \leqslant_e C \equiv^* D$ folgt $A \leqslant_e D$. Wir können also sinnvoll für $a, b \in V$ $a \leqslant_e b$ durch $A \leqslant_e B$ definieren, wenn $A \in a$ und $B \in b$. Ebenso hängen die folgenden Definitionen nicht von der Wahl der Repräsentanten ab: (Sei $A \in a \in V$, $B \in b \in V$) $a \leqslant_{\text{ra}} b$, wenn $A \leqslant_{\text{ra}} B$; $A \leqslant_e b$, wenn $A \leqslant_e B$; $A \leqslant^* b$, wenn $A \leqslant^* B$; $A \equiv^* b$, wenn $A \equiv^* B$; $a \leqslant b^2$, wenn $A \leqslant^* B^2$ (vgl. 2.6).

Definition 2.2. 1. A heißt vollständig, wenn $\forall B \subset \omega$, $B \leqslant_e A \Rightarrow B \leqslant_1 A$.

2. a heißt vollständig, wenn für alle $b \leqslant_e a \Rightarrow b \leqslant a$ $(a, b \in V)$. (Wenn A r.a., ist A vollständig, gdw. A 1-vollständig im Sinne von ([24] S. 82) ist.)

Lemma 2.3. 1. *Ist A vollständig und $A \in a \in V$, so ist auch a vollständig.*

2. *Für jedes B gibt es ein vollständiges B^v mit $B^v \equiv_e B$. B^v ist bis auf rekursive Isomorphie eindeutig bestimmt.*

3. *Zu jedem $b \in V$ gibt es genau ein vollständiges $b^v \in V$ mit $b \equiv_e b^v$. Wenn $B \in b$, ist $b^v \equiv^* B^v$.*

4. *$A \leqslant_e B$ gdw. $A^v \leqslant_1 B^v$.*

Beweis. (2). Setze $B^v = \{\langle x, y\rangle \mid x \in W^e_y[B]\}$. Offenbar ist $B^v \leqslant_e B$. Wenn $W_y = \{\langle x, u\rangle \mid D_u = \{x\}\}$, ist $x \in B$ gdw. $\langle x, y\rangle \in B^v$. Also $B \leqslant_1 B^v \Rightarrow B \leqslant_e B^v$.

Sei $A \leqslant_e B^v$, also auch $A \leqslant_e B$ und daher $A = W^e_z[B]$. Aus $x \in A$ gdw. $\langle x, z\rangle \in B^v$ folgt $A \leqslant_1 B^v$.

Die anderen Teile des Lemmas folgen daraus leicht. □

In den nächsten drei Lemmas vergleichen wir $\leqslant^*$ mit zwei schwächeren Begriffen, die selbst stärker als $\leqslant_T$ sind. Aus $A \leqslant^* B$ folgt (a) $A \leqslant^1_e B$, $\omega \setminus A \leqslant^1_e B$ und (b) $A \leqslant_e B$, $\omega \setminus A \leqslant_{\text{ra}} B$. Sowohl aus (a) als auch aus (b) folgt $A \leqslant_T B$ (d. h. $A \leqslant_{\text{ra}} B$, $\omega \setminus A \leqslant_{\text{ra}} B$). Aber weder aus (a) noch aus (b) folgt $\leqslant^*$.

Lemma 2.4. *Für eine Teilmenge A von ω sind äquivalent:*

(a) *für alle B folgt $B \leqslant^* A$ aus $B \leqslant_e^1 A$ und $\omega \setminus B \leqslant_e^1 A$.*
(b) $\omega \setminus A \leqslant_e A$.

Bemerkung 2.5. 1. (a) bzw. (b) sind äquivalent zu (c): für alle B ist $B \leqslant_T A$ gdw. $B \leqslant^* A$.
2. Wenn A vollständig ist, gilt $\omega \setminus A \not\leqslant_e A$.

Beweis. (a)$\rightarrow$(b): Da $\omega \setminus A \leqslant_e^1 A$, $A \leqslant_e^1 A$ folgt aus (a) $\omega \setminus A \leqslant^* A$ insbesondere $\omega \setminus A \leqslant_e A$. (b)$\rightarrow$(c): Sei $B \leqslant_T A$. Aus (b) folgt mit II, 3.5 $B \leqslant_e A$ und $\omega \setminus B \leqslant_e A$, also erst recht $B \leqslant^* A$.

Beweis von 2.5.2: Wenn A vollständig ist, ist $A^v \equiv_1 A$. Es genügt also $\omega \setminus A^v \not\leqslant_e A$ zu zeigen. A^v sei wie im Beweis von 2.3.2. Aus $\omega \setminus A^v \leqslant_e A$ folgt $\bar{A} := \{x \mid \langle x, x\rangle \notin A^v\} \leqslant_1 \omega \setminus A^v \leqslant_e A \Rightarrow \bar{A} \leqslant_e A$. Sei $z : \bar{A} \leqslant_e A$. Dann ist für alle x $x \in \bar{A}$ gdw. $\langle x, z\rangle \in A^v$. Also $\langle z, z\rangle \notin A^v$ gdw. $\langle z, z\rangle \in A^v$. $\square$

Definition 2.6. A und B seien Teilmengen von ω.
1. $A^{\breve{n}} = \{\langle m_1, \ldots, m_n\rangle \mid \exists i\, m_i \in A\}$.
2. $A^{\breve{\omega}} = \{s \in {}^{\breve{\omega}}\omega \mid \exists i < l(s)\ s(i) \in A\}$.
3. $B \leqslant_e^2 A$ gdw. ex. z für alle $x \in \omega$
$x \in B$ gdw. $\exists u, w(\langle x, u, w\rangle \in W_z \wedge D_u \subset A \wedge D_w^2 \subset \omega \setminus A)$.

2.7. Man sieht leicht, daß $A \leqslant_1 A^{\breve{n}} \leqslant_1 A^{\breve{n+1}} \leqslant_1 A^{\breve{\omega}} \leqslant_e A^{\breve{n+1}} \leqslant_e A^{\breve{n}} \leqslant_e A$; $A \leqslant^* B \Rightarrow A^{\breve{\omega}} \leqslant^* B^{\breve{\omega}}$; $(A^{\breve{\omega}})^{\breve{\omega}} \equiv^* A^{\breve{\omega}}$; $B \leqslant_e^2 A \Leftrightarrow B \leqslant_e^1 A^2$; $B \leqslant_{\mathrm{ra}} A \leftrightarrow B \leqslant_e^1 A^\omega$; $B \leqslant_e^1 A \Rightarrow B \leqslant_e^2 A \Rightarrow B \leqslant_{\mathrm{ra}} A$.

Lemma 2.8. *A sei eine Teilmenge von ω. Dann sind äquivalent*
(a) *Für alle $B \subset \omega$ $B \leqslant_e A \wedge \omega \setminus B \leqslant_e^2 A \Rightarrow B \leqslant^* A$.*
(b) $A^{\breve{\omega}} \equiv^* A$.
(c) $\omega^2 \setminus A^{\breve{2}} \leqslant_e^1 A$.

(Für rekursive aufzählbares A wurde 2.8 in [3] bewiesen.) (Wenn (a) bzw. (b), (c) gilt, folgt $B \leqslant^* A$ aus $B \leqslant_e A$ und $\omega \setminus B \leqslant_{ra} A$.)

Beweis. (a)$\rightarrow$(c): folgt aus $A^{\breve{2}} \leqslant_e A$ und $\omega \setminus A^{\breve{2}} \leqslant_e^2 A$. (b)$\rightarrow$(a): Aus $\omega \setminus B \leqslant_e^2 A$ folgt $\omega \setminus B \leqslant_e^1 A^{\breve{2}} \leqslant_1 A^{\breve{\omega}} \leqslant^* A \Rightarrow \omega \setminus B \leqslant_e^1 A$. (c)$\rightarrow$(b): Wir müssen ${}^{\breve{\omega}}\omega \setminus A^{\breve{\omega}} \leqslant_e^1 A$ zeigen. Sei $z : (\omega^2 \setminus A^{\breve{2}}) \leqslant_e^1 A$, also für alle $x, y \in \omega$ $\langle x, y\rangle \notin A^{\breve{2}}$ gdw. $\exists u, w(\langle x, y, u, w\rangle \in W_z \wedge D_u \subset A, D_w^1 \subset \omega \setminus A)$. Wenn n die Länge von $s \in {}^{\breve{\omega}}\omega$ ist, folgt aus der letzten Beziehung durch $n-1$-maliges Anwenden: $s \notin A^{\breve{\omega}}$ gdw.

$$\exists u, w(\exists m_1, \ldots, m_{n-2}[(\exists u', w'\langle s(0), s(1), u', w'\rangle \in W_z$$

$$\wedge D_{u'} \subset D_u \wedge D_{w'}^1 \subset \{m_1\})$$

$\wedge (\exists u', w' \langle m_1, s(2), u', w' \rangle \in W_z \wedge D_{u'} \subset D_u \wedge D^1_{w'} \subset \{m_2\}) \wedge \cdots$

$\wedge (\exists u', w' \langle m_{n-3}, s(n-2), u', w' \rangle \in W_z \wedge D_{u'} \subset D_u \wedge D^1_{w'} \subset \{m_{n-2}\})$

$\wedge (\exists u' \langle m_{n-2}, s(n-1), u', w \rangle \in W_z \wedge D_{u'} \subset D_u)] \wedge D_u \subset A \wedge D^1_w \subset \omega \setminus A)$

Aus dieser Darstellung erkennt man leicht ${}^{\omega}\omega \setminus A^{\omega} \leq^1_e A$. □

Lemma 2.9. *Zu jedem $B \subset \omega$ gibt es ein A mit $B \leq_1 A$ und $\omega^2 \setminus A^2 \not\leq^1_e A$. (Wir werden in* VI *sehen, daß für "vollständig subgenerische" Mengen $\omega^2 \setminus A^2 \not\leq^1_e A$.)*

Beweis. Wir können annehmen, daß B eine Menge von ungeraden Zahlen ist. Wir definieren zwei aufsteigende Folgen $P_0 \subset P_1 \subset \cdots N_0 \subset N_1 \subset N_2 \cdots$ von endlichen Mengen von geraden Zahlen, so daß $N_i \cap P_i = \emptyset$ für alle i. Für A werden wir $B \cup \bigcup \{P_i \mid i < \omega\}$ nehmen. Wenn N_i und P_i schon definiert sind, unterscheiden wir zwei Fälle:

(a) Es gibt $a, b \in 2\omega$; $u, w \in \omega$ so daß $\langle a, b, u, w \rangle \in W_i$ oder $\langle b, a, u, w \rangle \in W_i$ und $(P_i \cup \{a\} \cup D_u \cup B) \cap (N_i \cup D^1_w \cup ((2\omega + 1) \setminus B)) = \emptyset$. Wir wählen dann solche a, b, u, w und setzen $P_{i+1} = (P_i \cup \{a\} \cup D_u) \cap 2\omega$ und $N_{i+1} = ((N_i \cup D^1_w) \cap 2\omega) \cup \{2k\}$ für ein $2k \notin N_i \cup P_{i+1}$.

(b) Wenn der Fall (a) nicht eintritt, wähle einfach $N_i \subsetneq N_{i+1} \subset 2\omega$ und setze $P_{i+1} = P_i$. Weil $B = A \cap (2\omega + 1)$, ist $B \leq_1 A$. Annahme: $i : \omega^2 \setminus A^2 \leq^1_e A$. Da wir die N_j bei jedem Schritt vergrößert haben, gibt es $a' \neq b'$ aus $2\omega \setminus (A \cup N_i)$. Da also $(a', b') \notin A^2$, gibt es u', w' mit $\langle a', b', u', w' \rangle \in W_i$ und $D_{u'} \subset A$, $D^1_{w'} \subset \omega \setminus A$. Da $a' \notin D^1_{w'}$ oder $b' \notin D^1_{w'}$, erfüllt a', b', u', w' oder b', a', u', w' die Bedingung von (a) bei der Konstruktion von P_{i+1}, N_{i+1}. a, b, u, w seien wie dort gewählt. Es folgt dann, weil $D_u \subset B \cup P_{i+1}$ und $D^1_w \subset ((2\omega + 1) \setminus B) \cup N_{i+1}$, daß (a, b) oder $(b, a) \notin A^2$, also $a, b \notin A$. Es ist aber $a \in P_{i+1} \subset A$. □

In ([24]) wird definiert: $A \leq_Q B$ gdw. es ein z gibt, so daß für alle x, $x \notin A$, gdw. $\exists n (\langle x, u \rangle \in W_z \wedge D^1_u \subset \omega \setminus B)$. Für rekursiv aufzählbare A und B stimmt $\leq_Q$ mit $\leq^*$ überein. In ([3]) wird $\leq_Q$ für r.a. Mengen für ähnliche Zwecke benutzt wie in dieser Arbeit $\leq^*$. Nach ([24]) gibt es r.a. A, B mit $A \leq_T B$ und $A \not\leq_Q B$. Nach 2.8 folgt daraus wie in ([3]) $B^2 \not\leq_Q B$, also $B^2 \not\leq^* B$.

Wir bemerken ohne Beweis:

Lemma 2.10. 1. *Für jedes nicht rekursive A gibt es ein B mit $A \leq^* B$ und nicht $A \leq^+ B$.*

2. *z und z' seien aus ω. Wenn es zu jedem B ein A mit*

$(z, z'): A \leqslant^* B$ *gibt, gibt es ein rekursives* $f: \omega \to \mathcal{P}_\omega(\omega)$ *mit* $(z, z'): A \leqslant^* B$ *gdw.* $f: A \leqslant^+ B$ *für alle* A, B.
(Vergleiche VI, 3.6.)

Folgende Verschärfung von 2.12 ist zugleich eine Verallgemeinerung des Satzes von Boone und Higman in ([4]):

Für eine endlich erzeugte Gruppe sind äquivalent:
(a) $\omega \setminus W(G) \leqslant_e W(G)$.
(b) *Es gibt eine endlich über G präsentierte Gruppe F und eine einfache Gruppe K mit* $G \subset K \subset F$.

(ohne Beweis)
Wir zeigen, wie das Hauptresultat von ([4]) folgt: "G hat lösbares Wortproblem gdw. ex. endlich präsentierte Gruppe F und eine einfache Gruppe H mit $G \subset H \subset F$".

Wenn G lösbares Wortproblem hat, ist $\omega \setminus W(G) \leqslant_e W(G)$. Wir wählen H und F wie in (b). $W(F)$ ist dann r.a. Also ist F in eine endlich präsentierte Gruppe einbettbar.

Wenn es umgekehrt eine einfache Gruppe H und eine endlich präsentierte Gruppe F gibt mit $G \subset H \subset F$, folgt aus (a), daß $\omega \setminus W(G) \leqslant_e W(G)$. Weil $G \subset F$, ist aber $W(G)$ r.a. Also ist auch $\omega \setminus W(G)$ r.a. und somit $W(G)$ rekursiv.

$*$-Grade einiger Wortprobleme

Lemma 2.11. *Für endlich erzeugte Gruppen F, G ist*

$$W(F \times G)/\equiv^* = \sup(W(F)/\equiv^*, W(G)/\equiv^*).$$

Beweis. F, G seien durch $\vec{f}$, $\vec{g}$ erzeugt. Wir ordnen jedem Wort $V_i(\vec{x}, \vec{y})$ die Wörter $V_i(\vec{x}, \vec{e}) = V_{i'}(\vec{x})$ und $V_i(\vec{e}, \vec{y}) = V_{i''}(\vec{y})$ zu. Es ist dann $i \in W(F \times G; \vec{f}, \vec{g})$ gdw. $\{2i', 2i''+1\} \subset W(F) \vee W(G)$. Also ist $W(F \times G) \leqslant^* \sup(W(F)/\equiv^*, W(G)/\equiv^*)$. Umgekehrt ist natürlich $W(F) \leqslant^* W(F \times G)$, $W(G) \leqslant^* W(F \times G)$. Daraus folgt die Behauptung. □

Zusammen mit 1.5.3 und 1.7 haben wir damit

Folgerung. *$F, G_0, \ldots, G_n$ seien endlich erzeugt. Dann ist* $W(F) \leqslant^* \sup(W(G_0)/\equiv^*, \ldots, W(G_n)/\equiv^*)$ *gdw. in alle a.a.Gr., in die all* G_i *einbettbar sind, auch F einbettbar ist.*

Lemma 2.12. *Wenn die e.e. Gruppe G einfach ist, ist* $\omega \setminus W(G) \leqslant_e W(G)$.

Beweis. Sei G von $\vec{g}$ erzeugt und $g_0 \neq e$. Dann ist $f \neq e$ gdw. g_0 im Normalteilererzeugnis von f liegt. Aus der Beschreibung $W(\vec{g}) \neq e$ gdw. ex. $W_1, \ldots, W_n, \tilde{W}$ mit $g_0 = \tilde{W}(W_1 W W_1^{-1}, \ldots, W_n W W_n^{-1})(\vec{g})$ erkennt man, daß $\omega \setminus W(G) \leqslant_e W(G)$.

Folgerung. *Wenn G, F e.e. Gruppen sind, G einfach, ist* $W(F) \leqslant_T W(G)$ *gdw. F in alle a.a. Grupgen einbettbar ist, in die G einbettbar ist.*

Lemma 2.13 (F, G seien endlich erzeugte Gruppen).

1. *Wenn je zwei nicht triviale Normalteiler von F nicht-trivialen Schnitt haben, ist* $W(F)^{\omega} \equiv^* W(F)$.
2. *Wenn* $F, G \neq E$, *ist* $W(F * G) \equiv^* (W(F) \vee W(G))^{\omega}$.
3. ($H \neq E$ *habe lösbares Wortproblem*) *Es sind äquivalent*
   (a) $W(F)^{\omega} \equiv^* W(F)$.
   (b) $W(F * H) \leqslant^* W(F)$.
   (c) *Für alle a.a. Gr.* M, $F < M \Rightarrow F * H < M$.
   (d) *Für alle a.a. Gr.* M *und alle* $G, F < M$, $W(G) \leqslant^* W(F) \Rightarrow F * G < M$.

(2.13 enthält Resultate von ([3]) über Gruppen mit r.a. Wortproblem.)

Beweis. 1. Eine Folge $a_1, \ldots, a_n \in F$ enthält genau dann nur Elemente $\neq e$, wenn der Schnitt der von den a_i jeweils erzeugten Normalteilern nicht-trivial ist. Also ist (wenn $F = \langle \vec{f} \rangle$) $W_1(\vec{f}) \neq e$, $W_2(\vec{f}) \neq e$ gdw. ex. $U_1, \ldots, U_k, \bar{U}_1, \ldots, \bar{U}_r, \bar{W}_1, \bar{W}_2$ mit $e \neq \bar{W}_1(U_1 W_1 U_1^{-1}, \ldots, U_k W_1 U_k^{-1})(\vec{f}) = \bar{W}_2(\bar{U}_1^{-1} W_2 \bar{U}_1^{-1}, \ldots, \bar{U}_r W_2 \bar{U}_r^{-1})(\vec{f})$. Das zeigt, daß $\omega \setminus W(F)^2 \leqslant_e^1 W(F)$.

2. Zunächst has $F * G$ die Eigenschaft von 1: Den Fall $|F| = |G| = 2$ brauchen wir nicht zu behandeln, weil dann die Behauptung von 2 ohnehin gilt. Sei $F \geqslant 3$. Ein Element $h = f_0 g_1 f_1 \cdots g_n f_n$ ($n \in \omega$, $f_i \in F \setminus E$, $g_i \in G \setminus E$) von $F * G$ heißt F-Element. Jedes Element h' von $(F * G) \setminus E$ läßt sich eindeutig in der Form (i) h oder (ii) gh oder (iii) hg oder (iv) $g_1' h g_2'$ oder (v) g schreiben, wobei h ein F-Element und $g, g_1', g_2' \in G \setminus E$ sind. Jedes Element h' aus $(F * G) \setminus E$ sind und einem F-Element konjugiert, denn, wenn $f \in F \setminus E$ und im Fall (iii) $f \neq f_0^{-1}$ und im Fall (ii) $f \neq f_n$ ist, wenn h' nicht selbst F-Element ist, $fh'f^{-1}$ ein F-Element. Wenn h_1, h_2 aus $(F * G) \setminus E$ sind und ah_1a^{-1}, bh_2b^{-1} F-Elemente, $g \in G \setminus E$, so vertauschen $g(ah_1a^{-1})g^{-1}$ und bh_2b^{-1} nicht. Der Kommutator dieser beiden Elemente liegt dann

sowohl im Normalteilererzeugnis von h_1 als auch im Normalteilererzeugnis von h_2 und ist nichttrivial. Also ist $W(F*G)^{\wp} \equiv^* W(F*G)$. Wegen $F, G \subset F*G$ ist $W(F), W(G) \leqslant^* W(F*G)$. Also $(W(F) \vee W(G))^{\wp} \leqslant^* W(F*G)^{\wp} \leqslant^* W(F*G)$. Weil in $F*G$ nur die Gleichungen gelten, die aus den Gleichungen von F und G folgen, ist $W(F*G) \leqslant_e (W(F) \vee W(G))$. $W(\vec{f}, \vec{g})$ ist $\neq e$ in $F*G$ gdw. eine Folge von Wortern $W_1, U_1, \ldots, W_n, U_n$ existiert mit $W(\vec{f}, \vec{g}) = W_1(\vec{f})U_1(\vec{g}) \cdots W_n(\vec{f})U_n(\vec{g})$ und $W_1(\vec{f}), U_1(\vec{g}), \ldots, U_n(\vec{g}) \neq e$ (etwas vereinfacht). Also ist $\omega \setminus W(F*G) \leqslant_{\mathrm{ra}} (W(F) \vee W(G))$, d. h. $W(F*G) \leqslant_e^1 W(F) \vee W(G))^{\wp}$.

3. (b)$\leftrightarrow$(c) folgt aus 1.8.1.

(a)$\rightarrow$(d) $W(F*G) \leqslant^* (W(F) \vee W(G))^{\wp} \leqslant^* (W(F))^{\wp} \leqslant^* W(F)$

(d)$\rightarrow$(c) $W(H) \leqslant^* W(F)$.

(b)$\rightarrow$(a)

$W(F)^{\wp} \leqslant^* (W(F) \vee W(H))^{\wp} \leqslant^* W(F*H) \leqslant^* W(F) \leqslant^* W(F)^{\wp}$. □

Das nächste Lemma zeigt, daß die Voraussetzungen in 1.3 notwendig sind.

Lemma 2.14. *$U \subset F, G$ seien Gruppen. F, G endlich erzeugt. Dann sind äquivalent:*

(a) $(W(F \mid U) \vee W(F)) \leqslant^* W(G)$.

(b) *In jedes a.a. $M \supset G$ ist F zweimal einbettbar: $F, F' \subset M$ mit $F \cap F' = U$, $F \cong_U F'$.*

(c) *In jedes a.a. $M \supset G$ ist F so einbettbar $F \subset M$, daß es ein $h \in M$ gibt mit $U = \{f \in F \mid hf = fh\}$.*

Beweis. (a)$\rightarrow$(c) folgt aus 1.3 und 1.4.

(c)$\rightarrow$(b): Sei $G, F \subset M$ und für ein $h \in M$, $U = \{f \in F \mid hf = fh\}$. Ein $g \in M$ erfüllt genau dann das rekursive System von Implikationen (F sei von $\vec{f}$ erzeugt)

$$\{\boldsymbol{h} W(\vec{\boldsymbol{f}}) \doteq W(\vec{\boldsymbol{f}})\boldsymbol{h} \rightarrow x W(\vec{\boldsymbol{f}}) x^{-1} \doteq W(\vec{\boldsymbol{f}}) \mid W \text{ Wort }\}$$
$$\cup \{x W_1(\vec{\boldsymbol{f}}) x^{-1} \doteq W_2(\vec{\boldsymbol{f}}) \rightarrow \boldsymbol{h} W_2(\vec{\boldsymbol{f}}) \doteq W_2(\vec{\boldsymbol{f}})\boldsymbol{h} \mid W_1, W_2 \text{ Wörter}\},$$

wenn $\tau_{g|U} = \mathrm{id}_U$ und $F \cap \tau_g[F] = U$. Da es solch ein g nach I, 4.4 in einer Obergruppe-von M gibt, gibt es nach II, 2.7 auch eine Lösung g' in M. Setze $F' = \tau_{g'}[F]$. (b)$\rightarrow$(a): Wir werden später (3.4) sehen, daß es zu jeder Menge $A \subset \omega$ eine e.e.Gr. H gibt mit $W(H) \equiv^* A$. Sei $W(H) \equiv^* W(F \mid U)$. Sei M eine a.a.Gr., die G enthält und sei also F, $F' \subset M$ mit $F \cong_U F'$, $F \cap F' = U$. Sei $F = \langle \vec{f} \rangle$ und vermöge des

Isomorphismus $F' = \langle \vec{f}' \rangle$. Dann ist für jedes Wort $W(\vec{f}) \in U$ gdw. $W(\vec{f}') = W(\vec{f})$. Also ist $W(F \mid U) \leqslant_1 W(\langle F, F' \rangle; \vec{f}, \vec{f}')$. Daraus folgt $W(H) \leqslant^* W(\langle F, F' \rangle; \vec{f}, \vec{f}')$ und daher nach 1.4 $H < M$. H liegt also in jeder a.a. Gruppe, in der G liegt, das bedeutet nach 1.8 $W(H) \leqslant^* W(G)$. $\square$

Im folgenden Lemma berechnen wir, wie "schwierig" es ist, ein F' mit $F \cong_U F'$, $F \cap F' = U$ in einer a.a. Gruppe zu finden, indem man $F *_U F$ einbettet.

Lemma 2.15. *U sei eine Untergruppe der e.e. Gruppe F. Dann ist* $W(F *_U F) \equiv^* W(F) \vee (W(F \mid U))^\wp_e$.

Beweis. F sei von f erzeugt und $F' = \langle f' \rangle$ eine isomorphe Kopie über U. Zunächst ist $W(F *_U F') \leqslant_e W(F) \vee W(F \mid U)$. Denn in $F *_U F'$ gelten genau die Gleichungen, die aus $\mathrm{Gl}(F, \vec{f}) \cup \mathrm{Gl}(F', \vec{f}') \cup \{W(\vec{f}) \doteq W(\vec{f}') \mid W(\vec{f}) \in U\} \cup T^G$ folgen.

Aus dem Normalformsatz für das amalgamierte Produkt sieht man: $W(\vec{f}, \vec{f}') \neq e$ gdw. ex. $W_1, \ldots, W_k$, $U_1, \ldots, U_k$, so daß $W(\vec{f}, \vec{f}') = W_1(\vec{f}) U_1(\vec{f}') \cdots W_k(\vec{f}) U_k(\vec{f}')$ und $W_i(\vec{f}), U_i(\vec{f}') \notin U$. (Etwas vereinfacht) *oder* ex. $\tilde{W}$ mit $W(\vec{f}, \vec{f}') = \tilde{W}(\vec{f}) \neq e$. Also ist $\omega \setminus W(F *_U F') \leqslant_e^1 W(F) \vee (W(F \mid U))^\wp$. Das ergibt zusammen $W(F *_U F') \leqslant^* W(F) \vee (W(F \mid U))^\wp_r$.

Weil $F \subset F *_U F'$ ist $W(F) \leqslant^* W(F *_U F')$. Weil $F \cap F' = U$ folgt aus dem letzten Lemma, daß $W(F \mid U) \leqslant^* W(F *_U F')$ und daher $W(F \mid U)^\wp \leqslant_e W(F *_U F)$.

Wir unterscheiden zwei Fälle:

(a) $F : U = 2$. Dann ist $W(F \mid U) = W(F/U)$ rekursiv, und es folgt $W(F \mid U)^\wp \vee W(F) \equiv^* W(F) \leqslant^* W(F *_U F')$.

(b) $F : U > 2$. Dann gibt es in $F *_U F'$ für alle $g \in F \setminus U$ $g' \in F' \setminus U$, $h \in (F *_U F') \setminus U$ ein $x \in F *_U F'$, so daß $[h, xg'gx^{-1}] \notin U$. (Wenn zum Beispiel $h = kk'$, $k \in F \setminus U$, $k' \in F' \setminus U$, wähle $y \in F \setminus (U \cup Ug)$ und $y' \in F' \setminus (U \cup (k')^{-1} U)$ und setze $x = y'y$.) Für $g \in F$ sei g' das entsprechende Element beim Isomorphismus $\langle f \rangle' \cong \langle f' \rangle'$. Dann ist $g \notin U$ gdw. $g' g^{-1} \neq e$. Weiter ist $g_0, g_1 \notin U$ gdw. ex. $x \in F *_U F'$ mit $[g_0' g_0^{-1}, x g_1' g_1^{-1} x^{-1}] \neq e$ usw. Also $g_0, \ldots, g_n \notin U$ gdw. ex. $x_1, x_2 \cdots x_n \in F *_U F'$, so daß

$$[[\cdots[[g_0' g_0^{-1}, x_1 f_1' f_1^{-1} x_1^{-1}], x_2 f_2' f_2^{-1} x_2^{-1}], \ldots,], x_n f_n' f_n^{-1} x_n^{-1}] \neq e.$$

Also ist $\omega \setminus W(F \mid U)^\wp \leqslant_e^1 W(F *_U F')$. $\square$

Satz 2.16. *M sei eine algebraisch abgeschlossene Gruppe. Es sind äquivalent*

(a) *Für alle* $G \subset F$ *und* $G \subset H$ *aus* $\mathrm{Sk}(M)$ *mit* $F \cap H = G$ *gibt es ein* $K \in \mathrm{Sk}(M)$ *mit* $F \cup H \subset K$.

(b) *Wenn* $H, F \in \mathrm{Sk}(M)$ *und* G *eine e.e. gemeinsame Untergruppe von* H *und* F *ist, ist* $H *_G F \in \mathrm{Sk}(M)$.

(c) *Für alle* $G \in \mathrm{Sk}(M)$ *und e.e.* H *ist* $W(H) \leqslant_e W(G) \Rightarrow H \in \mathrm{Sk}(M)$.

Bemerkung. Für algebraisch abgeschlossene Gruppen M mit der Eigenschaft von 2.16 gilt: Jede Gruppe N mit $\mathrm{Sk}(N) \subset \mathrm{Sk}(M)$ ist in einer a.a. Gruppe N' enthalten, die zu M partiell isomorph ist. Insbesondere gibt es beliebig, große zu M partiell isomorphe Gruppen. Beweis der Bemerkung: $S(\vec{g}, \vec{x})$ sei über N lösbar. G sei von den $\vec{g}$ erzeugt. Wenn H von S über G präsentiert wird, ist $W(H) \leqslant_e W(G)$ und also $H \in \mathrm{Sk}(M)$. Man sieht leicht, daß $\mathrm{Sk}(N *_G H) \subset \mathrm{Sk}(M)$. Auf diese Weise kann man N algebraisch abschließen.

Beweis. (b)$\rightarrow$(a) is klar.

(c)$\rightarrow$(b). Aus II, 3.3 folgt $W(H \mid G) \leqslant_e W(H)$ und $W(F \mid G) \leqslant_e W(F)$. Wie im Beweis von 2.15 folgt $W(H *_G F) \leqslant_e W(H) \vee W(F) \equiv^* W(H \times F)$. Weil $H \times F \in \mathrm{Sk}(M)$, ist also $H *_G F \in \mathrm{Sk}(M)$.

(a)$\rightarrow$(c). Wenn (a) gilt, ist $W(F \mid G) \leqslant^* W(F)$ für alle $G \subset F$ aus dem Skelett von M. Das folgt aus 2.14. Wir brauchen eine Konstruktion, die uns noch später nützlich sein wird: c, b seien Erzeugende einer Gruppe $\mathfrak{A}$. Wir definieren $b_k = c^{-k} b c^k$ für $k \in \mathbf{Z}$ und $a_i = b_{i+1} b_0 b_{i+1}^{-1} b_0^{-1}$ für $i \in \omega$. $\mathfrak{A}$ sei durch die Relationen $\boldsymbol{c}\boldsymbol{a}_i \doteq \boldsymbol{a}_i\boldsymbol{c}$, $\boldsymbol{a}_i\boldsymbol{a}_j \doteq \boldsymbol{a}_j\boldsymbol{a}_i$, $\boldsymbol{a}_i^2 \doteq \boldsymbol{e}$, $\boldsymbol{a}_i\boldsymbol{b} \doteq \boldsymbol{b}\boldsymbol{a}_i$, $i, j \in \omega$, präsentiert. Aus den Relationen folgt $a_i b_k = b_k a_i$, $b_{k+i+1} b_k = a_i b_k b_{k+i+1}$ für alle $i \in \omega$, $k \in \mathbf{Z}$. Man sieht leicht, daß man jedes Element von $\mathfrak{A}$ in der Form $c^k b_{k_1}^{n_1} \cdots b_{k_m}^{n_m}$ schreiben kann. Daraus gewinnt man eine Darstellung jedes Elementes von H in der Form $c^k a_{i_1} \cdots a_{i_n} b_{k_1}^{n_1} \cdots b_{k_m}^{n_m}$ mit $i_1 < i_2 < \cdots i_n$, $k_1 < k_2 < \cdots k_m$, $k, n_i \in \mathbf{Z}$, $n, m \in \omega$, $n_m \neq 0$. In ([29]) wurde (implizit) gezeigt, daß diese Darstellung eindeutig ist (siehe auch ([3])). $\mathfrak{B}$ sei die von den a_i erzeugte Untergruppe von $\mathfrak{A}$. $\mathfrak{B}$ liegt im Zentrum von $\mathfrak{A}$ und ist direkte Summe der zyklischen Gruppen der Ordnung 2 $\langle a_i \rangle$. Jede Untergruppe von $\mathfrak{B}$ ist Normalteiler von $\mathfrak{A}$. Sei nun G endlicherzeugte Untergruppe von M and $W(H) \leqslant_e W(G)$. Wir können $G \neq E$ annehmen. Dann gibt es eine rekursive Funktion $f : \omega^2 \rightarrow \mathscr{P}_\omega(\omega)$ mit

$$i \in W(H) \quad \text{gdw.} \quad \text{ex. } k \text{ mit} \quad f(i, k) \subset W(G).$$

Wir indizieren die a_i doppelt vermöge einer rekursiven Bijektion zwischen ω und ω^2. Es gibt also eindeutig j, k mit $a_{j,k} = a_i$, und umgekehrt kann man zu j, k genau ein i mit $a_i = a_{j,k}$ finden. Die Untergruppe N von $\mathfrak{B}$ sei erzeugt von

$$\{a_{i,j} \cdot a_{i,k}^{-1} \mid f(i,j) \subset W(G), f(i,k) \subset W(G)\}.$$

Wir betrachten $\mathfrak{A}/N$. Die Erzeugenden cN and bN nennen wir $\bar{c}$ und $\bar{b}$. Ebenso bezeichenen wir a_iN mit $\bar{a}_i$ und b_iN mit $\bar{b}_i$. Wenn $k \neq 0$ oder $n_m \neq 0$, und $k_1 < k_2 < \cdots$ ist $\bar{c}^k \bar{a}_{i_1} \cdots \bar{a}_{i_n} \bar{b}_{k_1}^{n_1} \cdots \bar{b}_{k_m}^{n_m} \notin \mathfrak{B}/N$.

Wir nehmen nun eine isomorphe Kopie $\mathfrak{A}'$ von $\mathfrak{A}$, die von c' und b' erzeugt wird. $\bar{A}$ bezeichne die von den a'_i für $i \in W(H)$ erzeugte Untergruppe von $\mathfrak{B}'$. Wenn $a'_i \in \bar{A}$, gibt es ein $k \in \omega$ mit $f(i,k) \subset W(G)$; wir identifizieren a'_i mit $\bar{a}_{i,k}$ (Wenn $f(i,j) \subset W(G)$, ist $\bar{a}_{i,k} = \bar{a}_{i,j}$) und bilden das amalgamierte Produkt $\mathfrak{B}/N *_{\bar{A}} \mathfrak{B}'$.

Das folgende System von Gleichungen und Ungleichungen in den "Unbekannten" $\boldsymbol{b}, \boldsymbol{c}, \boldsymbol{b}', \boldsymbol{c}'$ gilt offenbar in $\mathfrak{B}/N *_{\bar{A}} \mathfrak{B}'$. Die Menge der Gleichungen ist aufzählungsreduzierbar auf $W(G)$, die Menge der Ungleichungen 1-aufzählungsreduzierbar auf $W(G)$. Nach Satz II, 3.15 gibt es eine Lösung des Systems in M. Die $\boldsymbol{a}_i, \boldsymbol{a}_{i,j}, \boldsymbol{a}'_i, \boldsymbol{b}_{k'}, \boldsymbol{b}'_{k'}$ fassen wir als Wörter in $\boldsymbol{c}, \boldsymbol{b}, \boldsymbol{c}', \boldsymbol{b}'$, auf. $(i, j, k, i_1, \ldots i_n \in \omega;\ k_1 < k_2 < \cdots < k_m \in \mathbf{Z})$

0. $\boldsymbol{a}_{i,k} \doteq \boldsymbol{a}'_i$ wenn $f(i,k) \subset W(G)$.
1. $\boldsymbol{a}_i^2 \doteq \boldsymbol{e}, \boldsymbol{c}\boldsymbol{a}_i \doteq \boldsymbol{a}_i\boldsymbol{c}, \boldsymbol{a}_i\boldsymbol{a}_j \doteq \boldsymbol{a}_j\boldsymbol{a}_i, \boldsymbol{a}_i\boldsymbol{b} \doteq \boldsymbol{b}\boldsymbol{a}_i$.
2. $\neg\, \boldsymbol{c}^k \boldsymbol{a}_{i_1} \cdots \boldsymbol{a}_{i_n} \boldsymbol{b}_{k_1}^{n_1} \cdots \boldsymbol{b}_{k_m}^{n_m} \doteq \boldsymbol{a}'_i$ wenn $k \neq 0$ oder $n_m \neq 0$.
3. $\neg\, \boldsymbol{a}_{j,k} \boldsymbol{a}_{i_1} \cdots \boldsymbol{a}_{i_n} \doteq \boldsymbol{a}'_i$ wenn $i_1, \ldots i_n \neq (j,k)$, und $f(j,k) \not\subset W(G)$.
4. $\neg\, \boldsymbol{a}'_{i_1} \cdots \boldsymbol{a}'_{i_n} \doteq \boldsymbol{a}'_i$ wenn $i \notin \{i_1, \ldots i_n\}$.

Wir ändern unsere Bezeichnungen und bezeichnen mit b, c, b', c' eine Lösung des Systems in M. Wir zeigen, daß $i \in W(H)$ gdw. $a'_i \in \langle b, c \rangle$. Daraus folgt dann die Behauptung mit $W(H) \leqslant_1 W(\langle b, c, c', b' \rangle \mid \langle b, c \rangle)$ und nach unserer Bemerkung am Anfang $W(\langle b, c, c', b' \rangle \mid \langle b, c \rangle) \leqslant^* W(\langle b, c, c', b' \rangle)$ aus 1.4. Sei $i \in W(H)$. Dann gibt es ein k mit $f(i,k) \subset W(G)$. Wegen 0 ist $a'_i = a_{i,k} \in \langle b, c \rangle$. Sei umgekehrt $a'_i \in \langle b, c \rangle$. Weil 1 gilt, ist $a'_i = c^k a_{i_1} \cdots a_{i_n} b_{k_1}^{n_1} \cdots b_{k_m}^{n_m}$ für geeignete $k, i_1 \ldots, n_1 \ldots, k_1 \cdots$. Aus 2 folgt $k = 0$ und $m = 0$, also $a'_i = a_{i_1} \cdots a_{i_n}$. Wegen 3 kann man schreiben $a'_i = a_{j_1, m_1} \cdots a_{j_n, m_n}$ für $f(j_r, m_r) \subset W(G)$ $(r = 1, \ldots n)$. Aus 0 folgt $a'_i = a'_{j_1} \cdots a'_{j_n}$. Nach 4 muß $i \in \{j_1, \ldots j_n\}$ sein, d. h. $i \in W(H)$. □

3. Ideale von ∗-Graden und a.a. Gruppen

Definition 3.1. Wir ordnen jeder Gruppe M die Menge $W_*(M) \subset V$ der ∗-Grade aller endlich erzeugten Untergruppen von M zu. $X \subset V$

ist durch $\bigcup X$ eindeutig bestimmt: $X = \{a \in V \mid a \subset \bigcup X\}$. Für $\bigcup W_*(M)$ schreiben wir $W^*(M)$.

Aus 1.4 schließt man sofort

Lemma 3.2. *M sei algebraisch abgeschlossen. Dann ist für alle e.e. F* $F \in \mathrm{Sk}(M)$ *gdw.* $W(F) \in W^*(M)$.

Mit diesem Lemma können wir I, 2.10/2.11 für a.a. Gruppen anders formulieren.

Satz 3.3. *M, N seien Gruppen, M algebraisch abgeschlossen.*
1. $N <_p M$ *gdw.* $W_*(N) \subset W_*(M)$.
2. *Wenn N abzählbar ist,* $N < N$ *gdw.* $W_*(N) \subset W_*(M)$.

Sei auch N algebraisch abgeschlossen.
3. $N \cong_p M$ *gdw.* $W_*(N) = W_*(M)$.
4. *Wenn N und M abzählbar sind,* $N \cong M$ *gdw.* $W_*(N) = W_*(M)$.

$W_*(M)$ soll an die Stelle des Skeletts ω-homogener Strukturen treten. Ebenso, wie wir in I, 3 untersucht haben, welche Klassen als Skelette vorkommen, wollen wir jetzt die Teilmengen von V bestimmen, die von der Form $W_*(M)$ für ein algebraisch abgeschlossenes M sind.

Zunächst zeigen wir, daß alle $*$-Grade als Wortproblem einer endlich erzeugten Gruppe vorkommen.

Satz 3.4. *Für alle* $A \subset \omega$ *gibt es eine von zwei Elementen erzeugte Gruppe F mit* $A \leqslant_1 W(F) \leqslant^+ A$.

Dieser Satz wurde (unabhängig) in ([3]) und [29]) bewiesen.

Beweis. $\mathfrak{A}$ sei wie im Beweis von 2.16. $\bar{A}$ bezeichne jetzt die von den $a_i, i \in A$ erzeugte Untergruppe von $\mathfrak{B}$. Setze $F = \mathfrak{A}/\bar{A}$. Weil $c^k a_{i_1} \cdots b_{k_m}^{n_m} \in \bar{A}$ gdw. $\{i_1, \ldots i_n\} \subset A$ ist $W(F) \leqslant^+ A$. Weiter ist $f : A \leqslant_1 W(F)$ für $f(i) =$ Gödelnummer von a_i. Wir fassen a_i dabei als Wort in b, c auf. $\square$

Folgerungen 3.5. 1. *Für alle* $a \in V$ *gibt es ein e.e. F mit* $W(F) \equiv^* a$.
2. *Es gibt* 2^ω *von zwei Elementen erzeugte Gruppen.*
3. *Es gibt* $W(F) \leqslant_T W(G)$ *und eine a.a.Gr. M mit* $G < M$, $F \not< M$. *(Wähle* $\omega \setminus A \not\leqslant_e A$, $W(G) \equiv^* A$, $W(F) \equiv^* \omega \setminus A$, *M nach* 1.7.)
4. *Es gibt e.e.* $F < M$ *a.a., so daß für kein* $H \neq E$ $F * H < M$. *(Wähle A mit* $A^\wp \not\leqslant^* A$ (2.9), $W(F) \equiv^* A$, *wende* 2.13.3 *an.)*

Bemerkung 3.6. In [29] und [30] wird gezeigt, daß man Satz 3.5 nicht verschärfen kann, indem man $\leqslant^+$ durch schärfere Reduzierbarkeitsbegriffe — zum Beispiel $\leqslant_m$ — ersetzt. Es gibt ein nichtrekursives r.a. A, so daß für keine endlich erzeugte Gruppe F mit nicht lösbarem Wortproblem $W(F) \leqslant_{\mathrm{btt}} A$, [30]. ($\leqslant_{\mathrm{btt}}$: beschränkte wahrheitstafel Reduzierbarkeit.)

Lemma 3.7. *Wenn M algebraisch abgeschlossen ist, ist $W_*(M)$ ein Ideal in $(V, \leqslant)$.*

Beweis. Sei $b \in W_*(M)$, also $b \equiv^* W(G)$ für ein $G \in \mathrm{Sk}(M)$. Wenn $a \leqslant b$ für ein $a \in V$, wählen wir ein e.e. F mit $W(F) \equiv^* a$. Dann ist $W(F) \leqslant^* W(G)$ und also nach 1.4 $F < M$, also $a = W(F)/{\equiv^*} \in W_*(M)$. Wähle für $a, b \in W_*(M)$ $F, G \in \mathrm{Sk}(M)$ mit $W(F) \in a$, $W(G) \in b$. Nach 1.5.2 ist $F \times G < M$ und nach 2.11 ist $\sup(a, b) = W(F \times G)/{\equiv^*} \in W_*(M)$. □

Sicherlich gehört nicht jedes Ideal, z. B. $\{\emptyset/{\equiv^*}\}$ nach II, 2.11, zu einer algebraisch abgeschlossenen Gruppe. Wir wollen jetzt geeignete Bedingungen für das Ideal definieren. Dazu brauchen wir einen "rekursionstheoretischen Ersatz" für endliche Gleichungssysteme über Gruppen: r.a. Hornklassen.

Definition 3.8. 1. Eine Klasse $\mathcal{H} \subset \mathcal{P}(\omega)$ heißt Hornklasse, wenn

(a) $\mathcal{H}$ ist abgeschlossen in der Produkttopologie von 2^ω.

(b) $\mathcal{H}$ ist abgeschlossen unter Durchschnitten, d. h. $\emptyset \neq \mathcal{A} \subset \mathcal{H} \Rightarrow \bigcap \mathcal{A} \in \mathcal{H}$.

2. Eine Π^0_1-Klasse $\mathcal{H}$ heißt rekursiv aufzählbare (r.a.) Hornklasse, wenn $\mathcal{H}$ durchschnittsabgeschlossen ist.

Bemerkungen und Definitionen. Die Hornklassen sind die Klassen der Form $\bar{\mathcal{H}}_W = \{X \in \mathcal{P}(\omega) \mid \exists u, w \langle u, w\rangle \in W \wedge D_u \subset X \wedge D^1_w \subset \omega \setminus X\}$ für $W \subset \omega$. Die Relation $A \in \bar{\mathcal{H}}_W$ (zwischen A und W) ist arithmetisch (Π^0_1).

Die r.a. Hornklassen sind von der Form $\bar{\mathcal{H}}_W$ für rekursiv aufzählbare $W \subset \omega$. Statt $\bar{\mathcal{H}}_{W_i}$ schreiben wir $\bar{\mathcal{H}}_i$.

Die Relation $X \in \bar{\mathcal{H}}_i$ (zwischen X und i) ist Π^0_1. i ist eine Gödelnummer von $\bar{\mathcal{H}}_i$. Einer Hornklasse $\mathcal{H} \subset \mathcal{P}(\omega)$ ordnen wir die *Hornklasse* $\mathcal{H}^n = \{(X_1, \dots X_n) \mid (X_1 \vee \cdots \vee X_n) \in \mathcal{H}\}$ zu. Damit können wir weitere Hornklassen bilden: wenn $\mathcal{H}$ eine Hornklasse ist und $A_1, \dots A_{n-1} \in \mathcal{P}(\omega)$, definieren wir die Hornklasse $\mathcal{H}[A_1, \dots, A_{n-1}] = \{X \in \mathcal{P}(\omega) \mid (A_1, \dots, A_{n-1}, X) \in \mathcal{H}^n\}$. Typische

Beispiele für r.a. Hornklassen sind $W_z^e[X] \subset Y$ (damit meinen wir $\{(X, Y) \mid W_z^e[X] \subset Y\}$) und $Y \cap W_z^1[X] = \emptyset$. Umgekehrt ist jede r.a. Hornklasse von der Form $\{0\} \cap W_z^1[X] = \emptyset$.

Zu Hornklassen gehören Mengen von aussagenlogischen Implikationen. Wir betrachten Formeln, die sich aus den Aussagenvariablen $q(0), q(1), \ldots, q(i), \ldots$ $i < \omega$, und Konstanten $\top$, $\bot$ mit $\wedge$, $\vee$, $\neg$, $\rightarrow$ aufbauen. $A \subset \omega$ erfüllt die Formel φ, wenn bei der Wahrheitswertbelegung, die $q(i)$ *wahr* zuordnet, wenn $i \in A$, und *falsch*, wenn $i \notin A$, φ den Wahrheitswert *wahr* bekommt. Wir schreiben $A \models \varphi$; und für $\mathcal{F} \subset \mathcal{P}(\omega)$ und eine Menge T von Formeln $\mathcal{F} \models T$, wenn $A \models \varphi$ für alle $A \in \mathcal{F}$, $\varphi \in T$. Zur Hornklasse $\bar{\mathcal{H}}_W$ definieren wir die Menge von Implikationen

$$\hat{\mathcal{H}}_W = \{ \wedge \{q(j) \mid j \in D_u\} \rightarrow \vee \{q(i) \mid i \in D_w^1\} \mid \langle u, w \rangle \in W\}.$$

($\hat{\mathcal{H}}_i$ ist dann eine r.a. Menge von aussagenlogischen Implikationen.) Wir haben $A \in \bar{\mathcal{H}}_W$ gdw. $A \models \hat{\mathcal{H}}_W$. Man sieht umgekehrt leicht, daß man jede Menge von Implikationen in dieser Form schreiben kann und eine r.a. Menge von Implikationen in der Form $\hat{\mathcal{H}}_i$.

Hornklassen $\bar{\mathcal{H}}_W^n \subset (\mathcal{P}(\omega))^n$ ordnen wir entsprechend eine Menge $\hat{\mathcal{H}}_W^n$ von Implikationen in den Aussagenvariablen $q^1(i), q^2(i), \ldots, q^n(i)$, $i < \omega$, zu, so daß für alle $A_1, \ldots, A_n \subset \omega$ $(A_1, \ldots, A_n) \in \bar{\mathcal{H}}_W^n$ gdw. $(A_1, \ldots, A_n) \models \hat{\mathcal{H}}_W^n$. Dabei bedeutet $(A_1, \ldots, A_n) \models \varphi$, daß φ bei der Wahrheitswertbelegung: "$q^j(i) \mapsto$ *wahr* gdw. $i \in A_j$" den Wert *wahr* bekommt. Auf diese Weise gehören die r.a. Systeme von Implikationen in den Aussagenvariablen $q^j(i)$, $j = 1, \ldots, n$, $i < \omega$ zu den r.a. Hornklassen $\mathcal{H}^n$.

Ein System von (gruppentheoretischen) Implikationen I entspricht einer Hornklasse $\mathcal{H}$ für die $(G, \vec{g}) \models I$ gdw. $W(G, \vec{g}) \in \mathcal{H}$. Im nächsten Lemma fassen wir einige nützliche Eigenschaften der Hornklassen zusammen. Wir vermerken dabei analoge Sätze über Gruppen, die wir früher bewiesen haben. In einigen Fällen sind die gruppentheoretischen Sätze Spezialfälle der Ergebnisse über Hornklassen. Dazu benützt man, daß die Klasse der Wortprobleme von Gruppen eine r.a. Hornklasse ist (3.9.9).

Lemma 3.9. 1. *Der Durchschnitt einer Familie von Hornklassen ist eine Hornklasse. Der Durchschnitt einer r.a. Familie von r.a. Hornklassen ist eine r.a. Hornklasse (d. h. für alle r.a. A ist $\bigcap\{\bar{\mathcal{H}}_i \mid i \in A\}$ eine r.a. Hornklasse).*

2. *$\mathcal{F}$ sei eine Familie von Hornklassen. Wenn der Schnitt von je endlich vielen Mitgliedern von $\mathcal{F}$ nichtleer ist, ist der Schnitt von $\mathcal{F}$ nichtleer.*

3. *Wenn* $\mathscr{H} \models q(n_1) \vee \cdots \vee q(n_k)$, *gibt es ein i mit* $\mathscr{H} \models q(n_i)$ (*siehe* II. 1.4).

4. $\{X \mid \mathscr{H}[X] \neq \emptyset\}$ *ist eine Hornklasse (siehe* II, 1.6) *Wenn* $\mathscr{H}$ *r.a., ist auch* "$\mathscr{H}[X] \neq \emptyset$" *r.a.* (II, 2.1). $\{i \mid \bar{\mathscr{H}}_i \neq \emptyset\}$ *ist* Π_1^0-*Menge.*

5. $\mathscr{H}$ *sei r.a. und* $A \subset \omega$. *Dann ist* $\bigcap \mathscr{H}[A] \leqslant_e A$ (II, 3.2). *Weiter ist* $\omega \setminus \bigcup \mathscr{H}[A] \leqslant_e^1 A$.

6. $B \leqslant^* A$ *gdw.* $\{B\} = \mathscr{H}[A]$ *für eine r.a. Hornklasse* $\mathscr{H}$ (III, 1.6.2).

7. *Die Klassen der Form* $\mathscr{H}[A]$ *für r.a.* $\mathscr{H}$ *sind gerade die von der Form* $\{X \mid X \models I \cup J\}$, *wobei I bzw. J Mengen von positiven bzw. negativen Implikationen mit* $I \leqslant_e A$, $J \leqslant_e^1 A$ *sind* (II, 3.13).

8. $\bar{\mathscr{H}}_A \subset \bar{\mathscr{H}}_B$ *ist eine* Π_2^0-*Eigenschaft von A, B.*

9. $\mathscr{W}_n := \{(W(F; f_0, \cdots, f_n) \mid F \text{ von } \vec{f} \text{ erzeugt}\}$ *ist eine r.a. Hornklasse* $\{(X, n) \mid X \in \mathscr{W}_n\}$ *ist* Π_1^0.

10. *s seine eine endliche Teilmenge von* ω, $A \subset \omega$. *Wenn* $i \in \omega$, *bezeichnen wir mit* $g(i)$ *die Gödelnummer des Wortes in* $x_0, x_1, \ldots$, *das aus* $V_i(x_0, x_1, \ldots)$ *dadurch hervorgeht, daß man die Variablen* x_j *mit* $j \notin s$ *durch* **e** *ersetzt. Wir schreiben* $A \downarrow s$ *für* $g^{-1}[A]$. (*Wenn F durch* $f_0, \ldots$ *erzeugt ist, ist also* $W(F; f_0, \ldots) \downarrow n = W(\langle f_0, \ldots, f_{n-1}\rangle)$.) $\{(X, Y) \mid X = Y \downarrow s\}$ *ist eine r.a. Hornklasse* Π_1^0 *in X, Y und der Gödelnummer von s.*

Beweis. 1. Für eine Familie $(U_i \mid i \in I)$ ist $\bigcap\{\bar{\mathscr{H}}_{U_i} \mid i \in I\} = \bar{\mathscr{H}}_{\cup\{U_i \mid i \in I\}}$.

2. folgt aus dem Kompaktheitssatz der Aussagenlogik.

3. Wenn die Behauptung von 3 nicht stimmt, gibt es für jedes i ein $A_i \in \mathscr{H}$ mit $A_i \not\models q(n_i)$ — (also $n_i \notin A_i$). Dann ist $A_1 \cap A_2 \cap \cdots \cap A_k \in \mathscr{H}$ und $A_1 \cap \cdots \cap A_k \not\models q(n_1) \vee \cdots \vee q(n_k)$. Wid.

4. T sei die Menge aller Implikationen φ in den Aussagevariablen $q^1(i)$, $i < \omega$, $\mathscr{H}^2 \models \varphi$. (Wenn $\mathscr{H} = \bar{\mathscr{H}}_j$, ist T r.a.) Aus $(A, B) \in \mathscr{H}^2$ folgt $(A, B) \models T$, und daher $A \models T$. Sei andererseits $\mathscr{H}[A] = \emptyset$. Die Hornklasse

$$\mathscr{H}^2 \cap \bigcap\{\{(X, Y) \mid a \in X\} \mid a \in A\} \cap \bigcap\{\{(X, Y) \mid b \notin X\} \mid b \notin A\}$$

ist leer. Nach 2 gibt es $a_1, \ldots, a_k \in A$, $b_1, \ldots, b_m \notin A$ mit $\mathscr{H}^2 \models q^1(a_1) \wedge \cdots \wedge q^1(a_k) \rightarrow q^1(b_1) \vee \cdots \vee q^1(b_m)$. Eine Anwendung von 3 liefert ein i mit $\mathscr{H}^2 \models q^1(a_1) \wedge \cdots \wedge q^1(a_k) \rightarrow q^1(b_i)$. Diese Implikation ist in T. Also ist $A \not\models T$. Wenn $\hat{\mathscr{H}}_W = T$, ist somit $\{X \mid \mathscr{H}[X] \neq \emptyset\} = \bar{\mathscr{H}}_W$.

Die letzte Behauptung gilt, weil $\{i \mid \hat{\mathscr{H}}_i \nvdash \bot\}$ Π_1^0 ist.

5. Definiere $A^+ = \{q^1(a) \mid a \in A\}$ und $A^- = \{\neg q^1(a) \mid a \notin A\}$. Dann ist $\bigcap \bar{\mathscr{H}}_i[A] = \{n \mid \hat{\mathscr{H}}_i^2 \cup A^+ \cup A^- \vdash q^1(n)\}$. Nach 3 ist das das gleiche wie $\{n \mid \hat{\mathscr{H}}_i^2 \cup A^+ \vdash q^1(n)\}$. Also $\bigcap \bar{\mathscr{H}}_i[A] \leqslant_e A$. $n \notin \bigcup \bar{\mathscr{H}}_i[A]$ gdw. $\hat{\mathscr{H}}_i^2 \cup A^+ \cup A^- \vdash \neg q^1(n)$. Das gilt nach 3 gdw. ex $b \notin A$ mit $\hat{\mathscr{H}}_i^2 \cup A^+ \cup \{\neg q^1(b)\} \vdash \neg q^1(n)$. Daraus folgt die Behauptung.

6. Wenn $(m,n): B \leqslant^* A$, ist $\{B\} = \{X \mid W^e_m[A] \subset X \wedge X \cap W^1_n[A] = \emptyset\}$. Ist umgekehrt $\{B\} = \mathcal{H}[A]$, so ist $B = \bigcap \mathcal{H}[A] = \bigcup \mathcal{H}[A]$.

7. Wenn $\mathcal{H}_i[A]$ gegeben ist, wähle für I bzw. J die Menge der positiven bzw. negativen Implikationen in $q^2(j)$, $j < \omega$, die aus $\hat{\mathcal{H}}^2_i \cup A^+$ bzw. $\hat{\mathcal{H}}^2_i \cup A^+ \cup A^-$ folgen. Die gewünschte Eigenschaft folgt nun leicht aus 3 wie in 4. Wenn $z : I \leqslant_e A$, $z' : J \leqslant^1_e A$, wähle $\mathcal{H}_i$ so, daß $\hat{\mathcal{H}}^2_i$ die Vereinigung von $\{\bigwedge D^+_u \to \varphi \mid \langle \ulcorner\varphi\urcorner, u\rangle \in W_z\}$ und $\{\bigwedge (D^+_u \cup (\omega \setminus D^1_{u'})^-) \to \varphi \mid \langle \ulcorner\varphi\urcorner, u, u'\rangle \in W_{z'}\}$ ist. (Wir fassen dabei I und J als Mengen von Implikationen in den Variablen $q^2(i)$, $i \in \omega$ auf.)

8. Man erkennt die Richtigkeit der Behauptung aus $\bar{\mathcal{H}}_A \subset \bar{\mathcal{H}}_B$ gdw. $\forall \varphi \in \hat{\mathcal{H}}_B\ \hat{\mathcal{H}}_A \vdash \varphi$.

9. $\mathrm{Fr}(g_0, \ldots, g_n)$ sei die freie Gruppe in den Erzeugenden $\vec{g}$. $\mathcal{W}_n$ ist die Menge aller $A \subset \omega$ mit

(a) Wenn $V_i(g_0, \ldots) = e$ (in $\mathrm{Fr}(g_0, \ldots, g_n)$), ist $i \in A$.

(b) Wenn $i, j \in A$ und $V_i(g_0, \ldots, g_n) V_j^{-1}(g_0, \ldots, g_n) = V_k(g_0, \ldots, g_n)$ (in $\mathrm{Fr}(g_0, \ldots)$), ist auch $k \in A$.

(c) Wenn $i \in A$ und für ein $h \in \mathrm{Fr}(g_0, \ldots, g_n)$ $hV_i(\vec{g})h^{-1} = V_j(\vec{g})$, ist $j \in A$.

Denn $W(F)$ erfüllt natürlich (a), (b), (c). Ist anderseits (a), (b), (c) erfüllt, ist $N := \{V_i(\vec{g}) \mid i \in A\}$ ein Normalteiler von $\mathrm{Fr}(\vec{g})$. Sei $(F; f_0, \ldots, f_n) = (\mathrm{Fr}(\vec{g})/N;\ g_0 \cdot N, \ldots, g_n \cdot N)$. Aus der Definition von N folgt $W(F, \vec{f}) \supset A$. Wenn umgekehrt $j \in W(F, \vec{f})$, folgt $V_j(\vec{g}) \in N$ und daher $V_i(\vec{g}) = V_j(\vec{g})$ für ein $i \in A$. Wegen (c) ($h = e$) folgt $j \in A$. Also ist $W(F, \vec{f}) = A$.

10. g ist rekursiv. Das System T von aussagenlogischen Implikationen $\{q^1(n) \to q^2(g(n)) \mid n \in \omega\} \cup \{q^2(g(n)) \to q^1(n) \mid n \in \omega\}$, für das $A = B \downarrow s$ gdw. $(A, B) \models T$, ist also r.a. □

Definition 3.10. Ein Ideal $I \subset V$ heißt abgeschlossen, wenn es zu jedem $A \in \bigcup I$ und jeder r.a. Hornklasse $\mathcal{H}$, für die $\mathcal{H}[A] \neq \emptyset$, ein $B \in \bigcup I$ mit $B \in \mathcal{H}[A]$ gibt.

Bemerkung 3.11. 1. $\mathcal{K} \subset \mathcal{P}(\omega)$ sei nichtleer. $\mathcal{K}$ ist genau dann Vereinigung eines abgeschlossenen Ideals, wenn

(a) Für alle $A, B \in \mathcal{K}$ ist $A \vee B \in \mathcal{K}$; und, wenn $\mathcal{H}[A] \neq \emptyset$ für ein r.a. $\mathcal{H}$, gibt es ein $C \in \mathcal{K}$ mit $C \in \mathcal{H}[A]$.

oder

(b) Für alle $A, B \in \mathcal{K}$ und r.a. $\mathcal{H}$ mit $\mathcal{H}[A, B] \neq \emptyset$ gibt es ein $C \in \mathcal{K}$ mit $C \in \mathcal{H}[A, B]$.

2. Wenn I abgeschlossen ist, $C \in \bigcup I$, $A \leqslant_e C$, $B \leqslant^1_e C$, gibt es, wenn $A \cap B = \emptyset$, ein $D \in \bigcup I$, das A und B trennt.

Zum Beweis von 1 benützt man 3.9.6 und überlegt, daß es ein r.a. $\mathscr{H}$ gibt, sodaß $\mathscr{H}[A, B] = \{A \vee B\}$ für alle A, B. 2 gilt, weil "$W_z^e[X] \subset Z \wedge \emptyset = Z \cap W_{z'}^1[X]$" eine r.a. Hornklasse ist.

Es ist fraglich, ob aus der Eigenschaft 2 allein die Abgeschlossenheit von I folgt.

Satz 3.12. 1. *Wenn M a.a.Gr. ist, ist $W_*(M)$ ein abgeschlossenes Ideal.*

2. *Die abzählbaren abgeschlossenen Ideale von V sind gerade die Mengen der Form $W_*(M)$ für eine abzählbare a.a.Gr. M.*

3. *Es gibt genau dann eine algebraisch abgeschlossene Gruppe M der Mächtigkeit ω_1 mit $W_*(M) = I$, wenn $|I| \leq \omega_1$ und I ein abgeschlossenes Ideal ist.*

4. *(CH) Die Mengen der Form $W_*(M)$ für eine a.a.Gr. M sind gerade die abgeschlossenen Ideale von V.*
(Für alle M ist $|W_*(M)| \leq \min(2^\omega, |M| + \omega)$.)

(3.12) folgt aus dem nächsten Lemma: 1. Wenn M a.a. ist M ω-homogen (I, 1.10). Wegen I, 3.2.1/3.7. erfüllt $\mathrm{Sk}(M)$ daher U, JEP und AA. Aus 3.2 folgt, daß $\mathrm{Sk}(M) = S(W_*(M))$, also ist nach 3.13 $W_*(M)$ ein abgeschlossenes Ideal.

2, 3, 4 erhält man aus dem Lemma mit I, 3.8. Dazu überlegt man, daß aus 3.5.1 folgt, daß für jedes M $\mathrm{Sk}(M) = S(I) \Rightarrow W_*(M) = I$. Für 3 benützt man, wenn I abzählbar ist, I, 4.8.2.

Lemma 3.13. *Für $I \subset V$ sei $S(I)$ die Klasse aller e.e.Gr. F mit $W(F)/\equiv^* \in I$. Dann erfüllt $S(I)$ genau dann U, JEP und AA, wenn I ein abgeschlossenes Ideal ist.*

Beweis. $S(I)$ erfülle U, JEP und AA. Wir zeigen, daß $\bigcup I$ 3.11.1(a) erfüllt. Sei dazu $A, B \in \bigcup I$. Wir finden ein abzählbares J mit $A, B \in \bigcup J \subset \bigcup I$, für das $S(J)$ U, JEP, AA genügt. M sei — nach 13.8.2 — eine a.a.Gr. mit $\mathrm{Sk}(M) = S(J)$. Da — wegen 3.5.1 — $W_*(M) = J$, ist J Ideal (3.7). Daher ist $A \vee B \in \bigcup J$ und also $A \vee B \in \bigcup I$. Für die r.a. Hornklasse $\mathscr{H}$ sei $\mathscr{H}[A] \neq \emptyset$. Wir wählen ein $G \subset M$ mit $W(G) \equiv^* A$. Wir beschreiben $\mathscr{H}[A]$ durch zwei Mengen I' bzw. J' von aussagenlogischen Implikationen mit $I' \leq_e A$ und $J' \leq_e^1 A$ wie in 3.9.7 und ersetzen dann in I' und J' die Aussagenvariablen $q(i)$ durch die Gleichungen $N_i(x, y) = \boldsymbol{e}$. Auf diese Weise erhalten wir zwei Systeme $\boldsymbol{I}(x, y)$, $\boldsymbol{J}(x, y)$ von positiven bzw. negativen Implikationen mit $\boldsymbol{I} \leq_e W(G)$, $\boldsymbol{J} \leq_e^1 W(G)$, die genau dann auf Elemente f_1, f_2 einer Gruppe zutreffen, wenn $\{i \mid N_i(f_1, f_2) = e\} \in \mathscr{H}[A]$. Weil $\mathscr{H}[A] \neq \emptyset$, ist nach II, 2.3 $\boldsymbol{I} \cup \boldsymbol{J}$ lösbar. Nach II, 3.12 gibt es also auch eine Lösung

$f_1, f_2 \in M$. Wir setzen $C = \{i \mid N_i(f_1, f_2) = e\}$. Dann ist $C \in \mathcal{H}[A]$ und $C \leqslant_1 W(\langle f_1, f_2 \rangle) \in \bigcup J$. Also $C \in \bigcup I$.

Sei I ein abgeschlossenes Ideal. Wir zeigen, daß $S(I)$ U, JEP und AA erfüllt. **U** Wenn $G \subset F$ und $W(F)/{\equiv^*} \in I$, folgt wegen $W(G) \leqslant^* W(F)$ $W(G)/{\equiv^*} \in I$ aus der Idealeigenschaft von I. **JEP** Wenn $W(G), W(F) \in \bigcup I$, ist auch $\sup(W(G)/{\equiv^*}, W(F)/{\equiv^*}) \in I$. Nach 2.11 also $F \times G \in S(I)$. **AA** Für die von $f_0, \ldots, f_{n-1}$ erzeugte Gruppe F sei $W(F) \in \bigcup I$ und $S(\vec{f}, \vec{x})$ ein endliches Gleichungssystem, das in einer Obergruppe G von F durch $g_0, \ldots, g_m$ gelöst wird. Dann ist $W(G: \vec{f}, \vec{g}) \in \{X \mid X \in \mathcal{W}_{n+m} \wedge W(F; \vec{f}) = X \downarrow n \wedge Q \subset X\}$, wenn $S(\vec{f}, \vec{x}) = \{V_i(\vec{f}, \vec{x}) \doteq e \mid i \in Q\}$. Nach 3.9 ist die eben beschriebene Menge von der Form $\mathcal{H}[W(F)]$ für eine r.a. Hornklasse $\mathcal{H}$. Wegen der Abgeschlossenheit von I gibt es ein $C \in \bigcup I$, $C \in \mathcal{H}[W(F)]$. Weil $C \in \mathcal{W}_{n+m}$, ist $C = W(H; f'_0, \ldots, f'_{n-1}, h_0, \ldots, h_m)$ für eine Gruppe H. Aus $W(F) = C \downarrow n$ folgt $(F, \vec{f}) \cong \langle f'_0, \ldots, f'_{n-1} \rangle'$. Wir können also H als Obergruppe von F auffassen. Da $Q \subset C$ ist $h_0, \ldots, h_m$ eine Lösung von $S(\vec{f}, \vec{x})$ in H. Da $C \in \bigcup I$, ist $H \in S(I)$. □

4. Anwendungen

Durch 3.3 und 3.12 kann die Theorie — zumindest der abzählbaren — algebraisch abgeschlossenen Gruppen auf die Theorie der abgeschlossenen Ideale zurückgeführt werden. Zum Beispiel ist das Analogon von Satz I, 1.5.1 "Jede aufsteigende Vereinigung von abgeschlossenen Idealen ist ein abgeschlossenes Ideal". (Ein Analogon zu I, 1.5.2 — und dafür zunächst den Begriff "elementare Unterstruktur" für Ideale — werden wir im nächsten Kapitel kennenlernen.) Als weiteres Beispiel beweisen wir Satz 1.7 noch einmal, ohne über Gruppen zu sprechen.

Satz 4.1. *Das höchstens abzählbare Ideal I und die höchstens abzählbare Teilmenge Q von V seien disjunkt. Dann gibt es ein höchstens abzählbares abgeschlossenes Ideal $I \subset J$, $J \cap Q = \emptyset$.*

Wir führen den Beweis nur in dem einfachen Fall, daß $|Q| = 1$ und I ein Hauptideal ist. Wir brauchen vier Hilfssätze.

(1) *Sei $\mathcal{H}_1$ r.a. und $\{B\} \neq \mathcal{H}_1[A]$. Dann gibt es ein r.a. $\mathcal{H}_2 \ni A$, so daß für alle $C \in \mathcal{H}_2$ $\{B\} \neq \mathcal{H}_1[C]$.*

Beweis. Wenn $B \notin \mathcal{H}_1[A]$, gibt es u, u', sodaß $D_u \subset A \vee B$, $D^1_{u'} \subset \omega \setminus A \vee B$ und für alle A', B' $D_u \subset A' \vee B'$, $D^1_{u'} \subset \omega \setminus A' \vee B' \Rightarrow B' \notin \mathcal{H}_1[A']$. Setze

$\mathcal{H}_2 = \{X \mid 2\omega \cap D_u \subset 2X,\ 2\omega \cap D^1_{u'} \subset 2(\omega \setminus X)\}$.

Wenn $B, B' \in \mathcal{H}_1[A]$ für $B \neq B'$, sei $b \in B \setminus B'$ oder $b \in B' \setminus B$. $\mathcal{H}_2 := \{X \mid \mathcal{H}_1[X] \cap \{Y \mid b \in Y\} \neq \emptyset,\ \mathcal{H}_1[X] \cap \{Y \mid b \notin Y\} \neq \emptyset\}$ ist nach 3.9.1 und 3.9.4 eine r.a. Hornklasse.

(2) Wenn für ein r.a. $\mathcal{H}$, $\mathcal{H}^2[A] \neq \emptyset$, und für alle $C, D \subset \omega$, $(C, D) \in \mathcal{H}^2[A] \Rightarrow C = B$, ist $B \leqslant^* A$.

Beweis. Nach 3.9.4 ist $\mathcal{H}^2_1 := \{(X, Y) \mid \mathcal{H}[X, Y] \neq \emptyset\}$ eine r.a. Hornklasse. Die Behauptung folgt nun aus 3.9.6, weil $\{B\} = \mathcal{H}_1[A]$.

(3) Für ein r.a. $\mathcal{H}$ sei $\mathcal{H}[A] \neq \emptyset$ und $C \not\leqslant^* A$. Dann gibt ein $B \in \mathcal{H}[A]$ mit $C \not\leqslant^* A \vee B$.

Beweis. Wir konstruieren eine Folge $\mathcal{H}_0 \supset \mathcal{H}_1 \supset \mathcal{H}_2 \supset \cdots$ von r.a. Hornklassen, für die $\mathcal{H}_i[A] \neq \emptyset$, und wählen dann $B \in \bigcap\{\mathcal{H}_i[A] \mid i < \omega\}$ nach 3.9.2. Für $\mathcal{H}_0$ nehmen wir $\mathcal{H}$. Sei $\mathcal{H}_i$ bereits konstruiert. Wäre für alle $D' \in \mathcal{H}_i[A]$ $\{C\} = \bar{\mathcal{H}}_i[A, D']$, würde aus (2) $C \leqslant^* A$ folgen. Es gibt also ein $D \in \mathcal{H}_i[A]$ mit $\{C\} \neq \bar{\mathcal{H}}_i[A, D]$. Wir wenden (1) an und bekommen ein r.a. $\mathcal{H}_*$, so daß $(A, D) \in \mathcal{H}^2_*$ und für alle $(A', D') \in \mathcal{H}^2_*$, $\{C\} \neq \bar{\mathcal{H}}_i[A', D']$. Wir setzen nun $\mathcal{H}_{i+1} = \mathcal{H}_i \cap \mathcal{H}_*$. Wenn dann $B \in \bigcap\{\mathcal{H}_i[A] \mid i < \omega\}$, ist für kein $i < \omega$ $\{C\} = \bar{\mathcal{H}}_i[A, B] = \bar{\mathcal{H}}_i[A \vee B]$. Nach 3.9.6 bedeutet das $C \not\leqslant^* A \vee B$.

(4) Wenn $A_1 \leqslant^* A_2$, gibt es zu jedem i ein j, so daß $\bar{\mathcal{H}}_i[A_1] = \bar{\mathcal{H}}_j[A_2]$.

Beweis. Sei — nach 3.9.6 — $\{A_1\} = \mathcal{H}[A_2]$ für ein r.a. $\mathcal{H}$. Wähle für $\bar{\mathcal{H}}_j[A_2]$ — die nach 3.9.1 und 3.9.4 — r.a. Hornklasse $\{X \mid \mathcal{H}[A_2] \cap \{Y \mid X \in \bar{\mathcal{H}}_i[Y]\} \neq \emptyset\}$.

Beweis von 4.1. Sei $Q = \{C/\equiv^*\}$ und I von $\{A_0/\equiv^*\}$ erzeugt. Wir konstruieren eine Folge $A_0 \leqslant^* A_1 \leqslant^* A_2 \leqslant^* \cdots$ von Mengen mit $C \not\leqslant^* A_i$. A_i sei bereits definiert. Wenn $i = \langle k, n \rangle$ und $\bar{\mathcal{H}}_k[A_n] \neq \emptyset$, wählen wir nach (4) $j \in \omega$, so daß $\bar{\mathcal{H}}_j[A_i] = \bar{\mathcal{H}}_k[A_n]$. Nach (3) gibt es ein $B \in \mathcal{H}_j[A_i]$ mit $C \not\leqslant^* A_i \vee B$. Setze $A_{i+1} = A_i \vee B$. Wenn die Voraussetzungen nicht gelten, setzen wir $A_{i+1} = A_i$. Das von den A_i erzeugte Ideal hat die gewünschten Eigenschaften. □

Lemma 3.9:5 liefert uns eine neue Methode zur Konstruktion abgeschlossener Ideale (und damit algebraisch abgeschlossener Gruppen):

Lemma 4.2. 1. *Für das Ideal $I \subset V$ gelte: $a \in I$, $b \leq_e a \Rightarrow b \in I$. Dann ist I abgeschlossen.*

2. *Sei $Q \subset V$. Dann ist*
$\tilde{Q} := \{a \mid \text{ex. } b_1, \ldots, b_n \in Q,\ a \leq_e \sup(b_1, \ldots, b_n)\}$ ein abgeschlossenes Ideal.

Beweis. 1. Wenn $A \in \bigcup I$ und $\mathcal{H}[A] \neq \emptyset$ für eine r.a. Hornklasse $\mathcal{H}$, ist nach 3.9.5 $\bigcap \mathcal{H}[A] \in \mathcal{H}[A] \cap \bigcup I$. Für 2 überlegt man, daß aus $A_i \leq_e B_i$, $i = 1, 2$ $A_1 \vee A_2 \leq_e B_1 \vee B_2$ folgt.

Folgerung. *Es gibt 2^{ω_1} viele (nicht partiell isomorphe) alg. abgeschlossene Gruppen der Mächtigkeit ω_1.*

Beweis. Man überlegt leicht, daß es ein $\mathcal{K} \subset \mathcal{P}(\omega)$ gibt mit $|\mathcal{K}| = 2^{\omega}$, so daß für alle $A \neq A_1, \ldots, A_n \in \mathcal{K}$ $A \not\leq_e A_1 \vee \cdots \vee A_n$. Wenn also Q und R verschiedene Teilmengen von $\mathcal{K}$ sind, ist $\widetilde{Q/\equiv^*} \neq \widetilde{R/\equiv^*}$. Ist $|Q| = \omega_1$, so auch $|\widetilde{Q/\equiv^*}| = \omega_1$. Wir haben also so viele abgeschlossene Ideale der Mächtigkeit ω_1 wie Teilmengen von $\mathcal{K}$ der Mächtigkeit ω_1. Die Behauptung folgt also aus 3.12. □

Definition 4.3. Sei $A \subset \omega$. Wir bezeichnen mit M_A die — eindeutig bestimmte — abzählbare algebraisch abgeschlossene Gruppe mit $W^*(M_A) = \{B \mid B \leq_e A\}$. (Es ist also $W_*(M_A) = \{\widetilde{A/\equiv^*}\}$.)

Satz 4.4. 1. *$M_A \cong M_B$ gdw. $A^v \equiv_1 B^v$. $A^v/\equiv^*$ ist das größte Element von $W_*(M_A)$.*

2. *Sei F endlich erzeugt und $W(F) =^* A^v$ (Für jedes A gibt es solch ein F nach 3.5). Dann ist M_A die — dadurch eindeutig bestimmte — kleinste algebraisch abgeschlossene Gruppe, in die F einbettbar ist; d. h. o.E. ist $F \subset M_A$, und wenn $\mu : F \to M$ eine Einbettung in eine a.a. Gruppe M ist, gibt es eine Fortsetzung $\mu \subset \nu : M_A \to M$.*

3. *Wenn $W(F)/\equiv^*$ vollständig ist, gibt es eine kleinste a.a. Gruppe, die F enthält.*

4. *$M_\emptyset$ ist minimale a.a. Gruppe; d. h. jede a.a. Untergruppe von $M_\emptyset$ ist zu $M_\emptyset$ isomorph.*

5. *In jeder Gruppe M_A gibt es eine endlich erzeugte Untergruppe, in die jede e.e. Untergruppe von M_A einbettbar ist. "M_A besitzt eine universelle e.e. Untergruppe".*

Bemerkungen 4.5. Zu 1: Nicht jede abzählbare a.a. Gruppe, deren zugehöriges Ideal Hauptideal ist, ist von der Form M_A (z. B. endlich generische Gruppen, vergleiche 4.4.5 mit V, 3.4). Daß $W_*(M_A)$ ein größtes Element besitzt, folgt auch aus 5.

Zu 3: Nach I, 1.3 ist jede Gruppe in eine a.a.Gr. einbettbar. Nicht jede e.e. Gruppe ist in eine kleinste a.a.Gr. einbettbar. Denn wenn z.B. F lösbares Wortproblem hat, ist $F < M_\emptyset$. $\mathrm{Sk}(M_\emptyset)$ enthält ein G mit nichtlösbarem Wortproblem. Nach 1.8.2 gibt es eine a.a.Gr. M' in die G nicht einbettbar ist. F ist in M' einbettbar (1.8.2), es gibt aber keine a.a.Gr. M, die sowohl in $M_\emptyset$ als auch in M' einbettbar ist. Denn wegen 4 wäre $M \cong M_\emptyset$, das widerspricht $G < M_\emptyset$.

Zu 4: $M_\emptyset$ is offenbar die in I, 3.9.2 konstruierte abzählbare a.a. Gruppe M_0, deren Skelett die Klasse $\mathcal{K}_0$ aller e.e. Gruppen mit r.a. Wortproblem ist. Wir werden später noch andere minimale a.a. Gruppen kennenlernen: die endlich generischen Gruppen. Wie wir in der letzten Bemerkung gesehen haben, ist $M_\emptyset$ nicht in alle a.a. Gruppen einbettbar.

Zu 2, 3 und 4 vergleiche man I, 4.7.1: 4.7.1: Jede abzählbare a.a.Gr. ist zu einer echten Untergruppe isomorph, die eine vorgegebene e.e. Untergruppe enthält.

Zu 5: Man findet, wegen II, 2.4.2, sogar eine universelle e.e. Untergruppe, die von zwei Elementen erzeugt wird. Andererseits ist eine Untergruppe einer a.a.Gr. schon universelle e.e. Untergruppe, wenn sich jede von zwei Elementen erzeugte Untergruppe in sie einbetten läßt. Es is fraglich, ob alle abzählbaren a.a. Gruppen, die eine universelle e.e. Untergruppe besitzen, von der Form M_A sind.

Beweis von 4.4. 1. $M_A \cong M_B$ gdw. $W^*(M_A) = W^*(M_B)$ gdw. $A \equiv_e B$ gdw. (2.3.4) $A^v \equiv_1 B^v$. Nach 2.3 ist für alle C, $C \leqslant_e A$ gdw. $C \leqslant^* A^v$.

2. F ist in M_A einbettbar, weil $A^v \leqslant_e A$. Wenn F in die a.a. Gruppe M einbettbar ist, ist $A^v \in W^*(M)$ und daher $W^*(M_A) \subset W^*(M)$. Aus 3.3.2 folgt $M_A \subset M$; man kann M_A sogar über F in M einbetten, weil M ω-homogen ist.

3. folgt aus 2: Setze $A = W(F)$. Wenn $W(F)$ vollständig ist, ist nach 2.3 $W(F) \equiv^* A^v$.

Für 4 brauchen wir das folgende Lemma, das auch noch später nützlich sein wird.

Lemma 4.6 [32]. *Es gibt zwei disjunkte rekursiv aufzählbare Mengen $\tilde{A}$, $\tilde{B}$, so daß jede rekursiv aufzählbare Menge, die $\tilde{A}$ und $\tilde{B}$ trennt, vollständig ist. ($\tilde{A}$ und $\tilde{B}$ sind also insbesondere nicht rekursiv trennbar.)*

Nun zum Beweis von 4.4.4. Sei M a.a. Untergruppe von M_0. $W^*(M)$ besteht nur aus r.a. Mengen. 3.11.2 und 3.12.1 lehren, daß $\tilde{A}$ und $\tilde{B}$

von 4.6 durch ein — also r.a. — C aus $W^*(M)$ getrennt werden. C ist also vollständig und $W_*(M) = W_*(M_0)$ ist das von $C/\equiv^*$ erzeugte Ideal. $M \cong M_0$ folgt nun aus 3.3.4.

Wir beweisen 4.4.5: Wähle ein $G = \langle g_1, \ldots, g_n \rangle$ mit $W(G) \equiv^* A$. $(S_i(\vec{g}, x_1, x_2) \mid i < \omega)$ sei eine effektive Durchzählung aller endlichen Gleichungssysteme mit zwei Variablen. Wir schreiben $\mathrm{Gl}(G, \vec{g})$ in der Form $I(\boldsymbol{g}_1, \ldots, \boldsymbol{g}_n)$. Wir zerteilen die Folge der Terme $N_i(y_1, y_2)$ in eine Folge $N_1^{(i)}(y_1, y_2), \ldots, N_{n+2}^{(i)}(y_1, y_2)$, $i < \omega$, von endlichen Folgen von $n+2$ Termen. $H = \langle h_1, h_2 \rangle$ sei die durch die Gleichungen

$$\bigcup \{ I(N_1^{(i)}(\boldsymbol{h}_1, \boldsymbol{h}_2), \ldots, N_n^{(i)}(\boldsymbol{h}_1, \boldsymbol{h}_2)) \cup$$

$$\cup\, S_i(N_1^{(i)}(\boldsymbol{h}_1, \boldsymbol{h}_2), \ldots, N_n^{(i)}(\boldsymbol{h}_1, \boldsymbol{h}_2), N_{n+1}^{(i)}(\boldsymbol{h}_1, \boldsymbol{h}_2), N_{n+2}^{(i)}(\boldsymbol{h}_1, \boldsymbol{h}_2)) \mid i < \omega \}$$

präsentierte Gruppe. Offenbar ist $W(H) \leqslant_e W(G)$ und daher $H < M_A$ nach 3.3.2. Wenn $F < M_A$, ist $W(F) \leqslant_e W(G)$ und daher F einbettbar in eine endlich über G präsentierte Gruppe F' (II, 3.10). Wir können F' als von zwei Elementen erzeugt annehmen. F' sei durch $S_i(\vec{g}, \boldsymbol{f}_1, \boldsymbol{f}_2)$ über G präsentiert, $F' = \langle \vec{g}, f_1, f_2 \rangle$. Dann ist $F < F' \cong \langle N_1^{(i)}(h_1, h_2), \ldots, N_{n+2}^{(i)}(h_1, h_2) \rangle \subset H : H$ ist die gesuchte universelle e.e. Untergruppe von M_A. $\square$

IV. Elementare Aussagen

Eine Theorie besitzt genau dann einen Modellbegleiter, wenn die existentiell abgeschlossenen Modelle dieser Theorie eine elementare Klasse bilden. Der Modellbegleiter ist dann die Theorie dieser Klasse ([6]). So ist die Theorie der a.a. Körper der Modellbegleiter der Körpertheorie. Hält man die Charakteristik fest, ist diese Theorie vollständig.

Wir werden zeigen, daß die Klasse der a.a. Gruppen nicht elementar ist (die "Gruppentheorie" bestzt also keinen Modellbegleiter). Eine Klasse $\mathcal{K}$ von L-Strukturen ist genau dann elementar, wenn sie mit einer Struktur auch jede elementar äquivalente enthält und kompakt ist, d. h. wenn jede Menge von Aussagen (aus $L_{\omega,\omega}$), deren endliche Teilmengen jeweils ein Modell aus $\mathcal{K}$ haben, ein Modell aus $\mathcal{K}$ hat. Die Klasse der a.a. Gruppen erfüllt beide Bedingungen nicht. Im ersten Abschnitt geben wir zu jeder a.a. Gruppe eine elementar äquivalente Gruppe an, die nicht algebraisch abgeschlossen ist. (Also kann sogar keine Klasse von a.a.Gr. elementar sein.) Wir benützen dabei, daß sich in a.a.Gr. "$a \in \langle b \rangle$" elementar beschreiben läßt, d. h. daß es eine Formel $\varphi(x, y)$ aus $L^G_{\omega,\omega}$ gibt, so daß für alle a, b aus einer a.a.Gr. M $a \in \langle b \rangle$ gdw. $M \models \varphi(\boldsymbol{a}, \boldsymbol{b})$. Aus der Nicht-kompaktheit der Klasse der a.a.Gr., die wir im dritten Abschnitt zeigen, folgt sofort, daß es unendlich viele paarweise nicht elementar äquivalente a.a.Gr. gibt, insbesondere ist also die Theorie der a.a.Gr. nicht vollständig. Beim Beweis nützen wir aus, daß sich in a.a. Gruppen ein großes Fragment von $L^G_{\omega_1,\omega}$ elementar beschreiben läßt (2. Abschnitt). Wir geben dieses Fragment in ersten Abschnitt auf zwei Arten an: Als schwache zweite Stufe L^* mit "eingebauter Zahlentheorie" und als die Eigenschaften von Gruppenelementen, die sich durch Quantifizierung aus "rekursiven" Eigenschaften von Gruppenelementen ergeben, die "arithmetischen" Eigenschaften. Das beantwortet die Frage aus ([14]) nach einem Fragment von $L_{\omega_1,\omega}$ mit "rekursiver" Konjunktion, das in a.a. Gruppen elementar beschreibbar ist.

Diese Antwort ist in gewissem Sinn natürlich. Denn die mit L^* ausdrückbaren Eigenschaften a.a. Gruppen entsprechen gerade den durch L^2 beschriebenen elementaren Eigenschaften des zu jeder a.a. Gruppe M gehörenden ω-Modells $\omega(M) = (\omega, +, \cdot, W^*(M), \in)$ (1. Abschnitt. Das gilt eigentlich für alle ω-homogenen Gruppen). Im zweiten Abschnitt zeigen wir dann — und hier wird die algebraische Abgeschlossenheit erst wirklich gebraucht — daß sich die elementaren Eigenschaften von M und $\omega(M)$ gegenseitig bestimmen. Das entspricht dem im letzten Kapitel begonnenen Programm: die Untersuchung a.a. Gruppen wird zurückgeführt auf die Untersuchung der zugehörigen abgeschlossenen Ideale.

Nicht jede Aussage aus $L^G_{\omega_1,\omega}$ läßt sich in a.a.Gr. elementar beschreiben. Denn zwei abzählbare $L_{\omega_1,\omega}$-äquivalente Strukturen sind isomorph; es gibt aber elementar äquivalente, nichtisomorphe abzählbare a.a. Gruppen. Aber auch ein anderes Extrem kommt vor: abzählbare a.a. Gruppen, die sich eindeutig (unter allen anderen abzählbaren a.a. Gruppen) durch eine elementare Aussage charakterisieren lassen. Zum Beispiel gibt es für jede arithmetische Menge A eine elementare Aussage φ, so daß für jede abzählbare a.a. Gruppe M $M \models \varphi$ gdw. $M \cong M_A$ (3. Abschnitt). Wir erhalten so explizit abzählbar viele nicht-elementar äquivalente a.a. Gruppen. Aus der Existenz abzählbar vieler unabhängiger r.a. Turinggrade gewinnt man abzählbar viele bzgl. a.a. Gruppen unabhängige $\exists_3$-Aussagen. Also auch 2^ω viele a.a.Gr., die paarweise nicht $\exists_3$-äquivalent sind. (Das löst ein Problem aus ([14]).) Und verschärft I, 1.9: es gibt 2^ω viele nichtisomorphe abzählbare a.a. Gruppen.

Diese Beispiele aus dem dritten Abschnitt zeigen, wie modelltheoretische Probleme für a.a. Gruppen auf rekursionstheoretische Probleme zurückgeführt werden können:

Arithmetische Eigenschaften von M werden in L^2-Eigenschaften von $\omega(M)$ übersetzt, L^2-Eigenschaften von $\omega(M)$ übersetzt in elementare Aussagen über M. So läßt sich z. B. durch eine elementare Aussage ausdrücken, daß $W_*(M)$ ein Hauptideal ist. Diese Übersetzung geschieht mit den Methoden von Kapitel II, beruht also auf dem Satz von Higman, dessen Beweis so kompliziert ist, daß die Übersetzung kaum effektiv ist. Im vierten Kapitel zeigen wir, daß man $\omega(M)$ auf natürliche Weise in M interpretieren kann. Wir geben die interpretierenden Formeln explizit an, die dann eine effektive Übersetzung von L^2-Aussagen in elementare Aussagen über M gestatten.

1. Arithmetische Eigenschaften a.a. Gruppen

Lemma 1.1 ([6]). *Wenn U ein nichttrivialer Ultrafilter auf ω ist, und M eine a.a. Gruppe ist, ist M^ω/U nicht algebraisch abgeschlossen.*

Beweis. Nach I, 4.4 (siehe auch I, 4.3 oder II, 3.14) ist für Elemente $b_0, \ldots, b_n$ von M b_0 aus der von $b_1, \ldots, b_n$ erzeugten Untergruppe, gdw. $M \models E_n(\boldsymbol{b}_0, \ldots, \boldsymbol{b}_n)$. Dabei ist $E_n(x_0, \ldots)$ die Formel aus L^G (siehe [14]),

$$\forall x\,(xx_1 \doteq x_1x \wedge xx_2 \doteq x_2x \wedge \cdots \wedge xx_n \doteq x_nx \rightarrow xx_0 = x_0x).$$

(Da wir keine anderen Sprachen betrachten werden, schreiben wir in Folgenden für L^G — die Sprache der Gruppentheorie — einfach L.) M^ω/U ist ω_1-saturiert, alle unendlichen definierbaren Teilmengen sind also überabzählbar. Als Obergruppe einer algebraisch abgeschlossenen Gruppe besitzt auch M^ω/U ein Element b_1 von unendlicher Ordnung. Die von b_1 erzeugte Gruppe ist nicht definierbar, also auch nicht durch $E_1(x_0, \boldsymbol{b}_1)$. □

Die Klasse der algebraisch abgeschlossenen Gruppen ist also nicht elementar. Wir geben später noch einen anderen Beweis dafür an, indem wir zeigen, daß die Klasse der a.a.Gr. sogar nicht kompakt ist (3.5).

Wir haben im dritten Kapitel gesehen, daß das Ideal $W_*(M)$ die algebraisch abgeschlossenen Gruppe M bis auf $L_{\infty,\omega}$-Äquivalenz eindeutig bestimmt. Wir wollen nun zeigen, daß entsprechend der "elementare Typ" von $W_*(M)$ den elementaren Typ von M bestimmt. In welcher Sprache beschreiben wir $W_*(M)$? Es genügt — vermutlich — nicht die elementaren Eigenschaften des Halbverbandes $(W_*(M), \leqslant)$ zu betrachten. Wir ordnen daher jeder Teilmenge I von

V das ω-Modell $(\omega, +, \cdot, \bigcup I, \in)$ — für das wir kurz $(\omega, \bigcup I)$ schreiben — zu; auf diese Weise gehört also zu $W_*(M)$ das ω-Modell $\omega(M) =: (\omega, W^*(M))$. Die elementare Sprache für diese ω-Modelle ist L^2, die elementaren Eigenschafte von $W_*(M)$ sind also die Eigenschaften, die sich mit L^2-Aussagen über $\omega(M)$ beschreiben lassen.

Ein abgeschlossenes Ideal zu sein ist zum Beispiel eine elementare Eigenschaft von $W_*(M)$. Denn $\emptyset \neq \mathcal{K} \subset \mathcal{P}(\omega)$ ist genau dann Vereinigung eines abgeschlossenen Ideals, wenn

$$(\omega, \mathcal{K}) \models \forall X, Y \forall v_1 \exists Z_1, Z_2[Z_1 = X \vee Y \wedge (\bar{\mathcal{H}}_{v_1}[X] \neq \emptyset \rightarrow Z_2 \in \bar{\mathcal{H}}_{v_1}[X]].$$

Zur Rechtfertigung dieser Schreibweise erinnern wir daran, daß "$A = B \vee C$", "$\bar{\mathcal{H}}_n[A] \neq \emptyset$", "$C \in \bar{\mathcal{H}}_n[A]$" arithmetische Eigenschaften von A, B, C, n sind, die somit in L^2 ausdrückbar sind. Wir nennen diese $(\omega, \mathcal{K})$ algebraisch abgeschlossen. Mit L^2 können wir die elementaren Eigenschaften der partiellen Ordnung $(I, \leqslant)$ beschreiben. Denn "$A \leqslant^* B$" ist eine arithmetische (Σ^0_3) Relation. Zum Beispiel ist das Ideal I ein Hauptideal, gdw. die L_2-Aussage *max*: $\exists X \forall Y\ Y \leqslant^* X$ in $(\omega, \bigcup I)$ gilt.

Satz 1.2. *Zu jeder $L_{\omega,\omega}$ Formel $\rho(x_0, \ldots, x_n)$ kann mann eine L^2-Formel $\bar{\rho}(X)$ angeben, sodaß für alle $a_0, \ldots, a_n$ aus einer a.a. Gruppe M $M \models \rho(\boldsymbol{a}_0, \ldots)$ gdw. $\omega(M) \models \bar{\rho}(W(\langle a_0, \ldots a_n \rangle'))$.*

Folgerungen 1.3. *Für alle algebraisch abgeschlossenen N, M*

1. *Wenn $\omega(N) \equiv \omega(M)$, ist $N \equiv M$.*
2. *Aus $\omega(N) < \omega(M)$ und $N \subset M$ folgt $N < M$.*
3. *Wenn N elementar in M eingebettet werden kann, ist jede Einbettung von N in M elementar.*

(3 gilt für alle ω-homogenen Strukturen.)

Beweis. Genau genommen hängt $\bar{\rho}$ noch von der Wahl der $x_0, \ldots$ ab. (Die x_i müssen nicht alle frei in ρ vorkommen.) Wir verzichten auf diese Genauigkeit, weil, wenn $\rho(x_0, \ldots, x_n) = \rho(x_0, \ldots, x_n, x_{n+1}, \ldots, x_k)$ und

(a) $M \models \rho(\boldsymbol{a}_0, \ldots, \boldsymbol{a}_n)$ gdw. $\omega(M) \models \rho_1(W(\langle a_0, \ldots a_n \rangle'))$, ist $M \models \rho(\boldsymbol{a}_0, \ldots \boldsymbol{a}_k)$ gdw. $\omega(M) \models \rho_1(W(\langle a_0, \ldots a_k \rangle') \downarrow (n+1))$. Wenn andererseits

(b) $M \models \rho(\boldsymbol{a}_0, \ldots, \boldsymbol{a}_k)$ gdw. $\omega(M) \models \rho_2(W(\langle a_0, \ldots a_k \rangle'))$, gilt (denn man setzt einfach alle $a_{n+1}, \ldots, a_k$ gleich e) $M \models \rho(\boldsymbol{a}_0, \ldots, \boldsymbol{a}_n)$ gdw. $\omega(M) \models \rho_2(W(\langle a_0, \ldots, a_n \rangle'))$.

Wir konstruieren nun $\bar{\rho}$ durch Rekursion über den Aufbau von ρ.

Wenn $\rho(x_0, \ldots, x_n)$ atomar ist, also o.E. von der Form $V_i(x_0, \ldots, x_n) \doteq \boldsymbol{e}$, ist für alle $a_0, \ldots, a_n \in M$ $M \models \rho(\boldsymbol{a}_0, \ldots)$ *gdw.* $i \in W(\langle a_0, \ldots, a_n \rangle')$. Wir nehmen daher für $\bar{\rho}(X)$ die L^2-Formel $i \in X$.

Für $\overline{\rho_1 \wedge \rho_2}$ wählen wir $\bar{\rho}_1 \wedge \bar{\rho}_2$, für $\overline{\neg \rho}$ $\neg \bar{\rho}$. Weiter ist (wir brauchen eigentlich nur den Fall $k = n$) $M \models \exists x_n, \ldots x_k\ \rho(\boldsymbol{a}_0, \ldots, \boldsymbol{a}_{n-1}, x_n, \ldots, x_k)$ gdw. ex. $a_n, \ldots a_k \in M$ $\omega(M) \models \bar{\rho}(W(\langle a_0, \ldots, a_k \rangle'))$ gdw. es eine von $a_0, \ldots, a_k$ erzeugte Obergruppe F von $\langle a_0, \ldots a_{n-1} \rangle$ gibt mit $F \in \mathrm{Sk}(M)$ und $\omega(M) \models \bar{\rho}(W(\langle a_0, \ldots, a_k \rangle'))$, gdw. ex. $W \in W^*(M)$, $W \downarrow n = W(\langle a_0, \ldots, a_{n-1} \rangle)$, $W \in \mathscr{W}_k$ mit $\omega(M) \models \bar{\rho}(\boldsymbol{W})$.

Wir nehmen also für $\exists x_n \cdots x_k \rho$ die L^2-Formel $\exists Y(Y \in \mathscr{W}_k \wedge Y \downarrow n = X \wedge \bar{\rho}(Y))$ — man beachte: "$A \in \mathscr{W}_k$" und "$A \downarrow n = B$" sind arithmetische Eigenschaften (Π^0_1). □

Bemerkung 1.4. Wir haben beim Beweis von 1.2 nicht wirklich die algebraische Abgeschlossenheit von M gebraucht, sondern lediglich die ω-Homogenität. Auch auf die genaue Definition von $W^*(M)$ kommt es nicht an; weil III, 1.4 und III, 3.2 nicht mehr gelten, ist für beliebige ω-homogene Gruppen $W^*(M)$ ohnehin nutzlos. Wir haben aber für alle $\rho(x_0, \ldots), a_0, \ldots \in M$, M ω-homogen, $\mathscr{S} \subset \mathscr{P}(\omega)$ mit $\mathrm{Sk}(M) = \{F \in \mathscr{G} \mid W(F) \in \mathscr{S}\}$ (das gilt z. B. für $\mathscr{S} = W^*(M)$ oder $\mathscr{S} = \{W(F) \mid F \in \mathrm{Sk}(M)\}$), daß $M \models \rho(\boldsymbol{a}_0, \ldots, \boldsymbol{a}_n)$ gdw. $(\omega, \mathscr{S}) \models \bar{\rho}(W(\langle a_0, \ldots \rangle))$.

Die Sprache L^*

Der Satz 1.2 gilt nicht nur für Formeln ρ aus $L_{\omega,\omega}$. Wir geben eine stärkere Sprache an, die sich in a.a. Gruppen immer noch in L_2 Formeln übersetzen läßt. Wir werden sehen, daß sich auch umgekehrt L^2 in L^* ausdrücken läßt. L^* ist cinc Art "schwacher zweiter Stufe". Es gibt drei Sorten von Variablen: Zahlvariable $v_0, v_1, \ldots, w_0, w_1, \ldots$; Variable für Gruppenelemente $x_0, x_1, \ldots, y_0, z_0, \ldots$ und Variable $\sigma, \tau, \ldots$ für endliche Folgen von Gruppenelementen.

(Wir werden hier nur den Fall $L = L^G$ behandeln. Viele der folgenden Ergebnisse hängen von dieser besonderen Wahl von L nicht ab.) Zahlterme werden mit $+$ und $\cdot$ aus den Zahlvariablen, den Konstanten **0**, **1** fur die Zahlen 0, 1 und $l(\delta), l(\tau), \ldots$ gebildet. ($l(\sigma)$ gibt die Länge der Folge σ an.) Individuenterme (für Gruppenelemente) setzen sich mit $\cdot$ und $^{-1}$ aus den Variablen $x_0, \ldots z_0, \ldots$, der Konstanten $\boldsymbol{e}$ und $\sigma(t)$ für eine Folgenvariable σ und einen Zahlterm t zusammen ($\sigma(n)$ ist das $n+1$-te Folgenglied, wenn $n < l(\sigma)$. Sonst $= e$.) Atomare Formeln sind $t_1 \doteq t_2$ und $g_1 \doteq g_2$ für Zahlterme t_i und Individuenterme g_i. Die Formeln von L^* bauen sich aus den atomaren Formeln mit $\wedge$, $\neg$ und drei Arten von Quantoren auf: $\exists v$, $\exists x$ und $\exists \sigma$. Es ist klar wie die Formeln von L in einer Gruppe interpretiert werden sollen. Man kann die Aussagen von L^* auch als elementare Aussagen über ein dreisortiges System $((\omega; +, \cdot), (M; \cdot, ^{-1}, e), {}^{\omega}M)$ (M eine Gruppe oder allgemeiner eine L-Struktur) mit Funktionen l: ${}^{\omega}M \to \omega$ (Länge der Folge) und $\lambda\sigma\lambda v \sigma(v): {}^{\omega}M \times \omega \to M$ (v-tes Folgenglied) auffassen.

Mit L^* läßt sich "$a \in \langle b \rangle$" in jeder Gruppe ausdrücken: durch

$$\exists \sigma (\sigma(\mathbf{0}) \doteq \boldsymbol{b} \wedge \forall v_0(\sigma(v_0 + \mathbf{1}) \doteq \sigma(v_0) \cdot \boldsymbol{b} \vee \sigma(v_0 + 1) \doteq \boldsymbol{e}) \wedge$$
$$\wedge \exists v_1 (\sigma(v_1) \doteq \boldsymbol{a} \vee \sigma(v_1) \doteq \boldsymbol{a}^{-1})).$$

Wir können L^* als Teilsprache von $L_{\omega_1,\omega}$ ansehen: Jede L^*-Formel $\varphi(x_0, \ldots, x_n)$ ist gleichbedeutend mit einer Formel $\tilde{\varphi}(x_0, \ldots)$ aus $L_{\omega_1,\omega}$. Man gewinnt $\tilde{\varphi}$ aus φ, indem man beim Aufbau von φ die Quantoren $\exists v \rho(v)$ durch $\bigvee \{\rho(n) \mid n \in \omega\}$ und $\exists \sigma \rho(\sigma)$ durch $\bigvee \{\exists x_0, \ldots, x_n \rho(x_0 x_1 \cdots x_n) \mid n \in \omega\}$ ersetzt. Zwei partiell isomorphe Gruppen erfüllen also dieselben Aussagen von L^*.

Mit einem ähnlichen Beweis wie bei 1.2 zeigt man

Satz 1.5. *Zu jeder L^*-Formel $\rho(v_0, \ldots, v_k; x_0, \ldots, x_n; \sigma_0, \ldots \sigma_m)$ kann man eine L^2-Formel $\bar{\rho}(v_0, \ldots, v_k, w_0, \ldots, w_m; X)$ angeben, so daß für alle $n_0, \ldots, n_k \in \omega$ und $a_0, \ldots, a_n$ und $\vec{b}_0, \ldots, \vec{b}_m$ aus einer a.a. Gruppe M $M \models \rho(\boldsymbol{n}_0, \ldots, \boldsymbol{n}_k; \boldsymbol{a}_0, \ldots, \boldsymbol{a}_n; \vec{\boldsymbol{b}}_0, \ldots, \vec{\boldsymbol{b}}_m)$ gdw.*

$$\omega(M) \models \bar{\rho}(n_0, \ldots, n_k, l(\vec{b}_0), \ldots l(\vec{b}_m); W(\langle a_0, \ldots, a_n, \vec{b}_0, \ldots, \vec{b}_m \rangle)).$$

Folgerung. *Zu jeder L^*-Aussage ρ kann man eine L^2-Aussage $\bar{\rho}$ angeben, sodaß für jede a.a.Gr. M $M \models \rho$ gdw. $\omega(M) \models \bar{\rho}$.*

Wie in 1.4 gilt 1.5 in entsprechender Formulierung in allen ω-homogenen Gruppen.

Wir wollen zeigen, daß L^* und L^2 für a.a. Gruppen dieselbe Ausdruckskraft haben. Dazu untersuchen wir zunächst die Ausdruckskraft von L^*.

Eine Eigenschaft P einer Folge $n_0, \ldots, a_0, \ldots, \vec{b}_0, \ldots$ von natürlichen Zahlen, Elementen einer Gruppen und endlichen Folgen von Gruppen-Elementen nennen wir *rekursiv*, wenn man durch einen Algorithmus aus einer gegeben Folge $n_0, \ldots, a_0, \ldots, \vec{b}_0, \ldots$ "ausrechnen" kann ob sie die Eigenschaft P in einer Gruppe M hat oder nicht. Der Algorithmus operiert mit der Folge der Gruppenelemente, indem er z. B. aus zwei Gruppenelementen durch Multiplikation ein drittes bildet oder indem er prüft ob ein bei der "Rechnung" produziertes Gruppenelement $= e$ ist, oder nicht. Folgende Präzisierung bietet die Rekursionstheorie an:

$P(v_0, \ldots, x_0, \ldots, \sigma_0, \ldots)$ ist rekursiv, wenn es eine rekursive Relation $R \subset \omega^f \times \mathcal{P}(\omega)$ gibt, sodaß für alle $n_0, \ldots \in \omega$, $a_0, \ldots, \vec{b}_0, \ldots$ aus einer Gruppe M P in M auf $n_0, \ldots, a_0, \ldots, \vec{b}_0, \ldots$ genau dann zutrifft, wenn $R(n_0, \ldots, l(\vec{b}_0), \ldots; W(\langle a_0, \ldots, \vec{b}_0, \ldots \rangle))$. Aus den rekursiven Eigenschaften erhalten wir die *arithmetischen* Eigenschaften durch Quantifzierneung. Σ_0^g und Π_0^g Eigenschaften sind die rekursiven Eigenschaften. Wenn $P(v, \ldots)$ ein Π_n^g (Σ_n^g) Eigenschaft ist, ist "nicht P" eine Σ_n^g (Π_n^g) Eigenschaft, und "ex. v_0 P", "ex. x P" und "ex. σ P" Σ_{n+1}^g. Man sieht leicht, daß man jede Σ_n^g Eigenschaft $P(v_0, \ldots x_0, \ldots \sigma_0, \ldots)$ in der Form $\exists \tau_1, w_1 \forall \tau_2, w_2 \exists \tau_3, w_3 \cdots Q_n \tau_n$ $R(v_0, \ldots w_1, \ldots 1(\sigma_0), \ldots 1(\tau_1), \ldots; W(\langle x_0, \ldots \sigma_0, \ldots \tau_1, \ldots \rangle))$ schreiben kann, wobei R aus Π_1^0 bzw. Σ_1^0 (je nachdem ob Q_n ein Allquantor oder ein Existenzquantor ist) ist. Ein Σ_1^0 bzw. Π_1^0-Index von R ist ein Σ_n^g-Index von P. Der nächste Satz stellt einige Eigenschaften der eben definierten Hierarchie zusammen, deren Beweise man leicht aus den Beweisen der entsprechenden Sätze der Rekursionstheorie gewinnt.

Satz 1.6. 1. *Wenn P_1 und P_2 Σ_n^g sind, sind $P_1 \wedge P_2$ und $P_1 \vee P_2$ Σ_n^g.*

2. *Wenn P Σ_n^g, so ist P auch Σ_{n+1}^g und Π_{n+1}^g.*

3. *Wenn P Σ_n^g, ist $(\forall v_0 < v_1 P)$ Σ_n^g.*

4. *$V_i(\sigma) \doteq \boldsymbol{e}$, $l(\sigma) \doteq v_0$ sind rekursiv.*

5. *Wenn $R(v_0, \ldots w_0, \ldots; X)$ eine Σ_n^0-Relation ist, ist $R(v_0, \ldots 1(\sigma_0), \ldots; W(\langle \sigma_0, \ldots \rangle))$ eine Σ_n^g Eigenschaft.*

6. *Wenn $P(v_0)$ Σ_n^g und $f: \omega \to \omega$ rekursiv, ist auch $P(f(v_0))$ Σ_n^g.*

7. *Wenn $P(x_0)$ Σ_n^g, ist $P(V_{v_0}(\sigma))$ auch Σ_n^g.*

8. *Für jedes n gibt es eine universelle Σ_n^g Eigenschaft Q: die Σ_n^g-Eigenschaft mit dem Index i trifft auf $v_0, \ldots x_0, \ldots \sigma_0, \ldots$ genau dann zu, wenn Q auf $i, v_0, \ldots x_0, \ldots \sigma_0 \cdots$ zutrifft.*

Folgerung aus 8. *Die Konjunktion einer "arithmetischen Familie" von Σ_n^g Eigenschaften ist arithmetisch. (Dabei wird eine arithmetische Familie durch eine arithmetische Menge von Σ_n^g-Indizes beschrieben.)*

Beispiel 1. "Algebraisch abgeschlossen" ist Π_2^g. Zum Beweis definieren wir $\mathrm{Gl}(A) := \{V_i(x_0, \ldots) \doteq \boldsymbol{e} \mid i \in A\}$. "$\mathrm{Gl}(A) \cup T$ widerspruchsfrei" ist eine Π_1^0-Eigenschaft von A, T. M ist genau dann algebraisch abgeschlossen, wenn es die folgende arithmetische Eigenschaft hat:

$$\forall \sigma \forall v (\text{"Diag}(\langle \sigma \rangle') \cup \mathrm{Gl}(D_v) \cup T^G \text{ widerspruchsfrei"} \to$$

$$\to \exists \tau D_v \subset W(\langle \sigma, \tau \rangle'))$$

Mit Hilfe von 1.6 rechnet man leicht nach, daß diese Eigenschaft Π_2^g ist.

Beispiel 2. Die Eigenschaft MAX: "... besitzt eine universelle e.e. Untergruppe" (siehe III, 4.4.5) ist Σ_4^g. MAX läßt sich durch $\exists\sigma_0\forall\sigma_1\exists\sigma_2\,(\sigma_2\in\langle\sigma_0\rangle\wedge\langle\sigma_2\rangle'\cong\langle\sigma_1\rangle')$ ausdrücken. Daraus folgt die Behauptung, weil, wie man leicht überlegt, $\sigma\in\langle\tau\rangle$ (d. h. es gibt $i_0, i_1,\dots$ sodaß $V_{i_0}(\tau)=\sigma(0)$, $V_{i_1}(\tau)=\sigma(1),\dots$) Σ_1^g, und $\langle\sigma\rangle'\cong\langle\tau\rangle'$ (d. h. $W(\langle\sigma\rangle)=W(\langle\tau\rangle))$ Π_1^g ist.

Satz 1.7. *Die Formeln von L^* beschreiben gerade die arithmetischen Eigenschaften.*

Folgerung. *Zwei partiell isomorphe Gruppen haber dieselben arithmetischen Eigenschaften. Aus Beispiel* 1 *folgt also noch einmal die Folgerung* I, 3.8.1.

Beweis. Zunächst ist klar, daß die Formeln von L^* arithmetische Eigenschaften beschreiben, denn offenbar beschreiben die atomaren Formeln von L^* rekursive Eigenschaften und durch Anwenden von $\exists v$, $\exists x$, $\exists\sigma$, $\wedge$, $\neg$ gehen arithmetische Eigenschaften in arithmetische Eigenschaften über.

Da die arithmetischen Eigenschaften aus Σ_1^g Eigenschaften der Form $R(v_0,\dots 1(\sigma_0),\dots;\ W(\langle x_0,\dots\sigma_0\cdots\rangle))$ — R Σ_1^0 — durch Anwenden von $\exists v$, $\exists x$, $\exists\sigma$, $\neg$ hervorgehen, brauchen wir nur zu zeigen, daß die Σ_1^g-Eigenschaften der angegebenen Form sich durch L^*-Formeln ausdrücken lassen. Eine Σ_1^0-Relation $R(v,X)$ ist aber von der Gestalt $\exists u,w\,(S(v,u,w)\wedge D_u\subset X\wedge D_w\subset\omega\backslash X)$ für eine rekursive Relation S. Da sich rein zahlentheoretische Formeln schon in L^* befinden, müssen wir noch zeigen, daß $D_u\subset W(\langle\sigma\rangle)$ und $D_w\subset\omega\setminus W(\langle\sigma\rangle)$ in L^* beschreibbar sind. Diese Aussagen sind aber äquivalent zu $\forall v\in D_u\ V_v(\sigma)\doteq \boldsymbol{e}$ und $\forall v\in D_w\ \neg V_v(\sigma)\doteq\boldsymbol{e}$. Also genügt es zu zeigen, daß $V_v(\sigma)\doteq\boldsymbol{e}$ zu einer L^*-Formel äquivalent ist.

$V_s(x_0\cdots)$ ist eine Folge von Variablen x_n und x_n^{-1}, die wir als eine Folge von $2n$ und $2n+1$ beschreiben. s ist die Gödelnummer dieser Folge. Wenn $a_0, a_1,\dots$ eine Folge von Gruppenelementen ist, ist also $V_s(a_0,\dots)=e$ gdw. es eine Folge $b_0, b_1,\dots$ von Gruppenelementen gibt (die "Zwischenergebnisse bei der Berechnung" von V_s) sodaß $b_0=e$ und $b_{l(s)}=\boldsymbol{e}$ und für alle $j<l(s)$

$$b_{j+1}=\begin{cases} b_j\cdot a_n, & \text{wenn } s(j)=2n\\ b_j\cdot a_n^{-1}, & \text{wenn } s(j)=2n+1.\end{cases}$$

Diese Darstellung zeigt, daß $V_s(a_0,\dots)=e$ in L^* ausdrückbar ist. □

Wir können nun 1.5 in 2 des nächsten Satzes umkehren. 1 ist eine Verschärfung von 1.5.

Satz 1.8. 1. *Zu jeder* Σ^g_n *Eigenschaft* $P(v_0, \dots x_0, \dots \sigma_0 \cdots)$ *läßt sich eine* $\tilde{\Sigma}^1_{n+1}$*-Formel* $\bar{P}(v_0, \dots w_0, \dots, X)$ *von* L^2 *angeben, so daß für alle* $n_0, \dots \in \omega$ *und* $a_0, .. \vec{b}_0, \dots$ *aus einer a.a. Gruppe M*

(*) *P genau dann auf* $n_0, \dots a_0, \dots \vec{b}_0, \dots$ *zutrifft, wenn* $\omega(M) \models \bar{P}(n_0, \dots l(b_0), \dots W(\langle a_0, \dots \vec{b}_0, \dots \rangle))$.

2. *Zu jeder* $\tilde{\Sigma}^1_n$*-Formel* $S(v_0, \dots X_0, \dots)$ *aus* L^2 *gibt es eine* Σ^g_n*-Eigenschaft* $\check{S}(v_0, \dots, \sigma_0, \dots)$, *sodaß für alle* $n_0, \dots$ *und* $\vec{b}_0, \dots$ *aus einer a.a. Gruppe M*

(**) $\check{S}$ *genau dann auf* $n_0, \dots \vec{b}_0, \dots$ *zutrifft, wenn* $\omega(M) \models S(n_0, \dots W(\langle \vec{b}_0 \rangle), \dots)$.

Bemerkung 1.9. 1. 1.8.1 gilt auch für ω-homogene M und für — statt $\omega(M)$ — $(\omega, \mathcal{S})$ für irgendein $\mathcal{S} \subset \mathcal{P}(\omega)$ mit $\mathrm{Sk}(M) = \{F \mid W(F) \in \mathcal{S}\}$. 1.8.2 gilt für beliebige M, für $\omega(M)$ braucht man nur ein $(\omega, \mathcal{S})$ mit — z. B. — $\mathcal{S} = \{f^{-1}(W(F)) \mid F \in \mathrm{Sk}(M)\}$, f rek.

2. Eine Σ^g_n Eigenschaft nennen wir eine $\tilde{\Sigma}^g_n$ Eigenschaft, wenn sie in der Form $\exists \tau_1, w_1, \forall \tau_2, w_2, \exists \tau_3, w_3 \cdots Q_{n-1}\tau_{n-1}, w_{n-1}$

$$R(v_0, \dots w_1 \cdots l(\sigma_0), \dots l(\tau_1), \dots; W(\langle x_0, \dots \sigma_0, \dots \tau_1, \dots \rangle))$$

darstellbar ist, wobei R eine Π^0_1 bzw. Σ^0_1 Relation ist, je nachdem, ob Q_{n-1} ein Existenz- bzw. Allquantor ist. MAX ist ist z. B. eine $\tilde{\Sigma}^g_4$-Eigenschaft. Der Beweis von 1.8.1 zeigt daß es zu jeder $\tilde{\Sigma}^g_n$ Eigenschaft P eine $\tilde{\Sigma}^1_n$-Formel $\bar{P}$ aus L^2 gibt, für die (*) gilt.

Beweis. 1. Induktion über n: Wenn P Σ^g_0 Eigenschaft ist, existiert $\bar{P}$ mit (*) nach Definition der rekursiven Eigenschaften. Die Σ^g_{n+1} Eigenschaft P läßt sich in der Form $\exists \tau, w$ $\neg S(v_0, \dots w, x_0, \dots x_n, \sigma_0, \dots \sigma_k, \tau)$ für ein Σ^g_n S schreiben. Zu S gehört eine $\tilde{\Sigma}^1_{n+1}$ Formel $\bar{S}$ aus L^2 mit (*). Wie im Beweis von 1.2 sieht man, daß die Formel

$$\begin{aligned} \bar{p}(v_0, \dots w_0, \dots, X) &= \\ &= \exists Y \exists w \exists i, j (Y \in \mathcal{W}_j \wedge \\ &\quad X = Y \downarrow (w_0 + \cdots w_k + n + 1) \wedge \\ &\quad \neg \bar{S}(v_0, \dots w, w_0, \dots w_k, i, Y) \wedge \\ &\quad j = w_0 + \cdots w_k + n + i) \end{aligned}$$

die gewünschten Eigenschaften hat.

2. Wenn f die rekursive Funktion im Beweis von III, 3.4 ist, ist

$W^*(M) = \{f^{-1}(W(F)) \mid F \in \mathrm{Sk}(M)\}$ für alle a.a. Gruppen M. (Das folgt aus III, 1.4 und III, 3.4.) Wir beweisen 2 durch Induktion über n. Wenn S rekursiv ist, beschreibt $S(v_0, \dots W(\langle\sigma_0\rangle), \dots)$ eine rekursive Eigenschaft. Eine $\tilde{\Sigma}^1_{n+1}$ Formel $S(v_0, \dots X_0, \dots)$ Formel aus L^2 läßt sich in der Form $\exists Y_0, \dots \exists w \neg P(v_0, \dots w, X_0, \dots Y_0 \cdots)$ schreiben, P $\tilde{\Sigma}^1_n$. Dann ist auch $P'(v_0, \dots w, X_0, \dots Y_0, \dots) = P(v_0, \dots w, X_0, \dots f^{-1}(Y_0), \dots)$ $\tilde{\Sigma}^1_n$. Zu P' gehöre die Σ^g_n Eigenschaft $\check{P}'$, so daß (**) für P', $\check{P}'$ gilt. Sei M a.a. $n_0, \dots \in \omega$ und $\vec{b}_0, \dots$ aus M. Dann ist
$\omega(M) \models S(n_0, \dots W(\langle\vec{b}_0\rangle), \dots)$ gdw. ex. m und $c_0, \dots \in M$ mit
$\omega(M) \models \neg P(n_0, \dots m, W(\langle b_0\rangle), \dots f^{-1}(W(\langle c_0\rangle), \dots)$ gdw. die Σ^g_{n+1} Eigenschaft $\exists w \exists \tau_0, \dots \neg \check{P}'(v_0, \dots, w, \sigma_0, \dots \tau_0, \dots)$ auf $n_0, \dots \vec{b}_0, \dots$ zutrifft. □

2. Elementare Aussagen

Wir zeigen, daß sich in algebr. abg. Gruppen die L^2-Eigenschaften von $\omega(M)$ durch elementare Aussagen über M ausdrücken lassen. Im Hinblick auf den letzten Satz sind also alle arithmetischen Eigenschaften von M elementar ausdrückbar.

Wir betrachten spezielle $\tilde{\Sigma}^1_n$ formeln von L^2: Wenn A r.a. ist, $n \geq 2$ ist $S^A_n(X)$ die Formel

$$\exists Y_1 \forall Y_2 \cdots Q_{n-2} Y_{n-2} (\neg) \exists w \in A(X, Y_1, \dots, Y_{n-2}) \in \bar{\mathscr{H}}^{n-1}_w.$$

Wenn n ungerade ist, (ist Q_{n-2} ein Ex.-quantor) steht das Negationszeichen; wenn n gerade ist, steht kein Negationszeichen. Wenn A endlich ist, ist $S^A_1(X)$ die Π^0_1-Formel von L^2

$$X \in \bigcup \{\bar{\mathscr{H}}_i \mid i \in A\}.$$

Satz 2.1. 1. *Für jede $\exists_n$-Formel $\rho(x_0, \dots x_m)$ (aus $L_{\omega,\omega}$, $n \geq 1$) gibt es ein r.a. bzw. endliches $A \subset \omega$, so daß für alle $a_0, \dots a_m$ aus einer a.a. Gruppe M*

(*) $\quad M \models \rho(\boldsymbol{a}_0, \dots \boldsymbol{a}_m)$ *gdw.* $\omega(M) \models S^A_n(W(\langle a_0, \dots a_m\rangle))$.

2. *Für alle $m \in \omega$, $n \geq 1$ und r.a. bzw. endliche A gibt es eine $\exists_n$ Formel $\rho(x_0, \dots x_m)$ mit (*).*

Folgerung. *Zu jeder $\exists_n$-Aussage ρ gibt es ein r.a. bzw. endliches $A \subset \omega$ mit $M \models \rho$ gdw. $\omega(M) \models S^A_n(\omega)$ (*) für jede a.a. Gruppe M. Umgekehrt gibt es für alle $n \geq 1$, r.a. bzw. endliche $A \subset \omega$ eine $\exists_n$-Aussage ρ mit (*).*

Beweis. 1. $n = 1$: Die Existenzformel $\rho(x_0, \dots x_m)$ hat die Gestalt

$$\exists y_0, \dots y_q (\wedge S_0(x_0, \dots y_0, \dots) \vee \wedge S_1(x_0, \dots) \vee \cdots \vee \wedge S_k(x_0, \dots))$$

wobei die S_i endliche Systeme von Gleichungen und Ungleichungen sind. Für $a_0, \ldots a_n \in M$ ist $M \models \varphi(\boldsymbol{a}_0, \ldots)$ gdw. eines der Gleichungssysteme $S_i(\boldsymbol{a}_0, \ldots y_0 \cdots)$ in M — und, wenn M a.a., über M — lösbar ist. Für jedes i gibt es eine r.a. Menge von Implikationen $I_i(c_0, \ldots c_m)$, sodaß — für alle $a_0, \ldots, a_m$ aus einer Gruppe M — $S_i(\boldsymbol{a}_0, \ldots y_0, \ldots)$ genau dann über M lösbar ist, wennn $M \models I_i(\boldsymbol{a}_0, \ldots)$. (Denn in II, 1.6 ist die Menge I von Implikationen r.a., wie in II, 2.1.) $M \models I_i(\boldsymbol{a}_0, \ldots)$ kann man auch mit $W(\langle a_0, \ldots \rangle) \in \mathcal{H}_i$ für eine r.a. Hornklasse $\mathcal{H}_i = \bar{\mathcal{H}}_{n_i}$ ausdrücken. Wir setzen also $A := \{n_0, \ldots, n_k\}$.

$n = 2$: Die $\exists_2$-Formel hat die Gestalt $\exists y_0, \ldots y_q \neg \varphi(x_0, \ldots y_0 \cdots)$ für eine Existenzformel φ. Wir wenden den eben bewiesenen Fall an und bekommen r.a. Hornklassen $\bar{\mathcal{H}}_{n_0}, \ldots \bar{\mathcal{H}}_{n_k}$, so daß für alle $a_0, \ldots b_0, \ldots$ aus einer a.a.Gr. M

$$M \models \varphi(\boldsymbol{a}_0, \ldots \boldsymbol{b}_0, \ldots) \quad \text{gdw.} \quad W(\langle a_0, \ldots b_0, \ldots \rangle) \in \bar{\mathcal{H}}_{n_0} \cup \cdots \cup \bar{\mathcal{H}}_{n_k}.$$

$M \models \rho(\boldsymbol{a}_0, \ldots)$ gdw. $\omega(M) \models \exists Y(Y \in \mathcal{W}_{m+q+1} \wedge Y \downarrow m+1 = W(\langle a_0, \ldots \rangle) \wedge Y \notin \bar{\mathcal{H}}_{n_0} \cup \cdots \cup \bar{\mathcal{H}}_{n_k})$ folgt daraus wie im Beweis von Satz 1.2. Für alle $u_0, \ldots u_k, w_0, \ldots w_k \in \omega$ ist $\{Y \mid D_{u_0} \cup \cdots \cup D_{u_k} \subset Y \wedge (D^1_{w_0} \cup \cdots \cup D^1_{w_k}) \cap Y = \emptyset\}$ eine r.a. Hornklasse $\mathcal{H}$, deren Index wir mit einer rekursiven Funktion g aus $u_0, \ldots w_k$ berechnen: $\mathcal{H} = \bar{\mathcal{H}}_{g(u_0, \ldots w_k)}$. W ist genau dann nicht in $\bar{\mathcal{H}}_{n_0} \cup \cdots \cup \bar{\mathcal{H}}_{n_k}$, wenn es $\langle u_0, w_0 \rangle \in W_{n_0}, \ldots, \langle u_k, w_k \rangle \in W_{n_k}$ gibt mit $W \in \bar{\mathcal{H}}_{g(u, \ldots w_k)}$. B sei die Menge aller $g(u_0, \ldots w_k)$ für $\langle u_0, w_0 \rangle \in W_{n_0}, \ldots, \langle u_k, w_k \rangle \in W_{n_k}$. B ist r.a. Für jedes $w \in \omega$ ist $\{(X, Y) \mid Y \in \mathcal{W}_{m+q+1} \wedge Y \downarrow m+1 = X \wedge Y \in \bar{\mathcal{H}}_w\} = \bar{\mathcal{H}}^2_{h(w)}$ eine r.a. Hornklasse, deren Index rekursiv von w abhängt. Es ist $M \models \rho(\boldsymbol{a}_0, \ldots)$ gdw. $\omega(M) \models \exists w \in B(\exists Y \in \bar{\mathcal{H}}_{h(w)}[W(\langle a_0, \ldots \rangle)])$. Weil $\omega(M)$ abgeschlossen ist, gibt es genau dann ein $W \in W^*(M)$ $W \in \bar{\mathcal{H}}_{h(w)}[W(\langle a_0, \ldots \rangle)]$, wenn $\bar{\mathcal{H}}_{h(w)}[W(\langle a_0, \ldots \rangle)] \neq 0$. Nach III, 3.9 ist die Menge aller W' mit $\bar{\mathcal{H}}_{h(w)}[W'] \neq 0$ eine r.a. Hornklasse $\bar{\mathcal{H}}_{h'(w)}$. Der Beweis von III, 3.9 zeigt, daß wir h' rekursive annehmen können. Es ist also $M \models \rho(\boldsymbol{a}_0, \ldots)$ gdw. $\omega(M) \models \exists w \in B(W(\langle a_0, \ldots \rangle) \in \bar{\mathcal{H}}_{h'(w)})$. Wenn wir $A := h'[B]$ setzen, gilt (*).

(Dieser Beweis zeigt auch, wie man, statt wie im Beweis für $n = 1$ mit den Methoden von Kapitel II, mit den Sätzen über abgeschlossene Ideale und r.a. Hornklassen arbeiten kann.)

$n \geqslant 3$. Der Beweis geht durch Induktion über n. Die $\exists_n$ Formel $\rho(x_0, \ldots x_m)$ habe die Form $\exists y_0, \ldots y_q \neg \varphi(x_0, \ldots y_0, \ldots)$ für eine $\exists_{n-1}$ Formel φ. Die Induktionsvoraussetzung liefert eine r.a. Menge A', so daß für alle $a_0, \ldots, b_0, \ldots$ aus einer a.a. Gruppe M $M \models \varphi(\boldsymbol{a}_0, \ldots \boldsymbol{b}_0, \ldots)$ gdw. $\omega(M) \models S^{A'}_{n-1}(W(\langle a_0, \ldots b_0, \ldots \rangle))$. Also ist wie früher $M \models \rho(\boldsymbol{a}_0, \ldots)$ gdw.

$$\omega(M) \models \exists Y (Y \in \mathcal{W}_{m+q+1} \wedge Y \downarrow m+1 = W(\langle a_0, \ldots \rangle) \wedge \neg S_{n-1}^{A'}(Y)).$$

Wir schreiben das in der Form $\omega(M) \models S(W(\langle a_0, \ldots \rangle))$ für eine L^2-Formel $S(X)$. Wir zeigen, daß $S(X)$ für ein r.a. $A \subset \omega$ äquivalent — in allen ω-Modellen — zu $S_n^A(X)$ ist.

1. Fall: n gerade. Jedem w ordnen wir die r.a. Hornklasse

$$\bar{\mathcal{H}}_{g(w)}^{n-1} = \{(X, Y, Y_1, \ldots, Y_{n-3}) \mid Y \in \mathcal{W}_{m+q+1} \wedge Y \downarrow m+1 = X \wedge (Y, Y_1, \ldots, Y_{n-3}) \in \bar{\mathcal{H}}_w^{n-2}\}$$

zu. Wir finden ein rekursives g. Offenbar ist $S(X)$ äquivalent zu

$$\exists Y \forall Y_1 \exists Y_2 \cdots Q_{n-3} Y_{n-3} \exists w \in A'(X, Y, Y_1, \ldots Y_{n-3}) \in \bar{\mathcal{H}}_{g(w)}^{n-1}.$$

Nun sieht man, daß diese Formel für $A := g[A']$ zu S_n^A äquivalent ist.

2. Fall: n ungerade. Die r.a. Hornklasse $\{(X, Y) \mid Y \in \mathcal{W}_{m+q+1} \wedge Y \downarrow m+1 = X\}$ sei $\bar{\mathcal{H}}_W^2$ für ein r.a. W. Wir ordnen effektiv jedem k eine r.a. Hornklasse $\bar{\mathcal{H}}_{g(k)}^{n-1}$ zu. g also rekursiv. Wenn $k = 2s$, sei $\bar{\mathcal{H}}_{g(k)}^{n-1} = \{(X, Y, Y_1, \ldots Y_{n-3}) \mid (Y, Y_1, \ldots Y_{n-3}) \in \bar{\mathcal{H}}_s^{n-2}\}$. Wenn $k = 2s+1$ und $s = \langle u, v_0 \rangle$ sei

$$\bar{\mathcal{H}}_{g(k)}^{n-1} = \{(X, Y, Y_1, \ldots Y_{n-3}) \mid D_u \subset X \vee Y \wedge D_{v_0}^1 \cap (X \vee Y) = \emptyset\}.$$

Dann ist $S(X)$ äquivalent zu

$$\exists Y \forall Y_1 \exists Y_2 \cdots Q_{n-3} Y_{n-3} \neg \exists k \in (2A' \cup (2W+1))(X, \ldots Y_{n-3}) \in \bar{\mathcal{H}}_{g(k)}^{n-1}.$$

Wir wählen also für A $g[2A' \cup (2W+1)]$.

2. f sei wieder die rekursive Funktion aus dem Beweis von III, 3.4, für die $W^*(M) = \{f^{-1}(W(F)) \mid F \in \mathrm{Sk}(M)\}$ (wenn M a.a.Gr.).

$n = 1$: Sei $A = \{n_0, \ldots, n_k\}$. Jede der Hornklassen $\bar{\mathcal{H}}_{n_i}$ gehört zu einer r.a. Menge von Implikationen $I_i(c_0, \ldots c_m)$, sodaß für alle $a_0, \ldots a_m$ aus einer Gruppe M $M \models I_i(\boldsymbol{a}_0, \ldots)$ gdw. $W(\langle a_0, \ldots \rangle) \in \bar{\mathcal{H}}_{n_i}$. Aus II, 3.13 (für $G = E$) oder aus II, 2.6 folgt, daß es endliche Systeme $S_i(\boldsymbol{a}_0, \ldots y_0, \ldots)$ gibt, die genau dann in der a.a. Gruppe M lösbar sind, wenn die I_i auf die $a_0, \ldots$ zutreffen. Also ist $\omega(M) \models S_1^A(W(\langle a_0, \ldots \rangle))$ gdw. $M \models \exists y_0, \ldots (\bigwedge S_0(\boldsymbol{a}_0, \ldots y_0 \cdots) \vee \cdots \vee \bigwedge S_k(\boldsymbol{a}_0, \ldots y_0, \ldots))$.

$n = 2$: Sei A r.a. Jedem $w \in \omega$ ordnen wir effektiv ein endliches System $S_w(c_0, \ldots, c_m, y_0, y_1)$ zu, sodaß für alle $a_0, \ldots$ aus einer Gruppe M $(W(\langle a_0, \ldots \rangle) \in \bar{\mathcal{H}}_w$ gdw. $S_w(\boldsymbol{a}_0, \ldots y_0, y_1)$ über M lösbar ist, S_w besteht aus Gleichungen und höchstens einer Ungleichung (II, 3.13). Dann ist für alle $a_0, \ldots$ aus der a.a.Gr. M $\omega(M) \models S_2^A(W(\langle a_0, \ldots \rangle))$ gdw. es ein $w \in A$ gibt mit $M \models \exists y_0 \exists y_1\ S_w(\boldsymbol{a}_0, \ldots y_0, y_1))$. Weil die S_w höchstens eine Ungleichung enthalten, ist $I(c_0, \ldots d_0, d_1) = \{\neg \bigwedge S_w(c_0, \ldots d_0, d_1) \mid w \in A\}$ eine r.a. Menge von Implikationen. Damit gilt $\omega(M) \models S_2^A(W(\langle a_0, \ldots \rangle))$ gdw. ex. $b_0, b_1 \in M \not\models I(\boldsymbol{a}_0, \ldots \boldsymbol{b}_0, \boldsymbol{b}_1)$.

Wir wählen ein endliches System $S(c_0, \ldots d_0, d_1, \vec{z})$ von Gl. & Ungleichungen, das genau dann in M lösbar ist, wenn I gilt. Also ist

$$\omega(M) \models S_2^A(W(\langle a_0, \ldots \rangle)) \quad \text{gdw.} \quad M \models \exists y_0, y_1 \forall \vec{z} \neg \wedge S(\boldsymbol{a}_0, \ldots, y_0, y_1, \vec{z})$$

$n \geqslant 3$: Beweis durch Induktion über n. Sei $A \subset \omega$ r.a. $S_n^A(X)$ ist bis auf Umbenennung gebundener Variable $\exists Y \neg S_{n-1}^A(X \vee Y)$. Man rechnet leicht nach, daß für jedes $w \in \omega$

$$\{(Z, Y_1, \ldots Y_{n-3}) \mid ((Z \downarrow m+1) \vee f^{-1}(Z \downarrow \{m+1, m+2\}), \\ Y_1, \ldots Y_{n-3}) \in \bar{\mathscr{H}}_w^{n-2}\}$$

eine r.a. Hornklasse ist, deren Index $g(w)$ rekursiv von w abhängt. Sei $A' = g[A]$, und $\varphi(x_0, \ldots x_{m+2})$ eine $\exists_{n-1}$ Formel, sodaß für alle $a_0, \ldots a_{m+2}$ aus der a.a.Gr. M $M \models \varphi(\boldsymbol{a}_0, \ldots)$ gdw. $\omega(M) \models S_{n-1}^{A'}(W(\langle a_0, \ldots \rangle))$. Dann gilt für alle $a_0, \ldots a_m$ aus der a.a.Gr. M $\omega(M) \models S_n^A(W(\langle a_0, \ldots \rangle))$ gdw. es ein $W \in W^*(M)$ mit $\omega(M) \models \neg S_{n-1}^A(W(\langle a_0, \ldots \rangle) \vee \boldsymbol{W})$ gibt gdw. ex. $a_{m+1}, a_{m+2} \in M$ $\omega(M) \models \neg S_{n-1}^A(W(\langle a_0, \ldots \rangle) \vee f^{-1}(W(\langle a_{m+1}, a_{m+2} \rangle)))$ (nach II, 3.4) gdw. ex. $a_{m+1}, a_{m+2} \in M$ mit $\omega(M) \models \neg S_{n-1}^{A'}(W(\langle a_0, \ldots a_{m+2} \rangle))$ gdw. ex. $a_{m+1}, a_{m+2} \in M$ $M \models \neg \varphi(\boldsymbol{a}_0, \ldots, \boldsymbol{a}_{m+2})$ gdw. $M \models \exists x_{m+1}, x_{m+2} \neg \varphi(\boldsymbol{a}_0, \ldots, \boldsymbol{a}_m, x_{m+1}, x_{m+2})$.

$\exists x_{m+1}, x_{m+2} \neg \varphi(x_0, \ldots, x_{m+2})$ ist die gesuchte $\exists_n$ Formel.

Beweis der Folgerung: Man wählt $a_0 = e, \ldots, a_m = e$, dann ist $W(\langle a_0, \ldots \rangle) = \omega$. □

Wir zeigen nun, daß jede L^2-Formel äquivalent zu einer S_n^A Formel ist. Um n möglichst klein zu halten, klassifizieren wie die L^2-Formeln noch etwas genauer. Zunächst definieren wir die $\tilde{\Pi}_n^1$ bzw. Σ_1^0 Formel $P_n^A(X)$ für ein r.a. A (bzw. endliches A) als die Negation von S_n^A. Ebenso wie in 2.1 die $\exists_n$-Formeln zu den S_n^A gehören, gehören dann die $\forall_n$-Formeln von $L_{\omega,\omega}$ zu den P_n^A.

Definition 2.2. Eine S_1-Formel von L^2 ist eine Formel der Gestalt $s^A(x_1, \ldots, X_k) = \exists u, w \langle x_1, \ldots x_m, u, w \rangle \in A \wedge D_u \subset (X_1 \vee X_2 \vee \cdots \vee X_k) \wedge D_w^1 \subset \omega \setminus (X_1 \vee \cdots \vee X_k)$ für ein r.a. A. Wenn $m = 0$, sagt diese Formel gerade $(X_1, \ldots, X_k) \notin \bar{\mathscr{H}}_A^k$. Ist $k = 0$, reduziert sich die Formel auf $\langle x_1, \ldots, x_m \rangle \in A$. Sonst drückt diese Formel, wenn $A = W_i$, $\langle x_1, \ldots, x_m \rangle \in W_i^1[X_1 \vee \cdots \vee X_2]$ aus. Die S_n Formeln haben die Gestalt

$$\exists Y_1^1, \ldots Y_{r_1}^1 \exists y_1^1, \ldots y_{s_1}^1 \forall Y_1^2 \cdots Q_{n-1} Y_1^{n-1} \cdots Y_{r_{n-1}}^{n-1} Q_{n-1} y_1^{n-1} \cdots y_{s_{n-1}}^{n-1} \\ (\neg)\ \varphi(x_1, \ldots, x_m, y_1^1, \ldots y_{s_{n-1}}^{n-1}, X_1, \ldots, X_k, Y_1^1, \ldots Y_{r_{n-1}}^{n-1})$$

wobei φ eine S_1-Formel ist. Wenn n gerade ist (wenn also $Q_{n-1} = \exists$ ist), steht das Negationszeichen. Wenn n ungerade ist, ist $Q_{n-1} = \forall$ und das Negationszeichen fällt weg. Die P_n Formeln sind die negierten S_n Formeln.

Im nächsten Satz bedeutet $\varphi \in \boldsymbol{S}_n$ bzw. $\in \boldsymbol{P}_n$, daß es eine S_n-Formel bzw. P_n-Formel gibt, die in allen algebraisch abgeschlossenen ω-Modellen zu φ äquivalent ist.

Satz 2.3. *Mit* $\varphi_i^n(x_1, \ldots x_m, X_1, \ldots X_k)$ *bzw.* $\psi_i^n(x_1, \ldots X_k)$ *seien* S_n *bzw* P_n*-Formeln bezeichnet,* $i = 0, 1$.

1. *Für alle* n *ist*

(i) $\exists X_1 \varphi_0^n$, $\exists x_1 \varphi_0^n$, $\varphi_0^n \vee \varphi_1^n \in \boldsymbol{S}_n$ *und* $\forall X_1 \psi_0^n$, $\forall x_1 \psi_0^n$, $\psi_0^n \wedge \psi_1^n \in \boldsymbol{P}_n$.

(ii) $\neg \varphi_0^n \in \boldsymbol{P}_n$, $\neg \psi_0^n \in \boldsymbol{S}_n$.

(iii) $\varphi_0^n \in \boldsymbol{S}_{n+1}, \boldsymbol{P}_{n+1}$ *und* $\psi_0^n \in \boldsymbol{S}_{n+1}, \boldsymbol{P}_{n+1}$.

2. *Für alle* $n \geq 2$ *ist*

(i) $\varphi_0^n \wedge \varphi_1^n \in \boldsymbol{S}_n$ *und* $\varphi_0^n \vee \psi_1^n \in \boldsymbol{P}_n$.

(ii) *Für ein r.a.* A *ist* $\varphi_0^n(x_1, \ldots, X_k)$ *äquivalent mit* $S_n^A(\{x_1\} \vee \cdots \vee \{x_m\} \vee X_1 \vee \cdots \vee X_k)$. $\psi_0^n(x_1, \ldots, X_k)$ *ist für ein r.a.* B *mit* $P_n^B(\{x_1\} \vee \cdots \vee X_k)$ *äquivalent. Wenn* $m, k = 0$ *meinen wir* $S_n^A(\omega)$, *bzw.* $P_n^B(\omega)$. *Umgekehrt, wenn* A *r.a., ist* $S_n^A(\{x_1\} \vee \cdots \vee X_k) \in \boldsymbol{S}_n$ *und* $P^A(\{x_1\} \vee \cdots \vee X_k) \in \boldsymbol{P}_n$.

3. (i) $\forall X_1 \varphi_0^1 \in \boldsymbol{S}_1$ *und* $\exists X_1 \psi_0^1 \in \boldsymbol{P}_1$.

(ii) *Jede endliche Konjunktion (Disjunktion) von Formeln aus* $\boldsymbol{S}_1$ $(\boldsymbol{P}_1)$ *ist für ein endliches* A *äquivalent zu* $P_1^A(\{x_1\} \vee \cdots \vee X_k)$ $(S_1^A(\{x_1\} \vee \cdots \vee X_k))$. *Umgekehrt sind diese Formeln äquivalent zu endlichen Konjunktionen (Disjunktionen) aus* $\boldsymbol{S}_1$ $(\boldsymbol{P}_1)$.

4. *Für alle* $n \geq 1$ *ist jede* $\tilde{\Sigma}_n^1$ *Formel aus* $\boldsymbol{S}_{n+1}$ *und jede* $\tilde{\Pi}_n^1$*-Formel aus* $\boldsymbol{P}_{n+1}$.

Bemerkung. Wir brauchen die algebraische Abgeschlossenheit von $(\omega, \mathcal{S})$ nur in 2(ii), 3(i). Es genügt sonst in 1(i) für $\exists X_1 \varphi_0^1 \in \boldsymbol{S}_1$ und $\forall X_1 \psi_0^1 \in \boldsymbol{P}_1$ und in 4 für $n = 1$, daß in den betrachteten ω-Modellen $(\omega, \mathcal{S})$ $\mathcal{S}$ alle endlichen Mengen enthält. Diese Bedingung reicht auch in 2(ii) zusammen mit "$A \vee B \in \mathcal{S}$ gdw. $A, B \in \mathcal{S}$" aus, um zu zeigen, daß φ_0^n — in allen diesen Modellen — äquivalent zu einem $S_{n+1}^A(\{x_1\} \vee \cdots)$ ist. Ohne die algebraische Abgeschlossenheit bekommt man in 3(i) nur $\forall X_1\ \varphi_0^1 \in \boldsymbol{P}_2$.

Beweis. 1(i) Daß $\exists x_1 \varphi_0^n \in \boldsymbol{S}_n$, ist klar für alle n, ebenso folgt $\exists X_1 \varphi_0^n \in \boldsymbol{S}_n$ für alle $n \geq 2$ sofort aus der Definition. Sei $s^A(x_1, \ldots, X_k)$ eine S_1-Formel wie in 2.2. Wir formen die Formel um und erhalten zwei r.a. Mengen A', A'' sodaß s^A äquivalent ist zur Disjunktion der Formeln

$$\exists u_1, u_2, w\langle x_1, \ldots x_m, u_1, u_2, w\rangle \in A' \wedge D_{u_1} \subset (X_2 \vee \cdots \vee X_k) \wedge D_{u_2} \subset X_1 \wedge D^1_w \subset \omega \setminus X_1$$

und

$$\exists u_1, u_2, w\langle x_1, \ldots x_m, u_1, u_2, w\rangle \in A'' \wedge D_{u_1} \subset (X_2 \vee \cdots \vee X_k) \wedge D_{u_2} \subset X_1 \wedge D^1_w \subset \omega \setminus (X_2 \wedge \cdots \wedge X_k).$$

Aus dieser Darstellung sieht man, daß es genau dann "ein X_1 gibt mit $s^A(x, X_1, \ldots)$", wenn es "ein endliches X_1 mit s^A" gibt gdw.

$$\text{“}\exists u_1, u_2, w\langle \vec{x}, u_1, u_2, w\rangle \in A' \wedge D_{u_1} \subset (X_2 \vee \cdots \vee X_k) \wedge D^1_w \subset \omega \setminus D_{u_2}\text{”}$$

(Wähle $X_1 = D_{u_2}$!) *oder*

$$\text{“}\exists u_1, u_2, w\langle \vec{x}, u_1, u_2, w\rangle \in A'' \wedge$$

$$D_{u_1} \subset (X_1 \vee \cdots \vee X_k) \wedge D^1_w \subset \omega \setminus (X_2 \vee \cdots \vee X_k)\text{”}$$

(Wähle dann $X_1 = D_{u_2}$). Setzt man nun

$$B = \{\langle \vec{x}, u_1, w\rangle \mid \exists u_2, w'\langle \vec{x}, u_1, u_2, w'\rangle \in A' \wedge D^1_{w'} \subset \omega \setminus D_{u_2} \wedge D^1_w = \emptyset$$

oder $\exists u_2\langle x, u_1, u_2, w\rangle \in A''\}$, so sind in allen algebraisch abgeschlossenen ω-Modellen $s^B(\vec{x}, X_2, \ldots X_k)$ und $\exists X_1 s^A$ äquivalent. Denn jede endliche Menge ist als rekursive Menge durch eine Hornklasse beschreibbar und somit in jedem a.a. ω-Modell enthalten. Durch Übergang zu den negierten Formeln erhalten wir aus dem Vorangehenden, daß f.a. n $\forall X_1 \psi^n_0$, $\forall x_1 \psi^n_0 \in \boldsymbol{P}_n$. Da $s^A \vee s^B$ zu $s^{A\cup B}$ äquivalent ist, folgt zunächst $\varphi^1_0 \vee \varphi^1_1 \in \boldsymbol{S}_1$ und $\psi^1_0 \wedge \psi^1_1 \in \boldsymbol{P}_1$. Weiter ist $s^A \wedge s^B$ aus $\boldsymbol{P}_2$. Denn wenn

$$C = \{\langle 2x_0, \vec{s}\rangle \mid x_0 \in \omega, \vec{s} \in A\} \cup \{\langle 2x_0 + 1, \vec{s}\rangle \mid x_0 \in \omega, s \in B\}$$

ist $s^A(x_1, \ldots) \wedge s^B(x_1, \ldots)$ äquivalent zu $\forall x_0\, s^C(x_0, x_1, \ldots)$. Wir haben also $\varphi^1_0 \wedge \varphi^1_1 \in \boldsymbol{P}_2$ und $\psi^1_0 \vee \psi^1_1 \in \boldsymbol{S}_2$. Durch Induktion über n zeigen wir, daß f.a. $n \geq 2$ $\varphi^n_0 \vee \varphi^n_1 \in \boldsymbol{S}_n$, $\varphi^n_0 \wedge \varphi^n_1 \in \boldsymbol{S}_n$, $\psi^n_0 \vee \psi^n_1 \in \boldsymbol{P}_n$, $\psi^n_0 \wedge \psi^n_1 \in \boldsymbol{P}_n$ (Damit ist dann auch 2(i) bewiesen). Für $i = 1, 0$ sei $\varphi^n_i = \exists X_1, \ldots x_1 \ldots \psi^{n-1}_i$ oder abkürzend $\varphi^n_i = \exists X_1 \psi^{n-1}_i$. Dann ist $\varphi^n_0 \vee \varphi^n_1$ $(\varphi^n_0 \wedge \varphi^n_1)$ äquivalent zu $\exists X_1(\psi^{n-1}_0 \vee \psi^{n-1}_1)$ $\exists X_1, X'_1(\psi^{n-1}_0 \wedge \psi^{n-1}_1(\cdots X'_1 \cdots)))$. Nach Induktionsvoraussetzung ist $\psi^{n-1}_0 \vee \psi^{n-1}_1$ $(\psi^{n-1}_0 \wedge \psi^{n-1}_1)$ zu einer P_{n-1}-Formel oder, falls $n = 2$, zu einer S_n-Formel (P_{n-1}-Formel) äquivalent. Daraus folgt sofort, daß $\varphi^n_0 \vee \varphi^n_1$ $(\varphi^n_0 \wedge \varphi^n_1)$ aus $\boldsymbol{S}_n$ sind. Die anderen zwei Behauptungen folgen durch Übergang zu den negierten Formeln. 1(ii) folgt sofort aus den Definitionen. 1(iii) $\varphi^n_0 \in \boldsymbol{P}_{n+1}$ und $\psi^n_0 \in \boldsymbol{S}_{n+1}$ folgt durch Einführen "blinder Variable". Wir zeigen den Rest der Behauptung durch Induktion. Sei $A = \{\vec{x} \mid \exists y\, R(\vec{x}, y)\}$ für ein rekursives R. Dann ist $R(x_1, \ldots x_m, u, w, y) \wedge D_u \subset (X_1 \cdots) \wedge D^1_w \subset \omega \setminus (X_1 \cdots)$ äquivalent zu einer P_1-Formel ψ. s^A ist äquivalent zu $\exists u, w, y\psi$ und also aus $\boldsymbol{S}_2$. Daraus folgt, daß auch $\psi_1^0 \in \boldsymbol{P}_2$. Es sei nun $\varphi_0^n = \exists X_1 \psi_0^{n-1}$. Nach Induktionsvoraussetzung ist $\psi_0^{n-1} \in \boldsymbol{P}_n$, also $\varphi_0^n \in \boldsymbol{S}_{n+1}$. Ebenso folgt $\psi_0^n \in \boldsymbol{P}_{n+1}$.

3(i) Wenn A r.a. ist, können wir $x_1, \dots x_m$ effektiv den Index $g(\vec{x})$ einer r.a. Hornklasse $\bar{\mathcal{H}}^k_{g(\vec{x})}$ zuordnen, sodaß das Zutreffen von $\neg s^A(\vec{x}, X_1, \dots, X_k)$ durch $(X_1, \dots, X_k) \in \bar{\mathcal{H}}^k_{g(\vec{x})}$ oder $X_k \in \bar{\mathcal{H}}_{g(\vec{x})}[X_1, \dots X_{k-1}]$ beschrieben werden kann. Weiter finden wir für jedes $\vec{x}$ eine r.a. Hornklasse $\bar{\mathcal{H}}^{k-1}_{h(x)}$, so daß $(X_1, \dots, X_{k-1}) \in \bar{\mathcal{H}}^{k-1}_{h(x)}$ gdw. $\bar{\mathcal{H}}_{g(\vec{x})}[X_1, \dots, X_{k-1}] \neq \emptyset$. Da $(\omega, \mathcal{S})$ algebraisch abgeschlossen ist, ist also $\exists X_k \neg s^A$ zu $(X_1, \dots X_{k-1}) \in \bar{\mathcal{H}}^{k-1}_{h(\vec{x})}$ äquivalent. Dazu gibt es aber wieder ein r.a. B — $B = \{\langle \vec{x}, u, w\rangle \mid \langle u, w\rangle \in W_{h(\vec{x})}\}$ — für das $\neg s^B(\vec{x}, X_1, \dots, X_{k-1})$ zu $(X_1, \dots) \in \bar{\mathcal{H}}^{k-1}_{h(\vec{x})}$ äquivalent ist. Wir haben gezeigt, daß $\exists X_k \psi_0^1 \in \boldsymbol{P}_1$. Daraus folgt $\forall X_k \varphi_0^1 \in \boldsymbol{S}_1$.

Für 2(iii) und 3(ii) überlegen wir, daß die $\boldsymbol{P}_1$-Formeln gerade die L^2-Formeln sind, die für eine r.a. Hornklasse $\mathcal{H}$ äquivalent zu $(\{x_1\}, \dots, X_k) \in \mathcal{H}^{m+k}$ sind. Denn wenn wir für ein r.a. A die P_1-Formel $\neg s^A(x_1, \dots, x_m, X_1, \dots X_k)$ betrachten, ist

$$\{(Y_1 \vee \cdots \vee Y_m \vee X_1 \vee \cdots \vee X_k) \mid \forall x_1 \in Y_1 \cdots \forall x_m \in Y_m \neg s^A(x_1, \dots X_k)\}$$

die gewünschte Hornklasse. Ist umgekehrt $\mathcal{H}$ gegeben, so ist für alle $x_1, \dots x_m$ $\{(X_1, \dots X_k) \mid (\{x_1\}, \dots X_k) \in \mathcal{H}^{m+k}\}$ eine r.a. Hornklasse $\bar{\mathcal{H}}^k_{g(\vec{x})}$, deren Index rekursiv von $x_1, \dots x_m$ abhängt. Wie im Beweis von 3(i) bekommen wir ein r.a. A mit $\neg s^A(\vec{x}, X_1, \dots X_k)$ gdw. $(X_1, \dots) \in \bar{\mathcal{H}}^k_{g(\vec{x})}$.

3(ii) folgt unmittelbar aus dem eben Bewiesenen.

Eine Variante der letzten Überlegung zeigt, daß für jede r.a. Hornklasse $\mathcal{H}$ und jedes r.a. B $x_0 \in B \wedge (\{x_1\} \vee \cdots \vee \{x_m\} \vee X_1 \vee \cdots \vee X_k) \in \bar{\mathcal{H}}_{x_0}$ aus $\boldsymbol{P}_1$ ist. Daraus folgt der zweite Teil von

2(ii): Für alle r.a. B ist $S^B_n(\{x_1\} \vee \cdots \vee X_k)$ aus $\boldsymbol{S}_n$. Die Umkehrung beweisen wir durch Induktion über $n \geq 2$.

$n = 2$: Aus 3(i) folgt, daß man φ_0^2 in der Form $\exists y_1, \dots y_s \neg s^C(x_1, \dots, x_m, y_1, \dots, y_s, X_1, \dots X_k)$ schreiben kann, C r.a. Man findet leicht ein r.a. B, so daß $s^C(\vec{x}, y_1, \dots, y_s, \vec{X})$ und $s^B(\vec{x}, \langle y_1, \dots, y_s\rangle, \vec{X})$ äquivalent sind. φ_0^2 ist also äquivalent zu $\exists y \neg s^B(\vec{x}, y, \vec{X})$. Nun sehen wir wie früher, daß es eine rekursive Funktion gibt, für die $\neg s^B(\vec{x}, y, \vec{X})$ gdw. $(\{x_1\}, \dots, \{x_m\}, X_1, \dots, X_k) \in \bar{\mathcal{H}}^{k+m}_{g(y)}$. Setzt man $A = g[\omega]$, ist dann φ_0^2 äquivalent mit $S_2^A(\{x_1\}, \dots X_1, \dots)$. Entsprechend folgt die Behauptung für ψ_0^2.

$n > 2$: Sei $\varphi_0^n = \exists Y_1, \dots Y_r \exists y_1, \dots y_s \psi_0^{n-1}(x_1, \dots x_m, \vec{y}, X_1, \dots X_k, \vec{Y})$. Da $(\omega, \mathcal{S})$ alle einelementigen Mengen enthält, ist — in diesen ω-Modellen — $\exists \vec{y} \psi_0^{n-1}(\vec{x}, \vec{y}, \vec{X}, \vec{Y})$ äquivalent mit

$$\exists \vec{Z}\,(Z_1 \neq \emptyset \wedge \cdots \wedge Z_s \neq \emptyset \wedge \forall y_1 \in Z_1 \cdots \forall y_s \in Z_s \psi_0^{n-1}(\vec{x}, \vec{y}, \vec{X}, \vec{Y})).$$

In der Klammer steht eine P_{n-1}-Formel, denn $Z_i \neq \emptyset$ ist aus $\boldsymbol{S}_1$. Die Formel nennen wir $\psi(\vec{x}, \vec{Z}, \vec{X}, \vec{Y})$. Man sieht leicht, daß es eine P_{n-1}-Formel $\psi_1^{n-1}(\vec{x}, \vec{X}, Y)$ gibt, sodaß $\psi(\vec{x}, \vec{Z}, \vec{X}, \vec{Y})$ und $\psi_1^{n-1}(\vec{x}, \vec{X}, Z_1 \vee \cdots \vee Z_s \vee Y_1 \vee \cdots \vee Y_r)$ äquivalent sind. Da in algebraisch abgeschlossenen $(\omega, \mathcal{S})$ $A, B \in \mathcal{S}$ gdw. $A \vee B \in \mathcal{S}$, ist φ_0^n äquivalent zu $\exists Y \psi_1^{n-1}(\vec{x}, \vec{X}, Y)$. Wenn nach Induktionsvoraussetzung ψ_1^{n-1} für ein r.a. A mit $P_{n-1}^A(\{x_1\} \vee \cdots \vee X_1 \vee \cdots \vee Y)$ äquivalent ist, sind φ_0^n und $S_n^A(\{x_1\} \vee \cdots \vee X_1 \vee \cdots)$ äquivalent.

4. Wir brauchen nur zu zeigen, daß alle $\tilde{\Sigma}_1^1$-Formeln aus $\boldsymbol{S}_2$ sind. Eine $\tilde{\Sigma}_1^1$-Formel $\varphi(\vec{x}, \vec{X})$ hat o.E. die Gestalt

$$\exists \vec{Y} \exists u, w \langle \vec{x}, u, w \rangle \in A \wedge D_u \subset (X_1 \vee \cdots Y_1 \vee \cdots) \wedge D_w \subset \omega \backslash (X_1 \vee \cdots Y_1 \vee \cdots),$$

A r.a. .

$$\{(X_1, \ldots Y_1) \mid D_u \subset (X_1 \vee \cdots Y_1 \vee \cdots) \wedge D_w \subset \omega \backslash (X_1 \vee \cdots Y_1 \vee \cdots)\}$$

ist eine r.a. Hornklasse, deren Index rekursiv von u und w abhängt. Es gibt also ein ψ aus $\boldsymbol{P}_1$, so daß φ mit $\exists \vec{Y} \exists u, w \langle \vec{x}, u, w \rangle \in A \wedge \psi(u, w, \vec{X}, \vec{Y})$ äquivalent ist. Da $\langle \vec{x}, u, w \rangle \in A$ aus $\boldsymbol{S}_1$ ist, folgt die Behauptung aus 1 und 2. □

Folgerungen 2.4. 1. *Für jede S_n- (P_n-) Formel $\varphi(X)$, $n \geq 2$, $m \in \omega$, gibt es eine $\exists_n$- ($\forall_n$-) Formel ρ (aus $L_{\omega,\omega}$), sodaß*

(*) *für alle $a_0, \ldots a_m$ aus einer a.a.Gr. M $M \models \rho(\boldsymbol{a}_0, \ldots)$ gdw. $\omega(M) \models \varphi(W(\langle a_0, \ldots, a_m \rangle))$.*

Und umgekehrt.

2. *Für jede S_n- (P_n-) Aussage φ, $n \geq 2$, gibt es eine $\exists_n$- ($\forall_n$-) Aussage ρ (aus $L_{\omega,\omega}$), sodaß*

(**) *für alle a.a.Gr. M $M \models \varphi$ gdw. $\omega(M) \models \rho$.*

3. *Zu jeder Konjunktion (Disjunktion) von S_1- (P_1-) Formeln $\varphi(X)$ bzw. Aussagen φ gibt es eine $\forall_1$- ($\exists_1$-) Formel bzw. Aussage ρ, sodaß (*) bzw. (**). Und umgekehrt.*

4. *Zu jeder $\tilde{\Sigma}_n^1$- ($\tilde{\Pi}_n^1$-) Formel $\varphi(X)$ bzw. Aussage φ gibt es eine $\exists_{n+1}$- ($\forall_{n+1}$-) Formel bzw. Aussage ρ mit (*) bzw. (**) ($n \geq 1$).*

5. *Zu jeder L^2-Formel $\varphi(X)$ bzw. Aussage φ gibt es eine Formel bzw. Aussage ρ aus $L_{\omega,\omega}$ mit (*) bzw. (**); und umgekehrt.*

6. *Zwei a.a. Gruppen M, N sind genau dann elementar äquivalent, wenn $\omega(M)$ und $\omega(N)$ (bzgl. L^2) elementar äquivalent sind. Wenn M Untergruppe von N ist, ist N genau dann elementare Erweiterung von M, wenn $\omega(N)$ elementare Erweiterung von $\omega(M)$ ist.*

7. *Jede $\tilde{\Sigma}^g_n$-Eigenschaft von Gruppenelementen ist in a.a. Gruppen zu einer $\exists_{n+1}$-Formel äquivalent.*

8. *Jede Σ^g_n-Eigenschaft von Gruppenelementen ist in a.a. Gruppen zu einer $\exists_{n+2}$-Formel äquivalent.*

9. *Jede arithmetische Eigenschaft von Gruppenelementen ist in a.a. Gruppen einer elementaren Formel äquivalent.*

10. *Jede Formel von L^* ist in a.a. Gruppen einer elementaren Formel äquivalent.*

2.4.9 und 2.4.10 wurden unabhängig von [33] gefunden. Die Methode von [33] ist allgemeiner anwendbar, liefert aber nicht unsere genaue Angabe des Präfixtypes. In [33] wird bewiesen: In einer Struktur $\mathfrak{A}$ gilt genau dann 2.4.9 oder 2.4.10, wenn es eine $L_{\omega\omega}$-Formel $\varphi(x, y, \vec{w})$ gibt, mit der man jede endliche partielle Funktion $f \subset A \times A$ in der Form $f = \{(a, b) \mid \mathfrak{A} \models \varphi(\boldsymbol{a}, \boldsymbol{b}, \vec{\boldsymbol{c}})\}$ für ein $\vec{c} \in A$ schreiben kann.

Zwei Beispiele 2.5. 1. Dies Beispiel soll zeigen, wie genau man mit Hilfe von 2.3 L^2-Formeln klassifizieren kann. "Algebraisch abgeschlossen" drückt sich durch $\forall X, Y \forall v_1[\exists Z_1, Z_1 = X \vee Y \wedge (\bar{\mathcal{H}}_{v_1}[X] \neq \emptyset \rightarrow \exists Z_2 \in \bar{\mathcal{H}}_{v_1}[X])]$ aus. $Z_1 = X \vee Y$, $\bar{\mathcal{H}}_{v_1}[X] \neq \emptyset$ und $Z_2 \in \bar{\mathcal{H}}_{v_1}[X]$ sind aus $\boldsymbol{P}_1$. Wegen 2.3.3(i) sind also auch $\exists Z_1\ Z_1 = X \vee Y$ und $\exists Z_2\ Z_2 \in \bar{\mathcal{H}}_{v_1}[X]$ aus $\boldsymbol{P}_1$. Der Ausdruck $[\cdots]$ ist nach 2.3.2(i), aus $\boldsymbol{P}_2$. Also ist $\forall X, Y \forall v_1[\cdots]$ aus $\boldsymbol{P}_2$. "a.a" ist also äquivalent zu $P_2^A(\omega)$. Dies ist eine arithmetische Aussage, deren Zutreffen in $(\omega, \mathcal{S})$ nicht von $\mathcal{S}$ abhängt. (Natürlich erfüllen alle a.a. ω-Modelle "a.a.")

2. Die L^2-Aussage $\mathbf{max}\ \exists Y \forall X\ X \leqslant^* Y$ ist, wie man leicht nachrechnet, eine $\tilde{\Sigma}^1_5$-Formel, entspricht also einer $\exists_6$-Aussage. Nun sind aber $x \in W^e_z[Y]$, $x \in W^1_{z'}[Y]$ und $x \in X$, $x \notin X$ aus $\boldsymbol{S}_1$. Daher ist $\psi := (x \in X \leftrightarrow x \in W^e_z[Y]) \wedge (x \notin X \leftrightarrow x \in W^1_{z'}[Y])$ und somit auch $(z, z') : X \leqslant^* Y$ d. h. $\forall x \psi$ aus P_2. $\mathbf{max}$ ist also aus $\boldsymbol{S}_5$, und entspricht daher einer elementaren $\exists_5$-Aussage $\mathbf{max}$, die genau in den a.a. Gruppen M gilt, für die $W_*(M)$ ein Hauptideal ist.

Um arithmetischen Eigenschaften möglichst einfache elementare Formeln zuzuordnen, definieren wir:

Definition 2.6. Eine Eigenschaft $P(v_0, \ldots, x_0, \ldots, \sigma_0, \ldots)$ von natürlichen Zahlen $(v_0, \ldots)$, Gruppenelementen $(x_0, \ldots)$ und endlichen Folgen von Gruppenelementen heißt S^g_1-Eigenschaft, wenn es ein r.a. A gibt, sodaß für alle $n_0, \cdots \in \omega$ und $a_0, \cdots \vec{b}_0$ aus einer Gruppe M P genau dann auf $n_0, \ldots a_0, \ldots \vec{b}_0, \ldots$ in M zutrifft, wenn $s^A(n_0, \ldots, l(\vec{b}_0), \ldots, W(\langle a_0, \ldots \vec{b}_0, \ldots \rangle))$. P^g_1-Eigenschaften sind

Negationen von S_1^g-Eigenschaften. Ist P eine S_n^g bzw. P_n^g-Eigenschaft, so ist $\forall v_0, \ldots \forall x_0, \ldots \forall \sigma_0, \ldots P$ bzw. $\exists v_0, \ldots \exists x_0, \ldots \exists \sigma_0, \ldots P$ ein eine P_{n+1}^g bzw. S_{n+1}^g Eigenschaft.

Der nächste Satz folgt leicht aus 2.3, 2.4 und den Beweisen von 1.2, 1.8 und 2.1. $\in \boldsymbol{S}_n^g$ bedeutet: zu einer S_n^g-Eigenschaft äquivalent. "Äquivalent" heißt in 1 und 2: in allen Gruppen äquivalent; in 3, 4: in allen a.a. Gruppen äquivalent.

Satz 2.7. (*P und P' sind S_n^g-Eigenschaften.*)

1. *Für alle n ist $\exists v_0 P$, $P \vee P' \in \boldsymbol{S}_n^g$; $\neg P \in \boldsymbol{P}_n^g$; $P \in \boldsymbol{P}_{n+1}^g$.*
2. *Für alle $n \geqslant 2$ ist $P \wedge P'$, $\exists x_0 P$, $\exists \sigma_0 P \in \boldsymbol{S}_n^g$.*
3. *Für $n = 1$ ist $\forall x_0 P$, $\forall \sigma_0 P \in \boldsymbol{S}_1^g$.*
4. (i) *Jede endlich Konjunktion von S_1^g-Eigenschaften ist zu einer $\forall_1$-Formel äquivalent.*
   (ii) *Für alle $n \geqslant 2$ ist P zu einer $\exists_n$-Formel äquivalent.*

Beispiele 2.8. 1. "$a_0 \in \langle a_1, \ldots, a_n \rangle$" ist S_1^g-Eigenschaft (siehe Beispiel 2 nach 1.6), und daher in a.a.Gr. durch eine $\forall_1$-Formel (z. B. E_n von 1.1) beschreibbar. $\langle \vec{a} \rangle' \cong \langle \vec{a}' \rangle'$ ist P_1^g und durch "ex. Innerer Automorphismus..." (eine $\forall_1$-Formel) beschreibbar.

2. MAX ist, wie man aus der Darstellung im Beispiel 2 nach 1.6 sieht, S_4^g und daher durch eine $\exists_4$-Aussage beschreibbar: In ([14]) ist diese Aussage explizit angegeben.

3. Anwendungen

Satz 3.1. 0. "*$\langle a_0, \ldots a_m \rangle$ unendlich*" *ist in a.a. Gruppen durch eine $\exists_1$-Formel ausdrückbar (siehe auch* [2]).

1. *Daß $\langle a_0, \ldots a_m \rangle$ einfach (nicht nilpotent) ist, ist in a.a.Gr. jeweils durch eine $\forall_2$-Formel ausdrückbar* ([14, 2]).

2. "*$\langle a_0, \ldots a_m \rangle$ hat lösbares Wortproblem*" *ist in a.a. Gruppen mit einer $\exists_3$-Formel ausdrückbar.*

3. ([2]) *Sei G eine endlich erzeugte Gruppe mit lösbaren Wortproblem. Dann ist in a.a.Gr.* "*$\langle a_0, \ldots a_m \rangle$ ist in G einbettbar*" *durch eine $\exists_2$-Formel ausdrückbar.*

Beweis. 1 $\langle a_0, \ldots, a_m \rangle$ ist genau dann einfach, wenn es *für alle* $i = 0, 1, \ldots m$ und Wörter W, für die $W(\vec{a}) \neq e$, Wörter $\tilde{W}, W_1, \ldots W_n$ *gibt* mit $a_i = \tilde{W}(W_1 W W_1^{-1}, \ldots W_n W W_n^{-1})(\vec{a})$ (siehe auch den Beweis von (III, 2.12)). Aus dieser Darstellung erkennt man, daß "$\langle a_0, \ldots, a_m \rangle$ einfach" eine P_2^g-Eigenschaft ist.

Die Klasse der n-nilpotenten Gruppen ist gleichungsdefiniert, durch eine Gleichung $\mathcal{S}_n$. Da "$\langle a_0, \dots a_m \rangle$ erfüllt $\mathcal{S}_n$" eine P_1^g-Eigenschaft von $n, a_0, \dots$ ist, ist "nilpotent" eine S_2^g-Eigenschaft.

0. $\langle a_0, \dots a_m \rangle$ ist genau dann endlich, wenn es Wörter $W_0, \dots W_k$ und Zahlen $n_{i,j}$, $(i, j \leqslant k)$, gibt mit $W_0(\vec{a}) = a_0, \dots W_m(\vec{a}) = a_m$ und $W_i W_j^{-1}(\vec{a}) = W_{n_{i,j}}(\vec{a})$ f.a. $i, j \leqslant k$. Das ist aber eine S_1^g-Eigenschaft.

2. Wir müssen zeigen, daß "X rekursiv" aus $\boldsymbol{S}_3$ ist. Da aber $\varphi = (v \in X \leftrightarrow v \in W_z) \wedge (v \not\in X \leftrightarrow v \in W_{z'})$ P_2-Formel ist, ist $\exists z, z' \forall v \varphi \in \boldsymbol{S}_3$.

3. G sei von $\vec{g}$ erzeugt. Dann ist "$\langle a_0, \dots a_m \rangle < G$" äquivalent zu: "*ex.* Wörter $W_0, \dots W_m$, sodaß *für alle* W $W(a_0, \dots a_m) = e$ gdw. $W(W_0, \dots W_m)(\vec{g}) = e$ (in G)". Wie man sieht, ist das eine S_2^g-Eigenschaft. □

Wir haben schon gesehen, daß die a.a. Gruppen M, deren zugehöriges Ideal $W_*(M)$ ein maximales Element hat, durch eine $\exists_5$-Aussage und die a.a. Gruppen, die eine universelle endlich erzeugte Untergruppe besitzen, durch eine $\exists_4$-Aussage beschrieben werden können. Eine noch kleinere Klasse von a.a. Gruppen, die Klasse aller Gruppen, die partiell isomorph zu einer Gruppe M_A sind, $A \subset \omega$, ist ebenfalls "elementar":

Satz 3.2. *Es gibt eine $\exists_5$-Aussage φ, die in einer a.a. Gruppe M genau dann gilt, wenn es eine Menge A gibt, so daß $M \cong_p M_A$. φ gilt also in einer abzählbaren a.a.Gr. M genau dann, wenn M isomorph zu einer Gruppe M_A ist.*

Beweis. Wir müssen zeigen, daß die L^2-Formel

$$\exists X\, [(\forall z\, \exists Y\, Y = W_z^e[X]) \wedge (\forall Y\, \exists z\, Y = W_z^e[X])$$

aus $\boldsymbol{S}_5$ ist. Dazu überlegt man, daß $Y = W_z^e[X]$ aus $\boldsymbol{P}_2$ ist. □

Die abzählbaren a.a. Gruppen, deren Ideal ein Hauptideal ist, sind in gewisser Weise ω-kategorisch: Jede abzählbare a.a. elementare Erweiterung ist wieder zur Gruppe selbst isomorph. Denn sei M abzählbar a.a. und $W_*(M)$ von $B/\equiv^*$ erzeugt. Wenn N eine a.a. elementare Erweiterung von M ist, ist $\omega(N)$ elementare Erweiterung von $\omega(M)$. Also gilt in $\omega(N)$ ebenso wie in $\omega(M)$ die L^2-Aussage $\forall Y$ $Y \leqslant^* \boldsymbol{B}$. Da $W_*(N)$ also auch von B erzeugt wird, ist $W_*(M) = W_*(N)$ d. h. $M \cong_p N$. Aus I, 4.8.1 folgt, daß es immer echte elementare Erweiterungen einer a.a. Gruppe gibt. Natürlich gibt es a.a. Gruppen mit nicht isomorphen abzählbaren a.a. elementaren

Erweiterungen. Denn M_1 sei eine Gruppe mit überabzählbaren Skelett — z. B. eine ω-universelle a.a. Gruppe (I, 3.9) — und M eine abzählbare elementare Unterstruktur. N sei eine abzählbare elementare Unterstruktur von M_1, die M enthält, aber ein größeres Skelett als M hat. Dann sind (I, 1.5.2) M and N algebraisch abgeschlossen und $M \prec N$. Aber natürlich nicht $M \cong N$.

Der nächste Satz zeigt, daß die M_A für arithmetisches A sogar in folgendem Sinn "ω-kategorisch" sind: Jede zu M_A elementar äquivalente a.a. Gruppe ist zu M partiell isomorph. Dann geben wir noch ein Beispiel für eine ω-kategorische Gruppe, die nicht von der Form M_A ist, deren Ideal noch nicht einmal Hauptideal ist. Wenn $\mathcal{S}^a$ die Menge aller arithmetischen Mengen ist, ist $(\omega, \mathcal{S}^a)$ nach III, 4.2.1 algebraisch abgeschlossen. $\mathcal{S}^a$ ist abzählbar, also gibt es bis auf Isomorphie genau eine abzählbare a.a. Gruppe M^a mit $W^*(M^a) = \mathcal{S}^a$.

Satz 3.3. 1. *Wenn A implizit arithmetisch definierbar ist (also z. B. arithmetisch ist), gibt es eine Aussage φ^A aus $L_{\omega,\omega}$, die genau in den a.a. Gruppen gilt, die zu M_A partiell isomorph sind.*

2. *Wenn A durch eine Σ_k^0 (Π_k^0)-Relation implizit definiert ist, finden wir für φ^A eine $\exists_n$-Aussage mit $n = \max(k+1, 5)$ ($n = \max(k+2, 5)$). Wenn A eine Δ_k^0-Menge ist, finden wir für φ^A eine $\exists_n$-Aussage, $n = \max(k+1, 5)$. M_0 ist durch eine $\forall_4$-Aussage beschreibbar.*

3. *Es gibt eine $\forall_5$-Aussage, die genau in den a.a. Gruppen gilt, die zu M^a partiell isomorph sind.*

Beweis. Wenn $\{A\} = \{X \mid R(X)\}$ für ein arithmetisches R, ist M genau dann partiell isomorph zu M_A (d. h. $W^*(M) = \{B \mid B \leqslant_e A\}$) wenn $\omega(M) \models \exists X\, (R(X) \wedge \forall Y\, \exists z\; Y = W_z^e[X] \wedge \forall z\, \exists Y\; Y = W_z^e[X])$. Da diese Aussage eine L^2-Aussage ist, folgt 1 aus 2.4.5. Wenn man ausnützt, daß $Y = W_z^e[X]$ aus $\boldsymbol{P}_2$ ist und daß, wenn R Σ_k^0 (Π_k^0), $R(X)$ aus $\boldsymbol{S}_{k+1}$ ($\boldsymbol{P}_{k+1}$), berechnet man leicht, daß diese Aussage aus $\boldsymbol{S}_n$ für die angegebenen n ist. Der erste Teil von 2 folgt damit aus 2.4.2. Wenn A eine Δ_k^0 Menge ist, ist $X = A$ d. h. $\forall v\, (v \in X \leftrightarrow v \in A)$ aus $\boldsymbol{P}_k$. Wenn wir in der oben angegebenen Aussage $R(X)$ durch $A = X$ ersetzen, erhalten wir eine Aussage aus $\boldsymbol{S}_n$ für $n = \max(k+1, 5)$.

Nach III, 4.4.4 (und III, 3.3.2) ist eine a.a.Gr. M genau dann zu M_0 partiell isomorph, wenn $W^*(M)$ nur aus r.a. Mengen besteht. Denn wenn $W^*(M)$ nur aus r.a. Mengen besteht, ist eine (jede) abzählbare a.a. Untergruppe N von M in M_0 einbettbar. Daraus folgt $N \cong M_0$ und daher $W_*(M_0) \subset W_*(M)$, d. h. $W_*(M) = W_*(N)$. $\mathcal{S}$ enthält genau dann nur r.a. Mengen, wenn $(\omega, \mathcal{S}) \models \forall X\, \exists z\, (X = W_z)$. Da $X = W_z$ aus $\boldsymbol{P}_2$, ist diese Aussage aus $\boldsymbol{P}_4$. Damit ist 2 bewiesen.

3. Die vollständigen Σ_n^0-Mengen $\emptyset^{(n)}$ sind implizit Π_2^0-definierbar: Es gibt eine Π_2^0 Relation R, so daß für alle n $\{\phi^{(n)}\} = \{X \mid R(n, X)\}$([24] S. 344). Die arithmetischen Mengen sind die auf ein $\phi^{(n)}$ 1-reduzierbaren, oder die auf ein $\phi^{(n)}$ aufzählungsreduzierbaren. Also ist $W^*(M) = \mathcal{S}^a$ gdw. $\omega(M) \models \forall z\, \exists X\, R(z, X) \wedge \forall Y\, \exists z\, \exists X\, (R(z, X) \wedge Y \leqslant_e X)$. Diese Aussage ist, weil R aus $\boldsymbol{P}_3$ und $Y \leqslant_e X$ aus $\boldsymbol{S}_3$ ist, aus $\boldsymbol{P}_5$. □

Wir haben unendlich viele nicht elementar äquivalente a.a. Gruppen gewonnen, z. B. sind, wenn A arithmetisch ist und $A \not\equiv_e B$, M_A und M_B nichtelementar äquivalent. Wenn $n < m$, so gilt z. B. in $M_{\phi(m)}$ die $\exists_4$-Aussage "$\phi^{(m)} \in W^*(\cdots)$", nicht aber in $M_{\phi(n)}$. ("$\phi^{(m)} \in W^*(\cdots)$" ist in a.a. Gruppen durch eine $\exists_4$-Aussage ausdrückbar, weil das gerade $\omega(M) \models \exists X\, R(m, X)$ — für R wie im Beweis von 3.3.3 — bedeutet. R ist Π_2^0 und also $\in \boldsymbol{P}_3$.) Algebraisch abgeschlossene Gruppen, in denen verschiedene $\exists_4$-Aussagen gelten, wurden zuerst in ([14]) konstruiert; dort wurde zum Beispiel die $\exists_4$-Aussage MAX untersucht. Bei den bis jetzt betrachteten Gruppen, gilt MAX in den M_A, nicht aber in M^a oder ([14]) in a.a. ω-universellen Gruppen. In M^a oder in ω-universellen Gruppen gilt noch nicht einmal **max**, denn es gibt keinen maximalen arithmetischen $*$-Grad und keinen maximalen $*$-Grad (weil es keinen maximalen arithmetischen T-Grad und keinen maximalen T-Grad gibt). Es blieb in ([14]) offen, ob es $\exists_3$-Aussagen gibt, durch die sich a.a. Gruppen unterscheiden. Wir können jetzt leicht eine solche Aussage angeben: Wenn A eine r.a., nicht-rekursive Menge ist, ist "$A \in W^*(\cdots)$" $\exists_3$-ausdrückbar; denn die L^2-Aussage $\exists X\, X = A$ ist aus $\boldsymbol{S}_3$. Wegen III, 4.1 (oder III, 1.8.2) gibt es algebraisch abgeschlossene Gruppen M, für die A nicht in $W^*(M)$ vorkommt. Andererseits gilt aber "$A \in W^*(\cdots)$" in allen M_B, $B \subset \omega$. Im nächsten Satz zeigen wir auf ähnliche Weise, daß es sogar 2^ω a.a. Gruppen gibt, die sich paarweise durch $\exists_3$-Aussagen unterscheiden.

Aus dem Vorigen ergibt sich die Nichtkompaktheit der Klasse aller algebraisch abgeschlossenen Gruppen auf folgende Weise: Wir betrachten die Menge der $\exists_4$-Aussagen "$\phi^{(m)} \in W^*(\cdots)$" für $m \in \omega$ und die $\exists_5$-Aussage "ex. m $\phi^{(m)} \notin W^*(\cdots)$". (Diese Aussage ist $\exists_5$, weil M genau dann diese Eigenschaft hat, wenn (für das R aus dem Beweis von 3.3.3) $\omega(M) \models \exists z\, \forall Y \neg R(z, Y)$.) Diese Menge ist offensichtlich nicht erfüllbar; je endlich viele dieser Aussagen sind aber in einer a.a. Gruppe gültig. Denn in $M_{\phi(n)}$ gilt "ex. m $\phi^{(m)} \notin W^*(\cdots)$" und für alle $i \leqslant n$ "$\phi^{(i)} \in W^*(\cdots)$". Wir geben im nächsten Satz nicht erfüllbare, aber endlich erfüllbare Mengen von Aussagen kleineren Präfixtyps an.

Es gibt abzählbar viele rekursiv aufzählbare Mengen, deren

Turinggrade paarweise unvergleichbar sind ([24] S. 175). Auf ähnliche Weise kann man eine Folge $(A_i \mid i \in \omega)$ von r.a. Mengen konstruieren, deren Turinggrade "unabhängig" sind: Wenn $i \notin \{i_1, \ldots, i_n\}$, ist $A_i \not\leq_T A_{i_1} \vee A_{i_2} \vee \cdots \vee A_{i_n}$. (Das folgt auch aus ([31]).) Die Konstruktion liefert sogar eine r.a. Familie, d. h. $\{\langle x, i\rangle \mid x \in A_i\}$ ist r.a. Wir wählen uns für jedes i eine $\exists_3$-Aussage aus $L_{\omega,\omega}$, φ_i, die genau dann in einer a.a. Gruppe gilt, wenn $A_i \in W^*(M)$. $\exists z\, \forall Y\; Y \neq A_z$ ist eine L^2-Aussage aus $\boldsymbol{S}_4$. Es gibt also eine $\exists_4$-Aussage φ aus $L_{\omega,\omega}$, die genau dann in einer a.a. Gruppe gilt, wenn es ein A_i gibt, das nicht in $W^*(M)$ vorkommt. Wir wählen uns noch eine $\exists_3$-Aussage ψ, die für eine a.a. Gruppe aussagt, daß es ein i mit $A_i \in W^*(\cdots)$ gibt.

Satz 3.4. 1. *Die Folge der $\exists_3$-Aussagen φ_i, $i \in \omega$ ist in a.a. Gruppen unabhängig: Für jedes $B \subset \omega$ gibt es eine a.a. Gruppe M mit $B = \{i \mid M \models \varphi_i\}$.*

2. *Sei $T_1 = \{\varphi_i \mid i \in \omega\}$ und φ die oben definierte $\exists_4$-Aussage. Dann hat zwar jede echte Teilmenge von $T_1 \cup \{\varphi\}$ ein algebraisch abgeschlossenes Modell, es gibt aber keine a.a. Gruppe M mit $M \models T_1 \cup \{\varphi\}$.*

3. *Sei $T_2 = \{\neg\varphi_i \mid i \in \omega\}$ und ψ die oben definierte $\exists_3$-Aussage. Dann hat jede echte Teilmenge von $T_2 \cup \{\varphi\}$ ein a.a. Modell, $T_2 \cup \{\varphi\}$ aber nicht.*

Folgerung 3.5. 1. *Es gibt 2^ω viele a.a. Gruppen in denen paarweise verschiedene $\exists_3$-Aussagen gelten.*

2. ([16]) *Es gibt 2^ω viele verschiedene elementare Typen von a.a. Gruppen (vgl.* [28]).

3. *Die Klasse der algebraisch abgeschlossenen Gruppen ist nicht kompakt.*

Beweis. 1. Sei $B \subset \omega$ und I das von den $A_i/\equiv^*$, $i \in B$ erzeugte Ideal. I ist abzählbar. Wenn $j \notin B$, ist $A_j/\equiv^*$ nicht aus I; denn sonst gäbe es $i_1, \ldots i_n$ aus B mit $A_j \leq^* A_{i_1} \vee \cdots \vee A_{i_n}$ und somit $A_j \leq_T A_{i_1} \vee \cdots \vee A_{i_n}$, was der Unabhängigkeit der $A_i/\equiv_T$ widerspricht. III, 4.1 liefert uns nun ein höchstens abgeschlossenes abzählbares Ideal J, $I \subset J$, das kein $A_j/\equiv^*$, $j \notin B$ enthält. Nach III, 3.12.2 gibt es eine abzählbare a.a.Gr. M'_B mit $W_*(M'_B) = J$. Es gilt $B = \{i \mid A_i \in W^*(M'_B)\}$.

2. Es ist klar, daß keine algebraisch abgeschlossenen Gruppe $T_1 \cup \{\varphi\}$ erfüllt; denn φ sagt ja gerade "es gelten nicht alle φ_i". Da z.B. M_0 ein Modell von T_1 ist, genügt es zu zeigen, daß für jede echte Teilmenge S von ω $\{\varphi_i \mid i \in S\} \cup \{\varphi\}$ ein a.a. Modell besitzt. Solch ein Modell ist aber — in der Bezeichung des Beweises von 1 — M'_S.

3. ψ sagt, daß nicht alle $\neg \varphi_i$ gelten, es gibt also kein algebraisch abgeschlossenes Modell von $T_2 \cup \{\psi\}$. Sei S eine Teilmenge von ω. Dann ist $M'_{(\omega \setminus S)}$ ein Modell von T_2, wenn $S = \omega$, und von $\{\neg \varphi_i \mid i \in S\} \cup \{\psi\}$, wenn $S \neq \omega$. □

Bemerkungen 3.6. 1. 3.5.1 ist optimal: In allen algebraisch abgeschlossenen Gruppen gelten dieselben $\exists_2$-Aussagen (siehe [14]). Es gilt sogar für jede $\exists_2$-Formel $\varphi(x_0, \dots x_n)$: Für alle a.a.Gr. $M, N, a_0, \dots a_n \in M$, $b_0, \dots b_n \in N$ mit $\langle a_0, \dots \rangle' \cong \langle b_0, \dots \rangle'$ ist $M \models \varphi(\boldsymbol{a}_0, \dots)$ gdw. $N \models \varphi(\boldsymbol{b}_0, \dots)$. Das ist leicht direkt zu beweisen. Man kann das Problem aber auch in L^2 übersetzen. Nach 2.1 gehört zu φ ein r.a. A, für das wir $\omega(M) \models S_2^A(W(\langle a_0, \dots \rangle))$ gdw. $\omega(N) \models S_2^A(W(\langle b_0, \dots \rangle))$ zeigen müssen. S_2^A ist aber eine Formel ohne Mengenquantoren (Σ_2^0) und $W(\langle a_0, \dots \rangle) = W(b_0, \dots \rangle)$.

2. Für Mengen von $\exists_3$-Aussagen ist die Klasse der a.a. Gruppen kompakt. Es gilt sogar: Jede $\exists_3$-Aussage, die in einer a.a. Gruppe erfüllbar ist, gilt in jeder a.a. ω-universellen Gruppe. Da eine a.a.Gr. M genau dann ω-universell ist, wenn $W^*(M) = \mathcal{P}(\omega)$, müssen wir wegen 2.4.2 gerade zeigen, daß jede S_3-Aussage, die in einer a.a. Unterstruktur von $(\omega, \mathcal{P}(\omega))$ gilt, auch in $(\omega, \mathcal{P}(\omega))$ gilt. Wir zeigen allgemeiner: "$(\omega, \mathcal{S}_1) \subset (\omega, \mathcal{S}_2)$ seien zwei algebraisch abgeschlossene ω-Modelle, $\rho(X)$ aus $\boldsymbol{S}_3$, $B \in \mathcal{S}_1$. Dann folgt aus $(\omega, \mathcal{S}_1) \models \rho(\boldsymbol{B})$, daß $(\omega, \mathcal{S}_2) \models \rho(\boldsymbol{B})$." Beweis: Wegen 2.3.2(ii) kann man $\rho(X)$ in der Form $S_3^A(X)$ für ein r.a. A annehmen. Wenn es also ein $C \in \mathcal{S}_1$ mit $(\omega, \mathcal{S}_1) \models \neg \exists w \in A \ (\boldsymbol{B}, \boldsymbol{C}) \in \bar{\mathcal{H}}_w^2$ gibt, so erfüllt C auch $(\omega, \mathcal{S}_2) \models \neg \exists w \in A \ (\boldsymbol{B}, \boldsymbol{C}) \in \bar{\mathcal{H}}_w^2$ d.h. $(\omega, \mathcal{S}_2) \models S_3^A(\boldsymbol{B})$.

3. Die Klasse der a.a. Gruppen ist auch bzgl. $\forall_3$-Aussagenmengen kompakt — 3.5.3 ist also optimal. Wir werden nämlich später zeigen, daß jede $\forall_3$-Aussage, die in einer a.a. Gruppe erfüllbar ist, in jeder endlich generischen Gruppe gilt.

Die bis jetzt konstruierten $\exists_3$-Aussagen waren alle schon in M_0 gültig, also auch (man vergleiche 2 der letzten Bemerkung) in allen M_A, $A \subset \omega$, und M^a. Wir werden jetzt $\exists_3$-Aussagen angeben, die erfüllbar sind, in M^a aber nicht gelten.

Ein Baum ist eine Menge von Gödelnummern von endlichen Folgen von natürlichen Zahlen, die mit der Gödelnummer einer Folge auch die Gödelnummern der Anfangsstücke dieser Folge enthält. Ein unendlicher Zweig eines Baumes ist eine Teilmenge der Form {Gödelnummer von $(f(0), \dots, f(n-1)) \mid n \in \omega\}$ für eine Funktion $f: \omega \to \omega$.

Satz 3.7. *Zu jedem r.a. Baum T kann man eine $\exists_3$-Aussage φ_T angeben, die genau dann in einer a.a. Gruppe M gilt, wenn T einen unendlichen Zweig aus $W^*(M)$ besitzt.*

Beweis. k sei die Gödelnummer der leeren Folge. Für Gödelnummern von Folgen bedeute $s_1 \operatorname{unv} s_2$, daß s_1 und s_2 keine gemeinsame Fortsetzung haben; $s_1 \operatorname{anf} s_2$ bedeute, daß s_1 ein echtes Anfangsstück von S_2 ist. Die folgenden Formeln sind aus $\boldsymbol{S}_1$: $v \in Y \rightarrow v \in T$, $k \in Y$, $(v_0 \operatorname{unv} v_1 \wedge v_0 \in Y) \rightarrow v_1 \notin Y$, $v_0 \in Y \rightarrow \exists v_1 \in Y\ v_0 \operatorname{anf} v_1$, $(v_0 \operatorname{anf} v_1 \wedge v_1 \in Y) \rightarrow v_0 \in Y$. Also sind $Y \subset T$, $\psi_1(Y) = \forall v_1, v_0((v_0 \operatorname{unv} v_1 \wedge v_0 \in Y) \rightarrow v_1 \notin Y)$, $\psi_2(Y) = \forall v_0(v_0 \in Y \rightarrow \exists v_1 \in Y\ v_0 \operatorname{anf} v_1)$ und $\psi_3(Y) = \forall v_0, v_1((v_0 \operatorname{anf} v_1 \wedge v_1 \in Y) \rightarrow v_0 \subset Y)$. Formeln aus $\boldsymbol{P}_2$. B ist ein unendlicher Zweig von T gdw. $\psi(\boldsymbol{B})$ gilt, wobei ψ die P_2 Formel $Y \subset T \wedge k \in Y \wedge \psi_1(Y) \wedge \psi_2(Y) \wedge \psi_3(Y)$ ist. Wenn M a.a.Gr. ist, gibt es also genau dann einen unendlichen Zweig aus $W^*(M)$, wenn $\omega(M) \models \exists Y \psi(Y)$. Da $\exists Y \psi(Y)$ eine S_3-Aussage ist, folgt nun die Behauptung aus 2.4.2. □

Folgerungen 3.8. 1. *Es gibt eine $\exists_3$-Aussage, die in M^a nicht gilt, aber auf alle a.a. ω-universellen Gruppen zutrifft.*

2. *Die $\forall_3$-Theorie der a.a. Gruppen ist eine vollständige Π^1_1-Menge. D. h. die Menge der Gödelnummern der $\forall_3$-Sätze, die in allen a.a. Gruppen gelten, ist eine vollständige Π^1_1-Menge.*

3. *Die elementare Theorie der a.a. Gruppen ist vollständig Π^1_1.*

4. *Die elementare Theorie der a.a. Gruppen läßt sich nicht durch eine Menge von $\forall_2$- und $\exists_2$-Aussagen axiomatisieren.*

Beweis. 1. T sei ein rekursiver Baum, der einen unendlichen Zweig besitzt, aber keinen arithmetischen Zweig. φ_T hat die gewünschten Eigenschaften (siehe ([24] S. 419)).

2. Aus ([24] S. 396) folgt, daß die Menge der Gödelnummern (d. h. der Σ^0_1-Indizes) der r.a. Bäume ohne unendlichen Zweig eine vollständige Π^1_1-Menge $\mathcal{T}$ ist. Wir haben in 3.7. jedem r.a. Baum T eine $\exists_3$-Aussage φ_T zugeordnet. T hat einen unendlichen Zweig gdw. es eine a.a. Gruppe gibt in der φ_T gilt. Die Gödelnummer des Baumes T gehört also genau dann zu $\mathcal{T}$, wenn $\neg \varphi_T$ in allen a.a.Gr. gilt. Da die Zuordnung $T \mapsto \varphi_T$ effektiv ist und leicht injektiv gemacht werden kann (injektiv auf den Gödelnummern), ist somit $\mathcal{T}$ 1-reduzierbar auf die $\forall_3$-Theorie der a.a. Gruppen.

2 und 3 sind also nachgewiesen, wenn wir zeigen können, daß die Theorie der a.a. Gruppen Π^1_1 ist. Man kann jede abzählbare Teilmenge

von $\mathscr{P}(\omega)$ in der Form $\bar{A} := \{\{i \mid \langle i, n\rangle \in A\} \mid n \in \omega\}$ für ein $A \subset \omega$ darstellen. Wir können nun jeder L^2-Aussage φ eine arithmetische Eigenschaft $R_\varphi(X)$ von Mengen zuordnen, so daß für alle $A \subset \omega$ $(\omega, \bar{A}) \models \varphi$ gdw. $R_\varphi(A)$. Dabei ersetzen wir einfach überall in φ den Quantor $\exists X \cdots X \cdots$ durch $\exists n \cdots \{i \mid \langle i, n\rangle \in A\} \cdots$. φ gilt nun in allen a.a. ω-Modellen, wenn für alle A $R_{\text{"a.a."}\to\varphi}(A)$. Die L^2-Theorie der a.a. ω-Modelle ist also Π^1_1. Wegen 1.2 ist also auch die elementare Theorie der a.a. Gruppen Π^1_1.

4. Man kann jeder $\exists_2$-Aussage ρ effektiv eine r.a. Menge A zuordnen, sodaß ρ in einer (allen) a.a. Gruppe(n) gilt, wenn $S^A_2(\omega)$. Ebenso ordnet man jeder $\forall_2$-Aussage $\neg S^A_2(\omega)$ zu. Die $\exists_2$-Theorie der a.a. Gruppen ist also Σ^0_2 (sogar vollständig Σ^0_2), die $\forall_2$-Theorie Π^0_2. Die Menge der Folgerungen aus der $\forall_2 \cup \exists_2$-Theorie der a.a.Gr. ist Σ^0_3; es gibt also sogar $\forall_3$-Aussagen, die in allen a.a.Gr. gelten, aber nicht aus der $\forall_2 \cup \exists_2$-Theorie der a.a.Gr. folgen. □

Bemerkung. Wir werden später sehen, daß die $\exists_3$-Theorie der a.a. Gruppen vollständig Σ^0_3 ist.

4. Eine Interpretation von $\omega(M)$ in M

Im ersten Satz dieses Abschnitts betten wir $\omega(M)$ in M ein. (M a.a.Gr.). Dann geben wir Formeln an, die diese Einbettung elementar beschreiben, und bekommen so einen neuen Beweis für 2.4.5. Diesen Satz beweisen wir am Schluß noch einmal, indem wir die Formeln von L^* in (in a.a.Gr.) gleichbedeutende elementare Formeln übersetzen (siehe 2.4.10). 2.4.5 folgt dann mit 1.8.2 und 1.7.

Da **Z** lösbares Wortproblem hat, ist **Z** in jede a.a.Gruppe M einbettbar (II, 2.8). Es gibt also in M Elemente a unendlicher Ordnung. $|a\rangle$ sei die von a erzeugte Halbgruppe $\{a^n \mid n \in \omega\}$. Durch $a^n \oplus a^m = a^{n+m}$ und $a^n \odot a^m = a^{n\cdot m}$ definieren wir zwei Operationen auf $|a\rangle$. Für alle $c, b \in M$ setzen wir $S_{c,b} = \{a^n \in |a\rangle \mid c(a^n b a^{-n}) = (a^n b a^{-n})c\}$. (Das entspricht der Konstruktion in ([28]).)

Satz 4.1. $(|a\rangle, \oplus, \odot, \{S_{c,d} \mid c, d \in M\}) \cong \omega(M)$.

Beweis. Wenn $\bar{S}_{c,b} = \{n \mid a^n \in S_{c,b}\}$ $(= \{n \mid c(a^n b a^{-n}) = (a^n b a^{-n})c\})$, müssen wir zeigen, daß $W^*(M) = \{\bar{S}_{c,b} \mid c, b \in M\}$. Einerseits ist klar, daß für alle $c, b \in M$ $\bar{S}_{c,b} \leqslant_1 W(\langle a, b, c\rangle)$ und also $\bar{S}_{c,b} \in W^*(M)$. Sei anderseits $A \in W^*(M)$ und $A \equiv^* W(G)$ für eine e.e. Untergruppe von M. Fr(2) — die von zwei Elementen erzeugte freie Gruppe — hat lösbares Wortproblem und ist somit in M einbettbar. Da M ω-homogen ist, ist Fr(2), das wir als Obergruppe von $\langle a\rangle$ auffassen, über

$\langle a\rangle$ in M einbettbar. Wir erhalten so ein $b \in M$, so daß a, b $\langle a, b\rangle$ frei erzeugen. Wir setzen $d_n = a^n b a^{-n}$. Die Folge $(d_n \mid n \in \mathbf{Z})$ ist frei und jedes Element $W(a, b)$ von $\langle a, b\rangle = F$ läßt sich eindeutig in der Form $a^z W'(\vec{d})$, $z \in \mathbf{Z}$, schreiben. Wenn U die von $\{d_n \mid n \in A\}$ erzeugte Untergruppe von F ist, ist $W(a, b) \in U$ gdw. $z = 0$ und in $W'(x_0, \dots)$ nur die x_n mit $n \in A$ vorkommen. Also ist $W(F \mid U) \leqslant^+ A$. Nach III, 2.14 gibt es ein $c \in M$ mit $U = \{f \in F \mid fc = cf\}$. Es ist dann $n \in A$ gdw. $d_n \in U$ gdw. $cd_n = d_n c$ gdw. $n \in \bar{S}_{c,b}$. □

Satz 4.2 (siehe [28]). *Wir definieren die folgenden Formeln*

$$\varphi_0(x) := \exists w_1 (w_1 x w_1^{-1} \doteq x^2) \wedge \neg E_1(x, x^2) \quad (\textit{siehe Beweis } \mathrm{V},\ 1.1)$$

$$\varphi_+(y_1, y_2, z) := y_1 \cdot y_2 \doteq z$$

$$\varphi_\cdot(x, y_1, y_2, z) := \exists w\, (wxw^{-1} \doteq y_1 \wedge w y_2 w^{-1} \doteq z) \vee (y_1 \doteq \boldsymbol{e} \wedge z \doteq \boldsymbol{e})$$

$$\varphi_\omega(x, y) := \exists y_1 \cdots y_4 \exists w_1 \cdots w_4\, y \doteq w_1 \cdot w_2 \cdot w_3 \cdot w_4 \wedge$$

$$\bigwedge_{i=1}^{4} (E_1(y_i, x) \wedge \varphi_\cdot(x, y_i, y_i, w_i))$$

$$\varphi_\varepsilon(y, w_1, w_2) := w_1(y w_2 y^{-1}) \doteq (y w_2 y^{-1}) w_1$$

Dann gilt für alle a.a. Gruppen M und $a \in M$

1. *a hat genau dann unendliche Ordnung, wenn $M \models \varphi_0(\boldsymbol{a})$.*

Wenn a unendliche Ordnung hat, ist für alle $b, c \in M$, $n, m \in \omega$.

2. *$b \in \mid a\rangle$ gdw. $M \models \varphi_\omega(\boldsymbol{a}, \boldsymbol{b})$*
3. *$c = a^n \oplus a^m$ gdw. $M \models \varphi_+(\boldsymbol{a}^n, \boldsymbol{a}^m, \boldsymbol{c})$*
4. *$c = a^n \odot a^m$ gdw. $M \models \varphi_\cdot(\boldsymbol{a}, \boldsymbol{a}^n, \boldsymbol{a}^m, \boldsymbol{c})$*
5. *$a^n \in S_{c,b}$ gdw. $M \models \varphi_\varepsilon(\boldsymbol{a}^n, \boldsymbol{c}, \boldsymbol{b})$.*

Beweis. 1. a hat unendliche Ordnung gdw. $\langle a^2\rangle \cong \langle a\rangle$ und $\langle a^2\rangle$ eine echte Untergruppe von $\langle a\rangle$ ist d. h. $a \notin \langle a^2\rangle$. 3. ist trivial. Wenn $a^n \neq e$, gibt es in M einen inneren Automorphismus τ, der a in a^n überführt. Es ist dann $\tau(a^m) = a^{n \cdot m}$. Aus dieser Überlegung folgt 4. φ_+ und $\varphi_\cdot$ definieren sogar Addition und Multiplikation auf $\langle a\rangle$ und machen so $\langle a\rangle$ isomorph zum Ring der ganzen Zahlen. In diesem Ring sind aber die natürlichen Zahlen die Summen von vier Quadraten. Das beweist 2. 5 ist trivial. □

Folgerung 4.3 (siehe 2.4.5). *Man kann für jede L^2-Formel $\rho(\vec{v}, \vec{X})$ eine $L_{\omega,\omega}$-Formel $\check{\rho}(\vec{y}, \vec{w}, \vec{w}', x)$ angeben, so daß für alle a.a. Gruppen M, $\vec{n} \in \omega$, a, $\vec{b}$, $\vec{c} \in M$, wenn a unendliche Ordnung hat,*

$$\omega(M) \models \rho(\vec{n}, \bar{\boldsymbol{S}}_{b_0, c_0}, \bar{\boldsymbol{S}}_{c_1, b_1}, \dots) \quad \text{gdw.} \quad M \models \check{\rho}(\boldsymbol{a}^{n_0}, \boldsymbol{a}^{n_1}, \dots, \vec{\boldsymbol{c}}, \vec{\boldsymbol{b}}, \boldsymbol{a}).$$

Die Aussage ρ *gilt also genau dann in* $\omega(M)$, *wenn* $M \models \exists x\,(\check{\rho}(x) \wedge \varphi_0(x))$.

Beweis. Wir definieren $\check{\rho}$ induktiv: Wir können dabei annehmen, daß ρ nur atomare Formeln der Form $v_1 + v_2 \doteq v_3$, $v_1 \cdot v_2 \doteq v_3$ und $v_0 \in X_0$ enthält. Wir setzen dann

$$(v_1 + v_2 \doteq v_3)^\vee = \varphi_+(y_1, y_2, y_3), (v_1 \cdot v_2 \doteq v_3)^\vee = \varphi_\cdot(x, y_1, y_2, y_3)$$

$$(v_0 \in X_0)^\vee = \varphi_\varepsilon(y_0, w_0, w'_0), (\neg\rho)^\vee = \neg\check{\rho},$$
$$(\rho \wedge \rho')^\vee = \check{\rho} \wedge \check{\rho}', (\exists X_0\rho)^\vee = \exists w_0, w'_0\check{\rho}$$

und

$$(\exists v_0\,\rho)^\vee = \exists y_0(\check{\rho} \wedge \varphi_\omega(x, y_0)). \quad \square$$

Wir wollen eine Übersetzung von L^*-Formeln in elementare Formeln angeben. Dazu übersetzen wir zunächst L^* in eine neue Sprache L^{**}. Diese Übersetzung nützt aus, daß wir in algebraisch abgeschlossenen Gruppen jede endlich Folge $b_0, \ldots, b_n$ in der Form $N_0(c_1, c_2), \ldots N_n(c_1, c_2)$ schreiben können. L^{**} hat Variable $v_0, \ldots$ für natürliche Zahlen und $x, y, \ldots$ für Gruppenelemente. Zahlterme werden aus 0 und den Zahlvariablen mit $+$ und $\cdot$ gebildet.
Individuenterme aus $\boldsymbol{e}$, den Variable für Gruppenelemente durch "Gruppenmultiplikation", und wenn g ein Individuenterm und t ein Zahlterm ist, ist g^t ein Individuenterm (mit der Interpretation $g \cdot \cdots \cdot g$ -t mal). Die Formeln bauen sich wie üblich aus den atomaren Formeln $g_1 \doteq g_2$ und $t_1 \doteq t_2$ (g_i Individuenterme, t_i Zahlterme) auf. Offenbar beschreiben die Formeln von L^{**} arithmetische Eigenschaften von Gruppenelementen. Also ist nach 1.7 (in allen Gruppen) jede L^{**}-Formel durch eine L^*-Formel ausdrückbar. In a.a. Gruppen gilt auch die Umkehrung:

Lemma 4.4. *Zu jeder* L^*-*Formel* $\varphi(v_0, \ldots x_0, \ldots \sigma_0 \cdots)$ *gibt es eine* L^{**}-*Formel* $\varphi^*(v_0, \ldots w_0, \ldots x_0, \ldots z_0, \ldots z'_0, \ldots)$, *so daß für alle a.a. Gruppen* M, $a_0, \ldots \in M$, $c_0, \ldots \in M$, $c'_0, \ldots \in M$ *und* $n_0, \ldots, m_0, \ldots \in \omega$
$M \models \varphi(\boldsymbol{n}_0, \ldots \boldsymbol{a}_0, \ldots, (\boldsymbol{N}_i(\boldsymbol{c}_0, \boldsymbol{c}'_0) \mid \boldsymbol{i} < \boldsymbol{m}_0), \ldots)$ *gdw.*
$M \models \varphi^*(\boldsymbol{n}_0, \ldots \boldsymbol{m}_0, \ldots \boldsymbol{a}_0, \ldots \boldsymbol{c}_0, \ldots \boldsymbol{c}'_0, \ldots)$.

Beweis. Wir ersetzen in φ die Folgenvariable σ_i durch die Variablen z_i, z'_i, w_i mit der Idee, daß $l(\sigma_i) = w_i$ und $\sigma_i = N_0(z_i, z'_i) \cdots N_{w_i - 1}(z_i, z'_i)$. Wir nehmen an, daß die atomaren Formeln von φ nur entweder rein "zahlentheoretisch" sind oder atomare Formeln von $L_{\omega,\omega}$ oder von der Form $\sigma_i(v_j) \doteq x_r$ oder $l(\sigma_i) \doteq v_j$ sind. Für zahlentheoretische atomare Formeln und atomare Formeln setzen wir $\varphi^* = \varphi$. Wir definieren

$(\sigma_i(v_j) \doteq x_r)^* = (v_j < w_i \wedge N_{v_j}(z_i, z'_i) \doteq x_r) \vee (w_i \leqslant v_j \wedge x_r \doteq \boldsymbol{e})$ und $(l(\sigma_i) \doteq v_j) = w_i \doteq v_j$. ($N_v(x, y)$ ist der Individuenterm $[[x, y^{2v+1}], x]$ aus L^{**}.) Wir gewinnen nun φ^* durch die rekursive Definition $(\neg\varphi)^* = \neg\varphi^*$, $(\varphi \wedge \psi)^* = \varphi^* \wedge \psi^*$, $(\exists v_j \varphi)^* = \exists v_j \varphi^*$, $(\exists x_r \varphi)^* = \exists x_r \varphi^*$ und $(\exists \sigma_i \varphi)^* = \exists w_i \exists z_i, z'_i \varphi^*$. □

Satz 4.5. *Zu jeder L^{**}-Formel $\varphi(v_0, \ldots x_0, \ldots)$ kann man eine $L_{\omega,\omega}$-Formel $\hat{\varphi}(y_0, \ldots x_0, \ldots x)$ angeben, so daß für alle $n_0, \ldots \in \omega$ und $a, a_0, a_1, \ldots$ aus einer a.a. Gruppe M, a von unendlicher Ordnung, $M \models \varphi(n_0, \ldots \boldsymbol{a}_0, \ldots)$ gdw. $M \models \hat{\varphi}(\boldsymbol{a}^{n_0}, \ldots \boldsymbol{a}_0, \ldots \boldsymbol{a})$. Die Aussage φ gilt also genau dann in M, wenn $M \models \exists x\,(\hat{\varphi}(x) \wedge \varphi_0(x))$.*

Folgerung. *Zu jeder L^*-Aussage kann man eine in algebraisch abgeschlossenen Gruppen äquivalente elementare Aussage angeben.*

Beweis. Wir übersetzen zuerst die Formel $x_r^{v_j} = x_s$: Nun ist aber, wenn a unendliche Ordnung hat, $b^n = c$ gdw. $\langle b, c\rangle'$ ein homomorphes Bild von $\langle a, a^n\rangle'$ ist. In II, 2.5 wurde explizit ein endliches Gleichungssystem $H_2(\boldsymbol{d}_1, \boldsymbol{d}_2, \boldsymbol{d}_3, \boldsymbol{d}_4, z_1, z_2)$ angegeben, das in einer Obergruppe genau dann lösbar ist, wenn $\langle d_3, d_4\rangle'$ homomorphes Bild von $\langle d_1, d_2\rangle'$ ist. Wir setzen also $(x_r^{v_j} \doteq x_s)^\wedge = \exists z_1, z_2 \bigwedge H_2(x, y_j, x_r, x_s, z_1, z_2)$. Wir können annehmen, daß φ sonst nur noch atomare Formeln der Form $v_i + v_j \doteq v_k$, $v_i \cdot v_j \doteq v_k$ und $x_i \cdot x_j \doteq x_k$ enthält. Wir setzen $(v_i + v_j \doteq v_k)^\wedge = \varphi_+(y_i, y_j, y_k)$, $(v_i \cdot v_j \doteq v_k)^\wedge = \varphi_\cdot(x, y_i, y_j, y_k)$ und $(x_i \cdot x_j \doteq x_k)^\wedge = (x_i \cdot x_j \doteq x_k)$. Wir definieren dann rekursiv über den Aufbau von φ $(\neg\varphi)^\wedge = \neg\hat{\varphi}$, $(\varphi \wedge \psi)^\wedge = \hat{\varphi} \wedge \hat{\psi}$, $(\exists x_i \varphi)^\wedge = \exists x_i \hat{\varphi}$ und $(\exists v_j \varphi)^\wedge = \exists y_j\,(\hat{\varphi} \wedge \varphi_\omega(x, y_j))$. Man sieht leicht, daß die so definierten $\hat{\varphi}$ die gewünschte Eigenschaft haben. □

V. Generische Gruppen

"Forcing in der Modelltheorie" wurde in ([1, 14, 15, 23]) benutzt, um a.a. Strukturen (a.a. Gruppen) zu konstruieren. Während ein großer Teil dieser Konstruktionen durch die einfachen "schrittweisen" Methoden der Kapitel I und III ersetzt werden kann, (siehe z. B. I, 3.5, I, 4.7, die Konstruktion von M_0 (I, 3.9), III, 1.7) sind generische Gruppen weiterhin wegen ihrer relativ einfach zu bestimmenden elementaren Eigenschaften von Interesse (siehe z. B. V, 3.4, VI, 2.9, VI, 3.3.7, VI, 4.1(2), 4.4(2), 4.5(2)).

Im ersten Abschnitt von V behandelen wir die unendlich-generischen Gruppen. Das bekannte Resultat, daß die unendlich-generischen

Gruppen gerade die elementaren Substrukturen der a.a. ω-universellen Gruppen sind, führt zu einer einfachen Kennzeichnung: (1.5) Beim Übergang zu $\omega(M)$, dem zur a.a. Gruppe M gehörenden ω-Modell, entsprechen die unendlich-generischen Gruppen gerade den elementaren Unterstrukturen von $(\omega, \mathcal{P}(\omega))$. Dieser Satz macht die Untersuchung der ∞-generischen Gruppen sehr leicht. Wir erhalten z.B., wenn $V = L$, eine kleinste ∞-generische Gruppe M^0. Das Skelett von M^0 besteht aus den e.e. Gruppen mit analytischem Wortproblem (1.8).

Die Untersuchung der (endlich-) generischen Gruppen beginnen wir im zweiten Abschnitt. Wir geben eine neue Definition der Erzwingungsbeziehung $\Vdash$: Eine Bedingung p (eine endliche Menge von atomaren und negiert atomaren Aussagen aus $L^G(C)$, die mit T^G verträglich ist) erzwingt die Eigenschaft $\mathcal{A}$, wenn im dem Spiel, in dem zwei Spieler I und II abwechselnd Elemente einer aufsteigenden Folge von Bedingungen $p = p_0 \subset p_1 \subset p_2 \subset \cdots$ wählen, I eine Strategie hat, die gewährleistet, daß — wie auch II spielt — die von $\bigcup\{p_i \mid i \in \omega\}$ beschriebene Gruppe die Eigenschaft $\mathcal{A}$ hat.

Dieser Zugang hat den Vorteil, daß keine syntaktischen Überlegungen vorkommen. Man kann z. B. formulieren: $0 \models$ "... ist generisch" (2.4). Außerdem wird der Zusammenhang mit den "schrittweisen" Methoden klar.

Aus 2.6 folgt, daß für elementare Eigenschaften $\mathcal{A}$ unsere Definition mit der üblichen Definiton von $\Vdash$ übereinstimmt.

Im dritten Abschnitt bestimmen wir die durch "$\forall x_0, \ldots x_m$ $S_2^A(W(\langle x_0, \ldots x_m \rangle))$" ausdrückbaren Eigenschaften generischer Gruppen. (Das sind für r.a. A gerade die durch $\forall_3$-Aussagen beschriebenen elementaren Eigenschaften.) Als Folgerung bekommen wir den Satz aus ([14]), daß in generischen Gruppen nicht MAX gilt: es gibt keine universelle e.e. Untergruppe.

Schließlich geben wir noch zwei Charakterisiereungen der generischen Gruppen, ohne modelltheoretische Begriffe zu benützen: Die Gruppe M ist generisch, wenn jede "dichte" arithmetische Menge von endlichen Gl. & Ungl.systemen ein lösbares System enthält (3.8). Auf ähnliche Weise kann man die endlich erzeugten Untergruppen der generischen Gruppen (die "subgenerischen" Gruppen) charakterisieren. Die generischen Gruppen sind dann die a.a. Gruppen, deren endlich erzeugte Untergruppen subgenerisch sind (3.11, 3.12).

Im VI Kapitel werden wir die generischen Gruppen durch rekursionstheoretische Eigenschaften des zugehörigen ω-Modells kennzeichnen.

1. Unendlich generische Gruppen

Algebraisch abgeschlossene Gruppen sind "große" Gruppen. Ein Gleichungssystem, $S(\vec{a}, \vec{x})$, das über $\langle \vec{a} \rangle$ lösbar ist, ist schon in der Gruppe selbst lösbar. Wir werden einige Verstärkungen dieser Definition behandeln.

Die stärkste derartige Forderung ist, daß jeder Isomorphietyp einer endlich erzeugten Obergruppe von $\langle \vec{a} \rangle$ schon in M realisiert wird. Diese M sind gerade die a.a. ω-universellen Gruppen. Denn aus I, 2.3.1 und I, 3.9.1 folgt

Lemma 1.1. *Eine Gruppe M ist genau dann a.a. und ω-universell, wenn sich für alle $\vec{a} \in M$ alle endlich erzeugten Obergruppen von $\langle \vec{a} \rangle$ über $\langle \vec{a} \rangle$ in M einbetten lassen.*

Weil es 2^ω endlich erzeugte Gruppen gibt, hat jede ω-universelle Gruppe mindestens die Mächtigkeit 2^ω. Aus I, 1.4 folgt, daß sich jede Gruppe in eine a.a. ω-universelle Gruppe einbetten läßt (man wählt in I, 1.4 $\mathcal{K}$ so, daß jede endlich erzeugte Gruppe zu einer Gruppe aus $\mathcal{K}$ isomorph ist). I, 2.11.5 zeigt, daß man zu jedem G eine a.a. ω-universelle Obergruppe M finden kann mit $|M| = \max(2^\omega, |G|)$.

Wir suchen abzählbare a.a. Gruppen, die ähnlich "groß" sind wie a.a. ω-universelle Gruppen. Die endlich erzeugten Untergruppen $\langle a_0, \ldots a_n \rangle$ sollen in diesen Gruppen dieselben elementaren Eigenschaften haben wie in ω-universellen a.a. Gruppen. Diese elementaren Eigenschaften hängen nur vom Isomorphietyp von $\langle a_0, \ldots \rangle'$ ab; denn aus I, 2.10.1(a) folgt:

Wenn M, N a.a., ω-universell sind, $\vec{a} \in M$, $\vec{b} \in N$, so ist $(M, \vec{a}) \cong_p (N, \vec{b})$, also auch $(M, \vec{a}) \equiv (N, \vec{b})$, falls $\langle \vec{a} \rangle' \cong \langle \vec{b} \rangle'$.

(Wenn M, N beliebige a.a. Gruppen sind, gilt nur $(M, \vec{a}) \equiv_{\exists_2} (N, \vec{b})$ (IV, 3.6.1).)

Für endliche erzeugte Gruppen F und $\vec{a} \in F$ können wir also sinnvoll definieren: ($\varphi(\vec{x})$ eine Formel aus $L_{\omega,\omega}$) $F \Vdash \varphi(\vec{a})$ gdw. $\varphi(\vec{a})$ in einer (allen) a.a. ω-universellen Obergruppe(n) von F gilt. Mit folgendem Schema können wir durch Rekursion über den Aufbau von φ "berechnen", ob $F \Vdash \varphi(\vec{a})$:

Lemma 1.2. 1. *Wenn φ quantorenfrei ist, ist $F \Vdash \varphi(\vec{a})$ gdw. $F \models \varphi(\vec{a})$.*

2. *$F \Vdash \exists \vec{x}\, \varphi(\vec{a}, \vec{x})$ gdw. es eine e.e. Obergruppe $G \supset F$ und $\vec{b} \in G$ gibt mit $G \Vdash \varphi(\vec{a}, \vec{b})$.*

3. *$F \Vdash \varphi(\vec{a}) \wedge \psi(\vec{a})$ gdw. $F \Vdash \varphi(\vec{a})$ und $F \Vdash \psi(\vec{a})$.*

4. *$F \Vdash \neg \varphi(\vec{a})$ gdw. nicht $F \Vdash \varphi(\vec{a})$.*

Folgerung. *"$\langle \vec{a}\rangle \Vdash \varphi(\vec{\boldsymbol{a}})$" ist für jedes φ eine analytische Eigenschaft von $W(\langle \vec{a}\rangle)$. Das beweist man leicht durch Induktion über den Aufbau von φ, ist aber auch auf folgende Weise einzusehen: Nach* IV, 1.2 *gibt es eine L^2-Formel $\bar{\varphi}(X)$, so daß für alle a.a. ω-universellen Gruppen M und alle $\vec{a} \in M$ $M \vDash \varphi(\vec{\boldsymbol{a}})$ gdw. $(\omega, \mathcal{P}(\omega)) \vDash \bar{\varphi}(W(\langle \vec{a}\rangle))$. Die genaue Angabe von $\bar{\varphi}$ in* IV, 2.1.1 *zeigt, daß — wenn φ eine $\exists_n$-Formel ist — "$\langle a\rangle \Vdash \varphi(\vec{\boldsymbol{a}})$" eine Σ^1_{n-2}-Eigenschaft von $W(\langle \vec{a}\rangle)$ ist $(n \geqslant 3)$.*

Definition 1.3. M heißt unendlich generisch (∞-generisch), wenn für alle $\vec{a} \in M$ und alle Formeln $\varphi(\vec{x})$ $M \vDash \varphi(\vec{\boldsymbol{a}})$ gdw. $\langle \vec{a}\rangle \Vdash \varphi(\vec{\boldsymbol{a}})$.

Satz 1.4. 1. *N sei Untergruppe der ∞-generischen Gruppe M. N ist genau dann ∞-generisch, wenn N elementare Unterstruktur von M ist.*

2. *N ist genau dann ∞-generisch, wenn N elementare Unterstruktur einer a.a. ω-universellen Gruppe ist.*

3. *∞-generische Gruppen sind algebraisch abgeschlossen.*

4. *Jede Gruppe G is in eine ∞-generische Gruppe der Mächtigkeit $|G| + \omega$ einbettbar (es gibt also 2^ω viele abzählbare ∞-generische Gruppen).*

5. *M ist genau dann ∞-generisch, wenn für alle $\vec{a} \in M$ und alle $\varphi(\vec{x}, \vec{y})$, für die $\langle \vec{a}\rangle \Vdash \exists \vec{y}\, \varphi(\vec{\boldsymbol{a}}, \vec{y})$, $\vec{b} \in M$ existiert mit $\langle \vec{a}, \vec{b}\rangle \Vdash \varphi(\vec{\boldsymbol{a}}, \vec{\boldsymbol{b}})$.*

6. *Alle ∞-generischen Gruppen sind elementar äquivalent.*

Folgerung aus 6. *∞-generische Gruppen erfüllen nicht* ***max***, *es gibt also auch keine universellen endlich erzeugten Untergruppen. Jede $\exists_3$-Aussage, die in einer a.a. Gruppe gilt, gilt in allen ∞-generischen Gruppen. (Man vergleiche dazu* IV, 2.8.2, *die Bemerkung nach dem Beweis von* IV, 3.3 *und* IV, 3.6.2.)

Bemerkung zu 5. Wegen IV, 3.6.1 gilt in allen a.a. Gruppen M, $\vec{a} \in M$, für alle $\exists_2$-Formeln $\varphi(\vec{x})$ $M \vDash \varphi(\vec{\boldsymbol{a}})$ gdw. $\langle \vec{a}\rangle \Vdash \varphi(\vec{\boldsymbol{a}})$. Umgekehrt sind die Gruppen mit dieser Eigenschaft algebraisch abgeschlossen. Ähnlich wie in 5 gilt: Die Gruppe M ist genau dann algebraisch abgeschlossen, wenn für alle $\vec{a} \in M$ und alle $\exists_2$-Formel $\varphi(\vec{x}, \vec{y})$, für die $\langle \vec{a}\rangle \Vdash \exists \vec{y}\, \varphi(\vec{\boldsymbol{a}}, \vec{y})$, $\vec{b} \in M$ existiert mit $\langle \vec{a}, \vec{b}\rangle \Vdash \varphi(\vec{\boldsymbol{a}}, \vec{\boldsymbol{b}})$.

Beweis. 1 folgt unmittelbar aus der Definition. 2 folgt aus 1, weil a.a. ω-universelle Gruppen ∞-generisch sind und jede Gruppe in eine a.a. ω-universelle Gruppe einbettbar ist. 3 folgt mit I, 1.5.2 aus 2. 4: Man bettet G zuerst in eine a.a. ω-universelle Gruppe ein. Die gesuchte Gruppe ist eine elementare Unterstruktur von geeigneter Mächtigkeit, die G enthält und mit dem Satz von Löwenheim–Skolem gewonnen wird. 6 folgt sofort aus der Definition. 5: M sei Untergruppe der ∞-generischen Gruppe N. M ist unendlich generisch gdw. $M < N$ gdw. (Nach einem Kriterium von Tarski) für alle $\varphi(\vec{x}, \vec{y})$, $\vec{a} \in M$

$$N \models \exists \vec{y}\, \varphi(\vec{a}, \vec{y}) \Rightarrow \text{ex.}\, \vec{b} \in M\ N \models \varphi(\vec{a}, \vec{b}).$$

Daraus ergibt sich die Behauptung. □

1.4.2 liefert eine sehr einfache Beschreibung der ∞-generischen Gruppen. (Man vergleiche auch [28].)

Satz 1.5. 1. *Eine algebraisch abgeschlossenen Gruppe M ist genau dann ∞-generisch, wenn $\omega(M) < (\omega, \mathcal{P}(\omega))$.*

2. *Sei $(\omega, \mathcal{S}) \prec (\omega, \mathcal{P}(\omega))$. Dann gibt es eine ∞-generische Gruppe M mit $\omega(M) = (\omega, \mathcal{S})$ und $|M| = |\mathcal{S}|$. Wenn $\mathcal{S}$ abzählbar ist, ist M eindeutig bestimmt.*

Beweis. Eine a.a. Gruppe M ist genau dann ω-universell, wenn $W^*(M) = \mathcal{P}(\omega)$. 1 folgt so aus 1.4.2 und IV, 2.4.6. Sei $\mathcal{S}$ wie in 2. $(\omega, \mathcal{S})$ ist a.a. (vgl. Bem. vor IV, 1.2). Sei $(G_i \mid i \in I)$ eine Familie von e.e.Gr. mit $\mathcal{S}/{\equiv^*} = \{W(G_i)/{\equiv^*} \mid i \in I\}$. Setze $N_0 = \bigoplus(G_i \mid i \in I)$. Da $\mathcal{S}/{\equiv^*}$ ein Ideal ist, ist $W^*(N_0) = \mathcal{S}$. Sei N_i schon konstruiert mit $W^*(N_i) = \mathcal{S}$. $S^j(\vec{x}^j)$, $j \in J$ seien alle endlichen Systeme von Gleichungen über N_i, $|J| = |\mathcal{S}|$. Wir bilden das amalgamierte Produkt aller freien Lösungen $N_{i+1} = *_{N_i}((N_i * \mathrm{Fr}(\vec{x}^j))/\langle S^j(\vec{x}^j)\rangle^N \mid j \in J)$. Wegen 1.6.4 ist $W^*(N_{i+1}) = \mathcal{S}$. Setze $M = \bigcup\{N_i \mid i \in \omega\}$. □

Folgerungen 1.6. 1. *Wenn M ∞-generisch ist, ist* $\mathrm{Th}(M) \equiv_1 \mathrm{Th}(\omega, \mathcal{P}(\omega))$.

2. *F und G seien endlich erzeugte Gruppen, $W(F)$ analytisch in $W(G)$. Dann ist F in jede ∞-generische Gruppe einbettbar, in die G einbettbar ist* (*vgl.* III, 1.4).

3. *M^a ist in jede ∞-generische Gruppe einbettbar.*

4. *$U \subset F$, $U \subset G$ seien e.e. Untergruppen der ∞-generischen Gruppe M. Dann ist $F *_U G < M$.*

Beweis. 1. Nach IV, 2.4.5 lassen sich die Aussagen über M und $\omega(M)$ effektiv ineinander übersetzen.

2. gilt, weil, wenn $(\omega, \mathcal{S}) < (\omega, \mathcal{P}(\omega))$, jede Menge, die analytisch in einem Element von $\mathcal{S}$ ist, selbst Element von $\mathcal{S}$ ist.

3. Da alle arithmetischen Mengen analytisch in $W(E)$ sind, ist für jede ∞-generische Gruppe N $W^*(M^a) \subset W^*(N)$. Die Behauptung folgt nun aus III, 3.3.2.

4. Wenn $W(F) \leqslant_e W(G)$, ist $W(F)$ analytisch in $W(G)$. 4 folgt also aus 2 und III, 2.16.

Der letzte Satz gestattet uns eine weitere Charakterisierung der ∞-generischen Gruppen, die zeigt, daß ∞-Generizität eine natürliche Verstärkung der Algebraischen Abgeschlossenheit ist.

Satz 1.7. *Die Gruppe M ist genau dann ∞-generisch, wenn es zu jeder analytischen Klasse $\mathcal{J} \subset \mathcal{P}(\omega)$ und für alle $\vec{a} \in M$, für die es $\vec{b}$ in einer Obergruppe von M gibt mit $W(\langle \vec{a}, \vec{b} \rangle) \in \mathcal{J}$, $\vec{c} \in M$ mit $W(\langle \vec{a}, \vec{c} \rangle) \in \mathcal{J}$ gibt.*

Bemerkung. Nimmt man für die $\mathcal{J}$ in 1.6 nur r.a. Hornklassen, so charakterisiert die Bedingung von 1.6 gerade die a.a. Gruppen.

Beweis. Sei die Bedingung für M erfüllt. Wir zeigen, daß M die Eigenschaft von 1.4.5 hat. Sei $\vec{a} \in M$ und $\langle \vec{a} \rangle \Vdash \exists \vec{y}\, \varphi(\boldsymbol{a}, \vec{y})$. $\langle \vec{a}, \vec{d} \rangle \Vdash \varphi(\vec{\boldsymbol{a}}, \vec{\boldsymbol{d}})$ ist eine analytische Eigenschaft von $W(\langle \vec{a}, \vec{d} \rangle)$. Da für eine Obergruppe $\langle \vec{a}, \vec{c} \rangle \supset \langle \vec{a} \rangle$ $\langle \vec{a}, \vec{c} \rangle \Vdash \varphi(\vec{\boldsymbol{a}}, \vec{c})$ und man wegen der Amalgamierungseigenschaft der Klasse aller Gruppen $\vec{c}$ aus einer Obergruppe von M wählen kann, existiert nach Voraussetzung ein $\vec{b} \in M$ mit $\langle \vec{a}, \vec{b} \rangle \Vdash \varphi(\vec{\boldsymbol{a}}, \vec{\boldsymbol{b}})$.

Wir zeigen nun, daß umgekehrt alle ∞-generischen Gruppen die angegebene Eigenschaft haben. M, $\mathcal{J} \subset \mathcal{P}(\omega)$ und $\vec{a}$ seien wie in 1.7. $\mathcal{J}$ werde durch die L^2-Formel $\varphi(X)$ beschrieben, d.h. $A \in \mathcal{J}$ gdw. $(\omega, \mathcal{P}(\omega)) \models \varphi(\boldsymbol{A})$. Daß für eine Obergruppe $\langle \vec{a}, \vec{b} \rangle$ von $\langle \vec{a} \rangle$ $W(\langle \vec{a}, \vec{b} \rangle) \in \mathcal{J}$ bedeutet (wenn $\vec{a} = a_0, \ldots a_{k-1}$, $\vec{b} = a_k, \ldots a_n$) $(\omega, \mathcal{P}(\omega)) \models \exists Y\, (Y \downarrow k = W(\langle \vec{a} \rangle) \wedge Y \in \mathcal{W}_n \wedge \varphi(Y))$. Nach 1.5 ist $\omega(M) \models \exists Y\, (Y \downarrow k = W(\langle \vec{a} \rangle) \wedge Y \in \mathcal{W}_n \wedge \varphi(Y))$. Sei also ($M$ ist ω-homogen, man beachte den Beweis von IV, 1.2) $\vec{c} \in M$ mit $\omega(M) \models \varphi(W(\langle \vec{a}, \vec{c} \rangle))$. Dann ist wieder wegen 1.5 $(\omega, \mathcal{P}(\omega)) \models \varphi(W(\langle \vec{a}, \vec{c} \rangle))$, d.h. $W(\langle \vec{a}, \vec{c} \rangle) \in \mathcal{J}$. □

Satz 1.8 ($V = L$). 1. *Es gibt eine kleinste ∞-generische Gruppe M^0: M^0 ist in jede ∞-generische Gruppe einbettbar.* ($W^*(M^0)$ *besteht gerade aus den analytischen Mengen.*)

2. *Für e.e. F, G sind äquivalent:* (a) *$W(F)$ ist analytisch in $W(G)$*, (b) *F ist in jede ∞-generische Gruppe einbettbar, in die G einbettbar ist* (*vgl.* III, 1.8.1).

Bemerkungen. M^0 ist durch die angegebenen Eigenschaften eindeutig bestimmt. Es gibt keine kleinste a.a. Gruppe (III, 4.5 zu 3). ($V = L$) $W(F)$ analytisch gdw. F in alle ∞-generischen Gr. einbettbar.

Beweis. 1. Wie in 2 folgt aus $V = L$, daß $(\omega, \mathscr{A}) < (\omega, \mathscr{P}(\omega))$ — $\mathscr{A}$ die Klasse der analytischen Mengen. M^0 sei nach 1.5.2 die abzählbare ∞-generische Gr. mit $W^*(M^0) = \mathscr{A}$. Aus 1.6.2 folgt, daß M^0 in jede ∞-generische Gruppe einbettbar ist.

2. Aus $V = L$ folgt: R sei eine Π^1_n-Relation zwischen Mengen. Wenn für ein $A \subset \omega$ $\{X \mid R(X, A)\} \neq 0$, gibt es ein B, das Π^1_{n+1} in A ist und $R(B, A)$ erfüllt. Wenn nun $W(F)$ nicht analytisch in $W(G)$ ist, ist nach dieser Bemerkung für $\mathscr{K} = \{X \mid X$ analytisch in $W(G)\}$ $(\omega, \mathscr{K})$ eine elementare Unterstruktur von $(\omega, \mathscr{P}(\omega))$. Nach 1.5.2 gibt es ein ∞-generisches M mit $W^*(M) = \mathscr{K}$. F ist nicht in M einbettbar. Damit ist (b)$\rightarrow$(a) bewiesen. (a)$\rightarrow$(b) folgt aus 1.6.2. □

2. Forcing in der Gruppentheorie

Wir haben früher (III, 1.7) eine algebraisch abgeschlossene Gruppe M, die eine vorgegebene e.e. Gruppe G mit nicht-lösbarem Wortproblem nicht enthält, auf folgende Weise konstruiert: M war eine Lösung der Vereinigung einer aufsteigenden Folge $p_0(\vec{c}) \subset p_1(\vec{c}) \subset \cdots$ von endlichen Mengen von Gleichungen und Ungleichungen. Wir mußten bei der Wahl der p_i dafür sorgen, daß alle endlichen Gleichungssysteme $S_i(\vec{c}, \vec{x})$, die ev. später in einer Obergruppe von M lösbar sind Lösungen bekommen und daß, wenn $G = \langle \vec{g} \rangle$, für jede endliche Folge $\vec{t}_i(\vec{c})$ von Termen $(G, \vec{g})$ nicht isomorph in $(M, \vec{t}_i(\vec{c}))$ eingebettet werden kann. Wir numerieren diese Forderungen F_i, $i = 0, 1, \ldots$ und wählen, wenn p_{i-1} schon vorgegeben ist, p_i so, daß, egal wie weiter konstruiert wird, M die Forderung F_i erfüllt. Da wir dabei nicht ausnutzen, daß p_{i-1} "richtig" gewählt war, ist es möglich, mit dieser Konstruktion noch mehr Forderungen zu erfüllen. Die Sicherheit mit der dieses Verfahren zum Ziel führt, kann man auch dadurch beschreiben, daß man sagt, daß I ein Spiel der folgenden Art immer gewinnen kann.

B sei die Menge aller Gleichungen und Ungleichungen ohne freie Variable aus $L(C)$ (die Menge der basischen Aussagen), P die Menge aller endlichen Teilmengen von B, die mit T^G konsistent sind. Die Spieler I und II wählen abwechselnd Elemente einer aufsteigenden Folge $p_0 \subset p_1 \subset \cdots$ von Elementen aus P. Sei $\mathscr{A}$ eine Klasse von Teilmengen von B und eine Folge (ein Spiel) $p_0 \subset p_1 \subset \cdots$ gewählt. Wenn $\bigcup\{p_i \mid i \in \omega\} \in \mathscr{A}$, ist "$\mathscr{A}$ gewonnen". Eine Gewinnstrategie von I für $\mathscr{A}$ ist eine Folge $(f_i \mid i \in \omega)$, $f_i : P \rightarrow P$, mit $\forall i, p\ f_i(p) \supset p$, so daß in allen Spielen $p_0 \subset p_1 \subset \cdots$, in denen I nach dieser Strategie spielt, d.h. für alle $i > 0$ $f_i(p_{2i-1}) = p_{2i}$ und $f_0(\phi) = p_0$, $\mathscr{A}$ gewonnen ist. Ähnlich definiert man Gewinnstrategien von II für $\mathscr{A}$: eine Folge von

Funktionen $f_0, f_1, \ldots$ von P nach P, so daß in allen Spielen $p_0 \subset p_1 \subset \cdots$, für die f.a. i $p_{2i+1} = f_i(p_{2i})$, $\mathscr{A}$ gewonnen ist.

II hat eine Gewinnstrategie für $\mathscr{A}$ gdw. I für jedes $p \in P$ eine Gewinnstrategie $(f_i \mid i \in \omega)$ für $\mathscr{A}$ mit $f_0(\phi) = p$ hat ($\vec{f}$ "beginnt mit p").

p ist eine (I-) Gewinnposition für $\mathscr{A}$, wenn I eine Gewinnstrategie für $\mathscr{A}$ hat, die mit p beginnt. Wir schreiben dann $p \Vdash \mathscr{A}$ (p erzwingt $\mathscr{A}$). $p \in P$ ist eine II-Gewinnposition für $\mathscr{A}$, wenn es ein $p' \supset p$ mit $p' \Vdash \mathscr{A}$ gibt.

$\mathscr{A}$ heißt determiniert, wenn jedes $p \in P$ Gewinnposition für $\mathscr{A}$ oder II-Gewinnposition für $\mathscr{P}(B) \setminus \mathscr{A}$ ist (p kann nicht gleichzeitig Gewinnposition für $\mathscr{A}$ und II-Gewinnposition für $\mathscr{P}(B) \setminus \mathscr{A}$ sein. Alle $\mathscr{A}$, die wir später betrachten, werden determiniert sein).

Bemerkung. Es gibt zwei andere Begriffe für "Gewinnstrategie" für $\mathscr{A}$, eine stärkere und eine schwächere. Eine starke Gewinnstrategie von I für $\mathscr{A}$ ist eine Funktion $F : {}^{\omega}P \to P$ mit $p_i \subset F((p_0, \ldots, p_i))$ f.a. i und $p_0, \ldots, p_i$ aus P, so daß jedes Spiel $p_0 \subset p_1 \subset \cdots$ mit $p_{2i} = F((p_0, \ldots, p_{2i-1}))$ f.a. i $\mathscr{A}$ gewinnt. Eine schwache Gewinnstrategie von I für $\mathscr{A}$ ist eine Funktion $f : P \to P$ mit $\forall p\ f(p) \supset p$, sodaß $(f \mid i \in \omega)$ eine Gewinnstrategie von I für $\mathscr{A}$ ist. Aus jeder Gewinnstrategie von I für $\mathscr{A}$, $(f_i \mid i \in \omega)$, erhält man eine starke Gewinnstrategie, indem man $F((p_0, \ldots, p_{2i-1})) = f_i(p_{2i-1})$ setzt. Man kann sich nun überlegen, daß man aus einer starken Gewinnstrategie eine schwache Gewinnstrategie gewinnen kann. Die drei Begriffe sind also äquivalent.

Beispiele. 1. Sei G eine e.e. Gruppe mit nicht-lösbarem Wortproblem und $\mathscr{A}$ die Klasse aller Teilmengen von B, die mit T^G konsistent sind und für die jedes Modell, das von den Interpretationen der c_i erzeugt wird, algebraisch abgeschlossen ist und G — bis auf Isomorphie — nicht enthält. Der Beweis von III, 1.7 zeigt, daß $\phi \Vdash \mathscr{A}$.

2. φ sei eine atomare Aussage von $L(C)$. Dann ist $\phi \Vdash \{G \subset B \mid \varphi \in G$ oder $\neg \varphi \in G\}$. Denn wenn II $\emptyset \subset p_1$ wählt, so kann I $p_2 \supset p_1$ so wählen, daß $\varphi \in p_2$ oder $\neg \varphi \in p_2$. (Bei der Gewinnstrategie von I kommt es also nur auf f_1 an.) Statt $p \Vdash \{G \subset B \mid \cdots G \cdots\}$ schreiben wir auch $p \Vdash$ "$\cdots G \cdots$".

Lemma 2.1. *$\mathscr{A}, \mathscr{A}_0, \mathscr{A}_1, \ldots$ seien Teilmengen von $\mathscr{P}(B)$, $r, p, q \in P$.*

1. *Wenn $p \Vdash \mathscr{A}$, gibt es ein $G \in \mathscr{A}$, $G \cup T^G$ konsistent, $p \in G$.*

2. *$p \cup q \notin P$ (p, q unverträglich) gdw. $p \Vdash$ "$q \not\subset G$". "$q \subset G$" ist determiniert.*

3. *Aus* $p \Vdash \mathcal{P}(B)\setminus\mathcal{A}$ *folgt* $\forall q \supset p\ q \nVdash \mathcal{A}$. *Wenn* $\mathcal{A}$ *determiniert ist, ist auch* $\mathcal{P}(B)\setminus\mathcal{A}$ *determiniert und* $p \Vdash \mathcal{P}(B)\setminus\mathcal{A}$ *gdw.* $\forall q \supset p\ q \nVdash \mathcal{A}$.

4. $p \Vdash \bigcap\{\mathcal{A}_i \mid i \in \omega\}$ *gdw. für alle i* $p \Vdash \mathcal{A}_i$. *Wenn alle* $\mathcal{A}_i$ *determiniert sind, ist auch* $\bigcap\{\mathcal{A}_i \mid i \in \omega\}$ *determiniert.*

5. *Aus* $\forall q \supset p\ \exists r \supset q\ \exists i \in \omega\ r \Vdash \mathcal{A}_i$ *folgt* $p \Vdash \bigcup\{\mathcal{A}_i \mid i \in \omega\}$. *Wenn alle* $\mathcal{A}_i$ *determiniert sind, ist auch* $\bigcup\{\mathcal{A}_i \mid i \in \omega\}$ *determiniert und*

$$\forall q \supset p\ \exists r \supset q\ \exists i \in \omega r \Vdash \mathcal{A}_i \quad \text{gdw.} \quad p \Vdash \bigcup\{\mathcal{A}_i \mid i \in \omega\}.$$

6. *Wenn* $p \subset q$, $p \Vdash \mathcal{A}$, *so auch* $q \Vdash \mathcal{A}$.

Beweis. 1. Man gewinnt G als $\bigcup\{p_i \mid i \in \omega\}$ aus einem Spiel $p_0 \subset p_1 \subset \cdots$, bei dem I seine bei p beginnende Gewinnstrategie für $\mathcal{A}$ anwendet.

2. Wenn p und q unverträglich sind, ist jede Strategie, die bei p beginnt, eine Gewinnstrategie für "$q \not\subset G$". Wenn p und q verträglich sind, kann II auf die Wahl $p_0 = p$ von I mit der Wahl $p \cup q$ antworten. Also ist $p \nVdash$ "$q \not\subset G$" und p ist II-Gewinnposition für "$q \subset G$". "$q \not\subset G$" ist also determiniert. Nach 3 ist also auch "$q \subset G$" determiniert.

3. Sei $p \Vdash \mathcal{P}(B)\setminus\mathcal{A}$ und $q \supset p$. Wenn I eine bei q beginnende Gewinnstrategie für $\mathcal{A}$ hat, und II nach dieser Strategie spielt, gewinnt jedes Spiel $p \subset q \subset p_2 \subset \cdots\ \mathcal{A}$. Wid. Sei $\mathcal{A}$ determiniert, $p \nVdash \mathcal{P}(B)\setminus\mathcal{A}$. Wenn also I $p_0 = p$ wählt, kann II $p_1 = q \supset p$ so wählen, daß q keine II-Gewinnposition für $\mathcal{P}(B)\setminus\mathcal{A}$ ist. q ist dann I-Gewinnposition für $\mathcal{A}$.

4. Jede Gewinnstrategie für $\bigcap\{\mathcal{A}_i \mid i \in \omega\}$ ist auch eine Gewinnstrategie für jedes $\mathcal{A}_i$. Sei umgekehrt für jedes i $(f^i_j \mid j \in \omega)$ eine Gewinnstrategie von I für $\mathcal{A}_i$, die mit p beginnt. $((i_k, j_k) \mid k \in \omega)$ sei eine Durchzählung von ω^2 mit $j_0 = 0$ und $\forall k\ \exists k' > k\ (j_{k'} = j_k + 1, i_k = i_{k'})$. $(f^{i_k}_{j_k} \mid k \in \omega)$ ist dann eine Gewinnstrategie von I für $\bigcap\{\mathcal{A}_i \mid i \in \omega\}$, die bei p beginnt. Denn wenn I diese Strategie beim Spiel $p = p_0 \subset p_1 \subset \cdots$ angewendet hat, gibt es für jedes i eine Teilfolge $p = p_0 \subset p_{r_1} \subset f^i_1(p_{r_1}) \subset p_{r_2} \subset f^i_2(p_{r_2}) \cdots \subset p_{r_s} \subset f^i_s(p_{r_s}) \subset \cdots$. Die Vereinigung der p_{r_s} liegt aber in $\mathcal{A}_i$.

5. Sei $\forall q \supset p\ \exists r \supset q\ \exists i \in \omega\ r \Vdash \mathcal{A}_i$. Dann hat I die folgende Strategie für $\bigcup\{\mathcal{A}_i \mid i \in \mathcal{A}\}$: I beginnt mit p; wenn II $q \supset p$ wählt, wählt I ein $r \supset q$ mit $r \Vdash \mathcal{A}_i$ für ein i und spielt mit einer Strategie für $\mathcal{A}_i$, die bei r beginnt, weiter. Also ist $p \Vdash \bigcup\{\mathcal{A}_i \mid i \in \omega\}$. Der Rest von 5 folgt aus 3, 4 und der Darstellung $\bigcup\{\mathcal{A}_i \mid i \in \omega\} = \mathcal{P}(B)\setminus(\bigcap\{\mathcal{P}(B)\setminus\mathcal{A}_i \mid i \in \omega\})$.

6. Wenn $(f_i \mid i \in \omega)$ eine Gewinnstrategie von I für $\mathcal{A}$ ist, die bei p beginnt, ist $(f'_i \mid i \in \omega)$ mit $f'_0 = q$ und $f'_i = f_i$ sonst eine Gewinnstrategie von I für $\mathcal{A}$, die bei q beginnt. □

Beispiel 2.2. Wenn $G \subset B$, bezeichnet M_G die von den Gleichungen in G präsentierte Gruppe. Ist $G \cup T^G$ konsistent, gelten alle Aussagen von G in M_G. $c_0, \dots d_0, \dots$ seien in M_G durch $g_0, \dots h_0, \dots$ interpretiert. Es ist dann

$$\emptyset \Vdash \text{“}M_G \text{ ist algebraisch abgeschlossen”}.$$

Nach 2.1.4 müssen wir zeigen, daß für jedes endliche Gleichungs- & Ungl.-system $S(\vec{c}, \vec{x})$

$$\emptyset \Vdash \text{“Wenn } S(\vec{g}, \vec{x}) \text{ über } M_G \text{ lösbar ist, hat } S(\vec{g}, \vec{x}) \text{ eine Lösung in } M_G\text{”}.$$

I hat folgende Gewinnstrategie: p_1 sei von II gewählt; wenn $p_1 \cup S(\vec{c}, \vec{x})$ (mit T^G) konsistent ist, wählt I $p_2 = p_1 \cup S(\vec{c}, \vec{d})$ für Konstanten $\vec{d}$, die in S und p_1 noch nicht vorkommen. Auf die weiteren Züge von I kommt es nicht mehr an.

$\mathcal{K}$ sei eine Klasse von determinierten Teilmengen von $\mathcal{P}(B)$. Wir nennen $G \subset B$ $\mathcal{K}$-generisch, wenn G Ergebnis eines Spiels ist, bei dem "um jedes Element von $\mathcal{K}$ gespielt wurde". Das soll bedeuten:

Definition 2.3. $G \subset B$ heißt $\mathcal{K}$-generisch, wenn $G \cup T^G$ konsistent ist und für alle $\mathcal{A} \in \mathcal{K}$ $G \in \mathcal{A}$ gdw. $\exists p \subset G\ p \Vdash \mathcal{A}$.

Lemma 2.4. *Wenn $\mathcal{K}$ abzählbar, ist $\emptyset \Vdash$ "G ist $\mathcal{K}$-generisch". (Also gibt es nach* 2.1.1 *$\mathcal{K}$-generische Mengen.)*

Beweis. In Anbetracht von 2.1.4 müssen wir zeigen: Für alle $\mathcal{A} \in \mathcal{K}$,
1. $\emptyset \Vdash$ "$G \in \mathcal{A} \Rightarrow$ es gibt $p \subset G\ p \Vdash \mathcal{A}$" und für alle p mit $p \Vdash \mathcal{A}$,
2. $\emptyset \Vdash$ "Wenn $p \subset G$, ist $G \in \mathcal{A}$".

1. Wir geben eine Gewinnstrategie von I an: Wenn II p_1 wählt, und es ein $p \supset p_1$ mit $p \Vdash \mathcal{A}$ gibt, setzt I $p_2 = p$ (in dem Spiel ist dann offenbar "es gibt $p \subset G$, $p \Vdash \mathcal{A}$" gewonnen). Wenn es solch ein p nicht gibt, ist $p_1 \Vdash$ "$G \notin \mathcal{A}$". I spielt nun eine Gewinnstrategie von "$G \notin \mathcal{A}$", die mit p_1 beginnt.

2. Sei p_1 gegeben. Wenn p_1 und p verträglich sind, ist $p_1 \subset p_1 \cup p \Vdash$ "$G \in \mathcal{A}$". Sonst ist $p_1 \Vdash$ "$p \not\subset G$". □

Lemma 2.5. *$\mathcal{K}$ sei eine Klasse von determinierten Teilmengen von $\mathcal{P}(B)$. Wenn $\mathcal{A} \in \mathcal{K}$, sei auch $\mathcal{P}(B) \setminus \mathcal{A} \in \mathcal{K}$. Dann ist für alle $p \in P$ und $\mathcal{A} \in \mathcal{K}$ $p \Vdash \mathcal{A}$ gdw. für alle $\mathcal{K}$-generischen G $p \subset G \Rightarrow G \in \mathcal{A}$.*

Beweis. Wenn $p \Vdash \mathcal{A}$, G $\mathcal{K}$-generisch, $p \subset G$, $\mathcal{A} \in \mathcal{K}$, ist nach Definition $G \in \mathcal{A}$. Sei andererseits $p \nVdash \mathcal{A}$. Dann gibt es ein $q \supset p$ mit

$q \Vdash \mathscr{P}(B) \setminus \mathscr{A}$. Da $q \Vdash$ "G ist $\mathscr{K}$-generisch", gibt es ein $\mathscr{K}$-generisches G, das q enthält. Da $\mathscr{P}(B) \setminus \mathscr{A} \in \mathscr{K}$, ist $G \notin \mathscr{A}$. □

Wir interessieren uns für elementare Eigenschaften von Gruppen, also für jede Aussage $\varphi \in L(C)$ für die Klasse $A_\varphi = \{G \subset B \mid M_G \models \varphi\}$. Wir schreiben $p \Vdash \varphi$ für $p \Vdash A_\varphi$. In folgendem Lemma geben wir an, wie man $p \Vdash \varphi$ rekursiv "berechnen" kann.

Lemma 2.6. *φ, ψ seien Aussagen aus $L(C)$, $p, q, r \in P$, $\vec{t}$ konstante $L(C)$-Terme.*

1. *Wenn φ quantorenfrei ist, ist $p \Vdash \varphi$ gdw. $p \vdash^G \varphi$.*
2. *$p \Vdash \neg\varphi$ gdw. $\forall q \supset p\ q \nVdash \varphi$.*
3. *$p \Vdash \varphi \wedge \varphi$ gdw. $p \Vdash \varphi$ und $p \Vdash \psi$.*
4. *$p \Vdash \varphi \vee \varphi$ gdw. $\forall q \supset p\ \exists r \supset q\ r \Vdash \varphi$ oder $r \Vdash \psi$.*
5. *$p \Vdash \forall \vec{x}\, \varphi(\vec{x})$ gdw. für alle $\vec{t}$ $p \Vdash \varphi(\vec{t})$ gdw. für alle $\vec{c}$ $p \Vdash \varphi(\vec{c})$.*
6. *$\emptyset \Vdash$ "Es gibt c, $M_G \models t \doteq c$".*
7. *Alle A_φ sind determiniert.*
8. *Wenn $p(\vec{c}) \Vdash \varphi(\vec{c})$, ist $p(\vec{t}) \Vdash \varphi(\vec{t})$ (falls $p(\vec{t}) \in P$).*

Folgerung. *"$p \Vdash \varphi(\vec{c})$" ist für jedes φ eine arithmetische Relation zwischen (den Gödelnummern von) p und $\vec{c}$. Man rechnet leicht nach, daß, wenn $\varphi \in \forall_n$, $n \geq 1$, ist, diese Relation Π^0_{n+1} ist.*

Beweis. 1: Wenn $p \vdash^G \varphi$ und das Spiel $p_0 \subset p_1 \subset \cdots$ mit p beginnt, ist $\bigcup\{p_i \mid i \in \omega\} \in A_\varphi$. Also ist $p \Vdash A_\varphi$. Sei $p \nvdash^G \varphi$. Dann gibt es ein $q \supset p$ mit $q \vdash^G \neg\varphi$, also $q \Vdash$ "$G \notin A_\varphi$". Daraus folgt $p \nVdash \varphi$ und die Determiniertheit von A_φ. 2, 3, 4, 7 und der erste Teil von 5 folgen sofort aus 2.1. 6: Sei $p_1 \in P$. Wenn c weder in p_1 noch in t vorkommt, ist $p_1 \cup \{t_1 \doteq c\} \in P$. Aus $p_1 \cup \{t \doteq c\} \Vdash t \doteq c$ folgt die Behauptung. Wir zeigen den zweiten Teil von 5: Sei für alle $\vec{c}$ $p \Vdash \varphi(\vec{c})$ und $\vec{t}$ eine endliche Folge von konstanten Termen. Nach 6 ist dann $p \Vdash$ "Es gibt c mit $M_G \models \vec{t} \doteq \vec{c} \wedge \varphi(\vec{c})$". Daraus folgt $p \Vdash \varphi(\vec{t})$. 8: Es ist klar, daß für eine Bijektion $\pi: C \to C$ $p(\vec{c}) \Vdash \varphi(\vec{c})$ gdw. $p(\pi(\vec{c})) \Vdash \varphi(\pi(\vec{c}))$. Sei nun $p(\vec{c}) \Vdash \varphi(\vec{c})$ und $p(\vec{t})$ gegeben. $q \in P$ sei eine beliebige Erweiterung von $p(\vec{t})$. Für neue Konstanten $\vec{d}$ ist $p' = q \cup \{t_0 \doteq d_0,\ t_1 \doteq d_1, \ldots\} \cup p(\vec{d})$ aus P. Die Bemerkung am Anfang zeigt $p' \Vdash \varphi(\vec{d})$ und daher $p' \Vdash \varphi(\vec{t})$. □

Wir nennen G endlich generisch, wenn G $\mathscr{K}$-generisch für $\mathscr{K} = \{A_\varphi \mid \varphi$ Aussage aus $L(\vec{c})\}$. Das bedeutet also

Definition 2.7. 1. $G \subset B$ heißt endlich generisch, wenn $G \cup T^G$

konsistent ist und für jede $L(C)$-Aussage φ $M_G \models \varphi$ gdw. es ein $p \subset G$ mit $p \Vdash \varphi$ gibt.

2. Eine Gruppe M heißt (endlich) generisch, wenn für alle Formeln $\varphi(\vec{c})$, $\vec{a} \in M$ $M \models \varphi(\vec{a})$ gdw. es $\vec{b} \in M$ und ein $p(\vec{c}, \vec{d}) \in P$ gibt mit $M \models p(\vec{a}, \vec{b})$ und $p(\vec{c}, \vec{d}) \Vdash \varphi(\vec{c})$.

Lemma 2.8. 1. *$G \subset B$ sei mit T^G konsistent. Dann ist G genau dann endlich generisch, wenn M_G generisch ist und für jede atomare Aussage φ $G \vdash \varphi$ oder $G \vdash \neg \varphi$.*

2. *$(g_i \mid i \in \omega)$ sei ein Erzeugendensystem der Gruppe M und G die Menge aller Aussagen aus B, die in $(M, \vec{g})$ gelten. Dann ist M genau dann generisch, wenn G endlich generisch ist.*

3. *$p(\vec{c}, \vec{d}) \Vdash \varphi(\vec{c})$ gdw. für jede generische Gruppe M $\vec{a}, \vec{b} \in M$ $M \models p(\vec{a}, \vec{b}) \Rightarrow M \models \varphi(\vec{a})$.*

Beweis. 1. G sei generisch, $\vec{a} \in M_G$, $M_G \models \varphi(\vec{a})$. Da M_G von den Interpretationen der $\vec{c}$ erzeugt wird, gibt es Terme $\vec{t}(\vec{d})$, Konstanten $\vec{d}$ aus C, die in M_G durch $\vec{h}$ interpretiert werden, mit $\vec{a} = \vec{t}(\vec{h})$. Da $M_G \models \varphi(\vec{t}(\vec{d}))$, gibt es ein $q(\vec{d}, \vec{d}') \subset G$ mit $q \Vdash \varphi(\vec{t}(\vec{d}))$. Natürlich ist $M_G \models q(\vec{h}, \vec{h}')$. Wenn $\vec{c}$ neue Konstanten aus C sind, ist $p = q \cup \{t_0 \doteq c_0, t_1 \doteq c_1, \ldots\}$ aus P. Dann ist $p \Vdash \varphi(\vec{c})$ und $M_G \models p(\vec{a}, \vec{h}, \vec{h}')$. Wenn $M_G \models p(\vec{a})$, $p(\vec{c}) \Vdash \varphi(\vec{c})$ folgt $M_G \models \varphi(\vec{a})$. Denn sonst gibt es $\vec{b} \in M_G$, $q(\vec{c}, \vec{d}) \in P$, $M_G \models q(\vec{a}, \vec{b})$, $q \Vdash \neg \varphi(\vec{c})$. Da aber p und q verträglich sind, würde $p \cup q \Vdash (\neg \varphi \wedge \varphi)(c)$ folgen. Wid.

Sei nun umgekehrt M_G generisch und erfülle G die genannte Bedingung. Sei $p \subset G$ und $p \Vdash \varphi$. Dann ist $M_G \models p$ und somit $M_G \models \varphi$. Sei umgekehrt $M_G \models \varphi$. Dann gibt es ein $q(\vec{c}, \vec{d}) \Vdash \varphi$ mit $M_G \models q(\vec{c}, \vec{b})$ für $\vec{b} \in M$. Wir können annehmen, daß die $\vec{d}$ von den $\vec{c}$ verschieden sind. Es sei $\vec{b} = \vec{t}(\vec{g}')$ für die Interpretationen $\vec{g}'$ der Konstanten $\vec{c}'$. Aus 2.6.8 folgt $q(\vec{c}, \vec{t}(\vec{c}')) \Vdash \varphi$. Da $M_G \models q(\vec{c}, \vec{t}(\vec{c}'))$, ist $G \vdash q(\vec{c}, \vec{t}(\vec{c}'))$. Also gibt es $p \subset G$ mit $p \vdash \bigwedge q(\vec{c}, t(\vec{c}'))$. $p \Vdash \varphi$.

2. Folgt aus 1, weil $M = M_G$.

3. Die eine Richtung der Behauptung folgt sofort aus der Definition. Wenn $p(\vec{c}, \vec{d}) \nVdash \varphi(\vec{c})$, gibt es ein endlich generisches G mit $p \subset G$ und $M_G \nvDash \varphi(\vec{c})$. Es ist aber $M_G \models p$. □

3. Endlich generische Gruppen

In diesem Abschnitt behandeln wir zuerst einige einfache Eigenschaften generischer Gruppen. Dann geben wir verschiedene Charakterisierungen der generischen Gruppen.

Satz 3.1. 1. *Alle generischen Gruppen sind elementar äquivalent.*

2. *Generische Gruppen sind algebraisch abgeschlossen.*

3. *Die Theorie der generischen Gruppen ist rekursiv isomorph zu* $\emptyset^{\omega}$. ([28]).

Beweis. φ sei eine Aussage aus $L_{\omega,\omega}$, $p(\vec{c}) \Vdash \varphi$. Wir zeigen $\emptyset \Vdash \varphi$; Es gibt sonst $q(\vec{d}) \in P$, $q(\vec{d}) \Vdash \neg\varphi$. Wenn für die Permutation π von C $\pi(\vec{c})$ von $\vec{d}$ disjunkt ist, sind $p(\pi(\vec{c}))$ und q verträglich. Aber $q \cup p(\pi(\vec{c})) \Vdash \neg\varphi \wedge \varphi$. Wid. Damit ist 1 bewiesen.

2. Das endliche Gl. & Ungl.system $S(\vec{a}, \vec{x})$ sei über der generischen Gruppe M lösbar. Wenn S keine Lösung in M hat, gibt es $\vec{b} \in M$, $p(\vec{c}, \vec{d}) \Vdash \forall\vec{x} \neg \bigwedge S(\vec{c}, \vec{x})$, $M \models p(\vec{a}, \vec{b})$. Da $S(\vec{a}, \vec{x})$ in einer Obergruppe von $\langle \vec{a}, \vec{b} \rangle$ lösbar ist, sind $p(\vec{c}, \vec{d})$ und $S(\vec{c}, \vec{c}\,')$ für neue c' verträglich. Es ist aber $p \subset p \cup S(\vec{c}, \vec{c}\,') \Vdash \exists\vec{x} \wedge S(\vec{c}, \vec{x}\,')$. Wid.

3. Beim Beweis von 1 haben wir gesehen, daß eine elementare Aussage genau dann in allen generischen Gruppen gilt, wenn sie von $\emptyset$ erzwungen wird. Also ist φ genau dann aus T^f, der Theorie der generischen Gruppen, wenn die arithmetische Aussage "$\emptyset \Vdash \varphi$" gilt. Daraus folgt $T^f \leqslant_1 \emptyset^{\omega}$. Umgekehrt läßt sich nach IV, 2.4.5 jeder arithmetischen Aussage eine gruppentheoretische Aussage zuordnen, die genau dann in einer — allen — a.a. Gruppen gilt, wenn die arithmetische Aussage wahr ist. Also ist, wegen 2, $\emptyset^{\omega} \leqslant_1 T^f$. □

Folgerung 1. *Die arithmetische Eigenschaft* $R(x_0, \ldots)$ *trifft genau dann in einer generischen Gruppe* M *auf* $a_0, \ldots$ *zu, wenn es* $b_0, \ldots \in M$ *und* $p(\vec{c}, \vec{d}) \in P$ *mit* $M \models p(\vec{a}, \vec{b})$ *und* $p \Vdash$ "$g_0, \ldots$ *in* M_G *haben die Eigenschaft* R" *gibt. Das folgt aus* IV, 2.4.9, *weil generische Gruppen a.a. sind.*

Folgerung 2. *Keine generische Gruppe enthält eine endlich erzeugte Untergruppe, deren Wortproblem arithmetisch, aber nicht lösbar ist. Denn* (*Beispiel* 1 *vor* 2.1) *es gibt eine generische Gruppe, die eine solche e.e. Gruppe mit nicht-lösbarem Wortproblem nicht enthält. Da also auch alle elementar äquivalenten a.a. Gruppen* (*siehe* IV, 3) *diese Gruppe nicht enthalten, folgt die Behauptung aus* 1.

Keine der Gruppen M_A, M^a und keine ∞-generische Gruppe ist also generisch.

Mit dem folgenden Satz können wir viele arithmetische Eigenschaften generischer Gruppen herleiten.

Satz 3.2 (siehe [14]). A_i, $i \in \omega$ *sei eine Folge von Teilmengen von* ω, $m \in \omega$. *Dann sind äquivalent:*

(a) *Es gibt eine generische Gruppe M, sodaß für alle* $i \in \omega$ *und alle* $a_0, \ldots a_m \in M$ *gilt* $S_2^{A_i}(W(\langle a_0, \ldots a_m \rangle))$ (*vgl.* IV, 2 *für die Definition*).

(b) *Jedes endliche Gleichungs- & Ungleichungssystem* $S(\vec{x}, \vec{y})$, *das lösbar ist, hat für alle i eine Lösung* $\vec{a}$, $\vec{b}$ *in einer Gruppe H, so daß* $S_2^{A_i}(W(\langle a_0, \ldots a_m \rangle))$.

(c) *Für alle i gibt es eine a.a. Gruppe M, so daß für alle* $a_0, \ldots a_m \in M$ $S_2^{A_i}(W(\langle a_0, \ldots a_m \rangle))$ *gilt.*

Zusatz. *Wenn alle* A_i *arithmetisch sind, sind* (*a*), (*b*), (*c*) *äquivalent zu* (d). *Für alle generischen Gruppen M, alle* $i \in \omega$, $a_0, \ldots \in M$ *gilt* $S_2^{A_i}(W(\langle a_0, \ldots a_m \rangle))$.

Beweis. Wenn die A_i arithmetisch sind, folgt (a)$\leftrightarrow$(d) weil "f.a. $a_0, \ldots S_2^{A_i}(W(\langle a_0, \ldots \rangle))$" arithmetische Eigenschaften sind, die sich auf elementar äquivalente Gruppen übertragen.

(a)$\rightarrow$(c) ist klar. Um (c)$\rightarrow$(b) einzusehen, geben wir uns ein $i \in \omega$ und ein endliches Gl. & Ungl.system $S(\vec{x}, \vec{y})$ vor. S hat eine Lösung $\vec{a}, \vec{b}$ in der a.a.Gr. M, wo $S_2^{A_i}(W(\langle a_0, \ldots \rangle))$ gilt.

(b)$\rightarrow$(a): Wir zeigen $\emptyset \Vdash$ "f.a. i ex. $n \in A_i$ $W(\langle g_0, \ldots \rangle) \in \bar{\mathcal{H}}_n$" ($g_0, \ldots$ sind die Interpretationen der $c_0, \ldots$ in M_G). Das bedeutet

$$\forall i \in \omega \, \forall p \, \exists q \supset p \, \exists n \in A_i \; q \Vdash \text{"} W(\langle g_0, \ldots \rangle) \in \bar{\mathcal{H}}_n \text{"}.$$

Sei also $p(c_0, \ldots c_m, \vec{d}) \in P$ und $i \in \omega$ gegeben. Wegen (b) ($S(\vec{x}, \vec{y}) = p(x_0, \ldots \vec{y})$) gibt es $a_0, \ldots \vec{b} \in H$ mit $H \models p(\boldsymbol{a}_0, \ldots \vec{\boldsymbol{b}})$ une ein $n \in A_i$ mit $W(\langle a_0, \ldots a_m \rangle) \in \mathcal{H}_n$. Es gibt ein endliches System $S(\boldsymbol{a}_0, \ldots \vec{z})$ von Gl. & Ungl., das über H genau dann lösbar ist, wenn $W(\langle a_0, \ldots \rangle) \in \bar{\mathcal{H}}_n$ (siehe Beweis von IV, 2.1.2, $n = 1$). $q = p \cup S(c_0, \ldots \vec{d}')$ (für neues $\vec{d}'$) ist aus P, weil $S(\boldsymbol{a}_0, \ldots)$ über H lösbar ist. Andererseits ist $q \Vdash$ "$W(\langle g_0, \ldots \rangle) \in \bar{\mathcal{H}}_n$". Wie in 2.6.8 folgt nun $\emptyset \Vdash$ "f.a. $a_0, \ldots$ aus M_G, f.a. i $S_2^{A_i}(W(\langle a_0, \ldots \rangle))$". Da auch $\emptyset \Vdash$ "G generisch", gibt es ein generisches G, so daß M_G (a) erfüllt. □

Folgerung 3.3 (Bezeichnungen wie in 3.2). *Aus* 1 *und* 2 *folgt jeweils, daß* (a), (b), (c) *des letzten Satzes zutreffen.*

1. *Für alle* $i \in \omega$ *und Erzeugende* $a_0, \ldots a_m$ *einer Gruppe mit r.a. Wortproblem gilt* $S_2^{A_i}(W(\langle a_0, \ldots a_m \rangle))$.

2. *Kein* A_i *ist durch eine r.a. Menge von* $T_m := \{n \mid \mathcal{W}_m \subset \bar{\mathcal{H}}_n\}$ *trennbar.*

Beweis. Wenn 1 gilt, trifft für jedes i (c) von 3.2 auf M_0 zu; denn alle e.e. Untergruppen von M_0 haben r.a. Wortproblem.

2. Wir zeigen (b). Sei also $i \in \omega$ und $S(\vec{x}, \vec{y})$ gegeben.

Zu S gehört eine r.a. Hornklasse $\mathcal{H}$, die genau dann $W(\langle a_0, \ldots a_m \rangle)$ enthält, wenn $S(\vec{a}, \vec{y})$ in einer Obergruppe lösbar ist. Wir setzen $D = \{n \mid \bar{\mathcal{H}}_n \cap \mathcal{H} \cap \mathcal{W}_m = \emptyset\}$. D ist r.a. Wenn wir S als lösbar annehmen, folgt $D \cap T_m = \emptyset$. Es muß also $A_i \not\subset D$ sein. Daß für ein $n \in A_i$ $\bar{\mathcal{H}}_n \cap \mathcal{H} \cap \mathcal{W}_m \neq \emptyset$ bedeutet aber, daß es eine Gruppe $\langle a_0, \ldots a_m \rangle$ gibt mit $W(\langle a_0, \ldots \rangle) \in \bar{\mathcal{H}}_n \cap \mathcal{H}$, d.h. $S_2^{A_i}(W(\langle a_0, \ldots \rangle))$ und $S(\boldsymbol{a}_0, \ldots)$ lösbar über $\langle a_0, \ldots \rangle$. □

Beispiel 3.4 ([14]). Generische Gruppen erfüllen MAX nicht (siehe IV, 1.6 Beisp. 2).

Beweis. ε sei die Menge aller endlichen Systeme $S(x_0, \ldots)$ von Gl. & Ungl., die höchstens eine Ungleichung enthalten. Jedem $S \in \varepsilon$ können wir effektiv eine r.a. Hornklasse $\bar{\mathcal{H}}_n$ zuordnen, die genau dann das Wortproblem einer Gruppe $\langle a_0, \ldots a_m \rangle$ enthält, wenn S in $\langle a_0, \ldots \rangle$ nicht lösbar ist; n berechne sich durch $g(S)$ rekursiv aus S. ε_1 sei die die Menge der lösbaren Systeme von ε. Da jedes System von ε_1 in jeder a.a. Gruppe lösbar ist, muß auch jedes System von ε_1 in jeder universellen e.e. Untergruppe einer a.a.Gr. lösbar sein. In generischen Gruppen gibt es keine e.e. Untergruppen mit dieser Eigenschaft: Wenn $a_0, \ldots a_m$ Elemente einer generischen Gruppe sind, gibt es ein $S \in \varepsilon_1$ mit $W(\langle \vec{a} \rangle) \in \bar{\mathcal{H}}_{g(S)}$. Wenn $A = g[\varepsilon_1]$, heißt das $S_2^A(W(\langle a_0, \ldots \rangle))$. Um das zu zeigen, zeigen wir, daß A nicht durch eine r.a. Menge von T_m getrennt werden kann, und wenden dann 3.3.2 an. Nehmen wir an, D sei r.a. und trenne A von T_m. Da g $\varepsilon \setminus \varepsilon_1$ in T_m abbildet, wäre dann aber $\varepsilon_1 = g^{-1}(D)$ d.h. ε_1 r.a. Das widerspricht der Unlösbarkeit des Wortproblems für Gruppen. □

Die generischen Gruppen sind eine "elementare" Klasse von a.a. Gruppen:

Satz 3.5 (siehe [33]). *Es gibt eine rekursive Menge von elementaren Aussagen, die genau dann in einer a.a. Gruppe gelten, wenn die Gruppe generisch ist.*

Bemerkung. Da alle generischen Gruppen elementar äquivalent sind, ist das — von der Rekursivität abgesehen — dasselbe wie: Wenn $N \equiv M$ a.a. und N generisch, ist M generisch.

Beweis. Wir wählen eine Gödelnumerierung $(p^i \mid i \in \omega)$ von P. Dann ist für jedes $\varphi\{i \mid p^i \Vdash \varphi\}$ arithmetisch. "$(M, \vec{a}) \models p^i$" ist in M eine arithmetische Eigenschaft der $a_0, \ldots$ und i. Also ist $\forall \vec{x}\,(\varphi(\vec{x}) \leftrightarrow \exists v\, \exists \vec{y}\, \text{“}(\ldots; \vec{x}, \vec{y}) \models p^v\text{”} \wedge p^v \Vdash \varphi)$ eine arithmetische Eigenschaft von Gruppen. In a.a. Gruppen sind diese arithmetischen Aussagen durch elementare Aussagen beschreibbar. Wir nehmen für jedes φ die zugehörige elementare Aussage.

Wir geben jetzt andere Charakterisierungen für generische Gruppen.

Lemma 3.6. *Die Gruppe M ist genau dann generisch, wenn es für alle $\vec{a} \in M$, $p \in P$ mit $(M, \vec{a}) \models p$ und alle φ, ψ aus $L(C)$ ein $q \in P$ und $\vec{b} \in M$ mit $p \subset q$ und $(M, \vec{a}, \vec{b}) \models q$ gibt, so daß $p \Vdash \varphi \vee \varphi \Rightarrow q \Vdash \varphi$ oder $q \Vdash \psi$ und $p \Vdash \exists x\, \varphi(x) \Rightarrow$ ex. $c \in C$ $q \Vdash \varphi(c)$.*

Beweis. Die eine Richtung folgt sofort aus der Definition. Wenn die Bedingung erfüllt ist, zeigen wir durch Induktion über den Aufbau von $\varphi \in L(C)$, daß für alle $\vec{a} \in M$, $p \in P$ $(M, \vec{a}) \models p$, $p \Vdash \varphi \Rightarrow (M, \vec{a}) \models \varphi$.

Wir können annehmen, daß φ sich aus atomaren und negiert atomaren Formeln mit $\wedge$, $\vee$, $\forall x$, $\exists x$ aufbaut. Für quantorenfreie φ ist die Behauptung klar (siehe 2.6). Der Beweis ist beim Induktionsschritt für $\wedge$, $\forall x$ sehr einfach und bei $\vee$ ähnlich wie bei $\exists x$. Sei $(M, \vec{a}) \models p$ und $p \Vdash \exists x\, \varphi(x)$. Nach Voraussetzung gibt es $q \supset p$, $\vec{b} \in M$, mit $(M, \vec{a}, \vec{b}) \models q$ und $c \in C$ mit $q \Vdash \varphi(c)$. Nach der Induktionsvoraussetzung ist $(M, \vec{a}, \vec{b}) \models \varphi(c)$. Also gilt $\exists x\, \varphi(x)$ in $(M, \vec{a})$.

Wir müssen noch zeigen, daß es, wenn $(M, \vec{a}) \models \varphi$, ein $p \in P$ $\vec{b} \in M$ mit $p \Vdash \varphi$ und $(M, \vec{a}, \vec{b}) \models p$ gibt. Nun ist aber $\emptyset \Vdash \varphi \vee \neg\varphi$. Also gibt es $\vec{b} \in M$ und $\emptyset \subset p$ mit $(M, \vec{a}, \vec{b}) \models p$ und $p \Vdash \varphi$ oder $p \Vdash \neg\varphi$. Aus $p \Vdash \neg\varphi$ würde aber $(M, \vec{a}, \vec{b}) \not\models \varphi$ folgen, also ist $p \Vdash \varphi$. □

Definition 3.7. Eine Familie $\mathscr{F}$ von endlichen Gleichungs- und Ungleichungssystemen mit Koeffizienten $g_0, \ldots, g_n$ aus einer Gruppe G heißt *dicht* über G, wenn zu allen $g_{n+1}, \ldots, g_k \in G$ und jeder endlichen Menge $S(g_0, \ldots g_k)$ von Gleichungen und Ungleichungen, die in G gelten, es ein $F(g_0, \ldots, g_n, \vec{x})$ aus $\mathscr{F}$ gibt, sodaß $S \cup F \cup T^G$ widerspruchsfrei ist.

Bemerkung. $\mathscr{F}$ ist also dicht über G, wenn für kein $q \in P$, $\vec{g} \in M$ $(M, \vec{g}) \models q$ und $q \Vdash \neg \bigvee_{F \in \mathscr{F}} \exists \vec{x}\, F$.

Beispiel. Wenn das endl. Gl. & Ungl.system S' über G lösbar ist, ist $\{S'\}$ dicht.

In der nächsten Charakterisierung der generischen Gruppen kommt die Erzwingungsrelation nicht mehr vor.

Satz 3.8. *Eine Gruppe M ist genau dann generisch, wenn es für jede arithmetische, über M dichte Familie $\mathcal{F}$ ein $F \in \mathcal{F}$ gibt, das eine Lösung in M hat.*

Beweis. Die Bedingung sei erfüllt. Mit 3.6 zeigen wir, daß M generisch ist. Sei $(M, \vec{a}) \models p(\vec{c})$ und $p(\vec{c}) \Vdash \exists x \varphi(x)$. Die Familie von endlichen Systemen von Gleichungen und Ungleichungen über M $\mathcal{F} := \{q(\vec{\mathbf{a}}, \vec{x}) \mid q(\vec{c}, \vec{d}) \in P,\ p \subset q,\ p \Vdash \varphi(d'),\ d' \in C\}$ ist arithmetisch. Sei $\vec{a}' \in M$ und $M \models S(\vec{\mathbf{a}}, \vec{\mathbf{a}}')$ für eine endliche Menge $S(\vec{\mathbf{a}}, \vec{\mathbf{a}}')$ von Gleichungen und Ungleichungen. Dann sind p und $S(\vec{c}, \vec{c}')$ verträglich und es gibt ein $q \supset p \cup S(\vec{c}, \vec{c}')$ mit $q \Vdash \varphi(d')$ für ein $d' \in C$. $\mathcal{F}$ ist also dicht und es gibt ein $q(\vec{\mathbf{a}}, \vec{x})$ aus $\mathcal{F}$, das eine Lösung $\vec{b} \in M$ hat. Das wurde gerade in 3.6 verlangt. Der Fall $\varphi \vee \psi$ wird ebenso behandelt.

Sei M generisch und $\mathcal{F}(\mathbf{g}_0, \ldots \mathbf{g}_n)$ eine arithmetische Familie von endlichen Gl. & Ungl.systemen. $M \models \exists \vec{x}\ \bigvee \{ \bigwedge F(\vec{\mathbf{g}}, \vec{x}) \mid F \in \mathcal{F}\}$ ist eine arithmetische Eigenschaft von $M, g_0, \ldots$; wenn $M, g_0 \cdots$ diese Eigenschaft nicht hat, gibt es $p(c_0, \ldots, c_k) \in P$ $g_{n+1}, \ldots g_k \in M$ mit $M \models p(\mathbf{g}_0, \ldots \mathbf{g}_k)$ und $p \Vdash$ "$M_G \models \forall \vec{x}\ \bigwedge \{\neg \bigwedge F(\vec{c}, \vec{x}) \mid F \in \mathcal{F}\}$". Also ist für alle $\vec{d} \in C$ und alle $F \in \mathcal{F}$ $p \Vdash \neg \bigwedge F(\vec{c}, \vec{d})$. Das bedeutet aber, daß $p(\mathbf{g}_0, \ldots \mathbf{g}_k) \cup F(\mathbf{g}_0, \ldots \mathbf{g}_n, \vec{x}) \cup T^G$ für alle $F \in \mathcal{F}$ inkonsistent ist. $\mathcal{F}$ ist also nicht dicht. □

Nach 3.5 ist jede zu einer generischen Gruppe partiell isomorphe Gruppe wieder generisch. Die generischen Gruppen müssen sich also unter den a.a. Gruppen durch ihr Skelett auszeichnen lassen. Dazu definieren wir:

Definition 3.9. Ein Gruppe G heißt subgenerisch, wenn jede arithmetische Familie $\mathcal{F}(\mathbf{g}_0, \ldots \mathbf{g}_n)$ von endlichen Systemen von Gleichungen und Ungleichungen über G, die in folgendem Sinn "dicht" ist:

> Zu jedem endlichen Gl. & Ungl.system $S(\mathbf{g}_0, \ldots \mathbf{g}_k, \vec{y})$, das über G lösbar ist, gibt es ein $F(\mathbf{g}_0, \ldots \mathbf{g}_n, \vec{x})$ aus $\mathcal{F}$, so daß $F \cup S \cup T^G$ widerspruchsfrei ist.

ein Mitglied besitzt, das über G lösbar ist.

Bemerkung 3.10. Nach 3.8. ist eine a.a. Gruppe genau dann generisch, wenn sie subgenerisch ist. Aus I, 1.2 folgt daß jede Untergruppe einer subgenerischen Gruppe wieder subgenerisch ist.

Satz 3.11. *Eine algebraisch abgeschlossene Gruppe ist genau dann generisch, wenn jede endlich erzeugte Untergruppe subgenerisch ist.*

Beweis. 3.11 folgt aus 3.10. Denn eine Gruppe ist, wie man leicht sieht, genau dann subgenerisch, wenn jede e.e. Untergruppe subgenerisch ist. □

Folgerung. *Jede a.a. Untergruppe einer generischen Gruppe ist generisch.*

Satz 3.12. *Jede abzählbare subgenerische Gruppe ist Untergruppe einer generischen Gruppe.*

Beweis. Es sei $G = \{g_i \mid i \in \omega\}$ subgenerisch. Wir denken uns die Menge der Konstanten C disjunkt zerteilt in $\{\mathbf{g}_i \mid i \in \omega\}$ und eine unendliche Menge C'. Wir konstruieren eine aufsteigende Folge $p_0 \subset p_1 \subset \cdots$ von Elementen aus P, die mit $\mathrm{Diag}(G, \vec{g}) \cup T^G$ verträglich sind. Die generische Obergruppe M von G wird dann eine von den Interpretationen der $c \in C$ erzeugte Lösung von $\mathrm{Diag}(G, \vec{g}) \cup \bigcup\{p_i \mid i \in \omega\}$. ψ_i, $i \in \omega$ sei eine Numerierung aller Aussagen aus $L(C)$. Sei p_i schon gewählt und $\psi_i = \varphi_1 \vee \varphi_2$ (oder $= \exists x\, \varphi(x)$). In ψ_i mögen nur die Parameter $\mathbf{g}_0, \ldots, \mathbf{g}_n$ vorkommen. Wir betrachten die arithmetische Familie $\mathcal{F} = \{q(\mathbf{g}_0, \ldots \mathbf{g}_n, \vec{x}) \mid q \supset p_i$, $q \Vdash \neg\, \psi_i$ *oder* $q \Vdash \varphi_1$ oder $q \Vdash \varphi_2$ (*oder* $q \Vdash \varphi(c)$ für ein $c \in C)\}$. $\mathcal{F}$ ist im Sinn von 3.9 dicht. $q(\mathbf{g}_0, \ldots \mathbf{g}_n, \vec{x}) \in \mathcal{F}$ sei über G lösbar. Wir setzen dann $p_{i+1} = q(\mathbf{g}_0, \ldots \vec{c}\,') \cup p_i$ für neue Konstanten $\vec{c}\,'$ aus C'. Das so konstruierte M erfüllt offenbar die Bedingungen von 3.6. □

Bemerkung. Wir werden sehen, daß für generische M $W^*(M)$ abzählbar ist, G ist also genau dann partiell in eine generische Gruppe einbettbar, wenn G subgenerisch ist und $W^*(G)$ höchstens abzählbar. Wir werden im nächsten Kapitel die endlich erzeugten subgenerischen Gruppe auf einfache Weise durch ihr Wortproblem charakterisieren. Das direkte Product zweier subgenerischer Gruppen ist i.A. nicht subgenerisch.

Problem. Ist $W^*(G)$ für subgenerische G immer höchstens abzählbar?

VI. Generische ω-Modelle

Wir bestimmen die generischen Gruppen durch die zugehörigen ω-Modelle. Zuerst geben wir eine einfache rekursionstheoretische Beschreibung der subgenerischen Gruppen: Eine Menge von natürlichen Zahlen heißt subgenerisch, wenn sie Element der Vereinigung jeder "dichten" Familie von r.a. Hornklassen ist (1.1). Die e.e. Gruppe F ist subgenerisch gdw. $W(F)$ subgenerisch ist (1.11). Da mit der Menge G auch jedes H mit $H \leq^* G$ subgenerisch ist, ist die a.a. Gruppe M genau dann generisch, wenn $W^*(M)$ nur aus subgenerischen Mengen besteht (2.4). Wir nennen ein ω-Modell daher generisch, wenn es algebraisch abgeschlossen ist und nur subgenerische Mengen enthält. Die generischen Gruppen entsprechen dann gerade den generischen ω-Modellen.

Im zweiten Abschnitt definieren wir eine Erzwingungsrelation für ω-Modelle: eine r.a. Hornklasse $\mathcal{H}$ erzwingt die L^2-Formel $\varphi(X)$, wenn für alle generischen $(\omega, \mathcal{S})$ und alle $A \in \mathcal{S} \cap \mathcal{H}$ $(\omega, \mathcal{S}) \models \varphi(\mathbf{A})$ (2.7).

Wenn man nun ausnützt, daß r.a. Hornklassen endlichen Gleichungssystemen, L^2-Formeln Formeln aus $L^G_{\omega,\omega}$, generische ω-Modelle generischen Gruppen entsprechen, und bemerkt, daß (2.7) dem Lemma V, 2.5 entspricht, sieht man, daß unsere neue Erzwingungsrelation die Übertragung der Erzwingungsrelation von V auf ω-Modelle ist. Aus (der Definition) V, 2.7 kann man also schliessen:

In einem generischen ω-Modell $(\omega, \mathcal{S})$ gilt $\varphi(\mathbf{A})$ genau dann, wenn eine r.a. Hornklasse $\mathcal{H}$ mit $A \in \mathcal{H}$ $\varphi(X)$ erzwingt (2.8).

Wir beweisen 2.8 aber nicht auf diese Weise, sondern direkt, ohne die Resultate von V über generische Gruppen zu benutzen. Ebenso zeigen wir "nocheinmal" direkt die Existenz generischer ω-Modelle (1.3, 2.5). Das zeigt weitere Möglichkeit generische Gruppen einzuführen (nämlich analog zur Einführung der generischen ω-Modelle): Man definiert generische Gruppen durch V, 3.8 und die Erzwingungsrelation analog zu 2.7. Die Theorie der generischen Gruppen läßt sich dann wie in VI entwickeln.

Als erste Anwendung zeigen wir, daß alle in a.a. Gruppen erfüllbaren $\forall_3$-Aussagen in allen generischen Gruppen gelten (2.10). Man kann also generische Gruppen "klein" nennen, denn $\forall_3$-Aussagen, die in einer a.a.Gr. gelten, gelten auch in jeder a.a. Untergruppe. In diesem Sinn sind ∞-generische Gruppen "groß": Eine $\forall_3$-Aussage, die in einer ∞-generischen Gruppe gilt, gilt in allen a.a. Gruppen.

Durch diese "Kleinheit" werden die generischen Gruppen nicht charakterisiert. Denn eine zu einer generischen Gruppe elementar äquivalente a.a. Gruppe ist zwar generisch (V, 3.5). Für jedes n gibt es aber eine nicht-generische a.a. Gruppe, in der alle $\exists_n$-Aussagen gelten, die in generischen Gruppen gelten (3.5).

Der Beweis von 3.5 benützt schon das Hauptresultat des dritten Abschnitts: Zu jeder generischen Gruppe M gibt es eine (bis auf rekursive Isomorphie eindeutig bestimmte) Menge $B \subset \omega$, so daß $W^*(M) = \{A \subset \omega \mid A \leq_1 B\}$. Die so vorkommenden B (die also M bis auf partielle Isomorphie eindeutig bestimmen) lassen sich sehr einfach rekursionstheoretisch beschreiben: Es sind (bis auf rek. Isomorphie) die subgenerischen Mengen, die die rek. untrennbaren r.a. Mengen $\tilde{A}$, $\tilde{B}$ von III, 4.6 trennen (3.3). Dieser Satz führt also die Untersuchung der generischen Gruppen zurück auf die Untersuchung dieser Mengen (der "v.s.g." Mengen).

Für generische Gruppen M ist also $W_*(M)$ ein Hauptideal. Wir zeigen in 3.7, daß $W_*(M)$ immer unendlich ist. Im vierten Abschnitt zeigen wir, daß es in $W_*(M)$ sowohl $*$-Grade a mit $a^2 \not\leq a$ als auch nicht-rekursive $*$-Grade b mit $b^2 \leq b$ gibt (4.4, 4.5). Für a wählt man dabei den maximalen $*$-Grad in $W_*(M)$. Da c^2 arithmetisch in c ist, bedeutet das gerade nach 3.6, daß $a^2 \notin W_*(M)$ und $b^2 \in W_*(M)$; denn, wenn d arithmetisch in $c \in W_*(M)$ ist, ist (für generisches M) $d \in W_*(M)$ gdw. $d \leq c$ (3.6). Es gibt also in jeder generischen Gruppe M eine endlich erzeugte Untergruppe F, sodaß für kein $H \neq E$ $F * H$ nicht in M einbettbar ist. Es gibt allerdings auch immer e.e. Untergruppen F mit nichtlösbaren Wortproblem, so daß für alle endlichen H $F * H$ und alle $F * F$, $F * F * F, \ldots$ in M einbettbar sind.

Das steht im Gegensatz zu 4.1: Wenn M generisch ist und $G \in W^*(M)$, ist $\omega \setminus G \in W^*(M)$ gdw. G rekursiv ist. Daraus folgt das Resultat aus ([14]), daß alle e.e. einfachen Untergruppen einer generischen Gruppe lösbares Wortproblem haben.

1. Subgenerische Mengen

Die im folgenden betrachteten "subgenerischen" Mengen, entsprechen den Wortproblemen endlich erzeugter subgenerischer Gruppen.

Definition 1.1. 1. $A \subset \omega$ sei arithmetisch. Die "arithmetische" Familie $\{\mathcal{H}_i \mid i \in A\}$ von r.a. Hornklassen heißt dicht, wenn es zu jeder nichtleeren r.a. Hornklasse $\mathcal{H}$ ein $i \in A$ mit $\mathcal{H}_i \cap \mathcal{H} \neq \emptyset$ gibt.

2. Eine Menge G von natürlichen Zahlen heißt subgenerisch, wenn es in jeder arithmetischen dichten Familie von r.a. Hornklassen eine Hornklasse gibt, die G enthält.

Beispiele 1.2. 1. Jede rekursive Menge ist subgenerisch. Denn, wenn G rekursiv ist, ist $\{G\}$ eine r.a. Hornklasse. Wenn $\mathcal{F}$ eine dichte Familie von Hornklassen ist, ist also $\{G\} \cap \bigcup \mathcal{F} \neq \emptyset$, d.h. $G \in \bigcup \mathcal{F}$.

2. Jede subgenerische arithmetische Menge ist rekursiv.

$$\mathcal{F} = \{\{X \mid i \in X\} \mid i \notin G\} \cup \{\{X \mid i \notin X\} \mid i \in G\}$$

ist, wenn G arithmetisch ist, eine arithmetische Familie von r.a.

Hornklassen. G ist in keinem Element von $\mathcal{F}$ enthalten; wenn G subgenerisch ist, ist $\mathcal{F}$ also nicht dicht. Es gibt also eine r.a. Hornklasse $\mathcal{H}$, nicht-leer, die von $\bigcup\mathcal{F}$ disjunkt ist. Weil $\bigcup\mathcal{F} = \mathcal{P}(\omega)\setminus\{G\}$, folgt $\mathcal{H} = \{G\}$. G ist also rekursiv.

Aus dem nächsten Satz folgt, daß es nichtrekursive subgenerische Mengen gibt.

Satz 1.3. *Jede nichtleere r.a. Hornklasse enthält eine subgenerische Menge.*

Beweis. $(\mathcal{F}_i \mid i \in \omega)$ sei eine Aufzählung aller arithmetischen dichten Familien von r.a. Hornklassen, $\mathcal{H}_0$ eine nichtleere r.a. Hornklasse. Wir konstruieren eine absteigende Folge $\mathcal{H}_0 \supset \mathcal{H}_1 \supset \mathcal{H}_2 \supset \cdots$ von r.a. nichtleeren Hornklassen, so daß $\mathcal{H}_{i+1} \subset \bigcup\mathcal{F}_i$, $i = 0, 1, 2 \cdots$. Wenn $\mathcal{H}_i$ gegeben ist, finden wir ein $\mathcal{H} \in \mathcal{F}_i$ mit $\mathcal{H} \cap \mathcal{H}_i \neq \emptyset$. Wir setzen $\mathcal{H}_{i+1} = \mathcal{H}_i \cap \mathcal{H}$. Nach III, 3.9.2 ist $\bigcap_{i\in\omega}\mathcal{H}_i \neq \emptyset$. Jedes Element des Durchschnitts ist subgenerisch. □

Bemerkungen 1.4. 1. Ist B_i, $i \in \omega$ eine Folge von nichtrekursiven Mengen und $\mathcal{H}_0$ eine nichtleere r.a. Hornklasse, gibt es es eine subgenerische Menge aus $\mathcal{H}_0$, die von allen B_i verschieden ist. Denn man kann im Beweis von 1.3 in der Aufzählung der $\mathcal{F}_i$ für jedes j eine Familie $\mathcal{F}'_j$ von r.a. Hornklassen mit $\bigcup\mathcal{F}'_j = \mathcal{P}(\omega)\setminus\{B_j\}$ vorkommen lassen (siehe 1.2.2).

2. Da es nichtleere r.a. Hornklassen gibt, die keine rekursiven Mengen enthalten, gibt es nichtrekursive subgenerische Mengen. (Eine solche Hornklasse ist z.B. $\{X \mid X \text{ trennt } \tilde{A} \text{ und } \tilde{B}\}$ für die $\tilde{A}$, $\tilde{B}$ aus Lemma III, 4.6.)

Für diese Hornklassen gilt sogar

Satz 1.5. *Jede nichtleere r.a. Hornklasse, die keine rekursiven Mengen enthält, enthält 2^{ω} subgenerische Mengen.*

Beweis. Die nichtleere r.a. Hornklasse $\mathcal{H}_0$ habe keine rekursiven Elemente. $(\mathcal{F}_i \mid i \in \omega)$ sei eine Aufzählung aller arithmetischen dichten Familien von r.a. Hornklassen. Wir konstruieren für jede endliche Folge $\sigma \in {}^{\omega}2$ eine nichtleere r.a. Hornklasse $\mathcal{H}_\sigma$ mit (a) $\sigma \subset \tau \Rightarrow \mathcal{H}_\sigma \supset \mathcal{H}_\tau$, (b) Wenn $\sigma \in {}^{n+1}2$, ist $\mathcal{H}_\sigma \subset \bigcup\mathcal{F}_n$, (c) $\mathcal{H}_{\sigma^\frown\langle 0\rangle} \cap \mathcal{H}_{\sigma^\frown\langle 1\rangle} = \emptyset$. Dazu wählen wir, wenn $\sigma \in {}^{n}2$, $\mathcal{H}_\sigma$ gegeben ist, eine nichtleere r.a. Hornklasse $\mathcal{H} \subset \bigcup\mathcal{F}_n \cap \mathcal{H}_\sigma$. Weil $\mathcal{H}_0$ keine rekursiven Mengen enthält, gibt es in $\mathcal{H}$ zwei verschieden Mengen, von denen die eine sagen wir k enthält — und die andere nicht. Wir setzen $\mathcal{H}_{\sigma^\frown\langle 0\rangle} = \{X \mid k \in X \wedge X \in \mathcal{H}\}$ und $\mathcal{H}_{\sigma^\frown\langle 1\rangle} = \{X \mid k \notin X \wedge X \in \mathcal{H}\}$. Für jedes $f \in {}^{\omega}2$, wählen wir ein $G_f \in \bigcup\{\mathcal{H}_{f|i} \mid i \in \omega\}$. Die G_f sind subgenerisch und alle verschieden. □

Bemerkung. Wir können wieder erreichen, daß alle G_f nicht in einer vorgegebenen Folge von nichtrekursiven Mengen vorkommen.

Definition 1.6. Sei $\mathcal{A} \subset \mathcal{P}(\omega)$. Eine r.a. Hornklasse $\mathcal{H}$ erzwingt $\mathcal{A}$ ($\mathcal{H} \Vdash \mathcal{A}$), wenn alle subgenerischen Mengen aus $\mathcal{H}$ in $\mathcal{A}$ sind. Statt $\mathcal{H} \Vdash \{X \mid \cdots X \cdots\}$ schreiben wir $\mathcal{H} \Vdash$ "$\cdots X \cdots$".

Beispiel 1.7. $\mathcal{H}_0$, $\mathcal{H}_1$ seien r.a. Hornklassen. Dann ist $\mathcal{H}_0 \Vdash \mathcal{H}_1$ gdw. $\mathcal{H}_0 \subset \mathcal{H}_1$.

Beweis. Sei $\mathcal{H}_1 = \bar{\mathcal{H}}_W$ und $A \in \mathcal{H}_0 \setminus \mathcal{H}_1$. Dann gibt es $\langle u, w\rangle \in W$ mit $D_u \subset A$ und $D^1_w \subset \omega \setminus A$. Die r.a. Hornklasse $\mathcal{H} = \mathcal{H}_0 \cap \{X \mid D_u \subset X \wedge D^1_w \subset \omega \setminus X\}$ ist nichtleer, und disjunkt zu $\mathcal{H}_1$. Eine subgenerische Menge aus $\mathcal{H}$ ist in $\mathcal{H}_0$, aber nicht in $\mathcal{H}_1$, also $\mathcal{H}_0 \nVdash \mathcal{H}_1$. Die andere Richtung ist trivial. □

Satz 1.8. 1. *$\mathcal{A} \subset \mathcal{P}(\omega)$ sei arithmetisch, G subgenerisch. Dann ist $G \in \mathcal{A}$ gdw. es eine r.a. Hornklasse mit $G \in \mathcal{H}$, $\mathcal{H} \Vdash \mathcal{A}$ gibt.*

2. *$R(v_0, \ldots, X)$ sei eine arithmetische Relation. Dann ist $\bar{\mathcal{H}}_i \Vdash$ "$R(n_0, \ldots, X)$" eine arithmetische Relation zwischen $i, n_0, n_1, \ldots$.*

Bemerkung. 3. Für jede Familie $\mathcal{A}_i$, $i \in I$ gilt $\mathcal{H} \Vdash \bigcap\{\mathcal{A}_i \mid i \in I\}$ gdw. für alle $i \in I$ $\mathcal{H} \Vdash \mathcal{A}_i$. 4. Wenn $\mathcal{A} \subset \mathcal{P}(\omega)$ die Behauptung von 1 erfüllt, gilt $\mathcal{H} \Vdash \mathcal{P}(\omega) \setminus \mathcal{A}$ gdw. für alle $\emptyset \neq \mathcal{H}' \subset \mathcal{H}$ $\mathcal{H}' \nVdash \mathcal{A}$.

Beweis. 3 ist klar. Wir zeigen 4: Wenn $\mathcal{H} \Vdash \mathcal{P}(\omega) \setminus \mathcal{A}$, ist für alle $\mathcal{H}' \subset \mathcal{H}$ $\mathcal{H}' \Vdash \mathcal{P}(\omega) \setminus \mathcal{A}$. Also, wenn $\mathcal{H}' \neq \emptyset$, $\mathcal{H}' \nVdash \mathcal{A}$. Sei umgekehrt $\mathcal{H} \nVdash \mathcal{P}(\omega) \setminus \mathcal{A}$. Dann gibt es eine subgenerische Menge $G \in \mathcal{H} \cap \mathcal{A}$. Wegen 1 gibt es ein $\mathcal{H}'' \Vdash \mathcal{A}$, das G enthält. Dann ist aber $\emptyset \neq \mathcal{H}' = \mathcal{H} \cap \mathcal{H}'' \Vdash \mathcal{A}$.

(a) Aus 1.7 folgt, daß 1.8.1 und 2 für r.a. Hornklassen d.h. $R(v, X) = X \in \bar{\mathcal{H}}_v$ gelten.

Für eine Relation $R(v_0, \ldots X)$ formulieren wir 1 noch einmal:

5. "Für alle $n_0, \ldots \in \omega$ und alle subgenerischen Mengen G ist $R(n_0, \ldots G)$ gdw. es eine r.a. Hornklasse $\mathcal{H}$ mit $G \in \mathcal{H}$ und $\mathcal{H} \Vdash$ "$R(n_0, \ldots X)$" gibt."

(b) Wenn $R(v_0, \ldots X)$ 2 und 5 erfüllt, erfüllt auch $\neg R(v_0, \ldots X)$ 2 und 5.

Denn aus 5 folgt 4: $\bar{\mathscr{H}}_i \Vdash$ "$\neg R(n_0, \ldots X)$" gdw. $\forall j\,(\bar{\mathscr{H}}_j \neq \emptyset \wedge \bar{\mathscr{H}}_j \subset \bar{\mathscr{H}}_i) \Rightarrow \bar{\mathscr{H}}_j \nVdash$ "$R(n_0, \ldots X)$". Das ist, wegen 2 und III, 3.9 arithmetisch. Also erfüllt $\neg R$ 2. Sei G subgenerisch und $\neg R(n_0, \ldots G)$. Die Familie $\{\bar{\mathscr{H}}_i \mid \bar{\mathscr{H}}_i \Vdash$ "$R(n_0, \ldots X)$" oder $\bar{\mathscr{H}}_i \Vdash$ "$\neg R(n_0, \ldots)$"$\}$ ist dicht (— denn wenn $\mathscr{H} \nVdash$ "$\neg R(n_0 \cdots)$" ist $\mathscr{H}' \Vdash$ "$R(n_0, \ldots)$" für ein $\emptyset \neq \mathscr{H}' \subset \mathscr{H}$). G ist also in einem Element dieser Familie enthalten. Weil $\neg R(n_0, \ldots G)$, gibt es daher ein $\mathscr{H} \Vdash$ "$\neg R(n_0, \ldots)$", $G \in \mathscr{H}$. Damit ist auch 5 nachgewiesen.

(c) Wenn $R(v_0, \ldots X)$ 2 und 5 erfüllt und B arithmetisch ist, erfüllt auch $\forall v_0 \in B\; R(v_0, v_1, \ldots X)$ 2 und 5.

Denn aus 3 folgt, daß $\bar{\mathscr{H}}_i \Vdash$ "$\forall v_0 \in B\; R(v_0, n_1, \ldots X)$" gdw. für alle $n_0 \in B$ $\bar{\mathscr{H}}_i \Vdash$ "$R(n_0, n_1, \ldots X)$". Weil für R 2 vorausgesetzt war, folgt aus dieser Darstellung, daß $\forall v_0 \in B\; R(v_0, \ldots)$ 2 erfüllt. Sei G subgenerisch und $\forall v_0 \in B\; R(v_0, n_1, \ldots G)$. $\mathscr{F}$ sei die Familie aller r.a. Hornklassen $\mathscr{H}$, die für ein $n_0 \in B$ "$\neg R(n_0, \ldots X)$" erzwingen oder "$\forall v_0 R(v_0, \ldots X)$" erzwingen. Da $\neg R$ nach (b) 5 erfüllt, gibt es, wenn $\mathscr{H} \nVdash$ "$R(n_0, \ldots X)$" ein $\emptyset \neq \mathscr{H}' \subset \mathscr{H}$ mit $\mathscr{H}' \Vdash$ "$\neg R(n_0, \ldots X)$". Die Familie $\mathscr{F}$ ist also dicht und wegen 2 und (b) arithmetisch. Sei für ein $\mathscr{H} \in \mathscr{F}$, $G \in \mathscr{H}$. Dann ist $\mathscr{H} \Vdash$ "$\forall v_0\, R(n_0, \ldots X)$". Satz 1.8 folgt aus (a), (b) und (c), weil man jede arithmetische Relation aus r.a. Hornklassen durch Anwenden von "$\neg$" und "$\forall v_0 \in B \cdots$" erhalten kann. □

Der nächste Satz entspricht V, 3.2. Wir bestimmen die Erzwingungsrelation für eine einfache Klasse von Relationen. Dazu erinnern wir an die Bezeichnungen von IV, 2 und V, 3.2: G erfüllt genau dann $S_2^A(X)$, wenn $G \in \bigcup\{\bar{\mathscr{H}}_i \mid i \in A\}$. G ist also subgenerisch gdw. G jedes $S_2^A(X)$ erfüllt, für alle arithmetischen A, für die $\{\bar{\mathscr{H}}_i \mid i \in A\}$ dicht ist.

Satz 1.9. 1. *Sei A arithmetisch. Dann ist $\mathscr{P}(\omega) \Vdash$ "$S_2^A(X)$" gdw. die Familie $\{\bar{\mathscr{H}}_i \mid i \in A\}$ dicht ist.*

2. *Die Relation "$\bar{\mathscr{H}}_k \Vdash S_2^{W_j}(X)$" ist Π_3^0 (in k, j).*

Beweis. 1: $\mathscr{P}(\omega) \Vdash$ "$S_2^A(X)$" gdw. $\forall \mathscr{H} \neq \emptyset\; \mathscr{H} \nVdash$ "$\neg S_2^A(X)$" gdw. $\forall \mathscr{H} \neq \emptyset$ $\exists i \in A\; \mathscr{H} \nVdash$ "$X \notin \bar{\mathscr{H}}_i$" gdw. $\forall \mathscr{H} \neq \emptyset\; \exists i \in A\; \exists \emptyset \neq \mathscr{H}' \subset \mathscr{H}\; \mathscr{H}' \Vdash \bar{\mathscr{H}}_i$ gdw. $\{\bar{\mathscr{H}}_i \mid i \in A\}$ dicht.

2: Die Relation ist äquivalent zu:

$$\forall \mathscr{H}\,(\mathscr{H} \cap \bar{\mathscr{H}}_k \neq \emptyset \Rightarrow \exists i \in W_j\; \mathscr{H} \cap \bar{\mathscr{H}}_i \neq \emptyset).$$

Daraus erkennt man leicht die Gültigkeit der Behauptung. □

Folgerung 1.10. *A sei arithmetisch. Wenn $S_2^A(B)$ für alle r.a. B, ist* $\mathcal{P}(\omega) \Vdash$ "$S_2^A(X)$".

Beweis. Jede r.a. Hornklasse $\neq \emptyset$ enthält eine r.a. Menge.

Wir wollen zeigen, daß endlich erzeugten subgenerischen Gruppen die e.e. Gruppen mit subgenerischen Wortproblem sind. Der Beweis benützt das folgende Lemma:

Lemma 1.11. $(G \subset \omega)$ *G ist genau dann subgenerisch, wenn jede arithmetische Familie* $\mathcal{F}$ *von r.a. Hornklassen mit*:

Wenn die r.a. Hornklasse $\mathcal{H}$ *G enthält, ist* $\mathcal{H} \cap \bigcup \mathcal{F} \neq \emptyset$.

$G \in \bigcup \mathcal{F}$ *erfüllt.*

Beweis. Eine Richtung ist trivial. Sei G subgenerisch und $\mathcal{F}$ eine Familie von r.a. Hornklassen mit der angegebenen Eigenschaft. $\mathcal{F}'$ sei die Familie aller r.a. Hornklassen $\mathcal{H}$ mit $\mathcal{H} \subset \bigcup \mathcal{F}$ oder $\mathcal{H} \cap \bigcup \mathcal{F} = \emptyset$. $\mathcal{F}'$ ist arithmetisch und dicht. Sei $\mathcal{H} \in \mathcal{F}'$ mit $G \in \mathcal{H}$. Dann ist $\mathcal{H} \cap \bigcup \mathcal{F} \neq \emptyset$, also $\mathcal{H} \subset \bigcup \mathcal{F}$ und daher $G \in \bigcup \mathcal{F}$. □

Satz 1.12. *G sei endlich erzeugte Gruppe. G ist genau dann subgenerisch, wenn W(G) subgenerisch ist.*

Beweis. Sei G subgenerisch, G erzeugt von $g_0, \dots g_n$. $\mathcal{F}$ sei eine arithmetische dichte Familie von r.a. Hornklassen. Jedem $\mathcal{H}_i \in \mathcal{F}$ ordnen wir ein endliches System von Gleichungen und Ungleichungen $S_i(c_0, \dots c_n, \vec{x})$ zu, so daß $S_i(\boldsymbol{h}_0, \dots, \vec{x})$ genau dann über einer Gruppe H lösbar ist, wenn $W(H; h_0, \dots) \in \mathcal{H}_i$. Wir erhalten so eine arithmetische Familie $\bar{\mathcal{F}}(c_0, \dots c_n)$ von Gl. & Ungl.systemen. Wir zeigen, daß $\bar{\mathcal{F}}(\boldsymbol{g}_0, \dots \boldsymbol{g}_n)$ dicht im Sinn von V, 3.9 ist. Sei also $S(\boldsymbol{g}_0, \dots \boldsymbol{g}_n, \vec{y})$ über G lösbar. Zu S gehört eine r.a. Hornklasse $\mathcal{H}$, so daß $S(\boldsymbol{h}_0, \dots, \vec{y})$ genau dann über einer Gruppe lösbar ist, wenn $W(H; h_0, \dots) \in \mathcal{H}$. Da $W(G) \in \mathcal{H} \cap \mathcal{W}_n$, gibt es ein $\mathcal{H}_i$ aus $\mathcal{F}$ mit $\mathcal{H} \cap \mathcal{W}_n \cap \mathcal{H}_i \neq \emptyset$. Sei $W \in \mathcal{H} \cap \mathcal{W}_n \cap \mathcal{H}_i$. Dann gibt es ein $H = \langle h_0, \dots h_n \rangle$ mit $W(H) = W$. Sowohl $S_i(\boldsymbol{h}_0, \dots \vec{x})$ als auch $S(\boldsymbol{h}_0, \dots \vec{y})$ sind über H lösbar. $s_i(\boldsymbol{g}_0, \dots \vec{x}) \cup S(\boldsymbol{g}_0, \dots \vec{y}) \cup T^G$ ist also widerspruchsfrei. Da G subgenerisch ist, ist ein $S_i(\boldsymbol{g}_0, \dots \vec{x})$ aus $\bar{\mathcal{F}}(\boldsymbol{g}_0, \dots)$ über G lösbar. Also ist $W(G) \in \mathcal{H}_i$.

Sei umgekehrt $W(G)$ subgenerisch. $W(G)$ hat also die Eigenschaft von 1.11. $\mathcal{F}(\boldsymbol{g}_0, \dots \boldsymbol{g}_n)$ sei eine arithmetische Familie von endlichen Gl. & Ungl.systemen $S_i(\boldsymbol{g}_0, \dots \boldsymbol{g}_n, \vec{x})$, dicht im Sinn von V, 3.9. Zu jedem $S_i(c_0, \dots \vec{x})$ gehört eine r.a. Hornklasse $\mathcal{H}_i$, sodaß für alle $h_0, \dots \in H$

$S_i(\boldsymbol{h}_0, \ldots \vec{x})$ genau dann über H lösbar ist, wenn $W(H) \in \mathcal{H}_i$. $\bar{\bar{\mathcal{F}}}$ sei die Familie der so gewonnen Hornklassen. $\bar{\bar{\mathcal{F}}}$ ist arithmetisch. $\mathcal{H}$ sei eine r.a. Hornklasse, die $W(G)$ enthält. Das endliche Gl. & Ungl.system $S(c_0, \ldots \vec{y})$ sei in einer Obergruppe lösbar gdw. das Wortproblem zu $\mathcal{H}$ gehört. $S(\boldsymbol{g}_0, \ldots \vec{y})$ ist also über G lösbar. Für ein S_i aus $\mathcal{F}$ ist also $S_i(c_0, \ldots \vec{x}) \cup S(c_0, \ldots \vec{y}) \cup T^G$ widerspruchsfrei. Es gibt also ein $H = \langle h_0, \ldots h_n \rangle$, über dem $S_i(\boldsymbol{h}_0, \ldots)$ und $S(\boldsymbol{h}_0, \ldots)$ lösbar sind. Daher ist $W(H) \in \mathcal{H}_i \cap \mathcal{H} \neq \emptyset$. Wir haben gezeigt, daß $\bar{\bar{\mathcal{F}}}$ die Bedingung in 1.11 erfüllt. Also ist $W(G) \in \mathcal{H}_i$ für ein $\mathcal{H}_i$ aus $\bar{\bar{\mathcal{F}}}$. $S_i(\boldsymbol{g}_0, \ldots \vec{x})$ ist somit über G lösbar. $\square$

Folgerung. *Wir haben einen neuen Beweis für die Folgerung* 2 *von* V, 3.1: *Da arithmetische subgenerische Mengen rekursiv sind* (1.2.2), *haben alle endlich erzeugten Untergruppen generischer Gruppen lösbares oder nicht-arithmetisches Wortproblem.*

2. Generische ω-Modelle

Wir werden sehen, daß die generischen ω-Modelle gerade die zu generischen Gruppen gehörenden ω-Modelle sind.

Definition 2.1. Ein ω-Modell $(\omega, \mathcal{S})$ heißt generisch, wenn es algebraisch abgeschlossen ist und $\mathcal{S}$ nur aus subgenerischen Mengen besteht.

Ist also M a.a. und $\omega(M)$ generisch, so ist M generisch. Zur Konstruktion generischer ω-Modelle brauchen wir das folgende Lemma. Eine Folge $(A_0, \ldots, A_n)$ von Mengen heißt subgenerisch, wenn $A_0 \vee A_1 \vee \cdots \vee A_n$ subgenerisch ist.

Lemma 2.2. 1. *Wenn (G, H) subgenerisch ist, sind auch G und H subgenerisch.*

2. *Ist für eine r.a. Hornklasse $\mathcal{H}$ und eine subgenerische Menge G $\mathcal{H}[G] \neq \emptyset$, gibt es ein subgenerisches $(G, H) \in \mathcal{H}^2$.*

Anmerkung. Wenn G und H subgenerisch sind, ist i.A. (G, H) nicht wieder subgenerisch. 1.3 folgt aus 2.2.

Beweis. 1. Wir zeigen, daß G subgenerisch ist. Sei $\mathcal{F}$ eine arithmetische dichte Familie von r.a. Hornklassen. Wir ordnen jedem $\mathcal{H}$ aus $\mathcal{F}$ die r.a. Hornklasse $\tilde{\mathcal{H}}^2 = \{(X, Y) \mid X \in \mathcal{H}\}$ zu. Die so erhaltene Familie ist dicht. Denn wenn $\mathcal{H}_0^2 \neq \emptyset$, gibt es, weil $\mathcal{F}$ dicht ist, ein $\mathcal{H} \in \mathcal{F}$ mit $\{X \mid \exists Y\, (X, Y) \in \mathcal{H}_0^2\} \cap \mathcal{H} \neq \emptyset$. Dann ist $\mathcal{H}_0^2 \cap \tilde{\mathcal{H}}^2 \neq 0$. Es gibt nun ein $\mathcal{H} \in \mathcal{F}$ mit $(G, H) \in \tilde{\mathcal{H}}^2$. Also ist $G \in \mathcal{H}$.

2. $(\mathcal{F}_i^2 \mid i \in \omega)$ sei eine Aufzählung aller arithmetischen dichten Familien von r.a. Hornklassen $\mathcal{H}^2 \subset (\mathcal{P}(\omega))^2$. Wir konstruieren eine absteigende Folge $\mathcal{H}^2 = \mathcal{H}_0^2 \supset \mathcal{H}_1^2 \supset \cdots$ von r.a. Hornklassen mit $\mathcal{H}_i[G] \neq \emptyset$ und $\mathcal{H}_{i+1}^2 \subset \bigcup \mathcal{F}_i^2$. Wir brauchen dann H nur aus dem Schnitt aller $\mathcal{H}_i[G]$ zu wählen. Für die Konstruktion verwenden wir: "$\mathcal{F}^2$ sei eine arithmetische, dichte Familie. $\mathcal{H}_0^2$ eine r.a. Hornklasse mit $\mathcal{H}_0[G] \neq \emptyset$. Dann gibt es ein $\mathcal{H}_1^2 \in \mathcal{F}^2$ mit $(\mathcal{H}_0 \cap \mathcal{H}_1)[G] \neq \emptyset$."

Beweis. Wenn $\mathcal{H}^2$ eine Hornklasse ist, bezeichnen wir mit $P(\mathcal{H}^2)$ die Hornklasse $\{X \mid \exists Y\, (X, Y) \in \mathcal{H}^2\}$. $\tilde{\mathcal{F}}$ sei die Familie aller $P(\mathcal{H}_0^2 \cap \mathcal{H}_1^2)$ für $\mathcal{H}_1^2$ aus $\mathcal{F}^2$. $\tilde{\mathcal{F}}$ erfüllt die Bedingung von 1.11: Sei $\mathcal{H}$ eine r.a. Hornklasse, die G enthält. $\tilde{\mathcal{H}}^2 \cap \mathcal{H}_0^2$ ist nicht-leer (siehe 1). Also gibt es ein $\mathcal{H}_1^2 \in \mathcal{F}$ mit $\tilde{\mathcal{H}}^2 \cap \mathcal{H}_0^2 \cap \mathcal{H}_1^2 \neq \emptyset$. Das bedeutet $\mathcal{H} \cap P(\mathcal{H}_0^2 \cap \mathcal{H}_1^2) \neq \emptyset$. Nach 1.11 gibt es also ein $\mathcal{H}_1^2$ aus $\mathcal{F}$ mit $G \in P(\mathcal{H}_0^2 \cap \mathcal{H}_1^2)$, wie gewünscht. □

Bemerkung 2.3. Man kann 2.2 auf drei Arten verschärfen ($\mathcal{H}^2$ r.a. Hornklasse).

1. Sei G subgenerisch, $\mathcal{H}[G] \neq \emptyset$ $(B_i \mid i \in \omega)$ eine Folge von $B_i \subset \omega$ mit $B_i \not\leqslant^* G$. Dann gibt es ein subgenerisches $(G, H) \in \mathcal{H}$ mit $B_i \not\leqslant^* G \vee H$ für alle i (siehe 1.4.1 und III, 4.1 Bew. 3).

2. Sei G subgenerisch, $\mathcal{H}[G] \neq \emptyset$, $\mathcal{H}[G]$ enthalte kein B mit $B \leqslant^* G$. Dann gibt es 2^ω viele H mit (G, H) subgenerisch und $(G, H) \in \mathcal{H}^2$ (siehe 1.5).

3. Sei $(G_i \mid i \in \omega)$ eine Folge von $G_i \subset \omega$. Für alle $i \in \omega$ sei $(G_0, \ldots G_i)$ subgenerisch. Wenn $\mathcal{H}[G_0] \neq \emptyset$, gibt es ein H, sodaß $(G_0, H) \in \mathcal{H}^2$ und für alle $i \in \omega$ $(H, G_0, \ldots G_i)$ subgenerisch ist.

Folgerung 2.4. 1. *Wenn $H \leqslant^* G$ und G subgenerisch, sind auch (G, H) und H subgenerisch.*

2. *Die a.a. Gruppe M ist genau dann generisch, wenn $\omega(M)$ generisch ist.*

Weil man $\{H\}$ in der Form $\mathcal{H}[G]$ schreiben kann, folgt 1 aus 2.2. Wenn M generisch ist, müssen wir für 2 zeigen, daß alle H aus $W^*(M)$ subgenerisch sind. Es gibt aber ein $H \in \mathrm{Sk}(M)$ mit $H \leqslant^* W(G)$. Da G subgenerisch, ist $W(G)$ subgenerisch.

Aus V, 3.12 können wir nun schließen, daß jede subgenerische Menge G zu einem generischen ω-Modell gehört. Denn, wenn F eine e.e.Gr. mit $W(F) \equiv^* G$ ist, ist $W(F)$ und damit F subgenerisch. Wir betten F in die generische Gruppe M ein. G gehört dann zu dem generischen ω-Modell $\omega(M)$. Wir beweisen dieses Resultat noch einmal mit 2.2, ohne auf V zurückzugreifen.

Satz 2.5. *Jede subgenerische Menge ist in einem generische ω-Modell enthalten.*

Beweis (siehe auch den Beweis von III, 4.1). Sei G_0 subgenerisch. Wir konstruieren eine Folge von Mengen G_i, $i \in \omega$ für die $(G_0, \dots G_i)$ subgenerisch ist. G_i sei bereits definiert und $i = \langle k, n \rangle$. Wir setzen $m = \min(i, k) + 1$. Wenn $\bar{\mathcal{H}}_n[G_0, \dots G_m]$ leer ist, setzen wir $G_{i+1} = G_i$. Sonst schreiben wir $\bar{\mathcal{H}}_n[G_0, \dots G_m]$ in der Form $\bar{\mathcal{H}}_{n'}[G_0, \dots G_i]$. Nach 2.2 gibt es ein $G_{i+1} \in \bar{\mathcal{H}}_{n'}[G_0, \dots G_i]$, für das $(G_0, \dots G_i, G_{i+1})$ subgenerisch ist. $(\omega, \{G_i \mid i \in \omega\})$ ist generisch. □

Bemerkung 2.6. 1. Aus 1.5 folgt mit 2.5, daß es 2^ω viele generische ω-Modelle gibt. (Das ist die genaue Anzahl, denn, wie wir sehen werden, ist jedes ω-Modell abzählbar.) Es gibt also 2^ω viele abzählbare generische Gruppen ([15]).

2. (siehe 2.3.1). Ist G subgenerisch und B_i, $i \in \omega$, eine Folge von Mengen mit $B_i \not\leq^* G$, gibt es ein generisches ω-Modell, das G aber kein B_i enthält.

3. $I \subset \mathcal{P}(\omega)$ sei höchstens abzählbar, für alle $G_0, \dots G_n \in I$ sei $(G_0, \dots G_n)$ subgenerisch. Dann ist I in einem generischen ω-Modell enthalten.

Definition 2.7. Die r.a. Hornklasse $\mathcal{H}^{n+1}$ erzwingt die L^2-Formel $\varphi(X_0, \dots X_n)$ $(\mathcal{H}^{n+1} \Vdash \varphi(X_0, \dots))$, wenn für alle generischen $(\omega, \mathcal{S})$ und $A_0, \dots A_n \in \mathcal{S}$, mit $(A_0, \dots A_n) \in \mathcal{H}^{n+1}$, $(\omega, \mathcal{S}) \models \varphi(\mathbf{A}_0, \dots \mathbf{A}_n)$.

Bemerkungen. 1. Für arithmetische L^2-Formeln (also ohne gebundene Mengenvariable) stimmen 2.7 und 1.6 überein: $\mathcal{H}^{n+1} \Vdash \varphi(X_0, \dots)$ (im Sinn von 2.7) gdw. für alle subgenerischen $(A_0, \dots A_n)$ aus $\mathcal{H}^{n+1}$ $\varphi(A_0, \dots A_n)$ gilt. (Das folgt aus 2.5.)

2. $\varphi(X_0, \dots X_n)$ enthalte nur die Variablen $X_0, \dots X_m$, $m < n$. Wenn $\mathcal{H}_0^{n+1} \Vdash \varphi(X_0, \dots, X_n)$ und $\mathcal{H}_1^{m+1} = \{(X_0, \dots X_m) \mid \exists X_{m+1} \cdots X_n \ (X_0, \dots, X_n) \in \mathcal{H}_0^{n+1}\}$, ist dann $\mathcal{H}_1^{m+1} \Vdash \varphi(X_0, \dots X_m)$.
(Das folgt aus der algebraischen Abgeschlossenheit der gen. ω-Modelle: $(A_0, \dots A_m) \in \mathcal{H}_1^{m+1}$ gdw. ex. $A_{m+1}, \dots A_n \in \mathcal{S}$ mit $(A_0, \dots A_n) \in \mathcal{H}_0^{n+1}$.)

Satz 2.8. *$\varphi(X_0, \dots X_n)$ und $\psi(v_0, \dots X_0, \dots X_n)$ seien L^2-Formeln.*

1. *Für alle $A_0, \dots A_n$ aus einem generischen ω-Modell $(\omega, \mathcal{S})$ ist $(\omega, \mathcal{S}) \models \varphi(\mathbf{A}_0, \dots)$ gdw. es eine r.a. Hornklasse mit $(A_0, \dots) \in \mathcal{H}^{n+1}$ und $\mathcal{H}^{n+1} \Vdash \varphi(X_0, \dots)$ gibt.*

2. $\tilde{\mathcal{H}}_i^{n+1} \Vdash \psi(n_0, \ldots X_0, \ldots)$ *ist eine arithmetische Relation zwischen* $i, n_0, n_1 \cdots$.

Der Beweis geht durch Induktion über den Aufbau von φ wie der Beweis von 1.8. Wir behandelen nur den Fall "$\forall X_n$". Zuvor bemerken wir noch, daß, wie in 1.8, aus 1 folgt

3. $\mathcal{H}_0^{n+1} \Vdash \neg\varphi(X_0, \ldots)$ gdw. für alle $\emptyset \neq \mathcal{H}_1^{n+1} \subset \mathcal{H}_0^{n+1}$ $\mathcal{H}_1^{n+1} \nVdash \varphi(X_0, \ldots)$.

Wir nehmen an, daß 2.8 für $\varphi(v_0, \ldots X_0, \ldots X_n)$ und $\neg\varphi(v_0, \ldots)$ gilt und zeigen die Gültigkeit von 2.8 für $\forall X_n \varphi(v_0, \ldots)$. Daß 2 gilt, folgt aus $(\{X_0, \ldots X_n) \mid (X_0, \ldots X_{n-1}) \in \mathcal{H}^n\} = \tilde{\mathcal{H}}^{n+1})$

4. $\mathcal{H}^n \Vdash \forall X_n \varphi(X_0, \ldots)$ gdw. $\tilde{\mathcal{H}}^{n+1} \Vdash \varphi(X_0, \ldots X_n)$ (klar).

Wir zeigen, daß 1 gilt. Sei $(\omega, \mathcal{S})$ generisch, $A_0, \ldots A_{n-1} \in \mathcal{S}$ und $(\omega, \mathcal{S}) \models \forall X_n \varphi(\boldsymbol{A}_0, \ldots X_n)$. Wir gebrauchen die Abkürzung $P(\mathcal{H}^{n+1})$ für die r.a. Hornklasse $\{(X_0, \ldots X_{n-1}) \mid \exists X_n\, (X_0, \ldots X_n) \in \mathcal{H}^{n+1}\}$. Die Familie $\mathcal{F} = \{\mathcal{H}^n \mid \tilde{\mathcal{H}}^{n+1} \Vdash \varphi(X_0, \ldots X_n)\} \cup \{P(\mathcal{H}^{n+1}) \mid \mathcal{H}^{n+1} \Vdash \neg\varphi(X_0, \ldots X_n)\}$ ist arithmetisch und dicht (weil 3 für $\neg\varphi$ gilt). $(A_0, \ldots A_{n-1})$ ist subgenerisch und daher in einem Element von $\mathcal{F}$ enthalten. Wenn $(A_0, \ldots) \in P(\mathcal{H}^{n+1})$, gibt es aber ein A_n aus $\mathcal{S}$ mit $(A_0, \ldots A_n) \in \mathcal{H}^{n+1}$. Also muß $(A_0, \ldots A_{n-1})$ in einem $\mathcal{H}^n$ mit $\tilde{\mathcal{H}}^{n+1} \Vdash \varphi(X_0, \ldots X_n)$ liegen. □

Folgerung. *A sei Element der beiden generischen ω-Modelle $(\omega, \mathcal{S}_i)$, $i = 0, 1$. Dann ist für jede L_2-Formel $\varphi(X)$ $(\omega, \mathcal{S}_0) \models \varphi(\boldsymbol{A})$ gdw. $(\omega, \mathcal{S}_1) \models \varphi(\boldsymbol{A})$. Insbesondere gelten in allen generischen ω-Modellen dieselben L^2-Aussagen.*

Die L^2-Formel $\varphi(X)$ "spricht nur vom Isomorphietyp von X" wenn für jede rekursive Bijektion $\pi : \omega \to \omega$ $\mathcal{P}(\omega) \Vdash \varphi(X) \leftrightarrow \varphi(\pi(X))$. Die r.a. Hornklasse $\mathcal{H}$ ist vollständig, wenn es für alle r.a. Hornklassen $\emptyset \neq \mathcal{H}_i \subset \mathcal{H}$ $i = 0, 1$ rekursiv isomorphe $A_i \in \mathcal{H}_i$ gibt.

Lemma 2.9. *$\mathcal{H}$ sei vollständig, $\varphi(X)$ spreche nur vom Isomorphietyp von X. Dann ist $\mathcal{H} \Vdash \varphi(X)$ oder $\mathcal{H} \Vdash \neg\varphi(X)$.*

Beweis. Sonst gibt es $\emptyset \neq \mathcal{H}_i \subset \mathcal{H}$, $\mathcal{H}_0 \Vdash \varphi(X)$, $\mathcal{H}_1 \Vdash \neg\varphi(X)$. Für eine rekursive Bijektion π sind $\mathcal{H}_0$ und $\mathcal{H}_3 = \{X \mid \pi(X) \in \mathcal{H}_1\}$ verträglich. Es ist aber $\mathcal{H}_0 \cap \mathcal{H}_3 \Vdash \varphi(X) \wedge \neg\varphi(\pi(X))$. Wid. □

Beispiel. $\mathcal{V}$ sei die r.a. Hornklasse aller X, die $\tilde{A}$ und $\tilde{B}$ trennen (III, 4.6). Wenn dann $\emptyset \neq \mathcal{H}_i \subset \mathcal{V}$, sind $\bigcap \mathcal{H}_0$ und $\bigcap \mathcal{H}_1$ Elemente von $\mathcal{H}_0$ bzw. $\mathcal{H}_1$, r.a. und rekursiv isomorph. $\mathcal{V}$ ist also vollständig.

Satz 2.10. 1. *Eine P_3-Aussage (siehe* IV, 2.2), *die in einem a.a. ω-Modell gilt, gilt in allen generischen ω-Modellen.*

2. *Eine $\forall_3$-Aussage, die in einer a.a. Gruppe gilt, gilt in allen generischen Gruppen.*

3. *Die $\exists_n$-Theorie der generischen Gruppen ist vollständig Σ_n^0, $n \geqslant 3$.*

4. *Die $\exists_3$-Theorie der a.a. Gruppen ist vollständig Σ_3^0.*

In IV, 3.6.2 haben wir gezeigt, daß eine $\forall_3$-Aussage, die in einer a.a. Gruppe gilt, auch in allen a.a. Untergruppen gilt. In diesem Sinn zeigt also 2.10.2, daß generische Gruppen "klein" sind.

Beweis. Nach IV, 2.3.2(iii) ist jede P_3-Aussage äquivalent zu $\forall X S_2^A(X)$ für ein r.a. A. Wenn diese Aussage in dem a.a. ω-Modell $(\omega, \mathcal{S})$ gilt, gibt es für jede r.a. Hornklasse $\mathcal{H} \neq \emptyset$ ein $B \in \mathcal{H} \cap \mathcal{S}$ und ein $i \in A$ mit $B \in \bar{\mathcal{H}}_i$. $\{\bar{\mathcal{H}}_i \mid i \in A\}$ ist also dicht. Nach 1.9 ist also $\mathcal{P}(\omega) \Vdash S_2^A(X)$, d.h. $\mathcal{P}(\omega) \Vdash \forall X S_2^A(X)$. Damit ist 1 bewiesen. 2 folgt aus 1 mit IV, 2.1.1, 2.

Mit IV, 2.2 übersetzt man jede Σ_n^0-Aussage über $\omega(M)$, in eine (für a.a. M) äquivalente $\exists_n$-Aussage über M, $n \geqslant 2$. Also läßt sich jede Σ_n^0-Menge 1-reduzieren auf die $\exists_n$-Theorie der generischen Gruppen. Um 3 zu beweisen, müssen wir noch zeigen, daß die $\exists_n$-Theorie der generischen Gruppen Σ_n^0 ist. Das folgt aus dem nächsten Lemma und IV, 2.2. (Zur Definition von $S_n^A(X)$, $P_n^A(X)$ siehe vor IV, 2.1 und IV, 2.2.)

Lemma 2.11 ($n \geqslant 3$). *Die Relation "$\bar{\mathcal{H}}_k \Vdash P_n^{W_j}(X_0)$" ist Π_n^0 in k, j.*

Beweis. Aus der Behauptung folgt, daß "$\bar{\mathcal{H}}_k \Vdash S_n^{W_j}(X_0)$" eine Π_{n+1}^0-Relation ist. Denn "$\cdots$" ist äquivalent zu $\forall i\,(\bar{\mathcal{H}}_i \cap \bar{\mathcal{H}}_k \neq \emptyset \Rightarrow (\bar{\mathcal{H}}_i \cap \bar{\mathcal{H}}_k) \nVdash P_n^{W_j}(X))$. Für $n = 2$ ist das 1.9.2, unser Induktionsanfang. 2.11 gelte für n. Aus der Darstellung $\bar{\mathcal{H}}_k \Vdash P_{n+1}^{W_j}(X_0)$ gdw. $\bar{\mathcal{H}}_k \Vdash \forall X_1 S_n^{W_j}(X_0 \vee X_1)$ gdw. $\{X \vee Y \mid X \in \bar{\mathcal{H}}_k\} \Vdash S_n^{W_j}(X_0)$ erkennt man, daß dann 2.11 für $n+1$ gilt. □

3 gilt nun, weil man jeder $\exists_n$-Aussage ein j zuordnen kann, derart, daß die Aussage genau dann zur $\exists_n$-Theorie der generischen Gruppen gehört, wenn in allen generischen $(\omega, \mathcal{S}) \models S_n^{W_j}(\omega)$ d.h. $\{\omega\} \nVdash P_n^{W_j}(X_0)$.

4. Eine $\exists_3$-Aussage gilt genau dann in allen a.a. Gruppen, wenn ihre Negation nicht a.a. erfülbar ist, d.h. (nach 2) wenn die Negation in generischen Gruppen nicht gilt. Die $\forall_3$-Aussagen, die in generische Gruppen gelten, bilden eine vollständige Π_3^0 Menge. Also bilden die $\forall_3$-Aussagen, die nicht gelten, eine vollständige Σ_3^0-Menge. □

M_0, die abzählbare a.a. Gruppe, deren Skelett gerade die e.e. Gruppen mit r.a. Wortproblem sind, ist zwar nach III, 4.4.4 minimal, aber nicht klein im eben angegebenen Sinn: Es gibt $\forall_3$-Aussagen, die in generischen Gruppen, aber nicht in M_0 gelten. Denn für jede r.a. Menge B gibt es eine $\exists_3$-Aussage φ, die genau dann in einer a.a. Gruppe M gilt, wenn $B \in W^*(M)$ (siehe IV, 3.4 Beweis). Wenn B nicht rekursiv ist, ist nach der Folgerung 2 aus V, 3.1 $\neg\varphi$ in allen generischen Gruppen gültig. Andererseits ist immer $M_0 \models \psi$.

In 3.5 werden wir zeigen, daß es a.a. Gruppen gibt, die "klein" sind (die alle $\forall_3$-Aussagen, die in generischen Gruppen gelten, erfüllen) und nicht generisch sind.

3. Die Ideale generischer Gruppen

Für generische Gruppen M zeigen wir:

$W_*(M)$ ist ein Hauptideal.

Für $A, B \in W^*(M)$ ist $A \leqslant^+ B$ gdw. $A \leqslant^* B$ gdw. A arithmetisch in B.

$W_*(M)$ ist unendlich.

Definition. 3.1. $G \subset \omega$ heißt vollständig subgenerisch (v.s.g.), wenn G subgenerisch ist und $H \in \mathcal{V}$ für ein $H \equiv_1 G$ (s. Beispiel zu 2.9).

Aus 1.5 folgt, daß es 2^ω v.s.g. Mengen gibt.

Lemma 3.2. *(H, G) sei subgenerisch, G v.s.g. Dann ist $H \leqslant_1 G$.*

Vergleiche 2.2.1 und 2.4.1. Aus 3.2 folgt: Zu jedem v.s.g. G gibt es ein subgenerisches H, so daß (H, G) nicht subgenerisch ist; denn es gibt nur abzählbar viele H mit $H \leqslant_1 G$.

Beweis. *Toti* sei die Menge aller i, für die f_i — die i-te partiell rekursive Funktion — total und injektiv ist. *Toti* ist arithmetisch. Jedem $i \in Toti$ ordnen wir effektiv die r.a. Hornklasse $\bar{\mathcal{H}}_{g(i)} = \{(X, Y) \mid f_i : X \leqslant_1 Y\}$ zu. Dann wählen wir ein r.a. C, sodaß $\{(X, Y) \mid Y \notin \mathcal{V}\} = \bigcup\{\bar{\mathcal{H}}_i \mid i \in C\}$. Wir setzen $A = C \cup g[Toti]$. B_1, B_2 seien r.a. Wenn für kein $i \in C$ $(B_1, B_2) \in \bar{\mathcal{H}}_i$, ist B_2 aus $\mathcal{V}$, also vollständig r.a. Für ein $i \in Toti$ ist dann $f_i : B_1 \leqslant B_2$. Wir haben $S_2^A(B_1, B_2)$ gezeigt. Aus 1.10 folgt $\mathcal{P}(\omega)^2 \Vdash S_2^A(X, Y)$. Das sollte bewiesen werden. □

Satz 3.3. 1. *In allen generischen ω-Modellen gibt es eine — bis auf rekursive Isomorphie — eindeutig bestimmte v.s.g. Menge.*

2. *Wenn $(\omega, \mathcal{S})$ generisch ist und $B \in \mathcal{S}$ v.s.g., ist* $\mathcal{S} = \{X \mid X \leqslant^* B\}) = \{X \mid X \leqslant_1 B\}$.

3. $(\omega, \{X \mid X \leqslant_1 B\})$ *ist genau dann generisch, wenn* B *v.s.g. ist.*

4. $(\omega, \mathcal{S}_i)$ *seien generisch,* $B_i \in \mathcal{S}_i$ *v.s.g. Dann ist für jede* L^2*-Formel, die nur über den Isomorphietyp von* X *spricht,* $(\omega, \mathcal{S}_0) \models \varphi(\boldsymbol{B}_0)$ *gdw.* $(\omega, \mathcal{S}_1) \models \varphi(\boldsymbol{B}_1)$.

5. *Ist* $(\omega, \mathcal{S}_0) \subset (\omega, \mathcal{S}_1)$, $(\omega, \mathcal{S}_0)$ *algebraisch abgeschlossen,* $(\omega, \mathcal{S}_1)$ *generisch, so ist* $\mathcal{S}_1 = \mathcal{S}_0$.

6. *Generische* ω*-Modelle sind abzählbar.*

7. *In generischen* ω*-Modellen gilt* ***max*** (*siehe Beispiel vor* IV. 1. 2).

Beweis. 1. Das generische ω-Modell $(\omega, \mathcal{S})$ ist algebraisch abgeschlossen. Es gibt also ein $B_1 \in \mathcal{S} \cap \mathcal{V}$. B_1 ist v.s.g. Wenn $B_2 \in \mathcal{S}$ v.s.g., ist (B_1, B_2) subgenerisch und nach 3.2 $B_1 \leqslant_1 B_2$ und $B_2 \leqslant_1 B_2$.

2. Sei B v.s.g. aus dem generischen $(\omega, \mathcal{S})$. In allen a.a. ω-Modellen ist $\{X \mid X \leqslant_1 B\} \subset \{X \mid X \leqslant^* B\} \subset \mathcal{S}$. Sei $C \in \mathcal{S}$. Da (C, B) subgenerisch ist, ist $C \leqslant_1 B$.

3. Wenn $(\omega, \{X \mid X \leqslant_1 B\})$ generisch ist, gibt es ein v.s.g. $C \leqslant_1 B$, (B, C) ist subgenerisch, also $B \leqslant_1 C$. Ist B v.g.s., gibt es ein generisches $(\omega, \mathcal{S})$ mit $B \in \mathcal{S}$. Aus 2 folgt $\mathcal{S} = \{X \mid X \leqslant_1 B\}$.

4. folgt aus 2.9.

5. $\mathcal{S}_0$, $\mathcal{S}_1$ seien wie in 5. Da $(\omega, \mathcal{S}_0)$ a.a., gibt es ein $B \in \mathcal{V} \cap \mathcal{S}_0$ Weil $B \in \mathcal{S}_1$, ist B v.s.g., $\mathcal{S}_1 \subset \{X \mid X \leqslant_1 B\} \subset \mathcal{S}_0$.

6 und 7 folgen aus 2. □

Folgerungen 3.4. 1. *Wenn* B *v.s.g. ist, gibt es eine — eindeutig bestimmte — abzählbare a.a. Gruppe* M^B *mit* $W^*(M^B) = \{X \mid X \leqslant_1 B\}$. M^B *ist generisch.*

2. *Wenn* B_1 *und* B_2 *v.s.g. sind, ist* $M^{B_1} \cong M^{B_2}$ *gdw.* $M^{B_1} < M^{B_2}$ *gdw.* $B_1 \equiv_1 B_2$ *gdw.* $B_1 \leqslant^* B_2$.

3. *In jeder generischen Gruppe* M *gibt es eine e.e. Untergruppe* G, *deren Wortproblem v.s.g. ist. Es ist dann* $M \cong_p M^{W(G)}$.

4. *Eine generische Gruppe ist partiell isomorph zu jeder a.a. Untergruppe. Abzählbare generische Gruppen sind also minimal.*

5. *Generische Gruppen erfüllen die* $\exists_5$*-Aussage* ***max*** (*siehe* IV, 2.5.2).

6. *Es gibt zwei e.e. subgenerische Gruppen, die nicht gemeinsam in eine generische Gruppe einbettbar sind.*

Beweis. 1. Wenn B v.s.g., ist $(\omega, \{X \mid X \leqslant_1 B\})$ a.a. und abzählbar. Wegen III, 3 (3.4 und 12.2) gibt es eindeutig eine abzählbar a.a. Gruppe M mit $W^*(M) = \{X \mid X \leqslant_1 B\}$. Weil $\omega(M)$ generisch ist, ist M generisch (2.4.2).

2. $M^{B_1} \cong M^B$ gdw. $M^{B_1} < M^{B_2}$ folgt aus 4. Aus $B_1 \equiv_1 B_2$ folgt

natürlich $M^{B_1} \cong M^{B_2}$. Daraus folgt $B_1 \leqslant^* B_2$. Wenn $B_1 \leqslant^* B_2$ ist (B_1, B_2) generisch, also $B_1 \equiv_1 B_2$.

3. $B \in W^*(M)$ sei v.s.g. Es gibt ein $G \in \mathrm{Sk}(M)$ mit $B \leqslant_1 W(G)$. $W(G)$ ist dann v.s.g. und $B \equiv_1 W(G)$.

4. folgt aus 3.3.5, 5 aus 3.3.7, 6 aus der Bemerkung zu 3.2. □

Nach V, 3.5 lassen sich die generischen Gruppen unter den a.a. Gruppen durch eine elementare Satzmenge auszeichnen, es gilt aber:

Satz 3.5. *Für kein n gibt es eine Menge von* $\exists_n$*-Aussagen, die genau dann in einer a.a. Gruppe gilt, wenn die Gruppe generisch ist.*

Beweis. (Skizze) Sei n gegeben.

(a) Es gibt ein $m \in \omega$ mit: Für jede S_n-Aussage φ aus L^2 gibt es eine Σ^0_m Eigenschaft $R^\varphi(X)$, sodaß für alle $B \subset \omega$ $(\omega, \{X \mid X \leqslant_1 B\}) \models \varphi$ gdw. $R^\varphi(B)$. Wir nennen $B \subset \omega$ k-subgenerisch (k-s.g.), wenn für jede dichte Σ^0_k-Familie $\mathcal{F}$ von r.a. Hornklassen $B \in \bigcup \mathcal{F}$. Wir schreiben $\mathcal{H} \Vdash_k R(X)$, wenn $R(B)$ für alle k-s.g. B aus $\mathcal{H}$. Aus dem Beweis von 1.8 erkennt man.

(b) Es gibt ein $k \in \omega$, so daß für alle Σ^0_m-Eigenschaften $R(X)$ und alle r.a. Hornklassen $\mathcal{H}$ $\mathcal{H} \Vdash_k R(X)$ gdw. $\mathcal{H} \Vdash R(X)$. Mit einer leichten Änderung des Beweises von 1.3 kann man zeigen:

(c) Es gibt eine arithmetische k-s.g. Menge $B \in \mathcal{V}$. Es sei $\mathcal{S} = \{X \mid X \leqslant_1 B\}$. Wenn wir $n \geqslant 4$ annehmen, ist $(\omega, \mathcal{S})$ a.a. Denn wenn φ die P_3 (also auch S_n) - Aussage "a.a." ist, ist nach 3.3.3 $\mathcal{V} \Vdash R^\varphi(X)$. Da $\mathcal{V} \Vdash_k R^\varphi(X)$, ist $R^\varphi(B)$. Wir finden nun eine a.a. Gruppe N mit $W^*(N) = \mathcal{S}$. N ist nicht generisch, weil B arithmetisch und nicht rekursiv ist. Wir zeigen aber, daß alle $\exists_n$-Aussagen ρ, die in generischen Gruppen gelten, in N gelten. Zu ρ gehört nach IV, 2.4.2 eine S_n Aussage φ, die genau dann in $\omega(M)$ gilt, wenn ρ in der a.a.Gr. M gilt. Es ist also, wenn ρ in allen generischen Gruppen gilt, φ in allen generischen ω-Modellen, also allen $(\omega, \{X \mid X \leqslant_1 G\})$ für subgenerisches $G \in \mathcal{V}$, gültig. Aus $\mathcal{V} \Vdash R^\varphi(X)$ folgt aber $\mathcal{V} \Vdash_k R^\varphi(X)$ und $R^\varphi(B)$. Also ist $(\omega, \{X \mid X \leqslant_1 B\}) \models \varphi$ und somit $N \models \rho$. □

Der nächste Satz schließt die Lücke zwischen 1.2.2 (Jede arithmetische subgen. Menge ist rekursiv) und 2.6.2 (Wenn G subgenerisch ist, und $H \not\leqslant^* G$, gibt es ein generisches ω-Modell, in dem G, aber nicht H liegt).

Satz 3.6. (G, H) *sei subgenerisch. Dann sind äquivalent*

(a) *H ist in G implizit arithmetisch definierbar,*

(b) $H \leqslant^* G$,
(c) $H \leqslant^+ G$ (*falls* $G \neq \omega$).

Beweis. (c)$\rightarrow$(b)$\rightarrow$(a) ist klar.

(a)$\rightarrow$(b): Sei $R(X, Y)$ arithmetisch und $\{H\} = \{Y \mid R(G, Y)\}$. Nach 1.8 gibt es eine r.a. Hornklasse $\mathcal{H}^2$ mit $(G, H) \in \mathcal{H}^2$ und $\mathcal{H}^2 \Vdash R(X, Y)$. Wenn $H \not\leqslant^* G$, gibt es ein $H' \neq H$ mit $(G, H') \in \mathcal{H}^2$. Wegen 2.2 können wir annehmen, daß (G, H') subgenerisch ist. Dann würde aber $R(G, H')$ folgen. Wid.

(b)$\rightarrow$(c): (G, H) sei in der r.a. Hornklasse $\mathcal{H}^2$, für $r, s \in \omega$ sei $\mathcal{H}^2 \Vdash (r, s) : X \leqslant^* Y$. Wir wählen $g \in \omega \setminus G$. Wir definieren $W^i = \{u \mid \langle i, u \rangle \in W_r\}$ und bilden die r.a. Hornklassen $\mathcal{H}_i^2 = \{(X, Y) \mid i \notin W_s^1[Y]\}$ und für jedes $u \in W^i$ $\mathcal{H}_{i,u}^2 = \{(X, Y) \mid D_u \not\subset Y\}$. Wenn $(A, B) \in \mathcal{H}_i^2 \cap \bigcap\{\mathcal{H}_{i,x}^2 \mid x \in W^i\}$, ist $i \notin W_r^e[B]$ und $i \notin W_s^1[B]$, also $(r, s) : A \not\leqslant^* B$. Für jedes i ist also

$$(*) \qquad \mathcal{H}^2 \cap \bigcap\{\mathcal{H}_{i,x}^2 \mid x \in W^i\} \cap \mathcal{H}_i^2 = \emptyset.$$

Wenn $C \in \mathcal{H}^2 \cap \mathcal{H}_i^2$ und für $u \in W^i$ $C_u \in \mathcal{H}^2 \cap \mathcal{H}_i^2 \cap \mathcal{H}_{i,u}^2$, wäre $C \cap \bigcap\{C_x \mid x \in W^i\}$ im Durchschnitt $(*)$. Es gibt also eine Funktion $f : \omega \rightarrow \mathcal{P}_\omega(\omega)$ mit: $f(i) = D_u$ für ein $u \in W^i$ mit $\mathcal{H}^2 \cap \mathcal{H}_i^2 \cap \mathcal{H}_{i,u}^2 = \emptyset$ *oder* $= \{g\}$ und $\mathcal{H}^2 \cap \mathcal{H}_i^2 = \emptyset$. Wir können f rekursiv wählen. Es ist $f : H \leqslant^+ G$. □

Folgerung. *G und F seien e.e. Untergrupgen der generischen Gruppe M. Wenn $W(G)$ implizit arithmetisch in $W(F)$ definierbar ist, ist $W(G) \leqslant^* W(F)$.*

Gruppen mit lösbarem Wortproblem sind in jede generische Gruppe einbettbar. Wenn eine v.s.g. Menge denselben $*$-Grad wie das Wortproblem der endlich erzeugte Gruppe G hat, ist G in genau eine abzählbare generische Gruppe einbettbar. Gibt es e.e. Gruppen mit nicht lösbarem Wortproblem, die in verschiedene (nicht partiell isomorphe) generische Gruppen einbettbar sind? Diese Frage ist äquivalent mit der Frage, ob die Ideale $W_*(M)$ für generische M nur aus zwei Elementen bestehen. Denn wenn B v.s.g. und für ein $G < M^B$ $G \not\equiv^* B$, also $B \not\leqslant^* W(G)$, gibt es eine generische Gruppe N mit $G < N$ und $B \notin W^*(N)$ (2.6.2).

Satz 3.7. *Für alle generischen Gruppen M ist das Ideal $W_*(M)$ unendlich.*

Zum Beweis definieren wir:

Ein $*$-Grad a wird durch die r.a. Hornklasse $\mathcal{H}$ *beschrieben*, wenn $\mathcal{H} \neq \emptyset$ und jedes r.a. Element von $\mathcal{H}$ aus a ist. Der $*$-Grad einer vollständigen r.a. Menge wird z. B. durch $\mathcal{V}$ beschrieben. Wir brauchen ein Lemma:

Lemma 3.8. *a_1 bzw. a_2 seien durch $\mathcal{H}_1$ und $\mathcal{H}_2$ beschrieben, und $a_1 \not\leq a_2$. Wenn dann (G, H) subgenerisch ist, $G \in \mathcal{H}_1$, $H \in \mathcal{H}_2$, ist $G \not\leq^* H$.*

Beweis. Sei $G \leqslant^* H$ und also für ein rekursives f $f: G \leqslant^+ H$ (3.6). Nach 1.8 ist $\mathcal{H}^2 \Vdash f: X \leqslant^+ Y$ für eine r.a. Hornklasse mit $(G, H) \in \mathcal{H}^2$. Es gibt r.a. $(A, B) \in \mathcal{H}^2$ mit $A \in a_1$ und $B \in a_2$. Es ist also $f: A \not\leqslant^+ B$. Sei $i \in A \not\leftrightarrow f(i) \subset B$ für ein $i \in \omega$. (A, B) ist in der r.a. Hornklasse $\mathcal{H}_0^2 := \{(X, Y) \mid i \in A \leftrightarrow i \in X \wedge f(i) \subset B \leftrightarrow f(i) \subset Y\}$. Also $\mathcal{H}^2 \cap \mathcal{H}_0^2 \neq \emptyset$. Es kann aber keine subgenerischen (C, D) in $\mathcal{H}^2 \cap \mathcal{H}_0^2$ geben. Wid. □

Satz 3.7 folgt nun aus dem nächsten Lemma: Wir wählen für jeden der $*$-Grade eine beschreibende r.a. Hornklasse $\mathcal{H}$ und ein Element aus $\mathcal{H} \cap W^*(M)$. Diese Elemente haben dann alle verschiedenen $*$-Grad.

Lemma 3.9. *Es gibt eine absteigende unendliche Folge von beschreibbaren $*$-Graden.*

Beweis. Wir brauchen aus der Rekursionstheorie:

I ([24]). Jede nichtrekursive r.a. Menge läßt sich disjunkt in zwei r.a. Mengen zerlegen, die unvergleichbare Turinggrade haben (S. 175, Sacks).

II ([24]). Es gibt maximale r.a. Mengen R. D.h. R ist r.a., $\omega \setminus R$ unendlich, für alle r.a. A folgt aus $R \subset A$, daß $A \setminus R$ oder $\omega \setminus A$ endlich ist (S. 235, Friedberg).

Wir benützen nur eine Folgerung aus I:

III. *Jede nichtrekursive r.a. Menge A' läßt sich disjunkt in zwei nichtrekursive r.a. Teilmengen A, B mit $A <^* A'$ zerlegen.*

Beweis. Wir finden nach I A und B mit unvergleichbaren Turinggraden. A und B sind somit nichtrekursiv. Weil A r.a., ist $A \leqslant_e A'$. $\omega \setminus A \leqslant_e^1 A'$ gilt, weil $x \notin A$ gdw. $x \in B$ oder $x \notin A'$. Also $A \leqslant^* A'$. Wäre $A' \leqslant^* A$, würde $B \leqslant^* A$ folgen.

Wir wenden nun III sukzessive auf die maximale r.a. Menge R an und bekommen zwei Folgen A_i, B_i von nichtrekursiven r.a. Mengen mit $R = A_0 \dot{\cup} B_0, \ldots A_n = A_{n+1} \dot{\cup} B_{n+1} \cdots$, $R^* > A_0^* > A_1^* > A_2 \cdots$. Alle $A_n/{\equiv^*}$ sind beschreibbar:

Setze $\mathscr{H} = \{X \mid A_n \subset X \wedge X \cap (B_0 \dot\cup B_1 \cdots \dot\cup B_n) = \emptyset\}$. Offenbar ist $A_n \in \mathscr{H}$. Sei $B \in \mathscr{H}$ r.a. Dann ist $B \dot\cup B_0 \dot\cup \cdots \dot\cup B_n \supset R$. Wäre $\omega \setminus (B \dot\cup B_0 \dot\cup \cdots \dot\cup B_n)$ endlich, wäre $B_0 \dot\cup \cdots \dot\cup B_n$ rekursiv, also $A_n \equiv^* R$. Also ist $(B \dot\cup B_0 \dot\cup \cdots \dot\cup B_n) \setminus R = B \setminus A_n$ endlich. Daher $A_n \equiv^* B$. □

Folgerung. *Es gibt eine endlich erzeugte Gruppe mit nicht-lösbarem Wortproblem, die in zwei generische Gruppen M, N $M \not\equiv_p N$ einbettbar ist.*

Kommen in jeder a.a. Gruppe unendlich viele $*$-Grade vor?

4. Drei Eigenschaften generischer Gruppen

Die Turingreduzierbarkeit unterscheidet sich von der $*$-Reduzierbarkeit dadurch, daß zwar für alle A $\omega \setminus A \leqslant_T A$ und $A^2 \leqslant_T A$, im allgemeinen aber nicht $\omega \setminus A \leqslant^* A$ und $A^2 \leqslant^* A$. Wir zeigen $(G \subset \omega)$:

Ist G nichtrekursiv und subgenerisch, so ist $\omega \setminus G \not\leqslant^* G$.

Ist G v.s.g., so ist $G^2 \not\leqslant^* G$.

Es gibt nichtrekursive subgenerische G mit $G^2 \leqslant^* G$.

Satz 4.1. *Wenn $(G, \omega \setminus G)$ subgenerisch ist, ist G rekursiv.*

Beweis. Sei $(G, \omega \setminus G)$ subgenerisch und G nichtrekursiv. Nach 1.8 gibt es eine r.a. Hornklasse $\mathscr{H}^2$ mit $(G, \omega \setminus G) \in \mathscr{H}^2$ und $\mathscr{H}^2 \Vdash (Y = X \setminus \omega) \wedge$ "X nicht rekursiv". Aus 1.7 folgt $\mathscr{H}^2 \subset \{(X, Y) \mid Y = X \setminus \omega\}$. Wenn A, B r.a. und $(A, B) \in \mathscr{H}^2$, sind A und B rekursiv (also auch subgenerisch). Daraus folgt $\mathscr{H}^2 \nVdash$ "X nicht rekursiv". □

Folgerung. 1. *Wenn G subgenerisch ist und $\omega \setminus G \leqslant_e G$, ist G rekursiv.*

2. ([14]) *Jede endlich erzeugte einfache Untergruppe einer generischen Gruppe hat lösbares Wortproblem.* (*Aus* IV, 3.1.2 *folgt, daß sich diese Eigenschaft der generischen Gruppen in a.a. Gruppen durch eine $\forall_4$-Aussage ausdrücken läßt.*)

Beweis. 1. Wenn $\omega \setminus G \leqslant_e G$, ist $\omega \setminus G \leqslant^* G$. Nach 2.4.1 ist daher mit G auch $(G, \omega \setminus G)$ subgenerisch. 2 folgt aus 1 weil nach III, 12 für einfache F $\omega \setminus W(F) \leqslant_e W(F)$. (Es gibt nichtrekursive subgenerische G, für die auch $\omega \setminus G$ subgenerisch ist.)

Definition 4.2. Eine r.a. Hornklasse $\bar{\mathscr{H}}_i$ heißt *ordnend*, wenn für alle n, m $\hat{\mathscr{H}}_i \vdash q(n) \rightarrow q(m)$ oder $\hat{\mathscr{H}}_i \vdash q(m) \rightarrow q(n)$. ($\mathscr{H}$ ist also genau dann ordnend, wenn $\mathcal{H}$ (bzgl. $\subset$) eine Kette ist: für alle $A, B \in \mathcal{H}$ ist $A \subset B$ oder $B \subset A$.)

Lemma 4.3. 1. *Wenn* $G \in \mathcal{H}$, $\mathcal{H}$ *ordnend, ist* $G^2 \leqslant^* G$.
2. *Wenn* G *subgenerisch,* $G^2 \leqslant^* G$, *gibt es ein ordnendes* $\mathcal{H}$, $G \in \mathcal{H}$.

Beweis. 1. $\bar{\mathcal{H}}_i$ sei ordnend und $G \in \bar{\mathcal{H}}_i$. Dann ist $(x, y) \notin G^2$ gdw. $x \notin G$ und $y \notin G$ gdw. $\hat{\mathcal{H}}_i \vdash q(x) \rightarrow q(y)$ und $y \notin G$ oder $\hat{\mathcal{H}}_i \vdash q(y) \rightarrow q(x)$ und $x \notin G$. Das zeigt, daß $\omega \setminus G^2 \leqslant_e^1 G$.
2. Sei G subgenerisch und $\omega \setminus G^2 = W_i^1[G]$. Es gibt eine r.a. Hornklasse $G \in \mathcal{H}$, $\mathcal{H} \Vdash \omega \setminus X^2 = W_i^1[X]$. $\mathcal{H}$ ist ordnend. Denn sei $n, m \in \omega$ und $\hat{\mathcal{H}} \nvdash q(n) \rightarrow q(m)$. $\hat{\mathcal{H}} \nvdash q(m) \rightarrow q(n)$. Dann gibt es subgenerische Mengen $G_1, G_2 \in \mathcal{H}$ mit $n \in G_1$, $m \notin G_1$, $m \in G_2$, $n \notin G_2$. Da $(n, m) \in G_j^2$, ist $(n, m) \notin W_i^1[G_j]$ $(j = 1, 2)$. Also ist $G_1 \cap G_2 \in \mathcal{H} \cap \{X \mid (n, m) \notin W_i^1[X] \wedge n \notin X \wedge m \notin X\} =: \mathcal{H}_0$. Für alle $A \in \mathcal{H}_0$ ist aber $\omega \setminus A^2 \neq W_i^1[A]$. Wid. □

Satz 4.4. *Wenn* G *v.s.g., ist* (G^2, G) *nicht subgenerisch.*

Folgerungen. 1. *Wenn* G *v.s.g.,* $H \equiv^* G$, *ist* $H^2 \nleqslant^* H$.
2. *In jeder generischen Gruppe* M *gibt es eine e.e. Untergruppe* F, *sodaß für kein* $H \neq E$ $F * H$ *in* M *einbettbar ist.*

Beweis der Folgerungen. 1. Aus 2.4.1 folgt $G^2 \nleqslant^* G$. Wenn $A \equiv^* B$, ist aber immer auch $A^2 \equiv^* B^2$. 2. Man wählt F so, daß $W(F)$ v.s.g. ist. Nach III, 2.13.2 ist $W(F)^2 \leqslant^* W(F * H)$.

Zum Beweis von 4.4 konstruieren wir zunächst eine r.a. Menge B, die in keiner ordnenden r.a. Hornklasse liegt. Wir wählen dazu eine rekursive Relation R, so daß für alle i, n, m aus ω $\hat{\mathcal{H}}_i \Vdash q(n) \rightarrow q(m)$ gdw. $\exists k\, R(k, i, n, m)$.

$$B := \{2i \mid \exists k\, (R(k, i, 2i, 2i+1) \wedge \forall j < k \neg R(j, i, 2i+1, 2i))\}$$
$$\cup \{2i+1 \mid \exists j\, (\forall k \leqslant j \neg R(k, i, 2i, 2i+1) \wedge R(j, i, 2i+1, 2i))\}$$

B ist r.a. Sei $\bar{\mathcal{H}}_i$ ordnend. Wir wählen k (ev. $= \infty$) minimal mit $R(k, i, 2i, 2i+1)$ und j minimal mit $R(j, i, 2i+1, 2i)$. Da $\bar{\mathcal{H}}_i$ ordnend ist, ist k oder $j \neq \infty$.

Wenn $k \leqslant j$, ist $2i \in B$, $2i+1 \notin B$, $\hat{\mathcal{H}}_i \vdash q(2i) \rightarrow q(2i+1)$. Wenn $j < k$, ist $2i+1 \in B$, $2i \notin B$, $\hat{\mathcal{H}}_i \vdash q(2i+1) \rightarrow q(2i)$. In beiden Fällen folgt $B \notin \bar{\mathcal{H}}_i$.

Sei nun G v.s.g. und (G^2, G) subgenerisch. Da $G^2 \leqslant_T G$, folgt aus

3.6, daß $G^2 \leqslant^* G$. G ist also in einer ordnenden r.a. Hornklasse $\mathcal{H}$ enthalten. Wir können o.E. $G \in \mathcal{V}$ annehmen. Sei nun A r.a. und $A \in \mathcal{H} \cap \mathcal{V}$. Dann ist A vollständig, und es ist $f: B \leqslant_1 A$ für eine rekursive Funktion f. B ist dann ein Element der ordnenden Hornklasse $\{X \mid f[X] \in \mathcal{H}\}$. Wid. □

Satz 4.5. *In jedem generischen* $(\omega, \mathcal{S})$ *gibt es ein nichtrekursives* $G \in \mathcal{S}$ *mit* $G^2 \in \mathcal{S}$.

Folgerungen. 1. *In jedem generischen* $(\omega, \mathcal{S})$ *gibt es ein nichtrekursives* G *mit* $G^2 \leqslant^* G$.

2. *In jeder generischen Gruppe* M *gibt es eine e.e. Untergruppe* F *mit nichtlösbarem Wortproblem, sodaß alle* $F * F$, $F * F * F, \ldots, F * H$ *für e.e. Gruppen* H *mit lösbarem Wortproblem in* M *einbettbar sind.*

3. *Es gibt nicht-rekursive subgenerische* G, *für die auch* $\omega \backslash G$ *subgenerisch ist.*

Beweis der Folgerungen. Da $G^2 \leqslant_T G$, ist $G^2 \leqslant^* G$, wenn (G, G^2) subgenerisch ist (3.6). Also gilt 1.

2 folgt aus III, 2.13.2, weil $W(F * F)$, $W(F * H) \leqslant^* W(F)^{\omega}$. Man wählt $F < M$ mit $W(F) \equiv^* G$ für ein $G \in W^*(M)$ mit $G^2 \leqslant^* G$. Aus III, 2.8 folgt $G^{\omega} \equiv G$. 3 Man überlegt leicht: Wenn G in einer r.a. ordnenden Hornklasse ist, ist G subgenerisch gdw. $\omega \setminus G$ subgenerisch.

Beweis von 4.5. $\equiv$ sei die r.a. Äquivalenzrelation von 4.6. Wir identifizieren ω mit Q' und definieren die r.a. Hornklasse $\mathcal{H} := \{X \subset Q' \mid 0 \in X,\ 1 \in X,\ \forall r \in X\ \forall s\, ((s < r \vee s \equiv r) \to s \in X)\}$. $\mathcal{H}$ ist offenbar ordnend, nichtleer (denn $0/\!\equiv\ \in \mathcal{H}$) und enthält keine rekursive Menge. Wenn $(\omega, \mathcal{S})$ generisch, wählen wir $G \in \mathcal{H} \in \mathcal{S}$. Dann ist $G^2 \leqslant^* G$ und also $G^2 \in \mathcal{S}$.

Lemma 4.6. *Auf der Menge* Q' *der rationalen Zahlen aus dem Intervall* $[0, 1]$ *gibt es eine r.a. Äquivalenzrelation* $\equiv$ *mit*

(i) *Die Äquivalenzklassen sind konvex, d.h.* $r < s < t$, $r \equiv t \Rightarrow r \equiv s$.

(ii) $0 \not\equiv 1$.

(iii) *Es gibt keine rekursive Teilmenge* $B \subset Q'$ *mit* $0 \in B$, $1 \notin B$, *f.a.* $r, s \in Q'$, $r \in B$, $s \equiv r \Rightarrow s \in B$.

Beweis. $n \mapsto (n_1, n_2)$ sei eine rekursive Bijektion von ω mit ω^2. $f: \omega \to Q'^2$ sei eine partiell rekursive Auswahlfunktion für $R(n, r, s)$: gdw. $n \in \omega$, $r, s \in Q'$, $r < s < r + \dfrac{1}{2^{n+1}}$, $r \in W_{n_1}$, $s \in W_{n_2}$. D.h. wenn

$f(n)=(r,s)$, ist $R(n,r,s)$; und wenn $R(n,r,s)$, ist $f(n)$ definiert. $\boldsymbol{J}=\{[r,s]\subset Q' \mid \text{ex. } n\ f(n)=(r,s)\}$ ist eine r.a. Menge von abgeschlossenen Intervallen. Wir defininieren $r\equiv s$ gdw. es gibt $J_0,\dots J_k\in\boldsymbol{J}$ mit $r\in J_0$, $s\in J_k$ und für $i=0,1,\dots k-1$ $J_i\cap J_{i+1}\neq\emptyset$. $\equiv$ ist offenbar r.a. und die Äquivalenzklassen sind konvex. Weiter ist $0\not\equiv 1$, denn die $J\in\boldsymbol{J}$ können 0, 1 nicht überdecken, weil ihre Gesamtlänge kleiner als
$\frac{1}{2}+\frac{1}{4}+\cdots\frac{1}{2^{n+1}}+\cdots=1$ ist.

Sei nun $B\subset Q'$, B rekursiv, $B=W_{n_1}$, $\omega\setminus W_{n_2}$. Wenn $0\in B$ und $1\notin B$ gibt es ein $r'\in B$, $s'\notin B$ mit $r'<s'<r'+\frac{1}{2^{n+1}}$. $f(n)$ ist also definiert und sei $=(r,s)$. Dann ist $r\in B$, $s\notin B$ und $[r,s]\in\boldsymbol{J}$ d.h. $r\equiv s$. Damit ist das Lemma bewiesen. □

Literatur

[1] J. Barwise und A. Robinson, Completing theories by forcing, Annals of Mathematical Logic, Vol. 2 (1970) 119–142.

[2] O.V. Belegradek, Definability in algebraically closed groups, Mathematical Notes of the Academy of Sciences of the USSR, Vol. 16, No. 3 (1974) 813–816.

[3] O.V. Belegradek, Über algebraisch abgeschlossene Gruppen, Algebra i Logika 13, No. 3 (1974) 239–255 (Russian).

[4] W.W. Boone und G. Higman, An algebraic characterisation of groups with soluble word problem, J. Austral. Math. Soc. 18 (1974) 41–53.

[5] C.C. Chang und H.J. Keisler, Model Theory (North-Holland Publishing Co., Amsterdam, 1973).

[6] P. Eklof und G. Sabbagh, Model-completions and modules, Annals of Mathematical Logic, Vol. 2 (1970) 251–295.

[7] R. Fraissé, Sur l'extension aux relations de quelques proprietés des ordres, Ann. Sci. Ecole Norm. Sup. 71 (1954) 540–542.

[8] C. Higman, B.H. Neumann und H. Neumann, Embedding theorems for groups, Journal of the London Mathematical Society, Vol. 24 (1949) 247–254.

[9] C. Higman, Subgroups of finitely presented groups, Proc. Roy. Soc. London (A) 262 (1961) 455–475.

[10] J. Hirschfeld und W.H. Wheeler, Forcing, arithmetic, division rings, Springer Lecture Notes in Mathematics Vol. 454 (1975).

[11] C. Karp, Finte quantifier equivalence, in: The theory of models, Proc. of the 1963 Symposium at Berkeley (North-Holland Publishing Co., Amsterdam, 1965).

[12] H.J. Keisler, Forcing and the omitting types theorem, preprint.

[13] D.W. Kueker, Definability, automorphisms and infinitary languages, in: Syntax and semantics of infinitary languages, Springer Lecture Notes in Mathematics, Vol. 72, Berlin, 1968.

[14] A. MacIntyre, On algebraically closed groups, Annals of Mathematics Vol. 96 (1972) 53–97.

[15] A. MacIntyre, Omitting quantifier-free types in generic structures, Journal of Symbolic Logic Vol. 37 (1972) 512–520.
[16] A. MacIntyre, On algebraically closed division rings.
[17] A. MacIntyre, Martin's axiom applied to existentially closed groups, Mathematica Scandinavica, Vol. 32 (1973) 46–56.
[18] C.F. Miller III, The word problem in quotients of a group, unpublished.
[19] B.H. Neumann, Some remarks on infinite groups, Journal of the London Mathematical Society, Vol. 12 (1937) 120–127.
[20] B.H. Neumann und H. Neumann, Embedding theorems for groups, J. London Math. Soc. 34 (1959) 465–479.
[21] B.H. Neumann, A note on algebraically closed groups, Journal of the London Math. Soc. Vol. 27 (1952) 247–249.
[22] B.H. Neumann, The isomorphism problem for algebraically closed groups, in: Word Problems (ed. by W.W. Boone et al.) (North-Holland Publishing Co., Amsterdam, 1973).
[23] A. Robinson, Infinite forcing in model theory, Proc. of the Second Scandinavian Logic Symposium, Oslo, 1970 (North-Holland Publishing Co., Amsterdam, 1971).
[24] H. Rogers, Theory of recursive functions and effective computability, New York, 1967.
[25] P.E. Schupp, Some reflections on HNN extensions, in: Proc. of the Second Intern. Conference on the Theory of Groups, 1973, Springer Lecture Notes in Mathematics, Vol. 372 (1974) 611–632.
[26] W.R. Scott, Algebraically closed groups, Proc. of the American Math. Soc., Vol. 2 (1951) 118–121.
[27] H. Simmons, The word problem for absolute presentations, Journal of the London Math. Soc., Vol. 6 (1973) 275–280.
[28] W.H. Wheeler, Algebraically closed division rings, forcing and the analytical hierearchy, Diss. Yale Univ. 1972.
[29] M. Ziegler, Gruppen mit vorgeschriebenem Wortproblem, Math. Ann. 219 (1976) 43–51.
[30] M. Ziegler, Ein rekursiv aufzählbarer btt-Grad, der nicht zum Wortproblem einer Gruppe behört, Zeitschrift für Math. Logik und Grundlagen der Math. 1976.
[31] G.E. Sacks, Degrees of unsolvability, Ann. of Math. Studies No. 55, Princeton, 1963.
[32] R.M. Smullyan, Theory of formal systems, Ann. of Math. Studies, Princeton, 1961.
[33] M.Y. Trofimov, Definability in algebraically closed systems, Algebra i Logika (14) 1975.
[34] S. Shelah und M. Ziegler, Algebraically closed groups of large cardinality, Journal of Symbolic Logic 44 (1979) 130–140.
[35] A. MacIntyre, Existentially closed structures and Jensen's principle, Israel J. Math. 25 (1976) 202–210.
[36] K. Hickin, A MacIntyre, Algebraically closed groups: Embeddings and centralizers, Proc. Oxford Logic Conf., Word Problems II, this volume, pp. 141–155.
[37] K. Hickin, Maximal subgroups of algebraically closed groups (preprint).
[38] S. Shelah, Existentially closed groups in $\aleph_1$ with special properties, Bull. of the Greek Math. Soc. (submitted).
[39] S. Shelah, Existentially closed groups in continuum (preprint).
[40] O.V. Belegradek, Elementare Eigenschaften algebraisch abgeschlossener Gruppen (in Russian), Fund. Math. XCVIII (1978) 83–101.

S.I. Adian, W.W. Boone, G. Higman, eds., Word Problems II

PROBLEMS

P.M. COHN
Bedford College, London

The following is a list of open problems relevant to the topic of the working conference Decision Problems in Algebra. Some were obtained in discussion with others at this conference, some elsewhere.

1. (a) Let K be a skew field and A an $n \times n$ matrix over K. Show that there is an extension field L of K and $\alpha \in L$ such that $A - \alpha I$ is singular (i.e. α is a 'singular eigenvalue' of A).

(b) If moreover K is a k-algebra, where k is an algebraically closed commutative field, and only extensions that are k-algebras are admitted, show that A has a non-zero singular eigenvalue unless A is triangularizable over k.

Note: For 2×2 matrices (a) and (b) have been verified, cf. P.M. Cohn, Skew field constructions, LMS Lecture notes, No. 27 (Cambridge University Press, 1977). There it is also shown that the conditions are needed.

2. As a counterpart to 1, if K is an infinite skew field with finite centre k and A is an $n \times n$ matrix over K, does there exist $\alpha \in K$ such that $A - \alpha I$ is non-singular?

Note: If K is finite, such α may not exist (e.g. for a suitable diagonal matrix A). If k is infinite, the reduction theory of matrices over $K[t]$ shows that such α always exists in k.

3. (Asked by A. Macintyre) Find an existential sentence about skew fields which is true in an existentially closed skew field K precisely if K has characteristic 0.

Note: In the commutative case one cannot have such a sentence because the class of algebraically closed commutative fields admits ultraproducts (so a suitable ultraproduct of algebraically closed fields of finite characteristic will be algebraically closed of characteristic 0).

If one does not insist on an existential sentence one can proceed as follows: The sentence

$$W(x): \exists y, z\,(xy = yx^2 \wedge x^2z = zx^2 \wedge xz \neq zx \wedge y \neq 0)$$

(due to W.H. Wheeler) expresses the fact that (in an existentially closed field) x is transcendental over the ground field. The sentence

$$B(x): \exists y (xy - yx = 1)$$

due to M. Boffa and P.V. Praag, does the same in characteristic 0. In finite characteristic, $B(x)$ holds if and only if x is either transcendental or purely inseparable over (but not in) the ground field k.

Now Wheeler also has a sentence $W(x, x')$ which expresses (in an existentially closed field) that x, x' are independent commuting indeterminates, and

$$B_1(x): \exists y, z (W(z) \wedge \neg W(x, z) \wedge xz = zx \wedge yz = zy \wedge xy - yx = 1)$$

expresses the fact that for some z, purely transcendental over k, x is algebraic but not separable over $k(z)$. So $\exists x B_1(x)$ holds precisely when K has characteristic $\neq 0$.

4. (Asked by S. Shelah) Let (K_λ) be a family of skew fields, all containing E as subfield, and denote by $P = *_E K_\lambda$ their coproduct (= free product) over E. If a single relation

$$u_1 u_2 \cdots u_r = 1, \qquad u_i \in K_{\lambda_i}, \lambda_i \neq \lambda_{i+1}$$

is imposed, under what conditions is the resulting ring $\bar{P}$ (i) an integral domain, (ii) embeddable in a skew field?

Note: J. Lewin and T. Lewin (J. Algebra, 52 (1978) 39–74) have proved that if a group with a single defining relation is torsion free then its group algebra is embeddable in a skew field.

5. (Asked by S. Eilenberg) Is every finitely generated group which is embeddable in a finitely presented semigroup also embeddable in a finitely presented group?

Note: V.L. Murskii (Mat. Zametki 1 (1967) 217–224) has proved the following analogue of Higman's embedding theorem: A finitely generated semigroup is embeddable in a finitely presented semigroup if and only if it is recursively presented. The proof of Murskii's embedding theorem is much easier than that of Higman's embedding theorem and the above question is of interest because a positive answer obtained without using Higman's result would yield a new proof of Higman's embedding theorem. Of course the answer to question 5 is "Yes" — for this follows by Higman's result trivially.

6. (Asked by E. Formanek) Does every skew field contain a free subgroup of rank two?

Note: For finite-dimensional division algebras this result was proved by J. Tits, J. Algebra 20 (1972) 250–270.

7. (Asked by Y. Zalcstein) Is every finitely generated periodic subgroup of the multiplicative group of a skew field finite?